Sincerely

L.C. Baird.

BAIRD'S HISTORY

OF

CLARK COUNTY INDIANA

By CAPTAIN LEWIS C. BAIRD

President of the Clark County Historical Society, Assisted by
Well Known Local Talent.

ILLUSTRATED

B. F. BOWEN & COMPANY, PUBLISHERS
INDIANAPOLIS, INDIANA
1909

The reproduction of this publication has been made possible though sponsorship of the Howard Steamboat Museum, Inc. 1101 East Market St., P.O. Box 606, Jeffersonville, IN 47130

Windmill Publications, Inc.
6628 Uebelhack Rd. Mt. Vernon, IN 47620

NINETEEN HUNDRED NINETY SEVEN

AUTHOR'S PREFACE

In the preparation of this history, the author has endeavored to carry out the following design, viz: to give only the most important and interesting events, and to place them before the reader in not only an attractive but systematic form. The chronological arrangement of the history proper from the traditional period to the present time, is treated in decades, as by this method, the gradual development of the people and the resources of the county can be best appreciated. Following this will be found separate chapters on such phases of our history as deserve individual treatment. The military annals, the churches, the secret societies, the ship-building industry, the car works, banks and banking, the bench and bar, etc., etc., have been described from data furnished by men most capable and most intimately acquainted with these subjects.

If some of our frailties have been exposed, the account of our material development, and the high character and ability of our earlier leaders more than overbalance the weaknesses of those periods, and should serve to direct and enthuse the lives and efforts of this and succeeding generations. The author has endeavored most conscientiously to make this work authentic and complete and has freely consulted authorities both local and otherwise.

He is indebted to many persons in the preparation of the chapters following the decades as well as in writing the body of the work, and believes that the facts thus presented may be relied upon as being authentic. To John Owens, of Charlestown, he wishes to give the greatest credit for the facts procured from the storehouse of his memory and his library, and for the suggestions he has made. Col. Reuben T. Durrett, of Louisville, Hon. Jonas G. Howard and Dr. D. L. Field, both of Jeffersonville, and others have added greatly to the value of the work. English's "Conquest of the Northwest," Dillon's "Indiana," Dunn's "Indiana," and other volumes have furnished much. In fact every precaution has been taken to record the history of the county correctly and the author is profoundly grateful for the encouragement he has received.

LEWIS C. BAIRD.

PUBLISHER'S PREFACE

All life and achievement is evolution; present wisdom comes from past experience, and present commercial prosperity has come only from past exertion and suffering. The deeds and motives of the men that have gone before have been instrumental in shaping the destinies of later communities and states. The development of a new country was at once a task and a privilege. It required great courage, sacrifice and privation. Compare the present conditions of the residents of Clark county, Indiana, with what they were one hundred years ago. From a trackless wilderness and virgin prairie it has come to be a center of prosperity and civilization, with millions of wealth, systems of intersecting railways, grand educational institutions, marvelous industries and immense agricultural productions. Can any thinking person be insensible to the fascination of the study which discloses the incentives, hopes, aspirations and efforts of the early pioneers who so strongly laid the foundation upon which has been reared the magnificent prosperity of later days? To perpetuate the story of these people and to trace and record the social, political and industrial progress of the community from its first inception is the function of the local historian. A sincere purpose to preserve facts and personal memoirs that are deserving of preservation, and which unite the present to the past is the motive for the present publication. The work has been in the hands of able writers, who have, after much patient study and research, produced here the most complete biographical memoirs of Clark county, Indiana, ever offered to the public. A specially valuable and interesting department is that one devoted to the sketches of representative citizens of this county whose records deserve perpetuation because of their worth, effort and accomplishment. The publishers desire to extend their thanks to these gentlemen who have so faithfully labored to this end. Thanks are also due to the citizens of Clark county for the uniform kindness with which they have regarded this undertaking, and for their many services rendered in the gaining of necessary information.

In placing "Baird's History of Clark County, Indiana" before the citizens, the publishers can conscientiously claim that they have carried out the plan as outlined in the prospectus. Every biographical sketch in the work has been submitted to the party interested, for correction, and therefore any error of fact, if there be any, is solely due to the person for whom the sketch was prepared. Confident that our efforts to please will fully meet the approbation of the public, we are,

Respectfully,

THE PUBLISHERS.

TABLE OF CONTENTS

CHAPTER I.

TRADITIONAL EARLIEST INHABITANTS OF CLARK COUNTY.

CHAPTER II.

EARLY HISTORY OF CLARK COUNTY BEFORE ORGANIZATION.

CHAPTER III.

THE ILLINOIS GRANT.

CHAPTER IV.

ORGANIZATION OF CLARK COUNTY—THE FIRST DECADE 1801-1810.

CHAPTER V.

THE SECOND DECADE—1811-1820.

CHAPTER XI.

THE EIGHTH DECADE—1870-1880.

CHAPTER XII.

THE NINTH DECADE—1880-1890.

CHAPTER XIII.

THE TENTH DECADE—1891-1900.

CHAPTER XIV.

THE ELEVENTH DECADE—1900-1910.

CHAPTER XV.

THE MILITARY HISTORY OF CLARK COUNTY—1786-1844.

CHAPTER XVI.

THE MILITARY HISTORY OF CLARK COUNTY—1844-1860.

CHAPTER XVII.

CHAPTER XVIII.

THE MILITARY HISTORY OF CLARK COUNTY.

CHAPTER XIX.

THE MILITARY HISTORY OF CLARK COUNTY.

CHAPTER XX.

FREE MASONRY IN CLARK COUNTY.

TABLE OF CONTENTS

CHAPTER XXI.

ODD FELLOWSHIP, PYTHIANS AND OTHER SECRET SOCIETIES IN CLARK COUNTY.

CHAPTER XXII.

HISTORY OF ST. PAUL'S PARISH, JEFFERSONVILLE, THE ONLY EPISCOPAL CHURCH IN THE COUNTY.

CHAPTER XXIII.

THE METHODIST CHURCH IN CLARK COUNTY.

CHAPTER XXIV.

THE PRESBYTERIAN CHURCH IN CLARK COUNTY.

CHAPTER XXV.

THE ROMAN CATHOLIC CHURCH IN CLARK COUNTY.

CHAPTER XXVII.

THE CHRISTIAN CHURCH IN CLARK COUNTY.

THE SEVENTH DAY ADVENT CHURCH IN CLARK COUNTY.

CHAPTER XXVIII.

THE REFORMED CHURCH IN CLARK COUNTY.

CHAPTER XXIX.

THE BENCH AND BAR OF CLARK COUNTY.

CHAPTER XXX.

BANKS AND BANKING IN CLARK COUNTY.

CHAPTER XXXI.

THE RIVER—STEAMBOAT BUILDING AND STEAMBOATING—FLATBOATING AND FALLS PILOTING—HARBOR IMPROVEMENTS AND THE NINE FOOT STAGE.

CHAPTER XXXII.

HOSPITALS AND HOMES.

CHAPTER XXXIII.

PUBLIC UTILITIES.

INDEX

HISTORICAL

INDEX

BIOGRAPHICAL

INDEX

HISTORICAL

CHAPTER I.

TRADITIONAL EARLIEST INHABITANTS OF CLARK COUNTY.

That the country north of the Falls of the Ohio and adjacent to the river was inhabited by a strange people many years before the first recorded visit of a white man, there can be no doubt. The relics of a former race are scattered throughout this territory, and the many skeletons found buried along the banks of the river below Jeffersonville are indisputable evidence that a strange people once flourished here. Of all the legendary stories told of pre-Columbian visitors to the American continent, the Madoc tradition takes precedence. The Atlantis tradition, twelve thousand years old; the Phoenician tradition, dating from three quarters of a century before the Christian era; the Chinese tradition of the Buddhist priest in the fifth century; the Norse tradition of the tenth century; the Irish tradition of the eleventh century; and the Madoc tradition of the Welshmen in America near the close of the eleventh century, all lay claim to the honor of being accounts of the first visit of white men to the North American continent. The greatest probability of truth seems to attach to the Madoc tradition, and the evidence from many different sources gives it a greater credibility than any of the other accounts.

This tradition is to the effect that a colony of Welshmen, who had emigrated to America in 1170, found their way finally to the Falls of the Ohio, and remained there for many years, being finally almost exterminated in a great battle with "Red Indians."

Owen Gwyneth, Prince of Wales, died in 1167, and left seventeen sons. Disputes and contentions arose among them as to who should succeed the father, and Madoc, one of the sons, thinking it better prudence to try his fortune elsewhere, set sail with a good company of Welshmen and traveled westward until he reached the shores of another continent. The new land offered such a fair and alluring prospect that Madoc returned to Wales and brought back a considerable number of Welsh to join his colony in the "New World." Where they landed is conjecture, but the testimony of many authorities, and the stories and traditions of many of the early settlers of this west-

2

ern country prove to a greater or less degree of probability that white Indians, who spoke an almost pure Welsh tongue, existed in several localities.

In 1582 the first account of this Welsh emigration to America appeared in "Hakluits's Divers Voyages Touching the Discovery of America," etc., and his authority was Gutton Owen, a Welsh bard, who flourished during the reign of Henry VII. The account also appears in an addenda to Caradoc's "History of Wales," which was translated into English in 1584. In America the first mention of the Madoc tradition belongs to Captain John Smith, who gives it as the only discovery prior to that of Columbus (See "Generall Historie of Virginia, New England and the Summer Isles," London, 1624, page 1), but the personal evidence corroborative of this tradition begins with a statement by the Rev. Morgan Jones, in 1685. (See Gentlemen's Magazine, London, 1740, page 103). The Rev. Mr. Jones was sent out by Governor Berkeley, of Virginia, as chaplain of an expedition to South Carolina. Arriving at Port Royal on April 19, 1660, they lay at a place called Oyster Point for about eight months, at which time, being almost starved by their inability to procure provisions, he set out with five companions through the wilderness. His narrative continues as follows: "There the Tuscarara Indians took us prisoners because we told them we were bound for Roanoke. That night they carried us to their town, and shut us up close, to our no small dread. The next day they entered into a conversation about us, which after it was over, their interpreter told us that we must prepare ourselves to die the next morning. Thereupon being very much dejected and speaking in the British (Welsh), tongue, 'Have I escaped so many dangers that I must now be knocked on the head like a dog?' His words were understood by one who seemed to be a war captain, and through his intervention the six prisoners were spared." These men remained with the Indians for four months, and, the minister states, "During which time I had the opportunity of conversing with them familiarly in the British (Welsh) tongue, and did preach to them three times a week in the same language."

Captain Isaac Stewart, an officer in the Provincial Cavalry of South Carolina, in 1782 was captured by Indians and taken westward of Fort Pitt. He and a Welshman named John Davy were kept in bondage for over two years and were finally taken up the Red river to an Indian settlement. Davy understood and conversed with this tribe of white Indians in his native tongue. (See American Museum, Vol. 2, page 92, July, 1787).

The Rev, John Williams, LL. D., in a book entitled "An Inquiry into the Truth of the Tradition Concerning the Discovery of America by Madog," published in London in 1796, gives the testimony of numerous persons who had been among the Welsh Indians in America. These incidents are too lengthy to relate here, but they show that enough testimony relating to White Indians who spoke the Welsh language has been collected by writers in the past to give the story more weight than attaches to the Norse, the Chinese, the Irish or the Phoenician traditions of pre-Columbian discovery.

In later years historians have delved deep into this subject, and George Catlin, who published "Letters and Notes on the Manners of the North American Indians" in 1857, says that the Mandan Indians, among whom he lived and studied their history and peculiarities, were descendants of the Welsh colony established in America by Prince Madoc in the twelfth century. This entire tribe of Welsh Indians was almost wiped out of existence by the small-pox in the summer of 1838. In 1842 Thomas S. Hinde, an antiquarian of more than local reputation, gave some valuable information touching the Madoc tradition. In answer to inquiries made by John S. Williams, editor of The American Pioneer, he wrote as follows:

"Mount Carmel, Illinois, May 30, 1824. Mr. J. S. Williams: Dear Sir— Your letter of the 17th, to Major Armstrong, was placed in my hands some days ago. The brief remark and hints given you are correct. I have a vast quantity of western matter, collected in notes gathered from various sources, mostly from persons who knew the facts. These notes reach back to remote periods. It is a fact that the Welsh under Owen Ap Zuinch, in the twelfth century, found their way up the Mississippi, and as far up the Ohio as the Falls of that river at Louisville, where they were cut off by the Indians; others ascended the Missouri, were either captured or settled with and sunk into Indian habits. Proof I. In 1799, six soldiers' skeletons were dug up near Jeffersonville. Each skeleton had a breastplate of brass, cast with the Welsh coat-of-arms, the Mermaid and Harp, with a Latin inscription, in substance, 'virtuous deeds meet their just reward.' One of these plates was left by Captain Jonathan Taylor with the late Mr. Hubbard Taylor, of Clark county, and when called for by me in 1814 for the late Dr. John P. Campbell, of Chillicothe, Ohio, who was preparing notes on the antiquities of the West, by a letter from Mr. Hubbard Taylor (a relative of mine), now living, I was informed that the breast-plate had been taken to Virginia by a gentleman of that state, I supposed as a matter of curiosity. Proof II. The late Mr. McIntosh, who first settled near this and had been for fifty or sixty years prior to his death, in 1831 or 1832, a western Indian trader, was in Fort Kaskaskia prior to its being taken by General George Rogers Clark, in 1778, and heard, as he informed me himself, a Welshman and an Indian from far up the Missouri speaking and conversing in the Welsh language. It was stated by Gilbert Imlay, in his history of the west, that it was Captain Abraham Chaplain, of Union county, Kentucky, that heard this conversation in Welsh. Dr. Campbell, visiting Chaplain, found it was not he. Afterwards the fact was stated by McIntosh, from whom I obtained other facts as to western matters. Some hunter, many years ago, informed me of a tombstone being found in the southern part of Indiana with the initials of a name, and '1186' engraved upon it.

The Mohawk Indians had a tradition among them respecting the Welsh, and of their having been cut off by the Indians at the Falls of the Ohio. The late Colonel Joseph Hamilton Davis, who had for many years sought for information on this subject, mentions this fact, and of the Welshman's bones being found buried on Corn Island."

The early pioneers of Kentucky, in their intercourse with the Indians, who frequently visited the Falls of the Ohio for the purposes of trade, got from them the tradition of Madoc, and Colonel Reuben T. Durrett, the president of the Filson club, of Louisville, in the 23d publication of that society, gives an account which was related to him by an aged Welshman named Griffin in the early sixties. Griffin related as follows:

"On the north side of the river, where Jeffersonville now stands, some skeletons were exhumed in early times with armor which had brass plates bearing the Mermaid and Harp, which belong to the Welsh coat-of-arms. On the same side of the river, further down, a piece of stone supposed to be part of a tombstone was found, with the date 1186 and what seemed to be a name or initials of a name so effaced by time as to be illegible. If that piece of stone was ever a tombstone over a grave, the party laid beneath it must have been of the Welsh colony of Madoc, for we have no tradition of any one but the Welsh at the Falls so early as 1186. In early times the forest along the river on both sides of the Falls for some miles presented two kinds of growth. Along the margin of the river the giant sycamores and other trees of the forest primeval stood as if they had never been disturbed, but beyond them was a broad belt of trees of a different growth, until the belt was passed, when the original forest again appeared. This indicated that the belt had been deprived of its original forest for agricultural or other purposes and that a new forest had grown up in its stead. He said, however, it was possible that the most important of these traditions learned from the Indians concerned a great battle fought at the Falls of the Ohio, between the Red Indians and the White Indians, as the Welsh Indians were called. It has been a long time since this battle, but it was fought here and won by the Red Indians. In the final struggle the White Indians sought safety on the island since known as Sand Island, but nearly all who sought refuge there were slaughtered. The remnant who escaped death made their way to the Missouri river, where, by different movements at different times, they went up that river a great distance. They were known to exist there by different parties who came from there and talked Welsh with the pioneers. Some Welshmen living at the Falls of the Ohio in pioneer times talked with these White Indians, and although there was considerable difference between the Welsh they spoke and the Welsh spoken by the Indians, yet they had no great difficulty in understanding one another. He further said, concerning this tradition of a great battle, that there was a tradition that many skeletons were found on Sand Island, mingled promiscuously together as if left there unburied after a great battle, but that he had examined the island a number of times without finding a single bone, and that if skeletons were ever abundant there they had disappeared before his time."

John Filson, the author of the first history of Kentucky, published in 1784, was a believer in the Madoc tradition, and while in Louisville collecting material for his history, discussed the subject with such men as General George Rogers Clark, Major John Harrison, Colonel Moore and others. At a meeting of a club of prominent citizens in that city about this time Filson was invited to attend, and the subject of the Madoc tradition was brought up for discussion. General Clark spoke first, and confined himself to what he had learned from a chief of the Kaskaskia Indians concerning a large and curiously shaped earthwork on the Kaskaskia river, which the chief, who was of lighter complexion than most Indians, said was the house of his ancestors. Colonel Moore spoke next, and related what he had learned from an old Indian about a long war of extermination between the Red Indians and the White Indians. The final battle, he said, between them, was fought at the Falls of the Ohio, where nearly the whole of the White Indians were driven upon an island and slaughtered. General Clark, on hearing this statement by Colonel Moore, confirmed it by stating that he had heard the same thing from Tobacco, a chief of the Piankeshaws. Major Harrison spoke next, and told about an extensive graveyard on the north side of the Ohio, opposite the Falls, where thousands of human bones were buried in such confusion as to indicate that the dead were left there after a battle, and that the silt from inundations of the Ohio had covered them as the battle had left them.

The testimony of many living men of Clark county today bears out the statement about the number of skeletons to be found in the vicinity of the Big Eddy. The late Dr. Beckwith, of Jeffersonville, had in his possession a skull from this graveyard at the Falls, and he pronounced it not the skull of an Indian. The White Indians, or, as some of the other Indian tribes called them, the "Stranger People," were possibly the builders of the mysterious fortifications on the hill crest, two hundred and fifty feet above the river, at Fourteen Mile creek. It is without doubt the most elaborate and extensive work of defense erected by the vanished race. It is the only one of its kind in the United States. It has an area of about ten acres and has the remains of strong fortifications along its exposed front. These fortifications consisted of a wall with watch mounds or towers at intervals, five of which can yet be traced. Students and antiquarians have shown that it was not built by North American Indians, but its origin, like the battle at the Falls, is made obscure by the hazy lapse of centuries, and we can only surmise as to what it was and who built it, whether by the Stranger People or the Mound Builders; but that it was of a race previous to the Indians is certain. Bones of a race antedating the Red Indians are frequently found in the mounds in this vicinity. As an historical and antiquarian curiosity its ruins are far more remarkable and interesting than the dilapidated castles along the German Rhine.

Among the traditional or semi-traditional accounts of early white explorers to the Falls of the Ohio, the visit of the French explorer, La Salle, may be mentioned. The Indiana country was claimed by the French by virtue of his discovery of the Ohio river. The account of this voyage is as follows:

Robert Cavelier Sieur de la Salle in 1669 started on a voyage of discovery down the Ohio, and it is said that he floated as far down as the Falls of that river, where his guides and crew deserted him. Not daunted by this misfortune, he made his way back to the French settlements to the north. An iron hatchet which he left here in a small tree on the bank of the river is said to have been found imbedded in the tree one hundred and thirty-nine years afterward. La Salle is credited with being the earliest white man ever in this vicinity, but his discovery amounted to nothing. From shortly after his supposed visit other explorers began to periodically discover the river, until the settlers came and the "Beautiful river" became a highway for travel, rather than an entrance into a mysterious land.

Note: I am indebted to Colonel Reuben T. Durret, President of the Filson Club, of Louisville, Kentucky, for much of the material in this chapter.

CHAPTER II.

EARLY HISTORY OF CLARK COUNTY BEFORE ORGANIZATION.

From the discoveries of Robert Cavelier Sieur de la Salle and the earlier voyage of the Jesuit Fathers Charemonot and Breboeuf, France claimed all of the Indiana, Ohio and Illinois country as early as the seventeenth century. The Iroquois nation also claimed it, but France was an aggressive power, and the wars of the Indians against her encroachments availed nothing. At the treaty of Utrecht, April 11, 1713, Louis XIV renounced in favor of England all claims except those to the St. Lawrence and Mississippi valleys. Both nations claimed the region west of the Alleghany Mountains, along the Ohio river, and the resultant squabble was that war known as the French and Indian war, 1754 to 1763. The Treaty of Paris ended this war and Indiana, together with all of the other territory east of the Mississippi claimed by France, was ceded to England. This territory, of which Clark county was a part, thus passed to the rule of the British nation, to remain a colony until the war of the Revolution was terminated by the Treaty of Paris, September 3, 1783. In the year of 1766 the British parliament insisted upon the Ohio river as the southwestern boundary and the Mississippi river as the western limit of the dominions of the English crown in this quarter. By this measure the entire northwest, or so much of it as afterwards became the Northwest Territory, was attached to the Province of Quebec, and the tract that now constitutes the state of Indiana was nominally under its local administration.

Virginia began to lay early claim to the vast area beyond her western border, but government was still nominal, and the few white settlers and Indians were generally a law unto themselves. In 1769 Virginia, acting upon the authority of her royal grants, by an enactment, extended her jurisdiction over all the territory northwest of the Ohio river, and by that act the county of Botetourt was organized and named in honor of Lord Botetourt, governor of the colony of Virginia. It was a vast country, about seven hundred miles long, with the Blue Ridge for its eastern and the Mississippe for its western boundary. It included large parts of the present states of West Virginia, Ohio, Indiana, and Illinois, and was the first county organization covering what is now Clark county. After the conquest of the Indiana and Illinois country by General George Rogers Clark, in 1778, the county of Illinois was erected by the Virginia legislature (in October of the same year) out of the great county of Botetourt, and included all the territory between the Pennsylvania line, the Ohio, the Mississippi, and the northern lakes. Colonel John Todd was appointed the first county lieutenant and civil commandant of the county. He perished in the battle of Blue Licks, August 18, 1782, and Timothy de Montbrun was named as his successor.

The close of the war of the Revolution found the American states deeply involved in debt and with no resources in prospect, except such as might be derived from the sale of their lands west of the Alleghanies. Some of the states claimed that the title to this vast unsettled domain to have vested in the various colonies whose charters had extended their limits indefinitely to the west, and there was a special claim from Virginia on account of her conquest and the retention of possession through George Rogers Clark. Other states objected to this, but on October 20, 1783, Virginia authorized a cession to the Federal government, and on March 1, 1784, our country passed from Virginian rule to that of the United States of America. A plan for the division of this vast tract was taken up immediately and a scheme for the formation of ten states out of it was reported. The names of the states as proposed were as follows: Sylvania, Chersonesus, Michigania, Washington, Saratoga, Metropotamia, Assenisipia, Illinoia, Polypotamia and Pelisipia. These last two names concern Clark county, as it lay partly in both as proposed. Both of these states lay south of the thirty-ninth parallel and north of the Ohio river, and their dividing line was a meridian drawn through the rapids of the Ohio. Pelisipia was to be the eastern state and Polypotamia the western. To think that our mail might have been addressed to Charlestown, Pelisipia, or to Borden, Polypotamia, may appear strange, but such was the plan of the early fathers. However, the plan failed to carry, and the name of Indiana was finally given our great state when the territory was organized, and the illustrious name of Clark given the county when it was created in 1801. No legislative measures ever enacted meant so much to Clark county as the Ordinance of 1787. This celebrated act, entitled "An ordinance for the government of the territory of the United States northwest of the river Ohio," was passed by Congress July 13, 1787. By this great organic act—"the last gift," as Chief Justice Chase said, " of the congress of the old confederation to the country, and it was a fit consummation of their glorious labors"— provision was made for various forms of territorial government to be adopted in succession, in due order of the advancement and development of the western country. The sixth article provided that, "There shall be neither slavery nor involuntary servitude in the said territory, otherwise than in the punishment of crimes, whereof the party shall have been duly convicted. This question of slavery was a bitter one, and within a few years was to become the chief issue in the politics of the territory of Indiana, but it was a bulwark behind which the best men of the time stood, and even the action of a legislature was powerless to have this paragraph changed. The settlement made at

Clarkesville, mentioned in a succeeding chapter, and the building of the fort at Jeffersonville in 1786 were the beginning of the settlements of Clark county. This period of the history of the county will be more fully treated in the chapter on the military annals.

In 1793 the first of the great floods ever recorded overtopped the banks of the Ohio and the few settlers who had built their cabins in the rich low-lands were forced to retreat to higher ground for safety, while their fences, and, in some cases, their cabins, floated away. This flood was not as great as the flood of 1832, but no record of the stage of the water is in existence.

CHAPTER III.

THE ILLINOIS GRANT.

The grant of land by the state of Virginia January 2, 1781, to General George Rogers Clark and his men was a fitting recognition of the value of their services in the "Conquest of the Northwest." Around this grant and the events leading up to it cluster nearly all the early history of Indiana Territory and the Northwest Territory. The events leading up to this grant of land to Clark and the Illinois regiment date from the instructions he received from Patrick Henry, then governor of Virginia, January 2, 1778. Two sets of instructions were given to Clark, one intended for the public eye, as follows:

"Lieutenant Colonel George Rogers Clark:

"You are to proceed, without loss of time, to enlist seven companies of men, officered in the usual manner, to act as militia, under your orders. They are to proceed to Kentucky, and there obey such orders and directions as you shall give them, for three months after their arrival at that place; but to receive pay, etc., in case they remain on duty a longer time, etc., etc., etc.

"Given under my hand at Williamsburg, January 2, 1778. "P HENRY."

The private instructions given into the hand of Clark are, in part, as follows:

"Virginia Sct. "In Council Williamsburg, January 2, 1778. "Lieutenant Colonel George Rogers Clark: "You are to proceed with all convenient speed to raise seven companies of soldiers to consist of fifty men each, officered in the usual manner, and armed most properly for the enterprise, and with this force attack the British post at Kaskaskia. It is conjectured that there are many pieces of cannon and military stores to a considerable amount, at that place, the taking and preservation of which would be a valuable acquisition to the state. If you are so fortunate, therefore, as to succeed in your expedition, you will take every possible measure to secure the artillery and stores, and whatever may advantage the state. For the transportation of the troops, provisions, etc., down the Ohio, you are to apply to the commanding officer at Fort Pitt for boats, and during the whole transaction you are to take especial care to keep the true destination of your force secret; its success depends upon this. Orders are therefore given to Captain Smith to secure the two men from Kaskaskia.

"It is earnestly desired that you show humanity to such British subjects,

RESIDENCE OF GENERAL CLARK AT CLARKSVILLE.

From "Conquest of the Northwest." Copyright 1895. Used by special permission of the publishers, The Bobbs-Merrill Company.

and other persons as fall into your hands. If the white inhabitants of that post and neighborhood will give undoubted evidence of their attachment to this state, for it is certain they live within its limits, by taking the test prescribed by law, and by every other way and means in their power, let them be treated as fellow citizens, and their persons and property be duly respected. Assistance and protection against all enemies, whatever shall be afforded them, and the commonwealth of Virginia is pledged to accomplish it. But if these people will not accede to these reasonable demands, they must feel the consequences of war, under that direction of humanity that has hitherto distinguished Americans, and which it is expected you will ever consider the rule of your conduct, and from which you are in no instance to depart. The corps you are to command are to receive the pay and allowances of militia and to act under the laws and regulation of this state now in force as to militia. The inhabitants of this post will be informed by you that in case they accede to the offers of becoming citizens of this commonwealth, a proper garrison will be maintained among them, and every attention bestowed to render their commerce beneficial; the fairest prospects being opened to the dominions of France and Spain. It is in contemplation to establish a post near the mouth of the Ohio. Cannon will be wanted to fortify it. Part of those at Kaskaskia will be easily brought thither or otherwise secured as circumstances make necessary. You are to apply to General Hand, at Pittsburg, for powder and lead necessary for this expedition. If he cannot supply it, the person who has that which Captain Sims brought from New Orleans, can. Lead is sent to Hampshire by my orders, and that may be delivered to you. Wishing you success, I am your humble servant, "P. HENRY."

It will be seen from the above that the campaign was to be of such a character that the men themselves were not to know more than that the service was to be on the frontier and against the Indians and British, as they well knew the British were secretly in league with the Indians and furnishing them with the munitions of their cruel and treacherous warfare.

Thus was the expedition launched and the organization of his forces begun. The end of May, 1778, found the little army encamped on Corn Island, a long narrow strip of land reaching from what is now Fourth street to Fourteenth street, Louisville, Kentucky, and laying very near the south side of the river. On June 24, 1778, they embarked in the boats which had been prepared—shot the falls, and in the sombre shadow of an almost total eclipse of the sun began the first part of their expedition against the British posts at Kaskaskia. Their voyage down the river to the mouth of the Tennessee, and the march of one hundred ad twenty miles through the wilderness, towards Kaskaskia without pack horses, wagons or other means of conveying their munitions of war, baggage or provisions than their own robust selves, was a feat of endurance that tried their hardihood.

Through forest dark, dense and tangled, across glades of intervening prairie lands which were often covered with reed-like grasses, higher than the head of the tallest among them, over hill and through valley, often withiut water for hours, save only that which each man carried, under the blazing of a Southern Illinois summer sun, without transportation of any kind, no horses, no wagons, no tents, no baggage, no artillery: this band of heroes led by a hero, pressed on. When in the confines of what is now Williamson county, Illinois, the guide, Saunders, became confused and lost his bearings and the troops believing he was betraying them, were on the point of wreaking summary punishment on him for his suspicioned treachery, when he recognized a point of timber which he said marked the way to Kaskaskia.

The little band pressed on with clothes ragged and soiled with the wear of the march, and faces scratched and bruised by brambles and briars, footsore and weary with the labor of forced marching and want of proper rest, with only the sod for a bed, and the canopy of heaven for a covering when at night they lay down for a few hours' sleep in strict silence, not a shot being fired for fear its echoes might be heard by some prowler and the news of their approach carried to the enemy. Arriving withn a few miles of Kaskaskia on the evening of July 4, 1778, no time was lost in effecting the capture, and when the morning of. July 5th broke the town was Virginian and not Britsh. Clark immediately hastened to send a detachment of troops to take possession of Cahokia, St. Phillips and Prairie du Rocher, on the Mississippi. The fort and town of Vincennes, having been left by Abbott, the English Governor, virtually in the hands of the French inhabitants, was garrisoned, the American flag raised and Capt. Leonard Helm put in command.

Clark being now in possession of all the military posts, turned his attention at once to making the best terms he could with the numerous Indian tribes. Helm continued in command at Post Vincennes, but his force was small, and Fort Sackville was described as "wretched," "a miserable stockade without a well, barrack, platform for small arms, or even a lock to the gate."

General Hamilton, the commandant at Detroit, headed an expedition against Helm at Vincennes, and on December 17, 1778, Fort Sackville and the ancient town of Vincennes again came into possession of the British. Helm and his twenty-one men demanded and received all the honors of war upon their surrender to an enemy, which numbered between five hundred and six hundred men. In February, 1779, Clark began his memorable march from Kaskaskia against Vincennes. After incredible difficulty and severe exposure, marching and wading through the icy water of swamps and overflowed streams, with an insufficieney of provisions and baggage, the worn and wearied expedition appeared before the town, and Clark, with his usual generalship, compelled Hamilton to surrender, and the final downfall of the British in the Wabash and Illinois country was accomplished.

When Clark marched his little army from Massac to Kaskaskia, across the glades and timberlands of Southern Illinois, it was summer time. Soft winds wafted the perfume of flower-sprinkled prairies, and the fragrance of the woodlands about the marching troops, the water of the streams was comparatively low, and the swamp lands were firmer to the tread of their moccasin-clad feet. The canopy of sky and cloud was covering enough by night, and while the blazing of a June sun was far from soothing to spirts or temper, it was not to be compared to the hardships to which the troops on the march to the capture of Vincennes were to encounter.

At the crossing of the Little Wabash, Clark cheered them on, and called to his aid an Irish drummer, celebrated for his fund of droll and comic songs, the singing of which, at a time when the men were chilled almost to freezing by the icy waters through which they had been wading, sometimes for an hour, up to their armpits, would put new life into the men, and again they would struggle on. What a picture! What melody can equal the living picture of this band of heroes or the song of this wild Irishman's singing? The painters of the picture have passed away. The song of the singer is stilled forever, but truly their works live after them.

The party on the 18th heard the morning gun at Fort Sackville, at Vincennes, and when they reached the Wabash, below the mouth of the Embarass river, they were exhausted, destitute and starving—literally starving, with no means of crossing the river, which was overflowed and was several miles wide. On the 20th of February a party of French, in a boat, was hailed and came to the little army. From them Clark learned that the French of Vincennes were true to the oath of Vincennes, which they had taken the previous summer, and that the British garrison had no knowledge of the approach of the expedition, indeed, had no knowledge that an expedition had even been planned, much less had they thought it possible that men would undertake so hazardous an expedition, and one which, if undertaken must, as they thought, result in the death of every soldier from the hardships of the march. And now, with the facts before us it seems to us they accomplished the impossible. By wading and rafting they managed to cross to the highlands below Vincennes. Clark immediately sent the following notice to citizens of Vincennes: "To the inhabitants of Post Vincennes: Gentlemen: Being now within two miles of your village, with my army, determined to take your fort tonight, and not being willing to surprise you, I take this method to request such of you as are true citizens, and would enjoy the liberty I bring you, to remain, still, in your houses. Those, if any there be, that are friends to the King, will instantly repair to the fort and join the hair-buyer general, and fight like men, and such as do not go to the fort and shall be discovered afterwards, they may depend on severe punishment. On the contrary, those that are true friends to liberty shall be treated as friends deserve. And once more I request them to keep out of the streets, for everyone I find in arms on my arrival I shall treat as an enemy:

"G. R. CLARK."

Clark's army, consisting of one company from Cahokia, commanded by Captain McCarty, and one company from Kaskaskia, commanded by Captain Charleville, and were composed of French, and the rest, about seventy men, were Americans of his old command, in all not over one hundred and seventy men, were made to appear to the villagers' minds as much greater by this peculiar note, and to still further deceive them and to make the garrison believe a large force was about to attack them, Clark marched his men back and forth among some mounds in the prairie, changing the flags, so that the British believed many times the true number of fierce Kentuckians were about to assail them, as the British only knew them as Kentucky bordermen, and had no thought that more than half were Illinois French. At about sunset on February 23d, Lieutenant Bayly was sent with fourteen men to make an attack on the fort. He led his men to about thirty yards of the fort, where they lay concealed behind a bank of earth, protected from the guns of the fort. Every one of the Americans was an expert rifleman, and whenever a porthole was opened a storm of bullets whistled in, killing or wounding the men at the guns, so that none would work the cannon. At nine in the morning of the 24th, while his men were eating the first breakfast they had had for several days, Clark sent the following note to the British commandant:

"Sir: In order to save yourself from the impending storm which now threatens you, I order you immediately to surrender yourself, with all your garrison, stores, etc. If I am obliged to storm, you may depend upon such treatment alone, as is justly due a murderer. Beware of destroying stores of any kind, or any papers or letters that are in your possession, or hurting one house in town, for, by heaven, if you do, there shall be no mercy shown you.

"G. R. CLARK."

This note may seem brutal to modern minds, but when it is remembered that it was addressed to a man who was paying a bounty to the merciless savage as a reward for the murder, not only of the American men, but of helpless women and innocent children, it is not too harsh. Governor Hamilton was deeply impressed by this note, it is certain, by the meek reply returned by him, which is as follows:

"Governor Hamilton begs leave to acquaint Colonel Clark that he and his garrison are not to be awed into any action unworthy of British subjects."

About midnight of the 23d Clark had cut a ditch near the fort, and in it, secure from the guns of the fort, the riflemen lay, with watchful eye and unerring aim. They poured in a steady fire, and in fifteen minutes had silenced two pieces of artillery and killed every gunner approaching them or had driven them away from their guns, horror-stricken at the certainty of death or of wounds, if but the smallest portion of their person was exposed but for an instant. This terrible fire was kept up for eighteen hours. This incessant fire convinced the garrison that they would be destroyed, and Governor Hamilton sent Clark the following note:

"Governor Hamilton proposes to Colonel Clark a truce of three days, during which time he promises that there shall be no defensive work carried on in the garrison, on condition that Colonel Clark will observe, on his part, a like cessation of offensive works, that is, he wishes to confer with Colonel Clark, as soon as can be, and promises that whatever may pass between them two and another person, mutually agreed on to be present, shall remain secret until matters be finished, as he wishes whatever the result of the conference may be, it may tend to the honor and credit of each party. If Colonel Clark makes a difficulty of coming into the fort, Lieutenant-Governor Hamilton will speak to him by the gate.

"HENRY HAMILTON."

February 24, 1779.

Clark replied:

"Colonel Clark's compliments to Governor Hamilton, and begs to say that he will not agree to any terms other than Mr. Hamilton surrendering himself and garrison at discretion. If Mr. Hamilton wants to talk with Colonel Clark, he will meet him at the church, with Captain Helm."

A conference was held and Clark demanded a surrender, otherwise he threatened to put the leaders to the sword for the gold paid for American scalps. He was in earnest and the garrison so understood. In an hour Clark dictated the following terms of surrender, which Hamilton accepted:

"First—Lieutenant-Governor Hamilton agrees to deliver up to Colonel Clark, Fort Sackville and all the stores, etc.

"Second—The garrison to deliver themselves as prisoners of war, and to march out with the arms and accoutrements.

"Third—The garrison to be delivered up by tomorrow, at ten o'clock.

"Four—Three days are allowed the garrison to settle their accounts with the inhabitants and traders.

"Fifth—The officers of the garrison are to be allowed their necessary baggage.

"Signed at Post Vincennes, this 24th day of February, 1779.

"Agreed to for the following reasons: First, remoteness from succor; second, state and quantity of provisions; third, the unanimity of the officers and men in its expediency; fourth, the honorable terms allowed, and lastly, the confidence in a generous enemy.

"HENRY HAMILTON."

Lieutenant-Governor and Superintendent."

On the 25th this surrender took place. Fifty thousand dollars' worth of arms and stores were turned over to Clark. Governor Hamilton, Major Hay and some other officers were sent under guard to the capital of Virginia. Seventy-nine prisoners were paroled and sent to Detroit.

An expedition up the Wabash, under command of Captain Helm, resulted in the capture of seven British boats which were manned by about forty men and loaded with valuable goods and provisions, intended for Fort Sackville, worth at least fifty thousand dollars. Thus was consummated the scheme of conquest which originated in the brilliant mind of the genius, Clark. Dillon says, "With respect to the magnitude of its design, the valor and perseverance with which it was carried on, and the momentous results which were produced by it, this expedition stands without a parallel in the annals of the valley of the Mississippi. English says: "Measured by the standard of great results, the map of the magnificent territory, acquired mainly through his agency, speaks louder in behalf of General Clark and his little army than any words of praise." When compared with other portions of the United States, the five states of Indiana, Ohio, Illinois, Michigan, Wisconsin, and part of Minnesota comprise the very heart of the Republic. The resolution of the General Assembly of Virginia, January 2, 1781, provided that a gratuity of land not to exceed one hundred and fifty thousand acres should be given the officers and men of Clark's army. In 1783 another act was passed "for locating and surveying the one hundred and fifty thousand acres of land, as follows:

"Be it enacted by the General Assembly, That William Flemming, John Edwards, John Campbell, Walker Daniel, gentlemen, and George Rogers Clark, John Montgomery, Abraham Chaplin, John Bailey, Robert Todd and William Clark, officers in the Illinois regiment, shall be, and they are hereby constituted a board of commissioners and that they or the major part of them, shall settle and determine the claims to land under the said resolution. That the respective claimants shall give in their claims to the said commissioners on or before the first day of April, 1784; and, if approved and allowed, shall pay down to the said commissioners one dollar for every one hundred acres of such claim, to enable them to survey and apportion the said lands. The said commissioners shall appoint a principal surveyor, who shall have power to appoint his deputies, to be approved by the said commissioners and to contract with him for his fees. That from and after the said first day of April, 1784, the said commissioners, or the major part of them, shall proceed with the surveyor to lay off the said one hundred and fifty thousand acres of land on the northwest side of the Ohio river, the length of which shall not exceed double the breadth; and, after laying out one thousand acres at the most convenient place therein for a town, shall proceed to lay out and survey the residue, and divide the same by fair and equal lot among the claimants; but no lot or survey shall exceed five hundred acres. That the said commissioners, in their apportionments of the said land, shall govern themselves by the allowances made by law to the officers and soldiers in the Continental Army. That the said commissioners shall, as soon as may be, after the said one hundred and forty-nine thousand acres shall be surveyed, cause a plat thereof, certified on oath, to be returned to the register's office, and thereupon a patent shall issue to the said commissioners or the survivors of them, who shall hold the same in trust for the respective claimants; and they, or the major part of them, shall thereafter, upon application, execute good and sufficient deeds for conveying the several portions of land to the said officers and soldiers."

The frontage of the "grant" upon the Ohio river extended from a point about midway between Silver creek and Falling run, up the r'ver to a point opposite the upper end of eighteen Mile Island, and lay almost wholly in Clark county. The divisions of this tract of land are unlike the regular United States survey of the public lands, which is based upon lines running at right angles to the cardinal points of the compass. The lines here run northeast and southwest. Why this survey was made in this position it is impossible to tell, unless it resulted from trying to make the lines run perpendicular to the Ohio river when the survey commenced.

At the preliminary negotiations for peace in Paris in November, 1782, between England and her revolted, successful American colonies, both France and Spain, for similar reasons of discovery and partial occupancy, filed their protests against the claim of either of the lately contending parties to "the Illinois country." It cannot be too often repeated, to the everlasting honor of General Clark, that it was his conquest in 1778 that determined the controversy in favor of the infant republic, and carried the lines of the new nation to the Mississippi and the northern lakes. Otherwise the east bank of the Ohio, or possibly even the Alleghanies, would have formed its western boundary in part. The final convention signed at Paris, September 3, 1783, confirmed the claim of the United Colonies as made good by the victories of Clark. On August 3, 1784, the commissioners met in Louisville for the purpose of allotting the land of the grant, and to decide who was entitled and who was not.

The state of Virginia appointed William Clark, a cousin of the general, as surveyor. He selected his assistants as follows: Edmund Rogers, David Steel, Peter Catlett, and Burwell Jackson. This cession or grant was made by Virginia; but she relinquished soon after her right to the United States, on condition that the previous donation would be respected. From this time Virginia has not retained ownership of land north of the Ohio river. William Clark and his party divided themselves into companies. Some of his men were poor engineers, and many mistakes occurred. Peter Catlett was especially notorious for inaccuracies. He surveyed that portion of the county now occupied by Oregon, a row of five-hundred-acre tracts off the west side of

3

Washington, and the greater part of Owen. From his mistakes resulted many lawsuits, when in later days land became more valuable. Says William Clark: "I discovered several errors by Catlett in going into his district to subdivide some of the five-hundred-acre tracts." They were principally made in laying down watercourses. David Steel surveyed that part of the county now occupied by Charlestown, Utica, and Union townships; and his surveys are almost without errors. Burwell Jackson surveyed the township of Silver Creek, a part of Monroe, and besides assisted in laying off Clarksville. Edmund Rogers and William Clark surveyed the remaining part of the county.

The area of some of the tracts in the grant instead of being five hundred acres, as intended, miss that figure by one hundred acres.

The provision for a town in the grant was made by the following act:

That a plat of said land (one thousand acres) be returned by the surveyor to the Court of Jefferson which was then in Louisville, to be by the Clerk thereof recorded and thereupon the same shall be and is hereby invested in William Flemming, John Edwards, John Campbell, Walker Daniel, George Rogers Clark, John Montgomery, Abram Chaplin, John Bailey, Robert Todd, and William Clark. The lots are to be laid off into one-half acre each, with convenient streets, and the same shall be and is hereby called Clarksville.

On each lot there was to be built a good dwelling house, at least eighteen feet by twenty feet, with a brick or stone chimney, to be completed three years after the deed with received. If these terms were not complied with the commissioners had the right to sell again the lot and use the money in public improvements. After some time, however, it was found necessary to enlarge this provision in order to give the young colony a chance to grow, and induce early settlers to make it their residence.

However, the inducements did not seem to induce, and Clarksville's claim to greatness lies in her history rather than in her prospects.

The grant outside of the town of Clarksville was allotted to those entitled, and from this allotment originate all the titles to property in the tract at the present day.

William H. English, in his "Conquest of the Northwest," has the only authentic roll of officers and soldiers who "assisted in the reduction of the British forts," and the following is a copy with their allotments. Each number represents five hundred acres, unless otherwise indicated. Where a letter precedes a number it indicates that that tract is subdivided and the subdivisions lettered.

OFFICERS.

Clark, George Rogers, Brigadier General—Nos. 27, 56, 62, 84, 165, 168, 185, 208, 212, 223, 227, 229, 242, 285, 288, 297; four acres in 74, and forty-five acres in 141. Total, 8,049 acres.

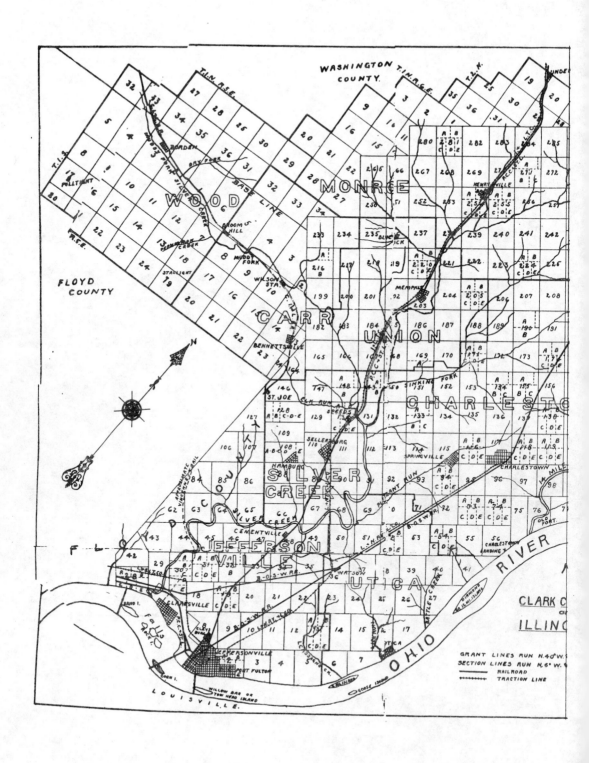

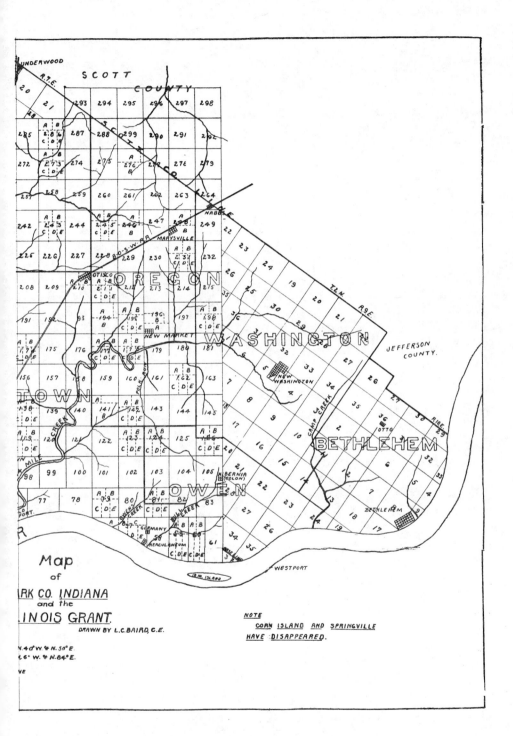

Map
of
ARK CO. INDIANA
and the
ILINOIS GRANT.
DRAWN BY L.C.BAIRD, C.E.

N.4°W.& N.50°E.
6° W.& N.84°E.
NE

NOTE
CORN ISLAND AND SPRINGVILLE
HAVE DISAPPEARED.

Montgomery, John, Lientenant Colonel—Nos. 35, 40, 51, 143, 167, 202, 239, 270, 283 and B141, 351 acres. Total, 4,851 acres.

Bowman, Joseph, Major—Nos. 5, 49, 97, 125, 140, 186, 193, 237, and B32, 312 acres. Total, 4,312 acres.

Lynn, William, Major—Nos. 12, 93, 105, 132, 181, 217, 218, 291 and B216, 312 acres. Total, 4,312 acres.

Quick, Thomas, Major—Nos, 21, 70, 163, 204, 215, 233, 265, 284, and B276, 312 acres. Total, 4,312 acres.

CAPTAINS.

(3,234 acres each.)

Bailey, John—Nos. 16, 22, 24, 81, 225, 226, and A194, 234 acres.
Brashear, Richard—Nos. 68, 111, 112, 114, 134, 236 and B194, 234 acres.
George, Robert—Nos. 17, 137, 146, 159, 172, 275 and A149, 234 acres.
Herrod, William—Nos. 91, 99, 164, 234, 261, 264, A148.
Helm, Leonard—Nos. 66, 147, 201, 266, 269, 279, 149.
Kellar, Abraham—Nos. 71, 120, 156, 173, 238, 295, B148.
McCarty, Richard—Nos. 63, 80, 90, 228, 251, 259, A190.
Rodgers, John—Nos. 11, 72, 207, 235, 282, 296, A248.
Ruddell, Isaac—Nos. 14, 34, 77, 110, 153, 179, B190.
Shelby, James—Nos. 42, 43, 88, 89, 95, 249, B248.
Taylor, Isaac—Nos. 109, 129, 144, 151, 253, 293, 101.
Todd, Robert—Nos. 3, 36, 48, 55, 122, 203, A246.
Williams, John—Nos. 9, 75, 115, 152, 166, 240 and 101.
Worthington, Edward—Nos. 33, 67, 69, 131, 176, 199 and B246.

LIEUTENANTS.

(2,156 acres each.)

Bowman, Isaac—Nos. 1, 158, 213, 289 and A32.
Calvit, Joseph—Nos. 41, 50, 61, 161, and A216.
Carney, Martin—Nos. 38, 192, 250, 263, and C154.
Chaplin, Abraham—Nos. 145, 180, 222, 267 and A276.
Clark, Richard—Nos. 15, 18, 191, 274, and part 160.
Clark, William—Nos. 96, 103, 272, 287, and part 160.
Dalton, Valentine—Nos. 76, 104, 206, 247, C155.
Davis, James—Nos. 39, 136, 187, 257, and B154.
Floyd, Henry—Nos. 65, 107, 230, 280, and A154.
Gerault, John—Nos. 82, 117, 175, 189, and A133.

Harrison, Richard—Nos. 102, 135, 139, 183, and B133.
Merriweather, James—Nos. 26, 92, 150, 214, and A106.
Montgomery, James—Nos. 6, 83, 127, 252, and C133.
Perault, Michael—Nos. 23, 78, 256, 277, and C106.
Robertson, James—Nos. 25, 200, 260, 294, and B106.
Slaughter, Lawrence—Nos. 8, 58, 157, 221, and A271.
Swan, John—Nos. 37, 98, 100, 209, and B156.
Todd, Levi—Nos. 29, 46, 87, 290, and C271.
Williams, Jarrott—Nos. 197, 241, 258, 268, and part 160.
Wilson, Thomas—Nos. 10, 45, 47, 298, and A169.

ENSIGN.

(2,156 acres.)

Vanmeter, Jacob—Nos. 7, 64, 182, 232, and 156 acres in B155.

CORNET.

(2,156 acres.)

Thurston, John—Nos. 53, 244, 278, 292, and 156 acres in A155.

SERGEANTS.

(216 acres each.)

Brand, John—16 acres in 169 and 200 acres in D and E130.
Brown, James—16 acres in 169 and 200 acres in D & E273.
Crump, William—16 acres in 169 and 200 acres in A184.
Dewit, Henry—16 acres in 196 and 200 acres in 121.
Elms, William—16 acres in 169 and 200 acres in 108.
Irby, James—16 acres in 169 and 200 acres in A and B138.
Kellar, Isaac—16 acres in 169 and 200 acres in C and D245.
Key, Thomas—16 acres in 194 and 200 acres in B and E245.
Merriweather, Wm—16 acres in 169 and 200 acres in 4.
Miles, Michael—16 acres in 169 and 200 acres in A and B85.
Moore, John—16 acres in 169 and 200 acres in A and B126.
Morgan, Charles—16 acres in 196 and 200 acres in 178.
Oreer, John—16 acres in 160 and 100 acres in C211 and 100 acres in 31.
Parker, Edward—16 acres in 169 and 200 acres in part of 4.
Patterson, Robert—16 acres in 169 and 200 acres in D and E177.
Pittman, Buckner—16 acres in 169 and 200 acres in D and E171.

Prichard, William—16 acres in 169 and 200 acres in C and D124
Rubey, William—16 acres in 169 and 200 acres in C and D118.
Strode, Sam—16 acres in 169 and 200 acres in 19.
Treat, Beverly—16 acres in 169 and 200 acres in A and B142.
Vaughn, John—16 acres in 196 and 200 acres in 178.
Walker, John—16 acres in 169 and 200 acres in A and B130.
Williams, John—16 acres in 169 and 200 acres in B and E124.`

PRIVATES.

(108 acres each.)

Allen, David—8 acres in 196 and 100 acres in 188.
Anderson, Joseph—8 acres in 210 and 100 acres in C178.
Ash, John—8 acres in 210 and 100 acres in 19.
Asher, William—8 acres in 210 and 100 acres in C59.
Bailey, David—8 acres in 210 and 100 acres in B195.
Barnet, Robt.—8 acres in 210 and 100 acres in C162.
Batten, Thos.—8 acres in 210 and 100 acres in A273.
Baxter, James—8 acres in 210 and 100 acres in C273.
Buckley, William—8 acres in 208 and 100 acres in D162.
Bell, William—8 acres in part of 210 and 100 acres in 184.
Bell, Sam—8 acres in 210 and 100 acres in A162.
Bentley, James—8 acres in 196 and 100 acres in 184.
Bentley, John—8 acres in 196 and 100 acres in 184.
Bethey, Elisha—8 acres in 210 and 100 acres in E108.
Bigger, James—8 acres in 210 and 100 acres in 262.
Bilderback, Charles—8 acres in 210 and 100 acres in D85.
Blackford, Sam'l—8 acres in 196 and 100 acres in 20.
Blankenship, Henry—8 acres in 210 and 100 acres in B162.
Booton, Travis—8 acres in 248 and 100 acres in C85.
Booton, William—8 acres in 48 and 100 in B44.
Bowen, Ebenezer—8 acres in 210 and 100 acres in A128.
Boyles John—8 acres in 210 and 100 acres in C60.
Bryant, James—8 acres in 196 and 100 acres in 188.
Bulger, Edward—8 acres in 210 and 100 acres in A195.
Burk, Nicholas—8 acres in 210 and 100 acres in 113.
Bush, William—8 acres in 196 and 100 acres in 219.
Cameron, Angus—8 acres in 210 and 100 acres in C281.
Camp, Reuben—8 acres in 196 and 100 acres in 86.
Campbell, John—8 acres in 248 and 100 acres in D60.
Camper, Moses—8 acres in 169 and 100 acres in E52.

Camper, Tilman—8 acres in 210 and 100 acres in C52.

Conore, Andrew—8 acres in 210 and 100 acres in A170.

Chapman, William—8 acres in 210 and 100 acres in A205.

Chenowith, Richard—8 acres in 101 and 100 acres in C30.

Clark, Andrew—8 acres in 196 and 100 acres in 231.

Clark, George—8 acres in 210 and 100 acres in E205.

Clifton, Thomas—8 acres in 196 and 100 acres in 188.

Cofer, William—8 acres in 210 and 100 acres in B286.

Choheren, Dennis—8 acres in 210 and 100 acres in C231.

Copland, Cornelius—8 acres in 210 and 100 acres in A60.

Consule, Harman—8 acres in 210 and 100 acres in C205.

Cowan, John—8 acres in 210 and 100 acres in A231.

Cox, Richard—8 acres in 210 and 100 acres in B59.

Cozer, Jacob—8 acres in 210 and 100 acres in B205.

Cozer, Peter—8 acres in 210 and 100 acres in B52.

Craze, Noah—8 acres in 210 and 100 acres in A52.

Crosley, William—8 acres in 169 and 100 acres in D52.

Curry, James—8 acres in 210 and 100 acres in D205.

Curtis, Rice—8 acres in 210 and 100 acres in B60.

Davies, Asael—8 acres in 246 and 100 acres in C220.

Davis, Robert—8 acres in 141 and 100 acres in E59.

Dawson, James—8 acres in 210 and 100 acres in 113.

Doherty, Frederick—8 acres in 141 and 100 acres in A220.

Doherty, Neal—8 acres in 101 and 100 acres in D30.

Doran, Patrick—8 acres in 141 and 100 acres in E220.

Dudley, Amistead—8 acres in 210 and 100 acres in E60.

Duff, John—8 acres in 141 and 100 acres in 86.

Elms, James—8 acres in 141 and 100 acres in 86.

Elms, John—8 acres in 141 and 100 acres in D220.

Evans, Charles—8 acres in 141 and 100 acres in B220.

Faris, Isaac—8 acres in 141 and 100 acres in B94.

Fear, Edmund—8 acres in 141 and 100 acres in C73.

Finley, Samuel—8 acres in 32 and 100 acres in D30.

Finn, James—8 acres in 32 and 100 acres in E 94.

Flanaghan, Dominick—8 acres in 141 and 100 acres in A73.

Floyd, Isham—8 acres in 196 and 100 acres in 188.

Foster, William—8 acres in 32 and 100 acres in A30.

Freeman, William—8 acres in 141 and 100 acres in E73.

Flogget, William—8 acres in 32 and 100 acres in 121.

Frost, Stephen—8 acres in 141 and 100 acres in B73.

Funk, Henry—8 acres in 141 and 100 acres in D73.

Garrot, Robert—8 acres in 169 and 100 acres in C224.

Gaskins, Thomas—8 acres in 276 and 100 acres in B273.
Gagnia, Lewis—8 acres in 196 and 100 acres in 113.
Gaylor, Gasper—8 acres in 194 and 100 acres in D224.
Gilmore, George—8 acres in 276 and 100 acres in C94.
Glass, Michael—8 acres in 196 and 100 acres in 121.
Glenn, David—8 acres in 216 and 100 acres in 20.
Godfrey, Francis—8 acres in 276 and 100 acres in A94.
Goodwin, William—8 acres in 196 and 100 acres in 262.
Gray, George—8 acres in 216 and 100 acres in E224.
Greathouse, William—8 acres in 216 and 100 acres in B224.
Green, John—8 acres in 276 and 100 acres in D94.
Grimes, John—8 acres in 196 and 100 acres in A124.
Guthrie William—8 acres in 216 and 100 acres in A281.
Gwin, William—8 acres in 74 and 100 acres in A224.
Hacker, John—8 acres in 148 and 100 acres in B28.
Hammet, James—8 acres in 133 and 100 acres in E138.
Hardin, Francis—8 acres in 133 and 100 acres in D138.
Harland, Silas—8 acres in 190 and 100 acres in D13.
Harris, James—8 acres in 190 and 100 acres in D28.
Harris, John M—8 acres in 106 and 100 acres in E128.
Harris, Samuel, Sr.—8 acres in 106 and 100 acres in D128.
Harris, Samuel, Jr.—8 acres in 106 and 100 acres in C128.
Hatten, Christopher—8 acres in 148 and 100 acres in A28.
Hayes, Thomas—8 acres in 196 and 100 acres in 198.
Henry, David—8 acres in 154 and 100 acres in A57.
Henry, Hugh—8 acres in 154 and 100 acres in B57.
Henry, Isaac—8 acres in 154 and 100 acres in A13.
Henry, John—8 acres in 154 and 100 acres in B13.
Higgins, Barney—8 acres in 190 and 100 acres in D57.
Holmes, James—8 acres in 160 and 100 acres in E13.
Honaker, Henry—8 acres in 133 and 100 acres in C57.
Honaker, Peter—8 acres in 133 and 100 acres in E57.
Hooper, Thomas—8 acres in 149 and 100 acres in part 19.
House, Andrew—8 acres in 148 and 100 acres in E28.
Hughes, John—8 acres in 148 and 100 acres in C28.
Humphris, Samuel—8 acres in 190 and 100 acres in C13.
Isaacs, John—8 acres in 271 and 100 acres in B123.
James, Abraham—8 acres in 155 and 100 acres in D198.
January, James—8 acres in 271 and 100 acres in C198.
Jarrald, James—8 acres in 155 and 100 acres in B128.
Johnson, John—8 acres in 271 and 100 acres in E170.
Johnston, Edward—8 acres in 196 and 100 acres in part 113.

Jones, Charles—8 acres in 169 and 100 acres in A198.

Jones, David—8 acres in 271 and 100 acres in C138.

Jones, John—8 acres in 194 and 100 acres in B198.

Jones, Mathew—8 acres in 169 and 100 acres in C170.

Joynes, John—8 acres in 196 and 100 acres in 219.

Kendall, Benjamin—8 acres in 155 and 100 acres in 245.

Kendall, William—8 acres in 196 and 100 acres in D44.

Kenton, Simon—8 acres in 155 and 100 acres in E198.

Key, George—8 acres in 246 and 100 acres in C79.

Leare, William—8 acres in 196 and 100 acres in A54.

Lemon, John—8 acres in 196 and 100 acres in A119.

Levingston, George—8 acres in 196 and 100 acres in 86.

Lindsay, Arthur—8 acres in 196 and 100 acres in D79.

Lockart, Pleasant—8 acres in 196 and 100 acres in D54.

Lovell, Richard—8 acres in 196 and 100 acres in 219.

Lunsford, George—8 acres in 196 and 100 acres in 86.

Lunsford, Mason—8 acres in 246 and 100 acres in E44.

Lunsford, Moses—8 acres in 246 and 100 acres in E119.

Lusado, Abraham—8 acres in 196 and 100 acres in A79.

Lutterell, Richard—8 acres in 169 and 100 acres in B79.

Lines, John—8 acres in 196 and 100 acres in C119.

Lyne, Joseph—8 acres in 196 and 100 acres in E79.

McBride, Isaac—8 acres in 74 and 100 acres in D130.

McDermet, Francis—8 acres in 196 and 100 acres in B54.

McDonald, David—8 acres in 248 and 100 acres in A211.

McGar, John—8 acres in 196 and 100 acres in 219.

McIntire, Alexander—8 acres in 101 and 100 acres in C130.

McManus, George—8 acres in 74 and 100 acres in A286.

McManus, John, Sr.—8 acres in 74 and 100 acres in D286.

McManus, John, Jr.—8 acres in 74 and 100 acres in C286.

McMullen, Samuel—8 acres in 196 and 100 acres in A254.

McNutt, James—8 acres in 196 and 100 acres in E126.

Mayfield, Micajah—8 acres in 196 and 100 acres in D184.

Mahoney, Florence—8 acres in 74 and 100 acres in E281.

Manifee, Jonas—8 acres in 106 and 100 acres in E254.

Marr, Patrick—8 acres in 196 and 100 acres in 219.

Martin, Charles—8 acres in 74 and 100 acres in B254.

Mershorn, Nathaniel—8 acres in 74 and 100 acres in C254.

Millar, Abraham—8 acres in 196 and 100 acres in C54.

Montgomery, John—8 acres in 196 and 100 acres in 231.

Monroe, James—8 acres in 169 and 100 acres in D254.

Moore, John—8 acres in 196 and 100 acres in C126.

Moore, Thomas—8 acres in 196 and 100 acres in A123.
Murphy, John—8 acres in 196 and 100 acres in 86.
Murry, Edward—8 acres in 196 and 100 acres in E54.
Myers, William—8 acres in 196 and 100 acres in D126.
Nelson, Enoch G—8 acres in 74 and 100 acres in E85.
Newton, Peter—8 acres in 196 and 100 acres in 20.
Oakley, John—8 acres in 74 and 100 acres in 4.
O'Harrow, Michael—8 acres in 149 and 100 acres in B211.
Oreer, Daniel—8 acres in 160 and 100 acres in 31.
Oreer, Jesse—8 acres in 160 and 100 acres in 31.
Oreer, William—4 acres in 210, 4 in 196 and 100 in 31.
Osburn, Ebenezer—8 acres in 74 and 100 acres in E211.
Oundsley, Charles—8 acres in 74 and 100 acres in D211.
Pagan, David—8 acres in 196 and 100 acres in 19.
Paintree, John—8 acres in 74 and 100 acres in B177.
Patten, James—8 acres in 101 and 100 acres in B30.
Paul, John—8 acres in 74 and 100 acres in 123.
Peters, John—8 acres in 74 and 100 acres in B281.
Phelps, Josiah—8 acres in 74 and 100 acres in A177.
Pickens, Samuel—8 acres in 74 and 100 acres in 121.
Piner, Jesse—8 acres in 74 and 100 acres in B171.
Prather, Henry—8 acres in 74 and 100 acres in C171.
Priest, Peter—8 acres in 74 and 100 acres in A171.
Pruitt, Josiah—8 acres in 74 and 100 acres in D170.
Purcell, William—8 acres in 196 and 100 acres in 123.
Pulford, John—8 acres in 74 and 100 acres in E31.
Ramsey, James—8 acres in 74 and 100 acres in D119.
Ray, William—8 acres in 74 and 100 acres in B118.
Rubey, William—8 acres in 74 and 100 acres in A118.
Ruddle, Cornelius—8 acres in 74 and 100 acres in E118.
Rulison, William—8 acres in 74 and 100 acres in C177.
Ross, Joseph—8 acres in 196 and 100 acres in 113.
Sartine, John—8 acres in 74 and 100 acres in D116.
Sartine, Page—8 acres in 74 and 100 acres in C116.
Saunders, John—8 acres in 74 and 100 acres in A174.
Severns—Ebenezer—8 acres in 74 and 100 acres in D174.
Severns, John—8 acres in 196 and 100 acres in 195.
Shepard, George—8 acres in 74 and 100 acres in A116.
Shepard, Peter—8 acres in 196 and 100 acres in 195.
Sitzer, John—8 acres in 74 and 100 acres in E2.
Sitzer, Michael—8 acres in 74 and 100 acres in B2.
Simpson, Thomas—8 acres in 74 and 100 acres in B59.

Slack, William—8 acres in 74 and 100 acres in E174.

Smith, George—8 acres in 149 and 100 acres in A2.

Smith, William—8 acres in 196 and 100 acres in C44.

Sworden, Jonathan—8 acres in 74 and 100 acres in E116.

Snow, George—8 acres in 74 and 100 acres in C174.

Spear, Jacob—8 acres in 74 and 100 acres in B174.

Spilman, Francis—8 acres in 74 and 100 acres in D2.

Spilman, James—8 acres in 196 and 100 acres in 262.

Stevens, Shep—8 acres in 196 and 100 acres in 108.

Stephenson, Samuel—8 acres in 74 and 100 acres in E286.

Swan, William—8 acres in 74 and 100 acres in A44.

Swearingen, Van—8 acres in 74 and 100 acres in B116.

Talley, John—8 acres in 74 and 100 acres in D142.

Taylor, Abraham—8 acres in 74 and 100 acres in C142.

Teall, Levi—8 acres in 74 and 100 acres in B170.

Thompson, William—8 acres in 74 and 100 acres in 262.

Thornton, Joseph—8 acres in 74 and 100 in C2.

Tygert, Daniel—8 acres in 196 and 100 acres in 108.

Taylor, William—8 acres in 74 and 100 acres in E142.

Vance, Hanley—8 acres in 74 and 100 acres in D243.

Vanmeter, Isaac—8 acres in 74 and 100 acres in C243.

Venshioner, George—8 acres in 74 and 100 acres in B119.

Walker, Thomas—8 acres in 74 and 100 acres in A210.

Watkins, Samuel—8 acres in 74 and 100 acres in A243.

Walen, Barney—8 acres in 74 and 100 acres in E255.

Welch, Dominique—8 acres in 149 and 100 acres in B255.

White, Layton—8 acres in 74 and 100 acres in D255.

White, Randall—8 acres in 196 and 100 acres in E195.

Whitecotton, James—8 acres in 74 and 100 acres in 123.

Whitley, William—8 acres in 74 and 100 acres in 262.

Whitehead, Robert—8 acres in 196 and 100 acres in 20.

Whitehead, William—8 acres in 196 and 100 acres in 20.

Wilson, Edward—8 acres in 74 and 100 acres in A255.

Williams, Daniel—8 acres in 74 and 100 acres in E243.

Witt, Robert—8 acres in 74 and 100 acres in B243.

Wood, James—8 acres in 169 and 100 acres in C255.

Yates, Isaac—8 acres in 74 and 100 acres in B210.

Zockledge, William—8 acres in 210 and 100 acres in E162.

RECAPITULATION.

1 Brigadier General	8,049	acres
1 Lieutenant Colonel	4,851	acres
3 Majors—4,312 acres each......................	11,936	acres
14 Captains—3,234 acres each....................	45,276	acres
20 Lieutenants—2,156 acres each.................	43,120	acres
23 Sergeants—216 acres each....................	4,968	acres
1 Ensign	2,156	acres
1 Cornet	2,156	acres
236 Privates—108 acres each....................	25,488	acres
300 Men	149,000	acres

The following table will show the number of the tract upon which the various cities, towns and villages were located, and the name of the soldier to whom same was allotted:

Charlestown, 117, Lieutenant John Gerault.
Charlestown Landing, 56, General George Rogers Clark.
Hamburg, 108, Sergeant William Elms and others.
Henryville, 254-5, Private James Monroe and others.
Herculaneum, 57, Private David Henry and others.
Hibernia, 105, Major William Lynn.
Jeffersonville, No. 1, Lieutenant Isaac Bowman.
Marysville, 248, Private Travis Booton and others.
Memphis, 203, Captain Robert Todd.
New Market, 196, Sergeant John Vaughan and others.
Otisco, 210, Private John Biggar and others.
Petersburg, 130, Private Isaac McBride and others.
Port Fulton, 2, Private Francis Spilman and others.
Sellersburg, 110, Captain Isaac Ruddle.
Springville, 94, Private Isaac Faris and others.
Utica, 16, Captain John Bailey; 17, Captain Robert George.
Watson, 36, Captain Robert Todd.
Clarksville, opposite the falls, just below and adjoining Jeffersonville.
Old fort above Fourteen Mile creek, 76, Lieutenant Valentine Dalton.

The deed for the Illinois grant was not recorded by the commissioners until about 1823. It appears on page 270 of Deed Record No. 30 in the deed records of Clark county. It is a peculiar coincidence that General Clark had a double title to the land which became his in the Illinois grant. After the close of his memorable campaign, where he had fairly earned the title "the Hannibal of the West," he lost no time in pacifying the Indians.   The loyal Piankeshaws held a council and insisted on presenting the General with a tract of land two and one-half leagues square, on the west side of the falls of the Ohio, the location of his subsequent grant from Virginia.

General Clark was a citizen of Clarksville for many years and took an active part in elections and public affairs, but being a bachelor, he divided his time between Indiana and Kentucky.   As early as 1783 a number of log houses had been built in Clarksville and a town government was organized, pursuant to the charter.   In the record book of the Trustees of Clarksville, pages 66 and 67, appears a resolution to confirm the title of the following persons, as they were the original settlers in the town:

David Owens, John Owens, brothers.
Levi Theel (Teall), private in Illinois regiment.
William Burgoe.
Robert George, captain in Illinois regiment.
William Clark.
Martin Carney.
John Jackson.
Valentine T. Dalton (lieutenant in Illinois regiment).
John Martin.
George Clear.
Christopher Hewet.
William Burge.
Jacob Miner.
John Cleghorn.
Joseph Cleghorn.
Joseph Sprolsman.
Philip Walkes.
Nancy Smith.
Buckner Pitman.

This resolution is dated August 7, 1784.   The town, however, did not prosper, and in 1797 there were but twenty houses in the place.   The Captain Robert George mentioned above had brought a party of settlers out to the "grant" from Pennsylvania, and some of the names in the resolution were of his party.   Mrs. Nancy Smith's daughter, aged twelve, was shot and scalped by the Indians in 1790.   She had gone to the spring about a quarter of a mile from the stockade for water, and after the Indians had scalped her they left her for dead.   The men in the fort brought her in and to the surprise of all, she finally recovered.   The hair on her head grew in again, but very coarse and snow white. She married a man named Pitman, who, with his family, afterwards emigrated down the river and settled on an island about twenty miles above Natchez, Mississippi, called Fairchild's Island.

The Valentine Dalton in the resolution drew the old stone fort at Fourteen Mile creek in the allotment of land in the grant.

The place selected by General Clark for his residence was at the upper end of the village on a point later on called General's Point. Here he had a full and delightful view of the falls, but he took little pains to improve the site, having raised only a small cabin. His lonely life here was enlivened at one time by a party of jovial hunters, who left him at the end of their visit in the best of spirits. Shortly after their departure he was stricken with paralysis and fell into the fire, burning one of his legs badly. This burn finally made amputation necessary and Dr. Ferguson performed the operation amid surroundings that are probably without a parallel. It was before the day of anaesthetics and a fife and drum corps marched around the cabin playing during the operation, and it is said that the old General kept time to the music with his fingers, and when the music finally stopped asked, "Well, is it off?"

He died at the home of his sister, Mrs. Lucy Croghan, at Locust Grove, Kentucky, February 13, 1818, and is buried in Cave Hill cemetery, Louisville, Kentucky.

CHAPTER IV.

ORGANIZATION OF CLARK COUNTY.

THE FIRST DECADE.

William Henry Harrison, the first Territorial Governor of the Territory of Indiana, created Clark county by gubernatorial proclamation February 3, 1801. Emigrants had begun to settle at many points along the Ohio river, and for the convenience of these settlers it became necessary to establish a new county by cutting off a portion of Knox county. Clark county was the first to be created out of the territory included within the original limits of Knox, so that she has the proud distinction of belonging to the second generation of Indiana counties. Knox county was organized June 20, 1790, by proclamation of General Arthur St. Clair, Governor of the Northwest Territory. This county not only included all of what is now Clark county, but nearly all of what is now Indiana. The new county which was to bear the name of the illustrious George Rogers Clark was a state in itself. The proclamation creating Clark county was dated February 3, 1801, and the description of the tract is as follows: Beginning on the Ohio at the mouth of Blue river, now the boundary line between Harrison and Crawford counties, up the said river to where the trail leading from Vincennes to the Ohio Falls crosses said river; thence by direct route to the nearest point on (the east fork) White river; thence up said river to the branch thereof which runs towards Fort Recovery, and from the head springs of said branch to Fort Recovery; thence along the boundary line between Indiana Territory and the Northwest Territory, south to the Ohio river; thence down said river to the place of beginning. It may be difficult to trace these lines at the present day, but the point on Blue river where the line left the stream was about where the town of Fredericksburg is located in the southern part of Washington county. The line runs almost north through the entire length of Washington county until it strikes the east fork of the White river. This stream is followed in a northeastwardly direction through Jackson, Bartholomew, Shelby, Rush and Henry counties. The line runs from a point at the head springs of this stream in a straight line northeastwardly through Randolph and Jay counties to Fort Recovery, which is situated just across the Ohio state line, about opposite the center of Jay county. The line returns to the Ohio river at the mouth of the Kentucky river and thence down the Ohio to the point of beginning. Here indeed was a magnificent scope of territory. It included either in whole or part the following counties: Harrison, Floyd, Clark, Washington, Jackson, Scott, Jefferson, Jennings, Ripley, Decatur, Franklin, Bartholomew, Shelby, Rush, Fayette, Union, Henry, Randolph, Wayne and possibly part of Jay and Switzerland counties.

No other name could have been applied to this noble tract of land which included within its bounds not only the town of Clarksville, but also the grant of land given to General Clark, his officers and men by the state of Virginia, January 2, 1781.

At this early day there were but few families residing in the wilderness which is now embraced in the bounds of Clark county. One family resided at the present site of Charlestown—a few more south and southeast of here, and a few more six miles east at a place called "Armstrong's Station."

Clark county at its creation embraced about one-fifth of the present area of the state of Indiana. It would have been appropriate if Clarksville could have been chosen as the countyseat, but geographical considerations had to be remembered, so the town of Springville was selected April 7, 1801, as the new seat of justice.

Springville was a rising and prosperous little town, about four miles from the river, and about one mile southwest of Charlestown. As early as 1799 a Frenchman kept a store at the place where Springville was afterwards located. One of the principal traders was a man named Tully, and for this reason the Indians called the place Tullytown. The town of Springville was platted about the year 1800 and in 1802 it was a thriving little village of probably one hundred bona fide inhabitants. It was on the old Indian trail from the falls of the Ohio to the Indian nations of the north, west and east. Being the first camping station north of the falls, it naturally prospered. It was laid off almost wholly on survey No. 115 of Clark's Grant. (See plat.) The streets running north and south were seventy feet wide and those running east and west were one hundred feet wide. The lots were one hundred feet front and two hundred feet deep. In 1801 the prospects of the little town were brightest. There were two taverns, one kept by John Ferguson and the other by Nicholas Harrison, who also had a store. The latter was also a Justice of the Peace. There was a blacksmith shop, a wheelwright shop, a hatter shop, etc. Old Dr. Vale was the physician. Even Shelby county surveyor, etc. Near by a still house operated. A short distance west lived Jonathan Jennings, the first Governor of Indiana. Just below the town on Pleasant run John Bottorff carried on the milling business. The location of the still houses and trading posts made Springville a great rendezvous for Indians, and this, together with its location on the trail, made it a very prosperous village for those days.

The settlers in this locality were often alarmed by the drunkenness and insolence of the Indians, who had traded and bartered at Tullytown. Here the red men were swindled out of their skins, venison and bear meat by the villainy of the Frenchmen and the small price which they received for their goods was usually invested in whisky, ruinous to themselves and dangerous to the settlers. They would generally get no further from Springville on their way homeward than where Charlestown is now situated, and their drunken revels would make night hideous and usually resulted in bloodshed.

Springville and vicinity was at this time the only purely American settlement in Indiana off of the river, although there were Americans scattered all through the French settlements elsewhere.

After the county seat was removed to Jeffersonville, June 9, 1802, the town began to dwindle away until within a few years it had wholly disappeared. Not a vestige of it now remains to tell the curious where it stood, and where once was heard the sound of simple industry, where once the leading men of early days met to transact the necessary business of the courts, nothing remains but a rural scene, a winding country road and the song of birds above the growing crops.

On April 7, 1801, the first court in Clark county was held at Springville. It was named the Court of General Quarter Sessions of the Peace, and it was created by the Governor, William Henry Harrison. It was composed of Justices Marston, Green Clark, Abraham Huff, James Noble Wood, Thomas Downs, William Goodwin, John Gibson, Charles Tuley and William Harwood. The men composing this court were the leading citizens of the county at the time, and nearly all have left their mark upon some phase of our early history.

The first and most important work of the court was to divide the county into townships, so that the administration of justice might begin an active operation. The boundaries of the three townships of Clarksville, Springville and Spring Hill, into which the county was divided, were given as follows:

The first to begin on the Ohio, opposite the mouth of Blue river; thence up the Ohio to the mouth of Peter McDaniel's spring branch; from thence in direct course to Pleasant run, the branch on which Joseph Bartholomew lives, and down that branch to the mouth thereof; thence down Pleasant run to where the same enters into Silver creek; thence a due west course to the western boundary of this county; to be called and known by the name of Clarksville township.

The second to begin at the mouth of Peter McDaniel's spring branch; thence up the Ohio to the mouth of Fourteen Mile creek; thence up the main branch thereof to the head; and from thence a due west course to the county line, and from thence with the same to Clarksville township, and with the line thereof to the Ohio at the place of beginning; to be called and known by the name of Springville township.

The third one began at the mouth of Fourteen Mile creek; thence with

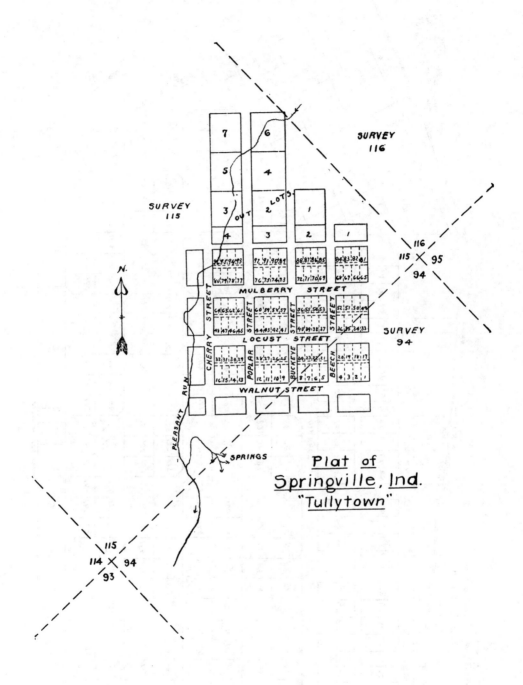

SURVEY
116

SURVEY
115

SURVEY
94

N.

OUT LOTS

7   6
5   4
3   2   1
4   3   2   1

116
115 X 95
94

MULBERRY STREET

CHERRY STREET

POPLAR STREET

BUCKEYE STREET

BEECH STREET

LOCUST STREET

WALNUT STREET

PLEASANT RUN

SPRINGS

115
114 X 94
93

Plat of
Springville, Ind.
"Tullytown"

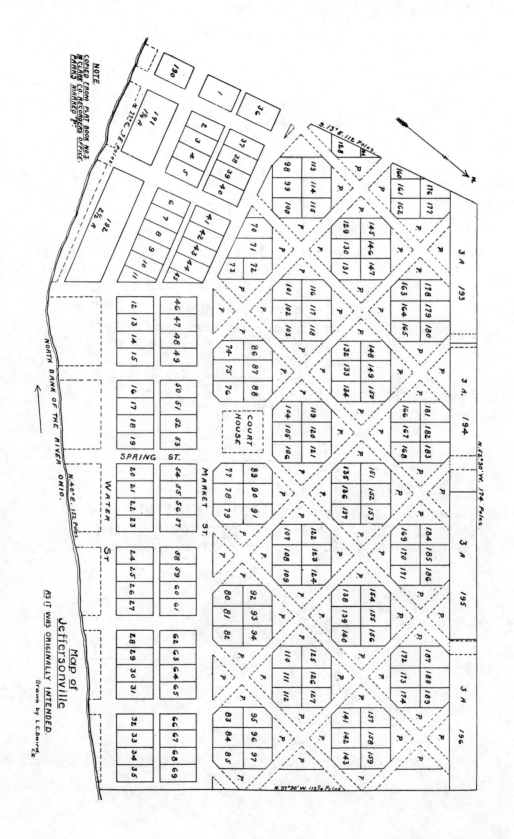

Map of
Jeffersonville

AS IT WAS ORIGINALLY INTENDED.

Drawn by L.C.Baird,
C.E.

NOTE
COPIED FROM PLAT BOOK No.3
IN CLARK CO. RECORDERS OFFICE.
PARKS MARKED "P".

the line of Springville township to the county line; thence with the same to the Ohio river; and thence down the same, to include the remaining part of the county, to the place of beginning; to be called and known by the name of Spring Hill township.

From these three original townships the number has grown to twelve. Jeffersonville, Utica, Charlestown, Owen and Bethlehem townships border upon the river; Union is in the center; Carr and Silver Creek are on the west; Monroe and Wood are on the north and northwest; Washington and Oregon are in the northeast.

The first "constables of the county" were Charles Floyd for Clarksville township, William F. Tuley for Springville and Robert Wardel for Spring Hill.

The court transacted a great amount of business and appointed all the necessary officers for the county. Samuel Gwathmey was appointed Protho-notary Clerk of the several courts: Jesse Rowland, Judge of Probate; Davis Floyd, Recorder; Thomas Douns, Treasurer; Marston G. Clark, Surveyor; Samuel Hay, Sheriff; Peter McDonald, Coroner.

On December 24, 1803, Davis Floyd and John Owens were appointed and commissioned pilots on the Falls. August 14, 1802, the court ordered the first jail built at Jeffersonville. It was built by William Goodwin, with Davis Floyd on his bond of nine hundred dollars.

This was a most vigorous beginning for the young county, but the re-moval of the county seat to Jeffersonville sounded taps to Springville's hopes as well as reveille to the ambition of the little village on the banks of the Ohio. However, Springville remained a village as late as 1810.

Jeffersonville had grown to be a scattering border of houses and stores along the river front, extending up from old Fort Steuben. On June 23, 1802, Isaac Bowman, who owned tract No. 1 of Clark's Grant, disposed of part of it to Marston Green Clark, William Goodwin, Richard Pile, Davis Floyd and Samuel Gwathmey as trustees to lay off a town and sell lots. The tract con-tained one hundred and fifty acres and John Gwathmey laid it off according to a design said to have been devised by Thomas Jefferson, for whom the town was named. The original plan resembled a checker-board; the black squares to be sold in lots, the red squares to be crossed diagonally by streets, leaving four triangular spaces for parks in each square through which the streets passed. This design was not adhered to, and the present plan was adopted in 1817. The boundaries of the original town of Jeffersonville are as follows: Beginning at a point on the north bank of the Ohio river at low-water mark, eighty-eight feet west of the west line of Fort street; thence parallel with the west line of Fort street to a point on Ohio avenue fifty feet south of the south line of Court avenue; thence with a line parallel to the south line of Court avenue and fifty feet from it to the west line of Watt street; thence with the

4

west line of Watt street to a point on the north bank of the Ohio river a low-water mark; thence with the meanderings of the north bank at low-water mark to the beginning; containing about one hundred and fifty acres.

About this time settlements began to be made in Bethlehem township, and the Plaskets, Rodgers, Giltners, Hamiltons, Kellys, Thislers, Abbotts and Simingtons began to improve their new farms. Jacob Giltner, Sr., came from Kentucky to Clark county about 1808, but was born in Pennsylvania in 1767. His wife, Elizabeth Donagan, was from Lancaster county, of the same date. When the family came to Clark county there were four in the household—two daughters, Elizabeth and Mary, and Mr. and Mrs. Giltner.

Jacob Giltner bought three quarter sections of land at the land office in Jeffersonville. For many years after becoming a resident of the township he ran a distillery in connection with farming. By trade he was a linen stamper, when goods were made of that kind by the pioneers. During the War of 1812 he was drafted, but on account of a physical disability was exempted. He was a member of the Lutheran church, and died in 1859. Mrs. Giltner died a few months after her husband, in the same year.

William Kelly, Sr., was born in Virginia, but was taken to Kentucky by his parents when a child, and came to Clark county in 1806. He married Margaret Kelly, who bore him thirteen children, four dying in infancy, the remaining nine growing up to maturity. He located one mile and a half northwest of Bethlehem village, before the land was surveyed. When the surveys were completed he attended the public sale in Jeffersonville in 1809, but previously had made no clearing, on account of the uncertainty of getting the land desired. He bought two quarter sections, and began the work of improvement. He died June 27, 1837. Mrs. Kelly died September 13, 1854.

William Kelly, Jr., was born August 12, 1812, and married Elizabeth Starr, whose maiden name was Hammond, May 4, 1858. There are but few of the Kelly's left in the county.

William, son of Archibald and Sarah Hamilton, was born near Frankfort, Kentucky, October 10, 1790. When twenty-two years of age he emigrated with his mother and two sisters to Bethlehem township, landing at the mouth of Knob creek March 25, 1812. The Ohio river at that time made landing easy by the backwater up these small streams. He immediately opened a tannery on one of the branches of Knob creek, which he ran till his death in 1845. His son, John T., continued in the business of his father up to 1865, when the old tannery was abandoned for more lucrative employment. William Hamilton married Margaret Byers (who was born near McBride's Mill, Woodford county, Kentucky, April 4, 1795, and who came to Jefferson county, Indiana, in 1816), October 30, 1821. Mrs. Hamilton died May 9, 1875, near Otto.

Robert Simington was a settler and an owner of land in the township in 1805, though his claim was subject to dispute after the public sales in 1809.

He owned seven hundred and fifty acres in fractional sections 32 and 33. Simington left in 1817, after selling most of his property, and settled one mile beyond Hanover, in Jefferson county, Indiana, where he died in 1849.

The Abbotts were among the first men of their day, considered in the light of sportsmen. John Abbott was the ancestor of the Abbotts in this county, and from him descended many of the same name.

John Thisler began clearing off land below Bethlehem at an early day. The old farm now runs up close to the village.

Moses Rodgers was among the first and most successful of the early settlers.

Lucas and William Plaskett, the latter a flat boatman, were here during the first decade.

All these men, with their wives and families, took an active part in preparing the way for future generations; and to their credit it can be truly said, they did their work well. Let us see that posterity shall improve on the past.

The first settler in Monroe township was Robert Biggs, who came here in 1806 from Kentucky. He settled on Biggs's fork of Silver creek. Biggs lived and died in sight of Henryville. He took much pleasure in hunting, and was considered a superior marksman.

Joseph Miller settled in sight of Henryville about 1806, or, what is more probable, a year or two afterwards; for Robert Biggs must have married one of his daughters. Miller was from Kentucky; his family consisted mostly of daughters, the only son dying many years since, and of course the family name is now extinct. He died about 1830.

Nicholas Crist, a brother-in-law of Abner Biggs, settled about one mile west of Henryville in 1808 or 1810. He was born in Pennsylvania, but came here from Kentucky. He married a daughter of Robert Biggs. Crist removed to Clay county, Indiana, in 1830 or 1831, and died at an extreme old age.

Robert Carns, who was from Pennsylvania by way of Kentucky, settled one mile east of Henryville about 1810. He carried on farming.

Zebulon Collins, who was no doubt a brother of the famous scout and hunter, William Collins, settled a year or two before the Pigeon Roost massacre one mile and a half east of Henryville. Here he began to operate a still house, and finally a way tavern on the Charlestown and Brownstown road. During a part of his life he was chosen as a justice of the peace. It was at his tavern that the first polls were opened in the township, and from this fact the township derived its first name, that of Collins. The township was abolished afterwards and the territory was taken into other townships. It was here that a company of soldiers was stationed in 1813 when Mr. Huffman was killed by the Indians, to protect the frontier. Collins was originally from Pennsylvania.

Mr. Huffman was an emigrant from Pennsylvania and settled on the west bank of Silver creek, one and a half miles from Henryville, three or four years before his death, in 1813.

Among the later settlers who came after Indiana was admitted as a state were James Allen and David McBride, brothers-in-law, from Pennsylvania. Juda Hemming, who emigrated from Kentucky, and Islam McCloud, of South Carolina, were the only early settlers in the township in the extreme south side.

The most prominent family in the extreme west was that of Lawrence Kelly, who came from Pennsylvania, and was here as early as 1810. His sons were Hugh, John, Abram, William and Davis, who lived in the township till their deaths. Martha Kelly married John Lewis, Sr., of Monroe township. Another daughter married William Blakely, a Virginian, but here from Kentucky. One of the daughters married William Patrick, whose descendants are quite numerous in the county at this time.

John Deitz and wife, both Germans, came to Monroe from Kentucky while the grant was yet in its infancy.

On the west side of the township, near the Oregon line, William Beckett, of Pennsylvania, settled about 1810. His family was very large, and consisted mainly of sons. He died many years ago. There are now but few of the family, with their descendants, in this section.

Josiah Thomas settled in the same section years ago, marrying one of the Beckett girls.

During the years when the other townships were filling up with settlers rapidly, Monroe was left out in the cold. There were no early permanent settlers between Henryville and the Pigeon Roost settlement.

William E. Collins, by birth a Pennsylvanian, was one of the first white men in the neighborhood of the northwestern corner of the township. He came secondarily from the interior of Kentucky, whither he had gone from Louisville in quest of game. Learning that game was abundant in this region —the Pigeon Roost ground—he came hither. His son Henry met his death from the hands of the Indians. Kearns, one of the oldest sons of the family, settled near the old battleground in 1813, where he resided until his death.

Seymour Guernsey was born in Connecticut, and emigrated to Utica township, Clark county, in 1817. From Olean Point, on the Ohio river, about one hundred and fifty miles above Pittsburg, the family took passage in a boat, on which they made the entire trip to their place of landing. Mehetabel Beardsley, his wife, was born in New Haven, Connecticut, and bore him before arriving here two sons—Burritt and Seymour—and one daughter—Malinda Ann. After remaining in the vicinity of Utica for one year and raising a crop he removed to Monroe township, where he and his wife died. The marriage produced four sons and two daughters.

One of the most prominent families in this township is the Willey family. Barzillai Willey was a soldier of the Revolution, and was born in New York, and came to Cincinnati in 1808 from Utica, in that state. All the land below the city at that time belonged to the Harrisons and Sedams. After remaining here for two years, accumulating a boatload of produce, he started for New Orleans. Arriving at the Falls of the Ohio, he found them impassable, and anchored on the west side. After waiting here some time for the river to rise, and having his merchandise damaged considerably by the cold weather, he sold his load to the best advantage possible and made Jeffersonville his home for one year. In 1811 he moved to Monroe township and settled near Memphis; but at that time there was no such township as Union in the county. After a life of much hardship and ripe experience, he died at the residence of his son, J. F. Willey, in the township of Utica, n 1854.

Colonel John Fletcher Willey, the son of Barzillai Willey, was one of the foremost Union men in Southern Indiana during the war of the Rebellion.

In Oregon township the Henthorns, who settled in the vicinity of New Market, came from Virginia. Robert Henthorn, the founder of the village, was a prominent man in the affairs of his time.

The Coverts came from Pennsylvania in 1798 and settled near the old site of Work's mill. The family was composed of Bergen, Daniel, Peter and John Covert.

In 1817 James A. Watson came to Clark county and settled on grant No. 59. He moved to Oregon township in 1850, and settled on the bottoms of Poke run.

One of the early and most prominent families in Oregon was the Henlys. They rose to occupy some of the highest positions in the gift of the people. Thomas J. Henly represented the third district of Indiana in congress for two or three terms. In 1842 he and Joseph L. White fought a hard battle for congressional honors. This district being overwhelmingly Democratic, it was almost impossible for a Whig to secure a prominent office. White lost the election and Henly went to congress.

In the northwest corner of Oregon township the early settlers were made up of John Taflinger and family, John Todd and family, Alexander McClure and James Beckett, with their wives and families. Many of their descendants are now living in this part of the township, well-to-do farmers and artisans.

In Silver Creek township the Poindexter family was quite an early one. C. S. Poindexter, a native of Virginia, was born in 1797, and came to New Albany with his father's family at an early age. After remaining in New Albany for a short time, he removed to the vicinity of Sellersburg, where he had previously bought a tract of land from Absalom Littell. Nancy (Holland) Poindexter, his wife, was born in Virginia and died in Sellersburg in 1854, at an advanced age. By this marriage were born seven children, five sons and two daughters.

The Littell family came from Pennsylvania and settled on Silver creek, one mile east of Petersburg. There were five sons and two daughters.

The Wellses were from North Carolina. They settled on Camp run as early as 1800. There were four daughters and five sons.

William Adams was of Scotch-Irish extraction. He had a large family, and settled on Camp run.

An early statistician says there were five hundred voters in Clark county in 1840 by the name of Bottorff. John Bottorff was the father of twenty-six children. They were long-lived people, and from them descended a numerous posterity, who now live in nearly every state in the Union.

In 1794 James Noble Wood and his wife settled in Utica township on the present site of Utica. He established the first ferry there in 1795. He was the foremost man in the township in early days, and had a reputation of being a great hunter. Wood made three trips to New Orleans, the first in 1805, when the whole country from Louisville to Natchez was an unbroken wilderness. On returning he walked through the country of the Choctaw and Chickasaw nations. The second trip was made in 1806, and the third in 1807. James Noble Wood was present when most of the treaties were made with the Indians at Vincennes. He saw Tecumseh and his brother, the Prophet (Tuthnipe), and the chief Meshecanongue. In 1805 he met Aaron Burr at Jeffersonville, and with him was much pleased.

Judge Wood's character is evidenced by the active part he took in the affairs of his time. He died near Utica, March 25, 1826. He was a fine historian, a faithful citizen, a devoted husband, and withal a man of many excellent parts. Margaret Wood was of fine physique and very handsome. She had musical talents of no ordinary degree; she was also a fine swimmer. Her heart seemed to overflow with kindness and generosity, and in the world she had no enemies.

Basil R. Prather, the father of all the Prathers in the township, came here from North Carolina in 1801. His sons—Thomas, William, Walter, Basil R., Jr., Judge Samuel, Lloyd, John and Simon—were all married when they came here, except the last named. They settled throughout the township, and formed a class of men possessed of many admirable qualities.

Jeremiah Jacobs came here with his family from North Carolina in 1800, and settled near the old fort. His family was large, and its increase steady. A goodly number of his descendants are now living in this vicinity, respected and hospitable citizens.

In the fall of 1802 Matthew Crum, from Virginia, settled within one-half mile of the Union Methodist Episcopal church. He married his wife, Miss Margaret Spangler, near Louisville in 1800, who bore him one child, William S., born October 28, 1801, before coming to this township. The marriage of Matthew Crum and Margaret Spangler resulted in a family of ten sons and two daughters.

In 1819 John Lewman came to Utica township from North Carolina with his father. In this family were four brothers and three sisters.

Hezekiah Robertson was born in Maryland, and came with his father's family to this township when fifteen years of age. In the family there were six brothers and two sisters. They immediately began the work of clearing, living here the most of their lives.

In the year 1802 John and Elizabeth Schwartz came from Pennsylvania with a family of four children and settled five and a half miles above Jefferson-ville. His vocation was farming. In Indian wars he took an active part, but on account of his age did no fighting. His death was caused by an accident in June, 1824. Mrs. Schwartz lived to be over seventy years of age.

The Bottorffs settled in Utica township about the year 1815. In all affairs of the township they took a prominent part, and are now among the substantial people of the county.

The Lutz family came to Utica township from North Carolina and are now scattered over the township in considerable numbers.

There is no record of the first permanent settlement in Wood township. Whether George Wood was the first white man who settled in the township we cannot say; but it is quite certain he was among the first. Wood emigrated north in 1802 and settled near Charlestown, where he resided till 1807. He then removed to the Muddy Fork valley and settled for life one and a half miles below where New Providence was afterwards located. George Wood was a native of South Carolina; he died ten or twelve years after removing to this township.

After Wood came John and Robert Burge, James Smith, Matthew Barnaby, Moses Harman, Elijah Harman, James Warman and Simon Akers. To protect themselves from the savages a block house was erected on George Wood's farm in 1808. After this means of defense became generally known, John Giles, Jonathan Carr and Samuel Harrod came, accompanied by their families. In 1810 John McKinley, of Shelby county, Kentucky, settled in the same valley; in 1811 Samuel Packwood came from Shenandoah county, Virginia. The Burges, Harmans, Smith and Barnaby emigrated from North Carolina; Giles and Akers were from Kentucky; likewise Warman and a man named Frederick Gore and others. Carr and Harrod were from Pennsylvania. Harrod had two sons, William and Henry. The former was by trade a miller, and for many years owned a notable mill on Silver creek. Henry for several years was Clerk of Clark county.

In 1813 came James McKinley, brother of John, whose name we have already mentioned. William Packwood, brother of Samuel, came in 1819. These were the parents and grandparents of many sons and daughters now in this region, and well known far and near.

Among the other early settlers were Charles Robertson, James Baker and

brother Jesse, Micaiah Burns, Thompson Littell, William Kelly, Michael Borders, Christopher Morris, William Gibson, James Johnson and brother Lance-
lot, James Brown (who came from North Carolina in 1824 at six years of age
and settled in the Silver creek valley with his father's family), John Bell,
George Brock, Isaac Baggerly, Cyrus Bradford, George Goss and his brother
David, John Goss, Matthew West, Thomas Halow, mostly from the south.
Robertson was from Virginia, and the Bakers from South Carolina; Burns
was from Vermont; Littell and Bradford were from New York state; the remaining ones whose names have been mentioned were from North Carolina.

Among other early families in the county can be mentioned the Absalom
Little family, near Sellersburg; James, John and Charles Beggs, near Charlestown; John and David Owens, near Charlestown; the Pettitt family, near Solon; Nathan Robertson, near Charlestown; the Hay family and Parson Todd's
family, near Charlestown; Henry Bottorff, James Garner, David Lutz and
Mathias Hester, near Charlestown; Amos Goodwin, near Utica, and the
Amicks, Cortners and Clapps, in Oregon township. The customs of these
early people was simplicity and plainness of dress and address. Their lack of
wealth prevented the introduction of superfluity, and their dependence upon
each other seemed to endear them in their several associations.

During the first decade of Clark county history the settlements along the
river at Bethlehem, Utica, Jeffersonville and Clarksville, and those back at
Charlestown, Springville and New Providence, were the only ones in the county
where more than three or four families had congregated. Charlestown was
then the second town in the county, a population of probably four hundred people, in and near the place.

The land at this time was covered with an almost unbroken forest and
with canebrakes of vast extent. Game was unlimited, and the settlers had only
to venture into the forest to obtain an ample supply. The presence of a salt
lick attracted the denizens of the forest, and the fox, the panther, the cata-
mount, the wildcat, the bear, the black and gray wolf and the wild hog made the
journey through the forest extremely hazardous. Deer of several kinds, the
raccoon, the opossum, the otter and the mink were numerous, while the squir-
rels in some instances became a pest. Migratory fowls, such as the wild goose,
wild ducks, brant and sandhill cranes, were found in profusion, and the forests
were enlivened by the brilliant-hued plumage of thousands of paroquets. The
wild animals were to be feared next to the Indians, and more than one story
testifies to their ferocity when brought to bay or attacked.

James Anderson, who lived on Becket's Fork of Silver creek, shot at two
panthers while in the forest a short distance from his cabin, killing one. The
other attacked him ferociously and in the melee he lost his gun and his knife.
He fell on the beast and managed to get its face down, but not until it had

terribly lacerated him. After he had strangled the animal he recovered his rifle and killed it, but not until he was about hors de combat from loss of blood.

Up to the year 1800 it was unsafe to venture far from the settlements without weapons. Buffalo were reported by some of the early pioneers, Bull Creek being so named because a buffalo bull was killed near its mouth by one of the early settlers. One ambitious sportsman of this period declared that he had witnessed the last mastodon crossing the river from Kentucky near Fourteen Mile creek.

As early as 1794 a mill had been built on the Mill Run creek. It is mentioned in a deed recorded in Record No. 11, pages 188 to 190. This is evidently the earliest mill in the county. In 1800 Spencer Collins built a grist mill on Muddy Fork, near where the village of Petersburg now stands. It came into the hands of Samuel and Peter Bottarff in 1815. Montgomery's mill, one and three-fourths miles above Petersburg on Elk Run, was about the earliest mill in the northern part of the county. Some time between 1802 and 1804 John Schwartz put up a water mill in Utica township, on Six Mile creek. Straw's mill on Silver creek was put up not long after this date by Rezen Redman. In 1808 George Wood built the first mill in Wood township.

William Pervine was next to John Work in the milling business. He established a mill on Fourteen Mile creek about 1808. He did a big business, but sold out to a Mr. Walker in 1815. This mill was finally made into both a grist and saw mill and did many years service. These mills were among the earliest necessities of the settlers and their builders not only reaped their reward from the business, but added to the attractiveness of the county by building them.

In 1803 Samuel Gwathmey built the first frame house in Jeffersonville. Before this time log houses sheltered the seven hundred inhabitants of the village. The first licensed ferry at Jeffersonville was established in 1803 by Marston G. Clark. In 1808 a Mr. Sullivan established and ran a ferry between Bethlehem and Westport, Kentucky. With the early settlers of Clark county the matter of schools and churches was not wholly forgotten. In subsequent chapters both the schools and the various churches will be treated fully. It is worthy of note here that the first Methodist church in Indiana was built near Charlestown in 1807, and the building, "old Bethel meeting house", built of logs, still stands. The year 1806 is memorable as the date of the visit and scheeming of Aaron Burr, and his use of the canal project to cover his political designs in the West. On August 24, 1805, the Territorial Legislature of Indiana, passed an act incorporating the Indiana Canal Company for the purpose of digging a canal around the Falls of the Ohio at Jeffersonville and Clarksville. The incorporators were Aaron Burr, John Brown, George Rogers Clark, Jonathan Dayton, Davis Floyd, Benjamin Hovey, Josiah Stevens, William Croghan, John Gwathmey, John Harrison, Marston G. Clark and Samuel

C. Vance. The project was a most important one for Jeffersonville and Clarksville, and was commented upon by several travelers of that period as the beginning of a period of prosperity and growth. The line as surveyed seemed more practical than the one marked off on the Louisville side of the river. The attempt of Burr, Hovey and others to secure the canal for Indiana led the Kentuckians to try their chances, and with governmental aid their project was carried to completion. The inability of the Indiana incorporators to finance their scheme no doubt gave their competitors a great advantage, and the arrest of Burr on a charge of treason in 1807 made the success of the undertaking an impossibility. The estimates of the cost of this canal are amusing.

The total cost was estimated at two hundred and fifty-two thousand six hundred and thirty-eight dollars. This included the purchase of two hundred negroes at six hundred dollars each, making a total of one hundred and twenty thousand dollars. That amount would be increased by their clothing, subsistence, loss by desertion and mortality to one hundred and eighty thousand dollars. It was calculated that when the canal was finished the company would have on hand one hundred and eighty negroes valued at five hundred and fifty dollars each, or a total value of ninety-nine thousand dollars. This would reduce the cost of labor to eighty-one thousand dollars. If the plan had succeeded it would have made the country around Jeffersonville, New Albany and Clarksville one great city. Victor W. Lyon and other engineers still ably contend that a canal is a practical possibility on the Indiana side. This proposed canal should start near Six Mile island, and by following the course of Lacasagne creek, a natural channel would be found to connect with Mill Run creek. This creek could be followed to Silver creek and thence across low lands southwestwardly to the lower end of New Albany. The ambitions of Burr's friends were to have him become a citizen of Indiana and to return him to congress. His trip to Vincennes, under the assumed name of Colonel Burnham, was to see Francis Vigo, who had been very prominent in a previous scheme to have Indiana and Kentucky break off from the Union and unite with the Spanish provinces west of the Mississippi. An agent was appointed to select several five hundred acre estates for Burr to choose from, one of which was on the Ohio river just above Jeffersonville. The idea of returning him to congress fell through with, but Burr continued to visit some of his adherents in Jeffersonville, and caused several boats to be built there. It was never established that any of his Clark county friends knew of his designs against the Spanish authority either in Texas or Mexico, but the probabilities are that they were privy to his whole scheme. Before the scheme was fully ripe the militia at Jeffersonville, acting on information of his treason, seized the boats that had been built there for him, and Davis Floyd, his host, while visiting the village, was arrested and tried as an accomplice in the crime of his friend.

At this time, 1807, Charlestown had not been laid off, Springville was already declining, Clarksville had but four or five houses, and Jeffersonville not more than forty houses.

A Mr. Josiah Espy, who was here in 1805, found Clarksville in the same state of decay which affected Springville later on, but with not such fatal results. He says, "At the lower end of the Falls is the deserted village of Clarksburgh, in which General Clark himself resides. The general has not taken much pains to improve the commanding and beautiful spot, having only raised a small cabin. While the villages and settlements throughout the country were weak the people themselves, in common with the rest of the territory, were strong in the advocacy of their political beliefs. The sixth article in the Ordinance of 1787 prohibited slavery in the Northwest Territory. In 1807 the pro-slavery party had grown strong and were petitioning congress to suspend this article. The anti-slavery element became aroused to the danger, and in Clark county a mass meeting was called for October 10th, at Springville, to take action on the legislative resolution which the pro-slavery people had been strong enough to put through. There was a large attendance and a general harmony of sentiment. John Beggs was elected chairman and Davis Floyd secretary. A committee composed of Absalom Little, John Owens, Charles Beggs, Robert Robertson and James Beggs was appointed to draw up a memorial against the Legislature's resolution. James Beggs was evidently the author of the memorial, which after briefly reviewing the history of the slavery controversy in Indiana, proceeds: "And although it is contended by some that at this day there is a great majority in favor of slavery, whilst the opposite opinion is held by others, the fact is certainly doubtful. But when we take into consideration the vast emigration into this territory, and of citizens too decidedly opposed to this measure, we feel satisfied that at all events Congress will suspend any legislative act on this subject until we shall, by the Constitution, be admitted into the Union, and have a right to adopt such a constitution, in this respect, as may comport with the wishes of a majority of the citizens. . . The toleration of slavery is either right or wrong, that it is inconsistent with the principles upon which our future constitution is to be formed, your memorialists will rest satisfied, that, at least, this subject will not be by them taken up until the constitutional number of citizens of this territory shall assume that right." This petition was presented to the senate on November 7, 1807, and was referred to Messrs. Franklin, of North Carolina; Kitchell, of New Jersey, and Tiffin, of Ohio. They reported on the 13th that it was inexpedient to suspend the sixth article, and a resolution to that effect was adopted on the 17th. The house received this same communication on the 6th and referred it, but no action was taken after the report in the senate. It was during the strife over the question of slavery that there appeared a new champion in the field in the person of Jonathan Jennings. In 1806 Jonathan Jennings emigrated to Indiana, and for a short time stopped in Jeffersonville, but soon after pushed on to Vincennes. He soon afterward returned to Charlestown and adopted that place as his home. His slogan was, "No slavery in Indiana," and throughout his long and brilliant career he kept the slavery question to the front. Jonathan Jennings was a man of the people, and owed much of his brilliant success in politics to his peculiar knack of keeping close to them. Anecdotes of his doings were treasured up—how he used to take an axe and "carry up a corner" of a log house; how he took a scythe in the field and kept ahead of half a dozen mowers; and other deeds which appealed to the hearts of the men among whom he was campaigning. He was the political sage of Southern Indiana, and his home the mecca of many aspiring politicians, who sought his advice on public questions. Clark county has produced no more brilliant character. His incorruptible integrity, his refusal to bow to political expediency, his hospitality, his thorough understanding of the lives and needs of the people, and his firmness of character place him in the front rank among Indiana's great men. Clark county had the honor to furnish both candidates in the first campaign for governor in the new state.

Thomas Posey, the territorial governor, and pro-slavery standard bearer, was a resident of Jeffersonville, as Jennings was a resident of Springville.

In the year 1808 a new town was laid off a short distance north of Springville. The original proprietors were Barzillai Baker and James McCampbell. John Hay and Charles Beggs were the surveyors, and the town, like many other places, derived its name, Charlestown, from one of its surveyors. What induced the founders to lay off a new town back in the woods, as it was then situated, will never become known. Charlestown is situated upon grant number 117, and in the original plat there were one hundred and fifty-nine lots and about ninety-five acres of land. The lots were eighty by two hundred feet, and the founders of the town donated the proceeds of the sale of thirty lots for public buildings. In the central part of the new town a plat of about three acres was reserved for a public square.

The excellent location for a town, and the decadence of Springville were both a help to Charlestown, and the original town was enlarged from time to time. The first addition lay north of Thompson street and comprised about thirteen acres. James Ross added forty-two acres, and James McCampbell twenty-nine acres some time afterwards. John Naylor added twelve acres. Barzilla Baker added twenty-eight acres and James Garner six acres. Charlestown now contains nearly three hundred acres.

The early milling history of Charlestown township is without a parallel in Indiana history, and this honor belongs to John Work. He settled near Charlestown, on Fourteen Mile creek, in 1804, and found a mill already in operation on the one hundred acres which he purchased from John and James Bate. Mr. Work operated the mill until his conception of the tunnel project in 1814. He was a man of great mechanical and mathematical talents,

JONATHAN JENNINGS, OF CHARLESTOWN, INDIANA.
FIRST STATE GOVERNOR.
FROM A MINIATURE OWNED BY MR. WILLIS BARNES.

and the calculations and actual work which he performed stamp him as a genius. His old mill was discontinued and a new one erected. The new mill was begun in 1814 and will be described in a subsequent chapter. Among the early families who settled in Clark county in the first decade of her history besides those mentioned previously were Jonathan Jennings, in Charlestown; the Yarborough family in Jeffersonville; the Wood, Burge, Smith, Barnaby, Harman, Warman, Akers, Giles, Carr and Herrod families in Wood township; the Adams and other families in Washington township; the Slider, Warman and other families in Carr township; the Hutchings and other families in Owen township; the Crist, Carns, Connel, Becket and other families in Monroe township. With the advent of settlers still-houses began to appear, and from their number it seemed as if they were thought as necessary as mills. In Bethlehem township Joseph Jones, Jacob Giltner and George Sage distilled the juice of the corn. In Carr, Charles Goatman; in Charlestown, Jonathan Jennings and others; in Monroe, Zebulon Collins; in Owen, Mr. Levi, a Mr. Needham and Samuel Struseman; in Utica, Samuel Prather; in Washington, Jacob Bear, Fitch, Helterbridle, Samuel Montgomery and William Fisher; in fact the distillation of whisky and brandy seemed to be among the first undertakings of the pioneers. Nearly every farmer had something to do with the manufacture of spirits, yet strange to say, there is no record of much drunkenness. Keeley cures were unknown, and the chief executive of the state saw nothing in the widespread manufacture of "John Barleycorn" to excite his wrath. Barrels of whisky with the heads knocked in were the usual thing at liberal public gatherings, but, as one writer says, "It was not such whisky as we get now." It is a matter of pride to the people of the county now that there is not a brewery nor distillery within our boundary. January 1, 1906, there were one hundred and sixteen saloons in the county, drawing their heavy supplies of beverages from outside sources. The end of the first decade of Clark county history finds little of the land cultivated and the people still primitive and simple. The dangers which they faced in beast and savage foe remained, and the second decade was to be ushered in with a massacre as brutal as that of the valley of the Wyoming in 1778.

In 1810 the population of Clark county was five thousand, six hundred seventy.

CHAPTER V.

THE SECOND DECADE—1811-1820.

With the increase in her population by the advent of new settlers, Clark county began to dwindle in area by the organization of new counties from her territory. Jefferson county was cut off and organized in 1810; Washington in 1814; Floyd in 1819, and Scott in 1820. One of the signs of a coming population was the opening up of new roads between the settlements. Perhaps the most useful as well as the earliest road in the county was the Jeffersonville and Charleston road, laid out in the year 1810. It passed through the Fry settlement and on to Charlestown by way of Springville. Before the township of Utica was organized there were three roads leading from Charlestown to Jeffersonville, all of which passed through the township as it now is. They were designated as the Western, Middle and Eastern roads. The Fry settlement road was and is still known as the Middle road; the Eastern road ran over to Utica and thence down the river to Jeffersonville. It is now known as the Utica pike. That which led to Springville cut off a small slip of the northwest corner of the township. It has long been discontinued.

The danger of the Falls gave the ferry at Utica the advantage over the Jeffersonville ferry. The latter place had long been considered dangerous by those who knew it best. Many boats with their cargoes had gone to the bottom on the Falls as the result of inexperience and lack of care. Between the years 1800 and 1825 the ferry at Utica did an immense business. Emigrants were streaming into the interior counties like bees, and the white covered wagons were as familiar as steamboats are now. These emigrants took the Charlestown road, passed by way of New Washington on to the Wabash or beyond, through the dense forests which then covered the land. In 1811 a ferry was established at Bethlehem which has continued to this day with various degrees of success.

In 1812 Aaron Hoagland kept a ferry about one mile below Bethlehem. In 1815 there were ten ferries in Clark county. With the establishment of ferries, roads were opened up and in 1818 a road was built from Bethlehem to Madison. This was the first road in this township. It ran over the best and highest land between the two places, and at Bethlehem it descends to the town from the top of a bluff nearby, two hundred feet above the river. The approach and view of Bethlehem from this road presents an interesting picture with the fertile valley spread out below and the majestic river with steamboats and other water craft in the distance. It was not long before roads were built to Charlestown and to New Washington. Charlestown being the early county seat there were roads leading into the town from all parts of the county. One road which led to Charlestown landing is in use yet, but not of much consequence. At the latter place existed a ferry which was established about 1796 by a Peter McDonald. In 1817 there were two roads leading from Charlestown to Salem, called the upper and lower Salem roads. A later road was built to the mouth of Bull creek, where a ferry had been kept from early times by the Pettitt family. The ferries at Jeffersonville had been running since 1802, when Marston G. Clark was granted a license. In 1807, Joseph Bowman was granted a ferry license. The ten ferries in existence in 1815 were owned by Marston G. Clark, William Clark, Joseph Bowman, Peter McDonald, John Pettitt, Richard Astor, Robert Patterson, N. Scribner, James Noble Wood and William Plaskett.

The second decade of the century still found Clark county wild, primitive and sparsely settled. Emigrants were attracted to the locality, and during this period settlements began to appear here and there and the small patches of cultivated land relieved the weary stretch of forest and cane brakes. The Yarborough family came to Jeffersonville in 1810. At this time the village had only a few log houses and very little else to recommend it as a place of residence. In Wood township Samuel Packwood emigrated from Virginia in 1811, and Carr and Herrod in 1810, from Pennsylvania. Herrod had two sons, William and Henry. William became a miller, and for many years owned a notable mill on Silver creek. Henry was a politician and for several years was Clerk of the Clark County Circuit Court. In 1813 came James McKinley, a brother of John McKinley, mentioned before. In 1819 came William Packwood, a brother of Samuel, and at various times during this period came Charles Robertson, James and Jesse Baker, Mica Burns, Thompson Little, Amos Little, William Kelley, Michael Borders, Christopher Morris, Wiliam Gibson, James Johnson, James Brown, John Bell, George Brock, Isaac Bagerly, Cyrus Bradford, George Goss, David Goss, John Goss, Mathew West and Thomas Harlowe. These emigrants were mostly from the south. The settlement in Wood township was made within easy distance of Wood's blockhouse. The Indians often visited these new settlements in the county, and generally appeared friendly, but they were treacherous to the core, and the settlers were never safe so long as the savages were with them. The visitors loved whisky, and the owners of the still houses were foolish enough to sell to them. Their love for strong drink would prompt them to declare the most undying affection for the white man. On one occasion a gallon of whisky brought a man out of captivity, and to receive it the Indians brought their prisoner to Clarksville from the far north.

One diversion of the settlers was to shoot at a target, a sport which the

Indians were particularly fond of, and when the pale faces were beaten in the contest, which was often purposely permitted, the joy of the red skins was unbounded. This condition of affairs existed throughout the county until 1812, and up to the time of Harrison's victory at Tippecanoe. It was not long after this that the Indian began to take up his march to find less civilized but more congenial homes and hunting grounds far to the west. With this ever present sword of Damocles removed from over their heads the pioneers breathed their first free air and went forth unarmed to their labors.

In 1817 John Borden and Stephen Borden came to Wood township from Rhode Island, together with Henry Dow from Connecticut.

Dow purchased land; so also did John Borden. Dow returned to his home in Connecticut. Borden having laid out the town of New Providence, naming it after Providence, Rhode Island, returned home also. In 1818, leaving his children, two or three in number, with relatives in his old state, accompanied by his wife and Joseph Cook—a young man of influence and respectability, and by trade a blacksmith—he removed to this so-called land of promise. Dow came in 1819, bringing with him John Fowler, a son-in-law, and an unmarried daughter, also two sons unmarried, and Henry, a son who was married—altogether about sixteen men, women, and children. William Brannan, a man of wealth and respectability, with a large family, came soon after Dow, from New York. Bannannel Shaw and family from Rhode Island, soon followed Brannan. Then came Thomas Bellows. His family was composed of his mother, then a widow; two sisters, Lydia and Laura; a brother, David, and of course his wife and children. The company in which the Bellowses came was composed of Samuel Hallett and Silas Standish, with their families; Joseph Durfy and Peleg Lewis, without families, all from New London county, Connecticut.

The Bordens took the lead in affairs at New Providence, John being the first storekeeper. He engaged in blacksmithing, farming and sheep raising, and kept an inn, and his wife continued the business from the time of her husband's death in 1824, until 1851.

The first school taught in Wood township was in 1811 by Moses Wood, a brother of George. Samuel Packwood started the first tannery in Wood township in 1812. The first saw mill was erected in 1820 by Henry Dow, Sr. On the opposite side of the county Willis Brown established the first store at Bethlehem in 1815. Abram Kimberlain established possibly the earliest tannery in the county near Knobbs Station. It was in operation in 1812.

The establishment of mills and tanneries was continued even in the face of Indian troubles. After the battle of Tippecanoe the commercial and agricultural life of the county grew apace, and as conditions permitted new settlements were made and schools, churches, mills and tanneries followed as a matter of course. Distilleries continued to be profitable until the government taxed the product, when they disappeared.

In 1812 the village of Bethlehem was platted. W. C. Greenup was the surveyor, and the town was laid out with streets parallel to the river, and a reservation was made for a public square in the center. Much of the land upon which Bethlehem is built was owned by John Armstrong of Revolutionary fame. In the original plat there were one hundred and twenty-four lots.

Jeffersonville in 1812 was a sleepy little town of possibly five hundred people. In this year the question of the *removal of the county seat* to Charlestown came up and was settled; and the next year the first and original courthouse was built at Charlestown. In September of 1812, the people of the county were thrown into a panic of fear by the Pigeon Roost Massacre (see Military Annals). Many people crossed the river to Kentucky for safety, but after a few weeks regained courage. Several block-houses were built as a result of this scare, but it had little or no effect on the new settlers who continued to come in. In Washington township several block-houses were built Jesse Henly erected one on what is now the Charlestown and New Washington road, two miles and a half south of New Washington village in 1812. The house stood near the mouth of Henly's cave from which a plentiful supply of water was furnished. After the excitement went down the block-house was abandoned. It has entirely disappeared.

Mr. Pervine put up a fort on Fourteen-mile creek near his mill. It, too, has long since passed away.

On Frederic Fisher's farm, one mile north of New Washington, a block-house was erected in 1812. There was one also in a little settlement called Hookertown, but which has entirely disappeared.

Colonel Adams himself put up a private block-house. In it the family lived for a year or two, and then returned to their old but more comfortable log cabin.

The Indians seldom gave the white settlers in Washington township any trouble, except a few petty thefts which they committed, and which, fortunately, the settlers were always able to bear. In 1811 the Adams family removed to Clark county from Terre Haute.

General Harrison was engaged at that time in trying to conciliate the Indians on the frontier. It was on this account that the family moved to Washington township. In the spring of 1813, Col. Martin Adams enlisted as a ranger to fight the Indians on the borders, and made several campaigns. On the 18th of August, 1825, he married Miss Jane H. Davis. The Davises came from Kentucky and settled in Jefferson county, Indiana. The title of colonel he received from his service with the Rangers.

John Russell lived in Washington villige in 1811. He was a Revolutionary soldier, and died many years ago.

5

Henry and William Robinson came from Nelson county, Kentucky, in 1814, in company with father, mother, five brothers and three sisters. The former was born December 31, 1803; the latter February 9, 1806. The family settled on the road leading from New Washington to Bethlehem on their arrival.

Jesse Henly was one of the wealthiest men in the township in 1811. He bought his land in most instances from the government. At the time of his death he owned twenty-one hundred acres.

William Montgomery, a man who took much interest in all township questions, was the father of ten sons and three daughters. A large number of his descendants are now living in this county.

The Foutses came from North Carolina; their descendants are scattered in many parts of the United States.

In 1811 the Willey family took up their residence on a farm near where Memphis is now located. Barzillai Willey, the father, became a local preacher and was engaged in the milling business for several years. He left a family of eleven children, all of whom, except one son, John Fletcher Willey, emigrated farther west. John Fletcher Willey is the head of the numerous Willey family in Clark county.

In 1813 Jeffersonville became the seat of Indiana government temporarily.

Governor Posey did not like Corydon as a place of residence. On December 27, 1813, he sent a communication to the legislative council stating that he had gone to Jeffersonville, where he could be near his physician, who lived in Louisville. He added that if the Legislature had any business with him it could be sent on to the former city. This communication evidently did not please the Legislature, for on January 6, 1814, a preamble and resolution was adopted criticising Governor Posey for leaving the seat of government. The resolution in part reads: "Whereas, the expense of near fifty dollars a day doth arise to the people of the territory by reason of the Legislature being kept in session, all of which evil and inconvenience doth arise from the Governor leaving the seat of government and going to Jeffersonville," etc., it was resolved to adjourn *sine die,* that the people might not be put to the extraordinary expense of fifty dollars a day by the members remaining at Corydon.

Governor Posey did not get offended at the Legislature and resign. He remained in office until November 7, 1816. Most of the time he lived in a "mansion" at Jeffersonville. This old-fashioned house stood until about 1836.

The above mentioned breed of legislator is no more. He has gone the way of the cave-bear, the three-toed horse and the ichthyosaurus.

In 1812 the first Presbyterian church in the county was established in Charlestown. In 1814 Silver Creek township was organized. This township is the smallest in the county and takes its name from Silver Creek, the

GOVERNOR POSEY'S RESIDENCE.

From "Conquest of the Northwest." Copyright 1895. Used by special permission of the publishers, The Bobbs-Merrill Company.

largest stream in the county. In early days Silver Creek township was covered with a magnificent growth of oak, hickory, beech and poplar trees of immense size. These forest trees furnished great sources of income to the early settlers, and gave employment to many hands, and to the farmers during the winter season in cutting and hauling it to market. Much of this early timber was hauled to the creek and taken to the river on freshets. A great deal of the lumber from this timber was used in steamboat building, a rising industry at that time.

In 1816 the County Commissioners met at Charlestown and proceeded to separate the northeastern part of the grant and that portion of territory which had been annexed to it into four townships, one of which was Washington. This same year the town of Utica was laid out, August 9th, marking the culmination of a long anticipated hope. In the original survey there were two hundred and twenty lots, one hundred feet square. Lot number one was in the southwest corner, from which all the rest were numbered. Five lots were given for public purposes by those having the matter in charge—James Noble Wood, Samuel Bleight and John Miller. The shape of the town is that of a rectangle and the streets run parallel to the river. Front street is seventy feet wide; Walnut street is forty-three feet; Mercer and Warren thirty; and all others are sixty feet in width.

Doctor Bleight contracted with a James Ferguson, of Louisville, in 1816, to build one hundred log cabins with clapboard roofs at twenty-five dollars each. In 1817, when Samuel Morrison arrived in Utica, he found all of these cabins built and some of them occupied. The original plan of Jeffersonville, in which every other lot was lost for business purposes, was changed in 1817. An act of the Legislature in that year authorized the town board to replat all that part north of Market street, and J. K. Graham platted that part of the city as it is now laid out. New deeds of conveyance were given to all the property holders, who held property under the original deeds of 1802. The new plan had in lots numbered from one to two hundred and forty-six, and out lots numbered from two hundred and forty-seven to two hundred and fifty-three.

Originally Mulberry street was Front street; Pearl street was First; Spring street was Second; Wall street was Third, etc. This is the plan of that part of the original town at the present day with the exception of the names of the streets. Charlestown, the county seat, had meanwhile been pushing ahead and the industry and ambitions of her citizens received favorable comment from travelers.

Mr. Palmer, the Englishman who journeyed through the Ohio valley in 1817, has this to say in his subsequent book of travels in the United States:

"Charlestown, the seat of justice for Clark county, is situated in the center of a rich and thriving settlement, thirty-two miles southwest from Madison, two miles from the Ohio river, and fourteen from the Falls. This village, like many others in the Western country, has sprung up suddenly by the magical influence of American enterprise, excited into action by a concurrence of favorable circumstances."

The following notice of the place in contained in Dana's Georgraphical Sketches on the Western Country, published in 1819:

"Charlestown, the county seat of Clark, is situated two miles from the Ohio, twenty miles south of west from Madison, and fourteen miles above the Falls. It is one of the most flourishing and neatly built towns in the state; contains about one hundred and sixty houses, chiefly of brick, a handsome court-house, and is inhabited by an industrious class of citizens. There are numerous plantations around this town, consisting of good land, and better cultivated, perhaps, than any in the state. This tract is within the grant made by the state of Virginia to the brave soldiers, etc., etc. Charlestown's first postmaster was Peter G. Taylor, of New York."

Down to 1849 the mail came three times a week by way of Louisville, from Cincinnati. The steamboats brought the mail in most cases down the river. From the villages along the Ohio mail routes led off to the county seats and little post-offices in the townships. Mails were carried to all the villages of any importance in the county, on horseback, in a pair of saddle-bags. A mail-carrier was a person whom all persons delighted to see. Letters then, more than now, were precious articles.

On February 26, 1819, the County Commissioners advertised for bids to build a jail at Charlestown. Daniel P. Faulkner erected the building, and all necessary out buildings. The jail was of logs.

The first court-house was built on the northeast side of the present square about 1817, just between the building and the fence.

In the spring of 1813 a party of Indians came to within nine miles of Charlestown on a raid, and concealed themselves near the house of a Mr. Hoffman, on the banks of Silver creek. They fired upon and killed Hoffman and then shot his wife, inflicting a wound supposed to be fatal, but from which she finally recovered. They took his grandson, aged nine years, a prisoner, and kept him about nine years until the Federal Government was prevailed upon to take the matter of his return up and redeem him. During this time he had become almost savage and it was with some difficulty that he could be prevailed upon to leave the savage tribes and return home to his friends. At this time there were soldiers camped within a short distance of Hoffman's, but it being Sunday, they were visiting a family some distance away. From the number of horses stolen by these savages, and from other signs it was evident that they had visited several different parts of the county, but they were never caught, as their skill in retreating down rivulets and streams made this difficult to do.

This was the last of the Indian atrocities in Clark county, with a few minor exceptions of the abductions of children and the theft of horses and cattle. The braves who at earlier times roamed their hunting grounds with lordly mien, had now become thieving, begging varmints and their hegira to newer and wilder lands in the boundless West called forth no tears nor resolutions of regret from the settlers on the creeks and runs of Clark county.

In Washington township there was no regularly laid out village at this time. Its isolated situation seemed to preclude any idea of future greatness. But there naturally sprang up a desire to have a township center, a place where people could vote, where ammunition and groceries could be bought, and where Christmas shooting-matches could be held. David Copple, Bala Johnson and Adam Keller, who owned land in the vicinity of New Washington, were the first persons who made a successful attempt to found a village. New Washington is admirably situated. It was laid out in 1815 by the three persons above-mentioned. There were one hundred and twenty-eight lots, each ninety by one hundred and fifty feet. Eight lots were given for public purposes, and the proceeds of their sale turned into a fund for churches, schools and the grading of streets. They were located on the first square northeast of the center of the town—for it was a town of size which they had planned. In 1819 Johnson made an addition on the west side of nine lots of the same size as those surveyed at first. Mr. Todd made an addition of thirty-three inlots and twelve outlots, in 1879, on the south side, the former ninety by one hundred feet.

Adam Keller, who came from Wales, with his wife and a part of his family, was one of the first citizens of New Washington. He afterwards moved to Shelby county, Indiana, where he died.

Bala Johnson came from Kentucky, farmed for a living, and, after a life of much fruitfulness, died near his ideal village.

David Copple was a farmer. He came from one of the Carolinas. Absolom Frazier, another early citizen, a wheelwright and edge-tool-maker, was here before 1820. He erected a steam grist mill eighty odd years ago in the village, to which he afterwards attached a saw-mill. He was a man of considerable ability, and aided much in the improvements of New Washington.

In a few years after the village had been laid out it became a thriving place. This resulted mainly from its location on the great thoroughfares which led to Madison and Lexington, over which hundreds of emigrants passed yearly.

In 1817, two years after New Washington was laid out, the town of New Providence was laid out in Wood township by Stephen, John and Asa Borden. In the center of the village is a public square, which lies at right angles with the Muddy fork of Silver creek. It is situated on the Monon Railroad about eighteen miles from New Albany. In 1816 Bethlehem township was organized. It lays wholly outside the famous Clark grant in the extreme northeastern part of the county. Like Washington township it derived its name from a village which had been laid out within it before there was a separate organization and township lines were fixed definitely. That village was Bethlehem, platted in 1812, and situated on the Ohio river. The township is bounded on the north by Jefferson county; on the east by the Ohio; on the south by the Ohio river, Owen and Washington townships.

On February 10th, 1817, Jeffersonville township was organized. At that time it included much more territory than it does at present. The first election was ordered for the second Monday of March of that year, at the house of Charles Fuller on Front street. James Lemon was appointed inspector of the election, and three Justices of the Peace were elected. On May 12th of the same year the township was reduced in size by the formation of a new township as follows:

Ordered; That all that part of said township (Jeffersonville) west of Silver creek, lying and being between the said creek and Greenville township, do constitute and form one new township, and that the same be called and known as New Albany township.

The organization of new townships and the laying out of towns during this decade would argue prosperity and growth, but not so with the old town of Clarksville. John Palmer, in his Journal of Travels in the United States, recording his journeyings of 1817, said:

Clarksville lies at the lower end of the Falls, and, although commenced as early as 1783, does not contain above forty houses, most of them old and decayed. It has a safe, capacious harbor for boats.

In Doctor McMurtrie's Sketches of Louisville, published in 1819, the following not over-flattering notice is given of Clarksville:

"Although this was one of the earliest settled places in the state of Indiana being established in 1783 by the Legislature of Virginia, as part of the Illinois grant, yet it is at the present moment far behind them all in every possible respect. A few log houses of one story comprise the list of its dwellings, and from their number and appearance I should suppose that they do not contain altogether one hundred inhabitants. It is, however, pleasantly situated at the foot of the Indiana Chute, and immediately opposite Shippingport. It is said to be very unhealthy, which is more than probable, from the number of marshes that are in the vicinity."

This condition, however, did not prevail elsewhere in the county. McMurtrie seemed to be soured on the territory across from Louisville, particularly on the canal project as revived again in 1818.

A Mr. Palmer, who was in Jeffersonville in 1817, said: "Jeffersonville stands on the banks of the Ohio, nearly opposite Louisville and a little above the Falls. It contains about one hundred and thirty houses of brick, frame and hewn logs. The bank of the river is high, which affords a fine view of Louisville, the Falls and the opposite hills. Just below the town is a fine eddy for boats. A post-office and a land-office for the sale of United States lands, are established and it promises to become a place of wealth, elegance and extensive business. The most eligible boat channel is on the Indiana side of the Ohio."

The year 1814 is noteworthy as the date of the commencement of the tunnel on Fourteen Mile creek for the tunnel mill. John Work owned a mill on the creek, but he conceived the idea that instead of repairing the old one he would build a new mill. A tunnel was to be made through a spur of a hill, around which the creek ran, to act as a mill race, and therefore always gave a good supply of water. Nature had fitted Work peculiarly for the work of his life. His natural mathematical and mechanical talents were great, and to these natural accomplishments he added an indomitable will and a tireless mind.

Fourteen Mile makes a long curve in the form of a pear, leaving a body of land resembling a peninsula, which included, perhaps, twenty acres. The distance through at the narrowest point was a little over three hundred feet. But the obstacles were of mammoth proportions. The hill, for such it was, rose to one hundred feet from the bed of the creek. It was made up of solid rock. After mature deliberation and a few surveys, he began the work. From the old mill-site he began tunneling, and also at the same time on the opposite side, or where the new mill was to stand. His implements were rude; his experience in blasting and making powder limited. The work began in 1814 and lasted three years. During this time three men were constantly engaged. Six hundred and fifty pounds of powder were used, and the cost of the work is estimated at three thousand, three hundred dollars. The race was six feet deep and five wide, and was ninety-four feet below the summit.

The work which he performed in driving the tunnel, and the calculations necessary to its successful completion seem almost incredible. The two ends of the tunnel met accurately when the work was finished. The day of completion was a gala day for the surrounding country. John Work invited all his customers to partake of his hospitalities. A great dinner was provided. A man who weighed over two hundred pounds rode through the tunnel on horseback. At each end was a barrel of prime whiskey, with the head knocked out. Speeches were made and a glorification had which to this day is remembered with many affectionate regards.

Henceforward this was called the Tunnel mill. At the end of the race an overshot wheel was put up. The two buhrs ran by a never-failing water supply, with a fall of twenty-four feet. The mill is frame, and is fifty by thirty-five feet. The wheel is twenty feet in diameter, though twenty-six feet could be used, if necessary. There were originally two wheels. John Rose acted here as second engineer, and Wood and Proctor as tool-sharpeners and gunsmiths.

The first bank in Clark county was started in Jeffersonville in 1817 by Beach and Bigelow. The currency which it issued was a great convenience to people of the town and surrounding country at that time. This institution continued in business until after the failure of the canal project.

An important event in the second decade of Clark county's history was the project inaugurated in 1818 to build a canal around the Falls of the Ohio on the Indiana side of the river. The Jeffersonville Ohio Canal Company was incorporated in January, 1818, with a capital stock of one million dollars, and the articles of incorporation permitted the officials to raise one hundred thousand dollars by a lottery. The charter was to run to 1899, but the canal was to be completed and in use by 1824. The maps of Jeffersonville at this time have the line of the canal marked plainly upon them. By May, 1819, surveys had been made of the line of the proposed work and some contracts had been let for the excavation. Work was commenced and a ditch dug the entire length. The upper end of the canal was at the south end of Meigs avenue (Canal street then) and ran northwestwardly across Market street at the intersection of Walnut street. The remains of the old ox pond, a great skating place for the boys before the levee was built in the eighties, was one of the scars left by the canal seventy-odd years before.

The route cut through the block under the present location of St. Paul's church, and left it at the mouth of the alley on Locust street, between Market street and Chestnut street. It ran from here to the intersection of Chestnut street and Wall street, and thence to Spring street. It crossed Spring street at No. 437 and 438, and ran thence to Court avenue, where it struck the street about one hundred feet east of Pearl street. From here the route was across Court avenue to the intersection of Kentucky avenue and sixth street; thence to Michigan avenue and Seventh street; thence to Ohio avenue and about one hundred and fifty feet south of Eighth street; thence to Broadway, about one hundred feet north of Eighth street; thence to Ninth street about half way between Broadway and Illinois avenue; thence to Missouri avenue about one hundred feet south of Tenth street; thence diagonally through out lots 21 and 22 of Clarksville, to Cane Run creek, striking the Ohio river at the upper end of General's Point. It was to empty into the whirlpool through the ravine about one mile below the Pennsylvania bridge. At a point about where the junction is located a lock was to be constructed and another set of locks was to be located at the lower end of the canal where it emptied into the river. It was to be two and one-half miles long, one hundred feet wide at the top and fifty feet wide at the bottom. It was to have an average depth of forty-five feet and a fall of twenty-three feet. The upper one-fourth of the excavation was to be made in earth, but in the lower three-fourths ten or twelve feet of solid rock would have had to have been blasted out, entailing an enormous expenditure of time and money. The great fall through two and one-half miles of the canal was to furnish unlimited power to drive machinery for shops and factories along the line. It was the idea of the projectors that the ditch if started would soon wash itself out, and a rise in the river was expected to demonstrate the far sightedness of the engineers. A large log did travel almost the entire length of the ditch during high water, but as it came up from the lower end where the water backed up in the "canal" the scheme stood somewhat discredited. Unfortunately also, the water failed to wash out the ditch to the required depth, but left a layer of mud in it which had never been there before.

Finances ran low, the proper backing could not be found and more progressive people of Louisville and Philadelphia formed a company to dig a canal on the Kentucky side of the river. The Jeffersonville canal project was fought with vigor and the scheme died a natural death. For many years afterward the route of this canal could be easily traced but the marks have all been obliterated at the present day. While the idea of a canal was occupying the mind of Jeffersonville, Bethlehem thought of roads, and in 1818 the road leading to Madison was established.

The old cemetery at Charlestown, where so many of the men of prominence in our affairs sleep, was laid out in 1818. In the early part of the century it was used by the public generally and was the most noted of any in that part of the county. Here Jonathan Jennings was buried, and here nearly every early family of the county is represented.

In 1819 the first steamboat was built in Jeffersonville. Her name was the "United States," and she was owned by Hart and others. In a succeeding chapter, the boat building industry of Jeffersonville and Clark county will be treated separately and fully.

In 1820 the first brick house was built in Charlestown which was somewhat pretentious for those days. On June 26, 1819, Clark county was honored by a visit of the president, James Monroe, at Jeffersonville. James Flint, a traveler here at that time, wrote: "On the 26th (June) the President arrived. A tall pole with the striped flag was displayed on the bank of the river, a salute was fired and a large body of citizens awaited his coming on shore. To be introduced to the President was a wish almost universal, and he was subjected to a laborious shaking of hands with the multitude. A public dinner was given and this, too, was an object of ambition.

"Grocers left their goods and mechanics their work-shops to be present at the gratifying repast. The first magistrate appears to be about sixty years of age. His deportment is dignified, and at the same time affable. His countenance is placid and cheerful. His chariot is not of iron, nor is he attended by horse-guards or drawn swords. His protection is the affection of a free and a represented people."

In 1320 Jeffersonville was remarked in Gilleland's Geography of the States and Territories west and south of the Alleghany mountains, appended to the Ohio and Mississippi Pilot, published at Pittsburg, as "the largest town in the State and from the advantages of its situation, will probably continue to be so."

An incident which occurred in Charlestown about 1820, recalls a case of Indian brutality. Mathias Hester, one of the pioneers of Clark county, while in Kentucky in 1793, was employed in teaming between Louisville and Shelbyville, with a man named Leatherman. On one trip when they had passed "Benney Hughes' " Station on the way to Shelbyville, they were fired upon by a party of Indians. Leatherman managed to escape, but Hester was shot with a rifle ball from a distance of four paces, the ball striking him above the left eye, breaking his skull. He fell from his horse, but started to escape by running. He was prostrated three times in running one hundred and seventy yards by the pain and being blinded by the blood, his last fall happening when his pursuers were so close behind him that he decided to feign death and submit to their torture. The first Indian struck him a glancing stroke on the head with his tomahawk and the second saluted him likewise. They scalped him and during the performance of this horrible act repeatedly speared him in the back as he lay upon the ground. After their butchery they took the horses and rode away. Hester, wonderful to say, recovered, and in the fall of 1799 he removed to the Illinois grant and took up his residence beyond Springville, at what is now Charlestown.

The Indians were accustomed to stop at his house and ask for lodging, when returning north from trading at the French store at "Tullytown". On one night two Indians applied for and received quarters for the night, and as they had a jug of whiskey, it was not long before Hester was obliged to send his little son to a neighbor's house for help, meanwhile secreting one of their large butcher knives in a crack in the wall. After the arrival of the neighbor, who had asked to smoke with the tomahawk of one of the Indians, the savage became suspicious and when he missed his knife immediately wrenched the tomahawk from the neighbor's hand and assaulted Hester with it. The Indians were finally prevailed upon to desist by kind expressions and signs and peace prevailed in the Hester household. Such incidents as these did not create a great love for the Indians in the breast of the elder Hester.

About 1820 a sale or gathering of some sort was held near Charlestown, and Hester, with most of the inhabitants of the town was in attendance. Some Indians were as usual in attendance and one old buck approached Hester, and looking at the scalp wound on the top of his head solemnly remarked, "Me thought me kill you." It was the wretch who had scalped him years before in Kentucky, and it is said that the victim of that operation became so violent towards the savage that it required the united persuasion of all of his friends to prevent his shooting him on the spot.

One of the most noted institutions in Clark county at this time was "The Jeffersonville Springs". This resort was located beyond Eleventh street and to the north of Spring street, including about thirteen acres in the grounds. In 1819 Doctor McMurtrie, of Louisville, in his history of that city, speaks as follows of these wonderful springs:

"About a mile from this town are several valuable springs, mineralized by sulphur and iron, where a large and commodious building has lately been erected by the proprietor, for the reception of those who seek relief either from physical indisposition, their own thoughts, or the disagreeable atmosphere of cities during the summer season. In a word, he is preparing it for a fashionable watering place, to which there is nothing objectionable but its proximity to Louisville; its being so near requires neither equipage nor the expense of a journey to arrive there, things absolutly required to render every place of the kind perfectly a la mode. It is, however, one of the most powerful natural chalybeate waters I have ever seen or tasted, and will no doubt prove very serviceable in many complaints, particularly in that debility attended with profuse cold sweats, which are constantly experienced by the convalescent victim of a bilious fever, so common to the inhabitants of this neighborhood."

The land where this resort was located was owned by a Swiss, named John Fischli. He discovered the wonderful properties of the water in the springs and conceived the idea of making it a health and pleasure resort. He improved and cultivated the ground, laid out roads and walks, made a puzzle garden, etc.

Fountains were arranged, bath-houses were erected, bowling alleys were established and all the attractions possible were made to catch the public. Cottages were built at various places in the grounds, where visitors and their families could spend the season and enjoy the brilliancy and attractiveness of the society which repaired to this mecca from all over the South. In the summer season it was the gayest place in this part of the world. The manager of the "Springs" in 1820 was one Gutsel and his reputation as an entertainer was wide spread. He had provided all sorts of amusement devices, and the gambling here became in after years very heavy. There were rooms for faro, poker and every other conceivable sort of game except bridge whist. All of these games were public and visitors were welcome to view or participate as they chose. The great men of the South in those days and until 1850 were wont to repair here for rest and pleasure. R. M. Johnson, Vice President under Van Buren; Henry Clay, Thomas Marshall, Humphrey Marshall, Ben Hardin, General Jackson and many other celebrities of the day besides the lesser lights, added to the gaity of the resort.

In 1838 the owners built a big hotel at the foot of Broadway, near the river bank, and it was the finest hotel in Indiana or Kentucky when completed. A good wharf was built and Broadway was graded out to the Springs.

Carriages were always waiting to transport the seeker for health or pleasure to his goal, and many a dollar did the lucky owner of a rig gather in during a season. The end of the second decade of Clark county history found a healthy growth and substantial condition of affairs.

The Indian question had been settled for all time. The outlaying parts of the county were being taken up and cultivated. The territory had become a sovereign state. The population in 1820 was eight thousand, seven hundred and nine.

CHAPTER VI.

THE THIRD DECADE—1820 to 1830.

The period of 1820 to 1830 was the first peaceful epoch in the history of the county. The improvement of farms, the building of mills and the establishment of new settlements in the remoter parts of the county, all bespoke a welcome period of freedom from Indian or other conflicts, and the people began to till their farms, to plant new orchards, to erect school-houses and churches, to build hamlets, and to engage, with some degree of ardor in the various peaceful pursuits of civilized life. A sense of security pervaded the minds of the people. The hostile Indian tribes, throughout the state having been overpowered, humbled and impoverished, no longer excited the fears of the settlers who dwelt in safety and security in their plain log cabin homes, and cultivated their small fields without the protection of armed sentinels. The numerous temporary blockhouses and stockades, which were no longer required as places of refuge for the pioneers, were either converted into dwelling houses, or suffered to fall into ruin, and the people turned their attention to the substantial development of their resources.

In 1820 Jacob Giltner erected a saw-mill near Otto, and it was continued by him and his sons until 1848. It later on passed into other hands, but under his management was a valuable factor in the development of the surrounding country. The streams of Bethlehem township are small and have either rapid or tortuous currents and there were very few favorable mill sites. Peter Mikesell's horse mill, which stood near the old Antioch church, was erected in 1828, and for many years ground most of the grain of the county. It continued to run until about 1844.

The mills of Owen township were generally small affairs, on account of the scattered settlements. When Leonard Troutman erected the first water mill in the township, on Bull creek, there was not enough custom work to keep him grinding all the time. From 1820, the year of its erection, until 1825, it ground most of the grains for the farmers in this region. After that date Jacob Bear put up a horse mill in the "Possum Trot" district. Here he carried on his trade for ten or more years. Previous to the abandonment of the horse-mill Mr. Bear had erected an overshot grist-mill on its mouth, one mile above Bull creek. This was about 1826 or 1827. He engaged in milling on this site for a number of years. As time went by and the Tunnel mill rose to be considered the best on the northern side of the county, mills in Owen township were left to struggle with a small income. Trade was uncertain. Business was unprofitable, and this branch of industry soon went into non-existence. It was useless to compete with John Work, the founder of the famous Tunnel mill.

In Carr township Lewman Griswold had an overshot wheel on Muddy Fork, two and one-half miles below Bridgeport, as early as 1830. The Hughes-Palmer mill on the river bank in Clarksville was built in 1827, and remained in service until it was washed away by the great flood of 1832. In 1908 the mill-stones lay where they fell seventy-six years before as good as when they were in use.

Previous to the year 1820, George Smith and Nathaniel Bolton published the first newspaper in Clark county, at Jeffersonville. Its name is lost and a copy is not known to exist. The printing office for the paper was located on Front street, in the residence of the editors. In 1821 they removed to Indianapolis, where they established the first newspaper in that city.

In the fall of 1821 the first state prison was established in Jeffersonville at the corner of Ohio avenue and Market street. Capt. Seymour Westover was the first lessee, the prison at that time being leased by the state. The prison was then a primitive affair, built of logs at a cost of about three thousand dollars, the greater part of which had been subscribed by Jeffersonville people. Previous to the opening of the prison, prisoners had been punished at the whipping-post. The law was so changed that all persons who committed a crime for which they should receive not to exceed thirty-nine lashes on the bare back, should be sent to prison for a term not to exceed three years. Where formerly the punishment was one hundred stripes, a term not to exceed seven years was imposed. Captain Westover was a blacksmith and had a shop on West Market street. Upon his release of the lease, he went to Texas, in 1826, and was reported to have been killed with Crockett at the Alamo. The old prison had fifteen cells built in a row. They were made of logs ten inches square, dovetailed at the ends. The doors were four inches thick and covered with strap iron, and throughout the building there was little or no attention paid to sanitation or health. This institution, now called the Indiana State Reformatory, will be treated in a separate chapter later on.

In 1823 an industry was started at New Providence, which has been a valuable asset to the town ever since. At that time the tanning for the community was done by Samuel Packwood, Sr., and his pit was a large poplar log trough. A regular tannery was established by John Borden, Sr., with Butler Dunbar as principal workman. It passed into the hands of James McKinley later on and has remained in this family ever since. That the good people of New Providence had not lost sight of the necessity of spiritual training for their children in their endeavor to develop their settlement is attested

by the opening of the first Sunday school in 1824. It was taught by Mrs.
Sabra White and Miss Laura W. Bellows. These and other minor events
serve to illustrate the steady growth of the outlying districts of Clark county.
The chief event of the decade, however, was the visit of Lafayette May 11,
1825.

At various times Clark county has been honored by visits of civil and
military heroes, but never has a more notable gathering of this kind taken
place, and never a more spontaneous outpouring of the people to welcome and
honor a patriot, than that of May 11, 1825, when Major General Marie Jean
Paul Roch Yves Gilbert Motier, Marquis De Lafayette—soldier, statesman
and patriot in the cause of liberty, the friend and comrade of Washington,
visited this county, while making a tour of the United States at the invitation
of a grateful nation.

His official visit to Indiana soil was at Jeffersonville, and he was received
with the same demonstrations of popular enthusiasm which made his progress
through the twenty-four states of the Union resemble a continuous triumphal
procession.

His tour was under the supervision of the Federal Government, and
preparations had been perfected for his reception by the Indiana State authorities long before he arrived at Louisville. The Legislature had taken up the
matter early in January, 1825, and the resolutions adopted at that time express their sentiments in the following language:

"The committee to whom was referred a joint resolution of the General
Assembly, directing them to take into consideration the propriety of the General Assembly's expressing their sentiments in reference to Major General Lafayette, respectfully report the following preamble and resolutions:

"The Senate and the House of Representatives of the State of Indiana,
in General Assembly convened, would be deficient in respect to the feelings of
their constituents, and unmindful of their obligations to a distinguished benefactor did they fail to join in the pean of national gratitude and unanimous
welcome to Major General Lafayette on the occasion of his late arrival in
the United States. It is scarcely necessary for them to say that they unanimously accord with the sentiments expressed towards their illustrious friend
by the chief magistrate of the Union, and cordially add their sanction to the
provision in his favor recently enacted by Congress. The latter they view
as the smallest return for his pre-eminent services and sacrifices, the American
people could make, or the guest of the nation receive. It is the dignity of a
spectacle unparalleled in the history of man, which they particularly feel and
admire. Ten millions of hearts spontaneously offering the homage of their
gratitude to a private individual, unsupported by rank, or power, for services
long past, of the purest and most exalted character; whilst they furnish con-
soling evidence that republics are not ungrateful, also carry with them the de-

lightful conviction that the sons of America have not degenerated from their fathers of the Revolution.

"In pausing to contemplate with appropriate feelings this sublime example of popular gratitude, united with respect for character and principles, the General Assembly learns with peculiar satisfaction that it is the intention of General LaFayette to visit the western section of the United States. The felicity denied by a mysterious providence to the father of his country has, it is hoped, been reserved by his adopted son. What the immortal Washington was permitted to see only through the dark vista of futurity, will be realized in the fullness of vision, by his associate in arms and glory.

"The General Assembly hails with inexpressible pleasure the prospect of this auspicious visit. They cannot, they are aware, receive their benefactor in the costly abodes of magnificence and taste, nor vie with their sister states in the embellishments of a hospitality more brilliant than it is theirs to offer; but not more sincere.

"But they can, and do, in common with the whole American people, welcome him to a home in their hearts. They feel persuaded that he will take a deep interest in this part of our country, which though not the actual theatre of his generous labors, has emphatically grown out of the glorious results of his Revolutionary services. On the west of the Alleghany mountains, our illustrious guest will behold extensive communities of freemen, which within the period of his own recollection, have been substituted for the trackless wilderness. Where, forty years ago, primeval barbarism held undisputed sway over man and nature; civilization, liberty and law wield the mild scepter of equal rights; it is here that our illustrious friend will find his name, his services, and we trust his principles, flourishing in perennial verdure. Here, too, may he enjoy the exulting prospect of seeing them, in the language of a favorite son of the West, "transmitted with unabated vigor down the tide of time, to the countless millions of posterity."

In accordance with the preceding sentiments, the General Assembly adopted the following resolutions:

"*Resolved*, That this General Assembly, in common with their fellow citizens of the state and Union, have the most heart-felt gratitude for the services of Major General LaFayette, and most cordially approve of every testimonial of kindness and affection he has received from the people and Government of the United States.

"*Resolved*, That in the opinion of this General Assembly, it would afford the highest gratification to the citizens of Indiana, to receive a visit from their revered and beloved benefactor, the only surviving general of the American revolution; and that the Governor of this state be requested, without delay, to transmit to General LaFayette this, with the preceding resolution and preamble, accompanied by an invitation to visit this state, at the seat of Government, or such town on the Ohio river as the General may designate.

"*Resolved,* That the Governor of the state, together with such officers and citizens as may find it convenient to attend at the point selected by General LaFayette, do receive him with the honors due to the illustrious guest of the state and nation, and that the Governor draw on the contingent fund, for the payment of all expenses incurred in executing these resolutions.

"*Resolved,* That the Governor be requested to transmit a copy of the foregoing preamble and resolutions to the President of the United States, and to each of our Senators and Representatives in Congress".

On the arrival of General LaFayette at Louisville, May 10th, Colonel Farnham, one of the aids to the acting Governor, in conjunction with Messrs. Gwathmey, Samuel Merriwether, Beach and Burnett, waited upon him with the congratulations of the state. To which the General most affectionately replied that a visit to Indiana, where he should have an opportunity in person to express his sensibility to her Executive, representation and citizens, for their very kind invitation and generous expression of regard, was among the fondest wishes of his heart, and appointed the following day on which to make his visit to the state, at Jeffersonville.

The country from New Providence to Bethlehem turned out to welcome him. Never before had such a multitude thronged the streets of the village of Jeffersonville. The state Legislature and officers, together with those of equal rank from neighboring states, assembled to honor the patriot.

At 11 o'clock, a. m., on Thursday, the 11th, the above named committee waited upon him on board the steamboat, General Pike, to which he was escorted by the Committee on Arrangements and Marshals of Louisville and Jefferson county. The General was greeted on the Indiana shore, by a salute of thrice twenty-four guns, discharged from three pieces of artillery, stationed on the river bank, at the base of three flag staffs, each seventy feet in height, bearing flags with appropriate mottoes.

He was received by Gen. Marston G. Clark, of Jeffersonville, and Gen. John Carr, of Charlestown, marshals of the day, and escorted by a detachment of three artillery companies, commanded by Captains Lemon, Melford and Booth. Captain Parker's infantry company of Charlestown, and other military organizations, to the pleasant mansion house of the late Governor Posey, on the west corner of Front and Fort streets overlooking the river and the city of Louisville beyond.

On his arrival at the entrance to the Governor's house, the General was welcomed by his Excellency James B. Ray, to which the General returned the following answer:

"While I shall ever keep the most gratified and grateful sense of the manner in which I have been invited by the representatives of Indiana, it is

6

now to me an exquisite satisfaction to be, in the name of the people, so affectionately received by their chief magistrate, on the soil of this young state, and in its rapid progress to witness one of the most striking effects of self-government and perfect freedom.

"Your general remarks on the blessings which I have had to enjoy, in this continued series of popular welcomes, and delightful feelings; as they sympathize with my own inexpressible emotions, so the flattering personal observations you have been pleased to add, claim my most lively acknowledgments, never more, sir, than when you honor me with a mention of my name, as being the filial disciple of Washington, and the fond admirer of Bolivar.

"Be pleased to accept the tribute of my thanks to you sir, to the branches of the representations of Indiana, and my most devoted gratitude and good wishes for the people of this state."

The General was then conducted to chambers provided with refreshments, and presented to a numerous company of ladies assembled to welcome him, and to several hundreds of citizens, including a few venerable relics of the "times that tried men's souls."

The citizens at this reception, besides meeting the General, had the pleasure of being presented to Col. George Washington De LaFayette, his son, who accompanied his father as an aid.

One incident occurred during the reception that served to relieve the proceedings of any stiffness which might have appeared. Capt. John Parker, of Charlestown, had brought his militia company down to Jeffersonville to form part of the large military escort, and to give his men an opportunity to see the illustrious visitor.

During the presentation he took several of his men up to be introduced. One strapping young militiaman stepped forward to shake the General's hand and politely raised his hat, when out fell several large crackers which he had thoughtfully provided for a lunch during the exciting duties which he might have been called upon to perform. The General adroitly relieved him of his embarrassment and mortification by congratulating him on being a good soldier, in carrying his rations with him.

At 3 o'clock in the afternoon the General was conducted to dinner under a military escort accompanied by a band of music. The table was handsomely prepared under an arbor, about two hundred and twenty feet in length, well covered and ornamented throughout, with the verdure and foliage of the forests, among which roses and other flowers were tastefully interwoven by the ladies of Jeffersonville. This table was set in the woods just above the Governor's house, about one hundred feet above Fort street, and in constructing the arbor or covering, as was usual in that day on such occasions, the branches of the surrounding beech trees were used.

At the head of the table, a transparent painting was hung, on which was inscribed: "Indiana welcomes LaFayette, the Champion of Liberty in Both Hemispheres!" over which was a flag, bearing the arms of the United States. At the foot of the table was a similar painting, with the following inscription: "Indiana in '76 a wilderness—in 1825, a civilized community! Thanks to La Fayette and the soldiers of the Revolution!"

The company was honored by the presence of many distinguished gentlemen from Kentucky, Tennessee and other states, among whom Governor Carroll and suite; Hon. C. A. Wickliffe, Judges Barry and Bledsoe; Atty. Gen. Sharp, Colonel Anderson, the Hon. John Rowan, with the committee of arrangements of Louisville and Jefferson county, Major Wash, Mr. Neilson, etc.

After dinner, the following toasts were drank with entire unanimity of applause:

1. Our country and our country's friends—One gun.
2. The memory of Washington.
3. The Continental Congress of the thirteen United Colonies and their illustrious coadjutors.
4. The Congress of 1824—They have expressed to our benefactor, the unanimous sentiment of our hearts.
5. The President of the United States—A vigorous and fruitful scion from a Revolutionary stock.
6. Major General LaFayette, united with Washington in our hearts—We hail his affectionate visit with a heart-cheering welcome—Three guns, drank standing.

The above was received with three times three heart-moving cheers. As soon as the emotion subsided General LaFayette returned his thanks in the most affectionate manner, to the state of Indiana and company present, for the honor conferred upon him, and begged leave to offer the following sentiment: "Jeffersonville and Indiana—May the rapid progress of this young state, a wonder among wonders, more and more evince the blessings of republican freedom."

General LaFayette, on being invited to propose a toast, gave "The memory of General Greene".

At six o'clock General LaFayette left the table, and was re-escorted to the General Pike, where the committee of arrangements from Kentucky, resumed the honor of their special attendance in which they were joined by the Governor of Indiana and suite, the Marshals and Indiana committee of arrangements, who accompanied him to Louisville, and enjoyed the gratification of being near his person until his departure on the next morning for Frankfort.

Thus terminated a day that reflected luster on the annals of Indiana, and should be a subject of grateful recollection, not only to that generation, but to posterity.

The simple fact of this visit, and the incidents connected with it, are now unknown to most of the people of our locality, but if there be aught in the life and deeds of the Marquis De LaFayette in offering his life, his fortune and his sacred honor in the cause of principle in a foreign land, we should keep green the memory of his visit to our hospitable state, as a perpetual reminder of a high and patriotic character for emulation.

History relates that but for one man, in all probability Jeffersonville would have been the state capital after it was decided to quit Vincennes, where the original territorial government was established May 7, 1800. It was not, however, until July 29, 1805, that the first session of the General Assembly of the territory was called to meet at Vincennes. This was when Governor Harrison issued a proclamation to that effect. The first session of the third General Assembly met at Vincennes on November 12, 1810, and James Beggs, of Clark county, was made president of the body. Mr. Beggs and his relatives had large landed interests in the vicinity of where Charlestown now stands, and the removal of the county seat from Springville to Jeffersonville in 1802 had left a sore spot in the breast of Mr. Beggs, even after he became a member of the Legislature. Charles Beggs had laid out Charlestown, which was named for him in 1808, and James Beggs conceived the idea that with the county seat at Jeffersonville, the town would never thrive. With these thoughts foremost in his mind, he never lost an opportunity to vote against anything that would benefit Jeffersonville. The first session of the fourth General Assembly decided to remove the capital from Vincennes to some more central point, and it was agreed that the new location should be either Corydon or Jeffersonville, at the Falls of the Ohio.

Corydon had been laid out by R. M. Heth in 1808, the same year as Charlestown. There was a spirited contest over the location and when the vote was taken it resulted in a tie. As presiding officer, Mr. Beggs had the deciding vote and he lost no time in joining the Corydon forces. The second session of the fourth General Assembly met at Corydon as a result of this vote cast by Mr. Beggs, but it is safe to say that had Mr. Beggs stood by his own county, Jeffersonville would have remained the state capital, after becoming so and would, in all likelihood, have been a much larger place at the present time than Louisville.

Its location and the country between Jeffersonville and Charlestown, offers a magnificent site for a city. A splendid harbor, an excellent drainage condition, an absence of swampy or low grounds and a generally level surface would all have added to its attractiveness and possibly even now Charlestown would have been a part of the city, the residential suburb. But let us draw the veil. Jeffersonville had at the time a population of about six hundred inhabitants. In 1825 the first tavern was established in Carr township. It was kept by John Slider and "Slider's Hotel" was a prominent stopping place for travelers, between Jeffersonville and Vincennes. It was located on the Vincennes road, in sight of Bennettsville.

The original tavern was built of logs. As business increased, Mr. Slider made a frame addition to the log house, converting the only room above into six sleeping compartments. The style of public houses in those days was to have but one room in the upper story. Here all travelers were put, and among the promiscuous sleepers there was always some notorious rake, who delighted to disturb the tired and worn-out emigrant. Slider was here fifteen or twenty years. During that time all the marketers, teamsters, hog-drivers, many of the public men and the public generally, stopped with "Old John Slider."

The settlement and advancement of that part of Clark county to the north led to the erection of a new township, some time previous to 1830.

The commissioners of Clark county in 1824 were John Owens, John M. Lemmon and Robert Robertson. From the surname of the first of these men the township derived its name. As nearly as can be ascertained Owen township was organized a year or two after Owens vacated his office, which makes it about 1830. The minutes of the commissioners of the grant are obscure up to 1816. The old-fashioned paper has lost nearly all its retaining power, and dates and minutes of regular meetings are very difficult to decipher. Nothing is indexed. Town plats are stowed away carelessly, and nearly all original documents and legal papers are torn or disfigured. From these circumstances the exact year the township was placed under a separate organization cannot be positively fixed.

Monroe is a township lying in the northwestern corner of Clark county. The first mention made in the records of this, the second largest township in the county, which has over thirty-five thousand acres, is under date of January 1, 1827, when Andrew McCombe and I. Thomas were appointed fence-viewers. Previously, and in fact for a number of years afterwards, the boundaries were indefinite. The surface precluded strictly established lines. It was known that the upper side of the township bordered on the line between Scott and Clark counties, and that the south side was adjacent to Charlestown township. Beyond this there seemed to be no fixed boundaries. The west side was described as "extending to the county line," but even that line was imaginary. On the dividing line between Wood and Monroe there was no dispute. That question was settled in 1816, when the former township was organized. The reason why boundary lines were so indefinitely located was in the hilly surface, poor soil, few settlements, and general unimportance of the township. On its first organization it went by the name of *Collins township;* and it was only in 1827 that its name was permanently settled. It was probably named in honor of President Monroe, who had only vacated his office a few years before; or, what is more likely, the township name was changed about the year 1826, but no mention of it was made in the records until a year after, when we find record of the two men above named as fence-viewers.

In New Providence the first post-office was established in 1826. Tilly H. Brown was the first postmaster. He was a Presbyterian minister, and was succeeded by Samuel Hallett, a member of one of the oldest families in the county.

In 1827 the first Presbyterian church was erected in Charlestown. Here also, in 1830, Doctor Baker founded a famous school. He was an Englishman by birth and held his school in the old Masonic hall. This seminary consisted of three large rooms, and had, sometimes during the fall terms, as many as three hundred students.

The second school-house in Wood township was established in New Providence in 1827. In the last two years of this decade two flourishing little villages of Clark county were laid out.

Herculaneum was surveyed for William L. Pettitt in 1830, by John Beggs. It is situated on tract number fifty-seven of the Illinois grant, below the mouth of Bull creek. The streets run at right angles with the river. There are twenty-two lots, which number from the lower right hand corner.

Germany was laid out by Jacob Bear, Sr., in 1829. It has nineteen lots and is crossed by two streets, Main and Main Cross streets. Both these villages are now of little consequence. Bull creek with its high bluffs passes close by, and almost makes one village out of two—if villages they can be called. The main business of the station is to ferry people across the river, as they come from New Market and Stricker's corner.

These villages took their names from the German people who early made the narrow bottoms their home. Standing on the high banks of Bull creek and looking down in the valley which follows it, the places can hardly be called either neighborhoods or hamlets. They are just between the two, and will, apparently, stay where they are for a number of years to come.

Among the notices of Jeffersonville for this period we find the following in Flint's "Condensed Geography and History of the Western States":

"Jeffersonville is situated just above the Falls of the Ohio. The town of Louisville on the opposite shore, and the beautiful and rich country beyond, together with the broad and rapid river, pouring whitened sheets and cascades from shore to shore, the display of steamboats, added to the high banks, the neat village, and the noble woods on the north bank, unite to render the scenery of this village uncommonly rich and diversified. It is a considerable and handsome village, with some houses that have a show of magnificence. It has a land-office, a post-office, a printing-office, and some of the public buildings. It was contemplated to canal the Falls on this side of the river, and a company with a large capital was incorporated by the Legislature. In 1819 the work was commenced, but has not been prosecuted with the success that was hoped.

The completion of the canal on the opposite side will probably merge this project, by rendering it useless. One of the principal chutes of the river in low water, is near this shore; and experienced pilots, appointed by the state, are always in readiness to conduct boats over the Falls. Clarksville is a small village just below this place".

In 1829 there was not a church in the city; the ferry to Louisville was nothing but a skiff, and there was not a house on Spring street.

The population of Clark county in 1830 was 10,686.

CHAPTER VII.

THE FOURTH DECADE—1830-1840.

From the accounts of the various phases of life in Clark county during this decade, we learn that it was a period of prosperity. Townships and towns were laid out and the reports of travelers are bright with prophecies. In 1833 both Charlestown and Jeffersonville received favorable notices in the State Gazetteer, as follows:

"Charlestown, a post-town and seat of justice of Clark county, situated on a high table-land between the waters of Fourteen-mile creek and those of Silver creek, about two and a half miles from M'Donald's ferry, on the Ohio river, from which there is a direct road and well improved to the town, thirteen miles from the Falls of the Ohio and one hundred and six miles southeast of Indianapolis. It is surrounded by a body of excellent farming land, in a high state of cultivation. Charlestown contains about eight hundred inhabitants, seven mercantile stores, one tavern, six lawyers, four physicians, three preachers of the gospel, and craftsmen of almost all descriptions. The public buildings are a court-house, a jail, an office for the Clerk and Recorder, and a market-house, all of brick; in addition to which the Episcopal Methodists, the Reformed Methodists, the Baptists, and the Presbyterians have meeting-houses, all of brick, and an extensive brick building has lately been erected for the purpose of a county seminary. In the immediate vicinity of the town a flouring-mill and oil-mill have been recently erected, which are propelled by steam power. The situation is healthy, and supplied with several springs of excellent water. There are in Charlestown about sixty-five brick dwelling-houses, and about one hundred of wood. There are also carding-machines, propelled by horse or ox-power.

"Jeffersonville, a town on the Ohio river, in Clark county. It is a beautiful situation, on a high bank above the highest water-mark, and extends from the head of the Falls up the river, so as to include a deep eddy, where boats of the largest size can approach, at all stages of the water, within cable-length of the shore. From this town there is a delightful view of Louisville and of the landing at the mouth of Beargrass. It also affords the most advantageous landing for boats descending the river and intending to pass the Falls through the Indiana chute. It is laid out on a large and liberal plan, and must, from its local advantages, become a place of great commercial importance. The state prison is located at this place; and there are in its immediate vicinity two steam mills, a ship-yard, an iron foundry; and in the town there are six mercantile stores, three taverns, and a steam grist and saw mill, and numerous mechanics of all trades. * * * Its present population amounts to six hundred or seven hundred inhabitants, three of whom are physicans."

The smaller towns of Bethlehem, New Washington and Utica were mentioned also and given favorable notices, as follows:

"Bethlehem, a pleasant village on the bank of the Ohio river, in the county of Clark, about fifteen miles northeast of Charlestown. It contains about three hundred inhabitants, amongst whom are mechanics of various kinds.

"Utica, a pleasant, thriving post-village in Clark county. It is situated on the bank of the Ohio river, about eight miles south of Charlestown. It contains about two hundred inhabitants, three mercantile stores, and a variety of mechanics.

"Washington is a post-town in Clark county, about twelve miles northeast from Charlestown. It has about one hundred and fifty inhabitants, two taverns, three mercantile stores, and several mechanics of various trades."

In 1831 the old hand ferry at Jeffersonville was discontinued and the first steam ferryboat began to run. This boat ran but a short while, its boiler exploding in 1832, killing seven men. The company soon replaced this boat by another and better one, and continued the business. Wathan and Gilmore, who were the proprietors of the ferry at this time, sold out to Shallcross, Strader & Thompson in 1838. The ferryboats at this time ran from the foot of Spring street directly across the river to a place called Keiger's landing, the island not having attained its present size, offering no obstacle.

The township of Utica was established November 7, 1831, the line adjoining Jeffersonville being as follows: "Commencing on the Ohio river on the line dividing Nos. 5 and 6; thence on a straight direction to the line of No. 13, at the corners of Nos. 22 and 23; thence on the line dividing said Nos. 22 and 23, and on the line between Nos. 35 and 36, 49 and 50, and 67 and 68 to Silver creek," etc.

The village of Hibernia sprang up in the early thirties, David Hostetler being one of the earliest settlers. The Charlestown and Bethlehem road crossed the Boyer's landing and Otisco road at the corner of his property. The northeast boundary of the grant passes through the village, and its principal street is on this line.

Hostetler came here in 1828 and bought land of Daniel Kester from tract number one hundred and five. Thomas Applegate and William Pangborn were neighbors. William Pangborn was from New Jersey and emigrated to Indiana after serving throughout the Revolutionary war. After a few years others gathered here, and hence the place naturally took the form of a village. Hostetler soon opened a store, and was the first to carry on this branch of industry in the village. He was also the first postmaster, as the mails were carried to Bethlehem from Charlestown. His store was used many years as the voting-place for Owen township. John Roland, James Lee Stricker, and Isaac Crumm were storekeepers during the early experience of Hibernia.

Hamburg, the oldest village in Silver Creek township, is located on Grant No. 108. It was laid out in 1837 by Abram Littell and Thomas Cunningham, and had thirty-one lots of various sizes. The original plat resembles a triangle, and the ordinary size of the lots is sixty by one hundred and twenty feet. "Lot number three, on School street and in the forks of the same, is donated to the Christian congregation, or the Church of Jesus Christ, for a meeting-house, and for that use forever, never to be transferred. Lot number four is donated for school purposes, and for that use forever, the same given by Absalom Littell." The proprietors also donated land for a market-house—a good idea, but never realized; they also gave land for school purposes, "and for that use forever".

Mr. Littell, who was a Christian minister and who owned quite a large tract of land in this vicinity, a man of considerable foresight and remarkable energy, was the first to bring the idea of founding a town at this point to a successful termination. A combination of influences decided the matter. The old stage route between Jeffersonville and Salem, established as early as 1830, had for a stopping place John A. Smith's, two miles above the present site of Hamburg. This line made three trips each way every week. Four horses were used, and the business done was considerable.

These circumstances induced Mr. Littell to lay off the town. But previous to 1837 the post-office had been established, with William Wells as first postmaster. His office was in a little log house on "Jeff street," as it was generally called by the people. Sometime after he kept the office in a frame building on the southwest corner of the cross-roads. The year the town was laid out David Young served as postmaster. His place of doing business was in a small log house on Jeff street. William Thompson came next, keeping the office in Well's old place. Then came John W. Jenkins, in the same building. Reuben Hart followed Jenkins in a frame house on the northwest corner of the cross-roads.

Hamburg never attained much size or prominence, and its prospects to become metropolitan are remote.

In 1837 all that part of Grant No. 1 not being in Jeffersonville, and belonging to the Jeffersonville Association, was platted by a Mr. Barnum, of Cincinnati. The association rejected all of that part of his map north from Court avenue and east of Spring street, and employed Edmund F. Lee to replat it. It was replatted by Lee, lithographed by T. Campbell, of Louisville, and printed by C. R. Milne, of the same city, and erroneously called Milne's map. This plat consists of blocks, not lots, or squares numbered from one to

154, and also of Commercial Square at the south end of Broadway; of Central Park, laying on both sides of Broadway, between Indiana avenue and Illinois avenue, and bounded on the north and south by North and South Fourth streets. Rose Hill school occupied one part of Central Park, and Rader Park the other part. The Milne map also has Washington Square on each side of Broadway, between North and South Eighth streets, and from alley to alley; also Franklin Square, just above the Court House lot; also Jefferson Square, bounded on the north by Vernon (Sparks) avenue, on the east by Canal (Meigs) street, on the south by Eleventh street, and on the west by Watt street.

This public square is now the northwest quarter of the United States quarter-master depot. Milne's map also calls for Market Square, which is bounded by New Market (Court avenue) street, Wall street, and the alley east of Kentucky avenue. It includes Park street, and Park, and the triangle where the engine house and the police station are now located. That part of Market Square lying east of Spring street is now divided up into Park street, Warder Park, Flynn avenue, and the Plaza. No other city in the state has a "Plaza." Shallcross Block, or Shipyard Block, lying east of Meigs avenue, to a point sixty feet east of Mechanic street, and from the river to the alley north of Market street is also a separate unnumbered part on Milne's map. The fact that the land adjacent to Jeffersonville was platted, was no sign that there had been a great influx of settlers. In 1840 there were only five hundred voters in the city.

In 1839, Dr. Nathaniel Field, who then represented Clark county in the Legislature, introduced a resolution authorizing the incorporation of Jeffersonville as a city, and an act in conformity to this resolution was passed. In April of this year an election was held and Isaac Heiskell was elected the first Mayor. The first Councilmen of the city were: First ward, L. B. Hall and James G. Read; Second ward, John D. Shryer and Samuel Merriweather; Third ward, A. Wathen and J. B. McHolland; Fourth ward, Nathaniel Field and James Slider; Fifth ward, Daniel Trotter and C. W. Magill. John Mitchell was the first Treasurer, and Thomas Wilson was the first Clerk. Jackson Hulse was the first Marshal. The population of the city at this time was five hundred and eighteen.

Two events in the year 1832 are worthy of note. The great flood came that year, the greatest ever known up to that time. Havoc was wrought along the river by the washing away of property. One account of the damage done to this locality as related by a Louisville historian, is as follows:

"In 1832 a new calamity came upon the city. This was an unparalleled flood in the Ohio. It commenced on the 10th of February and continued until the 21st of that month, having risen to the extraordinary height of fifty-one feet above low-water mark. The destruction of property by this flood was immense. Nearly all the frame buildings near the river were either floated off or turned over and destroyed. An almost total cessation in business was the necessary consequence; even farmers from the neighborhood were unable to get to the markets, the flood having so affected the smaller streams as to render them impassable. The description of the sufferings by this flood is appalling. This calamity, however, great as it was, could have but a temporary effect on the progress of the city, as will be seen hereafter."

The height of fifty-one feet given here does not tally with the official record. The water reached its greatest height on February 19th—forty-five and four-tenths feet. The Hughes-Palmer mill, in Clarksville, was swept away by this flood.

Cholera was epidemic in 1832. While people were succumbing to the disease everywhere, Clark county lost very few, if any. They died by scores in Louisville, but we were almost completely immune from it. At Salem there were sixty deaths in one night. In 1833 the disease was very bad, but there was none in 1834; in 1835, however, it was worse than ever before and there were many deaths. Besides the great flood of 1832, the county was subjected to a great drouth during the summer months. It remained the worst on record until that of 1854. In 1834, James Howard built his first steamboat in Jeffersonville, the first of a vast fleet of water craft turned out from these yards since that time. In 1832 the first foundry was started by Robert C. Green, who came from Cincinnati. Charles C. Anderson, who had learned the foundry business with Mr. Green, in Cincinnati, started a small machine shop, which he operated successfully on a growing scale up to the time of his death. In this year also a project for a bridge across the river was inaugurated and James Guthrie, Samuel Gwathmey and Daniel McAllister, of Louisville, went to Indianapolis to receive the incorporation of a company by the Indiana Legislature to aid in the building. One charter had already been granted by the Kentucky Legislature, but another one seemed necessary to push the scheme to completion. This project made apparent progress.

The Kentucky charter was deemed sufficient and contracts for the construction of the bridge were let. The corner stone on the Kentucky side was laid September 7, 1836, with great solemnity and ceremony near the foot of Twelfth street, two squares above the present Pennsylvania bridge. On the Jeffersonville side the abutments were commenced also, but financial difficulty arose, the contractor failed to proceed with the work and the project finally fell through and forty years elapsed before it was broached again.

The first fair in Clark county was held in 1836, in Charlestown, on Denny's lots, southeast of the court-house. Thomas J. Henly, John Denny, and John W. Long were instrumental in its success. Nothing was exhibited of special attraction, except Dr. James Taggart's Durham bull, the first in the county. Avery Long was their president, and Campbell Hay, treasurer.

July 26, 1834, ex-Governor Jonathan Jennings died at his home on the picturesque banks of Sinking Fork surrounded by his family and friends, and beloved by all. His body was taken to Charlestown for interment and laid in an unmarked grave. During the pioneer age schools were imperfectly managed and even down to later days this is true in some parts of the county. In Bethlehem township the school antedated the church.

Before the Antioch church had been thought of, a school was carried on near where the church now stands. The house was sixteen by eighteen feet, and had a door which swung to the outside—a very rare thing, even in those backwoods days. Cyrus Crosby was the first teacher. After him came Thomas J. Glover; Dr. Solomon Davis, Rev. Benjamin Davis, a local Methodist preacher; and perhaps a few others. In 1832 Mr. Martin Stucker taught in a new hewed-log house. Then came Charles Smith, of New York state; Samuel C. Jones, of Kentucky, but at this time a citizen of the county, and who had been here as one of the very earliest teachers. Joel M. Smith came soon after Jones; he was a native of New York, but came with his father's family when a boy and settled near Charlestown. Thomas S. Simington taught in 1839 and 1840, and it was during his term that the old school-house burned down. Very soon thereafter another building was put up, in which George Matthews acted as teacher. After the new school law came into force a new district was created, and another building erected in a different place.

Although the town of Bethlehem was on the mail route from Jeffersonville to Vevay, she had no postmaster. This route was begun about 1827, and was continued until 1840. George Monroe carried the mail over the route in 1834-1838. William G. Armstrong was the first postmaster and he was succeeded in 1835, by Asa Abbott.

Bennettsville, in Carr township, is the only place in that township which claims to be a village, and its population is not so seething that you would notice it. It was laid off in September, 1838, by H. O. Hedgecoxe, county surveyor, for Baily Mann. The first name given to the newborn village was New Town. After several years the name was changed, Bennettsville being thought preferable to the name of New Town. Benedict Nugent, who was the first store-keeper in the village, probably had much to do indirectly with the changing of the name. The evidence is that Mr. Mann removed to some other locality, and that Mr. Nugent being the most prominent man in the place, the citizens, for some reasons peculiar to a pioneer people, almost unawares gave it the name of Bennettsville, a prolongation of Mr. Nugent's given name.

The original plat does not give the width of the streets and avenues. In finding the direction which Washington street takes with reference to section lines, subtract the variation five degrees and fifty minutes from field note north thirty degrees and forty-five minutes west.

Bennettsville is located on the railroad. It has few features which attract attention.

The village of New Market was laid out by Robert Henthorn in 1839. The streets are sixty feet wide, avenues thirty feet, alleys ten feet. It is situated in the southern part of survey or tract number one hundred and ninety-six on the west bank of Fourteen-mile creek. In 1850 Gabriel Phillippi made an addition of twenty-two lots on the southeast corner of the original plat. Round about the village the country is rolling. In the northern part of the first plat the ground is broken and not well adapted for a thriving business place. The eastern half of the village juts out on the high banks of Fourteen-mile creek. Here the road leads up the bluffs as it follows up the dividing line between the tracts.

For many years previous to 1839 New Market was a rendezvous for market wagons, which made it a stopping point on their way to the towns on the Falls. People soon learned to bring their produce here—eggs, butter, poultry, calves and dressed hogs—and to receive in exchange groceries and dry goods. From this fact the village derived its name of New Market. The first man who engaged in buying and selling country produce, and who lived in New Market and sold all the articles common in country stores, was Anderson Ross. After him came Wesley Bottorff, Mr. Garner, J. W. Haymaker, Dr. Benson and Alexander Ruddell. Between 1840 and 1850 there were three stores in the town at the same time. There was an old-fashioned saloon here about 1845, which dealt out all kinds of drinks, from hard cider to Kentucky "Bourbon." A prosperous blacksmith and cooper shop about the same time gave the village an appearance of considerable business. In the place now there is but one store.

The resort known as the Jeffersonville Springs was in the heyday of its existence at this time. Its patronage came from all points of the South and West. In 1838 the management built a large and handsome hotel at the foot of Broadway and the street out to the resort was graded and became a highway for the equipage of fashion and wealth.

Jeffersonville had never been satisfied with the manner in which the county seat had been taken away and removed to Charlestown. There had been no controversy upon the county seat question in the election of the Representatives to the Legislature, and they had acted wholly upon their own personal feelings and wishes in the matter. The people of Jeffersonville bided their time to take back the county seat and get their revenge at the same time. In 1838 the county seat removal question was raised again, and both sides to the question prepared for a pitched battle. A Senator and two Representatives of the Legislature were to be elected and the candidates were chosen on that issue.

The anti-removal candidates put in nomination for Senator were Benjamin Ferguson, and for the Lower House Col. John S. Simonson and Thomas J. Henly. Those in favor of removal to Jeffersonville put forward William G. Armstrong for the Senate, and Dr. Nathaniel Field and Major Henry Hurst for Representatives. This was a noted contest in the political history of Clark county as the nominees were all men of ability and of great personal popularity. The canvass was hot and the contest, as it always is on questions of county seat removals, was bitter. The removalists, the Jeffersonville party, elected their candidates, but the victory was barren of fruits: the Legislature refusing to the people of Clark county their wishes on that subject, and Charlestown still retained her hold upon the county seat. But the strength of the removal feeling had been tested and it showed that a majority of the people were in favor of it. They were defeated but not discouraged. After a lapse of forty years the fight was renewed.

The Hon. James G. Howard gives a measure of the period as follows: "At that time school-houses were not very plentiful. The only one that we had in Jeffersonville was a little old unused clerk's office. They had the court-house here then, but the county seat was at Charlestown; and the first school I went to when I came here was to that little clerk's office. The people did not have many opportunities for an education those days. They were not generally well educated; but there was a class of men here at that early day— quite a number of them, that with all the disadvantages that surrounded them would compare favorably with any I have ever met. So far as the morals of the community at that time are concerned, I do not think the period between 1830 and 1850 has ever been surpassed. It is astonishing that the intelligence, the judgment and stamina that constitute vigorous manhood should have been consolidated in men of those days of hardship and few advantages; and when I undertake to compare the present with the past, I think that the men of those days would compare most favorably with those of our present time. I believe that every man, so far as I can remember, was a church-going citizen. There was a stability of character pervading the community at that time that almost astonishes me when I think of it. And more especially was this true of the farmers; nearly every farmer was a church-going man." The population of Clark county in 1840 was fourteen thousand five hundred ninety-five.

CHAPTER VIII.

THE FIFTH DECADE—1840 TO 1850.

On January 23, 1841, Jeffersonville expanded once more. The Jefferson-ville Association, Dr. Nathaniel Field, agent, promoted the eastern division enlargement. This division extended from the river with the line of Port Fulton (which is the dividing line of C. and D. of tract No. 2, of the Illinois grant) to Eighth street, thence with Eighth street to within six hundred and sixty-five feet of Fulton street (which is the east line of Benson's addition) thence with this line to the Ohio river, comprising blocks one to sixteen including Chestnut Grove cemetery.

A flouring mill, tannery and foundry were started in Jeffersonville at this period. In 1847 Samuel H. Patterson and James Callahan erected a brick flouring mill on Spring street. This was the first steam flouring mill in the city and was run for two or three years when Mr. Patterson bought out the interest of his partner and soon after sold the business to John F. Howard, of Louisville. In 1841 James Lemaire started a tannery at the corner of Eleventh street and Broadway. He carried on this business until 1848, when he sold out to John A. Ingram and J. M. Ross.

The Anderson foundry which was carried on in a small shop near the ship yard, was moved, about 1844, to a location on Spring street. This firm, consisting of Charles C. Anderson, James Keigwin, Hamilton Robinson and Richard Goss, did business at this location for a number of years, but finally in 1860 removed to their present plant on Watt street, between Maple and Court avenue. The necessity for a better wharf prompted the city council of Jeffersonville to have the present wharf between Spring and Pearl streets graded down in 1843. Originally the ground stood some six or seven feet higher than the pavement on Front street and extended out nearly two hundred feet level. On this plat of ground was a row of large trees at the edge of the bluff, while just to the rear of them was an old graveyard which had been used by the garrison of Fort Steuben in 1790 for their burials. Harvey McCampbell had the contract to grade down the earth and the city council had the bodies of the old soldiers there removed to the Mulberry street cemetery. At different times during this decade Clark county was the host for several of the national political leaders. July 5, 1842, Gen. William Henry Harrison visited Jeffersonville and Charlestown. At the latter place he made a speech describing the battle of Tippecanoe and refuting several charges which had been made as to his mismanagement of the troops in this battle. While here he spoke in the most commendatory manner of a great many officers who had fought at Tippecanoe, but never mentioned Bigger or Beggs. These officers had performed valiant service, and during the whole campaign had done their duty in a brave and honorable manner. The General's neglect of recognition to these officers not only in his speeches but in his reports of the campaign and the battle was noticed. It was and is a matter of regret that these officers and the men who fought under them in this memorable action, did not receive the public recognition which was their just due.

Richard M. Johnson came, too, in the course of the fall, and delivered his speech to attentive listeners. He was received by a committee, and from here went to Salem, in Washington county. At the foot of the knobs he cut hickory canes for the committee, which were preserved as relics of much value. Thomas J. Henly delivered the reception speech in behalf of Clark county. In 1844 James K. Polk visited Jeffersonville. He had been elected President, and had been brought across the river to Jeffersonville, to a reception given in the old Methodist church on Wall street. President Polk was on his way east and his escort wore scarlet coats. When the boat landed at the foot of Spring street, there was a great crowd to receive him, a band was playing, and cannon were booming. In the crowd was a raw-boned individual, named Maybe, who was an ardent Polk man. Some one made a slighting remark about the scarlet coats and a fight ensued in which Maybe whipped about twenty men. Such encounters as this were common in those days, all men were plucky and were as willing to fight as to eat.

In 1844 also Ben Hardin, of Kentucky, was the speaker at a great Henry Clay meeting held at the "Springs." About four thousand people were here to hear him, and the "Springs" which were then in the glory of their popularity, was crowded to the gates. In 1849 Gen. Zachary Taylor visited Jeffersonville and was received in the church on Market street, between Spring and Pearl. He was on his way to Washington to be inaugurated President. Millard Fillmore spoke in Jeffersonville in 1850 from the small porch in front of the building on the southwest corner of Market and Spring streets.

In 1845 Charlestown and Clark county suffered the loss of one of its oldest and most prominent citizens, Gen. John Carr. In the Southern Indianian, a county paper published at Charlestown by William S. Ferrier, is the following account:

"It becomes our painful duty in this week's paper to announce the death of Gen. John Carr, who died on the 20th instant (January 20, 1845) after a long and very painful illness. His death created a space which cannot soon be filled. General Carr was a man of no ordinary character. He had long occupied an elevated standing among his fellow men. He was born in Fayette

7

county, Pennsylvania, on the 6th of April, 1793, and had at the time of his death nearly completed his fifty-second year. He emigrated from that state with his father to the then territory of Indiana, in the spring of 1806, having been a citizen of this county ever since—a period of thirty-nine years. During the summer of 1811 he was engaged in several scouting parties on the frontier, and in watching and guarding against the approach of the Indians, who were then known to entertain hostile feelings toward the settlers. At this time he was but eighteen years of age. In the fall of the same year he joined the Tippecanoe expedition, with Captain Bigger's company of riflemen, and was engaged in that memorable and bloody conflict, which occurred on the 7th of November of that year. On the declaration of war in 1812 he was appointed a lieutenant of a company of United States rangers, authorized by an act of Congress and organized for the defense of the western frontiers. During the years of 1812 and 1813 he was actively engaged in several important and fatiguing campaigns, which were attended with extreme hardship and peril. The Mississinewa and Illinois or Peoria campaigns were particularly distinguished for their many privations, difficulties and hairbreadth escapes; in all of which he participated. During much of his time the command of his company devolved upon him, in consequence of the absence of the captain. Though then but a youth he was equal to any emergency.

After the war he filled successively several military offices. Among these were brigadier and major-general of the Militia of Indiana. The latter office he held at the time of his death. General Carr was repeatedly honored with the confidence of his fellow-citizens in the election to several civil offices of trust and honor. He filled at various times the offices of Recorder, agent for the town of Indianapolis, Clerk of Clark County Circuit Court, to which he was re-elected, and Presidential Elector on the Jackson ticket in 1824. All these duties he discharged with honor to his country and himself. In 1831 he was elected a member of the House of Representatives of the Twenty-first Congress of the United States, and continued to serve in this body for six consecutive years. In 1837 he retired, but was re-elected for the fourth time in 1839, and served two years more, making in all eight years' service in that body. His Congressional career was noted for industry, efficiency and usefulness. He originated the sale of lands in forty-acre lots, thus bringing within the reach of all the home that so many needed. He assisted in passing the pension act, by which so many of the old Revolutionary soldiers received pensions and afterward aided many of them in establishing their claims to this hard-earned bounty of their Government. In private, as well as in public life, he was distinguished for his nice sense of honor and the uprightness of his conduct. Of him it may be said in truth that he was one of God's noblest works, an honest man." Carr township was named for General Carr.

In 1843 there appeared in the heavens a great comet which almost rivaled the splendor of the sun itself. It became visible in America on March 6, 1843. As observed in this country the greatest length of the tail was about fifty degrees, and its size and brilliancy may be imagined when we learn that it was visible at midday, near the sun, with the naked eye. It remained within vision about a month and caused the greatest excitement, as its appearance was coincident with the prophecy of William Miller that the millenium would be in 1843.

William Miller was born in Massachusetts in 1782 and held a captain's commission in the War of 1812. He held peculiar views concerning the second advent of the Saviour, and began to preach his doctrine in 1833. In 1840 the first general conference of the Second Advent believers was held in Boston, and the work spread with rapidity from that time on. All the calculations of the sect were to the effect that in the year, 1843 was to be the great day when the faithful were to be caught up in the air and enter into the realms of celestial bliss forevermore. In Clark county this sect had many followers. Mordecai and Christopher Cole in Charleston and Dr. Nathaniel Field, of Jeffersonville, were the leaders in the Millerite following in these localities. April 14, 1843, was the revealed date and as the great day approached, many of the believers in Clark county, as well as elsewhere, were waiting in their white ascension robes to be caught up in the air, or were on the house-tops or in the grave yards watching. Many disposed of their worldly goods. For some days preceding this time, their secular business was, for the most part, suspended, and those who looked for the advent, gave themselves over to the work of preparation for that event, as they would have done if they had been on a bed of sickness expecting death. Notwithstanding the ridicule heaped upon them by the public, they continued to maintain their societies even after their great disappointment, and the Second Adventists still have churches in the county.

Sellersburg was laid out in 1846, by Moses W. Sellers and John Hill. Sellersburg is very irregularly laid off. None of the forty-two lots have a right angle. It resembles an isosceles triangle pressed together from its base. One writer says, "Sellersburg resembles a box twisted and squeezed together." Sellersburg together with Cementville and Speeds is a great shipping point for cement, an industry which will be treated later on.

New Market became a post-office about 1845. Mails were formerly carried through the eastern end of Oregon township on their way to Bethlehem and Madison, from Charlestown. Poke Run was the only office for many years in the township. Dr. John Covert was postmaster here for fourteen years. The way of carrying mails was on horseback with a pair of saddlebags; or in summer, a light vehicle was sometimes used, when a passenger might be picked up along the route. After the Ohio & Mississippi branch was built, Poke Run ceased to be a post-office. New Market had grown sufficiently to gain the right of having an office within her limits. Accordingly the old route was abandoned and a new one established, which ran from Charlestown to New Washington via New Market. The first postmaster was John W. Haymaker. After him came Sisney Conner, D. M. Turner, and James A. Watson.

The first post-office in Union township was established at Sylvan Grove, one-quarter of a mile south of Memphis, on the route which led from Charlestown to Bedford, in Lawrence county, Indiana. The office was established in 1847, with John Y. Wier as the first post-master, and who held the office for many years. Some time in 1860 this route was abolished and the office taken to Memphis. The first postmaster in Memphis was J. F. McDeitz; then came U. S. Reynolds, A. P. Jackson, Daniel Guernsey, and John D. Coombs. Blue Lick was established about 1842 by the efforts of the Thompsons, Guernseys, McDietzes, Kelleys and Hawses, with Thomas McDietz, Sr., as the postmaster.

But few of the smaller post-offices established in this decade remain. The rural free delivery has wiped them out of existence, and has replaced them with a service far superior to what was given before.

In Jeffersonville the state prison was changed from its old location to the present in 1845, and the wall and buildings at the corner of Ohio avenue and Market street were torn down, and the brick sold to various purchasers in Jeffersonville. The old house at the southwest corner of Market and Locust streets was built from these old prison brick. The State Reformatory is in Clarksville, not Jeffersonville. The first warden of the prison south in its new location was William Lee. This institution from its log cells at Ohio avenue and Market street to its new location, and its change in management and principle, will be described in a separate chapter. In 1845 the historic old Governor's mansion at Fort and Front streets burned down. It was here that Governor Posey retired when he left Corydon, and it was here that General LaFayette was received in 1825.

In 1847 the second great flood swept down the Ohio valley leaving waste and destruction in its path. It reached its highest December 18th, and rose to the height of forty and eight-tenths feet, only four and six-tenths feet below the record of February 19, 1832.

The idea of building a canal around the Falls of the Ohio, which seems to have had a periodical recurrence in Jeffersonville, took on a tangible form again in 1848. On December 6th, of that year an act to incorporate the "Indiana Canal Company" was passed by the Legislature and the following were named as incorporators: Athanasius Wathen, William D. Beach, William G. Armstrong, Samuel H. Patterson, John D. Shryer, Thomas J. Howard, Samuel Merriwether, George F. Savitz, of Clark county; Sheppard Whitman,

James Brook, Randal Crawford, John Brown, Somerville E. Leonard, Henry H. Royse, John Austin, William A. Weir, of Floyd county; John Law, of Knox county; William Carpenter, of Vanderburgh county; Richard W. Thompson, of Vigo county; Abijah W. Pitcher and John Woodburn, of Jefferson county; George H. Dunn, of Dearborn county; James Morrison, of Marion county; Jacob Burnet and Josiah Lawrence, of Cincinnati, Ohio; Benjamin Loder, of New York City; Erastus Corning, of Albany, New York, and Henry B. Stone, of Boston, Massachusetts. The capital stock was five hundred thousand dollars, but the directors had power to increase this amount by the sale of additional shares as they thought necessary. The tolls which were to be charged were as follows: For steamboats, sea vessels, barges or keel boats, any sum not exceeding seventy cents per ton; for each flat boat, not exceeding twenty dollars; for each raft of timber, plank or other lumber, not exceeding twenty dollars, for each sixty feet in length and twenty feet in width. The state of Indiana (not the United States) was given the right to transport troops, munitions of war and provisions free of toll in time of war.

On June 16, 1849, the directors met at Jeffersonville and elected James C. Hall as president; Amos Lovering, secretary, and William D. Beach, treasurer. William J. Ball was appointed chief engineer and he made a voluminous report dated January 1, 1850. He enumerated several schemes, the first of which is the opening of a navigable channel in the middle of the river; second, the digging of a canal from the head of the middle chute to the foot of the Kentucky chute; third, a canal near the Indiana side to the head of big eddy, thence with locks through Goose Island; fourth a canal through Goose and Rock Island, but with a dam across the river at the head of Goose Island instead of the canal from that point up to the head of the Falls; fifth, a new canal on the Indiana side from Jeffersonville to just below the point of rocks, to be fed from the upper pool of the Ohio; sixth, a new canal to be built on the Indiana side from Jeffersonville to "Falling Run," canal to be fed from the upper pool of the river; seventh, a new canal built on a high level, to be fed by a navigable feeder from Columbus, Indiana, to Jeffersonville, eighty miles in length. The plan adopted was a canal from one hundred feet to two hundred feet wide, extending from above the drift of the Falls to the whirlpool, at which point the locks were to be located. From this lower end the natural channel was to be improved.

The length of this proposed canal was one and three-fourths miles, the lockage twenty and twelve one hundredths feet, and the total cost was to be six hundred and eighty-eight thousand thirty-three dollars and sixty-five cents. The project never got beyond the paper period, and the idea of transporting boats around the Falls was allowed to sink into innocuous desuetude until another genius conceived the new idea of building a railroad from the head to the foot of the rapids and hauling steamboats around on cars.

The Mexican war period in Clark county like other counties throughout the state was one of excitement, particularly so to this county because the regiments all came to the southern part of the state to embark on their journey. Fort Clark, called Camp Joe Holt in the War of the Rebellion, was the scene of rendezvous of the Fourth Indiana Volunteer Infantry, and as they embarked on steamboat here the war was brought very near to home. In the chapters of the military annals of Clark county, appear accounts of these events.

Following the Mexican war the gold fever occupied the minds of the more adventurous and some few left to try their fortunes in the far West.

Cholera appeared again in 1849, but with far less mortality than in 1835. A not very bright description of the sanitary and health conditions of Jeffersonville is given in Doctor Drake's treatise published in 1850.

"It stands about a mile above the Falls of the Ohio, on a terrace, the south or river side of which is forty feet above low water, and about four hundred and twenty feet above the sea. This terrace, like most others along the Ohio, declines from near the river and is liable to inundation, so that in high floods the town becomes inundated. Both above and below it there are small streams entering the Ohio, which are the channels by which these overflows are effected. To the north and northeast, near the town, there are ponds skirted with marsh, one of which has lately been drained. The surface, like that of the plain on which Louisville stands, on the opposite side of the river. is argillaceous, and retains the water which rains or flows upon it. It will be observed that all the insalubrious surface lies to the summer leeward of the town, but the flats and stagnant waters near the mouth of Beargrass creek. on the opposite side of the Ohio, are directly to the windward of this town, with only the river intervening. Jeffersonville is also to the leeward of the Falls. and exposed therefore to any insalubrious gases which may be liberated by the agitation of the waters. Two miles north of the town a watershed, between the Ohio river and Silver creek, commences and runs to Charlestown, thirteen miles north. At its commencement this terrace is sixty feet above the level of the town, and its rise afterward is about ten feet per mile. Doctor Stewart, to whom I am indebted for several of the facts in this article. informs me that autumnal intermittents and remittents are decidedly prevalent in Jeffersonville and its vicinity. The penitentiary in the state of Indiana. stands in the western part of Jeffersonville (not so—in Clarksville). Doctor Collom, its physician, informs me that the convicts are every year invaded by autumnal fever, but in a degree rather less than the inhabitants of the town." This condition, we are happy to say has been obliterated and Jeffersonville together with the rest of Clark county has a good health record.

On April 23, 1839, John Fleming surveyed the west half of C of Grant No. 2, of the Illinois grant, and the plat was certified to on May 17, 1848.

This addition to Jeffersonville lay between Fulton street and the west line of the eastern division, and from the Ohio river to Eighth street. It was called Benson's addition and was divided into blocks numbered from one to twelve. In Benson's addition Fleming gave names to all the alleys, as follows: Wagoner, Cherry, Virgin, Cypress, Sassafras and Wood.

In both Charlestown and Jeffersonville schools of no small merit were established in the latter part of the decade. In Charlestown the Rev. H. H. Cambern, in 1849, bought up the old Masonic hall, or rather the original seminary, made additions and erected boarding houses, and opened a female seminary for the first time in Charlestown. Rev. George J. Reed was the first teacher. In this school all the higher branches were taught, the ladies leaving, in many instances with a diploma. Cambern's seminary lasted for fifteen or twenty years. The Rev. Mr. Reed was succeeded by John F. Lindley, of Frederickstown, Ohio. He was succeeded by Zebulon B. Sturgus about 1859. Sturgus had previously been teaching in a frame building on upper Thompson street in what was known as the Charlestown boys' school. Here Sturgus made considerable reputation, his students coming from different states along the Ohio river. But in course of time changes were made. Untoward circumstances threw the old teacher out of his position. Students gathered here from all sections, and the faithful old teacher had the pleasure of seeing in after years some of them quite distinguished lawyers, statesmen and philanthropists. Henry Crawford, one of the prominent lawyers of Chicago, and Senator Booth, of California, received much of their early education from Mr. Sturgus. The old teacher was a strict disciplinarian. Tobacco-chewers and swearers were not allowed among his students. It is related that when the first locomotive passed over the Ohio & Mississippi Railroad, he whipped all the scholars for imitating the engine. Sturgus is no more; the old schools are gone, and the present generation is reaping their golden grain.

In Jeffersonville a Mr. Hibben established a seminary on the north side of Market street, just below Pearl street about 1850. This school was a high class institution and had quite a reputation, receiving scholars from a distance and for that day giving them an education above the average. In Professor Wylie's history of Indiana University in Bloomington, appears the following: "He (Hibben) completed his sophomore year at Jefferson College, Pennsylvania, and was graduated at Transylvania University September 1, 1848, from which university he received the degree of A. M. He then began his career as a teacher in Jeffersonville, Indiana." This school lasted until in the fifties and was known as the Jeffersonville Seminary. In 1850 the population of Clark county was fifteen thousand eight hundred twenty-eight.

CHAPTER IX.

SIXTH DECADE—1851-1860.

This period in Clark county was marked by no events of importance to history. The quiet pursuits of peace gave employment to the minds and energies of the people, and the political tension which was beginning to be drawn everywhere throughout the country gave a prominence to national affairs which dwarfed local issues.

Townships, towns and villages were laid off, a fact which testifies to the progress of the county which otherwise would not be evident. Broom Hill in Carr township was begun in 1851 by Thomas Littell, who lived in this immediate neighborhood. Here he began the making of brooms, and from this circumstance the village derived its name. But Littell was not the first settler in this locality by any means, though he built the first house in the village and opened the first store. Littell's house stood on the north side of the railroad. Previous to Littell, about the year 1809, one Michael Burns, of Connecticut, settled here and built a cabin on the site of Broom Hill, on the south side of the railroad. Austin Rowe was a storekeeper after Littel.

Broom Hill has had many small manufactories. William Leighton, in the former part of its history, put up a shingle machine. He also erected a grist-mill and afterwards attached to it a stave factory. At one time a thriving portable saw-mill was run by the Bussey brothers. It lasted for a few years only. After the Bussey brothers, William McKinley and Michael Burns erected a saw-mill. The business done at this mill was considerable.

Blacksmith shops, shoemaker shops, and the various trades have been carried on in the village, though never on a very extended scale. Broom Hill is noted as once being the seat of extensive railroad supplies. During the first few years of the railroad the village furnished more wood than any other station on the road.

Bridgeport, much like Broom Hill, came into existence about the time the railroad was built. The section hands created a demand for many of the coarser wares, and hence, as a result, Samuel Plummer, of this section, began to sell various things, such as shovels, picks, spades, drills and crowbars, to the men employed by the railroad. Mr. Plummer died before the road was completed, and the store fell into the hands of his brother, Charles. Soon after it was finished James Warman erected a warehouse on the north side of the track. Here were stored various grains, the house serving as a kind of "depot for supplies" for the people round about. Wesley Warman was a storekeeper here about this time.

The village of Henryville is situated in the center of Monroe township. Many years before the place was laid out there was an old Indian trail running through the village, much as the Pennsylvania railroad now runs. It is located on Wolf run and Miller's fork of Silver creek, the former a tributary stream of Silver creek, which derived its name from the great rendezvous it furnished wolves forty years before Henryville was platted. The village lies in a beautiful valley, with hills on the east side, and in sight of the famous mounds. A little further east, on a high hill, is where the red man of forest manufactured his darts, implements of war, and hunting utensils. Formerly the village was known by the name of Morristown, which name it retained for three years. It was laid out in 1850, and in 1853 was named Henryville, in honor of Col. Henry Ferguson. The Pennsylvania Railroad passes through the village, going almost due north, and leaves the place in a very irregular shape.

Joseph Biggs was the first storekeeper in Henryville. He kept his stock in a little frame house on the west side of the railroad. A Mr. Overman came next, but stayed only for a short time. He kept in a little frame house on the east side of the railroad. Henry Bussey and David Fish followed.

The post-office was established immediately after the railroad was built. The first postmaster was Mr. Overman, second, Harvey Bussey; third, Mr. Lewis; fourth, John Bolan, who acted in this capacity two years.

Memphis is the only village regularly laid out in Union township. It was platted by Thompson McDeitz in 1852. The lots are at right angles with Main street. There have been several additions made, the most important of which is J. F. Willey's, of very awkward shape, made so because of the location of the land. Generally the town is shaped ungainly. The railroad passes through the principal street, while the business houses are on either side. Memphis is wholly in tract number two hundred and three, of the Illinois grant. Neither of the founders of the village ever lived here permanently. McDeitz was a resident of Blue Lick, and Colonel Willey of Utica township. Tract number two hundred and three was originally owned by heirs in Virginia.

Previous to 1852 the citizens of what is now Oregon were included in the township of Charlestown. People residing in the northeastern part of the latter township found it inconvenient to attend elections at the county seat, or even nearer home. The old, original place of voting was constantly losing much of its regular business, and other towns and villages were gaining what she lost. So the residents naturally desired to be struck off from the old township, and to have a separate organization of their own. These and many more influential people finally induced a petition to be circulated for signers, and to be presented to the honorable board of County Commissioners, praying for a new township organization. The petition was written by Dr. John Covert, a distinguished resident of New Market, and mainly through his efforts the plan succeeded. Within the same year, 1852, the County Commissioners granted the request, and hence the present township of Oregon. It was struck off the northeastern side of Charlestown, and is four tracts wide from northeast to southwest and ten from northwest to southeast, making in all forty five-hundred-acre tracts, if they were wholly in Clark county. But the county line between Scott and Clark counties cuts off the northeastern corner of the township, and throws three or four tracts into the county of Scott. From this fact the tract which would naturally belong to Oregon extending further in a northeasterly direction than any of those in other townships, the name was derived. The Territory of Oregon was then the most distant body of land lying in the northwest which belonged to the United States; since there seemed to be a striking coincidence between the two sections, it was mutually agreed that the new township should be named after the new territory.

The site of Otisco was formerly owned by Thomas Cowling; but after his death his son, Samuel, inherited the property. They were of English extraction, and came here about 1830, when the upper part of the township was a dense forest. Immediately after the railroad was built, which was in 1854, the village was laid out.

Carr township lies in the western half of the county. It was organized in 1854, being struck off almost entirely from the eastern side of Wood. It has an area of nearly twenty-seven square miles, or over seventeen thousand acres, one third of which is knobs. It is bounded on the north by Wood, Monroe, and Union townships; on the east by Union and Silver Creek townships; on the south by Floyd county; and on the west by Wood township. The boundaries are very irregular on the north and east sides. They are set forth in language something like the following:

Beginning on the line which divides Clark from Floyd county, and on the line which divides sections nineteen and twenty, and from thence running north until it strikes the southwest corner of section thirty-two; thence east and thence north to where tracts numbers two hundred and fifty, two hundred and thirty-four, and two hundred and thirty-five corner; thence south, with variations, until it strikes the Muddy fork of Silver creek; thence with that stream, with its meanderings, to the south side of tract number one hundred and sixty-six; thence west, with variations, to the county line of Floyd, near St. Joseph's Hill, and thence with the dividing line between Clark and Floyd counties to the place of beginning.

This township is composed mostly of sections, though there are four or five of the Grant tracts lying along the eastern side of the township.

Petersburg, one of the little villages of Silver Creek township, was laid out about the year 1854, by Lewis Bottorff. The survey was made by Daniel H. McDaniels. Owing to some irregularity in the Recorder's office the plat was never recorded. There were eighteen lots fifty by two hundred feet, and the village was named in honor of Peter McKossky, a Russian who lived near by on the Muddy fork.

Union township, covering an area of nearly thirteen thousand acres, occupies the central portion of the county, and according to the census of 1900 has a population of nine hundred and sixteen. It was organized in September, 1858, mainly through the efforts of Col. John Carr. It is the newest of all the townships of the county, and takes its name from the fact that it was made up from a union of parts of other townships. Monroe bounds it on the north, except a narrow strip on the east side, where the township of Charlestown forms also the eastern boundary; the townships of Carr and Charlestown bound it on the south; Monroe and Carr form the western boundary. The township as it now is was erected out of Monroe, Charlestown and Carr townships. The extreme northern end of Silver Creek township and the extreme southern corner of Union unite in the middle of Silver creek, near the southwest corner of tract number one hundred and sixty-six; also the extreme portions of Carr and Charlestown townships—the only instance of the kind in the county.

In the late forties the town of Jeffersonville became interested in the construction of a rairoad. The Jeffersonville Railroad Company was incorporated by an act approved January 20, 1846, which empowered the company to build a road from Jeffersonville to Columbus, and also to use the tracks of the Madison and Indianapolis Railroad. The company organized under the name of the Ohio & Indiana Railroad Company, on the 17th of March, 1848, with James Keigwin, Samuel Merriwether, William G. Armstrong, A. Walker, Woods Maybury, Benjamin Irwin, J. B. Abbott, J. D. Shryer, W. A. Richardson, W. D. Beech, and Samuel McCampbell as directors, and William G. Armstrong, president; Samuel McCampbell, secretary, and J. G. Read, treasurer, as its officers. The name of the corporation was changed to the Jeffersonville Railroad Company in 1849, and in the fall of 1852 the road was completed.

The two roads were consolidated subsequent to 1862 as the Jeffersonville, Madison & Indianapolis Railroad Company. This consolidation was a practical absorption of the older by the younger road, as the officers and directors of the Jeffersonville Railroad Company were retained in office. This railroad now exists under the name of the Pennsylvania, having been absorbed by that company in 1873.

In September, 1853, the Fort Wayne & Southern Railroad was first discussed in the Jeffersonville council. This discussion finally culminated in

April, 1855, in the purchase of two hundred thousand dollars' worth of stock in the company. The route of this road after it entered the county about where the Pennsylvania now crosses Silver creek was up Front street in Clarksville and Jeffersonville to the foot of Pearl street, where the terminal was to be located. The efforts of such men as William G. Armstrong, James Keigwin, Samuel Merriwether, J. D. Shryer, Woods Maybury and James G. Read did much to advance the interests of Jeffersonville, although the heritage of the Fort Wayne & Southern investment is nothing to create much pleasure in the breasts of the present tax-payers of the city.

The periodical recurrence of the scheme to get steamboats over the Falls appeared again in 1852. The movement began with the organization of a company which intended to take steamboats out of the water at Jeffersonville and transport them by rail around the Falls, depositing them again upon the bosom of the stream below the Falls. This company was chartered May 11, 1852, and was called the "Ohio Falls Marine Railroad Company." The seal of the company depicts the ease with which this feat was to be performed. The boat resting gracefully upon the cars "en train" is shown with smoke pouring out of her chimneys, and from the steam issuing from her escape pipes her engines are evidently still at work. Among the citizens of Jeffersonville who subscribed money for the scheme were Sidney S. Lyon, L. D. Clemmons, John P. Cox, B. F. Marsh, Joseph Lank, Warren How, George L. Swartz and David H. Lane. They each subscribed for forty shares. This ship railroad was to be "wholly in Clark county," and was "to begin at a place in the town of Jeffersonville a short distance from the Jeffersonville ferry landing, as at present established, and to terminate at a place called Whirlpool, as estimated to be one and three-fourths miles below the Jeffersonville landing, the length of said road being as near as may be, a mile and three-fourths." Although surveys were made and plans drawn the road was never built and the project still hangs unplucked by the promoter.

The conditions of the transportation facilities on our railroads and ferries, as well as the attractions of Jeffersonville, are told by a traveler who arrived in 1858. His account ends as follows:

"After no less than four accidents to our train on the Ohio & Mississippi Railway, happily involving no other evil consequences than the smashing of the company's engine and two or three cars, the sacrifice of many valuable hours, and the loss of an amount of patience difficult to estimate, though once possessed by all the passengers, myself included, we arrived at the miserable village, though called a city, of Jeffersonville, in Indiana, nearly opposite to Louisville, in Kentucky, on the River Ohio. The train was due at an early hour in the afternoon, but did not reach Jeffersonville until half past nine in the evening, long before which time the steam ferry-boat had ceased to ply, and the captain of which refused to re-light the fires of his engines to carry the passengers across. We saw the lights of the large city gleaming temptingly across the stream, but, there being no means of conveyance, we were all reluctantly compelled to betake ourselves to the best inn at Jeffersonville—and bad, very bad, was the best. We had had nothing to eat or to drink all day, in consequence of the accident to our train having befallen us in an out-of-the-way place and in the very heart of the wilderness; and such of us as were not teetotalers looked forward to a comfortable supper and glass of wine or toddy, after our fatigue and disappointments. But, on asking for supper and wine at the hotel, we were told by mine host that we were in a temperance state, and that nothing in the way of drink would be served except milk, tea, coffee and lemonade. A thoughtful friend at Cincinnati had given us on starting a bottle of Bourbon whiskey twenty years old; and we told mine host that if he would provide us with glasses. hot water, sugar and a corkscrew, we should enjoy his meat, find our own drink, and set Fate at defiance."

Happily, we of later years are not compelled to be victims of such conditions, and the fact that the traveler was tired, hungry and disappointed upon his arrival. and possibly recovering from his above mentioned drink when he drote this description, may account for the beautiful tribute which he has paid Jeffersonville. The city, however, seemed to be considered important enough to notice even earlier than this. In 1852 General Scott visited Jeffersonville to deliver a speech against Franklin Pierce. Pierce had served under Scott in the Mexican war and had risen to the rank of brigadier-general. The presence of Mexican war veterans in Clark county prompted the visit of the old general, but it availed him nothing, and Pierce was elected to the Presidency.

In 1852 the public school system was inaugurated in Jeffersonville. The new constitution made education compulsory and free in the state. Two new school-houses were built at this time, both of which have disappeared. The first was on Mulberry street about opposite the end of Chestnut street, and was called the Mulberry street school. The other stood on the northwest corner of Maple and Watt streets and was called the "Blue" school-house. They were two-story brick structures and served admirably for the purposes for which they were constructed, yet they stand in great contrast to the newest addition to the schools of the city of Jeffersonville. The first school trustee of Jeffersonville was Jonas G. Howard, still an active factor in the politics and business life of the county. The establishment of the public school system in Indiana provided good schools, but there still seemed to be an opening for private institutions. In 1852 the Methodist church purchased the Springs property, where formerly the beauty and society of the South were wont to disport itself, and where gambling and conviviality were the pastimes of gentlemen. The "Palaces of Sin" were torn down or converted into school buildings, and quite a number of young ladies were enrolled as students in the new "Seminary." It prospered but a short while. Soon after the lapse of gaity at "The Springs," the hotel which stood at the foot of Broadway, burned (1857).

The establishment of a branch of the Bank of the State of Indiana in Jeffersonville in 1855 inaugurated the banking system in Clark county. It remains today, under the name of the Citizens National Bank, the oldest bank in the county.

In 1855 the question of lighting the city of Jeffersonville with gas was discussed in the Council, and in 1859 a company was chartered for that purpose. Mains were laid and within a year the streets were lighted and the residences were piped for the safer and more desirable illumination.

In Utica the first addition to the town was made in 1854 by James H. Oliver. It was on the northwest corner of the town.

In Bethlehem a great fire in 1856 burned down one entire block, including some of the oldest and largest houses in the town.

In Sellersburg the first post-office was established in 1852. In 1856, the Clark County Fair which had been held regularly in the vicinity of Charlestown, was held at Jeffersonville, but remained here but a few years, when it was taken back to Charlestown.

In the year 1853 the proceedings of the Common Council of the city of Jeffersonville show that the town of Port Fulton was annexed to Jeffersonville, but the action was premature as the annexation was never consummated. The solons of Jeffersonville were evidently wide awake at this period, for in January, 1855, the Council took up the question of the removal of the county seat from Charlestown. In February of this year Judge Read reported to the Council that he had been to Indianapolis to push the matter, and in January, 1856, a committee of three was appointed to advance the idea—four hundred dollars being appropriated for their expenses. As the county seat remained at Charlestown for twenty years after this attempt, it is evident that the project was salted away for future use.

In 1854 Clark county was visited by a great drouth, lasting from July to October. The crops were ruined, springs went dry, and the river reached an unprecedented low stage. The temperature during this period hovered about one hundred degrees for one hundred days. The following year the river reached an exceedingly low stage, and as there was no dam on the Falls the upper harbor extending past Madison suffered greatly. There was an early winter that year and during the latter part of November the river froze over, and on account of the shallow places froze to the bottom. About December 20th there was a period of mild weather and the owners of steamboats, supposing that navigation could be resumed, started out with their crafts. There was a sudden cold snap and between Fourteen Mile creek and

Twelve Mile Island five large steamers loaded with freight and passengers were caught in the ice and held fast.

The only new industry started in the city of Jeffersonville during this decade was a woolen mill. This mill was a large two-story brick building near the river bank just below Mechanic street. It was built by Samuel H. Patterson. This mill he placed in the hands of J. W. L. Mattock, who had formerly managed a mill of like kind in Danville, Indiana. In 1863 the mill was sold to Moses G. Anderson, who ran it some two years. In 1865 it was bought by J. L. Bradley, Dillard Ricketts and S. H. Patterson, who conducted it under the firm name of Bradley & Company. During the following year and a half the firm lost considerable money, and closed up the mill, selling the machinery to various persons. This building stood vacant for many years and was torn down in the eighties.

In 1860 occurred the trouble between the citizens of Jeffersonville and the convicts of the Prison South. The warden of the prison had contracted to furnish brick for the Louisville water works, then building, and the convicts were marched through the city streets to the brick works above the city. The fact that these men were taken through the streets chained together, and that they competed with free labor aroused the people to the injustice of the practice and a mob was formed to compel its discontinuance. The convicts were driven back to the prison, and since that time have never performed any labor outside the walls.

Politically the people of Clark county were comparatively quiet during the early fifties, but the election of 1854 stirred up feeling which engendered much bitterness. The Whigs and the Democrats had fought their political battles before this, and had then forgotten their differences, but this campaign produced a new feeling. Members of both the Whig and Democratic parties formed the People's party and in their meeting at Charlestown they promulgated their beliefs, among which was "temperance." Within this party was organized a secret organization, which went by the name of "Know Nothing." It was created for the purposes of waging a political war against the Roman Catholics and foreigners. At the time of the election riots occurred in the city of Jeffersonville when these citizens were assaulted to prevent their voting. No serious injuries resulted and the feeling in Clark county subsided. However, the movement which was nation-wide, appeared in Louisville the next year, 1855, and the memorable "Bloody Monday" resulted

While the political atmosphere of the county became agitated in '54, and during the last year or two of the decade, the social and commercial conditions presented a calm and unruffled surface. The people both in the country and in towns were a quiet, contented and industrious class. In the rural districts the farmers were far more contented and possibly had more reason to be so than at later periods. Previous to 1850, the county was covered with a thick forest, and the land was owned by settlers who, besides farming a small part of their forty or fifty acre tract, made considerable profit out of the manufacture of staves, hoops and barrels. There were few, if any, large farms at this time, and the division of the land into small parcels, each with its cabin or more ostentatious residence upon it, made a neighborhood of every farm, and no one was isolated or without near neighbors. The cooperage plants and the shipping of the output as well as the hoop-poles gave occupation to a very large population outside of the cities and towns. It is a matter of fact as well as astonishment to know that the rural population of Clark county at that time was greater than at the present day. The timber disappearing, the population followed, either moving to the city of Jeffersonville or the various towns situated northwardly. The small farms became a part of larger ones, and where twenty or thirty families had lived and flourished, the present day presents extensive tracts of pasture, or cultivated fields of an extent unknown in those days.

The larger rural population made the country far more attractive than it is in some localities at present, and the simpler habits and customs of the people made for contentment, and the desire for wealth which has spoiled the simple happiness of many of the present day farmers had not become as marked then as later on.

The farmers raised their crops and marketed them; were independent and happy. The spring, summer and fall gave occupation to all and the winter evenings were more given to reading and study than at the present day. As a rule they were a religious, God-fearing people. The farmer who did not attend church was the exception. Political, religious and general information was the rule, and although papers and magazines were far less plentiful than at present, these mediums were perused with interest and the topics of the day were studied and understood. The Christian Advocate, The Louisville Journal, edited by George D. Prentice, and the Louisville Democrat, edited by Harney, together with the Cincinnati Enquirer, were the journals subscribed for. The country churches were the centers of neighborhood activities, and the visit of a preacher always resulted in an all-day gathering. It has been said that almost every neighborhood had men so familiar with the Bible that if the book had been destroyed they might have reproduced it from memory. A social and friendly spirit seemed to pervade each countryside, and the simple religion of the pioneers remained to brighten and lighten the lives of those who chose to live in the free air and cheerful light of heaven. Nearly every family had prayers in the evening and a chapter read from a well-thumbed Bible became a part of the devotions. The Bible was the one book which was familiar to almost every country man. To this familiarity with the Book may be attributed the high tone which marked the character of the men of the day.

Previous to 1850 it was impossible to procure and keep harvest hands unless whiskey was served in the field, but this habit disappeared and with it the incident features which had helped to lower the standard of morality. Industry, prosperity and success marked the lives of the men who tilled the soil. The religious phase of their lives had none of the deadening influences which marked Puritan England in the sixteenth century, nor did as violent a reaction follow. The country dances and social gatherings were not affected by Puritanical views of such things. The intercourse between the people of Jeffersonville and Charlestown was most cordial. The road leading to Jeffersonville from the county seat was a very busy highway, and although there was neither railroad, electric line, or telephone, the incidents and events in one locality were subjects of interest elsewhere almost as quickly as at present. A 'bus running between Charlestown and Jeffersonville over the old Charlestown road brought the city and town in close touch.

The exciting questions which arose during the last year of the decade concerned the issues in national affairs, and but few months of the new decade had passed until the storm of war broke upon the nation, and Clark county, like the remainder of the loyal state of Indiana, entered with heart and soul in the duty of upholding the government founded by their forefathers in 1776. In the year 1860 the population of Clark county was twenty thousand five hundred and two.

8

CHAPTER X.

THE SEVENTH DECADE—1861-1870.

The seventh decade of the history of Clark county was the most momentous of all. The War of the Rebellion had deluged the land with blood for more than half of this period, and although Clark county never became the scene of actual combat, yet no city in the Union, large or small, had more of the outward and visible signs of war than did Jeffersonville. Beyond the river lay the Southland, whose legions surged to and from the border, while from the North came untold blue-clad thousands to preserve the Union established by our fathers. Jeffersonville being one of the principle gateways to the South, became the scene of martial display and military activities, which made every other business here sink into insignificance. Troops of all arms of the service, either arriving, camping here, leaving, or in hospitals, gave an importance to the city, the adjacent country, and the lines of transportation leading out of it that has never been known either before or since. The county itself presented a scene of activity in bearing its burden of the weight of war, and the raising of troops together with the many other activities co-ordinate with it kept the people alive to the condition of affairs both national and local. The farmer, the mechanic, the professional man and the tradesman, those who found it impossible to volunteer, still followed their vocations, but *War* was the dominating question, *War* was the principal theme, and *War* was the chief basis of business. In other chapters of this volume will be found recorded the events of interest connected with Clark county, and the War of the Rebellion, under the title of "Military Annals." Of disloyal organizations there were fortunately few within the borders of Clark county, but these few let no opportunity slip to advance the rebel cause or to gain friends for the Southern Confederacy. Their meetings were secret, as were their activities, but they made themselves felt at times and their machinations added spice to the times, if not to the honor of a loyal county.

In the early sixties the city of Jeffersonville established her first gas plant and the streets were lighted. The Patterson wharf was built and a new ferry company was started. This company, however, consolidated soon afterward with the older company.

The Car Works was established in 1864. The First National Bank was established in 1865. The Charlestown and Utica pike was opened in 1866. The first steam mill in Wood township was built in 1868.

In 1864 one hundred and fifty thousand dollars were appropriated by Congress to build the United States Quartermaster Depot at Jeffersonville. There being no provision for the purchase of the ground, the citizens of the city took the matter up and a committee headed by S. B. Diffenderfer, finally found means to get the location. This was under the administration of Levi Sparks as Mayor of the city, and the city after paying eleven thousand dollars for the ground donated it to the United States for the purpose of erecting a permanent depot. The buildings were begun soon after and the permanent location of the quartermaster depot was assured for Jeffersonville.

Up to the year 1860 there had never been a legal hanging in Clark county, but this year the Sheriff executed a man sentenced by the Clark Circuit Court. There has only been one other legal hanging since.

In 1865 Congress, by act, authorized the Louisville, Nashville & Jeffersonville Railroad Companies, who were stockholders in the Louisville Bridge Company to construct a railway bridge across the Ohio at the head of the Falls. The erection of the superstructure was begun in May, 1868, and on February 1, 1870, the spans were connected. The first train passed over on February 12, 1870. This bridge cost two million three thousand six hundred ninety-six dollars and twenty-seven cents. In the various accidents during the construction of this work there were fifty-six men killed and eighty wounded.

The winter of 1866-1867 was a very severe one. The cold was intense, and the river so low that it froze up early in the winter. The coal supply gave out, and the people suffered for want of fuel. What little there was on hand went to 60 cents per bushel. Previous to this period there were two ferry lines, one of which had a landing at the foot of Clay street, Louisville, and after fighting for some months they consolidated, but part of the agreement was that a boat should continue to land at Clay street. The fuel famine became so serious that Phil Tompert, who was then Mayor of Louisville, was appealed to by the people to ask the boats to stop running, a channel having been cut between Louisville and Jeffersonville, so that the coal they were consuming could be distributed among the sufferers. There was practically no trouble in getting the boat landing at Clay street to stop, as it was not paying, and from that day to this it has never made a trip. There was threatened litigation, but this never amounted to anything, and the present ferry company gained its monopoly of the business through the demand for coal stopping the other boat.

In 1870 the Ohio & Mississippi Railroad, the main line of which runs between Cincinnati and St. Louis, built what is now the Watson connection. At that time some good coaches were used on the Watson line, but they have become slightly worn since then. This road now operates under the title, Baltimore & Ohio Southwestern.

In the year 1870 the mill known as the Gathright Mill was built just below the Pennsylvania bridge. This mill was operated by a turbine water-wheel, except during high water, and was successfully operated for many years. It burned about 1906.

The end of this decade finds Clark county back to a normal condition after the war. The population of the county in 1870 was twenty-four thousand seven hundred seventy.

CHAPTER XI.

THE EIGHTH DECADE—1871-1880.

An epoch of commercial, political and religious activities was that of the seventies. The temperance question, the county seat removal, the glass works and car works questions, the panics and strikes, and a general condition of material improvement marked this decade as war had marked the preceding one. The various departments and offices of the United States quartermaster were still scattered over the city of Jeffersonville, but work was soon commenced upon the new buildings which were to contain all of the offices and storehouses under one roof. In 1870 was launched the steamer, James Howard, at the Howard ship yards in Jeffersonville. She was the largest inland river steamer ever built on western waters.

The village of Marysville, containing about one hundred inhabitants, was laid out by W. W. Tevis, civil engineer, in 1871, for Patrick H. Jewett. It is located on the Baltimore & Ohio Southwestern Railroad, between Otisco and Nabbs. It is on both sides of the railroad and has forty lots. The village is located on the south side of tract number two hundred forty-eight, about midway from the north and south line. Marysville was named after Miss Mary Kimberlain, the wife of A. Q. Abbott, of Oregon township. During the years which have elapsed since the village was regularly platted, very little has been done in the way of improvement.

On January 31, 1871, the city of Jeffersonville ceded all jurisdiction over the four blocks purchased by the United States Government for a quartermaster's depot, to the United States Government. At meetings held in several places in the county immediately following the Chicago fire, substantial donations were made for the benefit of the sufferers.

On the 6th of July, 1871, the city council passed an ordinance providing for a steam fire department, to consist of one engineer, two drivers, and four hosemen for each engine and hose-cart. In September of the same year a committee was appointed to buy the necessary engine, hose-cart, hose, etc. An Amoskeag engine was bought at a cost of four thousand five hundred dollars; hose cart, five hundred fifty dollars; one thousand feet of hose and three horses, six hundred dollars, and harness, eighty-four dollars and twenty-five cents, making a total cost of seven thousand two hundred twenty-four dollars and twenty-five cents. Previous to this the department consisted of a hand engine and fires were often the occasion of a fight or a frolic.

On September 22, 1872, Horace Greeley, nominee of the Democrats and Liberal Republicans for the Presidency, visited Jeffersonville and spoke to an immense crowd on Spring street. His speech was delivered from the small iron balcony in front of the second floor of the old hotel at Spring and Market streets. In this year also occurred a great disaster to the city of Jeffersonville in the burning of the shops of the Ohio Falls Car and Locomotive Company. The company had just made extensive improvements, but everything was swept out of existence. Fortunately a heavy insurance was carried and the building of the present magnificent system of fire-proof and isolated structures was begun. The improvements were still incomplete when the panic of 1873 came and the long period of financial depression which followed completely paralyzed the car building business.

In December, 1872, the office of the County Treasurer at Charlestown was robbed, and although the amount of actual county funds stolen finally turned out to be small, the robbery caused great excitement. A gang of toughs had terrorized Charlestown for several years, and the robbery was of their doing. They were captured, however, soon afterward.

In both Charlestown and Jeffersonville fairs were held this year to raise funds to be used for the relief of the poor who were suffering as a result of the panic. Mosart Hall was the scene of the fair in Jeffersonville. This building, at the southwest corner of Spring and Court streets, served for many years for gatherings of this kind, and held the unique position of being the only available hall of its size in the city, during a period when such fairs and social gatherings were far more frequent than at the present day.

During the winter of 1872 smallpox was epidemic throughout the county, and reached such a stage that the council of Jeffersonville ordered that red flags be displayed before each house containing a case. The papers of the time tell of Sam Hedge being ill with the disease, and of how he had decorated the whole front of his house with myriads of red flags to warn away everybody.

Building a new school-house at Utica was a warm subject in 1873, in that township. However, after extended debate and much feeling, but no casualties the building was ordered built.

In this year on October 8th all the female convicts at the prison were sent to Indianapolis. Previous to this the Prison South received female as well as male prisoners as no special provision had been made by the state up to that time for their separate incarceration. Previous to this, in February, 1873, the citizens of Jeffersonville had held a meeting and adopted a most inexplicable resolution. They worked and used every influence to get the prison removed from Jeffersonville to Michigan City, but fortunately failed.

A new company was incorporated this year to construct a bridge across the river from the foot of Clay street in Louisville. Among the incorporators were Barrett, Dennis Long, W. Ray, Doctor Green, T. Bradley and others. The following subscribed stock:

Chesapeake & Ohio...$200,000.00
Ohio & Mississippi 200,000.00
City of Jeffersonville 100,000.00
City of Louisville 100,000.00

The fact that Jeffersonville subscribed as much as Louisville shows either a financial healthfulness or a desire to be so that was commendable. That she was abreast of Louisville in some ways was evidenced by the existence of three banks, all in a flourishing state of prosperity. The Citizens' National Bank, the First National Bank and Mr. Barnaby's Faro bank.

In 1873 the village of Bethlehem made application for incorporation. It had been laid out in 1812, and since that time had seen varying changes of fortune.

In 1873 began the agitation against the liquor traffic. The movement began as did the one in 1907 and 1908, and gathered momentum as it advanced. In the year 1874 the actual warfare against the saloon and the whiskey business in general was begun by the women of Jeffersonville.

Dr. Sallie C. Jackson was president of the woman's society which was battling against the rum demon. Mrs. Winesburg, of the Presbyterian church, was elected vice-president, and Mrs. Martha Cook, treasurer. These women, numbering sometimes a hundred, would meet at the Methodist church, and after prayers, would march out in column of twos to the various saloons in the city.

Their first meetings were held in the saloons of Alonzo Fouts and the Falls City hotel, where they were treated with great discourtesy. At the saloon in the Strauss Hotel, on the corner of Front and Spring streets, meetings were held, but whatever results may have come at that time have wholly disappeared as this place still dispenses old Tambo over the bar in satisfactory quantities.

At John Sittle's emporium the ladies were attacked by the proprietor's wife with tubs of water. Although drenched to the skin, they stood their ground and one of the party of crusaders, glorying in her condition, cried out in her ecstacy, "Bless God, I am a Baptist!"

These efforts culminated in the formation of the Woman's Christian Temperance Union in Jeffersonville, and the reputation of the crusaders of this city went abroad in the land. A paper of the day has this item concerning the effects of their efforts:

"The ladies of the Temperance Union of this city have been now about four weeks engaged in active work against the liquor traffic. All the druggists but one in the city have signed the pledge to sell liquor only upon the prescription of a regular physician. All the physicians but two have signed pledges to use iquor in their practice only in cases of emergency. Pledges not to sign applications for a renewal of license have been widely circulated among the voters and have met with such favor that it is believed that a renewal of license could not now be obtained in any ward in the city. There has been such an awakening on the subject of temperance as was scarcely if ever known before. The traffic has been reduced at least sixty per cent."

During the time of the crusaders the women held one hundred fifty-two street prayer meetings, besides visiting saloons, offering pledges and praying and talking to saloon-keepers.

In 1874 another fine school-house, the Rose Hill school in Jeffersonville, was finished. The question concerning the removal of the county seat from Charlestown to Jeffersonville resulted in one of the bitterest political fights ever known in Clark county. The fight which was made in 1838 and won by the removalists, the Jeffersonville party, resulted in nothing as the Legislature refused the people of the county their wishes on that subject.

During the sixty-six years, while Charlestown had been the county seat, Jeffersonville had passed her in population, and had acquired an envy of her only great possession. After a lapse of forty years from the first attempt the fight was renewed.

Jeffersonville township, including the city of Jeffersonville, now had near-ly one-half of the whole population of the county, and it seemed just that the majority should rule. As early as March, 1874, the papers of the time con-tain accounts of meetings held to discuss this subject. At this time one meet-ing was held at Charlestown, and a united effort was decided on to prevent the removal. Discussion became bitter, letters, circulars and newspaper articles appeared. About January 1, 1876, the City Council of Jeffersonville, headed by its then recently elected Mayor, the Hon. Luther F. Warder, decided to inaugurate a determined effort to regain the long lost county seat. The ground was donated for the site of the court-house and thirty thousand dol-lars was voted, raised and deposited with the County Treasurer as a donation to the county to build a court-house in case removal was made. The people of Charlestown met the movement at the beginning and fought it with vigor and determination. The people in the upper end of the county joined them. The contest ran into bitter personal animosities and hostility between the two sections of the county. Animosities were engendered that perhaps will never he healed, and the newspapers of the time present some rich and racy reading. Political affinities were destroyed and the removal question dominated every other and all other questions of public interest. The Board of County Com-missioners met at Charlestown court-house on the first Monday in March, 1876, and the petitions for removal, containing a clear majority of all the voters in the county were presented, but every effort was made to defeat them. It was charged that a large portion of the signatures were fictitious, but the anti-removalists were met at every point. The case was pressed through the Commissioners' court and then appealed to the Circuit Court. A change of venue was taken to Floyd county and a special judge was agreed upon. Judge Perkins, of Indianapolis, was sent to try the case. At length the anti-removalists had reached the end of their resources and were compelled to submit to the inevitable. On September 23, 1878, the order was made to remove the county records to Jeffersonville, and during the month of October they were brought to the new county seat and placed in the new and commodious court-house, which had been built to receive them. After a lapse of sixty-seven years, Jeffersonville again became the county seat of Clark county, and it is hardly probable that the removal question will ever arise again.

The affairs at the Prison, South, occupied a great deal of attention in 1874, on account of the frequent escapes of a genius namer Rodifer, who was serving time there. An investigation of conditions at the prison was made soon after, and the report of the investigating committee was to relieve Shuler, the warden, for gross mismanagement.

In 1875 a great revival of religion swept over the county.

In May, 1875, the first notices of the new glass works began to appear in the papers, and it was stated, "Work will be started if twenty thousand dollars worth of stock can be subscribed. On November 1, 1876, work was started on the plant. The company was chartered under the name of the Ford Plate Glass Company, with a capital stock of one hundred twenty-five thousand dollars. The city donated five hundred feet of ground on Market street, east, extending to the river front, to secure the location of this industry in Jeffersonville. John F. Read was chosen president of the company. In February, 1880, the name was changed to the Jeffersonville Plate Glass Company, the incorporators being at this time, John F. Read, S. Goldbach, Felix Lewis, Edward Howard, James Burke, Edward Ford, Warren Horr, Joshua Cook, Frederick Herron, Abraham Frye, Jonas G. Howard. S. Goldbach was elected president, H. T. Sage, secretary and treasurer and E. L. Ford, superintendent. After the reorganization of the company one hundred feet front was added. Two hundred men were employed and the business was confined to the manufacture of plate glass. This industry was a valuable addition to the city of Jeffersonville, and as it was one of the first glass works in the United States, its output was easily disposed of. An article of that time described the plant as follows:

"So great is the demand for plate glass that the works in Jeffersonville are driven to their fullest capacity, and find it difficult to fill their orders. They have two large furnaces, each with a capacity for eight crucibles holding fifteen hundred pounds of melted glass. One furnace is opened in the morning, the other in the afternoon, and sixteen large plates are rolled each day. As soon as possible after pouring, the plates are removed from the iron bed on which they are made and transferred to the annealing ovens, where they are allowed to gradually cool. They then pass through the various stages of grinding, polishing and cleaning, and are ready to be packed. The entire process requires the greatest care and accuracy, owing to the brittle character of the article, and breakages are not infrequent.

"The table on which the molten mass is poured is eleven by twenty-two feet and glass can be made of nearly this size, the largest being one hundred ten by two hundred thirty inches. The time required to melt the metal in the crucibles, and allow it to cool sufficiently to pour, is twenty-four hours."

In the year 1881 the sales of the company amounted to two hundred fifty thousand dollars. The finished plate glass was worth at that time about one hundred dollars and sixty cents per square foot.

The year 1876 being an election year as well as the centennial year, the usual enthusiastic demonstrations during the compaign took place, and the torch-light processions of this and the succeeding campaigns of 1880 and 1884 were evidence of the great interest which the masses took in the issues of the day.

On April 24, 1876, the great steamer, the Robert E. Lee, was launched at Howard's ship yard. It was an occasion which drew great crowds, not only because of the name of the boat, but on account of her size. The shipyards at this time were in the most prosperous period of their existence, but the founder and head of this industry, Capt. James Howard, was drowned on October 14th by his buggy backing off of the ferry boat.

An amusing incident occurred during the early part of 1876. A baby was found on a doorstep in Jeffersonville with a note attached, giving the information that its father was a councilman. Col. James Keigwin, always a great joker, discussed the matter at a council meeting, and together with Capt. William Northcutt and William S. Goldbach, other members, furnished amusement to the people of the city for some time.

In Jeffersonville the Orphans' Home was founded this year, and the work of raising a building fund was begun. This year also the town of Watson was laid out. J. B. Speed was the moving spirit in the new village. In 1871 the cement mill had been erected in this vicinity and it was this fact which brought the village into existence. In 1872 the post-office here was established.

Following the election of Mr. Hayes to the Presidency, after the hot campaign of the fall, came the violent dissatisfaction of those who voted the other way, and Clark county added her mite to the cause by holding meetings at several points to protest. At New Washington the Democrats and Republicans clashed and engaged in a rough and tumble fight, but no casualties resulted.

The panic and strikes in 1877 affected the industries of Clark county materially. The threats of members of the mob in Louisville, that they intended coming to Jeffersonville to seize the stores and arms at the quartermaster's depot, was the occasion of much concern, and the Jeffersonville Rifles, the local militia company, was held under arms for quite a while. Cannon from the Government building were kept in readiness, but the mob never came.

In 1877 the question of water works for Jeffersonville was agitated, and in the latter part of the year a company was organized, called the Jeffersonville Water Works Company. Dennis Long, of Louisville, was president; John C. Howard, John Read, D. S. Barmore and other were interested, but the company failed to make good.

The visit of President Hayes to Jeffersonville and his enthusiastic reception, September 17, 1877, was evidence that the people of Clark county had forgotten the animosities created by the campaign and in the election squabble.

On September 23, 1878, the final order was given for the removal of the records from Charlestown to the new court-house at Jeffersonville.

The town of New Washington was increased in size in 1879 by the addition of thirty-three in-lots, and twelve out-lots. On Thursday, September 18, 1879, the Most Worshipful Grand Master of the Masons of Indiana, Calvin W. Prather, of Jeffersonville, laid the cornerstone of the Jeffersonville Orphans' Home with great ceremony.

As a whole the decade of 1870-1880 was one in which Clark county showed material advancement in many ways. Her industrial, her social and her religious life had each their revivals, and the year 1880 opened with a people happy, prosperous and ambitious. The population of the city of Jeffersonville in 1880 was ten thousand six hundred sixty-six; that of Clark county was twenty-eight thousand six hundred ten.

CHAPTER XII.

THE NINTH DECADE.—1881-1890.

Outside of the commercial activity, which marked this decade and the floods which threatened to ruin the city, nothing of great importance occurred. In 1881 the block bounded by Court avenue, and between Spring street and Wall street was divided by a thirty-foot street known as Park street. The part laying between Park street and Court avenue was laid out as a park and improved with walks, trees and shrubs and christened "Warder Park," in honor of the mayor, the Hon. Luther F. Warder.

In 1881 Sweeney's foundry was moved to its present location. It was originally established in 1869 by Michael A. Sweeney and Chris. Baker, who opened a small shop on Pearl street, near Court avenue. Mr. Baker retired from the firm in 1870, Mr. Sweeney continuing the business alone. In 1872 he moved to Court avenue, and in March, 1876, admitted James Sweeney as a partner. The business was continued here until March, 1881, when the firm purchased nine acres of ground from Guthrie, Marlin & Company, of Louisville, and as soon as buildings could be erected, moved their works to the place they now occupy. They have a river frontage of nine hundred sixty-five feet, and since their purchase of this property have made extensive improvements. For a number of years they have engaged in boat-building, and have launched quite a number of handsome steamers in late years. The principal work of this firm, however, is engine building, although all kinds of machinery is constructed. This firm still remains one of the important industries in Clark county. The most important incident, or rather series of incidents, which collectively made one great calamity in the eighties, were the floods of 1883 and 1884.

In the year 1883 the river reached such a stage that a large part of Jeffersonville was flooded and great damage done, but in 1884, when on February 15th, the river reached the unprecedented stage of 46.7 feet, the city of Jeffersonville suffered a blow to her hopes—her industries and her business which took years to repair. The water on this date covered Port Fulton up to the Utica pike, as far down at Jefferson street, out to High street, down to Division street, out to Chestnut street, down Chestnut street, out Penn street, down Court avenue, out Fulton street, thence to Ninth street and Walnut, thence east to Walnut and Watt streets, thence to Tenth street and Locust, thence to Eleventh and Wall, to Thirteenth and Walnut, to Locust and Fourteenth, thence southwardly to Sparks avenue, east to Spring street, thence to Spring and Broadway, thence west to the city line, between Eleventh and Sparks avenue. The water reached the point where Eighth street crosses the west line of Jeffersonville, thence to Missouri avenue and Seventh street, thence to Seventh and Broadway, thence to Sixth and Indiana avenue, thence to Court avenue, east of Indiana avenue, thence to Fourth street, east of Indiana avenue, thence to Ohio avenue and Fourth street, thence to Third and Ohio avenue, thence to Market and Fort street, thence with Fort street to the alley, between Market and Front streets, thence to Clark street, thence to Mulberry and Market streets, and thence to the river front.

The city of Jeffersonville contained two hundred fourteen blocks, of which ninety-three were wholly submerged, forty-three partly submerged, and seventy-eight were dry. Some of the measurements taken at that time by Victor W. Lyon, C. E., show the following depths of water February 15, 1884:

Spring and Front streets .... 3.14 feet
Pearl and Market streets .... 1.42 feet
Pearl and Chestnut streets .... 4.51 feet
Pearl and Maple streets .... 6.82 feet
Pearl and Court avenue .... 8.12 feet
Michigan avenue and Court avenue .... 8.86 feet
Fifth street and Ohio avenue................. 9.05 feet
Sixth street and Ohio avenue .... 2.95 feet
Seventh street and Ohio avenue .... 9.19 feet
Eighth street and Ohio avenue .... 9.31 feet
Eighth street and Michigan avenue .... 11.42 feet
Ninth street and Spring street .... 8.11 feet
Eleventh street and Spring street .... 7.89 feet
Front street and Locust street .... 5.18 feet
Market street and Locust street .... 6.21 feet
Chestnut street and Locust street .... 6.30 feet
Walnut street and Maple street .... 6.58 feet
Walnut street and Court street .... 4.98 feet
Walnut street and Seventh street .... 6.66 feet
Walnut street and Eighth street .... 8.54 feet
Walnut street and Market street .... 10.00 feet
Locust street and Ninth street .... 11.88 feet
Ekin avenue and Indiana avenue .... 13.70 feet
Ekin avenue and Illinois avenue .... 12.31 feet
Eleventh street and Illinois avenue .... 16.18 feet
Missouri avenue and Tenth street .... 14.15 feet

Missouri avenue and Eleventh street .... 13.74 feet
Missouri avenue and west line of city .... 16.53 feet
Indiana avenue and Ninth street .... 11.98 feet
Maple street and Watt street .... 5.07 feet
Wall street and Ninth street .... 13.61 feet
Market street and Division street .... 7.00 feet
Chestnut street and Graham street .... 1.50 feet

This flood caused great suffering in Jeffersonville and along the whole length of the river, but relief in abundance was received from all over the country. Soon afterward the levee was built under Government supervision and with a Government appropriation. Jeffersonville stands now well protected against the recurrence of such a disaster and during the great flood of 1907, the highest since 1884, Jeffersonville was the dryest town or city along the whole Ohio valley.

In the eighties also the oil and gas fever struck Clark county and a company was formed in Jeffersonville to open wells. J. V. Reed was president, Willis Goodwin, secretary and J. H. McCampbell, treasurer. Stock was greedily bought and six or seven wells were sunk near Jeffersonville. The one in Ferguson's woods struck a good flow of gas and the stockholders, in their elation, held a celebration at the well and the whole city turned out. The gas was lighted and night was turned into day. The stockholders refused to sell their holdings to less fortunate friends, but their dream was short lived, as the gas soon gave out. Luther F. Warder formed another company to sink wells but they met with no better success.

The political campaigns of '84 and '88 were the most enthusiastic since the Civil war. Cleveland and Hendricks marching clubs vied with the Blain and Logan clubs and the county presented about an equal number of marchers in the many torch-light processions which marked the campaign in this locality. The campaign of 1888, between Cleveland and Harrison, was equally as strenuous and the Clark county citizens maintained their reputation for keeping things warm until the night of the election.

In 1884 one of the most philanthropic acts in the history of the county was performed by Prof. William W. Borden, of Borden, in erecting and starting the Borden Institute, a school which he maintained for a number of years, and which has furnished good educations to hundreds of young men and women of Wood township.

In Jeffersonville the water works system was completed in 1888 and accepted. The population of Clark county in 1890 was thirty thousand two hundred fifty-nine.

CHAPTER XIII.

THE TENTH DECADE—1891-1900.

On March 27, 1890, the city of Jeffersonville and the southern part of the county was visited by the most destructive cyclone in the history of the city. About seven o'clock p. m. it broke with all its fury, demolishing buildings and sweeping away property, but fortunately killing no one. In Louisville, however, scores of people were killed and the destruction of property was tremendous. In Jeffersonville many buildings were unroofed, many were partly down, and many were so badly damaged that they had to be pulled down. About two hundred houses were ruined in the city alone, and at the time the damage was estimated at five hundred thousand dollars. The force of the wind was terrific, large timbers being blown across the river from wrecked buildings in Louisville. A skiff in the river was blown out of the water and into a house on Front street.

In 1891 the Car Works and other industries of Clark county were enjoying a period of great prosperity. At that time the Car Works was employing two thousand men, and this year turned out five thousand and eight cars, valued at two million nine hundred thousand dollars, or one car for every thirt-five minutes. The sixty-three acres of the plant, with its five miles of track, was one of the busiest places around the Falls, the saw mill alone turning out ten million feet of lumber per year.

The Big Four bridge, which had been in course of construction for several years, had reached that stage where the spans were being placed on the piers. In December, 1892, during a heavy gale, the large center span fell and shortly afterward the span on the Kentucky side followed. The collapse of the center span carried a score of men to death, but the fall of the second span resulted in no casualties. Three years previously several lives were lost by accidents in the caissons, but the Phoenix Bridge Company repaired the damage and the bridge was finished and opened for traffic in September, 1895.

In the fall of 1895 the twenty-ninth annual reunion of the Grand Army of the Republic was held at Louisville, and Jeffersonville prepared to help entertain the old soldiers. Enough lunch stands and sleeping quarters were prepared to care for five thousand visitors, but the sandwiches went uneaten, the coffee undrunk and the cots undisturbed by sleepers. Half the population expected to make money during the festivities and half the population were disappointed. The owner of one impromptue lunch stand had ordered five hundred pies per day and he disposed of one pie. One genius erected five thousands seats on the river bank to seat the crowds during the display of fire works one night and he had one customer. The reunion was not a season of happiness so far as Jeffersonville was concerned.

In this decade another addition was made to Jeffersonville, called Ingram's addition. It consisted of blocks one to four and lays in Grant No. 8.

From 1890 to 1900 the transportation of Jeffersonville citizens was on a celebrated system of mule cars. This line of cars, which ran the whole length to Market street, was the butt of all jokers, but it was a great convenience to many and paved the way for the present system of electric cars, which has added so materially to the attractiveness of the city.

In 1893, a bill, presented to the Legislature by Willis Barnes, of Charlestown, was passed appropriating five hundred dollars for a monument to Gov. Jonathan Jennings. Jennings' remains had laid in the old cemetery south of Charlestown since June 27, 1834, but they were moved to the new cemetery in 1894, and the monument erected to mark his final resting place.

In September, 1891, a great fair was held in Charlestown. The exhibits being of great interest, were viewed by thousands of visitors.

From 1892 to 1893 Clark county had the first company of the National Guard since 1877. The officers of this company were: Captain, L. C. Baird; first lieutenants, C. H. Kelly, W. W. Crooker and H. H. Thacker; second lieutenants, W. W. Crooker and H. E. Barrett. The company was called into active service during the strike and riots of 1893 and upon their return from Sullivan county were received by a great crowd of friends.

In 1898 the Spanish war found Clark county without a company for the first call, but this was caused by the call being filled by militia regiments. The second call was responded to by a splendid company recruited from nearly all parts of the county. Their service in the One Hundred Sixty-first Indiana Volunteer Infantry will be found in the chapters on the military history of Clark county. Their return from foreign service May 3, 1899, was the occasion of a great demonstration.

In October, 1899, was held a carnival of flowers on the occasion of the meeting of the Southern Indiana Press Association in Jeffersonville. The display of beautifully decorated carriages was a delight to the many visitors here at that time.

On September 4, 1899, a great labor day celebration was held in Jeffersonville.

In October, 1899, the corner stone of the school-house in Howard Park was laid with appropriate ceremonies.

On December 10, 1899, Father Andran, the beloved priest of St. Augustine's Roman Catholic church, died. His death removed the friend and coun-

CLARK COUNTY COURT HOUSE.

sellor of many and a wonderfully successful worker from the Christian church.

In this decade Jeffersonville and Clark county enjoyed all the advantages which belonged to other places similarly situated with the exception of street car and interurban service, but the next decade produced a service second to none.

In 1896 Jeffersonville spent nearly ten thousand dollars on street improvement.

In 1897 the city was one of the best lighted cities in the country, having sixty arc lights on the streets.

The population of Clark county in 1900 was thirty-one thousand eight hundred and thirty-five.

9

CHAPTER XIV.

THE ELEVENTH DECADE—1901-1910.

This last decade of Clark county history is the centennial decade, not only of the county, but of Jeffersonville and of Charlestown.

On February 3, 1801, William Henry Harrison, the first Territorial Governor, created Clark county by gubernatorial proclamation. The centennial of this date was marked by no celebration, but the celebration of the centennial of the founding of Jeffersonville, June 23, 1902, was an event of county wide interest. A great parade of societies, exhibits, bands and citizens was a feature of the day, followed by exercises at the court-house, where Col. James Keigwin, Hon. Jonas G. Howard, and Hon. Frank Burke delivered speeches.

To the ladies of the Daughters of the American Revolution belong all the credit for this centennial. The parade in the morning was divided into divisions and were commanded by Jeffersonville soldiers. Col. John Ingram, a veteran of the Mexican war, commanded one division. Col. James Keigwin, Capt. John Hoffman, Col. Isaac Brinkworth, and Capt. C. W. Coward, veterans of the War of the Rebellion, commanded other divisions; while Maj. D. C. Peyton, Capt. L. C. Baird, and Capt. James W. Fortune, of the Spanish war, commanded others. In the evening a concert by a military band was given on Front street, and this was followed by a display of fire works from a barge anchored in the river.

On September 19, 1903, the corner stone of the new Jeffersonville Carnegie Library was laid by the most worshipful grand lodge of Free and Accepted Masons of Indiana, with imposing ceremonies. Fifteen thousand dollars had been provided by Mr. Carnegie for the building of this structure, and one thousand five hundred dollars per year had been pledged for its support. At the ceremonies, Grand Master William E. English, of Indianapolis, presided, and Brother E. L. Powell, of Louisville, made the principal address.

The following is a list of articles deposited in the corner stone:

City directory of 1903.
One copy of Daily Courier Journal, dated September 19, 1903.
One copy of Daily Herald, September 19, 1903.
One copy of Daily Evening Star, September 19, 1903.
One copy of Daily Evening News, September 19, 1903.

One copy of Weekly Clark County Republican, September 19, 1903.

Copy of Masonic directory, 1902.

Roster of officers and members of Clark Lodge, Free and Accepted Masons, September 19, 1903.

Roster of officers and members of Grand Lodge, Free and Accepted Masons, Indianapolis, 1903.

Roster of officers and members of the Forty-ninth Indiana Volunteer Infantry in war of 1861-5, furnished by (and in his own writing) Col. James Keigwin, its commanding officer.

Roster of officers and members of Company E, One Hundred Sixty-first Indiana Volunteer Infantry, in war of 1898-99, by Capt. Lewis C. Baird.

List of city officers for 1903.

List of county officers for 1903.

List of township officers for 1903.

Roster of post-office officials, carriers, etc., 1903.

List of officers of new library (Carnegie's), 1903, and copy of resolutions on death of Miss Hannah Zulauf, one of the original founders.

List of officers of Walnut Ridge cemetery.

List of officers of First Presbyterian church, 1903, with history of the organization of the church and photograph of the Rev. John S. Howk, pastor.

List of officers of Wall Street Methodist Episcopal church, 1903, and photograph of Rev. Charles E. Asbury, pastor.

List of officers and rector of St. Paul's Episcopal church, 1903.

List of officers and members of the Methodist Episcopal church, South (Morton Chapel), and its history from the organization, by Rev. J. B. Butler, pastor.

List of officers of First Christian church.

List of officers of First Baptist church.

List of officers of Advent Christian church.

List of members of Bar of Clark county.

Invitation to exercises of dedication.

Program of exercises of dedication.

Almanac of 1903.

Proclamation of Mayor for half-holiday.

Municipal reports of city, 1898, Alfred H. Bamber.

The Delineator, a magazine of fashion, 1903.

Buttericks's fashion patterns, October, 1903.

Roster of teachers of city schools, 1903, and photograph of Alexander C. Goodwin, superintendent.

Nickel of coinage of 1903, by Thomas B. Bohon.

Confederate bill of denomination of ten dollars, dated February 17, 1864.

History of Jeffersonville township public library, by Miss Eva Luke.

Copy of contract and specifications for new library building, by Clark and Loomis, architects.

Photograph of Arthur Loomis, architect.

Photograph of Mrs. Carrie Loomis.

Roster of A. A. S. R. for 1902, Valley of Indianapolis, by Thomas W. Perry.

Roster of Murat Temple, 1902, A. A. R. Shrine, by T. W. Perry.

Photograph of Hon. James K. Marsh, Judge of the Circuit Court.

Photograph of Thomas W. Perry, secretary of school board.

Photograph of W. A. Davis, president of school board.

Photograph of Simeon S. Johnson, past grand master Masons of Indiana.

Card of Timmonds and Stancell, makers of deposit box.

In December, 1903, St. Augustine's Roman Catholic church was burned with a loss of about thirty-five thousand dollars. The congregation immediately took steps to rebuild and on Sunday, October 2, 1905, it was dedicated by Bishop Francis Silas Chatard.

In February, 1904, occurred the death of a distinguished educator of Indiana, Prof. A. C. Goodwin, the superintendent of the Jeffersonville public schools.

On May 1, 1904, the last mule car was seen in Jeffersonville; the line was discontinued for a short time, and a new electric equipment was installed. This line extended up Market street to Jackson street, Port Fulton, and down Market street to Ohio avenue. There was also a line on Spring street from Front to Court avenue, up Court avenue, to Meigs avenue, and out Meigs to the government depot.

On July 12, 1904, the City Council of Jeffersonvlile granted a franchise to build an approach to the Big Four bridge from Court avenue, and on September 13, 1905, the first car was taken over the bridge.

In August, 1904, the re-dedication of the old Bethel meeting house, three miles south of Charlestown, took place in the presence of a large concourse of Methodists. Bishop Walden, of Cincinnati, presided.

In May, 1903, the state of Indiana acquired two thousand acres of land near Henryville and established a state forestry reservation. This tract of land was acquired to show that seven hundred thousand acres of so-called worthless knob land in Southern Indiana could be made of value. Here also were to be raised seedling trees to distribute all over Indiana to make the state again an extensive and commercial hardwood producer, and thereby retain many of the wood working concerns which would have to eventually leave the state unless a new supply of timber could be grown. It was also established to teach forestry. On the summit of the knob in this tract six hundred feet above the plains of northern Clark county and one thousand twenty-six feet above sea level one can look down on the most promising farm lands of the state. This undertaking on the part of the state promises to be of great value and has already borne fruits.

On August 25, 1904, Jeffersonville lost one of her oldest and best known citizens in the death of Col. James Keigwin, late of the Forty-ninth Indiana Volunteer Infantry. Always proud of Jeffersonville and Clark county he belonged to that class of men who made a community better by living in it. He was a gallant soldier and in his day was widely known and connected with most of the enterprises of the city.

In August, 1904, the Jeffersonville and New Albany Chautauqua Assembly was held at Glenwood Park. As the president and seven out of eleven directors were Jeffersonville men it may fairly be called a Jeffersonville enterprise. This meeting was held at Glenwood Park on the bank of Silver creek and a program of entertainment for eleven days was offered. This Chautauqua has been held every year since and it affords clean, wholesome and intelligent entertainment at a very reasonable cost.

In September, 1904, the new Spring Hill school was opened in Jeffersonville. This school is a modern, handsome, commodious and convenient building, and marks an epoch in school building in Clark county. The standard of excellence set here is to be surpassed by the erection of a new high school at a near date. Two of the old original schools of Jeffersonville were torn down about this time. The old Mulberry street school, at the lower end of Chestnut street, was torn down in the fall of 1904, and the old Blue school on Watt and Maple, was demolished later.

September 12, 1905, the first electric car was run over the Big Four bridge, thus opening the whole of Southern Indiana to Louisville. The trip across the bridge was the occasion of a great demonstration by the officials of the three cities.

In December, 1906, Judge C. P. Ferguson's death removed from the bar of Clark county a distinguished jurist. A friend and companion of many of the early leaders both in law and politics, and a student of men and measures, he rose to the front of the profession in Clark county.

In 1906 Charlestown celebrated her centennial with appropriate ceremonies. This old county seat town, and one of the most attractive towns in Southern Indiana retains the quiet refinement and characteristic sedateness which befits its age. A more picturesque place than Charlestown does not exist, and with the historic memories of her past and the many points of interest in her near vicinity there is no reason why the little town on Falling Run could not be made a summer resort of great popularity. Fern Grove, on the river at the mouth of Fourteen Mile creek, is but two miles away and here a continual stream of excursionists are found all through the summer. Other attractions near Charlestown are:

Buffalo Lick, lithia springs half mile.

White sulphur wells, one mile.

Tunnel Mill, over a century old, old-style water mill, still running, two miles.

Stockwell cave, two miles.

Delaware Indian cave, adjoins town.

Halcyon Hill, overlooking town.

Cave of the Silver Find, three miles.

Remains of Mound Builders' Fort, near Ohio river, two miles.

Fourteen Mile creek, fine fishing, one mile.

Monument and tomb of Jonathan Jennings, first Governor of Indiana.

Quaint architecture dating from 1806 to the War of 1812.

On July 31, 1905, the old Utica "bus" made its last trip from Jeffersonville to Utica, and on August 1st the first rural free delivery of the mail in Clark county was inaugurated on the route formerly covered by the "bus."

In the year 1907 the city of Jeffersonville made three improvements, the Seventh street sewer, Maple street sewer and Spring street improvement. W. O. Sweeney was the contractor in each case. The following shows the interesting figures connected with each, the total cost of all improvements amounting to forty thousand two hundred and sixty-six dollars and eighty-one cents:

Seventh street sewer: Material, vitrified tile; length, one thousand seven hundred and ninety feet; cost, two thousand seven hundred and fifty-six dollars and forty cents; contract approved November 5, 1907; final assessment approved February 1, 1908; covers sixty-nine property descriptions, effects forty-four property owners; city share, two dollars and twenty-seven cents.

Maple street sewer: Material, vitrified tile; length, two thousand fifty-five feet; cost, two thousand one hundred and forty-four dollars and fifteen cents; contract approved August 29, 1907; final assessment approved January 10, 1908; covers one hundred two property descriptions, affects sixty-five property owners; city share, one hundred sixteen dollars and fifty-six cents.

Spring street, from Court to Fourteenth: Material, vitrified brick; length, six thousand four hundred thirty-seven and twenty-six hundredths feet; total cost, thirty-two thousand three hundred sixty-six dollars and twenty-six cents; cost per lineal foot, two dollars seventy-eight cents; contract approved April 29, 1907; final assessment January 15, 1908; cover two hundred seventy-five property descriptions, affects one hundred eighteen property owners.

Appropriations of twelve thousand dollars for purchasing the turnpike running from Jeffersonville to Charlestown, and fourteen thousand two hundred fifty for buying the toll road between Jeffersonville and Utica and to a point a few miles beyond there, where it intersects the first named highway for an outlet to Charlestown, was made by the County Council of Clark county in April, 1907.

The appropriation is practically a loan, and eventually Jeffersonville, Utica and Charlestown townships will pay it back.

On February 10, 1908, a limited car service was established between Louisville and Seymour, Indiana. These cars ran every two hours, and the running time between Jeffersonville and Seymour was one hour and thirty-nine minutes.

In November, 1907, the famous Chalybeate Springs, which once made famous the "Springs" in Jeffersonville in the forties and fifties, were destroyed by the Big Four Railroad in making improvements.

July 18, 1907, the corner stone of the new county poor asylum was laid by the grand master of Masons of Indiana, Calvin W. Prather, acting grand master presiding. This ceremony was under the auspices of Blazing Star Lodge, No. 226, Free and Accepted Masons. The building when completed cost twenty-five thousand dollars, and is one of the finest in the state of Indiana.

August 25, 1907, the first car from Scottsburg, on the Indianapolis & Louisville Traction Company lines, arrived in Jeffersonville.

One of the important dates of late years was that of 1907. The river had reached a high but not dangerous stage. The residents of the lower end of Jeffersonville had been alarmed at reports of the weakness of the Pennsylvania fill at the junction, and at the ringing of the fire bell, when a break seemed imminent, pandemonium broke loose. Wagons, carts, buggies, wheelbarrows and every other available vehicle was pressed into service to haul household and other goods to high ground. It was the record breaking evacuation, notwithstanding the fact that the water would have reached few of the houses should the fill have broken. When the river had subsided the town of Clarksville, together with the Pennsylvania Railroad, reinforced the dike and Jeffersonville is today the safest and dryest river town from Pittsburg to Cairo.

In the centennial decade Charlestown began the improvement of her streets with granitoid sidewalks, and besides adding to the beauty, attractiveness and convenience of the town, it has added to the value of real estate. The spirit of municipal progress which gave Charlestown improved streets, a fine creamery, an electric lighting plant, good telephones, cement and wall plaster factory, and electric cars, will manifest in other lines, and the coming generation may expect to see the most beautiful residential suburb around the Three Falls cities. Her old attraction will always remain, and to the lovers of rural beauty and historical association she will always remain one of the choicest spots on Indiana soil.

Borden in like manner is growing in prominence on account of its industries and improvements, but particularly from its strawberry shipments. This town has become one of the principal berry shipping points in the West, no less than twenty thousand gallons being shipped to Chicago annually.

The shipment of fruits and berries to other cities is growing and this trade will soon be one of far-reaching importance to this section of the state.

Improvement seems to be the order of the day throughout Clark county, and Jeffersonville has within the last year taken great strides towards rejuvenating herself and advertising her advantages in every quarter. With the resumption of business at the car works and the returning confidence of the people in the stability of business in other lines Clark county and her various towns have indeed a bright future before them.

CHAPTER XV.

THE MILITARY HISTORY OF CLARK COUNTY.

1786-1844.

The earliest history of Clark county is military. The settlement at Clarksville had as its nucleus a stockade called Fort Clark, and within easy distance of its protecting walls were clustered the cabins of the settlers. However, the growing hostility of the Northwestern Indian tribes, collectively known as the Wabash Indians, and the grave political situation which had arisen among the people south of the Ohio river, because of the failure of the Union to protect the frontiers, and open the Mississippi river to commerce led the Government to establish and garrison the fort just above the rapids of the Ohio. The Indian situation was about as bad as it could be, and reports of murder and robbery were almost daily. The trapper or hunter who ventured back into the dense forests and canebrakes was compelled to match the cunning of the savage or pay the penalty with his life. The settler could at no time feel safe from the murderous attacks of a foe whom our English cousins had armed and incited to deeds of the most revolting cruelty.

Gov. Patrick Henry, of Virginia, was well informed as to conditions, and on May 16, 1786, presented the subject so strongly to Congress that action was soon taken, and on June 30, 1786, the Executive of Virginia was notified that the United States had ordered their commandant on the Ohio to detach two companies to the rapids of the Ohio, with request that the militia of that district be required to co-operate with them in defense of the frontier. Instructions were sent to Colonel Harmar as to the disposition of his forces, under date of June 27, 1786. These were received by him at Fort Pitt, July 13, 1786, by the hand of Major North. Colonel Harmar replied in part as follows: "That in obedience to instructions, he should detach two companies to the rapids of the Ohio, to protect the inhabitants from the incursions of the Indians." He thereupon proposed to detach Finney's and Ziegler's companies from Fort Finney, at the mouth of the Miami, to the rapids, and close the post at the Miami, there being no trouble below the Muskingum.

Fort Finney had been built in the fall of 1785, but the ground near the mouth of the Miami was very low and the trouble occasioned by floods was so great that it was never used again.

Colonel Harmar again reports to Secretary Knox, under date of August

4, 1786, in which he states that, "Agreeable to order of Congress, he had detached two companies to the rapids of the Ohio." This seems to fix conclusively the birth of the new fort, the 1st of August, 1786.

The site chosen for the new work was on the north bank of the river, and near the head of the rapids, in what is now the lower end of Jeffersonville. It was named in honor of Major Walter Finney, as was the work closed at the mouth of the Miami. Fort Steuben was a small work about thirty miles below Fort McIntosh on the Ohio. This was abandoned in June, 1787, and soon after Fort Finney at Jeffersonville was re-named Fort Steuben, in honor of that Revolutionary hero of Prussian birth.

The location selected by Major Finney was at the lower end of what later on became the original town of Jeffersonville, on a point about forty feet below what is now the foot of Fort street, and on a level piece of land lying between Front street and the river. It commanded a view up the river for some distance, as well as a view of the Falls, and it was here that the first organized body of white men made their habitation in Jeffersonville. Beyond the fact that it was in the year 1786, neither the war department nor other sources can give us any information. The first commander was Major Walter Finney, 1786 to 1787, and his company with that of Captain Zeigler the first garrison. Following Major Finney came Major Wyllys, who was afterward killed in action with the Indians on the Miami river October 22, 1790.

It became an important garrison and remained under the command of Capt. John Armstrong, U. S. A., until 1790, he having been ordered here from Fort Pitt (now Pittsburg). In shape the fort appears to have been a square affair of both wood and earthwork. A deep trench was cut from the south side of the work to the river, and this was covered with logs and earth, making a tunnel through which water could be brought and by which escape could be made, if necessary. During the few years of Fort Steuben's existence as a garrisoned fort the little village around it was the scene of more than one military display. Up to 1786 the head and center of military action seems to have been mostly on the Kentucky side of the river, but it shifted to Fort Steuben when that garrison was established and remained here until 1791.

In the year 1787 Colonel Harmar was at Fort Steuben, accompanied by Lieutenants Beatty and Pratt, and about June 1st, of this same year, Captain Strong and his company from Fort Harmar arrived to reinforce the garrison. The presence of Colonel Harmar can be accounted for by the fact that he was the commanding officer of the First U. S. Regiment, of which organization the garrison of Fort Steuben was a part. On June 10th Lieutenant Denny, Captain Smith and his company, Ensign Sedam with part of Captain Mercer's company, Lieutenant Peters and Doctor Elliott arrived, and on July 2d, Strong's, Mercer's and Smith's companies crossed the Ohio to the Virginia side and marched down to encamp below the Falls. The next day Captains Finney and Zeigler, with their companies, left the fort and joined the others in camp. These troops, together with Captain Ferguson's battery of artillery from Fort McIntosh, formed the body of a peaceful expedition from Fort Steuben to Post Vincennes, under command of Colonel Harmar and Major Hamtramck, and it was upon their return to Fort Steuben on October 28, 1787, that Harmar received his commission as a brigadier-general. Soon after this all of these, with the exception of Major Wylly's with Finney's and Mercer's companies, who remained to garrison the fort, left for Fort Harmar.

The depredations of the Indians became so bold north of the Ohio that settlement was hazardous in the extreme, and to give better protection to that tract known as Clark's grant and its vicinity, General Harmar sent reinforcements back to the garrison of Fort Steuben in 1788.

On August 26, 1789, about two hundred mounted troops, under Col. John Hardin, left the Falls to attack the Indian towns on the Wabash, and returned on September 28th, of the same year, without the loss of a man.

A day of martial display, no doubt, was that of January 8, 1790, when Gov. Arthur St. Clair and Winthrop Sargeant, secretary of the territory, arrived on their way to the Illinois country. This official party seems to have made Fort Steuben their headquarters, for the Governor's letters to Major Hamtramck, the commanding officer of Post Vincennes, are dated from here. The Governor and his party remained at Fort Steuben until January 27, 1790, and while here made the following appointments:

"William Clark, of Clarksville, Justice of the Peace and Captain of the Militia, in the Town and Vicinity."

"John Owens, Lieutenant of Militia."

It was in this same year that the Governor, being vested with power by President Washington, called for one thousand militia from Virginia and five hundred from Pennsylvania. Kentucky (which was still a part of Virginia) sent one hundred and twenty-five men from Lincoln county and fifty men from Jefferson county to Fort Steuben. These troops assembled here on September 12th, and soon after left for Vincennes for action against the red men.

On June 14, 1791, Brig.-Gen. Charles Scott arrived at Fort Steuben at the head of eight hundred mounted and armed men, having finished a successful expedition against the Wabash tribes. He delivered to Captain Ashton, of the First U. S. Infantry commanding the fort, forty-one prisoners of war. This was the largest body of mounted troops in this vicinity during this period, and even at the present day it would be no inconsequential force. Their approach to Fort Steuben was either by way of that trail that led westwardly from the fort past the whirlpool to the Vincennes trail, or by the upper trail, leading back through the virgin forest a short distance above the fort, and afterward named Spring street. Their triumphal return from a successful campaign against a savage foe so feared by all, with forty-one braves as prisoners of war, was no doubt an imprising entry, and brought a feeling of satisfaction and safety to the minds of those who lived in almost daily dread of capture, murder or torture. On August 21st of this same year Brig.-Gen. James Wilkinson arrived at Fort Steuben with five hundred and twenty-five men, having made an expedition similar to that of General Scott, and equally as successful. These troops, although small in number, and armed with old flint-lock muskets, were a formidable body for those days, and their march to the old fort must have been a great event in the little hamlet so unused to scenes such as these.

In May, 1791, the garrison was reduced to sixty-one men. The seat of trouble having moved northward and other forts having been established closer to the northern boundary, the old fort was soon after discontinued as a garrisoned post. The last mention of a garrison is that Captain Ashton, of the First U. S. Infantry, was in command, and then we find that on July 15, 1791, "the whole of the First U. S. Regiment" arrived at Fort Washington to participate in an expedition which established several forts to the north-ward. This evidently was the last garrison of regular troops, for the fort is never mentioned as such again, although the month after this (August 21st) was the date of the arrival of Wilkinson's expedition.

Travelers have mentioned the fort after this date as being still in existence, i. e., Francis Baily, an English traveler in Louisville in 1797, writes: "The Ohio here is nearly a mile wide and is bounded by an open champaign country, where there is a fort kept up for the protection of the infant colony and called Fort Steuben." But its garrison was no doubt part of the militia of the territory, as this organization was a very effective body at that time. The commanding officers of Fort Steuben were Major Walter Finney, who constructed it, but who remained only a year: Maj. David Wyllys, Capt. John Armstrong, and then for a short while Capt. Joseph Ashton.

Capt. John Armstrong, although an officer in the regular establishment, returned to Clark county and settled here after a long and honorable career in both the military and civil service of his country. He is buried on a farm opposite the Grassy Flats, in Clark county, and a monument marks his last resting place, inscribed as follows:

"Sacred to the memory of Col. John Armstrong, who was born April 20, 1755, and died February 4, 1816. He entered the Army of the United States at the commencement of the Revolutionary war and served his country seventeen years as a soldier and an officer. During his services in the army he was in thirty-seven skirmishes and four general actions, among which were the battles of Trenton, Stony Point, Monmouth, and the Siege of Yorktown.

"The deceased came to the western country with the first troops sent thither and was in Harmar's and St. Clair's campaign, and commanded the garrison (Fort Steuben) at the Falls of the Ohio for several years, making frequent excursions against the Indians. At an early day he selected for a farm the tract of land where his remains are interred, and formed a settlement on it of several families in the year 1796."

The family still remains in Jeffersonville, one of the oldest pioneer families, and his great-grandson, Capt. Frank Spear Armstrong, a native and a citizen of Clark county, and a graduate of West Point, is at present an officer in the regular army on his second long period of foreign service in the Philippines with his regiment, the Ninth Cavalry.

The soldiers of the garrison of Fort Steuben who died while stationed there were given burial in a little plot of level ground that extended out in front of the present ferry office. They lay here undisturbed by the march of civilizaton for many years. In 1843, when Harvey McCampbell was engaged in grading down the bank to make a wharf which would meet the requirements of a growing town, and which would afford access to the river, it became necessary to dig away the whole of this sacred spot. In accordance with the dictates of decency and respect, Dr. Samuel Merriwether, a member of the City Council, offered a resolution on October 12, 1843, to remove the bodies to the old Mulberry street cemetery, and the work was ordered done. The grave is now marked by an oak tree planted by the ladies of the Daughters of the American Revolution.

Old Fort Steuben, with its earthworks and its tunnel, its garrison and its equipment, its quarters and its supplies, disappeared many years ago, and not the slightest trace of its location remains, nor can a single relic of its existence be found. The scene of the usual routine of a garrisoned fort, it more than once furnished the characters for stirring acts, and was often the center of excitement when expeditions were leaving, or of great demonstrations upon their triumphal return. Even the plot of ground upon which it was erected has been swept away by the turbulent floods of the river, and only an occasional account serves to remind us that at Front and Fort streets veterans of the Revolution guarded the lives and property of the dwellers in the little village around them, or boldly forced their way northward through the forests to drive back the savages and claim the territory for their own race and flag.

From the abandonment of Fort Steuben by the United States troops, in 1791, until the battle of Tippecanoe, the record of the militia in and around Jeffersonville is meagre, the appointment of officers being about the only beacons by which we know of the existence of such a body. The old militia law of July 25, 1788, was the authority by which all the military organizations in the state were governed. This law required all citizens between the ages of sixteen and fifty to be enrolled in the militia. They were divided into two classes, the senior and junior. The senior class was composed of all who had held commissions in the U. S. army or were graduates of military schools. The law required every man to provide himself with "musket and bayonet or rifle, cartridge box and pouch or powder horn, and bullet pouch, with forty rounds of cartridges, or one pound of powder and four pounds of lead, priming wire and brush, and six flints." The companies usually consisted of sixty-four men rank and file, one captain, one lieutenant, one ensign, four sergeants, four corporals, one drummer and one fifer. Eight companies formed one battalion and two battalions one regiment.

Clark county was the fifth county to organize her militia under the new law of December, 1800. Governor Harrison turned his attention to military affairs February 6, 1801, by the appointment of his staff, and the first aid-de-camp commissioned was Henry Hurst. On September 20, 1803, the militia of the county was organized and Marston G. Clark was commissioned lieutenant-colonel commanding. Joseph Bartholomew was appointed major and five companies were organized with the following officers First company, captain, John Owens; lieutenant, William Plaskett; ensign, David Owens. Second company, captain, George Wood; lieutenant, Isaac Shelby; ensign, Barzillai Baker. Third company, captain, William Goodwin; lieutenant, Robert Burge; ensign, William Stacy. Fourth company, captain, William Smith; lieutenant, William Prather; ensign, John Morris. Fifth company, captain, Davis Floyd; lieutenant, John Jackson; ensign, Rezin Redman.

On September 22, 1804, John Berry and Matthew Rider were commissioned lieutenants, and Josiah Ekin an ensign in the First Regiment of Clark county. On May 25, 1805, James Bland was appointed captain and Thomas Bland, ensign, to succeed John Owens and David Owens, resigned. In this same year a new company was organized with William Herrod as captain, George Newland as lieutenant, and Joel Comly, as ensign. In December, 1805, Lieut. Col. Marston G. Clark removed from the county, and Maj. Joseph Bartholomew succeeded him.

On January 10, 1806, Lieut. William Prather was promoted to the captaincy made vacant by the death of William Smith, and John Work, Jr., was appointed a lieutenant vice Rider, resigned. On this same day Davis Floyd was promoted major.

On August 16, 1806, the first troop of horse in Clark county, and the second in the state, was organized in Jeffersonville with Charles Beggs as captain, Aaron Prather, first lieutenant; James Lemon, second lieutenant, and Peter Bloom, cornet.

On this same day John Owens was made major of the second battalion. On November 18th, Ensign Rezin Redman was commissioned captain, vice Goodwin, resigned, and Robert Robertson was promoted captain, vice Wood, resigned, and Josiah Aiken was promoted captain, vice, Owens, promoted. John Anderson was appointed captain; John McCoy was appointed lieutenant; Eli Robertson was appointed lieutenant; Jacob Fouts was appointed lieutenant,

Absalom Hart was appointed ensign; Thomas Chappell was appointed ensign; Joseph Bowman was appointed ensign, and David Fouts was appointed ensign, all on November 18, 1806.

On April 18, 1807, John Johnson and Enoch Boon were commissioned captains; John Smith and Paul French, lieutenants, and James Hickman and Robert Denbow, ensigns. On July 8, John Shields was appointed captain; William Smith, lieutenant, and Fielding Cromwell, ensign. On August 22, Gresham Lee was made captain; Joseph Howard lieutenant, and John Griffin ensign. On November 3, 1807, several promotions were made on account of resignations, and a new company was mustered into the service with William Herrod as captain, George Newland as lieutenant and Joel Combs, as ensign.

On March 25, 1808, the names of Lieutenants George Roberts and James Hickman appears in the promotions, and William Pennington and John Hickman in the appointments. On July 6, 1808, the commission of Maj. Davis Floyd was revoked. No cause can be found for this action in the records but as he had been associated with Aaron Burr in his treasonable acts, this was undoubtedly the real cause. Burr's forces lay at Jeffersonville during the winter of 1807 and 1808, and his secret scheming, carried on while seemingly working in the interests of a canal around the Falls of the Ohio on the Indiana side, was a matter of very great concern to the territorial authorities. Charles L. Byrns was appointed captain, vice Johnston, resigned, and Robert Denbo and Elijah Hurst were appointed lieutenants. John Parkinson and Robert Rusk were appointed ensigns.

On October 22, 1808, Capt. William Prather received his majority, vice Davis Floyd, relieved, and Samuel Latton was appointed cornet in the Jeffersonville troop of horse. On March 7, 1809, Major Owens and Major Bartholomew recommended the following commissions: Robert Evans to be captain; Jacob Fouts to be captain; John Norris to be captain; John Thompson to be captain; Peter Covert to be lieutenant; William Kelly to be lieutenant; John Crockett to be ensign; John McNaught to be ensign; John McClintock, Jr., to be ensign. On November 29, 1809, Rezin Redman received his majority, and Samuel Smock was appointed captain; John Blenard, lieutenant; Squire Hall, lieutenant and Andrew Gelvick lieutenant. On October 10, 1810, a new Clark county company was organized with James McFarland as captain, Booth Thomas, lieutenant, and James Gaddass, ensign.

The various companies were called together on certain days, called "muster days," for drill and instruction, but these days became times of such drinking and carousing that on December 10, 1810, the Legislature passed a law which forbade officers treating their men with "ardent spirits" and prohibited the sale of such within two miles of the muster place, except in licensed inns.

On April 5, 1811, the following appointments were made: William

Patrick, captain; John McCoy, captain; William Montgomery, captain; James Bigger, captain; John Jenkins, lieutenant; John Herrod, lieutenant; Henry Socles, lieutenant; John Chuns, lieutenant; Thomas Jacobs, ensign; Joseph Carr, ensign; Joseph Bowers, ensign; Joseph Stillwell, ensign. Walter Taylor was commissioned captain; George Twilley, lieutenant, and Joseph Stroud, ensign. The last mention of county regiments was made when Robert Robertson was commissioned as colonel of the Clark county regiment April 13, 1812.

The year 1811 was made memorable to the people of Clark county, by the battle of Tippecanoe, Tecumseh and his brother, the Prophet, had formed a confederacy of Indian tribes, and their strength and depredations had become such that an aggressive policy was decided on by Governor Harrison. A considerable number of troops were assembled and a march on the Prophet's town was decided on while Tecumseh was in the South. The part that Clark county took in this memorable campaign is one that reflects the highest credit on the soldiers who went from here. The following is a list of officers from Clark county, who served through the expedition:

Major Henry Hurst, A. D. C.
Brigade Inspector Marston G. Clark.
Lieut. Col. Joseph Bartholomew (wounded).
Major Rezin Redman.
Surgeon's Mate Andrew P. Hay.
Adjutant Davis Floyd.
Capt. John Norris (wounded).
Capt. James Bigger.
Capt. Charles Beggs.
Lieut. John Herrod.
Lieut. John T. Chunn.
Lieut. John Thompson.
Ensign Joseph Carr.
Ensign Joseph Stillwell.
Cornet Mordecai Sweeney.

The expedition consisted of about eleven hundred men and officers, organized as follows: Nine companies of U. S. Infantry (Fourth Regiment); Six companies of Indiana militia; three companies of Indiana mounted riflemen; two companies of Indiana dragoons; one company of Indiana riflemen; two companies of Kentucky mounted riflemen; one company of scouts; a total of twenty-four companies, of which Indiana had thirteen companies of militia. Of this force two hundred and seventy men were mounted. Col. John P. Boyd brought his regiment, the Fourth U. S. Infantry, from Pittsburg to the Falls and marched from there to Vincennes. Captain Geiger's company from Jefferson county, Kentucky, passed through Jeffersonville September 11th on their way to Vincennes. Clark county furnished three full companies, besides the officers on staff duty. Captain Norris's company of infantry was a drafted company. It was raised between Charlestown, Jeffersonville and Utica, and was sworn in at Springville. Captain Bigger's company was raised in Charlestown and vicinity and was sworn in at Charlestown. Captain Beggs's company was mounted. They were raised in Jeffersonville and vicinity and were sworn in at Jeffersonville. That these companies were in the thick of action their casualties show. Norris's company had three killed and one wounded; Bigger's company had two killed and three wounded and Beggs's company had one killed.

Shawnee Indians were chief among the tribes in the confederacy, both Tecumseh and Elkswatawa (The Prophet) being Shawnees. There were besides the Shawnees at the battle, Wyandottes, Kickapoos, Ottawas, Chippewas, Pottawatomies, Sacs and Miamis. This campaign had the effect of increasing the interest in the militia, and aroused the people to a keener sense of their danger from the Indians. The part played by Clark county officers was not small.

Marston G. Clark was one of the first settlers in Jeffersonville. He was a Virginian by birth, and a cousin of Gen. George Rogers Clark. He held many offices in Clark county and was brigade inspector on the staff of General Harrison at the battle of Tippecanoe. As a soldier, he was said to have been insensible to fear, often leading men in the pursuit of Indians who had committed depredations. He served as Indian agent under President Jackson and was appointed messenger to carry the electoral vote of Indiana to Washington in 1840. He is buried at Salem, Indiana. He was one of two officers who were sent forward by General Harrison to select the camping ground the night before the battle. The general said of him in his report to the Secretary of War eleven days after the battle: "Brigade Major Clark was very serviceably employed."

Maj. William Henry Hurst was an aid-de-camp on the staff of General Harrison and Dr. Samuel Merriwether was acting as surgeon, although not appearing on the official rolls as such at Washington. General Harrison, in a letter, said: "My two aids-de-camp, Majors Hurst and Taylor afforded me essential aid as well in the action as throughout the campaign." The admiration of the general for these two aids-de-camp caused him to have them act as his personal escort when he rode through the streets of Washington to the capitol to be inaugurated President of the United States. Hurst and Merriwether resided in Jeffersonville for many years afterward, examples of honor, integrity and civic virtue which we of later years could emulate with benefit to ourselves and the city.

Governor Harrison in his report of the battle, says: "Col. Joseph Bar-

10

tholomew, a very valuable officer, commanded, under Colonel Boyd, the militia infantry. He was wounded early in the action and his service lost to me." He was one of the foremost citizens of the county for many years and received many marks of honor and esteem at the hands of the citizens of the county. Harrison said of one of Clark county company, "Norris's company also behaved well."

Davis Floyd, the adjutant, has the proud distinction of being the best advertised man in his day and locality. Nothing seemed to dishearten him for he always bobs up serenely after any difficulty, and usually takes the most prominent position in whatever is going on. A prominent militiaman, he was an important officer at Tippecanoe. He represented Clark county in the Legislature in 1805. He kept a tavern and operated a ferry in Clarks grant. He was appointed Recorder of Clark county in 1801 and Sheriff in 1802 by General Harrison. He became involved in Aaron Burr's conspiracy and was sentenced to three hours in jail. He served as secretary of the Springville Anti-Slavery convention. In the Legislature he was elected Clerk of the House, and was a member of the Constitutional Convention in 1816.

General Harrison was severely criticised by many of his political enemies after the battle of Tippecanoe, who claimed that it was an unnecessary campaign, and that even when he had reached the vicinity of the Indian town he allowed the enemy to select his camping ground. The general visited Jeffersonville and Charlestown in 1835 and at the latter place, in answer to a request for a speech on "Tippecanoe," said: "When I left Vincennes for the Indian country on the Tippecanoe, it was under positive instructions from the War Department not to attack them if they showed a willingness to comply with the demands of the General Government. As to the Indians selecting my encampment, there is not a particle of truth in that statement. Gen. Marston G. Clark and Col. Davis Floyd were detailed to select the ground."

In those days a keen eye for the peculiarities of the red brother was quite necessary, and precautionary measures were still kept up in the outlying districts. The militia garrison, which from meagre accounts, seems to have been kept in old Fort Steuben for several years after its abandonment by the U. S. troops, was not the only defense available. As late as 1807 a letter by Waller Taylor (afterwards A. D. C. on General Harrison's staff) written to Governor Harrison, January 12th, in speaking about Burr's mysterious doings in Jeffersonville and the excitement occasioned by his presence, says: "There are stationed at this place about two hundred militia, who examine all boats that descend the river."

On the bank of the Ohio, at Whirlpool Point, was a stockade which was used as an outpost for Fort Steuben. Another outpost of Fort Steuben was about where the "junction" is situated. It was a place for the soldiers to meet on their rounds, and here the settlers used to come for safety when fear of the

Indians drove them from their cabins and clearings. This point was called the "Corner Post" for many years after. The last settler murdered by the Indians in the first decade of the century was a trapper named Springer. He had traps set on Springer's Gut (now in New Albany) and was surprised and slain by Wyandottes and Pawpaws, while running them.

The Indian phase of the War of 1812, which was no small thing to the western settlers, was of more moment to them than a consideration of danger from purely British sources. To be sure, the atrocities of the savages, to a great extent, were instigated by the British to the north, but from British troops themselves, no real danger was ever anticipated. The Pigeon Roost massacre, September 3, 1812, was the last trouble ever experienced in this vicinity, but it had the effect of awakening the settlers to the danger of unpreparedness and resulted in the establishment of a line of some fifteen or twenty stockades, beginning at the one called the "Corner Post" and extending by Charlestown back to the Ohio at the east of the town.

The Pigeon Roost massacre was not an Indian raid as has been so often stated. The Indians passed through the little hamlet which was the nucleus of Vienna and never harmed a soul, while there. There had been bad blood between the Collins family and the Indians for some time. The Collins boys had stolen a fawn from the Indians and refused to give it up, and from this cause and possibly some other, the whole trouble originated. Those other than Collinses were killed only because they lived in that neighborhood. Neither before nor after the massacre were other white people harmed, showing conclusively that it was only a local fight and giving no cause for alarm to other settlers.

The Indians, who were Delawares and Shawnees, are said to have crossed White river at Sparksville. They crossed three or four at a time and after all had crossed formed together and directed their way to the spot now hallowed in the memory of the early victims. During the afternoon of the same day they reached their destination, and Jeremiah Payne, who lived near Vienna, was warned of danger when his cows came bellowing home with arrows stuck in their sides. Taking his wife and only son to the fort at Vienna, the father started on foot to warn his brother, Elias, but when he arrived at the cabin he found the dead and mutilated bodies of the wife and seven children. Elias and his brother-in-law, Isaac Coffman, were in the woods at the time hunting bee trees. They were surprised by ten or twelve Indians and Coffman was instantly killed and scalped. Payne was pursued over two miles before he was overtaken and mortally wounded. Mrs. Richard Collins and her seven children soon fell victims to the redskins' thirst for blood, and Mrs. Henry Collins, although pregnant, was murdered and scalped and the child taken from the womb and scalped, and then laid across her breast. The incentive to such a diabolical deed was the five dollar British reward offered for each scalp. The fiends later massacred the mother, wife and only child of John Morris, and the escape of other settlers was almost miraculous.

A part of Clark county militia under Maj. John McCoy and Captain Devault pursued the Indians and killed one. In June, 1813 some Clark county militia, under Col. Joseph Bartholomew, went on an expedition to punish Indians who were hostile, and returned without any casualties.

At the close of the War of 1812 the militia of Clark county, as in the rest of the state, was in excellent condition. The Second Regiment was originally the Clark county Regiment, and as such it was under the command of Col. Robert Robertson. It was one of the most complete regiments in the service and included many special organizations, one of which was the only artillery company mentioned in the territorial records.

Colonel Robertson resigned in 1811 and Maj. Joseph Bartholomew was commissioned to succeed him October 21st, of that year. Colonel Bartholomew served until March 30, 1814, when Joel Combs was commissioned colonel. Rezin Redman was lieutenant-colonel, and was commissioned as such June 10, 1813.

In 1814, the Ninth Regiment, which was composed of companies in Clark county, was commanded by Col. John Depau, with headquarters in Jeffersonville, and the records report it as being one of the best organized in the state.

With the passing of the Indian the subjects considered by the Legislature concerning the militia seem to have materially changed. In 1815, an act was passed restricting the militia age to eighteen to forty-five and specified the uniform for the officers. Major and Brigadier Generals should "wear a French military hat, blue cloth coat turned up with buff or scarlet, with gold epaulettes, white small clothes, also boots and spurs." Muster days were Saturdays in April and September. The interest and energy which had formerly been directed against the Indians was now turned to clothes, and the citizen soldiery was neglected and allowed to become a dormant and practically useless body.

For about two years after the battle of Tippecanoe, the territorial Government maintained several companies of rangers to protect the people of the state from the depredations of marauding bands of Indians. One of these companies was composed of Clark county men, and was commanded by Capt. James Bigger, of Tippecanoe service, and he had as first lieutenant, John Carr, and as second lieutenant, James Curry.

In the month of June, 1813, an expedition composed of about one hundred and thirty-seven mounted men under the command of Col. Joseph Bartholomew, moved from Valonio toward the Delaware towns on the west fork of the White river, with the intention of surprising and punishing some hostile Indians, who were supposed to be lurking about those villages. All or a larger part of Captain Bigger's company was in this expedition, and they destroyed a great deal of corn found in the half-burned and deserted villages along the river. Colonel Bartholomew said of this: "We conceived it was more necessary to do this as the corn would, if not destroyed, enable considerable bodies of the enemy to fall upon and harass our frontier."

On July 1, 1813, Col. William Russell of the Seventh United States Regiment, at the head of a force amounting to five hundred and seventy-three men, set out on an expedition against the Indian villages, which were situated at and about the mouth of the Mississinewa river. As Colonel Bartholomew and several companies of rangers were in this force, evidently Bigger's company was among them. They found no Indians and the rangers returned home. The service of these companies of rangers was most valuable and should be given the same prominence in history that the Tippecanoe campaign received, for their service was equally as hazardous and equally as valuable to the settlers who lived in the remoter parts of the territory.

We hear little of the militia of Clark county from this time on. That the organization of state troops was kept up there can be no doubt, but their duties were nil, and the only milestone we have to guide us through this period are the mention of events where the militia turned out to do escort duty to some prominent visitor or for some gala occasion. In May, 1825, several companies of militia were under arms, and acted as the escort to General LaFayette when his official visit to Indiana was paid at Jeffersonville. Captain Parker's company from Charlestown was one of these, and the cracker story of one of his men has been passed down as classical. From the fact that cannon were used in saluting our illustrious visitor, we might infer that Clark county possessed artillery, but of this we are not certain.

By the treaty of 1804, the Sacs and Foxes had sold all of their land in Illinois to the United States. The provisions of this treaty were confirmed by Keokuk, their head chief, in subsequent treaties in 1822 and 1830; but Black Hawk refused to consider these treaties valid. The British agents assured him that the Indians still owned the land and this, together with the fact that he had become the leader of the wildest braves in the tribe, led to events which culminated in what is known as the Black Hawk war in 1832. This Indian war was fierce and sanguinary, but affected either Clark county or Indiana but little. However, there was a company of United States mounted rangers raised around Charlestown by Capt. Lemuel Ford, and they served until after the middle of 1833. This company was commanded by Capt. Lemuel Ford; first lieutenant, Meedy Shields, and second lieutenant, John Gibson. When this body of men left Charlestown July 1, 1832, it numbered one hundred and fifteen men. They assembled in the court-house yard and started on their campaign with the plaudits of an admiring crowd of citizens, many of whom remembered the earlier cruelties of the savages in Clark county. They camped near Memphis, the first night out, and then started north, marching to within twenty-five miles of Fort Dearborn (now Chicago) where a halt of three weeks was made on account of the prevalence of Asiatic cholera at the fort, where General Scott with the Regulars was waiting for the arrival of the rangers. The route taken by the rangers was changed to lead to Dixon's ferry on Rock river, Illinois. The company was inspected and mustered in by Captain Anderson, U. S. A., later of Fort Sumpter fame. The march was then taken down the river to within one and one-half miles of the mouth, and three miles below Rock Island or "Old Fort Armstrong," where they crossed to the north side of Rock river and marched up to the island. There the rangers met their commanding officer, Colonel Dodge, and General Winfield Scott, commanding the expedition. The cholera was very bad then at Fort Armstrong and the company lost three men: Peter Hall, Doctor Johnson and Shelby.

It was at this point that General Scott in his round of inspection of camp and hospital, berated the medical staff roundly and threatened to hang some of the M. D.'s for neglect of duty toward the stricken. He went into the tents and examined patients with his own hands, and elevated the abode of his satanic majesty, as only the old general could.

The command crossed into Iowa Territory and then back into Illinois, following the Mississippi river to Quincy, and thence to Jefferson City, Missouri, then a town of about five hundred. From here they marched to Booneville, forty miles above, and from there to Fort Gibson, Indian Territory, one mile above the mouth of Grand river. They went into winter quarters for the winter of '32-'33, one mile below the mouth of Grand river on the Arkansas river in log cabins. On May 6, 1833, they received marching orders, and the command consisting of Captain Ford's company from Indiana, Captain's Beem's company from Arkansas and Captain Boone's company from Missouri, all under the command of Colonel Manny, U. S. A., with about three hundred regulars, took a southwesterly course to Red river. It was on this march that the great buffalo hunting was done. The Captain Boone here mentioned was the son of Daniel Boone, of pioneer Kentucky fame.

These troops returned to Fort Gibson July 1, 1833, where the rangers were mustered out, disbanded and started for home and arrived at Charlestown just when the cholera was at its worst. The officers and a partial list of the members of this Clark County company were as follows:

Captain Lemuel Ford.
First Lieutenant Meedy Shields.
Second Lieutenant John Gibson.

Sergeant John C. Huckleberry.
Sergeant Campbell Hay.
Private W. M. Garner.
Private James Drummond.
Private Eden Combs.
Private David H. Wheeler.
Private Henderson Davis.
Private John Hanlin.
Private Charles Mathes.
Private William J. Owens.
Private William B. Shelley.
Private Joseph Davis.
Private John M. Pound.
Private George Reynolds.
Private Benjamin Chrissman.
Private George Christopher.
Private Wesley G. Hammond.
Private Eph Washburn.
Private Hugh Hartley.
Private Peter Hall.
Private Alford Huckleberry.
Private John Chrissman.

They saw little or no active service so far as extended fighting was concerned, but their long marches and their hardships entitle them to a high place in the early military annals of Clark county. They served until Black Hawk had been captured. The service which they gave was the last ever given by a Clark county organization in Indiana warfare. Black Hawk stands in history as the "Last native defender of the soil of the Northwest."

The ominous clouds of war hanging like a pall over the land were not necessary to influence the manhood of Clark county to enlist. The officers who had served during the Black Hawk war knew the temper of our Hoosiers, and that they made soldiers second to none. Capt. Lemuel Ford, in 1836, came to Charlestown to recruit men for the United States Dragoons. In the issue of "The Indianian," of Charlestown, dated Friday, October 28, 1836. appears the following: "Wanted for the First Regiment of United States Dragoons, able bodied citizens between the ages of eighteen and thirty-five years, being not less than five feet, six inches high, of good moral character, and of respectable standing among their fellow citizens. None need apply to enter the service but those who are determined to serve the period of their enlistment, which is only three years, honestly and faithfully.

"LEMUEL FORD."

It is needless to say that his rendezvous at Charlestown was a popular place, and that he received many recruits.

CHAPTER XVI.

THE MILITARY HISTORY OF CLARK COUNTY—1844-1860.

The first uniformed military company of which we have any record, after the twenty-five years of dormancy, from 1819 to 1844, was in Jeffersonville in 1844. It was called the Jeffersonville Blues, and its captain was a man named Charles Hensley. He was one of several brothers, and he had the reputation of being the most popular man in town. This company had for a drill master a refugee from Poland, who lived and died on a farm just this side of Sellersburg. His name and title was Col. J. J. Lehmonoski, and while drilling the men he wore the uniform of a high officer in the Polish army. His history is most interesting. Lehmonoski was a colonel of the Polish Lancers, the bodyguard of the great Napoleon, and had participated in two hundred and three battles. He carried fourteen wounds on his person as a result of his service. He was at the sieze of Toulon, at the victory of Austerlitz, he fought on the plains of Egypt, and witnessed the ocean of flame which rolled over Moscow. The disaster of Waterloo drew him to the United States in 1816, and for a while he traveled as an evangelist with the approval and sanction of Lyman Beecher and others. He finally settled in Clark county and died here. Under his instruction the company became very proficient and turned out two or three times each week to parade or drill, and everybody in town was very proud of "our company."

Col. James Keigwin in his memoirs says of this company:

"They were invited to attend an encampment of the Kentucky militia at the old Oakland race course in Louisville, and Colonel Lehmonoski took great delight in preparing them for the contest for some of the prizes to be contested for at the encampment, and of course every citizen of our town was anxious that 'our company' should bring home a trophy of their soldierly qualities and good behavior while in camp. But you can imagine our disappointment on their return home. Some of the officers and men were addicted to the too free indulgence of 'John Barleycorn,' and the report came daily from those of their admirers who visited them that a majority of the company spent a greater part of their time in the guard house charged with the too free use of 'ardent,' and with disorderly conduct.

"One incident I will relate that occurred after they crossed the river. In those days of slavery the negroes had learned from their masters that everybody who lived in that little town across the river was nothing but 'poor white trash' and that it was a dangerous place for a black face to be seen in, and that if a negro valued his life he had better keep away from it. The owners of slaves, for protection to that old-time property, instilled into the young darkies' minds that we were not only poor white trash, but that we would steal them and sell them to cotton planters down South, and the young darkies believed that as firmly as ever a white child believed in old Santa Claus. The company was handsomely uniformed, well drilled and armed with old flint-lock muskets. Their head dress was a tall leather hat or cap, surmounted by a handsome pompon that looked very much like a paint brush. When the company was passing out the streets of Louisville with the drum corps beating that favorite tune, 'The Girl I Left Behind Me,' every one of the company feeling that all eyes were centered on him, and that he carried the honor and reputation of old Jeff in his knapsack, determined to win laurels and fame for our little city. They were feeling elated at seeing so many people, both black and white, lining the streets to hear the music and look at a company of Hoosier soldiers. You can imagine our mortification when we heard a cry from the little darkies on the sidewalks: 'Look at dem poah white trash from Jeffersoville with paint brushes in dar hats.' It is needless to relate that no prizes were carried home at the completion of the tour of duty."

It is a matter of regret that complete rosters of these old militia companies of our early history have been lost, for to them belongs the credit of keeping alive, to a great extent, that spirit which found such eloquent expression here during the War of the Rebellion. The feeling among some misguided and un-American citizens of our present day of belittling our state troops by denunciation as well as a refusal to serve, is not the spirit which prompted such service in those days or in the times that tried men's hearts during the sixties.

These old militia companies filled a place, no doubt, and although some of them may not have performed any actual service for the state, it lessens their value none.

The general condition of the militia of Indiana, including that of Clark county, during the period just preceding the Mexican war, is described by Adjutant General Reynolds, November 29, 1845. He was greatly discouraged and wrote as follows: "It is true, however, that while our system has undergone a partial paralysis, the martial spirit is not extinct, but exhibits itself in the form of a number of energetic companies of independent militia, as well as a few regiments of district militia which have survived the general disorganization. It would seem also, if not quite impossible to revive military discipline, unless some exigency should demand an active service. War, with its thrilling incidents, could alone, we believe, fully accomplish it; and no state in the Union would more fearlessly and promptly respond to even its first notes of preparation than Indiana.

Six months after the unexpected happened. War was declared May 13,

1846, and Indiana was called upon for three regiments of infantry. On May 22d Governor Whitcomb issued his call for the thirty companies required, and by June 10th, or in eighteen days, the entire quota had been reported, and twenty-two additional companies were clamoring for admission.

The beginning of the Mexican war found the spirit of Mars strongly manifesting itself throughout the county, but to Charlestown, the county seat, belongs the honor of furnishing the only organizations. Individual enlistments in Kentucky and Indiana regiments were made from various parts of the county, and in Jeffersonville there was quite an enthusiastic movement started to raise a company of volunteer infantry for one of the regiments then forming, but it began and ended in talk. Col. James Keigwin has an account of one of their public meetings in the old market house on Market street, between Spring street and Pearl street, as follows:

"At this time they were trying to recruit the company, and, by the way, I attended all the meetings, as I was big enough to be a soldier myself. At that time there was but one saloon in the town, kept by one of the best bachelors that ever lived. Charles Cunningham was his name, and his saloon was on Front street, four doors below Spring street. It was in front of this saloon where the drums beat the assembly. All those who were the leaders were fond of their toddies, and whisky at that time being only worth six dollars a barrel, Charley, the saloon keeper, as he was called, being a patriotic lover of his country and anxious to have his own town represented in the war, said that he would give all who volunteered all they wanted to drink free of charge, so you can understand that by the time all the patriotic residents and barefooted boys had assembled in front of the saloon that the promoters of the company would be pretty full and would feel as if they could lick a regiment of 'greasers' by themselves.

"The organizers of the company were Amos Lovering, afterward one of the judges of one of our courts; William Buchanan and Richard Peacely, studying law with Judge Lovering, and John F. Read, who had just graduated from Hanover College. After the party had sampled Charley's whisky to their satisfaction, we were ordered to fall in and march to the market house, where we would have speeches from Read and others. Well, we fell in and marched to the market house, and Read was boosted up on the butcher's block by Peacely and Buchanan, who held to John's legs to steady him. He was making a very patriotic and convincing speech as to our duties to the best government in the world, and how we would lick old Santa Anna and his Mexican horde off of Texas soil, and then he pictured to us the humiliation we would feel if Jeffersonville failed to have a company in the war. John's father, the old judge, heard the racket in the market house, and as he came near and saw his hopeful in the condition he was, you can imagine his surprise. Just then Peacely and Buchanan discovered the judge's presence and began to pull

John's legs and tell him to close, when John blurted out in one of his sophomoric flights he had brought home from college: 'Yes, my fellow citizens, the government will furnish you all with plenty of the very best kind of clothes.' The meeting was a failure and it is unnecessary to add that our old town failed to be honored with a military company in the war with Mexico."

In Charlestown men responded to the call with alacrity, and the trouble was with the excess rather than the insufficiency of material. The first and second regiments had no Clark county companies in them, but the third regiment had a company from Charlestown and vicinity. This company was raised by Thomas W. Gibson, of that town, and he took as his lieutenants First Lieutenant Harrison Daily, and Second Lieutenant Daniel L. Fouts. The raising of this company was accompanied with the greatest enthusiasm, and the drum corps and martial music added to the excitement of the town. This company was to enlist for one year, and the prospect of service in Mexico, and the sights and adventures of such a campaign was more than the young men of the county seat could stand. The men were rapidly enlisted, and when they were not drilling in the court-house yard, they were skirmishing in the bottoms of Pleasant run. They were quartered in the house now known as the Badger house on Main street, near Spring street, and in their "barracks" as the house was called, they remained about a month. The day of departure of this company for the rendezvous at Camp Whitcomb, on the river just below the mouth of Silver creek, was one of intense excitement. Mothers and fathers, sisters and brothers, sweethearts and wives, assembled to wish the departing company well. They left Charlestown in wagons, and upon arrival at camp, began an active preparation for the campaign before them. They were mustered into the United States service ninety-four strong, on June 22, 1846, by Col. S. Churchill.

Captain Gibson's company served throughout their term of enlistment with an honorable record. The regiment was engaged in the battle of Buena Vista, and other actions, and upon their return home, found themselves covered with glory. The return of Gibson and his company to Charlestown was the occasion for a great demonstration. A great reception and barbecue was given them in Hammond's woods, and at the present day the trenches still remain where the beef was roasted whole. The citizens were proud of their soldiers, as well they might be.

On April 24, 1847, Governor Whitcomb called for one additional regiment to fill the quota required by the President's proclamation of April 19th. His proclamation ends as follows: "And in conformity with the suggestion of the Secretary of War, that a place of rendezvous be appointed on the Ohio river for the several companies as fast as they shall be organized, the ground near or adjacent to 'Old Fort Clark', near Jeffersonville, on the south is hereby designated for that purpose". May 30th the regiment was filled, and from that time on they were drilled and "licked" into shape for the service ahead of them.

The companies which were to form this new regiment arrived during the latter part of May and the first part of June, 1847. They reached Jeffersonville in the following order, and upon their arrival encamped just above the whirlpool on the bank of the Ohio, at a point later known as Camp Joe Holt, and not at Fort Steuben, as some authorities state:

Company A, Marion, Captain Dodd, arrived May 31, 1847.
Company B, Gosport, Captain Alexander, arrived June 8, 1847.
Company C, Lawrenceburg, Captain Payne, arrived May 28, 1847.
Company D, Indianapolis, Captain Landers, arrived May 28, 1847.
Company E, Rockport, Captain Graham, arrived June 8, 1847.
Company F, Columbus, Captain Fitzgibbon, arrived June 12, 1847.
Company G, Bloomington, Captain Lunderman, arrived June 10, 1847.
Company H, Terre Haute, Captain Cochran, arrived June 12, 1847.
Company I, Plymouth, Captain Fravell, arrived June 14, 1847.
Company K, Lawrenceburg, Captain Dumont, arrived June 7, 1847.

These companies, so the muster rolls state, were "called into the service of the United States" as they arrived. The regiments embarked on steamboats at the wharf, between Spring and Pearl streets, June 28th, and nearly everybody in Clark county was in town that day to witness the departure and wish them a safe return.

Three steamboats lay at the wharf and the martial spirit was in the very air. The steamer "Saladin" carried companies A, B, C and D, under command of Col. Willis A. Gorman. The steamer "Franklin" carried companies E, I and G, under Lieutenant Colonel Dumont, and the steamer "General Hamer" carried companies H, F and K, under Major McCoy.

On the day preceding the embarkation the regiment proceeded from their camp near the Big Eddy to Jeffersonville, and was drawn up in solid column for the purpose of receiving from the ladies of the city a splendid stand of regimental colors. This gift from the fair and patriotic ladies of Jeffersonville was received into hands strong to protect it in every emergency, and by hearts warm and ardent to appreciate its value. The adjutant general of Indiana supported the flag, and Capt. Edward Lander, in behalf of the ladies, delivered an eloquent address, which on behalf of the regiment, was responded to by the colonel, Willis A. Gorman. One newspaper account ends thus: "A fine band attached to the regiment then struck up 'The Star Spangled Banner' as the troops whirled into open column under the sound of instrumental harmony that breathed heroic ardor to adventurous deeds", and the regiment proceeded to its camp at Fort Clark.

While the Fourth Regiment remained at Jeffersonville, Company D,

Captain Landers, was the recipient of a splendid flag presented by the ladies of Indianapolis. The presentation took place in front of the old Bowman house, and was the occasion of quite a demonstration of patriotism.

On August 31, 1847, Governor Whitcomb issued his proclamation authorizing the raising of the Fifth Regiment. It was to be composed mostly of men who had seen service in Mexico in earlier regiments. This regiment rendezvoused at Madison, and Clark county was represented by a fine company of men under the command of Capt. George Greene. His lieutenants were Philip J. Roe, first lieutenant; James M. Ross, second lieutenant, and Henry Hensley, additional second lieutenant. Captain Greene at various times was a resident of both Jeffersonville and Charlestown, and his company, called the "Rough and Ready Guards", was recruited from in and around both places.

The Fifth Regiment embarked on steamboats at Camp Reynolds, Madison, on November 1, 1847, and arrived at Jeffersonville the same day. The steamers "Wave", "Ne Plus Ultra", and "Phœnix", carried them to New Orleans, arriving there on the 6th. Their service after arriving at Vera Cruz was equal to that of the other regiments, and upon their return home the Clark county soldiers were received with great demonstrations and were the heroes of the day.

Capt. Lemuel Ford, of Charlestown, recruited a company of United States Dragoons for the regular service from in and around that town, and with this troop performed valiant service in Mexico. He was brevetted major October 19, 1847, for gallant and meritorious conduct in the affair at Atlixco, and the service both he and his company of Clark county men gave was of the highest class.

Capt. John S. Simonson, of Charlestown, who was in the regular army, raised a company of mounted dragoons in and around Charlestown for service in Mexico, and besides the many creditable reports from him and his company while in the land of the "Greasers," he was brevetted major September 13, 1847, for gallant and meritorious conduct in the battle of Chapultepec.

In Captain Gibson's Company I, of the Third Regiment, was a sergeant named Jefferson C. Davis. He got his commission of second lieutenant after meritorious service—remained in the regular army after the war with Mexico —was in Fort Sumpter with Major Anderson when the war of the Rebellion opened with this "strange contest between seventy men and seven thousand". He rose to be brigadier general of volunteers and during this war was brevetted major, lieutenant-colonel, colonel, brigadier general and major general, for gallant and meritorious services.

Besides the men credited to Clark county, there were others who enlisted elsewhere.

There were four Jeffersonville men, so far as we can find, who joined the

Louisville Legion, and they served faithfully with their command during the war. These four Jeffersonville men were Benjamin P. Fuller, Simeon P. Bell, James A. Thompson and Francis M. Schell. They were all privates in Company A, First Regiment of Kentucky Foot Volunteers, known as the Louisville Legion. They were mustered in May 17, 1846, at the old race track on the Seventh street road, in Louisville, and were all mustered out at the New Orleans barracks May 17, 1847, with the exception of Francis M. Schell, who was discharged for disability at Camargo, Mexico, August 27, 1846.

The interest in things Mexican seems to have pervaded the whole county, for a great demonstration was projected when it was learned that President-elect Gen. Zachary Taylor was to pass through Louisville on his way to Washington. On Monday, February 5, 1849, the mayor of Jeffersonville, William F. Cullom, offered the following resolution, and it was unanimously adopted:

"Resolved, By the Mayor and Common Council of the city of Jeffersonville, that in consideration of the service rendered to his country by Gen. Zachary Taylor, President-elect of the United States, and in consideration of the exalted station to which he has been called to occupy by his fellow citizens, that he be invited to visit our city on his way to Washington, and partake of our hospitality".

The general saw fit to accept our invitation and visited Jeffersonville in February, 1849, and was received with a great demonstration of enthusiasm. The reception ceremonies were held in the small Presbyterian church on Market street, between Spring and Pearl streets, where he delivered a speech. This building still remains one of the old landmarks of the city, being occupied now by the German Reformed congregation as a place of worship.

After the regiments returned home from Mexico we would suppose that the ardor of some of the young soldiers would have prompted them to place Clark county in a better position than she was at the beginning of the war, but they seemed to have had all the military they desired in their campaign against the land of the Montezumas. There was, however, a company of young lads in Jeffersonville in the year 1853 or '54, with James Schell as captain, and they were uniformed and equipped. Their chief duty, so far as hearsay tells us (and that is our only authority) was to drill very often for the edification of their friends. Joseph Reign was color bearer, but of the other members we can find nothing.

From this time on until the period of the War of the Rebellion we find Clark county like the rest of the state, without much enthusiasm concerning things military.

CHAPTER XVII.

THE MILITARY HISTORY OF CLARK COUNTY DURING THE WAR OF THE REBELLION.

No part of the history of Clark county was so thoroughly saturated with military life as the period of the War of the Rebellion. The record of her enlistments, and the service of her soldiers leave no doubts of her loyalty, but of honest Southern sympathizers there were enough to add a spice to even those strenuous times. The towns, villages and farms contributed their share of loyal men to the armies in the field, but the city of Jeffersonville, from her situation, was the center of activities. From the rugged hills of Utica, along the border lands of the Ohio, to the peaceful village of Bethlehem, men needed but to gaze at the "dark and bloody ground" beyond the silent waters to receive the inspiration to do and die for their country, as did their forbears of 1876, when Paul Revere aroused them to heroic deeds at Concord and Lexington. From the heights and valleys of the knobs of Borden, from the undulating farms and country sides, from the old pioneer town of Charlestown and the country to the north, from the banks of Silver creek and Pleasant run, from Clarksville to New Washington, the trumpet call for volunteers was answered by fathers, sons and brothers. With the hosts of the nation's chivalry in the South the question of equipment and subsistence was no small task for those still left at home, and thus sprang up a labor of a magnitude undreamed of, when the struggle began. Jeffersonville being at one of the principal gateways of the South, she became the scene of an ever changing panorama of troops of all arms of the service either passing through the city, camping here awaiting orders, or returning north decimated and mangled after their bloody campaigns, bound for the great hospitals or their homes beyond. During this period nearly every man and boy in the city was connected at one time or another with the army in some capacity, and the vast storehouses, shops, factories, offices, hospitals and barracks were to be found scattered over all parts of Jeffersonville and its vicinity.

The tramp of marching men and horses and the heavy rumble of artillery were not the only outward and "visible signs" of the great struggle then in progress. Jeffersonville was the base from which all troops and supplies for the Union army were transported to points south of Louisville. Infantry, cavalry and artillery, ordnance, quartermaster, commissary and medical stores had to be transported across the river from the J., M. & I. depot at Court avenue and

Wall street to the Louisville and Nashville Railroad depot in Louisville by the ferry, and this, together with the various army institutions which were maintained in Jeffersonville during almost five years, gave the little city the busiest period of her history. Camp Joe Holt, the camping place of many regiments on their way south, was situated just above the Big Eddy, on the river bank. This historic camping ground extended back from Front street to Todd street, and north past Montgomery street almost to the present location of the P. C. C. & St. L. tracks and Cane Run creek. It derived its name from Gen. Joseph Holt, Secretary of War under Buchanan, and later judge advocate general. Being a native of Kentucky, he was sent to that state to influence her people towards loyalty, but his mission failed and the state declared for neutrality. Lovell H. Rosseau, a prominent lawyer of Louisville, believing that many Kentuckians were prevented from enlisting by this neutrality, accepted a colonel's commission from President Lincoln and began to organize his regiment across the river on Indiana soil, and in honor of the eloquent Kentuckian named his camp "Joe Holt".

One of Rousseau's captains was Edward J. Mitchell, of Louisville, who later became a citizen of Clark county. He commanded Company F, of the Second Kentucky Cavalry, and recruited several men for his company whose homes were in Clark county. James M. Patterson, his brother-in-law, went out with him as his first lieutenant. Companies A and C, of the Sixth Kentucky Infantry, were the only companies mustered into the United States service at camp Joe Holt, although there were other companies forming there at that time. Battery A, of the First Kentucky Light Artillery, was organized there at that time, all of these organizations constituting the force under the command of General Rousseau. Captain Mitchell's company was the only one, so far as we know, that drew men from Clark county, and we should congratulate ourselves on this fact, because from the records of the Kentucky adjutant general's office we would infer that Battery A was not as gallant a body as the "Twelve Hundred" or "The Old Guard". There were one hundred and twenty desertions from it. Rousseau's force crossed the river on the night of September 15, 1861, being the first troops to move south.

After the camp ceased to be used as rendezvous, a hospital was established and maintained until early in 1864, when the new Jefferson General Hospital was put in commission. The camp, however, was used almost continually until near the close of the war by regiments arriving or leaving at various times. The hospitals there consisted of a number of frame buildings for wards, offices and a chapel, the latter being purchased by St. Paul's parish of the Episcopal church, and moved to a lot on the lower side of Mulberry street between Chestnut and Maple, where it stood for many years, being used by the congregation as a place of worship until 1892. This building at Camp Joe Holt was situated on the west side of what is now Front street, and lay at the extreme west end of Montgomery street.

THE JEFFERSON GENE

AL HOSPITAL IN 1864.

One of the largest and most important government institutions in the city was the Jefferson General Hospital. Adjoining the village of Port Fulton to the east lay a beautiful farm reaching to the water's edge, the property of the Hon. Jesse D. Bright, at that time United States Senator from Indiana. Gently rolling to the southward and separated from the river bottom by a bluff of some fifteen feet, with a sufficient depth of water and a good landing the year around, a mile and a half from the Louisville ferry and about as far from the old J., M. & I. depot, it afforded an ideal location for the establishment of a hospital. Senator Bright had forsaken his congressional duties and had cast his fortunes with the Southern Confederacy. The Federal government had seized the land and here they erected a plant which was one of the finest in the United States for the care of their wounded and sick from the camps and battlefields in the South. It was the third largest hospital in the country, and was built on the plan of the Chestnut Hill Hospital in Philadelphia. From a great circular corridor, exactly one-half of a mile in circumference and eight hundred and forty feet across, under roof and enclosed by sliding glazed sash, there radiated outwardly like spokes from a hub, twenty-seven spacious buildings, each one hundred and seventy-five feet long and twenty feet wide. Twenty-four of these were wards, each containing fifty-three beds for patients and one for the ward master. The walls were high, the roof ribbed, without ceiling, the comb being open for ventilation. The windows, of which there was one between every two beds, extended from a foot above the floor to the eaves, so that there was a complete absence of hospital odor summer and winter, day and night, and every bed had a sunbath every day the sun shone. One of the remaining "spoke" buildings was equipped as a carpenter and repair shop for such emergencies as chanced to arise. The other two "spoke" buildings were of two stories each and were used for storage and supplies, with quarters over one of them for the women nurses. As an equator to the circle from north to south was a covered passage way, but not enclosed.

Each of the wards had its mess room and buttery in front and opening out on the circular corridor, while at the outer end of each building, in a small ell, was located a ward master's room, bath and toilet.

Just between the extreme outer ends of each two wards was an open coal bin, from which supplies were drawn during the winter to heat the buildings. Each ward was supplied with four large cast iron stoves, and they were sufficient to make the rooms comfortable. The large building located inside the circle was the much used little chapel and reading rooms, one hundred and fifty feet long by forty feet wide, and the small addition joining it on the north was the chaplain's office. The operating room lay just beyond, while farther in the distance was located the headquarters, a building two hundred and ten feet north and south, and thirty feet wide. The full and light diet kitchens, engine room, and machine shop in a building one hundred and

II

eighty feet long by thirty feet wide; the mess rooms and nurses sleeping apartments in another building one hundred and seventy-five feet by thirty feet, and the commissary department in a building one hundred and seventy-five feet long by fifty feet wide, were situated at the extreme western side of the circle near the baggage room and guard house. On each side of the circle were located two large hot water tanks, while just above, and to the east of the grounds, was located the pumping station, which furnished an ample supply of water from a well sunk to a great depth. It may be a matter of interest to know that one of these tanks is still in use at the circular saw-mill at Howard's shipyard (1909).

In the circle were also located the post-office, drug and instrument house and the dead house. In the distance and to the left was the river with Louisville beyond, while to the right and the distance among the trees could be seen the stables, and back of that Price's ditch, a great skating pond for Port Fulton boys up to a few years ago.

The drainage system was most complete, rarely requiring the plumber's attention.

Barracks for soldiers guarding the hospital and doing necessary police duty were situated near by, and the great laundry was located on the river bank, about a quarter of a mile above the present pumping station of the Jeffersonville water works.

The hospital was opened for the reception of patients on February 21, 1864, and was closed in December, 1866. Long before the war closed the capacity of the institution was found to be unequal to the demand and several tent divisions were in constant use. At one time, after Hood's defeat before Nashville, in the dead of winter, with snow of unusual depth, it became necessary to close the sash of the circular corridor and transform it into an immense ward. At that time the hospital had five thousand two hundred (5,200) beds, and they were all occupied. Besides the large number of soldiers and male nurses employed there was a corps of women nurses under the supervision of Mrs. Arbuckle, as chief nurse. The chief surgeon during the life-time of the hospital was Dr. Middleton Goldsmith, who in civil life had been a surgeon of large experience and great success. The position of executive officer, second in command, was at different times filled by Dr. W. T. Okie, United States Army; Dr. J. C. Happersett, Dr. A. B. Prescott and Dr. F. A. Seymour. There were but two chaplains, who, with equal rank remained throughout—Chaplain Chauncey W. Fitch, an Episcopal clergyman and the father of Col. Edw. W. Fitch; and Chaplain L. G. Olmstead, a Presbyterian. They were men of great heart as well as brain, and Chaplain Olmstead being a great lover of flowers was responsible for adding materially to the beauty and attractiveness of the grounds by planting many trees and flower beds to cheer the homesick sufferers.

During the existence of the hospital sixteen thousand, one hundred and twenty patients were cared for, and in providing wholesome rations for so vast a family great care and economy were necessary. It is doubtful if ever a meal was late. During this time there were served two million six hundred and sixty-four thousand three hundred and thirty-six meals, or what was equivalent to that many meals for one person. The economical disposal of the waste resulted in the saving of seventy-one thousand dollars, which in turn was applied to the purchase of provisions and medicines, some of which were not obtainable on the government supply list.

After the hospital was discontinued in 1866, the ground and buildings were turned over to the state of Indiana for the purpose of converting them into a soldiers' home, but after two months' possession the proposed home was moved to Knightstown, Ind., and the property was reconveyed to the United States. From this time on until 1874 the buildings were used as store houses for clothing, blankets, etc., and hundreds of thousands of these articles were kept here for use. The small brick house just above the stand pipe in Port Fulton, is the only remaining building which was connected with the hospital during the war. It was used by Doctor Goldsmith as his private quarters, and is now known as the old Zulauf house.

There were several camps of soldiers during the war in and around Jeffersonville besides Joe Holt and the hospital camp, but they had no permanent existence. The following institutions were housed in the city, and were a part of its life and business during the progress of hostilities.

During the early part of the war a bakery or hard tack factory was established in what is now Warder Park. The three buildings which composed this plant faced Spring street, ran back to Wall street, and filled the present area of the park. Here much of the hard tack for the army was made until near the close of the war and its necessity ceased.

On Wall street, between Eighth and Ninth, were four large warehouses of the usual size (about fifty feet by two hundred feet) for ordnance and magazine purposes. Other buildings of the same size, ten in number, were situated between Market street and the river and just above Mechanic street, and were used for storing commissary stores. There were two government fire engine houses for the protection of these buildings. One called the "Ever Ready No. 1" was on the northeast corner of Wall and Eighth streets for the magazines just beyond, and one called "No. 2" was on the northwest corner of Market and Penn streets for the warehouses on the opposite side of the street. A third company of eigh men, making twenty-four in the whole government department, with Billy Patterson as chief, constituted a hook and ladder company, and was stationed at the Jefferson General Hospital above Port Fulton.

The present site of the court-house lot was a wagon yard and sort of wagon hospital, there being a large frame building in the southeast corner which was used for the manufacture of harness and wagons, with a blacksmith shop attached. The government stables were situated on the upper side of Meigs avenue, between Seventh and Eighth. Farther down Court avenue, on the northwest corner of Walnut street, stood the feed and grain warehouses. On the west side of Spring street, the second door south of Chestnut street, the building, including the upper floors, was used as a hospital for convalescents. All of the quartermaster store houses and offices were finally consolidated and now constitute the United States Quarter Master depot. During the year 1864 the passage of troops and munitions of war became so heavy (all having to be transported across the river by the ferry boat) the engineers constructed a pontoon bridge, the Jeffersonville end striking the bank at the foot of Fort street. This bridge was kept here for about fifteen months, and over it were transported thousands of troops of all arms of the service.

On the northeast corner of Wall and Front streets the quartermaster's offices were located, and the three-story brick building on the west side of Spring street, near Front street, was used for hospital purposes. For many months early in the war a company of infantry was kept in barracks built on the lot at the corner of Wall and Maple streets, now owned by the German Roman church.

In 1863-64 it became necessary to resort to the draft system in order to fill out the quotas of many parts of the state. Before this time the state had furnished troops as required by the simple process of enlistment, but under the draft system the Federal government took charge and provost marshals were appointed for each congressional district. The provost marshal for this district was James Merriwether, and his headquarters were located in a large building belonging to Judge Read, standing on the west corner of Front and Mulberry streets. Here the names of all citizens between the ages of eighteen and forty-five were placed in a wheel, and the required number drawn out. Physical disability being a satisfactory excuse from service, it is said that a perusal of the records of this district, now filed in the archives at Washington, would show a most alarming and appalling list of diseases and ailments which then afflicted many of our citizens who favored the quiet walks of peace to the clash of arms or tented field.

On the present site of Ebert's flour mill, corner of Wall and Park streets, stood a large two-story brick building which was temporarily used for a hospital; and the brick building just in the rear of the new Citizens' Bank on Court avenue was used for a like purpose until the government had provided better quarters for her sick and wounded.

Of all the institutions and industries maintained by the Federal government in the city of Jeffersonville during the War of the Rebellion but one remains, and that is the Jeffersonville depot

THE UNITED STATES QUARTERMASTER DEPOT
INTERIOR VIEW.

of the United States Quarter Master Department. Work was begun in the spring of 1871 on the buildings which were to be used for the consolidation of the ware houses and offices still scattered around the city, and the commodious and spacious brick building covering the four city blocks from Tenth to Twelfth and from Watt to Mechanic streets were first occupied in 1874. The general plan of the depot was designed by Brevet Major General M. C. Meigs, quartermaster general U. S. army at that time. It is eight hundred one feet and four inches on each front, and its inside dimensions are six hundred and ninety-six feet each way. The building is of brick with metal roof, and is divided into forty compartments, each about fifty feet deep and giving a total storage capacity of two million seven hundred thousand cubit feet. In the center is the commanding officers's office, a brick building, originally surmounted by a tower one hundred feet high, which was torn down in 1902.

This quarter master's depot has steadily grown in importance since its beginning, until it has become one of the principal supply stations of the quarter master's department of the United States army.

The business of the institution consists of the manufacture and issue of army clothing, and the issue of quarter master supplies of all kinds to the army throughout the United States, the Philippines, Cuba, Porto Rico and the Hawaiian Islands. The commanding officers of the depot since its completion in 1874 have been as follows:

Col. James E. Ekin.. 1872 to 1883
Col. Rufus Saxton.. 1883 to 1887
Col. Henry C. Hodges.. 1887 to 1894
Col. A. G. Robinson .... 1894 to 1897
Col. Charles W. Williams .... 1897 to 1898
Lt. Col. Charles R. Barnett................................. 1898 to Sept., 1901
Col. James M. Marshall .... July, 1904, to Jan., 1903
Lt. Col. Sam R. Jones....................................... April 1903 to Dec. 1903
Col. C. A. H. McCauley...................................... Dec. 1903 to July 1904
Col. James M. Marshall...................................... July 1904 to Jan. 1908
Col. George Ruhlin .... Jan., 1908 to .....

One of the phases of military life in Clark county which should not be overlooked, was the draft. This horrible nightmare to some men stalked through the state, carrying nervous prostration and stage-fright to more than one poor thing who should have been at the front. It is said that if the records at Washington could be examined that it would disclose a roster of men who had the worst and most varied collection of ailments ever known to the medical profession.

A poor excuse was better than none, and it is a wonder that the officers in charge of the draft did not call a convention of the local M. D.'s to behold, for once at least, this galaxy of athletic cripples and sound decrepits.

From the Mexican war period there was little of the military spirit manifesting itself throughout the country; but from the response to the heavy calls for men to put down the Rebellion, it is evident that the spirit was dormant and not dead. The relations between the North and South had reached a state of strain bordering on rupture. In Jeffersonville a meeting was called for the purpose of organizing a military company in March, 1860. At the next meetning, March 8, 1860, held in the Mayor's office, which seems to have been the same building on Front street where the first meeting was held, the organization was effected by the election of John N. Ingram, captain; Nathaniel Field, first lieutenant; Robert F. Bence, second lieutenant; James G. Caldwell, third lieutenant; William M. Darrough, orderly sergeant, and John S. McCauley, secretary. A careful survey of their old minute book, and inquiry among those who still survive, show a roster of seventy names.

At the organization the following non-commissioned officers were appointed, the first sergeant having been elected, as were the commissioned officers:

Second Sergeant—William Howard.
Third Sergeant—Francis Berresford.
Fourth Sergeant—David Bailey.
Ensign—Gabriel Poindexter.
First Corporal—George H. Kram.
Second Corporal—Samuel Beach.
Third Corporal—James Patterson.
Fourth Corporal—William Thompson.

The "Indiana Greys" was the euphonious name selected, and it was also recorded that it was the express wish of the company that their uniforms should be a "grey suit trimmed with black, and that the buttons on the suit should be a silver color with an eagle on the face." The drill hall selected was known as Pratt's Hall, and was located on Spring street about one hundred and fifty feet from Front street, and about opposite Strauss' Hotel.

There seems to have been more or less enthusiasm at the early meetings of the Indiana Greys. New members were proposed and elected, various committees were appointed to attend everything imaginable, and fines were assessed and collected; but the spurt did not last, and the company decided on May 30, 1860, to "suspend operations until January 1, 1861." The awakening, however, which did not take place until February 21, 1861, seems to have been an entirely new move, as a mass meeting was called for the purpose of organizing a military company. This company elected the following officers, re-electing the captain of the former company on account of his experience in the Mexican war:

Captain—John N. Ingram.
First Lieutenant—Nathaniel Field, Jr.
Second Lieutenant—James Keigwin.
Third Lieutenant—James G. Caldwell.
Secretary—James N. Patterson.
Treasurer—John W. Kane.
Orderly Sergeant—John W. Kane.
Second Sergeant—James Wathen.
Third Sergeant—J. W. Jacobs.
Fourth Sergeant—David M. Dryden.
Fifth Sergeant—J. T. Davis.
First Corporal—George H. Kram.
Second Corporal—Moses Nahm.
Third Corporal—James Patterson.
Fourth Corporal—Forbes Redman.

Shortly afterward John Kane was elected third lieutenant and Gabriel Poindexter to be second lieutenant. The name selected by the company was the "Clark Guards" and they began their service, which was carried on during such critical times and which reflected so much credit on them. Some of their first meetings were held at the residence of David Dryden, on Walnut street, but very soon afterward they procured Spark's Hall on Wall street, between Market and Chestnut, and used it for a drill hall and assembling place as long as they remained in the state service. This building remained here until the summer of 1903, when it was torn down to make room for a modern dwelling, having been used at different times for hall, armory, theater, Methodist church, dance hall and stable. The City Council gave the company three hundred dollars with which to procure uniforms, and the purchase of these, the purchase of a keg of powder, three thousand gun caps, and the manufacture of paper cartridges, etc., etc., fitted the men out in true military style. The uniform adopted was a frock coat, so states the minutes, but even this scanty and abbreviated costume was only decided upon after various pros and cons between it and "a hunting shirt with stiff collar." "A cap similar to the National Blues of Louisville" was added to their apparel by almost unanimous vote, the only one voting against it being William Howard, and he held out for a "tall cap."

There being practically a total lack of military knowledge in Jeffersonville, as well as elsewhere in the Union at this time, it was deemed advisable to get instruction from some outside source. A committee which had been appointed to attend to the matter reported on March 13, 1861, that Captain Woodruff, of Louisville, would give the company twenty lessons for seventy-five dollars. Considering the time and the condition of the country, this offer seems anything but patriotic. This gentleman afterward became a brigadier general in the Union army.   In the early fall of this year Captain Woodruff was succeeded by Captain Mussey, of the regular army.   He was here on recruiting service at the time and his instructions were gladly given to the company without pay.   He brought them to a high state of efficiency.   Among other fancy drills which he taught them was the "bayonet drill," an exhibition which made the company very popular at fairs, etc.   The organization was in a remarkably prosperous condition when the Legislature enacted a new militia law, which necessitated a reorganization.   On June 5, 1861, the Deputy Adjutant General of Indiana, J. W. Ray, mustered the company into the state service and the records at Indianapolis contained the following roster of the Clark Guards, officers and non-commissioned officers:

Captain—John N. Ingram.
First Lieutenant—James G. Caldwell.
Second Lieutenant—Gabriel Poindexter.
Ensign—John W. Kane.
Orderly Sergeant—Henry F. Miller.
First Sergeant—Alford Lee.
Second Sergeant—H. H. Reynolds.
Third Sergeant—J. W. Jacobs.
Fourth Sergeant—B. R. Prather.
First Corporal—J. M. Ruddell.
Second Corporal—Ed A. Heller.
Third Corporal—A. W. Hamlin.
Fourth Corporal—William Northcutt.
Company Clerk—G. F. Miller.

There were sixty-five privates enrolled at muster.

J. Chap Collum afterward became secretary and Ed A. Heller was promoted to be second lieutenant.

From the organization of the Clark Guards in Jeffersonville up to the summer of 1862 the company did excellent work, at a time when the armies-to-be were evolving themselves from chaos, and when guards such as these were sorely needed.   They served until the volunteer regiments began to be formed and were relieved by them of much of their work, and most of their men and officers.

This company continued to exist through the whole period of the War of the Rebellion, and together with the other but later Clark county companies performed a valiant and valuable service. It later on became part of the Eighth Regiment, Indiana Legion.   Clark county at the beginning of the War of the Rebellion was in a similar condition to the rest of the state.   Although there were a few independent companies such as the Clark Guards, here and there, there was no organized militia anywhere when the war had actually commenced.

There were less than five hundred stands of effective first class small arms in the state, and eight pieces of weather-worn and dismantled cannon. Throughout the various counties there was an unknown number of old flint-locks, altered to percussion cap muskets which had been issued to militiamen years before, but these were useless, except for drilling purposes. The nucleus of the newly organizing regiments and brigades was the few independent companies which already existed. The Clark Guards became one of the three original companies in the Eighth Regiment, Second Brigade, Second Military Division, when Col. James Keigwin was commissioned to the command of the regiment August 30. 1861, the other two companies being Ben Lutz's company, the Battle Creek Guards, from just this side of Charlestown, and Ben Henderson's company, the "Union Company," from Hibernia. The resignation of Colonel Keigwin soon afterward to become lieutenant colonel of the Forty-ninth Indiana Volunteer Infantry, caused John N. Ingram, the captain of the Clark Guards, to be promoted and commissioned colonel October 6, 1861.

This Eighth regiment was augmented by the addition of several other companies from Scott and Clark counties and was considered a very fair organization. Generals Mansfield and Lane were at the head of the state troops at this time, and among the most efficient officers on the southern border of the state were James Keigwin, John N. Ingram and John F. Willey.

Colonel Willey succeeded to the command of the Eighth Regiment October 13, 1862, and at this time had seventeen companies under his command, of which twelve were in Clark county.

The field and staff of the Eighth Regiment were as follows:

Colonel—James Keigwin.
Colonel—John N. Ingram.
Colonel—John F. Willey.
Lieutenant Colonel—Warren Horr.
Lieutenant Colonel—Samuel C. Taggart.
Lieutenant Colonel—Thomas D. Fouts.
Adjutant—Josiah W. Gwin.
Adjutant—James Ryan.
Quartermaster—Melvin Weir.
Surgeon—David H. Combs.

The Jeffersonville Artillery, one of the units of the regiment, was only a paper company; the officers were George L. Key, captain; Reuben Wells, first lieutenant; James Wathea, second lieutenant. This battery was supposed to hail from Jeffersonville, but no record exists of its service. The Battle Creek Guards, an infantry company from Utica township and from the south of Charlestown, was a loyal and efficient organization.

The Battle Creek Guards was about the only one beside the Clark Guards that saw a great deal of active service during the war. Their organization was kept up from the date of muster all through the war period, and it was a service not wholly of the nature of the service of Home Guards elsewhere. In October, 1861, the company was called into service and was taken down the Ohio by steamboat to the mouth of Salt river. Here they volunteered to cross the river, although their legal service did not extend beyond the state of Indiana. They here formed a part of quite a force of volunteers and were engaged, a part of the time, in collecting all the boats on Salt river. Their service here lasted about ten days, and while here they were quartered on a steamboat. They were on active service during Morgan's raid and added in no small way to the effectiveness of the militia force sent out to meet the invader.

The officers of this company, during its term of service, were Captains Benjamin F. Lutz, John F. Willey and Dennis F. Willey; First Lieutenants, Isaac M. Koons, George W. Luman and Oscar F. Lutz; Second Lieutenants, Alban Lutz and S. L. Jacobs.

The Union Home Guards was recruited from Memphis and vicinity. Its officers were Captains, James M. Gwin, Josiah W. Gwin and Joseph C. Drummond; First Lieutenants, William C. Combs, and Second Lieutenant John C. Peden.

The Oregon Guards, from Oregon township, had as officers: Captains, Francis M. Carr and Jesse Summers; First Lieutenants, William W. Watson and Wilshire Minor; Second Lieutenants, Cornelius B. Ruddle and Joseph Carr.

The Ellsworth Zouaves, of Jeffersonville, was one of the phantom companies of the Eighth Regiment. It existed only on paper. Its officers were: Captain, William W. Caldwell; First Lieutenant, Thomas Gray, and Second Lieutenant, George W. Brown.

The Union company was recruited from the vicinity of Hibernia. Its officers were: Captain, Benjamin Henderson; First Lieutenants, John D. Noe and Jacob P. Bare; Second Lieutenants, Paron Crop and Calid Scott.

The Henryville Grays was an infantry company, with officers for its two years of service as follows: Captain, Cyrus M. Clark; First Lieutenants, J. S. Ryan, Luke S. Becket and James V. Herron; Second Lieutenants, J. A. C. McCoy, H. H. Prall and Alexander G. Biggs.

The Hoosier Guards were from New Hope and vicinity and added their quota of strength to the defense against the Morgans who might dare invade Clark county soil. The officers were: Captains, John T. Hamilton and John J. Baur; First Lieutenant, Chesterfield Hutsell; and Second Lieutenants, Edward W. Thawley and William K. Matthews.

The Utica Rough and Ready Guards came from the hills and valleys of Utica. Jesse Combs was captain, Moses H. Tyler, first lieutenant and Thomas J. Worrall, second lieutenant.

The Silver Creek Guards came from Sellersburg. E. W. Moore was captain, George Bottorff was first lieutenant, and P. J. Ash, second lieutenant.

The Charlestown Cavalry was commanded by Captain Warren Horr.
Isaac Koons was first lieutenant, and Benjamin Perdue was second lieutenant.
This troop completes the roster of companies in the Clark county regiment.

Besides the service which these companies gave, "they were a prolific
nursery for the volunteer service, a quickener of the patriotic impulse and a con-
servator of genuine loyalty." The service given by this regiment is summed up
in the report of Colonel Willey for 1863-64 as follows:

"We had five battalions, and were called into service by order
of the Governor, June 20th, to meet the raid under Captain Hines;
July 6, 1863, called into service by Adjutant General Noble; rendezvoused at Jeffersonville; July 7th, dismissed the command; July 8th, met
at Jeffersonville to repel Morgan raid; were in line of battle but no
enemy came; July 15th relieved from duty and command dismissed; June
9, 1864, called into service by order of the Governor to meet a raid from Kentucky by Morgan; dismissed June 25th; August 10th called companies A and
H to picket the Ohio river in the vicinity of the Grassy Flats to stop guerrillas
under rebel Jesse from crossing; pickets fired on guerrillas, fire returned, but no
one hurt; dismissed August 20, 1864. We had two battalion drills in April,
1864, one regimental drill in May and one in October. The regiment is well
drilled for militia, and is ready and willing to turn out whenever called on."

Such was the temper, character and service of the regiment of Clark county militia.

The Morgan raid across the southern part of the state in July, 1863, was
the cause of an abnormal activity among both the active and sedentary militia,
and although it amounted to nothing so far as active service was concerned, it
caused more or less patriotism to suddenly appear in the breasts of the stay-at-
homes and an outward and visible sign of a desire to fight that must have been
gratifying if not amusing to the boys in blue at the front.

A movement was commenced to intercept Morgan at Vienna on the afternoon of the 10th by sending a brigade of infantry and a battery of artillery from
Jeffersonville by rail, and the troops were already embarked on cars, in high
spirits, when an order from General Boyle, to whom the military "post" at Jeffersonville belonged, stopped them. The militia, as stated in Colonel Willey's report, were called to duty July 9th for the same purpose, but the public
mind was in such a wrought-up state that these United States volunteers and
militia did not give satisfactory assurance of perfect safety from the dreaded
bugaboo, so a volunteer force was raised besides. This force appeared in the
shape of a so-called regiment of men from Jeffersonville, which seemed to
spring, mushroom-like, out of the ground over night. The "raiders" were
coming and everybody was ready to fight. This hurry-up organization amount-

ed to from six hundred to eight hundred men, besides two "quick" troops of cavalry (if the historian may be pardoned for so designating them), the above mentioned bodies having about all the able bodied men of Jeffersonville in their ranks.

The battle of Corydon was an inspiration to the luke-warm, so the advance of this body of men to the rear of the city was an imposing one so far as numbers went. The first night out they camped in Taylor's woods, and then moved out near the springs property on Spring street, near Twelfth, there to welcome the dread invader "with bloody hands to hospitable graves." The fact that although they had been armed with muskets, yet had been issued no ammunition, never dawning upon them until after the scare. They remained on duty about six days, but it is stated by some that when the remnant of the regiment returned to the city at the end of their duty they found that the largest portion had already arrived before them, not having waited for such an inconsequential thing as an order or permit to leave and return homeward.

Among these brave defenders was one Isaac Gaither, a brother of Perry Gaither, the Falls pilot. He was a most enthusiastic shouting Methodist and a leader in the Wall Street church. The night being cool when Morgan was expected, and the anticipation of a fight being rather trying to many, a bottle of that "licker" commonly called "spirits frumentii," was circulated among the boys, and Gaither was persuaded to take a pull for his health's sake. As the spirits in the bottle lowered the spirits of the men rose, especially Gaither's, and he finally seized his gun, jumped into the middle of the road, raised the weapon to his shoulder and shouted, "John Morgan, if you're coming, come on NOW!" This show of spirits did not seem to appeal to some and touched the risibles of none, for one of them, "Bill" Jackson by name, replied in a stage whisper, "Shet up, you damned fool, some of Morgan's men might be out there and hear you."

This body of Jeffersonville soldiery disappeared as it came, and its history is only what can be gleaned from the tales told by the survivors at this day.

The citizen soldiery of Charlestown lost no opportunity to perfect themselves in the art of war, and night after night found them drilling in the courthouse. During the winter of 1860 and 1861, these drills were kept up, Harry Daily being the drill master. During the period of nervous prostration which General Morgan had caused to be an epidemic in Clark county, and when the militia had assembled to repulse the invader, about five hundred rebels started to cross the river at Twelve-Mile Island, but a gunboat opened fire on them and only one boat load of forty-six succeeded in reaching the northern shore, or rather in escaping to it. At this time there was a deep-laid, well-organized conspiracy throughout the southern part of the state to assist Morgan in every way possible. That treasonable, disloyal and infamous secret society, called the "Knights of the Golden Circle," had plotted and planned to make Morgan's raid successful. Clark county was unfortunate enough to have within her borders men who were traitors to their country and flag, and to these men the invaders at Twelve-Mile Island looked for support. Of the forty-six who succeeded in invading Clark county, hardly a one escaped capture, while Morgan's force itself went around to the north. The militia force returned home, and the country-side guards who had, like Putnam of old, left field or team to defend their homes, returned once more to peaceful pursuits.

One of the earliest organizations of men in Clark county formed for the purpose of entering into active service in the great conflict, was headed quite naturally by that patriotic citizen of Jeffersonville, whom every one knew and everybody liked, James Keigwin, later the gallant colonel of the Forty-ninth Indiana. When the President had issued his first call for 75,000 men, April 15, 1861, to put down the rebellion, Jeffersonville, like every other city and town in the state of Indiana, had its company of men ready in a few hours after receiving the news. This company consisted of about sixty men and they were quartered temporarily in Spark's Hall, on Wall street, where stoves to cook upon and bedding and provisions were provided, not, however, by the State or Federal Government, but out of the private purse of the man raising the organization. Indiana's quota being filled almost as soon as the call was made, the men whom Keigwin had assembled sought other fields and the only reward or satisfaction he received for his patriotism at that time was a knowledge that he had done his duty, the three hundred dollars spent for subsistence being credited to profit and loss.

A company of first-call men was raised in Charlestown the same time that Keigwin raised his Jeffersonville company. Clark county made her initial bow in this conflict as early as any other county in the state, and the standard which she set at the outset was kept up throughout the period. When Sumter was fired on, several young men at the county-seat began the organization of an infantry company, and Henry Ferguson assumed the leadership in the movement. J. B. Roland was slated for first lieutenant and Isaac Haymaker for second lieutenant. A drum and fife corps was made up, and these officers, together with a few others, started out to visit the neighboring villages near Charlestown to recruit their company. Vesta, Solon, New Washington, New Market and other places were visited and the temper of the men was shown by a roster of one hundred and thirty-eight enlistments. The recruits marched to Charlestown and camped in the public square, but they were doomed to the same disappointment which Keigwin met, and their offer of service was refused, as those companies nearer Indianapolis had already been accepted. David Daily was not discouraged, however, and took seventy-eight of these men up to Indianapolis on a special train, marched them up to the State House and offered their services to Governor Morton. It was too late, but the men had only to wait a short while before an opportunity was given for them to offer their services in newer regiments.

The next body of men raised in Jeffersonville was headed by David M. Drydan, the pilot. An old riverman named Jesse J. Stepleton had interested Drydan in raising a company for immediate service. Stepleton had been a mate on one of the river boats and Drydan very naturally fell in with his plans, and raised a good-sized squad of men in and around Jeffersonville. For this work he was made a second lieutenant when the company was mustered in.

Drydan's squad consisted of twenty-seven men from Jeffersonville, Utica, Charlestown and vicinity. These men, with a number from Louisville, aggregating about one hundred and six, embarked on the mail boat and were taken to Cincinnati, Ohio, where they were mustered in as Company F, First Kentucky Volunteer Infantry, by Major S. Burbank, of the First Infantry, U. S. A., at Camp Clay, June 4, 1861. Captain Stepleton resigned soon afterward, it is said, from fear of his men, whom he had treated with great brutality, and Drydan was promoted to fill his place. The regiment was ordered to the Department of West Virginia and performed much valuable service in the early part of the war. From there it was ordered to the Department of the Cumberland in January, 1862, and took active part in the advance on Nashville and participated in the following engagements: Gauley Bridge, Red House and Peytonia, Virginia; Shiloh, Tennessee; Corinth, Mississippi; Stone River, Tennessee, and Chickamauga, Georgia.

These men composed the first body of soldiers to go into the army, and as they went into a Kentucky regiment, neither Indiana nor Clark county received the credit for them. They served until mustered out at Covington, Kentucky, June 18, 1864.

The first volunteers from Clark county to go into an Indiana regiment were Company D, of the Twenty-second Indiana Volunteer Infantry, from Charlestown. This was the regiment commanded by Col. Jeff C. Davis. Colonel Davis was promoted brigadier general of the United States Volunteers, December 18, 1861, and brevetted major general, August 8, 1864. The organization and muster of this company was but the prelude to that proud chapter in Clark county's history, wherein is written the patriotic service of her sons in many regiments.

"How they went forth to die!
Pale, earnest thousands from the dizzy mills,
And sunburnt thousands from the harvest hills,
Quick, eager thousands from the city's streets,
And storm-tried thousands from the fisher's fleets,
How they went forth to die!"

Company D, of the Twenty-second Regiment Indiana Volunteers, was headed quite naturally by David W. Dailey, who had made such strenuous efforts to force his earlier company into the service. William H. Ratts went out as first lieutenant, and Isaac N. Haymaker as second lieutenant. Dailey rose to the lieutenant colonelcy after the death of John A. Hendricks at the battle of Pea Ridge, March 6, 1862. During the service of this company, David W. Dailey, Isaac N. Haymaker, James M. Parker, Thomas H. Dailey and Patrick H. Carney, served as captain; William H. Ratts, James M. Parker, Samuel H. Campbell, Thomas H. Dailey, Patrick H. Carney and George G. Taff as first lieutenants and Isaac N. Haymaker, Samuel H. Campbell, Thomas H. Dailey, Patrick H. Carney, David N. Runyan and Charles J. Giles second lieutenants.

The company was rendezvoused in Charlestown, the squads of recruits camping in the court-house yard. The movement to raise this body of men was not coincident with the organization of the Twenty-second Regiment, most of the men being the remains of Dailey's old company who had been kept together and drilled from time to time. The regimental rendezvous was at Madison and here, on July 15, 1861, they were organized, and soon after left for Indianapolis, where they were mustered into the United States service, August 15, 1861, for three years.

The battle of Pea Ridge, Siege of Corinth, pursuit of Bragg, Perryville, Stone River, the charge up Mission Ridge, and Sherman's "Marching Through Georgia," were all part of its history, and Company D's return to Charlestown after muster-out at Washington, D. C., in June, 1865, was the occasion of well merited congratulations.

The next troops were Companies B and I, Twenty-third Indiana Volunteer Infantry. Most of the men in B company were from Jeffersonville and vicinity, while those in I company were from Charlestown. One of the prime movers in organizing Company B, besides William W. Caldwell, was James B. Merriwether, who later on served as lieutenant colonel of the Thirty-eighth Indiana, vice Walter Q. Gresham, resigned, and still later as provost marshal of the second district. The company was organized in their own camp at Taylor's Woods, just back of Jeffersonville, and was mustered in at New Albany, July 29, 1861. In February, 1862, several men of this company lost their lives on the ill-fated gunboat Essex, eleven guns, when her boilers blew up, Lieut. Daniel Trotter being one of the unfortunates.

Caldwell took out with him William M. Darrough as first lieutenant and Daniel Trotter as second lieutenant. Darrough was promoted captain and was killed at Vicksburg and Trotter was killed at Fort Henry in 1862.

Company I was recruited in Charlestown during the month of June, and on July 8th received orders from Gov. O. P. Morton to proceed to Camp Noble at New Albany. On July 27th they were mustered into the United States service, and on August 15th left Camp Noble for St. Louis.

The battle of Shiloh, the Siege of Corinth, the capture of Iuka, Thompson's Hill, Raymond, Champion Hill, Jackson, Vicksburg, the Atlanta Campaign, the pursuit of Hood, with Sherman to Savannah, the campaign of the Carolinas and the battle of Bentonville, is a record that any regiment could be proud of, and our companies of the Twenty-third did their share of duty. The officers of Company B were as follows:

William W. Caldwell, Captain.
William M. Darrough, Captain.
Michael Whalen, Captain.
Frederick Wilkens, Captain.
William M. Darrough, First Lieutenant.
Michael Whalen, First Lieutenant.
Henry C. Foster, First Lieutenant.
Philip Pflanzer, First Lieutenant.
Daniel Trotter, Second Lieutenant.
Henry C. Foster, Second Lieutenant.
Martin Muthig, Second Lieutenant.
The officers of Company I were as follows:
Henry C. Ferguson, Captain.
Benjamin F. Walter, Captain.
James N. Wood, Captain.
Benjamin F. Walter, First Lieutenant.
Joshua W. Custer, First Lieutenant.
David Moore, First Lieutenant.
Joshua W. Custer, Second Lieutenant.
Henry C. Dietz, Second Lieutenant.
Francis M. Crabtree, Second Lieutenant.
Claiborn M. Delton, Second Lieutenant.

When the Thirty-eighth Regiment Indiana Volunteers was organized it had two companies from Clark county, Company H, of Jeffersonville, and Company F, of Charlestown. Company H was raised by Capt. Gabriel Poindexter, who at the breaking out of the War of the Rebellion, was in the hardware business on Spring street, near Front. During this company's term of service it had the following Clark county officers: Gabriel Poindexter, Victor M. Carr and Andrew J. Crandell, captains; Victor M. Carr, Andrew J. Crandell and Joseph L. Leach, first lieutenants, and Andrew J. Howard and Victor M. Carr as second lieutenants.

About three o'clock on a beautiful afternoon in the early part of September, 1861, the men composing the company assembled and took wagons for New Albany. The leave taking of soldiers was still new to the city, and a goodly crowd assembled to witness their departure. The road that led to New Albany in those days was on the present right of way of the Pennsylvania Railroad. They were not mustered in until September 18th, but before that time one of their number died. His name is not to be found now on mortal rolls, but all the honors of war were accorded him in his funeral obsequies. Besides the officers and men who composed this company and who hailed from Jeffersonville, there were James B. Merriwether, lieutenant colonel of the regiment; Joshua B. Jenkins, major, and T. C. Mercer, of Utica, assistant surgeon. In Charlestown the company for this regiment was raised by Wesley Connor. There was no lack of enthusiasm, and the quota was filled without trouble. Wesley Connor, Joshua B. Jenkins and William M. Pangburn served as captains; Stephen S. Cole, Joshua B. Jenkins, William M. Pangburn and Thomas R. Mitchell served as first lieutenants, and Joshua B. Jenkins, Thomas H. Adams and Elias Daily as second lieutenants. The men composing this company were recruited from the vicinity of Charlestown, Otisco, New Market and New Washington, and as was usual in those days, rode to the place of rendezvous at New Albany in farmers' wagons. The history of these companies was the history of the regiment throughout the war. They served in the campaigns in Kentucky, 1861; Tennessee and Kentucky in 1862; pursuit of Bragg, 1862; Rosecrans' campaign in Tennessee, 1863; against Chattanooga, 1863; against Atlanta, 1864; pursuit of Hood, 1864; Sherman's march to the sea, 1864, and through the Carolinas in 1865. They were sent to Louisville in 1865 and remained there until the middle of July of that year. The two companies of Clark county men were mustered out with the regiment July 15, 1865, participated in a public reception at Indianapolis July 18th, where they were addressed by Governor Morton. During the service of this regiment it covered an immense amount of territory in its marches. After the campaign in the Carolinas it marched to Washington, D. C., a distance of one hundred and ninety-two miles in six days, an average of thirty-two miles per day. The sum total of its service is more than creditable.

12

CHAPTER XVIII.

THE MILITARY HISTORY OF CLARK COUNTY.

FORTY-NINTH INDIANA.

The Forty-ninth Regiment of Indiana Volunteers was organized at Camp Joe Holt, Jeffersonville, Indiana, on the 18th day of November, 1861, and mustered into service November 21, 1861, for three years or during the war. The staff officers for the whole term of their service were as follows:

Colonel.	Residence.	Date of Com.
John W. Ray	Jeffersonville	November 18, 1861.
James Keigwin	Jeffersonville	October 18, 1862.
James Leeper	Charlestown	December 1, 1864.
Lt. Colonel.		
James Keigwin	Jeffersonville	November 18, 1861.
Joseph H. Thornton	Leavenworth	October 11, 1862.
Arthur J. Hawhe	New Albany	July 28, 1863.
James Leeper	Charlestown	December 1, 1864.
James A. Gardner	Rome	September 6, 1865.
Major.		
Joseph H. Thornton	Leavenworth	November 25, 1861.
Arthur J. Hawhe	New Albany	October 13, 1862.
James Leeper	Charlestown	July 28, 1863.
John A. Hamacher	Vienna	September 26, 1865.
Adjutant.		
James M. Gwin	Memphis	November 22, 1861.
George W. Riddle	Leavenworth	April 15, 1862.
Beverly W. Sullivan	Jeffersonville	February 22, 1865.
Quarter-master.		
Charles H. Paddack	Jeffersonville	September 25, 1861.
George W. Pettit	Jeffersonville	April 1, 1865.

Chaplain.
William Maple.........Salem ....December 5, 1861.
L. M. Hancock.........   May 1, 1862.
L. L. Hazen...........   June 17, 1863.
    Surgeon.
Charles D. Pearson.....Indianapolis ....November 19, 1861.
James R. Munroe.......Seymour ....March 11, 1862.
John A. Ritter.........Orleans ....October 18, 1862.
Emanuel R. Hawn......Indianapolis ....February 20, 1864.
Edward F. Buzzett.....Jeffersonville ....April 1, 1865.
    Assistant Surgeon.
J. A. C. McCoy.........Jeffersonville ....December 27, 1861.

The non-commissioned staff was George F. Howard, sergeant major; Elisha L. Trueblood, quarter-master sergeant; Beverly W. Sullivan, commissary sergeant; Samuel Lingle and Preston C. Worrell, principal musicians. The Forty-ninth was the first and only regiment organized in Clark county for the War of the Rebellion, and had so many Clark county men as field and line officers, besides the rank and file that it may be truly called a Clark county regiment. Colonel Ray resigned after commanding the regiment from its muster into the service, November 21, 1861, until the following June, when he left it, and from that time until the regiment served out their full term of enlistment of three years it was commanded by Col. James Keigwin. A part of the regiment re-enlisted in Texas and Captain Leeper was made lieutenant colonel, and served with the veterans up to the close of the war, when they were mustered out of the service at Louisville, Kentucky, September 13, 1865, having served their country three years and ten months as gallantly and faithfully as any soldiers that ever left the state. It would require a large volume to record the battles, skirmishes and hardships the old Forty-ninth endured during its long and faithful service for their country and flag. The enlistments, first and last, of officers and men, numbered twelve hundred and sixty-eight, of whom two hundred and thirty-eight gave up their lives for their country. The regiment performed the duties required of it by army regulations, and obeyed with alacrity all orders from superior officers, and were ready every hour of their three years and ten months' service to kill the enemies of their country and flag, or be killed in defense of them. And well may Clark county be proud of her boys who wore the blue and performed their part so well in saving and making the greatest nation on the globe. "A government of the people, by the people and for the people."

One of the most amusing things occurred at the time the Forty-ninth was in camp at Joe Holt, and was published in all the papers in the country after its occurrence. Many of the recruits came from a dark corner of our state, and were not up to the fashions, etiquette and polished ways of the present day. They might have been called green if the hayseed in their hair had not been faded to a light dust color. They were told by their friends when they started for camp to wear the oldest and worst clothes they had, and throw them away when they drew their uniforms, which would save them the trouble and expense of sending their clothes home after they had drawn their uniforms. I can truthfully say that they accepted the advice of their friends, and any sort of a judge of man's dress would say that they wore their worst clothes when they came to camp. On account of some delay of the quartermaster, the uniforms did not arrive as soon as expected, and the poor boys had to wear those "worst clothes" for a week or more, which was a great disappointment to the whole regiment. Colonel Keigwin recounts the following: "All the young ladies in Jeffersonville were casting wistful eyes at the young officers of the regiment, and using every endeavor to make their stay in camp as pleasant as possible. One of the debutantes of our city concluded that she would cast her hook into the military fish pond to catch a soldier, if possible, by giving to the officers of the regiment a reception at her home on Market street. (In our day it would be called a 'function' or some other Newport name.) The debutante wrote the invitations to the 'function' herself and it read: 'The pleasure of your company is invited to attend a party to be given by Miss ————, at her home on Market street, on —— day, —— hour, to the defenders of our flag and country.' The captain of the company that came into camp with their worst clothes on understood the invitation for him to appear with his company, and he came. I, being a distant relative of the young lady, of course it was my duty to make things go off as pleasantly as possible for the company, and to be the first on the ground to receive them. Just as it was getting dark I went to the front gate and looked down market street, and you can judge of my surprise when I saw the captain with his full company in their rag-tag motley garments they had left home in. Well, just at that time I was worse rattled than I ever was when forming the regiment in line for battle. Jack Fallstaff and his famous company were well dressed as compared with that crew. Well, we did the best we could with them, inviting them into the parlors which we had taken so much pains to decorate with pictures of Washington and Jackson and other famous fighters of early times. The walls were decorated with flags and other ornaments suitable for a regimental 'function' in 1861. Refreshments for all that number? you ask. Well, we just cut the bits of cake which were small enough for one into two pieces and added a little more water to the lemonade, and all returned to camp well satisfied that he had learned what a real reception in Jeffersonville was forty years ago. The captain who brought all of his company to the reception has been dead for more than twenty-five years previous to this writing (1904), and it is to be hoped that the function he is now enjoying is of a different sort from the one he attended in Jeffersonville with his Fallstaffian company. Many hundreds of years ago a multitude of five thousand were served with five loaves and two fishes, and after all were satisfied there remained twelve baskets full of loaves and fishes, but I can truthfully say that not a crumb as big as a buck-shot was left after the well dressed company of the Forty-ninth Indiana had been served at that 'debutante function' on Market street in Jeffersonville forty-two years ago."

The Forty-ninth Regiment left their camp at Joe Holt, Jeffersonville, December 11, 1861, and made their first march through Louisville and out the Bardstown Pike. At that time Jeffersonville had a brass band, and they volunteered to escort the regiment across the river and through Louisville, where at that time, as many cheered for Jefferson Davis as shouted for Lincoln. William H. Fogg, Professor John Johnson, Henry Ewing, Abraham Carr and others were members and they tooted their horns vigorously marching through the city with one thousand armed men following them, but the danger of getting back with their horns exposed after escorting a Yankee regiment through the streets of a rebel city, was too great to be risked, and they deposited their instruments in a house on the outskirts of the city and sent a wagon to haul them home. This trip was the last toot the band ever made on those horns.

The regiment reached Bardstown on the 13th of December, and went into camp at the fair grounds, where they devoted all their time to drilling and fighting mouth battles, telling how they would lick the Johnnies and return to their homes in a few months to receive from their friends the palm of victory. They did not know as much about war then as they learned later. Col. James Keigwin's account of their service is as follows: "One thing which added greatly to our courage was the good old Nelson county Bourbon whiskey which was sold at that time for twenty-five cents per gallon, which brought it in reach of the most impecunious soldier in the regiment. The only total abstinence man that I knew in the regiment at that time was Col. John W. Ray, who spent most of his time talking about the comforts of home as compared to those of camp life, and admonishing us of the great danger of a too free use of "old Tambo" (as it was then called by the men in the regiment), and praying that Jeff Davis and his followers would soon find the folly of trying to break up the Union and trying to lick such loyal fighting men as he had in the Forty-ninth Indiana. Our colonel was from his boyhood days a better talker than a fighter, and he almost convinced me in some of his oratorical flights that the war could not last six months longer, and I was almost afraid that I would never have a chance to witness or take part in a battle. One beautiful, crisp, frosty moonlight night I suggested that we have a false alarm in camp to teach the men that when they lay down for the night to always put their arms, accoutrements and clothing where they could put their hands on them no matter how dark it might be, or under all sorts of danger or excitement, when called out in the night. No one knew that there would be an alarm but Ray, myself and Major Thornton. About twelve o'clock we called up the drum corps and ordered them to beat the long roll, that the enemy was but a few miles from us, approaching on the Lebanon pike. They beat the roll earnestly, and we three field officers ran up and down the company streets commanding in a loud voice 'turn out! fall in on the color front,' that the Johnnies were advancing on the pike and were but a few miles away. Well, it was one of the most excitable and amusing scenes I have ever witnessed. After getting them on the color front we found some of them with only one shoe on, some without a gun and others without a cartridge box; in fact they would have put up a poor fight in the condition they were in. We double-quicked them out of the fair grounds, down the pike, formed line of battle and told them that there was no armed enemy within fifty miles of the place, and explained to them what the alarm was given for, and I can truthfully say that the regiment never forgot the lesson it learned that night. We had the roll called and found thirty "coffee coolers" absent. Next day we held a court martial and found that all of the absentees had some sort of an excuse for his absence. I will never forget the excuse of a Company A man, who was the tallest in the company, which gave him the honor of marching in the first four at the head of the regiment. He had an idea that regiments went into battle endways and as the front files fell the others followed up until all were killed or wounded to the left of the regiment. He denied being absent and his excuse was that he was at the taller end of the regiment, that he thought the enemy might 'tak us at 'tother end and he wanted to be first in the fight. His excuse was so novel we had a good laugh over it and he was excused without punishment.

"The regiment left Bardstown January 12, 1862, under orders to reinforce General Thomas, who was watching General Zollicoffer, who was threatening Kentucky with another invasion, he having been defeated at Wildcat and driven through Cumberland Gap by our forces a few months before. The regiment marched through Springfield, Danville and Lebanon, Kentucky, reaching a point five miles south of Lebanon, where it received the news of General Thomas' victory at Mill Springs, Kentucky. We marched from Lebanon to Cumberland Ford, Kentucky, arriving there February 15, 1862, and remained there until the following June. While camped at this place the regiment was severely scourged by disease, losing by death a large number of its members. On the 14th of March, 1862, I took part of the regiment to Big Creek Gap, Tennessee, where we had a skirmish with the First Tennessee Cavalry, capturing their battle flag, which is now in the state library at Indianapolis, and Lieutenant Colonel White, Captain Winston, a lieutenant and thirty-two men and seventy-five horses. We returned to the Ford and took part in an ineffectual attempt to take Cumberland Gap. The regiment marched with

Gen. George W. Morgan's force over the Cumberland mountains into Powell valley, Tennessee, toward Cumberland Gap, and on the 18th of January, 1862, we occupied it, the enemy having evacuated it the same day. The regiment remained at Cumberland Gap, engaged in building fortifications, and having almost daily encounters with the enemy, by whom we were surrounded a greater part of the time until the night of the 17th of September, 1862, when the works were abandoned, the enemy having cut off all communication with the rear, preventing reinforcements and supplies from reaching the garrison.

"The first man killed in the regiment was Corporal Henry H. McCullum, in a skirmish near Cumberland Gap, August 25, 1862. The regiment was engaged in a number of skirmishes near Cumberland Ford and the Gap with only a few wounded. One incident that occurred while we were invested at the Gap I shall never forget because it brought to me a very valuable piece of property in the form of a fine black stallion, which was the property of Colonel Alston, a son of Governor Alston, of South Carolina. Gen. Samuel P. Carter, who commanded the first troops that reached Cumberland Ford, wanted to purchase the horse and asked me what I would take for him. I told him the horse was worth five hundred dollars, but in the locality in which we were at that time soldiering, and poor facilities for running away in case the Johnnies got the better of us in a fight, we were about to be engaged in, that I would not trade nor sell the horse for a steamer Jacob Strader, at that time the finest boat on the western rivers. I do not want my friends to think that I stole that horse from the government, to whom he belonged at the time of the capture so I must tell you the story of how I came by the horse honestly:

"We had an old Tennessean, a sergeant in the Second Tennessee Regiment of Infantry, who was the most reliable scout in the command. He knew every path and road through the mountains of East Tennessee, and every man who kept a stallion in that part of the state. He never returned from a scouting expedition that he was not mounted on a horse of that kind. He was a great friend of the Forty-ninth Indiana, and seemed to have more confidence in Hoosier soldiers than those from his own state. He would often come to me to get a detail of men to go with him on some of his dangerous journeys. He was known by all of the command as "Stud Reynolds." One day at my quarters I said to him jokingly, 'Stud I wish the next time you leave camp you would bring me a fine stud horse.' He laughed and said the next one he found he would bring to me. He said that his business at that time was to get some of my men to go with him down to Baptist Gap, five miles distant from our camp, to try to trap some rebels who had been crossing the mountains in our rear, and a few days before had killed Turkey Joe Turner, a Union man for giving us information in regard to the 'Johnnies' at the Gap. I told him to take as many as he wanted, and to take the choice of any in the regiment. He selected twenty men and moved along the bench of the mountain to Baptist Gap and divided his men, placing ten of them about half way to the top of the mountain and the others he kept with him about two hundred yards nearer the foot of the mountain. All of the men were concealed in the thick shrubbery of the mountain side. He was there but a short time when he heard the clatter of horses' hoofs in the valley below. Soon they were ascending the path up the mountain gap. Stud kept quiet until Colonel Alston and five of his men rode past him when he charged into the path in their rear and ordered them to surrender. The squad charged into the path from above and there was no escape for the colonel and his men. Colonel Alston at first refused to surrender to a private soldier, and demanded that they send for an officer before he would consent to give up his sword and dismount. Stud again ordered him to dismount, but the haughty South Carolinian began to parley about the matter, when Stud ordered, 'Ready! Take aim,' which brought the noble scion down from the saddle in short order. Stud mounted the black stud, ordered them to march in front, and brought them into camp, the most woe-begone looking cavaliers that ever left the state which fired the first shot at 'Old Glory,' waving over Fort Sumter and the emblem of the freest people on earth. Of course we rejoiced when the son of one of the aristocratic governors of that state, which was the first to secede from the Union, had been captured by private soldiers in the Union army. Stud Reynolds rode the black stallion up in front of my quarters, saluted and said, 'Colonel, here is your stud horse.' Our chief quartermaster, Major Garber, from Madison, an old friend of mine, whose duty it was to take care of all captured property and report the number of horses on his rolls, had told me that anything in his corral that had four legs and a tail counted for a horse, and having one of that sort on hand at that time I just turned him into the corral and rode Colonel Alston's horse through the states of Kentucky, Tennessee, West Virginia, Mississippi and Louisiana, and I never mounted him but I thought that I was riding the state of South Carolina with sabre at my side and spurs on my heels.

"While at Cumberland Ford a part of the Forty-ninth Indiana (Company B, under command of Capt. James Thompson) and a part of the Second Regiment East Tennessee Infantry, made a raid against Cumberland Gap, which was heavily fortified and occupied by a large force of the enemy under General Raines, C. S. A. Colonel Carter of the Second East Tennessee Infantry, with myself in charge of the above troops, was sent to Big Creek Gap which was blockaded and guarded by the First Tennessee Confederate Cavalry, Colonel Rodgers in command. Colonel Carter left Cumberland Ford on the morning of the 14th of March, 1862, without a wagon or any artillery, and the paths through which our guides were to lead us could only be trodden in places single file, and the officers, horses and thirty cavalrymen we had with us would often be several miles ahead of the main column to find a path through which to lead their horses. I think that the route the guides took us was about sixty-five miles from the ford to Big Creek gap, our objective point. We left the ford with all the provisions we could carry in our haversacks and were absent on the expedition eleven days, passing through a country scantily supplied with provisions in times of peace so you will understand that many of the boys went hungry a greater part of the time on the trip. When we reached the foot of the mountain after crossing it, we turned into the fields in the valley with only two hundred men left of our original command, the remainder being lost somewhere up in the mountains. It being nearly time for reveille, we decided to attack with our force and Colonel Carter and I both taking half, he attacking the part of the enemy camping at the school-house and I that at Sharp's residence. It was just beginning to get light when we made the attack and I could see the Johnnies skedaddling up the bluff bank in the rear of their tents and running toward Jacksborough, where the rest of their troops were camped. There was a young lieutenant in the Second Tennessee with about thirty men, who stayed with me and I ordered him to charge down the road, which he did in gallant style, capturing some of the enemy that would have escaped. Capt. J. W. Thompson with Company B, of the Forty-ninth Indiana, who was left on the mountain, heard the firing and he and his men came on the run, Steve Gibbs leading the van, and when he got near to me he called out, 'Here we come, where do you want us?' After it was all over we formed the command across a field facing Fincastle. We could hear plainly the clatter of the horses' feet a long time before they came in sight and when our line fired they turned and returned to Fincastle as fast as they came. We broke ranks and it was a jolly sight to see our boys gathering the spoils of war. Plenty of corn meal, flour, sugar, coffee and tobacco, two hundred double-barreled shot guns, seventy-five horses with saddles and equipment. We also captured Lieutenant Colonel White, one lieutenant, thirty men and the regimental battle flag which was captured by Capt. James W. Thompson, Company B, Forty-ninth Indiana Infantry. The captain gave me the flag and I had it deposited in the state library at Indianapolis, where it still remains, the first trophy of the valor of the Forty-ninth Indiana. This was the maiden fight of the regiment. We then advanced to Jacksborough where we captured Captain Winston and two other soldiers and the camp supplies and camp equipage, the force having run away from us as we approached. We returned to Cumberland Ford and finding that the army had gone to the Gap, we followed, arriving there in time to see the first unsuccessful attempt to capture that stronghold. General Carter honored me by detailing me with a detail of men from the Forty-ninth to take the prisoners to the Louisville military prison, which was quite a treat to us as it enabled us to get to our homes once more and have a time with our friends.

"The Forty-ninth Indiana was located at Cotteral Spring, three miles south of Cumberland Gap, and while there General Morgan ordered me to take a squadron of cavalry to go on to picket post to learn the nature of the flag of truce. The General instructed me that after the business of the truce was over to go toTazewell, Tennessee, with the rebels if they invited me. When I had concluded the business with the Confederate officer and we were about to separate, he invited us to go to Tazewell and spend the night. I thanked him, accepted the invitation and dismissed my escort of cavalry from which I had detailed two to act as orderlies. Maj. S. S. Lyon, topographical engineer on General Morgan's staff, and Lieutenant Montgomery, one of my aids, accompanied me, which made five of us and forty-one Confederates in the party. The rebels had, previously to this, approached our picket post several times and fired on it. Col. James Carter, of the Second East Tennessee Infantry, with Company F, of the Forty-ninth Indiana, set a trap to kill and capture them. On the night that I received a flag of truce at the ford, General Morgan sent a messenger to Colonel Carter to notify him that a flag of truce was there, but the messenger failed to find him in the woods, so the colonel kept on to a point on the road that the flag of truce party had taken. He inquired of a native whether he had seen any 'Johnnies' lately and was told that a company had gone to the ford about an hour before. Colonel Carter, in selecting a place to kill or capture the party, placed part of his men, in four ranks, with bayonets fixed, across the road to impale the horses should any reach that point. The remainder of his eight hundred men he deployed along the roadside. Company F, of the Forty-ninth Indiana was on his right side with orders to fire and wheel across the road in our rear to prevent escape that way. Our party came jogging along nicely; I was riding at the head of the column with Doctor Compton on my right and the Confederate sergeant with the flag of truce on my left. No one had a thought of the trap we were riding into, and the first intimation we had of danger was a volley from about eighty rifles so close to us that the fire from the muzzles reached past us. Down went about half of our party. The horse that I was riding got a flesh wound in the first fire which caused him to run in spite of all I could do to stop him. He carried me along that line of men who were not more than fifteen feet from the middle of the road in which the horse was running, followed by some of the riderless horses of the party. On we went, and every man by the roadside took a crack at us till the horse had run the gauntlet with me on his back, and no less than five hundred guns had been emptied at us as we flew by them. The horse carried me to within two hundred feet of the men with fixed bayonets across the road, when a volley from about twelve guns flashed their fire past us, and the last thing I remember was dropping my feet out of the stirrups and the horse and I came down with a crash on the hard turnpike road. I must have fallen on my head for I was knocked senseless. I was trodden on the back by the riderless horses following me, which paralyzed both of my legs for several weeks after it happened. It was several hours afterwards that

I was found and the men who found me said that I was lying on my face apparently dead. They doubled their blankets and carried me to a log house near where they had gathered all of the wounded. It was daylight before I was brought to consciousness and Major Lyon and I were placed side by side and hauled by ambulance over the rough roads, six miles to the Gap. It was reported that I was dead and Major Lyon seriously wounded. His wounds received that night finally caused his death, and here I am writing about it forty-one years afterward. The retreat of the army through the mountains of Eastern Kentucky was a long and arduous one, the troops subsisting mostly on green corn during the entire distance of two hundred and fifty miles, occupying seventeen days and nights of almost constant marching and fighting. The regiment reached Greenupsburg, Kentucky, on the Ohio river on the night of October 4, 1862, and proceeded from there to Oak Hill, Ohio, where they received a new outfit, all their camp and garrison equipage having been destroyed when we evacuated the Gap. At Oak Hill I received my commission as colonel of the regiment on my birthday, October 18, 1862. From Oak Hill the regiment marched to Gallipolis, Ohio, and crossed into Western Virginia, going up the Kanawha river as far as Cole's Mouth, where it went into winter quarters, but in a few days received marching orders and proceeded down the river to Point Pleasant where, on the 17th of November, 1862, it embarked on transports for Memphis, Tennessee, arriving there the 30th of the same month. We embarked at Point Pleasant on the steamers, Sunny Side and New York. Nothing of importance occurred on the trip until we got almost in sight of old Jeffersonville, and I well knew that there was not a soldier in the regiment who would not be delighted to take one more look at Spring street before continuing his journey. When we left Cincinnati, I requested the Secretary of War to permit me to let the men, who nearly all lived near the bank of the river, to let me land and furlough them home for three days to see their families and sweethearts before continuing our journey. The secretary declined to grant the request. I knew that if I landed at either Louisville or Jeffersonville, nearly all of the regiment would go to their homes in spite of all that I could do, so I concluded to anchor the boats near the middle of the river, double the guard and trust to luck. The bar-keeper on the Sunny Side had a barrel of whiskey on the boiler deck in front of his bar. Just as we could see the lights of Jeffersonville the boys got that barrel of whiskey down to the lower deck, had it back in the deck room with the head knocked in, and were taking it straight and filling their canteens. I called the officers to me and we made haste to the barrel where the men were as thick as flies around a molasses barrel in summer. We threw it overboard, searched all the canteens and poured out all the whiskey we could find. Without this precaution there was no telling what the men would have done to the boats that night. They did cut the anchor line on the New York, but it was discovered in time to save her from the Falls of the Ohio.

"There was a small covered opening on the top of the wheel house of the Sunny Side that I knew nothing about and failed to guard it. As soon as we dropped anchor there appeared all of the skiffs in Jeffersonville, loaded with all the old soldiers' friends and cronies from Jeffersonville. When they found that they would not be permitted to take their friends ashore, they hid their skiffs under the wheelhouse and Steve Gibbs, Tom McCawley, Beverly Sullivan, Jim Wheat and about twenty other Jeffersonville boys went down through the wheel, and from what I heard, had a high old time in Jeffersonville that night. They had all returned for roll call in the morning. The next day we passed through the canal, where we took aboard the soldiers' wives, friends, and sweethearts. One of the most heroic deeds that I have ever witnessed in saving a life occurred as we were passing through. Lieutenant Thomas Bare, Company B, was an officer of the guard that day, and I must say that no braver or more generous soldier ever wore Uncle Sam's blue than Tom Bare. There was a soldier in his company from our old town, named Thomas Smith, who had married a few months before his enlistment. During his absence from home his wife bore him a little babe; it was natural that his wife should want the husband to see the child, and of course the husband was anxious to see it. She crossed the river and walked from the ferry boat down to the canal, carrying the young babe, wrapped in a red shawl in her arms. The river was low and as the boat bumped along the sides of the canal many stepped from the shore to the boat, and Bare and the men were assisting them to get aboard. When Mrs. Smith arrived the boat was swinging away from the wall, and Lieutenant Bare told her to hand him the little child and that the men would assist her in getting aboard. She passed the little one to the lieutenant and as he took it the boat swung away from the wall about three feet. Bare thought he had the urchin secure, but it was so small that it slipped out of the shawl into the canal. Down the poor little fellow went and Bare, with uniform, sash and sword, after him. Down he went under the water, he scooped up the little one in his arms, passed it up, saved its life, and was hauled out of the water by his comrades. The mother fainted, fell on the shore, the boat was stopped, she was brought aboard, restored to consciousness and you can imagine that meeting of husband and wife and the darling babe whose life had been saved by the brave and generous Lieutenant Bare, and you can imagine the cheers that went up from a thousand men for the officer's brave act. He lived to be eighty-three years old, and died during the Spanish war. The father, Samuel Smith, never saw the child after that day; he was killed at Vicksburg on the 19th of May, 1863. I never heard of the widow afterward. After the boats passed through the canal, I ordered them to land at New Albany, and ordered the soldiers' families and friends ashore. After they were sent ashore the boats ran down the river about twenty miles and dropped anchor for the night. A short time afterwards an officer approached me and told me that there were two women from New Albany with their sweethearts, Thomas Killick and Charles Yack, hidden abaft the ladies' cabin. I went back and found them sitting as close together as lovers are apt to get on all occasions at that happy period of man and woman's life, when they don't care if all the world knows they are lovers. I approached them and said: 'Ladies, did you not hear the order for all persons to go ashore at New Albany?' The girls spoke up and said that they had heard the order, but they were engaged to be married to the boys, that they were going to Memphis with us, and would get married down there. I said, 'You will not go to Memphis with us, for I will put you on the first boat we meet going up or at the first town we come to in the morning.' They seemed to be so disconsolate over the order that I left them alone until after supper and found that they were in earnest about going to Memphis with us and marrying the two young soldiers. I thought about the matter for a while and concluded that it would be better for them to marry that night and prevent a scandal upon the good morals and virtues of the best regiment in the service; a regiment that had always up to that time been noted for its good conduct and piety. What could we do? We had a good chaplain who could perform the ceremony that would make four souls with but a single thought, four thoughts that beat as one, happy, if not for life, at least for the time being. I finally came to the conclusion that they ought to marry and save their reputations, and that of the regiment I had such a fatherly care over. We had the minister, but where could we get the license for parties to be joined together in 'holy wedlock,' anchored amid the stream with the nearest court-house twenty miles away? I took the matter under careful consideration, and finally came to the conclusion that as all the laws of the land were in a chaotic state, and not strictly observed in the territory where the boats were anchored, I concluded to make the joining of the couples a military necessity, and issued an order to my chaplain to perform the ceremony. He objected at first to the proposition, but finally consented to join the couples in the holy bonds of matrimony, provided all the officers of the regiment signed a request for him to perform the ceremony, which they willingly did. He said he wanted the paper to protect himself from charges that might be brought against him in the conference to which he belonged. The tables were put out of the way in the cabin, and the parties called forth and joined together as husband and wife. Two of the best rooms in the ladies' cabin were assigned them, and we all retired for the night feeling certain that we had four happy souls aboard, regardless of the dangers and hardships we knew were to follow. Arriving at Memphis the newly wedded pairs got boarding for their wives in the city and were permitted to spend their time with them. The young soldiers had plenty of money which they expended freely on their wives for clothing and jewelry and seemed well satisfied with the choice they had made for life partners. It is an old adage that absence conquers love, and it seems to have been true in their case.

"The regiment fought its way down the Mississippi river to New Orleans and from there to Texas. About eighteen months after the happy event had taken place I received a letter from one of the ladies saying that she had consulted a lawyer and that he said she was not legally married and if I did not let the soldier come home and marry her she would prosecute me to the extent of the law, and wound up the missive with the old adage, 'A word to the wise is sufficient.' About a month after my letter was received, her husband received a letter stating that she had found a man she loved better than him, and had married him. I am no lawyer, but it has always been a question in my mind whether or not the lady was guilty of bigamy. The other lady remarried a short time after and the young soldiers have long since joined the 'invisible caravan,' who have passed on before, and I have made up my mind that in making military laws for matrimony, I haven't proved a success.

"On the 19th of December, 1862, the regiment embarked with General Sherman's army on the first campaign against Vicksburg, landing at Chickasaw Bayou on Christmas day, and engaging in the seven days' battle that followed, in which its losses in killed and wounded were quite severe (fifty-six). The attempts to take the enemy's works were unsuccessful, and I will never forget the jollification the "rebs" had that beautiful, frosty, moonlight night, when all the citizens of Vicksburg, including the ladies, came out to jollify over our defeat. You can imagine how we felt in the bottom, below the works, where we could hear every word the speakers uttered, the cheers of the men and the ringing laughs of the ladies as they rejoiced over the bravery of their soldiers, who had proved conclusively by that day's fighting that one 'Johnnie' could lick five 'Yanks' every day in the week.

"The regiment re-embarked on the transports and left Chickasaw Bayou on the 2d of January, 1863, and proceeded to Young's Point, Louisiana, from where it went on the expedition against Arkansas Post, Arkansas. In the capture of that stronghold on the 11th of January, 1863, with General Churchill and over five thousand prisoners of war, the Forty-ninth performed gallantly their part. The day of the battle was a beautiful, warm day, and after the prisoners had been corralled on the bank of the river, many of them without coats or blankets, it commenced raining and then followed the hardest snow storm that ever fell in that latitude. It then turned very cold and froze everything stiff as pokers. Our men suffered severely from the cold and you can judge of the suffering of those five thousand prisoners, their clothing first soaked by rain and then frozen to their skins. This was a big victory for our army at that time, and following so soon after the licking we got at Chickasaw Bayou, it removed some of the humiliation we felt after the Chickasaw Bayou campaign.

"After the capture of the Arkansas Post, the regiment returned to Young's Point, Louisiana, and assisted in digging Grant's famous canal or ditch across the point, by which he hoped to turn the Mississippi river away from Vicksburg, in order to pass our naval fleet and transports out of reach of the fortifications at that place. The canal was a failure and all the labor expended on it was in vain. The regiment remained at Young's Point until April 2, 1863, when it moved with Grant's army down the west bank of the river to a point opposite Grand Gulf, Mississippi, which the army had strongly fortified. Admiral Porter fought the river batteries for five and one-half hours and withdrew from the contest with his fleet badly disabled. The army marched down the river, passing Grand Gulf to Dishroon's plantation, five miles below. During the night the army and navy transports ran the blockade at the gulf, landed alongside the army and bivouaced on the levee. The next morning the army went on board gunboats and transports, which took them to the landing at Bruinsburg, near the mouth of Bayou Pierre.

"It was on the 30th day of April, we crossed the river to the side of the enemy in Mississippi. Rations were issued and the army left the river about 4 o'clock, marching on the road to Port Gibson. The enemy at the Gulf spiked their guns, destroyed their magazines and other property, marched to Port Gibson and down the road we were marching on, meeting our army about four miles from Port Gibson at 2:00 o'clock, a. m., May 1st. The battle opened at daylight, and continued until 4 p. m., when the enemy retired from the field, and our army scored the first victory on Mississippi soil. The Forty-ninth Indiana Volunteer Infantry was the first to open the battle on the left of an army at Thompson's Hill, or Port Gibson, Mississippi. It was the Forty-ninth Indiana that killed Confederate General Tracy. Early in the morning they were relieved after firing all of their ammunition but six rounds, by the Forty-Second Ohio, Colonel Pardee. They supported the First Wisconsin battery until about 3 p. m., when they were ordered by General Osterhouse to charge the rebel battery in front that had held its position on the field near a farm house filled with rebel sharpshooters, who had sent many of our comrades to eternal rest during the day. The battery was called the 'Botetourte Virginia Artillery.' The charge of the Forty-ninth Indiana on that battery is so indelibly photographed on my memory that I can see it every time I think of it. At this writing (1903), forty-one years afterward, I can see the Forty-ninth with bayonets fixed, in column by division on the center. I can see the ravine in front, across which we were to charge the battery on the other side. I can still hear my voice command, 'Attention! Battalion! Forward, March!' The left foot of every man steps off and we are off to capture that battery or die in the attempt. After moving a short distance I gave the command, 'Deploy into line on center division; campanies right and left face, double quick, march!' The companies obeyed the command and performed the evolution as nicely and quickly as they would have performed it on drill, with no enemy near them. As the companies double quicked into line on the center division, the next command is given: 'Forward! Double quick! March!' We are now near enough to hear the officers order the pieces loaded with canister. On, on, the Forty-ninth go in the face of shot and shell with their victorious shouts—over the battery and beyond it to the house where they capture seventeen sharpshooters between the upper tier of joists and rafters, who had removed enough shingles to give them a clear view of our battle line. About forty feet in the rear of the house was another valley about two hundred yards wide, beyond it an open field about two hundred yards to a dense forest. The Forty-ninth passed the house and about thirty feet in the rear of it was a high rail fence, running along the bank at the top of the valley, up which the Sixth Missouri Regiment was marching in as soldierly a manner is if on dress parade. Not more than thirty or forty men were up with the colors at the time we met the Sixth Missouri, with nothing but the fence to separate us. As soon as the colonel of the regiment saw that we had captured the battery and the house we had been fighting for all day, he halted and ordered them to fire and they did it without wounding a man in the Forty-ninth, faced about and down they went into the valley, where half of them threw down their guns and fell on their faces in token of surrender. The rest of them followed their colonel, a gallant fellow, who lay flat over the front of his saddle, hugging his horse's neck tighter than he ever hugged his sweetheart in his young days. The colonel and about half of his men escaped to the woods on the other side of the field. I never was so busy as I was at that time, urging the men to load and fire at that colonel and his men as they were running before us. Many fell in crossing the field, killed or wounded. After the firing was over General Osterhouse rode up and standing in his stirrups shouted, 'Put that Forty-ninth flag on the top of the house; no other shall go up there,' and up it went to the chimney top, where it could be seen all over the field, giving notice that the battle was won and the enemy on the run to Port Gibson. We followed them as fast as we could with that jubilant feeling that no one can describe after the battle is won, a sensation the evangelist tells us the sinner feels after life's cares are over and he has reached the portals of that Heavenly abode of rest. On the contrary when the battle is lost and you are on the skedaddle and the enemy following at your heels, it is like that hot place with the short name where the wicked and weary are never at rest. After the Forty-ninth Indiana had made that charge which ended the battle of Thompson's Hill and the men had halted, it was then that General Grant rode up, raised his hat and saluted the regiment and said, 'Men, I thank you for what you have just accomplished.'

"May 2d, we reached Port Gibson, crossed Bayou Pierre and with the advance division of the army commanded by Gen. Peter J. Osterhouse, we drove the Confederate army before us as far as Raymond, Mississippi, where the enemy offered battle and were defeated by Gen. John A. Logan's division.

The Forty-ninth took an active part in that engagement as well as those that followed at Champion's Hill, May 16th, losing twenty men killed and wounded there. At Black River bridge, May 17th, the Forty-ninth Regiment was ordered by General Lawler to support his brigade, which was going to charge. Before I had reached the regiment after receiving the order, his men sprung up like magic and were off. Just as they started an aid on the general's staff rode up and said that the general desired that I go in the charge and the Forty-ninth and Sixty-ninth Indiana were off like race horses when the button is touched that throws up the barrier across the track on the race course. Myself and Adjutant George W. Riddle being the only mounted officers on that part of the field our men being nearest to the rifle pits, from where we started gave us some advantage in being the first to reach it. There was a small bayou running parallel to the rifle pits with about a foot of water in it and full of fallen trees. We knew nothing of this obstacle until we were close to it. Fortunately for us, just before we reached it our rebel friends ceased firing and in token of surrender pulled little tufts of cotton from the cotton bales along the rifle pits and put it between the rammer and the muzzle of their guns, which plainly indicated to us that they had quit firing for that day, which was one of the loveliest Sundays I have ever seen. On we went over them, Riddle's horse and mine jumping over their heads, and the Forty-ninth colors being the first inside the works. As soon as the enemy on the bridge and boats saw that we had captured the place, they first got their artillery horses across, then fired both bridge and boats leaving on our side of the river one thousand seven hundred prisoners and seventeen pieces of fine artillery, which some of the men in the Forty-ninth who were well drilled in artillery tactics turned upon the enemy and fired all the ammunition in the limber chests at them on the other side of the river. The pontoon was laid across the Big Black river just above the burnt bridge and we crossed on the morning of May 18, 1863, and marched ten miles which brought us in sight of the enemies' fortifications at Vicksburg and the Forty-ninth took an active part in the actions here, including the assaults on the 19th and 22d of May.

"At 2 p. m., on the 19th of May, 1863, our brigade (First Brigade, Ninth Division, Thirteenth Army Corps) under command of General Lee was deployed in line of battle, followed by the Second Brigade as a supporting column. We moved to the top of the hill in our front, where we discovered the enemy waiting for us and ready to give us a hot reception by a salute from all the guns on our front with an accompaniment of small arms that made a racket which would put a Fourth of July celebration to shame. On we went until we reached the top of a hill, which left another valley between us and the enemy. Just as we started to go across the valley, General Lee fell, seriously wounded. The brigade went a short distance further and concluded that discretion was the better part of valor, halted and opened fire on the enemy. This

13

continued until the 22d day of May, 1863, when General Grant assaulted the works with the whole of his army. He was repulsed with great slaughter, and then began the siege which lasted until the 4th day of July, when the army surrendered thirty-five thousand prisoners to General Grant. After the surrender of Vicksburg July 4, 1863, the regiment marched to Jackson, Mississippi, and took an active part in the seven days' fighting at that place and vicinity. Returning to Vicksburg the regiment embarked August 10th for Port Hudson, from whence it proceeded to New Orleans, when it was assigned to the Department of the Gulf. From New Orleans the regiment was transported on cars to Brasher City on Berwick's Bay or Atchafalia Bay, and took part in the expedition up the Tesche, going as far as Opelousa, Louisiana, passing through the towns of Pattersonville, Franklin and New Iberia, on that river. I must relate another characteristic event that occurred when the regiment was in camp at Carrion Crow Bayou, Louisiana, November 1st to November 15, 1863, with the Thirteenth Army Corps under command of Major Gen. E. O. C. Ord. We camped on that bayou about four weeks and I don't think there was an officer or soldier in the command who knew what we were there for, as there was no enemy within two hundred miles of the place. It is an old saying that idleness is the devil's workshop, and I am certain that he had personal supervision over the shop at that time. It seemed to me that the corps became somewhat demoralized about that time. Old Nick started a gambling epidemic in his shop, and the consequence was that all, from the highest officer to the lowest private in the rear rank engaged in the sport. The disease became so violent a type that it became necessary to check it if possible. The soldiers could hardly be kept in line long enough for roll call. They raced our horses, fought cocks, played chuck-a-luck, honest frank, old sledge, euchre, draw poker, faro, red and black, in fact all the games that could be played with cards or dice. I often think what an unfortunate thing it was for our poor soldiers of the Civil war that craps was unknown to the gambling fraternity at that time. The mania became such a nuisance that Col. Thomas Bennett, of the Sixty-ninth Indiana Infantry and myself went to General Ord and requested him to issue an order prohibiting all sorts of gambling in the corps. He issued the order; it was read that night on dress parade, and cast a gloom over the men of the command as great as if half of their comrades had been killed and wounded in battle. The order, however, had the effect of stopping the gambling. A few days after this order was promulgated, Colonel Bennett and I were walking together and noticed quite a number of soldiers under the shade of a tree. Colonel Bennett said, 'I wonder if those fellows have a chuck-a-luck game running over there?' I replied, 'No, I don't think the boys would dare violate General Ord's order.' 'Let us go over,' said he 'and see what they are doing. As we approached them, I said, 'Hello, boys, playing chuck?' One of them spoke up and said,

'You stopped the only amusement we had in camp and we have found a new game that does not violate the order.' I said, 'What is it?' The soldier answered, 'We are running louse races.' 'Well,' said Colonel Bennett, 'that's one of the games I never heard of; how do you play it?' Come into the ring and we will show you,' replied the soldier. We stepped in and found a cracker box in the center of which was a circular piece of paper about ten inches in diameter, fastened to the box by a pin in the center. Those who entered for the race just put up a quarter of a dollar in the judge's hands, and when the pool was made up those in the race searched under their shirt for the gamest-looking thoroughbred grey-back he could find and then held it over the pin in the center of the paper. When the judge said, 'Go!' they let the grey-back drop and the first off the paper got the pot. The game being novel to both Bennett and I, being somewhat sporty ourselves, we concluded to take a hand, and I said, 'Bennett, I'll bet you five dollars that a Forty-ninth thoroughbred can beat a Sixty-ninth one over the course.' Colonel Bennett said it was a go. We put the money in the judge's hands and I said to a Forty-ninth soldier, 'Now get me a thorough-bred.' The Sixty-ninth man had his ready, the judge said 'Go!' and the Sixty-ninth greyback won the money for Colonel Bennett. There had always been a rivalry between the two regiments and when the Sixty-ninth bug won the money, they cheered as loudly as they ever did when they put the Johnnies to flight. The Forty-ninth boys were as mum as they ever were when the "Johnnie Rebs" won the victory. About a week after the race, the Forty-ninth soldier, who entered the greyback in the race for me, having some business at my quarters, I discovered a large greyback on the collar of his blouse, and was reprimanding him for his carelessness about the care of his person. He looked the bug over very carefully, picked him up and put him under his shirt, remarking, 'Why colonel, I've had that fellow in training for the last week to beat that Sixty-ninth Indiana fellow and win back that five dollars from Colonel Bennett that he won from you the other day.'

"The regiment, after leaving camp at Carrion Crow Bayou, was ordered back to New Orleans, from whence, on December 19, 1863, it embarked on steamers for the coast of Texas, reaching Decroe's Point, Matagorda Peninsula, on the 14th of December, 1863, after a rough voyage across the Gulf of Mexico. From Decroe's Point the regiment crossed Matagorda Bay to Indianola, where, on the 3d of February, 1864, one hundred and sixty-seven men and four officers re-enlisted for three years, or during the war. In March the regiment moved to Fort Esperanza, on Matagorda Island, where it remained until April 19th, when it re-embarked and crossed the gulf back to New Orleans, where it took passage on the steamer, 'Emma,' for Alexandria, Louisiana, to re-inforce General Bank's army on Red river, which had met with disastrous defeat on that river campaign. The regiment, after arriving at

Alexandria, were moved to the front and engaged thirteen days in driving the enemy from the vicinity of where our army was constructing dams on the falls of that river, where our naval fleet had been left above them by low water. After the gun boats were safely landed below the falls, the regiment on May 13, 1864, retreated with the army to Morganza Bend on the Mississippi river. From Morganza Bend the regiment was again ordered to New Orleans, and went into camp at Chalmette, Jackson's old battle ground below the city, from whence in a few days the veteran portion of the regiment proceeded to Indiana on veteran furlough, reaching Indianapolis July 9, 1864. At the expiration of their furlough, the veterans were ordered to Lexington, Kentucky, passing through Jeffersonville. The citizens of the city gave them a royal reception; the tables were loaded with everything to tickle the palate and stomach of an old soldier. They were waited on by all the loyal matrons and beautiful lassies in the city, and the veterans have not to this day forgotten the reception given to them by the patriotic loyal women of Jeffersonville. The tables were on the ground where the city hall now stands, which makes that spot of ground hallowed above all others in my native town, except the place of my birth, a few hundred feet below on the same street. That good, patriotic, loyal old citizen of Jeffersonville, known to every one in the city, Dr. Nathaniel Field, made the reception address, which was cheered and applauded by all the old veterans and their friends who turned out to welcome them. That good woman, Mrs. J. H. McCampbell, one of the pioneers of our old town, who had known me all of my life, claimed the honor of waiting on your humble servant at the table and it is unnecessary to say that I was well served, in fact all the ladies of old Jeffersonville did everything in their power to make the reception pleasant for the boys, and the boys enjoyed and fully appreciated their efforts.

"The veterans were sent to Lexington, Kentucky, where they had light service the remainder of their enlistment, serving as provost guards, and in charge of the military prisons in that city until the war closed. On the 7th of September, 1865, they were ordered to Louisville and from thence to Indianapolis, where on September 13, 1865, they were finally discharged from the United States service after serving their country honorably three years and ten months. Well may the survivors and friends of the Forty-ninth be proud of the old regimental organization that was raised and officered by so many natives of our loyal old city, who served their country so faithfully and honorably through four years of bloody war in defence of the old flag, the emblem of our nationality, that floats triumphantly over the greatest and freest people on the face of the earth.

"After the departure of the veterans from Chalmette in July, 1864, the non-veteran portion of the regiment was ordered to Algiers, Louisiana, just across the river from New Orleans, where it did garrison duty in the city until November 5, 1864, when it embarked on an ocean steamer for New York City, arriving there November 20th, after a rough voyage. From New York the regiment went by rail to Indianapolis, where on the 29th day of November, 1864, it was honorably discharged from the service of the United States, having served three years, one month and eight days. On the voyage from New Orleans to New York one man died, and Black Ann, a company cook, had a child born on the voyage. Our surgeon, Dr. Emanuel R. Hawn, reported to the health officer at New York that the regiment was all present or accounted for—one died and one born, which made the number they started out with from New Orleans correct. The doctor was a great wag, and it would take a volume to tell all the amusement he furnished for the regiment."

Thus ends the history of the largest and most notable military organization that Clark county ever furnished. At this writing (1908) but few of the survivors remain and another decade will find the roster of living members of the gallant Forty-ninth but a blank, yet they have indelibly inscribed their names on the roll of fame of their city and county, and history will forever record their hardships and deeds, their victories and ultimate success, and the Clark county citizen of years to come must needs remember that this brave band of men who went out from our borders to fight and die for the cause of liberty and justice and the Union did not suffer in vain, and though they have passed through the valley of the shadow of death, have crossed the river and rest under the shade of the trees, their deeds live after them.

> "On Fame's eternal camping ground,
> Their silent tents are spread,
> And Glory guards with solemn round
> The bivouac of the dead."

James Keigwin, their colonel, was a man of the highest patriotic ideals, of bravery unquestioned, and the peer of any in gallantry. A high type of the American soldier he lived and died beloved of all, a fitting character for emulation among the younger men at arms of later days.

CHAPTER XIX.

THE MILITARY HISTORY OF CLARK COUNTY.

STERLING'S BATTERY.

Immediately following the organization of the Forty-ninth Regiment of Indiana Volunteer Infantry the Twelfth Battery of Indiana Light Artillery was recruited. George W. Sterling, who was a blacksmith in Jeffersonville became enthused when he received a contract to build the wood and iron work for several batteries of artillery. He was joined in his efforts by Wilford Walkins, M. Stradler, Benjamin Lutz and Samuel Glover. The organization left for Indianapolis December 19, 1861, one hundred and fifty-six strong, officers and men, and were mustered in January 25, 1862. Their equipment consisted of six brass twenty pounders, one hundred and twelve horses and seventy-six mules and the battery was in excellent condition when it went south. Captain Sterling resigned and the lieutenants did likewise soon after the battle of Shiloh. Governor Morton, who was there soon after, commissioned James E. White, captain; George Leach, Sr., first lieutenant; Moody Dustin, Jr., first lieutenant; James Dunwoody, Sr., second lieutenant, and Joseph Shaw, Jr., second lieutenant. The battery was engaged before Nashville and was in the battle incident to the great victories at Lookout Mountain and Missionary Ridge. For the rest of the war they remained as the garrison in Fort Negley at Nashville. They returned to Indianapolis July 1, 1865, one hundred and eleven strong, and were mustered out of the service July 7th. This battery was a Clark county organization and though their service was confined to few actions, yet their record measures up to the standard set by Clark county men elsewhere in the great struggle.

When the Fifty-third Regiment of Indiana Volunteers was organized at New Albany in January, 1862, Company D represented Clark county's quota. This company was organized by Seth Daily, one of the most popular men of Charlestown. He established his headquarters in the old Zed Griffith hotel, which stood on the corner of Main and Market streets, and here he received his recruits. The Clark county officers of this company were as follows: Captains, Seth Daily, of Charlestown and William Howard, of Jeffersonville; Howard was commissioned second lieutenant, May 23, 1863, and was promoted captain July 23, 1864. The colonel of this regiment was Walter Q. Gresham. This organization served in Tennessee; with Grant in Mississippi;

was at the siege and capitulation of Vicksburg; in the Atlanta campaign, with Sherman to Savannah, and in the Carolinas. It was mustered out at Indianapolis in July, 1865.

The Sixty-sixth regiment, which was organized at Camp Noble, New Albany, in August, 1862, had two Charlestown men to serve it as quartermasters—Campbell Hay, Jr., the nephew of the Black Hawk war veteran, and Thomas C. Hammond. Dr. Nathaniel Field, of Jeffersonville, went out as surgeon, and Dr. James C. Simonson, of Charlestown, returned with the regiment as surgeon.

The Seventy-seventh had one company from Clark county; Company D, from Charlestown, recruited by Warren Horr and Edmund J. Davis. This company was officered by first class material, two of its captains being promated majors, and one lieutenant was brevetted captain. The regiment was organized at Indianapolis, August 22, 1862, as the Fourth Cavalry. It served in Kentucky and Tennessee in 1862 and 1863, and participated in Chickamauga, Fayetteville, Mossy Creek, Talbots, Dandridge, the Atlanta campaign, and back into Tennessee in 1865. The Clark county officers were as follows: Warren Horr, captain; promoted major. Samuel E. W. Simonson, captain; promoted major of the Seventh Cavalry. Richard F. Nugent, captain, all of Charlestown. Thomas B. Prather, first lieutenant, of Jeffersonville, brevetted captain. Edmund J. Davis, second lieutenant, of Charlestown; Enoch S. Boston, second lieutenant, of Jeffersonville; Isaac M. Koons, second lieutenant, of Charlestown; Albert Taggert, second lieutenant, of Charlestown. Besides these officers Dr. John F. Taggert, of Charlestown, went out as assistant surgeon, and he was afterward promoted regimental surgeon.

When Captain Caldwell of the Twenty-third Indiana resigned March 28, 1862, and returned to Jeffersonville, it was not to remain long. In August the Eighty-first was organized, and he was made adjutant, and eight days later promoted colonel, there having been no commander commissioned. Andrew J. Howard (Jack) resigned as second lieutenant of Company H, Thirty-eighth Indiana, July 16, 1862, and returned home to raise a company for this new (Eighty-first) Regiment, and re-entered the service as its captain. A sketch of this regiment is doubly interesting from the fact of it being commanded by a Clark county man, and having a Jeffersonville and a Charlestown company in it. "Jack" Howard began to recruit his company in the city and several meetings were held in Sterling's old blacksmith shop, on Spring street. Sterling having left with his battery, the Twelfth, some time previous. Some time prior to this William D. Evritt, John Carney and John Schwallier, of Charlestown, had begun the systematic organization of a company of men for the Sixty-sixth Indiana. Schwallier had gone to New Albany, where the regiment was forming, while Evritt and Carney went out in the county around Charlestown after recruits, sending them to Schwallier as fast as found. A total of fifty-eight men was recruited, but the company was refused, as its roster was too short, and because there were other full companies ready to enter the service, already organized. John C. McCormack, of Charlestown, had raised fifty men for the Eighty-first, then forming, and the earlier company, spliced with his, made a full company and was mustered in as Company I. The men of this organization were from Charlestown, New Washington and Bethlehem, and were a well organized and thoroughly efficient company. The regiment was mustered in at New Albany, at Camp Noble, August 29, 1862, left there and marched up the old plank road, the present route of the "dinky" track, to Jeffersonville, where they received their equipment at the Jeffersonville, Madison & Indianapolis depot. They then marched to the river, took the ferry to Louisville, and camped that night south of the city at Camp Neffler. After moving camp several times, they returned to Louisville, when Kirby Smith was reported to be marching on the city. They afterward crossed to Jeffersonville on their way to Cincinnati, Ohio, but their orders were countermanded and the regiment went into camp just above Port Fulton, on the top of the river bluff above the deep diggings, where the present water works pumping station is located. Details from Company B were made to guard the ferry boat, while at Camp Gilbert, as it was called, but outside of this duty the men spent an enjoyable period while here, receiving from their friends and relatives much to help out their usual camp fare. They moved south again about the middle of September, 1862, and acted as support for artillery during the battle of Perryville. Company B was selected at almost every opportunity for picket duty, the first mention of this duty being near Lebanon, Kentucky. The regiment remained in Kentucky until the early part of November, when they moved into Tennessee, where they lost Lieutenant Morgan, of Company B, at the battle of Stone River. While the regiment lay at Nashville, Corporal John J. Gallager, of Company B, was appointed ordnance sergeant and with him were detailed Neil McClellan and Mel Bruner of the same company. They were all captured by the rebels, but afterwards, being paroled, were exchanged October 7, 1863. In the roll of honor published at this time appear the names of a number of men from both Company I and Company B.

In August, 1863, Lieutenant Schwallier of Company I commanded a company of the Pioneer Corps and assisted in constructing a pontoon bridge over four hundred feet long across the Tennessee river. During a skirmish outside of Murfreesboro, Sergeant James M. Mitchell of Company B was mortally wounded and died on the field. The latter part of the summer of 1863 the regiment was engaged in the advance upon Chattanooga, and it was while they were camped at Winchester that Colonel Caldwell and Capt. A. J. Howard of Company B left the service. Lieutenant Northcutt (Bill) was wounded at Chickamauga, and Lieut. Eugene Schell, who was acting as regimental adjutant at the time, received some very high compliments for his actions during the same engagement. From this time on, all through the campaigns in Georgia, Companies B and I had a great deal of hazardous duty. Detail after detail, as skirmishes, pickets, flankers, advance and rear guard were given them, and on March 31, 1864, Company B was detailed to guard Confederate prisoners. At the siege of Atlanta, the men were under fire for twenty-four days. On June 20, 1864, Joseph Kenner, of Company B, was wounded while on the skirmish line, and had to be left on the field, but on June 22, the enemy having been driven back somewhat, Lieutenant Schell, with two men volunteered to undertake the very dangerous duty of going out to find him. They were successful and brought him in after he had lain on the field two days and one night. He had been robbed of everything he had, and had been refused food and water by the rebels. He was sent to the hospital at Chattanooga for care and treatment, but died a few weeks later.

About July 24, 1864, Captain Northcutt rejoined the regiment, after a furlough home, but resigned soon after and Schell, that "bravest of the brave," was commissioned captain. Soon afterward he was granted a well earned leave and returned home, rejoining the regiment, however, October 31, 1864, the command then being beneath the shadow of Lookout Mountain. His services from this time on were but a continuation of that manliness and dignity which had marked him before. His personal bravery and gallantry had already been proven, and his actions at the battle of Nashville were but a repetition of those which had marked him ever since he had won an enviable reputation and practically his commission at the battle of Stone River. At Nashville, the Eighty-first Indiana, with Schell leading Company B, charged a hill beyond Fort Negley and captured part of the Thirty-fifth Mississippi. The action was won, but at the cost of a life of great promise, Captain Schell falling, and dying on the field. It is no reflection upon the other soldiers which Clark county has furnished to laud this brave and gallant young officer. His reputation among his associates in the army and among his home people before he entered the service was one of great promise, and it is to be regretted that his life was not spared for the successes and honors which would undoubtedly have been his had he lived. The regiment was mustered out of the service June 13, 1865, and arrived at Indianapolis June 15. During its term of service it participated in the following engagements: Perryville, Liberty Lick, Rocky Face, Dallas, New Hope Church, Kenesaw Mountain, Peach Tree Creek, Jonesboro, Franklin, Stone River, Chickamauga, Resaca, Kingston, Bald Knob, Marietta, Siege of Atlanta, Lovejoy's Station, Nashville. The following are the Clark county officers of the Eighty-first Indiana:

William W. Caldwell, colonel.—Jeffersonville.
William D. Everett, major.—Charlestown.
William W. Caldwell, adjutant.—Jeffersonville.

John J. Gallagher, adjutant.—Jeffersonville.

Andrew J. Howard, captain, Company B.—-Jeffersonville.

William H. Northcutt, captain, Company B.—Jeffersonville.

Eugene M. Schell, captain, Company B.—Jeffersonville.

Leonard Tuttle, captain, Company B.—Utica.

William H. Morgan, first lieutenant Company B.—Henryville.

William H. Northcutt, first lieutenant, Company B.—Jeffersonville

Eugene M. Schell, first lieutenant, Company B.—Jeffersonville.

Leonard H. Tuttle, first lieutenant, Company B.—Utica.

James Wilson, first lieutenant, Company B.—Utica.

George W. Alpha, first lieutenant, Company B.—Jeffersonville.

George W. Clark, second lieutenant, Company B.—Henryville.

William H. Northcutt, second lieutenant, Company B.—Jeffersonville.

Eugene M. Schell, second lieutenant, Company B.—Jeffersonville.

Charles Ashton, second lieutenant, Company B.—Utica.

William D. Evritt, captain, Company I.—Charlestown.

John Carney, captain, Company I.—Charlestown.

John C. McCormack, first lieutenant, Company I.—Charlestown.

John Carney, first lieutenant, Company I.—Charlestown.

John Schwallier, second lieutenant, Company I.—Charlestown.

George T. Peters, second lieutenant, Company I.—Charlestown.

COMPANY E, ONE HUNDRED TWENTY-FIFTH (TENTH CAVALRY).

The next time Clark county appears as furnishing a company was in December, 1863, and the movement was headed by one John W. Bradburn, an erstwhile Jeffersonville man, who had been authorized to raise a company or rather a troop for the One Hundred and Twenty-fifth Indiana, better known as the Tenth Indiana Volunteer Cavalry. He opened a recruiting office in a little frame building on the east side of Spring street about one hundred and fifty feet north of Front. The only enlisted man from Jeffersonville was Walter Eversole, and in procuring recruits and taking care of them he seemed to be the chief cook and bottle washer. With hardly an exception all the other enlisted men were Southerners, hailing as Eversole says, from Georgia, Tennessee, Alabama and Mississippi. At this time there were many refugees from the South coming north, and Jeffersonville being on one of the main lines of travel in that direction, many of them reached there. Some of the travelers had procured jobs as wood-choppers in the woods which then stretched away from the hospital buildings in Port Fulton. A few of these refugees were inveigled into the new company by the promise of three hundred dollars bounty by the county. Bradburn, however, not being satisfied with this, offered four hundred dollars (for which he had no authority) and many additional recruits were received. They were usually met at the ferry boat by Eversole, and sent to the office on Spring street, where Bradburn administered the oath. The recruits were quartered in the large brick house which stands on the north side of Market street between Meigs avenue and Walnut street, and were sent in squads of twenty from here to the fair grounds in New Albany, where the company was mustered in. The other companies of the regiment were organized and mustered in elsewhere.

This conglomerate mass of soldiers, many of whom, according to Eversole, had served in the rebel army, constituted the worst company which is credited to Clark county. Their past record was not open to inspection, and the history of the company reflected no honor on either themselves, the county, state or nation. Their incomparable act in the military tragedy of Clark county, was a melodrama. It opens with a brilliant display, where their officers as stars appear on the stage playing the natural parts of the most damnable ignorance, viciousness and general cussedness, which it will be next to impossible to duplicate in any other Indiana organization. It is a matter of regret that Walter Eversole ever pulled the fair name of Clark county into this aggregation by going into it, and although the county is credited with this quota of men, she should not be held responsible for their acts in the service. Bradburn, the captain of this crew, is not remembered by the older citizens of Jeffersonville with a great deal of pleasure for some reason or other, and his record together with that of his first and second lieutenants, who hailed from Jeffersonville also, would lead the unprejudiced mind to conclude that they were not what officers should be. Terrell's reports give the following record of their services: Bradburn was compelled to resign for the good of the service, November 29, 1864. First Lieutenant John T. Dunlap was dismissed from the service for general worthlessness April 12, 1865, and F. G. Wall, second lieutenant, was sent to the penitentiary before he was mustered and his commission revoked. The enlisted men themselves showed a complete lack of that careful early training which tends to elevate and ennoble the mind. The regiment passed through Jeffersonville on their way south, and at Louisville they were given mounts, and what more appropriate mounts could have been selected than the old reliable army mules which they received, a few horses being thrown in for variety's sake. Bradburn and Company E, together with one other company, were detached from the regiment and ordered to Pulaski, Tennessee, arriving in time for the fight there. Their actions here were quite noteworthy in that they ran like the Old Harry at the first few shots, Bradburn in the lead, and they never lost a man, although it is quite possible that some of the warriors were pretty well blown when they reached town. This was the only fight they ever got near enough to smell smoke, but their fear of being captured by their former comrades in the Confederate army must be remembered and accepted as the reason of their successful retreat.

After Pulaski the regiment went south on steamers to New Orleans and thence on transports to Mobile, where they were stationed for some time on courier duty, no doubt on account of the great speed they had shown previously in the service. They must have been saturated with the spirit of courier duty for they allowed nothing to interfere with it in the least. In climbing aboard their mules most of the men found that their sabres would get tangled up in their legs, and they forthwith threw them (the sabres and not their legs) away. Even the mules were sold and the money used by the fortunate seller to indulge his fancy as his fancy saw fit. This, however, was always fixed up with the captain, and an accounting of some sort made to the government. From Mobile the regiment moved to Vicksburg, where they were mustered out of the service and sent to Indianapolis to get their pay and discharge papers. Many of the men deserted to remain in the land of their birth, and Indiana was relieved of their citizenship, which at least should be entered to their credit. By the testimony of reliable citizens, not a single member of this foreign crew has ever been seen in Jeffersonville since.

So endeth the lesson extending from December 30, 1863, to August 31, 1865. Let us, therefore draw the veil and proceed to further chronicles of better men. The historian feels justified in reciting this wonderful tale. For fear that the narrative of brave men and brave deeds may become tiresome, he has recited this history in full as a change. It is true, unfortunately. Walter Eversole and General Terrell had no reason to misrepresent.

The Thirteenth Cavalry, One Hundred Thirty-first Regiment, was the last cavalry organization raised in the state. Company M of this regiment was recruited from Charlestown by Dillon Bridges and George P. Bunce, of that town, as captain and first lieutenant. James M. Ross, of Charlestown, was promoted first lieutenant in June, 1865. Company M was unmounted until after the battle of Nashville, in which it participated, but after receiving an entirely new equipment the regiment embarked on transports for New Orleans February 11, 1865. Here they re-embarked for Navy Cove, Mobile Bay, arriving there in time for the operations against the defences of Mobile. They were mustered out at Vicksburg, Mississippi, November 18, 1865.

When the One Hundred Thirty-seventh Regiment was organized in May, 1864, Thomas D. Fouts, of Jeffersonville, was commissioned as lieutenant colonel, although there was no Clark county company in the command.

The month of January, 1865, saw the organization of a movement to raise the last Clark county troops for the war. It might have been argued that the county had already furnished enough, but evidently her citizens thought otherwise, for both Jeffersonville and Charlestown appear in the roster of companies. John F. Wilson took the lead in organizing the Jeffersonville company although he was sadly lacking in military knowledge. The men were examined by Doctor Collum, and sent by squads to Indianapolis.

The officers of this company were Henry H. Ewing, captain, and John F. Wilson, first lieutenant, both of Jeffersonville. The company was designated as Company G, One Hundred and Forty-fourth Regiment Indiana Volunteers. Company H was commanded by Stephen S. Cole, of Charlestown. The regiment was sent to Harper's Ferry, Virginia, and was subsequently engaged in guard duty in Virginia and Maryland, until mustered out August 5, 1865.

From the close of the War of the Rebellion until 1876 Clark county remained without a military organization of any kind. This condition can hardly be criticised as the county had responded so often to calls that were necessary regardless of the cost it entailed during the progress of the war that the spirit of war had about run out. Besides this the tame attractions of a militiaman's life were so far below that of the service just finished in the South that few if any recruits could have been secured. It was only when a new vintage of youths had reached maturity that a company became possible.

JEFFERSONVILLE RIFLES, 1876.

The period immediately preceding the Presidential campaign of 1876 seems to have been a time when the martial spirit of the young men of Jeffersonville demanded expression. The movement to organize a military company met with an enthusiastic response, for an organization of eighty-two men was the result. They elected their officers and organized on the night of November 1, 1876. This meeting was held in the old council chamber at the corner of Spring and Court avenue, where the engine house now stands. "Bill" Carter was appointed temporary chairman, and in the election of officers which ensued, J. P. Wallace was elected captain, W. H. Carter (Bill), first lieutenant, and James B. Young, second lieutenant. The non-commissioned officers were as follows:

William C. Glossbrenner, orderly sergeant.
Lloyd White, first duty sergeant.
Pink Schell, second duty sergeant.
Peter Miller, third duty sergeant.
James Pierson, fourth duty sergeant.

John P. Wallace, the captain, was a veteran of the Civil war, having been chief of scouts under both Burnside and Sherman. He was retained in the service after the war and was in Custer's regiment. He seems to have been an excellent soldier, but the company fell to pieces after he left it in 1877.

"Bill" Carter is still a fixture of Jeffersonville, having filled various positions in the city's political business for many years. At his election to the first lieutenantcy he knew nothing of his duties but by study became a fairly good militia officer of that time. He owed his election solely to the fact that he had worked hard to bring the organization to a consummation. The men composing the company, with possibly one exception, were all Jeffersonville citizens, and an article in the Jeffersonville Evening News, of November 15, 1876, speaks of them as being composed of "clever and brave men," and predicted that with their enthusiasm they would soon be the "best military company in the state." The number of their members certainly speaks well for their prospects for the writer well knows that eighty-two men in 1876 were an indication of enthusiasm, when in 1895 fifty members were as many as could be induced to go into the state's service. The Jeff Blues were mustered in as an Independent company November 27, 1876. The city of Jeffersonville helped the company in various ways in their organization. On November 22, 1876, a resolution was adopted "That we hereby tender our hearty thanks to the Honorable Council and City of Jeffersonville, for the kind encouragement extended to us in perfecting our organization; that we will endeavor to show in some measure our appreciation of their kindness by trying to make it the 'crack company of the state.' " Soon after this, on December 6, 1876, one hundred breech-loading 45-caliber Springfield rifles were received from Indianapolis.

The armory of the company was the lower floor of the Odd Fellows' building, at the corner of Market and Wall streets, and here the weekly drills were held except when they used the streets or commons. The large open commons below Graham street and extending on either side of Maple street were used most frequently for drills and marching, while the commons just above the Pennsylvania bridge fill, between the state prison and the river, were used for target practice and turkey shooting, the fill making an excellent abutment in which to fire, ranges up to two hundred and fifty yards being laid out. These target practices were frequent occurrences, the state furnishing the ammunition. Washington's birthday, 1877, was the occasion of the largest turkey shooting. This was held at the usual place, the target being placed against the fill and a range of one hundred and fifty yards laid off. A large crowd of friends attended the "shoot," among their number being several soldiers from the garrison of the government buildings. These regulars had arrived here, Company I, Second Infantry, U. S. A., January 7, 1877, to protect the military stores from harm by the hot heads during the great strikes of this year. Later on, July 26, 1877, Company B and Company C, of the Eighteenth Infantry, U. S. A., arrived.

During the whole time of this company's service it was only once under arms for actual duty. At that time, during the great strikes, when President Standiford's house in Louisville was stoned by reckless men, the rumor had become current that the mob intended to seize the old ferry boat, Wathen, come to Jeffersonville and capture the rifles which they thought were stored at the quartermaster's depot. The company remained under arms for forty-eight hours at their armory, but the rioters never appeared; whether it was because they had heard of the ferocious warriors awaiting them, or other reasons, no one ever knew.

On September 20, 1877, the enthusiasm had waned to such an extent that a meeting at was held by the citizens to raise money for uniforms for the entire company. This mass meeting at their armory was followed by an appeal in the Evening News, and an entertainment was projected, but as the efforts of the citizens did not seem to be appreciated the subject was dropped. From this time on interest lagged and the organization gradually went to pieces, the arms being returned to the government depot.

The company at one time took a practice march to New Albany, participating in a parade while there, and marching back later in the day. They were also invited to Louisville to join with the Louisville Legion and some regular troops in the parade at the opening of the first Louisville exposition at Fourth and Chestnut streets. The boys were first taken to the Galt house, where they were given their dinner, after which the parade took place.

A company from Louisville, named the "Clark Rifles," challenged the Jeffersonville Rifles to a turkey shooting match, at the range of the latter. The result was a tie, and Captain Wallace, of the Jeffersonville Rifles, and Captain Clark, of the Clark Rifles, shot to decide it. Wallace won and saved the day. The return match was shot at Lion Garden on Preston street, between St. Catharine and Kentucky, and at this match Jeffersonville won, and was given a supper and dance. These and other like occasions enlivened the existence of the organization, but it went the way of many others, where there was so little inducement to serve the state in a military capacity, and Jeffersonville remained without a military organization until 1892.

COMPANY G, FIRST REGIMENT INDIANA NATIONAL GUARD.

On October 11, 1892, a company of the National Guard was mustered in at Jeffersonville, about sixty strong, as Company G, First Infantry Indiana National Guard. The officers at muster were Captain L. C. Baird; First Lieutenant C. H. Kelly, and Second Lieutenant H. H. Thacker. Lieutenant Thacker was promoted first lieutenant, vice Kelly, resigned, and First Sergeant W. W. Crooker was commissioned second lieutenant, vice Thacker, promoted. Later on H. E. Barrett was commissioned second lieutenant, vice Crooker, resigned. This company was armed with Springfield 45-caliber rifles, and uniformed in the regulation army uniform. Captain Baird had shortly before resigned as midshipman of the United States Navy from Annapolis. Lieutenant Thacker had served in the Louisville Legion, but aside from these two, there were no others who had had any military training. The company made an excellent reputation for discipline and drill, and on June 3, 1894, they reported near Princeton, Indiana, on active service in the strikes of that year. Their record here was excellent although their duties were trying. They, with other troops, were engaged in restoring law and order near Shelburn, Farmersburg and Alum Cave until June 18th. The only casualty was when Captain Baird was accidentally shot in the foot while Company G was left in charge of the train at Alum Cave. After two weeks in the field they were ordered home, the lawlessness having been subdued, and were received by a great demonstration on the part of friends, mothers and sweethearts.

In June, 1893 the company attended the state encampment at Terre Haute and in June, 1895 at Fairview Park, Indianapolis. Visits to New Albany and Scottsburg, dances in their armory on Pearl street near Court avenue, and several picnics at Fern Grove added an interest and helped to cement the organization. When the Twenty-ninth Annual Encampment of the Grand Army of the Republic was held at Louisville, Company G invited some six or eight companies down to partake of her hospitality and participate in a sham battle at Four Mile Springs, just above Jeffersonville. The battle was a roaring success. In the summer of 1893 a rifle range was established at Four Mile Springs, and practice was given the men in target shooting.

The various inspections held by the regimental and brigade officers were always passed with flying colors and the company acquired a more than local reputation for soldierly qualities. On October 11, 1895, the three year term of enlistment having expired, the company was mustered out of service and the arms and equipment reshipped to the state quartermaster general at Indianapolis. During the three years' service of this company there were all told eighty-five enlistments.

WAR WITH SPAIN—1898-1899.

The National Guard of Indiana filled the state's quota in the first call of President McKinley for troops. The second call found Clark county waiting and ready. May 28, 1898, a meeting was held in Jeffersonville, officers elected, and enlistment lists opened. The company was recruited above the maximum. On the evening of June 30, 1898, the ladies of Jeffersonville presented the company a stand of colors, and on July 1st, the boys left for Indianapolis, with the following officers: Captain Lewis C. Baird, First Lieutenant James Fortune, and Second Lieutenant W. W. Crooker. Captain Baird and Lieutenant Crooker had had experience in military training. Lieutenant Fortune had served as a Columbian guard at the World's Fair at Chicago. Edward McCawley, the first sergeant, was afterward commissioned second lieutenant, upon the promotion of Lieutenant Crooker. He and John Van Liew, the new first sergeant, were both old Company G men.

On July 1st, the company arrived at the regimental rendezvous at Indianapolis. While camped at the old fair grounds here the different companies were quartered in the barns on the grounds. The Clark county company was designated as Company E, and the regiment as the One Hundred and Sixty-first Indiana Volunteer Infantry. They were mustered into the United States service July 12, 1898, and remained in Indianapolis until August 11th, when they moved south. At Jacksonville, Florida, the regiment was made a part of the Seventh Army Corps under the command of Major-General Fitzhugh Lee. Leaving Camp "Cuba Libre" October 24th, the regiment moved to "Camp Onward," at Savannah, Georgia, and remained there two months. While camped there the Clark county company was detached and Captain Baird was placed in command of the Avondale Rifle range as range officer. On December 12th, the regiment boarded the United States transport, Mobile, and arrived in Havana, Cuba, December 15th, going into camp at Camp Columbia, near Mariana, about eight miles beyond Havana, on a beautiful table-land overlooking the gulf. The regiment remained in Cuba until March, 1899, when they were ordered home for muster out, and they were finally mustered out and discharged April 30, 1899, at Savannah, Georgia.

Clark county also furnished another officer to the volunteer army in the appointment of Dr. David C. Peyton as major and brigade surgeon.

There was no active duty for the One Hundred and Sixty-first Regiment to perform during its term of service, and there were no casualties; but its "foreign service" was performed with credit and pleasure and it returned to Indiana with an honorable record to its name. This regiment together with all other troops in the province of Havana, participated in the impressive ceremonies of January 1, 1899, when the flag of Castile and Aragon was lowered from the staff over Moro Castle, and the stars and stripes run up, thus terminating Spanish rule in the New World, and placing the United States before humanity as the greatest benefactor ever known among nations.

In 1902 an effort was made to organize a company of the National Guard in Jeffersonville by James Fortune, but it resulted in a discouraging fizzle. Later on others took up the matter and a roster was quickly made up. John Van Liew, late first sergeant of Company E, One Hundred and Sixty-first Indiana Volunteer Infantry, in the Spanish war, and Dr. George Twomey, a late member of the same company, headed the movement, and to their ability and management may be attributed the successful organization. There being no vacancy the company was not accepted until 1906. It was mustered into the state service February 9, 1906, in a store room on the west side of Spring street, about four doors south of Market street. John R. Van Liew was commissioned captain; George Twomey, first lieutenant, and William W. Fitch second lieutenant. The company procured the third floor of Spieth's hall on

14

Spring and Chestnut streets for their drill hall, and also a large room on the second floor which they fitted up as gun rooms, and for gallery target practice. These quarters were used as a club room and were attractively furnished for the use of members of the organization. The company was designated as Company M, First Infantry Indiana National Guard, and was assigned to the First Battalion, commanded by Maj. W. J. Coleman, of New Albany.

Lieutenant Twomey was detailed and appointed battalion adjutant October 12, 1906; Fitch was promoted first lieutenant; and First Sergeant Francis B. Shepherd was commissioned second lieutenant. Captain Van Liew resigned June 19, 1908, and Lieutenant Fitch July 1, 1908. Lieutenant Shepherd was promoted captain; First Lieutenant Leon Harrell was transferred from Company C, First Infantry, and Private Lawrence G. Smith was commissioned second lieutenant.

The company participated in the maneuvers at Fort Benjamin Harrison in 1906 and 1908, and in the state encampment in 1907. They formed part of the military display at the Madison Centennial, July 4, 1906, and at the dedication of the soldiers' monument at Madison, May 29, 1908. In marksmanship this company has made an enviable reputation, being the third best in the state and the first in the regiment. In 1907 it had two expert riflemen, four sharpshooters and five marksmen. The personnel of the company is good, the officers earnest and hard-working, and the rank and file composed of men who seem to realize the character of the service in which they have enlisted. The present membership is sixty-eight.

A recital of the things military in Clark county, and of the men military who were her citizens would be incomplete if mention were not made of the fact that hundreds of sturdy youths and young men had enlisted in the regular service of their country, afloat and ashore. During the War of the Rebellion and since, there has been a small but steady stream of enlistments in the army and navy which is large in the aggregate.

Lemuel Ford in the thirties, Jefferson C. Davis and John S. Simonson, in the sixties, were prominent men in the regular army and were all Clark county men. Richard S. Collum was appointed a lieutenant in the Marine Corps, United States Navy, in 1865. Frank Spear Armstrong entered West Point from Jeffersonville in 1887, and is at present in the Philippines as captain in the Ninth Cavalry. Jonas Howard Ingram, ensign in the United States Navy who was with the battle ship fleet that circumnavigated the globe, is a native of Jeffersonville. These and others, besides the large number of enlisted men, present a most creditable showing, and indicate that despite the foolish and un-American refusal of some workingmen to serve in the state troops, there underlies a mighty stream of patriotism which has only to be tapped to bring forth companies, regiments and brigades, if necessary.

CHAPTER XX.

FREEMASONRY IN CLARK COUNTY.

The legal establishment of Masonary in Clark county took place when Blazing Star Lodge, No. 36, was established at Charlestown in 1816, by authority of the Grand Lodge of Kentucky. The charter of this lodge is dated August 28, 1816, and her lineage, which is also that of the other lodges in the county, as well as that of the Grand Lodge of Indiana, adds distinction to an already distinguished society. They derive their Masonic authority from the Grand Lodge of Kentucky. That Grand Lodge was the offspring of the Grand Lodge of Virginia, and the Grand Lodge of Virginia was composed of lodges which had been chartered by the Grand Lodge of England. At the organization of the Grand Lodge of Indiana at Madison, January 12, 1818, Alexander Buckner, of Charlestown, was elected first grand master, and two other Clark county men from Charlestown were elected to offices in the Grand Lodge. Samuel C. Tate was elected grand treasurer and Isaac Howk was elected senior grand deacon. Charlestown was then selected as the site of the Grand Lodge until legally changed agreeably to the rules and regulations governing such matters.

Blazing Star Lodge, No. 3, of Charlestown, in 1818, at the time of the organization of the Grand Lodge of Indiana, had the following officers: Alexander Buckner, master; Joseph Bartholomew, senior warden; George Leas, junior warden; Isaac Howk, secretary; Evan Shelby, treasurer; John Meriwether, senior deacon; William Boven, junior deacon, and William Duerson, steward and tyler. The high regard in which Masonry was held by men of prominence at that time is shown by the character of her officers and members. Alexander Buckner became the first grand master; Isaac Howk, later on speaker of the Indiana house of representatives; Evan Shelby, Colonel Joseph Bartholomew, was wounded at the battle of Tippecanoe; John Owens, Jonathan Jennings, the first Governor of Indiana, and others, who considered it not beneath their dignity to meet within the tiled recesses of the lodge. From 1830 to 1835 this lodge was stricken from the list of subordinate lodges by a resolution of the Grand Lodge, but its charter was not arrested. Nine years later, in 1844, the Grand Lodge remitted all the dues and arrearages of Blazing Star Lodge and reinstated her with all powers as if no forfeiture of her chartered rights had taken place. Her new officers were installed on May 15, 1845, by Brother Levi Sparks.

During the years 1846 and1847 the lodge made no report, her charter was forfeited, and her number, 3, was given to Carlisle Lodge. In 1857 the Grand Lodge granted a dispensation to form another lodge at Charlestown by the name of Blazing Star, No. 226, and in 1858 a charter was granted, with Asa Glover as master; Andrew J. Hay, senior warden, and David W. Dailey, junior warden. Since then the lodge has pursued the even tenor of her way. The following is a list of the past masters of Blazing Star Lodge:

John Miller, Alexander Buckner, first most worshipful grand master 1818; Henry L. Miner, Jonathan Jennings, most worshipful grand master 1823 to 1825; Joseph Bartholomew, Isaac Howk, most worshipful grand master 1826 to 1827; Asa Glover, James Morrison, Hugh Lyle, William M. Steele, Isaac Naylor, John S. Simonson, George Green, William Duerson, Asa Glover, Andrew J. Hay, most worshipful grand master in 1877; Alfred Hough, S. L. Robinson, James Oldham, Francis M. Runyan, William Work, Joseph Cotton, Cadwalder Jones, Edward C. Hughes, McDowell Reeves.

It will be noticed that this lodge has been honored above any lodge in the state in having four of its masters elected grand master of the Grand Lodge of Indiana. In 1908 it has about sixty members and numbers among them the most prominent and influential citizens of Charlestown township.

Clark Lodge, No. 40, of Jeffersonville, is the next oldest Masonic lodge in the county. She was preceded in Jeffersonville by Posey Lodge, No. 9, which was chartered by the Grand Lodge September 14, 1819. This lodge was named in honor of Governor Posey, and Samuel Gwathmey was the first master. Gwathmey was a distinguished citizen of Southern Indiana, and was one of the trustees who laid out Jeffersonville in 1802. Posey Lodge was a weak organization from the beginning, and in 1829 its charter was arrested and it ceased to exist. The first Mason to be made in Jeffersonville was James Nesmith. He was initiated in Posey Lodge October 2, 1819. The annual communication of the Grand Lodge met in Posey Lodge hall September 11, 1820.

Clark Lodge, No. 40, was organized January 26, 1835, and chartered December 17th the same year, with Thomas D. Lemon as master. The following is a list of past-masters with years of service:

Samuel J. Stuart, (U. D.) 1835
Thomas D. Lemon (U. C.)................................... (a) 1836
William M. Steele... (b) 1836
Daniel Trotter.. (a) 1837
.......(b) 1837, (a) 1838, (b) 1838, (a) 1839, (b) 1839,
(b) 1840, (a) 1841, (b) 1842, (a) 1843, (a) 1846, (b) 1846,
.... (a) 1847, (b) 1847, (a) 1848
Robert H. Read.. (a) 1840
Robert Curran... (b) 1841

Levi Sparks...(a) 1842
Burdette C. Pile...........................(b) 1843, (b) 1848
R. S. Heiskell....................(a) 1844, (b) 1844—1863—1865
Henry French..(a) 1845
John Mitchell..(b) 1845
James G. Caldwell...(a) 1849, (b) 1849, (a) 1850, (b) 1850, (b) 1851—1853
H. W. Heaton.............................(a) 1851, 1857 1858
John W. Ray ....1852, '54, '55, 1856
William H. Fogg 1861
Archibald Cameron 1859
John Ware ....1864—1866
Reuben Wells ....1860—1862
W. H. Snodgrass... 1867
Simeon S. Johnson........1868, '69, '70, '71, '72, '84, '85, '86, '87. 1888
(M. W. Grand Master 1898—1899.)
John L. Delahunt............................1873, '74, '76, '82, 1883
Thomas Sparks.. 1875
Fountain Poindexter 1877 1878
John P. Glossbrenner...............................1879—1880
Jabez R. Cole... 1881
Robert W. Wood... 1889
Harvey G. Eastman.. 1890
William N. Northcutt.................................. 1891 1892
Floyd Parks... 1893
Walter L. Twoomey...............................1894, '95, '96
John W. Stratton.. 1897
Nelson B. Hartwell.. 1898
Thomas W. Perry.. 1899
Lewis C. Baird.....................................1900, '01, '02
William H. Humphreys....................................... 1903
Horace Dunbar.. 1904
George M. Crum... 1905
Joseph A. McKee...................................1906 '07
Thomas B. Bohon.. 1908

Note.—From 1835 to 1852 officers were elected semi-annually; (a) shows first half of year and (b) second half of year.

The first meeting place of Clark Lodge was in the old county court house, which stood on the north side of Market street, about where the present city hall is located; then on October 2, 1840, they moved to a building on the east side of Spring street, adjoining the north side of the alley between Market and Front streets. It then occupied the upper floor of a building on the northwest corner of Chestnut and Pearl streets.   While occupying this building it burned, Sunday, March 3, 1861, and her charter was the only thing saved.   The third floor of the building on the northeast corner of Spring and Chestnut streets was then used for a Masonic hall until 1898, when the third floor on the southeast corner of Spring and Maple streets was fitted up.   This hall is now used by all the Masonic bodies in Jeffersonville.

Clark Lodge laid the corner stone of the Jeffersonville Orphans' Home, and was instrumental in having the Grand Lodge lay the corner stone of the Jeffersonville Carnegie Public Library September 19, 1903.   On May 20, 1886, Clark Lodge was honored with a visit and lecture by Brother Robert Morris. The first Masons made by Clark Lodge were Brothers B. C. Pile, Robert S. Heiskell and John Mitchell.   They were initiated on April 21, 1835.   Brothers Pile and Heiskell were raised in New Albany at 2:00 p. m. in the Grand Lodge of the state there assembled, June 24, 1835.

New Washington Lodge, No. 167, is located at New Washington.   This lodge was organized December 12, 1854, and chartered May 30, 1855, with Thomas S. Faltinburg as master.   It is the only lodge in Washington township, but is an energetic and loyal supporter of the tenets of Freemasonry.   The following is a list of her past-masters:

Thomas S. Faltinburg...................................1855, 1856
Thomas D. Fouts.....................1857, '58, '59, '60, '61, 1862
Thomas Davidson................................1863, ,64, '65—1870
Felix B. Campbell..1866, 1867
Andrew M. Fisher....1868, '69—1873, '4, '6, '7, '8, '9, 1880, '1, '2, '3,
      ....'4, '5, '6, '7, '8, 1890, '2, '3, '4, '5, '9, 1900, '1, '2, '4, '5, '6—1907
George E. Taflinger..1871, '72
John C. Fouts...1875
James R. Russell...1888
Wright R. Wells..1891
Thomas W. Sample.......................................1896, '97
Wilton F. Blackford...1898
Otis B. Fifer...1903

New Washington Lodge has about fifty members in 1908.

New Providence Lodge, No. 237, is located at Borden, Wood township. It was organized January 26, 1859, and chartered May 24, 1859, with David W. Voyles as master.   The following is a list of her past-masters:

David W. Voyles..........................1859 '60 '61 '62 '63 '64 '67
G. M. Lockmiller.......................................1865 '66
W. H. Bright...1868 '69 '70
............................'71 '72 '74 '75 '76 '77 '78' 79 '80

J. W. Elrod.. 1873
B. F. Stalker.......................... 1881 '82 '83 '85 '86
.... '87 '88 '89 '90 '95 '96
J. N. Charles.. 1884
S. W. Burns.............. 1891 '92 '94 '96 '97 '98 '99 1900 '02
J. M. Herle... 1893
Jesse E. McKinley.................................... 1901
A. G. Littell....................................... 1903
S. W. Burns... 1904
John Hallet... 1905
Willard Todd.. 1906
F. M. Brock... 1907

It has about fifty-five members at present.

Utica Lodge, No. 337, is located at Watson. The lodge originally held her meetings at Utica, but owing to the change of residence of many of her members moved to Watson. Utica Lodge has suffered much loss from fires in the past, but a no more loyal body of Masons can be found in the state. It has had the honor of having one of its past-masters, Brother Calvin W. Prather, elected most worshipful grand master of Indiana. Brother Prather is now the grand secretary of the Grand Lodge. A lodge that makes Masons like Calvin W. Prather can certainly hold no mean place in the estimation of the fraternity throughout the state. The following is a list of her past-masters:

H. W. Fulton 1866-1867
S. R. Wilcox................................. 1868
Calvin W. Prather.............. 1869, 1870, 1871, 1872, 1873
        Most Worshipful Grand Master................ 1880—1882
Thomas J. Brendle.................... 1874—1881 1884 1885
Stephen W. Belknap 1875, 1876, 1877, 1878, 1879
George Zinck 1880
James H. Hazzard............................. 1882
Lewis L. Williams......................... 1883—1886
C. Ezra Bushfield.......................... 1887
Sarvis M. Howes............................. 1888
John D. Curran.............................. 1889
Nathaniel C. Noe.............. 1890, 1893, 1894, 1895, 1899
Robert L. Russell........................... 1891
Basil E. Myers......................... 1892 1904 1905
Erasmus T. Sage......................... 1896—'97
Aaron P. Scott.............................. 1898

Washington M. Hunt 1900
Edward A. Snodgrass.. 1901
Edward Dold 1902, 1903
Lewis F. Roller.. 1906 '07

This lodge has about fifty-five members at present.

Jeffersonville Lodge, No. 340, is located in Jeffersonville. She was organized August 1, 1866, and chartered May 29, 1867, with William H. Fogg as master. Jeffersonville Lodge is an offshoot of Clark Lodge, having been formed by a number of members of that lodge. Brother Calvin W. Prather, past grand master, and our present grand secretary, is also a past master of Jeffersonville Lodge. This lodge is the second largest Masonic body in Clark county, having about one hundred and twenty members. The following is a list of her past masters:

William H. Fogg ....1866, '67, '69, '70, '71
J. Chapline Cullom... 1868
Edward J. Tuttle...................................... 1782 1873
George T. Anderson.....................................1874 '75 '76
Harry T. Sage...........................1877 '78 '79 '80 '81 '82 '83 '85
Edward A. Austin...................................... 1884
Calvin W. Prather.......................................1886 '87
(Most Worshipful Grand Master in 1880 '81 and present Grand Secretary.)
A. D. Scott 1888
C. H. Walden... 1889
Norval G. Felker... 1890
Thomas J. Fires..1892
U. B. Lewis 1892
A. M. Thias... 1893
George W. Meaders.....................................1894 '95 1900
Charles E. Louis.. 1896
George Dunham.......................................1897 '98
Thomas B. Rader 1899
Edward Page... 1901
Benjamin C. Watts.......................................1902
William B. Thornley...................................... 1903
John P. Barsha... 1904
William G. Young.................................. 1905 '06 '07 '08

Buckner Lodge No. 631, is located at Sellersburg, in Silver Creek township, and was organized May 31, 1900. It was chartered on May 28, 1901, with Edward N. Wicht as master.

The following is a list of her past masters:

Edward N. Wicht, (U. D.).. 1900
Edward N. Wicht, (U. C.).. 1901
Walter J. Leach... 1902 '03
John T. Smith... 1904
John M. Meloy...1905—6
William E. Lines.. 1907

Buckner lodge has about thirty-five members.

Henryville Lodge No. 651, of Henryville, was organized March 30, 1903, and chartered May 27, 1903, with Michael U. Harbold as master. It has about forty members. The following is a list of its past masters:

Michael U. Harbold... 1903 '04
H. Ray Hamacher... 1905 '07
Harry C. Raymond... 1906

HOREB CHAPTER NO. 66 ROYAL ARCH MASONS.

Capitular Masonry made its official advent into Clark county when Horeb Chapter, Royal Arch Masons, was organized January 26, 1867. This chapter was chartered on May 23, 1867, with James S. Caldwell as high priest.

The history of Capitular Masonry in Clark county shows that it has attracted to its fold the most prominent and influential men of the county. The high standing of these members and the enthusiasm with which they labor, reflects credit on the community in which they live. Their apartments in the Masonic Hall are tastefully and appropriately furnished, and bear witness to the enthusiasm they have for this branch of Masonry. The following is a list of the past high priests:

James G. Caldwell...1867, 70
Theo W. McCoy.. 1868
John G. Briggs... 1869
Jabez R. Cole.. 1871
Simeon S. Johnson...1872, '73 '74
            (Most Excellent Grand High Priest in 1878:)
Edward J. Tuttle..1875, '76
George T. Anderson... 1877 '78
Calvin W. Prather... 1879
            (Most Excellent Grand High Priest in 1888.)
Harry T. Sage... 1880
John L. Delahunt.. 1881
Henry Voigt... 1882
Simon Goldbach 1883

Richard L. Woolsey.........................1884, '85, '86, '87, '88
Fernando H. Miller...............................1889
Floyd Parks.....................................1890
Arthur Loomis...................................1891
John Rauschenberger.............................1892
John H. Hoffman.................................1893
George Pfau.....................................1894
William H. Harper.........................1895, 1903
Alfred M. Thias.................................1896
Harvey E. Eastman........................1897, 1902
John C. Lewman.................................1898
Walter L. Twomey...............................1899
Jarvis M. Howes................................1900
George A. Dunham.........................1901, 1906
Andrew P. Williams.............................1904
Porter C. Bottorff.............................1905
George A. Scheer...............................1907

This chapter is in a most flourishing condition and has about eighty members.

JEFFERSONVILLE COUNCIL NO. 31, ROYAL AND SELECT MASTERS.

Cryptic Masonry is represented in Jeffersonville by Jeffersonville Council No. 31, Royal and Select Masters. This council was organized May 23, 1867, and chartered October 20, 1869, with William H. Fogg as illustrious master. The following is a list of past illustrious masters: William H. Fogg, 1867, '68, '69, '70. S. S. Johnson, 1871, '72, '73, '74, '75, '76, '78, '79, '80, '81, '82, '83, '84, '85, '86, '87, '88, '89, '90, '91, '92, '93, '94, '95, '96, '97, '98, '99, 1900, '01, '02, '03, '04, '05, '06, '07 and '08, and illustrious grand master in 1894. Edward J. Tuttle, 1877.

The Council has about forty members.

JEFFERSONVILLE COMMANDERY, NO. 27, KNIGHTS TEMPLAR.

Jeffersonville Commandery No. 27, Knights Templar, was organized August 28, 1875, and chartered April 26, 1876. The history of the commandery shows the high standing of the men who have been attracted to chivalric Masonry in Clark county. The following is a list of past eminent commanders: Simeon S. Johnson, 1875, '76. '80, '86, and right eminent grand commander in 1883. R. L. Woolsey, 1877, and right eminent grand commander in 1883. Calvin W. Prather, 1878, '82, '89;

Harry T. Sage, 1879; John P. Glossbrenner, 1881; Henry Voigt, 1883; John L. Delahunt, 1884; Herman H. Heaton, 1885; Jacob Loomis, 1887; Charles H. Walden, 1888; Edward C. Eaken, 1890; Fernando H. Miller, 1891; John H. Hoffman, 1892; Arthur Loomis, 1893; John Rauschenberger, 1894; Alfred M. Thias, 1895, '96, 1902, '03, '06, '07, '08; William H. Harper, 1897; Harvey G. Eastman, 1898; Jarvis M. Howes, 1899, 1900; Silas Carr, 1901, Andrew P. Williams, 1904; Porter C. Bottorff, 1905. The commandery has about seventy-five members.

On October 27, 1905, Jeffersonville Chapter, Order of the Eastern Star, was organized, and on April 26, 1906, a charter was granted by the Grand body at Indianapolis. The few years that the Order of Adoptive Masonry has been in existence in Jeffersonville have proved its popularity, and their roster shows about forty members.

Clark county also has a goodly number of Masons who have received the degrees of the Ancient Accepted Scottish Rite, Valley of Indianapolis.

Freemasonry throughout the county has existed from the earliest times, and a full history of the order would be a history of the county and its most distinguished citizens.

CHAPTER XXI.

ODD FELLOWSHIP—PYTHIANISM AND OTHER SECRET SOCIETIES IN CLARK COUNTY.

INDEPENDENT ORDER OF ODD FELLOWS.

The Odd Fellows organized their first lodge in Clark county at Jeffersonville, September 11, 1837, and named it Jefferson Lodge. It appears as No. 3 on the roster of lodges of the state, and this number indicates that Clark county was only behind two other places in the state in organizing. Jefferson Lodge was chartered on application of C. H. Paddox, Thomas Humphries, John Applegate, Benjamin Riggles and Nicholas Kearns. It now has two hundred and thirty-four members, and Don D. Walker is noble grand.

The next lodge of Odd Fellows to be organized in Clark county was Tabor Lodge, No. 92, also at Jeffersonville. Tabor Lodge now has one hundred and forty-eight members, and Ernest E. Jacobs is noble grand.

Charlestown Lodge, No. 94, was organized the same year, February 20, 1851, at Charlestown. This lodge has at present seventy-nine members. Milliard A. Badger is noble grand.

The next year saw the birth of Odd Fellowship among the rugged hills of Utica. Utica Lodge, No. 112, was organized May 29, 1852. It has thirty-eight members and J. M. Worthington is noble grand.

Tell Lodge, No. 272, was organized in Jeffersonville on January 16, 1867. Its present membership is eighty-eight, and Ernest Rauth is noble grand.

Cement Lodge, No. 494, was organized at Prather, July 2, 1875, and named after the industry which has added so much to the business life of the county. Cement Lodge has a membership of forty-nine at present. E. C. Long is noble grand.

Sellersburg Lodge, No. 702, was organized at Sellersburg, December 28, 1893. George W. Morgan is the present noble grand. Its membership is eighty-seven.

Marysville Lodge, No. 714, was organized at Marysville, June 13, 1895. Its present membership is ninety-nine, and B. K. Stoner is the noble grand.

Henryville Lodge, No. 794, was organized at Henryville, November 15, 1902. Homer Wills is the present noble grand, and the membership is one hundred and two.

The total membership of these Clark county lodges is nine hundred and twenty-four.

Rebekah Lodge, No. 8, Daughters of Rebekah, was instituted in Jeffersonville, March 1, 1869, with Herman Preefer, Mary Preefer, R. H. Timmonds, M. C. Timmonds, H. N. Holland, J. T. Davis, James W. Jacobs and others as charter members. This lodge is for the benefit of the wives and daughters of Odd Fellows, and it gives them the fraternal ties which bind their husbands and brothers in the bonds of friendship, love and truth. Rebekah Lodge has two hundred and four members. The noble grand is Lola Hodson.

Gold Knob Lodge, No. 701, Daughters of Rebekah, is located at Henryville. It was instituted January 27, 1906. Mamie Ferguson is the noble grand.

Excelsior Encampment, No. 14, Independent Order of Odd Fellows, was organized several years ago. The membership at present is about seventy. S. L. Huff is chief patriarch.

The lodges now existing in the county are enthusiastic and energetic in pushing the principles of Odd Fellowship. Thomas H. Stradley is the present district deputy grand master.

Clark county has furnished several distinguished Odd Fellows to their grand lodge. William Cross, a member of Jefferson Lodge, was grand master in 1844.

William H. Dixon, a member of Tabor Lodge, was grand master in 1861.

John P. Sanders, a member of Jefferson Lodge, was grand master in 1867, and John Dixon, of Jefferson Lodge, was grand secretary in 1846-47.

Some years ago William Beach erected a two-story brick building on the southeast corner of Market and Wall streets. The Odd Fellows added a third story for their use as lodge rooms in 1856; and later on, on the death of Mr. Beach, they purchased the lower part of the building. This they rent, retaining the upper floors for their own use.

THE KNIGHTS OF PYTHIAS.

The Knights of Pythias of Clark county are a numerous and progressive organization. The oldest lodge in the county is Hope Lodge. No. 13, founded on July 7, 1871. It was instituted by Grand Chancellor Hazelton, assisted by other grand officers, and Friendship Lodge, No. 10, of New Albany. It had twenty-five charter members, and the following were the first officers: S. B. Halley, P. C.; W. H. Northcutt, C. C.; T. B. Sharp, V. C.; J. Davis, Jr., K. of R. S.; C. H. Kelly, M. of F.; Herman Preefer, M. of E.; John Howard, M. A.; Brother LeClare, I. G.; Brother Bowman, O. G.

The membership December 31, 1907, was three hundred and sixteen.

Jeffersonville has another lodge of Knights of Pythias, Myrtle Lodge, No. 19. It was chartered July 24, 1872, by A. L. Eggleston, C. H. Kelly, W. H. Bowman, J. B. Piper, O. W. Rogers, G. W. Prather, W. E. Rose and about thirty others who came out of Hope Lodge to organize this additional lodge. It is in a prospering condition.

Sampson Lodge, No. 32, was organized by members of the two previous named lodges on July 22, 1873. Among those who were the earliest and most enthusiastic members were William H. Myers, W. S. Bowman, W. W. Crooker, R. M. Hartwell, J. E. Finch, Charles Rossler, G. W. Ware, E. A. Barnett and M. Myers. This lodge has ceased to exist.

The Endowment Rank, Knights of Pythias, was organized in Jeffersonville December 29, 1877, by William T. Myers, R. M. Hartwell, Alexander Sample, Charles H. Kelly and ten others.

The Uniform Rank, No. 9, Knights of Pythias, was organized and mustered in on July 27, 1882, by H. T. Rawlings. John M. Glass was the first captain, Samuel Perrine the second, Thomas B. Rader the third, W. W. Crooker the fourth and Fielding Wilson the fifth and present commanding officer. This organization has been a most enthusiastic and hard working body and has the reputation of having won prizes at every competition which they entered.

At Cincinnati, August 3, 1882, they won the silver cup. At Seymour, Indiana, they took the second prize; at Washington they took the thirty dollar prize; at Indianapolis they took the fourth prize of three hundred dollars; at Detroit they took the third prize of six hundred dollars; at Indianapolis, in 1904, they won the prize, a fine sword; and at Louisville they won a prize of three hundred dollars.

The company at present has a membership of twenty-seven and with the excellent accommodations afforded by the spacious armory just completed will evidently prosper.

This armory, completed at a cost of twenty thousand dollars, is the largest and best hall in the city of Jeffersonville. Built upon the site of the old Wigwam armory, which burned several years since, it occupies a convenient position, and from a financial standpoint the attractiveness of its auditorium will make of it a valuable investment and reflect credit on the order which made it possible. The floor of this armory is one hundred two by fifty-nine feet; the stage is thirty by twenty-three feet; the lodge room is sixty by forty feet and is located in the third floor.

Henryville Lodge, No. 532, Henryville, Indiana, was instituted April 6, 1907, with thirty-five (35) members. It was instituted with the following officers: J. H. Walker, C. C.; J. C. Hainincher, V. C.; T. F. Huffman, prelate; M. H. Dunlevy, M. of W.; J. W. Bailey, K. of R. S.; T. F. Prall, M. of F.; Ed. Hostettler, M. of E.; J. A. Smith, M. at A.; Frank Masters, I. G.;

Fred Metzgar, O. G.; Trustees, Dave Dunlevy, Fred Hallimbach and Ira Smith. Officers, June 30, 1908: James D. Dean, C. C.; Frank Mastin, V. C.; Aaron Cummings, prelate; Otto Guernsey, M. of W.; M. H. Dunlevy, K. of R. S.; T. F. Prall, M. of F.; James A. Smith, M. of E.; J. W. Bailey, M. at A.; Charles Enterman, I. G.; Charles Francke, O. G.; Trustees, I. L. Smith, Zack Taylor and Fred Kallenbuck.

Bethlehem Lodge, No. 498, Bethlehem, Indiana, was instituted July 19, 1902, with twenty-nine (29) members. It was instituted with the following officers: George Schowe, C. C.; Amie Clemmons, V. C.; Harry Baird, prelate; James Smith, M. of W.; Samuel P. Kelly, K. R. S.; Thomas Stevens, M. of F.; U. S. Berry, M. of E.; John S. Smith, M. at A.; Aaron Baker, I. G.; Judson Hineline, O. G. A. Hollenbeck, J. W. Jackson and William Woodward, Trustees.

Officers, June 30, 1908, are: J. E. Farmer, C. C.; E. M. Matthews, V. C.; A. B. Clemmons, prelate; C. Y. Priest, M. of W.; S. P. Kelby, K. R. S.; U. S. Berry, M. of F.; C. E. Pernet, M. of E.; Tracy Smith, M. at A.; C. E. Strausberry, I. G.; R. L. Beach, O. G. D. E. Pernet, D. W. Jessup and T. R. Stevens, trustees. In 1908 there were one hundred eighteen members.

Jennings Lodge, No. 418, Charlestown, Indiana, was instituted June 6, 1895, with thirty-seven (37) members. It was instituted with the following officers: Eli Runyan, C. C.; Charles Lanz, Jr., V. C.; C. M. Bottorff, prelate; B. T. Buler, M. of W.; L. L. Chapman, K. R. S.; Joseph W. Morrow, M. of F.; E. O. Hostettler, M. of E.; J. L. Cole, M. at A.; W. G. Conn, I. G.; Gustav Beuler, O. G.; E. B. Bentley, J. O. Johnson and D. K. Coombs, Jr., trustees.

Officers, June 30, 1908: E. G. Runyan, C. C.; James Morrow, V. C.; E. L. Boyer, prelate; Royal Boyer, M. of W.; A. W. Yager, K. R. S.; William Frickhoeffer, M. of F.; Joseph W. Morrow, M. of E.; William Noe, M. at A.; H. H. Floyd, I. G.; William Nickles, O. G. J. B. Carr, James Morrow and J. J. Cole, trustees.

Sellersburg Lodge, No. 417, Sellersburg, Indiana, was instituted May 22, 1895, with thirty-one, (31) members. It was instituted with the following officers: William O'Connell, C. C.; William Pass, V. C.; Earl Piercy, prelate; Elias Dodd, M. of W.; Will H. Sierf, K. R. S.; Walter Hyatt, M. of F.; Edward Dodd, M. of E.; John W. Piercy, M. at A.; Walter Carson, I. G.; Pat Nevils, O. G. John M. Nickles, Stephen Allen and Michael Moore, trustees.

Officers, June 30, 1908: Charles Werle, C. C.; C. J. Eismann, V. C.; Louis Dodd, prelate; William Seitz, M. of W.; L. F. House, K. R. S.; Benjamin Beyl, M. of F.; O. F. Davis, M. of E.; E. E. Seibel, M. at A.; C. P. Hartling, I. G.; W. M. Cleveland, O. G. M. F. Nickles, Elias Dodd, William Seitz, trustees.

Valley Lodge, No. 57, Utica, Indiana, was instituted December 22, 1874, with thirteen (13) members. Officers June 30, 1908: Charles Ruddle, C. C.; Charles Colvin, V. C.; Henry Deairk, prelate; William Carmney, M. of W.; W. B. Sims, K. R. S.; S. N. Wood, M. of F.; Louis Meyers, M. of E.; Tood Woods, M. at A.; F. C. Colvin, I. G.; J. C. Grimes, O. G. F. C. Colvin, D. W. Deairk, J. C. Grimes, trustees.

Bethlehem Temple, No. 325, Pythian Sisters, was instituted February 2, 1906, at Bethlehem, with thirty-three charter members. Since the organization of the Temple there have been sixteen members admitted.

THE BENEVOLENT AND PROTECTIVE ORDER OF ELKS.

This order was organized February 5, 1897, with the following officers: James W. Fortune, exalted ruler; Joe E. Bottorff, esteemed leading knight; M. Z. Stannard, esteemed loyal knight; C. C. Foster, esteemed lecturing knight; James E. Burke, treasurer and William C. Pfau, tyler. The thirty charter members in 1897 has grown to one hundred fifty members in 1908, and since the organization the following have served as exalted ruler: James W. Fortune, 1897; Joseph E. Bottorff, 1898; Edgar Howard, 1899; G. A. Scheer, 1900; James E. Burke, 1901; W. A. Ruby, 1902; M. H. Gascoign, 1903; W. J. Schwaninger, 1904; Orlando Chandler, 1905; James W. Taylor, 1906; Harry C. Sharp, 1907; Thomas J. Piers, 1908.

During the summer of 1901 and 1902 the Elks gave a street fair and carnival for the purpose of raising money to build a "Home." With the fund thus started the project was carried to a successsful culmination in 1904. On November 17th of that year the handsome Elks' hall at 242 Spring street was dedicated in the presence of a large number of Elks and their friends from the three falls cities. The cost of the building was eighteen thousand dollars, and the whole of the upper floor is given up to lodge rooms, the first floor being used for a store room. Jeffersonville Lodge, No. 262, Benevolent and Protective Order of Elks, is in a flourishing condition, and the comfortable and commodious club rooms offer a convenient and attractive lounging place for the members and their friends at all times.

THE MODERN WOODMEN OF AMERICA.

The Modern Woodmen of America, a fraternal organization, entered Clark county about 1896. Sellersburg Camp, No. 3896, was organized at Sellersburg January 30, 1896. The first venerable consul was M. L. Smith, the present is A. E. Snodgrass. The present membership is one hundred thirty-five.

Hoosier Camp, No. 3594, was organized February 21, 1896, at Jeffersonville. The first venerable consul was Henry Nachand, the present is Luther Childs. The present membership is two hundred twenty-eight.

Henryville Camp, No. 3761, was organized at Henryville in April, 1896. The first venerable consul was John Gray, the present is George Smallwood. The present membership is thirty-three.

Charlestown Camp, No. 3823, was organized at Charlestown in May, 1896. The first venerable consul was Frank W. Carr, the present is John W. Whitlatch. The present membership is sixty-six.

Ivanhoe Camp, No. 3951, was organized at Utica in June, 1897. The first venerable consul was William Hobson, the present is Aaron Scott. The present membership is twenty-six.

Jeffersonville Camp, No. 12587, was organized at Jeffersonville in July, 1907. The first venerable consul was C. T. Brightwell, the present is C. T. Brightwell.

New Washington Camp, No. 4408, was organized at New Washington, in December, 1897. The first venerable consul was A. G. Knowles, the present is Charles Pierce. The present membership is fifty-six.

Ideal Camp, No. 4103, was organized at Borden, in March, 1898. The first venerable consul was A. E. Almstead, the present is Richard A. McKinley. The present membership is forty-five.

Otisco Camp, No. 6406, was organized at Otisco in August, 1903. The first venerable consul was Dr. C. P. Meloy, the present is S. L. Stoner. The present membership is forty-six.

THE KNIGHTS OF HONOR.

This fraternal and beneficial order was organized in Louisville, Kentucky, on June 30, 1873. It was originally composed of men only, but of late years members of both sexes are admitted, the age limits being eighteen to fifty-four years. The order soon spread to Clark county, and Eureka Lodge, No. 3, was organized in Jeffersonville November 6, 1873. Soon after this, on August 24, 1875, Barbarossa Lodge, No. 146, was organized in Jeffersonville. It was followed by Hope Lodge No. 308, organized at Charlestown, June 15, 1876; Ohio Falls Lodge, No. 405, organized at Ohio Falls November 15, 1876; Silver Creek Lodge, No. 1171, was organized at Sellersburg on August 8, 1878.

Up to the present date the Supreme Lodge has paid out death benefits for the following amounts:

Eureka, No. 3—36 deaths ....$58,000.00 received.
Barbarossa, No. 146—29 deaths .... 55,000.00   "
Hope, No. 308—14 deaths .... 26,000.00   "
Silver Creek, No. 1171—8 deaths.................. 13,000.00   "

Making a total of one hundred fifty-two thousand dollars paid to beneficiaries in Clark county.

15

GERMAN AID SOCIETY.

This society was organized May 16, 1887. Its object is as its name implies—aid to its various members as they may need it. It is composed of the most prominent German citizens of Jeffersonville, and since the date of its organization in 1887, to 1908, has received as dues and interest, nine thousand five hundred sixty-one dollars. There have been paid out as benefits, seven thousand one hundred fifty dollars, leaving two thousand four hundred eleven dollars in the treasury. A weekly sick benefit is paid each member, while ill, and in case of death of either a member or his wife a substantial sum is donated. Matthew Kilgus was the first president, F. X. Kern, the first secretary, and Herman Preefer the first treasurer. The presidents who have served since the organization are as follows: Matthew Kilgus, 1887-1888; G. T. Englehardt, 1889; F. X. Kern, 1890; Matthew Kilgus, 1891 to 1901; Andrew Kilgus, 1902 to 1908. The secretaries have been Frank X. Kern, Adam Laun, Hugo Alben and August Happel.

KNIGHTS AND LADIES OF HONOR.

Mystic Tie Lodge, No. 7, Knights and Ladies of Honor, was organized in Jeffersonville, December 12, 1877, with thirty-three charter members. At present it has a membership of ninety-eight.

Eden Lodge, No. 240, Knights and Ladies of Honor, was organized in Jeffersonville December 31, 1881, with twenty-five charter members. At present the membership is one hundred seven.

The railroad men of Jeffersonville have three organizations, as follows:

The Brotherhood of Railroad Trainmen have one lodge, Jeffersonville Lodge, No. 689. This organization is composed of railroad conductors, brakemen and yardmen, and the objects of the order are mutual protection and insurance. The lodge was organized in the eighties, and at present has one hundred sixty-five members.

The Brotherhood of Locomotive Firemen and Enginemen have one lodge, Clark Lodge, No. 297. This lodge was organized in 1886, and at present has one hundred twenty-five members. Its membership consists of Pennsylvania engineers and firemen, of the Louisville division. Its objects are mutual protection and insurance.

The Brotherhood of Locomtive Engineers have one lodge, Engineers' Division No. 712. It was organized in 1907, and at present has fifty members. Its objects are mutual protection and insurance. The Pennsylvania has fitted up a reading room and billiard room in the depot at Wall street and Court avenue, where their employes may spend their leisure time. The above named organizations meet regularly in the Elks' hall, on Spring street.

IMPROVED ORDER OF RED MEN.

Kwasind Tribe, No. 268, Improved Order of Red Men, was organized in Jeffersonville April 1, 1898, with a membership of fifty. The tribe has grown until it now has a membership of over three hundred. Harry Pfeiffer is the prophet. Thomas Hodson, a member of Kwasind Tribe, is district deputy grand sachem.

Okenuck Tribe, No. 476, Improved Order of Red Men, was instituted at Memphis, Indiana, August 22, 1908, with a membership of forty. Jack Cleveland is the prophet.

Mengive Tribe, No. 376, Improved Order of Red Men, was instituted at New Washington, Indiana, January 23, 1904, with twenty-three charter members, and Charles H. Jones as prophet. The tribe at present has a membership of thirty-two.

Agawan Tribe, No. 272, Improved Order of Red Men was instituted at Sellersburg July 8, 1899, with thirty-six charter members. John M. Meloy was elected sachem. The present membership of the tribe is eighty-six.

Abenaki Tribe, No. 367, Improved Order of Red Men, was instituted at Bethlehem, with thirty-six charter members. E. D. Giltner was the first sachem, and W. H. Patterson, the prophet. July 1, 1908, there were one hundred fifteen members.

There are councils of the Degree of Pocahontas at Charlestown and Bethlehem. The Bethlehem council is known as Silver Heels Council, No. 260. This degree of the order admits women, and these two localities are in a flourishing condition.

THE EAGLES.

Jeffersonville Aerie, No. 1527, of the Order of Eagles, was organized in 1907 with Lyman Parks, past worthy president; James Fortune, president, and Henry Miller as vice president. This order is a social and convivial organization and its popularity has resulted in a roster of over two hundred names.

THE ROYAL ARCANUM.

Clark Council, No. 1216, Royal Arcanum, is located in Jeffersonville. It was organized on December 9, 1889, with Herman Preefer as regent. At present it has a membership of forty-five. Clark Council is the only council of the Royal Arcanum in Clark county.

THE PATHFINDERS.

Jeffersonville Lodge, No. 403, was organized November 20, 1905, by Jacob Hoffman. George Kopp was the first president and the following have served as such: George Kopp, 1905-6; Emil Rauth, 1906, six months; Levi English, 1907, six months; Walter Grant, 1907, six months; Charles Clayton, 1908. The Pathfinders is an insurance and social organization. The lodge in Jeffersonville, the only one in the county, has at present eighty-five members.

UNITED ORDER GOLDEN CROSS.

The Grand Commandery United Order Golden Cross was instituted in Jeffersonville April 29, 1891, at which time William H. Buckley was elected past grand commander; Rev. E. L. Dolph, grand commander; Kate W. Dawson, grand prelate; William S. Tucker, grand treasurer; John C. Loomis and S. W. Evans, grand trustees; all these being residents of Clark county. The Rev. E. L. Dolph is at present prelate of the supreme commandery, and resides in Jeffersonville. Previous to this date there had been several commanderies in Clark county, Bain Commandery being the pioneer. This commandery was the first one to be organized outside the state of Tennessee.

Bain Commandery, No. 15, was organized on February 28, 1877, by the late George W. Bain, Kentucky's great temperance lecturer. Since its organization the commandery has had nearly five hundred members, sixty or more of which have died. At present the membership is one hundred fourteen.

Perpetual Commandery, No. 724, was organized at Ohio Falls, November 10, 1894, by Samuel Swartz, of Jeffersonville, who was the grand commander of the state. The commandery was organized with twenty-five charter members and since that time there have been initiated one hundred nineteen new members. At present the membership is forty-two.

Clark Commandery, No. 57, was instituted on June 7, 1877. At present the membership is thirty-six.

Charlestown Commandery, No. 454, of Charlestown, was instituted October 6, 1890. It is not a strong organization, having only ten members.

Banner Commandery, No. 456, was instituted October 28, 1890 It has a membership of ten.

Welfare Commandery, No. 746, was instituted February 5, 1897. It has a membership of twenty-three.

CHAPTER XXII.

HISTORY OF ST. PAUL'S PARISH, JEFFERSONVILLE, INDIANA, THE ONLY EPISCOPAL CHURCH IN THE COUNTY.

Few there are who do not take an interest in the beginning of a family, a town or parish; is it not interesting to know who were the first church people of Clark county, where they worshiped and who first administered to them of the Word and Bread of Life? The slow growth of the church in Indiana is no criterion to judge of its founding and growth elsewhere.

It is a matter of history that the first religious service in the English tongue, on this Western Continent, was that of the Church of England, conducted by the Chaplain of Sir Francis Drake on the California coast, in 1579, in commemoration of which George W. Childs has erected on the spot a beautiful Celtic cross of mammoth size.

The prayer-book services of the English colony of Jamestown, Virginia, were the first in the English language on the Atlantic coast.

The first religious service in Kentucky was a prayer-book service held under the trees, during the erection of the fort at Boonesborough.

The majority of the signers of the Declaration of Independence were members of the Church of England. Thomas Jefferson, who planned our city, was a regular attendant upon the services of the church.

In 1823, the Rev. Amos G. Baldwin, of New York, was sent here by the Domestic and Foreign Missionary Society. His report says he found in Jeffersonville, "members who welcomed him gladly." In 1835, the saintly Bishop Kemper paid Jeffersonville a visit, and also a second visit in 1836. The formation of the parish followed these visitations. The Rev. James G. Britton, who was assistant at Christ church during this time gave occasional services. The Rev. Benjamin O. Peers, a prominent presbyter and educator, officiated prior to this visitation of the bishop, and was present and presided at the organization of the parish, August 14, 1836. The record stands thus in the old register:

"Organization of St. Paul's church, Jeffersonville, Indiana.

"At a meeting of those desirous for the formation of an Episcopal parish in the town of Jeffersonville on Sunday, the 14th of August, 1836, the Rev. Mr. Peers was called to the chair and Mr. G. Stearns appointed secretary, the following preamble being adopted," etc. The Rt. Rev. Jackson Kemper was bishop of the diocese and the signatures were as follows: Robert Weimmer,

Charles Fisk, Samuel Merriwether, Francis Barnes, W. D. Beach, George-Stearns, Christopher Peaceley, Andrew Fite, David Grisamore, Ira Robinson, Georgiana Buchannan, Ann Idell, Mary Ann Idell.

At the first election of vestrymen, the Rev. Mr. Peers in the chair, the following were chosen: Charles Fisk, Andrew Fite, Francis Barnes, George Stearns, Ira Robinson. Mr. Stearns was elected secretary. In November of the same year, the Missionary Board appointed the Rev. Mr. Steele as First Missionary to the parish; he also had charge of St. Paul's parish, New Albany.

The congregation first worshiped in a school-house on Market street, but soon the lower room of the court-house was fitted up and afforded a convenient accommodation.

The Sunday school was organized in that year.

January 1, 1837, the Ladies' Guild was formed.

January, 1837, Rev. Mr. Steele removed to New Albany and confined his ministrations to that city; he was succeeded by Rev. Samuel R. Johnson.

In 1837 the primary convention to organize the diocese was held in Madison, and the Rev. Robert Ash is reported as pastor from Jeffersonville.

The first confirmation service was held July 1, 1838, when the following persons received the Apostolic Rite at the hands of Bishop Kemper: Mrs. Ira Robinson, Mrs. N. Kerms, Miss Mary Buchannan and Miss Mary A. V. Idell.

The first St. Paul's church was erected on a leased lot on Spring street, at what is now No. 238. Later a debt of three hundred dollars was paid off with the very kind aid of the ladies of Christ church, Louisville, Kentucky.

The Rev. Charles H. Page, who resided in Louisville, had charge of this parish from 1839 to 1849. He was a godly man and left his imprint upon the parish. He writes in the old parish register: "In 1839 the house of Ira Robinson was the only house where the minister was entertained, but now in 1849, there are eight families where the minister is kindly entertained. Upon the Rev. Mr. Hickox, my successor, may grace, wisdom and strength be multiplied."

Rev. Mr. Page says in the first published report of the parish, the Sunday school has twenty-five children and the church twenty communicants. The assessment for convention expenses was two dollars.

In 1841 there were twenty-six communicants.

Bishop Kemper consecrated St. Paul's church in 1840, the debt having been removed.

In May, 1843, the bishop says in his address, "The remainder of Sunday, January 15th, was devoted to Jeffersonville, where I found the congregation in a flourishing condition." He confirmed eight persons.

Rev. Mr. Page writes later, "A Sunday school has been reorganized, which commenced with twenty-five children." It is evident from this that the Sunday school formed in 1836 had died out, and from a resolution by the vestry at this time, we conclude that our parents were very bad children, or else that the vestry held very high notions with regard to the sancity of the building. The resolution was, "That the church be not used for the purpose of a Sunday school, it being considered by the vestry that the sanctuary should not be used for that purpose."

In 1843 a special meeting or convention was held in Indianapolis for the purpose of electing a bishop, and for the first time the parish had a representation in the person of Doctor Collum.

Bishop Kemper in 1844 writes, "I went to Jeffersonville with several clergymen November 30th, and preached to an attentive congregation."

During the winter the Rev. Mr. Hickox, of Madison, took charge of the parish and also of New Albany; but not receiving the encouragement he hoped for, he determined to go South for the benefit of his health, as he had an affection of the throat. He was, however, suddenly attacked by sickness which in three weeks' time proved fatal. He died Sunday morning May 5th, and was interred at New Albany.

In 1845 Messrs. Bottorff, Cookerly and Collum were appointed a committee to purchase a lot upon which to remove the church from Spring street, where it stood on leased ground. They purchased on Chestnut street, between Spring and Pearl streets, on which, still in 1897 stood the original building used for a kindergarten school. A vestryroom large enough to accommodate the Sunday school was erected and the church painted, all costing about four hundred dollars.

Mr. Page's report for 1844 was: Baptisms seven, confirmed four, communicants thirty-one, Sunday school teachers five and scholars twenty.

Report for 1846. Communicants twenty-eight, Sunday school scholars twenty-five. He regrets that the ground upon which the church stands has not yet been paid for, owing to the divided estate of the population, there being five different denominations and the too prevalent apathy to eternal things.

In 1845 the Rev. Mr. Page regrets that he cannot report the prospects of the church essentially improved. The congregation varies from thirty to fifty, teachers four, scholars twenty, communicants twenty-six, marriages five.

In 1848 he reports that it was difficult to sustain the Sunday school; teachers three, scholars twenty, communicants forty, contributions for missionary work fifteen dollars, diocesan assessment, two dollars, not paid. At the diocesan convention the apportionment made on Jeffersonville for the support of the bishop was twenty-five dollars or one thousand dollars to be raised.

In 1849 the Rev. R. M. Chapman came to the parish as rector. He was a man of fine character and education. In 1852 for the first time the parish was represented among the clergy. In 1854 the convention was held in New Albany, the Rev. Dr. Chapman and two lay delegates, W. F. Collum and H. P. Murry being present. Report: diocesan assessment or bishop's salary, twenty dollars; missionary fund fifteen dollars. Now the parish is beginning to show real life. In 1854 Doctor Chapman resigned his charge and confined himself to his duties as principal of a ladies' seminary.

On January 1, 1855, Rev. James Runcie took charge of the parish. He reports thirty-three communicants, Sunday school thirty-four, contributions thirty-three dollars. Rev. Mr. Runcie was elected alternate delegate to the general convention.

In 1855 the first convention was held in the parish, being that of Central Indiana, at which time the bishop ordained Rev. John B. Wakefield, who was chosen as rector of St. Paul's, Richmond, and as priest the Rev. W. G. Spencer, rector-elect of St. Stephen's, Terre Haute. This was the first ordination service held in the parish, offering for missions at convocation, thirty dollars.

In 1857 Mr. Runcie was appointed chaplain at the penitentiary. In 1858 a fund was started by the Ladies' Guild looking towards a new church, and the amount of one hundred and fifty dollars placed to its credit. The Rev. Mr. Githens assisted the rector during this year. In 1859 Rev. Mr. Runcie resigned the parish but still remained chaplain at the penitentiary.

The Rev. R. W. Trimble, deacon, officiated from April to November, 1859. This year the Ladies' Guild contributed two hundred and five dollars, most of which was used to repair the church. Deacon Trimble speaks of the Sunday school as being increased fourfold, and of the offering as being taken up weekly instead of monthly. The Rev. Mr. Runcie was a man of genial personality, and upon his departure left none but friends.

January 9, 1862, the Rev. P. Charlot took charge of the parish, but his stay was short as he was appointed chaplain of the Twenty-second Indiana Volunteers.

January 1, 1864, Rev. C. W. Fitch, D. D., took charge of the parish, rendering as his report says such services as did not interfere with his duties as chaplain to a U. S. Army hospital. In his time a committee was appointed to procure subscriptions for the erection of a new church, and four hundred and ten dollars was raised. Communicants thirty-eight, Sunday school fifty, burials three hundred and thirty-six. This extraordinary large number of burials was from the army hospital, where Mr. Fitch was chaplain. In 1866 Doctor Fitch removed to the diocese of Michigan.

March, 1867, Rev. F. G. Carver officiated in the parish, and then Doctor Davidson as lay reader. The latter was a Presbyterian minister, who came from New Albany. He was ordained deacon March 31, 1867.

November 4, 1867, Rev. Thomas R. Austin, LL. D., assumed the rectorship, being then only a deacon. He came from the Methodists and was ordained priest in New Albany, April 15, 1868. The vestry decided to purchase the Government chapel at Camp Joe Holt and a lot was procured from the Baptists on Mulberry street. They gave one hundred dollars for the old church and there was an even exchange of lots. For the chapel three hundred dollars was paid, and Hiram Wright received four hundred and fifty dollars for moving the building, repairs, furniture, etc., making the total cost two thousand eight hundred dollars. The Ladies' Guild gave one thousand three hundred and twenty-six, Judge Read one hundred dollars, Mrs. Childs two hundred and five dollars, Mr. Willacy one hundred dollars, Mr. Shryer one hundred and fifty dollars, Mrs. Merriwether one hundred dollars, the Misses Shryer eighty-five dollars and many smaller amounts. The church was consecrated by Bishop Talbot, April 16, 1868.

May 1, 1870, the pews were declared free. In this year the Rev. Dr. Austin went to St. Stephen's, Terre Haute, and the Rev. Thomas B. Bacon took charge of the parish; but in 1872 he went to Ohio. In 1872 Rev. Richard Totten took charge, but in 1874 went to the diocese of Easten.

On December 1, 1874, Rev. Dr. Chapman returned to the parish, but his health obliged him to remove to California.

December, 1875, Rev. G. W. E. Fisse was sent as *locum tenens;* he left in 1876. The parish being vacant for some time, the services were supplied by Rev. Dr. Chapman, Rev. John Girlow, of New Albany, and Rev. Dr. Fitch. At this time a bell was placed in the church, being borrowed from the Government Depot.

Rev. G. C. Waller, of Louisville, officiated part of 1878, until Rev. Charles A. Cary, of Mississippi, took charge as rector and remained five years, the longest pastorate to date. A reed organ was placed in the church, Mr. Frank Burke being organist.

In 1881 the first rectory was purchased principally with the bequest of one thousand dollars left by Mrs. Buchannan; it stood on Mulberry and Chestnut streets. In 1883 Rev. Mr. Cary resigned and went to Florida, when Rev. J. R. Bicknell took charge until 1885. In his pastorate the congregation began to look toward a new church, and a fund was commenced of one hundred and fourteen dollars.

In 1884 Bishop Knickerbacker, of blessed memory, was elected to the diocese. It was in the year of the great flood, and the first note of relief came from him; he sent fifty dollars and telegraphed, "How much more do you want?" Rev. Mr. Cary also sent a donation. In all the money donations amounted to five hundred and twenty-five dollars, which placed the church in good repair. There was over ten feet of water on the site of the present church. During the flood services were held on board the steamer, Grey Eagle, and in the O. F. Hall on Market street. Our services and those of our Roman Catholic brethren were the only ones held in those days.

December, 1885, Rev. F. C. Jewell, of the diocese of Chicago was called and assumed charge. The endowment fund of the diocese was started and this parish gave its bond for eight hundred dollars, which was paid in full in seven years. New additions were constantly made to the building fund. The parish was honored by the appointment of its senior warden, E. W. Fitch, as supplementary deputy to the General Convention.

A lot on which the present church now stands was finally purchased from James Burke, at a cost of two thousand five hundred dollars, five hundred dollars of which was provided by Miss Hannah Zulauf and five hundred dollars more provided in a manner unknown to the vestry, but which was supposed to have come from the same generous family. In 1889 the parish lost two old and valued communicants, Mrs. J. G. Reed and her daughter, Mrs. Merriwether. They remembered the parish liberally in their wills.

February, 1890, the old church and rectory were sold for two thousand dollars, with the privilege of using the church for two years and the ownership of the furniture. A terrible cyclone struck the town March 27th, causing loss to eleven church families, amounting to over twenty thousand dollars. Rev. Mr. Jewell resigned July, 1890, the state of the church being as follows: Communicants ninety-eight, Sunday school sixty, current expenses seven hundred and fifty-nine dollars, total expenses, one thousand three hundred and nine dollars and seventy-one cents.

October 12, 1890, Rev. W. H. Bamford became rector and remained for one year. Mr. Bamford insisted that the building of a parish house and rectory were of equal importance with the building of the church.

The Rev. A. F. Todrig succeeded Mr. Bamford as rector.

July, 1892, the plans of Arthur Loomis for church and parish house were accepted and the offer of Captain Ed. J. Howard for both, for the sum of fourteen thousand four hundred and sixty-six dollars and sixty cents, was accepted; this did not include the furnishing of the church which was about one thousand five hundred dollars. October 6, 1892, the corner stone was laid with appropriate ceremonies. The list of principal contributors to the new church, St. Paul's: Mrs. S. C. Ransom, four thousand dollars; Captain E. J. Howard, five hundred dollars; Joseph V. Reed, five hundred dollars; R. M. Hartwell, five hundred dollars; Mrs. Wilhelmina Zulauf, five hundred dollars; Miss Hannah Zulauf, five hundred dollars; John C. Zulauf, five hundred dollars; Mrs. John Read, five hundred dollars; E. W. Fitch, five hundred dollars; Misses Ellen and Georgiana Shryer, three hundred dollars each; Captain John Hoffman two hundred and fifty dollars; Ladies' Guild, three thousand six hundred and twenty-seven dollars; Arthur Loomis, the architect, contributed all the plans and superintendence of the work, which was in itself a large contribution. Words should fail to express the gratitude of the congregation to Mr. Loomis. Some of the other contributors were:

Thomas Sparks, M. Z. Stannard, P. C. Donovan, J. A. Jenkins, J. C. Lewman, S. D. Oglesby, Mrs. E. M. Myers, L. C. Baird, Mrs. C. Poindexter, H. Peter, G. W. Lewman, John Adams, Mrs. I. Myers, Mrs. S. Simmonds, Louis Girdler, J. D. Stewart, Eugene Frazer, J. E. Burke, Rev. Mr. Hutchinson, Mrs. J. L. Lewman.

Much praise is also due to Capt. Ed. J. Howard, the contractor, who has saved the congregation one thousand five hundred dollars or two thousand dollars in the cost of the church, and given more honest work than any other would.

March 1, 1894, Rev. Dr. C. Graham Adams accepted the rectorship of this parish, and came at a time when a pilot at the helm was sorely needed. A handsome rectory was erected next to the church at a cost of five thousand dollars.

Should the dead who took such an interest in the beginning and progress of the parish, but revisit the scenes of their toils and trials, or the familiar and cherished places which they loved on earth; should they be with us in the Holy Temple, and listen to the prayers and sermons, the chants and hymns, they would not think they labored in vain.

Easter, 1897, a beautiful pipe organ was placed in the church by the munificence of that ever-liberal and truly Christian lady, Mrs. S. A. Ransom. It was built by the Pibcher Organ Company, of Louisville. In the sanctuary of the church stands the beautiful white marble altar, the noble gift of the Zulauf family. The Stealey family placed a fine memorial window in the church. Many other gifts were given, as an altar rail, literary desk, pulpit, etc.

Comparison—A. D. 1821, church property, three thousand dollars; communicants, seventy-one; Sunday school average, forty; offering, eight hundred and eighty-three dollars.

A. D. 1891, church property, two thousand five hundred dollars; communicants, one hundred ten; offerings one thousand three hundred and nine dollars; Sunday school average, sixty.

A. D. 1893, church property, nine thousand eight hundred dollars; communicants, one hundred fifteen; current expenses, nine hundred and eighty-five dollars; Sunday school average, forty-six.

A. D. 1897, church property twenty-seven thousand five hundred dollars; communicants, one hundred eighty-five; Sunday school, the 28th of November, sixty-two present on the rolls; current expenses, one thousand five hundred and seventy-five dollars; total offering, three thousand six hundred and fifty dollars.

February 5, 1900, the Rev. C. Graham Adams resigned the rectorate, and the Rev. Frank N. Chapman, of Kirksville, Missouri, was called June 8th. Mr. Chapman served the parish about four years, resigning June 1, 1904. In October of this same year the Rev. Mr. Bamford, who had served the parish in 1891, but who had been in charge of St. Paul's at Madison since that time, was called to the rectorate. He remained in charge of the parish until February, 1908. During the two succeeding months the Rev. E. A. Neville, rector of St. Paul's, New Albany, gave such time as he could spare from his own church. The Easter offering while Mr. Neville was temporarily in charge, was a large one.

The Rev. A. Q. Bailey was called from Hartwell, Ohio, to assume the rectorship and took charge in April, 1908. Mr. Bailey seemed to be able to enthuse a new life in the people, and under his tactful and wise administration the church is building up and strengthening itself in all the different phases of parochial work. The vestry at present, 1908, is: J. Howard Fitch, senior warden; Thomas Sparks, junior warden; Thomas Bohon, treasurer; Lewis C. Baird, clerk; John C. Zulauf, A. T. Allmond, W. J. Schwaninger.

The church societies of St. Paul's, the St. Agnes Guild, the Woman's Auxiliary and the Ladies' Guild are earnest and enthusiastic bodies. The St. Agnes Guild was organized by the Rev. W. H. Bamford, during his first rectorate and was strictly an altar guild, but it became ambitious and branched out into other work besides its altar duties. This guild erected the brass railing in front of the organ, and also gave the stone wall around the church property. Part of the money for the wall was raised by entertainments, the remaining one thousand dollars being a bequest to the St. Agnes Guild for that purpose, by Miss Hannah Zulauf. Much of the best work of the parish has been accomplished by this guild. It has been a society of unmarried women, so the members were expected to leave as soon as they changed their names. The following are the officers at present: Miss Nora Whitesides, president; Miss Bess Hoffman, treasurer; Mrs. Bettie Allmond, secretary.

The Woman's Auxiliary of St. Paul's was organized during the rectorate of the Rev. F. C. Jewell. It is the missionary society of the church. After several years of activity it was discontinued, but was revived again by Doctor Adams. During the rectorate of Mr. Chapman it became a live factor in the activities of the parish and the diocese. At that time the officers were: President, Mrs. J. V. Reed; treasurer, Mrs. Thomas Sparks; secretary, Miss Lila Jewett. This society has the reputation of being one of the most active in the parish, and of being one of the best and strongest auxiliary branches in the diocese. It has given twenty-five dollars each year to the arch-deacon's salary, it has sent a number of very good boxes to different mission stations, besides responding to many special appeals. It has distributed missionary literature and in many ways has endeavored to interest the parish in missions. At present the work is being carried on by twenty-five members, with the following officers: President, Miss Lila Jewett; treasurer, Mrs. C. E. Poindexter; secretary, Mrs. Lewis Girdler.

The Ladies' Guild of St. Paul's was first organized January 1, 1837, and with very few breaks in its service has had a continuous history to the present day. This body of earnest women has accomplished a great deal for the parish in various ways. It has raised much money for different church purposes and is one of the strongest societies in the parish.

St. Paul's Sunday school has the most modern organization of any Sunday school in the county. The new method of adopting the graded system of the public schools for Sunday school work has worked wonders in the school, and the systematic study of the Bible, the church and the prayer book is carried on up clear through a high school course. The use of this new method and an excellent staff of enthusiastic teachers presages a bright future for this school. A system of home study for those who cannot attend regularly has just been organized, and will afford an opportunity to many to take up a study of church subjects and learn more of the church and her ways.

THE BAPTIST CHURCH IN CLARK COUNTY.

(By J. V. Biggert.)

The history of the Baptists in Clark county, Indiana, is most peculiar and sad, but withal, very interesting. It is peculiar and sad because of its many trials, discords and divisions, thereby weakening the local strength of the Baptists and their doctrines of faith and practice; interesting because of its early date in the history of the country, its continued existence through its many trials, and its influence for good in the cause of Christianity.

In the year 1765 representatives from Baptist churches met at Philadelphia and adopted what is commonly known among Baptists of today as the "Philadelphia confession of faith."

In the brief space alloted in this work it is impossible to give in detail the facts contained in this document, but it is probably sufficient to say that it declares the "Bible to be the only infallible, sufficient, certain rule of all saving knowledge, faith and obedience," and teaches the doctrine of regeneration as prerequisite to salvation, a principle peculiar to the Baptists and the promulgation of which relieves the Baptists of the unkind and unjust criticism of the term, "close communists" (communionists).

On November 22, 1798, the first evangelical church organized in the territory west of Cincinnati, Ohio, was called into existence by the announcement of the following constitution, which is copied from Elder William H. McCoy's pamphlet entitled, "The oldest church in Indiana":

"We, the church of Christ, on Owens creek in the county of Knox, and territory northwest of the Ohio river, in the Illinois grant, were constituted as a church on the principles of the Baptist Confession of Faith, adopted at Philadelphia in the year of our Lord 1765. Being constituted by Brother Isaac Edwards, we have hereunto set our hands this twenty-second day of November, 1798. John Fislar, John Pettet, Sophia Fislar, Cattern Pettet."

Thus two men and their wives constituted the first evangelical church in the Northwest Territory, "A Baptist Church," originally known as "Fourteen Mile Church," because of its location on Owens creek, which was soon afterwards and to this day, known as Fourteen Mile creek.

The church was subsequently called the Charlestown Baptist church and is now known more commonly as the Silver creek Baptist church. Isaac Edwards, who organized the church, was a Baptist preacher from Kentucky, but the records of the church show no further reference to him immediately following the organization.

The first recorded meeting of this church following its organization was held on February 16, 1799, at which time William Kellar was chosen moderator and John Pettet church clerk.

The former was at this time pastor of the church, being a Baptist preacher from Kentucky. On July 16, 1799, the first additions to the church are recorded, viz: James Abbett and Margaret Abbett by letter and Stephen Shipman by experience and baptism.

James Abbett was chosen pastor on March 13, 1802, and the same day the church "agreed to attend to communion and washing feet." However, at the meeting in the following June the records read, "that as considerable light was shown upon the thirteenth chapter of John by several of the members present, the matter of washing feet was deferred."

On December 11, 1802, James Abbett, the pastor, was excluded for the "heinous and abominable crime of falsehood."

On July 8, 1801, Elisha Carr was received by experience and baptism. For some time following, the meetings of the church were held at the residence of Elisha Carr, on Silver creek, near the present location of the Charlestown or Silver creek church. In April and May, 1803, the matter of building was considered and in December, 1804, an amount had been secured sufficient to erect a comfortable log house on "Silver creek, near the mouth of Sinking Fork," on ground donated for the purpose.

In 1818 the house had become too small and too old to be serviceable and it was agreed to build a brick house on a piece of ground donated by Elisha Carr, near the old house. This house was forty-six by twenty-eight feet and it was completed and ready for occupancy November 27, 1824, the trustees at the time of building being John McCoy, John Bowel and Jonah Harris. The church prospered greatly for thirty years, and was the leading church of all denominations in Clark and adjoining counties. It was also the "Mother Church" in all the surrounding territory, the following named churches in

Clark county being organized by members of the Charlestown church: New Providence (Borden), 1820; Jeffersonville, 1839; Utica (probably), 1844; Memphis, 1858. In addition to these, many of the Baptist churches in Washington and Scott counties as well as the church at New Albany were the result of aggressive work on the part of this church. In 1829 the first serious problems confronted the church in dealing with the questions advocated in the "Christian Baptist," edited by Alexander Campbell. The articles of faith on which the church was constituted were voted out, and a split resulted, the division taking place on May 23, 1829.

Each party met at the church, but the minority being aggrieved at the action of the majority and its continued persistence, on April 25, 1829, withdrew to the "shade" near a large basin not far from the church, and here it was that this minority received the approbrious epithet, "The Sink-Hole Elect." Here in the shade, with prayers and tears, they prepared a remonstrance and determined to stand fast, maintain the Baptist faith, ask their constitutional rights and declare themselves, "The Silver Creek Baptist church."

The two branches continued to occupy the house, alternately, until about 1834, when the majority built a commodious and neat house in Sellersburg and styled themselves the "Silver Creek Christian church." On December 4, 1858, the majority gave its entire right and title in the old meeting-house to the Charleston Baptist church. The schism of 1829 caused by the propagation of the principles advocated in the Christian Baptist resulted in the adoption of extreme views by those of the minority. However, the strict adherence of these few to what they believed to be the scriptural teaching regarding missionary activity soon led to renewed growth and for a number of years the little church was again prosperous. We find also that from this early church went out as missionaries to the Indians, Rev. Isaac McCoy, Christiana McCoy, Eliza McCoy and Sarah Osgood. At present the church house still stands, but is used very little except for funeral services. The location is rather isolated, the settlement being now along the railroad and in Sellersburg, and there is probably little future for the church. In Jeffersonville the Baptist church was organized on June 22, 1839, the meeting being held on Sunday afternoon in the Presbyterian church, the following being the constituent members: Mason J. Howell, Eleanor Howell, by letters from Spencer county, Indiana; Judith Halstead, by letter from Cincinnati, Ohio; Asa Marsh, by letter from Madison, Indiana; William McCoy, by letter from Charlestown, Indiana; Levi Hall, Esther Hall, Sarah Shryer, James Gill, baptized in the Ohio river at foot of Pearl street, Sunday, June 22, 1839.

Besides these there were present seven ministers and five laymen from points in Kentucky, Indiana, Missouri and Louisiana. Rev. William C. Buck was the first pastor, and the church met regularly on Saturday afternoon of each week in the Presbyterian church until a house was built on the southwest corner of Pearl and Market, where subsequent meetings were held.

Whether or not this house belonged to the organization or was only leased could not be learned, but some time later the organization built a house on leased ground on the south side of Market street between Wall and Locust streets, but owing to what was termed an exhorbitant rental for the real estate, the church bought a lot on the opposite side of the street where the residence of Capt. William Howard now stands, and the house was moved to this lot. Meetings continued here until some time in 1866, according to the best information, when the house was destroyed by fire. It is presumed that the records of the church were destroyed in this fire, as nothing can be found between October 21, 1856, and January 15, 1869. It is rather a peculiar coincidence that on the night of the fire a business meeting was held in the church and the matter under consideration brought about a division of the church, the minority organizing the Enon Baptist church. This latter organization held meetings for some time in the old engine house on West Maple street, until the present house on the square below was built in 1868.

This organization of the Enon Baptist church was wholly uncalled for and the church was doomed to failure. The pastor of this organization, taking advantage of the opportunity, solicited aid to rebuild the church which was destroyed by fire and used the money for the Enon church, and while the building was completed and occupied, the church was not sufficiently strong to live.

In the meantime the original organization had held meetings at various points throughout the city and soon purchased the property of the Episcopalians on West Chestnut street, near Pearl. Here many overtures were made to secure a union of the two churches, but all to no avail, as both sides were unwilling to make concessions, and finally after most of the Enon membership had returned, few at a time, to the parent church, the house passed to the control of Capt. Ed. J. Howard, from whom it was purchased by the First Baptist church on June, 1880.

While still holding meetings in the Chestnut street property the First church called to its pastorate a young man then at the Seminary in Louisville, Rev. Nelson B. Rariden, and during this pastorate perhaps greater progress was made than at any time in the previous history of the church.

The Rev. Mr. Rariden is now one of the prominent men of the denomination, being District Secretary of the American Baptist Home Mission Society, having charge of the work west of the Mississippi river.

Notably among the men who have served this church are the following: Rev. E. F. Strickland, who together with George C. Lorimer, was an actor playing an engagement in the old Third Street Theater in Louisville, when they were visited by a couple of the women and prevailed on to attend a service then being held in one of the Louisville churches. They were both converted and immediately went into the ministry, Rev. Strickland serving the church in Jeffersonville during his term in the seminary. He is now one of the prominent men in the denomination. Rev. F. C. McConnell, at present pastor of one of the largest churches in Kansas City and considered one of the ablest men in the Southern Baptist convention, served the First Baptist church in this city about 1880-1. With all of the difficulties and trials which the church appears to have experienced the organization is at the present time in a very prosperous condition, and, in fact, this is true with respect to the Borden church, which has had a seemingly peaceful existence. A peculiar thing is the fact that along the entire northern bank of the Ohio river in the state of Indiana, the Baptists are as a rule weak. Located as they are at Jeffersonville and the immediate surrounding country in the very pale of the Southern Baptist Theological Seminary at Louisville, it appears that they should be very strong, but for some unknown reason the seminary appears to have been a hindrance rather than a help. But with all the struggles and discouragements, the several churches are not satisfied; they seek enlargement; they desire to do even greater things for the cause of Christianity. They have been cast down, but not forsaken; discouraged, but not despondent. Through it all the spirit of the Master has inspired and lead, and with an unwavering faith in Him, they pray, labor and wait, looking forward with hope to the time, "when Christ shall come the second time without sin unto salvation."

16

CHAPTER XXIII.

METHODISM IN CLARK COUNTY.

Early in 1801 there came to Clark's grant a young man named Samuel Parker. He was not yet licensed to preach but deep in his soul he had felt the call of God to cross the river from his native Kentucky and preach the gospel of peace and love to the settlers in Indiana. He went from house to house, preaching and exhorting. Later he was joined by Edward Talbott, another earnest young Kentuckian, and the two held a great camp meeting at Springville, then the only town in the county, except Clarksville. This was the first seed sown.

The next year Benjamin Lakin, a traveling preacher of the Salt River and Shelby circuit of Kentucky, visited the Methodists in the grant and organized societies at Gazaway's, Robertson's and Jacob's, Gazaway's is now Salem, three miles southeast of Charlestown; Robertson's, Bethel, three miles northeast, and Jacob's, New Chapel on the plank road. These three societies were added to the Salt River circuit, which already embraced all of Kentucky, Northern Tennessee, and most of Illinois and Indiana, a district covering hundreds of miles of almost unbroken wilderness, and all traveled by one man. What his salary was we do not find recorded, but in 1815 the circuit preacher's munificent stipend was fifteen dollars and ninety-seven and one-fourth cents, and the presiding elder's nothing. Verily those were the days when men preached truth for truth's sake and esteemed the reward of conscience higher than the praise of men.

In 1803 Rev. Mr. R. Lakin was given entire charge of the circuit and in 1804 was succeeded by the noted Peter Cartwright. At the close of the year 1806 the grant was made into a separate circuit and named Silver Creek. In 1807 the first church was erected, old Bethel meeting house. It was a rude log cabin built on the farm of Nathan Robertson, one of five brothers, who were pioneers of Methodism in Clark county. Bethel meeting house is still in existence. It was used for fifty years, then sold and removed to the farm of John Stanger, where for many years it served as a stable. Fast falling into decay the old house was purchased in 1902 by a committee appointed by the Indiana Conference of the Methodist church, the intention being to place it on the old site and restore it as nearly as possible to its original condition. On the brow of the hill it stands again, while below on the sloping hillside sleep the men and women who long ago traveled the wilderness roads, gun in hand, to worship God in the old log church, and thus it serves as a fitting memorial of the days that are past and calls to the minds of the new generation, the sacrifices and toils of the fathers and mothers of Methodism.

In 1803 Ralph Lotsprech, a traveling preacher, was sent into the grant to assist Benjamin Lakin, and soon after William Huston was also employed in traveling and preaching in the grant.

Quoting from a letter of the Rev. George Knight Hester to his son, Asbury: "It is believed that the first society that ever was formed in the state was organized at old Father Robertson's. It has sometimes been supposed that the first society was formed at Gazaway's, but Brother Hezekiah Robertson distinctly recollects that the first society was formed at his father's, and Sister Gazaway has often been heard to say to female members when excusing themselves for their neglect in attending class-meetings on account of distance that she had uniformly gone to Nathan Robertson's to class every two weeks, a distance of four miles, which makes it evident that the first class was organized there. And this must have been done in the spring of 1803, when Lakin and Lotsprech, who were at this time traveling the Shelby circuit, came over the Ohio river and took them into their work, for there were a few scattered members in the wilderness, and these faithful pastors would gather them into the church fellowship at the earliest possible time, and this probably was done in the month of April or May of 1803."

These brethren were succeeded the following conference year by the Revs. A. McGuire and Fletcher Sullivan. Following these preachers came Benjamin Lakin and Peter Cartwright. Peter Cartwright was in Capt. David Robb's company at Tippecanoe. He was the man who ran against Abraham Lincoln for membership in the Illinois Legislature and defeated him.

In 1805 Lakin and Cartwright were succeeded by Asa Shin and Moses Ashworth, and they continued in charge until the fall of 1806.

In 1807 Joseph Olesley and Frederick Hood were the regular preachers. Hood did not continue long as there was some objection raised against him on account of his connection with slavery. He declined traveling in this circuit, but Olesley continued. At the close of the year 1807 it was thought best to strike off the Illinois grant into a separate circuit, and Moses Ashworth was sent to take charge in 1808. A two weeks' circuit was established and this was soon after changed to a three weeks' circuit. The boundaries and work of the circuit continued to grow until in 1815 it was an eight weeks' circuit, yet had only one traveling preacher. Ashworth's last year on Silver Creek circuit, as it was called, closed with a great camp meeting held near Robertson's. It was a novel affair and was attended by great multitudes of people.

The old Bethel meeting house, erected in 1807, was the first Methodist church erected in Indiana, and in this church the first Christian meeting perhaps ever held in this part of the state was held this year. James Garner preached on the occasion from the following text: "We have seen His star in the East, and have come to worship Him."

Up to 1809 local brethren supplied the newly settled country, but in 1809 and 1810 there were marked revivals of religion. Preaching was introduced into Charlestown in 1809, and strange as it may seem at this day, no house could be found large enough to accommodate the crowds. The early camp meetings of those days were occasions where scenes were enacted which seem strange to those of our time and age. The nervous and hysterical state to which many of the hearers were wrought produced an excitement which was intense. Men and women often rolled on the ground and lay sobbing or shouting. An affection called the "jerks" prevailed at many meetings, and while under the influence the victim would plunge and pitch about with convulsive energy. The nerves of many became uncontrollable, and they became affected with what was called the "holy laugh," in which the mouth was distorted with a hideous grin, while the victim gave vent to a maniac's chuckle, and every muscle and nerve of the face twitched and jerked in horrible spasms. The exhortations of the workers moving among the audience, and the shoutings of hysterical enthusiasts or "converted" sinners, produced an indescribable confusion and excitement. Scenes such as these, or sometimes worse, prevailed at most of the religious meetings of this kind in those days. Happily they have disappeared and a quiet and more serious reflection has superseded the nervous hysteria which marked the great assemblages for public worship in the early years of the nineteenth century.

The War of 1812, and the incident brutalities and butcheries, which our British cousins incited the Indians to commit, was a setback to the spread of the Gospel throughout the whole state of Indiana. The traveling preachers continued to travel some time after the Indian disturbances began, but at last they gave it up and left the country, and local preachers supplied. One quarterly meeting, held about this time, within five miles of Charlestown, had neither presiding elder nor circuit preacher, and but a handful of people.

In 1819 occurred the second great revival, and its results were felt throughout the whole of the circuit. Such a thing as a Sunday school was unheard of for many years by the first settlers of the county, and the first proposal to start one was met with great opposition, and by some too, who were official members of the church, as being a reflection on the citizens and citizenship of the locality, as not being able to school their own children.

In 1825 the Illinois Conference was held at Charlestown, and embraced the whole of the states of Indiana and Illinois. Bishop McKendree and Bishop Roberts were in attendance, as was also Peter Cartwright. About 1821 the Silver Creek circuit was united with the Charlestown circuit. James Armstrong served this circuit for about two years, but it had grown so large that it was impossible for one man to perform the work.

WALL STREET METHODIST EPISCOPAL CHURCH, JEFFERSONVILLE.

The churches in the circuit were gradually becoming stronger, and in 1833 the church in Jeffersonville was separated from the circuit and made a station, of which the celebrated Edward R. Ames became the first pastor. During the pastorate of Reverends Moore and McMurray, trustees had already been appointed for the First Methodist church, namely; James Keigwin, Charles Slead, Andrew Fite, David Grismore, Aaron Applegate and Nelson Rozzle. The date of the appointment of the trustees is June 25, 1833, but the deed of the first church was not made until after 1840, by William Heart to James Keigwin, Charles Slead, David Grismore, Leonard Swartz and William D. Beach, as trustees. The church was finished in 1835. This church stood on Wall street, between Chestnut and Market streets, south of the alley. James Keigwin laid all the brick in the building as his subscription.

In 1840 Wall street church had grown so that an addition was built, making the building like a "hemp rope factory," as Dr. T. M. Eddy, one of the early pastors, remarked. In 1858 the necessity for a larger and more commodious house of worship becoming apparent, the question was vigorously discussed and January 11, 1859, at a quarterly meeting, on motion of William L. Beach, a committee was appointed to report a plan and estimates for a new church. The question of a site was a very absorbing one, and many places were considered, especially the lots upon which St. Augustine's Roman Catholic church and George H. Holzbog & Bros.' carriage factory now stand, but at last all agreed upon the lot where stood the house in which the first society was organized. The deed was given by Mrs. Ann Tuley on May 6, 1859, and June 6, 1859, the corner stone was laid. In October of the same year the brick work was completed, and April 22, 1860 the basement was dedicated by Bishop Thomas Bowman. In November, 1863, the steeple, including belfry, clock tower and spire, surmounted by a cross, was erected. The erection of this cross caused considerable dissention among the members as it was unfortunately not usual for Protestant churches to be surmounted by the Christian symbol. The main auditorium was not dedicated until July 16, 1865, under the pastorate of the Rev. J. K. Pye. The dedicatory sermon was preached by the Rev. Dr. Thomas M. Eddy upon the subject, "Now is the Judgment of this World; Now Shall the Prince of this World be Cast Out."

The total cost of the new edifice was near twenty-five thousand dollars. The Board of Trustees was composed of B. C. Pyle, William D. Beach, R. S. Heiskell, Peter Myers and William S. Jacobs, of whom Mr. Jacobs is the sole survivor, and to this day a trustee and a member, whom everyone delights to honor. The present edifice was enlarged by the addition of an organ loft in 1892.

The church has had two parsonage properties. The first was erected during the pastorate of Dr. T. M. Eddy in 1850, and consisted of four rooms. It was built upon the west half of the lot at the southwest corner of Wall and Chestnut streets and the east half was sold to satisfy a claim for brick work on the house. A number of years afterward the house was remodeled and enlarged and is now owned and occupied by Mrs. Elizabeth Liston. The last parsonage was erected during the pastorate of Rev. V. W. Tevis, and is one of the most modern and beautiful homes in the city. Upon the death of Felix Lewis, the church was able to obtain the lot adjoining the church on the corner, and the whole is now a very valuable piece of property.

The pastors of the Wall Street church, beginning with Benjamin Lakin, are as follows:

Benjamin Lakin 1802
Adjet McGuire 1803
Peter Cartwright 1804
Asa Shin and D. Young..1805
Frederick Hood 1806
Moses Ashworth 1807
Josiah Crawford 1808
Sela Payne 1809
Isaac Lindsey 1810
Gabriel Woodfill 1811
William McMahon and Thomas Nelson............................1812
James Garner 1813
Charles Harrison and Elijah Sutton 1814
Shadrack Ruark 1815
Joseph Kincaid 1816
Joseph Purnal 1817
John Cord 1818
David Sharp 1819
Calvin Ruter and Job W. Baker................................1820
Calvin Ruter and William Cravens.............................1821
James Armstrong 1822-23
Samuel Hamilton and Calvin Ruter.............................1824
James Thompson and Isaac Verner..............................1825
Allen Wiley and James Randle.................................1826
Allen Wiley and James Garner.................................1827
George Lock, Calvin Ruter and Enoch G. Ward..................1828
I. W. McReynolds and James Scott.............................1829
James Scott and I. W. McReynolds.............................1830
James L. Thompson 1831
William Moore and D. M. Murray...............................1832

Edward R. Ames 1833
W. V. Daniels 1834
Zech Gaines and John W. Bayless.................. 1835
John W. Bayless.................................. 1836
John Kearns 1837
William H. Good 1838-1839
T. C. Holliday 1840-1841
William V. Daniels 1842
Hosier Durbin 1843
William Morrow 1844
James Jones 1845
Walter Prescott 1846-1847
T. M. Eddy 1848-1849
James Hill 1850-1851
Jiles C. Smith 1852
Enoch G. Wood 1853-1854
F. A. Hester 1855-1856
S. B. Falkenberg 1857
J. W. Sullivan 1858-1859
J. S. Tevis 1860
T. G. Beharrel 1861-1862
Elijah D. Long and John K. Pye.............. 1863-1864
John K. Pye 1864-1865
William H. Harrison 1866
G. P. Jenkins 1867-1868-1869
J. G. Cheffee 1870-1871
J. W. Locke 1872-1873
W. W. Snyder 1874-1875
Rev. E. L. Dolph....................... 1876-1877-1878
John S. Tevis 1879-1880-1881
George L. Curtiss 1882-1883
G. P. Jenkins 1884
R. Roberts 1885-1886-1887
J. H. Doddridge 1888-1889
Virgil W. Tevis 1890-1891-1892
Charles Tinsley 1893-1894-1895-1896
James T. O'Neal....................... 1897-1898-1899
George D. Wolff 1900
Charles E. Asbury 1901-1902-1903-1904
John S. Ward 1905-1906-1907-1908

Among the most prominent men who have been pastors of Wall Street church may be mentioned Edward R. Ames, who became missionary secretary and later bishop.

The Rev. Moses Ashworth built the Bethel meeting house, and the Rev. James Garner preached the first Christmas sermon in this part of Indiana. During the pastorate of the Rev. J. W. Sullivan the present church building was begun.

The greatest revival ever held in Wall Street church was in the year 1867, and continued for one hundred days, during which time there were two hundred sixty confessed conversions and three hundred forty-nine accessions to the church.

Among the early class leaders were Andrew Fite, James Keigwin, Robert Heiskell and Charles Slead.

Among the members who contributed much to the success of the Wall Street church was Dr. Robert Curran. Doctor Curran was a holy man and one who took a lively interest in the church.

Robert Heiskell, William D. Beach, B. C. Pile, John W. Ray, I. N. Ingram, Rev. Samuel Bottorff, Jonathan Johnson and wife and others were prominent in the affairs of the church for many years.

Wall Street church has had several off-shoots: Port Fulton was organized in 1849; the German Methodist Episcopal church had its first members, men and women, from Wall Street. In 1868, twenty-two members of Wall Street organized Morton Chapel, later on called Morton Memorial Church South. Wesley Chapel in Ohio Falls, and Harrison Avenue Chapel, in Howard Park are also offsprings.

In 1867 the first organ was placed in the church and although its advent was the cause of much talk, yet no division nor withdrawals took place. In 1891 the Epworth League was organized. In 1859 the Woman's Missionary Society was organized by Mrs. Seymour. The Young Ladies' Missionary Society was organized a few years later, and the Standard Bearers, a society for young folks, still later. As far back as 1850 there was a flourishing sewing society.

At present Wall Street church has seven hundred forty full members, twenty-nine probationers and four hundred thirty scholars in the Sunday school. The church building is valued at fifteen thousand dollars and the parsonage at five thousand dollars.

PORT FULTON METHODIST EPISCOPAL CHURCH.

The church was organized in the year 1849. Among its first members were the following: Rev. E. L. Dolph, Nancy French, Mrs. Ault, Henry French, Ann Buckley, William Prather and Ann Prather. There were early circumstances that led to the formation of this church that in this space it will be impossible to print. At the session of the Indiana conference of 1850, Rev. F. W. White was appointed to Port Fulton charge, which embraced the following appointments: Fort Fulton, Asbury chapel, Louisville, Kentucky, (known as the Point) and Preston Street church, three appointments.

The stewards met in Asbury church and fixed the amount of the pastor's salary at one hundred dollars, besides an allowance for board and traveling expenses, which was raised outside of the membership.

The second Sabbath of May, 1850, the first Sunday school was organized in the east end of the "double house on the hill," as it was then called. At that time it was owned by Henry French, but is now owned by the Moore family.

It was seated with second-hand school benches while a nicely covered dry goods box was used as a pulpit. E. L. Dolph was chosen as the first superintendent, a position he held for a number of years.

The teachers were the following: Mrs. Martha Howard Baird, Miss Sallie French, Miss Mary Prather, Miss Frank Ault, now Mrs. Josiah Dorsey, Mrs. Lightcap, Mrs. Mary Prather Holmes.

Although the room in which the church was organized was small, yet a very successful revival meeting was held.

One of the first converts was Aaron Wootan, whose conversion was so wonderful that its influence affected the whole community.

Reverend White took up a subscription to build a church, and so successful was he that early in the spring of 1851 the erection of the church was commenced and was completed in time for dedication in the following July. The dedication sermon was preached by Rev. Thomas M. Eddy. The building cost one thousand six hundred dollars. In 1851 Port Fulton was attached to Wall Street. Revs. James Hill and F. S. Potts were appointed to the charge. From that time on the church began to grow in numbers and financial strength.

After this came the following pastors: Sheets, Collins, Curtis, Marlatt, Wood, Maule, Sargent, Sheets, O'Beyrne, Ruddell, Machlan, Kinnear, Sheets, Mendall, Beharrell, McMillan, Kennedy, Farr, Murphy, Reynolds, Jones, Grigsby, Thomas, Smith, Henninger, Stout, Dolph and Jerman, now serving his third year.

In June, 1899, subscription lists were opened for the purpose of raising money to build a parsonage, and with the generous assistance of Capt. E. J. Howard, of the ship yards, who gave them a fine lot, the parsonage was soon completed. Captain Howard was also the donor of the bell which hangs in the belfry of the church. In May, 1900, the semi-centennial of the founding of the church was most appropriately held.

At present the membership of Port Fulton church is about one hundred sixty-five. Its Sunday school has one hundred and twenty-five scholars and sixteen teachers. The church building, on the northwest corner of Market and Jefferson streets, is worth two thousand four hundred dollars and the parsonage at No. 110 Market street is worth about one thousand five hundred dollars.

CHARLESTOWN.

The town of Charlestown has a very prosperous and influential congregation of Methodists. Of the later history of the Charlestown church but little can be learned, but its earlier history is that of the grant, as the earliest services held in this locality were held near Charlestown. The church here is one of the three full stations in Clark county, Wall Street in Jeffersonville, and Port Fulton being the other two. The church building at Charlestown is a substantial brick structure. It was dedicated in 1854 by Bishop Ames. There is also a good parsonage, offering a comfortable and convenient home for the pastor. It is valued at three thousand dollars. The congregation numbers about three hundred souls.

NEW WASHINGTON CIRCUIT.

The New Washington Circuit at present consists of six chapels: New Washington, Mount Zion, New Hope, Bethlehem, Salem and Shiloh. Salem Chapel is about three miles southeast of Charlestown and was originally Gazaways, one of the first three societies organized in the county by Benjamin Lakin. The congregation now numbers sixty. The New Washington church at New Washington is not very strong, having only thirty-seven members reported at the last conference. Mount Zion was reported as having ninety members; New Hope, twenty; Bethlehem, seventy, and Shiloh, fifty.

Shiloh lays between Westport landing and Hibernia. It is one of those temples which we all turn to intuitively; one whose history awakens the happiest and tenderest emotions. Its first members were Thomas Allen and wife, John Lever and wife, Job Ingram and wife, Jacob Bottorff and family, John Hutchins and wife. Calvin and John Rutter were the first preachers. They were brothers, men devoted to the work they had chosen. In 1854 the old house of worship was replaced by a better building. This society is fairly prosperous.

The church at Bethlehem is the only one in the extreme east end of the county. The Methodist church in this end of the county sprang from a long series of successful revivals. On the same section where Jacob Giltner ran his horse mill in 1808, but on the northeast corner, lived Melsin Sargent. His house stood on the road which led to New Washington, one and one-half miles from the present post-office of Otto. Sargent was one of the first Methodists in this end of the county, and at his house the services of the denomination were held for many years. His house was always open to preaching, and was the regular place of worship up to 1836. Sargent moved to Jefferson county, Indiana, and died many years ago. The people who gathered at Sargent's were of various religious professions. Many of the richest experiences of this class were enjoyed there, while the church was just beginning to feel the healthful currents of a sound body politic. From these meetings the New Hope Methodist Episcopal church sprang into existence; but during the time which elapsed previous to 1836, the year the church building was erected, services were often held in the dwelling houses of Michael Berry and Eli Watkins. The church was erected in the year above mentioned, and was the first church of this denomination put up in the township. The old house was used until 1871, when it was replaced by another frame, thirty by forty-two feet. Rev. Calvin Ruter was probably the first preacher. He was a man of great influence among the members, and afterwards became presiding elder. Rev. Samuel Hamilton succeeded Mr. Ruter as presiding elder. He also was much admired for his excellent character. Rev. James L. Thompson, John McRunnels, Thomas Scott, Allen Wylie, James Garner and George Lock came in succession after Hamilton. Then came Enoch G. Wood, a person of great influence and possessed of an unblemished character. Rev. Joseph Taskington and John Miller were here in 1833 and 1834, the latter a man of many fine parts. Rev. Zachariah Games and Thomas Gunn came next, Mr. Gunn preaching in 1835. Revs. George Beswick and McElroy (the latter an Irishman and by profession a sailor), John Bayless, W. V. Daniels, were all here in 1836-37-38. Rev. John Rutledge served one year. After him came Rev. Isaac Owens, who preached in 1839-40-41. In 1843 Charles Bonner served the people. Rev. Constantine Jones was their circuit preacher for one year. Rev. Lewis Hulbert, assisted by Elisha Caldwell, was the preacher in 1844.

Then came Revs. William McGinnis, L. V. Crawford, John Malinder, Doctor Talbott, E. Flemming, Amos Bussey, and William Maupin. These latter persons bring it down to 1854. The first members were Eli Watkins, Melsin Sargent, John Tyson, Daniel Ketcham, Levi Ogle, Michael Berry, John W. Jones and Samuel Whiteside, all with their wives and a portion of their families.

HENRYVILLE CIRCUIT.

The Henryville Circuit consists of five chapels and is at present under the charge of the Rev. W. H. Thompson. The chapels are located as follows: Henryville at Henryville, Memphis at Memphis, Underwood at Underwood, Mount Olive and New Chapel in the adjacent country. The first preaching place in this community was Little Union, a school-house, which was built about the year 1830. It was a hewn log building with an old-fashioned fireplace. This building we are told was used by all denominations then worshipping in this community. This house was built about one-half mile northwest of Henryville, on the ground now known as the Little Union graveyard.

About the year 1835 the Methodists organized and built what was known as the Mount Zion Methodist Episcopal church. It was built on the farm of the Rev. Seymour Guernsey in the plat of ground now known as the Mount Zion cemetery. This house was built of hewn logs, many of them poplar, and was perhaps twenty-four by thirty-six feet in size. In 1839 the west end of the house was sawed out and an addition of frame added. This house was used as a preaching place until some time in the sixties. Henryville had grown to have enough members of the Methodist church to reasonably expect that service should be held in the town, so by the consent of the Presbyterians, the Methodists used the Presbyterian church, a frame structure, standing on the bank of Wolf Run, a few rods east of the present Henryville seminary. The old Mount Zion church underwent some repairs about this time, and was used for a number of years as a shelter in time of storm for those who came to bury their dead. About the year 1871 the society got together and concluded to build a church in Henryville. They selected a mechanic, known as Uncle Sammy Williams, as foreman, and the house was dedicated early in the year 1872 with the name of Williams Chapel. In this house the people worshiped until the year 1908. The church having been remodeled through the instrumentality of the pastor, Rev. Lit Peck, was re-dedicated April 26, 1908.

The Mount Olive Methodist Episcopal class was first known as the Mount Moriah class, which was organized in 1828 some three and a half miles southeast of the present town of Henryville. In 1859 or 1860 the class was moved nearly a mile from the former place to Oakland school-house, where the people worshiped regularly until 1871, when Mount Lebanon Presbyterian church was built. The Methodists worshiped with them in the same building until 1899 under Rev. U. G. Abbott, when the people began building the present frame building called Mount Olive church about one mile north of the Mount Lebanon Chapel, and three miles southeast of Henryville. It was completed under Rev. J. L. Cooper and dedicated in 1900.

Willey's Chapel, Methodist Episcopal class, was organized in 1885, in the Forest Grove school-house by Rev. J. M. Norton, where the people worshiped until 1886, when the present frame building was erected and dedicated. It stands about five miles southwest of Henryville. The class around which the people at Willey's chapel rallied was a few survivors of the old "Bowery Chapel" church, erected in early times about one mile west of Memphis. When Bowery ceased to be used for church purposes this class erected the old "Gum Log" meeting house at Blue Lick, which served as a place of meeting for many years, but at this time, 1886, had gone to decay, and most of the members had either died or scattered. The few remaining ones constituted the first class at Willey's chapel. The leaders were Joel Rose and John King.

The Underwood Methodist Episcopal class was organized in the year 1883, and was known as the Summit class. During this same year the frame church building was erected, where the people worshiped regularly until November, 1908, when under the pastorate of the Rev. W. H. Thompson, Ph. B., the church was enlarged and completely remodeled. This building was re-dedicated by the Rev. M. B. Hyde, D. D., the district superintendent of Seymour district.

Memphis Methodist Episcopal church was built by the Baptist society in 1870, but was sold the same year at Sheriff's sale to Daniel Guernsey, who turned it over to the Methodist congregation, which was at that time worshiping in the school-house. It stands in the present town of Memphis, having escaped the fire in 1901, which destroyed nearly the whole town.

HISTORY OF THE OTISCO CHURCH AND CIRCUIT.

The Otisco society was organized early in 1870 in the school-house, with only eleven members, none of which are now living. It was organized by Rev. Peter H. Bottorff, as local elder. He is now living on a farm in Utica township, near Utica, Indiana. At that time Enoch G. Wood was presiding elder. The following pastors served while they worshiped in the school-house: In the fall of 1870 Rev. W. H. Widman was sent on the work; his year was completed by Rev. Jacob Ruddle. Rev. A. M. Louden served one year, from 1871 to 1872. Rev. Thomas Brooks served one year, from 1872 to 1873; Rev. A. G. Aldridge one year, from 1873 to 1874. Rev. Henry Morrow, one year, from 1874 to 1875. Then came the Rev. W. H. Burton, who served three years in all, from 1875 to 1878. During his first year's work in the school-house, he, with the help of others, erected and completed the church which is now standing, and in June, 1876, on the 25th day of the month, the church was dedicated for the public worship of God, by the Rev. F. A. Hester, D. D. Brother Ed Covert is now the oldest living member uniting with the Methodist Episcopal church, in March of 1870. Sister Emma Nevelle, being the next oldest living member, both of these united during the pastorate of Rev. P. H. Bottorff. Brother J. A. Kirk, now living at this place was licensed as a local preacher in 1878, during the pastorate of Rev. J. T. O'Neal, D. D., who served as pastor two years, from 1878 to 1880. Brother Ed Kirk was given an exhorter's license by Rev. George Church, who served one year, from 1901 to 1902. The following pastors have served the church faithfully and well:

Rev. W. H. Burton, three years—1875 to 1878.
Rev. James T. O'Neal, two years—1878 to 1880.

Rev. T. W. Conner, two years—1880 to 1882.

Rev. D. T. Hedges, two years—1882 to 1884.

Rev. Isaac J. Turner, one year—1884 to 1885.

Rev. J. M. Norton, three years—1885 to 1888.

Rev. J. P. Maupin, two years—1888 to 1890.

Rev. J. T. Davis, part of one year—1890 to 1891.

Rev. J. S. Campbell, two years and remainder of J. T. Davis's year from 1891 to 1893.

Rev. A. R. Jones, three years—1893 to 1896.

Rev. U. G. Abbot, one year—1896 to 1897.

Rev. W. P. Wallace, one year—1897 to 1898.

Rev. T. J. Tone, one year—1898 to 1899.

Rev. Charles Rose, two years—1899 to 1901.

Rev. George Church, one year—1901 to 1902.

Rev. J. P. Maupin, two years—1902 to 1904.

Rev. D. G. Griffith, two years—1904 to 1906.

Rev. James W. Trowbridge, two years—1906 to 1908.

Rev. James O. Scott came in 1908 and is the present minister sent by the conference held at Shelbyville, Indiana.

The church has continued to grow from her infancy with only eleven members until now, during the present minister's pastorate, Rev. J. O. Scott, she has reached almost one hundred members.

Other chapels in the Otisco circuit are: Pleasant Ridge, a class of sixty-five members; Beswick chapel, a class of thirty-nine members; Nabb's chapel at Nabbs, with a class of thirty-five members; New Bethel, a class with ninety members, and Lexington, a class with thirty-five members.

The church at Sellersburg and Pleasant Grove are in charge of the Rev. E. F. Schneider. Sellersburg has a well built frame church and a parsonage of a total probable value of six thousand dollars; two hundred ninety-four members of the church and two hundred and thirty members of the Sunday school. Pleasant Grove has a class of fifty-five members.

Sellersburg circuit consists of chapels as follows: Jacob's chapel, situated on the New Albany road between Sellersburg and New Albany, fifty-six members.

Ebenezer church stands three miles west of Memphis and fourteen miles west of New Albany. This church was built in 1842 and re-built in 1888. It has sixty members.

Bennettsville Methodist Episcopal church stands in the town of Bennettsville, ten miles northwest of New Albany, on the Monon Railroad. This church was built in 1852 and re-built in 1891. It has sixteen members.

Asbury Methodist Episcopal church stands five miles north of Jeffersonville on the Baltimore & Ohio Railroad, and two miles east of Cementville. This church was built in 1879. It has thirty-eight members.

The Jeffersonville circuit comprises chapels on Harrison Avenue in Howard Park, and Wesley Chapel, in Ohio Falls. Both of these chapels are flourishing and give promise of being influential factors in the growth of these localities.

UTICA CIRCUIT.

The Utica circuit consists of three chapels: Utica, New Chapel and Union. The date of the New Chapel church is not exactly known, but it is given as very near the date of 1800. It belonged to the oldest circuit in the state. As early as the year 1793 preaching had been held about a mile above Utica, and several Methodists from Louisville had their membership here on account of there being no church class at home.

The organization of the Utica class was effected at the residence of Basil R. Prather, whose house for a number of years before had furnished a place of worship. Bishop McKinley was the minister in charge on the day of ordination. About 1804 a round-log house was erected on an acre of land in tract number thirty-seven, deeded to the Methodist Episcopal church by Jeremiah Jacobs and Walter Prather. It was built by subscription, and worth, when completed, about two hundred and fifty dollars. It had but one window, clap-board roof and the old style of stone chimney. In 1811 the house was torn away, and a new hewed-log house erected twenty-two by thirty-six feet, one and one-half stories high. It had four windows, a shingle roof, stove, pulpit, comfortable seats, and so on. This house was also built by subscription, and cost two hundred dollars. In 1836 the hewed-log house was torn away and a third, built of brick, forty-five by fifty-five feet, took its place. It had eleven windows, was one and one-half stories high, had three doors, and an altar and pulpit. This house was also built by subscription, and cost one thousand three hundred eighty-two dollars. In 1867 the chapel was repaired at a cost of one thousand four hundred dollars.

Among the first preachers at the new chapel of the Methodist Episcopal church were Revs. Josiah Crawford in 1808, Silas Payne in 1809. Isaac Lindsey and Thomas Nelson in 1810-11, William McMahan and Thomas Nelson in 1812. James Garner, Elijah Sitters, Shadrick Rucker, Joseph Kincaid, Joseph Powel, John Schrader, David Sharpe, C. W. Ruter, Robert M. Baker and William Cravens, all before 1820.

The Utica Methodist Episcopal circuit was formed in 1843, with William V. Daniels as the first presiding elder. Rev. Charles Benner was the first traveling preacher. He was followed by Emmaus Rutledge in 1845 and James Hill in 1846; Rev. Elijah Whitten was in charge in 1847, and then for one year each the following persons: Revs. Lewis Hulbert, John A. Brouse,

Jacob Myers and Jacob Bruner. These men were all here before 1852. Rev. Mr. Daniels served as presiding elder until 1850, when he was succeeded by Rev. John Herns, who acted for one year. Revs. C. R. Ames and William Dailey were presiding elders in 1851-52.

Connected with the New Chapel church is a handsome cemetery, enclosed by a stone wall on the east side and at both ends. A number of fine monuments are scattered about. The graveyard looks decidedly neat, more so than any other in the county as far from Jeffersonville. The yard is a rectangle; has about four acres of land, and is in keeping with the church of which it forms a part. There is also a good Sunday school carried on at this point during the year. This church and Sabbath school are fair exponents of the people in this region. They are located about one mile northeast of Watson post-office.

New Chapel has at present one hundred twenty-two members. It was originally called Jacob's Chapel and was one of the three first classes organized by Benjamin Lakin.

The Union Methodist Episcopal church, in the northwest corner of the township, was composed formerly of members from the Lutheran church, by whom really the Methodist church was formed. Among the first members of the Lutheran church were Jacob Grisamore and wife and David Lutz, Sr., and wife. Rev. Mr. Fremmer, of New Albany, who traveled the entire country, was one of the first preachers. The original church building was a log structure. Some few years after 1830 a brick church was erected by the neighborhood, the old Lutheran members having moved off or died in many instances. This church derived its name from the fact that all denominations worshiped in the first house. After forty-odd years of use and much repairing, a proposition was made to buy or sell by both the Christian and Methodist Episcopal people, who were the leading denominations. At the sale the Methodists paid two hundred fifty dollars for the undivided half. The church was then repaired and used for a few years more, until it needed repairing again. At last a movement was made to build a new house. Money was solicited, a kiln of brick was burned on the ground, and now a handsome building is situated almost on the old site. The property is worth, including the cemetery, about eight thousand dollars. The land on which the church stands was originally deeded to the Lutheran denomination by Jacob Grisamore, but it has since become the property of the Methodists. Mathias Crum and wife, David Spangler and wife, Charles Ross and wife, were some of the first members of the Methodist class. For preachers they had, before 1810, Revs. Josiah Crawford, Silas Payne, Thomas Nelson and others, who preached at the New Chapel church. This class has now about ninety members.

In the western part of the county in the fall of 1891, Pomona Chapel was built as the result of a series of meetings held in the school-house near by.

MORTON MEMORIAL CHURCH, SOUTH.

For several years during the latter part of the sixties a little band of eleven Methodists met regularly and held services in the old engine house on Maple street between Pearl and Mulberry, and called themselves Southern Methodists. The names of the eleven charter members of the church are Mary E. Welburne, Edwin H. Welburne, J. R. Lingenfelter, Esther F. Lingenfelter, Sarah Potter, Martha Campbell, Caddie Bosworth, Judith A. Bellis, George McKensie, G. W. Baxter and Anna L. Guernsey. Of these four are still living, and are Mrs. Potter, Mrs. Bosworth, G. W. Baxter and Esther F. Lingenfelter. This was in 1868, and Rev. Samuel W. Speer, D. D., was the pastor from November 8, 1868, until July, 1869. At that time Rev. Silas Newton became pastor and remained until October of the same year. Rev. Jacob Ditzler was sent as pastor in 1869, but did not serve. In the year 1869 the idea of building a church edifice was conceived and carried out, and the first Southern Methodist church in Jeffersonville was erected at Maple and Mulberry streets and was dedicated March 13, 1870, by Bishop Kavanaugh. The first pastor for this new church was the Rev. R. D. Pool, who came July 21, 1870, and remained until the conference was held four months later, when the Rev. Thomas G. Bosley was sent October 1, 1870, to become pastor and he remained five months.

Irregular supply was furnished from March, 1871, for three months, and on July 30, 1871, John Lewis came as pastor and served three months. In October, 1871, Rev. F. G. Brodie became pastor and he remained six months, and was followed by Rev. J. E. Martin, who occupied the pulpit for six months also.

In October, 1872, Rev. Samuel Lovelace was installed as pastor and he served the church faithfully for three years and was followed by Rev. J. M. Phillips in October, 1875, who was pastor for two years. Rev. George Brush became pastor in October, 1877, and remained two years and the Rev. George Foskett came in October, 1879, and was pastor for four years and was greatly loved by all the members.

Rev. Granville Lyons served one year, coming in October, 1883, and he was followed by the Rev. John M. Crow in September, 1884, and he in turn was followed by the Reverend Gaines.

About this time the Big Four bridge was planned and the railroad company purchased of the church trustees the old building and the members concluded to build a larger and better church. For some time after the building was abandoned the church was used by a religious sect who called themselves the Feet Washers, or All Saints. Later, when a split occurred in the Christian church, some of the members secured the building and held services there for about two years, calling themselves the Second Christian church.

17

After this the colored people held church services in the building.

In 1893 the Morton Chapel Methodist Episcopal church was erected on Locust street, between Maple street and Court avenue, and the following ministers have served as pastors in the new edifice: Revs. Charles Crow, G. B. Overton, George Campbell, B. F. Bigg, J. M. Lawson, J. F. Cherry, J. B. Butler and S. M. Miller. In 1887 the membership consisted of three hundred sixty members and now over four hundred are enrolled on the church books.

At the time when the old church was in use the parsonage was at 100 Ohio avenue, at the foot of Maple street. When Morton chapel was erected a parsonage was erected adjoining the church.

The name Morton Memorial church was given after the death of Dr. David Morton, who was secretary of the church extension. He had been very active in raising funds for this church.

THE GERMAN METHODIST EPISCOPAL CHURCH, JEFFERSONVILLE.

This congregation was organized in 1845 by the Rev. Conrad Muth. The first church building was erected on Locust street in 1851 by the Rev. G. Heller. The second church building was erected on the site of the present building in 1877. at the corner of Maple and Watt streets by the Rev. Jacob Brockstahler. The congregation was organized originally from among the early German settlers, and it is still largely composed of the descendants of these people. At the present time the church is really more English than German, German preaching being retained only in the Sunday morning service. Its present membership is one hundred three. In 1908 a beautiful pipe organ was installed. The officers of the church are Jacob Schwaninger, C. C. Prinz, Charles Strauch, Charles Roth, John Francke, William Seibert, Albert Schwaninger, Albert Peters and Alfred Holzbog.

CHAPTER XXIV.

THE PRESBYTERIAN CHURCH IN CLARK COUNTY.

THE CHARLESTOWN CHURCH.

Presbyterianism in Clark county began with the organization of the church at Charlestown in 1812, by the Rev. Joseph P. Lapsley. This was the second Presbyterian church in the state, the first being "The Presbyterian church of Indiana," organized near Vincennes in 1806.

It is impossible to give any of the particulars of the early days of the Charlestown church, as there is no record of the first eight years of its life. The first book of records in possession of the church contains this statement on its first page: "Charlestown church was organized in the year 1812; but no record was kept of its proceedings until April, 1820, at which time there were thirty-nine members, of whom fourteen were the heads of families." The first minister was the Rev. John Todd, but of his origin or end we know nothing. He came out of the mists of obscurity, labored well in this field for a few years and then disappeared. He probably began his ministry in Charlestown in 1815 or 1816 and closed it in September, 1824. The Rev. John T. Hamilton came in the fall of this year and remained until April, 1827. In the spring of 1827 the Rev. Leander Cobb was called and remained until 1838. During his pastorate the church prospered and increased in membership from sixty-eight to ninety-three. In March, 1839, the Rev. William Orr took charge and remained until March, 1841. In August, 1843, the Rev. H. H. Cambern was installed as pastor and remained in charge until 1853. He was a man of strong character and made his influence felt in educational as well as spiritual matters. Under his leadership the "Barnett Academy" was built. This school was in existence for a number of years and during its life did much for the mental growth and advancement of the community.

In July, 1853, the Rev. John S. Hays came and remained until March, 1857. Mr. Hays was a young man, fresh from the seminary, this being his first charge. He was a genial, popular and earnest man and made a strong impression upon the community. His departure was regretted by all.

The Rev. Henry E. Thomas held the pastorate from 1857 until September, 1859. In his manner he was dignified, in his habits, studious and scholarly, and was careful and faithful in the discharge of his pastoral duties. The church was ministered to until October, 1862, by the Rev. J. L. Matthews, when he was succeeded by the Rev. C. B. Davidson. Mr. Davidson remained until the fall of 1864. The Rev. Henry Keigwin was in charge from April, 1865, until October, 1867. Mr. Keigwin was a brother of the late Col. James Keigwin, of the Forty-ninth Indiana Volunteer Infantry, during the War of the Rebellion.

In November, 1867, the Rev. William Torrance took charge of the church and remained until October, 1871. He was a man greatly beloved by all, both as a man and as a minister. Faithful as a pastor and eloquent as a preacher, he impressed himself most powerfully upon the church and community.

In January, 1872, the Rev. J. W. Blythe was called to the charge, and he served until his death in 1875.

The Rev. Samuel Barr came in November, 1875, and remained until the fall of 1879. Under his leadership the church prospered, the greatest result of his labors being the erection of the present beautiful and commodious brick church in 1877. The old church which this building replaced was built upon ground deeded to the Presbyterian church by John Work, one of the pioneers of Clark county, and one of the very early members of the church. The old building served for more than fifty years as a house worship and at one time was one of the best church edifices in Indiana. Among the prominent men who shouldered the burden of building this first church may be mentioned Samuel McCampbell, Judge James Scott, James McClung and Jacob Simmers.

Since the time of Mr. Barr the following ministers have served the Charlestown church: The Revs. M. E. McKillip, W. E. B. Harris, W. M. Cutler, J. C. Garrett, B. W. Tyler, S. D. Young, F. R. Zugg, E. O. Fry. The church has at present one hundred sixty-one members and a Sunday school of seventy-five scholars.

THE FIRST PRESBYTERIAN CHURCH IN JEFFERSONVILLE.

On February 16, 1816, a church of Presbyterians was organized at Jeffersonville, called the Union church of New Albany and Jeffersonville, and composed of residents of both places. It was organized by the Rev. James McGready, under commission of the General Assembly. In this church the Hon. Thomas Posey, Governor of Indiana, then residing here, was a ruling elder. The organization was only temporary and by the removal of the members to New Albany was afterward transferred to become the First church of that city.

The First Presbyterian church of Jeffersonville was organized by a committee of Salem Presbytery May 22, 1830, with twelve members. Samuel Merriwether was elected ruling elder. On June 1, 1830, the Rev. Michael Remley was received as stated supply, and remained with the church until

September 28, 1831. Many of the members were lost by death and removal, but not being discouraged, the remaining ones began the erection of a small brick church on lower Market street, now occupied by the German Reformed congregation. The church lot was donated by Dr. Samuel Merriwether, and the means to build the house were contributed by him in a large measure. James Keigwin, of the Methodist church, aided materially, and the corner-stone was laid September 24, 1832, by the Rev. Mr. Fleiner, pastor at that time.

Up to December, 1833, the church seems to have had no permanent minister, but on December 1, 1833, the Rev. Edward P. Humphrey, D. D., was called as stated supply, and served until the summer of 1835. At this time the membership was eighteen, only two of whom were male members.

On January 1, 1836, the Rev. P. S. Clelland began his ministry in this church, and remained until the troubles of 1837-1838, known as the New and Old School controversy, began. The pastor and two of the elders, Messrs. Heiskell and Rodgers, adhered to the new school body, and they carried with them almost the entire membership; but it was not long before they began to take letters to the churches of the other denominations in the town. Doctor Merriwether fitted up a room in his residence for the members of the old church to worship in. This body of Presbyterians finally purchased the church from the new school party, who had kept possession of it, and called the Rev. H. H. Cambern as pastor. He was an energetic, active, faithful man and served until the winter of 1841, when he resigned to accept a call to Charlestown. The Rev. John Clark Bayless was called and entered upon his labors here October 9, 1842, and was ordained and installed as pastor June 30, 1843. He resigned his pastorate in the summer of 1844. Mr. Bayless was a splendid preacher, strong mentally and a successful pastor, who endeared himself greatly to his congregation. The Rev. W. H. Moore was stated supply from 1845 to 1848. From the fall of 1848 to the fall of 1851 the Rev. W. W. Hill, D. D., of Louisville, supplied the church. On November 18, 1851, the Rev. R. H. Allen accepted a call as stated supply and on November 6, 1853, was called as pastor. The regular quarterly communions were established under his ministry and in 1853 the church had one of its greatest revivals. It was during these meetings that Doctor Merriwether died. April 13, 1856, Mr. Allen resigned and the Rev. Dr. Thomas E. Thomas supplied until November 8, 1856.

On May 13, 1857, the Rev. S. F. Scovel, a graduate from the seminary at New Albany was called as supply, and on September 6, 1857, was elected pastor, his ordination and installation taking place October 18, 1857. He had a prosperous pastorate, and it was during his ministry here that the present church was built. The foundations were laid in August, 1860, and the lecture room was dedicated to the worship of God in December, 1860. The complete building was dedicated in October, 1864, Dr. James Wood, of Hanover College, preaching the dedication sermon.

In the latter part of December, 1860, Mr. Scovel resigned, but regular services were kept up until the Rev. Thomas F. Crowe, D. D., began his ministry May 1, 1862. The pastorate of Doctor Crowe lasted until his death, January 13, 1871, and was one of healthy growth in numbers and influence.

Shortly after Doctor Crowe's death the Rev. J. M. Hutchinson was invited and on April 26, 1871, he was installed. Mr. Hutchinson's labors were abundantly rewarded, and his long pastorate lasting until his death, April 2, 1896, was one of sound growth in all lines of church work. His untimely death was a loss not only to the church, his family and his wide acquaintanceship, but to the city as well.

On June 10, 1896, Rev. J. P. Hearst, Ph. D., was elected pastor, and was installed October 7, 1896. Doctor Hearst resigned on the 11th day of April, 1899. On the 16th day of August, 1899, Rev. John Simonson Howk, D. D., was elected pastor and was installed October 19, 1899.

A church manse was begun February, 1900, and completed in the summer of that year. This building is situated in the rear of the church at No. 222 Walnut street, and furnishes the pastor a commodious, convenient and beautiful home.

Doctor Howk resigned as pastor October 1, 1908, and on the 23d day of December, 1908, Rev. C. I. Truby was elected pastor and occupied the pulpit for the first time January 31, 1909.

Among those who have taken prominent parts in church work may be mentioned Henry E. Thomas, an elder in the forties; William Lackey, an elder in the fifties, and Elders James W. Gilson, John G. Fenton, Charles Paddox, Abraham Carr, Dr. O. S. Wilson, W. H. Fogg, John S. Hall, Thomas Caise, George C. Zinck, William Smart, Prof. R. L. Butler and Charles D. Kiernan. But of those who bore the burden when it was heaviest and who labored the hardest for the upbuilding of the church no names can be written higher than those of Dr. Samuel Merriwether in early days, and James H. McCampbell, in later ones. Capt. Addison Barrett, an elder, and for many years the superintendent of the Sunday school, was an example of dignified Christian manhood and lovable character seldom encountered.

PISGAH PRESBYTERIAN CHURCH.

The old Pisgah Presbyterian church on Camp creek, three miles east of New Washington, was organized on the 27th day of February, 1816, at the house of Alexander Walker by the Rev. James McGready, a missionary under the direction of the General Assembly of the Presbyterian church. The Pisgah church was supplied by missionaries until the year 1819, when the members of the Pisgah church with the Rev. Samuel Shanon presiding, elected the Rev. John M. Dickey pastor, and appointed two of the elders to confer with the

New Lexington church in preparing a call.* This call was laid before the Louisville Presbytery of Kentucky in April by Mr. Walker and accepted by Rev. John M. Dickey, who was a regularly installed pastor of the two churches on the first Saturday of August, 1819, at Lexington, Scott county, Indiana, Rev. Isaac Reed preaching the installation sermon, Rev. David C. Banks presiding and giving the charge. J. M. Dickey settled in the bounds of New Lexington church and continued there until January, 1827. About the year 1837 the Presbyterian church divided, forming two separate congregations known as the Pisgah church, New School, and the New Washington church, Old School. The new school congregation retained the old church building, the old school going to New Washington. The early members of the Pisgah church were true, devoted Christian men, who were guided by a conscientious regard for law and justice. Among these early members were Alexander Walker, John Henderson and John Matthews, with their wives and families. The early life of the church was prosperous, but it received a set-back after the controversy arose which divided it into two parts, and Presbyterianism has never been very strong in that part of the county since.

THE MOUNT VERNON PRESBYTERIAN CHURCH, NEW MARKET.

The Mount Vernon Presbyterian church at New Market was organized in June, 1833, with fourteen members. The Rev. Enoch Martin preached to the settlers in this locality about the year 1830. Peter Amick and John Cortner were the first ruling elders and they also acted as deacons. It was owing to the labors of such men as these that the unity of the Presbyterian church was preserved, and the code of morals which she so untiringly maintains, kept to a respectable grade.

In 1839 the first Sunday school was started with John Covert and George Stith as superintendents, but the school has been allowed to die out. During the history of the church there have been received into membership about four hundred fifty members. At present the membership is forty. The present church was built in 1874, and it stands on the site of the old church. The list of the fourteen charter members of the Mount Vernon church represent some of the oldest families around New Market. They were Abraham Cortner, Levi Amick, John Covert, Gideon Amick, Daniel Cortner, Margaret Amick, Barbara Cortner, Mary Amick, Elizabeth Cortner, Catharine Cortner, Fama Cortner, Sophia Amick, Gilbert Ray and Elizabeth Ray.

THE OWEN CREEK PRESBYTERIAN CHURCH.

An application was made to Salem Presbytery in 1840. The Presbytery appointed a committee consisting of the Rev. James Wood and the Rev. William Orr, and William McMillan as elder. These men met on Saturday, June

13, 1840, and organized Owen Creek Presbyterian church, with the following charter members: William Crawford and his wife, Jane; Mary Ann Crawford, Catherine McNulty, William McGhee, father of the Rev. Clark McGhee, and his wife, Tamar, Charlotte Henderson, Martha McGhee, Jacob Bare and his wife, Polly; Harriet Taggart, Rebecca Ray, James McGhee and Joseph Bare. William Crawford and Jacob Bare were elected elders at that time. The Presbytery appointed the Rev. Samuel Orr as supply for the year, from May 1, 1840, and he was succeeded by the Rev. Josiah Crawford, who served from 1841 to 1848. The Rev. H. H. Cambern came next and supplied from 1848 to 1852, when the Rev. Josiah Crawford returned and served until 1887. The Rev. E. B. Harris came in 1887, Rev. William A. Cutler in 1889, Rev. W. B. Brown in 1892, Rev. J. M. Oldfather in 1896.

During the life of this church it has had three young men brought up under its care: Rev. C. R. McGhee, Dr. J. F. Baird and Dr. William Baird. The present brick church was erected about 1842, and the Sunday school was also started about this time. The present elders are C. L. Bare, W. W. Taggart and S. E. Taggart. The congregation numbers seventy-five.

THE NEW WASHINGTON PRESBYTERIAN CHURCH.

The early history of the New Washington church is identical with that of Pisgah. The memorable pastorate of the Rev. John M. Dickey is dear to to the New Washington church as well as Pisgah. It was under his pastorate that the commodious brick church was built, and his residence, a substantial hewed log house, plastered and weatherboarded, built in 1827, still stands in a good state of preservation on the farm now owned by his grandson, W. A. Britan. It was also under his pastorate that the branch church was erected at Bethlehem. He was a great believer in higher education and induced Thomas Stevens, a wealthy member of his church, to build a seminary or boarding school on his farm near Bethlehem. Teachers were brought from the East, and Mr. Dickey lived here for a number of years and boarded the teachers and some of his pupils. He was also instrumental in the founding of Hanover and Wabash Colleges. In the unhappy division of the Presbyterian church in 1838, about one-third of the membership of old Pisgah withdrew and formed another church under the name of the Old School church. Their first pastor was the Rev. James A. McKee, who was instrumental in building their church in 1841. It still stands, the home of the united church and a monument to their fidelity. The old Pisgah church building having become much cracked it was considered dangerous, and it was torn down, the brick being used in the home of W. A. Britan. The New School division also built a church in New Washington, a church and seminary building combined, the lower part for the church and the upper rooms for the school. It was used as such for a number of years until the public schools were started when it was sold to the township and for many years used by it for school purposes. The present high school build-ing stands on its site. Mr. Dickey served this church faithfully for thirty years, until his death in 1849. He rests with many of his fold in the old Pisgah cemetery. A simple marble slab marks his grave, on which is inscribed: "Rev. John M. Dickey; died May 21, 1849, aged fifty-nine years, eleven months and five days. A pioneer preacher of the Presbyterian church. He was a good man, full of faith and of the Holy Ghost, and many people were added unto the Lord." Some of the pastors after him were his son, Rev. N. S. Dickey, Rev. Enoch Martin, Rev. John Gerrish, Rev. Josiah Crawford, Rev. John Creath, Rev. Isaac More, Rev. W. H. Brown and the Rev. J. M. Old-father, D. D. In 1870 the two divisions were happily united, taking the name, "New Washington Church," and in 1902 the Bethlehem branch became a separate church, retaining the old church name, Pisgah. Since its organization eight hundred ten persons have been connected with it, and some of its mem-bers have become distinguished ministers of the Gospel, among these being the Rev. N. S. Dickey, whose son the Rev. S. C. Dickey, D. D., is the promoter and manager of the Winona Chautauqua; the Rev. J. L. Taylor, D. D., of Fairmount Park, New Jersey; the Rev. Joseph Taylor Britan, of Yonkers, New York, and the Revs. Homer and Virgil Scott.

Sunday schools were organized about 1850, and have continued until the present time, the membership being about forty. The church membership is now sixty-five.

Henry F. Schowe, James Graves and W. A. Britan are the elders, and John H. Ferry and Robert Brentlinger are the deacons.

THE BETHLEHEM PRESBYTERIAN CHURCH.

The Bethlehem Presbyterian church was founded some time in the thirties, while the Rev. John M. Dickey was pastor of the Pisgah church, near New Washington. Mr. Dickey had founded his seminary and boarding school on Mr. Stevens' farm near Bethlehem, and it was in active operation at an early day. The church building there must have been completed in 1842. In 1902 the Bethlehem branch became a separate church and it retained the old church name of Pisgah.

THE PRESBYTERIAN CHURCH AT NABBS.

In March, 1885, the session of the Lexington church decided to send the Rev. Frank M. Gilchrist to establish a preaching point here. He began by holding services in the school-house until the Rev. George Ernest came and held a series of protracted meetings. About twenty-five persons were received into membership and the church was organized December 5, 1885. The following were the charter members: Anna Belle Tilford, Lizzie Lukenbill, Rose Cole, Mary Izzard, Robert Henderson, Sarah Alice Henderson, Franklin Henderson, Addie Henderson, James C. Bussey, John M. Graves, William L. Tilford, John Boyd, Frank Bussey, Edwin Lukenbill, George Cyrus Bussey, Ella Bussey, John Tilford, Mary Tilford, Hugh R. Ursher, Mary Ursher and Mary E. Tafflinger.

August 19th, preceding the organization of the church, William Gray deeded a lot to the church and subscriptions were started toward erecting a building. With about four hundred and fifty dollars raised locally and further assistance from the board of church extension, a church was built and opened Saturday night, June 18, 1887. Rev. F. M. Gilchrist preached to a large congregation, but the happy anticipations of the dedication the next day were rudely broken by the complete demolition of the building by fire that night. Plans for rebuilding were made immediately and in May, 1888, the second church was dedicated, the Rev. T. G. Bosley preaching the dedicatory sermon. The following pastors have served this church since its organization:

Rev. George Ernest 1885-1886
Rev. F. M. Gilchrist 1886-1887
Rev. James Gilchrist 1887-1889
Rev. J. M. Montgomery...........................1889-1890
Rev. T. G. Bosley...............................1890-1891
Rev. W. C. Broady 1892-1900
Rev. D. B. Whimster.............................1901-1903
Rev. Trigg Thomas..............................1903-1904
Rev. W. D. Malcome   1904

The present church building was erected in the years 1887-1888. The Sunday school was started in 1884.

Previous to 1901 this church had been a branch of the Lexington church, but on March 25th of this year it was organized into a separate church with a membership of thirty-nine souls. A series of protracted meetings held at this time resulted in twelve additions. The first elders were John Kennedy, W. D. Tilford and Sanford K. Peck.

THE PRESBYTERIAN CHURCH AT UTICA.

April 10, 1839, when G. C. Zinck came to Utica, there was a small Presbyterian church here, consisting of Robert McGee and wife, Theophilias Robinson and wife, Jacob Middlecoff and wife and daughter, Elizabeth and Miss Sallie Byers. Messrs. Robinson, McGee and Middlecoff were then acting elders. The division in the Presbyterian church had taken place just before this in 1838, into the New and Old School. Mr. Robinson had identified himself with the New School church just before he moved here from New Washington, and after being elected elder here, attended Salem Presbytery, it being a New School Presbytery, and had this church enrolled with Salem Presbytery. The other members of the church were Old School in sentiment, and the New School Presbytery being short of ministerial strength, were not able to supply the church with preachers but very rarely. About 1841 John C. Bayless and family moved here from Louisville, he having been an elder in the First Presbyterian church for years and Dr. William Orr and family moved here from Covington, and being in the regular enjoyment of the means of grace felt the loss of it and would have been satisfied if the New School Presbytery could have supplied the church with preaching, but that could not be done. Mr. Bayless drew up a petition to the Old School Presbytery, of New Albany, which was signed by all the members of the church to be organized into an Old School church. New Albany Presbytery granted the request and appointed a committee to effect the organization and appointed Rev. Josiah Crawford the stated supply. He continued preaching here for seven years, every other Sabbath. Mr. Bayless and Doctor Orr were also elected elders in the new organization. Mr. Robinson declined to unite with the new organization. The church prospered and God visited the little church with a revival of wondrous power; by it the church more than doubled itself as to the eldership in the church. In the absence of the church records, the writer must speak from memory. Dr. Robert Sprowl came here from the Charlestown church. Some of the former elders having moved away, Doctor Sprowl was elected elder and was also a very efficient one. G. C. Zinck was elected shortly after and George Summers was elected in due time. N. B. Wood and Moses W. Tyler and a Mr. Patterson were the next called to the eldership and Marion Gunter followed. John Tyler is one of the present elders.

MOUNT LEBANON PRESBYTERIAN CHURCH, HENRYVILLE.

The Mount Lebanon church was organized on May 22, 1853, in the Steuart meeting-house near the Lexington road, and moved to the Mount Lebanon church in 1871. There were ten charter members, all from the Mount Vernon church; Mrs. Polly Nicolls was received by profession of faith. A committee of two, the Rev. J. G. Atterbury and Elder Haines, from the Salem Presbytery, assisted in the organization. William Hartman was elected ruling elder and Cyrus Park, deacon.

The Sunday school here was organized in the early forties, by the Cumberland church, and has continued down to the present day. The present church building was erected in 1871. There have been two hundred fourteen members of this church, all told, with a present membership of forty-five.

THE OTISCO PRESBYTERIAN CHURCH.

The Otisco church was organized December 11, 1875, with eighteen charter members. There have been received into membership of this church one hundred sixteen persons, with fifty on the roll at the present time. The building now occupied by this congregation was built by the German Lutherans in 1860. In 1882 the Sunday school was organized, its membership being fifty now. The following ministers have served this church since 1875:

Rev. John McCrae until.............................1879
Rev. Engstrom until 1880
Reverend Buck until 1881
Rev. M. E. McKillip until.........................1882
Rev. George Ernest until.........................1886
Rev. James Gilchrist until.......................1889
Rev. I. I. St. John until........................1890
Rev. Alexander Hartman until.....................1891
Rev. W. C. Broady until 1900
Rev. D. B. Whimster until........................1903
Rev. F. A. M. Thomas until.......................1904
Rev. W. D. Malcome until.........................1906
Rev. E. Fry, present pastor.

The first elders were William Hartman, M. J. Lewelln, and the first deacon was Francis Watt. The present elders are W. R. Hunter, M. J. Lewellen, W. T. Montgomery and P. R. Lewellen. The present deacons are P. C. Hartman, Phillip Dayes, W. T. Montgomery and John W. Bower.

MOUNT ZION PRESBYTERIAN CHURCH.

The Mount Zion church was organized at Pleasant Hill in 1876 with thirteen charter members. The church building was erected at this time, but it burned down in the fall of 1892, and was rebuilt at Mount Zion in 1893. It was dedicated November 12, 1893, by the Rev. Mr. Vandyke, of New Albany. The Sunday school was organized in early days. This church was first organized at Henryville, and its building was used as a place of worship for a great many years until the members became so scattered that it was abandoned. It was in after years that it was reorganized at Pleasant Hill by the Rev. John McCrae. The following ministers have served Mount Zion church: Revs. John McCrae, Theodore McCoy, George Ernest, W. C. Broady, W. E. Prather, Clinton H. Gillingham, John Engstrom, I. I. St. John, William Lewis, R. H. Bateler, J. M. Oldfather, D. D., and the Rev. L. V. Rule. The first elders were Thomas Lewellen, David Cass and William T. McClure. The first deacon was Charles Franke.

Since 1876 there have been received into this church about one hundred members, and at present the roll shows forty-three. The membership of the Sunday school is forty. The present elders are George F. Guernsey, Michael Fetter and T. J. McClure. The present deacons are C. S. Dunlevy and Charles Fetter.

HEBRON PRESBYTERIAN CHURCH.

The Hebron church was organized about three miles east of Underwood on November 17, 1894, with fifteen charter members. The first elders were William F. Zeller, Fred Ester, and the first deacon was Charles Does. There have been received into membership here sixty-six persons. The membership is at present thirty-eight. The Sunday school was organized in 1895, and has an average attendance of forty children. The pastors who have served Hebron are Rev. W. C. Broady, Rev. R. C. Hartman, Rev. W. C. Prather, Rev. R. H. Bateler, Rev. J. M. Oldfather, Rev. J. Gillingham and Rev. Lucien Rule, the present incumbent. The present building was erected in 1896. The present elders are William F. Zeller and J. W. Gladden. The present deacons are Joseph Clak and Edward Bolly.

CHAPTER XXV.

HISTORY OF THE HOLY ROMAN CHURCH IN CLARK COUNTY.

There are many difficulties in the way of writing an accurate history of the Catholic church in Clark county, since its organization as a county in 1801. Ever since 1783, when the State of Virginia ceded one hundred and fifty thousand acres of land to Gen. George Rogers Clark and his soldiers, for their valor in reducing the British Post at Vincennes, in February, 1779, there have been members of the Catholic faith resident in Clark county.

In Clark's "army" of one hundred seventy men, there were seventy privates and eighteen officers of Irish birth or descent, and quite a number of French. It is but fair to presume that many of these were of the Catholic faith. They took up the lands allotted to them by a grateful state, in what is known as the "Illinois Grant," which comprises most of Clark county, soon after 1784, when the lands were divided and alloted to each officer and soldier. Both the surname and Christian name of these soldier settlers, in many instances, indicate that they were of the Catholic faith.

Jesuit and other missionaries frequently passed through Clark county on their way from Bardstown to Vincennes. It is recorded that Father Benedict Joseph Flaget, afterward the first Catholic Bishop of Kentucky, read mass in a log church located at the foot of the Knobs, at St. Mary's, in what is now known as Lafayette township, Floyd county, soon after the year 1800. This was then a part of the county of Clark, for Floyd county was not organized until 1819. Father Theodore Stephen Baden, also made trips through Clark county on his way to Post Vincennes along about 1800, but whether he stopped to minister his divine office, or to shrive those of his communion, history does not record. There were Catholic churches, or at least Catholic priests, all the time in the early days, between 1702 and 1850, in Vincennes and Bardstown and at Louisville, Kentucky, and the devout Catholic residents of Clark county, in all probability either went to Kentucky or to Vincennes when they desired to perform their annual religious obligations.

It was not until 1850 that the Catholics of Jeffersonville requested the church authorities to send them a priest to offer up the holy sacrifice of the mass. In response to their request the Rev. Father Daniel Maloney came to the city and read mass at what was known then as the Hansley House, on the river front. It belonged to Capt. James Wathen, who operated the ferry line, and who was at that time the most prominent Catholic in the town. In

August, 1851, the Rt. Rev. Martin John Spaulding, Bishop of Louisville, laid the cornerstone of the first Catholic church in Jeffersonville. It was located on what was then known as Canal street, now Meigs avenue, near Maple street, and was a brick structure twenty-five by fifty feet. It was named in honor of St. Anthony. The first mass was said by Rev. Father Otto Jair, a Franciscan priest, from Louisville. In this church the English-speaking and also the German Catholics worshiped for years. Among the pastors of this unpretentious church, and who was really the first Catholic pastor in Jeffersonville, was Father August Bessonies, who afterward became vicar general of the diocese, and who took a prominent part in the civic affairs of the city of Indianapolis and of Indiana until his death. Father Bessonies came to Jeffersonville in March, 1854, and was accompanied by Bishop de St. Palais, who begun to take a deep interest in the spiritual welfare of the Catholics of Jeffersonville. Father Bessonies, who also attended seven other stations in Clark and Floyd counties, remained until 1857, when he was succeeded by Rev. William Doyle, who remained a year, and was succeeded by his brother, Father Philip Doyle, who remained until October, 1860. After that date the spiritual wants of the congregation were attended to by Franciscan priests from Louisville until December, 1861, when the Rev. G. Ostlangenberg was appointed pastor. By this time it became apparent that the little church on Canal street was inadequate to accommodate both the German-speaking and English-speaking Catholics, and by direction of Bishop de St. Palais, Father Ostlangenberg took steps to build a new church for the Irish or English-speaking Catholics, on ground donated by the Bishop and Father Bessonies, at the corner of Chestnut and Locust streets. On October 10, 1863, Rt. Rev. Bishop Martin John Spaulding, of Louisville, laid the cornerstone, and the Very Rev. Bede O'Connor preached the sermon. Father O'Connor, by the way, was an Irishman, educated in Germany, and a member of the Benedictine order. He spoke German with great fluency and power, and on several occasions gave missions in Jeffersonville, converting many to the faith and bringing back wayward church members to a sense of their religious obligations.

Father Andrew Michael became the pastor April 16, 1864, having succeeded Father Ostlangenberg, who left in December, 1863, the interim being filled by the Rev. William Doyle. As soon as Father Michael took charge he set to work to complete the foundation of St. Augustine's, and he accomplished the task during this year. In the meantime small-pox broke out among the soldiers in Jeffersonville, and in ministering unto them, he contracted the disease, but recovered, but his sister who was his housekeeper died of it. In 1866 the Bishop directed the Rev. John Mougin, of New Albany, to attend to the pastorate in connection with his other duties, and under his direction the walls of St. Augustine's were completed, and the first mass was said within the unfinished building by Rt. Rev. Bishop de St. Palais, on March 17, 1868. Rev. Father M. Fleischmann became pastor of St. Augustine's for a short time in that year, when the Bishop appointed the Rev. Ernest Audran, rector, on December 3, 1868, who remained pastor until his death, December 11, 1899. The name of Father Audran will forever be an inspiration to the Catholics of Clark county. For thirty-one years he looked after the spiritual, and at many times the temporal affairs of his flock. Born in France, of distinguished ancestry, Father Audran came to Vincennes when a young man, and studied theology under his uncle, the Rt. Rev. Bishop Celestine de la Hailandiere. For fifty-four years he was a priest, laboring incessantly in the cause of religion and morality. When he came to Jeffersonville there was nothing but the bare church walls. He built up schools, beside practically rebuilding the church. He was a man of strong individuality; firm, but kindhearted. He had the respect of the entire community, and was loved by Catholic and non-Catholic alike. At his death there was widespread sorrow throughout the city and throughout the county of Clark.

On the night of December 9, 1903, fire destroyed the church building completely, causing a loss of about forty thousand dollars, but Father O'Connell and the trustees, John B. Murphy, Dennis O'Hearn, Martin Fogarty, Redmond Stanton, James Marra and Thomas Donahue, pushed the movement to rebuild, and the result was the present handsome building designed by D. X. Murphy, of Louisville. The building is commodious and will seat about nine hundred persons. It is in the Spanish Renaissance style. The beautiful towers in the front are seventy-four and ninety-six feet high. On Sunday, October 2, 1905, the Rt. Rev. Bishop Francis Silas Chatard conducted the services of dedication, and once more the congregation of St. Augustine's had a home.

The little church of St. Anthony continued to prosper. In 1871 Rev. Avelin Szabo took charge, and during his time did much in the way of reducing the indebtedness contracted in the purchase of the new building site. In 1875 Father Leopold Mozygamba, who succeeded Father Clements Luitz, commenced the erection of the present place of worship on Maple street, just above Wall street. The church was built at a cost of between eight thousand and nine thousand dollars, under the supervision of Henry Nagle, Ferdinand Voigt, George Unser, Michael Recktenwald, Engelbert Spinner and Theobald Manny, building committee. The priests after Father Leopold came in the following order: Caesar Cuchiarian, 1877-78; Joseph Liesen, 1878-79; Pius Koetterer, 1879-81; Anthony Gehring, 1881-83; Bernard Ettensperger, 1883-87; Avelin Szabo, 1887-96; Francis Newbauer, February, 1896, to July, 1896; Lucius Matt, 1896.

Two school-houses, one for boys and the other for girls, have been built on the church lot, and the schools are flourishing under the supervision of the

Franciscan Sisters. There are at present about one hundred scholars for the two teachers.

During the pastorate of Father Liesen the cemetery just above the eastern cemetery was purchased, and also the lot at the corner of Maple and Wall streets.

In 1889 the church had ninety-nine families, and in 1909 has one hundred twenty-five families. The societies are the Knights of St. John, the Ladies' Sodality, the Poor Souls Sodality and the Young Ladies' Sodality. The Spanish has furnished two members to the priesthood, both of whom have joined the Franciscans, O. M. C. One is the Rev. F. M. Voigt and the other is the Rev. Otto Recktenwald.

St. Joseph's Hill, or St. Joe, as it is called, is situated near the dividing line of Clark and Floyd counties in Grant 146.

The early settlers were from Germany, coming to this country in 1846, and by their industry gained a home. After having provided for their bodies, they provided for their souls, mindful of the words of our Savior, "What does it profit a man, if he gain the whole world and loses his own soul?" by erecting a church in their midst. The building was of frame, eighty by thirty feet; it was commenced on the 11th day of June, 1853, and finished the same year. Martin Koerner and Joseph Eringer were the carpenters and contractors. They received for their labor two hundred seventy-five dollars. The leading men were Peter Biesel, Sr., Peter Renn, Sr., Frank Ackerman, Andrew Rank, Sr., Philip Strobel and Ludwig Herbig.

Rev. Father Neyron, the well known priest and physician, was the first missionary attending to their spiritual wants. He resided at St. Mary's, Floyd knobs. Father Bessonies, vicar general, attended to them afterwards. St. Joseph's was then attended by Rev. Ed Faller, of New Albany. After the congregation numbered about seventy families, they petitioned the Right Rev. Bishop for a residing priest, but their petition was not heard immediately, for the want of priests. In the year 1860 the first resident priest, Rev. Andrew Michael, arrived at St. Joseph's Hill. His arrival was announced by the ringing of bells, and the people rejoiced at the arrival of their spiritual director. He remained with them for four years. During his time he erected a large two-story brick parsonage, valued at one thousand five hundred dollars, he himself working like a laborer quarrying rock. His successor was Rev. Father Pauzer. He remained with them nearly nine years, and erected two large frame buildings, the one for a school-house, and the other for a teacher's dwelling.

In the year 1873 Rev. Joseph Dickman, a native of Indiana, took charge of the congregation. He paid all outstanding debts, and made preparations to erect the present splendid church, the old one having become too small. In 1880 he took up a grand subscription towards that building. He next had the

18

members to quarry rock for the foundation and haul logs to Peter P. Renn's mill, only a few hundred yards from the church, where all the lumber for the building was sawed. On the 18th day of October, 1880, the cornerstone was laid of the new church with great solemnity, by the Right Rev. Bishop. The foundation was completed that fall by Joseph Zipf, of Clark county, and Louis Zipf, of Floyd county. The new edifice, which is one hundred fourteen by fifty-two feet, and crowned by a spire of one hundred and thirty feet, was completed in 1881. It was dedicated by the Right Rev. Bishop, assisted by Rev. Joseph Dickman, the pastor; Rev. J. Stremler, D. D., of St. Mary's; Rev. J. P. Gillig, of St. John's, Clark county; Rev. Ubaldus, O. S. F., of Louisville, and Rev. J. Klein, of New Albany, on the 20th day of November, 1881. The cost of the building is estimated at twenty-seven thousand dollars. The congregation numbers one hundred families. The trustees who assisted the pastor deserve credit for their activity. They were Mathias Renn, Jacob Strobel, Lorenz Weidner, Joseph Zipf, Max Zahner and J. C. Schmidt.

St. Joseph's is the largest Catholic church in the county, outside of Jeffersonville. The situation is well adapted for regular religious growth. Everything is in a prosperous condition. Industry and public-spirited enterprise have made for St. Joseph's Hill a name which many other religious communities may well strive to attain.

The schools at St. Joseph's are taught by the Sisters of St. Francis, and about one hundred ten children attend them. There are over one hundred thirty families in the parish, mostly German.

ORDERS OF THE HOLY ROMAN CHURCH IN CLARK COUNTY.

THE CATHOLIC KNIGHTS OF AMERICA.

Branch No. 54 was organized in Jeffersonville April 4, 1879. The following is a list of presidents since that date: Dennis Kennedy, 1879-1880; T. J. Gilligan, 1881-1882-1883; Maurice Coll, 1884-1885; John B. Murphy, 1886-1887; John Miller, 1888; J. E. Thicksrun, 1889-1890; Patrick Tracy, 1891-1892-1893; John Miller, 1894-1895; Jacob Sedler, 1896-1897; J. E. Thickstun, 1898; Patrick Tracy, 1899-1900; J. E. Thickstun, 1901-1902; B. A. Coll, 1903-1904-1905; Maurice Coll, 1906-1907; John Kenney, 1908.

Since the organization of the branch the beneficiaries of deceased members in Jeffersonville have received fifty-eight thousand dollars. At present the membership is about fifty.

The Catholic Knights and Ladies of America Branch No. 13 was organized in Jeffersonville March 19, 1892. The following members have served as president since that date: John B. Murphy, 1892-93-94-95-96-97 and 98; Patrick Tracy, 1899-1900-1901 and 1902; Miss Maggie Ash, 1903; L. Constantine, 1904-1905; Mrs. Mary Burke, 1906-1907; Mrs. Ella Brooks, 1908. At present the membership is small.

THE ANCIENT ORDER OF HIBERNIANS.

Division No. 1 of Clark county was organized in Jeffersonville September 15, 1890. William McDonald was president; John Donahue, vice-president; George O'Neil, recording secretary; Stephen Hogan, financial secretary and Richard Flood, treasurer.

Since the date of organization the presidents have been as follows: William McDonald, 1892; John Mooney, 1893-94-95; James Cavanaugh, 1896-97; William P. Reilly, 1898-1899-1900; Robert Gleason, 1901-1902-1904-1905; Frank W. Hogan, 1903; John A. Kennedy, 1906-1907-1908. At present the membership of the branch is about one hundred.

THE KNIGHTS OF COLUMBUS.

Jeffersonville Council No. 1348 was organized June 28, 1908, with a charter membership of fifty-four. It is a subordinate council of the Knights of Columbus, incorporated at New Haven, Connecticut, March 29, 1882, and whose purpose is to more closely unite practical white, male members of the Roman Catholic church. It has insurance as well as social features. When organized Jeffersonville council elected the following officers, who are still holding office: Grand knight, James W. Fortune; deputy grand knight, John A. Kennedy; chancellor, John J. Hines; financial and recording secretary, Conway C. Samuels; warden, Lawrence Ford; advocate, Matthew Dolan; lecturer, Frank A. Lang; treasurer, Frank J. Braun; trustees, Martin Fogarty, Richard J. Kennedy, Martin A. Conroy; guards, Thomas F. O'Hern, John E. Cole, Jr.

KNIGHTS OF ST. JOHN.

St. George Commandery, No. 141, Knights of St. John, was organized May 2, 1882, with Anthony P. Karbel as its first president. This society is a semi-military, social Roman Catholic order, offering benevolent and insurance rates to its members. It has a present membership of fifty-four of the leading German Roman Catholics in Jeffersonville. It has paid out a sum exceeding eight thousand dollars for sick benefits to its members, besides doing a vast amount of charitable work. Its members belong to St. Anthony's Roman Catholic church. August Gatterer is the present president.

CHAPTER XXVII.

THE CHRISTIAN CHURCH—THE ADVENT CHRISTIAN CHURCH

(By. F. E. Andrews.)

THE CHRISTIAN CHURCH.

The Christian church, or the Church of Christ, began in Jerusalem at the great Pentecost, when the first Gospel sermon was so grandly proclaimed; but the current restoration movement began on September 7, 1809, at which time the famous address of Thomas Campbell was issued.

This movement has spread until it now numbers more than one million communicants. Its chief distinctive tenets are:

1.   The urgent need of the union of God's people.

2.   No government except God's word.

3.   The restoration of apostolic teaching and practice in all church ordinances and government.

In Clark county, Indiana, there are congregations at the following points: Jeffersonville, Charlestown, Borden, Pleasant Ridge, Muddy Fork, Sellersburg, Memphis, Blue Lick, Bethel, Hibernia, Olive Branch, Marysville, New Washington, New Market, Utica, Bethany, Stony Point. Several other congregations have been started in the county, but they disbanded and the members entered the other congregations near them.

One of the earliest organizations of this faith in the county was perfected July 7, 1832, on Camp Run, near Belknap's mill. It was organized by the adoption of the following resolution: Resolved, therefore, that we give ourselves to the Lord and to one another by the will of God and from this 7th day of July, 1832, consider ourselves standing in the relation of a church of Jesus Christ, professing to be built upon the foundation of the apostles and prophets, Jesus Christ himself being the chief corner stone; mutually agreeing and receiving the Scriptures of Divine authority and as such the only infallible rule, in both faith and obedience and agree to be governed thereby. The following were the charter members:

Joseph Cunningham, George B. Campbell, Clevias Poindexter, John Adams, Mary Littell, Charles Vandyke, Elizabeth Wilson, Jane Vandyke, Samuel Tilford, Ann Tilford, Francis Widener, Rachel Campbell.

In 1837 a meeting house was built in Hamburg. Some years after this the congregation moved to Sellersburg and of late years has not affiliated with the other churches of this name because of opposition to instrumental music and organized missionary work.

Another early church was organized at Stony Point, April 22, 1837. This congregation still meets near the point where it was organized, about midway between Memphis and Charlestown.

The earliest congregation of which any records can be found was organized in Jeffersonville on March 7, 1830, in the court-house. Elder Benjamin Allen, of Goose Creek church, Kentucky, was the organizer. The following were the charter members: Nathaniel Field, Christian Bruner, Elizabeth Bruner, Mary Phillips, Elizabeth Bennett, Eleanor Wright, Francis McGarrah, Maria McGarrah. To these were added by baptism the same day, Sarah Ann Field, Elizabeth Field and Elizabeth Knight. The original book of this organization is now in the possession of Henry Burtt. It is in a fair state of preservation, and is quite interesting to read. In those days many members were excluded for living in an unbecoming manner.

A congregation was started at Charlestown at a very early date but the exact time is not known since the records have been lost. In 1834 a member was received by letter in Jeffersonville from the Charlestown congregation; but how long before that the church was in existence is not known.

The Christian church is congregational in its government; but there is an annual meeting of the various county congregations, at which co-operative work is often considered. This meeting is held on the fourth Lord's Day in August.

THE ADVENT CHRISTIAN CHURCH.

Differences regarding doctrine in the Christian church having arisen in the early forties Dr. Nathaniel Field and eleven members of this church withdrew April 11, 1846. Shortly after this they organized a new church in the old court-house, on Market street, between Spring and Pearl. In 1850 Calvin Cook gave the new congregation a lot on Watt street, near Maple, and Doctor Field furnished the material and built the church. Doctor Field remained pastor of this church until his death, in the late eighties, and during the long time of his service never received pay. C. C. Anderson, Daniel Lanciskes and Mr. Wooley were the first trustees.

During the year 1897 and 1898 most of the members took their letters and united with the Advent Christian church in New Albany, at Silver Grove. After the death of the Rev. M. A. Stevens, who was pastor of both churches at that time, the members of the old church came back, reorganized, and in 1899 rebuilt the present church building, on Watt street. The Rev. Mr. Garberson is the present pastor.

CHAPTER XXVIII.

GERMAN REFORMED CONGREGATIONS, JEFFERSONVILLE AND SELLERSBURG.

ST. LUCAS GERMAN EVANGELICAL—REFORMED CONGREGATION, JEFFERSON-VILLE.

On May 13, 1860, a call was issued by a number of German citizens, signed by John A. Bachman, Daniel Eyer, Henry Sittel, I. L. Rockstroh, William Nanz, John Reuhl, Daniel Rieth, Christian Heyn, Valentine Wuergler, Ludwig Henzler, Jacob Angst, John Greiner, Henry Pfiester, Herman Preefer, Jacob Spielman, Joseph Stein, August Reipschlaeger, Jacob Eyer, Andrew Bauer, Christian Schlosser, Melchior Brændly, Fried, Renz, Philip Gœbal, Christian Hoffman, for the organization of a German Protestant church. At that first meeting officers were elected to perfect the organization: J. L. Rockstroh, president; John A. Bachman, secretary, and Henty Sittel, treasurer. As a result on June 22, 1860 the congregation bought the Presbyterian church, opposite the present city hall, for the sum of one thousand two hundred dollars.

At a regular legal meeting on July 12, 1860, the first officers were duly elected as follows: J. L. Rockstroh, president; Ludwig Henzler, secretary; John A. Greiner, treasurer. Henry Sittel, Valentine Wuergler, Christian Heyn, William Nanz and John Ruehl, trustees. In October, 1861 the first constitution and by-laws were adopted, signed by John L. Rockstroh, Henry Sittel, Ludwig Henzler, John Greiner, Christian Heyn, Valentine Wuergler, William Nanz, John Ruehl, Christian Selimer, Jacob Angst, Daniel Rieth, Andrew Bauer, John A. Bachman, Melchior Brændly, Christian Schlosser, Karl S. Spielman, John Best, Conrad Seelbach.

The first pastor to be called was a Reverend Grassow, and the congregation was known as "The German Evangelical." The next pastor was called on September 21, 1862, Reverend Hartly. In March, 1863, he was succeeded by Rev. I. N. U. Bradsh, of New Albany. On December 6, 1864, Reverend Wiehe was called, who was followed by the Rev. Carl Becker, of New Albany, who served to January 30, 1870. Then came a decided change, the congregation voted to affiliate with the Reformed Church, and called a graduate of the Mission College, Rev. Christian Baum, on May 1, 1870. Then began a new era. The new officers under Reformed church rules were: John Rauschenberger, president; H. Preefer, secretary; Andrew Bauer, treasurer; consistory, John Ehle, G. Woehrle, W. Same, Ludwig Roederer, A. Kern, W. Bueschemeyer. The first official action was to appoint a committee to buy a lot for a parsonage. The lot next to the church was secured at a cost of one thousand dollars, of John H. Read; and a parsonage at a cost of one thousand six hundred dollars built by C. Heyn (addition was since added thereto at a cost of six hundred dollars). The church was rebuilt and enlarged in 1882 at an expense of several thousand dollars.

Reverend Baum resigned April, 1873, and was succeeded by the Rev. H. Rieke, who on account of longing for the old country, resigned in the following year. Rev. H. Meiboom followed and served to July 10, 1876, to be succeeded by the Rev. C. F. Fleiner, who filled the pulpit to July 7, 1880. Next to take charge of the pastorate was the Rev. H. M. Gersman, to May, 1900, followed by Rev. Daniel Neuenschwander, who served one year, and was succeeded by J. G. Rees, of Chicago. In March, 1901, he resigned and was followed in the pastorate by Rev. W. G. Lienkaemper, who, on account of ill health resigned on November 13, 1903. Next, Rev. A. G. Gekler took charge in February, 1904. He served one year and resigned to again enter the mission field. On April 2, 1905, Rev. J. F. Vornholt took charge and served to August, 1908, and the pulpit is now filled by Rev. Ben E. Lienkaemper, the brother of a former pastor.

Over five hundred members have been taken into the church by confirmation, making it in point of membership the largest congregation in the city. A strong feature is its "Woman's Society," which is saving funds, with a view of building a church which modern conveniences for Sunday school and the young people. A beautiful pipe organ has been installed less than a year ago. The future for this church looks very promising. The church is officered at the present time by Rev. Benjamin E. Lienkaemper; consistory, John Rauschenberger, F. H. Miller, Peter Nachand, John Gienger, William Pfau, John Schlæfer, Andrew Schlosser, Jacob Woehrle, Charles A. Schimpff, secretary, since 1870, continuous. A flourishing Young People's Society was organized in June, 1891, that has sixty-five members, whose aim is to assist the church in the equipment of the new edifice in prospect.

A Sunday school with an enrollment of one hundred sixty-five has been in uninterrupted regular session since 1870, with Charles A. Schimpff as superintendent, with only a slight intermission of service. Another member with almost the same record is J. C. Reschar, a faithful teacher. John Rauschenberger has been a member of the consistory for a generation. Miss Lucy Steidinger has filled the position of organist for both church and Sunday school, continuous and faithful, since April, 1889. Great work is anticipated under the present new energetic pastor. A fitting semi-centinnial celebration would be the dedication of a new church in 1910.

ST. PAUL'S GERMAN EVANGELICAL REFORMED CONGREGATION, SELLERSBURG

St. Paul's Reformed congregation of Sellersburg. Indiana, belongs to the Reformed church in the United States, historically known as the German Reformed church.

The work of the Rev. J. H. Krueger, a minister of the Reformed church, who occasionally held religious services for the German Protestants living in the vicinity of Sellersburg, Indiana, resulted in the desire on their part to have an organized congregation and a house of worship for regular services. A meeting was held in the Baptist church at Sellersburg on March, 20, 1871, which was presided over by William Stickan, and of which Edward Haas was the secretary. An organization was effected under the direction of Rev. J. H. Klein, of Louisville. A constitution was adopted, and a consistory of three members was elected, one elder and two deacons, William Mueller being the choice for the office of elder and William Stickan and William Dreyer for that of deacons. Following are the names of those who signed the constitution at the time of organization: J. William Mueller, F. William Stickan, William Dreyer, Carl Schwengel, Frederic Loheide, Louis Utrecht, Christian Melcher, William Matteg, Carl Loheide, George Kranz, Edward Haas, William Krekel, H. Grossbach, Peter Mueller, August Koehler, Ernst Meyer.

A modest frame structure, twenty by thirty feet, was soon afterwards erected in which the congregation worshiped and in which were also held the sessions of its parochial school, until almost twenty years later a new and more commodious church was erected. The latter, located near the site of the old, was built during the pastorate of the Rev. Ph. Steinhage, in 1890, and dedicated on December 14th of that year.

For a number of years after its organization St. Paul's Reformed congregation, together with Reformed congregations at Charlestown and Otisco, Indiana, constituted one pastoral charge, these three being served successively by the following pastors: Revs. Julius Herold, Edward Gruenstein and Charles Hartmann. St. Paul's was then united with Immanuel Reformed congregation of Crothersville, Indiana, these together forming the Crothersville charge, under the care of one pastor, and now within the bounds of Kentucky Classis, Synod of the Northwest, of the Reformed church in the United States.

Since 1882 this charge has been served by the following pastors, successively: S. C. Barth, Ph. A. Steinhage, C. Wisner (1891-98). J. Gaenge 1898-1903), Caleb Hauser (1904-1906), P. G. Kluge, since May, 1907.

The number of young persons who have been received into the membership of St. Paul's since its organization is one hundred twenty-five. The membership of this congregation has at no time been large. This is due partly to the fact that it shares the fate of most churches in the small communities, which constantly lose from their membership those who remove to the larger towns and cities in search of greater opportunities and more remunerative employment, and also to this, that its activity has been more or less restricted to the German protestant population of the community in which it is located. But St. Paul's has always faithfully endeavored to discharge its duty of training those under its influence for a Christian life and church membership. Numerous members of churches in the nearby cities have received their early religious training and education while under its care. St. Paul's has always distinguished itself by charitable liberality, contributing freely for the support of missions and other benevolent causes. With regard to matters of language the present is a time of transition from the German into the English.

Membership (1909): Communicant members, eighty; unconfirmed members, sixty-nine. Organizations in the congregation: Sunday school, choir, Young People's Society of Christian Endeavor, organized in 1908; Ladies' Aid Society, organized 1908.

CHAPTER XXIX.

THE BENCH AND BAR OF CLARK COUNTY.

The profession of law in no part of the United States in early days had more brilliant intellects nor deeper students than did Clark county. Her judges upon the bench and the lawyers who practiced before them will compare with those of any other locality both as to depth and breadth of intellect.

Perhaps the most prominent early member of the bar in Clark county was Jonathan Jennings, the first Governor of Indiana under the state constitution. He was a native of Rockbridge county, Virginia, and was born in 1784. When a youth his father emigrated to Pennsylvania, and the boy having obtained some knowledge of Greek and Latin, commenced the study of law, but before being admitted to the bar removed to the Territory of Indiana, and was employed as clerk by Nathaniel Ewing, of Vincennes.

He returned to Charlestown soon after and adopted that place as his home. His slogan was "No Slavery in Indiana," and throughout his long and brilliant career he kept the slavery question to the front. Jonathan Jennings was a man of the people and owed much of his success in politics to his peculiar knack of keeping close to them. Clark county has produced no more brilliant character. His incorruptible integrity, his refusal to bow to political expediency, his hospitality, his thorough understanding of the people, and his firmness of character place him in the front rank of Indiana's great men.

In 1809 he was elected delegate to Congress, and remained as such until the formation of a state constitution. He was chosen president of the constitutional convention, and at the first state election, in 1816, was the choice of the people for Governor. He was again elected to the office in 1819, and in 1822 was returned to Congress from the Second district, continuing its representative until 1831, when he failed of a re-election. He died on his farm about three miles west of Charlestown, in 1834.

The following paper was written by the late Judge C. P. Ferguson, and is of particular value on account of his personal knowledge of the man of whom he writes:

THE BENCH AND BAR OF CLARK COUNTY, PRIOR TO THE CONSTITUTION OF 1851.

Early in the month of January, in the year 1801, William Henry Harrison, then twenty-eight years of age, arrived at Vincennes and entered upon the discharge of his duties as Governor of the Indiana Territory. At that time the boundaries of the territory included all that immense scope of country out of which the states of Indiana, Illinois, Michigan and Wisconsin were afterwards formed. So it remained until 1805, when Michigan Territory was struck off, and in 1809, Illinois Territory was organized, and from that time the territory of Indiana had the same boundaries as the state of Indiana now has.

As a part of the organization of the Indiana Territory, the law provided for an appointment by the President of the United States of a Governor, a Secretary and three Judges. John Gibson was appointed Secretary and served as such during the whole territorial period, and among the territorial judges acting under the commission of the President of 1813, and as United States Attorney for the territory in 1809, was a Charlestown man, who for a long period ranked as an important man under both the territorial and state governments. Of this man I have never seen in print any biographical sketch, and what I shall say of him I have gathered from his public acts, so far as they have become a part of the history of the state, and from what I knew of him personally in his old age.

I have reference to Judge James Scott. After serving as United States Attorney and United States Judge for the territory his next public service was a delegate from the county of Clark to the convention called for the purpose of framing a state constitution, in 1816. That constitution provided for the appointment, by the Governor, to be confirmed by the Senate, of three judges of the Supreme Court. Jonathan Jennings, the first Governor and also a Clark county man, appointed his friend and neighbor, Judge Scott, as one of the Supreme judges for the constitutional period of seven years. He served his first term and was re-appointed by Governor William Hendricks for a second term, serving altogether fourteen years and retiring in 1831. After retiring from the Supreme Bench, it would seem that he did not meet with much success as a member of the bar, for about the period 1834 we find him giving attention to the editing of a newspaper called "The Comet," printed in a little frame building which stood on a part of his residence lot, No 55, in Charlestown. At the head of his paper the following lines were kept standing as its motto: "Ask not to what doctor I apply, for sworn to no sect or party am I."

How long this newspaper was published, I am unable to say, but after Gen. W. H. Harrison was inaugurated as President, in 1841, Judge Scott was appointed as register of the land office, at Jeffersonville, and served as such until removed under the administration of President Polk.

After leaving this office he opened a school for girls in Charlestown. I could name several grandmothers, well known to some of you, who were under his tuition when they were frisky little girls. But the school did not last very long, and it seems this was the last effort he made for self-support.

He was old and poor and childless, and his wife had been dead for many years, but there was a lady living in Carlisle whom he had reared as an adopted daughter. In her house he sought a home and found it, and there he died. Judge Scott had the reputation of having a fine education and great learning. As to his ability as a jurist, his many opinions published in the Supreme Court reports in the hands of every Indiana lawyer, must speak for themselves. That he was an amiable, honest and devoted Christian man, I can testify of my own knowledge.

When the Indiana Territory was established by ordinance of Congress, the county of Knox included all the territory embraced in what is now the state of Indiana. Out of Knox county the county of Clark was formed, which included what is now Harrison county and by boundaries eastward and northward covered about one-fifth of the present state, and a court was established in the new county. Our court records show that the first court held in the county was held at Springville, April 7, 1801, by the following named persons as judges: William Goodwin, Marston G. Clark, Abraham Huff, Thomas Downs, and James N. Wood. Charles P. Tuley was also one of the justices of the court, but was not present. Samuel Gwathmey was the first Clerk and Samuel Hay the first Sheriff.

These first officials in the organization of the county took deep root. During their own lives they continued from time to time to fill important places and after them, their descendants have often filled places of honor and trust in the county. It may be interesting to note that after the lapse of nearly one hundred years, a great-grandson of one of these judges was the Judge of the Circuit Court, and another great-grandson of the same person was the Clerk of the court, and the grandson of the first Sheriff, as well as grand-nephew of one of those judges, was Recorder of the county, all holding office at the same time.

The laws governing these local courts were made by the Governor and Territorial judges appointed by the President, until the county arrived at what was called the second grade, when it became entitled to a Legislature, and this happened in 1805, when the first Legislature convened.

No trace of Springville, which was located a little more than a mile west of Charlestown, where the courts were held until July 6, 1802, can now be found, but like ancient Carthage, it has not only been destroyed, but the ground upon which it stood ploughed up and converted into a field.

On and after July 6, 1802, the courts were held at Jeffersonville until March 3, 1811, when the court was first held at Charlestown. These local county courts continued to exist for thirteen years, some new names appearing as judges from time to time; the name of Evan Shelby, Rezin Redman and John Miller appearing as judges at the close of 1813.

They had both criminal and civil jurisdiction and had a grand jury to present indictments. None of these judges pretended to be lawyers, but were plain, honest and intelligent men, acting under the appointment of the Governor, in fact, justices of the peace, with power to come together at certain times as a court. During the period of these courts and especially while they were held at Jeffersonville, the business was largely in the hands of Louisville attorneys, the names of Breckinridge, Harrison, Johnson, Fortunatus Cosby, Worden Pope, James Ferguson and other Kentucky names of distinction, often appearing in court proceedings.

Among the Indiana lawyers of this early period the names of Henry Hurst, Robert A. New, Jonathan Jennings, James Scott, Benjamin Park, Gen. Washington Johnson, Thomas Randolph and others appear in the records.

It may truly be said of Henry Hurst that he was in at the beginning, for at the second term of court held at Springville he made his appearance under the style of Deputy United States Attorney General, ready to indict and prosecute in the name of the United States all violators of the law. He settled himself at Jeffersonville and among the landmarks of that city still standing in a good state of preservation is his two-story brick dwelling, with high stone steps, at the top of the wharf directly fronting the ferry landing.

Major Hurst became one of the noted men of Indiana. He was an aid to General Harrison at Tippecanoe, and history has it that on the morning of the battle, the general had risen a little after four o'clock as usual, and was in his tent in the act of drawing on his boots in conversation with Major Hurst and Major Owens, when the unexpected attack was made. When President Harrison was inaugurated, on the 4th day of March, 1841, he rode on horseback at the head of the procession, through the streets of Washington, and at his request, Major Hurst, mounted on a white horse, rode at his right hand, while the officer who had been his aid at the battle of the Thames, rode at his left. Thus was Clark county, through one of her citizens, given the post of honor on a most notable occasion. Major Hurst, for a time, served as Clerk of the United States District Court, and in 1838 was a member of the Legislature from Clark county. He was of portly frame, with the dignified carriage of a gentleman of the old school, and his ivory headed cane, his bandana handkerchief and his snuff-box were his inseparable companions. He was blunt of speech, and was fond of a joke, liked his wine and delighted in a game of cards, but he was not a gambler. In the long ago when lawyers traveled the circuit he was generally with them, more for the pleasure of the association than the profits of his profession. The last important business he attended to was in settling the estate of John Fischli, as executor of the will. Mr. Fischli died in 1838, leaving the shortest will ever recorded in Clark county, the devising part occupying only three lines of record, yet those three lines controlled the largest estate ever disposed of in the county, up to that time, the settlement of which demanded the attention of the court for years, as well as requiring some special acts of the Legislature to preserve the rights of the devisees.

In 1814 the judicial system of the territory underwent a change; the territory was divided into three circuits, with a presiding judge for each circuit and two associate judges in each county, all appointed by the Governor.

In November, 1814, Jesse L. Holman appeared in Charlestown and took his seat as presiding Judge under the commission of Territorial Governor Posey, and William Goodwin and John Miller having also produced their commissions, took their seats at associate judges, and Isaac Shelby was the Clerk. This was the same Judge Holman who became one of the first Supreme judges under the state constitution, and unless I have been wrongfully informed, he was the father of William S. Holman, who was an Indiana Congressman almost continuously for thirty years. Judge Holman's commission being a territorial appointment, his services came to a close at the November term, 1816, Indiana having been admitted as a state and adopted a constitution. Under the constitution the state was divided into circuits, each circuit to have one presiding Judge, to be elected by the Legislature, and two associate judges for each county, to be elected by the votes of the respective counties, and term of all judges was seven years. At the commencement of this new era in Indiana history, the following named Clark county attorneys were permitted to continue in the practice by taking a new oath to support the constitution, and also the oath against duelling, required by law: Alex Buckner, John H. Thompson, Benjamin Ferguson, David Floyd, Craven P. Hester, Henry Hurst, John F. Ross, Isaac Naylor, Isaac Howk and James Morrison.

Many of the attorneys so named subsequently removed from the county. Mr. Buckner owned and kept his office on lot 1, in Charlestown, and while a resident here he was the very head and front of the Masonic Order in Indiana. He went to St. Louis and became United States Senator in 1831.

Mr. Thompson, after becoming Judge, removed to Salem. Mr. Ferguson retired from the practice and settled on a farm. Mr. Hester, the father of the late Judge James S. Hester, of Brown county, went to California.

Mr. Morrison removed to Indianapolis, became Judge of the Circuit Court and filled other important offices, among which was president of the State Bank. Mr. Naylor removed to Crawfordsville and became Judge of the Circuit Court. Mr. Howk, who was the father of the late Supreme Judge, George V. Howk, died at Indianapolis in 1833, and had been speaker of the House of Representatives. Mr. Floyd, formerly of Clark county, was already located in Harrison county. At this period Charles Dewey attended the Clark county courts, but was a resident of Paoli.

The first term of the Clark Circuit Court under the constitution was held in March, 1817. The court records show that David Raymond was the presiding Judge and William Goodwin and John Beggs the associates. Isaac Shelby produced his commission as Clerk for seven years and took the oath of office and oath against duelling. The June term, 1817, was held by the same judges. I have been unable to find out who Judge Raymond was and by what authority he held these two terms. The election for Judge should have been at the November session, 1816, when the United States Senators and state officers were elected by the Legislature. If Judge Raymon was the Judge elected why did he hold two terms only? So far as I have knowledge Judge Raymond is one of the lost judges.

At the October term, 1817, Davis Floyd took his seat as Judge of the Second Circuit, under a commission to hold the office for seven years from October 13, 1817. William Goodwin and John Beggs were the associate judges and John F. Ross Prosecuting Attorney.

The career of Judge Floyd, if written out in detail, would read like a romance. From the first organization of the county he seems to have been the liveliest man in it. A very tall and dark complexioned man, full of courage, he appears to have been in everything and ready for anything, and for twenty-five years he was a most prominent figure in the territory and state of Indiana. The records show that in 1801 he was deputy for Samuel Hay, the first Sheriff; was licensed to keep a tavern at Clarksville; said to have been a falls pilot and major of militia, and in 1803 was Sheriff and collector of public revenues, and was adjutant for Joe Hamilton Daviess at Tippecanoe, and admitted to the bar in 1812.

His name often appears in litigation in the earliest records sometimes as plaintiff, but generally as defendant, defending actions for·debt, actions for trespass, suits on his official bond, and sometimes indictments preferred against him. The first execution issued in the county, No. 1 on the docket, issued January, 1802, was in his favor against Aaron Bowman, for fifty dollars, and the criminal records show that on account of matters growing out of the execution of the writ, Mr. Bowman assaulted Sheriff Hay, for which he paid a fine of twenty dollars. With it all he seems to have been a very popular man, for at the first territorial Legislature, in July, 1805, he took his seat as a member of the House of Representatives from the county of Clark. Soon after the close of the Legislature he became involved in the mysterious and supposed treasonable movements of Aaron Burr, went to Blennerhasset's Island to meet Colonel Burr and received a special visit from him at Jeffersonville, and on December 16, 1806, some men he had in charge joined the expedition and proceeded down the river. For this little piece of fillibustering he was indicted in the United States General Court, held at Jeffersonville, June 2, 1807, by Judge Thomas T. Davis, tried by a jury, which found him guilty of carrying on a military enterprise against his Catholic Majesty, the king of Spain, and was punished by a fine of ten dollars and imprisoned for three hours. But this did not seem to set him back in the estimation of his fellow citizens, for we find him taking an active part in a historic meeting held at Springville, October 10, 1807, over which John Beggs presided as chairman and Mr. Floyd acted as secretary, the object of which was to remonstrate to Congress against the scheme of Governor Harrison, Walter Taylor, Thomas Randolph and other pro-slavery men, for the suspension of that part of the Ordinance of 1787, forbidding slavery in the territory. Of how many intervening legislatures Judge Floyd was a member, I am unable to say, but having been a member of the first territorial Legislature, he again turns up as a member of the first state Legislature, which convened November 4, 1816, he then appearing as a member of the House of Representatives from Harrison county, having previously been a delegate from that county in the convention which framed the constitution.

At this session the Governor was directed to procure a great seal for the new state, and it was upon the motion of Mr. Floyd that the device adopted by the Legislature was the same now in use, with which the school children are familiar—a woodman felling a tree, a fleeing buffalo and the setting sun. At the next session of the General Assembly he was elected Judge of the Second Circuit and after serving seven years on the bench went to Florida under the commission of President Monroe, to investigate some troubles growing out of land titles. Of his career afterwards scarcely anything is known with certainty, but old citizens of Harrison county are emphatic in the assertion that he never returned to Indiana. The Sheriffs of Clark county who served under Judge Floyd were John Weathers, Joseph Gibson, James Curry and John S. Simmonson.

Judge John F. Ross, a resident of Charlestown, was the successor of Judge Floyd. His first term of Clark Circuit Court was commenced in May, 1824, when he was thirty-six years of age. Willis W. Goodwin and Benjamin Ferguson took their seats with him as associates. Gen. John Carr had just commenced his first term as Clerk, and Gen. John S. Simonson was Sheriff.

Judge Ross, after serving one term of seven years, was re-elected and died about the middle of his second term, his last signature on the court record being May 24, 1834. He was a scholarly man, had been a soldier in 1812, served in a session of the Legislature, often was Prosecuting Attorney and of undoubted integrity as a Judge. His birthplace was Morgantown, Virginia, but in his infancy his parents moved to near Bardstown, Kentucky, where his father died when he was nine years of age. After his death his mother was careful to see that he, as well as the other children of the family, received a good education. Upon the death of Judge Ross the venerable Judge Scott, who had been his law preceptor, pronounced this eulogy: "His life was strictly moral, humility was one of the brightest traits of his Christian character. He was one of Indiana's purest statesmen. He was a strict, uncompromising temperance man, and fearless in advocacy of his views. Philanthropic in his aims, he was popular with the mass of the public. He always thought to promote the best interests of humanity. A gallant soldier, a finished scholar and a true gentleman, without fear or reproach."

During Judge Ross' administration several Clark county lawyers, not previously mentioned, were members of his bar, among whom were James Collins, father of the late Judge Thomas Collins, of Salem, Newton Laughberry, who married the daughter of Judge Evan Shelby, and Samuel C. Wilson. Mr. Wilson came from New York and located at Charlestown, married Miss Laura Maddock and afterwards removed to Crawfordsville, where he became a partner with United States Senator, Joseph E. McDonald, in the practice of law. Also, about this time, Lyman Leslis took up his residence at Charlestown.

The Sheriffs under Judge Ross, after General Simonson, were Thomas Carr and David W. Daily. When Judge Ross had been on the bench about one year he was called upon to perform a duty, the most painful of all duties required of a Judge of humane feelings, the pronouncing of the death penalty on a convicted criminal. A negro named Jerry killed ex-Sheriff Joseph Gibson at Charlestown Landing, in 1825, and was indicted, tried and sentenced to death by Judge Ross within two weeks after the killing. But Jerry did not hang, the Supreme Court gave a new trial, and upon the second trial he was sent to the penitentiary for fifteen years. Here I will digress a little to state that the sentence of death had been pronounced seven times in the Clark Circuit Court since its organization, but only two executions have taken place; that of William Hardin, who was executed by Sheriff T. F. Bellows, and Macy Warner, executed by Charles S. Hay. In territorial times there was no penitentiary and if the killing was not a hanging case, the punishment was by burning the letter M in the hand with a red hot iron.

Such was the punishment given Henry Bannister in 1811, who killed Moses Phillips, in Harrison county, who was tried in Clark. And to John Irwin, in 1812, who killed Joseph Malott near the road leading from Charlestown to the Ohio river. On November 8, 1809, at Jeffersonville, Walter Taylor, a United States Judge for the territory, and afterwards United States Senator, passed sentence that John Ingram, for stealing a horse worth ten dollars, "be hanged by the neck until he is dead, dead, dead," but afterwards, on the day set for the execution, the prisoner while on the scaffold, was reprieved.

In cases of theft generally, the punishment, in territorial times, was by compelling the restoration of the property, or its value, and by a designated number of stripes laid on the bare back.

After the death of Judge Ross, Governor Noble, on the 5th of July,

19

1834, appointed John H. Thompson Judge of the Second Circuit to serve until a Judge could be elected. Under this appointment, and a subsequent election, Judge Thompson presided for a period of over ten years. At the time he went upon the bench, he was a resident of Charlestown, but afterwards removed to Salem. In early life he had been a cabinet maker, but after he took to the law he became a successful practitioner at the bar and was Lieutenant-Governor of the state from 1825 to 1828. At the session of the General Assembly, which convened in December, 1844, a Judge for the Second Circuit had to be elected. And Judge Thompson was a candidate for re-election. At that time there was living in Brownstown a young lawyer by the name of William T. Otto, scarcely thirty years of age. At the previous Legislature he had been principal secretary of the Senate, proved himself to be an excellent officer, and became well known and popular, and when the election came off, he was elected over Judge Thompson. Judge Thompson took the defeat very much to heart, but it turned out to be the very best thing that could have happened to him. The same Legislature had to elect a Secretary of State, and the defeat of Judge Thompson for Judge aroused a sympathy for him, and he was elected Secretary of State. This office suited him admirably. His wife had been the widow of John Strange, the eminent Methodist minister, and in his family he had a step-son, William R. Strange, just arriving at manhood, who went into the office as deputy, and relieved the Judge of many of its burdens. Besides, a change of residence had to be made, causing the Judge to sell his Salem property, and to remove to Indianapolis and remain there, and the advance was so great that he was put at ease financially during the remainder of his life.

Among the attorneys who located in Clark county while Judge Thompson was on the bench, were the following: B. F. Clark, Joseph Evans, M. Y. Johnson, J. M. Stagg, William Newton, John C. McCoy, Charles Hensley, Silas Osborn, T. W. Gibson, a Mr. Ogden, Andrew C. Griffith, Amos Lovering, and George F. Whitworth, none of whom remained in the county very long except Mr. Gibson and Mr. Lovering. Major Griffith died in Charlestown in 1844.

While Judge Thompson was on the bench Lemuel Ford and Joseph Work served as associate Judges, after the expiration of the terms of Judges Carr and Prather, and Henry Harrod served as Clerk, as the successor of General Carr, who had been elected to Congress. Thomas Carr was the successor of General Simonson as Sheriff, and Joseph Moore succeeded Colonel Carr; then Carr came in again and was succeeded by George Green.

Judge William T. Otto first presided as Judge of the Clark Circuit Court at the May term, 1845. The associate judges were: Beverley W. James and Hezekiah Robertson. Eli McCauley was Clerk, and John C. Huckleberry was Sheriff, succeeded by John Stockwell. At the very start Judge Otto gave

JUDGE CHARLES DEWEY, OF CHARLESTOWN.

things a general shake-up. In many respects he revolutionized the practice, and let the members of the bar and the officers of his court understand that the go-easy methods they had been pursuing would not be tolerated; in fact, he assumed a crabbed air, as if to say that when he put his foot down every person must succumb without a word. But notwithstanding his apparent harshness, his splendid ability as presiding Judge, his quick comprehension of the law and clearness in decision soon developed themselves, and the bar, without exception, had the greatest admiration for him. It is safe to say that no Circuit Judge in Indiana was ever his superior. He was the last Judge of the Second Circuit elected by the Legislature. When his term expired, the constitution of 1851 was in force, and he was succeeded by Judge Bicknell, by election of the people. After Judge Otto retired from the bench he returned to the bar, secured a fair practice and was considered a formidable lawyer. But misfortune overtook him, his partner involved him into some financial troubles, which swept his means from him and turned him loose upon the world. Deciding to leave New Albany, the place of Assistant Secretary of Interior under Mr. Lincoln's administration was offered him and he accepted. After this he became official reporter of the decisions of the Supreme Court of the United States. This place he kept for many years, then gave it up, fickle fortune in the meantime smiled on him and placed him in independent circumstances. A few years ago he was living and I have not heard of his death. Judge Otto was never married, but in Brownstown cemetery there is a tombstone erected by himself which marks the grave of a lady, who doubtless would have become his wife had not death carried her away. [Note:—Judge Otto died in Philadelphia in November, 1905, at the advanced age of eighty-nine.]

The Clark County Bar, during Judge Otto's term, was a strong one. The resident attorneys were: Judge Charles Dewey, Capt. T. W. Gibson, Amos Lovering, Charles E. Walker, John D. Ferguson, J. G. Howard, Charles Moore, John F. Read, W. H. Hurst, Henry Foster Smith, C. T. Solas, W. W. Gilliland, and possibly some others whom I have overlooked. Besides every term of court was attended by some of the best lawyers of the adjoining counties. Randall Crawford, H. P. Thornton, James Collins, Judge W. A. Porter, Cyrus L. Dunham and Joseph G. Marshall, the sleeping lion, were regular in their attendance, as were also Humphrey Marshall and W. P. Thomasson, of Louisville, and sometimes in particular cases the most eminent of the Louisville lawyers would make their appearance. I know of one case, in 1848, memorable as the Clarksville Slip Case, in which Henry Pirtle, Charles M. Thurston, T. W. Gibson, James Guthrie and Randall Crawford all took their turn in making speeches to the Judge. It was a battle of giants. Mr. Thurston swaying like an aspen in a storm. Mr. Guthrie stood motionless as a statue, looked the Judge square in the face and talked to him as man talks to man, but made no gestures. Mr. Thurston had never seen the Judge before whom he was to appear. When he entered the court room finding Judge Otto in the act of charging a jury, he stopped in the lobby with the crowd until the charge was finished, then nodded his head and muttered, "A pretty smart Judge that."

Among the strong lawyers at Judge Otto's bar was Judge Charles Dewey, who returned to the practice after over ten years' service as Judge of the Supreme Court. He was a Massachusetts man and when he came to this state located in Paoli. He represented Orange county in the Legislature in 1821, and the journals show that he was an active member, and was conspicuous as the special friend and defender of Governor Jennings, when an attempt was made to censure him in regard to some transactions growing out of the Jeffersonville canal project. After this he came to Charlestown and became Supreme Judge in May, 1836, upon the resignation of Stephen G. Stephens.

While serving as Supreme Judge he was by the President tendered the appointment of United States Judge for the District of Indiana, as the successor of Benjamin Parke, but declined it on account of the difference of the salaries of the two offices. No previous Judge in Indiana had ever attained the celebrity that was given Judge Dewey while on the Supreme bench. I had known him from early boyhood, and when I heard him so often spoken of as a great man I was a little slow to comprehend it, for a boy never sees greatness in a person with whom he is familiar, but always looks for greatness in the distance. When I got older I got over that, and now, at that distant day, when I think of the kind of man he was, I am satisfied that no man of ordinary perception could have come into the presence of Judge Dewey without being impressed with the feeling that he was in the presence of no ordinary man. His superb frame, large features, swarthy complexion, protruding under lip and heavy brow indicated force of extraordinary character.

When Judge Dewey died I walked with Judge Otto to the family residence to take a last look at the corpse. I well knew of the high esteem Judge Otto had for the deceased, and was not surprised when he turned to me and said. "The equal of Daniel Webster is in that coffin today."

Hugh McCulloch, Secretary of the Treasury under three administrations, a few years ago wrote a very interesting book in which it is stated that when he came West, in 1833, seeking a location, he remained at Madison for a considerable time, and while there made the acquaintance of three of the most distinguished lawyers in Southern Indiana, and they were Charles Dewey, Isaac Howk and Jeremiah Sullivan.

And now at the close of this feeble effort to bring to your minds the memory of some of the men, now dead and gone, who assisted in establishing and building up your county and state, I want to say a few words in regard to one man whose long service at the bar and close identification with the people of the county, demand something more than a mere casual reference. I mean Thomas W. Gibson, who first came to Charlestown in 1837, over sixty long years ago. Young, handsome, active, full of pranks and frolicsome mischief, he soon became the life and soul of enjoyment among the young and middle aged people of the town, and from the start he attracted attention as a promising lawyer. After he became married and the head of a family, he soon established his reputation as an able attorney and counsellor, acquired a large practice and great influence among the people, which he retained to the last. After serving as an officer in the Mexican war he was sent as a delegate to the convention that framed the constitution adopted in 1851. Not only did he help make the constitution but for several sessions was a member of the Legislature which had before them the difficult task of making the laws in conformity with the constitution so adopted. Subsequently, while retaining his family and residence at Charlestown he opened an office in Louisville and was recognized as a leading lawyer in that city. In the war between the states he did not hold any commission, but was often called in consultation with men of high official positions, especially in regard to the organization of troops, munitions of war and the gun-boat service, and his counsel was valuable. He had been a cadet at West Point, a midshipman in the navy, and had seen service in the field. Not only was he learned in the law, but he was a great student and close observer, and his knowledge of things in general, small matters as well as great, was wonderful, and besides he had been a student of medicine before he turned his attention to law. As a companion Captain Gibson was the most entertaining of men, had a supply of jokes always on hand, and was as fond of a joke as Abraham Lincoln. He had a horror of gambling and drunkenness, was steadfast in friendship, and always on the lookout for an opportunity to confer a favor upon some friend or relieve the suffering of some fellow-being. Altogether he was certainly a remarkable man. Beneath the sod of Clark county are the remains of many men who were regarded as excellent lawyers and jurists; others who were distinguished as soldiers, and others who were justly classed among statesmen, but it might well be written upon the monument of this man, that the quality of the jurist, the statesman and the soldier were all combined in the same person.

The following paper by the Hon. Jonas G. Howard completes the history begun in Judge Ferguson's article:

THE BENCH AND BAR OF CLARK COUNTY, SUBSEQUENT TO THE CONSTITUTION OF 1851.

The Judicial District of Indiana, of which the Clark Circuit Court forms a part, was composed of the counties of Clark, Floyd, Harrison, Crawford, Orange, Washington, Jackson and Scott, until about the year 1876, when the counties of Clark and Floyd were formed into a Judicial District. Prior to the change in the districts there were but two terms a year in each district in the state, and the sessions for the transaction of business in each county were limited to from two to four weeks. This court was in session only in one county at the same time. The time fixed for the session to be held in each county was prescribed by law.

The Judge would go from county to county and hold court at the prescribed time, and the lawyers of the district, as a rule, would follow the court around the circuit and would take cases wherever offered. The lawyers did not then, as now, confine themselves in the practice of law to the counties in which they lived. Prior to 1850, when many streams were unbridged, the traveling was chiefly by horseback. From 1843 to the close of the year 1852, Judge William T. Otto presided over the Clark Circuit Court. Judge Otto was succeeded by George S. Bicknell, who presided over said court from 1852 to 1876. Judge Bicknell was succeeded by John S. Davis, who presided from 1876 to 1882, the time of his death, which occurred a few months before his term expired. Simeon K. Wolfe was appointed to fill out the unexpired term of Mr. Davis. Mr. Wolfe was succeeded by Charles P. Ferguson, who served on the bench from 1882 to 1894. Mr. Ferguson was succeeded by George H. D. Gibson, who served from 1894 to 1900. Mr. Gibson was succeeded by James K. Marsh, who served six years and was succeeded by Harry C. Montgomery, the present incumbent.

In 1852 a Common Pleas Court was created in the state of Indiana, with circuits composed of from two to four counties, with four terms a year. It had exclusive jurisdiction of all probate business and concurrent jurisdiction with the Circuit Court in all matters of contract and tort, where the amount in controversy did not exceed one thousand dollars, and in matters arising between landlord and tenant, where the title to real estate did not come in issue. For several years after the creation of this court, the counties of Clark and Scott formed a circuit and afterwards the circuit was enlarged by the addition of the counties of Floyd and Washington. Judge Amos Lovering was the first Judge to preside over the Common Pleas Court. He served from 1852 to 1862, when he resigned about the middle of the third term, when Melville C. Hester was appointed to fill the vacancy. In 1864 Judge Hester was succeeded by Judge Patrick H. Jewett, who held the office for eight years. In 1872 Judge Charles P. Ferguson succeeded Judge Jewett and held the office about four years and until the court was abolished.

Judge William T. Otto was the first Judge to preside over the Clark Circuit Court during the period above mentioned. It was claimed by Judge Otto's contemporaries that as a jurist and presiding judge he had no superior and by some that he had no equal.

The Honorable Alexander Dowling, Ex-Judge of the Supreme Court of Indiana, recently said that Judge Otto was the finest conversationalist, the best lawyer and the best judge he ever met; that he could talk law as no other man he ever heard of did, and would have been an ornament upon the bench of the Supreme Court of the United States.

The late Gen. Walter Q. Gresham, Ex-United States District Judge for Indiana; Ex-Postmaster-General under Arthur's administration and Ex-Secretary of State under Cleveland's second administration, said of Otto as a jurist and presiding judge that "he had no superior and few equals."

Judge Otto was born, reared and educated in Philadelphia. He was born in 1815 and came to Indiana about 1837, settled in Brownstown, Indiana, Jackson county, and commenced the practice of law. Soon his superior literary and legal attainments attracted the attention of the leading men of the state; that at the age of twenty-seven years he was elected by the Legislature Judge of the Clark Circuit Court and the District of which Clark county formed a part. This position he held until the close of the year 1852. During the period of his incumbency on the bench he spent his winter vacation in lecturing on law at the Indiana State University at Bloomington. While on the bench he won the reputation of being the ablest presiding Circuit Judge that was ever in the state. While on the bench his manner was imperious, austere and autocratic. He brooked no familiarity from young or old, and handled the most abtruse proposition of law as if a plaything and astonished the older members of the bar with the rapidity and ease with which he solved every legal question submitted for his consideration. Immediately after leaving the bar in 1853 he settled in New Albany in the practice of the law and at once his services were in demand to argue important cases pending before the Supreme Court. In 1855 he was employed by the Liquor League of Indiana, to test the constitutionality of the Maine liquor law, then but recently passed by the Indiana Legislature, in which his efforts were crowned with success. In person he was commanding; was about five feet and eleven inches tall; would weigh about 175 pounds; stout, sturdy and symmetrically built, with a head of medium size, well shaped, with a strong but handsome face, with features, every lineament of which was suggestive of a great strength and power; with a strong, full voice and fine flow of the choicest language. In arguing before the court or jury he stood straight up, motionless, without a gesture or any dallying with oratory, went direct to the controlling points of the case, and came down on his adversary with crushing power like an avalanche. His power was not in arousing the passions or feelings, but in convincing and carrying captive the judgment. I am now speaking of him as a lawyer. He never appealed to the passions or feelings of the court or jury. He seemed to have no use for any weapon other than that calculated to convince the judgment, and enlighten the understanding. His power and influence over a jury thus exerted, far surpassed the effect and influence of the impassioned class of orators. The effect of the impassioned speech may die with the passion, while the convincing power of logic will live.

In 1895, less than three years after Otto had left the bench, he was pitted against George G. Dunn, the "Henry Clay of the West," as he was called, in a noted murder trial at Corydon, in which Dunn spoke eight hours. Mr. John F. Reed, who was associated in the case with Mr. Dunn, said that Otto made the most powerful speech before the jury that he had ever heard and that there was no comparison between the power of the men before a jury; that Otto was by far the superior of the two; yet Dunn stood at the head of the bar in Indiana, as an advocate. I have seen Charles Dewey, Joseph C. Marshall and William T. Otto at the bar in Clark county at the same time and I never have seen three men at the bar of any court, or on the bench of the Superior Court of any state, or of the United States, that I thought equal to those three men.

Judge Otto was appointed Assistant Secretary of the Interior under Lincoln's administration in 1862, and left Indiana and never returned. He served in the position to which he was appointed through Lincoln's and Johnson's administrations and then served for ten years as Reporter of Decisions of the United States Supreme Court, after which he spent the remainder of his life traveling in foreign countries. He died about two years ago at the age of eighty-nine years.

George A. Bicknell was born, reared and educated in the city of Philadelphia and came to Indiana and settled in Scott county in about 1848, and was soon after elected Prosecuting Attorney for the Second Judicial District, and in 1852 was elected Judge of the same district and served for twenty-four consecutive years until 1876, when he was made a Representative in Congress, when he served until 1880, then he served several years as Commissioner as an assistant to the judges of the Supreme Court of the state, in deciding cases that had accumulated in said court from time to time, over and above what the regular judges could dispose of. After that he was elected Judge of the Floyd Circuit Court, which position he filled until his death in 1892. Here is a man who was scarcely ever a day out of office from 1848 to 1892, thirty-six years, yet he was never known to electioneer for any position he filled, a record almost, if not quite unparelleled in the history of the county. His long official career, without any apparent effort on his behalf to secure it, speaks volumes for the man. He was indeed a worthy successor to Judge Otto. Perhaps no man was ever on the bench who was more loved and respected by both bar and litigants. So popular was he upon the bench that it was not unusual for a whole term of court to pass without calling upon a jury to try a single civil suit. The Hon. Thomas W. Gibson said of him: "He never decided a case that he did not convince him he was right, even when the decision was against himself." In conclusion it may be said of him that he discharged every official trust reposed in him with distinguished ability and fidelity.

Judge John S. Davis was not a great jurist, yet he was a very formidable competitor at the bar. He possessed a large fund of common sense and was an excellent judge of human nature. He exercised a wonderful influence over men with whom he came in contact. In this regard, had he been more fortunate in his political aspirations, he may have rivaled Jesse D. Bright. In politics he was a Whig until that party passed away. He then became a Republican, which party ran him for Congress in 1860 against James A. Cravens, the Democratic nominee in a district Democratic by more than three thousand majority, and he came within about three hundred votes of being elected. This race demonstrated his power before the people. Had he remained in the Republican party he doubtless would have attained great political eminence, because his wonderful race for Congress in the stronghold of Democracy gave him a commanding position in his party, but during the War of the Rebellion he joined his fortune with the Democratic party, and sought the nomination for Congress in its convention in 1870, 1872, 1874 and 1876, and was defeated each time and for no other reasons than many Democrats had not forgotten the race he had previously made against them as a Republican. But in his own county, Floyd, where he came in daily contact with the people, he absolutely dominated the Democracy from the time he came into the party until his death. Anything his county could give him he could get. In 1874 Floyd county elected him to the Lower House of the Legislature, where in 1875, in the memorable race for the United States Senate, between Joseph E. McDonald and Benjamin Harrison, at a time when the Democracy lacked one vote of a majority on joint ballot and at a time when the Republicans were highly elated with the prospects of success, and the Democrats correspondingly depressed. In this emergency the last expiring hope of Democracy was centered in John S. Davis. Davis's management secured the needed vote and McDonald was elected to the United States Senate.

The situation at the time was such that no other man than Davis could have secured the vote that gave that important victory to the Indiana Democracy; hence it is fitting that Davis should be held in greateful remembrance by the Democracy of the state of Indiana and of Floyd county as well, for giving to the state the only man that could have done the work.

Simeon W. Wolfe served but a few months as Judge of the Clark Circuit Court, but long enough to show that he possessed great capacity for the business. Mr. Wolfe was born in Harrison county, about 1822, and was educated in the schools of his native county. He married at the age of twenty-one years and settled in Georgetown, Floyd county, Indiana. He engaged in making shoes and reading law until 1849, when he entered the law school of the Indiana State University in Bloomington, Indiana, and was graduated from that university in one term.   He then moved to Corydon, the county seat of Harrison county, and commenced to edit a newspaper and to practice law.   In 1852 he was Democratic Presidential elector for his district and canvassed the same with ability.   In 1860 he was a delegate to the Democratic National Convention at Charlestown, South Carolina.   In 1862 and 1864 he represented Harrison county in the State Senate.   In 1872 he was elected to Congress from his district and served with distinction.   In 1882 he was appointed Judge of the District, composed of the counties of Clark and Floyd.   After that he practiced law in New Albany, until his death in about 1889.   Of all the distinguished men that that magnificent county has given to the state, not one surpasses Simeon W. Wolfe in breadth and strength of intellect.   If his magnetism and social qualities had been equal to his ability, history would place him high up in the ranks of the great men of our state. He was not an attractive speaker, but as a logician and debater he ranked with the very best we had in the state.   In the campaigns of 1866, 1868, 1870 and 1872, I thought he made the ablest and most instructve speeches that were made.   With the severest logic he always went to the very bottom of every subject he discussed.

Judge Charles P. Ferguson, whose name deserves to be held by the people of Clark county in grateful remembrance, for if there ever was a faithful servant of the people Charles P. Ferguson was one.   It might have been truly said of him as Robert Ingersoll said of his brother, that if every person to whom he had done little acts of kindness were to put a rose upon his grave, he would sleep under a world of flowers.   Who can remember the poor people to whom in his long life he has given legal advice without money, and without price, who can number the men he has saved from vexations and fruitless law-suits by giving sound advice?   Of the sixty years he lived, after reaching mature manhood, thirty-six years were spent in the performance of official duties imposed upon him by the partiality of the people.

Mr. Ferguson was born in 1824 in Clark county, near Charlestown, Indiana.   He was educated in Charlestown at the time when it was celebrated for the proficiency of its schools.   At an early age he entered the office of the Clerk of the Circuit Court, as Deputy Clerk and as such served from 1844 to 1852, and in 1852 he was elected Clerk of said court for a term of four years.   In 1856 he was elected for a further term of four years.   In 1860 he began to practice law, and during the same year he was elected to the State Senate for four years.   He then practiced law until 1872, when he was elected Judge of the Common Pleas Circuit Court and served until the court was abolished four years later.   He then practiced law until 1882, when he was elected Judge of the Clark Circuit Court for six years.   In 1888 he was re-elected for six years more, and served until 1894. After that he practiced law until within about three years of his death. As a Judge he was able, faithful and conscientious. He performed every trust reposed in him with distinguished ability, fidelity and with an eye to the public welfare.

While in the strength and vigor of his days Judge Ferguson probably exercised more influence over the people of Clark county than any other man.

Judge Ferguson was well grounded in the principles of the law and always took care of his clients, and was a remarkably shrewd and able practitioner. Socially he was one of the most agreeable and pleasant companions, and generous hearted to a fault. In person he was about five feet and seven inches in height and weighed about one hundred and thirty-five pounds. He had a large and well formed head, with light hair, high and broad forehead, a pleasant expression and an intellectual cast of features indicating firmness and will power.

Patrick H. Jewett was a native of Georgia and came to Indiana about the year 1849 and settled in Lexington, Scott county, and commenced the practice of law and soon came into prominence at the bar. In the year 1854 he was elected Prosecuting Attorney for the Second Judicial District, composed of eight counties. He made an active, energetic prosecutor and discharged the duties of the office with commendable ability. In 1864 he was elected Judge of the common Pleas Court, the circuit being then composed of the counties of Clark, Floyd, Washington and Scott. In 1868 he was re-elected and filled the office, in all, eight years. He performed the duties of the office well and made a proficient judge. As a lawyer he was able, energetic and resourceful, and in the earlier days of his life, before ill health had impaired his native vigor, he was a formidable competitor at the bar and one of the most companionable of men.

Amos Lovering was the first Judge who presided over the Clark Common Pleas Circuit Court. He was a native of Massachusetts, was graduated in one of its colleges. He came to Indiana and settled in Jeffersonville in 1840. He was well grounded in the general principles of law, but never liked to practice it, consequently had but few clients. He had a great taste for literature and avoided the drudgery the law imposed upon him. He was elected Judge of the court in 1852 and served until 1862, when he resigned before the expiration of his third term. He made an excellent and able Judge, and seldom were any of his decisions reversed. He was popular with the people and the bar, and could have retained the office much longer had he so desired. In person he was six feet tall and weighed about one hundred and fifty pounds. He had a large, well shaped head, black hair and symmetrical and handsome features. He died in Louisville about 1877, and will long be remembered as a faithful public servant.

Melville C. Hester, who was appointed to fill out the unexpired term of

Judge Lovering, served about two years. He made a good Judge, and was an able lawyer. He was a native of Clark county and was educated at the Asbury University, Greencastle, Indiana. He belonged to a family noted for its scholarly attainments, and was a brother of several distinguished Methodist preachers, formerly of Southern Indiana. About 1881 Mr. Hester left Charlestown, where he was then living, and went to California, where he now resides. He was a worthy successor to Judge Lovering upon the bench.

Cyrus L. Dunham was born in Thompson county, New York, the 16th day of June, 1817. He was educated and studied law in that state, and came to Indiana and located at Salem in Washington county, in 1841, being then in the twenty-fourth year of his age, and commenced the practice of law, and soon ranked with the best attorneys at that bar. In 1844, at the age of twenty-seven, he took the stump and canvassed his district for James K. Polk for President. In that canvass he demonstrated his ability to successfully cope with any of his opponents. In 1845, at the age of twenty-eight, he was elected Prosecuting Attorney for his circuit and at once established the reputation of an able criminal lawyer. He appeared at the bar of the Clark Circuit at its first session after he was elected Prosecutor, rather shabbily dressed and being a stranger in that locality he made an unfavorable impression upon the people, all of which disappeared before the end of the first day of the session. On the docket for trial that day was a certain criminal case in which the prosecuting witness, after looking at Dunham, came to the conclusion that he had better hire another lawyer to help prosecute the case, plucked Dunham to one side and said, "Young man, had I better employ another lawyer to assist you in the prosecution of this case?" Dunham answered: "My friend, you can do as you please about that, but I tell you that I can prosecute that man as hard as he ought to be prosecuted." Which fact was subsequently verified to the complete satisfaction of the prosecuting witness. In 1846 Mr. Dunham was elected to the Legislature from Washington county and re-elected two years afterwards. In 1848 he was a presidential elector and stumped the state for Cass and Butler, the Democratic nominees for President. In 1849, at the age of thirty-two years, he made the race for Congress and defeated William McKee Dunn. In 1853 he was re-elcted to Congress over Rodger Martin. In 1852 he defeated Joseph G. Marshall, the "Sleeping Lion," for Congress. In 1859 he made the race for Congress and was defeated by George C. Dunn. This was the end of his Congressional career, which was most brilliant. Thus, before he had completed his thirty-fifth year, he had served two years as Prosecuting Attorney, four years in the Legislature and six years in Congress. In 1859 he was Secretary of State under the appointment of Governor Willard, to fill out the unexpired term of Daniel McClure, resigned. In 1860 he was a candidate before the Democratic Convention for Governor, and all the southern part of the state was for him. The northern part was for Hendricks and Dunham withdrew in favor of Hendricks and moved to make his nomination unanimous. In 1861 he raised the Fiftieth Indiana Remigent and was commissioned its colonel and went into the war, served for about one year with distinction, when ill health forced him to resign. In 1871 he was elected Judge of the Floyd and Clark Criminal Court Circuit. He then removed to Jeffersonville, where he lived until his death, November 21, 1877. At a meeting of the Jeffersonville bar, over which Jonas G. Howard presided, the following resolutions were adopted:

Resolved: That in the death of Colonel Dunham, our profession has lost a member possessed of imminent personal and rare legal attainments, guided always by a sense of duty, justice and right. His firmness and perseverance and independence in maintaining his convictions, won the confidence of all who knew him, either in professional, public or private life.

Unfortunately for Mr. Dunham's fame, that in 1854 after he served his six years in Congress, that he did not open a law office and return to the practice of law, for which he was so well equipped and admirably adapted, instead of spending the best years of life on a big thousand acre farm in White river bottoms, raising corn and hogs, a business in which he had had no experience.

Mr. Dunham, in strength and breadth of intellect, was a great man and could combat successfully with any adversary at the bar, or on the stump. Mr. Dunham was one of the few of our distinguished men of Indiana who combined the great persuasive power of eloquence with the crushing power of logic. As a rule these two elements are not found in a great degree in the same individual, as notable exceptions we will name Joseph G. Marshall and Jason B. Brown. Mr. Dunham was more than what is usually termed an advocate. He was intellectually capable of grapling successfully with the most difficult subjects the human mind is called upon to solve. Mr. Dunham, before he reached the meridian of manhood, had contracted irregular habits, which finally, long before his death sapped his intelluctual vigor and those who only knew him after he came out of the war, have but a faint conception of his intellectual power. Long before his death he was conscious of his waning strength and loss of influence. In a conversation with him in 1868, when he resided in New Albany, he complained that when Thomas A. Hendricks and Joseph E. McDonald visited his town, they never called on him; that when he went to their town he never failed to see them. In that conversation, the writer replied to him: "Dunham, if you would just hold up and be yourself again, you would have no trouble with Hendricks and McDonald. They would be glad to meet you, but I fear that you are too excitable to control yourself." He said: "Yes, I am too excitable." This ended the conversation on that subject and I afterwards felt that I ought not to have said what

I had to him. About two months after that conversation I received a note, a few lines, of which I yet have in my possession, which reads as follows, after the address: "Dear Sir:—I have concluded to take your advice and have cut off all supplies forever. Will soon be myself again, age and loss of time only excepted. Yours truly, C. L. Dunham."

In 1864, in the Indiana Legislature, Mr. Dunham was by odds the ablest debater in that body, as well as the most eloquent speaker, though this was some years after his powers began to wane. He appeared at his best in 1852 and 1854, in making his races for Congress with those two intellectual giants, Joseph G. Marshall and George D. Dunn. Once, while making a speech in the Legislature, he was advising against the habit of drinking, some member cried out: "Do you practice that?" Instantly came the answer: "Does the guide board point the way any less because it does not travel it? In the Mexican war there was an Irish gunner named Riley, in General Taylor's command, who deserted and joined the Mexican army. Afterwards, in 1854, during "Know Nothing Times," Dunham, in making a speech, was eulogizing the patriotism of the Irish and Germans, when some one in the audience called out, "Who was Riley." Instantly came the reply: "Riley was an Irishman and Benedict Arnold was an American." Dunham was one of the most gifted men and by nature designed for a better fate.

The names of the principal local attorneys who practiced law at the bar of Clark county, state of Indiana, from 1851 until the year 1900, to-wit: Charles Dewey, Thomas W. Gibson, John D. Ferguson, John F. Read, Charles Dewey, Jr., John Borden, Jonas G. Howard, Simeon S. Johnson, James B. Meriweather, Cyrus L. Dunham, Patrick H. Jewett, George H. D. Gibson, Henry A. Burtt, James E. Taggart, Jacob Buchannan, Thomas J. Gillian, M. Z. Stannard, Matthew Clegg, Park Dewey, Charles P. Ferguson, Melville C. Hester, James K. Marsh, James A. Ingram, George H. Voigt, Edgar A. Howard, James W. Fortune, Ward H. Watson, Edward C. Hughes, L. A. Douglas, F. W. Carr, F. M. Mayfield, T. J. Brock, Harry C. Montgomery, Frank B. Burke, H. W. Phipps and B. C. Lutz.

The names of non-resident attorneys, who for many years during said period appeared at the Clark county bar, are as follows, to-wit: William T. Otto, Joseph G. Marshall, Randall Crawford, Alexander Dowling, John H. Stotsenburg, Thomas M. Brown, D. C. Anthony and George V. Howk.

The bar of Clark county, between the years 1852 and 1862, was stronger than it has ever been since. At the close of that period it lost three of the greatest jurists, lawyers and intellectual giants that ever appeared in a court of justice, namely Charles Dewey, William T. Otto and Joseph G. Marshall, three men that in legal attainments and in intellectual grasp and power have never been surpassed and neither of whom has ever had an equal upon the bench of the Supreme Court of the United State since the days of John Marshall.

Dewey was born in Massachusetts in 1784, and was graduated at Williams College in that state, with first honors of his class. He studied law and came to Indiana in 1816 and located in Paoli, Orange county, and entered into the practice of law, but did not confine himself in the practice to a single county. His great ability brought him rapidly to the front and soon the field of his practice extended to the boundaries of the state. As most lawyers do, Mr. Dewey soon took to politics, and in 1821 was elected to the Indiana Legislature and served with such distinction as to attract the attention of the people throughout the state, and the next year the people of his district demanded that he should run for Congress. His district at that time comprised more than one-third of the state. He was a Whig in politics; his district was strongly Democratic, and he was beaten in the race. Two years after that, in 1824, he moved to Charlestown in Clark county, where he lived until his death, which occurred April 25, 1862, at the age of seventy-six years. At Charlestown he devoted himself assidiously to the practice of law and had the reputation of being the ablest lawyer in the state of Indiana. In 1852 he made the race for Congress against John Carr and was defeated, after which he never ran for an elective office. In 1856 he was appointed by the Governor, Judge of the Supreme Court of the state, which he occupied for eleven years, and honored it as few have done, and by universal consent was placed in the very front rank of Indiana's greatest jurists. Judge Dewey's associates on the bench were Judge Blackford and Jeremiah Sullivan, and it is universally conceded that at no time since the organization of the court has it stood so high as when Dewey, Blackford and Sullivan were its judges, but in strength of intellect and ability to grasp legal questions, Dewey was far superior to either of his distinguished associates. In 1886 Judge William T. Otto said that Judge Dewey was the equal of Daniel Webster, that he had never met a man that in strength of intellect and ability to grasp a legal proposition, was Judge Dewey's equal. That no man on the bench of the Supreme Court of the United States, except David Davis, of Illinois, approximated him. It will be remembered that when Judge Otto made this statement, that it was after Dewey had practiced for twelve years in the circuit of which Otto was Judge and after Otto had served eight years as Assistant Secretary of the Interior under Lincoln's and Johnson's administrations, and had served ten years as Reporter of Decisions of the United States Supreme Court, and several years traveling in Europe, visiting in the courts of England, France, Germany and other countries.

In person Judge Dewey was large and commanding. He was six feet high and weighed about two hundred pounds, his head was large, his forehead high and broad, his hair was black, his complexion dark, his face was large, his features irregular but wonderfully suggestive of intelligence, strength and will power. Judge Dewey was a great admirer of Clay and Webster, but he hated Andrew Jackson. He always condemned the American practice of deserving and selecting military chieftains for civil offices of government, instead of statesmen. He believed that statesmen for the forum and chieftains for the field were the safest for a republic. In 1861, on the day the news reached here that Fort Sumpter had been fired on, Judge Dewey came into the court-house at Charlestown, took a seat by the stove to await the opening of the court. It was a chilly April morning, and he sat there with bowed head and gloomy and apparent distress pictured on his countenance, surrounded by a small group of lawyers all still, not a word being spoken, suddenly he raised his crutch, which he held in his hand and broke the silence by exclaiming, "I wish old Jackson could be brought up out of purgatory just long enough to put down this rebellion, but then I would want him sent right straight back there again." Judge Dewey died on the 25th of April, 1862, and was buried at Charlestown in the town cemetery.

It was said of Marshall that in breadth and strength of intellect Indiana never had a superior and in ability to stir the passions and sway the feeling of the people he never had an equal. He was called the "Sleeping Lion" and fully aroused he was a lion indeed. On such occasions his oratory was like the hurricane that sweeps everything before it. Ordinarily this power was dormant, but when engaged in a case that enlisted his feelings and conscience his words were like hot shot from the cannon's mouth.

In his sketches of Indiana men Oliver H. Smith says of Mr. Marshall, "As a lawyer Mr. Marshall stood among the very first in the state. His great fort as an advocate was in the power in which he handles facts before the jury. At times I have thought him unsurpassed by any man I ever heard, in impassioned eloquence." It should be remembered that Mr. Smith had sat in the Senate of the United States and heard speeches from Clay, Webster and Calhoun. Colonel Abraham W. Hendricks, who for many years had practiced law at the Madison bar with Mr. Marshall in a recent address said of him, "He was the most transcendentally powerful advocate that ever figured at the Indiana bar in Indiana." His intellect was colossal. He seemed to know the lowly intuition; his logic was surrounded by a glowing atmosphere of passion. He could sweep through his subject like a tempest or crash through it like an avalanche. He was sometimes called the Webster of Indiana.

John L. King, of Chicago, once said in a letter that Mr. Marshall was by odds the greatest man Indiana ever produced, but Mr. Marshall himself and Judge Otto both believed that in breadth and strength of intellect that the honor belonged to Judge Dewey, but both men were too great to be envious of each other's fame. Marshall was large, raw-boned, over six feet high and weighed about two hundred pounds. He had a large head and face and sandy hair. His countenance indicated strength, power and determination.

Joseph G. Marshall was born in Fayette county, Kentucky, on January 18, 1800. He was graduated from the university in 1823. He read law in Kentucky. In 1828 he came to Indiana and settled at Madison, where he remained until his death in a town noted for strength of its bar. He soon obtained a lucrative practice and rose to eminence at the bar. Two years later after his arrival in the town he was elected Probate Judge, which office he filled with ability. In 1836, 1840 and 1844 he was on the Whig electoral ticket and each time made an active canvass of state. In 1846 he made the race for Governor and was beaten by James Whitcomb. In 1849 President Taylor appointed him Goernor of Oregon, but he declined the place. In 1850 he was elected Senator from his county and served the legal term. In 1842 he was nominated for Congress in his district, but was beaten by Cyrus Dunham. In addition to the offices named he represented his county several times in the lower branch of the State Legislature. Mr. Marshall had an ambition to go to the United States Senate, but his ambition was never gratified. In the Legislature in 1844 the Whigs had the majority on joint ballot. They nominated him for the Senate but the Democrats refused to go into the election. Each party had twenty-five votes in the Senate, and Jesse D. Bright, then Lieutenant Governor, gave the casting vote against going into the election. In 1854 the People's party had a majority of fourteen on joint ballot, but the Democrats had the majority in the Senate and refused to go into an election. Mr. Marshall was the nominee chosen of the Republican party and had the election been held he would have been chosen, thus it seems that he was twice prevented from going to the Senate by the refusal of the Democrats to go into an election.

John D. Ferguson was a native of Clark county, Indiana. He was born near Charlestown in 1822. His parents were Virginians, and came to Indiana early in the nineteenth century. He read law and was admitted to practice in the Clark Circuit Court at the age of twenty-one. In 1851, at the early age of twenty-nine, he had acquired a large and lucrative practice and was regarded the best lawyer of his age in Southern Indiana. At the time of his death, at the age of thirty-six, he was one of the leading lawyers of the county and at that time had the largest practice of any man in the county. He died in 1858, on the 25th day of April, with consumption. Had he lived until he was fifty years of age he would scarcely have had a superior at the bar in the state. He was a man of the very finest intellect, resourceful, with a wonderful capacity for work, and capable of grappling successfully with the most abtruse questions of law. He was not only a good lawyer, but he was well grounded in national politics. He studied thoroughly the writ-

20

ings of Jefferson, Madison, Hamilton, John Adams, Calhoun, Benton, Clay, Webster and other distinguished writers on political economy; hence he was well equipped at the time of his death for the leadership of his party, which leadership he had enjoyed for the ten years before his death. Absolute leadership was conceded to him by all the leaders of the Whig party in the county. The leaders of the Whig party in Jeffersonville and elsewhere in the county did not know, nor care to know, any other leader than John D. Ferguson. Willard never had a more absolute control over the Democracy of Floyd county than had John D. Ferguson over the Whig party of Clark county from 1850 until that party ceased to exist. He died soon after the Republican party was organized. Had he lived he doubtless would have cast his lot with that party, in fact the great majority of his old Whig friends went into the Republican party after the demise of the Whig party. Although he had never been a candidate for an office, yet no man in Southern Indiana was better equipped for the political arena than he, consequently he had a bright future before him, had his life been spared. He was a distinguished looking man, over six feet high and slender, but symmetrically made, would weigh about one hundred and sixty pounds when in health. He had a large head, a high broad forehead and a long, slim, well proportioned face, light hair, slightly sandy. In speech he had a good voice and an easy flow of language; in argument he was logical, convincing and persuasive; in temperament he was mild and genial. He reminded one of William McKinley in this, he made no enemies. Politically he was popular with both parties. He once said that at one time he had been an admirer of Hamilton, but that upon further investigation his mind had undergone a change and that he had reached the conclusion that Jefferson was the greatest statesman the age had produced.

Captain Thomas W. Gibson was educated at the Military Academy at West Point. He first studied medicine, then law. He came to Charlestown when quite a young man and engaged in the practice of law and soon rose to distinction. He was with General Scott in the war with Mexico. In 1851 he was elected to the Indiana State Senate. He was appointed by that body as one of a special committee to revise the code of practice and to make a new code of laws under our new constitution. These duties were discharged with honor to himself and credit to the state. In 1853 he opened a law office in the city of Louisville, but still retained his residence at Charlestown and attended the sessions of the court of that place in connection with his Louisville practice. His reputation had preceded him and he was employed soon after he arrived there in the prosecution of Mat Ward for killing Butler, a noted case that shook Kentucky from center to circumference, and well nigh turned Louisville upside down. Ward's father was a wealthy Louisville merchant. He was tried in Hardin county and acquitted. This so incensed the people of Louisville that a mob arose and stoned the father's residence, and the residences of some of the attorneys engaged in the defense of defendant. Upon the trial of the cause many able speeches were made on both sides. I read them all and reached the conclusion that Captain Gibson's speech was the ablest delivered on that occasion. Captain Gibson always ranked in strength and intellect with the ablest lawyers of our state. Captain Gibson differed from most lawyers of the present day in this, that outside of his profession he was full of valuable information upon almost any subject that might be broached. Joseph G. Marshall had great admiration for Captain Gibson, when he came to Louisville in 1850 to arrange to fight a duel with Senator Jesse D. Bright, he turned his back on all the other numerous friends of his in Indiana and came to Charlestown and took Captain Gibson with him to act as his second, but while the belligerents were getting ready for the conflict James Guthrie, Judge Pirtle, William O. Butler and other friends of both parties settled the matter so far as the fight was concerned, but the parties never spoke to each other afterward. In person Captain Gibson was a sturdy built man, about five feet, ten inches high and would weigh about one hundred and eighty pounds. He had a large head and face, with regular features, and light hair and complexion. His countenance indicated a man that would brook no insult nor quail before a foe. In 1846 and 1847 he served as captain of a company in the war with Mexico and with distinction. In 1853 he served Clark county in the Senate of the state and was chairman of the committee who made Indiana's code of practice under the constitution. Captain Gibson in breadth and strength of intellect ranked with the very ablest men of Indiana.

John F. Read was born in the county of Davis in the state of Indiana, in 1822. He was a son of James G. Read, a prominent politician of Indiana. Mr. Read came to Indiana with his parents about 1833. He was graduated at Hanover College in 1843, and then read law with Maj. Henry Hurst in Jeffersonville, and was admitted to the bar in 1845, and commenced practicing law in Jeffersonville. In 1853 he was elected to the Legislature and served one term. In 1853 he was appointed receiver of the land office located at Jeffersonville, and he filled that office for several years. After that he served several years as City Attorney. In 1866 Mr. Read and I formed a partnership for the practice of law and for certain enterprises in which we were engaged. Mr. Read was the most valuable man to the city of Jeffersonville that ever lived in it. Yes, he has done enough for the city of Jeffersonville without money and without price, to entitle him to a monument that would transmit his name in story and in song to the most distant posterity. He always contributed to every enterprise calculated to promote the general welfare, freely. The following are some of the enterprises he aided to promote and put his money in to aid in the advancement of the city of Jeffersonville, to-wit: In 1859 he insisted that for the interest of Jeffersonville a turnpike road should be built to the county seat at Charlestown. He aided in the organization and building of the Charlestown pike. In 1864 he insisted on building the Hamburg turnpike, with a view of inviting the trade of our county lying north of Silver creek, which had been going to New Albany to come to Jeffersonville. He helped organize the company and built that road. In 1867 he organized the Ohio Falls Hydraulic Company with the view of developing the water power of the Falls of the Ohio, which resulted in the building of the big flour mill at the Falls. About 1865 and for several years previous the shipyards had been building in Jeffersonville, about twenty-five steamboats a year, the machinery of all were furnished by New Albany foundries. Mr. Read insisted that Jeffersonville should have a foundry and have that work done at home and he organized a company for that purpose, with a capital stock of seventy-five thousand dollars, to which he subscribed ten thousand dollars. He got Dillar Ricketts, then president of the Jeffersonville, Madison & Indianapolis Railroad Company, and several Louisville capitalists interested in the enterprise, but the company failed in getting a competent man to run the business and the scheme was abandoned. Mr. Read then turned his attention to the Sweeney boys, who had started a small foundry on Pearl street, and encouraged them to enlarge their business and aided in raising money to buy machinery. He also encouraged and aided Plumadore in raising money to start his wagon and buggy factory on Pearl street. He assisted Henry Same to raise money to start and run his flour mill on Walnut street. In 1870 he helped organize and put in operation the Ohio Falls Wagon Company, with a capital stock of seventy-five thousand dollars, to which he subscribed five thousand dollars. He also got Belknaps and Avery, of Louisville, interested in the enterprise, and each put into it five thousand dollars, which company gave employment to about seventy-five men for about three years and when the panic of 1873 swept the country like a besom of destruction the company had shipped south several hundred of its wagons to be sold on commission from which it never received any returns. It, together with over twenty-five thousand similar enterprises, went to the wall. Among those that failed was the great Ohio Falls Car & Locomotive Company, capitalized at one million dollars, and the other car company operated in the Indiana State Prison, South. After the former had gone into bankruptcy a bid was offered to the company to buy and remove the plant from Jeffersonville to a neighboring city, and after Mr. Sprague, its president, had labored in vain for more than three months with the people of Jeffersonville to raise the money to re-organize the company and save it to Jeffersonville, and had given up all hope, and had concluded that it be sold and removed to New Albany, at this critical period Mr. Read sent for Mr. Sprague and told him that rather than have the works taken away from this place he would take the responsibility of raising the required amount of money to prevent its removal. In two days after that interview with Mr. Sprague the money was raised, the company re-organized and plans were being made for the resumption of business. This was thirty-five years ago and from that day to this that company has employed from fifteen hundred to three thousand men almost continuously until about one year ago. Again in 1876, in the hope of reanimating Jeffersonville, he organized the Jeffersonville Plate Glass Company, with a capital stock of one hundred and fifty thousand dollars, in which company he invested over sixty thousand dollars. He was president of the company, and at the same time was president of the Citizens National Bank. The company employed two hundred and twenty-five men for nine years, forty of them were experts who received four dollars per day for their labor. The men were paid off every Saturday night, and every glass was sold as fast as it was made. It made the largest plate glass made in the United States. For nine years the company brought into Jeffersonville twenty-five thousand dollars a month. Again when Mr. Barmore's big shipyard sawmill was burned and his shipyard business was lying prostrate and Mr. Barmore was contemplating a location elsewhere, Mr. Read sent for him and told him that he must not leave this city, that his mill must be rebuilt and that he would assist him to raise the money to do it, and he did. In all these enterprises through all these years Mr. Read was so quiet, so unassuming, so unostentatious, so undemonstrative, that the public seldom knew whence the power came. But this is not all, Mr. Read went more poor men's security and helped more men out of financial difficulties than all the other men in Jeffersonville, beside, for years he was on every Falls pilots bond, on the official bond of nearly every officer of the city, township and county. He never withheld help from the needy nor refused aid to the suffering. Through his management and skill the government building was secured to Jeffersonville. He brought on the fight for the re-location of the county seat from Charlestown and lead the fight for three long years and in it Jeffersonville had met such giants at bar as Judge Alexander Dowling, Jason B. Brown and John S. Davis. Jeffersonville had two lawyers besides Mr. Read. Mr. Brown said on several occasions that they would have won in the fight had it not been for that long head of John F. Read. Be that as it may, certain it is that Jeffersonville would not have won without him. In 1884 it was Read who had the men sent to Washington to get the appropriation to build the levee. Mr. Read was endowed with a great intellect and had he given one half the attention to the law that he bestowed upon these other affairs he would have been equal to the very best. In the thirty-five years that Mr. Read and I were associated together he spent in these different enterprises not less than one hundred thousand dollars, beside all these services in every public enterprise was given without compensation. In conclusion I will say that Jeffersonville is indebted to him for the government building, for the county seat, for the Car Works, for the levee and for the Big Four bridge.

In person Mr. Read was about five feet and ten inches high, and would weigh about one hundred and forty pounds; his body was symetrically formed, his head was large, his face well shaped with regular features, his hair was black, his temperament was cool and calculating. Nothing seemed to excite him. He never flew into passion nor used an oath. In speech he was rapid, with a good flow of language. His speeches were earnest, convincing and logical and always directly to the point. In logical power I belive he was unsurpassed.

Frank B. Burke was born in Jeffersonville, Indiana, December 26, 1856. He was a son of the late James and Cornelia Burke, of Jeffersonville. His father was a native of Ireland, and came to the United States in 1848. His mother was a native of Louisiana; her ancestors were French. Mr. Burke was educated at Nazareth, Kentucky. In 1876 he began to make speeches in the Presidential campaign of that year, being then in the twentieth year of his age. He studied law in Jeffersonville and attended law lectures at the Law University in Louisville. He was admitted to the bar in 1878. In 1880 he was elected Prosecuting Attorney of the district composed of counties of Clark and Floyd. In 1882 he was re-elected; from 1886 to 1890 he represented Clark county in the state Senate. In 1893 he was appointed, under Cleveland's second administration, United States District Attorney for the United States, District of Indiana. While in that office he distinguished himself and established the reputation of being a strong and able lawyer. In 1900 he was a candidate before the Democratic convention for Governor and was defeated by John Kern. In the same year he was nominated for Congress by the Democrats of the Indianapolis District and was beaten by his Republican opponent. Burke was a great thinker, but he never spent much time with the books. He did not like the drudgery the practice of law imposed upon him. He liked to examine great questions and discuss them from his own standpoint. He disliked the idea of having to obtain the meaning of the question from the conflicting opinions of a dozen or more different judges and then figure up which side had the majority. He possessed a wonderful capacity for learning and an astonishing ability to grasp the controlling points in a case. His power to arouse the passions and stir the feelings of an audience was almost unequaled. I think in that line he would have rivalled Joseph G. Marshall, the "Sleeping Lion." Once many years ago while he was making a speech to a jury in the prosecution of a man charged with murder in which the sympathies of the audience were with the defendant, at a time when he was coming down heavily upon him, the audience hissed him. He instantly turned to them and said, as no other man could have said it, "More than eighteen hundred years ago the multitude cried out, surrender unto us Barabas." It is said for ten seconds the silence was so intense that you could almost hear every person in the audience breath. Burke possessed great logical power as well as the gift of eloquence. In this he differed from many of our popular orators. As a rule the two elements are not in a marked degree combined in the same person. I claim that Joseph G. Marshall and Burke were exceptions to this rule, that Burke and Marshall's logical powers enabled them to grapple successfully, with any subject, however obtruse, with the ablest advocates in this country. This could not be said of the Henry S. Lane or the Ed. Hanigan type of orators. Cyrus L. Dunham was another of our distinguished men, who combined great logical and oratorical powers. In person Mr. Burke was commanding; he was six feet high and would weigh about one hundred and eighty pounds. He was stout built and symmetrically formed, his head and face were large, his features regular and his hair was black. In temperament he was cool, reserved and undemonstrative, and nothing seemed to excite him. In speech he had an easy flow of language and a voice that I am unable to describe. It differed from the voice of any other I ever heard; and all that I can say about it is that I have seen the passions and feelings of an audience swayed by it as I never witnessed from any other human voice.

Simeon Stephens Johnson was a native of Vermont. He was born at Athens, Windham county, July 22, 1836. He was educated at Newbury Seminary, and prepared for Yale College. His father's death changed his plans and he came to Jeffersonville in 1856, where his elder brother, Jonathan, was then located. He taught school for a year, clerked for a while in his brother's drug store and then entered the law office of the Hon. Jonas G. Howard, to read law. Mr. Johnson was admitted to the practice of his profession in 1859 and immediately entered into partnership with Mr. Howard. He later dissolved this connection and began to practice for himself. Under his instruction several young men of Jeffersonville, who have made their mark, read law, one of them being the Hon. George H. Voigt, one of the most prominent attorneys at the bar of the Clark Circuit Court. In politics Mr. Johnson was a staunch Democrat of the old school, and although he was not an office seeker, he served as City Attorney from 1863 to 1869 and from 1885 to 1887. From 1889 to 1891 he was a member of the City Council from the Second Ward. His services to the city of Jeffersonville were pitched on a high plane of civic and professional pride.

His paramount inclination was toward equity, fair dealing, kindness and charity. Simple and unostentatious he was recognized by all as a man of the most sterling character. In his professional character he was trusted because of his ability and strict adherence to the line of right. In his private relations his life was pure and unsullied.

In 1866 he entered Masonry, being initiated into Clark Lodge, No. 40, Free and Accepted Masons, of Jeffersonville. From this time until his death his whole life was wrapped in the study and practice of the principles of the institution. He was raised to the sublime degree of a Master Mason in May,

1866, and served as worshipful master for ten years, and as grand master in 1898-99. He received the Capitular degree in Horeb Chapter, Royal Arch Masons in 1867; served as high priest in 1872-74 and as grand high priest in 1878.

In Jeffersonville Council, Royal and Select Masters, he served as illustrious master thirty-seven years, and as illustrious grand master in 1894. He was knighted in New Albany Commandery, Knights Templar, in 1867, and served as eminent commander of Jeffersonville Commandery in 1875-76-80-86. He was right eminent grand commander in 1883.

He received the Scottish Rite grades, including the thirty-second degree in the Valley of Indianapolis in May, 1867, in the class with Hazelrigg, Howk and others. In Ancient Craft Masonry he was particularly well versed. He served on the committee on correspondence in the Grand Lodge of Indiana for four terms, from 1886 to 1890, and had the happy faculty to condense a report so that the average Mason could find time to read it. This epitome of Brother Johnson's Masonic record gives but a faint idea of his services for the good of Masonry for nearly half a century. His zeal and work did not abate in the least on retiring from official position, and he attended regularly all the bodies in which he held membership and cheerfully assisted in every way to promote the best interests of all of them. His thorough knowledge of the jurisprudence of Masonry made him a wise and safe counsellor at all times, both in the grand and subordinate bodies. His Masonic record, which has been duplicated in but few cases throughout the United States, indicates to what extent Masonry had entered into his life and to what extent it was appreciated by the craft.

His death in January, 1909, was a loss to Masonry, to the bar of Clark county, and to the city of Jeffersonville.

Sketches of the Judge of the Clark Circuit Court and his two predecessors will be found in the biographical part of this volume. Judge Montgomery, Judge Marsh and Judge Gibson have maintained the high standard of service, character and attainments, which was set in earlier days, but as the scope of this chapter is not intended to include the present membership of the bar of Clark county, a future historian must record their acts. However, one exception may be made to this determination. The Hon. Jonas G. Howard, the dean of the profession, for nearly sixty years a member of the bar, since 1850 prominently connected with nearly every great public movement in the county, and at present a vigorous and enthusiastic leader in public questions, deserves special mention. Jonas G. Howard was educated at Greencastle, read law with John F. Read and was admitted to the bar in 1852. In 1860 he and Simeon S. Johnson practiced together. In 1866 Mr. Howard and John F. Read formed a partnership for the practice of law and for certain enterprises in which they were both engaged. To recount the various enterprises in which he and Mr. Read became interested would be to recount the history of Jeffersonville for the last half century. One of the most important undertakings with which he was connected was the movement to span the river with a bridge. Against overwhelming odds the promoters of this enterprise had to contend; every river man on the Ohio river fought it; the ferry company and other transportation companies controlled the testimony of pilots and other employes, and this, together with affidavits and depositions of connected interests, presented a front well-nigh insurmountable opposition. The Big Four bridge stands today as a monument to the effectiveness of the work done by its promoters.

As a lawyer Mr. Howard will always hold a high place in the history of the Clark County Bar. He was especially noted for his fidelity to his clients, and even after an adverse verdict he was usually found redoubling his energies in endeavoring to secure a new trial. He was never known to give up a legal battle that he felt should be won. His arguments of questions of law were usually based on fundamental principles rather than on case law, and in his arguments before the jury he was particularly effective, oftentimes in an extended argument when warmed up he would take off his coat and continue his speech in his shirt sleeves. He had great success in defending criminal cases, but would never prosecute one. In the great controversy concerning the removal of the county seat from Charlestown to Jeffersonville in the seventies he was one of the leading lawyers on the winning side. In the practice of law the success of his case was his first consideration, the matter of fees being a minor and secondary matter. During the time he practiced law he was extensively engaged in farming, and even at the age of eighty-three he would frequently ride to his farm on horseback, as erect as a cavalryman, where during the harvest season he would be in the field helping to stack his hay. He retired from the practice of law several years ago, but still takes an active interest in politics. He has always been a strong and uncompromising Democrat, and during the third Bryan campaign was one of the most energetic men on the stump in the state, although in his eighty-third year. He still keeps posted on the political issues of the day, and at his present age there is not a better informed man on political affairs in the state. He served in Congress for four years as the Representative from the Third Indiana district, and has held other minor offices in Clark county.

Mr. Howard is public spirited and is interested in all the public enterprises which are for the advancement of the interests of Clark county or of Jeffersonville. Personally he is a most agreeable companion, very sociable and always with a good story to tell. His supply in this line seems to be inexhaustible, and his excellent memory never fails to furnish him with scenes and incidents of the early history of the county and state, especially of lawyers and public men. Physically Mr. Howard is of medium build, a fine specimen

of manhood, well preserved and claiming that the last twenty-five years of
his life were the healthiest.

(Note: Sketches of all the present members of the bench and bar of
Clark county will be found elsewhere in this volume.)

CHAPTER XXX.

BANKS AND BANKING IN CLARK COUNTY.

The first bank in Clark county was a private bank in Jeffersonville in 1817, called the Exchange Bank of Indiana. It was owned by Beach & Bigelow, but the location has been lost. The currency which they issued was a great convenience to the people and the institution was considered a substantial one. It continued in business for several years, but was discontinued shortly after the canal project of the early 'twenties fell through, and strange as it may appear, redeemed all bills that were presented, and some came in many years later. It is said that a passenger on one of the ferries inquired of a boatman if a ten dollar note he held on that bank was good. He was informed that he would do well to inquire of one of the original members of the firm, and on presenting it it was cashed without hesitation.

Jeffersonville suffered through the unlimited circulation of "wild cat" money for many years. But the history of these institutions is too well known to need repetition here. Their day is long past, and it is devoutly to be hoped that the time may never again come when such a system will be allowed to exist.

A few years after this bank ceased to exist a private bank was established by James Keigwin, Sr., Peter Myres and Judge Davis. James Keigwin was the president, and the banking room was the present ferry office on Front street. This bank ran with varying degrees of success until early in the forties, when it collapsed.

The next banking venture was the Bank of Jeffersonville, promoted by Samuel Judah, of Vincennes. George Savitz was the secretary of this bank, and the business was carried on in the room on Front street which had been used by the Keigwin bank. Felix Lewis, Levi Sparks, John Fry, Jacob and George Swartz were stock holders, and the institution was considered a sound one. After this bank went out of business their room was rented by the city of Jeffersonville for a treasurer's office on account of the vault which the management of the old Keigwin bank had built there. At this time it was the only vault in the city.

A branch of the Bank of State of Indiana was organized in Jeffersonville in 1855. This was one of many branches of the Bank of the State of Indiana which were being established throughout the state about that time.

The Board of Directors of the branch of the Bank of the State of Indiana were Messrs. Charles Howard, president; George F. Savitz, secretary and treasurer; W. F. Collum, Simon Bottorff and Thomas L. Smith. After the office of cashier was created, William H. Fogg became the first incumbent. The capital stock was $100,000.00 and it was subscribed by Maybury, Pile & Company, James G. Read, James Mitchell, Simon Bottorff, William F. Collum, George F. Savitz, A. S. Crothers, Levi Sparks, W. L. McCampbell and others.

The bank began business in a brick building on Spring street at what is now 316, and continued here until the institution was nationalized and became the Citizens' National Bank of Jeffersonville. The Citizens' National Bank of Jeffersonville was chartered March 14, 1865, with a capital stock of $150,000.00. It remained in the same location until 1868, when it moved to 219 Spring street. The first Board of Directors was James L. Bradley, president; John Adams, cashier; Dillard Ricketts, James G. Read, Samuel H. Patterson and Andrew J. Hay. This bank is wholly commercial and its sound management has made it the foremost institution of its kind in Clark county. A savings department offers an opportunity for those of small means to profit by patronizing the Citizens' Bank, and its success has shown the wisdom of the directors.

In March, 1907, the Citizens' Trust Company was organized with a capital stock of twenty-five thousand dollars. John C. Zulauf is president, Charles Poindexter, vice-president, and John D. Driscoll secretary and treasurer. The directors are H. M. Frank, Ed. J. Howard, Charles Poindexter, John C. Zulauf, M. Z. Stannard and John C. Rauschenberger. The capital stock was paid up by a special dividend from the Citizens' National Bank. The shareholders of the Citizens' Trust Company are the same as those of the Citizens' National Bank. The Trust company does a trust business exclusively and their building at the corner of Spring street and Court avenue is fitted with the finest vault in the city, and with safety vault boxes for those who wish them. The building was erected in 1908, and with its furnishings cost over twenty thousand dollars.

THE FIRST NATIONAL BANK OF JEFFERSONVILLE.

The First National Bank of Jeffersonville was organized and began business January 30, 1865, with a paid-up capital of one hundred thousand dollars. The organizers were James H. McCampbell, president; Woods Mabury, William L. McCampbell, Hiram Mabury, George W. Ewing, Peter Myers, Levi Silberman, John F. Willey, William W. Gilliland, Gabriel Poindexter and William H. Fogg, the latter leaving the Branch State Bank, where he was cashier, to become cashier of the new institution. All the directors were from Jeffersonville except William McCampbell, who was a resident of Louisville.

The first place of business was on the west side of Spring street, two doors north of the alley between Front and Market streets, and the vault built for their use still remains in this room. The first bank building was purchased from the Lentz estate for the sum of nine thousand dollars. The banking hours were from 10 a. m. to 2 p. m., except Sundays and holidays. In 1887 the capital was increased fifty thousand dollars, or to one hundred and fifty thousand dollars, as it still remains. Mr. Fogg resigned as cashier in 1882, and since that time H. E. Heaton has held that position.

The present location of the First National Bank at Spring and Market streets is a handsome brick and stone building erected about 1870 at a cost of over thirty thousand dollars. The present capital and surplus is over two hundred and twenty thousand dollars. This bank has always operated as a staunch and conservative institution, extending its influence along lines of safety and to the betterment of all classes in the city and county. It is legally known as a bank of discount and deposit, and has lately added a department for savings with liberal interest rates added as accrued.

THE BANK OF CHARLESTOWN.

The Bank of Charlestown was chartered August 15, 1891, and opened for business September 9, 1891, in the room on the corner of Main and Market streets. Its capital stock is twenty-five thousand dollars, divided into two hundred and fifty shares of one hundred dollars each. The stock holders were M. B. Cole, J. D. Sharp, Ward H. Watson and eleven others. Mordecai B. Cole was the first president, Wilfred M. Green, vice-president, and A. M. Guernsey, cashier. The Board of Directors were M. B. Cole, W. M. Green, Rev. J. F. Baird, J. D. Sharp and W. H. Watson.

This bank does a general banking business and has increased its business with the growth of banking elsewhere in the county. In 1898 the bank moved into its new location on the northwest side of the court-house square. This building, constructed to meet the needs of the business, has a handsome Hall vault, of a design similar to that in the Citizens' National Bank of Jeffersonville, and is equipped with safety vault boxes for the use of patrons.

THE FIRST NATIONAL BANK OF CHARLESTOWN.

The First National Bank of Charlestown was chartered September 11, 1903, and started in business in October of the same year at the corner of Main and Market streets. Its capital stock is twenty-five thousand dollars. The first Board of Directors was John C. Zulauf, McD. Reeves, J. S. Robertson, J. F. McCulloch and George W. Lewman, and the board remains the same now with the exception that George H. Gibson has succeeded Mr. Lewman. This bank does a general banking business, and is in a very prosperous condition, paying six per cent. dividends. The deposits amount to sixty-five thousand dollars, and at present there is an undivided surplus of four thousand five hundred dollars on hand.

THE HENRYVILLE STATE BANK.

The Henryville State Bank was organized February 11, 1904, and began business March 17, 1904. Hardin Wilson, of Louisville; E. L. Elrod, George Bollinger, John Scholl, Charles Genner, John Hamm, Zach Taylor, and many others were interested in its organization. The capital stock is twenty-five thousand dollars, and its present surplus and undivided profits are five thousand dollars. The first president was Edward L. Elrod, George Bollinger, vice-president and W. Wayne Wilson, cashier. The principal stockholders are Hardin Wilson, John J. McHenry, John W. Hamm, Edward L. Elrod, John S. Scholl, H. R. Hamacher, Henry C. Hamm, Elizabeth Corbett, Charles Genner, Zach Taylor and George Bollinger.

THE BORDEN STATE BANK.

The next bank organized in Clark county is located in the town of Borden, and was chartered by the State of Indiana. The Borden State Bank was organized October 20, 1905, with Samuel H. Karnes as president; G. M. Johnson, vice-president, and Murray S. Wilson, cashier, commencing business March 3, 1906. Opening with deposits the first day which showed the confidence of the public in the officers, the business of the bank has steadily grown into one of the strongest state banks in not only Southern Indiana, but, according to two of the state bank examiners, in the state. It has a capital stock of twenty-five thousand dollars.

During the first year of business the net earnings of the bank amounted to eight per cent. of the capital. The stockholders were paid a dividend of four per cent. and the remainder of the earnings carried to the surplus, it being the intention of the officers to put the institution on a sound basis independent of the stockholders' liability. At the close of business the second year the net earnings showed almost eleven per cent., of which amount an eight per cent. dividend was paid to the stockholders and the balance carried to the surplus. After six months of the third year it appeared that the earnings for the year would eclipse previous records. During the thirty months in operation not a single note has been accepted which has not been good for one hundred cents on the dollar. During the panic, so-called, of the fall of 1907 and the spring of 1908 the Borden State Bank did not suffer in the least from loss of confidence of the public, paying in full every check presented by a customer or friend.

At the beginning of the second year of business Charles E. McKinley was elected president to succeed Mr. Karnes, and Mr. McKinley has since retained the position. For four months in 1907 Mr. Wilson was absent from his post as cashier, the position being filled during that time by H. C. Woolf.

With average deposits of sixty-five thousand dollars, the bank in excellent conditions, is managed by the following officials: Charles E. McKinley, president; G. M. Johnson vice-president; Murray S. Wilson, cashier, J. M. Shoemaker, assistant cashier. The directors are Charles E. McKinley, G. M. Johnson, J. H. McKinley, H. B. Payne, George McKinley, Hardin Wilson, Nelson Morris, Sylvanus McKinley and Ben Hanka, Jr.

The Clark County Sentinel, of Borden, says of the Borden State Bank: "One of the excellent banking institutions of Clark county is the Borden State bank, which was established last spring. Its September statement shows strength and it is destined to become one of the leading financial institutions of the county." The officers of the bank seem to be very popular and to have the confidence of the people of Borden and vicinity. It has been a great convenience to the berry growers. Mr. Wilson, the cashier, reports that nearly fifty thousand dollars of berry money passed through the bank during the season of 1907, several thousand dollars' worth of small change having been paid out. It is estimated that ninety per cent. of the checks were under ten dollars, meaning that approximately eight thousand berry checks have been cashed at the bank without any expense to the grower. When this record is compared with that of the balmy days when it was a case of the odd cents off for cash, the grower can figure out what has been saved. That this bank is anxious to serve its customers is shown by it keeping open from six to seven in the evening to accommodate the berry growers who arrive too late for regular banking hours.

THE NEW WASHINGTON STATE BANK.

Early in 1908 the movement for organizing a state bank at New Washington took definite form, the articles of incorporation being as follows:

For the purpose of organizing an association to carry on the business of a bank of discount and deposit under the provisions of an act of the General Assembly of the state of Indiana approved February 7, 1873, and of the several acts amendatory thereof and supplementary thereto, the undersigned subscribe for the stock of said association to enter into the following articles of association:

Article 1.—The name of the Association shall be New Washington State Bank.

Article 2.—The place where the business of the bank is to be carried on is the town of New Washington, Clark county, Indiana.

Article 3.—Amount of Capital Stock of said bank shall be twenty-five thousand dollars, to consist of two hundred and fifty shares of one hundred dollars each.

Article 4.—Names and places of residence of shareholders and number of shares held by each is as follows, to-wit: N. H. Linthicum, New Washington, five; J. H. Dickey, Louisville, Kentucky, ten; J. L. Magruder, New Washington, thirty, and many others.

IN WITNESS WHEREOF, We, the undersigned, subscribe our names, this 3d day of March, 1908.

Signed by—

Henry Schowe, Marysville, Indiana, seven shares.

A. M. Fisher, New Washington, Indiana, ten shares.

S. K. Peck, Nabb, Indiana, five shares.

A. R. Miles, Bethlehem, Indiana, ten shares.

N. H. Linthicum, New Washington, Indiana, five shares.

R. S. Taggart, New Washington, Indiana, five shares.

J. C. Bower, Charlestown, Indiana, seven shares.

T. N. Manaugh, New Washington, Indiana, five shares.

T. R. Stevens, Bethlehem, Indiana, five shares; and others.

Henry F. Schowe was elected president and J. L. Magruder, cashier. Twelve thousand, five hundred dollars of the capital stock was paid in, being fifty per cent. of the total.

THE SELLERSBURG STATE BANK.

The last financial institution in Clark county was organized and the articles of incorporation sworn to November 27, 1908. It was organized under the name of "The Sellersburg State Bank. Its capital stock is twenty-five thousand dollars, consisting of two hundred and fifty shares at one hundred dollars each.

A directory of nine members guide the destinies of the bank. A partial list of the stockholders is as follows:

Ed C. Hughes, Charlestown, Indiana, thirty shares.

Oscar F. Lutz, Charlestown, Indiana, five shares.

Thomas T. Combs, Charlestown, Indiana, ten shares.

Samuel Lutz, Charlestown, Indiana, ten shares.

C. A. Prather, Memphis, Indiana, five shares.

Chris Weidner, Sellersburg, Indiana, five shares.

John T. Ross, Charlestown, Indiana, five shares.

Lemuel G. Bottorff, five shares.

T. A. Pass was elected president and Otis W. Scott, cashier. One-half of the capital stock has been subscribed and paid for.

STEAMER JAMES HOWARD.

CHAPTER XXXI.

THE RIVER.

STEAMBOAT BUILDING AND STEAMBOATING — FLAT-BOATING AND FALLS
PILOTING—HARBOR IMPROVEMENTS AND THE NINE-FOOT STAGE.

The frontage of Clark county upon the river, and the intimate relations
between the people of the river towns and the commerce of that great natural
highway, have brought boat building up to a high position in the business life
of the county.

Jeffersonville, from her location at the head of the Falls, and from the
fact that she possesses the best and deepest harbor between Pittsburg and
New Orleans, has been a place for water craft construction from very early
times. The history of her boat-building plants and her output of water craft,
beginning with the launching of the steamer United States here in 1819,
would be incomplete without a description of the forerunners of our present
floating palaces, the keel-boat and the flat-boat. To this subject may naturally
be added that of Falls piloting for Falls piloting was peculiarly a Jeffersonville
business, and Jeffersonville the home and headquarters of falls pilots.

In the latter part of the seventeenth, and the early part of the eighteenth
centuries, the Falls of the Ohio, and the region around about, was a center of
attraction; alluring to explorers, travelers, traders and emigrants; including
agents for capitalists, surveyors, engineers and scientists. These visitors left
copious notes of their observations, and some vivid predictions respecting the
future growth and prosperity of the settlements. The predictions then made
are now fully verified in the present numerous population, great wealth and
prosperity of the three Falls Cities. For had it not been for the Falls there
would now be no Louisville, no Jeffersonville, no New Albany.

As early as June, 1765, a Colonel Crogan, who was in the employ of an
English Indian agent, came down the river in small boats, called batteaux, to
the head of the Falls, where the boats were lightened and passed over. These
batteaux were small row-boats, and the navigators of them were sometimes
called batteau-men. Later on boats on the river were called keel-boats. Gen.
George Rodgers Clark in his memoirs mentions loading stores and ammunition, and embarking one hundred and fifty volunteers at Pittsburg, and
coming down the river to the head of the Falls, where his command encamped
on an island near the Kentucky shore, and that they left the island on June

21

24, 1778, and ran about a mile up the river in order to gain the main channel and shoot the Falls. The boats mentioned by him must have been keel-boats, modeled for rowing against the current, or they could not have run up a mile to gain the main channel.

In Dillon's History of Indiana is a mention that in the summer of 1786 provisions and stores were loaded in keel-boats at Louisville and Clarksville for the army at Post Vincennes. Obviously these keel-boats were partly load-ed above the Falls, and stores which had been taken by the portage route on the Indiana side to Clarksville were added to the cargo there, after passage of the Falls.

For many years after these events, keel-boating was the only mode for taking cargoes down the river. They were built with a keel, sharp bow and stern, modeled somewhat like a canal-boat, but lighter. They floated down with the current to destination, and were cordelled back. Getting back was the laborious part of the trip. In cordelling a part of the crew would walk up the shore, pulling the boat up stream with a long line attached to its bow, while others of the crew on the boat would help over obstacles and keep it off shore with long poles. In this way keel-boats were brought back from New Orleans to the Falls and points above; consuming sometimes the better part of the year to make the round trip.

Mr. James Flint, a Scotchman, was here in 1819. On May 19th of that year he wrote as follows: "The steamboat, Western Engineer, and a number of keel-boats descended the Falls today." So it is in evidence that keel-boats were still numerous on the river at that date. And he ought to be good authority for he appears to have been a close observer. He also wrote that there "were sixty-five houses, thirteen stores and two taverns in the town, and a steamboat on the stocks, measuring one hundred and eighty feet long, forty feet broad, estimated to carry seven hundred tons."

Living in Jeffersonville during the era of keel-boating was a roving, tumultuous character, named Marble Stone, or Rolling Rock, as he called himself when in his cups. When relating his river experiences in his sober hours, he always claimed that he had made thirteen trips on keel-boats to New Orleans and walked back, sometimes helping to cordelle the boats, and sometimes taking the shortest trail homewards. On one of these trips, the boat arrived at New Orleans soon after the battle had been fought and won by General Jackson, but in time for the crew to participate in the prevailing enthusiasm, and gather incidents of the fighting. While footing it home by a trail leading through Nashville, the party made up a song, replete with humor, laudatory to General Jackson and the Americans, and belittling to Lord Packingham and the British. On arriving at Nashville Stone tanked up to a hilarious condition, celebrating the occasion of his arrival by singing the song on the streets, and attracting unusual attention. As Tennessee was largely represented in that battle, the song naturally created much enthusiasm as well as amusement. The Legislature being then in session, Stone was brought to an informal meeting of the members, the sole object being to hear the song repeated. Stone's version of his reception was that he captured the whole crowd tooth and toe-nail, and was feasted and treated and sent home to his wife Polly in a stage coach. And he ever afterward asserted that he was the only keel-boatman ever entertained by a state Legislature.

As time rolled on Indians disappeared from the shores, or became friendly. Traffic on the river increased, flatboats, sometimes called broadhorns, succeeded keel-boats, because they were more economical. They were built for the down trip only, and in such a manner that they might be taken apart and sold with the cargo. The flatboat was a square bowed, square sterned box, like a scow, from twenty to eighty feet long. In its construction large timbers were used for gunwales, one for each side, curved upwards on the ends, and fastened together with strong cross timbers. The bottom was made by fastening heavy planks across from gunwale to gunwale, and tightly caulking the seams to prevent leaking. On this solid part of the boat or hull, a light freight house was built, in which to store the cargo. Upon the roof the oars were hung on iron oar pins, ready for use in landing, avoiding sandbars or the banks in short bends. In these flatboats the hay, grain, potatoes, salt pork and the like, produced in the upper country, so called, were floated to New Orleans, or peddled along the coast of the lower Mississippi river. Coal and salt boats were built in like manner, but with heavier timbers, and without housing or roofing. The early day coalboats were from eighty to one hundred feet long, twenty feet wide and eight feet deep inside, with perpendicular sides and ends, drawing when loaded about six feet of water. They floated in pairs, lashed together and were kept in the channel with ten oars, three on each side called sweeps, two on the stern ends, one on each boat, called steering oars, two on the bows called gougers. These double boats required a crew of eighteen men, which was increased to twenty-one in passing the Falls. Single boats in passing the Falls required thirteen hands including the pilot and assistants. Later on coal boats were enlarged to one hundred and eighty feet long, twenty-four to twenty-six feet wide and ten feet deep, drawing when loaded eight feet of water, leaving only two feet above water all around. They held twenty-five thousand or more bushels of bituminous coal, of nearly nine hundred tons weight. Consequently they were unwieldy and difficult to handle. During high stages of water they were taken safely over the Falls in pairs, but on scant coal-boat water were taken singly. But coal fleets generally came down the river on the crest of high water and such as were destined for markets below were rushed over with the least possible delay. One pilot, H. S. Barnaby, is reputed to have taken over twelve pairs in one day, earning fees amounting to one hundred and twenty dollars. This record, however, was made at a favorable time in June, 1855. There was plenty of water, but falling fast. A large fleet of all kinds of flat bottom boats was passing, and so anxious were boat owners to get over while the Falls water lasted that they crowded into the channel, following the leaders so closely that, at times, it looked to observers, like inviting destruction, but good luck was with them and the day passed without accident. A gentleman now living here drove Mr. Barnaby's buggy to Clarksville to meet him, from daylight until dark that day. He says that Mr. Barnaby would jump into the buggy at Clarksville, take the whip and lines and drive back at a furious pace to catch another pair of boats opposite the town, making the round trip in less than an hour. At this rate his day's work netted him ten dollars an hour.

The number of boats of all kinds going over the Falls, and the necessity of capable men piloting them gave the business a more than ordinary importance. River talk in those days was on every tongue. The interesting topics discussed were prospective rises, falls, water, character and efficiency of pilots, the treacherous currents and eddies, obstructions in the Falls, like Ruble rock, Aleck rock, Wave rock, Willow Point rock and Old Enoch. Ruble rock was considered the most dangerous; it was dreaded by owners, pilots and crew at certain stages of water. It lay under the surface, almost in the middle of the channel, a little below where the Louisville Railroad bridge now crosses to Fourteenth street. It could not be located accurately when the river was low by the waves and eddies caused by the resistance to the current. A generally credited report says that a Mr. Ruble was the owner of the first boat wrecked by striking it, hence the name of Ruble rock. It is also said that the names Aleck and Enoch rocks were attained for like causes. Aleck rock lay some five hundred feet below Ruble, on the left of the channel, projecting out into the chute, but not dangerous in low water as the channel then receded from it. Wave rock, about half a mile below, reached out some five hundred feet from the backbone side, causing the channel to turn sharply to the right, and creating the upper part of the Whirlpool bend. Willow Point rock, just below Wave rock, reached out from the Indiana side, about one hundred yards beyond the point of Wave rock, causing the channel to turn again sharply to the left, thus completing the Whirlpool bend. Some distance below this Enoch rock lay on the left of the channel. All of these then dangerous rocks have been removed under the supervision of the United States engineers.

In order to understand just how a flatboat passed through the Falls, you should imagine yourself in a position to follow one over with the eye. The boat is turned out into the channel from the harbor above, pilot, steersman, and oarsmen are aboard, the pilot assumes command and stations himself on deck in full view of the steersman and crew, and facing the head of the chute;

from there he indicates to the steersman the course to hold the boat with his right and left hands. The propelling oars are stoutly manned and vigorously plied to give the boat steering momentum. As she approaches the head of the chute she is held for the deepest water, which is in the left of the channel. She enters the chute speeding along with a ten or thirteen mile current, and, bearing a little to the left, with lively help of the oars, safely passes the dangerous Ruble rock, then bearing a little to the right she avoids Aleck rock, then a little to the left again to avoid the Little Eddy, she glides swiftly down Whirlpool point, where the current turns sharply to the right and carries her on past the point of Wave rock into the Whirlpool bend, where with active help she swings around the point and heads toward the Kentucky shore, now bearing up to the left to keep off Willow Point rocks which reached out from the Indiana side, she rushes past these and swings sharply around to the right again and is carried down into the Big Eddy, and into serene waters nearly opposite to old Clarksville, where the Falls crew leave her after a successful run of nearly a mile and a half.

Long before keel-boating had been relegated to the limbo of the past steamboats had become common. The earliest steamboats came from Pittsburg. The first steamboat to navigate the Ohio was one named the "New Orleans" and upon her first trip down the river she passed by Utica, between nine and ten o'clock at night, in October, 1811, creating much alarm. After she had passed, the reality appeared more like a dream On her arrival off Louisville, about 12 o'clock, the boat in letting off steam brought many people from their beds to witness the novel sight. The general impression was that a comet had fallen from the heavens into the Ohio. This boat made two trips between Louisville and Pittsburg, and then went south to stay. The New Orleans was built by Robert Fulton and Robert Livingstone, at Pittsburg. She had low pressure engines and was a little over three hundred tons. The next steamboat to pass down the river was the Comet. She was a stern-wheel boat of forty-five tons, built at Pittsburg by Daniel French. She was equipped with his patent vibrating cylinder and was considered a wonder. She made the voyage to Louisville in the summer of 1813 and to New Orleans in the spring of 1814. After this she made two voyages to Natchez, and was then sold.

The third steamboat to pass down the river was named the "Vesuvius." She was a boat of about three hundred and ninety tons and was built at Pittsburg. She passed down the river in 1814, bound for New Orleans. The fourth steamboat was the Enterprise, a boat of forty-five tons, built at Bridgeport, on the Monongahela river by Daniel French. She made two voyages to the Falls of the Ohio in the summer of 1814. On May 6, 1815, she left Pittsburg and reached Shippingsport May 30th (the same year), making the unprecedented time of twenty-five days. She was the first steamboat to come from New Orleans to the Falls of the Ohio. The fifth steamboat to visit our shores was the Aetna, three hundred and sixty tons, one hundred and fifty-three and one-half feet long, twenty-eight feet beam and 9 feet hold. She was built at Pittsburg by Fulton and Livingstone and came down the river in 1815. The sixth steamboat was the Dispatch, twenty-five tons; the seventh was the Buffalo, three hundred tons; the eighth was the James Monroe, ninety tons; the ninth was the Washington, four hundred tons. The Washington was the first boat to have her boilers on the main deck instead of in the hold.

The success of these boats and the advantages of Jeffersonville as a boat-building location led to the establishment of a yard here as early as 1819. The first steamboat built here was the United States, and she was launched this same year. She was owned by a Mr. Hart and others and was reported as being undoubtedly the "finest merchant steamboat in the universe." She had two separate engines which were built in England and drew but little water but was capable of carrying three thousand bales of cotton. She was one hundred and eighty feet long, forty foot beam and of seven hundred tons. In this same year another yard was established in Clarksville, and four boats were building there boats of from sixty to two hundred tons. Most of the timber for these craft was cut from the banks of upper Silver Creek and floated down by freshets.

As all steamboats burned wood in those days the establishment and maintenance of wood yards along the river was a necessity and, until the adoption of coal as a fuel the wood business was a large and important industry.

One of the early boat-builders of Clark county was Barzillai Willey, who lived near Silver Creek near Memphis. He was one of the earliest settlers there and was a great mill builder. He built a sixty-foot boat on his farm in 1813 or 1814 and floated her to the river on a freshet where he sold her. In 1824 he furnished a great deal of whip-sawed lumber to build a boat then on the stocks near the mouth of Silver creek. This boat was being constructed by a genius who conceived the idea that he could propel her by means of laying a steam pipe over her stern and allowing the steam to escape through it into the water. The three French brothers, William, George and Henry, engaged in boat building in Jeffersonville in 1829, and turned out several very fine boats, among which were the Diana, a side-wheeler, the Edward Shippen, a side-wheeler, the Louisiana and several others. Their yard was below the present Howard plant. The French plant was in existence for a number of years, and these boat builders ranked very high in steamboat construction. William was the genius of the family.

In 1831 or 1832 Robert C. Green had a small yard at the upper end of the city, where he made a few boats, but did not continue the business long. Green started a foundry where the glass works were in the eighties, and paid more attention to making engines and machinery than to boat building.

The methods of work in those days were in great contrast to the methods now. Where a great deal of the timber used in the construction of steamboats is transported by rail from a distance at present, all that used in the early days of steamboat building was rafted down the Ohio. For many years Alex Hanley and his sons furnished rafted timber to the Howard yards, and it is a matter of interest to know that the timber received from the earliest days to the present time has all come from the same locality—the Big Sandy, the Guyandotte rivers, and Twelve Pole creek. The logs were taken from the river and sawed into lumber by the most primitive methods. Whipsawing, as it was called, consisted of cutting the timber by hand power, using a long saw with a double handle on each end. The log was rolled over a pit where one man below and one above drew the saw up and down until it was reduced to timber of the dimensions needed.

Henry French and Peter Myers engaged in the boat building business in 1847, and turned out considerable good work in the five years they were associated. Mr. French attended to the ship-yard while Mr. Myers had charge of the saw-mill. The business was finally divided, Mr. Myers retaining the saw-mill, which he rented to French, Stratton and Logan, and some years later it burned. Logan, who was connected with the saw-mill, died and Stratton sold it to David S. Barmore in 1864. The French yard turned out about twenty boats, but a complete list of names or dimensions is impossible to secure Previous to the purchase of the lower boat plant by Barmore, Samuel King had come into control, but he retained it less than two years.

As the construction of water craft in Jeffersonville continued and increased the importance of falls piloting likewise grew. To a person standing on the river bank any balmy day in the fifties, when the river was up to full boating stage, the scene was intensely interesting. More than two miles of the channel was in plain view, produce boats, high hay boats, low salt boats, and family scows, following each other in a long line leading into the Indiana chute. On every boat was alertness and activity, along the shore pilots, steersmen and hands were hustling for trips, skiffs with crews were plying between the line of boats and the shore, horses with boy riders and light wagons were hurrying to and from the landings to bring pilots and crews back for other trips. These activities, together with the eager crowds of onlookers, completed a panorama-like picture not soon to be forgotten by the eye witness.

At such times when the river was full of boats, and all the pilots were busy, a few restless owners would turn out into the channel and follow boats known to be in charge of licensed pilots. It is probable that more would have done so, had their inclination to take the chance not been held in check by a clause in the cargo insurance policy, which required the presence of a licensed pilot on board. For some years the Jeffersonville Insurance Company issued policies for Falls risks. James Keigwin, Althanasius Wathen and other prominent citizens of the town, were the officers and owners of the stock. Its business office was in the building now occupied as the office of the superintendent of the Ferry Company, on Front street.

Dangerous as the Falls were considered to be, few lives were lost by accidents to descending flatboats, only one is now recalled. In 1837 Leonard Bowman, while steering for pilot William Bowman, was thrown overboard and drowned. He was standing by the steering oar, the blade of which was caught in an eddy or strong undercurrent. He was a highly respected young man, and it is said that his was the largest attended funeral seen in the town up to that time.

A much-talked-of incident occurred some years later. A coal-boat in going over the Falls, struck Ruble rock and tore a hole in the bottom from bow to stern, letting the coal out and the water in. Cyrus Wright was steering. When he saw the coal disappearing, he realized that the boat could not float many minutes, so he unshipped his oar to have something to float on. After the boat disappeared he found only himself and Isaac Gaither on the oar. Mr. Gaither was a very pious man, a loud and stirring exhorter at Methodist revivals, and a firm believer in the efficacy of prayer. He at once threw up his hands and began to call loudly on the Lord to save them. Mr. Wright was a very different character, he was a resolute man of action, and evidently thought that safety lay in their own exertions, and at once commenced paddling vigorously with both hands. On discovering that his companion was making no effort except to make his prayer heard above the roar of the Falls he became enraged and shouted to him to paddle. "Paddle, Gaither, paddle, damn you, paddle and pray afterwards." When Gaither's fright somewhat subsided and the true situation dawned on him, he did paddle as vigorously as he had prayed, and the oar was run safely to shore. People who were intimately acquainted with Mr. Wright credited him with language much more forcible than that here attributed to him. The others of the crew clung to floating planks and oars, and were rescued by fishermen who put out from the shore in skiffs. It was a very cold day in winter and their clothes froze on them soon after reaching the shore, and some of the weaker ones, being exhausted, were about to succumb to the cold, but Mr. Wright again arose to the occasion, and by vigorous swearing at them and pounding them in the back, kept them going, and they all reached town. His service as collector on the ferry boats for many years made him widely acquainted, and his free and unlimited use of adjectives on all occasions was alarming to the pious.

It is obvious that the law making powers were at an early date called upon to regulate falls navigation by statute. The first act was passed by the Kentucky Legislature in 1797. The next act found on record is the territorial law adopted by the Governor and two judges of the territory of Indiana, September 24, 1803.

Davis Floyd and John Owens, citizens of Clarksville, were appointed falls pilots December 14, 1803, nearly three months after the adoption of that law. Charles and Reuben Sleade, brothers, were appointed at a later date—they were known to be falls pilots in 1810.

The first state law was enacted by the General Assembly and approved February 7, 1825. By this act the number of pilots authorized was increased to four, who were required to each execute a bond in the sum of five thousand dollars. The pilotage fees were fixed at three dollars for a flatboat, except for family boats under thirty feet in length, for which two dollars should be charged. It provided for a fine of ten dollars for refusal by an authorized pilot to take a boat over on tender to him of the lawful fee, and a fine of twenty dollars for taking a boat over by an unauthorized person, except he be the owner. The pilots commissioned under this law, so far as ascertained, were Charles Sleade, Andrew Fite, Alexander Welch and John Weathers.

Later on another general law concerning falls piloting was passed—see revised statutes 1843. By this act the number of pilots authorized was increased to six. The fees were slightly changed, the same character of bond was required, the same forfeitures and penalties for violation of the law were re-enacted; also an additional clause that provided for forfeiture or license for wilfull neglect of duty, or removal from the vicinity of the Falls, and for demanding a greater fee than that fixed by law.

William Bowman, Charles Sleade, William Patrick, John Morgan, Thomas Powell, Samuel Cash, Angel Gill and Moody Dustin are remembered as Falls pilots acting under that law.

Another general law on the subject passed the General Assembly on June 15, 1852. By this act the Governor was authorized to appoint eight falls pilots for terms of four years each, and it provided that the fees for pilotage should be fixed by the Board of Clark County Commissioners.

A complete list of the pilots appointed under the act of 1852 is as follows: Aaron P. Sleade, April 28, 1853; John Lanceskes, April 28, 1853, re-appointed March 25, 1861; Charles Friend, April 28, 1853, re-appointed November 13, 1857, and June 9, 1863; Angel Gill, April 28, 1853, re-appointed October 20, 1857; David M. Dryden, April 28, 1853, re-appointed May 7, 1859, and June 9, 1863; H. S. Barnaby, April 28, 1853, re-appointed May 7, 1857; M. W. Veach, April 28, 1853; Moody Dustin, April 28, 1853, re-appointed May 7, 1857 and June 9, 1863; Samuel Cash, March 6, 1854; Joslan Reeder, April 30, 1857; Thomas Patterson, April 30, 1857; John Gibbs, October 20, 1857; George W. Lampton, March 5, 1858, reappointed March 6, 1862; Thomas Grey, March 5, 1859; John Lefevre, April 16, 1861, re-appointed November 30, 1865; Calvin Cook, March 4, 1862; W. H. H. Taylor, March 3, 1863; Solomon Partlow, April 30, 1865; W. B. Cox and Samuel Knight in 1869; Fountain Harness in 1873, Perry Gaither in 1873 and 1878 and 1882; John

Onion, March 1, 1874; Levi Reeder, March, 1874, and March 8, 1878; W. B. Carter in 1874 and John H. Hoffman in 1874.

The conditions are now so changed that any state law concerning falls piloting is absolutely useless. No more flatboats are passed over the Falls by pilots licensed by the state. Powerful towboats, owned by capitalized combinations, now handle all the coal boats and barges and other heavy products, over the Falls or through the canal, guided by the towboats' pilots, who obtain license from inspectors who are authorized to issue in accordance with laws of Congress. And the produce that in times past floated to Southern markets has been diverted from the river to the railroads, or is carried by steamboats. The old Falls pilots were a sturdy lot of men, and their occupation was one that called for a high class of efficiency, and the value of the cargoes and lives entrusted to their care bespeaks for them a reputation in their work the peer of any.

THE HOWARD SHIP YARDS.

The history of steamboat construction in Clark county is to a great extent the history of the Howard yards. James Howard, the founder of this great industry, was born near Manchester, England, September 1, 1814, and emigrated with his father, mother and brother, Daniel, to the New World, in 1819, landing in Brooklyn. In 1820 the family traveled overland to Wheeling, West Virginia, where they embarked on a flatboat for the city of Cincinnati, arriving there late that year. James worked for his father in wool-carding and cloth-dressing until he was fifteen years old, and then for a short time in the ship-yard of William Gordon. He was afterward apprenticed to William Hartshorn, a steamboat builder, to learn the trade of ship carpenter, and applied himself with such assiduity to his work that he was able to draft a boat when he was only nineteen years of age. After spending four years with his master he came to Louisville and succeeded in getting a contract to build a boat. Jeffersonville offering the most available location to meet his needs he established his yard on a small tract of land at the foot of Mechanic street. Here he laid the keel for his first boat and she was finished in 1834. She was named the "Hyperion," and was built to run on the Chattahoochee river in Alabama. She was a side-wheeler, one hundred and seven feet long, eighteen feet beam and eight feet hold, Captain Leonard. At that time and in fact for many years afterwards, the hull was the only part built by the contractor, the upper work and engines being separate contracts. During the years 1834 and 1835 he built two more boats—the "Black Locust," a center-wheel ferry boat, for the Jeffersonville & Louisville Ferry Company, and the "Tecumseh," a side-wheel boat one hundred and fifteen feet long, sixteen feet beam and five feet hold for the Arkansas river trade. In 1836 he moved his plant to Madison, where he built sixteen boats, but he discontinued the busi-

HOWARD'S

HIP YARDS.

ness there in 1844, and ran on the river until 1846. The boats which he built at Madison are as follows:

Irvington—a side-wheeler, built for Captain Brown.

Livingstone—a side-wheeler.

Hard Times—a barge one hundred and ten feet long, nineteen feet beam and six feet hold.

Natchez—a barge, same size as Hard Times.

Argo—a side-wheel steamboat for Kentucky river trade.

Robert Fulton—a side-wheel steamboat of two hundred and fifty tons burden, very fast.

Montezuma—a side-wheel steamboat, one hundred and fifty feet long, twenty-eight feet beam and six and one-half feet hold, and nine others whose names are lost.

In 1846 he established a yard at Shippingsport, but met with such loss in the great flood of 1847 that he moved his plant to the upper end of Louisville. While at Shippingsport he built six boats as follows:

Courier—a side-wheel steamboat.

Mobile—a steamboat.

Major Barber—a steamboat.

General Jessup—a side-wheel steamboat, for the United States Government, one hundred and fifty feet long.

Lavaca—a side-wheel snag boat one hundred and thirty feet long.

James Hewett, a side-wheel steamboat two hundred feet long.

His yard in the upper end of Louisville was about opposite Spring street, in Jeffersonville, and has held in partnership with John Enos. Enos died within four or five months and James Howard returned to Jeffersonville, the scene of his first venture and success, sixteen years previously. Daniel, his brother, had become interested with him at this time, and was left on the "Point" to finish such boats as were on the stocks, and saw up such timber as might remain, while James took charge of the new work being started in Jeffersonville. The work on the "Point," all told, consisted of seven or eight boats for southern rivers and when they were completed the yards there were discontinued.

The location of his new yard in Jeffersonville is still the scene of active and progressive boat building, and with the exception of about two years at the beginning of the War of the Rebellion, has added its yearly quota of water craft to the great rivers of the West. In 1848, his first year at his new location, he built five boats as follows:

Emperor, a side-wheel steamboat, two hundred and forty feet long, thirty-one feet beam and seven feet hold.

Louisiana, a steamboat two hundred and forty feet long, thirty-one feet beam and seven feet hold, for Captain Cannon.

Mary Foley, a steamboat two hundred feet long, thirty-one feet beam and seven feet hold.

Prairie Bird, a ferry boat one hundred feet long, thirty feet beam and four feet, six inches hold.

A dredge boat to be used in the canal.

In 1849, Daniel Howard became a member of the firm, and during that year the following boats were built:

Boat—Side-wheel.	Length.	Beam.	Hold.
St. Charles	230 ft. 0 in.	31 ft. 7 in.	7 ft. 0 in.
Isabella	175 ft. 0 in.	30 ft. 0 in.	7 ft. 0 in.
Falcon	220 ft. 0 in.	32 ft. 0 in.	6 ft. 6 in.
Fanny Smith	220 ft. 0 in.	32 ft. 0 in.	6 ft. 6 in.
Lexington	220 ft. 0 in.	32 ft. 0 in.	6 ft. 6 in.

In 1850 the following boats were built:

Boat—Side-wheel.	Length.	Beam.	Hold.
Empress (L.)	190 ft. 0 in.	29 ft. 0 in.	6 ft. 6 in.
Helen (L.)	180 ft. 0 in.	26 ft. 0 in.	6 ft. 6 in.
Cuba (L.)	180 ft 0 in.	29 ft. 0 in.	7 ft. 0 in.
Music (L.)	175 ft. 0 in.	29 ft. 0 in.	7 ft. 0 in.
Blue Wing	150 ft. 0 in.	30 ft. 0 in.	6 ft. 6 in.
John Simpson	180 ft. 0 in.	30 ft. 0 in.	6 ft. 6 in.
Wade Allen (L.)	175 ft. 0 in.	24 ft. 0 in.	6 ft. 0 in.
Terre Bonne (L.)	120 ft. 0 in.	24 ft. 0 in.	4 ft. 6 in.
S. W. Downs (L.)	175 ft. 0 in.	28 ft. 6 in.	6 ft. 6 in.
Swan	170 ft. 0 in.	28 ft. 0 in.	7 ft. 0 in.
United States Survey No. 1.			
United States Survey No. 2.			

During this year the last of the boats contracted for under the old partnership with John Enos were finished, those marked "L." in the above list having been constructed in Louisville. In 1851 the following boats were built:

Boat—Side-wheel.	Length.	Beam.	Hold.
Lucy McConnell	100 ft. 0 in.	28 ft. 0 in.	4 ft. 6 in.
Glendy Burk	245 ft. 0 in.	33 ft. 0 in.	8 ft. 0 in.
Southern Belle	240 ft. 0 in.	31 ft. 0 in.	8 ft. 0 in.
Frank Lyon	200 ft. 0 in.	31 ft. 0 in.	8 ft. 0 in.
Peter Dalman	200 ft. 0 in.	30 ft. 0 in.	7 ft. 6 in.

W. B. Clifton	225 ft. 0 in.	33 ft. 0 in.	6 ft. 6 in.
Trinity	175 ft. 0 in.	28 ft. 0 in.	6 ft. 0 in.
Doctor Smith	120 ft. 0 in.	30 ft. 0 in.	5 ft. 0 in.
Kate Sweeney	100 ft. 0 in.	30 ft. 0 in.	6 ft. 6 in.

In 1852 the following boats were built:

Boat—Side-wheel.	Length.	Beam.	Hold.
Brunett	180 ft. 0 in.	29 ft. 6 in.	6 ft. 0 in.
Octavia	180 ft. 0 in.	30 ft. 0 in.	6 ft. 0 in.
Sallie San	180 ft. 0 in.	30 ft. 0 in.	6 ft. 0 in.
Jennie Beale	185 ft. 0 in.	31 ft. 0 in.	6 ft. 0 in.
Magnolia	180 ft. 0 in.	31 ft. 0 in.	7 ft. 6 in.
H. M. Wright	210 ft. 0 in.	32 ft. 0 in.	8 ft. 0 in.
Messenger	180 ft. 0 in.	32 ft. 0 in.	7 ft. 0 in.
Sam Dale	210 ft. 0 in.	32 ft. 0 in.	7 ft. 6 in.
Athey Watchen, c'ter-wheel	150 ft. 0 in.	40 ft. 0 in.	5 ft. 6 in.
Francis	150 ft. 0 in.	28 ft. 0 in.	5 ft. 6 in.
Empress	280 ft. 0 in.	34 ft. 0 in.	7 ft. 6 in.
W. P. Sweeney	170 ft. 0 in.	29 ft. 0 in.	6 ft. 0 in.

In 1853 the following boats were built:

Boat—Side-wheel.	Length.	Beam.	Hold.
Geo. W. Jones	110 ft. 0 in.	29 ft. 0 in.	6 ft. 6 in.
S. S. Prentice	180 ft. 0 in.	29 ft. 0 in.	7 ft. 0 in.
Southerner	240 ft. 0 in.	34 ft. 0 in.	6 ft. 0 in.
Gopher	110 ft. 0 in.	29 ft. 0 in.	6 ft. 6 in.
C. B. Junior	200 ft. 0 in.	30 ft. 0 in.	7 ft. 6 in.
Runaway, stern-wheel	125 ft. 0 in.	26 ft. 0 in.	5 ft. 0 in.
Alice W. Glaze	140 ft. 0 in.	32 ft. 0 in.	7 ft. 0 in.
Josiah H. Bell	180 ft. 0 in.	36 ft. 0 in.	7 ft. 6 in.
Lucy Belle	180 ft. 0 in.	32 ft. 0 in.	6 ft. 0 in.
Ceres	185 ft. 0 in.	32 ft. 0 in.	7 ft. 0 in.
Atakapas	180 ft. 0 in.	32 ft. 0 in.	7 ft. 0 in.
James H. Lucas	230 ft. 0 in.	35 ft. 0 in.	7 ft. 0 in.

In 1854 the following boats were built:

Boat—Side-wheel.	Length.	Beam.	Hold.
Fanny Bullitt	245 ft. 0 in.	32 ft. 0 in.	7 ft. 0 in.
Rainbow	235 ft. 0 in.	35 ft. 0 in.	7 ft. 0 in.

Ben Franklin ....300 ft. 0 in.	40 ft. 0 in.	7 ft. 6 in.
Capital ....235 ft. 0 in.	35 ft. 0 in.	8 ft. 0 in.
National ....170 ft. 0 in.	30 ft. 0 in.	6 ft. 0 in.
Marion ....130 ft. 0 in.	30 ft. 0 in.	5 ft. 0 in.
David Tatum ....230 ft. 0 in.	32 ft. 0 in.	6 ft. 0 in.

In 1855 the following boats were built:

Boat—Side-wheel.	Length	Beam.	Hold.
P. C. Wallis..............160 ft. 0 in.	32 ft. 0 in.	5 ft. 6 in.
Barge ....130 ft. 0 in.	26 ft. 0 in.	4 ft. 6 in.
John Tompson, stern-wheel 160 ft. 0 in.	36 ft. 0 in.	6 ft. 0 in.
Victoria ....140 ft. 0 in.	30 ft. 0 in.	5 ft. 6 in.
R. S. Cobb..............160 ft. 0 in.	30 ft. 0 in.	4 ft. 6 in.
R. M. Patton, stern-wheel..160 ft. 0 in.	30 ft. 0 in.	5 ft. 6 in.
Carrier ....200 ft. 0 in.	33 ft. 0 in.	6 ft. 0 in.
Scotland ....225 ft. 0 in.	35 ft. 0 in.	7 ft. 6 in.
Diamond, stern-wheel ....155 ft. 0 in.	40 ft. 0 in.	5 ft. 6 in.

In 1856 the following boats were built:

Boat—Side-wheel.	Length.	Beam.	Hold.
W. J. Eaton.............220 ft. 0 in.	35 ft. 0 in.	6 ft. 6 in.
John Warner ....220 ft. 0 in.	36 ft. 0 in.	6 ft. 6 in.
Dove ....150 ft. 0 in.	30 ft. 0 in.	5 ft. 6 in.
Princess, stern-wheel ......155 ft 0 in.	30 ft. 0 in.	3 ft. 6 in.
Pete Whetstone ....225 ft. 0 in.	38 ft. 0 in.	7 ft. 6 in.
Kate Howard ....235 ft. 0 in.	36 ft. 0 in.	6 ft. 6 in.
Woodford ....250 ft. 0 in.	35 ft. 0 in.	6 ft. 6 in.
Governor Pease ....160 ft. 0 in.	32 ft. 0 in.	6 ft. 0 in.
Tom Peacock ....120 ft. 0 in.	30 ft. 0 in.	6 ft. 0 in.
W. R. Douglass.........145 ft. 0 in.	30 ft. 0 in.	6 ft. 0 in.
Col. Edwards ....155 ft. 0 in.	31 ft. 0 in.	6 ft. 6 in.
Silver Heels ....180 ft. 0 in.	29 ft. 0 in.	5 ft. 6 in.

The Kate Howard was built for Captain Moses Hilliard for the Mississippi river trade, and was named after the youngest daughter of her designer and builder, James Howard.

In 1857 the following boats were built:

Boat—Side-wheel.	Length.	Beam.	Hold.
Joe G. Smith............. 90 ft. 0 in.	28 ft. 0 in.	4 ft. 6 in.
Twilight ....215 ft. 0 in.	33 ft. 0 in.	6 ft. 0 in.

Barge	150 ft. 0 in.	26 ft, 0 in.	4 ft. 6 in.
Barge	150 ft. 0 in.	26 ft. 0 in.	4 ft. 6 in.
Alonzo Child	236 ft. 0 in.	38 ft. 0 in.	7 ft. 0 in.
Southwester	220 ft. 0 in.	36 ft. 0 in.	6 ft. 6 in.
New Orleans, center wheel.	120 ft. 0 in.	20 ft. 0 in.	4 ft. 6 in.
Jefferson, center wheel....	120 ft. 0 in.	30 ft. 0 in.	4 ft. 6 in.
Diana	275 ft. 0 in.	37 ft. 0 in.	7 ft. 6 in.
Music	190 ft. 0 in.	35 ft. 0 in.	7 ft. 0 in.
Platte Valley	226 ft. 0 in.	33 ft. 0 in.	6 ft. 0 in.
John D. Perry	220 ft. 0 in.	32 ft. 0 in.	6 ft. 0 in.

In 1858 the following boats were built:

Boat—Side-wheel.	Length.	Beam.	Hold.
St. Francis	160 ft. 0 in.	29 ft. 0 in.	6 ft. 0 in.
Rescue (stern wheel)	100 ft. 0 in.	24 ft. 0 in.	4 ft. 0 in.
Aline (center wheel)	120 ft. 0 in.	30 ft. 0 in.	6 ft. 0 in.
Judge Porter	140 ft. 0 in.	30 ft. 0 in.	6 ft. 0 in.
Grand Duke	205 ft. 0 in.	38 ft. 0 in.	8 ft. 0 in.

In 1859 the following boats were built:

Boat—Side-wheel.	Length.	Beam.	Hold.
D. F. Kenner	215 ft. 0 in.	37 ft. 0 in.	8 ft. 0 in.
Laurel Hill	200 ft. 0 in.	38 ft. 0 in.	8 ft. 0 in.
Lafourche	185 ft. 0 in.	34 ft. 0 in.	7 ft. 6 in.
Bayou City	165 ft. 0 in.	28 ft. 0 in.	5 ft. 0 in.
John M. Sharp	155 ft. 0 in.	30 ft. 0 in.	5 ft. 6 in.
J. D. Swain	150 ft. 0 in.	30 ft. 0 in.	6 ft. 0 in.
James Wood	257 ft. 0 in.	37 ft. 0 in.	7 ft. 0 in.

In 1860 the following boats were built:

Boat—Side-wheel.	Length.	Beam.	Hold.
Isaac Bowman	160 ft. 0 in.	39 ft. 0 in.	5 ft. 6 in.
Mary T.	185 ft. 0 in.	34 ft. 0 in.	8 ft. 0 in.
Little Sallie (stern wheel)..	100 ft. 0 in.	23 ft. 0 in.	3 ft. 6 in.
Memphis	260 ft. 0 in.	38 ft. 0 in.	7 ft. 0 in.
Arcadia	188 ft. 0 in.	35 ft. 0 in.	7 ft. 0 in.
J. F. Paragould	234 ft. 0 in.	38 ft. 0 in.	8 ft. 0 in.
Robert Campbell	236 ft. 0 in.	41 ft. 0 in.	6 ft. 0 in.
John A. Cotton	248 ft. 0 in.	48 ft. 0 in.	8 ft. 0 in.

In 1861 the following boats were built:

Boat—Side-wheel.	Length.	Beam.	Hold.
Major Anderson ....245 ft. 0 in.		36 ft. 0 in.	5 ft. 6 in.

In 1862 the following boats were built:

Boat—Side-wheel.	Length.	Beam.	Hold.
General Buell ....248 ft. 0 in.		36 ft. 0 in.	5 ft. 6 in.
Wren ....150 ft. 0 in.		30 ft. 0 in.	5 ft. 6 in.
Ruth ....273 ft. 0 in.		46 ft. 0 in.	8 ft. 0 in.
James Thompson ....155 ft. 0 in.		37 ft. 0 in.	5 ft. 0 in.

In 1863 the following boats were built:

Boat—Side-wheel.	Length.	Beam.	Hold.
Julia ....241 ft. 0 in.		41 ft. 0 in.	7 ft. 0 in.
Olive Branch ....283 ft. 0 in.		42 ft. 0 in.	8 ft. 0 in.
Bostona No. 3.........240 ft. 0 in.		36 ft. 0 in.	5 ft. 6 in.
Tarascon ....249 ft. 0 in.		36 ft. 0 in.	6 ft. 0 in.
Blue Wing No. 3........150 ft. 0 in.		30 ft. 0 in.	5 ft. 6 in.

In 1864 the following boats were built:

Boat—Side-wheel.	Length.	Beam.	Hold.
Ida Handy ....258 ft. 0 in.		45 ft. 0 in.	8 ft. 0 in.
Morning Star ....250 ft. 0 in.		36 ft. 0 in.	6 ft. 0 in.
Ruth No. 2 ....300 ft. 0 in.		49 ft. 0 in.	9 ft. 6 in.
Wharf Boat ....200 ft. 0 in.		50 ft. 0 in.	5 ft. 0 in.

This wharf boat is still used in 1909 as a landing place for the Cincinnati and Louisville packet boats at the foot of Fourth avenue in Louisville.

In 1865 James Howard took into the firm with him his younger brother, John C. Howard, and his son, Edmund J., as partners, the firm becoming James Howard & Co. This year there were built:

Boat—Side-wheel.	Length.	Beam.	Hold.
Virginia ....226 ft. 0 in.		42 ft. 0 in.	7 ft. 0 in.
North Missouri ....160 ft. 0 in.		30 ft. 0 in.	5 ft. 6 in.

In 1866 the following boats were built:

Boat—Side-wheel.	Length.	Beam.	Hold.
Stonewall ....224 ft. 0 in.		42 ft. 0 in.	7 ft. 0 in.
Galveston (a barge) ......120 ft. 0 in.		25 ft. 0 in.	6 ft. 0 in.
Belle of Memphis........260 ft. 0 in.		40 ft. 6 in.	7 ft. 0 in.

THE STEAMER JAMES HOWARD

RACE BETWEEN MAIL BOAT AND MOTOR BOAT

MOTOR BOAT UNDER WAY

GASOLINE BOAT

Birdie Brent (center wheel).112 ft. o in.	35 ft. o in.		4 ft. 6 in.
William Dwyer (a barge) 126 ft. o in.	25 ft. o in.		6 ft. o in.
Wm. R. Johnson (a barge).126 ft. o in.	25 ft. o in.		6 ft. o in.
Jessie (center wheel) ....132 ft. o in.	35 ft. o in.		5 ft. o in.
H. M. Shreve ....198 ft. o in.	35 ft. o in.		5 ft. 6 in.

In 1867 the following boats were built:

Boat—Side-wheel.	Length.	Beam.	Hold.
Dove No. 2 (stern wheel)..116 ft. o in.	26 ft. o in.	4 ft. 6 in.
Governor Allen ....217 ft. o in.	40 ft. o in.	8 ft. o in.
Early Bird ....125 it. o in.	25 ft. 6 in.	4 ft. 6 in.
Frank Paragould ....255 ft. o in.	41 ft. o in.	9 ft. o in.

In 1865 the following boats were built:

Boat—Side-wheel.	Length.	Beam.	Hold.
Belle of Alton..........227 ft. o in.	35 ft. o in.	6 ft. o in.
E. St. Louis (center-wheel).175 ft. o in.	53 ft. o in.	6 ft. o in.
Thomas M. Bagley ....166 ft. o in.	30 ft. o in.	6 ft. 6 in.
Trade Palace (screw prop.).150 ft. o in.	30 ft. o in.	5 ft. 6 in.
St. Frances No. 3........172 ft. o in.	32 ft. o in.	6 ft. o in.

In 1869 the following boats were built:

Boat—Side-wheel.	Length.	Beam.	Hold.
Ben Franklin, No 2.......255 ft. o in.	37 ft. o in.	6 ft. o in.
Gladiola (stern-wheel) ....136 ft. o in.	34 ft. o in.	4 ft. 6 in.
La Belle ....176 ft. o in.	35 ft. o in.	6 ft. 6 in.
Texas (stern-wheel) ......135 ft. o in.	35 ft. o in.	6 ft. o in.
Trenton (stern-wheel) ....130 ft. o in.	32 ft. o in.	4 ft. o in.
Big Sunflower (stern) ....125 ft. o in.	28 ft. o in.	4 ft. o in.
Texarkana (stern) ....135 ft. o in.	35 ft. o in.	5 ft. 6 in.

In 1870 the following boats were built:

Boat—Side-wheel.	Length.	Beam.	Hold.
Idlewild ....214 ft. o in.	35 ft. o in.	5 ft. 6 in.
Grand Tower (stern)......265 ft. o in.	42 ft. o in.	8 ft. o in.
Cherokee (stern) ....131 ft. o in.	32 ft. o in.	4 ft. o in.
City of Vicksburg........265 ft. o in.	42 ft. o in.	8 ft. o in.
Diana ....165 ft. o in.	32 ft. o in.	6 ft. o in.

22

City of Chester	241 ft. 0 in.	38 ft. 0 in.	7 ft. 0 in.
Jessie Taylor (stern)	156 ft. 0 in.	37 ft. 0 in.	7 ft. 0 in.
Howard (a barge)	125 ft. 0 in.	25 ft. 0 in.	6 ft. 0 in.

The James Howard was a side-wheel steamboat, three hundred eighteen feet in length with fifty-four feet beam and ten feet hold. This magnificent creation was one of the wonders of her day. She was the largest inland steamboat ever built up to or since her time. The steamer James Howard was a boat of three thousand four hundred tons. To the uninitiated in the mysteries of tonnage these figures may mean but little, but when we learn that the City of Louisville and the City of Cincinnati, the present mail boats between Louisville and Cincinnati, are less than one thousand tons, the size of the James Howard may be better understood. She was launched on October 8, 1870, and when finished ran in the New Orleans and St. Louis trade. The total cost of this boat and her equipment was one hundred and seventy-five thousand dollars. The launching of the James Howard was viewed by thousands of spectators, all drawn to the yards to witness the plunge of this leviathan into the bosom of the Ohio.

The contrast between this vessel and those of earlier times, which were in every particular frail and inferior boats, was like that which exists between the ocean greyhounds of today and the ships of forty or fifty years ago. The genius of a McKay, a Steers, a Cramp and a Webb invoked the change which is seen on the ocean; and the talents of a Howard have worked a like transformation on our mighty inland rivers. If by the first our foreign commerce has been enlarged and enriched, so by the second our domestic commercial interchanges have been promoted and made of increased value. The steamer, James Howard, still stands as the highest type of steam boat construction, and it was fitting that she should bear the name of the master-builder of western waters. During this year the following additional boats were built:

Boat—Side-wheel.	Length	Beam.	Hold.
John Howard	170 ft. 0 in.	40 ft. 0 in.	6 ft. 6 in.
Bayou City (a barge)	125 ft. 0 in.	25 ft. 0 in.	6 ft. 0 in.
Paul (a barge)	90 ft. 0 in.	24 ft. 0 in.	6 ft. 0 in.
James Wathen (center)	150 ft. 0 in.	37 ft. 0 in.	6 ft. 0 in.
Dixie (a barge)	125 ft. 0 in.	25 ft. 0 in.	6 ft. 0 in.

In 1871 the following boats were built:

Boat—Side-wheel.	Length.	Beam.	Hold.
Houston, a barge	125 ft. 0 in.	25 ft. 0 in.	6 ft. 0 in.
Otter, a barge	125 ft. 0 in.	25 ft. 0 in.	6 ft. 0 in.
Ferry, a barge	125 ft. 0 in.	25 ft. 0 in.	6 ft. 0 in.
Beaver, a barge	125 ft. 0 in.	25 ft. 0 in.	6 ft. 0 in.

Lee, a barge...............	125 ft. 0 in.	25 ft. 0 in.	6 ft. 0 in.
Rush, a barge	125 ft. 0 in.	25 ft. 0 in.	6 ft. 0 in.
Grey Eagle, a barge......	85 ft. 0 in.	18 ft. 0 in.	4 ft. 0 in.
Tarascon, a barge........	85 ft. 0 in.	18 ft. 0 in.	4 ft. 0 in.
Grey Eagle, side-wheel....	238 ft. 0 in.	38 ft. 0 in.	6 ft. 0 in.
Wharf boat	225 ft. 0 in.	45 ft. 0 in.	5 ft. 0 in.
Lizzie, side-wheel	165 ft. 0 in.	35 ft. 0 in.	5 ft. 0 in.
City of Helena, side-wheel	266 ft. 0 in.	42 ft. 0 in.	8 ft. 0 in.
Mary, stern-wheel	146 ft. 0 in.	34 ft. 0 in.	6 ft. 0 in.
John Howard, stern-wheel..	181 ft. 0 in.	36 ft. 0 in.	6 ft. 6 in.
Barge	100 ft. 0 in.	20 ft. 0 in.	4 ft. 6 in.

In 1872 the following boats were built:

Boat—Side-wheel.	Length.	Beam.	Hold.
Concordia	86 ft. 0 in.	25 ft. 0 in.	4 ft. 0 in.
Barge	120 ft. 0 in.	20 ft. 0 in.	4 ft. 6 in.
Wharf Boat	150 ft. 0 in.	36 ft. 0 in.	4 ft. 0 in.
Barge	210 ft. 0 in.	40 ft. 0 in.	8 ft. 0 in.
Barge	210 ft. 0 in.	40 ft. 0 in.	8 ft. 0 in.
R. T. Brierly, stern-wheel	150 ft. 0 in.	33 ft. 0 in.	4 ft. 6 in.
Wharf Boat	150 ft. 0 in.	36 ft. 0 in.	4 ft. 0 in.
James S. Bramsford, stern..	150 ft. 0in.	30 ft. 0 in.	4 ft. 0 in.
Longfellow, stern	112 ft. 0 in.	20 ft. 0 in.	4 ft. 0 in.
Little Fayette, a barge.....	130 ft. 0 in.	24 ft. 0 in.	4 ft. 6 in.

In 1873 the following boats were built:

Boat—Side-wheel.	Length.	Beam.	Hold.
Atlanta, a barge..........	160 ft. 0 in.	35 ft. 0 in.	5 ft. 0 in.
Dolphin, stern-wheel	135 ft. 0 in.	23 ft. 0 in.	4 ft. 0 in.
Barge No. 1.............	90 ft. 0 in.	18 ft. 0 in.	4 ft. 0 in.
Barge No. 2.............	90 ft. 0 in.	18 ft. 0 in.	4 ft. 0 in.
Barge No. 3.............	90 ft. 0 in.	18 ft. 0 in.	4 ft. 0 in.
Three States, center.......	150 ft. 0 in.	35 ft. 0 in.	4 ft. 0 in.
Pump Boat	45 ft. 0 in.	12 ft. 0 in.	3 ft. 0 in.
Arch P. Green, stern-wheel	110 ft. 0 in.	22 ft.0 in.	3 ft. 0 in.
Barge No. 49.............	213 ft. 0 in.	40 ft. 0 in.	8 ft. 0 in.
Barge No. 50.............	213 ft. 0 in.	40 ft. 0 in.	8 ft. 0 in
Z. M. Sherley, side-wheel..	153 ft. 0 in.	36 ft. 0 in.	6 ft. 0 in.
H. S. McComb, side-wheel..	195 ft. 0 in.	45 ft. 0 in.	7 ft. 0 in.
Little Nell, a barge........	135 ft. 0 in.	28 ft. 0 in.	5 ft. 6 in.

Red Cloud, stern-wheel....176 ft. o in.	34 ft. o in.	5 ft. o in.
John Howard, No. 3 barge.137 ft. o in.	27 ft. o in.	4 ft. 6 in.
B. H. Cook, stern-wheel...151 ft. o in.	30 ft. o in.	4 ft. 6 in.
Ida, screw propeller.......71 ft. o in.	14 ft. o in.	7 ft. 6 in.

In 1874 the following boats were built:

Boat.	Length.	Beam.	Hold.
Barge .... 75 ft. o in.	16 ft. o in.	4 ft. o in.
Barge .... 75 ft. o in.	16 ft. o in.	4 ft. o in.
Barge .... 95 ft. o in.	25 ft. o in.	7 ft. o in.
Fawn, a stern-wheel.......180 ft. o in.	34 ft. o in.	5 ft. o in.

In 1875 the following boats were built:

Boat.	Length.	Beam.	Hold.
Porter White, a barge.....135 ft. o in.	27 ft. o in.	6 ft. o in.
Barge ....135 ft. o in.	27 ft. o in.	6 ft. o in.
Chicago, a barge ....175 ft. o in.	37 ft. o in.	6 ft. o in.
Barge ....135 ft. o in.	28 ft. o in.	5 ft. o in.
Barge ....135 ft. o in.	28 ft. o in.	5 ft. o in.
Barge ....135 ft. o in.	28 ft. o in.	5 ft. o in.
Barge ....135 ft. o in.	28 ft. o in.	5 ft. o in.
Jas. S. Morgan, side-wheel.195 ft. o in.	45 ft. o in.	7 ft. o in.
Bonnie Lee, stern........165 ft. o in.	30 ft. o in.	4 ft. o in.
Rene McCready, side......140 ft. o in.	29 ft. o in.	4 ft. 6 in.
Timmie Baker, stern......100 ft. o in.	21 ft. o in.	3 ft. o in.
Assumption, stern ....150 ft. o in.	36 ft. o in.	6 ft. 6 in.
Kate Fisher, center........80 ft. o in.	18 ft. o in.	3 ft. o in.
Barge ....117 ft. o in.	28 ft. o in.	4 ft. o in.

In 1876 were built the following boats:

Boat.	Length.	Beam.	Hold.
Climax, stern-wheel ....140 ft. o in.	25 ft. o in.	3 ft. o in.
Walker Morris, stern......96 ft. o in.	19 ft. o in.	4 ft. o in.
Robert E. Lee, side.......306 ft. o in.	48 ft. o in.	10 ft. o in.
Yazoo Valley, stern.......180 ft. o in.	36 ft. o in.	6 ft. 6 in.
C. W. Anderson, stern.....160 ft. o in.	31 ft. o in.	4 ft. 6 in.
Alberta ....116 ft. o in.	25 ft. o in.	3 ft. 6 in.
E. B. Stahlman stern......145 ft. o in.	27 ft. o in.	3 ft. o in.

On October 14, 1876, James Howard was drowned by his buggy backing off of the ferry boat. The ship yards were continued by his son and brother until 1888, when John C. Howard retired, leaving E. J. Howard in control of the industry. The yards have continued to add their yearly quota of water craft to the great rivers of the West. Several contracts have been completed for boats in Central and South America, and the first large steam boats upon the Yukon river in Alaska were constructed at Howard's, knocked down and shipped to Dutch Harbor, where they were built and launched for the trade up that great river.

The following is a list of steamboats built at the Howard ship yard since 1877:

1877.

Headlight, steamer 140x24x3½
Delner, steamer 136x26x4
J. G. Fletcher, steamer....................................120x24x3½
Louis Hite, barge..100x20x4½
Allan Hite, barge..100x20x4½
Mattie Belle Hays, steamer..............................100x20x3½
J. Gumby Jordan, steamer................................120x25x3½
Dora Cablar, steamer....................................155x30x4½
Fashion, steamer 220x36x5
James Howard, schooner 110x26½x14
Four barges, No. 1, 2, 3, 4..............................100x18x3½
————, wharf boat 100x20x5
Barge 100x20x4½
Winnie, steamer 110x24x3½
James Guthrie, steamer 240x36x6

The schooner, James Howard, was built for the gulf trade and was a seaworthy, satisfactory vessel.

1878.

John W. Cannon, steamer................................252x43x9½
New Shallcross, steamer, ferry..........................158x37x6
Laura Lee, steamer 206x37x7
Jewel, steamer 174x33x5
B. S. Rhea, steamer......................................162x36x4½
Barges, No. 5 and 6......................................85x20x3½
Ed Richardson, steamer..................................300x49x11

1879.

City of Greenville, steamer..............................281x46x9½
Barge for Gulf, light, Victor............................115x27x7

C. N. Davis, steamer...................................140x27x3
City of Yazoo, steamer............................. 20x38x7
Rainbow, steamer 263x40x6
William Fagin, steamer 165x35x5
Charmer, steamer 185x34x6
Jesse K. Bell, steamer 218x40x8
Wash Gray, tug 87x18x6½
Wharf boat 150x36x5

1880.
Milwaukee, steamer 135x30x5
Ferry boat, steamer 70x53x5
Gus Fowler, steamer 160x29x5
City of Providence, steamer 270x44x8½
Concordia, steamer 90x25x5
Joseph Henry, steamer 180x32x6
Barge 165x32x7
Alberta, steamer 150x28x4
Barge 165x32x7
Clyde, steamer 180x32x5
Thomas D. Fite, steamer 150x29x4
Belle of Memphis, steamer.........................265x42x8½
Barge 195x32x6

1881.
W. Butler Duncan, steamer........................200x45x7
Jeff, ferry clock 112x22x4½
Ella, steamer 150x28x3
S. P. Ewald, steamer 150x30x4½
City of Vicksburg, steamer........................270x44x8½
J. P. Drouillard, steamer.........................165x31x5
City of New Orleans 285x48x9
City of Baton Rouge............................285x48x9
Barge 100x20x5½
Barge 110x20x5½
Derrick boat 60x30x3½
Crane boat (2 of these) 60x30x40
City of Nashville, steamer........................149x31x4½
Barge 203x36x5½

1882.
City of Cairo, steamer...........................278x44x8½
Barge (2 of these)...............................135x27x6

Charlie Depauw 125x23x4
Landing barge 95x18x5
J. H. Hillman, steamer....................................149x29x3½
Arkansas City, steamer 271x45x8½
J. G. Parker, steamer.................................140x28x4
Two barges 135x26x6
One barge 208x36x5½
S. H. Parrisot, steamer 225x41x7 2-3
W. C. Hite, ferry boat....................................156x36x6½
W. H. Cherry, steamer.....................................168x32x5
Gulf Lighter 140x26x6
Samuel J. Keith, steamer...............................160x32x5
City of St. Louis, steamer.................................297x49x9
Four barges 100x25x5

1883.
Alto, steamer 165x35x5
Barge 100x25x5
Eight pile drivers 80x20x4
General Gilmore, steamer 140x28x4
Barge 136x27x6
Three barges 120x30x6
Two barges 135x27x6½
Henry Sackman, steamer 220x46x6
C. C. Greeley, ferry boat.................................160x46x6
Barge 135x27x6
Oceola, steamer 133x24x4
Barge 135x27x6
W. F. Nesbit, steamer 200x35x6
Benton McMillan, steamer 155x33x5
W. H. Osborn, transfer boat...............................285x45x7
Lime boat 80x17x5

1884.
Barge 200x24x5
Pargoud, steamer 242x42x8
Four barges 140x277x6
Alberta No 2, steamer 145x28x4
Wharfboat.

1885.
City of Natchez, steamer..................................296x48x10
John Smith, steamer 70x14x2½

Ferry boat, steamer 170x48x6½
H. K. Bedford, steamer.................................... 148x27x4
Alert, steamer 135x24x4
Pump boat 50x14x3
City of Owensboro, steamer............................... 240x38x6
Grace V., steamer 80x18x4
Milton H. Smith, steamer.................................. 110x24x4
Steamboat 52x22x2½
Steamboat 155x28x4½
Steamboat 130x26x5

1886.
Two barges 165x32x8
Steamboat 125x25x5
William Porter, steamer 150x28x4½
B. F. Rhea, steamer...................................... 162x30x4½
Oliver Bierne, steamer 260x44x8
John J. Brown, steamer 110x25x5
Fanny Fern, steamer 135x31x5
Wharf boat 150x32x5
John Fowler, steamer 149x27x4
Teche, steamer 190x38x6
Blanche Cornwall, steamer 140x28x4

1887.
Coal float 140x28x2½
Mat F. Allen, steamer.................................... 160x28x4
New South, steamer 254x42x7
J. L. Stephens, steamer 102x28x4
Roy Lynds, steamer 85x25x4
Crystal City, steamer 230x40x7
Pearl, steamer 140x22x3½
E. G. Ragon, steamer..................................... 165x31x4½
Barge 170x32x8
City of Monroe, steamer.................................. 270x44x8
Hallette, steamer 160x30x4½

1888.
Barge 119x24x5
Barge 155x30x6
Crane boat 75x26x3½
Sunshine, ferry boat 170x36x5

BOAT LAUNCH AT HOWARD'S SHIP YARD.

Two theater boats 150x35x5
Three barges 120x28x7
Wharf boat 150x25x4
L. T. Armstrong 154x30x4
Joe Fowler 180x32x5
La Fourche, steamer 165x38x7
Garland, steamer 160x30x4½
Two barges 125x20x4
Paul Tulane, steamer 210x40x7
New Idea 125x26x4
Matt F. Dortch, steamer..........................160x30x3
Barge 170x33x8

1889.
Boat Club House (Louisville) 100x30x4
Florence, steamer 130x34x5
Aid, tug 51x12x6
Tell City, steamer 190x35x5
Kate Adams, steamer 240x34x7
Three barges 135x27x5
Cook boat 120x21x3
Coal float 55x20x4
Rush, steamer 115x36x4½
Lady Lee, steamer 165x35x5
E. B. Wheelock, steamer..........................160x30x4½
Two barges 120x20x4
C. E. Satterlie, steamer 150x30x4
City of Savannah, steamer........................190x32x5½
Three barges 120x20x4
Valley Queen 190x35x5½
Joe Trudeau, steamer 160x30x4½

1890.
Janie Rea, steamer 110x23x3
City of Hickman 285x44x9½
Two barges 225x36x9
Wharf boat 250x50x6
Two barges 285x35x6½
Rowena Lee, steamer 165x35x4½
Ouchita, steamer 185x38x6½
City of Sheffield, steamer 180x35x5
John W. Hart, steamer 165x28x4

Barge 120x28x6
Josie, steamer 80x25x9
Alex Perry, steamer 150x28x5½
Emily, steamer 90x32x3
Barge 135x27x6
Ora Lee, steamer 140x36x7
Mabel Comeaux, steamer 178x36x6
Natchez, steamer 225x40x8

1891.

H. L. Clarke, steamer 170x48x6½
Delta, steamer 226x45x7
City of Jeffersonville, steamer...........................150x34½x6
City of Paducah, steamer 190x33x5½
George Medill, steamer 265x45x7
Dolphin, steamer 150x30x4½
Two barges 190x35x6½
Santa Fe, steamer 65x16x3
T. P. Leathers, steamer 220x40x6½
Two barges 40x12x2½
Colbert, steamer 125x24x3
Two barges 165x30x4

1892.

Grey Eagle, steamer 250x40x6
Parlor City, steamer 125x26x4
City of Peoria, steamer 130x26x4½
Columbia, steamer 170x35x6
Madison, steamer 150x44x6
Landing Dock.
Two coal floats 87x21x7
W. K. Phillips, steamer 165x30x4
Thomas Pickles, steamer 130x65x7
Two coal floats 150x26x3
City of New Albany 225x35x6
Ashland City, steamer 120x20x4
Two coal floats 140x21x2½
Barge 240x22x5

1893.

Two barges 130x32x5½
Huntsville, steamer 125x24x4
A. C. Church, steamer 120x49x6

Crane boat 90x36x3
Coal float 140x22x3
City of Camden, steamer 175x35x5
Thirty-four barges 100x25x5½
Help, tug 60x18x5
Dredge boat
City of Little Rock, steamer 145x28x4
John Howard, steamer 180x37x6
Shawnee, steamer 35x8x3
P. D. Staggs, steamer 160x30x3
Six barges.
Four quarter-barges.

1894.
City of Louisville, steamer 300x42x7
General Barrios 90x20x4
Snag boat, steamer 116x24x3
E. R. Andrews, steamer 165x32x5
Barge 100x22x4
Clyde, steamer 175x33x5
De Koven, steamer 220x36x6
Four barges 200x31x6
Imperial, steamer 210x40x7
Four barges 135x28x5
Fritz, steamer 120x26x4
Four barges 80x18x3½

1895.
City of Warsaw, steamer 100x24x3
Three barges 110x22x4
Two scows.
Three barges 200x37x7
One dump scow 75x20x5
Rose Hite, steamer 150x28x3½
General H. L. Abbott, steamer 170x32x5
Will J. Cummings, steamer 160x30x4
Four barges 135x28x5
W. T. Scovell, steamer 160x31x3
Two barges 100x20x4
Patrol, steamer 130x30x5
Charlie Kerlin, steamer 87x18x3½
Barge 250x42x8

Wash Gray, tug 90x18x8
Two barges 110x24x3½
Tarascon, steamer 190x35x5

1896.
Verapas, steamer 90x18x3
Two barges 85x18x2½
Barge.
Major McKenzie, steamer 125x25x4½
El Peta, steamer 90x20x4
Two barges 65x18x2½
Steamer (tow-boat) 100x20x4
Lookout, steamer 110x25x3
Ollie, steamer 125x30x4½
Two barges 90x20x4
Istrouma, steamer 150x30x5
H. W. Buttorff, steamer 160x30x4
Bluff City, steamer 225x42x6
Eliza, steamer 110x25x3
Dredge boat.

1897.
Jim T. Duffy, Jr., steamer 120x26x4
Colonel Gillespie, steamer 110x25x3
Henry Haarstick, tug 115x22x10
Dolphin No. 3, steamer 156x36x6½
W. C. Hite, steamer 156x36x6½
Barge 230x28x7
Andrew Christy 176x48x7½
Bob Dudley 157x28x3½
Barge 120x40x4
Chiska, steamer 160x30x5
Robert E Lee, steamer 245x43x6½
Tennessee, steamer 170x32x5
Two scows.
Two steel dredges 160x40x6½
Electra, steamer 175x35x5
Sun Rise, steamer 180x36x5
John W. Thomas, steamer............................. 160x26x3½
James Lee, steamer 230x43x6½

1898.
Belle of the Bends, steamer 210x32x6
Cumberland, steamer 130x26x4

Georgia Lee, steamer 210x43x6
Julian Poydras, steamer 160x30x5
City of Memphis, steamer 200x36x6
Henry Harley, steamer 160x29x4
Gem, steamer 135x28x4
Two barges 100x20x3
Kate Adams, steamer 240x40x7
Arthur Hider, steamer 160x30x5
America, steamer 200x38x7
Richardson, steamer 165x30x4
Greenwood, steamer 130x28x4
Mary, steamer 177x32x4½
Boat House 70
Landing Dock.

1899.
City of Cincinnati, steamer...............................307x41x6½
Ouichita, steamer 140x32x4½
Red River, steamer 155x28x4
Wharf boat 165x35x4
Mary, steamer 100x24x3½
William R King, steamer 190x40x5
Three steamboats (Government) 1, 2, 3...................100x24x4
Two barges 160x32x5
Two barges 100x20x7
Six barges 200x33x6
Peters Lee, steamer 220x42x6
Rees Lee, steamer 220x42x6
Bayless Lee, steamer 190x38x6
Rowena Lee, steamer 190x38x6

1900.
Three barges.
Indiana, steamer 285x42x6
Col. A. McKenzie, steamer................................160x32x5
Two barges 108x18x4
M. W. Kelly, steamer 150x32x4
Alma, steamer 155x32x4
Two barges 110x22x4
One barge 240x22x5
E. T. Slider, steamer.....................................110x24x3½
Six barges.
Landing dock 60x20x3

1901.
Tow boat 120x26x4
Morning Star, steamer 225x38x6
J S., steamer 175x37x5
McClelland, steamer 150x38x4½
Barge 126x20x3½
Dredge boat 80x30x7
Gold Dust, steamer 170x34x5
Barge 175x35x3
Vega 104x18x3½
Steel Queen, steamer 125x28x4
A. D. Allen, steamer 125x27x3½
H. M. Carter, steamer................................. 155x28x4
G. W. Thomas, steamer................................ 150x28x4
Senator Cordill, steamer 170x34x5
Sadie Lee, steamer 140x31x5

1902.
Boat House 92x22x3½
Landing dock.
Stacher Lee, steamer 225x45x6
City of Savannah, steamer.............................. 200x38x6
Four barges 120x28x6
Shiloh, steamer 190x30x6
Life Saving Station.
Beauregard, steamer 128x30x4
Barge.
Sand Digger.
St. Genevieve, steamer 215x45x8
Ferry boat 120x37x7

1903.
Derrick boat.
Gunterville, steamer 150x30x4
Five barges 130x30x7
Coal float.
Steamboat 130x27x4
Dredge boat.
Lida, steamer 122x24x4
John, steamer 90x20x3
Henry, steamer 90x20x3
Two derrick boats.

Two mud scows.
Six barges.
Columbia for (N. O.) steamer.........................170x30x4½
Barge 110x26x6
Roberta, steamer 135x27x4
Bob Blanks, steamer 175x35x5
Handy, steamer 110x22x3
Frank Hayne, steamer 130x26x4
Charlie Jutte, steamer 150x27x4½

1904.
Two barges 150x30x5
Derrick boat 140x40x5
Barge 100x20x4
H. St. L. Coffee, steamer............................140x30x6
Two barges 100x30x7
Barge 120x28x6
Barge 80x20x6
Two barges 100x25x6
Kentucky 175x33x4½
Saltillo, steamer 200x36x6
M E. Rea, steamer................................ 40x10x3
Steam ferry boat 100x27x4
Barge 110x24x3
Bowling Green, steamer. 123x32x6
Nugent, steamer 120x24x4
A. Baldwin, steamer 125x30x7
Three States, steamer 150x30x4½
Derrick boat 100x26x4

1905.
Scimitar, steamer 135x26x4
L. H. Morero, steamer 119x30x7
Jennie Barber, steamer 110x28x4
White Oak, steamer 90x18x3
J. W. Thompson, steamer 125x30x5½
Barge 130x26x4½
Dredge boat.
Five barges 130x30x7
One barge 70x16x4

1906.
Alton, steamer 240x38x6
J. O. Cole, steamer 130x26x4½

J. O. Cole, steamer 130x26x4½
Edenborn, steamer 145x31x5
Two barges 120x28x6
One dredge 130x30x6
One barge 100x20x4
One gasoline boat 75x18x3
One pile driver 80x36x3
Concordia, steamer 150x30x5
Mary Anderson, steamer 100x28x3½
John A. Patton 165x32x4½
Barge 130x30x7
Wharf boat 150x40x6

1907.

Two snag boats, steamers, United States.
Humphrey and Randall 137x32x5
One coal float 150x26x2½
Wharf boat 150x40x5
John Quill, steamer 170x35x4
Two barges 135x34x6
One steel dredge 125x34x6
Merrill, steamer 115x22x3½
Kentucky, steamer 185x34x5
Barge 225x36x7

1908.

City of Muskogee, steamer 125x28x3½
Derrick boat 120x30x6
Northern, steamer 125x25½x4
Mammoth Cave (U. S. snag boat).....................140x34x5
Hiwasse, steamer 100x20x3
Chilhowee, steamer 100x20x3
Four barges 160x34x6
Fuel flat 100x20x6
Thomas Bigbee, steamer 100x28x5
R. C. McCalla, steamer 100x28x5
Two mat barges 135x34x5

This record of steamboat building is not equalled by any plant on the western rivers of the continent. The Howard boats, both as to construction and finish, have made the yards at Jeffersonville the peer of any inland plant in the world, and the reputation of the Howard boats for beauty, design and

THE JAMES LEE.

LAUNCH OF THE ROBERT E. LEE IN 1876.

VIEWS AT HOWARD'S SHIP YARD.

general satisfaction is known from Pittsburg to New Orleans and on tributary rivers. The impetus, which the personality and technical skill of James Howard gave the business, and which John C. and Daniel so thoroughly maintained, is still felt. Ed. J. Howard, the present head of the concern, is one of the best equipped and most thoroughly competent steamboat builders of the day. He is now president of the company, which includes shipyards or marine ways at Cincinnati, Madison, Jeffersonville, Mound City and Paducah. Clyde Howard is the secretary and treasurer of the company and James Howard the vice-president. James Armstrong, a nephew of Capt. E. J. Howard, is in charge of the books of the concern. The prospects of a 9-foot stage of water will, no doubt, give an impetus to boat building at all points along the river, and the Howard yards will be given many opportunities to furnish water craft to meet the new and larger demands upon the traffic which will result. The ultimate control of the river, and possibly its sources of supply, will not only have the effect of affording a steady boating stage, but will tend to a reduction of the dangers of the great floods which in the past have attained the following stages:

February 19, 1832, reached...................... 45.4 feet
December 18, 1847, reached...................... 40.8 feet
February 23, 1850, reached...................... 34.0 feet
January 24, 1862, reached....................... 33.0 feet
March 7, 1865, reached.......................... 33.0 feet
March 16, 1867, reached......................... 37.0 feet
January 20, 1870, reached....................... 34.0 feet
August 6, 1875, reached......................... 32.5 feet
February 22, 1882, reached...................... 37.5 feet
February 16, 1883, reached...................... 43.8 feet
February 16, 1884, reached...................... 46.7 feet
April 10, 1886, reached......................... 32.7 feet
February 6, 1887, reached....................... 32.5 feet
March 28, 1890, reached......................... 35.6 feet
February 27, 1891, reached...................... 32.4 feet
February 28, 1897, reached...................... 35.3 feet
March 30, 1898, reached......................... 36.3 feet
March 10, 1899, reached......................... 32.8 feet
April 28, 1901, reached......................... 33.2 feet

Beside the Howard yards in Jeffersonville, the Barmore yard, owned by David S. Barmore, turned out a number of very fine boats from 1869 until 1885.

David S. Barmore was engaged in the business with Samuel King in 1856, and in the firm of Stuart & Barmore in 1864. In 1869 Mr. Barmore

23

bought Stuart's interest, and continued the business alone until 1885, when his plant was destroyed by fire. He had a considerable yard and turned out many fine boats. During the war he built a number of boats for the Government. When first in business alone he built four boats, the Coosa Belle, Julia, Swan and Jesse K. Bell. Since that time he built the following steamers, some being side-wheel, stern and others center-wheel boats:

Lilly, Warren Belle, Sam Nicholas, Atlantic, Dexter, Belle Lee, John Lumsden, Mary Houston, Lizzie Campbell, W. S. Pike, Grand Era, Belle Yazoo, Seminole, Bradish Johnson, Wade Hampton, M. J. Wicks, C. B. Church, A. J. White, Lightest, Southwestern, Lucy Kevin, Ouichita Belle, Katie, Capitol City, Fannie Lewis, Emma C. Elliott, Maria Louise, Carrie A. Thorne, Sabine, Business, Silverthorn, Fowler, Fannie Keener, Mary, W. J. Behan, Yazoo, Ozark Belle, W. J. Lewis, Mattie, Belle St. Louis, May Bryon, Mary Lewis, Sunflower Belle, Lilly, Tensas, Tallahatchie, Baton Rouge, Barataria, Osceola Belle, Calhoun, Yellowstone, Southern Belle, Gold Dust, Little Eagle, J. Don Cameron, General Sherman, John Wilson, Alvin, Carrie Hogan, Mary Elizabeth, Little Bob B., New Mary Houston, Whisper, John H. Johnson, E. C. Carroll, Jr., Sunflower, Leflore, Deer Creek, St. John, Maggie F. Burke, Shields, W. P. Halliday, General Barnard, Richard Ford, Kwasind, E. H. Barmore, Napoleon, E. W. Cole, J. Bertram, Jack Frost, John F. Lincoln, City of St. Louis, John, Belle Crooks, Fanny Freeze, Polar Wave.

Besides the above, Mr. Barmore built the following wharf-boats, barges, coal boats, etc:

Wharf-boat, Hettie, Mary, Essetelle; flatboat, Eva; coal float, Missouri No. 1, Missouri No. 2, Charlie Hill, Saline No. 1, No name, Little Eagle No. 2, No. 60, 61, 62, 63, 64, 65, 66, Lime barge, Nos. 57, 58, 59, Engineer No. 1, Engineer No. 2, Khedive, Egypt, Saline No. 2, No. 67, 68, 69, 70, 71, 72, 73, 74, 75, 76, 77, 78, Saline No. 3; barges No. 26, 37, 36, 79, 80, 81, 82, 83, 84, 85, Saline No. 4; barges 86, 87, landing barge, four grading boats, eight pile drivers for the Government.

The value of the great water highway which passes Clark county is not fully appreciated by the larger part of those who live here. One of the noblest streams in the world, or as McMurtrie describes it in his History of Louisville, "By far the noblest river in the universe," it presents to the eye an everchanging panorama of beauty. The north side of the river in Clark county is as diversified as it is beautiful. From the lower end of the Illinois grant opposite the Falls where cluster the historic memories of George Rogers Clark, the banks are high and the land beyond level; offering an uninterrupted view of the country beyond and the knobs in the far distance. The bluffs and hills of Utica and the tableland opposite, Twelve Mile island, remind one of some scenes along the Columbia, while the precipitous cliffs and rugged hills in the vicinity of Fourteen Mile creek present a scene of grandeur not excelled on the Hudson. But the practical utility of the stream is its most interesting feature.

From the Falls of the Ohio to Madison, fifty miles above, the harbor is of inestimable value to the surrounding territory. With an ample depth of water at all seasons of the year it affords a harbor capable of floating the assembled water craft of the whole Mississippi valley. Along the Indiana side of the river is found the deepest water and the best harbor. Immediately below Six Mile Island is the famous Pumpkin Patch harbor for coal boats, while from the town of Port Fulton to Four Mile Springs the vast coal fleets find safe anchorage, and millions of bushels of coal are kept here in reserve. Along the front of Jeffersonville a depth of water sufficient for the launching or landing of the largest Mississippi steamers is found, a deeper and safer natural harbor than is found along the Kentucky side. The Falls, however, have ever been the great obstacle to navigation, and from early times have been one of the problems which has called for the deepest study and the expenditure of vast sums of money for its solution.

In 1820 Congress made an appropriation for a survey of the Ohio river from Louisville to the Mississippi river and down that river to its mouth. This survey was made in 1821 by Captains Young and Poussin, of the topographical engineers, and Lieutenant Tuttle of the engineers. In 1824 an appropriation of $75,000 was made for the improvement of certain sand bars in the Ohio and for the removal of snags from the Ohio and Mississippi rivers.

The plans for the improvement of the Falls of the Ohio include straightening and deepening the channel, and controlling the water flow in the Indiana chute.

This is the main channel of the river by which commerce passes over the Falls when the stage of water is such as to permit navigation via that route. Originally it was very crooked, with swift currents and whirls, filled with dangerous rocky points projecting from the sides and bottom, and it could be navigated only at stages of eleven feet or more, upper canal gauge.

The Federal Government has undertaken a plan which requires the expenditure of over $1,760,000 for improving the Indiana chute, the Louisville canal and the harbor above.

The Falls of the Ohio are formed by a mass of limestone rock extending across the river bed creating a fall of twenty-seven feet in two and one-half miles of the river.

The control of the water rushing over the obstruction is to be made by the erection of dams at the head of the chutes.

The dams constructed here and to be constructed are of the general type which will be employed throughout the river improvement scheme.

The types used are commonly known as the Boule and Chanoine dams: The Boule dam consists of an iron framework on levers, which are attached to a concrete base on the bed of the river. This framework is raised into a vertical position by steamboats built especially for this purpose. Owing to the fact that the water above the dam will flow freely through the framework the power required to raise them will not be of great volume. When in position the framework is filled in with wooden wickets or doors which, when in position, form a solid wall and hold back the water.

The Chanoine dam is somewhat similar but instead of presenting a vertical front to the water slants down stream. It consists of a series of heavy wooden wickets or doors, which are raised separately by steam power furnished by the type of boat referred to above. These wickets are attached to a concrete base fixed to the solid rock of the river bed and are raised by means of levers. When the stage of the river becomes sufficiently high so that the dam is no longer needed, the wickets are tripped by an ingenious arrangement and automatically fall back into place, affording a free passage way.

The appropriation made by Congress is being used in the construction of 500 feet of Boule dam in Middle Chute, 648 feet of Chanoine dam in Indiana Chute, and about 600 linear feet of concrete dam between Indiana Chute and the north bank of the river. These sections of dam constitute additions to the former projects, and are to have their crests at elevation +9 feet, upper canal gauge (412.004 feet above sea level). This height is such as will afford a minimum depth of 9 feet upstream to Madison, Ind., and a minimum depth of six feet on the lower miter sill at Lock No. 1, Kentucky river.

CHAPTER XXXII.

HOSPITALS AND HOMES.

THE JEFFERSONVILLE ORPHAN HOME.

In the fall of 1876 a supper was given by the Masons of the city, and at the close of the evening's entertainment it was found that quite an amount of eatables and some money were still in the hands of the committee. This was distributed to the widows and orphans. From this Mrs. S. H. Patterson, Mrs. Caldwell, and Mrs. McClure became interested in caring for the orphans of the place. A meeting was held at the home of Mrs. Patterson, where she was chosen president, Mrs. McClure secretary, and Mrs. Caldwell treasurer. In this manner was perfected the organization of the orphan asylum. The self-appointed officers rented a house on Front street for a term of three years, and opened the institution with a little foundling. In two weeks two more children were received, and during the three years of this lease quite a number of children had been assisted. At the expiration of the three years' lease sixteen children were inmates of the home. A noble-hearted lady, Mrs. Zulauf, donated to the cause three building lots, and on this a two-story brick house was built. This property consisting of the roomy and comfortable house and a large yard and playground is located at 832 Meigs avenue. The yard is about half an acre in extent. The institution is private, but it is supported by boarding the wards of Clark county. Its capacity is forty-five, but the present time there are only thirty-two wards being cared for. There are five persons employed at the home. During the history of the institution there has been five matrons, the second one, Mrs. Eliza Harrington, serving for twenty-five years. The present matron is Mrs. Julia Twomey.

THE JEFFERSONVILLE HOSPITAL.

In July, 1892, a meeting was called at the city hall, in Jeffersonville, to discuss the advisability of erecting a hospital in Jeffersonville. On July 26th of this year a second meeting was held at the residence of Mrs. Sarah Caldwell and the following directors were elected:

Mrs. David McClure, president; Mrs. Lucy Armstrong, vice-president; Mrs. Sarah Caldwell, treasurer; Miss Clara J. Loomis, secretary; Miss Hannah Zulauf, assistant secretary; Mrs. Ed Morris, Mrs. Barney Coll, Mrs. Herman

Preefer, Mrs. N. H. Myers, Mrs. John Rauchenberger, Mrs. Mary Gottwaller, Mrs. Martha Cook, Mrs. Charles Neeley, Miss Lizzie Hertzsch, Mrs. George Pfau, Sr., Mrs. Anna Shafer and Mrs. Al. Thias.

The institution was incorporated December 3, 1892, as the Jeffersonville Infirmary. On August 27, 1892, the old Myers home, at 415 East Front street, was purchased for four thousand and fifty dollars. Since then improvements to the amount of five thousand dollars have been added until the property is now worth about ten thousand dollars. The ladies who served on the first board deserve all the credit for making this institution a possibility, as it was only by their hard and unceasing labors that it lived through its first few years. Arthur Loomis, the architect, furnished all the plans and supervision for the improvements free of charge. The following furnished rooms and donated them to the hospital. Clark Lodge of Masons, Daughters of Rebekah, Mrs. A. T. Hert, Mrs. William W. Borden, Epworth League, Knights of Pythias, the Aid Society, and the old board of directors. The equipment is modern and complete, and the location is ideal, facing the river as it does and offering a view of ever changing interest to the patients who are able to occupy the spacious sun parlor across the front of the building.

The hospital was under the management of the deaconess of the Methodist church for several years and was carefully and efficiently conducted. The men of the city have taken charge in the last few years, one representative from each church being on the board of managers. The president is J. Howard Fitch.

MERCY HOSPITAL, JEFFERSONVILLE.

On Thanksgiving day, 1897, the Sisters of Mercy opened their first hospital in Jeffersonville, on upper Chestnut street. It was located in a small six room cottage at No. 623, East Chestnut, rented to them at fifteen dollars per month. Here under adverse conditions and with this poor and meager beginning was begun the institution which now crowns the hill at Twelfth and Missouri avenues.

Sister Mary Regina, the Mother Superior, and one sister were the only ones to shoulder the necessarily hard work of the organization and start the hospital, but their efforts were rewarded and in just one year and two weeks, on December 8, 1898, their new hospital building, at the corner of Twelfth and Missouri avenues, was occupied. This building is a substantial frame, formerly the residence of Mrs. Charles Rogers.

In less than three years, on September 30, 1901, the sisters had completed the sanitarium, a handsome brick building, located to the east of the hospital. The hospital is equipped for the care of the sick, medical and surgical cases; the sanitarium for the care of nervous and mental diseases. The latter building is a most substantial one, having all the inside walls of brick, with granitoid floors in basement, hard wood floors throughout the rest of the building, and heated with steam heat. This was erected wholly without outside aid and stands as a monument to the business sagacity of the Mother Superior.

At present this institution owns one whole city block between Twelfth and Thirteenth streets and Missouri avenue, an excellent site. It is owned by the Sisters of Mercy and is the headquarters of the sisterhood in the diocese of Indianapolis. Neither support nor direction is received from any outside authority, and it is self-supporting. The hospital at Columbus, Indiana, is a branch.

The plant is assessed at about forty-five thousand dollars, and with the growth of the city northward and the completion of extensive improvements and additions in the future Mercy Hospital bids fair to occupy a prominent place among the institutions of its kind in Southern Indiana. There are five sisters now ministering in the hospital and sanitarium. The former has a capacity of twelve, the latter of fifty. The institution is in a prosperous and substantial condition, and shows a healthy growth.

THE OLD LADIES' HOME.

On January 2, 1905, a meeting was held at the residence of Mrs. George Pfau, Jr., for the purpose of forming and perfecting plans for founding a home for persons who were without the means of providing themselves with the necessities and comforts of life. The first name selected for the institution was "Home for the Aged," but as this included both sexes, a condition contrary to law, the name was changed to "The Old Ladies' Home." Solicitors were appointed to see what amount could be raised, and they met with such success that at the next meeting a committee was appointed to draft a constitution, by-laws, and rules, i. e., Henry Burtt, Mrs. Sarah Ransom, Miss Clara J. Loomis and Miss Rose Beck.

A board of directors to serve one year was elected as follows: Mrs. George Pfau, Jr., president; Mrs. Sarah Ransom, first vice-president; Mrs. Agnes Zulauf, second vice-president; Miss Clara J. Loomis, secretary; Miss Rose Beck, treasurer; Miss Ada Bruner, Mrs. John Loomis, Mrs. Ed. Weber, Mrs. Daisy Kehoe, Mrs. C. E. Asbury, Mrs. William Lewis, Mrs. Jessie Bishop, Mrs. John Geinger, Mrs. I. F. Whitesides, and Mrs. William Seibert. The following gentlemen were appointed on the first advisory board: George H. Voight, A. A. Schwartz, W. B. Lewis, S. E. Mullings, John Best, George Holzborg, James H. Armstrong, George Pfau, Sr., Henry Burtt and John C. Zulauf.

In November, 1905, the Ward property at the northwest corner of Market street and Ohio avenue, was rented and prepared for the admission of applicants. Eight ladies were cared for in this home until late in 1906. In October, 1906, the property at 330 West Market street was purchased from George Pfau, Sr., and the ladies were moved to the new building in April, 1907.

In the purchase of this new property Mrs. Sarah Ransom donated one thousand dollars and Mrs. Jennie S. Cobb, the sister of the late William Stratton, of Colorado Springs, donated a like amount. The rest of the necessary amount was made up of small subscriptions.

Eleven ladies have been cared for in the new home. The institution is supported by hard work on the part of the ladies who manage its affairs, and on the generosity of friends. An aid society has been formed, and it affords much assistance to the managers in the matter of supplies and money. The present board is Mrs. Sarah Ransom, president; Miss Rose Beck, first vice-president; Mrs. John C. Loomis, second vice-president; Mrs. Daisy Kehoe, third vice-president; Miss Clara J. Loomis, secretary; Mrs. William Seibert, treasurer. The home has done much good in Jeffersonville and the ladies managing it deserve unstinted praise for their perseverance and success.

THE HAUSS SANITARIUM—SELLERSBURG.

In 1907 Dr. I. Robert Hauss, A. M., established a privte hospital at Sellersburg, Indiana, and its need was immediately manifest. The building is one of nine rooms, but is entirely inadequate. A larger and much more modern building is being planned at this time, which when completed will afford accommodations for more patients and for more conveniences possible in the present building. Doctor Hauss does a general practice, but his hospital work is largely surgical. All of the surgical cases at the sanitarium are drawn from the private practice of Doctor Hauss, and as this practice is one of the largest in the county the operations are numerous enough to testify to the need of an institution such as this in its locality. The operating room is one of the best in the county and the whole plant, in neatness and in keeping, is excellent. A head nurse is on duty at the institution all the time, extra nurses being called in as needed.

Doctor Hauss is a graduate of the Eclectic Medical Institute at Cincinnati, Ohio, had two years clinical instruction in the Cincinnati Hospital and had a special private course under the late Professor McDermott.

THE POOR FARM.

For many years the paupers of Clark county had been receiving almost as good care as some of the animals on farms surrounding the poor house, but public sentiment was aroused and public officials who had been guilty of this neglect finally undertook the task of building a new asylum. Amos W. Butler, secretary of the Indiana State Board of Charities, was responsible for the sanitary lines upon which the new building was constructed. When completed the building cost the county twenty-three thousand six hundred and sixty-nine dollars. The contractor was Clarence E. Howard and he turned it over to the county commissioners November 20, 1907.

The new asylum is complete in every detail and is two stories high. It fronts to the north and there is an east and west wing, each of which has a large porch. There are thirty-three rooms in the building, exclusive of the bathrooms, halls and clothing closets. The apartments to be occupied by the superintendent and his family are nicely finished and contain many modern conveniences, including bathrooms, kitchen and dining-room. The house throughout has hardwood floors made of Canada maple. The heat is supplied by steam and two large tanks in the attic furnish a supply of water for the building. The bedrooms are large, and there are lounging-rooms for the charges, many of whom have seen better days.

The structure is of brick. None of the inside walls have been plastered, but instead have been painted. This was done for the sake of keeping the place sanitary. There are broad stairways, and each step is so arranged that it can easily be cleaned. In this new building the sexes will be entirely separated, and will not even come face to face at meal times, each having different dining-rooms. The furniture will be plain, but good, all of the bedsteads being of iron, with good springs, besides which there will be a straw tick. The normal capacity of the building is sixty, but with little trouble one hundred could be easily accommodated.

It was only after several years of planning that the county finally secured the new asylum, there having been considerable opposition to building it. The County Council finally appropriated twenty-five thousand dollars for the building, and when bids were asked for putting up the structure the contract was given to Clarence E. Howard, who offered to do the work for twenty-three thousand six hundred and sixty-nine dollars. R. L. Plaskett, of New Washington, was appointed superintendent of the work and he saw that the contract was carried out in every detail. The building is looked upon as the best in the state of Indiana for the price. It is substantial from end to end and has been built with a view of service more than of beauty.

In appearance, however, it presents rather an imposing front. It is in full view of travelers to and from Charlestown on the interurban and no citizen of Clark county need be ashamed of this institution.

CHAPTER XXXIII.

PUBLIC UTILITIES OF CLARK COUNTY.

RAILROADS—TRACTION LINES—ELECTRIC LIGHTS—GAS—WATER—FERRIES—
TELEPHONES.

THE JEFFERSONVILLE WATER SUPPLY COMPANY.

The Jeffersonville Water Supply Company began to lay their mains and erect the pumping station in 1887. The pumping station is located above Port Fulton on the river bank and is a powerful and complete plant. The stand pipe is located just within the eastern limits of Port Fulton near the end of Market street. It is one hundred and fifty feet high, fifteen feet in diameter and has a capacity of a quarter of a million gallons.

The water works, as accepted December 14, 1888, had a total of ten miles of water mains, about one hundred and fifty subscribers, and represented on investment of about one hundred and fifty thousand dollars.

At the present time there are about fifteen miles of water mains, with about nine hundred subscribers. There are no mains smaller than six inches and none larger than fourteen inches. One hundred and thirty-four fire plugs located in all parts of the city furnish ample free fire protection, and the normal pressure of seventy-five pounds is sufficient for all ordinary fires. In extraordinary cases the pressure can be raised to one hundred and ten pounds in five minutes.

In 1906 this company began digging wells east of Fulton street and north of Tenth street, sinking thirty-two and striking copious flows of soft freestone water. The pumping station near the wells was erected at a cost of about thirty thousand dollars, and it is from this station that most of the water supply of Jeffersonville is derived. The daily consumption of water in Jeffersonville is one and one-half million gallons.

David Allen, the superintendent, has been connected with the Jeffersonville Water Supply Company from the first. With a larger pumping plant at the wells pumping station Jeffersonville will be supplied with as pure water as any city in the state of Indiana.

THE UNITED GAS & ELECTRIC COMPANY.

The first gas plant in Clark county was built in Jeffersonville, in 1855, the franchise being granted by the Council on February 7th of that year, to furnish gas at two dollars per thousand. J. M. Cooper and J. C. Belman were granted exclusive rights for twenty years and the company was known as the Jeffersonville Gas Company. At the end of this period, in 1875, the contract was renewed for ten years under the same name. On January 28, 1880, it was renewed again, and on January 3, 1882, the name was changed to the Electric Lighting, Gas Heating & Illuminating Company. The company at this time was composed of Simon Goldbach, John C. Howard, S. S. Johnson, E. W. McKenna, Felix R. Lewis and their associates.

In 1889 the name was changed to the Electric Lighting, Gas Heating & Coke Company. An electric plant was installed on Maple street between Spring and Wall streets, in 1890. It consisted of two fifty light arc machines for street lighting, one alternating machine for incandescent lighting, two one hundred horse power boilers and two one hundred horse power engines, and it was operated until 1900. In this year Charles S. Knight was at the head of a company which entered the field to develop the business in Jeffersonville. This company was called the Jeffersonville Light & Water Company, and they were granted the contract for city lighting, in February, 1900, with an understanding with the powers then at the head of affairs of the city that Jeffersonville would take over the property in time and would run it under municipal control. However, a change in the political complexion changed this plan and the unloading failed to materialize. The plant was erected at Sixth street and Kentucky avenue, and consisted of one two hundred and twenty-five horse power engine, one one hundred and seventy-five horse power engine, two eighty light arc machines, two two hundred and fifty horse power boilers, one three thousand light and one thousand light generator for alternating incandescent lights. This company furnished arc lights to the city at forty dollars per year. The Jeffersonville Light & Water Company went under within a short time and finally Frank Willey was appointed receiver. At this time the receipts from the commercial lighting would hardly pay the coal bills of the concern. The plant had deteriorated badly by the time the United Gas & Electric Company organized and bought it in 1900.

This new company also absorbed the Electric Lighting, Gas Heating & Coke Company, which owned the gas plant at Sixth street and Michigan avenue, in 1900.

The gas plant now occupies ground on Sixth street and Michigan avenue, one hundred and fifteen feet by three hundred and fifty feet, and consists of a retort house sixty feet by thirty feet, a meter and exhauster room twenty-three feet by eighteen feet, and the condensing house thirty-six feet by twenty-eight feet, all of these buildings being of brick construction with slate roofs. There is also a separate brick structure twenty feet by twelve feet, containing the oxide room, a coal storage shed with metal roof one hundred and four feet by thirty-one feet, and a coke crushing plant. The gas holder is built in a brick tank fifty-four feet in diameter, having a storage capacity of twenty-seven thousand cubic feet. This plant, technically known as a three bench coal gas plant, is equipped for a daily output of one hundred and fifty thousand cubic feet of gas, the maximum output now being one hundred cubic feet. It compares favorably with plants in cities larger than Jeffersonville, and the charge of one dollar per thousand cubic feet for gas seems reasonable.

The electric plant at Sixth and Kentucky avenue is now operated as a distributing and rotary converter substation, supplying an alternating current series, arc and commercial lighting and power service to Jeffersonville, Howard Park, Port Fulton and Clarksville, and distributing railway current to the Louisville & Northern Railway & Lighting Company, the Louisville & Southern Interurban Traction Company, and the local city lines. Besides the above named equipment at this station there is also a twelve hundred amphere fifty-five volt general electric booster, used in connection with a storage battery, which is located in an adjoining building. The battery consists of two hundred and sixty-four cells, chloride accumulators, with a capacity of six hundred amphere hours at the one hour rate of discharge. These storage batteries are charged from the main generation station and are used to boost over the hard pull of the day from five to seven o'clock p. m.

The change in the gas and electric light business in the last six or eight years has been phenomenal. In 1902 there were only five hundred gas customers in Jeffersonville, and only one hundred and fifty gas stoves.

In 1909 there are over one thousand five hundred customers for gas lighting; there are one thousand two hundred and sixty gas stoves, sixty water heaters, one hundred and twenty-five gas heaters (small stoves), and fifteen miles of gas mains.

In 1902 there were practically no incandescent subscribers, and unsatisfactory street arc lamps. In 1909 there are one hundred and sixty-five inclosed street arc lamps of the General Incandescent Company make, eight hundred subscribers to incandescent light, ten thousand two hundred and two sixteen candle power lamps for commercial lighting, six hundred and thirty-eight horse power motors, one hundred desk fans, twenty-five ceiling fans, twenty-three electric signs and two hundred and seventy-seven commercial arc light lamps, over two hundred of which are in the Car Works. This growth has all been made in less than seven years.

The Charlestown Lighting plant is small but efficient. It is owned by the Louisville & Northern Railway and Lighting Company, and has about seventy-five customers for incandescent lights and about thirty-six street arc lamps. This plant contains one forty kilo watt two hundred and fifty volt generator, belted to a sixty horse power high speed Atlas engine, one eighty horse power tubular boiler, and one one hundred and twenty horse power five hundred volt motor. The apparatus is so arranged that the generator can be engine driven or motor driven, as conditions may warrant. It was installed in 1904, by Clarence Hay.

In 1888 the Car Works installed four electric machines for lighting their shops, and they were continued in use until 1902, when the power began to be supplied by the United Gas & Electric Company. In 1893 Belknap Cement Mills, at Sellersburg, installed an electric lighting plant and have been operating it ever since.

Capt. Ed. J. Howard installed an eight hundred light electric plant for his ship yards and residence in 1894, and it is still in operation.

In 1894 Sweeney's Foundry installed an electric machine of their own make for lighting their shops. It is now used as a nickel plating system.

In 1901 Prof. W. W. Borden, of Borden, installed an electric plant, consisting of one ten horse power gasoline engine, one ninety light generator supplying four arc lamps of twelve hundred candle power and fifty-two sixteen candle power incandescent lamps.

John F. and Joseph Spieth installed an eight hundred light plant in their building at Chestnut and Spring streets for furnishing incandescent lights from Court avenue to the river. This plant was operated for three years.

In 1902 the Market street mule car line was converted into an electric line by Ham Duffy and was operated for two years as such, when it was purchased by the Louisville & Southern Indiana Traction Company.

In 1904 the Claggett Saddle Tree Company, at Market and Broadway, installed one fifty light electric machine for lighting their shops.

In 1905 a plant was installed at Speed's cement mill.

The Reformatory plant was installed about 1900.

In 1909 a two hundred light machine was installed by J. L. Pease & Company, of Howard Park.

THE LOUISVILLE & SOUTHERN INDIANA TRACTION COMPANY.

This company, which operates between Jeffersonville, New Albany and Louisville, also owns and operates the city railway in Jeffersonville. The equipment of this road is one of the best in the state of Indiana and the service of a thirty minute schedule between Jeffersonville and New Albany, and a fifteen minute schedule between Jeffersonville and Louisville is adequate for the travel, if not for the comfort of the passengers. From the county line at Silver Creek and Gleenwood Park the interurban line traverses a section destined to be an important and desirable residence location. The city lines on Spring street, Court avenue, Chestnut street to the upper end of Port Fulton, Market street west of Spring, Missouri avenue and Sixth street practically cover the entire city and furnish rapid and convenient transportation.

The approach to the Big Four bridge in Jeffersonville was completed in September, 1905, and electric inter-communication begun. This approach and bridge not only offer access to Louisville for the Louisville & Southern Indiana Traction Company, but the Louisville & Northern, and the Indianapolis & Louisville traction cars also.

The Louisville & Northern Railway and Lighting Company control and operate the lines from Jeffersonville to Charlestown and from Watson to Sellersburg. The Indianapolis & Louisville Traction Company operates the lines north of Sellersburg. Over this system of lines from Indianapolis run the local and limited cars to Louisville. An hourly schedule of trains from 6:30 a. m. to 8:30 p. m., with four limited flyers called the Hoosier Flyer and Dixie Flyer, offer exceptional facilities for rapid transit both local and through. The construction and equipment of these lines show a close adherence to the best standards of modern interurban railway work. Girder rails of ninety pounds Loraine section and T rails of seventy-five and seventy-seven and a half pound Carnegie sections are used, the ties being selected white oak. A deep filling of crushed stone ballast insures the stability of the roadbed, which is built in accordance with standard steam railroad specifications. The trolley circuits consist of double 3-o grooved wires and the feeder system of five hundred thousand c. m. insulated cable. Span construction is used throughout with thirty and thirty-five foot eight inch top poles. Numerous convenient waiting stations along the thirteen and twenty-six hundredths miles from Jeffersonville to Charlestown, three miles from Jeffersonville to Glenwood, four and thirteen hundredths miles from Watson to Sellersburg, and fourteen and sixty-three hundredths miles from Sellersburg to Underwood, mark the stopping places of the cars, and a large suburban, interurban and rural population is served.

Fifty-seven trains daily arrive from Louisville.
Thirty-five trains daily arrive from New Albany.
Eleven trains daily arrive from Indianapolis.
Eleven trains daily arrive from Charlestown.

The rolling stock of the Louisville & Southern Interurban Traction and the Louisville & Northern Railway and Lighting Company consist of forty-one interurban motor cars, trailers and express cars, one electric mogul car, repair cars, freight cars, express cars and sprinklers, besides the city cars. This equipment is all in excellent condition, and the interurban cars, built by the St. Louis Car Company and the American Car & Foundry Company, are of the latest design and construction, the motor cars being equipped with four fifty horse power G. E. motors. In Jeffersonville a commodious barn is located, where the cars are housed when not in service.

At Watson is located the sub-station. It is equipped with a three hundred kilo watt general electric rotary convertor, three sixty cycle one hundred ten kilo watt step down transformers and a two panel switch board. Current is taken from a four thousand volt transmission line, as in the case of the Jeffersonville sub-station, and after passing through the transforming and converting apparatus it reaches the direct current railway feeders at a pressure of about six hundred volts. This station is an excellent example of the latest engineering practice in railway sub-station construction.

THE PENNSYLVANIA RAILROAD.

Pittsburg, Cincinnati, Chicago & St. Louis Railway Company. The old Jeffersonville, Madison & Indianapolis railroad was a consolidation of two roads, the Jeffersonville and the older Madison & Indianapolis, taking the combined name. The former was originally the Ohio & Indianapolis Railroad, chartered by the Legislature of Indiana, January 20, 1846, and changed to the Jeffersonville Railroad three years after—January 15, 1849. It was first in full operation February 1, 1853. The other was chartered in June, 1842, and set in operation in October, 1847. It was afterwards sold under foreclosure, and reorganized March 28, 1862, as the Indianapolis & Madison Railroad Company. May 1, 1866, the companies became one, and merged their lines into a single one, from Jefferson to Indianapolis. January 1, 1873, the road became part of the Pennsylvania system.

The road from Jeffersonville, commonly called the Dinky line, was built in 1865 and a schedule of regular trains started.

The Pennsylvania Railroad has twenty-eight and nine hundredths miles of main line track in Clark county; nineteen and forty-one hundredths miles of siding, and two and six hundredths miles of second main track. The yards in Jeffersonville are the largest in the county; in them all north bound freight trains from Louisville and Jeffersonville are made up.

The Pennsylvania bridge across the river just below the city of Jeffersonville, although not wholly one of the public utilities of Clark county, is a part of the railway which bears the same name, and adds materially to the importance of the city. On February 19, 1862, the Kentucky Legislature passed an act "to incorporate the Louisville Bridge Company." Much time was consumed in settling the legal difficulties which arose, but finally the contracts were let. The piers were finished and the superstructure begun in May, 1868. After many accidents and delays the first connection of superstructure between the shares was made February 1, 1870; the railway track was laid and the first train passed over on the 12th of this same month. The bridge had cost, to the close of 1870, two million three thousand six hundred and ninety-six dollars and twenty-seven cents, including one hundred fourteen thousand five hundred and sixty-two dollars interest on the capital stock, and all other expenses. The construction account alone was one million six hundred forty-one thousand six hundred and eighteen dollars and seventy cents, reaching not greatly beyond the estimate of the chief engineer, January 1, 1868, which was one million five hundred thousand dollars. The partial year of operation in 1870 yielded the company a gross income of one hundred twenty-one thousand two hundred and sixty-seven dollars and fifty-five cents—eighty-four thousand six hundred and five dollars and ninety-eight cents tolls from railway freights, thirty-five thousand five hundred and fifteen dollars and ninety-seven cents from railway passengers, and one thousand one hundred and forty-five dollars and sixty cents tolls on the foot-walks. The operating expenses were ninety-one thousand twenty-three dollars and seventy-seven cents.

It has a single railroad track, and its total length between abutments is five thousand two hundred and eighteen and two-thirds feet. The spans commencing at the abutment on the Indiana, or north, shore are as follows: 99, 149.6, 180, 180, 180, 398¾ (Indiana Chute), 245½, 245½, 245½, 245½, 245½, 245½, 370 (Middle Chute), 227, 227, 210, 210, 180, 180, 149.58, 149.58, 149.58, 149.58, 132, 132 (draw over canal), 50, 50. These dimensions are from center to center of piers, and they are greater by the half-widths of two piers than the clear waterway. The trusses themselves are of the two styles patented by Albert Fink, the chief engineer of the bridge. The two channel-spaces are spanned by Fink triangular trusses, and all the others except the draw by Fink trussed girders. The approach to this bridge on the Indiana shore consists of a long and high embankment. This, however, does not properly belong to the bridge, and in accordance with the rule adopted for other bridges, we consider that we have reached the end of a bridge when we come to earth-work. Under this rule this bridge has no approaches, the entire space from abutment to abutment being waterway. This bridge originally had a six foot side walk for the use of pedestrians, but they were torn off in late years.

THE BIG FOUR BRIDGE.

This colossal structure, which is Jeffersonville's chief outlet to the south, was completed in August, 1895, seven years having been occupied in its construction. It is a single track railroad bridge and is used by the Big Four Railroad, the Louisville & Southern Interurban Traction Company, the Louisville & Northern Railway and Lighting Company, and the Indianapolis & Louisville Traction Company, for their interurban traffic. The length of the spans, beginning on the Indiana side, is as follows: One of 210 feet, two of 550 feet each, one of 553 feet, and two of 341 feet each. The piers are five hundred and fifty feet apart and the bridge is one thousand two hundred

THE BIG FOUR BRIDGE.

and twenty-four feet long between shore piers. Length of bridge proper is two thousand five hundred and forty-five feet, and with approaches is over nine thousand feet long. The clearance over the channel is fifty-three feet above high water. In round numbers the bridge cost five million dollars, of which one million eight hundred thousand dollars was spent in construction and three million two hundred thousand dollars for property on either side of the river for approaches.

For some years Jeffersonville and Louisville capitalists had endeavored to form a company to build a bridge between the cities, but in 1881 capitalists in New Albany formed a company to build the bridge there and the Jeffersonville scheme suffered a setback.

In 1885 began the long fight for the new bridge which finally resulted in the Big Four bridge. The fight that the river interests made against the construction of this work reflects no honor and little credit on the men who were in it either as river capitalists or river employes. In a small pamphlet published by the War Department the sworn statements of these river men appear and they are a sad commentary on the veracity as well as the intelligence of the men making them.

Every imaginable obstacle was thrown in the way of the scheme from the very beginning, in 1885. Senators and Representatives from every state bordering upon the river flung themselves into the fight to protect the interests of the river men. The promotors had prepared for this and had consulted all the leading pilots before settling on their plans, notably Pink Varble, a well known pilot, who nevertheless came in with an affidavit that the location of the bridge would ruin navigation.

After a long fight the plan went through and the building begun. Even then a snap vote was secured in Congress in the absence of Congressman Howard, stopping the work, but at last the opposition was overcome. In December, 1892, after several spans had been erected, a half span with the traveler fell into the river, carrying down a score of workmen to death. Later that night a complete span fell. Three years before this two accidents in the caissons when the piers were being constructed resulted in the death of sixteen men.

The scheme to build this bridge originated with James W. Baird. The first work was done October 10, 1888. After the loss of the span and a half amounting to over sixty thousand dollars, the bridge was thrown into the hands of the Big Four. It was completed and thrown open for business in September, 1895.

The Big Four Railroad owns no property in Clark county except the bridge and a yard. This yard, just in the rear of the United States government building, is one of the largest railroad yards around the Falls and contains about nine miles of track in its switches. The freight depot and

24

switch at Spring street and the bridge crossing completes the property. The approach for the traction cars in Jeffersonville was constructed in 1905.

THE BALTIMORE & OHIO SOUTHWESTERN.

This road was originally the Ohio & Mississippi, the present Jeffersonville branch from Watson being the main line, as the New Albany extension was not built until February, 1888. It was chartered by Indiana February 12, 1848; Ohio, March 15, 1849; and Illinois, February 12, 1851. It was built by two separate corporations, and completed in 1867, with a six-foot gauge, which has since been changed to standard. Since November 21, 1867, it has been operated under one management, two divisions. An act of the Indiana Legislature, March 3, 1865, provided for the branch from North Vernon, through Clark and other counties in that state, to Louisville, which was opened in 1868 and has since been successfully operated.

When the extension to New Albany from Watson was made it was known as the New Albany & Eastern. This extension constitutes the main line into Louisville now, the trains entering that city from New Albany over the Kentucky and Indiana bridge.

The Baltimore & Ohio Southwestern has about twenty-five miles of track in Clark county, and in Jeffersonville, at Market and Broadway, have yards of about one hundred cars capacity. The tracks of this road, from the limits of Jeffersonville northward, are used by the Big Four Railroad.

The business handled by the Baltimore & Ohio Southwestern in late years has been small and from present indications will never be much larger.

THE MONON RAILROAD.

The Chicago, Indianapolis & Louisville Railway Company. This road has twelve and eighty-two hundredths miles of main line track in Clark county. It passes through the extreme western end of the county, touching Borden in Wood township.

THE FERRY COMPANY.

All the ferries in early times were owned and managed by Jeffersonville men. On October 12, 1802, Marston Green Clark was granted a license to operate a ferry by William Henry Harrison, Governor of Indiana. This ferry was put in operation by Clark and was continued by him until March 4, 1815, when he sold his rights to James Lemon. Lemon ran the ferry, which until that time and for some years afterward was but a small row boat affair, until October 9, 1822, when he sold out to Robert Fray. Fray sold to George White on December 19, 1822.

George White had previously bought from Samuel Meriwether another ferry right, which had been confirmed by the Indiana Legislature to White, in December, 1820. At this time White owned two ferries and he continued to operate them until July 3, 1826, when he sold a half interest in both ferries to Charles Stead.

On the same day George White sold the remaining halves of the two ferries to Eliphalet Pearson, who on the same day sold his holdings in these ferries to Ephraim Gilmore. On July 3, 1826, Stead sold his undivided interest in the two ferries to Athanasius Wathen for six hundred dollars. Gilmore and Wathen continued to hold and operate the two ferries until July 22, 1835, when Gilmore sold his undivided half interest to John Shallcross, Charles M. Strader and James Thompson.

Meanwhile the ferry privilege had attracted other men and on July 2, 1807, Governor Harrison issued a license to Joseph Bowman. This ferry was to run from the foot of Spring street to the public road at the mouth of Bear Grass creek, in Louisville, this road being about where the foot of Second street is located now. Bowman operated this ferry until February 1, 1817, when he died, unmarried, and left his ferry rights to his brothers, Leonard and William, and sisters, Elizabeth and Susan. On December 10, 1825, James Fisler and his wife, Susan (Bowman's sister), sold their one-fourth share to Athanasius Wathen. On July 26, 1829, William Bowman sold his interest to A. Wathen. In May, 1821, Leonard Bowman died, leaving nine children, one of whom, Elizabeth, was the wife of Athanasius Wathen.

(The fact that Athanasius Wathen became insane before he died may be attributed to his efforts to figure out just how much of each ferry he did own.)

Wathen purchased the interests of the other eight of Leonard Bowman's children late in 1821 and became the owner of another one-fourth.

On May 13, 1823, John Wealthers and his wife Elizabeh (Bowman's sister) sold their one-fourth interest in the ferry to James Nesmith, and on July 4, 1825, Nesmith sold this one-fourth interest to Ephraim Gilmore. On July 22, 1829, Gilmore sold this one-fourth interest to John Shallcross, Charles M. Strader and James Thompson, who then became owners of one-half interest in all the ferries, Athanasius Wathen owning the other one-half interest in the three ferries.

In 1831 the old hand power ferry boats were discontinued and the first steam ferry boat began to run. In 1832 the boiler of this boat blew up, killing seven men, but a new and better boat was built and the business continued.

The ferry boats at this time ran from the foot of Spring street to a place called Keiger's landing, opposite, the island not having attained its present size at that time.

The name of this first ferry boat is lost, but the one which succeeded her was named the Black Locust. She was a double hull boat, with a center wheel. She had engines on each side and was about one hundred and fifty-five feet long. Long before the Black Locust had worn out the A. Wathen was built and put in the trade. The·two boats for many years ran on different routes, one of them running across the river, as stated above, to Clay street, the other to a landing about the foot of Second street. This double service continued until the severe winter of 1866-67. This winter was so cold that the river froze up early and the coal supply gave out and people suffered for the want of fuel. What little there was went to sixty cents per bushel. The famine became so serious that Phil Tommpert, who was then Mayor of Louisville, had the boats which ran to Clay street stop running so that the fuel they were consuming could be distributed to the sufferers. As this boat was not paying it was taken off and since that day there has never been a ferry to Clay street.

In 1862 the James Thompson was built by the Howards for the ferry trade and ran but a short time when she was sold to the United States government. She was bought back again at the close of the war and put on the Clay street ferry until the hard winter of 66-67. She was a boat of one hundred and fifty-five feet in length, thirty-seven feet beam and five feet hold. The old A. Wathen continued in the ferry to First street.

The Shellcross was built soon after the War of the Rebellion by Daniel Richards on the Louisville side, just below the island. She had her engine and boiler out on her guards, but afterwards they were moved in on the hull.

The Z. M. Sherley was built by the Howards in 1873. She was a side wheel boat, constructed to carry wagons on both ends, her cabin being upstairs. She was one hundred and fifty-three by thirty-six by six feet.

The new Shallcross was built in 1878 by the Howards and she was similar in construction to the Sherley. Her dimensions were one hundred fifty-eight by thirty-seven by six feet.

The W. C. Hite was built in 1882 and differed materially from her predecessors. Wagons were carried only on the forecastle, the after end being utilized for a cabin on the main deck. This boat was rebuilt in 1897 and a new hull substituted. She was one hundred fifty-six by thirty-six by six and one-half feet.

In 1888 the Sunshine, an excursion steamer, was launched at Howard's. She was one hundred seventy by thirty-six by five feet, and was built for the purposes of carrying excursions to Fern Grove, at the mouth of Fourteen Mile creek. The Columbia, another excursion steamer, one hundred seventy by thirty-five by six feet, was built at Howard's in 1892, for the same purposes.

A new ferry boat, the City of Jeffersonville, was built in 1891, and together with the Hite, still runs between the two cities. The Sunshine was sold in 1907.

The present ferry company, the Louisville and Jeffersonville, was chartered March 16, 1869, by the state of Kentucky, for a term of fifty years. Two hundred thousand shares of stock at one hundred dollars per share were subscribed, and this charter empowered them to purchase all other ferry privileges. In 1865 the North and South Ferry Company was chartered but it never began business.

THE HOME TELEPHONE.

In 1902 the Sellersburg Independent Telephone Company established an exchange at Sellersburg, with a few subscribers, and in 1903 the Louisville Home Telephone Company, of Louisville, acquired control of it.

This company has since that time extended its lines to Charlestown, Nabbs and Underwood, where they have pay stations, but no exchange. It has lines to St. Joe and for sixteen miles on the knobs beyond. Borden is in connection with New Albany. The Stromberg Carlson instruments are used, as in Louisville, and the service, though small at present, is excellent. The Sellersburg exchange has about one hundred subscribers.

Throughout the county there are several independent farmer's lines connected with the Home system.

THE CUMBERLAND TELEPHONE AND TELEGRAPH COMPANY.

The history of the development of the telephone utility in Clark county dates back to 1883, when the Ohio Valley Telephone Company, the Bell licencee operating in the Louisville district, then under the management of H. N. Gifford, extended its lines from New Albany, where it had just opened an exchange.

The first exchange in Jeffersonville was in the rear room, first floor of 215 Spring street, and remained there until it was washed out by the flood of 1884. It found temporary quarters in the second story of a building further north on the east side of Spring street, while a permanent office was being arranged for it on the second floor of 355 Spring street, now Franks' dry goods store. The room had a bay window overlooking the street, which was of great convenience to the operator in spying out persons who were wanted at the 'phone. The exchange closed at 6:00 p. m. It remained here until it was moved into quarters which were part of its present home.

Miss Leilla Houston was the first operator in Clark county, and she was assisted by her sister. Later Miss Nannie Burke, a well known and very popular young lady of Jeffersonville, succeeded Miss Houston and she had sole management of the company's business for many years, until the Cumberland Telephone & Telegraph Company absorbed the Ohio Valley Company, and put men in charge of its smaller exchanges. The service spread out very slowly in Clark county; the lines were extended to Sellersburg and Utica on account of the lime and cement industry in those places, and a line was built to Charlestown and finally to Madison. In 1897 the joint wisdom of the Ohio Valley Company in offering, and the citizens of Jeffersonville in accepting, good service at fair rates, with a single system saved the city from the sad and expensive experience of telephone duplication. Up to this time it had been a day service and the subscribers numbered fifty, but the business was extended and the equipment was modernized and the subscriptions rapidly increased.

Exchanges were soon built at Charlestown, Sellersburg, and Henryville, in 1900, and later at Utica and New Washington.

Generally speaking Clark county is well developed in a telephone way. All the towns in the county have 'phones and the farmers have considered it second only in importance to the railroads.

The Jeffersonville exchange, under the management of Charles Casperke, has ten operators and the free service extends all over the county, except Borden. The service to New Albany is free and these attractive conditions exist throughout the county. Quick, efficient and satisfactory service has brought the whole county together as nothing else could do. At present the Jeffersonville exchange has one thousand four hundred subscribers, Charlestown two hundred and thirty-one, Borden sixteen, Henryville one hundred and forty-two, Sellersburg one hundred and fourteen, Utica sixty-five, New Washington, one hundred and fifteen, and Bethlehem four.

INDIANA REFORMATORY ENTRANCE.

CHAPTER XXXIV.

THE INDIANA REFORMATORY AND THE AMERICAN CAR AND FOUNDRY COMPANY.

THE INDIANA REFORMATORY.

In the fall of 1821 the first state prison in the state of Indiana was established on the northeast corner of Ohio avenue and Market street, in the town of Jeffersonville. Previous to the opening of the prison, prisoners were punished at the whipping post. The law was so changed that all persons who committed a crime for which they should receive not to exceed thirty-nines lashes, should be sent to prison for a term not to exceed three years. Where formerly the punishment was one hundred stripes, a term not to exceed seven years was imposed. The old prison was a primitive affair built of logs at a cost of about three thousand dollars, the greater part of which had been subscribed by Jeffersonville people. It had fifteen cells in a row, made of logs ten inches square, dove-tailed at the ends. The doors were four inches thick covered with strap iron. There was no light or ventilation except what came through a space of about four inches at the top of the door. The roof was of heavy planks cut from the surrounding forest, and dressed by hand. The cell-house was surrounded by a stockade made of logs, and to get into this inclosure one had to pass through a massive door swung on hinges and strong enough to resist a battering ram. The office, guardroom and other apartments were in a two-story log house outside the stockade, and within the guard room was an ample supply of flint-lock guns and pistols. These were strewn around on tables and desks and some of them were hung on the walls in accessible places. Rawhides were used on the convicts then without mercy, and one dose was usually enough. The first lessee was Capt. Seymour Westover.

The first convict ever received was named Friend, and it is a singular coincidence that the oldest inmate at present in the Indiana Reformatory bears the same name. Captain Westover went to Texas in 1826 and was killed with Crockett in the Alamo. He was succeeded by James Keigwin, the father of the late Col. James Keigwin.

The prisons of Indiana have been conducted on three different principles. The first adopted at their inception and above referred to, was suited to the days when but a small number of persons were convicted, or confined, and may be designated as the boarding system. During its continuance the keeping of every prisoner was at the direct cost of the state, without any return and without any sufficient check upon the dishonesty and rapacity of keepers, who could abuse the men committed to their charge by semi-starvation and other measures of "economy."

So soon as the number of convictions in the state had so far increased as to warrant the change, prisons were erected at the cost of the people. In these the convicts were confined, building, prisoners and all, leased to private individuals who fed, clothed and maintained the prisoners, and paid a certain gross annual sum in addition for such labor as they could extract from them.

The third system adopted by the state consisted of renting the labor of the convicts to contractors, who paid a certain per diem for each man employed, while the discipline, control and personal care of the men was in the hands of a warden and other officials representing the state. This was commonly designated as the contract system. The curse of idleness was removed by the lessee system, but only to give place to abuses so horrible that it is a matter of congratulation that Indiana abandoned it as soon as she did. Under the lease system a warden was oppointed by the state for each prison, whose duty it was to see that the contract of the lessee was lived up to, but the convicts were body and soul in the hands of the contractors, and the warden had little power and too often less inclination to restrain those whose interest often led them to commit the greatest cruelties. The one aim of most of the lessees was to obtain from the convicts under their control the greatest possible amount of labor at the least expenditure for maintenance. Men were ill-fed, ill-clothed, punished by the lash with the utmost severity, for trivial derelictions, or for a failure to perform in full the daily allotment of labor, often when sickness and infirmity made it an impossibility to fulfill the requirement. The sick and disabled were neglected as if the consideration of life weighed lightly in the balance against the few cents daily necessary for their maintenance. The cells and corridors were foul, damp and unwholesome; swarms of vermin infested every corner, and thus overwork, cruelty, starvation, filth, the pistol and lash of the guard, all contributed to a wholesale murder of the weak, and to brutalizing the strong beyond the hope of redemption here or hereafter. The horrors of the prison systems before the lessee ceased to be the guardian of convicts were such as to better befit the days of the Spanish Inquisition than the enlightenment of the nineteenth century.

One great argument against the contract system was the fact that it worked in opposition to free labor.

The history of the old Prison South is one of many phases, and unfortunately the stories of cruelty and neglect were often true. The modern ideas of reformation and the square deal to the unfortunates incarcerated had not developed to a degree that resulted in any great benefit to them. With advanced ideas and improvements in every line of business and science, it was but natural that the students of criminology should advance likewise, and the metamorphosis of the old stockade of the Prison South into the present wonderful institution of the Indiana Reformatory bears testimony that Indiana is the peer of any state in handling such questions.

The growth of the number of inmates from 1821 until the present year is as follows:

For the year ending   Daily Average.

For the year ending	Daily Average
November 30, 1822	3
November 30, 1823	6
November 30, 1824	19
November 30, 1825	25
November 30, 1826	38
November 30, 1827	27
November 30, 1828	24
November 30, 1829	37
November 30, 1830	29
November 30, 1831	32
November 30, 1832	46
November 30, 1833	44
November 30, 1834	43
November 30, 1835	41
November 30, 1836	53
November 30, 1837	57
November 30, 1838	35
November 30, 1839	61
November 30, 1840	74
November 30, 1841	100
November 30, 1842	77
November 30, 1843	57
November 30, 1844	81
November 30, 1845	91
November 30, 1846	98
November 30, 1847	122
November 30, 1848	129
November 30, 1849	120
November 30, 1850	122
November 30, 1851	150
November 30, 1852	212
November 30, 1853	223
November 30, 1854	259
November 30, 1855	260
November 30, 1856	277

November 30, 1857 304
November 30, 1858 397
November 30, 1859 484
November 30, 1860 410
November 30, 1861 281
December 15, 1862 202
December 15, 1863 214
December 15, 1864 245
December 15, 1865 247
December 15, 1866 399
December 15, 1867 420
December 15, 1868 387
December 15, 1869 393
December 15, 1870 380
December 15, 1871 381
December 15, 1872 399
December 15, 1873 395
December 15, 1874 388
December 15, 1875 456
December 15, 1876 531
October 31, 1877 553
October 31, 1878 626
October 31, 1879 624
October 31, 1880 600
October 31, 1881 524
October 31, 1882 564
October 31, 1883 578
October 31, 1884 570
October 31, 1885 572
October 31, 1886 573
October 31, 1887 510
October 31, 1888 557
October 31, 1889 549
October 31, 1890 569
October 31, 1891 592
October 31, 1892 594
October 31, 1893 635
October 31, 1894 708
October 31, 1895 815
October 31, 1896 827
October 31, 1897 811
October 31, 1898 909

October 31, 1899 940
October 31, 1900 887
October 31, 1901 895
October 31, 1902 912
October 31, 1903 932
October 31, 1904 976
October 31, 1905 1,044
October 31, 1906 1,095
September 30, 1907 1,145
September 30, 1908 1,212

Hardly a year has passed since the present location was selected that improvements of some kind have not been made. In 1882 a large cell house was built at a cost of fifty thousand dollars, but the greatest number of improvements have been made since the institution became the Indiana Reformatory.

In April, 1897, an exchange of inmates was made between the Indiana Reformatory and the Michigan City penitentiary, to carry out the provisions of the new law which provided that all life-time men and those over thirty years of age should be confined in the latter place. At that time three hundred and sixty men were taken north and two hundred and ninety-seven men were received here. A. T. Hert, who was the last warden, became the first superintendent, and he remained as such for two years, to be followed by W. H. Whittaker. Among the many modern improvements which have been made at the new institution may be mentioned the new C cell house, constructed in 1901, from plans drawn by Arthur Loomis, of Jeffersonville. This cell house is one of the most modern in the United States. It is sixty cells long and five cells high, making a double stand of three hundred cells on each side of the center of the cell house. Each cell is about six feet wide by eight feet high, by ten feet deep and is equipped with running water, toilet and washstand, electric light, wire spring bed, shelf and chair. The total cell capacity is six hundred for C cell house; one hundred sixty-eight for B cell house, and two hundred for A cell house, making a total of nine hundred sixty-eight.

The present entrance was reconstructed during the wardenship of Mr. Patton, just preceding Mr. Hert. The foundry was built and burned in 1908; the hospital was built in 1898; the trade school building in 1895; the new laundry and bath house were built under Mr. Whittaker's superintendency, and the large drill ground was walled in in 1907. In 1909 about eight additional acres of land were obtained through condemnation proceedings. The roof garden for the hospital is one of the most valuable features in the whole plant. Here the men in the grasp of the white plague are made to sleep and exercise, and the results of this treatment have been excellent. The building containing the office of Mr. Barnard, the assistant superintendent, also contains the solitary cells. The last report speaks as follows of this feature:

"Our methods of discipline are humane. At no time is a man thrown into a dungeon or into a dark or poorly ventilated cell; but, whenever necessary to confine a prisoner for discipline, it is done in a well-lighted and well-ventilated cell, and for the first offense he is given two full meals a day while in punishment. We find we get just as good results from this method as we did from the old method of giving a man only eight ounces of bread per day and all the water he could drink while in punishment.

"I find that the best method of handling men of this character is to give them at all times fair treatment, and in no case should punishment be meted out to the offender unless he has wilfully violated some rule of the institution. In adhering closely to this rule and in giving to each fellow a "square deal," I find that far better results can be attained than by the old method of vindictive punishment, and where careful investigations were not always made before a prisoner was placed in punishment."

There are no dungeons at the reformatory now. The solitary cells are about eight feet by ten feet by twelve feet deep and are airy, clean and well lighted, every cell having an outside opening.

The library is of great benefit in offering good, clean instruction and pastime to the inmates and at the same time in furthering the reform idea. The library was burned on February 8, 1908, and three thousand and seventeen books out of a total of four thousand six hundred twenty-seven were destroyed. Since that time new books have been added until there are now six thousand, five hundred forty-nine. This library has an average monthly circulation of fifteen thousand seven hundred fifty-one volumes, or a total circulation of one hundred eighty-nine thousand and fourteen for the year.

On the second floor above the library is the chapel, with a seating capacity of one thousand fifty. Here every Sunday morning the inmates and officers gather for divine service, and the fact that the inmates contributed one thousand two hundred dollars towards the purchase of a pipe organ for this chapel indicates to what extent they are interested.

Among the minor features of the reformatory may be mentioned an excellent brass band of twenty-eight pieces, and also a newspaper, called the "Reflector," which each inmate finds in his cell every evening. For physical exercise, besides the daily work of the trade schools, the military idea has been adopted, and a drill for each day is held if possible. Under the instructions of Lieutenant Harrell, of the Indiana National Guard, the men have received excellent training in the sitting-up exercise and marching, as well as in discipline.

The central idea in the reformatory being reform, education is naturally used as the best means of accomplishing this result. The trade schools are not only teaching trades to the men but are a source of revenue to the institution. They are on an excellent basis. Instruction is given the men in the following trade schools: chain-making, shirt-making, foundry department, shoe-making, tinsmithing, blacksmithing, brickmasonry, broom and brush-making, cabinet-making, carpentering, tailoring, laundering, painting and printing.

The various other institutions in the state such as the insane asylums, etc., etc., are supplied with furniture, clothing, shoes, etc., from the reformatory and the receipts from this source reduce considerably the expense on the taxpayers for maintaining this institution. The shirt department clears about forty-five thousand dollars per year. In 1908 the institution cost one hundred ninety-six thousand eight hundred fifty-seven dollars and thirty-nine cents for maintenance in all departments including schools, library, parole and discharge of prisoners, supervision of paroled prisoners, salaries, food, clothing, fuel, etc., yet the trades schools made one hundred seventeen thousand three hundred twenty-one dollars and forty-four cents, leaving a very small remainder for the taxpayers to contribute towards the support of nearly one thousand three hundred of their delinquent citizens at less than eighteen cents per capita, when we remember, too, that over two hundred boys are kept in school under competent teachers more than nine months in the year. The fact that competent instructors are provided in all trades schools, and the fact that inmates are given military drill and moral instruction to help them physically and mentally, and the further fact that no contractor has a word to say as to the amount of work a boy must perform makes the system almost ideal. The trades schools are now furnishing all of the chairs, beds, mattresses, tinware and furniture for the new Southeastern Hospital for the Insane, being constructed at Madison.

In the educational department the men are given good practical instruction. If they are illiterate they are placed in the kindergarten department, where they are taught reading, writing, spelling and number work. In the next or primary department the men are taught reading, elementary language, arithmetic, history and geography. In the intermediate department, literature, grammar, physiology, civil-government, geography and arithmetic are taught. In the advanced department, arithmetic, English grammar, and ten lessons in algebraic equations.

There is also another department for weak minded boys, and also one for foreigners, another department of mechanical drawing, and a correspondence school, whereby the men may study in their cells. At present the school is able to offer arithmetic only by correspondence, but the demand for this work has been so large and the results so commendable that this course is to be made to include the other subjects.

The system as adopted in the reformatory is certainly a success, and each succeeding year demonstrates its value. Its idea is to correct rather than to punish. Although there is a complete lack of clap-trap sentimentality, there is no unswerving rigor in enforcing the regulations. The instructions are of practical benefit and the output is of practical benefit to some one. The ultimate intention is to produce everything required by the other state institutions. The system of paroling men has stood the test of time and its unquestioned value proven. The wonderful results evident in the management of the Indiana Reformatory could never have been produced with politics the sole qualification for service. The sixty-five to seventy officers and instructors are doing what the average politician could never do. W. H. Whittaker and M. Barnard, the superintendent and assistant superintendent, have given the state an exceptionally efficient service. Mr. Barnard came to the reformatory from the Michigan City penitentiary after eight years' service there as assistant superintendent. The other officers of the institution without an exception are imbued with an esprit de corps which argues well for the present and future management of the plant.

THE AMERICAN CAR AND FOUNDRY COMPANY.

June 1, 1864, the Ohio Falls Car and Locomotive Company was organized with a capital stock of three hundred thousand dollars, afterwards increased to four hundred and twenty-eight thousand five hundred dollars. The following were the first officers of the company: President, D. Rickets; secretary and general manager, Hiram Aldridge; treasurer, Jacob L. Smyser. Its first directors were D. Rickets, A. A. Hammond, J. L. Smyser, W. P. Wood and H. Aldridge.

On October 1, 1866, Mr. Joseph W. Sprague took charge of the works as president and general manager. The business of the company was not then of the best, its credit was questionable, and its stock selling far below par. Under Mr. Sprague's judicious administration a great change was wrought, the company was pressed with orders, the stock was brought up to par, and there was every prospect for a continued and increased prosperity.

So matters stood when one day in 1872 the works caught fire, and before anything could be done to prevent such a result, were completely swept out of existence. Fortunately a heavy insurance was carried, and the building of the present magnificent system of fire proof and isolated structures was commenced. These were still incompleted and the business of the company barely resumed, when came the panic of 1873, which, with the long period of financial depression that followed, completely paralyzed the building and equipment of railroads in the United States, and compelled the company to suspend, and ultimately to dissolve and offer its property for sale to cover its indebtedness.

THE AMERICAN CAR AND FOUNDRY COMPANY.

On the 7th day of August, 1876, was organized the Ohio Falls Car Company, with Joseph W. Sprague as president and general manager, and R. M. Hartwell secretary and treasurer. Its directors were J. W. Sprague, S. A. Hartwell, J. L. Smyser, J. H. McCampbell, and S. Goldbach, and its capital stock of eighty-eight thousand three hundred dollars, later increased to four hundred thousand dollars. The officers remained the same, with the exception of the appointment of R. S. Ramsey as general manager, made September 27, 1881, to relieve Mr. Sprague from overwork. The company purchased the lands, buildings, machinery, stock and tools of the old corporation, and at once began operations, first in a comparatively small way, gradually increasing to enormous proportions. The new company was made up of nearly the same stockholders as the old, and any losses made by the former failure were retrieved tenfold. The success of the institution was largely due to the enterprise and business tact of its managers, but not a little to natural advantages of location. The works are located about five hundred feet from the Ohio, and, being outside the city limits, a low rate of taxation is permanently secured.

The Ohio river affords the cheapest class of transportation for iron, coal, lumber and other supplies. The Pennsylvania Railroad, Baltimore & Ohio Southwestern, and the Louisville & Southern Indiana Traction Company enter the premises by switches. By means of the railroad bridge over the Ohio river, located half a mile below the works, immediate connection is made at Louisville with the southern network of railroads. Within a very small radius an ample supply of the quality of white oak, white ash, yellow poplar and black walnut used in construction can be obtained at reasonable prices. Empty cars returning from the South insure very low rates of freight on yellow pine, and the various brands of irons made from the rich ores of Alabama. Considering the convenience of receiving supplies and of the distribution of products, this location can hardly be surpassed for almost any branch of manufacture.

The real estate upon which the extensive institution is located embraces a large territory. The buildings which were first built are situated upon outlot No. 34, of Clarksville, containing an area of about nineteen and two-thirds acres. Part of outlot No. 23 containing about five and a half acres immediately west of outlot No. 34 is used as a lumber yard.

The river slip containing about thirteen thousand eight hundred square feet lies opposite the works upon the river bank. On this was located the engine house and pump for furnishing the water supply. This was before the installation of the water works system by the city of Jeffersonville, since which the company has used water from this source. Automatic sprinklers were introduced in all the shops, and fire hydrants were erected at a cost of over twenty thousand dollars. Lot No. 9, Jeffersonville, containing about five thousand sixty square feet, secures a connection with the Baltimore & Ohio South-western Railroad. Blocks No. 18, 19, 49 and 80, situated on the west side of Missouri avenue, were purchased by the company upon which to erect new shops. The beautiful residence for the superintendent was erected on the river bank in 1900. The buildings of the company, numbering over fifty, are all substantial and in good condition. With the exception of the office, the pattern lofts and cupola they are one story high. They are constructed of brick and the roofs are covered with the best quality of slate. These build-ings are arranged with high gables, with ample spaces between them and are substantially fireproof. They are all thoroughly lighted and most of them are amply provided with skylights of heavy plate glass. The machine shops in the freight and iron department are provided with gas from the city mains of Jeffersonville, and are wired for the necessary electric currents. Mr. Sprague took charge of the institution in September, 1866, and labored faith-fully for the interests of the company until about October, 1888, when he re-tired, selling his large stock interests to his associates. This was during the financial depression which commenced in 1884, and continued until the fall of 1889. Upon the resignation of Mr. Sprague, Jacob L. Smyser, of Louisville, Kentucky, was elected president. For about fifteen months during 1888 and 1889 the works were closed for lack of orders. General business was badly depressed, and this worked a terrible hardship upon the large force of men who had in the past relied upon this institution for their living and support of their families. Necessarily the business of Jeffersonville was seriously affected, but the gradual resumption which commenced late in 1889 soon relieved the situ-ation. The employees were called to their old places and in an unusually short time the works were in full blast. The business of the company became larger than ever before, with corresponding profits the results. New buildings and improved machinery were continually being added until 1892, the working force had reached a maximum of two thousand three hundred men, with a pay roll of seventy thousand dollars per month, nearly three thousand dollars per working day. These figures and facts are staggering, but serve to illustrate what location, energy and a comprehensive grasp and application of business principles can accomplish. In 1893 another panic swept over the country and the business of the company shared in the depression as a natural consequence. In the late fall active work was again suspended and was not resumed until about the beginning of 1895 and then only in a limited degree. During this period the banks of the country were under suspension, and currency was sell-ing as high as four per cent. premium, being paid for by certified check, payable only through the clearing houses of the various financial centers. Notwith-standing this severe tax upon the depositors to avail themselves of the balances they had in the banks, this company, at a great sacrifice met all of their ma-turing obligations without asking a single renewal.

Resumption of business was very slow; many railroads had to pass through long-drawn-out receiverships, and it was not until about 1898 that normal conditions had returned. In the interim, however, the car company, because of exceptional facilities and financial strength, had its full share of the business to be done, and continued its prosperity until 1899, when there was a merger of about thirteen car building companies of the country, of which this company became one, selling to the new corporation, the American Car and Foundry Company, at a very acceptable price its entire business and effects. The plant has been enlarged and improved by the same company, and it is generally understood that it has had a profitable career. The capital of this new company, the American Car and Foundry Company, is sixty million dollars, half preferred and half common shares. The preferred pays regular quarterly dividends of one and three-quarters per cent., equal to seven per cent. per annum. This common stock pays one per cent. quarterly. The last yearly statement of the American Car and Foundry Company, shows it to be one of the strongest and most prosperous industries in the country, having a net surplus of over twenty million dollars. For several years, up to 1908, John D. Ingram was the manager of this branch of the company. At present J. R. Scanland is the general manager.

In 1888, soon after J. L. Smyser had been placed in control, M. E. Duncan was made general manager of the Ohio Falls Car Manufacturing Company, and Jefferson D. Stewart, secretary and treasurer. They continued with the company until the time of the merger, excepting that during the depression after the panic of 1893, Mr. Duncan was otherwise engaged for about two years. When activity returned he resumed his former relations in the management. Mr. Smyser was a director in the new American Car and Foundry Company and so remained for about eight years, when he declined re-election.

This plant means much to the working people and general business of Jeffersonville, and it is to be hoped that its continued prosperity may reflect happiness and contentment on all those who depend upon it for employment or support.

25

CHAPTER XXXV.

JOURNALISM IN CLARK COUNTY.

In 1820 George Smith and Nathaniel Bolton published the first newspaper in Clark county, at Jeffersonville. This paper was published in their residence on Front street, but did not last long, as they removed to Indianapolis in 1821, where they established the first newspaper in that city. In the thirties the elder Keigwin published a paper in Jeffersonville called the "Humbug," but its life also was short.

In the early thirties Joe Lingen published a paper in Charlestown, but of its name, circulation or politics we know nothing.

In 1836 the Democratic party at the county seat, Charlestown, established a newspaper to expound the doctrine of their faith, and Thomas J. Henly was installed as editor. Henly was a brilliant man, well read and an eloquent speaker, but in strange waters when editing a newspaper. He later on served as a member of Congress from this district for two terms, but only remained in the editorial sanctum for a short while, turning it over to John C. Huckleberry. Huckleberry kept the paper alive until the summer of 1841, when he was obliged to close the office. The name of this paper was "The Southern Indianian."

In 1837 "The Jeffersonville Republican," a weekly political journal representing Democratic principles, was established in Jeffersonville by Robert Lindsey. Not having means sufficient to carry out this enterprise, Dr. Nathaniel Field and others became his sureties for the payment of the material needed, and at the end of five years of alternate disappointment and encouragement he was obliged to abandon his paper, which came into possession of Doctor Field as the principal surety. The doctor continued its publication some three years at a financial loss, though making a very acceptable journal. He then closed the establishment and sold the press to J. M. Mathews, of Bloomington, who moved it to that place, and for some time Jeffersonville had no paper published within its borders.

In the year 1840 Joseph Usher published a paper in Jeffersonville, called the "Ball of '40." It was a campaign paper, and an ardent Whig. That campaign was known as the hard cider campaign, and the "Ball of '40," added materially to the enthusiasm of the day in Clark county.

An early job office in Jeffersonville in 1841 was located on Spring street in the small two-story brick at No. 252. It was owned by a Mr. Tilden and a description of this plant may make some of the job offices of the present day sit up and take notice. There were four presses, and six to eight men were employed constantly. The presses were hand affairs, but they were capable of excellent work and during the early forties, besides the general run of job work, which kept them running night and day. Tilden printed the Louisville City Directory, a medical work for a Doctor Bright, containing about one thousand pages, and also an English grammar for a Doctor Benedict. William S. Ferrier, the dean of the profession, still living in Charlestown at a hale and hearty old age, set all the type for the grammar.

In the spring of 1842 Ferrier returned to Charlestown, and, although he was only a youth of seventeen, undertook to resuscitate the "Southern Indianian." A Mr. Donaldson assisted for three or four months and then left Ferrier to fight it out alone. He continued the publication of the "Southern Indianian" until 1846, when he sold out to Henry B. Woolls. This paper was a success and supported Thomas J. Henly, who was making the race for Congress on the Democratic ticket, the youthful editor accompanying Henly, and his opponent, Martin, on horseback throughout the district. Henly won and Ferrier returned from one of the hottest campaigns of those days to his paper at Charlestown.

In 1844 Thomas Wright published a Whig paper in Jeffersonville. He was a good writer, a printer by trade and put out a first-class journal.

In the year 1847 Ferrier returned to Charlestown from Ohio and bought out the printing plant of Judge James Scott. Judge Scott retired from the Supreme bench in 1831, and about 1834, or very soon after, began the publication of a newspaper called "The Comet," in a little frame building on Lot number 55. At the head of his paper he kept standing as its motto "Ask not to what doctor I apply, for sworn to no sect or party am I." Whether Judge Scott's paper was still published in 1847, or whether it was the outfit only which was purchased can not be told, but upon his purchasing the office Ferrier started the "Western Farmer." The name of the paper was finally changed to the "Clark County Democrat." In 1850 this paper was moved to Jeffersonville, where Ferrier continued its publication until 1853, when it was sold to William French. The building where this paper was published still stands in Jeffersonville and is now used as the ferry office.

The paper was published by French later in a building which stood on the northwest corner of Chestnut and Pearl streets, and here it received its baptism of actual fire. The building burned and the office together with the contents of the Masonic Hall on the upper floor was a total loss.

In 1862 Ferrier, who had established an office in Charlestown, moved his plant to Jeffersonville and published a paper in the building standing on the southwest corner of Spring and Chestnut streets. He remained as editor of this paper for about one year, and then sold out to a Republican syndicate, who moved it to New Albany.

In 1864 Ferrier was publishing another Republican paper in Jefferson-ville. It was published only a short while, but it lasted during the campaign. It was the first daily Republican newspaper in Jeffersonville. In 1869 Ferrier returned to Charlestown and started the Clark County Record. It was a Republican paper and continued as such until 1900, when it was sold and its politics became Democratic. It is still published and under the name of "Clark County Record and Hoosier Democrat," it proudly declares its age as forty-one years.

THE NATIONAL DEMOCRAT.

The "National Democrat," the oldest existing weekly newspaper in Clark county and the parent of the Evening News, the first daily newspaper ever established in Jeffersonville, was founded by William Lee, on November 11, 1854. It was a four-page eight-column sheet and was established to uphold the pure doctrine of Democracy. With Mr. Lee was S. R. Henry, and the publishing company was known as William Lee & Company. Mr. Henry withdrew after the first year and in the absence of Mr. Lee in Washington the burden of the publication devolved almost entirely upon Mrs. Kate Lee, his widow since November, 1902, and now resident at Ireland, Dubois county, Indiana, and well advanced beyond fourscore years.

After two years existence the paper and plant were sold to a number of citizens, all long since dead, who placed the late Capt. A. J. Howard in the editorial chair, but according to Mrs. Lee the verbal promises to pay were never more than partially redeemed. The office was on Front street, over the Ferry office. Messrs. Wiltse and Nixon were the next purchasers, the latter being the Hon. Cyrus J. Nixon, whose brother, Magistrate Benjamin F. Nixon, died a year ago. They soon transferred their property to Henry B. Woolls, who retained the paper for some years, but finally sold it to Reuben Dailey, who issued his first number on June 6, 1872. He retained the paper till his death and it is now jointly owned by his widow and son. Mrs. A. E. Dailey and Clarence I. Dailey. They also own the daily edition referred to which was started by the late Mr. Dailey on November 18, 1872.

It is to be regretted that the files were not retained intact in the office, but were kept by the parties who owned the paper from time to time, if indeed office files ever existed. Only the first two volumes, published by William Lee, are now in existence prior to the first volume published by Mr. Dailey.

The weekly edition was published by Mr. Lee in a building on the site now occupied by the Eaken building at Spring and Chestnut streets, while the opposition "Know Nothing" paper was published by William M. French, one square west at Chestnut and Pearl, his paper being known as the "Republican." Later the Democrat was published by Mr. Howard, on Front street, between Pearl and Spring streets, and by Woolls on Spring street, where Frank Spieth now has a meat store. Mr. Dailey assumed charge there, moved to West Chestnut street, then back to Spring street, and thence to Wall and Chestnut streets, where the paper withstood the flood of 1883. Before the more disastrous flood of the following year it had been moved to the News block, built by the proprietor, where it has been issued ever since, It has always been a Democratic paper.

The original "Evening News," but for which Jeffersonville like Newport and Covington, Kentucky, or Allegheny, Pennsylvania, also situated adjacent to large cities, might never have had a daily paper, was a four column sheet, twelve by nine inches, printed on one side only and sold for one cent a copy five days a week, no publication occurring on Wednesday, which was "weekly day." The paper had "ads." printed on the back soon after and for $1 the editor undertook to print his entire issue on the back of business circulars. However, the bantling grew and during the next two or three years we find it growing to four pages of even six columns, but one issue shrunk to two columns, four pages, and so it fluctuated until on March 17, 1873, the epoch-making decision was reached to fix the price at ten cents a week and the size was four columns, four pages at that time. A few years later it grew in size and is now seven columns, four pages, while the weekly contains from six to eight pages, eight columns.

The "National Democrat" missed an issue in its early days, so far as Mrs. Lee recollects, and certainly that of August 8, 1855, is not in the files. This was two days after a fierce election in which the "Know Nothings" figured largely and which was of such a character that the Louisville Journal, the predecessor of the present Courier-Journal, failed to appear on August 7th, and in the next issue, giving a full account of the riots of the previous day, alleged them as the cause of its failure to appear.

During the great flood of 1884, when the News office was flooded, only handbills, similar in size to the earliest issues of the paper, were published. Regular issues were resumed after one week.

THE JEFFERSONVILLE TIMES.

The Jeffersonville Times was started in the early eighties, by Lee Johnson and Joe Fitzpatrick. A. J. Howard, popularly known as Jack Howard, came into possession of the paper afterwards and used it as his political mouthpiece when he became warden of the Prison South. The Jeffersonville Times was a seven column, four page paper, and its first habitation was on the second floor at the northeast corner of Spring and Chestnut streets, in the rooms now occupied by the telephone exchange. Here the Rev. T. G. Bosley became the business manager. The offices were moved to the west side of Spring street two doors south of Maple. Here George Howard became business manager, but as he did not give his brother, Jack, complete satisfaction, he severed his connection and Devore Broy assumed the management and remained with it until it was carted away to the journalistic graveyard in 1886. Jack Howard, the editor, was one of the best known men in Southern Indiana, and in his day one of the most influential politicians in the state. His wide acquaintance and political sense, together with his newspaper, served to bring him into prominence. His paper, the "Times" was a good one, and in the political fights of the times was a rather dangerous weapon in the hand of its editor.

THE JEFFERSONVILLE GAZETTE.

In the early eighties George R. Brown established a Republican daily paper in Jeffersonville called the "Jeffersonville Gazette." It was a four page, six column sheet, and as it was published before the day of patent insides, it was filled with local and plate matter. It finally shared the fate of all other Republican newspapers in Clark county, and in 1885 it became a corpse in the building on the west side of Spring street, about two doors south of Market.

THE JEFFERSONVILLE WORLD.

In the early nineties the Small Bros., unwilling to learn by the ghastly array of defunct journals in Jeffersonville, began the publication of the "Jeffersonville World." Their office was located in the brick building at 244 Spring street, but they soon after moved to 216 Spring street. The Small Brothers sold the paper and Albert Small, one of them afterward became identified in publishing patent newspaper matter in Indianapolis. George Voigt finally got control of the paper and continued it as an expounder of the Democratic faith with George Johnson as business manager. The World finally ceased to live.

THE JEFFERSONVILLE JOURNAL.

The Jeffersonville Journal has been described as "a spasm." It was a small Republican paper published in the nineties by a Mr. Tevis, a son of a pastor of Wall Street Methodist church. The Journal worried along for a short while and then died a natural death with no near relatives and very few mourners at the demise.

THE PENNY POST.

In the eighties William Armstrong and Luther F. Warder started a new Democratic paper and called it the "Penny Post." It had a meteoric career across the journalistic heavens of Jeffersonville and finally fizzled out. It was a five column, four page sheet, and was published on the second floor, at the southeast corner of Spring and Chestnut streets.

A Mrs. Johnson published a temperance paper called the "Agitator," in Jeffersonville, probably in the seventies, but no record of its life or influence can be discovered. It is dead.

THE CLARK COUNTY REPUBLICAN AND JEFFERSONVILLE STAR.

The Charlestown Hustler was established by James Ruddell in Charlestown in 1891. In 1893 Lee L. Robinson and A. R. Schimpff leased the property from Ruddell for six months, and at the end of this term it again became the property of Ruddell. It was afterward purchased by William E. Robinson, and the name changed to "Clark County Republican."

In 1903 Bundy and Patchell purchased the plant and September 2d, of that year started the "Jeffersonville Star." On August 1, 1904, the plant went into the hands of a receiver and on December 1st it was sold to C. A. and A. R. Schimpff. In August, 1905, C. A. Schimpff sold out to A. R. Schimpff, who still publishes it. The first location of the Star in Jeffersonville was in the brick building on the north side of Chestnut street above Spring street. Charles Patchell was manager and Devore Broy, city editor. The present location of the Star at 115 West Maple street is a convenient and well appointed newspaper office. It is a staunch supporter of the Republican party and principles and, and its success in being the only Republican paper to exceed nine months in existence, is no doubt due greatly to its consistent and untiring support of these men and measures.

In the campaign of 1905 the Star had much to do in turning the city over to the Republicans.

THE CLARK COUNTY SENTINEL.

On November 1, 1893, the Clark County Sentinel was established at Borden, Indiana, by A. E. Olmstead and R. F. Mix. In March, 1894, the office was partially destroyed by fire, but the paper never suspended publication. In April of this year Olmstead purchased the one-half interest of R. F. Mix, and since that time he has edited and published it as a Democratic newspaper. It is a seven column, four page paper, well gotten up and has a circulation of about six hundred.

THE CLARK COUNTY CITIZEN.

The "Clark County Citizen," the Democratic weekly newspaper published at Charlestown, was founded in October, 1902, by Carl Brayfield, a well known newspaper man and versatile writer, who had previously been a political staff correspondent, traveling in Indiana and the South. The Citizen, from its inception, took a leading position in the political affairs of Clark county, and the Third Congressional district, its political opinions being widely quoted and republished in the press of the Hoosier State.

The Citizen occupies three rooms in the Russell block in Charlestown, and is in a prosperous condition. Its circulation is not confined to Clark county alone, but it is widely read by people of the Democratic faith throughout the nine counties of the Third district.

The "Clark County Citizen," in the first issue of its seventh year, October 7, 1908, has the following to say:

With this number The Citizen enters upon the seventh year of its existence in Charlestown—the fourteenth year of its age both here and in Henryville, at which last named place it was known as the Times.

When the material of the Times was removed from Henryville to Charlestown six years ago, two wagons were all sufficient to convey the entire plant, and the loads were not heavy.

Today the plant occupies three rooms in the Ruddell building, and has been more than quadrupled in size.

When the Citizen was established here six years ago, those who did not understand the situation, much less did not know the man at the helm, were profuse in their prediction of failure, and the prophecy was freely made that six months would, at most, see the end of its existence.

The Citizen has lived to see a number of newspaper changes in Charlestown since that bright day, October 3, 1902, when it made its first appearance here. Its Democratic rival, a venerable publication, dating its beginning from the days of the Civil war, after passing through various hands and leading a precarious existence, finally ceased to be, and was succeeded by a Republican paper, leaving the Citizen the sole Democratic occupant of this field.

The Citizen has grown in popularity, in business and in material worth, year after year, until now it is one of the permanent business enterprises of Clark county.

Its standing has been secured by its independence of character, by its hard work, and by refusing to become a mendicant for official and public favors. Whatever it has won has been earned by merit, and it has never prostituted a proud profession by marketing its space for political crumbs that fall from the tables of county officials.

A history of journalism in Clark county would be very incomplete without a mention of the two journals, one of which is still published under unusual circumstances. As far back as 1890 a prisoner in the old prison south, Joe Bush, issued a paper within the walls and called it "Hot Drops." It was an original and unique sheet, one copy being the whole issue, written in long hand, yet its fame spread far beyond the limits of its circulation. Its successor is the "Reflector." For several years this paper was issued from the Reformatory printing office as a weekly journal, but early in 1908 it began a daily issue and has succeeded beyond the expectations of its most sanguine friends. It is an exchange with every county paper in the state of Indiana, and a copy is issued to every man in the institution every evening. The weekly issue has a large circulation throughout the United States. The daily paper is a four page, four column sheet, and the weekly issue is six pages and four columns.

CHAPTER XXXVI.

SCHOOLS OF CLARK COUNTY.

BY S. L. SCOTT, COUNTY SUPERINTENDENT.

In common with the struggle for homes and for the necessities of life, the hardy pioneer also toiled for the establishment and maintenance of schools for his children. Rude almost as Indian wigwams, low and dark and gloomy, with greased paper for a window, and a split log for a seat, with a huge stone chimney built on the outside of the building. The log school-house, built in the wilderness of Indiana, served its purpose well, and was often the center around which clustered scores of cabin homes. It served the threefold purpose of an intellectual center for the community, a place for a general business meeting, and as a house of worship for its builders. No sooner had the hunter, the trapper and explorer opened up the road into the wilderness of Clark county late in the eighteenth century and prepared the way for a handful of early pioneer settlers than the itinerant school master, uncouth and uncultured, pitched his tent among them and boldly plead for patronage among the lads and lassies of the little settlement. Some of them came from Kentucky and Virginia, but many of them from New England. Often the double profession of preacher and teacher was practiced by some of these men. No qualifications, no experience, no training were required and only a very elementary education consisting of reading, writing and ciphering, was essential. Yet these men had lofty ideals, and much of the spirit of the real teacher. From these most humble beginnings amid conditions and surroundings unfavorable and unpromising, the early log school-house took its stand on the outskirts of civilization, on the borderland of the Indian savage. The curling smoke from the hut of Indian warriors gave place to the more cheerful fires of the log cabin school-house. The war-whoop of the Indian savage had not ceased to echo amid the hills and tree-tops of the Indiana forests until the glad shouts of the school children were ringing through the woodlands and fields of the settlement.

The foundation for the present system of education in Indiana was laid before Clark county was settled. As far back in history as the year 1785, after the conquest of the Northwest Territory by George Rogers Clark, Congress passed an ordinance which declared that one square mile in every township in the Northwest Territory should be set apart for the maintenance of public schools. Two years later in the "Ordinance of 1787," Congress declared that "religion, morality and knowledge are essential to good government and the happiness of a people, and that schools and the means of an education should forever be encouraged in the new territory." The famous "ordinance" passed before Indiana had either organization or a civilized people has been the basis from which grew one of the strongest and most practical school systems of modern times. And this is due in a very large measure, to the wisdom and foresight of the fathers of another century and of other states, the splendid school system the Clark county boy enjoys today. This ordinance, reaching down through more than six score years, has furnished the basis and inspiration for favorable school laws to the builders of two state constitutions and to the patriotic members of every General Assembly convened within her borders. As early as 1808 the territoritorial Legislature of Indiana passed a law giving courts the power to lease the lands which had been reserved in each township for school purposes. These leases were not to be for a longer period than five years, and the persons leasing the school lands were to clear not less than ten acres on every quarter section.

The constitution adopted in 1816, provided for township schools, county seminaries and state university, ascending in regular graduation, with free tuition and equally open to all. With these and many other favorable laws the school system had its beginning. The early years of progress were slow indeed. Buildings were poor, and teachers without training, and those who attended had tuition to pay. The day of free schools for all was still afar off. The earliest schools in Clark county were usually not taught more than three months in the year. The teacher's pay was small, indeed and he usually boarded around with the patrons, staying a week at each home.

As early as 1801 a school was kept in Silver Creek township by Richard Slider. This school was taught from six to eight weeks annually and was in existence for a number of years. Among the first teachers at the Slider school were James McCoy, Andrew McCafferty, George McCulloch and Spenser Littell.

In 1803 a school was opened on the old Hester farm near Charlestown, and was taught by a Mr. Epsy. Teaching then began with the rudiments of the language in Dilworth's spelling-book. Epsy was rather deficient, even in the knowledge of correct reading and pronunciation. His pupils were taught to give nonsensical names to vowels whenever one of them formed the syllable of a word. Reading books furnished little useful information, and were in no sense adapted to beginners. Two books which were used as readers were Gulliver's Travels and a dream book. The rigid discipline exercised, the cruel penalties inflicted upon delinquent pupils, and the long confinement to their books—from a little after sunrise to near sunset—are all now considered as detrimental to intellectual as well as physical advancement.

In 1811 in Utica township on the James Spangler farm, a rude log school-house took its place among the still ruder lob cabins of the early pioneers. Among the first teachers in this old log school-house were William Crawford, a Mr. Blackburn and a Mr. Scantlin. These men taught most of the children of the families in those days. As far back as 1820 a dwelling was converted into a school-house on the Charlestown and Utica pike road. It stood near where the residence of Peter H. Bottorff later stood. A Mr. Kincaid was one of the teachers. Perhaps the next school-house in Utica township was the one put up on E. B. Burtt's place some time in the thirties. The teachers who taught here were Messrs. Brown, Fellenwider, John Randolph, Jonas Raywalt and George Ross. It was at this school that the Swartzs, the Jacobs, the Epsys, the Patricks, the Spanglers, the Prathers, and the Ruddles, received their early instruction.

In 1830 Clark county had its first institution of higher learning located at Charlestown, and known as the "Charlestown Seminary." The school was opened by D. Baker, an Englishman, and was in the old Masonic hall. Mr. Baker was the father of Hon. E. D. Baker, afterwards United States Senator from Oregon. This school had rather a successful career covering a period of nearly twenty years. The annual enrollment reached at one time three hundred students. In 1849 the school was bought by the Rev. H. H. Cambern and was changed to a female seminary, under the supervision of Rev. George J. Reed. After a successful career of some fifteen years the school passed under the control of Prof. Zebulon B. Sturgus, a scholar of superior worth and attainments. Students were enrolled from several states along the Ohio river, and the school was in a prosperous condition during the active life-time of Professor Sturgus. He called the institution "Barnett's Academy."

One of the early schools in the county was in Wood township. Moses Wood, a brother of George Wood, the founder of the township was the first teacher. In 1825 a Mr. Ransom taught and he was followed in 1826 by Tilly H. Brown. In 1827 William Sparks had the school. Other early teachers were Joshua W. Custer, Charles A. Carpenter, Asa M. Bellows and Evan Baggerly.

In Bethlehem township a school was carried on before the Antioch church was thought of. It was very near the place where later the church was located, and was a log affair about sixteen by eighteen feet with a door which swung to the outside. Cyrus Crosly was the first teacher and after him came Thomas J. Glover, Dr. Solomon Davis, Rev. Benjamin Davis and others. In 1832 a new hewed log school-house was presided over by Martin Stucker. Charles Smith, Samuel C. Jones, Joel M. Smith and Thomas S. Simington followed, and it was while the last named was the pedagogue that the building burned. This was about 1840, and a new building was soon erected and the school presided over by George Matthews. The schools of this locality have kept abreast of the improvements made elsewhere in the county.

The second institution of higher learning in Clark county was Borden Institute, founded in 1884 by Prof. William W. Borden. This was located at the town of Borden, and had a very successful career for more than twenty years. Three distinguished educators have been at the head of the faculty of this institution: Prof. Francis Stalker, Dr. W. E. Lugenbeel and Prof. H. A. Buerk. This school ranked high among the better institutions of learning in the state. The museum in connection with this school had a collection of geological, mineral, archæological and historic specimens not surpassed by any other institution in Indiana. Under the present laws of the state the county school system has developed into a complete system of graded schools, including a four years' high school course in which tuition is free and attendance is compulsory. The minimum term in the district school is six months, and in some townships this is extended to eight months, while the town and city schools have a full term of nine months. Clark county has two commissioned high schools, one in the city of Jeffersonville, and one in the town of Charlestown. It also has one certified high school at New Washington and six other high schools doing two or more years' work.

The original public schools of Jeffersonville consisted of two buildings, both of which have disappeared. The old Mulberry street school which stood about opposite the end of Chestnut street, was a two-story brick building, built about 1850. It served its purpose until 1904, when it was torn down to make room for the interurban viaduct. The other school-house, a duplicate in design, stood on the northwest corner of Maple and Watt streets. It was torn down in 1907. In 1870 the oldest of the present school buildings was opened for use. It was built as a graded and high school and marks the beginning of the high school system of the city. For four years thereafter the girls and boys had separate high schools, but after that they were united and have remained so until the present time. W. H. Parsons was the first principal of this Chestnut street school, and held that and other positions in the public schools of Jeffersonville for years.

In 1874 the Rose Hill school was built and W. B. Goodwin became the first principal. The present high school building was erected in 1882 and for several years several of the grades were taught on the lower floor, but it is devoted wholly to high school use now.

In 1904 the Spring Hill building was opened for use, and its construction has marked a decided change in school matters of the city. Public sentiment has of late years been directed toward the sanitary and structural details of the school buildings and as a result these features have made notable improvement. The city of Jeffersonville of late years, under the management of Supt. A. C. Goodwin and more recently Supt. C. M. Markle, has developed one of the very best city school systems in Indiana. The graduates from the city high school take high rank in the higher institutions of learning in the state.

Clark county now has one hundred and two school buildings, which, together with equipment and grounds, are valued at more than a quarter of a million of dollars. Our enumeration of school children is now more than ten thousand, with an annual enrollment of five thousand nine hundred. Clark county employs one hundred and eighty-five teachers and pays them an annual salary of more than seventy-five thousand dollars. While many of our buildings are old and unsanitary, those built in recent years are beautiful, sanitary, modern in every particular. All of our teachers have had normal or college training and many of them are graduates of higher institutions of learning.

Our public schools have kept abreast of the progress of the age. Public sentiment supports them to the fullest extent. The people love and cherish our schools as they do no other institution of modern life. Next to the family hearth-stone in the hearts of our citizens is the little school home of our children. Within the walls of each school room, whether it be a modest building in a rural district, or a magnificent structure of beauty and convenience, we are striving to kindle and develop in the heart of every child who enters there the best that it is possible for it to experience. The tendency in recent years has been to make the school more natural; to make the school and the home work together for the same common end; to make school experiences real life experiences, and to include in the course of study in the public schools many of the problems of the real outside experiences of the child. With this thought in the mind of our ablest teachers we have faith that our success will be assured and that the citizens of the next generations in Indiana will be more practical and skillful; will be stronger, better and more able to fill their places in the destiny of the race that nature intended for them.

CHAPTER XXXVII.

THE LIME AND CEMENT INDUSTRY OF CLARK COUNTY.

LIME.

As early as 1818 the burning of lime was begun in the vicinity of Utica, and with varying degrees of success and profit was continued until 1907. The first lime burned by the early settlers was on brush and log fires and even at that early date was shipped down the river on flat boats. There must have been a good deal of lime burned in the early days of the industry. Soon after the possibilities of the business began to be apparent and the profits began to make it attractive, the settlers began to burn lime in kilns dug in the ground. The earliest lime burned at Utica was often shipped south as far as New Orleans, not however, as a separate cargo, but only to fill out and complete a load of flour, pork or whiskey. It was shipped in flour barrels and a barrel of lime often sold on the Mississippi river at the same price as a barrel of flour.

About the year 1826 a coal burning kiln was built here, on what is now known as the Nicholas Lentz place, one-half mile above Utica on the river front. The coal used in this kiln was brought from Pittsburg in flat-boats, carrying only five thousand bushels each, and this kiln was used until 1847, when it was abandoned.

A man named Starkweathers burned lime in this kiln shortly after 1826.

The first boat load of lime sent to New Orleans was sent south in 1850 and the cargo consisted of five thousand barrels.

About the year 1830 a man named Peabody came to Utica from Pennsylvania and introduced a better plan for burning lime in the "Ground Hog," or "Pot" kilns. His plan saved fuel and made the business more profitable besides turning out an excellent grade of lime. In 1849 or 1850 N. B. Wood made a great improvement in the kilns by erecting a temporary wall in front of the furnace, leaving a space for the fuel to go in over the top of the wall.

About 1830 Robert S. Wood, James Sweeney and William Brendel boated lime to Louisville. In the forties Allen Somers and James Sweeney, and later on James Hogg went into the business. In 1857 H. C. Emerke and Meshac James entered the boating trade to Louisville.

In 1868 Moses H. Tyler, who had been in partnership with P. Howes, built a patent kiln which added greatly to the output of lime. This kiln was so constructed that it burned continuously, the lime being drawn from below, the rock being fed on the top.

The lime industry was the life of Utica for many years, and the little town was known from Pittsburg to New Orleans on account of the commodity which she manufactured. The principle men who burned lime, both in the ground hog kilns and in the patent kilns, were the Woods, Sweeneys, Somers, Hogg, E. Emerke, James, Lyman Parks, Keys, Jack Howard, Floyd Ogden, T. Rose, Redford Perry and Jacob Robinson.

The principle men who were engaged in boating lime were Jacob Robinson, William Webb, Sweeney and Hobson, and a Mr. Barber, an up-river man.

About 1882 an up-river boatman loaded a boat at Utica for the Atakapas country, and this was the last of the flatboating. It was not until 1868 or 1870, however, that lime burning was considered a profitable industry here. The burnings previous to this time were on a limited scale. Within the above named year the Utica Lime Company, with headquarters at Louisville, erected two kilns, with a capacity of one hundred barrels per day, and valued at $10,000. This company was actively engaged during fifteen years in burning lime, employing from ten to twenty hands regularly. Wages averaged $1.50 per day. The lime stratum is fourteen feet in thickness here.

The first man prominently engaged in the manufacture of lime at Utica was M. H. Tyler, who had built a kiln and made additions until at last its capacity was about two hundred barrels daily. In 1870 the Louisville Cement Company bought out Mr. Tyler, also the firm of H. C. Emerke, whose capacity for burning was about one hundred and twenty barrels per day. This company had four kilns, two for coal, which turned out one hundred barrels daily, and two which burned wood, making in all a capacity of five hundred and twenty barrels a day. Lime was selling, December 1, 1881, at fifty-five cents per barrel. The cost of burning was twenty-five cents not including the stone. The property at that time was valued at twenty-five thousand dollars. Thirty-five hands were employed, wages ranging from $1.40 to $1.75 a day.

The rocks used for lime belong to the Niagara epoch. The following section of the Niagara group was obtained at Speed's quarry: Corniferous limestone, twelve feet; yellow rock, impure limestone, twenty feet; building stone, four feet; gray crystalline limestone, burned for lime, fourteen feet; upper bed crinoidal limestone, two feet; crinoidal bed containing *Caryocrinus ornatus,* etc., four feet; gray limestone, eight feet; magnesian limestone, five feet; total, ninety-six feet.

In May, 1907, the Speeds, who had secured control of the industry at Utica, ceased manufacturing lime here, and since that date all the lime burned by them has been at Milltown on Blue river.

The patent kiln was not responsible for the death of the lime industry in and near Utica; it was rather the ultimate result of the battle between the small burners and the wealthy company which finally controlled the industry.

The extent of the shipments of lime was wide. Utica lime was used in great quantities in Pittsburg in the early fifties; the Louisville and Kanawa packets carried great quantities of it on their up-river trips. A great deal went up into the state of Pennsylvania as far as water transportation could take it; and the down-river packets, the Cincinnati and New Orleans, and the Cincinnati and Memphis boats carried quantities. Those were the palmy days of steamboating and the excellent transportation facilities made Utica lime a standard article up the Wabash, Green, Cumberland, Tennessee, Red, and Arkansas rivers. It sold in the Atakapas country and in Texas, and eastward along the Louisiana, Mississippi, Alabama and west Florida gulf coast. The location of the strata of rock from which lime is made is peculiar. The layer of rock at Utica is the same as the top layer of rock found at the Falls at low water mark. At Charlestown landing the choice strata is about one hundred and sixty feet higher than at Utica; at Riley's Point, opposite Eighteen Mile island, this strata is still higher and only six feet thick. Three miles further up the river it is only four feet thick and it ends there.

CEMENT.

The first cement mill in Clark county was owned by William Beach and it was located in Clarksville, about opposite the Tarascon mill in Louisville. In 1866 the Falls City Cement Company started the manufacture of cement by the erection of a mill on the James Well's farm, about one-half mile south of Sellersburg This mill has been running ever since. In 1869 the Louisville Cement Company purchased land from Louis Bottorff at Speed's. In September, 1869, they purchased the mill of Sabine & Gilmore, about six miles north of Jeffersonville, and in 1870 moved this mill to Watson, where its remains still stand. In 1882 the mill at Speed's was enlarged and in 1890 it had a capacity of about four thousand five hundred barrels of natural cement per day. With the discovery of shale in 1905 a Portland plant was erected at Speed's, having a capacity of about five hundred barrels per day. At present the capacity of this plant is one thousand eight hundred barrels per day.

In 1870 the Black Diamond mill, near Cementville, was built by Bondurant and Todd, on the John Peet farm.

The next mill was the Silver Creek mill. Then came the Ohio Valley mill, the Kentucky and Indiana mill, the New Albany mill, the Clark county mill, the Indiana mill, the United States mill, the Hoosier mill, the Standard mill, the Golden Rule mill and the Queen City mill. Of these the Silver Creek

26

and the Queen City have been dismantled. The Falls City, th Clark county and the Speed's mill are the only ones in active operation at this time. In 1900 the output of these mills was over two million barrels, but on account of the advent of Portland cement in the market this output fell, in 1908, to about two hundred thousand barrels.

In 1898 there were seventeen mills in active operation in Clark county. The Speed's mill had a daily output of three thousand five hundred barrels, Belknap's one thousand eight hundred, Ohio Valley six hundred, Kentucky and Indiana six hundred, Watson one thousand, Standard four hundred, Globe three hundred, Clark County seven hundred, United States five hundred, Black Diamond one thousand five hundred and Gheens six hundred.

In 1870 the output was three hundred twenty thousand barrels.
In 1880 the output was six hundred twenty-seven thousand barrels.
In 1890 the output was one million eight hundred thousand barrels.

Originally the cement rock was quarried, but in later years tunneling was resorted to, and the caverns left by the companies are in some cases quite extensive. The quarrying in early days resulted in more or less rock being stripped off of the cement rock and this was used in building roads. During the busy epoch of the cement industry the Pennsylvania Railroad and the Baltimore & Ohio. Southwestern ran regular cement trains and employed scores of men to handle this class of freight.

In 1903 the Falls City mill made six hundred thousand barrels of natural cement, and in 1908 about forty thousand barrels.

The natural cement business in Clark county is about as dead as the lime business, but the Portland business is maintainig a steady growth to meet the demand for the supply. The new Portland plant at Speed's, running at its full capacity, and with the increased demand, will, no doubt, be enlarged to increase its output.

The remains of the old mills stand as mute landmarks to the glory of departed enterprise, and their abandonment has in many instances obliterated the little settlements which had sprung up around them. Their discontinuance was a severe blow to the localities in which they lay and it is to be hoped, for the sake of the county, that commercial enterprise enough may be created to revive the industry as a Portland business wherever it is possible and profitable.

CHAPTER XXXVIII.

PATRIOTIC SOCIETIES—ANN ROGERS CLARK CHAPTER D. A. R.—FORT STEUBEN
CHAPTER C. A. R.—GRAND ARMY OF THE REPUBLIC POSTS—
THE UNITED SPANISH WAR VETERANS.

Clark county has never been found wanting in patriotism, and in all matters where a spirit of pride and veneration for the deeds and lives of the founders and conservers of the state and nation has been possible, there were found those who gave their time and means to keep alive the record of the past.

To the ladies of Jeffersonville belongs the honor of having formed the highest type of patriotic society, the Ann Rogers Clark Chapter, Daughters of the American Revolution. This chapter was organized January 15, 1901, with Mrs. Nathan Sparks as Regent. The chapter had twenty charter members and with several losses to its membership has at present forty-five. This chapter has taken the lead in several things which reflects credit on the society. They initiated and carried out the centennial celebration of the founding of Jeffersonville, and they have undertaken, with the city's permission, to preserve and improve the old deserted Mulberry street cemetery. They formed a junior society called the Children of the American Revolution to instill into the younger minds a spirit of patriotism. To the ladies of Ann Rogers Clark Chapter Daughters of the American Revolution, and to them alone, belongs the honor of being instrumental in having the state erect a monument to the pioneer heroes massacred at Pigeon Roost. At a state conference of the Daughters of the American Revolution the local chapter initiated the movement, and the state body took it up and had the bill passed at the following session of the Legislature. The present Regent of the chapter is Mrs. Lewis C. Baird.

The Fort Steuben chapter, Children of the American Revolution, was organized in 1907. Its membership is restricted to those children who can trace back to an ancestor of Revolutionary service similar to that of the Daughters of the American Revolution. The society has twenty members and under the instruction of the ladies of the Daughters of the American Revolution, is becoming a well informed and enthusiastic body of little patriots. Such societies as these, where elevating study and the acquiring of useful knowledge is the object, stands in glaring contrast to the card clubs of present day popularity.

GRAND ARMY OF THE REPUBLIC.

Indiana furnished over two hundred thousand men to the Union armies during the War of the Rebellion, and the survivors who reside in Clark county have always striven to keep alive the memories and preserve the friendship of battle, camp, march and hospital. That men who patriotically served their country long and well should seek a closer companionship and comradeship after a return to civil life is but natural. The posts of Clark county have been composed of patriotic veterans who gave the strength and health of youth for the cause of liberty and union in the sixties, and yet in 1909 the flush of youth, the elastic step, the erect form, the clear eye and hearty grasp affected by the weight of years, their enthusiasm still rings as clear as it did in 1861. From the early eighties these veterans have maintained their organizations in Clark county, but the sun is setting behind the hills and ere another decade has rolled around taps will have been sounded over comrade and post, and their work bequeathed to the patriots of another generation and age. The following are the posts of Clark county:

Jeffersonville Post No. 86, organized July 26, 1882. Twenty charter members. Post commander, James Keigwin; senior vice, J. W. Thompson; junior vice, Jacob B. Pifer; officer of the day, James Whicher; officer of the guard, G. C. Watson; chaplain, E. G. Neeld; quartermaster, Philip Specht; adjutant, John Gallagher.

Samuel Simonson Post No. 226, Charlestown. Organized September 1, 1883, thirty-four charter members. Post commander, George W. Coward; senior vice, I. N. Haymaker; junior vice, James Bottorff; officer of the day, Thomas Stricker; officer of the guard, William McComb; chaplain, William Smith; surgeon, H. D. Rodgers; quartermaster, William A. Steirheim; adjutant, Thomas J. Huffman.

Dan Griffin Post No. 323, Sellersburg. Organized March 24, 1884; twenty-three charter members. Post commander, E. T. Leach; senior vice, George Robinson; junior vice, J. H. Smith; officer of the day, A. J. Acton; officer of the guard, Henry Harrold; chaplain, Silas Anson; surgeon, J. V. Robinson; quartermaster, J. L. Leach; adjutant, Henry C. Clark. This post has forfeited its charter and is not in existence.

Rosseau Post No. 351, Jeffersonville. Organized May 19, 1884; twelve charter members. Post commander, Wesley Brown; senior vice, Jefferson Henry; junior vice, Henry Craycroft; officer of the day, Robert Harris; officer of the guard, David Hill; chaplain, A. J. Spears; surgeon, Louis Trible; quartermaster, Charles Tinsley; adjutant, Nimrod Lewis. This post is the negro post of Jeffersonville.

General Lytle Post No. 416, Bethlehem. Organized October 10, 1885; eleven charter members. Post commander, Frank L. Dean; senior vice, J. L.

Dean; junior vice, James E. English; officer of the day, James L. McCoy; officer of the guard, William Hatcher; chaplain, William S. Dean; surgeon, B. F. Scull; quartermaster, William Young; adjutant, B. F. Scull. This post has had to forfeit its charter and suspend.

E. R. Mitchell Post No. 425, New Providence. Organized November 12, 1885; thirty-two charter members. Post commander, John A'. McWilliams; senior vice, B. F. Roerk; junior vice, John T. Kelly; officer of the day, J. M. Campbell; officer of the guard, John McCory; chaplain, J. M. Baxter; surgeon, B. F. Stalker; quartermaster, Ernest Schleicher; adjutant, T. S. Ransom.

Henry Clay Deitz Post No. 450, Memphis. Organized April 22, 1886; twenty-three charter members. Post commander, Cornelius D. Hunter; senior vice, Hiram G. Bridgewater; junior vice, Isaac M. Perry; officer of the day, Elam L. Guernsey; officer of the guard, John L. McCleary; chaplain, Zacharias Young; surgeon, Charles Henrite; quartermaster, Enoch A. McCoy; adjutant, James M. Gray. This post has ceased to exist.

Henryville Post No. 461, Henryville. Organized June 29, 1886; twenty charter members. Post commander, Amos T. Grey; senior vice, James Ryan; junior vice, H. H. Prall; officer of the day, William Sampel; officer of the guard, George R. Grey; chaplain, T. S. Brooks; surgeon, Miles Becket; quartermaster, George Luallen; adjutant, W. H. Williams.

Joel R. Spahr Post No. 580, Jeffersonville. Organized January 27, 1904; thirty-six charter members. Post commander, Charles W. Glossbrenner; senior vice, Joseph G. Snyder; junior vice, W. H. H. Clegg; officer of the day, George W. Coward; officer of the guard, Isaiah Higdon; chaplain, Samuel J. Gardner; surgeon, James W. Stanforth; quartermaster, Charles Stranch; adjutant, B. H. Robinson.

John Brown Post No. 585, Charlestown. Organized October 25, 1890; twelve charter members. Post commander, Robert Wilson; senior vice, Basil Van Cleave, junior vice, Hiram Colwell; officer of the day, Washington Lee; officer of the guard, Lewis Stone; chaplain, George W. Wilson; quartermaster, David Stone; adjutant, Richard Green. This last post was organized by negro soldiers, but its life was short and its charter has been surrendered.

THE UNITED SPANISH WAR VETERANS IN CLARK COUNTY.

Among the younger patriotic organizations represented within Clark county, Indiana, is the United Spanish War Veterans, which might be aptly termed "The Young Grand Army of the Republic," it being an organization somewhat along the lines of the Grand Army of the Republic. In membership the organization is composed of representatives from the North, East, South and West, who were engaged in the late war with Spain, which war, it is admitted on every hand has done more than all else to unite the two sections of the country, so long designated as the North and South, into one grand union of patriotic citizens with a love and admiration for one grand old flag, not surpassed by any nation on the globe. And this is but fitting, for upon the call of our country for volunteers to sustain its honor, the North and South vied with each other in sending forth their best sons, and those sons of the North and South fought shoulder to shoulder in the cause of their common country.

The object of the United Spanish War Veterans, as set forth in their constitution and by-laws, is as follows:

"Its object shall be to perfect and maintain national, state and local organizations; to keep alive the memories of the war with Spain; to promote the best interests of those who, in the service of the United States, took part in that war, and their dependents; to encourage and spread universal liberty and equal rights and justice to all men, as well as to inculcate the principles of freedom, patriotism and humanity. It shall be non-partisan."

Qualifications for membership in the organization are prescribed as follows:

"Active Members: All honorably discharged officers, soldiers and sailors of the regular and volunteer army and navy and marine corps of the United States, including acting assistant surgeons, who honorably served during the war with Spain, or in the incident insurrection in the Philippines, or participated in said war or insurrection prior to July 4, 1902, as an officer or enlisted man, in the United States Revenue Cutter Service, on any vessel assigned to duty under the control of the United States Army or Navy Departments during such war or insurrection, are eligible to membership.

"Honorary Members: Any person who performed distinguished and faithful service during the war with Spain may be elected an honorary member."

Shortly after the close of the Spanish-American War there was organized throughout the United States many organizations seeking to promote the welfare of the participants in that war in the service of the United States. Among these may be mentioned the Spanish-American War Veterans and the Spanish War Veterans, as probably having the largest membership.

The first camp of Spanish War Veterans to be organized within Clark county was the W. T. Durbin Camp No. 31 at Jeffersonville, affiliated with what was known as the Spanish-American War Veterans, that camp being named in honor of Col. W. T. Durbin, the regimental commander of the One Hundred and Sixty-first Indiana Volunteers, who afterwards became Governor of the state of Indiana. This camp was one of the first, if not the first camp organized within the state of Indiana, so Clark county may be given credit for being one of the leaders in the movement to organize the veterans of the Spanish war. Durbin camp was kept alive for several years by the strenuous efforts of a few faithful young veterans, and after finally being disbanded it was succeeded by Nathaniel Isler Camp No. 261, Spanish War Veterans, at that time a separate and distinct organization from the Spanish-American War Veterans. Isler camp was named in honor of Nathaniel Isler, of Jeffersonville, who met death in the battle of San Juan Hill, Cuba, in the late war.

After the organization of Nathaniel Isler Camp No. 261, Spanish War Veterans, a movement was inaugurated to amalgamate all societies composed of Spanish War Veterans, the first organizations to join forces being the Spanish War Veterans and the Spanish-American War Veterans, after which the combined organization gradually absorbed those outstanding until now the veterans of the Spanish war are organized into one united organization known as the United Spanish War Veterans.

During the course of the consolidation of all these societies Nathaniel Isler Camp of Jeffersonville has continued to exist, being taken into the United Organization as Nathaniel Isler Camp No. 13, United Spanish War Veterans.

By a perusal of the foregoing recitation of events as they transpired, it will be seen that Clark county has been represented within the ranks of this splendid patriotic organization from its inception until the present time, and the fact may be further mentioned that the state of Indiana was and has been since the close of the Spanish war, the leader in the movement to keep alive this organization, as it has in all patriotic organizations.

The United Spanish War Veterans, as mentioned in the foregoing part of this article, is much akin to the Grand Army of the Republic, and also to the United Confederate Veterans, being destined, in all probability, to be the successors of these two organizations of valiant and courageous veterans within the next few years. The grand old defenders of our Union and their worthy and courageous foes in the conflict of 1861-1865 are one by one succumbing to man's undefeated foe—death, and passing surely and silently into that great beyond, where there shall be no battles to fight and no foe to vanquish, but where all is peace and love. And it is fitting that this younger organization of veterans, composed as it is of the sons of the North and the South, should be the natural heirs and successors to the glory and honor bestowed upon these great old heroes. Was it not their blood coursing through the veins of the "Boys of '98" that carried these boys through the battles of Santiago, Manila Bay and others with such distinction to their country? Whom else but a man through whose veins flowed the rich red blood of American citizenship, when the enthusiasm of a great victory had not had time to subside, could have such compassion for his foe as he who uttered those now famous words, "Don't cheer, boys, those poor men are dying"? It was such magnanimity upon the part of the combatants of 1861-1865 that made easier the task of their sons to remove the feeling of bitterness and hatred between the North and South, as they did by fighting side by side in the Spanish-American war for the protection of that Union, the disruption of which had been the bone of contention between their sires. It is but meet and proper that an organization composed of their sons should be their successors in the effort to continue and protect a Union stronger than ever, of which it has been aptly said, "There is no North, no, East, no South, no West."

The constitution and by-laws of the United Spanish War Veterans provide that each local camp of that organization shall co-operate with the Grand Army of the Republic in all matters of import to those organizations, and in no other part of the country has there been such readiness on the part of the Grand Army to assist in every way possible the young veterans in everything they undertake, than within the County of Clark.

The United Spanish War Veterans is composed of a national organization, known as the National Encampment United Spanish War Veterans. The National Encampment is divided into what are known as departments, corresponding with the states, the departments being divided into local organizations known as camps.

The National Encampment United Spanish War Veterans is commanded by an officer known as the commander-in-chief, assisted by a staff of officers corresponding to the offices of secretary, treasurer, etc., in other organizations. The departments are commanded by department commanders, who also have a staff of officers assisting them, whose titles correspond to those officers of the National Encampment, with the additional designation of "department" added to their titles. The present department commander of Indiana is Maj. M. R. Doyon, of Kokomo, Indiana.

The local branches of the United Spanish War Veterans, or camps, are presided over by an officer known as a camp commander, assisted by a senior vice commander, junior vice commander, chaplain, officer of the day, officer of the guard, adjutant and quartermaster. The present officers of Nathaniel Isler Camp are: Commander, John W. Ware, senior vice commander, John F. Boyce; junior vice commander, John Morris; chaplain, Henry Barron; officer of the day, Warren Francisco; officer of the guard, James Smithers; adjutant, C. F. Faux; quartermaster, J. Henry Meiboon.

Nathaniel Isler Camp has among its members one department officer in the person of J. Henry Meiboon, senior vice department commander, who has risen steadily year after year from office to office, until at the present time he holds the next to the highest office within the gift of the Department of Indiana, having been elected to that office in July, 1908.

THE CLARK COUNTY HISTORICAL SOCIETY.

This society was organized on May 1, 1903. Its general purposes are the promotion of historical study and investigation of the County of Clark, through the discovery, collection, preservation, organization and publication of historical facts pertaining to said county; and by the collection and preservation of books, pamphlets, papers, maps, genealogies, pictures, relics, manuscripts, letters, journals, field books memoirs and any and all articles which will describe or illustrate the social, religious, political, industrial or educational progress of said county. L. C. Baird was elected president and has served as such continuously to the present time. The membership is composed of those who realize the value of historical research and preservation. The society has had read before its members many papers of historical value, and has preserved from loss facts and articles which may possibly be appreciated in the course of time. That it might come into closer touch with all the townships of the county, vice presidents were elected for each township. The society has met with but scant encouragement, but it stands ready to further any move which has as its object the preservation of the history of Clark county.

CHAPTER XXXIX.

PHYSICIANS AND SURGEONS OF CLARK COUNTY.

Without risking any unsupported claim, or indulging in any flattery, it can be truthfully said that the history of the medical profession, and its personnel, will compare favorably with any other profession in Clark county. Law has produced many distinguished jurists and practitioners on the bench and at the bar; but medicine has had as brilliant and eminent men in its ranks as can be claimed for the legal profession. Many medical men have distinguished themselves as authors, lecturers and surgeons. Clark county furnished a number of surgeons in the Civil war, who rendered services both on the battle field and in the tented hospitals. Such surgeons as the Doctors Fouts, Beckwith, Field, McCoy, Collins, Sheets, and Davis, saw arduous service both as regimental surgeons and in the hospitals. The late Dr. W. W. Goodwin was in charge of a hospital in Jeffersonville during the Civil war, and the late Dr. William Morrow was in charge of the government refugee eruptive hospital during the same period.

The present day physicians have no real conception of what hardships, exposure, and trials were the lot of the early physicians of Clark county. They were not blessed with macadamized roads, automobiles, coupes, depot wagons, taxicabs and closed carriages; but rode through thick and thin, hot and cold, at all hours of the day and night, on horseback, with the old time saddle bags strapped to their saddles. Some of the pioneer doctors would ride many miles over the county, in midwinter, leaving at daylight, and not returning till night, worn out from exposure, fatigue and nervous tension. It was characteristic of them to minister to the sick without reference to fee or reward, as the majority of the people were poor, and while honestly inclined, were unable to pay for medical attendance. I knew a physician, now gone to his reward, who practiced his profession from 1829 to 1888 and who estimated that he had done thirty thousand dollars' worth of medical service, for which he received neither cash, and many times, no thanks. While there is a spirit of grasping for lucre in all professions nowadays; yet the earlier practitioners seemed to take the practice largely from motives of philanthropy. It is one of the grandest of human offices to relieve suffering; to cheer the depressed; to succor from the assaults of diseases; and failing in this, to smooth the way to the inevitable tomb. There is no loftier mission; none which more closely assimilates the human with the divine. While the earlier physicians had to depend on the science as a means of livelihood, still they rose above the purely mercenary motive in their practice. Many of the pioneer doctors not only ministered to the body, but to the soul as well. Several practiced medicine, and "preached the Gospel to the poor." Notable among Clark county's physicians who combined preaching the Gospel with the practice of medicine, were the late Dr. Jacob Bruner, of Utica, and Dr. N. Field, of Jeffersonville. They, like the blessed "Master," preached the Gospel to the poor, free.

It is amusing and interesting to look back sixty years and see the character of service rendered, and fees charged in those days. The doctors worked hard, and were poorly paid for the ministrations. It was the period when cupping, leaching and bleeding were regarded as indispensable. The practice was carried to extremes by many, as the practice of vaccination was performed on those who had no blood to spare, and as a consequence it ceased. The diseases of early times were bilious, remittent, intermittent, and rarely— typhoid, and the cases of the latter were always grave and lasted for weeks and weeks. The old fashioned ague, where the victims almost shook themselves to pieces, was very common in the spring and fall, and good big draughts of Peruvian bark and whisky were the sheet anchors.

While the practice of medicine was regarded as the most honorable, and is yet, it was far from lucrative. In looking back we find some of the fees charged for medicines and professional service, and it must be remembered that doctors then dispensed their own medicines; the charge for visit in the town was one dollar, and for visits to the country, one dollar for the first mile, and fifty cents for each succeeding mile; bleeding fifty cents, two doses jalop fifty cents, box of pills twenty-five cents, extracting teeth twenty-five cents, one dose of calomel and one ounce of paregoric sixty cents. Accouchments five dollars, consultations three dollars. In surgery the fees were very moderate; strangulated hernia, fifty dollars; amputations, from ten to twenty-five dollars. Asepsis was unknown, and great stress was laid on "laudable pus." Diseases such as dysentery and fevers were attributed entirely to miasm, and visitations of sporadic and Asiatic cholera were common.

One doctor claimed great success in treating cholera, by the exhibition of: mustard, grains ten; calomel, grains ten; capsicum, grains ten; salt, grains ten, mixed. This palatable compound was forced down the patients throat with a cloth wrapped around a stick. It was wonderful what results followed, as many got well.

The physicians in early times were temperate, charitable, kind-hearted and self-sacrificing, and it ought to be said, long-suffering. No money could adequately compensate them for the sacrifice of comfort, pleasure, rest and even life itself. They were exposed to seen and unseen dangers.

The first medical society was organized in 1835, and to warn the present day physicians of the temptations and tendency to excesses in diet and spirituous beverages, which tends to cripple them professionally, as well as morally, not to speak of financial wreck; that the first society adopted and adhered to the following rules:

First. "Physicians should never neglect an opportunity to fortify and promote the good resolutions of patients suffering under the bad effects of intemperate and vicious lives; and in order to do so, their own lives should be such as to be blameless; as we regard a high moral character to be a prerequisite to an honorable stand in the profession."

The author is indebted to Dr. D. L. Field for the above information and for much that follows.

As near as can now be ascertained, Dr. Samuel Meriwether was the first physician to settle in Jeffersonville. He was a native of Jefferson county, Kentucky, and pursued his medical studies in Philadelphia under Doctor Rush. He married his cousin, Mary Meriwether, in Kentucky, and soon after marriage entered the army as surgeon's mate, serving during the War of 1812. For some time he was stationed at Vincennes, and for a period of three months was unable to communicate with his young wife, who was greatly alarmed for his safety. Finally, obtaining a short leave of absence, he visited his home and on his return to Vincennes was accompanied by his wife. The hardships of that lonely ride through the forest can only be appreciated by those who have had a similar experience, and they are few in these days.

Doctor Meriwether remained in the service until 1815, when he resigned on the urgent entreaty of his wife, though offered permanent service. Soon after resigning he settled for a time in Jeffersonville, remaining until 1823 or 1824, when he removed to Louisville. In 1830 he again returned to Jeffersonville and made this his permanent abode, becoming one of its best respected and most prominent citizens. As a medical practitioner he was very successful, and in addition to being well-read in matters pertaining to the healing art, he possessed the happy faculty of bringing relief to many sick beds by means of his cheerful ways. When a young man he became the owner, through inheritance, of several slaves, but believing the system wrong he gave them their freedom. He was an earnest Christian and a prominent member of the Presbyterian church, of which he was one of the first members and founders.

Doctor Stephenson came to Jeffersonville as early as 1821, or perhaps several years previous to that date. He continued in practice until the excitement consequent on the discovery of gold in California, when, with a party of some twenty-five persons, he departed on the overland route for the land of gold.

Dr. Nathaniel Field was born in Jefferson county, Kentucky, on the 7th day of November, 1805, and located in Jeffersonville, Indiana, in September, 1829. His father was a native of Culpeper county, Virginia; was a soldier in the Revolutionary war, was at the siege of Yorktown, and after the surrender of Cornwallis emigrated to Kentucky in the spring of 1783, taking up his quarters in the fort, at which was afterward Louisville, near the head of the canal. He was the first delegate from Jefferson county to the Virginia Legislature. He resided in that county until his death, in September, 1831.

Doctor Field came to Jeffersonville in 1829 and was thoroughly identified with the city until his death, in 1888. Though born in a slave state he was one of the first vice-presidents of the American anti-slavery society; was president of the first anti-slavery convention ever held in Indiana, and president of the Free-soil convention held in Indianapolis in the summer of 1850.

Notwithstanding his anti-slavery principles, he never would take any advantage of the slaveholder by advising his slaves to leave him and make their escape to Canada; nor did he take any part in what was called the "underground railroad." In a contest between the slave and his master on the question of freedom, he was neutral. He determined to abide by the law, creating and maintaining the institution, until abrogated by the moral sense of the masters themselves. He opposed slavery on moral and religious grounds, and appealed to the reason and conscience of the slaveholder and the slave.

He represented Clark county in the Legislature in 1838 and 1839. He served as surgeon in the Sixty-sixth Indiana Volunteer Infantry and rendered important service on several battle fields and in field hospitals. In 1868 he was president of the Indiana State Medical Society and was well and widely known as a writer upon scientific and religious subjects. Doctor Field was of the old school of physicians, and his visits to his patients, where he would compound his own prescriptions from a supply of drugs in his hand case, were occasions where his genial humor and fund of anecdote did much toward the recovery of the patient. His long experience in the practice of medicine placed him at the top of the profession in Clark county, and his hundreds of surgical operations in the army, including nearly all the operations known to military surgery, gave him the reputation of being one of the best surgeons in the state of Indiana. He was pastor of a church in Jeffersonville for more than half a century and would never receive a dollar for such service. He baptized nearly one thousand persons in the Ohio river during his pastorate. Doctor Field was a remarkable man, an original thinker and a firm defender of his views and opinions.

Dr. W. F. Collum was Mayor of Jeffersonville from 1848 to 1854, and was a councilman from the Third ward from 1845 to 1848, when he became Mayor, was a member of the Board of Health from 1855 and 1857, and from 1859 to 1865. He came to Jeffersonville in 1838, and practiced medicine and surgery till his death, which occurred in 1870. His death was caused by blood poisoning from a wound made in a post-mortem dissection. His oldest son was Capt. Richard Collum, who commanded a warship in the Civil war. Two other sons. William F. Collum and Chapman Collum, died in this city. His daughter, Sarah. married a Mr. Sellers.

Doctor Collum was one among the most capable and popular physicians of his time, and was a surgeon of eminence.

Doctor Holiday made his appearance some time about 1831. He came from Virginia in a boat containing his family, and on his arrival in Jeffersonville was in destitute circumstances. Chancing to call at the office of Dr. Nathaniel Field, he offered for sale some of his medical books, in order to procure funds to carry him to his destination in Illinois. He was persuaded to relinquish this plan, and instead, with the advice of Doctor Field that this was a good point for a physician, located in Jeffersonville, where he remained some five years. At that time he went on down the river and settled in Mississippi, where he died soon after.

Dr. H. N. Holland came here in 1849, in which year he graduated from the University of Kentucky. Originally a practitioner in the allopathic school, he became convinced that he could do humanity better service by giving medicine in small doses than in large, and after a few years' practice embraced homeopathy in 1853. Before coming to the city he was a resident of Scott county for nine years. In 1846-47 he was elected from that county to the state Legislature, and served with ability. He was first to introduce homeopathy into Jeffersonville, and was successful in building up an extensive practice. He served as school trustee and member of the council.

Doctor Farnsley, formerly a resident of Kentucky, located in Jeffersonville soon after 1840, and remained for a short time.

Dr. William Stewart settled here about 1850, but in a few years removed to Washington. D. C., where he became inspector of marine hospitals.

Dr. W. D. Fouts was a native of Scott county, Indiana, and read medicine with Dr. A. A. Morrison, of Lexington, Indiana, and in 1857 graduated from the University of Louisville. During the War of the Rebellion he was surgeon of the Eighty-first Indiana Volunteer Infantry, from which he was promoted to a brigade and finally to division surgeon. He was captured and confined in Libby prison for five months. At the close of the war he returned to Lexington and practiced medicine until 1871, when he located in Jeffersonville, remaining here until his death. The doctor was exceedingly popular with all classes and enjoyed a large practice.

Dr. C. R. McBride was a native of Clark county and passed his early life on a farm, which was near Dead Man's Hollow. At twenty years of age he began the study of medicine with the late Dr. N. Field, and in 1850 he entered the University of Medicine of Louisville, Kentucky, but did not graduate until later years—1866. All his life he practiced his profession in this city. He served as township trustee, was City Clerk for six years, physician to the State Prison and township physician for several years. In 1868 he was elected to the state Legislature, serving a regular term and a special session. Doctor McBride was a good physician and a man of versatile talents.

Dr. L. W. Beckwith obtained literary education at Greencastle, Indiana, and in 1849 began the study of medicine under Dr. Samuel Meriwether. In 1856 he entered the University Medical College in Louisville, from which he graduated in 1858. He began to practice in Harrison county, where he married, but subsequently located in Chicago. In the early part of the War of the Rebellion he was appointed surgeon of the Thirty-eighth Indiana Volunteer Infantry and served throughout the war. In 1865 he located in Jeffersonville and was equal in ability to the ablest physician about here, where he held his own. For five years he served as physician to the Indiana State Prison.

Dr. Isaac N. Griffith was a student under Dr. N. Field in 1834-35. He married a Louisville lady and removed to Louisiana, where he died eighteen months after he began the practice.

Dr. W. H. Sheets, a graduate of the Cincinnati College of Medicine and Surgery, entered the military service of the United States as acting assistant surgeon, and was assigned to duty at the United States Hospital at Madison, in 1862, immediately after leaving college. In 1865 he came to Jeffersonville and established a lucrative practice. He served for five years as physician to the Indiana Prison, South. In 1880 he was appointed pension examiner for this portion of the state. He has served as secretary of the Board of Health for several years.

Dr. W. N. McCoy pursued a course of medical study with Dr. Samuel Reid, of Salem, Indiana, and attended lectures at the University of Louisville in 1860. In his youth his opportunities were meager, and only by close application and persevering industry was he enabled to overcome obstacles that would have daunted many a man situated as he was. Early left with the care of a family resting on his shoulders, his success in his profession is all the more wonderful. After attending a course of lectures he engaged in practice in this county, at which he was quite successful. He entered the medical service of the United States as acting assistant surgeon, and was assigned to duty at New Albany. From that place he was sent to Jefferson barracks, Missouri, and thence to Mound City hospital at Cairo. He resigned in the spring of 1864, and soon after opened an office in Jeffersonville. In the winter of 1869-70 he attended a course of lectures at Bellevue Hospital Medical College, New York, from which he was graduated. In 1866 he was surgeon in charge of the military hospital at Jeffersonville, in which he remained most of the time until the hospital was condemned, and the business connected therewith closed. Doctor McCoy enjoyed a large practice for many years.

Dr. David McClure was a native of New York. He pursued his medical studies and was graduated from Fairfield and Geneva Medical College in 1837-38. In 1839 he came to Indiana, and in 1864 located in Jeffersonville. He had the confidence of the public to the extent that in 1843-44 and 1853-54 he represented Scott county in the state Legislature, and in 1880 was elected as a Demoratic Joint Representative of Clark, Scott and Floyd counties in the Legislature.

Dr. E. W. Bruner read medicine with his father at Utica, in this county, and attended lectures at the Miami Medical College in Cincinnati in 1866-67. After practicing in Sellersville, New Albany, and Utica, he came to Jeffersonville in 1879.

Dr. T. A. Graham, one of the most loveable, popular and successful physicians which Clark county has ever produced, studied medicine with Dr. D. S. Armer, of New Washington, after his graduation from Hanover College. He entered the Medical College of Ohio at Cincinnati in 1870, where he graduated in 1871. In 1872 he took the "ad eundem" degree at the University of Louisville. He began active practice in Oregon township and in 1872 removed to Jeffersonville, and purchasing the drug store of Isaac Brinkworth, he associated himself with his brother, T. A. Graham. Doctor Graham was an exceedingly popular man, and probably no physician before or since has enjoyed a more extensive and lucrative practice than was the deserving good fortune of this late lamented doctor. In his intercourse with his professional brothers he was high-minded, considerate, even affectionate, and the very soul of honor. The doctor's death in the very zenith of his usefulness, while yet a comparatively young man, was a crushing blow to his own household and a sad loss to the profession in Clark county. Doctor Graham was a member of the Indiana Legislature, and as a member of the Medical Association, among the most earnest and best.

Dr. O. P. Graham, a younger brother of Dr. T. A. Graham, and for a number of years associated with him, is a native of Clark county, was graduated from the medical department of the University of Louisville in 1890. Doctor Graham is one of the best known and most popular physicians in this section of the state and commands a large practice. He served two terms as County Health Officer, and is a member of the state and county medical societies.

Dr. D. C. Peyton is also a native of Clark county. He began the study of medicine in 1881 under the direction of Dr. J. M. Reynolds, and in 1882 attended the Ohio Medical College at Cincinnati. After practicing in Clark county for two years he entered the department of medicine of the University of Louisville and graduated in 1886. The same year he located in Jeffersonville and has built up a substantial practice. He has taken several courses in surgery, which in connection with his varied experience have given him a prominent position in the ranks of his profession. Doctor Peyton served for six years on the City Board of Health, for three years as secretary of the County Board of Health, for three years as surgeon of the old Prison South, and has also served as surgeon for the Car Works, the Baltimore & Ohio Southwestern Railroad, the Cleveland, Chicago, Cincinnati & St. Louis Railroad, and the Phoenix Bridge Company at the time the Big Four bridge was building. During the Spanish war Doctor Peyton was appointed major and brigade surgeon by President McKinley and had charge of all hospitals in the state of Pennsylvania.

Dr. David L. Field is a native of Jeffersonville and studied medicine under that eminent physician of Indianapolis, Dr. Thomas Harvey, and also under his father, Dr. N. Field, of Jeffersonville. He graduated from the department of medicine, University of Louisville, in March, 1868, and immediately began the practice of medicine in his native city, being associated with his father until the latter's death. In 1880 Doctor Field opened a drug store and conducted it in connection with his medical practice until 1894, when he sold it and devoted his whole time to his profession. He is a member of the State Medical Association, and the Clark County Medical Society, and he enjoys a large practice in the city of Jeffersonville. Doctor Field is a well read man, and his name is widely known among members of the medical profession throughout the country by reason of his valuable contributions to medical literature, many of which have been read and discussed before state and county associations. Doctor Field has inherited many of the genial and attractive characteristics of his father, and these together with his wide reading make him an interesting companion as well as a capable physician.

Dr. C. F. C. Hancock, a native of Clark county, began to read medicine under Dr. J. M. Reynolds, at Memphis, in 1885. He soon after entered the medical department of the University of Louisville, where he took first honors in a class of eighty-nine students. Later he entered the Ohio Medical College at Cincinnati, where he graduated in March, 1887. Doctor Hancock's first practice was in Jasper, Dubois county, where he formed a partnership with Dr. E. J. Kempf, of that city. In July, 1888, he located in Jeffersonville and here his success in his profession has been marvelous. His success may be attributed to his intense earnestness, which he has displayed throughout his medical career, and to his personality, which has won for him hosts of friends. Doctor Hancock has been a member of the county and city boards of health and also surgeon for the Pennsylvania Railroad Company. He has one of the largest practices in Southern Indiana and has been very successful in his business ventures as well as in his profession.

Dr. I. N. Ruddle, a graduate of the medical department, University of Louisville, in 1881, located in Jeffersonville soon after his graduation. With the exception of about six months in 1882, when he had removed to Illinois,

27

he has practiced in Jeffersonville ever since. Doctor Ruddle is one of the best informed practitioners in Clark county, and enjoys a very successful general practice. In his first year in Jeffersonville he served as the township physician. He later served as a member of the Board of Health of Jeffersonville several terms, and for twelve years has been on the examining board for pensions.

Dr. John H. Baldwin is a graduate of the Southwestern Hospital and College of Homeopathy in Louisville, Kentucky, class of 1897. He served as a house surgeon in the city hospital after his graduation and came to Jeffersonville in 1898, where he has carried on the practice of his profession ever since. For several years Doctor Baldwin was a lecturer in the school from which he graduated, and later became professor of the principles and practice of medicine. He has established a large and lucrative practice, and has identified himself prominently with things outside of his profession He is an elder in the Presbyterian church and is president of the Chautauqua Association, which has held such successful seasons for the last five or six years.

Dr. John Loomis, at present the oldest practicing physician in Jeffersonville, began the practice of his profession in 1861. He was a graduate of the Eclectic School of Homeopathy, of Philadelphia, and from the Homeopathic Medical University of Ohio. Although Doctor Loomis is now in his eighty-ninth year he enjoys the practice of medicine in Jeffersonville, Louisville and New Albany. He has written much for medical magazines throughout the country and in his practice was for many years the sole representative of the School of Homeopathy in Jeffersonville. Doctor Loomis' health and vigor at his age testify to his purity of life, and affords a valuable example for the younger generation of professional men to emulate.

Dr. Lewis L. Williams, a native of Jefferson county, Kentucky, began the practice of medicine in Jeffersonville in 1893. He had previously practiced in Utica, where he was for one term trustee, and in Spencer county, Indiana. Doctor Williams was a member of the state and county medical societies. During the Spanish war he was the examining surgeon for the enlistments for Company E, One Hundred Sixty-first Indiana Volunteer Infantry. Soon after he removed to Brazil, Indiana, and still remains in the practice of his profession.

In the late nineties two young men began the practice of medicine in Jeffersonville, who shortly sought other fields.

Dr. William L. Samuels, a graduate of the department of medicine of the University of Louisville established himself in Jeffersonville, but in 1897 was appointed superintendent of the county hospital at Eureka, Nevada. Doctor Samuels was a bright and studious young man and would have been an addition to the profession in Jeffersonville. He was educated in the public schools of his native city, and had served three years in the Indiana National Guard before starting to read under Dr. T. A. and O. P. Graham.

Dr. Terry Townsend, a graduate of the Jeffersonville high school, class of '94, read medicine under Doctor Hancock and later graduated from the medical department, University of Louisville. A student and an ambitious worker Doctor Townsend's future seemed bright. He removed to New York City soon afterward and built up an extensive practice.

Among the younger physicians of Jeffersonville are: Dr. George Twomey, Dr. Whayne Crum, Dr. Marshall Varble, Dr. Claude Crum, Dr. David Cohen, Dr. Austin Funk, and Dr. A. H. Seibert, whose sketches appear in this volume.

In the brief existence of Springville a disciple of Esculapius named Vale ministered to the people as long as the town remained a town, but of his personality we know nothing. Dr. Morrison James also practiced in Springville or Tullytown, as the Indians called it. He was a rough man of the period, and as was the custom, carried his medicine with him. His personality is likewise lost to history.

In later years Charlestown had the following doctors to minister to the wants of her sore and afflicted: Doctors Minor, A. P. Hay, Samuel Fowler, Hugh Lysle, H. I. Tobias, Alban Vernon, Andrew Rodgers, William G. Goforth, J. S. Athan, Leander Clemmens, Campbell, Hay, William Taggart, Samuel C. Taggart, D. H. Combs, R. Curran, J. E. Oldham, Josiah Taggart, and others.

Dr. Andrew P. Hay practiced medicine in Charlestown for many years, and during the last term of President Grant, he was appointed National Bank Examiner, and removed to Indianapolis, where he lived till his death, several years later. Doctor Hay was an eminent Mason, having been grand master of Indiana.

Dr. Campbell Hay also practiced his profession at Charlestown and was at one time Clerk of the County Circuit Court.

Charlestown was among the most prominent towns in Indiana from early times, and among her earlier physicians who added to the reputation of the place as a center of professional prominence were Drs. Samuel C. Taggart, David H. Combs, James S. Athan, J. E. Oldham, James Taggart, Robert Curran, etc., etc.

Doctor Athan was elected Secretary of State on the Democratic ticket in 1862.

In Owen township, among the prominent physicians who are now actively practicing medicine, are Drs. Josiah, William and Robert Taggart. They are all natives of the county and medical men of ability.

Among many of the doctors who shed lustre on their profession, and who have long since joined the "silent majority," may be mentioned, Drs. Abin Vernon, Leander Clemmens, H. J. Tobias, Andrew Rodgers, William G. Goforth, Hugh Lysle, Samuel Lawler and Samuel Work Those worthy doctors of Charlestown stood high in the community and enjoyed the love and esteem of all who knew them.

Clark county can claim to have many able and successful physicians, who are actively ministering to the sick and the afflicted. Among them may be mentioned Drs. Bottorff, D. H. Combs, C. Jones and Sidney Cortner, of Charlestown; Doctors Walker, Prall and others, of Henryville; Doctors Fountaine, Meloy, Q. R. Hause, J. M. Howes, of Sellersburg, and Drs. S. D. Hazzard and Frank Johnson, of Utica. Sketches of most of these men will be found in the biographical section of this volume.

There were always professional men in Bethlehem after its success as a village had become assured.

Doctor Fowler was one of the earliest, if not the very first physician to practice here. He located in the township about the year 1820. He did a large practice. The county being new, malarial fevers prevailed and during the fall months nearly everyone suffered from them.

Dr. M. Williams succeeded Doctor Fowler, between 1825 and 1830, and in 1828 Dr. Andrew Davis came to Bethlehem and he and Doctor Goforth practiced there during the early thirties. Doctor Taylor practiced in Bethlehem in 1834. Later Doctor Gilpin and Dr. George O. Pond were located here for a short time, Gilpin locating here in 1837. From 1840 to 1846 Doctor Cummings practiced medicine in Bethlehem. He removed to Chicago, but later returned to Bethlehem, and soon after died there. During the early fifties Dr. John Y. Newkirk practiced in the village.

Dr. Thomas Duerson and Doctor Fritzlen, both from Kentucky, located in Bethlehem in 1870. Doctor Fritzlen after practicing in Bethlehem a number of years removed to New Washington, where he died a few years later.

Dr. Thomas Duerson was the only one of the later physicians to remain long in Bethlehem. He was born and brought up on the Kentucky side of the river, nearly opposite Bethlehem. He studied medicine with his uncle, Doctor Deurson, of Kentucky, and after graduation, while still a young man, located at Bethlehem, and remained there until the end of his life, except for two or three short absences of but a few months each. He died in 1903. For many years he did a large practice in Bethlehem and surrounding country, but the small compensation he received compared with the large amount of work he did, was noted by all who gave the matter any attention. During Doctor Deurson's residence in Bethlehem and since his death a number of physicians have been located there each for a short time, among whom may be mentioned Doctors Mayfield, Hoddenshield and Muret. Each of them seems to have done a good deal of work there, but all agree in pronouncing it a hard place to practice in on account of the broken, hilly country, bad roads, etc. There are no physicians located at Bethlehem at the present time, the practice being done almost entirely by the New Washington physicians.

The physicians of Owen township have been few in number, but of long tenure. Dr. William Taggart began the practice in the township in 1833 or 1834, and from that date until 1870 was continuously engaged in the practice in the township, except the period from 1849 to 1858, during which he resided and practiced his profession in Charlestown. He did a large and laborious practice, always traveling on horseback. He often rode an average of fifty miles a day for weeks at a time during the late summer and fall months, besides visiting and prescribing for from fifty to sixty patients daily.

During the time Doctor Taggart resided in Charlestown Dr. Warren Horr lived and practiced medicine in Owen township for a few years. He is the only physician who was ever located in the township except the Taggarts (father and son), and except Dr. E. M. Bruner, who was located there for a few months in 1860, when he first began the practice.

Upon the retirement of Dr. William Taggart from the practice his mantle fell upon his son, Dr. John F. Taggart, who after serving through the war as surgeon of the Fourth Regiment, Indiana Cavalry, and surgeon of the Second Brigade, First Division Cavalry Corps, located in Owen township at his present residence, where he has been engaged in the practice of medicine to the present time.

Dr. Samuel Adair was the first physician to practice medicine in New Washington of whom we have any account. He was from Ohio and located here about 1820. He did a large practice in this and surrounding townships, and continued in the practice until near the end of his life. Dr. Phillip Jolly was another of the early physicians of the township. He also was from Ohio and for many years did a large practice in New Washington and vicinity. He subsequently removed to other parts, leaving Doctors Adair and Davis in the field. Dr. Solomon Davis was engaged in the practice of medicine in New Washington in the forties, but being engaged at the same time in merchandising and other occupations his medical practice was at no time extensive.

Immediately before and during the war Drs. T. Field and L. E. Eddy, sons-in-law to Doctor Adair, were practicing in New Washington. Doctor Eddy removed to Charlestown at about the beginning of the war, and there engaged in the drug business in connection with the practice of medicine, and later both he and Doctor Field removed to Louisville.

Doctor Armer was another physician who was engaged in the practice of medicine at New Washington during and for some time after the war. For a time he did a large practice, having little or no competition, until Dr. S. L. Adair, Jr., having in the meantime graduated in medicine, began the practice. After practicing a few years Doctor Armer removed to other parts and Dr. David S. Allhands located in New Washington, and a few years later Dr. George W Haymaker. The practice was then divided between Doctors Adair, Jr., Allhands and Haymaker. Doctor Haymaker did not remain long in New Washington. After a few years' practice in that place he removed to Charlestown and engaged in the practice at that place.

In 1894 Dr. R. S. Taggart began the practice of medicine at New Washington, and a few years later Doctor Allhands removed to Louisville. Doctor Adair, Sr., having turned over his practice to his son, Dr. S. L. Adair, Jr., nearly all the practice of New Washington township and much of the neighboring territory is done by him and Dr. R. S. Taggart.

For a number of years Henryville had two regular physicians—Dr. H. H. Ferguson and Dr. William Wisner.

Doctor Ferguson received his education principally at the Barnett Academy, in Charlestown, under the instruction of the principal, Mr. Z. B. Sturgus, a justly celebrated educator. His course of study preparatory to entering Hanover College was almost completed when the death of his father, in November, 1860, necessitated his leaving school; he was then only fifteen years of age. He was now thrown upon his own resources. During the winter of 1861, at the age of sixteen, he commenced the study of medicine, and attended lectures in Louisville the following winter, after which he stood a satisfactory examination and was appointed a medical cadet in the United States army, and stationed in a hospital at Louisville, Kentucky.

He continued to hold this position for two and one-half years, during which time he attended a second course of lectures and graduated as a doctor of medicine at the Kentucky School of Medicine in the spring of 1865. On the 16th day of October, 1865, he opened an office and commenced the practice of medicine at Henryville, his native town, not yet being twenty-one years of age. During the winter of 1866-67 he again attended a course of lectures and graduated at the Medical University in Louisville. After practicing five years he visited the city of New York and for six months devoted himself to the diligent study of his profession at the Bellevue Hospital Medical College, at which celebrated institution he also graduated. During his stay in that city he took private courses of instruction in medicine and surgery from some of the most eminent men of the profession, Frank Hastings Hamilton, Lewis A. Sayer, and Austin Flint. After his return from New York City he continued to do a large and successful practice, during which time he successfully performed many of the most difficult operations known to surgery. He performed successfully the operation for strangulated hernia on a man sixty-five years of age, and when the patient was in a condition of collapse, it being the only successful operation of the kind ever performed in the county. He continued in active practice in a constantly enlarging field until 1878, when he was nominated and elected Treasurer of the county over three competitors for the office, and in 1880 he was re-elected to the same office by the largest majority of any one on the ticket.

Dr. W. E. Wisner was born in New York state, Yates county, in 1832.

He was a son of H. Wisner, a prominent, active farmer of that county. When a young man the doctor became infatuated with the medical profession. At about the age of twenty-six he commenced studying under Dr. Samuel H. Wright, of Dundee, New York, with whom he principally read. He attended his first course of lectures at Geneva, New York. Several years were spent in pursuit of his medical education and in teaching. In the year 1862 he commenced his practice proper in Memphis, Indiana. In 1836 he moved to Henryville and built up an extensive practice. In 1880 he opened a drug store to be conducted in connection with his practice.

Dr. S. Z. Adair, Jr., graduated from the Kentucky School of Medicine in 1868, and later received a diploma from the Hospital School of Medicine. He shortly after located at New Washington, where he practiced for many years.

Dr. David Haymaker and Dr. David Allhands came later.

Although New Providence was one of the early settlements in Clark county it seems to have gotten along without a physician for a large part of its history. Dr. W. W. Britan, who had attended lectures at Cincinnati, began to practice medicine here in 1842. He remained but one year when he removed to Martinsburg. The village practically remained without a doctor until 1860.

About that time came Drs. Francis and M. Mitchell, both of New Albany. Prior to that time the people when sick were compelled to send to Greenville, in Floyd county, or to Martinsburg or Salem, in Washington county, the distance to the former being eight miles, to Martinsburg five miles, to Salem twelve. Mitchell having remained about four years, returned to New Albany, and Dr. William Bright, of Martinsburg, took his place. Doctor Bright remained a short time, returned to Martinsburg, and in 1866 was succeeded by Dr. Christopher C. Clark, of Washington county. Clark, having remained several years, became desirous to go west. He sold out to Dr. Benjamin F. Stalker, of Washington county, who in company with Dr. Cadwallader Jones, of Washington county, opened a drug store in New Providence.

Dr. T. V. Noaks, a son of Dr. T. J. Noaks, a noted physician of Breckinridge county, Kentucky, entered the office of Doctor Wisner and remained with him for about two years. He attended lectures in the Cincinnati hospital and was connected with the School of Medicine and Surgery there. He graduated at the Louisville University in 1874 and immediately began his practice at Otisco. Here he met with great success, but at the end of a year removed to LaPrairie, Illinois.

Dr. J. Bruner was born in Greene county, Tennessee, December 6, 1811. When five years of age he moved to Floyd county with his father, Jacob Bruner, who made that county his home three years, when he moved to Lawrence county, Indiana. His son accompanied him and remained at home until he was thirteen years of age, when he went to Brownstown, Jackson county, Indiana, and entered upon the study of medicine under Dr. Samuel P. Wirt, remaining two years, at the expiration of which time he engaged in the practice of medicine with great success. After a few years' practice he became a minister of the Methodist church and traveled on the circuit ten years, the town of Utica being his last appointment, in 1849. At this date he again resumed the practice of medicine and continued it nineteen years, when he gave up his practice on account of ill health. The closing of Doctor Bruner's practice was a matter of much regret to this community. His success in restoring to health the severely afflicted was remarkable. His competitors acknowledged his ability, and his practice was the largest in the county. He maintained the love and confidence of his patrons that only a faithful physician can possess.

Dr. James Madison Reynolds is a descendant of one of the early settlers of Union township, Clark county. His grandfather, Richard Reynolds, moved with his wife, Sarah, from Kentucky. Dr. Reynolds was born in 1851, nearly six months after his father died. He graduated from the Ohio Medical College at Cincinnati, in 1873, and began the practice of medicine at Memphis, Indiana.

Francis M. Carr, M. D., was born January 3, 1831, in Charlestown township, and has ever since resided in the county, with the exception of three or four years in Washington county. His father, Absalom, was a native of Fayette county, Pennsylvania. He came to Clark county in 1806 and was one of the early pioneers of Indiana. He was a brother of General Carr, and was a Tippecanoe soldier. He died in 1876. Doctor Carr graduated at the University of Louisville in 1855, and has ever since practiced in Clark county. He was married, in 1854, to Miss Martha E. Coctores, daughter of Daniel Coctores, of Oregon township.

David H. Combs, M. D., was born in Clark county, Indiana. He was a son of Jesse Combs, one of the pioneers, who died in 1857. Doctor Combs remained at home till seventeen years of age, when he entered Charlestown Academy, where he attended six sessions. From the time of his leaving this institution until his twenty-first year he spent in teaching and going to school. At that age he entered the office of Dr. James S. Athon, of Charlestown, with whom he remained three years as a student. He was one year in Louisville Medical University, and graduated at Jefferson Medical College, Philadelphia, in the spring of 1850. His first year he practiced in Salem, Indiana, after which, until 1876, he lived in Charlestown, where he enjoyed an extensive practice, more especially in the line of surgery. In 1876 he moved to his wife's farm, in Utica, and practiced his profession.

CHAPTER XL.

THE JEFFERSONVILLE CARNEGIE LIBRARY AND THE BORDEN MUSEUM.

THE JEFFERSONVILLE CARNEGIE LIBRARY.

An old township library had existed in Jeffersonville for many years and had in a small way catered to the wants of the public. It was in politics and was kept in the Trustee's office, usually a place where men loafed and smoked and discussed the issues of the day. It was no place where children or women could suitably visit. The Women's Literary clubs of the city became so aroused to the condition of affairs and the needs of the people that they determined to take the initiative and established a library which would be under better management and cater to a broader field than the old township library had done. At the suggestion of Miss Hannah Zulauf, a public spirited woman, a meeting was called at which each literary club in the city was represented by two delegates. Judge John F. Reed, a retired lawyer and a staunch friend of the project, gave aid and counsel which was invaluable. Under his suggestion the ladies raised one thousand two hundred dollars and proceeded to form a library association under an old law of 1852, which provided that when the citizens of any township had raised a fund of one thousand dollars and formed an association they might ask the Board of County Commissioners to turn the township library over to them. A technicality in the law was discovered and a wait until the winter of 1899 had to be endured when the Legislature passed a law satisfying the new association. Upon the expiration of the term of office of the Township Trustee then serving, December 1, 1900, the books to the number of one thousand four hundred volumes, and other property, were turned over to the association, and a room over the Citizens' National Bank was given, rent free, for their use. On December 17, 1900, the library was opened to the public under the name of the Jeffersonville Township Public Library, and the subscription money, as it was paid, was used for the purchase of new books. The income was from a tax levy of one cent on each one hundred dollars' worth of property assessed in the township, giving the library about five hundred and fifty dollars a year. At that time there were about one thousand seven hundred volumes upon the shelves. They were classified according to the Dewey system, and from the first the public has had access to all except fiction.

Miss Bertha Poindexter was secured as librarian and she has worked earnestly for the upbuilding of the library and in educating the public taste for good books rather than catering to a taste for worthless matter.

Soon after the library was established the idea of asking Mr. Carnegie for money with which to erect a building was conceived, and again Miss Zulauf took the initiative and a donation of fifteen thousand dollars was secured. Arthur Loomis, a citizen of Jeffersonville and an architect, drew the plans for the present beautiful and commodious building, and on September 19, 1903, the Most Worshipful Grand Lodge of Free and Accepted Masons of Indiana laid the corner stone; the Rev. E. L. Powell, of Louisville, delivering the address.

The library has at present an unusually fine collection of reference books for a library of its size. There are at present six thousand six hundred fifty-four volumes on the shelves; thirty-one periodicals on the reading tables; one thousand two hundred volumes in the children's reading room, and the number of borrower's cards in use amounts to two thousand six hundred eighty-five.

The popularity and recognition of the great value of the library has grown beyond the expectations of the most sanguine, an everage of one hundred nine volumes daily being issued this year. The public spirit evinced by Miss Zulauf, Judge Read and Mr. Loomis, and the philanthropy of Mr. Carnegie have added an institution to Jeffersonville whose worth can not be estimated.

THE BORDEN MUSEUM.

Ranking among the finest institutions of its kind in the state of Indiana, is the Borden Museum of Borden. It was founded by the late Prof. William W. Borden, one of the wealthiest and most public spirited men which Clark county has ever produced. A collector of interesting and valuable specimens all his life, he soon realized that to preserve them he must have a building of some kind, and to this end erected a substantial fire-proof building, on the site of his parents' home. The building which this museum replaced was a substantial two-story brick erected in 1819. The brick were made near the spot then, masons and carpenters were imported and its walls slowly arose. Window glass seven by nine was brought from Pittsburg. Such a house was a novelty in its day. The modern building is an ornate and handsome structure well adapted for the uses for which it was intended. The professor was always a collector and scattered throughout his valuables are curios of his early days of travel. After he had become financially able he began to buy collections systematically. His first collection bears the date of 1844, and it contains few inexpensive things. He added to this his own finds, particularly silver and other minerals, collected at Leadville in 1878 and 1879. In 1886 he bought the Knapp collection of Silurian and Devonian fossils and Indian relics. Doctor Knapp had spent thirty years in collecting relics, corals and crinoids from the Ohio Falls and Beargrass creek, Kentucky.

In 1887 he purchased the collection of Dr. S. H. Harrod, of Canton, Indiana. Living near Spurgeon's and Paynter's Hills, places rich in the fossils of the St. Louis group, Doctor Harrod had become possessed of the finest crinoidea these places could afford.

In 1889 the Doctor Lavette collection of fresh water shells was added to the museum. This collection was the result of a lifetime work. Shortly after this the Dr. C. C. Graham collection of bones of prehistoric animals was added. These remains had been unearthed at Big Bone Lick, Kentucky.

In 1897 a valuable collection of ancient pottery and culinary utensils of the Cliff Dwellers of Arizona and New Mexico, was purchased. In 1898 the G. L. Barnes collection of mound builders' remains was added to the museum. This addition was one of great value. Besides these larger additions the professor was continually acquiring single specimens and their aggregate is considerable.

In 1901 the G. K. Greene collection of over one thousand crinoids was purchased, making the Borden crinoid collection number over three thousand, and making it the largest in the state.

Besides the many books, pamphlets, etc., which are uncatalogued, the museum catalogue has a voluminous list of specimens arranged under the heads of Palæontology, minerals, marine shells, archæology and curios, and it represents one of the most valuable and instructive collections in the state of Indiana.

In his journeys to the Pacific and Atlantic coasts, through Canada, to Alaska and through Europe, the professor was continually adding to his collections, and the magnificent institution which stands as a monument to his memory, as well as a memorial to the memory of his parents, as he intended it should, represents a public spirit which flourishes far less verdantly in other parts of the county than at the quaint old town of Borden.

CHAPTER XLI.

INDUSTRIES AND STATISTICS.

That Clark county has within her borders industries of importance, possibilities of great value, and undeveloped resources of promise, only the most bilious hypochondriac will deny. The industrial and agricultural statistics of the county compare most favorably with other counties of similar size in the state. In 1905, the date of the last report of the Department of Statistics, there were eighty-five factories in Clark county, producing everything from steamboats to sewing machines. Although the Indiana Reformatory and the United States Quartermaster's depot are not industries *per se,* yet they are important industrially and add materially to the commercial importance of the county.

In Jeffersonville and the various towns of Clark county are manufactured castings, ice, bread, cruppers, lumber, saddle trees, cement, hominy, harness, flour, meal, spokes, grist, baking powder, extracts, carriages, wagons, cigars, canned goods, steamboats, small boats, chains, stoves, hollow ware, brick, kitchen cabinets, porch columns, wall plaster, brooms, tin and iron ware goods, fruit boxes, lard-oil, tile, wooden novelties, staves, cheese, hoops, electrical devices, steam engines, rattan and reed furniture, sewing machines and many other articles and commodities which a progressive and thriving county needs.

Her agricultural statistics show conditions and possibilities not realized by the average citizen. With an area of three hundred sixty-eight square miles, or of two hundred thirty-five thousand five hundred and sixteen acres, she has two thousand sixty-seven farms, of an average size of one hundred four and eight-tenths acres, and of an aggregate acreage of two hundred sixteen thousand five hundred twenty-six acres. Two thousand fifty-three farms are of less than five hundred acres, and fourteen are larger.

In 1906 Clark county was the largest tomato producer in the state—nine hundred seventy-four acres producing one hundred twenty-two thousand three hundred fifteen bushels.

She excells in the production of orchard grass, the yield in 1908 being about twenty-five thousand bushels.

Within the last few years the adaptability of the soil in certain parts of the county for tobacco culture has resulted in an increased acreage. In 1900 seventy-nine acres produced fifty-nine thousand five hundred fifty pounds of

THE COAL HARBOR ABOVE JEFFERSONVILLE.

tobacco. In 1909 the acreage was seven hundred acres and the product is the best grade light burley.

In 1900 there were eight hundred sixty-one acres in potatoes, and one thousand seventy-one acres in other vegetables. Seventeen acres in alfalfa, thirty thousand nine hundred two acres in corn, twenty-four thousand thirty-two acres in wheat, and one hundred six acres in strawberries.

The value of her yield of small fruits in 1900 was seventeen thousand five hundred and ninety-one dollars, and of her dairy products, one hundred sixty-one thousand ten dollars.

Her average temperature is fifty-seven and four-tenths degrees and her average rainfall is forty-three inches.

In 1900 the population of the county was thirty-one thousand eight hundred thirty-five, of which ten thousand seven hundred and seventy-four were residents of Jeffersonville, two thousand three hundred seventy in Clarksville, one thousand one hundred one in Port Fulton, nine hundred fifteen in Charlestown, seven hundred sixty-one in Sellersburg and one hundred sixteen in Claysburg.

There are fifty-eight saloons in the county, of which forty-three are in Jeffersonville, but the jail statistics for 1905 showing the ten counties with largest jail incarcerations do not include Clark county.

The value of her taxable property in 1905 was twelve million six hundred forty-three thousand nine hundred sixty-five dollars; that of her schools was two hundred forty thousand eight hundred fifty dollars, and her debt thirty thousand dollars.

There are twenty-one post-offices in Clark county and the intermediate points are well served by a rural free delivery. The old county seat town of Charlestown is one of the most interesting in the state. Historic memories of early state and territorial periods lend an attractiveness to the little town and her situation on the rolling hills of Pleasant Run make Charlestown an ideal spot. With all the inviting allurements of a quiet country town she has the advantages of being so closely connected with Jeffersonville and Louisville by traction lines that the advantages of the city are at her door. Charlestown promises to be one of the coming residental suburbs of Louisville.

Jeffersonville from her advantages needs but to possess energetic and progressive business men to develop the city into one of more than double the size.

With a natural deep water harbor on her side of the river she has unexcelled facilities for water shipments. The largest interurban center in Southern Indiana at present, she will constitute the junction point for a vast system of interurban diverging to every part of the state. Three trunk railroads enter the city and competitive freight rates with the river transportation, together with the cheapest coal in the west, make the city more than attractive for factories.

A public school system second to none, and wholly out of politics, a modern public library, many churches, many improved streets, a good sewer system, a police force and fire department, excellent in every detail, reasonable rents, moderate living expenses, fifteen minutes from the center of Louisville, with a five-cent fare, many desirable building lots in the city and many magnificent residence sites above the city overlooking the river, an abundant supply of clear, pure water, and a good health record, the city of Jeffersonville offers a multitude of inducements to those seeking a location either to engage in business or to reside. The Car Works, the Ship Yards, the United States Quartermaster's Depot and many other industries employ a large number of men, and it is a fact that all the wealthy men in the city made their fortunes at home.

An enthusiastic commercial club is aiding materially in advancing the interests of Jeffersonville and in advertising her attractions. The rich farming and dairy lands adjacent by reason of the excellent transportation facilities are just beginning to feel their natural development, and their proximity to the markets of Louisville give promise of large returns to those who develop them. The agricultural values of the northern and western parts of the county, the urban attractions of the southern part, the transportation and manufacturing advantages of the southern and souheastern parts, the intimate relations of all parts by means of the interurbans, the steam roads, the rural free delivery and the telephone make Clark county, as a county, one of the most desirable in the state, and her people, contented and prosperous and proud of her past history, her present advancement and her future possibilities.

James Howard

BIOGRAPHICAL

JAMES HOWARD.

James Howard, the founder of the famous Howard ship yards of Jeffersonville, Indiana, was born in Oldham, England, September 1, 1814. The son of a poor weaver, the expectations of his family could not have been particularly bright, yet he so employed the talents of character and manhood given into his keeping that at the end of his stewardship he left a heritage of high and unblemished character, of unsullied business integrity, and of strength of purpose that is treasured alike in the breasts of those who were attached to him by ties of affection as well as consanguinity. His first few years were spent at the scene of his birth, his baptism being registered in the parish register of St. Mary's church, Oldham.

In 1819 John Howard, the father, actuated by a desire to better his condition in life by seeking a home among the glowing possibilities of the New World, set sail with his good wife, Martha, and their two sons, James and Daniel, for the port of New York. After a rough and uncomfortable voyage of some six weeks they arrived at the metropolis of their land of promise and took up temporary residence in Brooklyn, remaining here the greater part of a year. In the spring of 1820, they joined a party bound for Wheeling, Virginia, traveling overland by wagon. This journey with its hardships and its trials no doubt had some effect in moulding the early character of the elder son. The mother was a woman of sterling worth and to her James owed much of his early ambition and determination.

The expenses of the trip westward being heavy for a poor family, each member of the party to be carried, being weighed and charged accordingly, the father decided to walk, but his determination was unfortunately shifted to other, but less sturdy, shoulders. He was taken ill when only a part of the journey had been accomplished, and his wife and James were forced to change places with him; James at that time, be it remembered, being not quite seven years of age. The family reached Wheeling the same year, 1820, and without tarrying embarked on a flat-boat, bound for the city of Cincinnati, far down the great river, reaching there late that year. Here the father erected a small mill and engaged in the occupation of wool carding and cloth dressing, and from the age of eleven to fifteen, James worked in the mill with him with an industry indicative of his future successes.

For a short while after leaving his father's mill he worked in William Gordon's ship yard, carrying water to the men, but was soon afterward apprenticed to William Hartshorn, a steamboat builder, of Cincinnati, to learn the trade of ship carpenter. While serving here he lost no opportunity to advance himself in the art of building water craft, and having a keen mind for mechanics he quickly mastered the principles and details of the business, draughting a boat himself when hardly nineteen years of age.

After spending four years under his master he came to Louisville, and in a few weeks after his arrival succeeded in getting a contract for building a steamboat. Jeffersonville offering the most available situation to meet his needs, he located his yards on a small tract of land on the river bank at the foot of Mechanic street, in 1834. His service under Hartshorn had been so loyal and he had displayed so much ability at his trade that his employer readily gave him the privilege of remaining where he was and building the boat. Starting here without a dollar in the world and with very few friends or acquaintances his success, won as it was only after years of unremitting toil, was one of those remarkable illustrations of what industry, integrity and ability can accomplish, and which should be a never-failing spring of inspiration to those who are bound to him by blood or affection. His first steamboat was the "Hyperion," and was built to run on the Chattahoochee river in Alabama. She was a side-wheel boat, for Captain Leonard, and was such a complete success that it was evident to all who saw her that the young boat-builder had a genius for his profession and was destined to make himself famous at it. When the spring came, his employer wished him to return to Cincinnati, and fill out the unexpired term of his indenture, but he obtained a release by paying Captain Hartshorn in full for leaving him before his time was out, and he finished two more boats at his yards in Jeffersonville during the years 1834-1835. A complete list of the boats built here will be found in the "History of Steamboating and Boat Building," elsewhere in this volume. In 1836 he decided that Madison offered better opportunities than Jeffersonville and located there, remaining until 1844.

On October 20, 1836, at Madison, Indiana, James Howard married Rebecca Ann Barmore, and of this union a family of four daughters and two sons resulted, namely: Martha Ann, who married James Baird; John Edmonds, who succeeded his father in the business; Lucy Matilda, who married John Armstrong; Kate Isabella, who married William A. Baird, and William French and Jeanette, who both died in infancy.

While at Madison, Mr. Howard built sixteen boats, all of which proved satisfactory to their owners, but the depression in business induced him to go on the river in 1844, and during the years of 1844 and 1845 he ran as engineer and as ship carpenter on the Ohio and the Mississippi rivers. His decision to run on the river was unfortunate, as it kept him from the work for which he was peculiarly adapted, however, he realized that his place was ashore constructing steamboats, and the spring of 1846 found him back in the harness at Shippingsport, a prosperous and promising location below Louisville. He constructed six boats here and for a short while was in charge of the docks in the canal.

In 1847 he had the misfortune to lose two boats by the great flood of that spring. The boats were on the stocks and were nearing completion, when carried away by high water.. This disaster did not dishearten him, but decided him to seek a new location for his yards, so he, in partnership with a man named John Enos, started a boat-building plant in the upper part of Louisville, on the point about opposite Spring street, Jeffersonville. Enos died within the first four or five months and James was obliged to give up the idea of further business at that location, and returned to Jeffersonville in 1849, the scene of his first venture and success, nearly sixteen years previous. His brother, Daniel, had become interested in the firm previous to this and after finishing six or seven boats on the "Point," the yards there were abandoned. The yards at Jeffersonville have added their yearly quota of water craft to the great rivers of the West and at present are still in active operation. His experience during the War of the Rebellion was most trying, but at the end of the conflict the demand for water craft gave an impetus to the business and until his death he continued actively to direct and supervise the work in all of its details, constructing two hundred and seventy-nine boats.

On October 14, 1876, James Howard was drowned from a ferryboat, by his buggy backing off into the water. The outpouring of thousands of people to his funeral testified to the high regard and love in which he was held. Doctor Craik, the Dean of Christ church cathedral, in Louisville, who conducted his funeral, said, "It was the grandest and most imposing funeral I ever witnessed. There were no societies, no music, no military display, the usual trappings of an imposing funeral, to mark the obsequies of this boat-builder. We have buried from this church the commander-in-chief of the United States, and all that the power and majesty of the great government could do to make the occasion grand and honorable was done, but it was nothing in comparison with the funeral solemnities of the simple, untitled citizen, James Howard."

Among the older citizens of Jeffersonville and among steamboat men from Pittsburg to New Orleans, he was known affectionately as "Uncle Jim." His unswerving integrity, his charity and his fair dealings with all, made his death a personal one to many as well as a public calamity to the city of Jeffersonville. It falls to the lot of few men to bequeath to posterity the name and reputation left by this master builder.

28

HON. JAMES K. MARSH.

This well known attorney at law and ex-Judge of the Fourth Judicial Circuit Court, is a native of Harrison county, Indiana, where his ancestors settled in an early day and with which part of the state both branches of his family have been closely identified from the pioneer period to the present time. His father, Jesse C. Marsh, a merchant and farmer, was born and reared in the county of Harrison and spent the greater part of his life at Laconia. He was a man of influence in the community, manifested a lively interest in whatever made for the advancement of the country and the good of his fellow citizens and his death, which occurred at the above town some years ago, was deeply lamented by the large circle of friends and acquaintances with whom he mingled. Elizabeth Shields, who became the wife of Jesse C. Marsh, was also born in Harrison county and, like her husband, belonged to one of the oldest and best known pioneer families of the community in which her ancestors settled. Of the three children born to this estimable couple James K. is the youngest and the only son, the others being Mrs. Eliza H. Miller, who lives near Corydon; and Anna, who married Dr. C. C. Mitchell, both now deceased.

James K. Marsh was born on the family homestead near Laconia December 9, 1844, and received his preliminary educational discipline in the public schools, later pursuing the higher branches of learning in the academy at Corydon. Actuated by an ambition to add still further to his scholastic knowledge he subsequently took a special course in Ashbury (now De Pauw) University at Greencistle and on leaving that institution entered the law office of Colonel C. L. Dunham, of New Albany, where under the direction of that able attorney, he fitted himself for the legal profession.

Mr. Marsh was admitted to the Clark county bar in 1867 and at once entered upon the active practice of his profession, overcoming in due time the obstacles and discouragements which usually interfere with the early progress of the young lawyer and forging to the front among the rising lawyers of Jeffersonville, by close application to business soon obtained his proportionate share of legal patronage and won the reputation of a capable and successful lawyer. In recognition of his ability he was elected in 1870 Prosecuting Attorney of the Criminal Circuit, composed of the counties of Clark and Floyd, and held the position four years, following which he served two years as Prospector of the Civil Circuit, retiring from the office in 1876. Meantime he had become greatly interested in public and political affairs and by reason of valuable services rendered the Democratic party of which for some years he had been a local leader, he was elected in 1876 to represent Clark county in the General Assembly.

As a member of that body Mr. Marsh made a creditable record and his efforts in behalf of his constitutents, as well as his activity in promoting measures for the best interest of the state, gained for him an honorable reputation as an able and discreet legislator and made him many warm friends throughout the county, irrespective of political allignment. He served on a number of committees where his opinions and counsel always carried weight and commanded respect and as a participant in the general deliberations of the chamber, he proved a strong debater, an influential leader and to him, as much as to say to any member was due the passage of a number of bills which had important bearing upon the subsequent history of the commonwealth.

His legislative experience terminating in 1878, Mr. Marsh devoted himself closely to his profession and for a number of years his name was connected with nearly every important case tried in the courts of Clark county and not infrequently were his services retained in other and distant courts. His habits of industry with other qualities which guarantee advancement won for him a commanding position at the bar, in recognition of which he was elected in 1898 Judge of the Fourth Judicial Circuit and during the ensuing six years he discharged the duties of that high and honorable position with credit to himself and to the satisfaction of the public, bringing to the bench the result of his many years of successful practice and filling it with the dignity becoming the learned and accomplished American jurist and his judicial career, like his professional record, is eminently above reproach. Since retiring from the bench Judge Marsh has devoted his attention to his profession, which as already stated, h takes very high rank. He also keeps in touch with the people, maintains a lively interest in whatever tends to the advancement of his city and county. He has been twice marrier, the first time in 1880 to Mrs. Mary A. Lutz, who died after a mutually happy wedded experience of four years, leaving one child, who followed its mother to the grave in 1885. His second marriage was solemnized with Ella L. Matthews, daughter of the late Nathaniel S. Matthews, an old settler and prominent citizen of Jeffersonville, the union being without issue.

Judge Marsh is a Mason of high standing, including the degree of Sir Knight, and an active and influential member of the Independent Order of Odd Fellows, besides being one of the oldest Knights of Honor in the city, taking great interest in all of his fraternal relations. In religion he is liberal in all the term implies, not being identified with any church organization, but believing in the sacredness of their mission and recognizing in every individual, however humble, the spark of divinity which bespeaks a heavenly origin and an immortal destiny. His character has ever been above criticism and in his relations with his fellow men he exemplifies his highest ideals of life and duty. He has kept himself free from contaminating influences and from the habits which pollute the body and degrade the mind, having never taken a drink of any kind of intoxicating beverage in his life, nor uttered a profane oath.

EDWARD N. FLYNN, M. D.

The "value of an ideal" was never more favorably illustrated than in the case of the present Mayor of Jeffersonville. Even as a boy he formed ambitious notions deciding, as boys often do, what he wanted to be, but unlike many other boys, he adhered to his resolutions until he saw his dreams fulfill. Undiscouraged by hardships and penury, the poor boy struggled manfully up to eminence. Besides being a fine sample of self-making, his career is invaluable as an encouragement to others inclined to falter in the weary journey that constitutes human life.

Edward N. Flynn was born in New Bedford, Massachusetts, in 1867, a son of John L. and Elizabeth Flynn. When two years of age his parents brought him to Jeffersonville, which was destined to be the theater of his life's work. He attended the public schools, proved to be an apt pupil and had finished the first grade of the high school, but at this point the exigencies of his situation compelled a temporary abandonment of study. He had always desired to become a doctor and as early as his twelfth year this idea had taken full possession of his mind. Manifestly, if he was to escape a life of drudgery, a better education was imperatively demanded and how to accomplish this was the big problem in his boyish mind. Poverty acting as a good, proved in this case, as in many others, something of a blessing in disguise, as the necessity for earning a living also brought the opportunity to continue his studies. Before he had completed his thirteenth year he secured a job as a lighter of signal lamps on the Pennsylvania Railroad, which, though the pay was small, furnished occupation and provided means for the passing day. When sixteen years old he started the learning of telegraphy, in time became a first class operator and when, after fourteen years service, he resigned, he was regarded as one of the most expert workmen in the service of the railroad company. All of his spare time was put to excellent use in preparatory medical study. Entering the Hospital Medical College in Louisville he devoted nine hours daily to mastering the theory and practice of the learned profession to which he had determined to devote himself. He was graduated from this institution in 1897 and immediately opened an office for practice in Jeffersonville, but owing to peculiar circumstances was not forced to wait so long for business as is usually the case with young graduates. During his preliminary studies he was in the habit of giving medical advice to many friends and acquaintances, especially among the poorer classes. Those who were benefited by his gratuitious assistance sounded his praises over the city, with the result that when he "hung out his shingle" he was by no means unknown, but had fourteen patients the first day. Here we have an instance somewhat out of the ordinary of a professional man whose reputation was established before graduation. In the meantime by his obliging disposition

and courteous manners he had been accumulating friends and a stock of popularity, which enabled him to realize another of his boyish ambitions which
was to become Mayor of his home town.   Though not a politician in the
ordinary sense of the term, Doctor Flynn had always taken an active part in
public affairs and was recognized among the leaders as good material for office.
In 1905 he was offered the nomination as candidate for Mayor on the Republican
ticket, and agreed to accept if it was the desire of the party, but he declined to
electioneer or ask any man for his vote.   He was given the nomination and
in due time triumphantly elected without using any of the arts or devices usually resorted to by candidates for office.   Thus the two fondest dreams of his
boyhood were realized—when he found himself Mayor of Jeffersonville, and
one of the city's most successful physicians.   Recently Doctor Flynn has erected
a new office building, which is regarded as one of the most complete of its
kind in the county.   It is fitted with reception, consultation and bath rooms,
each of which opens upon the entrance hall.   The consultation room is
equipped with the latest and most approved electric instruments for use in
that department of medical science known as electro-therapeutics.   All the
rooms are large and commodious, well lighted and finished in white tile.

Doctor Flynn is a valued member of the Advent Christian church in New
Albany and his fraternal relations embrace membership in the Knights of
Templar, Knights Pythias, Knights and Ladies of Honor and the Golden
Cross, Pathfinders and Elks.   Thus it will be seen that his activities cover
a wide field, embracing religious, political, professional, social and lodge duties
amid all of which the genial Mayor of Jeffersonville finds himself a very busy
man.

PROF. FRANCIS E. ANDREWS.

Professor Andrews, principal of the Jeffersonville high school and an
educator of much more than local repute, is a native of Morgan county, Ohio,
having been born in the town of McConnellsville on the 20th day of October,
1851. Seth Andrews, the professor's father, also a native of the Buckeye state,
was a farmer and teacher, in connection with which he also preached for a number of years for the Christian church, of which religious body all of his
family were members.   The maiden name of Mrs. Seth Andrews was Elvira
Thorla.   She was born in Noble county, Ohio, and, like her husband, traced
her genealogy to German-Scotch ancestry, who came to America at a very
early period, six generations having been represented in this country since
the original antecedents left their native land to seek a home amid the untried
conditions of a new world.   Of the six children born to Seth and Elvira Andrews, all but one are living, Francis E. being the fourth in order of birth.

Prof. Francis E. Andrews spent his early life in his native state and after a preliminary educational training in the public schools, was prepared for college under the tutorship of Prof. James G. May, of Salem, Indiana, following which he took the full classical course at Marietta College, Washington county, Ohio, where he took the literary honors when he was graduated in the year 1874. Meanwhile he had devoted considerable time to teaching and the better to fit himself for educational work he subsequently became a student of the Indiana State Normal at Terre Haute, in which institution he earned an honorable record and from which he was graduated with a high standing in all of his classes in 1894. Since the latter year Professor Andrews has devoted his entire attention to school work and attained eminent success in the line of his calling. As a matter of fact, however, his experience as an educator began several years prior to that date, for from the early seventies until completing his normal course he was alternately engaged in teaching and attending school, and it may be said that all of his mature years have been devoted to the profession which he now follows and in which his success has been so signal and continuous. He was principal of the public schools of Charlestown for three years and for a period of eleven years held a similar position at Sellersburg, where he established an honorable reputation as a capable teacher and manager of schools and gained recognition among the leading educators of his part of the state.

In the year 1886 Professor Andrews accepted a position in the schools of Jeffersonville, since which time he has been very closely identified with the educational interests of the city, passing through several promotions until reaching in 1903, the principalship of the high school, which honorable and responsible position he still holds, previous to that time having had charge of the Chestnut Street School. He is prominent in the religious circles of the city and as a member and elder of the First Christian church takes a leading part in the affairs of the organization, frequently filling the pulpit besides preaching with great acceptance to various congregations in other places.

He is also deeply interested in secret societies of fraternal and benevolent work, and belongs to several organizations of this character including the Masonic Order, Independent Order of Odd Fellows, Knights of Pythias, Modern Woodmen of America, all in Jeffersonville excepting the Pythian brotherhood, with which he holds membership at Sellersburg. Like all intelligent and progressive citizens the professor is a politician in the best sense of the term, but not a partisan, nor a seeker after honors or emoluments of office. On state and national affairs, in which he keeps thoroughly informed, he is a Republican, but in local matters, where no great questions or principles are involved, he votes as his judgment dictates, giving his support to the candidates best qualified for the positions they aspire to irrespective of political affiliation.

The domestic life of Professor Andrews dates from the year 1881, when he was married to Elizabeth Wells, a native of Indiana and a lady of high social and moral standing, to whom he is indebted for not a little of the success with which his career has been crowned. The pledges of this union are three children, namely: May, a graduate of the State Normal School and a teacher in the public schools of Connersville; Eva, a graduate of the Spencerian Business College of Louisville, at the present time is a stenographer in that city; and Ada, who is still at home with her parents, all being graduates of the Jeffersonville high school and young ladies of much more than ordinary intelligence and culture.

MAURICE COLL.

The subject of this sketch is a native of Ireland, where his birth occurred on November 27, 1833, having first seen the light of day at the ancestral home in County Donegal. His parents, John and Mary (Boyle) Coll, who were also born and reared in the above county, came to America in the prime of life, bringing a family of three sons and two daughters and settling in Pittsburg, Pennsylvania, where Mr. Coll secured renumerative employment as a machinist. Two of the children of this estimable couple died in Ireland, the following being the names of those who accompanied their parents to the new home in the United States and grew to maturity: Charles, who departed this life about the year 1903; Maurice, of this review, and Bernard J., who lives in Pittsburg and who served with an honorable record in the Civil war, being remembered by surviving comrades as an excellent soldier, ever ready for duty. He married Bridgett Burns, of Pittsburg, and has an interesting family of four children, who answer to the names of Charles, Mary, Eddie and Maurice. In early life Bernard J. Coll was a machinist and worked at the trade for a number of years in Pittsburg, but since the war has held various official positions under the municipal government of that city and is still in the public service. The two sisters of Maurice Coll died in early childhood, the only survivors of the family at this time being Bernard J. and Maurice.

Maurice Coll spent his early life in Pittsburg, where in due time, he became a skillful machinist, which trade he followed for a number of years as an employe of the Pennsylvania Railroad Company. After a long and arduous service with the above company at Pittsburg and Jeffersonville, Indiana, where he removed in 1869, he resigned his position with the railroad and entered the car works in this city and continued with the same until retiring from active life a few years ago.

Mr. Coll was married at Louisville, Kentucky, on the 8th day of March, 1860, to Maria Herron, a native of New Orleans, but reared in Louisville, to which city she was brought when a child. This marriage has been blessed by the birth of the following children: John P., a prosperous grocer of Jeffersonville; Bernard A., a shoe merchant of Jeffersonville, and one of the city's representative business men (see sketch); Annia M., wife of Cornelius McNamara, of Keokuk, Iowa; George, an attorney-at-law, practicing his profession in Dallas, Texas; Nellie, wife of Doctor Edelin, of Louisville; Edmund, a bookkeeper in that city; Ernest J., in the employ of the Louisville & Nashville Railroad, with headquarters in Louisville, and James, who is engaged in the drug business at Seymour, this state. Three sons are unmarried and still live with their parents and constitute a happy and prosperous household. All are practically educated, having wisely fitted themselves for the duties of life and are doing well in their respective lines of effort, two being prosperous business men, one a rising lawyer and the other three holding important positions in the railway service in one of the state institutions, and with a large business firm respectively. The daughters married men who stand high in their places of residence and are succeeding admirably in the fields of endeavor to which their time and energies are devoted.

Like his father, who was a leading Democratic politician and an active and influential campaigner, both in the ranks and on the stump, Mr. Coll has long devoted much attention to political and public matters, being a Democrat in all the term implies, an active participant in party affairs, but not a seeker after office, nor an aspirant for leadership.

Mr. Coll is by birthright a Catholic, and has ever been true to the church and its teachings, rearing his family under its influence. All of the family in Jeffersonville worship at the St. Augustine church, of which they are communicants and take an active part in all lines of good work under its auspices.

HON. JONAS GEORGE HOWARD.

This name suggests a flood of reminiscenses, carrying one back to the early settlement of Southern Indiana and the days of struggle, adventure and hardship, incident to the pioneer period. In fact, the Howard family was practically coeval with the organization of Clark county and have been prominently connected with all of its subsequent history and development. Jonas Howard, the pioneer founder, was a native of Vermont, of English descent and started for the West before Indiana had been admitted into the Union as a state. The route traveled was by way of the Allegheny river to Pittsburg and thence down the Ohio river on rafts and flat boats. When they landed at

Jeffersonville, the surrounding country was still clothed in primeval forests. Jonas Howard, who had been a farmer in his native state, lived but a few months after reaching Indiana Territory, his life being shortened by an attack of bilious fever. He, however, left a son and namesake, who was sixteen years old at the time of his father's arrival and proved worthy to take up and carry on to success the work mapped out by the old pioneer. Jonas Howard, Jr., remained in Clark county until 1824, when he removed to Floyd county and began farming. Six years later he returned to Clark county and engaged in the manufacture of brick, a highly important industry in the early settlement of a country. In association with a younger brother he made the brick that entered into the construction of the court-house at Louisville and the first and second buildings of the Galt house. In fact, the bulk of the brick used in building at Louisville during the late thirties came from the yards at Jeffersonville. Jonas Howard was also engaged quite extensively in farming and owned a large amount of land in Clark county. He died in 1849, at the comparatively early age of fifty-one years, after a life of unusual activity and business success. He married Margaret, daughter of George F. Helmer, a native of New York and of German parentage. He came to Clark county by the usual river route, but lived only a short time after arrival. His daughter, Margaret, who was born in Herkimer county, New York, was about fourteen years old when her parents disembarked from the flat boat at the Falls, after a long and tedious trip from the East. She survived her husband many years and died January 1, 1866. She was the mother of nine children, who grew to maturity, but of these only two are now living. Jonas George Howard, eldest of the sons, was born in Floyd county, Indiana, May 22, 1825, and was consequently about five years old when his father returned to Clark county. He was reared and educated in Jeffersonville, but spent much of his time on the farm, his early experiences being similar to thousands of other boys whose life began in the pioneer period of the state. When twenty years old he entered old Asbury University at Greencastle, Indiana, but after remaining there three years was called home while a senior on account of the ill health of his father. One of his classmates at Asbury was the afterwards celebrated Daniel W. Vorhees, between whom and Mr. Howard a friendship was formed which continued throughout their lives. Shortly after returning home Mr. Howard began reading law, but as the eldest child, much responsibility of taking care of the family fell upon his shoulders. In 1848 he entered the law school at Louisville and later was a student in the law department at Bloomington, Indiana, University, from which he was graduated in the class of 1851, being now the sole survivor of those who figured on that occasion. He immediately entered upon the active practice of his profession at Jeffersonville and continued without intermission until his voluntary retirement in 1905, at the age of eighty years. In 1867 he formed a partnership with John F. Reed, which during its continuance of thirty years, was one of the most successful legal firms in the state. Aside from their strictly professional work, Howard and Reed did much to promote the industrial development of Jeffersonville. A signal achievement in this line was their promotion of a corporation which finally resulted in building the bridge across the Ohio between Jeffersonville and Louisville, now known as the Big Four bridge. Another important industry promoted by this firm was the plate glass works, which was successfully operated for nine years under the presidency of Mr. Reed.

Mr. Howard's political career was in keeping with his achievements at the bar, as he has been recognized as one of the leaders of the Democratic party for over a half century. He was elected to the State Legislature in 1862 and re-elected in 1864, thus going through two of the stormiest sessions of that body during its history. In 1868, Mr. Howard was chosen as one of the Democratic electors and was given a similar honor during the exciting campaign of 1876. On both occasions he made a canvass of his district on behalf of his party. In 1884 he was nominated as Democratic candidate for Congress from the Third District and also again made the race as elector, this time being successful and having the pleasure of casting a vote for Grover Cleveland in the state's electoral college. After serving one term in Congress satisfactorily, Mr. Howard was re-elected in 1886 and ranked during the four years' service among the leading representatives in the Lower House. Since 1852 Mr. Howard has not missed canvassing his district in the interests of his party at every election period and always paid his own expenses. As late as the campaign of 1908, this old "wheel-horse" was still found in harness and at the age of eighty-three displayed all the vigor of his earlier years, making numerous speeches and keeping in good voice during addresses that consumed two hours' time. He is a man of remarkable vigor, one of the best preserved of all our older statesmen.

On November 23, 1854, Mr. Howard married Martha J. Roswell, a native of Clark county and member of an old pioneer family. Her parents, James and Drusilla (Dills) Roswell, came to Clark county from Virginia in 1829. To Mr. and Mrs. Howard three children have been born, the only survivor being Anna L., wife of William T. Ingram, of Jeffersonville. His first wife dying in 1872, Mr. Howard subsequently contracted a marriage with her sister, Elizabeth Roswell, by whom he has two children: Jonas G., Jr., who is an attorney at Jeffersonville, and Ethel, who remains at home with her father. Since his retirement from active practice Mr. Howard spends much of his time in reading, being especially interested in the study of history and politics, on which subjects his remarkably accurate memory makes him an authority.

EDWARD G. DAVIS.

Mr. Davis is a native of Kentucky, born at the town of West Point on February 11, 1874. His father, the late Dr. Jacob T. Davis, of Jeffersonville, for many years one of the most distinguished physicians and surgeons of Kentucky and Indiana, was born in Littleton, Wiltshire, England, February 24, 1833, received his literary education in the land of his birth and became a resident of the United States February 25, 1855, graduating from the Louisville Medical College at Louisville, Kentucky, in 1872. Previous to receiving his degree from the above institution, however, he practiced ten years including his service as assistant surgeon in the hospitals at St. Louis, Missouri, and at Madison and New Albany, Indiana, during the Civil war and also serving as assistant surgeon of field hospitals while attending the army in the field. In looking after the wounded at the battle of Perryville, Kentucky, he received a very severe wound and for two nights and one day lay helpless and unattended within the enemy's lines, suffering untold agony from pain and thirst until discovered by a comrade, John Marx, late of Madison, Indiana, who bore him to a place of safety and ministered to his necessities. After the war he practiced his profession with marked ability at West Point, Kentucky, and while there achieved honorable distinction for his success in fighting an epidemic of cholera which raged with terrific violence in various parts of the state in 1873, especially in the cities and towns along the Ohio river, and he was equally fortunate in his treatment of small pox patients during the epidemic of that dread disease a few years later. Doctor Davis was not only a learned and skillful physician but was profoundly versed in many subjects, possessing fine literary taste and the ability to express his ideas fluently and forcibly with the pen. He contributed frequently to the leading medical journals of the country besides writing on general topics. Many of his manuscripts on various subjects are now in the possession of his son who holds them beyond price. He was the originator of the Jefferson County, Kentucky, Medical Society at Jffersontown in 1876, and was elected its first president. After ministering to the ills of suffering humanity until infirmities of advancing age together with the pain from the injury received on the battle field, rendered the active practice of his profession difficult, the doctor, in March, 1873, was appointed by Governor Leslie, Judge of West Point, Kentucky, the duties of which with his office business brought him a very comfortable and satisfactory income. He was a man of strong religious convictions and a devout member of the Methodist Episcopal church, South, and a number of years ago entered the public ministry of that denomination, being ordained a deacon April 20, 1879, in Jeffersontown, Kentucky, by Bishop H. H. Kavanaugh, in which capacity he rendered effective service, preaching the Gospel among his fellow men. He was ordained elder by Bishop Joyce in Madison, Indiana, September 29, 1889, at a session of the Southeast Indiana Conference. About the year 1889 he removed to Jeffersonville, Indiana, where he continued his professional duties for a number of years, but finally on account of impaired health, due to exposure and injury while in the army he retired from the practice and from that time until his death on September 17, 1901, resided in Jeffersonville being sixty-nine years old.

Sarah Catherine Earhart was a native of Jefferson county, Indiana, and daughter of John and Rosanna Earhart. She bore her husband thirteen children, five sons and eight daughters, and departed this life in Jeffersonville on the 17th day of June, 1908, at the age of seventy years. Ten of the children born to doctor and Mrs. Davis are living, two daughters dying in infancy and one at the age of fifteen years. The oldest of the family, Flora R., wife of Burdette Golay, lives in the town of Wirt, Indiana. The following in order of birth are: Harriet M., who married Thomas O. Ogden, of Paris, Indiana; Annie Laurie, now Mrs. Charles H. Hurlbut, of Jeffersonville; John W., a hardware merchant and bicycle dealer of Indianapolis; Thomas W. G., a carpenter and builder of that city; Maud L., unmarried, who makes her home with Mrs. Hurlbut; Edward G., of this review; Daisy Catherine, wife of Charles R. Rigsby, of Jeffersonville; Nevaston F., a car accountant in the car accountant's office of the Louisville & Nashville Railroad, Louisville, and Almond H., city salesman for the Belknap Hardware & Manufacturing Company of the same city.

Edward G. Davis spent his childhood and early youth at West Point, Kentucky, and received the greater part of his educational discipline at North Madison high school, where he made rapid progress and earned an honorable record as a student. When fourteen years of age he became day clerk of the Madison Hotel, which position he held for a short time and then accompanied his parents to Henryville, thence subsequently came to Jeffersonville, where he secured employment with the American Car & Foundry Company, then the Ohio Falls Car works, with which he remained four years, during which time he worked in the decorating and finishing departments and became quite a skillful artisan. Severing his connection with the above company at the expiration of the period indicated he accepted a position in the finishing department of the Harland Pump Works at Louisville, where he remained one and a half years and then entered the employ of the Bee Hive Furniture & Manufacturing Company of Jeffersonville, beginning in an humble capacity, but by the end of the first year had worked up through various promotions until he became manager of the business.

Mr. Davis's rapid advancement indicates business ability of a high order and during the three and a half years he was at the head of the company's interests in Jeffersonville his management was marked by wise discretion and rare foresight, while his correct methods and well directed policy added much to the reputation of the firm in the city and elsewhere. At the end of the time mentioned resigning the position which he had so ably and faithfully filled he accepted the management of the branch store at Jeffersonville, owned by the Denhard Manufacturing Company. At the expiration of one year he purchased the business of the Bee Hive Manufacturing Company and engaged in the manufacture of picture frames and art novelties, in which during the last eight years he has built up an extensive business, his establishment being the only one of the kind in the city. He not only manufactures all kinds of frames, but also conducts an establishment for the overhauling and repairing of furniture and mattresses. Besides carrying full lines of goods for the retail and wholesale trade his place of business is complete in its every department and amply equipped to meet all the demands of the extensive trade which he now commands, and which is continually growing in magnitude and importance.

In connection with his business and industrial enterprises Mr. Davis has gained wide repute as the manufacturer of "Shinette," a furniture polish of superior quality which has an extensive sale and from which he derives no small share of his income.

The domestic history of the subject dates from the 30th day of December, 1897, when he contracted a matrimonial alliance with Ida May Smith, of Pee Wee Valley, Kentucky, daughter of the late James F. Smith of that place, the union being blessed with one child, Evelyn Christine, whose birth occurred on December 1, 1898.

In his fraternal relations Mr. Davis holds membership with the Knights of Pythias, the Independent Order of Odd Fellows and Woodmen of the World and is also identified with the Travelers' Protective Association. The Methodist Episcopal church represents his religious creed and at present he serves as vice-president of the Methodist Brotherhood of the Wall Street Methodist Episcopal church. In his political allignment he is a Republican, but not partisan in the sense of seeking public position. He also maintains a lively interest in military matters and served three years in Company G, First Regiment Indiana National Guard, under Capt. Lewis C. Baird, during which time he became skilled in the manual of arms.

BERNARD A. COLL.

During a continuous residence in Jeffersonville of nearly forty years, practically all of his active life, Mr. Coll has earned important official position and a liberal amount of this world's goods. For a number of years he has been actively interested in commercial pursuits and is now one of the leading business men of the community, his establishment at 406 Spring street being one of the largest and most successful of the kind in the city.

On the paternal side Mr. Coll is of Irish descent, his father, Maurice Coll, being a native of the Emerald Isle as was also his grandfather, John P. Coll, whose ancestors for many generations lived in County Donegal. John P. Coll spent the greater part of his life in the land of his birth and died from the effects of an accident at the ripe old age of ninety-eight years, his wife. Nancy, departing this life in Jeffersonville, when ninety-five years old.

Maurice Coll, whose birth occurred in 1833, came to the United States when young and spent a number of years in Pittsburg, Pennsylvania, where he worked as a machinist, removing in 1868 to Jeffersonville, where he has since resided. The maiden name of Mrs. Maurice Coll was Maria Herron, a native of New Orleans, Louisiana, and she has borne her husband the following children, all living and doing well in their respective spheres of endeavor: John P. is a grocer of Jeffersonville; Mrs. C. A. McNamara, of Keokuk, Iowa; Charles J., chief clerk at the Indiana Reformatory; Edmund J., bookkeeper for a wholesale grocery firm in Louisville; Ernest, a car builder employed at the Louisville & Nashville Railroad shops of Louisville, and James, a chemist at Seymour, Indiana; Bernard A.

Bernard A. Coll was born in Pittsburg, Pennsylvania, on the 22d of October, 1862, but at the age of seven years was brought to Jeffersonville by his parents and he has since made his home here. After attending the public schools of the city until completing the prescribed course of study he entered the grocery store of his uncle, Frank Voigt, where he remained for some time, subsequently engaging in the same capacity with another uncle by the name of P. Herron, in whose establishment he continued until engaging in business for himself. On resigning his clerkship he became a member of the grocery firm of M. Coll & Sons (consisting at the time of his father and brother), and was instrumental in building up the large and successful establishment at the corner of Chestnut and Fulton streets which his brother, John, now conducts and to which he devoted his attention until 1899. During the time thus engaged he made a careful study of the principles and ethics of mercantile life and laid the foundation upon which his subsequent success and present liberal fortune rest.

In the year indicated above Mr. Coll withdrew from the grocery firm to take charge of the County Treasurer's office, a position to which he was triumphantly elected in 1900 and the duties of which he discharged in an able manner for two terms, having been chosen his own successor in the year 1902.

At the expiration of his second term, January 1, 1905, he retired from office with the confidence and good will of the people of the county and accepting a position as traveling salesman with the wholesale firm of J. C. Hubinger & Brother, of Keokuk, Iowa, spent the ensuing two years on the road and built up an extensive patronage for his employers.

Severing his connection with the above house on January 1st of the year 1907, Mr. Coll purchased the boot and shoe store of J. R. Lancaster and has since devoted his attention to this line of merchandising, increasing his stock the meanwhile, and greatly extending his patronage until he now has the largest establishment of the kind in the city, having a well equipped store and giving employment to four regular clerks, a number he is obliged to increase during the busy seasons of the year. He owns in addition to his store a beautiful modern home and other valuable property, both real and personal, and is considered one of the solid and reliable men of the city whose credit has never been impaired.

As a representative Democrat few men in Clark county have been more influential. In party councils he has been a judicious adviser and in a number of hotly contested campaigns, it was by following his directions that victory was achieved. That his services have been fully appreciated by his co-workers is readily admitted and that he is entitled to still further recognition by his party is the general verdict of his many friends and fellow citizens.

Mr. Coll belongs to several fraternal organizations, in all of which he has been an influential worker besides holding important official positions from time to time. Among these societies are the Benevolent and Protective Order of Elks, Improved Order of Red Men and Ancient Order of Hibernians, Knights of Columbus, and Catholic Knights of America, the last three being largely under the auspices of the Catholic church and designed to inculcate a religious and patriotic spirit and make for a higher standard of manhood and citizenship. He was reared within the fold of the mother church, and has ever been one of its loyal sons and true to its teachings, his wife and family also being members of the same body.

Mr. Coll's marriage was solemnized with Carrie Meadows, of Jeffersonville, daughter of Galen Meadows, a well-to-do farmer and representative citizen of Clark county, the union resulting in the birth of three children: Edna, Louise and Bernard J., the oldest of whom is the only one living, the second dying at the age of eight years, and the youngest in infancy, at which time the mother was also called to her eternal rest. Edna, who is still a member of the home circle, was educated in the graded schools and high school of Jeffersonville, and is a young lady of pleasing personality and many admirable traits, being popular and moving in the best society circles of the city.

On September 1, 1904, Mr. Coll married his present wife, Mrs. Chrissie Anderson (nee Frank), the union being without issue.

RICHARD L. FLOOD.

At one time conditions in Ireland were such that large numbers of her citizens bade farewell to their native soil, bound for America, with the firm intention of making this land their permanent abiding place. Among the number were the ancestors of Richard L. Flood, one of the successful business men of Jeffersonville.

Mr. Flood was born in New Albany, Indiana, on the 21st of December, 1855, the son of Joseph and Alice (Neary) Flood, both natives of Ireland, where they grew to maturity, having married before migrating to America. They arrived here in due time and after casting about at various places, finally took up their abode at New Albany, where they lived out the remainder of their days, Mr. Flood departing this life in 1864, being survived by his wife until January 21, 1899.

Richard's boyhood days were spent under conditions that made him familiar with the rugged pathway that lies before the boy that must largely make his own way in the world. He was the only son in the family. Of the sisters, the following survive: Bridget, wife of William A. Elliott, a contractor in Jeffersonville; Mrs. Anna Gregg, a resident of Terre Haute; Kate, a trained nurse, having her home in Jeffersonville, being employed at the Mercy Hospital; Mrs. Benjamin Stallings, now residing at Dallas, Texas.

When approaching manhood Richard engaged in any kind of manual labor at which he could find employment. This often meant exceedingly hard work and small pay, but he never shirked his duty, nor went out of his way to avoid facing a hard day's task. For some time he was engaged at the Casting Hall Glass Works. After 1884 he became a salesman, and in 1887 went into business on his own responsibility, and has continued so ever since.

On June 5, 1888, he was joined in marriage with Annie M. Eagan, born in Jeffersonville. She was reared and educated in Kentucky, near the town of Morganfield. She has become the mother of four sons and one daughter, viz: Mary A., Richard L., Jr., Robert E., William P., and James A. These children, according to the custom among these families, have been educated in the Catholic Parochial School. Robert is taking a course calculated to fit him for subsequent work in the business world at the Bryant and Stratton's Business College in Louisville.

Mr. Flood and family are members of St. Augustine's Roman Catholic church, loyal in their support and zealous in their observance of all that their church represents. Our subject adheres, for the most part, to the tenets of the Democratic party, but has no aspirations for political preferment. His desires have rather been in harmony with the ideas consistent with an unassuming citizenship, believing that the ballot should be used only as an instrument for the advancement of the best interests of the community at large. He is a member of the Catholic Knights of America and the Ancient Order of Hibernians, being one of the charter members in the latter organization. He was the charter treasurer of the Ancient Order of Hibernians of Jeffersonville, and is held in high esteem by all who have had opportunity to make his close acquaintance.

AUSTIN FUNK, A. B., M. D.

This distinguished physician whose reputation is much more than local is a native of Harrison county, Indiana, born in the old historic town of Corydon, where he also spent his childhood and early youth. His father, Joseph P. Funk, who was of German descent, devoted the greater part of his life to educational work and achieved marked success as a teacher and school official. He was the first superintendent of the Lawrence county public schools, later served as superintendent of the schools of Corydon and for many years was principal of the New Albany high school, in which position he achieved much of his distinction as an educator. Mrs. Joseph P. Funk was of Scotch lineage and inherited many of the sterling qualities of head and heart for which that nationality has always been noted and which in a marked degree have been reproduced in her son, Austin.

Doctor Funk received his preliminary education in the public schools and after being graduated from the New Albany high school entered the State University, where he laid the intellectual foundation upon which his subsequent professional career has been builded, yielding to a desire of long standing by taking up the study of medicine, he became in due time a student of the medical department of the Louisville University and after completing the course of that institution began practice of his profession at New Albany, where his ability as a physician and surgeon soon brought him prominently before the public. Meanwhile the better to increase his efficiency in his chosen calling, he joined the Second Army Corps for service in the Spanish-American war, later was appointed acting assistant surgeon of the Marine Hospital at Cairo, Illinois, and afterwards was made a surgeon on S. S. Montreal of the British Naval Reserve during the Boer war.

Resuming his practice at New Albany on his return to the United States, Doctor Funk remained in that city until 1906, when he removed to Jeffersonville, where he has since devoted his entire attention to the treatment of diseases peculiar to the eye, ear, nose and throat, fitting himself for special work by taking a course in the Royal London Ophthalmic Hospital and in the Central London Throat and Ear Hospital, where he was instructed by some of the most distinguished specialists of the age.

Doctor Funk is a member of the Clark County Medical Society, the Indiana State Medical Association and the American Medical Association, taking an active interest in the deliberations of these distinguished bodies and contributing in no small degree to their influence in advancing the standard of professional efficiency. While devoted to his chosen calling and prosecuting his studies and researches with an enthusiasm characteristic of the man who aims to reach the highest possible standard in his profession and become a true healer of afflicted humanity he keeps in close touch with the trend of modern

29

thought and activity. Fraternally he is identified with the Masonic Order, and he also holds membership with the two college fraternities, the Phi Delta Theta, with which he united while a student of the Indiana State University, and the Phi Chi of the University of Louisville.

WILLIAM G. YOUNG.

This young business man, proprietor of one of the largest jewelry establishments in the city of Jeffersonville, is a native of Kentucky and the older of two children. Their parents were John and Charlotte Young, the former born in Harrison county, Indiana, and the latter in Germany. John Young was reared to maturity in his native county and state and when a young man located in Louisville, where he learned the machinist's trade and where in due time he married Charlotte Kraushaar. He still follows his chosen calling in that city and with his wife is highly esteemed by a large circle of friends and acquaintances, being a man of sterling worth and fully entitled to the confidence with which he is regarded. Besides William G. Mr. and Mrs. Young are the parents of a daughter who is the wife of Charles P. Crowder, a mail carrier of Louisville.

William G. Young was born in the above named city on the 4th day of May, 1874, and spent his childhood and youth under the parental roof, attending meanwhile the public schools and receiving a good practical education. At quite an early age he gave evidence of more than ordinary mechanical skill and having a decided liking for tools he began while still young to learn the jeweler's trade.

Animated by a determined purpose to become something more than a mere subordinate he addressed himself cheerfully to his labors and during the ensuing fifteen years was employed in Louisville and Jeffersonville and made substantial progress in his vocation. His great proficiency in the more skillful lines of work gave him an enviable reputation and within the period indicated his services were constantly in demand by the best jewelers of the city, with the result that he was never out of employment and always commanded the remuneration of an expert.

In 1903 he started the nucleus of his present establishment and within a comparatively brief period had all the work he could do in the way of repairing, besides building up quite a lucrative patronage in the commercial line. Of necessity he was obliged to begin in a somewhat modest way but it was not long until his business increased to such an extent that he was enabled to increase his stock and employ an assistant. Without detailing the growth of his business or noting specifically the various steps in his successful business career, his enterprise advanced not only steadily and substantially but rapidly until within the brief space of five years he became one of the leading jewelers of Jeffersonville, his establishment at this time being one of the largest and best stocked of the kind in the city and his patronage second to that of few others in the southern part of the state.

Mr. Young carries full and complete lines of watches, clocks, table cutlery, all kinds of jewelry from the ordinary priced to the most valuable on the market, also a large and varied assortment of cut glass and fine hand painted china-ware, making a specialty of the finer repair work on watches and jewelry. A skilled artisan himself he employs none but the most proficient workmen and guaranteeing everything that goes from the repair department, it is not strange that the best people of the city are among his patrons or that his reputation has become much more than local. Keeping fully abreast of the times in all matters relating to his calling, he is well informed concerning the making of jewelry and time-pieces of all kinds and thoroughly familiar with the trade, being a careful and judicious buyer and a successful salesman as well as an artisan of great ability and much more than ordinary artistic talent. Few men have achieved such signal success within the brief space of five years, advancing from a common work-bench and a kit of tools to become the head of one of the largest jewelry establishments in a populous center. His success financially has been commensurate with the energy and ability displayed in his chosen sphere of endeavor and today though comparatively a young man with the greatest part of his life in the future he occupies a conspicuous place among the substantial business men of his city with prospects of still greater success as the years go by.

Mr. Young is a married man and the father of four children, three of whom, Selma, Catherine and Dorothy are living, and one, a son, by the name of William G., died when eighteen months of age. Mrs. Young was formerly Dora Kreutzer, and the ceremony by which her name was changed to the one she now so worthily bears was solemnized on November 29th of the year 1898. She was born in New Albany, Indiana, and is the daughter of Jacob and Catherine (Bornwasser) Kreutzer, of German descent and both deceased.

For a number of years Mr. Young has taken an active interest in Masonry, joining Lewis Lodge, No. 191, in Louisville, at the age of twenty-three. Later in 1901 he transferred his membership to Jeffersonville Lodge, No. 340, and has since been one of its most active and influential members, besides being at intervals honored with important official positions, holding at the present time the high and responsible post of worshipful master, to which he was elected in 1904. He is identified with the Independent Order of Odd Fellows, belonging to Hope Lodge, No. 83, at New Albany and his name also occupies a prominent place on the records of Hope Lodge, No. 13, Knights of Pythias, in Jeffersonville. Politically he is a Republican, of which party he is a recognized leader in the ward in which he resides. In 1905 he was elected to represent his ward in the City Council, of which body he is still a member, his term expiring January 1, 1910, and in which he has been faithful, laboring earnestly for the general welfare of the municipality.

CHARLES EDGAR POINDEXTER.

The ancestors of Mr. Poindexter were of that sterling type which should excite the admiration of everyone, and many of their noble traits have descended to the present generation of the Poindexters. Charles Edgar Poindexter was born in Jeffersonville Indiana, December 4, 1853, the son of Gabriel and Mary F. (Willey) Poindexter. Barzillai Willey, grandfather of Charles Edgar, was a soldier in the Revolutionary war, from Connecticut. His son, John F. Willey, was born in June, 1809, where the city of Cincinnati, Ohio, now stands, and the following year he was brought to Clark county, Indiana, his father having moved near Memphis. The family came down the Ohio river before steamboats were in common use and landed at Jeffersonville, the Poindexters having come from Louisa county, Virginia, a year or two previously, this family having long been residents of the Old Dominion state, from which Clevias S. Poindexter's father, Gabriel Poindexter, Sr., went as a soldier in the Revolutionary war. Both the Virginia and Connecticut branch of this family were well known and influential in their day, all people of genuine worth.

Charles E. Poindexter is one of a family of four children now living, namely: Harry C. is Judge of the City Court in Jeffersonville; Bertha F. is librarian of the Carnegie Public Library in Jeffersonville; Frank C. is in the postal services in Indianapolis. The following are deceased: Fountin W., who married Emma Willey, of Madison, Indiana, left two children; Ella, who married Chester T. Berryman, and Randall; they both reside in Louisville. Mary A. married Dr. Edward L. Elrod, of Henryville, Clark couny; they both passed away early in 1908, leaving one daughter, Bertha Mary.

After leaving school Mr. Poindexter received his first business experience in the employ of the Adams Express Company in Jeffersonville, in which he remained for eight years, most of that time acting as agent for the company. He then went to the Louisville & Cincinnati Mail Boat Line, in whose employ he remained for a period of six years, giving the same unqualified satisfaction as he had his former employers, acting for the latter as cashier and agent in Louisville. After this he was freight agent for the Pennsylvania Railroad in the city of Jeffersonville for a period of eight years. Then in the year 1893 he was employed by the Citizen's National Bank of

Jeffersonville as cashier, which responsible position he still very creditably fills, having done much to increase the prestige of this institution through his able and conscientious service and courteous treatment of its patrons.

The matrimonial chapter in the life history of Charles E. Poindexter began in April, 1884, when he united in the bonds of wedlock with Ophelia Read, of Port Fulton. She is the daughter of John F. Read, who was born in Washington, Daviess county, Indiana, October 4, 1822. He was educated at Hanover College, studied law with the noted Humphrey Marshall, of the same family as Chief Justice Marshall of the United States. He made a subsequent record at the bar, serving one term in the Legislature. He was in the United States land office at Jeffersonville for a period of eight years. He was not only prominent in legal affairs but also in business circles, having been at one time president of the Ford Plate Glass Company of Jeffersonville; also president of the Citizens' National Bank of that city. In 1840 he married Eliza Keigwin, who died in 1852, and in 1855 Mr. Read married Eliza Pratt. One child was born to the first union and nine to the latter, the wife of Charles E. Poindexter being the eldest. Mr. Read is deceased and his widow lives with Mr. and Mrs. Poindexter. Mr. Read was a very prominent man in his day and one of the most useful in this county in both public and business life.

One son, James Edgar, has brightened the home of Charles E. Poindexter and wife. He is individual bookkeeper in the Citizens' National Bank, and is a young man of much promise.

In his fraternal relations Mr. Poindexter is a member of Clark Lodge, No. 40, Free and Accepted Masons; Horeb Chapter, No. 66; Jeffersonville Commandery, No. 27. H is a member of the Presbyterian church.

A. RUDOLPH SCHIMPFF.

Jeffersonville has reason to be proud of her newspapers, among the most progressive and ably conducted in the city as well as in the southern part of the state, being the Jeffersonville Star, which under its present management, has made rapid strides to the front and met with popular favor of a cumulative order and became an unfailing index of the civic pride and commercial and industrial prestige of the city.

A. Rudolph Schimpff is a native of Jeffersonville, Indiana, where his birth occurred on the 14th of November, 1875, of German descent, his grandparents on both sides of the family having been born in the Palatinate Rheumth, Bavaria. His father, Charles A. Schimpff, also a native of the Fatherland, came to the United States in 1858, at the age of eleven years and located with his mother, four brothers and three sisters, in Louisville,

Kentucky, where he remained until his removal ten years later to Jeffersonville, where he engaged in the confectionary business and in due time became one of the substantial men of the city. He married in 1873, Alvina Rossler, daughter of Charles and Caroline Rossler, and became widely known, not only in business circles but as an energetic man who took pride in the growth of his adopted city and did all within his power to foster and encourage all enterprises tending to this and other laudable ends.

A Rudolph Schimpff was reared to maturity in Jeffersonville, enjoyed the best educational advantages the city schools afforded and at an early age entered the office of the Star, with which paper he was connected for a period of fourteen months, during which time he served on the editorial staff and became skilled in nearly every department of newspaper work. At the expiration of the time indicated he took charge of the city circulation of the Jeffersonville Star and Clark County Republican, which position he held until January, 1903, when he became business manager of the two plants under the receivership.

In August, 1903, in partnership with Charles A. Schimpff, Mr. Schimpff purchased a half interest in the Star and Republican and on the 10th of December following became sole owner and publisher, this being the only Republican paper out of a total of nineteen in thirty-five years to weather the storms of discouragement and succeed. Under his able and judicious management the Star has made steady and substantial progress, meeting with a favorable reception from the time of his taking charge of the office and proving an alert, progressive and admirably conducted paper, attractive in make-up and latter press and an able exponent of the political principles to which it is pledged. Mr. Schimpff is not only an easy, graceful and forcible writer who impartially discussess the leading questions and issues of the day, whose editorials are widely quoted and copied, but is also an enthusiastic and enterprising newspaper man who has made the Star a credit to himself and an honor to the city. He has an office thoroughly equipped with modern machinery and appliances which with a large and constantly increasing circulation and a liberal advertising patronage, the plant is now one of the most valuable of the kind in the county, with every prospect of continuous growth in power and influence. Through the medium of his paper, Mr. Schimpff has advocated all worthy measures for the upbuilding of Jeffersonville and the advancement of Clark county.

As already indicated Mr. Schimpff is a Republican and by reason of his position as editor of the official organ of his party and vice-chairman of the County Central Committee, he has become one of its leaders in Clark county, and an influential factor in formulating and directing its policies, not only in local matters but in the larger and more extended affairs of district and state.

In his religious faith Mr. Schimpff is a member of the German Evangelical Lutheran church, belonging to the local congregation in Jeffersonville, known as St. Luke's church, his wife being identified with St. Augustine Roman Catholic church of this city. Fraternally he holds membership with Jeffersonville Lodge, No. 340, Free and Accepted Masons, Hope Lodge, No. 13, Knights of Pythias, in the latter of which he now holds the office of chancellor and for a number of years he has been one of the prominent workers in the Independent Order of Odd Fellows, belonging to Tabor Lodge. No. 92.

Margaret Fredricks, who became the wife of Mr. Schimpff on the 13th of April, 1898, was born at Port Fulton, Clark county, Indiana, August 20, 1880, being the daughter of Mr. and Mrs. E. J. Fredricks, well known residents of Jeffersonville. The pledges of this union are two interesting children, who answer to the names of Margaret and Alvina.

JOHN GIENGER.

John Gienger, wholesale dealer in produce and feed at Jeffersonville, Indiana, is a native of Wurtemburg, Germany, and the son of George and Katherine Gienger, both born and reared in that kingdom and descended from ancestors who, from time immemorial, lived and bore their parts in the affairs of the German nation and figured more or less conspicuously in their respective places of abode. George Gienger, in 1880, emigrated to the United States and settled at Jeffersonville, Indiana, where for seven years he conducted a successful dairy business, but at the expiration of that time disposed of his interests in this city and moved to the state of Oregon, where he continued dairying until retiring from active life at a comparatively recent date. Having acquired a competency he sold out his business and with his good wife is now enjoying the fruits of his many years of toil and judicious management in a comfortable home in the city of Portland.

John Gienger whose birth occurred on the 19th day of November, 1863, spent his early life in the land of his nativity and enjoyed the advantages of a good education in its schools. At the age of seventeen he accompanied his parents upon their removal to the New World and for some time thereafter assisted his father in the dairy at Jeffersonville, subsequently engaging in the produce trade upon his own responsibility and in due time building up a thriving business. Since the year 1887 he has devoted his attention to produce and feed, which he handles in immense quantities, supplying the local market and shipping to a number of tradesmen in neighboring towns, his wholesale house at 303 Court avenue, being the largest and most extensively patronized establishment of the kind in the city, and one of the best known in the southern part of the state. Mr. Gienger's business career has been eminently creditable and satisfactory, presenting a series of successes which have gained for him a conspicuous place among the progressive merchants of his city. He gives steady employment to five men every working day of the year and during the busy seasons it is found necessary to augment this force by several additional assistants, the demand for his goods being so great at times as to tax the establishment to its utmost capacity and keep the proprietor busy almost day and night in order to supply his numerous customers.

Mr. Gienger is a stalwart advocate of Democratic principles and policies and in the local ranks of his party he has been an active and valued worker. He has served in various positions of honor and trust and in very instance has proven worthy of the confidence of his fellow citizens as well as of the party to which he belongs. He represented his ward for some time in the City Council and as a member of that body was industrious and untiring in his efforts to promote the interests of the municipality, having introduced a number of important bills which became ordinances and in other ways made his influence felt as a safe and judicious local legislator. As a member of the local educational board he has done much to advance the schools of the city and make them among the best in the state. He is an active worker in the fraternity of Odd Fellows, the Benevolent and Protective Order of Elks, and in religion subscribes to the creed of the German reformed church, holding at this time the position of elder in the local congregation with which he is identified.

Mr. Gienger is essentially a business man and as such ranks among the most enterprising and successful of the city in which he lives. He has so managed and prosecuted his affairs as to acquire a liberal share of this world's goods, a third interest in two successful canning factories in Jeffersonville and is also interested in a similar enterprise in the town of Henryville, besides holding considerable valuable real estate in both city and country and a large amount of personal property to say nothing of private investments which add very materially to his income.

Mr. Gienger's domestic life dates from 1885, on November 5th of which year he was united in marriage with Catherine Mosser, whose birth occurred in Kentucky, but who for some time prior to the date mentioned lived with her parents in the city of Jeffersonville. This union has been blessed with one child, a daughter by the name of Amelia, who is now a young lady, the pride of her parents and popular in the social circles of the city. The Gienger family is highly esteemed socially and religiously and the name is closely identified with charitable work and benevolent enterprises through which the deserving poor and unfortunate receive assistance.

OSCAR THEODORE JOHNSON.

The family of which Mr. Johnson is a representative has been identified with the history of Clark county since the pioneer period, his grandfather, Stephen Johnson, having been among the early ministers of this part of the state and one of the first to preach the doctrines of Methodism to the few scattered settlers who subscribed to the faith of that church. Stephen Johnson was a man of good mind and sound practical sense, a devout Christian and an influential minister who hesitated not to declare the whole counsel of God as he understood it, and for a number of years his labors in this and other fields throughout Southern Indiana were greatly blessed. He not only visited the scattered pioneers in the wilderness and preached and otherwise instructed them in their humble cabin homes, but frequently conducted public worship in the towns, and to him belongs the credit of organizing a number of societies in a field which even at this date feel the effect of his teaching and the influence of his consecrated and God-fearing life.

John R. Johnson, son of Stephen and father of Oscar Theodore, was born in Clark county and grew to maturity in Oregon township, where he lived until about the year 1883, when he removed to his present place of residence in the village of Utica. In his young manhood he married Susan Fields, also a native of Oregon township, and in due time became the father of three children, two sons and one daughter, namely, Dr. J. W. Johnson, practicing physician of Utica; Oscar T., whose name introduces this sketch, and Stella, who married William Martin, of Louisville, Kentucky, and resides in that city.

Oscar Theodore Johnson, whose birth occurred on the 3d day of December, 1873, spent his early life in Oregon township and received his education in the public schools of Utica. While a mere lad he entered his father's barber shop in that town and under the latter's instruction soon became proficient in the trade, which he followed with gratifying success until the year 1898, when he accepted employment as guard of the Indiana Reformatory. After filling that position to the satisfaction of the management of the institution for a period of five and a half years, he resigned to become special officer in the employ of the Pennsylvania Railroad Company, the duties of which he discharged in a creditable manner for fourteen months, during which he devoted his attention closely to the interests of the corporation, proving faithful to the important trust reposed in him, and rising high in the esteem and confidence of his superiors. Severing his connection with the road at the expiration of the time indicated Mr. Johnson joined the police force of Jeffersonville and for a period of two years bore his full share in maintaining the peace and quietude of the city.

Resigning from the force at the expiration of two years Mr. Johnson was nominated by the Republican party for the office of Sheriff, being opposed by a popular candidate backed by a normal Democratic majority of four hundred. Notwithstanding the formidable strength of the opposition and his apparent hopeless outlook he entered boldly into the campaign and with his accustomed vigor and energy conducted a canvass which extended to every part of the county, resulting in triumph at the polls, defeating his competitor by 186 votes, running far ahead of his ticket and being the only Republican candidate elected that year. Mr. Johnson's nomination by acclamation and signal victory in a reliably Democratic county were complimentary to his sterling worth and personal popularity with the people irrespective of political allignment, and since taking charge of his office on January 1, 1908, his able and judicious course has fully justified the wisdom of his election.

Mr. Johnson on June 22, 1898, was married to Mollie Conlen, daughter of James and Winnie Conlen, of Jeffersonville, the father deceased, the mother still living in Clark county. Mr. and Mrs. Johnson have a pleasant and attractive home in Jeffersonville and move in the best social circles of the city, having many warm friends and admirers among those with whom they mingle and a popularity extending to the limits of their acquaintance.

Fraternally Mr. Johnson belongs to the Knights of Pythias, Modern Woodmen of America, and the Union Fraternal League, in all of which organizations he is active and influential, besides holding various positions of honor and trust. Mrs. Johnson is identified with the Women's Relief Corps and belongs to the Catholic church.

HENRY F. DILGER.

Mr. Dilger, a prominent local attorney, is a native of Perry county, Indiana, where his birth occurred on the 26th day of February, 1865, being the son of Joseph and Rosina (Brugger) Dilger. These parents came from Baden, Germany, a number of years ago, and were married about the year 1858 in Perry county, Indiana, where the father followed agricultural pursuits for a livelihood. Subsequently they removed to Michigan, thence to Spencer county, Indiana, where they spent the remainder of their days, the mother dying in 1884, the father in 1891. Their family consisted of three children, namely: John W., who lives in Missouri; Benjamin, a resident of Jeffersonville, engaged in the river trade, and Henry F., whose name appears above. By a previous marriage Mrs. Dilger had two sons and a daughter, whose names are as follows: Theodore H. Dilger, a farmer and miller of Spencer county, Indiana, and a large land holder in Alabama; Robert W. Dilger, a mechanic of Louisiana, Missouri, and Freda, who married Peter Weidner, a grocer of Jeffersonville.

Henry F. Dilger was educated in the schools of Michigan and Spencer county, Indiana, and spent his early life in close touch with nature on the farm. At the age of fourteen he began working for himself as a farm hand and later was employed for some time in a mill, the meanwhile husbanding his earnings with the greatest care for the purpose of adding to his scholastic knowledge. At the expiration of five years he was enabled to carry out a' desire of long standing by entering the Crawford county Normal School, which he attended until completing the prescribed course, thus fitting himself for teaching, a work to which he had long been favorably inclined. After teaching two years in the district schools of Crawford county he went to Kentucky, where he devoted one year to educational work but at the expiration of that time returned to Indiana and spent the ensuing two years in Jeffersonville, township schools, the meanwhile earning an honorable reputation as a capable and painstaking instructor.

Not caring to make teaching his permanent work Mr. Dilger in 1893 took up the study of law at Aurora, Indiana, in the office of McMullen & McMullen and later entered the law department of the Central Normal School at Danville, where he made substantial progress in the profession besides attaining a high standard as a close and diligent student. Returning to Jeffersonville he continued his legal studies under the directon of George H. Voigt, in whose office he remained until his admission to the bar in 1897, after which he devoted the greater part of the ensuing three years to educational work, not beginning the practice of his profession until 1901. In the latter year Mr. Dilger opened an office in Jeffersonville and in due time gained his proportionate share of legal patronage. With a spirit born of a determination to succeed Mr. Dilger persisted in the course upon which he set out and by ably and faithfully attending to such business as came to his office, he soon gained the reputation of a capable and thoroughly honorable attorney, with the result that in due time he succeeded in securing quite a number of patrons and building a safe and fairly lucrative business. Since the year 1901 his legal career has compared favorably with that of the majority of the members of the Jeffersonville Bar, and at the present time he has a large and lucrative practice in the courts of Clark county, being esteemed a safe and reliable counsellor, a judicious practitioner who spares no reasonable efforts in behalf of his clients and whose ability before judges and juries seldom fail to win verdicts for the causes he represents.

While devoted to his profession he is also interested in public matters and political affairs, being one of the influential Democrats of Jeffersonville and a leader of his party in both city and county. He has served several years as Treasurer of the County Central Committee and as a campaigner his services have been especially valuable, being a judicious adviser and aggressive worker. In May, 1904, he was made City Attorney of Jeffersonville and discharged the duties of the position with credit and ability until September of the year 1906, this being the only public office he has ever held or to which he has ever aspired.

Mr. Dilger is a member of the Tell Lodge, No. 272, Independent Order of Odd Fellows, Jeffersonville, in which he holds the title of past grand and ·in the general deliberations of which he takes an active and influential part, having served one term of three years as trustee and recently re-elected to that office. His domestic experience dates from the 28th day of December, 1898, at which time he was united in marriage with Annie L. Meyer, of Jeffersonville, daughter of Christopher and Elizabeth Meyer, natives of Germany and Indiana respectively, the union resulting in the birth of one son, Frank H., who first saw the light of day December 6th of the year 1899.

JOHN R. JOHNSON.

Now in the sixty-second year of his age Mr. Johnson can review with pride an unblemished business career, and a war record so meritorious that it won for him recognition from the great commonwealth of Indiana in the way of a medal of honor. Despite the crude educational facilities of his boyhood days he is regarded as one of the leading literary lights of the town in which he lives, Utica, Indiana, being a man of wide knowledge of the world.

John R. Johnson's native heath is Scott county, Indiana, having been born there August 14, 1846, the son of Stephen and Lavina (Williams) Johnson. Scott county was also the place of nativity of the parents, and they spent the greater portion of their lives there. The father, a farmer, and a Methodist preacher, died at the age of sixty-three years, his wife surviving him eleven years. They reared a family of four sons and four daughters. Sarah became the wife of John McClure, of Clark county; William spent four years as a soldier in the Civil war, being adjutant of his regiment, and he is now engaged in the manufacture of brick in Illinois; John R. and David are twins, and the latter has for the last thirty years been in the concrete business in Illinois; James is employed in the interurban service at Indianapolis; Caroline is the wife of Samuel Ferguson, of Kansas; Martha is the widow of John Smith, and also resides in Kansas; Mary is the wife of William Owens and lives on the old home farm in Scott county.

John R. was educated in a typical log school-house of the pioneer days, but as the result of a lifetime of study and investigation he is the possessor of a thorough education, few men with his limited opportunities being so well equipped intellectually. In May, 1864, he enlisted in the army as a member of Company K, One Hundred Thirty-seventh Indiana, and served one year. As stated in the introductory of this sketch he was presented a medal of honor by the state of Indiana as a recognition of his gallantry and valor on the field of battle. This medal is regarded as a sacred heirloom in the family. Returning from the army he engaged in business, and some time thereafter married Maria Susan Fields, a daughter of Milford and Samantha (Carroll) Fields, early pioneers of Clark county. The first home of the subject and his wife was at Marysville, Clark county, where they lived for about six years. In the year 1886 they moved to Utica, Clark county, and built their present pleasant and comfortable dwelling. Three children have been born to them: Dr. William Francis is practicing medicine in Utica with great success; Oscar Theodore is the present Sheriff of Clark county · Estella is the wife of William Martin, chief clerk of a large mercantile establishment in Louisville. Mr. and Mrs. Johnson attend the Methodist Episcopal church, and they are counted as among its most faithful members. Politically Mr. Johnson is a Republican, having been identified with that party all of his life. He is always to be found in the councils of his party, and is known as one of its leaders locally. He never sought but one political office, however, and that was during the Harrison administration when he applied for the postmastership of Utica and was appointed to the position. He had the hearty endorsement of the people of the community generally, without regard to their political affiliations and he discharged the duties of the office in a highly satisfactory manner. Mr. Johnson is very much interested in local literary work, and particularly in lyceums and debating clubs.

WALTER G. SHADDAY.

The Shadday family in this country lived originally in North Carolina and from that state migrated to Indiana in an early day, and located in Switzerland county, of which they were among the first pioneers. George Shadday, the grandfather of Walter G., was born in Switzerland county, but moved to the county of Ripley when a young man and there married and spent the remainder of his life. He served during the Civil war in the Forty-fifth Indiana Cavalry, participated in a number of campaigns and bloody battles and earned an honorable record as a brave and gallant soldier.

Walter G. Shadday, one of the leading real estate dealers of Clark county, also at the head of a thriving investment and insurance business, is a native of Indiana, born in the county of Ripley on the 3d day of December, 1882. His father, John H. Shadday, a well known contractor and builder of Jeffersonville, was for many years a resident of Ripley county and a man of much more than ordinary standing and influence in the community honored by his citizenship. John H. Shadday has devoted the greater part of his life to the business which he now successfully follows, first in Ripley county, later in Jeffersonville, to which city he moved when his son, Walter, was a child and in which, since 1903, he has been the successor of Henry Pollock, for many years one of the largest contractors and builders in the southern part of the state. The maiden name of the subject's mother was Arminta Spears; she became the wife of Mr. Shadday in Ripley county and bore him one child while living there, to-wit: Walter G., whose name introduces this review. In addition to his long and successful business career John H. Shadday has a military record of which he feels justly proud, having served five years in the regular army as an officer of Company A, Seventh United States Cavalry, during which time he experienced much active service in various parts of the country and earned honorable distinction by reason of duty ably and faithfully performed. Since retiring from the army he has devoted his attention exclusively to his business affairs, though always interested in civic matters and taking an active part in politics, being a pronounced Democrat, but not a partisan in the sense of seeking office or aspiring to leadership.

As already indicated Walter G. Shadday was a child when his parents transferred their residence to Jeffersonville and since three years of age his life has been closely identified with the city and its interests. After receiving a good education in the public schools he acquired a knowledge of practical affairs under his father's direction and in due time turned his attention to the lines of business in which he has since been engaged and in which he has achieved such marked financial success, namely, real estate, insurance and various kinds of investments, building up a large and lucrative patronage in Jeffersonville and vicinity, besides dealing extensively in real estate in Clark and other counties and states, all of which business resulted in liberal profits and gained for him an honorable reputation as a safe and reliable business man. His investments both in his own name and for others have invariably proven satisfactory and profitable, and in the matter of loans he has also been successful, placing a large amount of money on real estate and other first class security, his operations in this department alone representing many thousands of dollars, annually, and yielding a large share of his income. He is the local agent for a number of the largest and most reliable insurance companies in the United States and foreign countries and his very extensive business in this line is steadily growing in magnitude and importance, comparing favorably with that transacted by any other man or firm in the city similarly engaged.

He is a member of the Jefferson Social Club, and a prominent participant in its meetings and deliberations and his name is also found on the records of Lodge, No. 340, Free and Accepted Masons, in which ancient and honorable brotherhood he has risen to high standing, besides being honored at different times with important official positions. Although reared a Democrat his reading and investigations led him into the opposite political belief and ever since old enough to exercise the right of citizenship he has been an uncompromising Republican, believing the principles and policies of the party to be for the best interests of the American Republic and having faith that in the future as in the past the party will continue to fulfill the grand mission which its founders had in view. An active worker in the ranks and a judicious adviser in party councils he has never entered the political arena as an office seeker, but contents himself with voting for his favorite candidates. He is married and still an inmate of the parental home, to the maintenance of which he is a liberal contributor and to the attractiveness of which he adds greatly.

THOMAS J. BROCK.

The career of Mr. Brock, who, though a young man with but limited experience has made his example an inspiration to those who shall come after him and his presence a permanent benefit to those with whom he mingles. Thomas J. Brock, attorney-at-law, and one of the rising members of the Jeffersonville Bar, was born on a farm near Borden, Clark county, Indiana, July 9, 1876, being one of three children whose parents, Francis M. and Abigail I. Brock, were natives of Washington and Clark county, respectively. Francis M. Brock was born near Martinsburg, Indiana, on the 22d day of July, 1849, and his wife first saw the light of day on the family homestead near Borden, November 7th of the year 1854. The family of this estimable couple consisted of three children, the oldest of whom, a daughter by the name of Cora May, died when six years of age, Thomas J., of this review, being the second in order of birth and John B., the youngest.

The early life of Thomas J. Brock, in close touch with nature on the farm, was conducive to well rounded physical development and accustomed to habits of industry from childhood he grew up with well defined ideas of life, its duties and responsibilities. After acquiring an elementary education in the public schools he entered the Borden Institute, where he made commendable progress in the higher branch of learning and earned an honorable record as a student, graduating in the Teachers Scientific and Academic courses in the year 1892. During the six years following his graduation Mr. Brock taught in the public schools of Clark county and gained worthy prestige as a capable and enterprising instructor, popular alike with pupils and patrons as is indicated by his long period of service in but few places of labor. From 1896 to 1897 inclusive he was principal of the town school of Borden, and while holding this position he took up the study of law which he subsequently prosecuted in the Borden Institute, his progress being such that he was duly admitted to the bar in 1898, since which year he has been actively engaged in the practice of his profession in Jeffersonville.

In September, 1900, Mr. Brock was appointed City Attorney of Jeffersonville, and held the office to the satisfaction of all concerned until May, 1904, proving an able and judicious public servant who spared no pains in looking after the interests of the people. Since retiring from office he has devoted his attention very closely to his profession and at the present time has a large and lucrative practice, standing in the front rank of the successful members of the local bar and being held in high esteem by his professional brethren as well as by the public at large. In connection with his professional duties Mr. Brock is also largely interested in religious work, being a zealous member of the Christian church, and since February, 1892, an ordained evangelist of the same. He is an able and forceful speaker. He occupies no small place in public favor and enjoying the confidence and esteem of the people of his city, and with a promising outlook before him there is every reason to believe that the past is but an earnest of the higher honors which shall come to him by reason of duty ably and faithfully performed.

Mr. Brock is a member of four fraternal organizations and an active and influential worker in each, namely, the Free and Accepted Masons, Modern Woodmen of America, Knights of Pythias and Order of Eastern Star, and in politics he is stanchly and uncompromisingly Democratic.

On December 3d of the year 1894, Mr. Brock and Ada A. Littell, daughter of Milburn and Rachael Littell, were united in the holy bonds of wedlock, the union being blessed with two children, H. Curtis and Byron J., aged twelve and ten years, respectively.

CAPT. EDMONDS J. HOWARD.

Captain Edmonds J. Howard, president of the Howard Ship Yards Company, was born at Madison, Indiana, March 14, 1840. His father was the late Captain James Howard, the founder of the famous Howard yards, whose sketch appears elsewhere in this volume. His mother was Rebecca Barmore, a native of Hamilton county, Ohio.

The family located permanently at Jeffersonville in 1848, where the father was engaged in boat building, and here the son grew to manhood. He received his education in the public and private schools of Louisville, and afterwards attended the Kentucky Military Institute at Frankfort, Kentucky.

Before he had become of age he had entered business life, and following his father's example had turned to the river. In 1860 he went to the South

RESIDENCE OF CAPTAIN E. J. HOWARD, PORT FULTON.

and served as clerk on a steamboat running up Ouchita river. Here the breaking out of the War of the Rebellion found him, and realizing the need of his
presence at home he severed his connection with the boat and started North.
Reaching Jeffersonville after many difficulties he entered the employ of the
United States government as a clerk in the Ordnance Department, but remained there but a short while, leaving to become connected with his father's
yards. His career in the boat building business has not been one of easy success, but rather a fight to master the business from the first to the last detail.
He began as an apprentice and learned every department of boat building by
actual contact with the work. In 1865 the firm of James Howard became
James Howard & Company, by the addition of John C. Howard, a brother,
and Edmonds J. Howard. In 1876, upon the death of his father, he bought
all of his father's interest in the company and several years later also that of
his uncle John C. The firm was then known as the E. J. Howard, and as such
has turned out a vast fleet of magnificent steamers, as well as a large number
of smaller water craft for the Mississippi Valley and the Gulf coast rivers.
Boats have been built at his yards for the waters of Central America, and the
first large steamers to ply the Yukon river in Alaska were contsructed by him,
shipped to Dutch Harbor and put together there. For beauty, speed and construction the boats from the Howard yards at Jeffersonville stand as the peer
of any on the rivers of the West, and all show the result of the experience and
skill at the head of the business. Captain Howard's business ability is not
limited to the plant at Jeffersonville, for in 1905 he acquired the Marine
Ways at Cincinnati, Madison, Paducah, Kentucky; and Mound City, Illinois,
all operated under separate organizations except the plants at Madison and
Jeffersonville. At present this business, known as the Howard Shipyards
Company, is the most extensive inland ship building industry in the United
States. It has been in continuous operation since 1848 with the exception of
a short period in 1860. At times the ship yard at Jeffersonville has employed
as many as four hundred men, and it is considered one of the most successful
businesses of the kind in the United States.

Captain Howard was married to Laura Burke, a native of Louisville,
Kentucky, on January 6, 1863. Their two sons, Clyde and James, are both
interested in the business with their father, Clyde being the secretary and
treasurer of the concern and James the vice-president.

Besides Captain Howard's business at the local ship yards and Marine
Ways, he is a director in the First National Bank, and the Citizens' National
Bank of Jeffersonville.

In politics he is a Democrat, and while a resident of Jeffersonville, served
as Councilman from his ward for several years. During the War of the Rebellion he served as a member of the Home Guards, but participated in no

30

active service. He and his family are members of St. Paul's Episcopal church, where he served as vestryman for a number of years.

Captain Howard's residence in Port Fulton, just above Jeffersonville, and overlooking the ship yards, is one of the finest in Southern Indiana, and the grounds which surround it, including one whole city block, are evidence of a love of home which is one of his strong characteristics.

Elsewhere in this volume will be found the history of the Howard Ship Yards from 1834 to 1909.

REV. FRANCIS MARION BROCK.

This name is well known in Wood township, Clark county, where Reverend Brock has maintained his home all his life, where his parents were numbered among the pioneers.

Francis Marion Brock was born in Wood township in 1849, the son of Michael and Elizabeth (Stover) Brock. Michael Brock's father, George Brock, is believed to have come from North Carolina. He was a Baptist minister and a man of considerable prominence in his time. His wife was Elizabeth McKinley before her marriage. Elizabeth Stover was the daughter of Daniel Stover, of Virginia, who located in Jackson township, Washington county, Indiana, where he died, having reached the remarkable age of one hundred and four years. His wife was Polly Ann Carvia before her marriage. All these ancestors of Francis Marion Brock were influential in their respective communities and were people of much sterling worth, and many of the admirable traits which they manifested are today exemplified in the gentleman whose name introduces this sketch.

Francis Marion Brock has lived in Wood township all his life. He was educated in the public schools and at May's Academy at Salem, Indiana. He was an ambitious student and applied himself to his studies in the most arduous manner which resulted in his receiving a good education. Early in life he decided that his true "bent" was in teaching and accordingly began to prepare himself for this profession, which he followed with unqualified success for a period of seventeen years, at the same time preaching the Gospel in such a manner that he became one of the most useful men of his locality. His services as an educator were eagerly sought after and he was in constant demand in the various capacities of a minister. He is still a minister in the Christian church and is at this writing pastor of Chapel Hill church in Floyd county. He also preaches at Canton, Washington county, and at Old Zoah, Scott county. Wherever he preaches he is always greeted by large congregations.

Reverend Brock's domestic life began in 1872 when he was united in marriage with Abigail Brown, a native of Wood township. She is the daughter of Henry and Nancy Brown, and to this union three children have been born, namely: Thomas J. Brock, an attorney living in Jeffersonville and John B. Brock, who is teaching school in Wood township. One of the subject's children is deceased.

Reverend Brock is a member of New Providence Lodge, No. 237, Free and Accepted Masons. He is one of the oldest Masons in this lodge, and his daily life gives evidence that he believes in fostering the sublime principles taught by this ancient order. He has filled all the offices in the local lodge.

Mrs. Brock is the representative of a Southern family, her mother having been a native of Tennessee, and her father, who was the son of Isaac and Nancy Brown, were from North Carolina and Virginia, respectively. Mrs. Brock's mother's maiden name was Nancy Rippy. Her father was John Rippy, a native of Tennessee, and her mother was Elizabeth (Robinson) Rippy, also a native of Tennessee.

ELI M. LINDLEY.

The paternal branch of Mr. Lindley's family has been identified with the South from a very remote period, the genealogy being traced through a number of generations to the early history of Virginia and North Carolina, in both commonwealths the name appearing in connection with the founding and growth of various localities. Maternally he is descended from ancestors who moved from the North in an early day and settled in the Middle West and a few years prior to 1820 his mother's parents located in Clark county, Illinois, and became actively identified with the history of the old town of York on the Wabash, at that time the metropolis of the southeastern part of the state and a place of much importance and promise.

Abraham Lindley, Eli M.'s father, a native of Virginia, was born in 1801, married when still a young man, Maria Curtis, whose birth occurred at York, Illinois, in the year 1820, this couple spent the greater part of their married life in Powhattan, Arkansas, and it was there that their respective deaths occurred, the father's in 1865, the mother's in the year 1875. Of their family of five sons and two daughters but three are living, namely: Mrs. Callie McNaughton, of Jeffersonville, Indiana; T. J. Lindley, a successful merchant and prominent citizen of the same place, and Eli M. of this review.

Eli M. Lindley was born at Powhattan, Arkansas, on the 15th day of September, 1851, and until his sixteenth year, lived on a farm and became familiar with the rugged duties and wholesome discipline of outdoor life in the fields, meantime attending the public schools during the winter months and by diligent application made substantial progress in his studies but was unable to finish his education by reason of entering upon an apprenticeship at the age indicated to learn the tinner's trade. After serving five years at Powhattan and Pocahontas and becoming a proficient workman he was married on February 5, 1871, to Elvira Rainwater, of Alabama, but since her childhood a resident of Lawrence county Arkansas, immediately following which event he set up his domestic establishment on a farm and during the ensuing six years devoted his attention to the pursuit of agriculture. At the expiration of that period he discontinued tilling the soil and moving to Jeffersonville, Indiana, entered the employ of his brother, T. J. Lindley, who had preceded him to that city by ten years and who, during that time, had been engaged in the mercantile business.

After remaining with his brother two years Mr. Lindley in 1885 resigned his position and established the business in which he has since been engaged, the hardware trade, including stoves, house furnishings, tin and sheet iron and in connection with the commercial line he also conducts a large manufacturing establishment devoted to all kinds of tin and sheet iron ware and general repair work. He began operations by purchasing the stock of Gibson & Neal, who, at the time designated, had a fairly well established trade, but since then he has greatly enlarged the scope of the business, increasing the stock from time to time, adding new lines and building up a patronage second to no other enterprise of the kind in the city and earning much more than local repute in industrial and commercial circles. In addition to the lines of trade indicated above he is now doing an extensive and far-reaching business in the manufacture of pumps and pump fixtures, this with his other manufacturing interests affording steady employment for twelve mechanics, but during the busy seasons he is frequently obliged to employ a much larger force in order to meet the demands of the trade.

He has been one of the Democratic leaders of Jeffersonville and Clark county, having represented his city as City Treasurer for a period of four years besides rendering valuable service to his party during the progress of campaigns. Another evidence of his enterprising spirit is his membership with the ancient and honorable order of Masonry, in addition to which he also belongs to the Elks and Odd Fellows, having been honored with important official positions in their different fraternities. In his religious belief he subscribes to the creed of the Methodist Episcopal church, South, but is liberal in his views, believing all churches to be agencies in the hands of God for the redemption of the race and assisting by his means and influence in disseminating the Gospel among men both at home and abroad. In a financial way he has met with well earned success, being the possessor of an ample competence and admirably situated to enjoy the fruits of his many years of labor and good management, owning a beautiful and attractive home in Jeffersonville.

Mr. and Mrs. Lindley are popular in the social circle in which they move. Of their three children, two are living, a daughter by the name of Lillian, who is the wife of Jefferson D. Rainey, a business man of Jeffersonville. A son, Roy I., a young man of twenty-one, a graduate of the New Albany Business College and at the present time bookkeeper in his father's business establishment. William, the second in order of birth, died when five years old. Mrs. Rainey, the daughter, is not only an accomplished business women, but is also a lady of fine domestic tastes, besides being the mother of three bright and interesting children, who answer to the names of Fern, Josephine and Kenneth.

JAMES E. TAGGART.

A member of the law firm of Burtt & Taggart, Jeffersonville, and one of Clark county's native sons is James E. Taggart, who was born in Charlestown on the 1st day of July, 1858. His ancestors on both sides were among the early pioneers of Southern Indiana, his maternal grandfather, Samuel McCampbell, settling in Clark county about the beginning of the last century, the Taggart family moving to this part of the state some years later. James Taggart was the subject's paternal grandfather, a native of Ireland, came to the United States in 1817 and after a brief residence in the city of Philadelphia migrated to Tennessee, thence to Kentucky and about 1833 moved to Clark county, Indiana, locating on a farm near Charlestown, where he resided until his removal to that town in the year 1850. He was a physician by profession and practiced the healing art in Clark county from the time of his arrival until advancing age obliged him to retire to private life, after which he spent the remainder of his days in Charlestown, dying in that town when eighty years of age.

Samuel C. Taggart, son of James and father of the subject, was also a physician and followed his profession in Clark county for a number of years, meeting with encouraging success in his practice. He graduated from the Medical College in Louisville, Kentucky, after which he devoted his attention to his chosen calling for about thirty years, having long enjoyed an honorable reputation as an able and skillful physician and surgeon.

Cynthia E. McCampbell, daughter of Samuel McCampbell, was born in Clark county, became the wife of Samuel C. Taggart when a young man and bore him three children, Charles, James E., of this review, and Jennie, now Mrs. C. E. Lewis, of Charlestown, the first named dying in infancy. Samuel C. Taggart was a man of high social standing in his community and for many years bore an active and influential part in the affairs of Charlestown and Clark county, having been Clerk of the Circuit Court from 1880 to 1884, inclusive, besides serving ten years as president of the First National Bank at Jeffersonville. He was originally a Whig, but after the old party of that name had fulfilled its mission and passed out of existence he became a Republican and continued as such to the end of his days, wielding a strong influence in political circles and enjoying distinctive prestige as a leader of his party. He lived an active and eminently useful life and at the age of seventy-three was called from the scenes of his earthly trials and triumphs, his death being widely lamented and felt as a personal loss by all who were favored with his friendship and acquaintance. Mrs. Taggart, a lady of estimable character and fit companion and helpmeet to her distinguished husband, departed this life at the age of sixty-two years. This excellent couple were deeply religious.

James E. Taggart attended the public schools in his youth and later pursued the higher branches of study in Barnett Academy at Charlestown, the training thus received being afterwards supplemented by a course at Hanover College, where he laid the intellectual foundation upon which his subsequent success in one of the most responsible and exacting of the learned professions was based. Having decided to devote his life to the law he began the study of the same soon after completing his collegiate course and in due time entered the College of Law at Chicago, where he made rapid progress in the profession and earned an honorable record.

Mr. Taggart was admitted to the bar of Clark county county in 1885 and immediately thereafter became associated with Henry A. Burtt, of Jeffersonville, with whom he has since practiced, the firm thus constituted being one of the oldest law partnerships in the city as well as one of the best known and most successful. Ever since his admission to the bar his name has been connected with many of the important cases tried in the courts of Clark and adjacent counties. In his professional character he enjoys the confidence of his fellow members of the Jeffersonville Bar, and the general public, and his career, steady and substantial rather than spasmodic and brilliant, has been marked by continuous advancement and signal success.

His financial success has been commensurate with the ability and energy displayed in his professional career and he is today the possessor of an ample competency and one of the financially solid and reliable men of the city in which he resides.

The domestic chapter in the life of Mr. Taggart dates from 1885, on September 24th of which year was solemnized his marriage with Nettie B. Winesburg, of Jeffersonville, daughter of John P. Winesburg, a merchant of the city and one of its well known and substantial business men. Mr. and Mrs. Taggart are the parents of two children, Jennie and Samuel Clarence, both at home, the former being a graduate of the Jeffersonville high school, and the latter now in the fifth grade of the Jeffersonville schools.

In religious faith Mr. and Mrs. Taggart subscribe to the Calvinistic creed and for some years past they have been respected members of the First Presbyterian church of Jeffersonville, in which organization Mr. Taggart holds the position of elder.

CAPT. GEORGE W. COWARD.

A view at the strenuous and honorable career of Capt. George W. Coward, United States Claims Attorney, Jeffersonville, and one of the well known and highly esteemed men of the city, shows him to be a Kentuckian by birth and one of five children, whose parents were Joel Milton and Charlotte (Ellingsworth) Coward, natives of Tennessee and Indiana, respectively.

Joel M. Coward, whose birth occurred near Greenville, Tennessee, in the year 1815, was a mechanic in early life but later became superintendent of a large plantation in Jefferson county, Kentucky, in which capacity he served for a number of years. In 1854 he engaged in the hotel business at Jeffersontown, which he continued successfully until the breaking out of the Civil war when he located his family in Louisville in June, 1861, and the following September he became a member of Company D, Thirty-fourth Kentucky Infantry and was made second lieutenant, subsequently on account of meritorious conduct becoming captain of his company, which position he held until his discharge by reason of disability in March, 1864. Returning to Louisville on quitting the service he made that city his home the remainder of his days, dying August 26, 1873, from the effects of injuries received while in the army. Mrs. Coward survived her husband thirteen years, departing this life at Charlestown, Indiana, on the 9th day of August, 1886. Of the five children of this estimable couple that grew to maturity the oldest is Mrs. Louisa K. Knight, who lives in the town of Vesta, Clark county. Mrs. Millie J. Tyler, the second of the family, died at Louisville, Kentucky, in the year 1896; George W., of this review, being the next in order of birth; William Wallace, a farmer living near Vesta, is the second son, and Mrs. Jessie B. Winter, who died in 1897 in Louisville, was the youngest of the family.

Capt. George W. Coward, whose birth occurred in Jefferson county, Kentucky, on the 19th of October, 1842, received his early education in the subscription schools of his native state. Inheriting a tendency to study and an ardent love of books he availed himself of every opportunity to improve his mind, and while in the army he sought the assistance of those capable of instructing him in certain of the higher branches, besides devoting every leisure moment when not occupied to the perusal of such books as he was enabled to secure. He served an apprenticeship at stone and marble cutting and after becoming a proficient workman found employment in Louisville, where he was engaged until the breaking out of the rebellion, when he exchanged the tools of his trade for the death-dealing implements of war.

Soon after the beginning of hostilities Mr. Coward's employer, Lewis H. Ferrell, organized Company D of the Thirty-fourth Kentucky Infantry and was made captain of the same and it was in this command that George W. and his father enlisted, the latter serving with an honorable record for a period of three years and four months, during which time his regiment formed part of the Twenty-third Army Corps under General Schofield and took part in all of the skirmishes and battles of the East Tennessee campaign. George W. Coward was made a commissioned officer in April, 1863, and in due time rose to the command of his company before his twenty-first year, which fact speaks much for his efficiency as a soldier and for the trust reposed in him by his superiors as well as by the members of his company. In 1864, by unanimous vote of his company, he was chosen to command the same during the absence of the captain on detached service and held the position of captain and drew pay as such during the last six months of his service and in this as in other capacities proved a brave and gallant soldier until honorably discharged, January 28, 1865. His record is without a blemish and one of which any defender of the national honor might well feel proud.

On retiring from the army Captain Coward engaged in the contracting for street paving and other kind of stone work in Louisville, where he remained until 1875 when he removed to Charlestown. After continuing contracting for four years in the latter city he abandoned the business and turned his attention to the collecting and prosecuting of claims, pensions, back-pay and other legal work of similar character, in the meantime having been regularly admitted to practice before all the departments at Washington, D. C., and empowered to transact such business as came within the province of his profession. Since the year 1879 he has had all he could well do in the matter of claims, pensions, bounties, back-pay, etc., and his business is still large and lucrative and takes very wide range, his clients coming from all parts of Southern Indiana and Northern Kentucky and representing many thousands of dollars every year. In the prosecution of his business he is exceedingly careful and methodical, sparing no pains in looking after the interests of his clients and it's a compliment worthily bestowed to say that in no intsance has he proven unworthy of the trust which the people repose in his integrity and honor. Since July, 1900, he has maintained his office and residence in Jeffersonville.

Captain Coward was married on March 17th of the year 1870, to Lucy McGarvey, of Middletown, Kentucky, a union terminated by the death of the wife on July 14, 1873, after bearing him two children, Clyde S. and John Claude, both deceased. On September 7, 1886, the captain married his present wife, Iadna (Tyler) Oglesbey, daughter of William J. Tyler and widow of William H. Oglesbey. By her previous marriage Mrs. Coward had a son by the name of Tyler Oglesbey, who is now a lawyer practicing his profession in the city of Louisville.

In his political affiliations Captain Coward is a pronounced Republican and as such wields a strong influence for his party in Jeffersonville and Clark county. He is an active member of the local Grand Army of the Republic post, in which he has held every office within the gift of the organization and is also identified with the Order of the Golden Cross, in which he has been honored with important official positions from time to time. His activity and influence in the former society with which he has been connected for over twenty-five years has brought him prominently to the notice of the leaders in Indiana and other states, having held a number of offices in the department to which he belongs, including that of senior vice-commander of the department and attended many of the national encampments and other gatherings. Religiously the captain and his wife adhere to the Methodist faith and are members of the church in Jeffersonville.

CHARLES A. SCHIMPFF.

Charles A. Schimpff, the present efficient and popular comptroller of the city of Jeffersonville, was born March 18, 1847, in Rhenish, Bavaria, Germany, being one of eight children, whose parents, August Rudolph and Magdalena (Landes) Schimpff, were also natives of the Fatherland, as were their ancestors for generations beyond the memory of man. The father, a candle maker by trade and a most excellent citizen, departed this life on the 17th day of January, 1848, when but thirty-eight years of age; the mother survived him about eighteen years, dying at Louisville, Kentucky, in May, 1864, in her fifty-second year, having been a resident of that city from 1854 until her demise. Of the eight children born to August R. and Magdalena Schimpff, four survive, namely: Gustav A., confectioner, of Jeffersonville; Susan M., wife of Louis Spelger, of Louisville, Kentucky; Charles A., of this review, and August R., a bookkeeper for a real estate firm in San Diego, California. The deceased members of the family were Rudolph A., a member of "The Louisville Legion" in the Civil war, killed at the battle of Chickamauga; Adolph G., also a soldier in the army of the Union during the great rebellion, who died at Dayton, Ohio, from injuries received in the battle of Shiloh; Augusta Neeb died in Cincinnati, as did also a daughter by the name of Kate, who, at the time of her death, was the wife of Michael Schmitthenner.

Charles A. Schimpff spent the first eleven years of his life in the land of his birth and in 1858 came to America, locating at Louisville, Kentucky, where, during the ensuing two years, he attended the public schools and acquired a fairly thorough knowledge of the English language. At the expiration of the period indicated he entered a confectionery establishment for the purpose of learning the trade and by diligent attention and consecutive effort in due time became quite a skillful workman, besides becoming familiar with every other feature of the business with the object in view of making it his life work.

In 1868 he came to Jeffersonville and opened a confectinery establishment, which he conducted with fair success during the ensuing seventeen years, but at the end of that time closed out the business and engaged in the book trade, starting in 1885, which, under his efficient management, soon grew into a large and important concern and became one of the leading commercial enterprises of the place. To this line of business Mr. Schimpff has since devoted his attention the meantime building up a large and lucrative trade in books, stationery, wall paper, office supplies, etc., of which he carries full and complete lines and his place is now one of the best known in the city. From a somewhat modest beginning he has gradually enlarged the scope of his operations, adding to his stock to meet the demands of the trade and at the present time his patronage takes a wide range, his establishment being the largest and most successful of the kind in Jeffersonville and the center of supplies for a number of other tradesmen in the city and elsewhere. He takes great pride in his business and has spared neither pains nor expense to make it meet the popular demand. Financially his success has kept pace with the energy and enterprise displayed in his business affairs and he is now classed with the solid men of the community.

In public matters he has long been deeply interested and as a life long Republican and political worker his judicious counsel has tended greatly to the success of his party besides winning for himself the recognition which his services so well deserve. For a period of eight years he has held the office of Police Commissioner, to which he was first appointed by Governor Mount and later by Governors Durbin and Hanly successively and in recognition of his political services he was appointed as City Comptroller, the duties of which responsible position he has since discharged in the able and businesslike manner characteristic of the man.

Mr. Schimpff has been secretary of the German Reformed church of Jeffersonville since 1878 and superintendent of the Sunday school during the greater part of the interim, besides being otherwise actively engaged in religious and benevolent work.

Mr. Schimpff was married in the year 1873 to Alvina Roessler, of Louisville, who has borne him the following children, all living: Charles J., his father's business associate; A. Rudolph, manager of the Daily Star and Weekly Republican and one of the well known and successful newspaper men of Jeffersonville; Emma, wife of Prof. S. L. Scott, superintendent of the Clark county public schools; Alvin, chief draughtsman of the Cincinnati Car Company; Alma, Mrs. Fred Gehle, of Cincinnati; John, Mildred, William, Thomas G. and Edith are still members of the home circle.

Mr. Schimpff has traveled quite extensively in both the old and new world, visiting nearly every country in Europe and many places of historic interest there besides seeing all parts of the United States and becoming acquainted with its phenomenal resources and wonderful progress. He is a very close student and a great reader and is well informed on many subjects.

THOMAS W. PERRY.

Among the native sons of Clark county who have gained honorable recognition in business circles and high standing in the service of the public is Thomas W. Perry, the present efficient and popular City Treasurer of Jeffersonville. Mr. Perry was born September 7, 1860, in Utica township, and is a scion of one of the early families of that part of the county, his grandfather, a native of Pennsylvania, settling there many years ago and taking an active and influential part in the material development of the country. Redford R. Perry, Thomas W.'s father, accompanied his parents to Clark county when a boy and spent the remainder of his life in Utica as an enterprising and prosperous business man, dying in that town in 1881, at the age of sixty-one years. Letitia Robinson, wife of Redford Perry, was born and reared in Bethlehem township, Clark county, and, like her husband, was a descendant of one of the early settlers, her father, Rev. William Robinson, a native of Scotland, and for many years a well known Presbyterian divine, moving to Southern Indiana in pioneer times and locating a home in the township of Bethlehem. Mrs. Perry was a woman of beautiful character, a devoted wife and mother, and departed this life in the month of March, 1891, when seventy-four years of age.

Of the nine children born to Redford R. and Letitia Perry, two only are living, the subject of this review, who was the fifth in order of birth, and Samuel R., the youngest of the family, who is now engaged in the marble and granite business at Columbus, Indiana. Catherine R., who also grew to maturity, became the wife of Theodore Perry and was called from earth at the age of thirty-eight years. Gertrude lived to be twenty years old. The other five died in infancy.

Thomas W. Perry spent his early life in his native town of Utica and after obtaining a fair education in the public schools entered a school of pharmacy in Cincinnati, where in due time he completed the prescribed course and fitted himself for a business career. Beginning life for himself as a drug clerk when but seventeen years old, he soon acquired great proficiency in his chosen calling and by reason of his professional training, it was not long until he became manager of one of the largest and most successful pharmaceutical establishments in the city of Jeffersonville. After a three years' clerkship he engaged in the drug trade upon his own responsibility and during the ensuing twenty years built up a large and lucrative business in Jeffersonville.

Mr. Perry demonstrated marked ability as a business man and his success as such, together with his broad views and active influence in civic matters, in due time brought him prominently before the public with the result that he became a local leader of the Democratic party and one of the successful politicians of his city and county. Disposing of his business interests in 1900, he turned his attention to other matters until September, 1904, when he was elected City Treasurer of Jeffersonville, the duties of which responsible position he has since discharged in an eminently able and satisfactory manner, fully meeting the high expectations of his friends and justifying the wisdom of his choice. Personally, he commands the esteem of the people of the city, irrespective of political alignment, as a trusted official.

As a Democrat Mr. Perry takes a keen interest in the success of his party and in the general trend of national, state and local political events. His integrity of purpose is firmly established and his devotion to the public weal has been conspicuously demonstrated during his services thus far in one of the people's most important trusts. He was a member of the City Council from May, 1894, to May, 1898, and while in that body participated actively in all its deliberations, besides serving on a number of the leading committees and bringing about much important municipal legislation. For two years he was a member of the City School Board, resigning the latter position in 1904 to accept the treasureship. Fraternally he is identified with a number of secret and benevolent orders, belonging to Clark Lodge, No. 40, Free and Accepted Masons, Horeb Chapter, Royal Arch Masons, Jeffersonville Commandery, Knights Templar and Valley Lodge, No. 57, Knights of Pythias at Utica.

Mr. Perry's domestic experience dates from December, 1882, when he was united in marriage with Rosabel Bennett, a native of Clark county and daughter of S. J. Bennett, an enterprising farmer and respected citizen of Prather township, the union resulting in the birth of three children: Ethel M., now Mrs. Samuel Barrett, of San Diego, California; Irwin R. and Halbert. The mother of these children dying April 10, 1890, Mr. Perry on June 29th of the following year contracted a matrimonial alliance with Cora A. Swartz, of Utica, a daughter, Letitia, being the only child of this marriage. Mrs. Perry passed to her reward July 10, 1907. The third marriage of Mr. Perry occurred December 29, 1908, to Mrs. Nellie Field, daughter of Charles S. Ferguson, of Jeffersonville.

In his religious views Mr. Perry subscribes to the Presbyterian creed and with his wife worships with the church of that denomination in Jeffersonville. Both are well known in the best social circles of the city.

JEFFERSON D. GOYNE.

The family of this name are of old Virginia origin, and members of it have been long settled in the historic county of Henrico. As this locality adjoins Richmond it suffered much during the Civil war by the marching and countermarching of the contending armies. The old plantation that supported generations of Goynes is still in the possession of descendants, being owned undivided by two brothers, Joseph Goyne, who was of Scotch-Irish ancestry, married Martha Vaughn, of German descent, and several children were born to them, the only survivors being Allen, now in the West, and Jefferson D. The latter was born near Richmond, Virginia, May 15, 1866, and his mother died at his birth. Three years later he lost his father by death, but was provided with a home by John W. Barnhill, at Owensboro, Kentucky, with whom he lived until the completion of his majority. He was educated by his uncle Barnhill in the public and private schools of Kentucky and later was apprenticed to learn the trade of a machinist. As a journeyman he secured employment at the works of the American Car & Foundry Company in Jeffersonville, and remained there eight years in the tool dressing and saw filing departments. Subsequently he embarked in the mercantile business, but suffered a loss of some six thousand dollars as the result of fire that destroyed his entire stock of goods. After this disaster he returned to his old home farm in Henrico county, but eventually returned to Indiana to start life over again. He was Town Clerk of Port Fulton for over six years and in 1906 was elected Justice of the Peace for Jeffersonville township. He is a member of the Knights of Pythias, the Benevolent and Protective Order of Elks and the Modern Woodmen of America. His political affiliations have always been with the Democratic party and his religious connections with the Methodists.

In 1890 Mr. Goyne married Alice Eliza White, a resident of Port Fulton, but a native of New Albany. She is a daughter of William H. White, a well known citizen of Port Fulton, and graduated at the Jeffersonville high school.

Mr. and Mrs. Goyne have two sons and two daughters, Arminta, the eldest, was born April 25, 1892; Catherine, March 3, 1895; Erol Jefferson, April 5, 1899, and William C., March 15, 1904. Mr. Goyne is popular both as a citizen and an official. In all the positions he has held, whether political, clerical, judicial or business, he has so discharged his duties as to gain the reputation of being a conscientious, square-dealing man. In politics he is a good mixer and he has many friends among all classes of people who respect him for his upright life. He has the old Virginia cordiality of greeting and inherited from his ancestors a love of home and the hospitality that goes so far in making home life enjoyable.

GEORGE W. FINLEY.

Mr. Finley enjoys the distinction of being, with a single exception, the oldest photographer in the state of Indiana, having spent fifty consecutive years in his profession and achieved honorable distinction as an artist of merit and skill.

George W. Finley is a Southern man, hailing from Patrick county, Virginia, where his birth occurred on the 14th of November, 1831. His parents, George H. and Sallie (Penn) Finley, natives of the same county and state, were of Irish descent and representatives of old and highly esteemed families that figured auspiciously in the affairs of their respective places of residence, their antecedents migrating to this country at a very early period and becoming quite well known in the pioneer history of the above county. George H. Finley, a farmer by occupation, spent the greater part of his life in his native commonwealth and died when his son, George W., was in his seventh year; his wife survived him a number of years, departing this life in the town of Bainbridge, Ross county, Ohio, when but two days of the ninetieth anniversary of her birth. When fifteen years of age George W. Finley accompanied the family to New Petersburg, Ohio, and shortly after his arrival followed the bent of his early and cherished inclinations by entering a gallery to learn the art of photography.

After acquiring sufficient knowledge and skill to make the business a success Mr. Finley worked at different places until 1863, when he organized a company of carpenters for service in the Civil war, and spent the ensuing year in the employ of the government, devoting the greater part of the time to the construction of hospitals, quarter-master's buildings and other carpentry work at Camp Nelson, Kentucky. At the expiration of his period of service in 1864 he came to Indiana, but within a short time went to Danville, Kentucky, thence to Louisville, in 1865, where he followed his profession until his removal to Charlestown, Clark county, Indiana, two years later.

Mr. Finley in August, 1867, opened a gallery at Charlestown and conducted a very successful business until 1870, when he disposed of his establishment and sought a larger and more promising field for the exercise of his artistic skill, in the city of Jeffersonville, where he has since resided, the meanwhile building up a large and lucrative patronage.

During the fifty years which he has devoted to his profession he has been untiring in his efforts to keep in touch with the latest results of scientific research and prove himself an artist in the modern sense of the term. In common with the majority of men he has encountered discouragements and met with reverses of fortune, but in the main his career has been characterized by a series of advancements.

Mr. Finley has been twice married, the first time on December 15, 1863, to Kate Dawson, of Cincinnati, who bore him four children, two of whom are deceased, those surviving being Harry W. and Grace Young, both residing in Louisville. His second marriage, which was solemnized with Kate Hunter, of Canada, is without issue. Mr. and Mrs. Finley are highly esteemed among their neighbors and acquaintances and have many warm friends in the city and move in an eminently respectable social circle. They belong to the Presbyterian church, take an active part in all lines of religious and charitable work under the auspices of the local congregation with which identified and strive to make their daily lives correspond with the faith which they profess. Since the year 1864 Mr. Finley has been a member of the Masonic fraternity, but by reason of a partial deafness has recently been demitted, although still an enthusiastic believer in the truths of the order and a great admirer of the principles and precepts upon which it is based. In politics he is firm in his adherence to the Republican party, but has never sought office or aspired to any kind of public honors.

————

WENDELL BROWN.

Mr. Brown is an American by adoption, only, being a native of Germany, born on the 10th day of October, 1849, in Baden, grew to manhood and received his education in that kingdom, but in 1872 decided to try his fortune in the great republic beyond the sea, where he was satisfied better opportunities could be found than in the land of his birth. In the meantime his brothers, Ludwig and Rudolph, had found homes and employment in the United States and it was largely upon their solicitations that he was induced to bid farewell to the Fatherland and carve out a new career under new conditions in a country where the accident of birth cut little figure and the means of obtaining a competency were open to all.

In due time Mr. Brown rejoined his brothers who had located in Jeffersonville, Indiana, and it was not long until he secured employment at the ship yard at Port Fulton, where he was obliged to work at the hardest of manual labor to obtain a livelihood. About seven years after his arrival he was united in marriage to Mary Letzler, who is also of German birth, and from that time until 1892 devoted all his energies to manual toil with the result that his earnings, barely sufficed for the support of himself and growing family.

In the latter year Mr. Brown engaged in the liquor business at Port Fulton, and since that time has conducted a very decent, orderly establishment, and met with encouraging success. His patronage consists very largely of the employees of the ship yard and coal boatman, and his place has the reputation of being one of the most quiet and law abiding resorts of the kind in the city, being conducted in an eminently respectable manner, nothing of a disorderly nature being permitted on the premises.

It is worthy of note that Mr. Brown did not embark on his present business from choice, but rather from necessity, as he found it almost impossible to provide for the needs of his family at the poorly paid labor which he followed so long and which had he not abandoned in time would ultimately have undermined his health and physical strength, and reduced himself and those dependent upon him to dire poverty. As a means of bettering his condition he finally opened the place of which he is still proprietor.

Mr. Brown has so conducted himself as to gain the esteem of the public. He takes an active interest in municipal affairs and for about ten years represented his ward in the Common Council in which capacity he labored zealously for the city and proved an able and faithful servant of the people. In politics he is a Democrat, but not a partisan, and with the exception of the above office has never held nor aspired to public position. He owns a substantial home which is enlivened by the presence of his wife and four children, namely: Emma, Andrew, Harry and Clara.

In matters religious Mr. Brown and family adhere to the Catholic faith and belong to the German speaking church of that denomination in Jeffersonville. Among their many friends and acquaintances they bear an honorable name.

CHARLES A. SCHWANINGER.

Progressive in the broadest sense of the term, Charles A. Schwaninger, proprietor of the large drug and pharmaceutical establishment at 528 Spring street, Jeffersonville, Indiana, which bears his name, is a native of this city, and dates his birth from September 27, 1878. His father, the late Abraham Schwaninger, for many years one of the distinguished citizens of Clark county, held several important official positions in Jeffersonville, having served as Mayor of the city, and at the time of his death, October 16, 1906, was Judge of the Municipal Court, in both of which he acquitted himself with signal honor. As the name implies the Schwaninger family is of German origin, although Charles A.'s paternal ancestors lived for many generations in the Republic of Switzerland, of which country the above Abraham was a native. He was brought to the United States when quite young, and grew to maturity in Jeffersonville, where as a young man, he married Sarah A. Carwardine, whose birth occurred in England, but who, like her husband, spent nearly all her life in the city in which both became residents in childhood. Mrs. Schwaninger, who is still living at a good old age, is a woman of beautiful character and many sterling qualities of head and heart not a few of which have been reproduced in her children. Aneina, the oldest of the family, is the wife of Lewis Gridler, superintendent of the Belknap Cement Company, of Louisville; Williacy J., the second in order of birth, was formerly the business associate of Charles A., but is now proprietor of a drug house of his own in Jeffersonville, and doing a very successful business. Agnes, now Mrs. Emil Kiel, lives in the city of New Albany, where her husband is engaged in the tobacco trade; Edith married Walter E. McCullough and resides on a farm in Jefferson township, the next in order of birth is Charles Abraham, of this review, after whom comes Jacob, an employe of the Pennsylvania Railroad Company, with headquarters in Jeffersonville, all but Charles A., being married and all doing well at their respective vocations.

Charles A. Schwaninger was reared and educated in his native city and while still a young man formulated his plans for the future by deciding to become a pharmacist. To fit himself for this important and responsible profession he entered in due time the Louisville School of Pharmacy, where he earned a creditable record as a close and critical student and from which he was graduated in the year 1898, standing among the first in his class. Previous to taking his professional course, however, he obtained a practical knowledge of the business by entering in 1895 the employ of Hawes and Perry, the leading druggists of the city, and after receiving his degree he became a partner of the latter gentleman, Mr. Hawes, retiring from the concern in 1898. Before the expiration of the following year, W. J. and Charles A. Schwaninger purchased Mr. Perry's interest and under the firm name of Schwaninger Brothers conducted the business with success and profit during the ensuing five years, at the end of which time the subject bought the entire stock and became sole proprietor which relation he has since sustained and in which he has built up the trade until his establishment is now the largest and one of the most extensively patronized of the kind in the city with a reputation in business circles much more than local.

Since taking sole charge of the business September 1, 1907, Mr. Schwaninger has made commendable progress and the enterprise in which he is engaged has rapidly grown in magnitude. Being well fitted by careful professional training for his chosen calling and possessing business ability of a high order, his career thus far has been one of activity and steady advancement.

31

He carries a complete line of all goods essential to the make-up of a first class drug store, which are displayed to the best advantage in a room one hundred twenty by twenty-four feet in area and equipped with all the necessary appliances required by an up-to-date establishment. In addition to this large and well arranged apartment is a basement fifty by twenty-four feet in which are kept a full and complete stock of paints, oils and other goods, including a fine line of liquors for medicinal purposes and the legitimate trade, the building throughout being complete in all of its parts and admirably adapted for the purpose to which it is devoted. Mr. Schwaninger handles only first class goods and caters to a trade which will not be satisfied with any other kind, hence his customers include the best people of the community.

He holds membership with the Benevolent and Protective Order of Elks and the Independent Order of Odd Fellows, and is also actively identified with the Apollo Athletic Club of Jeffersonville. Politically he is a Republican, but not a partisan and religiously subscribes to the Protestant Episcopal faith, belonging to St. Paul's church, to the support of which he is a liberal contributor. He bears an enviabe reputation in all circles.

GEORGE H. HOLZBOG.

The manufacture of wagons, carriages and other vehicles has long been among the leading industrial interests of Jeffersonville, and the largest enterprise of this kind at the present time is that operated under the firm name of George H. Holzbog & Brother, which has added much to the city's reputation as an important business center. The business was estabished in 1854 by George J. Holzbog, and has been in continuous operation ever since, either by himself or members of his family, having grown from a modest beginning to its present leading position among the industries of the place, affording at this time employment for fifty skilled mechanics every working day of the year, and doing an annual business of not less than three hundred thousand dollars. George J. Holzbog, a native of Germany, immigrated to the United States in the early fifties and located at Louisville, Kentucky, thence, after a brief residence, removed to Jeffersonville, Indiana, and in the year above indicated established the business which still bears his name and which he conducted with marked success until succeeded by his sons some years later. He was a fine mechanic, a successful business man and stood high as a public spirited citizen, doing much to advance the industrial interests of Jeffersonville and lending his influence to all worthy enterprise for the general welfare. He reared a family of four children and died in this city, leaving to his sons not only a well established business, but an honored name, which they regard as a priceless heritage. Sophia, the oldest of the family, married W. F. Seibert, a contractor, and lives in Jeffersonville; George H., whose name introduces this sketch, being the second in order of birth; Alfred M., the second son, is secretary of the Todd Manufacturing Company, of New Albany; Henry J., is the junior member of the present firm of Holzbog & Brother, one child dying in infancy.

George H. Holzbog was born in Jeffersonville, Indiana, on the 15th day of January, 1862, received his educational discipline in the city schools and at an early age entered his father's manufacturing establishment where, in due time, he mastered the principles of the trade and became a skillful workman. Inheriting a taste for mechanical pursuits and reared under the tutilage of a master of his craft, it is not strange that young Holzbog made rapid progress in the trade to which his energies devoted and become familiar with the business matters, for which he also manifested a decided inclinaton while still a mere lad. After acquiring proficiency as a mechanic he took up the work of wagon and carriage making with his father, and continued in the latter's employ until given an interest in the business after which the plant was operated for some years, under the name of Holzbog & Son, and as already stated, forged rapidly to the front among the city's important industrial interests.

On becoming a partner in the concern George H. Holzbog took charge of the plant as manager in which capacity he demonstrated ability of a high order and contributed largely to the growth and far reaching influence of the business. Upon the death of his father he became the head of the enterprise and with his brother, Henry J., as his associate, the business has since been conducted under the name of George H. Holzbog & Brother, being one of the best known and most successful of the kind in Jeffersonville, and with a reputation second to none in the industrial and business circles throughout the country.

Mr. Holzbog's career as a business man has been eminently creditable, and he stands today among the leaders of industry in his city. By adhering to the safe and conservative policies laid down by his father, and using his well matured judgment in carrying the same into effect, he has built up an establishment which has made him widely known as a successful manufacturer.

Mr. Holzbog was married in 1889, to Anna M. Pfau, daughter of George Pfau, a prominent citizen of Jeffersonville, and for many years closely identified with its material interests. Mrs. Holzbog is a native of Jeffersonville, was carefully educated in the schools of the same and has spent her life within the limits of the city, being a lady of many estimable qualities, well known and highly esteemed in the social circles and respected by all with whom she comes in contact. To Mr. and Mrs. Holzbog two children have been born, the older a daughter by the name of Alma M., being a lady of culture and refinement, a graduate of the Jeffersonville high school and of the Semple School of Louisville. After finishing her studies in the latter institution, she entered the Young Ladies' Seminary at Tarrytown-on-the-Hudson, New York, where she completed the prescribed course and earned an honorable record as a diligent and painstaking student. Desiring to add still further to her scholastic knowledge, she subsequently became a student of the Cheevy-Chase, at Washington, D. C., where she is now prosecuting her studies and researches with the object in view of fitting herself for a useful position in the world. Chester Connette, the second in order of birth, now sixteen years of age, is a student of the Jeffersonville schools and has made commendable progress in his studies, standing among the highest in his classes.

Mr. Holzbog and family attend the Presbyterian church to the faith of which they subscribe, and are active in religious and philanthropic work, contributing liberally to the material support of the local church with which identified, and assisting in spreading the truths of the Gospel throughout the world. In his political affiliations Mr. Holzbog is a Republican, but in local matters is independent, voting for the man instead of the party. Fraternally he belongs to the Masonic Order, in which he has risen to high degrees, including those of the Royal Arch Mason and Sir Knight, and he is also an active and influential member of the Benevolent and Protective Order of Elks.

EDWARD B. CAIN.

Mr. Cain, who occupies the responsible position of assistant secretary of the Bauer Machine Company, of Jeffersonville, was born in Louisville, Kentucky, on the 24th day of April, 1878, and is the only child born to Edward A. and Addie (Byron) Cain. He has in his veins both Irish and French blood. His paternal grandparents were natives of Ireland, and in youth immigrated to this country, settling at Sellersburg, this county. Both are now dead, having reached advanced ages. The subject's maternal grandparents were of direct French descent. Edward A. Cain was born in this county and his wife was born in Louisville, Kentucky. The former was in early life a cabinet maker, but later became superintendent of a coffin manufactory in Kentucky. He died at the early age of thirty years, and his widow subsequently became the wife of Daniel Cameron, of South Louisville.

Edward B. Cain's life thus far has been spent in the city of his birth and in Jeffersonville. He received a good education in the public schools and prepared for a business career by taking a complete course in the New Albany Business College. He has occupied his present position during the past two years and is giving most faithful and efficient service to the company with which he is identified.

On the 12th of January, 1899, Mr. Cain was united in marriage to Cora Mitchell, the daughter of James R. and Elizabeth Mitchell, of Jeffersonville, both now deceased. To this union have been born a son and a daughter, Edwin B. and Dorothy E. Politically Mr. Cain is a stanch believer in the doctrines embodied in the platform of the Republican party, and fraternally he is a member of Clark Lodge, No. 40, Free and Accepted Masons. He and his family are members of the Methodist Episcopal church.

The Bauer Manufacturing Company is one of the leading industrial concerns of Jeffersonville and is devoted to the production of machinery for the manufacture of harness. The institution numbers among his stockholders some of the leading business men of the community, George H. Holzbog being president of the company, and representatives of the concern are sent to every part of the United States. They put out none but goods of the very highest quality and now control practically the entire field in their line. Mr. Cain has been a definite factor in the remarkable success which has come to this concern and is held in the highest esteem by his fellow officials and all who come in contact with him.

FRANK R. M. GILBERT.

The gentleman whose name forms the caption to this brief sketch is the proprietor of one of the leading livery and feed barns in Jeffersonville, his business being located at 120 Maple street.

Mr. Gilbert was born in Jeffersonville on December 8, 1843, and is a son of Frank R. M. and Elizabeth (Reynolds) Gilbert, both natives of Kentucky, the former born in Hardin county in 1821 and the latter in Lancaster. They were married in Jeffersonville in 1842 and resided here during the remainder of their lives, the father dying in September, 1903, and the mother on January 12, 1907. They became the parents of eleven children, of whom Frank R. M. is the eldest. Of these, three sons and two daughters are now living, namely: Laura A., Hallie A., the wife of Clarence Beeler, of Elizabethtown, Kentucky; James L., an engineer on the Pennsylvania lines, though residing in Jeffersonville; Aubrey resides in Knoxville, Tennessee, and is employed as chief clerk with the Louisville & Nashville Railroad.

The subject's paternal grandfather, Squire Gilbert, was a Canadian by birth and during the War of 1812 he was drafted into the British army. Not being in sympathy with the mother country, he and four comrades escaped and joined the American army in New York. After leaving the military service he "laid" his land warrant in Hardin county, Kentucky, where he lived until 1836, when he removed to Jackson county, Indiana. Here he spent the remainder of his days, dying in 1864 and leaving many descendants.

Frank R. M. Gilbert received his education in the public schools of Jeffersonville, and in 1870 began his business career here as a liveryman, to which line of activity he has since devoted his attention.   Socially he is a member of Clark Lodge, No. 40, Free and Accepted Masons, while in politics he is a Democrat.   In church relations the family is identified with the Methodist Episcopal church South.

On October 26, 1869, Mr. Gilbert was united in marriage with Florence, A. Boyer, of Charlestown, a daughter of James A. and Charlotte Temple (Daily) Boyer, both parents being members of old families in the vicinity of Charlestown.   The Boyer's especially have been very prominent in the history of Clark county.   To Mr. and Mrs. Gilbert have been born eight children, six of whom are living, namely: Rufus, who is engaged in business in Atlanta, Georgia, is married and the father of four children; Charlotte Temple is the wife of E. G. Holmes, of Indianapolis; Paul J., of Manchester, Iowa, who was formerly a minister of the Methodist Episcopal church, resigned his pastoral work in order to enter what is known as the "singing evangelist" work in the Young Men's Christian Association; he is married and is the father of two children; William B. is married and resides at Indianapolis where he is employed with the Merchants' Dispatch; Laura A., at home; Howard W., at home, and two who died in early life.

JOSEPH G. SNIDER.

The subject of this sketch, who conducts a successful livery, sale and feed stable at 124 East Maple street, Jeffersonville, is a native son of the old Hoosier state, having been born at Utica, Clark county, on the 25th day of February, 1843.   He is a son of William H. and Elizabeth (Nealy) Snider. His paternal grandfather, John A. Snider, who was a native of North Carolina, came to Barren county, Kentucky, in an early day and there lived the remainder of his life.   William H. Snider was born near Asheville, North Carolina, in 1807, and when a mere boy accompanied his father on his emigration westward.   They came over the mountains in wagons and crossed the Ohio river into Indiana at Utica.   He was one of the earliest settlers of Utica township and had much to do with the early development and organization of the varied interests of that locality.   He assisted in the organization of the first Sunday school in that township and for a long period of twenty years he was postmaster at Utica, being appointed to the office under President Pierce's administration.   He died in 1878 and his widow survived him four years, passing away in 1882.   She was born in Clark county, Indiana, in 1815.   They were the parents of eleven children, all of whom grew to maturity, and eight of whom are now living. These children were as follows: Sarah, who is the widow of M. S. Hobson, lives in Utica; John Alexander died July 5, 1907; Lucinda, Mrs. Benjamin Smith, of Utica; William H., of Utica; Mary, Mrs. Poillon, of Jeffersonville; Joseph G., of this review; Julia, now deceased, who was the wife of P. H. Weeks; Delilah, deceased, who was the wife of Charles VanPelt; Laura is the widow of the late Prof. S. A. Chambers, who was a prominent educator and minister at Graniteville, South Carolina; James is a farmer in Jeffersonville township, this county, and Emma, Mrs. Dunn, of Utica township.

Joseph G. Snider was reared on a farm and received his education in the common schools of Utica township. During the War of the Rebellion, and before he had attained his majority, Mr. Snider enlisted, on August 14, 1862, as a Union soldier, becoming a member of Company B, Eighty-first Indiana Volunteer Infantry, which command was assigned to the Army of the Cumberland, under the command of General Rosecrans. His first baptism of fire was at Perryville, following which they were almost daily engaged in battles and skirmishes up to the battle of Stone River, which lasted two days, terminating in the terrific struggle at Chickamauga. The command then went on the Atlanta campaign, during which they were under constant fire for twenty-four days and nights, including the pitched engagements at Buzzard's Roost, Resaca, Tullahoma, Marietta, Peach Tree Creek, Kenesaw Mountain, the siege and battle at Atlanta and the fierce fight at Jonesboro. Returning then to Atlanta, the Fourth Corps, to which Mr. Snider's command belonged, was assigned to General Thomas's army which then returned towards Nashville. During this march, practically all the way from Columbia to Franklin, the Union forces were engaged in conflict with the enemy, culminating in the general engagement at Nashville, which practically disorganized the Confederate army. The remnant of Hood's army was chased down to Huntsville, Alabama, where the Union troops went into winter quarters. In the spring of 1865 the brigade to which Mr. Snider's regiment belonged went to Asheville, North Carolina, and prepared for battle, but news was received of General Lee's surrender and that hostilities had practically ceased. Thereupon the troops were marched to Nashville, Tennessee, and, on the 29th of June, 1865. Mr. Snider was honorably mustered out of the military service. He had faithfully served his country in her hour of peril, but was glad to again see the dove of peace settle over the land.

Mr. Snider returned to the parental home in Utica township, where he remained until the spring of 1869, when he went to Kansas and during the four following years he was in various parts of the West, including Indian Territory, Arkansas, Missouri and Texas. With two companions he drove a wagon into Texas and visited fourteen counties endeavoring to find a suitable place to locate. In 1872-3 he assisted in grading the roadbed of the Missouri,

Kansas & Texas Railway from Red River to Sherman, Texas. Deciding that the East was, after all, the most desirable place in which to reside, he started home by wagon, having traveled overland nearly three thousand miles without mishap. During the following fourteen years Mr. Snider was engaged in farming in Jeffersonville township, this county, at the end of which time he relinquished rural pursuits and engaged in the livery business in Jeffersonville, and during the subsequent years he has remained at the same stand. During these years he has conducted the business in such a way as to insure for him a full share of the business in this line. His convenient and well-equipped stable has a frontage of seventy-one feet and a depth of two hundred and thirteen feet, with forty stalls and abundant space for carriages, etc. His horses and carriages are all as good as can be found in any livery, the very best of service being at all times possible. Mr. Snider enjoys the best class of patronage and has found his business profitable and satisfactory.

On December 28, 1875, Mr. Snider married Elizabeth Oglesby, a union blessed by the birth of two sons, Edgar O., a young man of much promise, who was a bookkeeper for a business house in Louisville, died in his twentieth year; and Ernest DeHaven, who is secretary and treasurer of Mooney's Tanning Company at Columbus, Indiana. The latter married Elsie Lyle, of Columbus, and they are the parents of a son, Edgar. Mrs. Elizabeth Snider died in December, 1895, and in 1897 Mr. Snider married Mrs. Elizabeth (Robbins) Donahue. Mrs. Snider was, by her first marriage, the mother of three children, all of whom reside in Jeffersonville.

Religiously Mr. Snider is in sympathy with the creed of the Methodist Episcopal church, in which faith he was reared. Politically he is a Republican, being the only member of his family to affiliate with that party. Fraternally he is a member of the Knights of Pythias, the Rathbone Sisters, the Lincoln League, the Union Veterans' Union and Joel R. Sparr Post, No. 580, Grand Army of the Republic.

JACOB EDGAR GLOSSBRENNER.

The president of the Louisville and Jeffersonville Ferry Company is Jacob E. Glossbrenner, with headquarters at 122 Front street in the latter city, who is a native of Clark county, Indiana, born in Utica township, November 25, 1866. His father, John P. Glossbrenner, whose birth occurred in Jeffersonville, in the year 1842, spent the greater part of his life in his native city and served in the Civil war as a private in Company C, Forty-ninth Indiana Infantry, devoting three and a fourth years to the service of his country, during which time he took part in a number of noted campaigns and battles, and earned an honorable record as a soldier. At the close of the war he returned to Jeffersonville, where he was employed for a number of years, in the government department with which branch of the service he was identified at the time of his death, on the 15th of April, 1882. Rachael Catherine Swartz, wife of John J. Glossbrenner, and mother of Jacob E., was also a native of Jeffersonville, where her birth occurred on February 25, 1845. She was married in this city and is still a resident of the same, being the mother of four children, three of whom are living, the only daughter, Cora C., dying in infancy; the names of the surviving members of the family are Jacob Edgar, Herbert M., of Indianapolis, and James C., who is secretary of the company of which Jacob E. is the executive head.

Jacob Edgar Glossbrenner was reared in Jeffersonville, where he received his early education in the public schools and from infancy to the present time has been identified with the city and interested in its advancement and welfare. His first practical experience was as a dry goods clerk with his uncle, A. A. Swartz, whose employ he entered at the age of fifteen, and with whom he continued for a period of five years, during which time he applied himself very closely to his duties and not only became an efficient and popular salesman but acquired a knowledge of business which proved of great value to him in after years. The better to fit himself for a business life he took a commercial course in Bryant and Stratton Business College from which he was graduated in 1887, and shortly thereafter entered the employ of the Louisville and Jeffersonville Ferry Company, beginning in a somewhat modest capacity, but soon rising by successful promotions to higher and more important positions.

Mr. Glossbrenner was well prepared for the duties which devolved upon him and displayed such ability and faithfulness in discharging the same that he was soon given work requiring much greater responsibility and trust. As already indicated he passed successively from one of the lowest and subordinate positions to the higher and more responsible posts, being made superintendent and secretary of the company on April 1, 1898, and served in this dual capacity until promoted to the presidency on July 7, 1908. He has been connected with the company for a period of twenty-one years, during which time he has managed its affairs in an able and businesslike manner. In his present position he is much in the public view, the passing years have continually added to his reputation as an official, while his high standing in social and business circles have gained for him a place among the enterprising citizens of the city in which he resides.

Mr. Glossbrenner, on the 16th day of January, 1895, contracted a matrimonial alliance with Estelle Lutz, daughter of George and Emma Lutz, of Clark county, the union being blessed with two children: Eugenia Mary, born December 9, 1896, and Edgar Lutz, whose birth occurred on September 4, 1900.

In his political views Mr. Glossbrenner is a pronounced Republican, but has never sought office at the hands of his fellow citizens, nor aspired to leadership, notwithstanding which he has held various positions in the municipality including among others, that of the School Board, of which body he is now serving as secretary. He is a firm believer in revealed religion, and holds to the Methodist Episcopal faith, himself and family being members of the church of that denomination in Jeffersonville, and interested in all lines of work under the auspices of the same.

ALBERT LeROY ANDERSON.

Mr. Anderson, who occupies the responsible position of City Clerk of Jeffersonville, and is also serving efficiently as the bookkeeper for the George S. Anderson Company, is a native son of the Buckeye state, having been born in Cleveland, Ohio, June 23, 1880. He is the son of Charles and Minerva (Addison) Anderson. The Anderson family has been for many decades prominently identified with the history of Clark county. The subject's paternal grandfather, Charles C. Anderson, a native of the state of New York, came to Jeffersonville in pioneer days and had much to do with the early development of this locality. He had four sons, George S., Robert C., John and Charles. Excepting John, the brothers remained here during their lives and were identified with the varied business interests of the community. There were also two daughters, Mrs. Mary Small and Mrs. Martha Lueders, both now residents of Philadelphia, Pennsylvania. Charles Anderson was born in Jeffersonville, Indiana, and his wife in Cleveland, Ohio.

Charles Anderson was married in 1868 to Minerva Addison, of Cleveland, Ohio, and to this union were born six children, namely: Neva May, the wife of James S. Hall, of Jeffersonville; Charles M., Deputy Sheriff of Clark county; Frank C., a moulder in his father's foundry, and also serving as a member of the City Council; Jesse H., Bishop of Jeffersonville; Albert LeRoy and Walter E., a mail carrier in Jeffersonville. Charles Anderson is a faithful member of the Advent Christian church, while his wife is a member of the Baptist church. Politically he is a Prohibitionist and has been very active along many moral and religious lines of activity.

The Anderson foundry and machine shop, with which Albert LeRoy is so closely identified, was established many years ago just north of the Falls City Hotel by Charles C. Anderson, the subject's grandfather, and his brother-in-law, Hamilton Robinson. There the plant was operated until 1855, when the old building was destroyed by fire, after which the shop was established at its present location on Watt street. In 1889 George S., Charles and Robert C. Anderson purchased the business from their father. William H. Lang was subsequently admitted as a partner. Two of the brothers are deceased and the business is now owned by Charles Anderson, Sarah Catherine, the widow of George S. Anderson, and Mr. Lang. The output of the plant consists chiefly of foundry and machine work and considerable attention is given to repair work, employment being given to about twelve men.

Albert LeRoy Anderson was brought to Jeffersonville when but two years old and received his education in the schools of this city. Upon completing his education he entered his father's office in the capacity of book-keeper and for eleven years he has remained in this position, performing his duties efficiently and faithfully and winning the warm regard of all with whom he is thrown in contact. Two years ago he was elected City Clerk of Jeffersonville, and to the duties of this office he gives the same careful and painstaking attention which he devotes to his regular employment. The duties of the office are multitudinous, but they are discharged in a manner that has won for Mr. Anderson the highest commendation.

On July 7, 1904, Mr. Anderson was united in marriage to Minnie Overton Cook, daughter of John and Marietta Cook, of Jeffersonville. Mr. Cook is a river engineer and is now attached to the steamer "Columbia." Mrs. Anderson was educated in the public schools. To this union have been born two sons, Bert Mitchell, born April 11, 1906, and Nelson Oscar, born July 24, 1907.

Politically Mr. Anderson is a zealous Republican, and fraternally is identified with Jeffersonville Lodge, Free and Accepted Masons, Jeffersonville Lodge, Independent Order of Odd Fellows, Myrtle Lodge, Knights of Pythias, and the Benevolent and Protective Order of Elks.

FRANK M. MAYFIELD.

Prominent among the leading legal lights of Clark county who have attained high standing at the Jeffersonville Bar and gained more than local repute as a successful practitioner is Frank M. Mayfield, ex-Prosecuting Attorney of the Fourth Judicial District and a man of influence among his profession brethren in the southern part of the state. Mr. Mayfield was born in Washington county, Indiana, July 21, 1870, the son of James H. and Mary (Hartley) Mayfield, the father a native of Tennessee and an early pioneer of Washington county, where for many years he was engaged in farming.

Frank M. Mayfield acquired his education in the public schools of Jeffersonville and the New Albany Business College and in 1896 entered the Indianapolis Law School, where he prosecuted his legal studies until completing the prescribed course and receiving his degree two years later. Immediately after his graduation he was admitted to the Clark County Bar, where in due time he won recognition as a capable and successful attorney and built up a large and lucrative practice in the local courts and elsewhere, having been retained as counsel in a number of important cases soon after engaging in his profession. He continued the general practice with gratifying success until 1900 when he was elected Prosecuting Attorney of the Fourth Judicial District, the duties of which position he discharged in such an able manner that at the ensuing election two years later, he was chosen his own successor by a very decisive majority.

Mr. Mayfield's official record is an honorable one and the ability displayed in looking after one of the people's most important interests gained for him great popularity as a faithful public servant. At the close of his second term he resumed the general practice and is now at the head of an extensive legal business with a large and appreciative clientele in Clark and neighboring counties, his continued success and advancement winning for him a conspicuous place among the rising young lawyers of the bar to which the greater part of his patronage is confined.

Mr. Mayfield is also interested in various other lines of activity and takes a prominent part in encouraging and furthering all projects and enterprises for the material advancement and general welfare of the city in which he resides. He is prominent and influential in a number of social and fraternal orders, among which are the Free and Accepted Masons, the Modern Woodmen of America, the Benevolent and Protective Order of Elks and the Union Fraternal League, in all of which he has been an active worker and from time to time an honored official. In politics he is a Democrat and for a number of years has been one of his party's able and judicious counsellors and an influential worker in a number of hotly contested campaigns.

On November 16, 1899, he was married to Julia L. Felker, the accomplished daughter of George W. and Lucretia Felker, of Jeffersonville, in which city she was for a period of twelve years a teacher in the public schools. Mr. and Mrs. Mayfield have a beautiful home, rendered especially attractive to them by the presence of a third inmate in the person of their only child, a daughter by the name of Helen. Mrs. Mayfield is a devoted member of the Methodist Episcopal church and interested in its various lines of effort. Although liberal in his religious views and tolerant of the views and opinions of others, Mr. Mayfield has profound regard for the church.

James H. Mayfield, the father of Frank M., was a soldier in the Civil war, enlisting in Company M, Sixty-third Indiana Infantry, with which he served with an honorable record until discharged on account of physical disability. He departed this life in 1891, his wife preceding him to the eternal world in the year 1874. Their family consisted of fourteen children, of whom five are deceased, the names of those living being as follows: Mrs. Laura Morgan, of Jeffersonville; Rufus, of Washington county, Indiana, a manufacturer and dealer in timber and lumber; Dorcas, wife of J. B. Blunt, of Jeffersonville; Joseph, a general merchant, of Washington county; Stella, now Mrs. John F. Davis, the husband a conductor on the Pennsylvania Railroad; Claude, who is also in the employ of that company, with headquarters at Clarksville; Ethel, who married Frederick Shannon, a railroad man living in the city of Louisville; Festus, a cartoonist, of Cincinnati; and Frank M., of this review. The deceased members of the family who were all older than the subject were: William, Emma, Harriet, Serrilda and John.

William W. Mayfield, the great-grandfather of Frank M., was a native of Virginia, a planter by occupation and at the breaking out of the War of the Revolution joined the American army and took part in a number of campaigns and battles, serving until independence was achieved. At the close of the struggle he returned to his estate in Virginia, where his death occurred a number of years ago. Both the Mayfield and Hartley families were from England, the latter emigrating to America direct from London and settling in Scott county, Indiana, in pioneer times. Rev. Wesley Hartley, a brother of Mrs. James H. Mayfield, was for many years a prominent minister of the Christian church and became widely known in religious circles throughout Central and Southern Indiana. He entered upon the duties of his holy office when but sixteen years old and after a continuous service of fifty-seven years, retired from his labors, dying at the old family homestead in Scott county, near the town of Scottsburg, at the advanced age of eighty-three.

FREDERICK W. DAVIS, D. D. S.

Standing at the head of his profession in Jeffersonville, Doctor Davis enjoys an excellent patronage. Frederick W. Davis has lived all his life in Indiana, having been born in Fulton county, this state, on October 11, 1873. He is the son of John M. and Catherine (Packer) Davis, who were both born in the state of Ohio. John M. Davis now occupies the responsible position of insurance inspector for Fulton county, an office under the jurisdiction of the state. He is a veteran of the War of the Rebellion, having enlisted in the regular army from this state, and being stationed during the greater part of his enlistment in New York, where he was assigned to the coast defense. He is a member of the Grand Army of the Republic and is also a Royal Arch Mason. To him and his wife were born the following children: Cyrus M., a merchant in Rochester, Indiana; Ostinella A., a successful attorney at Rochester; Henry A., a civil engineer in Michigan; Rosella who is the wife of Frank McKee, of Rochester; Frederick W., the immediate subject of this sketch; Charles A., an electrical engineer at Rochester; Vernon J., engaged in the manufacture of telephones and telephone supplies at Buffalo, New York; Marion L., who died at the age of four years.

Frederick W. Davis received his general education in the public schools of Rochester and then entered the University of Indianapolis, where he took a full course in dentistry, graduating with the class of 1900. He at once came to Jeffersonville and established himself in the active practice of his profession, in which he has been successful to a marked degree. He enjoys a constantly increasing practice among the best class of patrons. He has a well appointed suite of rooms and possesses a full line of the latest and most up-to-date mechanical appliances. He is a member of the P. G. C. Hunt Society, an organization closely allied to his professional work.

Politically the doctor is a stanch Democrat on national issues, though in local affairs he believes the man should be elected who is best qualified to fill the office. Socially he is a member of the Masonic Order, belonging to the Blue Lodge, Chapter and Commandery, and is also identified with the Knights of Pythias and the Benevolent and Protective Order of Elks. His professional relations are with the Indiana State Dental Society, the annual meetings of which he attends and in which he has taken some active part.

Doctor Davis has had a creditable military record as a member of the Indiana National Guard and the Spanish-American war volunteers. He enlisted in the Second Regiment of the National Guard on May 26, 1890, and gave efficient and faithful service, passing through all the grades from private to first sergeant. He then received special recognition, being "jumped" from first sergeant to first lieutenant. At the outbreak of the Spanish-American war, the subject's patriotism was aroused and, on April 12, 1897, he enlisted in Company B, One Hundred and Fifty-eighth Indiana Volunteer Infantry, and served until November 4, 1898. He was commissioned first lieutenant of his company, the greater part of the service being at Camp Thomas, Chickamauga Park, and at Camp Poland, Knoxville, Tennessee.

The apparent ease with which Doctor Davis has attained to his present position in his profession marks him as the possessor of talent, and, being a close student of professional literature, he keeps in close touch with the latest advances in his profession.

REV. JOHN S. WARD.

The gentleman who is serving efficiently and faithfully as pastor of the Wall Street Methodist Episcopal church in Jeffersonville is numbered among the leading clergymen of the city and wields a wide influence for good throughout the community. Rev. John S. Ward is a native son of Indiana, he having been born at Greenville, Floyd county, on Christmas day, 1876.

His father, Rev. J. A. Ward, was a native of Illinois and for forty years was engaged in active pastoral work as a member of the Indiana conference of the Methodist Episcopal church, having filled some of the leading pulpits of that denomination in this conference. He married Sylvinia Farmer. They now reside at Hymera, Sullivan county, Indiana, the father having retired from the active ministry.

The subject of this sketch received his preliminary education in the common and high schools, completing his education at that solid Methodist seat of learning, DePauw University. Having determined to enter the sacred ministry, he also during this time took the theological course of the conference itinerant school. In 1898 he was given his first appointment as an active pastor, though during the three years previously, while a student in college, he had done some preaching. During the first seven years of his ministry he held appointments at Indianapolis and vicinity and in 1905 he was appointed pastor of the Wall Street church, Jeffersonville, where he still continues. Excepting one church of this denomination at Evansville, the Wall Street church is the largest Methodist Episcopal society in Southern Indiana, having a membership of about seven hundred and fifty, and it requires abilities of high order to successsfully carry on the varied interests of so large an organization. When the fact is considered that Mr. Ward is the youngest member of the conference occupying so important a charge, and that he has been continued at this point four successive years, it stands in marked evidence of his strength not only in the pulpit but also as an administrator of the affairs of the church.

The Wall Street church is one of the most active and progressive religious bodies in the city and is a tower of strength in upbuilding the spiritual life of the community and maintaining a high moral standard. In connection with the main society, there are several healthy auxiliary organizations, among which may be mentioned the Sunday school, with an enrollment of three hundred and fifty members; the Methodist Brotherhood, of one hundred and sixty members, and of which Prof. C. M. Marble is the president; the Ladies' Aid Society; the Woman's Foreign Missionary Society; the Young Ladies' Society; the Standard Bearers, the King's Heralds and the Light Bearers, the latter being the strongest organization of its kind in Southern Indiana, the same being true of the Methodist Brotherhood; the Epworth League, one hundred and sixty-five members; the Junior Epworth League, one hundred and twenty-five members.

In 1896, at Greencastle, Indiana, the Reverend Ward was married to Hattie Combes, a native of Owen county, Indiana, and a daughter of Woodford C. and Lucinda Combes. To this union have been born three children, Ruth, Genevieve and John. Politically Mr. Ward is a Republican while his social affiliations are with the Masons, Knights of Pythias and Odd Fellows.

Reverend Ward is forcible in the pulpit, strong in his administrative ability, affable in his social relations and sincere and earnest in everything he does and says. Though comparatively young in years he has already received marked recognition in his church and there stand before him the open doors of a useful and successful career.

PROFESSOR WILLIAM W. BORDEN.

It is impossible within the circumscribed limits of this review to give more than a mere glance at the leading facts in the life of one of Indiana's most scholarly men, whose distinguished achievements in the realm of research attracted the attention of educational circles, and won for him an honorable position among the eminent scientific minds of the age in which he lived—nor was it by such achievements alone that he earned his fame and impressed his personality upon the minds of his fellows as a leader of thought and public spirited citizen. In the broadest and best meaning of the term he was a benefactor in that he ever labored for the material prosperity of this county and state and in his efforts to promote the intellectual advancement of the youth of the land, the institution which he founded and maintained will long stand as a monument to the noble purposes and high ideals by which his life was directed and controlled.

William W. Borden was born in the town of New Providence, or Borden, Clark county, Indiana, on the 18th day of August, 1823. His paternal antecedents were among the sterling Quaker yeomanry of New England, the branch of the family from which he is descended having located many years ago in Rhode Island.

His father, John Borden, whose birth occurred in Portsmouth, that state, near the close of the eighteenth century, was by occupation a blacksmith and machinist, having learned the former trade under his father and from a Mr. Low, of Waltham, Massachusetts. John amassed a competency by the manufacture and installing of spinning machinery and the building of factories. In 1816 he moved to Clark county, Indiana, and entered several tracts of land in what is now Wood township, and in due time became one of the leading farmers and public spirited citizens of the community. In addition to tilling the soil he operated a blacksmith and general repair shop, engaged quite extensively in sheep raising and managed an inn for several years besides establishing stores at New Providence and Salem, and in various other ways contributing to the material prosperity of the country and general welfare of the populace.

In a beautiful little valley surrounded by hills he platted a small village

Wm. W. Borden,

of a few blocks which he named New Providence, in honor of the metropolis of his native state, and which from that time to the present has continued to be an important local trading point and the center of a culure and refinement seldom found in villages of its size.

In May, 1822, John Borden married Lydia Bellows, of Groton, Massachusetts. She, too, was among the early pioneers of Clark county and accustomed to all the vicissitudes and hardships of life in a new and undeveloped country, nobly bore her part in establishing a home and looking after its mutual interests. In the little village founded by his father, William W. Bordon first saw the light of day on the date indicated above, but shortly after the first anniversary of his birth he was deprived of his father's loving care and guidance.

The death of John Borden on November 7, 1824, caused a feeling of gloom throughout the little community, as he was a leader among his fellow men and greatly esteemed by all who knew him. He left a widow and one child, the subject of this review, to battle with the world; a second son by the name of John, being born five months after his demise. With practical intelligence, sound judgment and rare tact the good woman took charge of the estate, and in addition to administering upon the same and attending to all her husband's unsettled business, also ran the hotel and so conducted her affairs as to add considerably to the value of her possessions. In his time Mr. Borden had conducted several lines of business, all of which his good wife assumed, and for a number of years she managed the interests of the estate in a safe and methodical manner, which gained for her a high reputation as a capable and far-sighted business woman. She also looked carefully after the early training of her children and until William had reached the age of nine years, sent them to the subscription schools of the neighborhood and did everything within her power to arouse in their young minds an interests in books and study.

Entering the Washington County Seminary at Salem, at the age indicated, young Borden took up the study of arithmetic, Latin, penmanship and several other branches and during the ensuing three years made such progress that at the expiration of that time he was able to matriculate at the Indiana State University, which institution he attended until finishing his scholastic course. Reared to agricultural pursuits he early manifested a liking for rural life and among the experiences of his youthful days, which he was often wont to recall, were the breaking of ground with a wooden plow, cutting grain with the hand-sickle and cradle, mowing the heavy hay crops with a scythe, then resting from his labors on a straw bed in an attic through the unplastered walls of which the breezes of summer fanned him to sleep and the snows of winter not infrequently covered his bed with a layer of virgin white. Under the direction of his mother who, as already stated, was a woman of uncommon energy, well read and conversant with the questions of the day, his

32

mind early took the proper bent, and while still a youth he became familiar with public matters and political issues, and in due time earned the reputation of being one of the most intelligent and studious boys of the neighborhood. When old enough he began to repay his mother for her useful devotion and as long as she lived he looked after her interests and comfort and ministered tenderly to her necessities, until her death, which occurred on the 2d of June, 1851.

It was in the year 1862 that an apparently trifling incident occurred which had a decided influence on the mind of Mr. Borden and very materially affected his subsequent career. While at New Providence on a professional visit Doctor Reid, of Salem, showed the young man several fossils which he had found, and in expaining their structure, formation, etc., aroused a keen interest in the young man, which from that time until his death increased to such an extent as to gain him a conspicuous place among the distinguished scientists of his day. At the doctor's suggestion the young man purchased a copy of Dana's Geology, the study of which, in connection with explorations in his own neighborhood, and later while guiding a number of professors of geology over various parts of the county, soon gave him a practical knowledge of this fascinating subject and gained him more than local repute as a critical and painstaking student and investigator. From the professors referred to he obtained many practical suggestions which proved of great value in his subsequent study and research, both of which he continued with unabated interest until the knowledge of his ability coming to the attention of the leading scientists of Indiana led to his appointment in 1873 as assistant to Professor Cox, the official geologist of the state.

During the three years spent in the above capacity Professor Borden assisted in making geological surveys of Clark county as well as numerous other counties, the published reports of which proved a valuable contribution to the scientific literature of the state, and in addition to his official work he also carried on investigations of his own in various parts of the country. In 1878 he was engaged in silver mining in Colorado with his brother and nephew and later became a member of the mining firm of Borden, Tabor & Company, the latter gentleman afterwards representing Colorado in the United States Senate, and a third partner, Marshall Field, becoming one of the merchant princes of Chicago.

Professor Borden's knowledge of geology proved of great advantage in the mining business and under his personal direction the company achieved great success and became one of the wealthiest corporations of the kind in the West. After obtaining a competency he disposed of his interest in the company and in 1880 returned to the old home in Clark county with the object in view of carrying out certain ideas for the benefit of his fellow men. Believing a liberal education the best preparation for a successful life, he encouraged the erection of the necessary buildings for a college in his native town and until the day of his death maintained the institution at his own expense and otherwise looked carefully after its welfare. The great value of this school to the community cannot be estimated and on one occasion when speaking of the hundreds of young men and women who had gone forth from its walls, equipped for the struggle of life, Professor Borden said, "When I think of them as good, honest citizens, playing their parts resolutely in the affairs of life, this alone is sufficient to reward me for all I have done."

Besides founding the college the professor established a museum on the site of his old home, an account of which, with its rare collections of minerals, fossils, archæological specimens, shells, bones of prehistoric animals, Indian relics and remnants of the handiwork of the Mound Builders, etc., is fully set forth in another part of this volume.

Professor Borden was married November 13, 1884, to Emma Dunbar, of New Albany, Indiana, daughter of John and Margaret (Whitson) Dunbar, and a lady who proved not only a faithful and loving wife and helpmeet, but who encouraged him in his scientific labors and heartily endorsed all of his enterprises for the moral and intellectual advancement of his fellow men.

The career of Professor Borden was fraught with great and permanent good to his fellow men, and few people so stamped their individuality on the mind and thought of the times. Few saw and took part in the great changes which so materially affected Indiana from the pioneer period to the present time as he did and among his contemporaries none contributed more to make such changes possible. He endured the hardships of the early settlers and lived to enjoy in full measure the great advantages of the present day civilization.

After traveling extensively over the greater part of his own country, including Alaska and other distant states and territories, he made tours through nearly all parts of Europe, visiting places of interest and making a careful study of the conditions of their peoples. In looking back over his varied experience, he said: "If a lesson can be drawn from my long life it is this: That all prosperity must rest upon an economical use of time and resources; that energy and perseverance, long continued, will eventually overcome all obstacles; that a poor boy or girl possessed of energy, honesty and frugality, will be sure to win a way in life; that the farmer who looks into the future as he holds the handles of his plow may succeed within his own environment, but will never break down its walls nor be of very great service to his fellow men."

Professor Borden broke down the walls of his environment and through the medium his scientific achievements and the institutions and influence which he established demonstrated his worth to the world and paved the way for still greater good to his fellow men in future years. Humanity grows through such lives as his and the County of Clark and the State of Indiana will always be proud to number him among their most scholarly and distinguished sons. He died on the 19th day of December, 1906, but still lives in the love and veneration of a grateful and appreciative public, which constitutes his enduring monument.

JAMES S. KEIGWIN.

This well known public official is a native of Clark county, Indiana, born in Jeffersonville, where he now resides, on January 5, 1865. His ancestors were among the early settlers of this part of the state and the name has long been identified with the history of the county, his grandfather, James Keigwin, having been a man of considerable prominence and the second warden of the state prison of Jeffersonville, where he was first to utilize the labor of convicts for the support of the institution. He established a large brick factory at Jeffersonville in an early day where were made the bricks of which the prison is constructed, and his establishment appears to have been extensively patronized for a number of years, proving the chief source of the considerable fortune which he amassed. Ephriam Keigwin, the subject's father, whose birth occurred in Clark county in the year 1831, was a farmer and merchant, and for a number of years a successful business man and prominent citizen of Jeffersonville. He was a man of strong character and strong judgment, served as Justice for Jeffersonville township and departed this life in the year 1898, honored and respected by all with whom he came in contact. He was twice married, the first time to Mary Morgan, who bore him three daughters, namely: Mrs. Susie Padgett, of New Albany; Mrs. Sallie Bishop, of Indianapolis, and Mrs. Mamie Dewees, of Jeffersonville. Some time after the death of the mother of these children, Mr. Keigwin married her sister, Josephine Morgan, which union resulted in the birth of James S., of this review, and Jessie, who died in infancy.

Ebenezer Morgan, the subject's great-grandfather, migrated from his native state of Connecticut to Clark county, Indiana, in an early pioneer day, and settled in Silver Creek township, where he developed a farm and became a successful agriculturist and influential man of affairs. Shortly after becoming settled in his new home in the forest he found it necessary to return to Connecticut, and in order to save expense made the trip there and back on foot, an experience fraught with many hardships and not a few dangers. This sturdy old pioneer took part in the various wars against the savages in an early day and later served as a soldier in the Black Hawk war. The old flint lock pistol which he carried during the border troubles has been handed down to his descendants, and is now in possession of James S. Keigwin, who prizes it greatly as a family relic. Sylvester Morgan, the maternal grandfather of Mr. Keigwin, came from Morgantown, Virginia, to Jeffersonville, Indiana, by flat boat, and in partnership with his father-in-law, kept one of the first taverns in the town which appears to have been quite extensively patronized. He also did a thriving business for a number of years, transferring people across the river to Louisville, and in connection with these two enterprises operated a stage line between Jeffersonville and Charlestown, which proved quite remunerative.

As already indicated the Morgans and Keigwins have long been identified with the history of Jeffersonville and neighboring towns, and both names are closely interwoven with the rise and growth of various important local enterprises. The Keigwins were intensely loyal during the rebellion, two of the subject's uncles, James and Albert Keigwin, serving from the beginning to the end of the war, the former as colonel of the Forty-ninth Infantry, the latter as captain of his company. After the war Colonel Keigwin was a business man of Jeffersonville for about thirty years and later was appointed superintendent of the National cemetery at Louisville, in which capacity he served untl his death. Albert Keigwin was for many years a distinguished minister of the Presbyterian church, but is now living a retired life in the city of New York.

James S. Keigwin, whose name introduces this article, was reared in Jeffersonville, enjoyed the best educational advantages the public schools of the city afforded, and when a youth in his teens began his career as driver for the Adams Express Company. This not being exactly to his liking, he resigned his place at the end of four months, and accepted a better and more lucrative position with the Louisville & Nashville Railroad with which he remained twenty-five years, his first post being that of mail boy, from which he rose by successive promotions to revising clerk, abstract clerk and inter-change clerk, each position of much greater importance than the preceding, as well as commanding a corresponding increase of salary. During his long period of service wth the Louisville & Nashville, Mr. Keigwin filled his several posts with ability.

Mr. Keigwin's principal reason for leaving the railway service was his appointment in January, 1907, as Justice of the Peace for Jeffersonville township, the duties of which he discharged in connection with his clerical duties for a period of one year, when he severed his connection with the road to devote his entire time to the business of his office. Since his election as justice, he has earned an enviable reputation as a capable and reliable official. The dignity with which Mr. Keigwin ties the nuptial knot has made him very popular with those matrimonially inclined and he is now widely known as the "marrying squire," having united eight hundred and fifty-four couples in the bonds of wedlock from January 12, 1907, to January 20, 1908, a record perhaps without parallel in the state.

On the 29th of December, 1886, Mr. Keigwin was united in marriage with Anna Nixon, whose birth occurred in Jeffersonville, Indiana, July 26, 1865. Her father, Benjamin T. Nixon, late of Jeffersonville, was born in Washington county, in the year 1826, and departed this life on the 2d day of July, 1908. The maiden name of Mrs. Nixon was Sarah Reese; she was born at Charlestown, Clark county, November 26, 1835, bore her husband five children, and died on July 27th of the year 1898. Of the five children who constituted the family of Benjamin T. and Sarah Nixon, Mrs. Keigwin and Mrs. Louise Small, of Philadelphia, are the only survivors.

To Mr. and Mrs. Keigwin seven children have been born, to-wit: Anna, Harold, Raymond, Homer, Nora, Warnock and Lillian, the last named dying in infancy.

Mr. Keigwin is a Democrat in his political affiliations and a leader of his party in Jeffersonville and Clark county. He is an active and influential member of the Independent Order of Odd Fellows, and Modern Woodmen of America fraternities and with his wife and family, except the two youngest children, belongs to the Presbyterian church. His attractive home, which he has occupied during the past fifteen years, is situated on a commanding eminence overlooking the Ohio river and portions of Louisville and Jeffersonville.

MARTIN A. CONROY.

The gentleman whose name appears above is a wholesale and retail dealer in flour and feed at the corner of Seventh and Spring streets, Jeffersonville, and is a native of Indiana, born in the town of Sellersburg, Clark county, March 9, 1856. His parents, Patrick and Elizabeth (Peters) Conroy, came from Queens county, Ireland, when young and married in New Albany, Indiana. They subsequently moved to Clark county and settled at Sellersburg, where the father died in middle life, the mother surviving him a number of years, dying in the city of Jeffersonville at the age of seventy-six. One son and two daughters constituted the family of this estimable couple, Martin A., of this review; Mary, who died in childhood, and Elizabeth, a Sister of Providence, under the church name of Mary Assumption, who met with a violent death some years ago in a street car accident in Indianapolis.

Martin A. Conroy was reared to habits of industry and received his educational discipline in the public schools and in the parochial schools of Jeffersonville, this training being afterwards supplemented by a course at an educational institution of higher grade by the name of St. Joseph's Hill. While still a mere youth he commenced working for himself in a brickyard, and after spending a few years in that capacity accepted a position in the Monon Railroad shops at New Albany, where he remained until taking service as a section hand sometime later. Severing his connection with that department of work he spent about seven years as a car builder, during which time he acquired great proficiency as a mechanic and earned the esteem and confidence of his employers. Not caring to make railroading his life work, Mr. Conroy, at the

expiration of the period indicated, discontinued the service and during the ensuing year was engaged in the boot and shoe trade at Jeffersonville, doing a
safe and satisfactory business. In 1892 he established the line of business to
which he has since devoted his attention, namely, the wholesale and retail flour
and feed trade in which his advancement has been rapid and continuous, his store
on the corner of Seventh and Spring streets consisting of a fine two-story brick
building with a ware house fifty by seventy-two feet in dimensions, being the
largest and best stocked establishment of the kind in the city. In addition to
the lines of merchandise mentioned, he also carries a fine stock of salt, paint,
painting supplies, hay and other commodities, and gives employment to an
average of five men every working day in the year, his patronage taking a
wide range and yielding him an income which long since placed him in independent circumstances.

The domestic life of Mr. Conroy dates from the year 1889, when he was
united in marriage with Mary O. Herron, of Jeffersonville, the ceremony being
solemnized according to the rites of the Roman Catholic faith in St. Augustine
church in this city. The only pledge of this union is a daughter by the name
of Mary, now a young lady of intelligence and refinement and her father's
assistant and bookkeeper. She was educated in the St. Augustine parochial
schools and later finished a commercial course in the Spencerian Business College of Louisville.

Mr. and Mrs. Conroy were reared in the Catholic faith and have ever been
true to the mother church, belonging with their daughter to the St. Augustine
congregation and are active in all of its various lines of religious and benevolent work. Mr. Conroy is one of the influential members of the Knights of
Columbus and the Travelers' Protective Association, and in politics gives his
allegiance to the Democratic party. He has never been a partisan in the sense
of seeking office.

EDWIN WILKES HYDRON.

The manufacture of wagons, carriages and other wheeled vehicles has
long been one of the important industries of Jeffersonville, and for some years
the leading establishment of the kind has been the one at 133 East Chestnut
street, conducted by the well known and enterprising business man whose name
furnishes the caption of this article. Edwin Wilkes Hydron, a native of New
Castle, Kentucky, was born November 23, 1867, and is a son of William and
Mary Frances (Schermerhorn) Hydron, the father an Indianian by birth, the
mother born about eight miles from Louisville, in Jefferson county, Kentucky.
William Hydron served with an honorable record in the Civil war and later
engaged in business pursuits at Jeffersonville, establishing a number of years

ago the wagon and carriage shops, now owned and operated by his son, the latter becoming a member of the firm of Hydron & Son in 1885. He also operated factories in Louisville and New Albany, and during the last thirty years of his life was one of the leading wagon and carriage makers of Jeffersonville, where he built up a large and lucrative patronage and earned an enviable reputation as a capable and skillful mechanic. He not only achieved marked success as a business man, but stood high as a citizen. After a strenuous and useful life he was called from the scenes of his activities and achievements on the 7th day of December, 1902, since which time the business he built up and conducted with such signal results has been carried on by his son, Edwin W.

William and Mary Frances Hydron reared a family of the following children, all living and well settled in life: Edwin W., the oldest of the number; Fred is engaged in the wholesale fruit business at Bakersfield, California; Harry, a railway engineer on the Pan Handle line; William, Jr., operates the Louisville & Jeffersonville Transfer Company, and is one of the well known citizens of the latter place; Belle married Charles Howard, a contractor of Louisville, and resides in Jeffersonville; Hattie is the wife of Frank Same, who is connected with the Louisville & Jeffersonville Transfer Company.

Edwin Wilkes Hydron spent his childhood and youth in New Albany, received his education in the public schools and high school of that city, and at the proper age he entered his father's factory to learn the wagon and carriage maker's trade. By diligent application and a determination to succeed, he made commendable progress and in due time became not only one of the most skilled mechanics in the establishment, but also his father's trusted assistant in conducting and managing the firm of Hydron & Son, which was carried on with signal success until the death of the father, since which time he has been sole proprietor of the establishment which is now one of the largest and best known in the city with much more than a local reputation in industrial circles.

In the management of his steadily increasing business, Mr. Hydron has displayed executive capacity of a high order; he oversees every detail of the establishment, doing nearly all of the finer painting himself and looking after the labors of his men. The products of his shops are of a high standard of excellence, and compare favorably with the best vehicles on the market. To supply the growing demand the factory is taxed to its utmost capacity, a number of mechanics being employed.

Although a Democrat in politics and interested in the success of his party, he is not an office seeker but keeps in close touch with the leading questions and issues before the people. Fraternally he holds membership with the Knights of Pythias and Knights and Ladies of Honor orders, and religiously he belongs to the Christian church, with which his wife is also identified, both being zealous and influential workers in the congregation in Jeffersonville.

Mr. Hydron on January 16, 1893, entered the marriage relation with Louise Gruber, of Jeffersonville, whose parents were for many years respected residents of this city. The mother is still living. The father died some years ago from disease contracted while in the army, having been a soldier in the war between the North and South.

To Mr. and Mrs. Hydron three children have been born: Edwin Stewart, who was born November 23, 1894, and died January 28, 1905, the other two being daughters, Helen Louise and Maxine.

JAMES H. BEARD.

This well known business man is a native of Gallatin county, Kentucky, where his birth occurred in the year 1845. His father, John Beard, a native of Butler county, Pennsylvania, was of Dutch extraction and his mother, also born and reared in the same county and state, bore the maiden name of Emily J. Morris and was of Irish descent. These parents moved to Kentucky a number of years ago and settled in Gallatin county, where Mr. Beard resided until his removal to Jeffersonville, in 1892, dying in the city four years later, Mrs. Beard having departed this life some time previously in Madison, Jefferson county, Indiana.

James H. Beard grew to maturity in his native county and state, received his education in the public schools and later fitted himself for a business career by taking a course in a commercial school in Cincinnati. He remained in Gallatin county until 1868, when by reason of an injury he gave up farming and removed to Markland, Switzerland county, Indiana, and engaged in the mercantile business, which he conducted in that town for a period of fourteen years. At the expiration of that time he disposed of his stock and moved to Louisville, Kentucky, where he accepted a position with a wholesale grocery house, subsequently severing his connection with the firm to enter the employ of the Adams Express Company. In 1892 he resigned his position with the company and changed his residence to Jeffersonville, Indiana, where he has since been engaged in various enterprises, devoting the greater part of the time to his duties as secretary of the Falls City Savings and Loan Association, one of the oldest and best known organizations of the kind in the southern part of the state, also one of the most successful, being capitalized at one million dollars and conducted by some of the most reliable business men of the city. In connection with the secretaryship he also deals extensively in real estate and insurance, in both of which lines he has built up a large and continually growing patronage, his business comparing favorably with that of any other man or firm in the city similarly engaged.

Mr. Beard was married in Gallatin county, Kentucky, in the year 1867, to Diana E. Satchvill, daughter of Joseph and Anna Satchvill, natives of that county, the union being blessed with two children, John T. and Emma D., the former an engineer in the city of Louisville, the latter the wife of Charles Banks, a soldier in the Spanish-American war, at the end of which he was given a position in the government work on the Panama Canal. Mr. Beard has been active in public affairs since becoming a citizen of Jeffersonville and is deeply interested in whatever tends to the material advancement of the city and the social and moral good of the populace. Previous to his removal to Jeffersonville he served for a number of years as a Justice of the Peace at Markland and earned the reputation of an able public servant. He takes an active interest in secret benevolent work and belongs to a number of fraternal orders, including Clark Lodge, No. 40, Free and Accepted Masons, Horeb Chapter, No. 66, Royal Arch Masons, Jeffersonville Commandery, No. 22, Knights Templar, Council, No. 13, Royal and Select Masters, and Jeffersonville Chapter, No. 327, Order of Eastern Star. He is also identified with Clark Assembly, No. 43, Union Fraternal League. In religion he subscribes to the plain simple teachings of the Christian church, and in politics supports the principles of the Democratic party.

PETER F. MYERS.

One of the leading lumber dealers of Jeffersonville is Peter F. Myers, a creditable representative of one of the sturdy old families of Clark county, and who to a marked degree inherits the sterling characteristics and amiable qualities of head and heart for which his antecedents were long distinguished. His father, Peter Myers, a native of Herkimer county, New York, came to Jeffersonville in an early day, figured prominently in the pioneer history of the city and over sixty years ago established the lumber business which has since been in the family name and which his son, Peter F. now owns and controls. About 1858 he discontinued business pursuits and from that time until his death at an advanced age, lived a life of honorable retirement, his sons, Peter F. and Charles H., being his successors, the latter dying in 1891, leaving the former sole proprietor.

Peter F. Myers was born in Jeffersonville, Indiana, June 21, 1846, and his life has been very closely identified with the city and its interests. His mother dying when he was a child, he was reared by his step-mother, Mrs. Rachael Myers, and remained with his father until the latter's death. He owes his present influential position in the business world as well as his earthly possessions, entirely to his persistent efforts to succeed. After he received an education in the public schools he underwent a practical training under the direction of his father, whose lumber business he entered at a comparatively early age and in due time became familiar with the trade in all of its details. His long connection with the lumber interest has made him one of the best informed and most experienced business men in this line in the city and his success has been continuous. As already stated he became sole proprietor in the year 1891, since which time he has gradually enlarged the scope of his operations, adding considerably to his stock and doing an extensive business in Jeffersonville and other places. At the present time his stock represents a capital of about eighteen thousand dollars, but as he handles an immense amount of lumber during the year in order to supply the large and constantly growing demand on the part of builders, contractors and tradesmen, this cannot be taken as a fair estimate of the magnitude and success of his enterprise. In connection with lumber he handles all kinds of building material, including full lines of building hardware, etc., and affords steady employment to from five to seven men and several trains, supplying a large number of patrons in Jeffersonville, besides commanding a firm and growing trade in the neighboring cities of Louisville and New Albany.

Mr. Myers has been twice married, the first time to Jennie Barnaby, of Jeffersonville, who bore him three children, viz., Alida, wife of William Harding, of Louisville; Nellie, now Mrs. Joseph Milheiser, of New Albany; and Claude, who is interested with his father in the lumber business. The last named is married and the father of one child, Sidney B., four years of age, whose mother was formerly Mattie Pottinger. The subject's second marriage was solemnized with Mrs. S. M. Cain, who became the mother of Dove, who is the wife of Doctor Varble, of Jeffersonville, and Daisy, who is still a member of the home circle, both being graduates of the city high school and otherwise well educated.

In politics Mr. Myers has been a life-long Republican. He was reared in the Methodist faith and subscribes to the creed of that church, to which religious body his wife also belongs and in the good work of which both manifest a lively and abiding interest.

REV. WILLIAM H. SHEETS, M. D.

This successful doctor of medicine and trusted spiritual guide is a native of Prince William county, Virginia, and the son of George John and Margaret (House) Sheets, both parents born in Baden, Germany, the father on November 1st of the year 1786, the mother a few years after that date. George J. Sheets and Margaret House were married in Diedersheim, Baden, in 1815 and two years later bade farewell to the land of their birth and sailed for the United States, landing at Baltimore after a long and arduous voyage of six months, during which time there was much suffering among the passengers by reason of the vessel being driven far from its course by the terrific storms which prevailed almost from the time of sailing until reaching port. Among the most poignant of the many sufferers during this strenuous and protracted voyage were Mr. and Mrs. Sheets, who lost sight of their own sad plight in trying to minister to the comfort of their sick child, but despite all of their efforts to relieve the little sufferer, it gradually grew worse until at last they were obliged to see its little body consigned to the waves of the mighty deep. The death of this, their only child, under peculiarly distressing circumstances had a very depressing effect upon the minds of the fond father and mother and finally when the vessel weathered the storms and came to anchor, they landed on the shores of a new world with heavy hearts and no very bright prospects for the future.

Mr. and Mrs. Sheets settled in Prince William county, Virginia, where they secured a good home. They became the parents of nine children, eight of whom grew to maturity, namely: Margaret, George, John, Frederick, Daniel, Catherine, William H. and David P., William H. being the only survivor of the once large and happy household. Having an aversion to slavery and decided objections to rearing his family under its baneful influence, George J. Sheets moved to Morgan county, Indiana, where he spent the remainder of an active and useful life, dying December 14, 1877, at the advanced age of ninety-one years, his wife preceding him to the eternal world in 1849, when fifty-six years old. The sons of this couple, with exception of William H., were tillers of the soil and business men and the majority of them spent their lives in Morgan county, George dying in the county of Hamilton. The parents were reared in the Lutheran faith in their native land, but after locating in Virginia and finding no society of that denomination near their place of residence, they united with the Presbyterian church. Later, on their removal to Indiana, where that church was not represented, their children united with the Methodist church, in which faith the family was reared, the parents, however, remaining Presbyterians to the end of their days.

William H. Sheets was quite young when his parents disposed of their interests in Virginia and moved to Morgan county, Indiana, where the future physician and divine spent his early life on a farm. From childhood he appeared religiously inclined and while still a mere youth he united with the Methodist Episcopal church and began laying his plans for the future in which the ministry figured as a prominent and controlling factor. Having decided to devote his life to this holy calling, he was licensed in 1850 while yet in his teens by Rev. Joseph Tarkington, presiding elder, and the same year was admitted to the Indiana Conference. In those days the life of such a minister meant hard work and little or no remuneration, and in speaking of the character of some of his early appointments, he often said they were as good as he deserved and much better than those the fathers before him had served. At the time of his admission, fifteen composed the class of whom fourteen have exchanged the church militant for the church triumphant, he being the sole survivor of this little band of noble consecrated servants of the Most High.

Doctor Sheets was ordained deacon by Bishop Janes and elder by Bishop Scott, at Shelbyville, Indiana, and served in the active pastorate for a period of twelve years, during which time he was instrumental in strengthening the churches under his care and winning many souls to the higher life. The Conference, at his own request, granted him a supernumerary relation, following which he took up the study of medicine in the office of Dr. R. E. Curran, of Jeffersonville, later adding to his professional knowledge by a course of lectures in the Old Medical University of Louisville and two sessions in the College of Medicine and Surgery at Cincinnati, graduating with the honors of his class at the latter institution about the time of the breaking out of the Civil war. Soon after receiving his degree he was appointed surgeon in the hospital department of the army and held the position to the close of the war, discharging his duties with ability and satisfaction, meeting the approval of his officers and soldier patients and proving faithful to every trust reposed in him. Doctor Sheets left the service at the cessation of hostilities with the rank of assistant surgeon and in 1865 located at Jeffersonville, where he has since resided in the active practice of his profession, building up the meanwhile an extensive patronage. During this time he has served as examining surgeon for pensions from President Hayes' term to the second term of President Cleveland, and was also physician for six years at the Indiana State Prison, South. He has been connected more or less, since 1882, with the health department of Jeffersonville and for the last eight years has been health officer of the city, in which capacity he has rendered valuable and effective service and added greatly to the efficiency of the department.

Ada M. Woodward, who became the wife of Doctor Sheets on the 12th day of November, 1868, was born at Hanover, Indiana, November 8th of the year 1844, and received a liberal education in Hanover College, one of the oldest and best known institutions of learning in the state. At the breaking out of the Civil war her parents moved from Hanover to Mooresville and it was at the latter place that she first met her future husband and it was there that the marriage was solemnized. Mrs. Sheets was reared a Presbyterian, but some time after her marriage she united with the Methodist Episcopal church and continued a faithful and zealous member of the same until called to the other world on October 31, 1906.

Ever since giving up the active pastorate Doctor Sheets has continued to preach when called upon, not only for his own denomination, but for others. His services are in frequent demand upon special occasions and it is stated with every semblance of truth that no man living or dead has conducted more funerals in Jeffersonville than he and he is also popular in the matter of solemnizing the marriage tie. In the year 1900 his conference granted Doctor Sheets a superannuated relation. He cast his first Presidential ballot in 1856 for John C. Fremont, since which time he has been pronounced in his allegiance to the Republican party. His church membership at this time attaches to the Wall Street church, Jeffersonville. He stands third on the Conference roll by seniority and is one of the best known Methodist divines of his day and generation in Southern Indiana.

CHARLES C. PEEL.

At 117 Chestnut street in Jeffersonville, the visitor will find a neat, well equipped, and carefully managed garage, owned by the gentleman whose name heads this biography. Mr. Peel was born at Wilmington, Dearborn county, Indiana, May 11, 1867. His father, Charles Peel, was a native of the Buckeye state, having been born in Cincinnati in 1846. His career was of short duration, having departed this life at the age of twenty-one years, having one son, Charles C. Martha (Bainum) Peel, mother of Charles C., remarried, her second husband being George Ward, a native of Dearborn county, Indiana. They removed to Jeffersonville in 1871, Mr. Ward finding here good opportunities for employment at his trade of car-building. He ended his days in this city in March, 1898. Since that time Mrs. Ward has made her home at St. Louis, Missouri. She became the mother of two children by her second husband, namely: Clarence, late of Lexington, Kentucky, died December 31, 1908, and Mrs. C. W. Williams, of St. Louis.

Mr. Peel was reared and educated in Jeffersonville and made that city his permanent home. After completing his common school education he felt that his life work would demand a greater knowledge of business methods than what he possessed and he therefore attended the New Albany Business College, continuing there until his graduation. For the next ten years he worked at car-building and painting, having first served as an apprentice, but soon became proficient and was rated as a skillful workman and able mechanic. In 1894 he established his present business and has followed it ever since. He does general repairing of bicycles, automobiles, and fine machinery. His equipment is ample and his work thorough and skillful. As a result he does a thriving business, and enjoys the confidence and good will of a host of friends and acquaintances. On the 8th of October, 1890, Mr. Peel was joined in marriage to Ophelia Masmer, daughter of Augustus Masmer, of Jeffersonville. Her parents were of English and German extraction, and constituted one of the oldest and best known families in the vicinity of Charlestown, this county, where Mrs. Peel was born and educated. She is a woman of refined demeanor and excellent tastes. She has become the mother of five children, only two of whom, however, are now living. These are Frank and Mary. The other three, Ward, Charles and Eva, died in early childhood.

Mr. Peel and family are members of the Presbyterian church. They take an active interest in religious work and contribute liberally of their time and means to the support of the Gospel in their own community. Mr. Peel has for several years acted as deacon in the church, and has been of great service in promoting the splendid spirit and wholesome atmosphere that characterizes that organization. He affiliates with the Republican party, but has never sought political prominence, preferring rather to be satisfied with his business affairs.

JOHN W. HOOVER.

It would appear that Mr. Hoover inherited a love for the business which is so closely allied with the profession of medical practitioner, for both his father and grandfather were engaged therein, and did much toward the alleviation of the sufferings of afflicted humanity. Mr. Hoover is one of the leading pharmacists of Southern Indiana, and his drug store at 731 East Chestnut street, Jeffersonville, Clark county, enjoys a liberal patronage. He has contributed not a little toward the material progress of Jeffersonville since he became a resident of the city about fifteen years ago.

Mr. Hoover is a native of Orange county, Indiana, having beeen born there July 22, 1851, the son of Charles Leonce Hoover, who first saw the light in Ohio county, Pennsylvania, November 30, 1823. He was a physician and came west in the forties, locating in Washington county, Indiana. He took a classical course at the State University of Indiana, and graduated with honors. Later he entered the Louisville College of Medicine, and received a diploma. He located at New Albany in the spring of 1853, and engaged in the wholesale drug business, continuing in that line of business for fifty years, being the oldest druggist in the state of Indiana, when he died in May, 1904.

The paternal grandfather of the subject, Leonce Hoover, was a native of Switzerland, and he and his sister were known to be the only members of the family that came to America. As a matter of fact the name of the subject was originally "Huber." Leonce Huber, the grandfather, studied medicine at

Paris, France, and had the honor of being commissioned a surgeon in the army under Napoleon. After having served in that capacity for some years he came to America and in 1849 went to California in search of gold, and was very successful in his quest therefor. He finally settled in Los Angeles and engaged in the manufacture of wines, having acquired a large and very productive vineyard. Later he engaged in the real estate business with his son, Vincent, dying when a very old man.

The mother of John W. Hoover was Mary Eliza Riley, born March 3, 1827, at Hardinsburg, Kentucky. She became the wife of Mr. Hoover's father November 11, 1847, and was the mother of seven children, only one of whom, Charles V., is dead, he having passed away in middle life. The others are John W., Mary Elizabeth Arnold, residing at Rockford, Illinois; James A., Stanley S., Emma, and Arthur K., all of New Albany.

Mr. Hoover was educated at the Morse Academy, New Albany, and when eighteen years old engaged in the drug business with his father, where he remained until the fall of 1894, when he removed to Jeffersonville, where he embarked in business for himself. Mr. Hoover was twice married, the first time October 13, 1881, one son being the result of this alliance, Charles Leonce, who died at the age of twenty years. The wife died August 5, 1897. The second marriage of the subject was to Mrs. Minnie (Conway) McGrath, the bride being a widow. She is the daughter of Joseph and Mary Conway, and was educated in the schools of Jeffersonville. Her maternal grandfather was the first white child born in Jeffersonville. His mother once cooked dinner for the Gen. George Rogers Clark party, when on their tour of the western wilds. The maternal grandmother of Mrs. Hoover was Mary Cunningham, a native of New York, and a niece of Robert Morris of Revolutionary war fame. The ancestors of Mrs. Hoover were closely identified with the Revolutionary period, and some of her family are connected with the Daughters of the American Revolution.

The Reily family, represented by the mother of John W. Hoover, were of Scotch-Irish descent. John M. Reily was a pioneer physician of Hardinsburg, Kentucky. He moved into Orange county in the early thirties, and died at New Albany at the age of seventy-eight. Mrs. Hoover has one daughter by her first husband, Helen Marguerite, who makes her home with her mother and step-father.

JOHN F. SPEITH.

The proprietor of one of the leading confectionary and bakery establishments in Southern Indiana, is a representative of an old and widely known pioneer family of Clark county. John F. Speith was born near the town of

Memphis, this county, on the 16th day of January, 1862. His father, Adam Speith, a native of Germany, came to the United States when a young man and, procuring a tract of land not far from the above town, cleared and improved a fine farm, and later in connection with agricultural pursuits, engaged in merchandising at Memphis and in due time built up an extensive business and became one of the successful men and leading citizens of the community. His wife, who bore the maiden name of Amelia Neumeister, was also a native of Germany, and like him came to America in her youth. This couple were married in Clark county, Indiana, and here reared their family, and achieved much more than ordinary success in their business affairs, Mr. Speith accumulating a handsome competence, his fine fruit farm two miles west of Memphis ranking among the best improved and most valuable places as well as one of the most attractive rural homes in this part of the state. Mr. Speith was a man of progressive ideas and tendencies, and to him as much as to any other is the town of Memphis indebted for its business and prosperity.

His death, which occurred on May 30th, of the year 1908, at an advanced age, was felt as a personal loss by the people with whom he had so long been associated.

Mrs. Speith, who survives her husband, makes her home in Jeffersonville, where she is well known and highly esteemed for her many sterling qualities. She is the mother of a family of eight children, seven sons and one daughter, whose names are as follows: Charles, Frank, George, Adam A., John F., Joseph, William, and Mrs. Laura Schenck, all living and doing well in their respective spheres of endeavor.

John F. Speith was reared and educated in his native county, and since early manhood his life has been closely interwoven with commercial pursuits. His business career in Jeffersonville has been eminently progressive and satisfactory and as proprietor of one of the most successful bakery and confectionary establishments in the city he commands an extensive and lucrative trade, his patronage being not confined to local custom alone, but taking a wide range and including a number of other towns which depend upon him for their supplies in the confectionery line.

Mr. Speith is identified with several lodges, being a member of the Masonic orders, in which he has taken a number of degrees, including that of Sir Knight and is also a member of the Independent Order of Odd Fellows, Hope Lodge, Knights of Pythias, the Benevolent and Protective Order of Elks, Improved Order of Red Men, and the Knights of the Maccabees. In his political views he is a Democrat.

Mr. Speith is a married man and the father of three children, whose names are William, a student at Purdue University, at Lafayette· Amelia, pursuing her studies in the Jeffersonville high school, and John P., a student

33

in the grade schools of the city. The mother of these children was formerly Lillie Stauss, daughter of the late William Stauss, of Jeffersonville, and for a number of years proprietor of the hotel which bore his name.

JOHN HEYN.

The family of this name has been identified with Clark county from a very early period and its members have long been well known in railroad circles. The founder was Christopher Heyn, who came from Germany during the first half of the nineteenth century and when a young man found his way to Southern Indiana in search of a way to procure a living. He had learned carpentering and had little difficulty in obtaining work at his trade after he reached Jeffersonville. Railroads were then in their infancy and crude affairs compared to the splendid efficiency now seen on all the great lines reaching to every point of the country. Young Heyn applied for a job to the company having charge of the road that has since become the Pennsylvania, and sixty years ago built the frame work of the present freight depot in Jeffersonville. In early manhood he was married to Carolina Bowman, a native of Dayton, Ohio, and one of his children is the subject of this sketch. John Heyn was born in Clark county in 1868 and as he grew up was taught a knowledge of mechanics, and learned not only how to work, but also to save his money. He attended the public schools of Jeffersonville and acquired the groundwork of an education which has served him well in his subsequent operations. Ambitious and industrious, he began work for himself before reaching his twentieth year and by diligence and close attention to business has made a success in life. His first railroad job was in 1887 when he secured employment as a repairer of freight cars at the car works in Jeffersonville. Proving apt in this line he had no trouble in securing further work and was engaged at different times by the Big Four, the Wabash and the Pennsylvania Railroad companies. At first working in a subordinate capacity he soon obtained promotion to the position of foreman of car repairers and since then has always held that place. At present he is foreman of car repairers, inspector and wreck master for a south end of the Louisville division of the Pennsylvania, a position of importance and responsibility. He was appointed to the place in October, 1900, and consequently has held it over eight years to the entire satisfaction of his employers. He is a painstaking workman, attentive to duty and always on hand when wanted. Among the numerous railroad employes at this center of railroad activity, none stand better in their respective roles than John Heyn.

In December, 1898, Mr. Heyn was married in Louisville to Josie, daughter of William and Mary Mallott, at Jeffersontown, Kentucky. They have one son whom they named John Geinger Heyn, and who is now attending the city schools. Mr. Heyn is a member of Clark Lodge, No. 40, Free and Accepted Masons and finds time from his business to indulge in social converse with his many friends. He has no political ambitions and gets his chief pleasure from his home and family, to whom he is warmly attached and for whose comfort he provides liberally and generously.

FRANK R. WILLEY.

The founder of the Clark county branch of the family of this name was Col. John F. Willey, born at Cincinnati, June 15, 1809. He achieved prominence as a fruit grower and a worker in the Methodist Episcopal church, of which he was a minister. On January 14, 1828, he was commissioned as an ensign in the Twenty-second Regiment, Indiana Militia, by Governor Roy and the year afterward was promoted to a captaincy, which he resigned in 1834. During the Civil war he was colonel in the Indiana Legion, with headquarters at Jeffersonville. In 1830 he married Pauline Garner, who died in 1875, and one of the children of this union was Dennis F. Willey, born December 27, 1834. On December 22, 1857, the latter married Rosalie H., daughter of Isaac Prather, a native of Clark county. Dennis F. Willey was commissioned captain in the Indiana Militia by Governor Morton, November 14, 1862, and captain of a company in the One Hundred and Thirty-seventh Regiment, Indiana Volunteer Infantry, May 26, 1864. In 1878 he was appointed by Governor Williams, Surveyor of Clark county and served two years. He died November 10, 1906, at his home in Jeffersonville.

Frank R. Willey, son of Dennis F. and Rosalie (Prather) Willey, was born in Utica township, Clark county, Indiana, in 1860. He remained on the farm until the completion of his twentieth year, meantime attending the local schools, the business college at New Albany and for a while at Purdue University. After holding several mercantile positions in Jeffersonville, he formed a partnership in September, 1885, with E. M. Coots in the undertaking business. This connection continued until 1899, when Mr. Willey, after a year in the insurance business, took charge of the Electric Light, Gas, Heating & Coke Company's interests in Jeffersonville. Through various changes and court complications of the Jeffersonville Light & Water Company, during which he acted for a while as receiver, the two concerns above referred to were finally purchased by and consolidated with the United Gas & Electric Company and in 1903 Mr. Willey was placed in charge of the business and has continued in control up to the present time. Aside from this his only public service was rendered during his membership of the City Council for two years. October 20, 1876, he married Ella, daughter of Col. John Ingram. The family of this name included a number of members who became prominent in the various walks of life.

WILLIAM THOMAS INGRAM.

William Thomas Ingram was born in Charlestown, Clark county, Indiana, December 7, 1857, his parents being William Austin and Nancy V. (Foutz) Ingram, who lived on Fourteen Mile creek, near New Washington. At the age of seven he was brought to Jeffersonville, which has ever since been his home. After a course in the public schools he studied law at the University of Louisville, but after leaving his studies engaged in the gravel business and farming. His brother, John Ellington Ingram, was at one time Clerk of Clark county. One of his sisters, who married Charles D. Armstrong, died in 1896. Julia Ingram, another sister, is a practicing physician in Louisville. In November, 1884, William T. Ingram married Anna L., daughter of Congressman Jonas G. Howard, and their children consisted of four sons, whose names are: Jonas Howard, Homer L., Warren T. and William A. The Ingrams have for years been regarded as among Clark county's best citizens. Whether holding civil or military positions and in the various lines of business to which they have turned their attention, their records have been good as men of efficiency and integrity.

COL. JOHN NELSON INGRAM.

This family name was familiar during the pioneer period, both in Kentucky and Southern Indiana as far back as the first quarter of the last century. James Ingram, who was born in Pennsylvania, February 5, 1790, came West in his youth and was married in 1815 in Oldham county, Kentucky, to Nancy, daughter of John and Eliza (Lindsay) Austin. John Austin served as a soldier of the patriot army during the entire period of the Revolutionary war. James Ingram fought under General Jackson at the battle of New Orleans. Later in life he removed to Jefferson county, Indiana, and died there, March 13, 1827, at the early age of thirty-seven. His children were Mary Elizabeth, William Austin, Malinda Jane, James Wesley, Julia Ann and John Nelson, of whom there are two survivors. Malinda J. is the wife of Alexander Chambers, of Danville, Indiana; Julia A. married John Ritchie and resides at Indianapolis.

John Nelson Ingram, the youngest of this family, was born in Jefferson county, Indiana, November 29, 1825, and died October 30, 1908. His early years were spent on a farm, with the usual attendance at the country schools during the winters. When about fourteen years old, he was apprenticed to Isom Ross, at Madison, to learn the tanner's trade. In 1846 he enlisted in Company G, Third Regiment, Indiana Volunteer Infantry, under command of Col. Hames H. Lane, for service in the Mexican war. He was in the battle of Buena Vista and other affairs in the progress of the American army to the capital of the Montezumas. After the war, receiving an honorable discharge, he returned to his tanner's trade at Madison. In 1848 he came to Jeffersonville and established a tannery. Being fond of military tactics, he organized in 1859 an independent company of militia, of which he was made captain. In 1862 Governor Morton authorized him to raise a regiment to be known as the Independent Legion, of which he was appointed colonel. Through inability to get equipment it was impossible to carry out the original design and after a year Colonel Ingram resigned to devote his time to the large tanning business he had established, turning over his military command to Colonel Willey. After the Civil war he dismantled his old tannery and with the machinery established a new one at Claysburg. In 1856 he was elected to the City Council from the second ward and served two years. He was re-elected in 1865, '77 and '79. In 1863 he was elected school trustee, which position he held for twenty-seven years. On February 14, 1848, he joined Monroe Lodge of Odd Fellows at Madison, and for some time he was the last surviving member of Tabor Lodge, No. 92, of the same order at Jeffersonville. He was a member of Wall Street Methodist church and was its stewart for many years.

In 1859 Colonel Ingram married Margaret E. McGonnigal, of Clark county. She was the daughter of Daniel McGonnigal, who was born in Columbia county, Pennsylvania, November, 1800, of Irish parentage. February 22, 1824, he married Hannah Herrin and removed to Tiffin, Ohio, using a wagon to haul their household goods and walking all the way. In 1833 he went to Jefferson county, Indiana, and in 1848 came to Jeffersonville. He built the first car for the old road in a small shop back of where St. Augustine's Academy now stands. It was hauled on a dray to the railway by Floyd Applegate. This venerable pioneer died in 1891 at the residence of Colonel Ingram. The latter had five children: Mary Olive died in infancy; James Austin, born December 2, 1853, died November 21, 1899; John, born November 11, 1855, died July 25, 1908; Elizabeth, born March 2, 1859, married Jacob S. Fry, one time Treasurer of Clark county, now living in Pomona, California; Ella, wife of Frank R. Willey, was born February 10, 1866. John D. Ingram was well known as district manager of the American Car & Foundry Company. He started as a water carrier and nail sorter and worked his way up step by step until he reached the position held at his death. His wonderful knowledge of every branch of car building made him a valuable man to his company. James Austin Ingram was educated at Greencastle, practiced law and was City Attorney in 1879 and 1881. Later he became a civil engineer in Texas, but afterwards returned to Jeffersonville, where he remained until his death. Mrs. Frank R. Willey, the youngest child of Colonel Ingram, has four children: Frank Ingram, Rosalie, Margaret and Walter Watts Willey, these being the only grandchildren.

JOHN L. GLASER.

In 1865 a young German in his twenty-first year and full of the spirit of adventure decided that he would cross the ocean and help the Federal army crush out the Rebellion. He was enthusiastic over the cause of the Union, opposed slavery and anxious to see the great western Republic free to realize its own grand destiny. Feeling this way it was with high spirits that he stepped on the docks of New York after the tedious ocean voyage and hastened to St. Louis, where he was directed to Jefferson barracks. Making known his desires the ambitious soldier was much chagrined when informed after taking the oath of allegiance that the war was over and his services would not be needed. The incipient hero thus foiled of his object was John L. Glaser, whose birth occurred at Weimar, Saxony, in 1844, his parents being Gottlieb and Dorothea Maria (Scheller) Glaser. Fortunately he had learned the trade of carpenter and builder in Germany and was thus not without a means of making a living in the strange land. He had no difficulty in getting a job, as he was a sober, industrious and expert workman, and he worked at his trade in St. Louis for nearly three years. Here also he met his "fate" as the story-writers would express it, as he became acquainted with a fine German girl, who subsequently became his wife. It was in 1868 that he married Anna, daughter of William and Rosena Teich. Removing to Louisville Mr. Glaser spent the next four years at his trade in that city and from there crossed the Ohio to Jeffersonville. Here he continued carrying on the business of building and in 1892 put up a structure which was intended for his own individual use. In this building, situated at Court and Mechanic streets, he placed a stock of groceries and put out his sign for trade. The business thus begun has proved prosperous and to it Mr. Glaser has since devoted all his time.

His marriage was blessed by the birth of a family of seven children, thus described: Minnie, wife of Charles Hoeffling, of Niles, Ohio; Amelia, wife of Edward Norton, of Jeffersonville; Max W., a carpenter and builder of the same city; Harry, a resident of Cincinnati; Rosa, wife of Fred Gepehart, likewise of Jeffersonville; Emma, who remains at home, and Ernest, who is employed in Cincinnati. Mr. Glaser is a member of the Independent Order of Odd Fellows and the Eagles. He at one time served in the City Council, and worships at the Lutheran church. Through his mother Mr. Glaser is an heir to the great Koller-Scheller estate at Bamberg, Bavaria, and the family have great expectations in this direction. It is often a topic of conversation at the family fireside and the children as well as the parents love to dwell on what they will do when this Bavarian money comes to enrich them. All of their friends, and they have many, hope to see them realize on this good fortune and feel sure that if it comes the Glasers will spend it with the prudence and wise frugality that is characteristic of people of the great German race.

THOMAS L. LeCLARE.

Jeffersonville has long been a producer of railroad men and many of them make their homes in this city. This sketch will tell something about one of the most popular of the younger generation in charge of the great transportation system of the country, carrying passengers and freight to every point and corner of the Union. The founder of the family here was Peter F. LeClare, a native of France, who came to this country many years ago. He married Susan Gardener. Their son, also named Peter F., married Mary, daughter of Thomas D. and Margaret (Bell) Lindsay, a family of Scotch-Irish descent, who came here from Northern Ireland. Thomas D. Lindsay was in the employment of the old Jeffersonville, Madison & Indianapolis Railroad during the Civil war. Peter F LeClare had four children, Thomas L., James N., Ida and Susie. Ida married Oscar Bateman, of Jeffersonville. The mother of this family had two sisters, one of whom married a Mr. Smith, an engineer, and the other a Mr. Harrod, who is a conductor, and both well known in railroad circles. Members of the Lindsay family have been in the employment of the local branch of the Pennsylvania Railroad ever since the beginning of the Civil war.

Thomas L. LeClare was born at Jeffersonville, October 28, 1870. After going through the public schools he learned the moulder's trade, but soon abandoned this to indulge in an inherited tendency for railroading. Ever since June, 1893, he has been with the Pennsylvania lines in one capacity and another until finally he reached the grade of conductor on the Louisville division. During the terrible floods of 1883, 1884, in the Ohio river he was newsboy and at considerable peril to his life courageously delivered his papers in a skiff. His father was a member of the police force and also street commissioner of Jeffersonville, in which positions he gained a wide acquaint- and achieved popularity as an efficient official.   Mr. LeClare belongs to Hope Lodge, Knights of Pythias, and Division No. 303, Order of Railway Conductors.

June 8, 1892, Mr. LeClare was married to Nora, daughter of Thomas J. and Elizabeth (Robbins) Donahew, who brought Mrs. LeClare here from Scott county when she was eight years of age.   They have one daughter, Inez. The parents are members of the Wall Street Methodist Episcopal church and popular figures in the younger social set.

JOSEPH C. DOUBET.

A number of French immigrants settled in the region around the Falls of the Ohio during the first half of the nineteenth century and their descendants may be found throughout Kentucky and Indiana.   Usually they seek the agricultural pursuits, especially fruit growing, though they are frequently found in connection with the mechanical arts, in which their nation is famous.   They seem to have a special talent for engineering and France has produced some of the greatest engineers of the world, both in civil and military life.   Jeffersonville has been fortunate in her citizenship of French extraction and in none more so than the young man whose name heads this sketch.   His ancestors were early domesticated in America, as it was as far back as 1827 that his grandfather, Peter Doubet, reached these shores.   He was a native of LeRoy, France, and a member of a social connection, widely known at that place in the older days.   Peter settled in Portland, Kentucky, and it was at that place that his son, Joseph P. Doubet, was born.   When a boy he removed to New Albany, where eventually he learned his trade and in due time became master mechanic in the employ of the Pennsylvania Railroad.   When the Civil war broke out he determined not to be out-done in patriotism by any of his neighbors, but to offer his services in the cause of the Union. With this end in view he enlisted in the Twenty-third Regiment and went to the front and served faithfully for three years.   Starting a private, he rose to the rank of first sergeant, and his comrades always spoke of him as a faithful soldier, who was always ready for his duty, however arduous it might be.   He married Mary B., daughter of Perry Wilson, a native of Orange county, Indiana, but removed to Clark county and lived there for some thirty years, north of Jeffersonville, engaged in farming.   It was at this country home that his daughter was married and here he resided until the day of his death.

Joseph C. Doubet was born in New Albany, November 28, 1873, but was brought to Jeffersonville by his parents during infancy, and has remained here ever since. He was educated in the public schools but also took a course in the business college at New Albany. Having a natural turn for the mechanical arts, he cultivated that faculty diligently until he became a licensed steam and electrical engineer. In 1889 he helped wire Jeffersonville for the first electric lights and has ever since been engaged with city lighting and contracting companies. He has built several electric lighting plants, including the one at Corydon. His brother, Morton Doubet, was killed on electric wires in Jeffersonville, August 17, 1903, the first accident of the kind in the city.

On March 18, 1897, Mr. Doubet married Roberta, daughter of William and Henrietta Simms, of Corydon, Indiana.

JOSEPH G. MOORE.

Wherever found the Englishman is able to hold his own with the best and usually he makes a good citizen, a good worker, and a reliable employe. A fine sample of the English working class is afforded by Joseph G. Moore, who was born near Bristol, England, January 7, 1841. He was still under age when he reached the shores of America and during the Civil war was employed on a steamboat engaged in the Lake Erie trade. At a later period he went to the new state of Nebraska, which was then sparsely settled and still decidedly of the "wild and woolly West." Omaha, however, already showed signs of becoming a city of importance and in this young town Mr. Moore secured work in the car shops of one of the railroads. He did not remain there long, however, but shortly after the close of the Civil war located at Jeffersonville, and was employed for a brief period for the American Car & Foundry Company. He then established a news agency and took charge of the circulation for the Indianapolis Journal, the Cincinnati Enquirer, Louisville Courier-Journal, Louisville Times and Jeffersonville Times. He built up a business in this line which yielded him a fair livelihood, and continued the business until the time of his death, August 29, 1906. For several years, while a resident of Port Fulton, he was a member of the school board, and at one time acted as its treasurer. He was a member of the Methodist Episcopal church at Port Fulton, and of Clark Lodge, No. 40, Free and Accepted Masons.

In 1883 Mr. Moore married Mrs. Mary E. Girdner, widow of John Girdner, of Greenville. She was the daughter of William and Thruza McClellan, of Memphis, Indiana, where the former ran a wool carding machine. Mr. and Mrs. Moore had two sons, Joseph Granville and Orville Frank, both quiet and unassuming boys of steady habits and excellent character. Joseph is a promising student at DePauw University, and Orville has charge of his father's business, which he is managing with good judgment and success. Granville McClellan, a brother of Mrs. Moore, is conductor on the Baltimore & Ohio Raliroad, and resides in Jeffersonville. Mrs. Amanda Huckleberry, Mrs. Moore's only sister, is a resident of Newburg, Oregon. Mrs. Moore's cozy little cottage shows by its neat appearance the presence of a good housekeeper and all the surroundings give indications of a happy and affectionate family.

EDGAR LEON CREAMER.

The founder of this name in Clark county was James Creamer, a native of North Carolina, who came to Floyd county, Indiana, in the early days, making the long trip overland in a wagon. His son, Benjamin J., married Harriet Cox, a woman of an excellent family and many domestic virtues. Her parents came from Sunset. Kentucky, and most of her male relatives were connected in one way or another with the river service. James Phillips, her brother-in-law, was an inventor of useful appliances connected with steamboat engines. He and one of the Cox brothers lost their lives by the explosion of the steamboat "Missouri," on which they were employed.

Edgar L. Creamer, a son of Benjamin J. and Harriet (Cox) Creamer, was born in Floyd county, Indiana. February 26, 1861. During his boyhood he resided in New Albany, but came with his parents to Jeffersonville in 1875. His father was a ship carpenter and an employee in Howard's ship yards for many years, until his death in 1905. Mr. Creamer learned the stove moulder's trade and followed it for seven years and then devoted his time for four years to car building. From this he went into the bakery business, which he has carried on for some eighteen years with fair success and also conducts a grocery in connection with the former. In addition to his other lines of work, he has had experience in blacksmithing and painting. He is a member of Myrtle Lodge. Knights of Pythias, in Jeffersonville. His brother, Walter Cox Creamer, removed to Alaska and has charge of a large amusement place at Dawson City.

On October 26, 1890, Mr. Creamer married Helena Marie F., daughter of Charles and Katherine Seitz. The father was born in Germany in 1835, and the mother was a daughter of Joseph Schraffenberger. Charles Seitz served four years as a soldier during the Civil war, and made a good record in the Federal army. Mr. and Mrs. Creamer have three children: Charles Benjamin, Leta Lucile and Catherine Cox. It will be seen that the Creamers are of excellent stock on both sides of the house and their relatives have done their full share in upbuilding the industries and transportation systems of the lower Ohio valley. As steamboat men, skilled mechanics, and in other lines of business the Creamers, Coxes and Seitzes have worked faithfully and successfully and have long been favorably known to those who do business on the great river and in the towns and cities along its banks. Edgar Leon Creamer has worked his way up through various useful employments until he is now able to live comfortably and independently on the resources he has earned as the result of a life of industry and saving. Still in the prime of life he may reasonably look forward to many years of happiness surrounded by a growing family and loving wife and a household possessed of all the comforts and many of the luxuries that make living enjoyable.

WILLIAM WEBER.

It was during the Civil war that a German family by the name of Weber came over and settled in Louisville. Three sisters of German birth by the name of Carl sought a home in the same city, where one of them married John Troxler, another, John Decker, while the third became the wife of John Weber, a son of the first mentioned immigrants. After marriage the latter couple settled in Jeffersonville, where the husband became an undertaker in the employ of the government to bury the soldier dead. They had eight children, all but one of whom are living. Nellie, the one who died, was the wife of John Yonkers, an engineer on the Pennsylvania Railway. The survivors are: Matilda, who married J. E. C. Eaken, of Jeffersonville; John, who married a Miss Shaw, and has earned a competence in California, where he resides; Edward, who married Mary Pillion, and is engaged in the wholesale grocery business in Jeffersonville; Anna, the wife of Thomas Gorman, resides in Borden, Indiana; William, our subject; Nora, at Bedford, Indiana; Henry, also married, is a resident of Los Angeles, California.

William Weber, who is number five in the above list, was born at Jeffersonville, March 23, 1863. At fourteen years of age he obtained a unique employment, which amusingly illustrates the progress of events during the last thirty years. His duty was to ride a horse down the track in front of trains and flag the people to get out of the way at crossings. Safety gates, towers and automatic switches were wholly unknown in those days and the roads had not even adopted the device of placing flagmen at the crossings. Young Weber got along very well as an outrider for trains until one day a team of mules, driven tandem and drawing a coal cart (a feature peculiar to Louisville), was ground up in the horrified presence of the boy. This was too much for his tender nerves so he threw up his job and quit the railroad life forever. After considerable experience in various mercantile lines and as traveling salesman for a wholesale grocery, Mr. Weber went into the grocery business for himself in 1886, and has prospered. His stand is on Spring street, and is now one of the best known business points in Jeffersonville. In addition to his regular line he does a large business as shipper of butter, eggs, poultry and other produce. He is energetic and progressive, a good buyer as well as seller of popular address and understands both how to get and how to keep customers.

November 28, 1907, Mr. Weber was married to Mrs. Theresa Laurie, an estimable and intelligent member of one of the city's substantial families. She was the widow of the late William Laurie, superintendent of the foundry for the American Car & Foundry Company of Jeffersonville.

WILLIAM QUICK.

In brief space is to be here reviewed a sample of the self-made and well made man. William Quick was born in Jeffersonville, March 18, 1861, and is still in the prime of life. His parents were Warren Thomas and Henrietta (Hyman) Quick, who were unable to do much for their promising boy and at an early age he was compelled to shift for himself. During his youth he obtained some valuable experience as a clerk in the grocery line. He was fortunate in securing the friendship of Eli Thompson, a well-to-do and methodical business man, whose advice and example proved valuable. After conducting concerns for two others successfully, Mr. Quick wisely determined to branch out for himself, realizing that no one ever gets rich working on a small salary. He was unfortunate, however, in choosing a poor locality and the venture proved unprofitable. The next move turned out better. While working for the wages of a day laborer he had been saving and the proceeds of this thrift enabled him to make an investment that turned out prosperously. Disposing of this at the right time he found himself in possession of a snug sum which only needed prudent investment to yield fair results. In November, 1897, he bought the place where he is at present located and where he has built up an excellent business. The establishment includes a large stock of groceries, combined with dry goods and notions, and is conducted with the skill and good judgment acquired during a lifetime of training in practical affairs. In this same place two others before him had failed in the effort to build up in the same line of goods and there was a general prediction that he also would fall a victim to the "hoodoo." Nothing daunted, he took hold and in three years has not only established a thriving mercantile plant, but has also acquired seventeen pieces of real estate, which is productive of a reliable income. All of this has been accomplished by hard work on limited resources and in spite of the obstacles which beset every venture in the world of trade.

July 1, 1886, Mr. Quick was happily married to Emma, daughter of Charles and Rosanna Schifler, of Jeffersonville. They have four children: Samuel H., Carrie B., Edwin I.., and Martha. They are all promising and show that they have inherited the qualities of their father. Mr. Quick is a member of the Kwasind Tribe of Red Men and affiliates with the Lutheran church. Though not a society man he has mingled much with those who carry on the business affairs of the city and being a good mixer has acquired a large acquaintance and many warm friends who admire his many excellent traits of character. Those who find life hard and are struggling against the difficulties of a cold world may take courage and a new resolution by referring to the career and achievements of William Quick.

JOHN B. MURPHY.

This sketch deals with one of the wealthiest as well as one of the most successful of the vast army of Irish who figured prominently in the development and progress of our transportation facilities.

John B. Murphy was born at Toledo, Ohio, June 29, 1852, his parents being Michael and Mary Murphy, who emigrated from Ireland a few years previously. Their son remained at the place of his birth until he reached the age of twenty-one, when he started out to seek his fortune. Coming first to Louisville he soon crossed over to the smaller town of Jeffersonville and succeeded in getting a job with the Pennsylvania Railroad on December 2, 1872. His first position was as night switchman in Louisville, and later in the same line of work at Jeffersonville, which was followed by promotion to the yard foremanship, in daytime. In 1879 he was made yard master in Jeffersonville and two years later was given the place of yardmaster at the Tenth street transfer station in Louisville. In November of the same year he was transferred to Jeffersonville as yardmaster, which he held until July, 1891, when he was promoted to the general yard mastership in Louisville, which position he still holds, showing a continuous service with the Pennsylvania of over thirty-six years. Mr. Murphy has been honored with various positions of trust both by election and appointment. He served in the City Council continuously from 1890 to 1900. In 1901 he was appointed a member of the Board of Metropolitan Police Commissioners by Governor Durbin, and was re-appointed on the expiration of his term in 1904. In 1907 Governor Hanly selected him as his own successor and he is now serving his third term in this important position.

In 1873 Mr. Murphy married Margaret E. McManus, by whom he has eight children, five reaching maturity: Frances Louisa, who is the wife of

Charles Kerrigan; James P., a resident of Louisville; Genevieve, John B., Jr., who is married and lives near his father's home, and Mary, the wife of Joseph Clem, of Jeffersonville. Mr. Murphy is a member of the Catholic Knights of America, the Knights and Ladies of America, Knights of Columbus, and the Ancient Order of Hibernians. The family are members of the St. Augustine Catholic church and are numbered among the esteemed people of the city, both in their social circle and in the industrial world, where Mr. Murphy has so long borne his share in the duties and responsibilities.

JOSEPH GOODMAN.

When Isaac Whiteside was just beginning his bakery in a simple way at Jeffersonville there came to him one day a young German seeking employment. The proprietor, who is a good judge of men, was pleased with the applicant and gave him a trial at moderate wages. This young man, like most of his countrymen who come over here "made good," to use one of our American colloquial terms. Born in Germany in 1860, son of Andreas and Mary Goodman, he had learned the baker's trade at an early age of fourteen years and soon began to long to try his fortune in the great Republic across the sea, of whose opportunities for gaining wealth he had often heard. He finally succeeded in his ambition and in 1882 found himself on the docks of the great city of New York. Determining that he could do better inland he lost little time in the East, but pushed resolutely toward the land of promise beyond the Alleghanies. It was in 1883 that young Goodman appeared before Mr. Whiteside, after a short service with whom he determined to branch out for himself. In the fall of 1884 he founded a partnership with Gottlieb Heilenman for the purpose of conducting a bakery, but this was soon dissolved and Mr. Goodman assumed sole charge of the business. In 1886 he moved to a more eligible situation, on Spring street near Court avenue, where he gradually added a stock of groceries and the two combined soon began to show signs of prosperity. After eleven years at this stand the store was established in a building across the street at the location which has become one of the well known features of the city. German thrift and industry never fail to produce results, and what was a very small affair at first has developed slowly and conservatively into a prosperous bakery and grocery in combination. Mr. Goodman, like all Germans, is sociable and companionable, with a fondness for fraternities and societies for improvement and recreation. He is a member of the Order of Modern Woodmen, treasurer of the German Aid Society and a devoted adherent of St. Anthony's Catholic church.

May 31, 1881, Mr. Goodman married Emma, daughter of Edward and

Rebecca (Nock) Kasper, and they have four children. The eldest took for his wife Lillie Belle Meisner and they have two children, Marvin Joseph and Emma Louise. The father is a plumber and dealer in plumbers' and pasfitters' supplies; Harry, Edward and Emma, the other three children, reside with their parents. The Goodmans have their residence in the same building as the store, which is open all the time and presided over by a family that never forgets to be affable and courteous. As in the typical German household, the good wife is a large factor, and Mrs. Goodman is no exception to this rule.

CAPT. WILLIAM HOWARD.

The prospects were not pleasing when George and Katherine (Hoke) Howard moved from their Kentucky home to the wilds of Clark county, Indiana. Their land of five hundred acres, situated about two miles from Charlestown, where the county asylum now stands, was almost a virgin forest. Great has been the transformation as today it is triangulated with railroads, a trolley line and a turnpike. With this pioneer couple came William Howard, a son, who was born in Jefferson county, Kentucky, and became a partner in a firm of contractors engaged in building Market street from the car works to the Howard Ship Yards. For two years he ran an omnibus line from the end of the Jeffersonville, Madison & Indianapolis Railroad to New Albany, and served as City Marshal from 1857 to 1861. In the latter year he enlisted as a private in a company of the Fifty-third Regiment Indiana Volunteer Infantry, but soon elected second lieutenant and at the battle of Atlanta obtained promotion to the captaincy. He took part in the battle of Chattahcochee river, the siege of Corinth, the engagements at Grand Gulf and Jackson, Mississippi, and maneuvers which drove the Confederates behind the walls of Vicksburg. During the siege that followed the Fifty-third Indiana was under fire of the enemy's guns for thirty-seven days and Captain Howard shared fully in all his regiment's dangers. After the surrender he helped to drive Gen. Joe Johnston's forces from Jackson and was with the triumphant Sherman in all the fighting from Chattanooga to Atlanta, during the memorable campaign of 1864. While at Chattanooga he was on detached service in command of a large force of men looking after the convalescents drafted and wounded. He was in the engagements of North Carolina, preceding the surrender of Joe Johnston and helped to give the final strokes to the dying Confederacy. After the war Captain Howard was employed for a while as a guard at the State Prison, South, and later was appointed Deputy Warden under Colonel Schuler. As a carpenter and inspector of goods he was employed for thirty years in the quartermaster's department but resigned in July, 1900, on account of ill health. The captain in retirement loves to talk of the older days, where his grandfather Hoke raised tobacco on a large farm near Jeffersontown, in Kentucky. His aunts worked in the field and made cigars which were retailed for ten cents a hundred, tied up in packages with a piece of bark. Captain Howard treasures as a curious heirloom two cigars which his aunts made over a hundred years ago. He also cherishes a big key, which opened his father's mill at Fisherville, Kentucky. His father, who came from the eastern shore of Maryland to the woods of Kentucky was bound out and learned the trade of millwright.

In 1846 Captain Howard married Nancy, daughter of Leven and ———— (Grismore) Howard, by which union there were four children: Rose A., who died in 1904; Lydia C., who died in 1860; Lucinda, who is her father's homekeeper, and Fannie Belle, wife of T. M. Dehoney, who resides in Chicago. The mother died in February, 1855, and when the father started to war it was with an aching heart that he left his four children with his parents as he marched away to fight his country's battles. In October, 1869, Captain Howard married Laura A. Porter, a native of Breckenridge county, Kentucky, who died in September, 1903. The ceremony was notable, being the first marriage that took place in the Presbyterian church at Jeffersonville. In 1845 the captain became a member of the Methodist Episcopal church and is at present a member of the Wall Street church, for whose construction he carried the first brick. Formerly he was for a time a member of the Presbyterian church and served as elder. He is a member of the Golden Cross and has been a staunch Republican since the organization of that party.

HON. REUBEN DAILEY.

A strong virile and picturesque personality, generous disposition and strong convictions on important questions, were the traits that made this veteran editor of Jeffersonville influential at home and widely known abroad. During the days of his activity his name was familiar all over the state and few of Indiana's newspaper men so impressed their individuality upon the public or were so frequently mentioned in the news columns. He was of foreign nativity of mixed English and Irish descent. Michael Dailey, the paternal grandfather, who was a native of Queen's county, Ireland, and a pronounced Roman Catholic, married a Miss Gibson, who was just as pronounced a Protestant, and reared all her sons in that faith. William Bird, the maternal grandfather, was an Englishman by birth and a shoemaker by trade,; was of very religious temperament, and composer of sacred music. He married Sarah Singleton, and Han-

REUBEN DAILY.

nah Bird, a daughter of this union, became the wife of Nicholas A., son of Michael Dailey, and this couple were the parents of the noted Indiana citizen, who constitutes the subject of this sketch.

Reuben Dailey was born at Tottenham, Middlesex county, England, March 6, 1844, being the youngest of a family of nine children, of whom the only daughter and four sons reached maturity. Reuben was strongly inclined towards a ministerial career, but his father offered violent opposition to this choice, his argument being that preachers should not be educated in the ordinary way, but depend on supernatural influence for their accomplishments. When still quite young Mr. Dailey came to the United States and spent some time at Pittsburg and Cincinnati, but was living at Newport, Kentucky, at the breaking out of the Civil war. He was eager to enlist, but met opposition on account of his youth, later, however, succeeding in enrolling himself as a member of Company F, Fifth Regiment, Ohio Volunteer Infantry, with which in due time he joined the Army of the Potomac. An illustration of his youthful ambition as well as the characteristic turn of his mind is found in the fact that in addition to his accoutrements he always carried with him a set of shorthand books. These he studied industriously in leisure moments, having made up his mind to become a reporter. Being religious and moral he avoided the ordinary dissipations of camp life, such as cards, profanity and drink and long before the end of his enlistment he had mastered the intricacies of shorthand reporting. During his service of three years and two months he was frequently employed as clerk for the company and the brigade surgeon being wounded in the face in an engagement that took place at Culpeper Court House, August 9, 1862, he was shortly afterwards detailed as clerk to General Halleck, subsequently acting as shorthand reporter for several court martial and military commissions. In April, 1865, Mr. Dailey became river reporter for the Memphis Argus, and retained this place for three years and a half, during which time he held the offices of magistrate and United States Commissioner, the latter by appointment of Judge Trigg.

By mere accident in January, 1869, he obtained a position as reporter on the Louisville Courier Journal, and was assigned to Jeffersonville and New Albany. Later he bought the National Democrat, a weekly publication, and on November 18, 1872, began the publication of the Jeffersonville Evening News, in handbill form. From that time until the close of his career, he was editor and publisher of this sprightly sheet, which was the first daily paper ever published in Clark county. He steadily improved the quality, while increasing the size of his paper, and achieved a financial success, which was chiefly due to his versatility and enterprising methods. Originally Republican in politics, Mr. Dailey's views underwent a change as a result of what he saw of the working reconstruction in the South, and he returned to Indiana as a

34

convert to Democracy. By his personal activity and strong editorial utterances he wielded a potential influence for his party in and around Jeffersonville, and was long regarded as one of the "wheel-horses." In 1892 Mr. Dailey was elected to the lower House of the State Legislature as Representative from Clark county and made a creditable record. For two years he served as chairman of the Democratic Central Committee of Clark county, and in this position exercised a large influence. Mr. Dailey was generous to a fault, never turning a deaf ear to any applicant, and though often imposed on readily forgave the impostor if occasion made it necessary. He kept what he called his museum, which contained objects purchased from mendicants merely as an excuse for giving. His last illness, which began in January, terminated fatally on April 8, 1906, and during the time he proved a very patient sufferer, never murmuring, however great the pain. Mr. Dailey's funeral occurred April 11th, and while his remains laid in state at the First Presbyterian church, of which he was a member at the time of his death, they were viewed by all the school children and nearly every man, woman and child in the city. Most of the leading business men at one time were carriers on his paper, the "News." His remains rest in the Eastern cemetery at Jeffersonville, Indiana, where, inscribed on his tomb are the words, "He lived for others."

On December 26, 1865, Mr. Dailey was married at Newport, Kentucky, to Anna Eliza Deviney, a native of Louisville, and the only surviving child of Captain Madison Deviney. There were five children by this union, as follows: Kate Middleton, Bird, Reuben Seymour, all deceased. Those surviving are a daughter by the name of Nahma, who married Nelson R. Bird, of the Art Engraving Company in London, England. She is quite accomplished as an artist and wood carver, having studied in Paris and also under Benjamin Pittman and Henry L. Fry, of Cincinnati. The latter was one of the carvers for the houses of parliament and the throne of England. Mrs. Bird has three children. Clarence Irving Dailey, the only son, now thirty-four years old, succeeded his father as editor of the Evening News and publishes the paper in connection with his mother. Mr. Dailey's home life was ideal, his hospitality unstinted and his affection for his household strong and tender. While stationed at Washington during the war, he professed religion in the Methodist church, and subsequently was baptized into the Christian church at Fulton, Ohio, although early in life he never had any fixed denominational belief. He was a member of Tabor Lodge, No. 92, Independent Order of Odd Fellows; Eureka Lodge, No. 3, Knights of Pythias; Falls City Lodge No. 8, Ancient Order United Workmen; Rain Commandery, No. 15, United Order of the Golden Cross, Veteran Odd Fellows' Association and the Grand Army of the Republic.

JAMES McGREGOR.

In a modest frame cottage on one of the residence streets of Jefferson-ville may be found an interesting man to talk to in his leisure hours. Large and well built, six feet four inches tall, his personality is unusually impressive, of quiet demeanor and unassuming, it is necessary to "draw him out" to talk of himself, though few have more entertaining stories to tell of the heroic days when the Union forces were opening the Mississippi. James McGregor was born in Beaver county, Pennsylvania, September 11, 1840, and was a son of Matthew and Ellen (Veasey) McGregor, the latter the daughter of an Irish mother and Vermont father. When four years old James was partly orphaned by the death of his father and being taken to Gallia county, Ohio, he spent the next eleven years in that locality. In 1855 the family removed to Henryville, Clark county, Indiana, and four years later he secured a job with the Jeffersonville & Madison Railroad Company as construction hand. He "stepped off" the distance for the setting of telegraph poles from Seymour to Columbus, walking all the way. He was thus employed when the Civil war broke out and in 1862 enlisted in the Forty-ninth Regiment, Indiana Volunteer Infantry, with which he went to the front and saw arduous service. He participated in the bloody affair at Haines Bluff, when the unsuccessful attack was made to break the lines at Vicksburg. He was with his command in the boat trip up White river and overland to Arkansas Post when that place was captured with seven thousand prisoners. The next severe engagement was at Port Gibson, whose capture forced the Confederates to abandon Grand Gulf. Sixteen days later Mr. McGregor was taken prisoner at the battle of Champion's Hill, but was exchanged several months later and took part in a four months campaign in Texas. After a trip up Red river he was assigned to guard duty in New Orleans and Algiers for four months. Next he was on an ocean steamer for fifteen days, guarding Confederate officers who were being taken to New York. The vessel was loaded with powder captured in the forts at Mobile and it stopped two days at Key West on the voyage to the North. His next service was as train guard on the Kentucky Central Railroad, which lasted until his muster out in 1865. Among Mr. McGregor's reminiscences is a story which establies his reputation as an excellent shot. A sharpshooter of the enemy, from a distant clump of brushes, was picking off men in the Union skirmish line, one at a time. Five had fallen, Mr. McGregor was the seventh in line and as his time was soon to come he determined to head off the dangerous "Johnny" if he could. Dropping to a knee he waited for the next puff of smoke and fired at this target in ambush. After the battle he found the dead sharpshooter at the place he had made so fatal to the Federals. On another occasion a group of rowdies tried to jostle him off the sidewalk, but bringing to bear his massive frame, he shouldered them into the gutter in quick succession and asked ironically if they had any friends who wished to meet him. Shortly after the war Mr. McGregor resumed his old position with the Indiana Railroad Company and in two months was appointed brakeman, then foreman and on May 15, 1870, was promoted to the place of engineer. He has been with this same company since and is probably the oldest continuous employe as he is now in the fiftieth year of his service.

On July 7, 1870, Mr. McGregor married Rebecca J., daughter of Joshua and Matilda Bennett, residents of Scott county, one mile east of Vienna. They have had six children: William H., the eldest, married a Miss Deark and was killed while engineering on the Pennsylvania Railroad, May, 1908, leaving two children; Belle is the wife of W. A. Poole, a monument dealer; Frank is an extra conductor on the Henderson route; James, Jr., died in childhood; Nellie married Charles Young and resides west of New Albany; Earl Bennett is with his brother-in-law in the monument business.

Mr. McGregor is a member of the Clark Lodge, No. 40, Free and Accepted Masons, of the Brotherhood of Locomotive Engineers, and the Christian church of Jeffersonville.

MAJ. BENJAMIN FRANKLIN BURLINGAME.

It has been nearly thirty years since he passed away, but hundreds still remember "Frank" Burlingame with feelings of regret. A brave, true man in all the relations of life he made and held friends as the result of his kindly accommodating disposition. He could fight when fighting was necessary, but preferred peace, and always dealt nobly with his fellow men. His children recall with delight the care and devotion he showed them and are justly proud of his memory. The flowers scattered on memorial day reach no mound that covers a braver soldier, a warmer friend or a more honest man than this dead comrade. Benjamin F. Burlingame was born in Syracuse, New York, in 1832, his parents being Benjamin F. and Adeline (Merrill) Burlingame. The latter located in Wilmington, Dearborn county, Indiana, when their son was a small boy and there he grew to man's estate. While a student at the Wilmington Seminary he was always a leader in the debates as well as the pranks so characteristic of abounding youth. He early developed a liking for the trades, was not afraid of work and before reaching his majority was able to secure good positions. One of these, which he filled acceptably, was as master mechanic of the Cochran shops, a large car manufacturing company in the suburbs of Aurora. At the outbreak of the Civil war he enlisted as a private in a company commanded by Captain Patterson, of Aurora, and the first military organization formed in Dearborn county for the Union. He rose to the rank of sergeant during the three months' service, re-enlisted as second lieutenant and was later promoted to the position of major. At the battle of Carrick's Ford Major Burlingame shot and killed General Garnett, the first Confederate officer of that rank who fell in the Civil war, the encounter taking place in a thicket. About the year after the close of the war Major Burlingame removed to Jeffersonville and took a position as foreman in the car works. He was later made superintendent and held this important place until his death, in 1880.

On March 25, 1862, Major Burlingame married Elizabeth, daughter of John P. and Rachael (Peynton) Rogers. Three of their children died in infancy and Frank, a promising son, passed away at the threshold of life, when eighteen years old. The surviving children are Paul, secretary to the Mayor of Louisville; Minnie, wife of Charles Rose, who resides in Jeffersonville, and Roger, a reporter for the Louisville Times. Elizabeth, who married Harry Bird, of the Jeffersonville News, died April 16, 1907, leaving one child, John Arthur. About 1890 Mrs. Burlingame removed to Greencastle in order to give her sons the advantage of an education at DePauw University. She engaged in business and through no fault of her own became involved in financial difficulties. Although in a position to refuse payment to creditors, like the high-minded woman she is, the opportunity was spurned, and she assumed bravely the entire obligation and by her own efforts earned the money to pay off every cent. Thus she preserved her financial honor unimpaired, besides proving herself a woman of excellent business qualities. This is precisely what her lamented husband would have desired her to do and in doing it she obtained the additional satisfaction of feeling that she had honored his hallowed memory, by leaving a stainless record for their children.

CAPT. HENRY DUGAN.

Mark Twain should have known this veteran boatman before he wrote his celebrated account of learning to be a pilot on the Mississippi. Captain Dugan could have given him pointers and furnished him lots of humor equal to that of Clemens himself. He was born in Switzerland county, Indiana, in 1853, his parents being William Perry and Mary (Wiley) Dugan, the latter a daughter of a Virginia farmer and the former a son of George Dugan, a Baptist preacher in Kentucky. While Henry was a small boy his family removed to Madison, and in 1862 to Jeffersonville. While at school one day he and his fellow pupils saw a lot of Confederate prisoners marching from the steamboat landing. The little boys showed their patriotism by throwing gravel at the "Johnny Rebs," among whom happened to be Simon Bolivar Buckner, destined to become a candidate of the Gold Democrats for President in a later day. When a little older the future steamboatman "played hooky" and worked for twenty-five cents an hour helping roll flour onto freight vessels. He also worked in the big government bakery, where they made "hard tack" for the army. A druggist who went to the war turned his store over to young Henry and an elder brother and the boys ran it with a rush until their father stopped them for fear they would poison someone. Before being thus called down they had done a land office business with the soldiers and officers camped east of Jeffersonville and were making money. An unamiable school teacher who was too zealous with the rod caused Henry to run away from home at the age of thirteen and join a steamboat crew as roustabout, bound for New Orleans. He soon became homesick from the cursings and thumpings received from his rough associates, but the pilots learning that his father was the well known captain on the Louisville mail boats rescued him from his pursecutors and taught him to steer the craft. On that trip he began his experience as pilot and engineer, the passion for which calling has kept him on the river ever since. He has been on the Ohio, the Mississippi and its tributaries in every capacity connected with steamboat work. He taught the business to his brothers and probably fifty other boys acquired the same knowledge from Captain Dugan. He is employed by the Louisville and Jeffersonville Ferry Company and for the past twenty years has had charge of their excursion boat, handling crowds that average one hundred and twenty thousand each summer. He has never had an accident for which the management was liable, a record for prudence and skill of which any captain might be proud. Captain Dugan has seen Jeffersonville grow from a small town, where nearly all the business was on the square of Spring street, from Market to the river. When he came here the square on which the city hall now stands was a public park. Near the present location of the city hall was the primitive log jail, which was in use until a prisoner set it on fire and caused its destruction.

December 24, 1876, Captain Dugan married Hanna, daughter of Charles and Adeline (Seibert) Deirflinger. Their six children are: Ida May, wife of Clarence E. Howard, a well known contractor and builder of Jeffersonville; Madison, who married Lina Schultz; Harry, who married Myrtle Stigwald; Georgia, wife of William Worral, of Jeffersonville; William Henry, assistant engineer of his father's boat; Raymond Scott, at home with his parents. Captain Dugan is a member of the Knights and Ladies of Honor, and the Odd Fellows. His wife is active in the Daughters of Rebekah, as well as in the Wall Street Methodist Episcopal church, of which both are members. Captain Dugan has represented the Fourth ward in the City Council and at present is a member of the County Council, which has the appropriation of all county funds.   He has been an active Democrat for several years, having served during the past campaign in the County Central Committee.

WILLIAM FLETCHER HOBSON.

In the death of the subject of this sketch there was presented to the world the sad story of an act of heroism that was seldom, if ever, paralleled in the state of Indiana, and those who saw William Fletcher Hobson deliberately sacrifice his life that others might be saved, will never be able to efface that scene from their memories.   Death in a terrible form came to this courageous man when he was in his prime and although he could have escaped it by deserting his post, this he refused to do, thinking only of the human freight for whose safety he felt himself responsible.   When the soul took leave of the mangled body it marked the passing of one of the truest friends and most honorable citizens of Jeffersonville, a man with a record that was open to the inspection of the world.

No servant of the corporation, in the service of which he met his untimely death, stood higher in the estimation of the officials than Mr. Hobson and none were more popular among the employes, for all of whom he ever had a cheery word and a hearty handclasp.

Mr. Hobson was born December 23, 1861, at Utica, Indiana.   His parents were Manlus and Sarah (Snider) Hobson.   Manlus was a school teacher and died when William was five years old.   The little boy then went to live with his grandparents, with whom he remained until November 10, 1885, when he was united in marriage to Eva Graves, daughter of Alfred and Cynthia (Strutt) Graves, of Charlestown.   Five children were the result of this marriage, Herbert, May, Otto, Roy and Leta.   Herbert and Otto are both in the employ of the Louisville & Southern Traction Company.   Herbert is married, his wife's maiden name being Nellie Blyth.   They have one son, Evan Fletcher Hobson.

When the first street cars were started in Jeffersonville William F. Hobson was placed in charge of one of them as motorman.   He operated the first cars that were run on the Chestnut and the Court avenue lines, and it was his car that hauled the first trailer from New Albany to Jeffersonville, and also that which was pulled from Jeffersonville to Charlestown.   For one year he served in the capacity of inspector for the local street railway system.   Death came to him on July 20, 1907, while at his post of duty, in a collision between his car and a big work car near Watson.   The work car, through a mistake of the motorman as to the time, was pushing along the rails of the main line at a great speed, when it should have been on the sidetrack, and the two cars met on a sharp curve. The subject had plenty of opportunity to jump and save his life, but instead of doing so he vainly endeavored to stop his car, but it had attained a rate of speed that made this impossible, and in the terrific crash that came his life went out.

Herbert Hobson, son of William F., had an experience in 1908 that would indicate that the young man has inherited some of the nerve that was possessed by his father. At the risk of his own life he snatched an elderly woman from in front of an approaching car when there seemed to be no chance, whatever, of saving her life.

Mr. Hobson was a lifelong and most earnest member of the Methodist church. He belonged to but one secret order, the Modern Woodmen. That he was a man of strong religious convictions was evidenced by the fact that a well worn Bible, in which many impressive passages were marked, was found on his mangled body. His record may prove a source of inspiration to others, and it is certainly a priceless heritage to his widow and children. His daily life was proof that he loved his fellow men and his heroic death was the fruits of such a life.

GEORGE M. RICKARD.

The story of the career of the gentleman of this review is that of a young man, who though confronted at almost every turn in his life with discouragements and obstacles, never faltered in his determination to reach the goal upon which his vision had been focussed since early boyhood. His early struggles to secure an education that he might go forth well equipped to take up the battle of life were, in a way, a true index to his sturdy character.

George M. Rickard was born in Toronto, Kansas, October 25, 1881, the son of Louis and Sarah E. Rickard, the latter's maiden name being Snyder. The parents of George M. had moved from Washington county, Indiana, to Kansas in 1876. They remained in the Sunflower state until George M. was seven years old, when they moved to Missouri. At the end of a period of three years they returned to Indiana, taking up their residence in Jeffersonville, where they have lived most of the time since. The paternal grandparents of George M. Rickard were George and Catherine (Motsinger) Rickard, and they at one time owned an entire section of land. The former helped build the Louisville and Portland canal. The great-grandfather of Mr. Rickard came to this country from Germany in 1777, settling in Pennsylvania. Later he made a trip to South America, where he remained for seven years, returning to Pennsylvania at the end of that time. The grandfather of the subject came west in 1810 and settled in Washington county, Indiana.

George M. Rickard completed a course in the public schools and then entered Borden College, graduating therefrom in 1900. While attending this institution he worked during his spare time in order to obtain funds to pay 'his expenses. Immediately after leaving college he took up the profession of teacher. He first taught the school at Nabb, Indiana, and later spent two years as a teacher in the schools of Jeffersonville township. He then became principal of the Port Fulton schools, has occupied that position for five years.

Mr. Rickard was married to Myra M. Grant, June 10. 1906, at Louisville, Kentucky. She is the daughter of Charles and Matilda Grant. Mr. and Mrs. Rickard are regular attendants at the Baptist church, and the former is an active worker in the cause of Democracy, although he has never held nor asked for any political offices. Mr. Rickard is a member of the Odd Fellows and the Knights of Pythias lodges.

CAPT. WILLIAM F. CISCO.

The career of Mr. Cisco has been marked by more thrilling experiences and narrow escapes from death than are crowded into the life of the average man, and the reputation of being one of the most courageous citizens of Southern Indiana is deservedly his. His occupations have been varied, but he can look back upon the days when he was serving the people of his municipality as an officer of the law at the most strenuous period in his existence. When he assumed the duties devolving upon the head of the police department 'crime was rampant in this community, there being a perfect epidemic of burglaries and robberies. In fact the conditions existing at that time might well have been likened unto a veritable reign of terror, but the advent of the subject into the office of Superintendent of Police signalized the beginning of the end of the operations of one of the worst gang of marauders that ever plied their nefarious vocation in the southern part of the state.

William F. Cisco was born in Boone county, Kentucky, in 1860, being the son of Francis and Elizabeth (Hedges) Cisco. Francis Cisco was the son of Hiram Cisco, who came from France to this country, and first settled in California, but later moved to Ohio. The name of his family was originally Francisco. The father of William F. is dead, but his mother still lives in Jeffersonville, his parents having come to this place when he was six years of age. He attended the public schools and showing a great aptitude for the absorption of knowledge graduated at quite an early age. Immediately after leaving school he accepted employment in a clerical capacity in the general store of John Bentel, remaining here until he had attained his twenty-second year. In 1889 he accepted a municipal appointment, being superintendent of pumps and wells in Jeffersonville. He held this position until the year of 1893, when he was made Chief of Police by a board that had been appointed by Governor Matthews, and it was in this capacity that he made a most enviable record, very early in his tenure of office demonstrating that he was a man absolutely without fear. When the foul murder of Stephen Gehr shocked an outraged community Captain Cisco declared that he would apprehend the negro who committed the brutal crime, and that it was no idle boast was evidenced by after events. There were ominous threats of lynching, but in order to prevent this blot from falling upon the good name of the community the fearless official placed his prisoner behind the bars of the state prison, where the would-be avengers of the negro's victim could not reach him. Among his other notable feats while directing the affairs of the police department was the capture of Gray and Gaynor, who killed a druggist at Reelsville, Indiana, and as a token of their appreciation of his success the authorities bestowed upon him a reward of goodly proportions. One of the many occasions when Captain Cisco showed his absolute fearlessness was when he prevented a prospective prize fight despite the fact that a mob of eight hundred men were at the ring side, who threatened the lives of him and Sheriff Davis. Later on he completely broke up an organized gang of thieves who were looting stores throughout the city, their leader a man named Chapman, alias Blackburn, subsequently sawing his way out of the Clark county jail.

At the conclusion of his term as Chief of Police Captain Cisco engaged in several different lines of business.

William F. Cisco was married to Lena Friend, daughter of Leonard and Elizabeth Friend. Three children were the fruits of this union: William B., Walter L., and Lila Margaret, the latter being the wife of LeRoy J. Hanna, traffic agent of the Indianapolis and Louisville line. Captain Cisco has always been an admirer of blooded horses, and for a long time had a number of fine racing equines, but recently disposed of them.

He is vice-president of the Knights and Ladies of Washington, in Kentucky, is a member in high standing of the Eagles, Red Men and Knights and Ladies of Honor. Captain Cisco has the respect and the confidence of the best people of Jeffersonville.

PETER CAMPBELL DONALDSON.

Although a young man, heavy responsibilities rest upon the shoulders of Peter C. Donaldson, but that he is eminently able to discharge them to the entire satisfaction of his superiors is attested by the great length of his service with the corporation which he represents. He is conversant with the minute details of the transportation business, possesses an active mind, rare good judgment, and the ability to solve any intricate problem that may arise in connection with the affairs of which he has charge. He embarked upon a business career before he had crossed the threshold of manhood, and his excellent qualifications for the position that he now occupies soon manifested themselves.

Peter C. Donaldson was born at Brownsville, Pennsylvania, June 15, 1879, his parents being Peter and Eliza Ford (Campbell) Donaldson. He was educated in the public schools of the place of his birth, and graduated with honor. At the age of twenty he went to Pittsburg and secured a position with a coal company, being connected with the transportation department. He came to Jeffersonville January 1, 1904, as the representative of the People's Coal Company, one of the largest concerns of the kind in Pittsburg. He has charge of what is known as the coal fleet, composed of a large number of great barges, on which coal is conveyed from Pittsburg into the Jeffersonville district. At the last named point the cargo of these barges is held for distribution to the dealers of the Falls cities. They have an average capacity of about eighteen car loads.

Mr. Donaldson is in close touch with the business community of Jeffersonville, and is regarded as a man of ability beyond his years. He takes a deep interest in both the business and social affairs of Jeffersonville, and has the happy faculty of making friends very readily, which largely accounts for his great popularity. He is a member of the Elks lodge. He lives in a commodious brick residence overlooking the Ohio river.

WILLIAM A. DAVIS.

Bereft of a father, who sacrificed his life in the service of his country in the Civil war, Mr. Davis, when he had barely entered his teens, practically began the struggle of life, being compelled to contribute to the support of his widowed mother, and the three other children, younger than himself. Working hard by day he attended school at night, pursuing a course in bookkeeping, paying his tuition from his pitifully small earnings. He was ambitious to rise from the depths, and this spurred him on to his best efforts. Despite the handicap of poverty and its attendant hardships and privations, he pushed bravely on, and the end of his course of study found him as well equipped from an educational standpoint as the average lad of that day.

William A. Davis was born January 25, 1859, at New Market, Clark county, Indiana, being the son of E. I. Davis, who was lieutenant of the

Eleventh Cavalry, Seventy-seventh Regiment, Indiana Volunteers, commissioned by Governor Morton. In 1863, while in the service he died of typhoid fever, leaving a wife and four children, three boys and a girl. Since attaining his majority the subject has been an active worker in the interest of the Democratic party, and that political organization has honored him with several offices. He is at the present time vice-chairman of the County Central Committee. He was a member of the Jeffersonville City Council for four years, representing the Fifth ward, and after that he served as trustee of Jeffersonville township. In the year of 1892 he was nominated for Sheriff of Clark county by the Democrats, and elected the following fall by over six hundred plurality. An event followed his induction into office which demonstrated beyond all question that he was a courageous official, with a determination to carry out the obligations of his oath, and enforce the statutes of Indiana without fear or favor. The information came to him that a prize fight, arranged by New Albany men, was to occur on the county line, and accompanied by Captain Cisco, then Chief of Police, he went to the place where the fight was to take place. This was on August 29, 1893, and when the two officers reached their destination they found a gathering of about eight hundred men, who declared that they would not permit of any official interference with the principals. Although they were surrounded by a threatening mob, some of whom were desperadoes, many of them under the influence of liquor, the officers showed not the slightest fear. They were the objects of curses and threats, but with revolvers in their hands they stood their ground, and when the members of the crowd saw that they were determined to uphold the law at any cost they changed their methods and held out inducements in the shape of bribes. These offers not having the desired effect they again resorted to abuse and threats, but finally the determined attitude of Sheriff Davis and his companion caused them to depart. Mr. Davis was also largely instrumental in ferreting out the slayers of Stephen Gier, and received much praise for his work on that celebrated murder case. After his term as Sheriff had expired Mr. Davis was named as the president of the Jeffersonville school board, serving in that capacity for nine years.

What is known as the Spring Hill school stands as a monument to the efforts of Mr. Davis. It was through his urgency and persistency mainly that this school was built. It is a modern structure, and considered one of the finest educational institutions in the southern part of the state.

In 1889 William Davis and Florence Dunn were united in marriage. Mrs. Davis was the daughter of Jonathan Dunn, of Utica township. Four children were born to them, two girls and two boys, namely: Alta, Lucy, Elmer and Edmund. The subject is a member and trustee of the First Christian church, and belongs to the Elks, Knights of Pythias, and the Modern Woodmen of America. At the present time he is engaged in the business of a contracting painter. When in the City Council he was always to be found on the side of any enterprise that had for its object the benefit of the interests of the people whom he represented. It was while he was in this body that the water works was built, and the electric light plant installed.

JOHN C. LEPPERT.

An adept at the trade that his father followed before him, John C. Leppert has, despite the sharp competition in his particular line in Jeffersonville, built up a patronage that brings in no mean financial returns, and it may be truthfully said of him that he is on the high road to prosperity. Mr. Leppert is a quiet, unassuming man of frugal habits, with a great love and devotion for his home and family. Although not a native of Jeffersonville, he has been engaged in the barber business in this city for a number of years. His establishment is modern in every respect, and this fact in connection with the surety of first class workmanship has been the means of insuring to him a liberal patronage from the best class of citizens.

Mr. Leppert first saw the light in Perry county, Indiana, October 31, 1865. His parents were John and Maria (Gartner) Leppert, and both of them were natives of Germany. When John C. was but nine years of age his parents removed from Perry county to Louisville, Kentucky, where his father engaged in the business of a barber. Very early in life the son went to work in the shop, and before he had reached his majority was complete master of the trade. On October 13, 1891, he married Clara L. Yester, of Claysburg. The father of Mrs. Leppert was born in Baden, Germany, in 1840, and came to this country in 1852, settling in New Albany, Indiana. Ten years later he married Wilhelmina Oehms, and they removed to Claysburg. There were born to them nine children, as follows: Mrs. Anna Morgan, William Yester, Mrs. Emma Bellis, Mrs. Minnie Robbins, George Yester, Mrs. Olive Whitlow, Mrs. Augusta Carr, Charles Yester, and Mrs. John C. Leppert.

Mr. Leppert is looked upon as a fixture in Jeffersonville, his shop being one of the oldest in the city and situated in the very heart of the business district. Being within easy access of their establishments it is patronized very liberally by men engaged in mercantile pursuits. Mr. and Mrs. Leppert and two sons, Carl and Clarence, live at the modest, but pretty residence of his father-in-law, Mr. Yester, in Claysburg, which is a suburb of Jeffersonville. He is a member of but one secret order, Myrtle Lodge, No. 9, Knights of Pythias. Mr. Leppert does not take part in affairs of a political nature, but is public-spirited and has the best interests of Jeffersonville at heart.

JAMES MARRA.

With a reputation for fair dealing in all of his business transactions James Marra naturally occupies a high place in the mercantile circles of Jeffersonville, and the history of his career is illustrative of the fact that an honorable life is not without its reward. Behind these attributes coupled with a keen knowledge of human nature, and the ability to read it in all its varied forms and phases, lies the secret of his succcess. Few men have applied more closely to their business the injunctions of the Golden Rule, and that their application thereto has been a source of benefit to Mr. Marra is shown by the liberal patronage that is accored him. He began the business of a grocer in an unostentatious manner, and from a small store it has developed into one of the largest establishments of the kind in the city, counting among its patrons some of the best people in Jeffersonville.

James Marra, the son of Michael and Mary B. Marra, was born in Jeffersonville, Indiana, in 1875. His parents were both natives of Tipperary, Ireland. He spent his boyhood in the public schools of Jeffersonville, and after completing his education secured employment in a grocery, where he clerked for nine years, mastering every detail of the business. Being of a frugal disposition he saved his money, and in 1896 opened a store for himself at Watts and Crut avenue. His patronage grew beyound his fondest hopes, and he was soon able to greatly increase his stock. He kept in close touch with the market, and regulated his prices accordingly. He is a careful buyer, and refuses to handle any but first class goods, hence at the end of a dozen years as a purveyor to the wants of the public he finds himself on the high wave of prosperity with bright promises for the future.

Mr. Marra is a devout Catholic, and interests himself greatly in the affairs of the church, being one of the trustees of St. Augustine, and is a member of the Jeffersonville Council of the Knights of Columbus. He is an unmarried man.

BENJAMIN FRANKLIN STALKER, M. D.

Clark county boasts of no finer family than the Stalkers, who have been identified with its interests for over thirty-five years. George Stalker, the emigrant ancestor, came from Scotland as far back as the middle of the eighteenth century, and settled in North Carolina, when that state was still a colony of Great Britain. He left a son named Eli, who removed from the old North state and became a pioneer of Southern Indiana Territory about 1808. He first located in Clark county, but two years later went to Washington county, where he entered government land. He married Parthenia, daughter of Simon and Elizabeth Carress, reared a family while going through the hardships incident to life in the wilderness and in the course of nature was gathered to his fathers at a ripe old age. His son, Benjamin F. Stalker, was born on the farm near Salem, Washington county, Indiana, December 16, 1845. His experience was that of all boys whose lot was cast in the agricultural regions of the West during the pioneer period. Hard work on the farm as long as daylight lasted in the summer and fall, endless chores around the house and barn evenings and mornings, with brief terms of school attendance in winter, when the weather was bad—such was the experience of millions of western boys, including the one who was destined in later life to become Doctor Stalker. He had entered his seventeenth year in 1863, and being full of patriotic ardor, determined to join the great army at the front that was fighting the battle of freedom. His first enlistment was with the One Hundred Seventeenth Regiment, Indiana Volunteer Infantry, and the second in the Fifth Indiana Cavalry. He saw service during the fall and winter campaigns in Tennessee during the years of 1863-4 and participated in the sharp engagements at Bean Station, Walker's Ford, Strawberry Plains, and other conflicts that occurred between the contending forces for supremacy in East Tennessee. After the war he attended school at Salem, under Professor James G. May, and the high school at Bedford, of which his brother, John M. Stalker, was a professor. After teaching school for five years he entered the medical department of the Louisville University in 1871, and two years later obtained his degree. Doctor Stalker, armed with his "sheep skin" and full of hope and ambition determined to try his fortunes in the promising town of Borden and during the summer of 1873 hung out his shingle at that place. He prospered from the beginning and soon became one of the prominent men of his community. From 1900 to 1904 he served as Trustee of the township and in the latter year was a candidate for the Legislature on the Republican ticket, but was defeated. Doctor Stalker is a member of the New Providence Lodge, 237, Free and Accepted Masons, and his religious affiliations are with the Baptist church. He is one of the best known and most popular of the county's physicians.

On December 25, 1872, he married Frances C. Norris, daughter of Thomas B. and Hannah (Peoples) Norris. The former was for many years a prosperous farmer near Salem, and long held the office of Justice of the Peace. He was of an old pioneer family in that locality. To the doctor and wife these children have been born: the oldest daughter, Isadene, died in 1907; the others are James B., Charles H. and John M., all members of the medical profession. James Bodine Stalker graduated in the medical department of the University of Louisville; Charles Homer and John Morton Stalker both graduated from the Hospital Medical College at Louisville. Dr. J. B. and Dr. Charles H. are practicing with their father at Borden,

Indiana, and in the surrounding country, while John M. is engaged in practice at the Pope Sanitorium in Louisville. All these are young men of good professional attainments and of the highest character as citizens.

LEWIS E. RICHARDS.

Among the younger generation in Indiana educational circles few give brighter promise of future usefulness than the modest and studious Professor Richards, who is descended from a remarkably virile ancestry, whose line is seldom equalled for longevity, strength of constitution and vigor to meet all the duties of life. His grandfather was Henry Richards, a pioneer "circuit riding" Baptist preacher, widely known in Southern Indiana and Northern Kentucky, as Elder Richards. He left eight sons and a daughter, all of whom are still living, the youngest being sixty-five, and the oldest ninety-five years of age, which is a circumstance perhaps unparalleled in any family of equal numbers. Three of these brothers served as oldiers during the Civil war and came through the ordeal entirely unscathed. Isaac Richards, the youngest of this interesting family, married Rebecca A., daughter of Jonathan Lyons, who came from Marietta, Ohio, in 1837 and settled in Grant county, Indiana, and there carried on his trade as a miller.

Lewis E. Richards, a son by this union, was born at Matthews, Grant county, Indiana, March 9, 1874. He grew up on his father's farm, went at an early age as a student in Fairmount Academy and completed his education at DePauw University. He was graduated there in the spring of 1902 and in the fall of the same year he took charge of the science department in Fairmount Academy. During the summer he had done post-graduate work at the university and when he finished was well equipped for his future educational career. He remained at Fairmount until March, 1904, when he resigned to take charge as professor of chemistry and physics in the high school at Jeffersonville. He has since retained this position and given entire satisfaction to his class, his patrons and the higher officials of the city's educational department.

On December 24, 1904, Professor Richards was married to Rose May, daughter of Rev. Henry and Caroline Watson. Mrs. Richard's father was long a Methodist minister, serving at various places, according to the itinerant system of that denomination and was well known in Northern Indiana. At the time of his death, in 1889, he was pastor in charge of the Methodist Episcopal church at Wabash, Indiana. The maiden name of his wife was Caroline Crow, and she was connected with one of the old time families who took part in rescuing Indiana from the primeval wilderness. Mr. and Mrs.

Richards have three children, Blyth W., Celestine Hope and Louverne Caroline. The family are members of the Wall Street Methodist church, are quite popular in their social circles and are welcome guests at the houses of the best people in the city. Personally Professor Richards easily makes friends, either professionally or socially. Studious by nature he is very fond of his books, especially those having a bearing on the department of education in which he is engaged. He has all the qualifications of a natural born educator and an ambition for success in the educational world, which his friends predict is sure to follow his studious habits and steady application to his duties.

SAMUEL McKINLEY.

The name of McKinley has of late years assumed something of a historic significance in this land of ours for it is linked in the public memory with the remembrance of a martyred President. It is but fitting that this should be so. And yet the family name and traditions go back beyond that towering figure of recent years, across the Atlantic and across the centuries, to find an ancestor of distinction and merit. The first to emerge out of the twilight of tradition with a definite record is the figure of a Scotch Covenanter, who, when the vicissitudes of the times made it necessary for him, went from his native land across to Ireland; thence in after years to the United States. Two of his sons, David and James McKinley, settled in Shelby county, Kentucky, and came in after years to the spot in Clark county, Indiana, where Borden now stands. David shortly after went northward to South Bend, and thence to Canton, Ohio, while James remained and made Wood township his future home. David McKinley, as may be surmised, was the great-grandfather of President McKinley. James McKinley reared six sons; James, John, Thomas, William, Jeremiah and Alexander. The first named son, James, was the father of the subject of our sketch. James married Jincy Packwood, a native of Virginia, the daughter of Samuel Packwood. Samuel McKinley had eleven children, of whom nine are yet living. They are: Edward, Fred, Charles, and Albert McKinley, and Mrs. Kate Minton, Mrs. Blanch Bell, Mrs. Lillie Bere, Mrs. Nettie Byerly, and Julia McKinley, all living in Borden with the exception of the three married sisters. Mrs. Kate Minton lives in Georgetown, Floyd county; Mrs. Blanche Bell lives in Jeffersonville, and the other married sisters in Louisville.

Samuel McKinley was born in Borden in 1836 and still resides at the family homestead. The tanyard, where he worked at his trade as a tanner, was first the property of his father. At a later period it belonged to an elder brother, and in 1866 our subject bought it and conducted a steady business

35

there until 1907, when ill health caused him to retire from the tanning business. Though advanced in years he is still active and deals very profitably in hides and furs. He is a prominent member of the Christian church and a man of importance in local affairs.

Samuel McKinley married Louise Scheicher, who was born of French parentage in Louisiana. Her father was Louis Scheicher, a native of the old province of France—Alsace-Lorraine; her mother, Catherine Scheicher, was also born in France.

On June 9, 1870, a son, Albert, was born to Samuel McKinley and wife. He is the popular postmaster of Borden. Albert McKinley was educated at the public schools and at Borden College and had a good college record. He was a precocious youth and at the age of fifteen started a small store, which developed into a large general store, which he sold at a good figure in May, 1906. At the age of twenty-one he was appointed postmaster of Borden, or New Providence, as it was then known, the appointment coming from President Harrison. He completed his term of office of four years in an admirable manner and was classed among those whose offices were excellently conducted. On July 27, 1897, he was re-appointed postmaster, a position which he has held ever since. In January of the year 1896 he married Eva M. Johnson, an event which marked the commencement of a happy married life. Four children have been born to them. They are: Carl, Ray, Robert and Mary Louise.

Albert McKinley is a prominent member of the Independent Order of Odd Fellows. In 1902 he was the Republican candidate for Representative but the county went, as it usually did, Democratic, and Albert McKinley accompanied his state ticket in the landslide. In 1904 he was elected chairman of the County Committee (Republican), and on going forward as a candidate for the Legislature he carried his own township and had the pleasure to be the first Republican on the county ticket to carry Wood township. For sixteen consecutive years ending in 1906 he has been a delegate to the state convention of his party, and has always found himself on the County Committee. During his County Chairmanship the county, usually six to eight hundred Democratic, went Republican.

Outside of politics Albert McKinley is quite as popular and successful. He has two fine farms and a beautiful home in Borden. He may be safely slated as a self-made man as he has been making his own way and making his presence felt in the community since his life reached the fifteenth and a half year mark.

His father, Samuel McKinley, is also extensively known and respected. Since his lapse into the less strenuous life of his present occupation he spends more time in the association of old acquaintances, which is one of his chief delights.

CHARLES W. DEAN.

Bartholomew Dean, familiarly known to his friends as "Bart," is a native of Ireland and a good representative of the genial, rollicking sons of the famous little country beyond the sea. He is sociable, always ready for a harmless joke, and knows how to make as well as hold friends. His parents brought him to America in 1840, when he was quite young and he had to shift for himself from an early period, but always managed to "get there" in whatever he undertook. After his father's death in New York, he came West and found himself in Illinois at the opening of the Civil war. Like most of the first immigrants he was patriotic and determined to offer his life in defense of the Union. Shortly after the first call for troops he enlisted in Company H, Thirteenth Regiment, Illinois Volunteer Infantry, and with his command was soon hurried to the front. He served four years, made a good soldier and after being honorably discharged came to Jeffersonville, where he has since made his home. He married Mary, daughter of Michael Halpin, who was born near Windsor, Canada.

Charles W. Dean, son of Bartholomew and Mary (Halpin) Dean, was born at Jeffersonville, in 1866, and as he grew up attended both the Catholic and public schools in his native city. After finishing his studies he learned the blacksmith's trade and worked at it until he was twenty-five years old. He then went into business for himself and has continued the same up to the present time. He is a member of the Eagles and of the St. Augustine's Catholic church. In personal appearance Mr. Dean is a tall, well built man, who looks younger than his years. His residence is in the same building where he carries on his business and as his disposition is social he has many friends. In 1890 he was married to Rosa Shane, of Madison, Indiana. Her father was Michael Shane and her mother before her marriage was Amelia Lichtenthaler. Mr. and Mrs. Dean have three children, Mary, Dora and Charles.

JOSEPH E. HADDOX.

When Longfellow wrote his famous poem on "The Village Blacksmith," which was read with delight by so many boys in the old McGuffey readers, he must have had in view men of the type of Mr. Haddox. This gentleman, long and favorably known in and around Borden, fills the bill exactly. He has the brawney arms like those of which Longfellow wrote, the kindly disposition, and the unpretentious industry which was so warmly praised by the poet as characteristic of the typical blacksmith. Perhaps the oldest of all the trades, it is also one of the most useful and it is well that all should be taught to respect those who pound out their living on the resounding anvil, to the harsh roar of the busy bellows. It is pleasing to speak a good word for men of this kind, and none deserve it more than Joseph E. Haddox, whose family sprang from what is now West Virginia, in the neighborhood of Wheeling.

Many years before the Civil war Elijah and Elizabeth (Smith) Haddox joined the tide of emigration that was setting in for the West, and after journeying down the Ohio for many miles concluded to land at Jeffersonville and locate in Clark county. With them came their son, John W. Haddox. who married Paulina, daughter of Southman Dietz, who lived at Blue Lick, near Memphis, since the early days. Joseph E. Haddox, who was one of the children by this marriage, was born near Memphis, Clark county, in 1860. School facilities were not of the best in those days but he managed to pick up some "book learning" during brief terms in the district school-house, mostly in winter time and then rather irregularly.

His father had been a blacksmith and accordingly he learned the trade under him and concluded to make it the business of his life. He opened a shop at New Providence in 1890 and now has the largest and best smithy at that point. He has prospered, owns his own home, is a good, quiet citizen, devoted to his family and daily duties and lives a happy life. He belongs to New Providence Lodge, Free and Accepted Masons, and the Modern Woodmen.

In 1878 Mr. Haddox and Barbara A., daughter of Christopher and Barbara A. (Frailey) Young, were married. The latter's father was Henry Frailey, one of the first settlers in Rockford, Indiana. Christopher Young was the son of Christopher C. Young, who came from Pennsylvania, settled in Ohio and later came to Clark county, arriving about 1840. Mr. and Mrs. Haddox have four children: Annetta, Ivareena, Lelia Belle and Nina Barbara. The parents belong to the Christian Advent church and are highly respected by all who know them.

EDWARD ARTHUR RYANS.

Many years ago three boys played together in Ireland. They attended school at Belfast and often talked of what they would do when grown to be men. Even then their eyes were turned westward toward the great Republic, the Eldorado and land of promise of all the oppressed people of the unhappy Emerald Isle. The names of these boys were Alexander Stuart, John Shillito and Lewis Ryans. They came over together in the same ship and the very mention of the first two recalls the two most celebrated merchant princes this county ever produced. Stuart established himself in the dry goods trade in New York, accumulated an immense fortune, and became world famous. Shillito was but little less successful in Cincinnati, where his name was long a household word. The third boy did not get so rich or famous, but he proved himself a man of talent with a decided aptitude in business lines. Lewis Ryans found his way to Indiana and became a contracting painter on a large scale at Jeffersonville. He manufactured his own paints and did work all over the Central West. He also had considerable talent as an artist and used to paint boats by contract at the ship yards. For a while he was in the wholesale paint business at Louisville, in a partnership under the firm name of Johnson & Ryans. He married Clara Bell Swoke, a native of Vienna. Scott county, Indiana, by whom he had the following children: John B., now employed as foreman painter for his uncle, John Ryans, a contracting painter in Louisville, was elected City Alderman in 1898: Charles L., a resident of Covington, Kentucky, is baggage master on the Baltimore & Southwestern Railroad and well known as a writer of several popular songs; Ada, the oldest daughter, is still under the parental roof; Emma, a young daughter, is assistant librarian at the Carnegie Library in Jeffersonville.

Edward Arthur Ryans, the other son, was born at Jeffersonville, September 8, 1874, and received the usual education in the city schools Shortly after laying down his books he entered the employment of the Adams Express Company, with which he remained only a short while, but long enough to master the details of the business. In 1902 he was placed in charge of the Jeffersonville office of the United States Express Company and has remained with this corporation ever since.

Mr. Ryans was married June 21, 1900, to Mabel, daughter of Henry and Mary Elizabeth (Wacker) Helt. The former was descended from one of the prominent pioneers of Harrison county and the latter's father was a well known Methodist minister. Mr. Ryans is a member of the Jeffersonville Lodge of Free and Accepted Masons and of the Maccabees. He is a young man of popularity and promise, being ambitious, sociable and industrious. The Ryans family, of which he is an honored member, has long been prominent in the business and social circles of the Falls cities and have contributed their full share to the development of the community in their various callings.

JAMES J. KENDALL.

Sergeant James J. Kendall, interurban line ticket agent at Jeffersonville, Clark county, now in his sixty-sixth year, is a man who by his steadiness, reliability and attention, achieved success and distinction during his services in the local police force. In his present sphere, since his retirement from active police work, he has been none the less popular and successful. He was born in Hamilton county, Ohio, on the 28th of July, 1842, and was the son of Thomas Kendall and his wife, whose maiden name was Isabelle Campbell. Both Thomas Kendall and his wife came of respectable families living in Ohio. When James J. had arrived at the age of twelve years his parents moved to near Charlestown, Clark county, and afterwards located permanently on Silver creek, in Monroe township. James J. remained on the farm until about thirty years of age. About the year 1865 he married Margaret E. St. Clair, who came from Washington, Pennsylvania, and whose father was Jesse St. Clair.

, James J. Kendall moved to Jeffersonville about the year 1872 and there he followed the carpenter trade for several years. He then became connected with the police force and was for about ten years a sergeant. On his retirement, on December 1, 1907, he was appointed ticket agent for the Interurban lines at Jeffersonville, a position which he still holds.

Sergeant James J. Kendall and his wife have led a happy and peaceable married life, clouded only by the demise of three out of the four children born to them, three daughters having died before reaching the age of maturity. Their son, James Thomas Kendall, is now married. He has one son, Lee, who is the pride of both parents and grandparents. James T. Kendall's family live in Jeffersonville though he is, himself, engaged in the painting trade in Louisville, Kentucky.

Sergeant James J. Kendall is well known in Masonic circles. He is a member of the Jeffersonville Lodge, No. 340, Free and Accepted Masons. As a citizen of Jeffersonville he has attained an enviable standing, being popular and respected by all the people, young and old, irrespective of creed or class. This, no doubt, has been due to his cheerful and kindly nature and the pains he has ever taken to guard and direct the rights of his friends and neighbors. As a sergeant of police he did much to uphold and maintain the dignity of the local force; and as a public servant, constancy and faithfulness to duty have been his twin virtues. He is yet hale and hearty and it is the heartfelt wish of the vast majority of his fellow citizens that he may be spared to public life for many years to come.

MITCHELL PETER SMITH.

Our subject, who is part proprietor of the Eagle Laundry, Jeffersonville, Clark county, is a man of large and extensive acquaintance, not alone in his township and county, but at the different points along the river touched upon during his career as a pilot, and in the northern part of Kentucky, where members of the Smith family have been known for many generations.

Mitchell Peter Smith was born in Utica, Clark county, in 1874, the son of George Dallas Smith and Mary Esther Howes, his wife. Both parents were born in Jefferson county, Kentucky. Mrs. Smith was the daughter of Mitchell P. Howes, who, during his lifetime, owned the well known Utica Limestone quarries from the kilns of which the famous Utica lime is manufactured. Mitchell Howes was a man widely known in his section of the county and was the possessor of a large fruit farm in addition to his limestone interests.

George Dallas Smith was the son of Peter Smith, proprietor of large milling interests in Kentucky. One of his mills was located just above where the Galt House now stands in Louisville. He had another at Harrod's creek, and one at Utica. He used to consign and ship flour by flat-bottom boats to New Orleans. It was his custom to personally superintend the shipping of his produce and he once suffered the experience of being blown into the river on the explosion of an old steamboat boiler.

George D. Smith and his father, Peter Smith, were, as we have before stated, widely known in Kentucky. Both were strong men in every sense of the world, of dominant will power and stern self-control. Previous to the Civil war they were also slave owners; Peter Smith having at one time had a thousand slaves. The Smiths, though men of large responsibility, were of a disposition kind and warm-hearted; and many stories of their generous traits are not yet forgotten.

Mitchell P. Smith was brought by his parents to Fort Fulton about 1878. Here his father, who kept a toll-gate, from that time until 1906, became widely known all through the county. Mitchell P. received an education suitable to meet the requirements of our day. He attended the public schools of Jefferson and of Port Fulton and also at the New Albany Business College. He then went on the river and learned the pilot's profession in all its phases. He piloted tow boats from Madison, Indiana, to New Orleans. His career on the river extended over many years and, as may be imagined, was not without many events and incidents of an exciting nature.

On November 6, 1908, Mitchell P. Smith and Dale Talkington started a laundry on East Chestnut street, Jeffersonville. It is equipped with the most up-to-date appliances to do laundry work of all kinds. It is known as the "Eagle Laundry," and has been a success both in the volume of its business and the quality of the work turned out. It is located on the old site of what is probably the only whetstone factory in the United States; the factory itself having been moved to Ohio.

Mitchell P. Smith is but thirty-four years old and is as yet unmarried. He has been industrious and active and as a pilot was well liked and respected. The tow boats which he piloted used to tow from six hundred thousand to one million bushels of coal at one trip on the river. He still lives with his parents. He is a man of commanding personal appearance and is of likable disposition.

———————————

THEODORE S. LONG.

Undoubtedly one of the best known restaurant proprietors in Clark county is Theodore S. Long, of Jeffersonville, the excellence of whose table has been voiced by many a bonvivant of the vicinity. In his present sphere he has studied all phases of the catering business in a desire to bring it to a high state of perfection. A man of varied experience, he brings to his present undertaking all the enthusiasm of former business conquests. He engaged for an extended period in the saw-mill industry and is conversant with its every detail. Previous to his engaging in his present occupation, ten years spent in the huckster trade gave him a readiness and a facility in meeting exacting business conditions which has been of the utmost importance to him. Mr. Long comes of good stock and inherits many of the dominant characteristics of his family. On the mother's side he is a descendant of the McCormicks, whose exploits in the pioneer days are well known in this section of the state. Charles McCormick, one of the prominent members of the family and an early settler, was grandfather of Theodore S. Further data of interest regarding the McCormick ancestry may be found by turning to another portion of this volume.

Theodore S. Long was born near Charlestown, Clark county, in October, 1855. He was the son of Benjamin F. Long and wife, whose maiden name was Jemima McCormick. Benjamin F. was born on the same farm as was his son and lived there practically all his life. His wife was likewise a native of the county and was born on the adjoining McCormick farmstead. Charles McCormick, the grandfather above referred to, was also born in the neighborhood. That family originally came from West Virginia some time in the earliest part of the last century and became important factors in the winning and progress of Indiana.

Theodore S. Long remained on the home place until his twenty-first year, his education having been received in the neighboring public schools. From the year 1879 till 1892 he engaged in the saw-mill business, owning and operating his plant himself. The period with the exception of two years in Western Kentucky and two years in Arkansas was spent in Clark county. Returning to Charlestown in 1892 he ran a huckster wagon for ten years. In 1905 he moved to Jeffersonville and bought a restaurant on Spring street in the heart of the business district of that thriving community. His huckstering experiences enabled him to buy wisely and of the best quality and consequently give good value to his patrons.

In November of the year 1879 Mr. Long married Mattie Hickman, daughter of Benjamin and Julia (Eastes) Hickman. Both parents were natives of Kentucky, though Mrs. Long herself was born in Indianapolis. Four daughters have been born to them, viz: Frankie, Nina, Julia and Clara. The Long family live a happy home life and all its members belong to the Wall Street Methodist Episcopal church. Theodore S. Long is now in his fifty-fourth year and has yet the promise of a long life before him. He is a quiet and unassuming man and though his father, Benjamin F. Long, was at one time a County Commissioner of Clark county, his own ambitions have never verged towards political preferment.

CHARLES ROBERT RIGSBY.

Young, energetic and ambitious, with an unlimited capacity for work, and with a determination to perform any task he may undertake in a thorough manner, Charles R. Rigsby advanced rapidly in his chosen avocation. Since he began carving his own way in the world he has neglected no opportunity to better his condition, and his efforts have not been without results. He is known in railroad and business circles as a rising young man. Owing to the active interest that he takes in the affairs of the several secret organizations, of which he is a member, he has a very extensive acquaintance among men in various walks of life, and his social disposition has made him scores of warm friends.

Charles Robert Rigsby is the son of Thomas D. and Lida (Latta) Rigsby, and was born in Jefferson county, June 8, 1880. He was about five years of age when his parents moved to Jeffersonville, and shortly thereafter began his education in the public schools of this city, also receiving instructions in connection therewith by private tutors. After completing his regular school term he attended business college at New Albany, thereby procuring a good commercial education. He studied shorthand, and became an expert stenographer, securing employment in the offices of the Louisville & Nashville Railroad at Louisville. Later he became a bookkeeper and then took up the vocation of a traveling salesman. He is at the present time serving in the capacity of cashier.

Mr. Rigsby was married to Daisy Catherine Davis, February 26, 1902. She was the daughter of Jacob Truman Davis and wife, of Jeffersonville. The maiden name of Mrs. Davis was Sarah Catherine Earhart. Mr. and Mrs. Rigsby have one son, Kenneth Hardin Rigsby.

Mr. Rigsby is a member of Myrtle Lodge, No. 19, Knights of Pythias, Travelers' Protective Association, Woodmen of the World, and the H.

T. A. He is the popular past chancellor of the first named, and also past grand representative. He was named as a member of the building committee, which has in charge the erection of the new Pythian hall and armory in Jeffersonville. He and his wife are members of the Methodist church at Port Fulton.

Mr. Rigsby is public-spirited and of a charitable disposition, as many unfortunates in Jeffersonville can testify. His home life is all that could be desired.

FRANCIS EUGENE PAYNE, JR.

Railroad companies entrust the control of their engines only to men of nerve and intrepidity on whom they have a well founded reason for the confidence imposed. Such a man is Francis Eugene Payne, Jr., who began when about twenty years of age as fireman on the Pennsylvania Railroad, and who, some eight years after, was promoted to the position of engineer which he held until he relinquished the same in February, 1908. He now resides with his wife and family in Jeffersonville, his native town, where his domestic life is serene and ideal.

Mr. Payne was born in 1875, and was the son of Francis Eugene Payne, Sr., and his wife, whose maiden name was Kate R. Lewis. Both were born in Clark county about the middle of the past century. Mrs. Payne was the daughter of Felix R. Lewis, whose father, Major Lewis, had charge of the land office under President Jackson. The Lewis family were originally from Ohio. Our subject's father was the son of Francis Marion Payne, whose father, William Payne, came from Virginia to Jeffersonville, Clark county, Indiana, in the early part of the nineteenth century. Francis Eugene Payne, Sr., was a soldier in the Civil war, serving in the One Hundred Ninety-first Ohio Volunteers. His father, Francis Marion Payne, was one of the pioneer steamboat engineers on the Ohio river. Our subject's father also followed that occupation.

Francis Eugene Payne, Jr., grew up in Jeffersonville and attended the public schools there. He began active business life as a clerk in a Louisville wholesale drug store and later in a retail drug store owned by Doctor Fields in Jeffersonville. When about twenty years of age railroad life seemed alluring to him and he became a fireman on the Pennsylvania line, promotion coming to him in March, 1903, as we have already stated. December 21, 1898, was the occasion of his marriage to Edith L. Smith, daughter of George and Kate (Jordan) Smith. The Smiths moved to Jeffersonville when Mrs. Payne was but ten years old. Four children have been born to Mrs. Payne and her husband. They were named consecutively: Catherine, Perry, Francis E. and Lewis Gordon. Mrs. Payne is an accomplished lady of domestic tastes who is constantly occupied with the affairs of her household and her four children. She is, however, a pianist of more than average ability and plays with something of the brilliancy and technique of the skilled artist. She is also the possessor of a cultivated voice which is the delight of her friends.

Mr. Payne is well known as a Mason and is a member of the Clark Lodge, No. 40, Free and Accepted Masons. He is also a member of the Brotherhood of Locomotive Engineers, and numbers a majority of the citizens of his native town among his friends.

HENRY J. VOLMER.

Henry J. Volmer, of Jeffersonville, Clark county, is one of the younger generation of business men, the product of our modern educational system—equipped in every way to grapple with the conditions of the present day—who of later years have been steadily obtaining a firm foothold in the business life of our towns and cities. Coming as he does of sturdy German ancestry, with racial and inherent talents developed and sharpened by a suitable course of study, he has made the most of his advantages, and so stands today well to the forefront in the business life of the community. He has shown himself already to be a citizen with a high conception of conduct; and, as freight agent for the large interurban traction interests he has proven exceptionally obliging and courteous.

Mr. Volmer was born in Evansville, Indiana, on the 16th of February, 1884, and was the son of Henry F. Volmer and his wife, whose maiden name was Elizabeth Blaser. Henry F. Volmer came from Evansville while his wife hailed from Springfield, Illinois, and both were of German extraction. Henry J. Volmer attended the public schools of Evansville and of Jeffersonville and passed through the Bryant and Stratton Business College in Louisville. In April, 1896, when in his twelfth year, his family moved to Jeffersonville. Here Henry F. Volmer, who was a printer, held a position for many years on the Jeffersonville Journal.

At the close of his business college course Henry J. Volmer entered the employ of Louis Zapp & Company, of Louisville, as bookkeeper, where he remained four and a half years. He then became tax clerk with the Allen-Bradley Distillery Company, a position of considerable responsibility. His early business experience was further supplemented in such large concerns as the Belknap Hardware & Manufacturing Company and the American Car & Foundry Company.

On June 1, 1906, Mr. Volmer became freight agent for the Louisville & Northern Railway and Lighting Company and the Louisville & Southern Indiana Traction companies, and also the Indianapolis & Louisville Traction Company. He was the first to hold this position in Jeffersonville. When he took hold there was but one traction line in operation in Jeffersonville, namely: the Louisville & Southern Indiana, the freight business of which was operated as an express company. A year later the Louisville & Northern entered the field. They were followed by the Indianapolis & Louisville. Mr. Volmer accordingly became freight agent for all three of them with headquarters for all combined and, as the express feature was not allowed by their charters, it was eliminated and the regular freight business carried on.

Henry J. Volmer is unmarried and lives in the family residence with his parents. In religion he is a member of the local Presbyterian church. He has always evinced much interest in fraternal affairs and is foremost in many societies. He is a member of the Jeffersonville Lodge, No. 340, Free and Accepted Masons; of the Hope Lodge, No. 13, Knights of Pythias; of the Knights and Ladies of Honor, Mystic Tie, No. 7, and of the Apollo Athletic Association, of which he is a charter member. In the Knights and Ladies of Honor he is now ending his second term as presiding officer. In October, 1908, he was one of their representatives at the Grand Lodge celebration in Indianapolis.

WALTER LEWIS LEMMON.

The family of this name, long well known in Clark county, came from a sturdy ancestry of Kentuckians and Ohioians. James H. Lemmon, who was a native of Frankfort, Kentucky, located in Jeffersonville about 1859. When the Civil war broke out he enlisted in the Twenty-first Indiana Artillery, with which he served two years and nine months. Being attacked by typhoid fever he was removed to a hospital in Washington City and after his recovery was mustered out of service. Returning to Jeffersonville he learned the bricklayer's trade, at which he worked most of the time during the remainder of his life. That he was a man of some prominence and popularity is known by the fact that he served from 1871 to 1875 as City Marshal. On November 26, 1867, he was married to Georgiana Lewis, in the Wall Street Methodist church at Jeffersonville. She was the daughter of Felix R. and Patience (Wood) Robinson Lewis, the latter a native of St. Clairsville, Ohio. Felix Lewis became prominent as a farmer and in later life resided at Jeffersonville. His father, Myron William Lewis, was a veteran of the War of 1812, and is buried in the old graveyard on Mulberry street, in Jeffersonville. His wife's maiden name was Sarah Antrim. James H. and Georgiana (Lewis)

Lemmon had three children: Walter L., James Harry and Elizabeth W. Elizabeth is now the wife of L. S. Wilbur; James H., commonly called Harry, is superintendent of J. B. Speed & Company's cement mills at Milltown, Indiana. He married Virginia Trotter, of Crawford county, and they have one son, Nicholas R.

Walter Lewis Lemmon, eldest of the family, was born at Jeffersonville, Indiana, May 29, 1871. He grew up and attended the public schools of his native town and his first job of work was on the folding machine in the mailing rooms of the Louisville Post. Subsequently he obtained a position in the press room of the Louisville Courier Journal. About 1889 he became a fireman on the Pennsylvania Railroad and retained this place for some seven years, changing in January, 1896, to the Baltimore & Ohio Railroad. In 1900 he was promoted to the position of engineer and has a run on the branch line between Jeffersonville and Watson. He is a good workman and has the confidence of his employers, as his long continued service with the same company amply proves.

On September 26, 1894, Mr. Lemmon married Mamie E., daughter of Fred and Anna B. (Pfeffer) Graham, both of Kentucky. Mrs. Lemmon is a native of Louisville. They have two children, George Henry and Anna Eugenia. Mr. Lemmon belongs to Jackson Lodge, No. 146, Free and Accepted Masons, of Seymour, and Division, No. 39, Brotherhood of Locomotive Engineers. He has a happy home circle and derives his chief pleasure from their company, his run being so arranged as to enable him to spend his nights at home.

JONAS DAVID BIGELOW.

In the older days the Bigelows were one of the substantial and well known families of New England. As in the case of many other families of that section they sent representatives to the West when the tide of emigration was settling in that section and in time the name became identified with states in the central Ohio valley. Jonas Dexter Bigelow, when a young man, decided to leave his home in Boston and seek fortune in the growing state of Indiana. He settled in Lafayette, married Sarah Smith, who was born in Ohio, but reared in the vicinity of Logansport, and engaged in business, but died early in the year 1854, before he had reached middle age. After his death his wife gave birth to a child, who was christened Jonas David Bigelow and who was born at Lafayette, Indiana, November 16, 1854. His mother remarried and brought him to Jeffersonville, during his boyhood. After leaving school he obtained a position at the car works, but after working there for a few years entered the service of the Pennsylvania Railroad

Company as a fireman. Later as the result of industry and attention to duty he was promoted to the other side of the cab and made an excellent record as a reliable engineer. Mr. Bigelow was an attentive reader of the press, and fond of good literature, with the result that his friends always found him well posted on current events and able to talk intelligently on many subjects. He held the honorable position of treasurer in the Brotherhood of Locomotive Firemen and enjoyed high standing among his brethren of the railway world. He also held membership in the Knights of Pythias and the Knights and Ladies of Security. Religious in his opinions, correct and moral in his habits, he was a devout member of the Presbyterian church. Fond of his home and much attached to his wife and children he was never so happy as when with his family and to them he gave all of his spare time.

On April 12, 1883, Mr. Bigelow married Elizabeth Jane Holden, a most excellent woman of a highly respectable family. She was the daughter of Thomas and Henrietta (Sherman) Holden, the latter a cousin of Gen. William Tecumseh Sherman, her birthplace being Coolville, Athens county, Ohio. Thomas Holden was a native of Baltimore, Maryland, but came to Ohio about 1851. In 1856 he brought his family to Louisville, Kentucky, and soon after removed to Jeffersonville. He obtained employment in the river part of the town and was working there when the call to arms was sounded in the fateful spring of 1861. At this time he was serving as mate on a boat which took part in the operations that led to the capture of Island No. 10, during which he had a taste of fighting on the Mississippi river. In 1864 he enlisted as a private in Company B, One Hundred and Forty-fourth Indiana Volunteer Infantry, with which he went to the front and served until the close of the war. A shoemaker by trade he had laid up a competence sufficient to provide for his family during his absence. In fact it was love for his family and desire that they would be above want that prevented him from entering the service at an earlier date. For sixteen years after the war he held a position at the government depot in Jeffersonville and was highly esteemed by his employers and those with whom he served. His daughter, Elizabeth, who afterward married Mr. Bigelow, was born on a farm in Ohio previous to the coming of her parents to Jeffersonville. By her marriage she became the mother of five children, in whom she took great pride, the chief desire of her life being to give them a good education. They proved unusually quick to learn and have fulfilled all expectations by the success with which they have met. Ella Jane, the eldest, is teaching in the Jeffersonville high school; Julia Alice, after studying physical culture and gymnastics at the Normal school of the North American Gymnastic Union in Milwaukee, Wisconsin, obtained a position at Menominee, Wisconsin, where she is now teaching these branches in the Stout Training School; Adeline is a graduate from the Jeffersonville high school, and Jonas David and Marguerite are pupils in the

Jeffersonville public schools. Mr. Bigelow died February 6, 1904, since which time his widow has looked after the children and her property interests in a way to show that she is not only a good mother, but a good business woman. She owns several pieces of real estate and is highly regarded by all who come in contact with her in a social way.

LOUIS SAUNDERS.

The founder of the Saunders family was an Irishman who came from Dublin early in the nineteenth century and lived to the phenomenal age of one hundred and fourteen years. He left a son who lived to complete his ninety-eighth year and in turn this octogenarian had a son who almost equalled his father's age. Thus it will be seen that the family is remarkably long-lived. The last mentioned was Charles Saunders, who established himself in the county in Kentucky of which Lexington is the county seat, and grew wealthy as a farmer and stock raiser. He married Zelphy Duncan, reared a family of robust children and passed to his reward in 1908, at the advanced age of eighty-seven years. Louis Saunders, the well known and popular hotel-keeper of Jeffersonville, was one of the children of this venerated Kentucky farmer and keeps up the reputation of the family for industry, geniality of temperament and faculty for getting along in the world. He was born at Lexington, Kentucky, July 31, 1859, and grew up on a farm in Jessamine county, Kentucky. Schools were poor in those days and Mr. Saunders had but limited opportunities for securing an education. It cost seven dollars a month and the chances for attendance seldom reached beyond three months of the year. There were academies in the county seats, but few of the country boys could take advantage of them, owing to expense and distance from their homes. When twenty-one years old Mr. Saunders went to Lexington and worked a year in the business of stair building. Not finding this very remunerative he established a saloon in Lexington and continued in this business for eight years.

In 1889 he disposed of his plant and went to Cincinnati, where he opened a saloon and restaurant and conducted them with fair success for six years. In September, 1895, he removed to Jeffersonville, where he was employed with the Prudential Life Insurance Company for nine months and then embarked in the installment plan furniture business, which occupied his attention for eight years. Rather accidentally he opened the Cottage Hotel in 1904, the beginning of it being the taking in of boarders during the National G. A. R. encampment at Louisville. This paid him so well that he decided to go into the business regularly and he has made a success of it.

Today he has one of the cleanest, most inviting and home-like hotels in Jeffersonville. His place was originally a large dwelling house, which he has thoroughly fitted up and adapted to hotel purposes. In good times he had two adjoining houses annexed to his main establishment and spent one thousand nine hundred dollars for furniture and fixtures for the extra rooms and equipment. Like all hotel-keepers he has had his ups and downs with periods of hard and flush times, but on the whole has prospered and established his reputation as a popular caterer.

In March, 1885, Mr. Saunders married Mary, daughter of Philip and Mary Koch, of Lexington, Kentucky. They have four children, Ora, Bloomfield, Emanuel and Letcher. Mr. Saunders is a member of the Knights of Pythias, Odd Fellows, Elks and the Christian church.

JOHN RAUSCHENBERGER.

Germany, celebrated for its manual training and industrial schools, has not only benefited greatly herself in all branches of manufacture and mechanical arts, but has sent her children to every country of the world as a precious contribution to that department of skilled labor most potential in adding to the wealth of nations. The United States has benefited greatly in this way and much of her commercial supremacy is due to the infusion of German blood. A fine sample is John Rauschenberger, whose life is now to be sketched in a manner all too brief for the merits of the subject. He was born in Unterwaldach, Wurtemburg, August 2, 1833, his parents being Michael and Eva (Broesamle) Rauschenberger. When nineteen years of age he came to Detroit, accompanied by his sister, Margaret, who married at Michigan City, Indiana, Andrew Kalmbach, also a native of Germany, subsequently coming to Jeffersonville, where her husband died in 1907. Mr. Rauschenberger was a proficient blacksmith and worked in a car and locomotive shop at Eslingen in Wurtemburg, while still a boy. After reaching Detroit he worked for a short time at his trade, but soon went to Michigan City because of the opportunities for better employment. Securing a position in the car works at that place he remained there twelve years and enjoyed that prosperity which always comes to the frugal and saving. In March, 1865, he came to Jeffersonville at the earnest solicitation of the founders of the car works and was placed in charge of the blacksmithing department. He had already established a home in Michigan City, and his former employers were loath to lose him, but after investigating the prospects he concluded to cast his fortunes with the city by the Falls of the Ohio. He remained with the car works until the plant was sold to the American Car & Foundry Company, when he resigned his

John Rauschenberger

position and retired in 1899. For a long time he had managed his department by contract, hiring his own men and having absolute control. In 1872 Mr. Rauschenberger had a very pleasant visit to his old home in the Fatherland. It was the first time he had been over in twenty years and many changes were noted since he, a poor and friendless boy, left home for the distant land of America. Although he had sent his relatives a picture of himself, surrounded by two hundred employes, here in the United States, they failed to recognize him, and for a pleasantry he pretended to be a lumber-buyer, in which role he transacted some business with them before making himself known.

He is a genial, kindly dispositioned man, and lives comfortably but unostentatiously in a cozy home facing the Ohio river, opposite Louisville.

In 1857 Mr. Rauschenberger married Mary, daughter of Bernhardt and Geneva Kastner, and born at Baden, Germany. They have had six children, of whom the survivors are: John, George, Maggie and Mary. The latter married W. W. Schwaninger, of Jeffersonville, and resides in Milwaukee. The other daughter lives with her parents and the two sons are also residents of Jeffersonville. Mr. Rauschenberger is a member of Jeffersonville Lodge, No. 340, Free and Accepted Masons, Horeb Chapter, No. 66, Royal Arch Masons, Jeffersonville Council, No. 31, Royal and Select Masters, and Jeffersonville Commandery, No. 27, Knights Templar. He is also a member of the German Lodge of Odd Fellows and St. Lucas German Reformed church.

JAMES L. MILLER.

Few men in Floyd county are better known than the old soldier who bears the above name. Born at Galena, in Floyd county, Indiana, in 1847, James L. Miller's whole life has been identified with the place of his nativity. His parents were Jacob B. and Isabelle (Smith) Miller, the latter being a descendant of Commodore Garrison, a Revolutionary soldier. Her mother, Experience Smith, had reached the advanced age of ninety-seven years at the time of her death. Jacob Miller and wife have several sons living. Charles W. Miller, the youngest, was Attorney-General of Indiana for several years and was recently appointed United States District Attorney for Indiana. Elmore S. Miller, another son, is living on a farm in Floyd county. When the Civil war broke out, in 1861, James L. Miller was only fourteen years old, but the boy as he was he burned to become a soldier and serve his country as best he could. Not being allowed to enlist he organized a company of boys, of which he was elected captain, but he was also the proud owner of a drum and beat it bravely when it was desired to get his command together. This juvenile organization was the first military company got

36

together in Floyd county, and though not accepted as such, many of the members managed at a later period to enlist as real soldiers. Captain Miller made several unsuccessful attempts to go to war without his father's consent and was so persistent that finally the latter helped him to become a member of ·Company A, One Hundred and Forty-fourth Regiment, Indiana Volunteer Infantry, which was part of the Army of the Potomac. Despite his youth Mr. Miller was appointed corporal and afterward was promoted to a sergeancy. He was present with his regiment when Lee surrendered. He was assistant Provost Marshal under Captain Hopper and later a member of Colonel Hancock's body-guard at White Sulphur Springs. He still cherishes as a precious heirloom the crape he wore for thirty days after Lincoln's assassination. In August, 1865, he received an honorable discharge and since has been justly proud of the record he made as a soldier of the Union. After the close of hostilities Mr. Miller returned to the old home farm in Floyd county and remained there until he was twenty-five years old. Removing to Jeffersonville he secured a position as carpenter in building cars at the local car works and continued in this employment until October 2, 1902. Securing a position two months later under the postmaster he delivered the first letter that was sent out by a mail carrier in Jeffersonville. He served as carrier under four different postmasters in the city, which shows that he was a diligent and reliable servant of Uncle Sam.

It is, however, as a member of the Grand Army of the Republic that Mr. Miller is best known. Twenty years ago he joined the Jeffersonville Post, No. 86, is past commander and ex-officio delegate to all state encampments. He was delegate to the Third (Indiana) Congressional District to the National Encampment at Denver, which elected Corporal Tanner commander-in-chief, and was honored by the appointment of aid on the commander's staff with the rank of colonel. He has been five times an aid, first on the staff of state Commander Lucas, and three times since has held similar positions. As in each case, he held the rank of colonel, he enjoys the unusual distinction of having enjoyed this rank five times, not counting the same title due him as past commander of the post. Before being elected commander Mr. Miller represented his post at state conventions at Louisville, Lafayette, Madison and twice at Indianapolis. When a delegate at Denver he was presented a beautiful badge, a combination of bronze silver and gold, that cost seventy-five dollars. Only one other man in Clark county has had the honor of being a delegate to the National Encampment. Though of limited means he spent two hundred dollars in order to go in proper style to the great national meeting of the organization he loves so well. In addition to his other honors he is a member of the Council of Administration for Indiana. As a citizen he does his duty with the same patriotism and conscientiousness that he manifested as a soldier in war.

On December 5, 1870, Mr. Miller married Clara E. Thurman, at Galena. Their only son, Homer L., is chief gauger under Elam B. Neal, Internal Revenue Collecter at Indianapolis. He has proven a competent official and is a worthy son of a worthy sire.

Mrs. Nettie M. Hazzard is Mr. Miller's only daughter, and the whole family enjoy the esteem which is well deserved by the manner in which they fulfill their respective duties in life.

FRANK H. SAME.

The family of this name is of German origin but has been identified with America for more than sixty years. William and Henry, sons of Franz Heinrich and Elizabeth (Scherer) Same, emigrated from Bielefeldt, Prussia, in 1847, spent eleven years at Cincinnati and in 1858 came to Jeffersonville. William Same married Elizabeth Gruber, a native of Baltimore, Maryland, who was brought to Jeffersonville. John A. Same, brother of Frank H., married Rose Pennington, who died in 1903, leaving four children.

Frank H. Same, the other son, was born at Jeffersonville, Clark county, Indiana, in 1866. After the usual course in the public schools he engaged in the grocery business as a clerk and subsequently became a proprietor for a time, being in partnership with H. L. Brendell at Walnut and Chestnut streets, Jeffersonville, but most of his life has been spent in carrying on a transfer business. He now owns and operates the Louisville and Jeffersonville Transfer Company, which keeps over thirty wagons in stock, some five of which are actively employed all of the time. About 1880 and for several years afterward his father and all the sons were public contractors engaged in building streets in Jeffersonville. Previous to this his father owned and operated a grist mill on Walnut street in Jeffersonville, but eventually sold it to his brother, Henry, who conducted it until its destruction by fire. There is a tragedy connected with the life of this family, involving one of those mysterious disappearances, which no detective work is able to explain. Franz Heinrich Same, who started to America to join his two sons, got as far as New York, where all trace of him was lost and he was never afterward heard of.

October 14, 1891, Mr. Same was married to Hattie M., daughter of William and Mary (Scammahorn) Hydron, by whom he has had two children, Monetta being the only one living. His father and Ethel, daughter of his brother John, are members of his household. His grandmother never left the old country. Mr. Same is a member of the Hope Lodge, Knights of Pythias, and of Eden Lodge, Knights and Ladies of Honor. The family occupy a modest home, comfortably but unostentatiously furnished, and Mrs. Same is regarded as a substantial and reliable business man.

GUSTAVE ADOLPH DENZLER.

Gustave Adolph Denzler is a native-born citizen of Jeffersonville, Clark county, who has all the requisite qualifications to enable him to maintain his present high standing in the community. His life record has marked him as one in whom uprightness and conscientious adherence to duty have ever been dominant traits; and his career of nearly twenty years as an employe of the Pennsylvania Railroad has been singularly free from unpleasant occurrences which occasionally cross the path of the locomotive engineer.

Mr. Denzler was born on the 22d day of May, 1869, and was the son of Casper and Verena (Bucher) Denzler. Both parents came from Switzerland. Casper Denzler was born in Diebendorf in the Swiss Canton of Zurich; while Rohr in the Canton of Aargau was the birthplace of his wife, Casper Denzler was born November 7, 1829, and his wife on December 12, 1832. Their marriage took place in 1854 in Louisville, Kentucky. Thirteen children were born of the union, of whom four survive. They are: Herman Denzler, who lives in Indianapolis, he is married and has a family of two boys and two girls; Caroline (Denzler) Wuerfel, wife of Martin Wuerfel, of Jeffersonville, who has two children; Emma, who married William Bastian, also lives in Jeffersonville and has one child.

Gustave A. Denzler is the youngest member of his family, and during his boyhood attended public school until his thirteenth year, when he went to work in the wall paper business. In his early years he obtained quite a varied business experience, being in turn a clerk in the post-office, an employe of the local car works and the Sweeney Foundry Company. He was also associated for a time with the Mississippi River Commission work. At the age of twenty-one he started as a fireman on the Pennsylvania road between Louisville and Indianapolis. Eight years later he attained the more responsible post at the other side of the cab, in which he still continues on the same division as engineer. On April 6, 1894, he married Cora Russ, the daughter of Christian and Anna Russ, of Jeffersonville.

Mrs. Denzler's father, Christian Russ, was a veteran of the Civil war. He was born in Germany on the 26th of October, 1843, and was the son of Christian and Amelia (Rose) Russ. In 1850 he came with his mother to Philadelphia, Pennsylvania, and after four years in that city migrated to Cincinnati. At the age of thirteen he came to Charlestown, Clark county, where he remained until his enlistment in Company F, Thirty-eighth Indiana Volunteers, on the 18th of September, 1861. He served until July 15, 1865, when he obtained his discharge. During his term of service he participated in the battles of Perryville, Chickamauga, Lookout Mountain, Missionary Ridge, Hoover's Gap, Chattahoochee, Rocky Ridge, Buzzard's Roost, Kenesaw Mountain, New Hope Church, Resaca, Atlanta, Jonesboro and

Bentonville and minor engagements. After the war, from which, though entering as a private he merged a first sergeant, he returned to Charlestown and learned the carpentry trade, which he has followed for the greater part of his life since. From 1876 to 1883, in partnership with John Hofmeister, he operated a brick yard in Jeffersonville. He was successful in his business ventures. On March 13, 1870, he married Annie Oetterer, daughter of Adam and Margaret Oetterer, of Jeffersonville. They had nine children. Christian Russ is a member of the Knights and Ladies of Security and in religious affairs he is an active member of the local Methodist Episcopal church.

Mr. and Mrs. Denzler have led a happy married life and five children have been born to them. They are: Annette R., Norma E., Clara May, Vivian and Charles Henry. Gustave Adolph Denzler in fraternal affairs belongs to the Brotherhood of Locomotive Engineers and the Brotherhood of Locomotive Firemen and Engine Men. He is a member of the Jeffersonville Lodge, No. 340, Free and Accepted Masons; the Hope Lodge, No. 13, Knights of Pythias; and the Horeb Chapter, No. 66, Royal Arch Masons. He and his family are members of the German Methodist church. They live in their comfortable cottage home anl number very many of the residents of Jeffersonville among their friends.

WILLIAM T. CLARK.

William T. Clark is a popular grocer and drygoods merchant of Clarksville, Clark county, and has many staunch friends in the community. He is a man who has had a singularly varied career and profited much thereby. In business life he is conservative and reliable and of an unobtrusive disposition. His grocery and dry goods store is one of the most up-to-date in the district and is ever found replete with a pleasing and varied stock of choice goods. He is esteemed as a citizen and has been entrusted with public offices both in Clarksville and Jeffersonville township and admirably performed his duties.

Mr. Clark was born in Floyd county, Indiana, on the 30th of April, 1848, the son of James J. Clark and Jennetta Lamb, his wife, both residents of the same county. When William T. was but a year old his parents moved to Crawford county. As a boy he attended the public school there and taught school for six or eight years. His father was Sheriff of Crawford county for four years and he became Deputy Sheriff under him. He also worked in stores during his teaching career. In addition he worked in the County Treasurer's and County Auditor's offices at Leavenworth. In the year 1881 he was appointed a guard at the Indiana State Prison, South, which position he held for ten years, during the Howard and Patton administrations. In 1891 he entered the grocery business on Woerner avenue, in Clarksville, immediately south of the Reformatory. In March of 1899 he moved one square nearer the river to his present location. On the first floor of his business place he carries a stock of groceries and notions and on the second a supply of dry goods.

On the 24th of October, 1872, Mr. Clark married Louisa M. Cole, of Crawford county. She was the daughter of William H. Cole. The marriage has proven a most happy one and four children, three of whom are living, were born to them. The eldest son, William H., married Clara Eaken, of Jeffersonville. He lives near Frankfort, Kentucky. Nellie B. married George R. McIntosh, of Leavenworth, Indiana. They live in Louisville, Kentucky, where he is the proprietor of a wholesale picture frame store, one of the largest in Louisville. They have two boys, William Roscoe and George Rowen. J. Raymond Clark resides with his parents and assists in the management of the business. He is a graduate of the Bryant and Stratton Business College and a young man of much business ability.

William T. Clark is a prominent member of the Masonic fraternity and belongs to Jeffersonville Lodge, No. 340, Free and Accepted Masons. Religion has always had a place in his life and he is a member of the Wall Street Methodist Episcopal church. In recognition of his worth as a citizen he was elected to fill two important public offices. He spent two terms as Trustee of Clarksville and was Deputy Assessor of Jeffersonville township for four years. He takes an intelligent interest in the political issues of the day and is a supporter of the Democratic party. William T. Clark is ably assisted in his business by Mrs. Clark. The couple, together with their son, live in comfort and security in the same building in which their business is carried on.

JOSEPH MOLCK.

The gentle and poetic business of floriculture has nothing about it suggestive of war and the last place one would expect to find a warrior would be amid the flowers of the greenhouse. Notwithstanding this, one who talks awhile with Jeffersonville's only florist, will find that he has been acquainted with war in its worst form, and supped to the full of its "pride, pomp and circumstance." Joseph Molck, as the result of experience in his young manhood, can tell of terrible battles in which he participated, of protracted sieges in which he bore a part and other blood-curdling incidents in one of the most tragic periods of the world's history. He was born in 1848 at Weisenburg, in the beautiful province of Alsace, then a part of France, but now a part of the German empire. His parents were Joseph and Madeline (Essig) Molck, and being in poor circumstances their son was compelled at an early age to look out for himself. When fourteen years old he left home for Strassburg, where he became an apprentice to the florist's trade. In the same line of work he also spent some time in Choullon, Nanzig, Versailles and Paris. When twenty years old he enlisted in the Seventh Regiment of French Artillery and had only two years to wait for military service of the most active kind. When the war between France and Germany broke out in 1870, the Seventh Regiment was serving under Marshal McMahon in Algeria, Africa, but this corps was ordered to the front to meet the German advance. Mr. Molck was taken prisoner by the enemy at Pont a Mouson, but escaped and went to Metz, where the French Marshal Bazaine was sustaining a siege. He arrived in August, 1870, and three days later the two armies were engaged at San Julia. August 15th Mr. Molck rode all day and on the 16th reached the battlefield of San Prival. The 17th was consumed in riding and on the 18th Mr. Molck took part in the great battle of Gravelotte. He was twice wounded, his horse killed under him and the cannon destroyed. He lay three days on the field until found by his brother, Capt. Jacob Molck, of the Twenty-sixth Regiment, who had him removed to the hospital, where he remained until Marshal Bazaine surrendered the city of Metz, and with one hundred and seventy-five thousand prisoners he was taken to Coblentz, Germany, where he was held for five months as a prisoner of war. Being released at the close of the war, he returned to his regiment and in 1871 marched under Marshal McMahon into Paris to confront the uprising of the Commune. The fighting was of the most terrible and heart-rending description. Families were divided and Mr. Molck's own brother was on the side of the Commune. Even the women and children were engaged in this fratricidal war and from nine o'clock in the morning until three o'clock in the afternoon the gutters ran red with blood. Thousands were driven into the river Seine, but despite their desperate resistance the Commune was eventually broken and defeated.

Being discharged shortly after these stirring events Mr. Molck spent two weeks at home and then embarked for America. Locating at Oil City, Pennsylvania, he established himself in the florist business and prosecuted it with fair success for thirteen years. In 1890 he removed to Jeffersonville and established a greenhouse in the northwestern portion of the city. Being the only florist in the place and growing steadily in patronage for eighteen years, he enjoys a large and lucrative business. Aside from his term in the army his whole life has been devoted to floriculture and few men understand plants and their propagation better than he. Having traveled extensively and speaking German, French and English he is interesting to talk to. He says the Germans outnumbered the French fourteen to one in the war of 1870, and the French were unprepared for war. Soon after arriving in Jeffersonville

Mr. Molck married Mary Peter, who was also a native of Weisenberg, Alsace. They have a son and daughter named, respectively, Frank and Mary. The family are members of St. Anthony's Catholic church and enjoy general respect among a wide circle of friends and acquaintances.

JOHN M. MAUZY.

As a locomotive engineer on the Illinois Central Railroad, in which capacity he has served for nearly twenty years, John M. Mauzy has established for himself a record of faithfulness and efficiency second to none. He was born in Jeffersonville, Clark county, on the 27th of June, 1850, the son of Andrew Jackson and Sarah (McLain) Mauzy. Both parents were natives of Kentucky. Andrew Jackson Mauzy moved to Salem, Washington county, Indiana, from his native state when a small boy, and in the year 1845 moved to Jeffersonville. Sarah McLain also came to Indiana at an early age. Andrew J. Mauzy was, during his lifetime, an influential member of the community. He became a captain in the Ninth Indiana Regiment of Militia. His military commission, which is still extant in the possession of John M. Mauzy, is dated 1842 and bears the signature of Governor Samuel Bigger. Of Andrew J. Mauzy's children, in addition to John M., there are two sisters living: Mrs. Mary L. Montgomery, the mother of Judge H. C. Montgomery, who resides at St. Angelo, Texas, and Mrs. Lillie H. Gould, who lives in Cincinnati, and who has one daughter, Mrs. Lillie Glazier. Besides Judge Montgomery, Mrs. Montgomery is the mother of three other children, Mrs. Jesse Abbott, of St. Angelo, Texas; Mrs. May Weir, of the same city; and Sarah Montgomery, who resides in New York City.

John M. Mauzy started upon his career as a railroad man at the age of seventeen years as a fireman on the old Jeffersonville, Madison & Indianapolis line. At the end of three years he was promoted and placed in charge of an engine, and in a short space of time was looked upon by his superiors as one of the most reliable of the younger engineers on the road. In the year 1890 he resigned his position on the Pennsylvania Railroad and associated himself with the Illinois Central, with which he has remained as an engineer ever since.

In the year 1873 Mr. Mauzy married Mary Belle Huston, of New Philadelphia, Washington county, Indiana. Mrs. Mauzy was the daughter of Robert Huston and his wife, whose maiden name was Mary Drain. Both parents were born in Kentucky, but spent their early days and after life in Indiana. Five children were born to John M. Mauzy and his wife, as follows: Mrs. Sallie Eberts, who is the widow of George Eberts and the mother of two boys and a girl, Norman, Edith and James; Mrs. Jennie Emery, who married Gus Emery, of Louisville, Kentucky, one daughter, Mary, being born to them; Charles Howard Mauzy, who married Jennie Daugherty, lives in Louisville, Kentucky, and has a family of a boy and a girl, Elizabeth and John; John Ernest and Wilbur Hancock Mauzy, who live with their parents in the family residence at Jeffersonville.

John M. Mauzy belongs to the Brotherhood of Locomotive Engineers, and is a prominent member of the local Myrtle Lodge, No. 19, Knights of Pythias. In the family circle he has always been known as a conscientious and considerate father and husband and one devoted to the interests of his family.

GEORGE NANZ.

A well known native born resident of Jeffersonville, Clark county, is George Nanz, whose family, of German origin, has for very many years been connected with the business and farming life of Clark county. He was born on November 12, 1866, and was the son of William and Elizabeth (Greiner) Nanz. Mrs. Nanz was the daughter of John Greiner, who came to Jeffersonville from Germany in the early days of Clark county. William Nanz was born in Germany and came to Jeffersonville, Clark county, about the middle of the last century. He and his wife were the parents of two children, George and William. William Nanz, senior, was in the saloon business in Jeffersonville in a large way prior to the Civil war. His sons, George and William, attended the Jeffersonville public schools in their youth. Subsequently William Nanz died in New Orleans and his wife and children were thrown on their own resources to make their way as best they could. His widow bravely faced the situation, and the two boys, when old enough, took up their share of the burden and went to work. William became a blacksmith at the local car works and George was also employed there.

In November, 1889, George Nanz started in the saloon business at Jeffersonville and about two years later bought a lot on Spring street, near Maple, and built a business and resident block. At its completion he moved in there and still continues in that location. In 1889 he married Barbara Herful, who died on the 19th of December, 1891. He again entered married life on the 20th of September, 1894, when his marriage with Katie Stemler took place. She was the daughter of Daniel Stemler and Katherine (Kanzinger) Stemler. Daniel Stemler was born in Germany, in 1823, and came to America about the year 1852. A farmer by occupation, he married, in 1858, Mrs. Katherine Baker, whose maiden name was Kanzinger. Mrs. Stemler was born in Baden, Germany, and came to Louisville in 1853. Four years later she moved to Jeffersonville. After her marriage in 1858 she and her husband lived on a farm about four miles from Jeffersonville. Ten children were born to them, seven of whom are living. They are: Henry, Will, George, Dan, John, Mary and Katie, wife of George Nanz. Henry Stemler married Amy Reichle and has nine children. Henry is in the dairy business in Jeffersonville as are also his brother, Dan, and other members of the family. Will Stemler married Annie Kreikle, has one child, and is in business for himself on Spring street. George Stemler married Mary Creamer, has four children, and is employed in the blacksmith department of the car works. Dan married Amelia Russ, has five children, and runs a dairy in Jeffersonville. John and Mary are unmarried and with their mother make up the home circle. They engage in the dairy work. Daniel Stemler, senior, died in 1902 and was a man who always took a great interest in the affairs of his family. The Stemlers all belong to the German Reformed church, of which they are active supporters.

George Nanz is a member of the Tell Lodge, No. 272, Independent Order of Odd Fellows; he also belongs to the Eagles. In religion he is a member of the German Reformed church. William Nanz, his brother, married on April 13, 1903, Mrs. Lizzie Metzger, who was the daughter of Phillip and Mary Hoffman, of Madison, Indiana. In October, 1904, he also entered the saloon business at 314 Spring street, where he still continues to do business with success. William Nanz belongs to the Eagles and to the Lutheran church in Jeffersonville. John Greiner, grandfather of the Nanz brothers, was one of the founders of the German Reformed church in Jeffersonvile. Previous to that time he used to cross the river in a skiff and attend church in Louisville.

FRANK WOERNER.

Jeffersonville, Clark county, has been the adopted home of Frank Woerner from the year 1881 to the present day, and his career there has met with much success. In recent years he has become deservedly popular with all classes as a business man of importance and a substantial resident. In all his business undertakings and financial ventures he has been ably counseled and assisted by his wife, who has been, since their marriage in the year 1876, a prime factor in increasing his store of wealth and an admirable supervisor of the affairs of the domestic hearth. Both come of thrifty German stock.

Frank Woerner was born in Louisville, Kentucky, March 31, 1857, and was the son of Conrad and Mary (Zwirman) Woerner, both of Germany. He was educated in the parochial and public schools. He learned the baker's trade, which he followed for several years. He then became a machinist and associated himself with that industry for fifteen years. About the year 1881 he came to Jeffersonville to work in the car works and located on the street immediately west of them. He put his earnings into property on that street and in time owned more of its real estate than anyone else. At this time there was a discussion as to whether the street should be named Smith or Smyser street, and an agreement was reached as a compliment to Mr. Woerner and it was renamed Woerner avenue.

Mr. Woerner was already married at the time of his arrival in Jeffersonville, having espoused in Louisville on October 8, 1878, Wilhelmina Jackel. She was the daughter of Leopold and Anna Mary (Roth) Jackel. Frank Woerner and his wife have had one son, Frank Paul, who was for nine years a salesman for the Belknap Hardware Company of Louisville. He now lives in Indianapolis, where he is associated with the Van Camp Hardware and Iron Company. Frank Woerner, Jr., married Geneva Sinex, of New Albany. They have one son, William Frank Woerner.

In June, 1894, Frank Woerner built a business block with residences attached, at the north end of Woerner avenue, and also started his grocery, which is said to be one of the neatest, cleanest, and most up-to-date in Jeffersonville. The Woerner grocery contains a varied assortment of high class fancy groceries and is also replete with a side-line of confectionery and notions, and has proved to be a most successful business venture.

On the 28th day of June, 1908, a local branch of the Knights of Columbus fraternity was established in Jeffersonville and Frank Woerner became one of the first and most active members. He also belongs to the Fraternal Order of Eagles and is a member of the Catholic Knights of America. Both he and his wife are influential members of St. Anthony's church. The Woerners have traveled much in other states and have been at different points from the Atlantic to the Pacific at various times.

Hand in hand Frank Woerner and his wife have built up the success that is theirs today, and their industry, thrift and business energy has not been without conferring a benefit on the community, and it is but a fitting recognition of their services that the street which has been the scene of most of their endeavors should bear their name.

WILLIAM HENRY FOSTER.

William Henry Foster, general foreman of the Pennsylvania Railroad shops at Louisville, Kentucky, is also prominent in his native town of Jeffersonville, in which he now resides. A machinist of skill and ability, his record as a loyal employee earned for him the gratitude and recognition he deserved. He comes from a family that has contributed much to the progress of Jeffersonville, for his father, as a builder and contractor, spent a lifetime of activity there. Our subject is essentially a self-made man, who, having had but scant educational facilities in his youth, which covered the stormy period of the Civil war, he had to depend to a large extent on his natural talents. His success under the circumstances is all the more appreciable.

He was born in Jeffersonville in 1858, the son of William Thomas Foster and Kate (Wesso) Foster. His mother came to America from her native Germany with her parents when young and was adopted by the Ewing family of Madison, Indiana, who at a later period located in Jeffersonville. William Thomas Foster was born in Franklin county, Kentucky, and came to Jeffersonville about 1856. Here he learned the bricklaying trade from George Ewing and boarded with his employer. In this connection it was but natural that he and the adopted daughter should become acquainted and their marriage ultimately resulted. Later William Thomas Foster launched out as a building contractor and erected many of the best known buildings in Jeffersonville. He made the brick and erected the building in which the First National Bank now stands. He also built the line of structures from there to the next alley north. Soon after the war the building at the northeast corner of Spring and Chestnut streets was erected by him and was thought to be the finest in the town. He interested himself in the contract work of the Government Depot and many other well known works. He helped to erect the Presbyterian church and the pest house. His earliest work was on the government bakery that stood on Warder Park during the war. He was an expert on brick baking ovens and did finished work of the kind at Evansville. He also built the "lodges" in the National cemeteries at Louisville, Lebanon, Kentucky, and at Grafton, West Virginia. Previous to his death he located in Cincinnati, where he died in 1886.

William H. Foster grew up in his native town and in the year 1876 started in as an employee of the Jeffersonville, Madison & Indianapolis shops, and learned the machinist's trade. In the winter of 1885 he was transferred to the Indianapolis department, where he remained until the fall of 1890. In September of that year he was made general foreman for the Pennsylvania road at Madison, Indiana. In 1895 he was changed to Louisville to take charge of the shops there and still holds the position.. Upon making his last change he located once more in Jeffersonville.

His marriage to Lida B. Luckett, of Franklin county, Kentucky, was performed in the year 1883. She was the daughter of John Luckett and his wife, whose maiden name was Frances Martin. Six children have been born to them. They are: Florence, who married Lee H. Adams, of Corydon Junction; she lives in Jeffersonville and has one child. Charles Thomas Foster married Lena Hutt; they reside in Jeffersonville and have one child; he is a fireman on the Pennsylvania Railroad as is also his brother, Wilbur Allen Foster. Graham Ray, Anna Irene and William E. Foster still remain at home with their parents. Susan J. Spicer is also a member of the family circle. She is the daughter of Mrs. Foster's deceased sister and was left an orphan at the age of three years.

William Henry Foster is well versed in the affairs of the Knights of Pythias. He is a member of Hope Lodge, No. 13. In religion he is a lifelong member of the local Presbyterian church. He lives on the same corner facing the Ohio river as did Governor Jennings when he resided in Jeffersonville.

JOSEPH THOMAS ENLOW.

The well known chief of the Jeffersonville fire department, Joseph Thomas Enlow, was born at Mauckport, Harrison county, Indiana, August 20, 1866, the son of John Emmett and Mary A. (Reynolds) Enlow, both branches of the family being well established and worthy representatives of Harrison county. In 1869 the Enlow family removed to Louisville, Kentucky, and in 1879 they removed to a farm near Underwood, Clark county, Indiana, our subject having remained on the farm until he was about eighteen years old, when he decided that better opportunities awaited him in the city than on the farm, consequently he went to Jeffersonville and secured employment in the car shops, having performed his services there in such a creditable manner that he at once attracted the attention of his employers and he was accordingly made foreman of the steel plant.

On September 3, 1906, Mr. Enlow was appointed chief of the Jeffersonville fire department, which appointment was for four years. He has succeeded in greatly strengthening the department in every respect and according to many of those in position to know, he is perhaps the best chief the department in Jeffersonville has ever had. When he took charge of the department it was equipped with only one "combination" wagon and one hose real, fifteen hundred feet of hose, and there were but four horses and five men. Now these are in addition to the city service combination ladder truck, which carries a chemical engine and one hundred and ninety feet of ladders, two hundred and fifty feet of hose; also an engine which was built especially for the Jeffersonville department. It has an Amoskeag pump, which is the very best design made, a Fox boiler, also highly efficient apparatus, in short, a most excellent fire fighting machine. Technically it was rebuilt from an old one that had been out of use for many years, but the old part is so insignificant as to hardly deserve mention. There is now a total of three thousand and two hundred feet of hose and eight horses and eleven men. A new house has also been erected and another house reconstructed on East Chestnut street.

The department as a whole has been more than doubled since Mr. Enlow took charge, which certainly speaks well of his executive ability and energy as a wide-awake fire chief, who is deserving of the high esteem in which he is held by the people of Jeffersonville.

Mr. Enlow was united in marriage on January 11, 1887, with Florence Austin, a native of New Albany, who passed to her rest in July, 1898, having become the mother of five children, namely: Grace, Laura, Florence, Mary and Ione.

The subject's father, who is the postmaster and a merchant at Underwood, Indiana, was a soldier in the Civil war, having been a member of the Thirty-fourth Kentucky Infantry. The Enlows bear an excellent reputation in the vicinity of Underwood and wherever else they are known.

Mr. Enlow is a member of the Independent Order of Odd Fellows, Lodge No. 3, of Jeffersonville. He is distinctively a fire fighter, seemingly singled out by nature for such work, a medium sized man with well knit frame, a square jaw, showing fortitude and determination. While in his every-day life is a kind-hearted and generous man, he has the dash and fire of a born leader of men when occasion requires, but is always cool and self-possessed.

CAPT. FRANCIS B. SHEPHERD.

In every community, large or small, there are a few men who, by their force of character, are intuitively recognized as leaders, men who are successful in whatever they undertake. In the thriving city of Jeffersonville, Indiana, there is a representative of this class found in Capt Francis B. Shepherd, a man who justly merits the high regard in which he is held by all who know him, if for no other reason, because of his past enviable record as a soldier, having performed his duty in the cause of humanity during the last wars of his country. He was born in White Sulphur, Scott county, Kentucky, in 1866, the son of Phillip B. Shepherd, a native of Mead county, Kentucky, and a man of many worthy attributes of character. The subject's mother was known in her maiden hood as Catherine Lee, daughter of Robert E. Lee, of White Sulphur, Kentucky, who had the distinction of serving in the War of 1812. Phillip B. Shepherd represented Mead county in 1849 and 1850 in the Kentucky Legislature, being the only Democrat ever elected from that county up to that time, which fact is indicative of popularity in his own locality. He afterward moved to Decatur, Illinois, and edited the first Democratic paper at that place. So faithfully did he defend the principles of Democracy that President James Buchanan appointed him postmaster of Decatur, in which capacity he served until the breaking out of the Civil war, when his sympathies for the Southern cause prompted him to sell out all his possessions and move to the South, where he at once joined Gen. Joseph Johnston's division of the Confederate army, in which he rendered efficient service. After the close of the war he was elected Judge in Grant county, Kentucky, in which capacity he served for a period of four years. Thus it is no wonder that Francis B. Shepherd should have naturally taken to army life, with the record of his ancestors so permeated with militarism.

Our subject remained at home (White Sulphur, the Blue Grass state) until he was eighteen years old, when, with his parents, he removed to Ft. Scott, Kansas, where he attended the Kansas Normal College during the first three years of his residence. After leaving school he enlisted in the Fourth United States Infantry, stationed at Ft. Omaha, Nebraska, and subsequently served all through the West. After his five years' term of enlistment expired he re-enlisted in the Seventh United States Cavalry, in which he served three years, by this time having made great progress in army discipline, and shortly afterward he gladly availed himself of an opportunity to go to Cuba, where he joined the Insurrectos, who were rising to throw off the yoke of Spanish oppression, two years before American troops were sent to that island. Mr. Shepherd's object in this new line of activity was to teach the Cubans tactics, drills, maneuvers, etc. So efficient was his work in this connection that he was promoted to the rank of major in the Cuban army. Leaving Cuba Mr. Shepherd went to South America, where he remained until the breaking out of the Spanish-American war, when he returned to the United States and enlisted in the Twentieth Infantry of the regular army, and was in the first expedition to land in Cuba, June 22 and 24, 1898, then fighting their first battle, in which President (then Colonel) Roosevelt was engaged. The subject was in Bates' Flying Brigade, and he also participated in the battles of El Caney and San Juan Hill, where this regiment did very effective work, returning to Montauk Point, then to Ft. Leavenworth, Kansas, after the close of hostilities. The regiment was then sent to Manila, Philippine Islands, leaving San Francisco on the transport Warren, which landed at Manila, February 12, 1899, that city still being practically on fire, resulting from the fierce fighting on February 5th.. Mr. Shepherd was detailed as personal orderly to Maj.-Gen. Lloyd Wheaton, and he participated in the following engagements: Guandaloupe Ridge, March 13, 1899; Pators, March 14th, advanced from San Fernando to Calulut, August 9th, following. Then the regiment with which the subject was connected engaged in skirmishes from Sandalon to Angeles, which place was reached on August 13th, and from whence they went to Porac, arriving there on September 28th, following, engaging in a skirmish; also at Lingayan Gulf, November 5th, remaining there until December 31st, when they captured Aguinaldo's mother and his secretary, but the famous insurgent leader escaped. From January 7th, to April 24,

1900, Mr. Shepherd was in Grant's expedition, which brigade invaded the Bulucan Mountains. They were in a battle at Balubad, June 11, 1900. There was almost constant fighting and skirmishing between these battles.

At the expiration of his term of service in 1901 Mr. Shepherd returned to Manila and was given the position of superintendent of land transportation under Col. C. P. Miller, and he remained there until 1904, when he was transfered to the classified service at the quartermaster's department in Jeffersonville, Indiana. He is messenger of Class C at the government depot and is captain of Company M, Indiana National Guard, at Jeffersonville. He is one of the best posted men in army and navy affairs in the state, receiving all general orders and keeping up-to-date in reference to military affairs. Captain Shepherd's personal appearance is that of a born soldier, portly and dignified. He is at present engaged in writing a book on the Cuban insurrection, which is awaited with great interest by his friends and army acquaintances, for it will doubtless be replete with stirring incident as well as valuable from a historical standpoint.

One of the leading incident's in the captain's life in the Philippines and one of the most important events of his life, was his marriage in Manila, on March 2, 1904, to Catherine Hogan, of Colorado Springs, Colorado, who made the long trip from her home to the Philippine capital that she might marry Captain Shepherd.

In his fraternal relations our subject is a member of the Independent Order of Odd Fellows, Tell Lodge, No. 272. He is also past commander of the Spanish War Veterans, making one of the most efficient leaders that body has ever had. Thus possessing as he does so many likable traits of character and such sterling worth, it is not strange that he is one of the popular men of his county.

LUTHER M. WORRELL.

The Worrells were originally a well established old family of Virginia, but representatives found their way west during the first half of the nineteenth century and became identified with different states. Martin B. Worrell, who was born in Harrison county, of the Hoosier state, enlisted as one of the Indiana soldiers during the Civil war, and made a good record while in the army. He married Margaret Hunsemacher, a native of Germany, who came to America in her childhood. Luther M. Worrell, one of the children by this union, was born at Jeffersonville, February 1, 1878. Mr. Worrell received the usual education in the common schools of the city. After finishing the course he studied electricity and worked in that line of business for four years. In 1898, when the Spanish-American war began, he determined to join the army, then enlisting for the defense of the country and do what he could to uphold her honor. With this end in view he joined Company E, One Hundred and Sixty-first Indiana Volunteer Infantry, with which he went to Cuba. Shortly after arriving in the island he was transferred to the Thirteenth Company of the United States Signal Corps, with which he served six months. This corps did valuable service for the government during the military operations in the island and Mr. Worrell is justly proud of the part he bore in the work.

After returning home Mr. Worrell secured a position as fireman on the Pennsylvania Railroad and gave such satisfaction that he was promoted to the post of engineer on August 1, 1906. He has since retained that place and is in active service with the Pennsylvania, being regarded as one of the company's most reliable locomotive engineers. He takes much interest in all that concerns the welfare of railroad men, and is one of the enthusiastic members both of the Brotherhood of Locomtive Firemen and Brotherhood of Locomotive Engineers.

On October 30, 1901, Mr. Worrell was married to Libbie Brinkworth, a young lady of refinement, who was born at Jeffersonville, but reared at Indianapolis. Her parents were George and Mary (Pepper) Brinkworth and natives of England, who came to Jeffersonville before the birth of Mrs. Worrell. They came to America in childhood and were reared near Madison, Indiana. Mr. Brinkworth enlisted at Madison in the Third Indiana Cavalry, and served with credit during the Civil war, on the side of the Union. Mr. and Mrs. Worrell have had three children, of whom George M. and Clara C. are living, the other having died in infancy. Mr. Worrell talks entertainingly of his experiences during the Spanish-American war. He was originally in Capt. Lewis C. Baird's company and after being transferred to the Signal Corps crossed over from Havana to Santiago, where the principal fighting took place. He learned much of the ways and peculiarities of the Cubans and also became acquainted with the large and varied assortment of annoying insects to be found in that part of the tropics. The family reside in a neat cottage in the best district of the city. Both Mr. and Mrs. Worrell are people of intelligence and refinement and their home life is ideally happy.

HENRY WATTERSON HARRISON, D. D. S.

The family of this name is of Kentucky origin and one branch of it at an early day settled in the county of Carroll. During the heated discussions preceding the Civil war, when Kentucky was rent with political, social and civic feuds, the Harrisons sided with the Democratic party and when the actual

37

clash of arms occurred were found in the ranks of the Confederates. R. F. Harrison, who was born in Carrollton, enlisted in the Southern army and went through many of the stirring scenes that distinguished this troubled period from the spring of 1861 until the surrender in 1865 brought comparative peace. That he was a man of prominence and popularity is proved by the fact of his election as Clerk of Carroll county, but still more by the fact that he held this important office for twenty-eight years. Under the old system prevailing in Virginia and Kentucky the county clerkship was practicularly a hereditary office, being handed down from father to son for generations. It was a position of great influence, combining in its incumbent great knowledge of the law as well as current business of the county, the clerk often figuring as guardian of children and administrator of estates. Some years before the Civil war a flatboat floated down the Ohio river, containing a New York family on their way to the Falls, where the parents hoped to better their condition in life. Kate E. Gibson, then a child of tender age, was a member of this family and when she reached Jeffersonville was adopted by Rev. Henry Smith, a minister and lawyer of the town. She grew to maturity, attended the public schools and finished her education at the Charlestown Academy. Subsequently she met and married R. F. Harrison, of Carrollton, and to this union we are indebted for the young dentist who is the subject of this brief review.

Henry Watterson Harrison was born at Carrollton, Kentucky, in 1872 and received his early education in his native county. About the time he reached his majority he entered the Pennsylvania College of Dental Surgery at Phildadelphia, from which he was graduated in March, 1893. He began practice at Carrollton, but after remaining there a year or two removed in April, 1895, to Rising Sun, Indiana. Remaining at this point for five years, he again changed location in 1900 and spent nearly two years at Evansville. In September, 1901, he removed to Jeffersonville, which has since continued the theater of his operations. He occupies an office and residence combined in the principal business part of the city. The neatness of the surroundings, the comfortable character and good taste displayed in the furnishings and the whole atmosphere of the place indicate that the young dentist is attending strictly to business and bids fair to make a success of his profession. Doctor Harrison is a member of the First Christian church of Jeffersonville and takes an interest in everything concerning its educational and charitable work. He has an inclination toward the fraternities and seems fond of lodge work, as is indicated by the numerous orders to which he belongs. These include Clark Lodge, No. 40, Free and Accepted Masons; Jefferson Lodge, No. 3, Independent Order of Odd Fellows; Hope Lodge, No. 13, Knights of Pythias, and the Modern Woodmen of America.

On October 10, 1894, Doctor Harrison was married to Hattie O., daughter of O. P. and Hannah J. Dailey, of Vevay, Indiana. They have two children, Hugh P. and Henry W., Jr. The family live quietly and modestly, enjoy respect in their circle of acquaintance and number on their list of friends many of the best people of the city.

ADOLPH I. FRANK.

The subject of this sketch, who is efficiently performing the responsible duties of Police Commissioner of the city of Jeffersonville, is one of the best known citizens of Clark county. His appointment to the position he now fills met with the approval of the public and he has abundantly fulfilled every expectation.

Mr. Frank is a native of Jeffersonville, Indiana, and was born on January 3, 1844. His father, John G. Frank, was born in Wurtemberg, Germany, in 1814, and received his education in the excellent public schools of his native land. In 1830 he emigrated to America, locating first in Canada, where he served an apprenticeship to the butcher's trade. In 1835 he came to 'the states," locating in Jeffersonville, where he remained during the remaining years of his life, his death occurring on the 10th of January, 1884. He had followed the meat business during his active life, retiring from active pursuits in 1870. He married Mary Oehm, who was born in Saxony, Germany, in 1818. In 1833 she came to America with her parents, who located near Charlestown, Indiana. The father, William Oehm, was an early settler and prominent farmer, but died in early life. Mrs. Mary Frank died on the 10th of June, 1890.

John G. and Mary Frank became the parents of eleven children, five of whom died in infancy, and but four of whom are now living. Those who lived to years of maturity are as follows: John W., who was a butcher in Jeffersonville, died May 10, 1900; Adolph I. is the immediate subject of this sketch; John H. is a butcher at Owensboro, Kentucky; H. M. runs a successful drygoods business in Jeffersonville; Lucretia, the wife of William H. Kehrt, a saddler and harnessmaker in Jeffersonville; Oliver J. died at the age of twenty-six years.

Adolph I. Frank received a good practical education in the public schools of Jeffersonville, and upon the close of his school days he served an apprenticeship in the drygoods business in Jefferonville two years. He was then for several years employed in a drygoods store in Louisville, Kentucky. In 1872 he entered into business on his own account in Jeffersonville, and so continued until 1890, when he entered the employ of his brother, H. M., in the same line. He has been fairly successful in all his business affairs, and, which is

better still, he has earned and retained the highest regard of all with whom
he has had business dealings.

On the establishment of the municipal office of Police Commissioner, in
1898, Mr. Frank was appointed to that office for four years. He then
remained free from political office for four years, but in 1906 was induced
to again accept an appointment to the same position, which he has since so
acceptably filled. He has also served four years as a member of the City
Council.

Politically Mr. Frank has always been an active Republican, and his fraternal affiliation is with the Independent Order of Odd Fellows. He is a member of the Methodist Episcopal church.

In 1866 Mr. Frank married Mary Robertson, a resident of this county,
though a native of Birmingham, Iowa. The Robertson family is an old one
and was prominently identified with the war of the Revolution. Mrs. Frank's
paternal grandfather, Hezekiah Robertson, was an early settler of Indiana
and assisted in hewing the logs for the erection of the first Methodist Episcopal church in the state. That was in 1800 and the church was located about
three miles north of Charleston. The deed to this property, which deed is
still in the possession of the Robertson family, conveys the land "to the M. E.
Church of the United States forever." Five children have been born to Mr.
and Mrs. Frank, namely: Ada W., who lives at home, is a graduate of De-
Pauw University, class of '98, and is now a teacher of Latin in the Jeffersonville high school; Clara K. died at the age of seven years; Laura O. is the
wife of S. H. McMullin, of Aurora, Indiana; Irwin R., of Cosmosdale, Kentucky, is the cashier of the Cosmos Cement Company; he married Gertrude
Hagerman; Olive died in 1906, unmarried.

NEWTON HUNT MYERS.

It was over ninety years ago, three years after Indiana was admitted as
a state, when the whole territory was clothed in original forest, when settlements were few and far between and towns found only at a few places on the
Ohio river, that Michael J. Myers left his home in Herkimer county, New
York, to seek his fortune in what was then known as the "far West." He
was a contractor by occupation, and his object in coming to Clark county in
1819 was to prosecute work on a then projected canal. Later he went to
Ohio, where he ended his career at a comparatively early age. With him at
the time of his arrival in Clark county was a son named Peter, then seven
years old, who after reaching manhood engaged in merchandising, shipbuild-
ing and the lumber business. He met with the usual fortunes attending such

ventures, but on the whole seems to have prospered during a long life that was terminated by death in January, 1886, in the seventy-fourth year of his age. He married Rachael, daughter of Thomas Jacobs, one of the earliest of the county's pioneers, who lived in Utica township. She died in 1893, when sixty-three years old. She became the mother of eight children. By a former marriage Peter Myers was the father of six children, and of his fourteen children, nine are still living.

Newton Hunt Myers, third of the children of the second marriage, was born at Jeffersonville, Indiana, December 27, 1857. After the usual preliminary attendance in the common schools, he was graduated from the city high school, in 1877, and was the second boy to receive that honor. After a course at Eastman Business College in Poughkeepsie, New York, he secured a position as bookkeeper in the Plate Glass Works at Jeffersonville, which he held for two years and then embarked in business on his own account. In partnership with Ed. Heller he established a mercantile firm to deal in clothing, hats and furnishing goods, but after the retirement of Mr. Heller within a year, he took sole charge and has since continued in the business. In 1892, in partnership with F. L. Rossbach he established a furnishing business in Chicago, known as the Washington Shirt Company, which proved a very successful venture. In addition to manufacturing the firm conducts three retail stores in Chicago. Several years ago a stock company was formed for the manufacture of wagons, kitchen cabinets and other household supplies, of which Mr. Myers became the largest owner and directing head. In addition to his business ventures Mr. Myers has found time for other activities and has become quite prominent in local politics. He is chairman of the Republican Central Committee and a member of the State Advisory Committee. In 1894 he was elected School Trustee, to serve four years, but resigned this position in February, 1898, to accept a higher honor. He was appointed postmaster by President McKinley and served acceptably during his first term, and was reappointed at the expiration of his term, in all completing a service of eight years. Mr. Myers' fraternal connections are numerous and conspicuous as they embrace membership in several of the best known fraternities. In the Masonic Order he is a Knight Templar, Scottish Rite and Shriner, an extrustee of the Knights of Pythias, and a member of the Benevolent and Protective Order of Elks.

On April 22, 1889, Mr. Myers was married to Elizabeth Means, a native of Louisville, Kentucky, and of English descent. Her parents, Edwin and Sarah Means, were born, reared and married in England, but came to this county in early life, the father dying January 10, 1908, aged eighty-six. and the mother died July 6, 1908, also at the age of eighty-six years. Mr. and Mrs. Myers have three children, Helen, Perin and Richard B. Mr. Myers ranks high in the business world as a man of affairs and action, who know how to get things done. He has taken the initiative in several enterprises of risk, but so managed them as to make valuable properties. In the political arena Mr. Myers has developed the skill and judgment that give value to those in active management and his associates rely on him as a wise advisor. He has filled such official positions as have been entrusted to his charge in such a way as to show integrity of character and a firm grasp on details. Socially his standing is among the best and he has developed the rare faculty of both making and holding friends.

HENRY F. BURTT.

Amasa Burtt purchased a tract of land in Utica township, Clark county, Indiana, July 21, 1821, which after the lapse of nearly one hundred years, is still in possession of his descendants. The original tract of one hundred seventy acres, mostly wild woodland, was increased by subsequent purchases until in the course of generations it was converted into a productive and valuable farm. Amasa Burtt, who became a prosperous farmer, spent his whole life in Utica township and finally ended his days in December, 1853, on the homestead he had established. He was succeeded as owner by his son, Eli, who spent the eighty years of his life on the place of his birth, and died there July 7, 1897. He married Pauline Hardin, a native of Oldham county, Kentucky, who came with her parents to Clark county when a girl. Her death occurred at the Utica township homestead, September 25, 1871, after becoming the mother of eleven children, of whom seven are living. These are: Mollie B., widow of Noah R. Dale; Henry A.; Laura, wife of Thomas Spaulding; Benjamin H.; Joseph B.; Balie L., and Rose T., wife of Daniel Holloway.

Henry Adolphus Burtt, second of this family, was born in Utica township, Clark county, Indiana, October 8, 1852. He grew up in the old homestead, established by his grandfather, got a limited education in the public schools, and when sixteen years old became a pupil at the Brownsboro Academy, in Oldham county, Kentucky, which he attended for two years. From there he went to the State University, at Bloomington, Indiana, and was graduated June 12, 1878. At intervals during his college life he taught school for several years, and the sickness and death of his mother caused protracted absence from college before he secured his degree. Immediately after this event he entered the law office of Ferguson & Marsh at Jeffersonville, but later took a course in the Louisville Law School, from which he was graduated with the class of 1880. On April 1st of the same year he opened an office at Jeffersonville and has been in continuous practice ever since.

In July, 1885, he formed a partnership with James E. Taggart, and this firm has never been dissolved. Burtt & Taggart are familiar names on all court dockets around the Falls Cities, as they have had their full share in all the important litigation. Mr. Burtt has always affiliated with the Democratic party, but while he has done his part of the work he has never been an aspirant for office on his own account, preferring to occupy that post of honor known as the private station. He is content to do his duties as a good citizen and has found ample employment for all his faculties as a devotee of that "jealous mistress," known as the law. He stands well in his profession and is regarded as well informed both as to the history and practice. He is competent as a trial lawyer and in that class of work which belongs to the office and as an all around practitioner is able to hold his own with the best. In 1904 Mr. Burtt was elected Mayor of Jeffersonville, but retired after serving two years.

In November, 1880, Mr. Burtt was married to Marietta Robertson, a native of Utica township and a descendant of one of the early settlers of Clark county. Her parents were William F. and Malinda (Carr) Robertson, who were born and reared near Charlestown, Clark county, Indiana, and ranked among the pioneer farmers to whom the agricultural development of this section is due. Mr. and Mrs. Burtt have six children: Ernest E., cartoonist on a Knoxville newspaper; Ella Irene, Eunice R., Amos Henry, Esther H. and Lora Josephine.

JOHN HUTCHINSON BALDWIN.

Few men of his age have accomplished more than the bright and popular young physician whose name heads this sketch. Though not much beyond his thirty-second year, he ranks among the successful practitioners of his community, and as a promoter and organizer of educational agencies for the general uplift and enlightenment of his fellow men. He has a natural talent as an organizer, one of the rare gifts among men and has made a success of everything he has undertaken in this line. In fact he is a feature of Jeffersonville social life and a factor of importance in all that concerns medical progress. Suave in manner, clean of life, full of energy and enterprise, he is valued as a counsellor and sought after by all who are contemplating movements along educational and progressive lines.

Edward Baldwin, the doctor's father, was a pilot on a Mississippi river gun-boat during the stirring days of the Civil war, when these vessels were causing such terror among our rebellious friends along the banks of the great "Father of Waters." It took a man of skill and courage to engineer one of these queer crafts up and down the streams that penetrated the Confederacy. Edward Baldwin proved equal to the task and did his full share in suppressing the great uprising that threatened the integrity of the Union. He married Susan E. Spitler, whose ancestry was German, but came to New Albany from Virginia.

John Hutchinson Baldwin, a child by this union, was born at New Albany, Floyd county, Indiana, in October, 1876. He went through the city schools and graduated from the high school in 1894. Shortly afterward he entered the Southwestern Homeopathic Medical College and Hospital, from which he was graduated at the head of his class in 1897. Being appointed interne at the Louisville City Hospital, he served there during the years 1897 and 1898, but in the summer of the latter year removed to Jeffersonville, where he has since actively engaged in the practice of medicine. In 1908 he built an office of concrete, the first erected in the city exclusively for office purposes. In the fall of 1903 Doctor Baldwin promoted the organization of the Jeffersonville Chautauqua Association and the first assembly was held from August 5th to 14th in 1904, continuing annually ever since. Speakers of national reputation and varied pursuits have spoken at this summer assemblage and make it one of the most notable of the West. Among the celebrities who have appeared on this platform are William Jennings Bryan, Champ Clark, Sam Jones, Maud Ballington Booth, Bishops J. R. McIntire and Edwin Holt Hughes, Lorado Taft, the sculptor, and other of world-wide reputation. Doctor Baldwin is president of the association, with Adam Heimberger, of New Albany, as vice-president; James E. Taggart, of Jeffersonville, as secretary, and George H. Holzbog as treasurer. Professor Charles A. Prosser, superintendent of the New Albany public schools, is superintendent, and the directors are John C. Zulauf, A. A. Swartz, H. M. Frank, and the general officers. The doctor's activities, social, religious and fraternal, are in keeping with his enterprising temperament. He is ruling elder in the Presbyterian church, member of Clark Lodge, No. 40, Free and Accepted Masons, and examining physician for Hoosier Camp of the Modern Woodmen of America. For ten years he has been a member of the faculty of the college from which he graduated and holds the important position of professor of the principles and practice of medicine. He is a member of the Indiana Institute of Homeopathy and for awhile held the position of vice-president of that institution. In addition to all this he is a member of the Falls City Homeopathic Medical Society, member of the staff at Deaconess Hospital and visiting physician at the Louisville City Hospital. Although among the younger physicians of Jeffersonville, none stand higher or are regarded as more useful than Doctor Baldwin. He has a large and extensive practice among the best people, who entertain profound respect for his professional opinions.

Doctor Baldwin owns and lives in a handsome home which he recently erected. As an organizer his qualities are such as to make him much sought after and in all his undertakings of a public character he has been recognized as a leader and usually becoming president of the association.

On January 30, 1900, Doctor Baldwin married Cora G. Peckenpaugh, a native of Leavenworth, Indiana, and daughter of Judge N. R. Peckenpaugh, who formerly presided over the Supreme Court of Alaska. They have three children, Edward Nicholas, Ruth Elizabeth and Dorothy May.

DAVID C. PEYTON, M. D.

Occupying an enviable position in the ranks of his profession and enjoying the respect and esteem of everyone in the community, the subject of this sketch merits personal mention in a work of the character of this volume. David C. Peyton was born near Charlestown, Clark county, Indiana, on October 12, 1860. He is a son of John M. and Susan (Clarke) Peyton, both also natives of this county. The father was a farmer and stood well among his fellow men. The paternal grandfather, Daniel Peyton, was commissioned a major of Indiana militia by Governor Jennings in 1816, the year that Indiana was admitted as a state, and the following year he was commissioned colonel of the Twenty-second Regiment, Indiana State Militia. He was a member of the rescue party at the Pigeon Roost massacre and had also taken an active part in the War of 1812. John M. and Susan Peyton were the parents of eight children, seven sons and one daughter, and of these four of the sons and the daughter are now living in Clark county, the brothers of the subject all being engaged in farming.

David C. Peyton received his preliminary education in the common schools of his native county and then took a three-years' course in a normal training school. He was engaged, for a year in teaching school, and then, having decided upon the medical profession as his life work, he took up his professional studies in the office of Dr. J. M. Reynolds, of Memphis, Indiana. He then entered the Ohio Medical College, of Cincinnati, Ohio, where he graduated two years later, and then entered the University of Louisville, where he graduated with the class of '86. He is also a graduate of the Medico-Chirurgical College of Philadelphia, class of '99. The doctor has besides taken much post-graduate work and is thus well fitted by training for the work which he has so successfully carried forward. He first entered upon the active practice of his profession at Henryville, Clark county, but a few months later came to Jeffersonville and has since been constantly in the practice here with the exception of nine months during the Spanish-American war. At the outbreak of that brief but decisive conflict the doctor was commissioned a major and brigade surgeon by President McKinley, his commission being issued in June, 1898. His first service was as assistant chief surgeon of the Second Army Corps at several points in Pennsylvania, and at Camp Meade, that state, he was relieved from that duty and transferred to Philadelphia, where he assumed the duties of chief medical officer of the state, performing these duties until the close of the war. He then returned to his practice at Jeffersonville, to which he has given an earnest attention and undivided interest, so that at this time he enjoys one of the most extensive medical practices in this section of the state. The doctor takes a deep interest in his profession and is a member of the Clark County Medical Society, the Indiana State Medical Society, the American Medical Association and the Mississippi Valley Medical Association. He is now serving as president of the state society, was a member for five years of the judicial council of the American Association, and a member for five years of the "house of delegates" from Indiana to the latter society. Among other positions of professional responsibility which he has held may be mentioned his membership on the city board of health and three years' service as secretary of the County Board of Health. He also served three years as surgeon of the Prison, South, now known as the Jeffersonville Reformatory. He was also surgeon for several corporations and railroad companies.

On June 26, 1883, Doctor Peyton married Henrietta S. Hay, a daughter of George W. and Susan Hay, of Charlestown, this county, where she was born. Mrs. Peyton was reared and educated there and is also a graduate of Barnett Academy. The doctor maintains fraternal relations with the Free and Accepted Masons, and has risen to the rank of a Knight Templar. His religious membership is with the Presbyterian church. Politically he is a zealous and active Democrat, though not an aspirant to political offices. He has, however, given six years efficient service as a member of the city board of school trustees.

A man of fine attainments and of strong social instincts, Doctor Peyton has won a host of warm personal friends. He is a constant and careful student of everything pertaining to his profession and keeps in close touch with the latest advances in the healing art.

THOMAS MULLEN.

When the tide of immigration was setting in strong during the middle decades of the last century, the Emerald Isle was contributing by the thousands to the bone and sinew so necessary to building up the great republic. Most of these emigrants became common laborers on the railways and canals then being constructed and others were scattered all over the country as mechanics in various industrial establishments. It was about 1852 that the elder Thomas Mullen, after marrying Bridget Castelo in Ireland, came with her to seek his fortunes in the states of North America. Two years later he found himself seeking employment in Jeffersonville, which he subsequently found at the big mill on the river west of the Pennsylvania bridge and here he remained at work until the time of his death. There were seven children by this marriage, of whom those now living are John, Thomas, Mary, James and Julia. John married Mary Cummings, of Jeffersonville, who died in 1908, leaving three children of her own, besides they had adopted one. Mary, James and Julia live with their mother at present, James being a pattern-maker at the car works.

Thomas Mullen, second in age of his father's surviving children, was born at Jeffersonville, Indiana, November 25, 1862, and as he grew up attended the Catholic schools of the city. Later he took lessons in mechanical drafting at Louisville and in 1878 secured a job at the car works to do general labor such as was suited to a boy. When he was older and more experienced he was put to work with tools as a car-builder, later made patterns and finally was promoted to the passenger car department. By degrees he rose to be assistant superintendent and has under his care all the work pertaining to passenger cars. He has held this position for ten years, has a large number of men under his charge and has given entire satifaction to his employers by his prompt and efficient discharge of duties assigned him. Mr. Mullen is a member of St. Augustine's Catholic church at Jeffersonville and is connected with the fraternal orders of the Elks and Knights of Columbus.

In 1900 Mr. Mullen married Julia B., daughter of Nimrod C. and Cynthia (Weathers) Beckham, and is a second cousin of the late Governor of Kentucky. Mrs. Mullen has reason to be proud of the long and honorable genealogy by which she can trace her ancestry through famous families of this and other countries. Her mother was a daughter of William and Elizabeth (Graham) Weathers, the former being a prominent citizen of Nelson county, Kentucky, where he owned two thousand acres of land. His wife was a sister of Dr. Christopher Columbus Graham, who was born October 10, 1784, and was more than one hundred years old at the time of his death, at Louisville, in 1885. He enjoyed the distinction of having been present at the marriage of the parents of Abraham Lincoln. His father was James Graham, a Deputy Sheriff of Augusta county, Virginia, when twenty years old, who afterwards came west with Gen. George Rogers Clark and fought with old warriors at Kaskaskia. One of his fellow soldiers was Colonel Edward Worthington, with whom after the military campaigns he settled in Boyle county, Kentucky, and later married the sister of Colonel Worthington.

James Graham traced his descent from the noble House of Montrose, so celebrated in the annals of England and Scotland, since the twelfth century. The Grahams, or Graeme, pedigree goes even farther back to the time when one member of the family fought so valiantly at the Roman Wall in the fifth century, that it was ever afterwards called after his name. Mrs. Mullen is a bright and intelligent woman, talks enthusiastically of the historic events connected with the history of her family, with which she has become familiar by reading and tradition. Mr. Mullen is faithful and reliable in business, a man of steady habits and much devoted to his home circle. Their only child is a boy, whom they have named Alvin, and who gives promise of being a worthy descendant of a distinguished ancestry.

HON. GEORGE H. VOIGT.

In no profession is there demanded a more conscientious and careful mental training or a more thorough appreciation of the absolute ethics of life than in that of law. In this profession success comes only as the result of capability and earnest and unremitting effort.

The subject of this sketch, who has in many ways become closely identified with the varied interests of Jeffersonville, has lived there all his life. He is the son of Ferdinand and Eva K. Voigt, natives of Germany, who came to this county early in life and lived in Jeffersonville many years.

George H. Voigt received a good preliminary education in the schools of Jeffersonville, and then, having decided upon the legal profession for his life work, entered the law department of the University of Louisville, where he graduated. Entering at once upon the active practice of his profession, Mr. Voigt met with immediate success and was quickly recognized as a young man of promise.

In 1885 he was elected City Attorney and discharged the duties of this position to the entire satisfaction of the people. In the following year he resigned to accept the office of Prosecuting Attorney of the Fourth Judicial Circuit, to which he had been elected. The circuit at that time comprised the counties of Clark and Floyd and the position was one requiring much work and responsibility. He performed the duties of the office without fear or favor and retired after serving a second term with a well earned reputation for absolute fidelity to the interests of the people.

Afterwards he was again elected City Attorney of Jeffersonville, but after several years of service resigned the office, the salary not justifying him in devoting the necessary time to the discharge of its duties.

For many years Mr. Voigt has enjoyed a large and lucrative business, his practice being a general one excepting, however, criminal law, the practice of which he discontinued some years ago. His law library is one of the largest and most carefully selected in the state.

Though busily engaged in the practice of his profession Mr. Voigt has become interested to a considerable extent in other lines of activity. He is a director of the First National Bank of Jeffersonville and interested in a number of other local enterprises.

A staunch Democrat in politics Mr. Voigt has always taken an active interest in the affairs of his party, being influential in its councils and advocating Democratic principles on the stump.

In 1890 he was elected a member of the House of Representatives of the Indiana Legislature from the district composed of Clark, Floyd and Jefferson counties. He was elected a Presidential elector in 1892 and in 1896 was sent to the Democratic National Convention as a delegate. Mr. Voigt takes a keen interest in the issues of the day and decided stand on the great questions before the American people.

He married Lora E. Hill, a daughter of William H. and Maria Hill. She is a native of Jeffersonville and a very attractive woman of rare accomplishments.

JAMES H. DUFFY.

Through sheer industry and close attention to the smallest details of the affairs of the big concern of which he is the head, James H. Duffy has placed the City Ice & Cold Storage Company, 955 Maple street, Jeffersonville, Indiana, in the front rank of establishments of this character. Although comparatively a young man Mr. Duffy possesses rare business acumen, and his career in the business world has been marked with signal success. He has been identified and contributed his moral and financial support to many projects that had for their purpose the betterment of the conditions of the community in which he has spent his life.

Mr. Duffy has passed the thirty-fourth anniversary of his birth, having been born in Jeffersonville township, October 22, 1874. He is the son of Captain James T. and Nora (Robinson) Duffy, a history of whom will be found upon another page of this volume. James H. Duffy is the eldest of a family of eight children, six of whom are living. He attended the public schools of the place of his nativity, and being an apt pupil with a full realization of the advantages of a good education advanced very rapidly. For the first ten years of his manhood he worked on the river in connection with his father's business, and being of a saving and economical disposition accumulated sufficient money to enable him to go into business for himself. In the year of 1900 he became the owner of his present plant, purchasing the same from the Jeffersonville Brewing Company. Immediately upon assuming control of the business he set about actively to making much needed improvements, and the business of the concern increased rapidly. Mr. Duffy is principally engaged in the business of manufacturing ice and his plant now turns out twenty tons daily, giving employment to four men. The cold storage department has a capacity of three thousand to four thousand barrels, and every inch of its space is in use the greater portion of the time.

The subject, on June 27, 1900, was married to Emma Howard, daughter of Thomas Howard, of Port Fulton. Mrs. Duffy is a native of New Orleans, but came to New Albany when a little girl, and was educated in the common schools of that city, and Louisville, Kentucky. One daughter was the result of this union, and she is now in the sixth year of her age, a bright child, who is idolized by her parents.

Mr. Duffy is very active in lodge work, being a member of the Elks and the Improved Order of Red Men. He is also a member of the Roman Catholic church, and takes a deep interest in religious affairs. He is an adherent of the principles of the Democratic party, having voted that ticket since he attained his majority. Because of his genial disposition and high sense of honor in dealing with his fellow men he is popular in Jeffersonville.

WILMER T. FOX.

Wilmer T. Fox, one of the rising members of the Clark County Bar and for over three years City Attorney of Jeffersonville, is the only living son of Prof. Charles F. and Mary P. Fox, and dates his birth from September 5th of the year 1881. His father was born at New Albany, Indiana, December 4, 1849, and is the son of Jacob Fox and Regina (Scholl) Fox. Jacob Fox was the son of George and Margaret (Householder) Fox and was born at Batchdorff, Alsace, France, on May 29, 1820, emigrating to America in 1838. Regina C. Scholl was the daughter of Fred Scholl and Katherine (Schumacher) Scholl, was born on November 30, 1813, at Upper Eslingen, Wurtemberg, Germany, and emigrated to this country in 1833. Her father was a soldier in the French army, served under Napoleon in the march against Moscow and on the return of the army from that expedition died from the effects of the terrible cold and exposure they had suffered.

Charles F. Fox received his early education in Clark county and later was graduated from the State Normal School at Terre Haute. For a period of thirty-six years he has devoted his life to educational work, being at this time one of the oldest teachers in active service in Clark county. He has held many important positions at different places and is now principal of the Rose Hill schools, one of the ward schools of Jeffersonville.

The maiden name of Mrs. Charles F. Fox was Mary P. Taylor. She is a daughter of Phineas and Mary J. (Allen) Taylor, and was born and reared in Clark county, being a descendant on the maternal side from a brother of Ethan Allen, of Revolutionary fame. Her great-grandfather on the maternal side of the family was Isaac McBride, who distinguished himself in the early border warfare and was a member of the expedition under General George Rogers Clark, when that intrepid commander passed through this part of Indiana on his way to capture the British stations of Kaskaskia and Vincennes and conquer an empire for the American cause. For services rendered during this and other expeditions he was subsequently awarded a large grant of land near the present town of Henryville, Clark county, and it is on this land that his remains were interred.

Wilmer T. Fox, whose birth occurred in Jeffersonville, spent his early life pretty much after the manner of the majority of city lads, entering the public schools at the proper age. He made commendable progress in his studies, completing the high school course on May 25, 1899, and on May 1st of the year 1900 he was graduated from the Spencerian Business College in Louisville, following which he was employed for three years as bookkeeper in that city. Having early manifested a decided taste for the legal profession, he began the study of the same in October, 1903, becoming a student of the Indiana Law School at Indianapolis, from which institution he was graduated May 24, 1905, and on August 1st of the same year he began the practice of his profession in Jeffersonville, where in due time he built up a large and lucrative practice.

Mr. Fox brought to his chosen calling a well disciplined mind and it was not long until he won recognition as a capable and painstaking lawyer, whose thorough professional training and ability and tact as a practioner caused his service to be much sought after by litigants.

On September 4, 1906, he was appointed City Attorney of Jeffersonville, the duties of which responsible position he has since discharged with credit to himself and to the satisfaction of the municipality.

Among his professional brethren Mr. Fox is held in the highest esteem and having the confidence of the public and the most loyal friendship of the many with whom he is accustomed to associate, it is not strange that his career thus far presents a series of continued successes, or that his future appears bright with promise. In his political affiliations he is a Republican and as such has rendered valuable services to his party in both city and country. He enjoys great personal popularity with the people irrespective of party alignment, many of his warmest friends and admirers holding views directly opposite to those he entertains.

Mr. Fox keeps in close touch with the trend of modern thought. He holds membership with the First Presbyterian church of Jeffersonville, is a ruling elder of the congregation and active in all lines of religion and benevolent work under its auspices, besides being influential in various movements and enterprises for the social advancement and moral welfare of the city. He is president of the Associated Charities of Jeffersonville and is also president and was the organizer of the Gentlemen's Literary Club, established in the year 1906, and since that time has been one of its most influential and active members, being untiring in his efforts to arouse and maintain an interest in the organization and make it answer the purpose for which intended.

While prosecuting his legal studies in Indianapolis Mr. Fox spent a part of his time as clerk to Judge Gillett of the Supreme Court and while thus engaged acquired a practical experience of great value to him in the subsequent practice of his profession.

Mr. Fox is a married man, his wife having formerly been Mary S. McKillip, of Charlestown, the ceremony by which they were united in the bonds of wedlock having been solemnized on the 24th day of October, 1907. Mrs. Fox is the only daughter of Mrs. Annie (Ford) McKillip and the late Rev. M. E. McKillip, and is a descendant of the best Southern families. She is a talented musician and a woman of personal charm.

GEORGE W. MARTIN.

Indiana was a territory of rough experiences and many dangers when the Martin family first settled here. The first arrivals were Jesse Martin and wife, who came from near Jamestown, Virginia, and settled in Washington county, when the Indians were still plentiful and occasionally hostile. A tradition is handed down to the effect that Jesse Martin, son of the above mentioned member of this family, was shot by an Indian, who, after friendly conditions prevailed came to the white settlement to see how badly his victim had been hurt. Manoah Martin, son of the elder Jesse, married Sarah Ann, daughter of George Wood, said to have been the first white settler in Wood township.

George W. Martin, one of the children by this union, was born in Washington county, Indiana, in 1847. In 1852 his parents removed to the old Hale farm in Clark county, a mile south of Borden. Here he remained until he reached manhood, meantime attending the local schools and completing his education by taking a commercial course at Hartsville College, in Bartholomew county. After leaving college Mr. Martin engaged in the manufacture of barrel staves, which he disposed of in 1882 to T. S. Carter. Later, for a number of years, he operated a spoke factory, saw, planing and flour mills on an extensive scale, which were burned in 1904, consuming twelve thousand

G. W. MARTIN.

dollars' worth of property, but he rebuilt and in 1906 sold to a corporation known as the Martin Milling Company, and is at present conducted by the Durham Tile & Lumber Company. In 1905 he established a general merchandise business at Borden, which he continues to conduct successfully, being altogether a very busy as well as prosperous man of affairs. He owns five fruit farms, one of which he manages in person and resides in a pleasant home at Borden, being regarded by his wide circle of acquaintances as a substantial and reliable citizen. He has for many years been a member of the Christian church, known as the Church of Christ.

In 1872 Mr. Martin married Belle, daughter of Robert and Elizabeth Huston, natives of Wood township. Mrs. Huston was a Miss Hallet before her marriage and her family lived near Utica, in Clark county. Of Mr. and Mrs. Martin's seven children only three are living. James Norman Martin, known by his friends as "Tay," has charge of a portable saw mill, which does a good business. He married Linnie Potts, a native of Wood township, and they have four children, James, John, Belle and Edward. Mr. Martin's two other living children are Georgia and Ralph Waldo. The entire family stand well among the industrious and prosperous citizens of Clark county, who in various lines of productive business have contributed to the growth and wealth of the community in which they live. Mr. Martin has been successful as a regular farmer, a fruit grower, a mill man and a manufacturer, giving employment to many men and enjoying the esteem of all as a fair manager who treats his employes with kindness and justice. His home is a place of meeting for many friends and all are treated with liberal and unostentatious hospitality.

GEORGE REMINGTON CLARKE.

It was many years ago that a young Englishman left his native land to seek his fortunes in the countries beyond the sea. Joseph Clarke, like most of the people of Great Britain, was much attached to the laws and institutions to which he had become accustomed and naturally gravitated towards a colony of "Old England" where the customs are much the same as those of the Fatherland. Directing his footsteps toward Ohio, there he met and married Claramond Shaw, a young woman of good family, whose native state was Ohio. George Remington Clarke, a son by this union, was born at London, Ontario, July 4, 1861. His father becoming dissatisfied with the outlook in Canada determined to look for betterment in some section of this great republic. With this end in view he gathered together his household goods and with his little family crossed lake Ontario and took passage for the distant state of Indiana. This was in 1865, when George Remington was about four

38

years old, and at this time his parents settled in Jeffersonville to make that city their home. George was sent at an early age to what was then known as the "Old Blue" school, well known as a part of the city's educational system. He remained in school, finishing the first year in the high school. His first venture in a business way was in a minor position at the office of the Howard Ship Yards. This he retained about one year and a half, when in April, 1879, he went with his brother-in-law, A. A. Swartz, the well known drygoods merchant on Spring street. This proved to be his life work, as he has remained in this mercantile establishment ever since, rising by gradual promotions until he has become a member of the firm, the old firm being changed to the Swartz Drygoods Company. Mr. Clarke developed a taste for politics in early manhood and attached himself to the Republican party and has taken an active interest in all the local campaigns. That he stands well in his political organization is proved by the fact that he was selected under Governor Mount as Republican member of the Board of Police Commissioners at Jeffersonville. He served satisfactorily and is esteemed as one of the local leaders, whose advice is worth listening to and whose work is valuable in helping the organization. He has long been a worker in religious circles and interested in the various charities, educational enterprises and missionary movements of his church. He is popular in all lines in which he has figured, being especially esteemed as a courteous and progressive business man. His address is agreeable, his manner affable and he has the faculty of making and holding friends.

On September 18, 1884, Mr. Clarke was married to Mildred, daughter of Mr. and Mrs. J. P. Winesburg, of Jeffersonville. Allen Winesburg Clarke is the only child of Mr. and Mrs. Clark. He is at present employed with the American Car & Foundry Company, of St. Louis. The family are members of the Presbyterian church, in which Mr. Clarke has served as deacon for ten years, or more. He ranks as a model citizen, a good neighbor, good friend and a public-spirited man, who is always ready to help any cause which promises to aid in the development of the city.

JOSEPH E. BOTTORFF.

A native son of Indiana, a representative of one of its prominent large pioneer families, and one who has been for many years identified with the industrial and material development of Clark county, a well known factor in the progress of this favored section of the commonwealth, is the gentleman whose life-history is herewith briefly outlined.

Joseph E. Bottorff was born in Harrison county, Indiana, in 1864, the son of Jacob S. and Matilda (LaDuke) Bottorff, the father a native of Clark county and the son of Louis Bottorff, both influential members of this old and well established Clark county family, and in many ways the subject evinces praiseworthy characteristics of his ancestors. He grew up in Elizabeth, Indiana, where he attended the public schools and laid the foundation for a good education. Early deciding to devote his life to the mercantile profession he came to Jeffersonville, in 1881, and entered the employ of Dennis Murphy, owner of a drygoods store on Spring street. Mr Bottorff gave evidence from the first that he possessed innate ability in the management of a concern like that of Mr. Murphy's and he made such rapid strides that he was enabled to buy out his employer in 1886, Mr. Murphy having been compelled by failing health to give up the business. Although then only about twenty-one years old, our subject assumed management of this store with ease and assurance, continuing to extend the trade of the same with most gratifying results. About 1904 his brother, Edward Bottorff, was taken in as a partner under the firm name of J. E. Bottorff & Company, since which time their trade has continued to increase, owing to the reliability of the managers and the fact that they handle a good grade of merchandise and always strive to give full value received, consequently never fail to please their customers. Their store is neatly kept and is equal to any of its kind in Jeffersonville. (The reader is respectfully referred to biographies of other members of the Bottorff family in this work for a history of the subject's ancestors.

Joseph E. Bottorff is the capable and efficient storekeeper at the quartermaster's department, which position he has held for a period of three years. Fraternally he is a member of the Benevolent and Protective Order of Elks, of which he has the distinction of being the past exalted ruler and he is a member of the grand lodge. Always abreast of the times Mr. Bottorff is a pleasant man to know and bears a reputation for integrity that is worthy of his ancestors.

CAPT. JOHN R. VAN LIEW.

Capt. John R. Van Liew is the scion of a respected and prosperous family of old Dutch stock and a man who has gained the position he holds today in the civic and business life of Jeffersonville, Clark county. As a militarist of the pronounced type ever since his term of service in the Spanish-American war he has done much to instill enthusiasm for a military calling into the younger citizens of the community.

Mr. Van Liew was born in Louisville, Kentucky, on October 15, 1876, the son of Dennis and Blanche (Weaver) Van Liew. When he had about reached his fourth year his parents removed to Jeffersonville across the river, and there his education was received, and the greater part of his life, since then, spent.   Upon leaving school he went into the box manufacturing business, in which he continued for eight years.   In 1893 he began a course of three years' service as sergeant of Company G, First Regiment, Indiana National Guard.   On the 4th of July. 1898, he enlisted in the One Hundred and Sixty-first Indiana Volunteer Infantry and was breveted with the rank of first sergeant in Company E, of which Lewis C. Baird, the editor of this work, was captain.   He preceded with his company from Indianapolis to Jacksonville, Florida, thence to Savannah, Georgia, and thence to Havana, Cuba. After seeing four and a half months' active service they returned via Savannah, were mustered out April 30, 1899, and returned to Jeffersonville through Washington, D. C.   The captain has been successful in building up the National Guard in his district and was captain of Company M, which he organized at Jeffersonville on February 9, 1906, for the period of two years. Since the close of his military career he is looked upon as an authority of importance in all things pertaining to army matters.

On his return from participation in the Spanish-American conflict Captain Van Liew was selected as an officer of the Indiana Reformatory, in June, 1899, and in consideration of his services as an officer of that institution was later promoted to the assistant superintendency of the shirt-making department, which position he still holds.

He was married on July 8, 1902, and selected as his wife, Emma Smith, the daughter of Augustus and Anna Smith, both natives of Louisville, Kentucky.   Mrs. Van Liew has borne her husband one child, Clarence P. Van Liew.

Captain Van Liew is a member of the Independent Order of Odd Fellows, the Modern Woodmen, and the Spanish-American war veterans.   He has numerous friends and is known to possess a kind and obliging disposition.   He is warmly attached to his family, and has a reputation for trustworthiness and efficiency in his present sphere of work.   At the present time he is no more than thirty-two years of age and, though his record in the past has been of the highest, his familiarity with business affairs are sure to win for him a larger share of recognition as a citizen of worth and probity.

ROBINSON PRATHER BOTTORFF.

There is a large and widely distributed family connection of this name in Clark county and for many years they have been engaged in developing this section.   Conspicuous in various walks of life, they are best known as farmers and devotees of the various mechanical arts.   They belong to the class of men that the essentially useful, doing those things which the people want done and obtaining success by doing them well. While none of the connection have accumulated great wealth, most of them have done well and laid by a competence. It is seldom indeed that a Bottorff is found who is not well-to-do and the name has become synonymous with thrift and industry. Originating in Germany representatives of this family became identified with Indiana at an early day. There has been a large increase by natural growth and inter-marriage and at present it ramifies through all parts of Clark county. William H. H. Bottorff, a son of Samuel, owned a farm near Utica for many years, but in 1884 disposed of his property and went to Kansas. One year later he died in the West and in 1888 the family returned to Clark county, locating in Jeffersonville. William H. H. Bottorff married Eliza, daughter of David and Edith (Prather) Grisamore, by whom he had eight sons, David, Nathan, Charles, Ruddle, Robinson P., Myron, Walter and Homer.

Robinson Prather Bottorff was born in Utica township, Clark county, Indiana, July 27, 1871. He remained on the farm until his parents went to Kansas and after returning secured a position in the car works. After a year in this line he began learning the trade of carriage trimmer, in which he soon became proficient. Two of his brothers also had jobs at the car works in different lines and developed into good mechanics. Myron learned black-smithing and now holds a responsible position with the American Brake Company at St. Louis. He is married and has one son. Walter learned carriage painting and at preent has charge of the Kentucky Buggy Company at Owensboro. Homer, the youngest of the boys, learned the carriage trimmer's trade under his eldest brother. All four brothers became employes at Jeffersonville, but in November, 1900, Robinson P. changed employment and took service with Rubell Brothers, carriage makers. In the spring of 1903 Mr. Bottorff, Robert O. Rubell and others organized the Falls City Buggy Top Company in Louisville and have made quite a success of this enterprise. Originally intending only to manufacture buggy tops the extensive use of automobiles suggested an opportunity to branch out in that line and in January, 1909, larger quarters were secured to afford room for making tops for autos, which has proved a profitable addition. Most of the stock is now owned by Messrs. Bottorff and Rubell and under their hustling management the business is increasing rapidly.

On September 3, 1896, Mr. Bottorff was married to Edna, daughter of Joseph and Emma (O'Neill) McPherson, of New Albany. Her father came from Pittsburg, Pennsylvania, but her mother is a native of Floyd county. They have had three children, those living being Iona and Roberta, two unusually bright girls of whom their parents are justifiably proud. Mr. Bottorff's fraternal relations are with the Red Men and Haymakers. He was three times a delegate to the Grand Council of Red Men at Indianapolis, and is one of the most influential and best known workers for the welfare of this popular order.

OSCAR H. DUFFY.

The family of this name in Clark county are of Scotch ancestry, their forefather's migrating across the English channel and settling in the north of Ireland, where several of the name rose to positions of prominence. A branch of the family emigrated to America about the first decade of the last century and in 1828 Maj. Andrew Duffy removed from there to Indiana, settling at Hanover Landing and became one of the early pioneers of Jefferson county. He dealt extensively in real estate and his grandson has papers in his possession signed by President Madison and James Monroe, when the latter was Secretary of State. Two of Major Duffy's uncles rose to higher rank as statesmen, both living bachelor lives and leaving large estates. Major Duffy was influential in Clark county affairs and served for a while as County Commissioner. His son, Thomas Duffy, gave additional luster to the family name during his long and useful life. He was born during his father's residence at Hanover Landing, but in childhood was brought to Clark county by his parents, Andrew and Kezziah Duffy, who settled at New Washington. After he reached maturity he engaged in farming for a while, but later removed to Jeffersonville and embarked in the grocery business. He was the first in the city to start a delivery wagon and for many years his establishment was the leading grocery of the county. For a long time he had charge of the poor of the township and established a reputation for charity, often giving out of his own store to relieve distress. During a small pox epidemic it was his duty to take provisions to the patients, which he performed bravely though daily exposed to infection. During the Civil war he remained a sturdy Democrat, though it cost something in those days, as men of that political faith were then rare in Southern Indiana. He and Jonas G. Howard voted together when the latter was threatened with violence for expressing his sentiment. While still a resident of New Washington, Thomas Duffy married Jane, daughter of Allen and Rebecca Rogers, and to this union we are indebted for the worthy gentleman who constituted the subject of this sketch.

Oscar H. Duffy was born at Jeffersonville, Indiana, in 1860, and six months later lost his mother by death. Wesley Duffy, an uncle, took charge of the babe and cared for him kindly at his home in Charlestown, until he reached the age of twenty-one. As he grew up he had the benefit of the public schools and during the intervals engaged in farming. When he became of age he located at Jeffersonville as a guest of his sister and for ten years was manager of a produce house in Louisville. In addition to being the purchasing agent and general superintendent of the business he also acted as traveling salesman for the firm. At later periods he engaged in various lines of work, being for three years with the T. J. Lindley hardware establishment in Jeffersonville, and the same length of time with the Belknap Hardware &

Manufacturing Company of Louisville. At present he is shipping clerk for the Indiana Chain Works, a manufacturing company at the Indiana Reformatory. Mr. Duffy began life at the foot of the ladder, always had to work his own way and rely on his own resources, but he has "made good' and proved a success in every line of business he has undertaken. He is a man of quick sympathies, of a kind and generous nature and enjoys a quiet life in a modest but comfortable cottage where his many friends are always welcome.

On October 25, 1905, Mr. Duffy married Mary Lucy Woodruff, a member of one of the old families and descendants of the early pioneers. Her father, James Woodruff, was a Virginian and her mother, Sarah Purdue, was a native of Scott county, Indiana. The latter's father was Nathan Purdue, who settled in Charlestown township, Clark county, in the early days and did his share in the hard work and development of pioneer times. Mr. and Mrs. Duffy are members of the Wall Street Methodist Episcopal church and he belongs to Hoosier Camp, Modern Woodmen of America.

JOHN LOOMIS, M. D.

Few families in American can boast so proud and ancient a lineage as that of the Loomises. As far back as the fifteenth century its members were famous both in England and Continental Europe. They were dissenters and the old records speak of a John Loomis who was burned for heresy at Canterbury, England, in 1856, for standing firmly by his religious convictions. Another, John Loomis, who was born before 1570, was a man of distinction at Braintree, England. His son, Joseph Loomis, a Puritan, some years after the landing of the Mayflower, came from Braintree to what is now Windsor, Connecticut. Perigrine White, the great-great-grandmother of Doctor Loomis, was the first white child born at Plymouth, Massachusetts. and the next child was Rebecca White. His grandfather and a number of others of the Loomis family bore a conspicuous part in the American Revolution. The family had a cost-of-arms, which bore devices that stand for loyalty to the king and country, for devoted self-sacrifice and whose motto means, "Yield not to adversity." The family in the United States, who are descendants from Joseph Loomis, the Puritan pioneer, number over twenty-eight thousand, many of them distinguished as scientists, soldiers, statesmen and members of the learned professions. They have endowed a college which stands on ground never owned by anyone but a Loomis since it was acquired by Joseph Loomis, in 1639. At that school any member of the Loomis family may be educated free of charge. It is a family, taken in its entirety that exemplifies the noble art of "plain living and high thinking," and seldom is one found who has not acquired a competency. Such is the noble lineage of a family which includes a number of representatives in Clark county, well worthy of the name.

Dr. John Loomis, chief patriarch and "head of the house" in Indiana, was born at Russell, Massachusetts, May 18, 1820. He is a graduate of both the eclectic and the homeopathic schools, and the oldest practicing physician in Clark county. Though over eighty-nine years old he is still engaged in his profession at Jeffersonville, where he has practiced since 1861. He was married October 17, 1843, to Clarissa Robinson, who was born in Pembroke, New Hampshire, in 1819, and died in Jeffersonville, Indiana. March 22, 1897, and is buried in Westfield, Massachusetts. He has reared an unusually interesting family, who have well sustained the proud escutcheon of the Loomises. John C. Loomis, the eldest son, was born at Westfield, Massachusetts, January 25, 1845, and came west with his parents in 1861. He attended high school in his native place, worked in railroad positions for two years, during which time he was conductor on the steam road between Jeffersonville and New Albany, and on the line to Indianapolis. Resigning this, in spite of the earnest requests of the management to remain, he went into the drug business in 1876 at Chestnut and Watt streets in Jeffersonville. Two years later he bought its site across the street from the first location and on that corner he still continues business. In 1906 he erected a fine new building which he now occupies, and enjoys the distinction of having the oldest continuing drug business and probably the oldest continuing mercantile business of any kind in the city. He is a graduate pharmacist and an analytical chemist of distinction. Twenty years ago he was appointed inspector of oils at the United States quartermaster's depot and now inspects everything there in the chemical line, which in an establishment of this kind are of great variety. In July, 1895, he married Mattie J., daughter of B. A. Johnson and wife, of Jeffersonville. He is a member of the Masonic lodge, of the Knights of Pythias, United Order of the Golden Cross, and elder in the Presbyterian church. His sister, Clara J. Loomis, conducts a private school in Jeffersonville and was one of the founders of the Jeffersonville Hospital, as well as the Old Ladies' Home. Jacob Loomis, the doctor's second son, is interested in the steel works at Wheeling, West Virginia; Herbert is associated with his brother in the drug business. Alice, the second daughter, is housekeeper for her father, elder sister and brother Herbert, who are still under the parental roof. Arthur Loomis, the youngest son and twin brother of Alice, is one of the best architects in Kentucky. In the line of his profession he designed the Todd building, the first sky-scraper in Louisville. He also designed the public library building and the beautiful new bank building at the corner of Spring and Court streets in Jeffersonville. The latter is the finest business building in the county. Kirke H., who died in 1878, in Westfield, Massachusetts, was a graduate of

Eastman Business College, at Poughkeepsie, New York, and became conductor on the Pennsylvania and later Louisville & Nashville Railroad. At the time of his death he was on his way to Canada to attend the annual meeting of the railway order of the United States and Canada, of which he was vice-president. Christia R., another daughter, married Homer Bush, and died in Westfield, Massachusetts.

BURDET CLIFTON PILE.

The lineage of the family of this name is ancient and honorable. The men on both sides served their country well both in war and peace and where-ever found were among the sturdy citizens of their respective communities. We first hear of Dr. Richard Pile, who lived in Virginia when she was a colony of Great Britain. His son and namesake was apprenticed to the sad-dler's trade but ran away to join the patriot army in the war of the Revolu-tion. He served for a time in the Eighth Virginia Regiment under General Jonathan Clark, and this body of troops rendered valiant service at the storm-ing of Stony Point. He was also with Washington as sergeant at Valley Forge. After the war he settled in Kentucky, where he married Rebecca Clif-ton, of the vicinity of Bardstown. Sometime before 1798 he moved to Spring-ville, near Charlestown, but later he removed to Jeffersonville. His wife was a famous cook and prepared the dinner for the surveyors who platted the town. One of his sisters married Evan, brother of Isaac Shelly, the first Governor of Kentucky. Another sister married an ancestor of Gen. Jefferson C. Davis, of Civil war fame. Richard Pile died in 1816, and about 1820 his widow married Thomas Morgan, of Jeffersonville, by whom she had one daughter, Elizabeth, who subsequently became the wife of Samuel Athey, and removed with him to Missouri. Richard and Rebecca (Clifton) Pile had four children: Marston Green Clark, Burdet Clifton, Mary and Margaret. The elder brother was the first white child born in Clark county, his native place being what was then called Fort Finney, but afterward Fort Steuben. Mary, the elder sister, married Moody Dustin, and Margaret became the wife of Thomas Powell, a native of New Jersey, who moved to Jeffersonville and made his home there until his death.

Burdet Clifton Pile, who enjoyed the pioneer honor of being Clark coun-ty's second white child, was born at Jeffersonville, Indiana, March 10, 1805. Early in life he became a brick manufacturer and later conducted a pottery at Port Fulton. About 1855 he became a partner in the firm of Maybury, Pile & Company, proprietors of a hardware store, but several years later he pur-chased the senior partner's interest and substituted his son-in-law, J. J. Con-way. He disposed of his mercantile interests in 1871, and two years later became Mayor of Jeffersonville, succeeding in that office, Levi Sparks, later brother-in-law to his daughter, Fannie Belle Sparks. Previous to his two years as Mayor Mr. Pile had served a number of terms in the city council and was trustee of the Wall Street Methodist church. He was director in the Ft. Wayne & Southern Railway Company, which projected a line through Clark county and built part of the road bed near Charlestown. In many ways Burdet Clifton Pile was a remarkable man. His early education was limited by lack of good schools, but he made up for this in after life by reading and observation. He was a close student of the Bible, had a retentive memory and could quote many fine passages from the good book. His vocabulary was extraordinary, his command of language never at fault and these qualifications made him an orator of ability. Above all he was a man of sterling character who earned and held the respect and high esteem of all who knew him. He was an active and enthusiastic member of the Masonic Order for many years and from time to time occupied all the official stations in the Blue Lodge and Chapter. He died March 17, 1885. January 29, 1834, Mr. Pile married Mary Ann Cunningham, the ceremony being performed by the minister, who was afterwards well known as Bishop Ames. Mrs. Pile was a daughter of David Cunningham and her birth occurred in Ontario county, New York, March 18, 1812. Her father's removal here was due to the fact that he was a sub-contractor in building the Louisville and Portland canal. He had five sons, all of whom were engaged with him on this important line of transportation. His wife was Anna, daughter of Peter Jennison, a Revolutionary soldier who responded to the Lexington alarm call. Her grandfather, Amos Singletary, served for eight years as a representative in the Great and General Court of Massachusetts. Robert Cunningham, a brother of Mrs. Pile, was in the battle of the Alamo under David Crockett, and his name appears among the other heroes on the monument erected in the state capital grounds at Austin, Texas. Mr. and Mrs. Pile had ten children. Maria T., the eldest, married Oliver N. Thomas, and her only daughter, Ida T., is now the widow of John H. Hause, who died in Jeffersonville about 1902. Mrs. Thomas having lost her husband by death, contracted a second marriage with William H. Buckley, a man of remarkable vitality, who at the age of eighty-eight is a foreman at the Howard Shipyards. Mary Ann, the second daughter of Mr. Pile, married Joseph Conway and after his death removed to St. Louis. They had eleven children, of whom three daughters and one son reside in Jeffersonville. Lucinda A., third daughter of Mr. Pile, married A. S. Gilbert, of Massachusetts. She and her son, Clifton S., are residents of Jeffersonville. Rebecca Virginia Pile, the fourth daughter, married Valentine Rose and died in Louisville. Sarah Eliza Pile, the fifth daughter, married Capt. George W. Kingsbury, of the United States Army, and both died at Clifton Springs, New York, there being one surviving child, who resides in Philadelphia. Rufus Moody

Pile, the eldest son, has been quite successful in the railway world, and is now assistant general passenger agent of the Pennsylvania systems, with headquarters at Philadelphia. William Clifton Pile, the second son, married Lizzie Barringer, and resides at St. Louis. Charles Burdet Pile, the third son, married Mary Durham, and lives at Wichita, Kansas. Fannie Belle, the youngest of the family, married Nathan Sparks, a sketch of whom appears elsewhere in this volume.

NATHAN SPARKS.

The gentleman whose name appears above is the representative of an old and well known family, members of which have been prominent in the martial affairs of this country since the days of the Revolution, and the present representative, Nathan Sparks, is eminently worthy to bear such a name. He has lived in Clark county for nearly three score years and his mind links the formative era with that of latter day progress in which he has taken a conspicuous part.

Nathan Sparks was born in Daviess county, Indiana. He came to Jeffersonville in 1850, where he has since resided. He is the son of Levi and Mary B. (Godwin) Sparks, both in Queen Ann's county, Maryland. They came overland to Daviess county, Indiana, about 1835, settling among the pioneers there. Soon after Nathan Sparks came to Jeffersonville, his sister, Mary Jane, and other members of the family also came for the purpose of attending the Jeffersonville schools, but, like the others, she remained to make her home here. About 1877 Mary Jane Sparks was married to Capt. James M. Phillips, of Jeffersonville, who was at that time stationed at Columbus, Indiana. Captain Phillips died in Texas in February, 1895, while superintendent of the Gulf, Colorado & Santa Fe Railroad. He was a native of Clark county, and he had already made his mark in the railroad world before going to Texas. Mrs. Phillips died in Jeffersonville July 17, 1897.

Nathan Sparks is one of six brothers, namely: George W., Levi, Joseph, Thomas, Nathan and James A. Of these Thomas, Nathan and Levi came to Jeffersonville. George W. lived at Wilmington, Delaware, until his death. Joseph lived in Clinton county, Indiana, and James A. lives in Daviess county, this state. Levi came to Jeffersonville in 1836 and followed mercantile pursuits. He was postmaster of Jeffersonville under President Franklin Pierce, and in the early seventies he was mayor of this city. For a period of twenty-one years he was connected with the city government, having been a rock-ribbed Democrat all his life. He took an active part in securing the government depot for Jeffersonville and he received well deserved credit for the part he took in the work. He died in 1875. Thomas Sparks came to Jeffersonville in 1847 to attend school, after which he remained. He always engaged in the mercantile business. He was a member of the City Council for eight years. He was also nominated by his party as candidate for Mayor of Jeffersonville.

Nathan Sparks came here in 1850, as already indicated, and he has since followed mercantile pursuits for the most part. He was long a member of the City Council and was United States Inspector at the government depot for four years under Cleveland and for two years under Harrison. He was a member of the School Board, part of the time as secretary and the balance of the time as president.

He was united in marriage October 21, 1879, to Fannie Belle Pile, daughter of Burdet Clifton and Mary Ann (Cunningham) Pile.

Mrs. Sparks is descended from soldiers of the American Revolution, both through her mother and her father, and she has good reason to be proud of her parentage. A sketch of her father, Burdet Clifton Pile, appears in this volume. Mr. Pile was Mayor of Jeffersonville, having succeeded Mrs. Sparks' brother-in-law, Levi Sparks.

Mr. and Mrs. Nathan Sparks have lived in Jeffersonville continuously since their marriage. Three children have been born to them, the first having died in infancy; the second, Levi Clifton, married Mary Josephine Burke, and they are the parents of one child, Mary Lee. The third child of Mr. and Mrs. Sparks is Janibelle.

Mrs. Sparks is a prominent member of the Daughters of the American Revolution. For seven years she was a teacher in the public schools at Jeffersonville and has always manifested a deep interest in promoting the welfare of the schools.

The Sparks residence in Jeffersonville is a homelike, cozy and well furnished one, where friends of the family often gather and where hospitality always reigns.

WILLACY JOSEPH SCHWANINGER.

Up-to-date and thoroughly reliable, Mr. Willacy J. Schwaninger has proved to the community his fitness for his chosen vocation—a pharmacist, and a call at his drug store at 458 Spring street, in Jeffersonville, will soon convince one of that fact. He has one of the best equipped and thoroughly stocked establishments in the city and is enjoying a flattering patronage.

Mr. Schwaninger was born in this city on the 7th of November, 1871, being the son of the late Judge Schwaninger, who filled the office of City Judge in Jeffersonville for many years, and was also Mayor of the city for one term. Judge Schwaninger was a native of Switzerland, came to Charleston in this county in early manhood, where he was married in this city to Sarah Ann Carwardine, who was a native of England. She is still living and enjoying the ripening years of her life with a reasonable share of health and vigor. Six children were born to this union, namely: Aniena R., wife of Lewis Girdler, of Jeffersonville; Willacy J., of this review; Mary Agnes, wife of Emil Keil, of New Albany, where he is engaged as a wholesale merchant; Edith H. married Walter E. McCullough, a farmer of this vicinity; Charles A., a druggist, being a former partner in business with our subject; and Jacob J., an employe on the Pennsylvania Railroad, and husband of Louisa Mahaffy.

Mr. Schwaninger received his early education in the public schools of this city and made a good record as a student. In order to prepare himself for his vocation, he attended the Louisville School of Pharmacy, and graduated from that institution with honors in 1890. He has been in business for himself for the last six years, devoting his entire time to the sale of proprietary medicines, drugs, and the filling of physicians' prescriptions, etc. He has the confidence of the public and the medical profession of the city, and stands high among the leading business men of his community.

In 1892 Mr. Schwaninger was married to Martha Leeper, who was born in Jeffersonville, being the daughter of Capt. James Leeper, deceased, and Mary (Phillips) Leeper. Two children have graced this union, Jeanne, Vance and Joseph L., aged fourteen and seven years, respectively. The former is now a sophomore in the Jeffersonville high school.

Mr. Schwaninger has made it his business to participate in the social and political activities of the community. He is a member of the Jeffersonville Lodge No. 362, Benevolent and Protective Order of Elks, and is past exalted ruler of the same. He warmly supplements the activities of this organization and is held in high esteem by his fellow members. His political affiliations have always been with the Republican party, and he is at the present time treasurer of the Clark County Republican Central Committee. In 1904, he was secretary of this organization. He also gives a share of his time and means to the discharging of the religious duties devolving upon him as a member of the St. Paul's Episcopal church, being one of the Board of Vestrymen.

JOHN JOSEPH CASEY.

In a beautiful and comfortably furnished home on the banks of the Ohio overlooking the head of the Falls, will be found an interesting man to talk to. He belongs to the class of inventors, the men who, perhaps, have done more to advance the industrial interests of the United States than any others. Especially is this true of those who have invented something of use in the mechanical arts inventions that accelerate business, increase work and make life better.

They are seldom rewarded as they ought to be, the benefits of their work usually going to others, who have the capital to manufacture them and promote their sale. The public, however, gets the benefit and it is to the inventors chiefly that the great republic owes its marvelous advance in wealth and power and glory. When in 1850 Michael and Mary (Nolan) Casey left their home at Galway, Ireland, for the land of promise across the sea, they brought along a baby who was destined to fill a useful role and make a name for himself in the country to which they were sailing. John Joseph Casey, the child in question, had been born at Galway in 1849 and was less than a year old when his parents reached the shores of America. They located at Troy, New York, and it was in the schools of that city that the Irish lad got his first taste of education. When nine years of age his parents removed to Louisville, Kentucky, and here John Joseph continued his studies in the public schools and one taught by the Christian Brothers. He was not destined, however, to continue long at his books as the exigencies of the case compelled him to seek a means of livelihood at the early age of thirteen. His first employment was with the Louisville & Nashville Railroad Company as a car-builder's apprentice and at the age of twenty he left home to take work at Huntsville. Alabama, with the Memphis & Charleston as car-builder, remaining one year and during that time acting as assistant foreman, going to Chattanooga, he took service with the Alabama and Chattanooga Railroad as gang foreman, from which he was speedily promoted to the general foremanship and before the end of the year had reached the important post of master car-builder. The following year Mr. Casey returned to Huntsville as general car- inspector for the Memphis & Charleston Railway, but in 1873 left this to accept the position of master car-builder for the St. Louis & Southeastern, now a part of the Louisville & Nashville System, with headquarters at Earlington. In 1874 he returned to the Memphis & Charleston road as general foreman of bridges and buildings and in 1878 was promoted master car-builder of the same line at Memphis, Tennessee. In 1882 he accepted a similar position with the Louisville, New Orleans & Texas Railroad, with headquarters at Vicksburg, Mississippi, but resigned in 1887 and took service as superintendent with the Missouri Car & Foundry Company at St. Louis, Missouri. In 1878 he resigned this place also to become superintendent of motive power for the Louisville, New Orleans & Texas at Vicksburg, and remained there until the road was absorbed by the Illinois Central, when he was transferred to Chicago as assistant superintendent of machinery of that system. In December, 1895, he resigned to accept the superintendency of the Haskell & Barker Car Company at Michigan City, Indiana, where he remained until July 1, 1905. and a few weeks later came to Southern Indiana to accept employment as superintendent of the Jeffersonville plant of the American Car & Foundry Company. He has retained this position and made his home at Jeffersonville up to the present time.

Though a very busy man, Mr. Casey found some time to devote to his inventions. One of these was a truck bolster that is now probably in use under more than two hundred thousand cars. It is known as the Pries & Casey bolster. Mr. Casey was also interested in another invention called the Williamson-Casey brake-beam, now used on hundreds of thousands of cars, besides many other useful inventions that are used on cars. He is recognized in the railroad world as a man of a high order of ability, with a genius for practical things.

He is of commanding presence and highly esteemed as an able and upright man, and in a remarkable degree the architect of his own fortunes. He is a member of the Elks in Michigan City, Knights of Columbus at New Albany and the St. Augustine Catholic church of Jeffersonville.

On November 5, 1873, Mr. Casey married Mary Agnes Rebman, of Huntsville, Alabama, and six children, four daughters and two sons, have been born to them. The latter are dead, and only three daughters survive.

WILLIAM SWEENEY.

By dint of sheer industry, and the faithful performance of the duties that devolved upon him, William Sweeney deservedly stands high in the estimation of the firm by which he has been employed for a number of years in the capacity of a salesman.

His youthful days were spent upon the farm, and although it was the hope of his father that the boy would follow in his footsteps and become an agriculturist, the lad entertained no such intentions, being filled with an ambition to enter upon a business life, but no opportunity to realize this desire offered, until he had reached the years of maturity, and he labored on the farm of his grandfather up to the time that he reached the sixteenth year of his age and then secured a position on the lime kilns at Utica.

Mr. Sweeney was born at Utica, Clark county, in 1861, his parents being James and Sarah Jane (Hobson) Sweeney, while his grandfather, with whom he spent much time, was Jacob Hobson.

William Sweeney has been married twice, his first wife being Martha Canter, of Utica, to whom he was wedded in 1884. Four children were the fruits of this alliance, as follows: Charles Oscar, Nellie, Arthur and William Earl. Nellie is the wife of Guy Daily, and they reside at the present time near Jeffersonville, while Charles wedded Agnes Elliott, daughter of William Elliott, of Jeffersonville. The death of Mrs. William Sweeney occurred December 22, 1894, immediately after the birth of her son, William Earl. Mr. Sweeney chose a second wife in March, 1897, when he espoused

Cora Howard, daughter of Thomas Jefferson Howard, generally known to his friends as "Jeff" Howard. He was a brother of Ex-Congressman Jonas Howard, a sketch of whose life appears elsewhere in this work. Mr. Sweeney has two daughters by adoption, Roberta Sweeney and May Howard Sweeney, both of whom live with their foster-parents.

Mr. Sweeney is a man of religious convictions, being a member of the Christian church of this city. He belongs to the Jeffersonville Lodge, Independent Order of Odd Fellows, and the Daughters of Rebekah. Besides this he is a Modern Woodman.

He has been in the employ of J. B. Speed & Company, Louisville, for many years, having commenced with this firm when he was thirty-three years of age. During the year 1892 his employers transferred him to their warehouse, Louisville, Kentucky, where he fills the position of salesman.

The domestic life of Mr. Sweeney is all that could be desired. The family live in a large house, comfortably and tastily furnished, and are highly respected by their neighbors. Both Mr. and Mrs. Sweeney are socially inclined, and have many warm friends in Jeffersonville and immediate vicinity.

J. HENRY MEIBOOM.

When Gregory H. Meiboom was united in marriage with Caroline Fuehrer there was a union between representatives of two of the most distinctive and progressive nationalities in the history of the world. The former was a native of Emden Ost Friesland, a province of Holland, and his wife was of German nativity, but came to America when a child of eight years. J. Henry Meiboom, their son, was born at Ironton, Ohio, January 27, 1872, and two years later was brought to Jeffersonville by his father, who received a call to the pastorate of the Evangelical Reformed church, of which he was a well known minister. Besides the usual course in the public schools of the city, Mr. Meiboom attended college at Franklin, Wisconsin, and soon after finishing his studies obtained employment at the Reformatory at Jeffersonville. Two years later he became instructor in shorthand and typewriting at the Graham Business College in Louisville, from which he went into the quartermaster's depot at Jeffersonville to take a position which he held until June 30, 1898. This was the year that witnessed the opening of the war between Spain and the United States, and the event appealed to the patriotism of young Meiboom. He was not without military experience, as he had been a member of Company G, of the Indiana National Guard, while employed at the Reformatory and took part in quelling the rioters in the strike of the miners of the block-coal district. Promptly after the declaration of war he enlisted in Company

E, One Hundred and Sixty-first Regiment of Indiana Volunteer Infantry, and served as sergeant under the command of Capt. Lewis C. Baird. The regiment was located for several months at Havana, Cuba, and did its full share in the liberation of that unhappy isle. Returning from the front at the conclusion of hostilities, Mr. Meiboom became bookkeeper for the Reliance Manufacturing Company at the Reformatory, but after ten months in this position he went into the employ of the Big Four Railroad Company and spent five years in their offices at Louisville and Jeffersonville. He then re-entered the government service as an official in the quartermaster's depot at Jeffersonville, where he has charge of the sample room. As a side line he conducts a grocery store in the city and is regarded as a young man of good business ability. He was instrumental in organizing the third camp in the state of Spanish-American war veterans, the same being called the W. T. Durbin Camp, No. 37. This organization was succeeded by the Spanish War Veterans, which was later by amalgamation with other organizations, changed to the United Spanish War Veterans, of which Mr. Mieboom is department senior vice-commander. His fraternal relations are confined to membership in the Woodmen of the World and the Improved Order of Red Men.

JOSEPH M. HUTCHISON, D. D.

Originating in Scotland the Hutchison family came to America in Colonial days and located in Pennsylvania. During the first quarter of the nineteenth century James and Ann Hutchison removed to Knox county, Ohio, where they ended their days as representatives of the early pioneers. Their son, Joseph Miller Hutchison, was born at Fredricksburg, Ohio, in 1831, and in early boyhood decided to become a minister of the Gospel. At the age of sixteen he began teaching school near his native town and despite his youth was successful in his first venture into the field of pedagogics. When about eighteen years old he entered the United Presbyterian Seminary at Xenia, and later, after a term at Monmouth College in Illinois, was given the degree of Doctor of Divinity. Subsequently he had charge of a mission in West Philadelphia, but remained there only six months and then started on an extended trip to the Holy Land, which consumed over a year and proved of great educational benefit. While abroad he made the acquaintance of Mark Twain and formed a warm friendship for that celebrated author and humorist. After returning from Europe Dr. Hutchison spent a short time in Philadelphia and was invited to Jeffersonville to preach for the congregation of the First Presbyterian church. He gave such satisfaction that he received a call as the regular pastor and remained in that capacity for nearly twenty-

39

five years. He was of charitable disposition, kind and lovable, and during his long residence in Jeffersonville was perhaps the most popular of the city's pastors, being revered by his congregation and highly respected by all the citizens. For many years he was a trustee of Hanover College and exercised a strong influence in religious circles. His useful and blameless life was closed on April 2, 1896, and his funeral was the most largely attended of any ever held at Jeffersonville up to that time. August 21, 1883, Dr. Hutchison was united in marriage with Annie McCampbell, a lady of distinguished parentage and many graces of character. The only fruit of this union was a son, christened James Harvey Hutchison, who died when five years old.

Mrs. Hutchison, who is spending the evening of life in a beautiful home in Jeffersonville, fronting the Ohio river, enjoys the love and respect of her husband's old friends and is admired by all who are permitted to share her gracious hospitality. Her parents were James Harvey and Letitia (Meriwether) Campbell, both names that recall many historic associations. Letitia was the daughter of Dr. Samuel Merriwether, a man of distinction, whose life left a strong impress upon the community in which he lived. He was the leader in founding the Presbyterian church, of which Dr. Hutchison became pastor, and for many years was its first and only elder and clerk. During the War of 1812 he was a surgeon in the United States army and subsequently was receiver of moneys for public lands sold in Indiana, acting as sub-treasurer at Jeffersonville. He was a descendant of Nicholas Meriweather, who came from Wales six generations ago and became the founder of one of the most distinguished families in America. Representatives of this name served as soldiers during the Revolutionary war, and one of them was with Washington at the time that young major of the Virginia militia endeavored to save General Braddock from his disastrous defeat on the bloody field near Pittsburg. Still others were with Gen. George Rogers Clark at Vincennes and Kaskasia, one served as Governor of Kentucky and they rose to places of distinction, both military and civil, under the Federal government and various states. Merriwether Lewis, one of the leaders in the historic exploration of the Northwest in 1803-04, known as the Lewis and Clark expedition, was a member of this distinguished family. James Harvey McCampbell, father of Mrs. Hutchison, was born at Charlestown, Clark county, Indiana, in 1817. His parents being Samuel and Jane (Tilford) McCampbell, both natives of Kentucky. He married Letitia Meriwether October 6, 1840. He came to Jeffersonville in boyhood and after growing up engaged in the dry goods business with John D. Woodburn. Shortly after his marriage he abandoned dry goods and joined Walter Meriwether in the retail drug business. In 1848 he was elected secretary and treasurer of the Jeffersonville, Madison & Indianapolis Railroad and continued with the company until its lease to the Pennsylvania, when he assumed the position of cashier. At the organization of the First National Bank of Jefferson-ville in 1865, Mr. McCampbell was elected as the president. In 1880 he left the railroad service and from that time devoted his whole attention to super-vising and directing the business of the bank. He served for a while as mem-ber of the city council and under all circumstances proved to be a large-minded, public spirited citizen. Throughout life he was a devoted member of the First Presbyterian church, holding the position of elder from 1846 until the time of his death, which ocurred February 16, 1888.

BASIL ROBINSON HOLMES.

Possessed of a strong individuality, endowed with an active brain, coupled with great energy, Basil Robinson Holmes, of Jeffersonville, is a true type of the successful business man of this day and age. He is an example well worthy of the emulation of the aspirant for honors in the world of commerce, who is now placing his foot on the first rung of the ladder that leads to fame and wealth, being identified with various gigantic interests, throughout the state of his nativity.

Basil Robinson Holmes was born in Jeffersonville December 2, 1862, the son of Hamilton and Mary Elizabeth (Prather) Holmes. His mother is the daughter of William Prather and wife, who live between Jefferson-ville and Utica. He received a good education in the public schools of Jef-fersonville, but did not enter college, preferring to enter upon a business career at once, and he was well equipped therefor, when, at the age of twenty-one years, he opened a grocery at the corner of Chestnut and Graham streets, Jeffersonville. Ambitious, and imbued with a desire to enlarge his scope he gave very close attention to his business from the very start and the rigid honesty which characterized his dealings with his customers, eventually brought its reward in the shape of a rapidly expanding patronage, with the result that the facilities of the little store were increased until it developed into one of the largest establishments of the character in the city. About three years ago a disastrous fire completely wiped out Mr. Holmes' place of busi-ness, and instead of sitting down and bemoaning his fate, as many of his weaker fellow-men would have done, he began to take the initial steps toward rebuilding before the smoking ruins had fairly cooled. This in itself marked him as a man of undaunted courage.

It was not long after the fire before a new structure, larger and more modern than its predecessor, stood upon the site of the old building, and the business that had been temporarily suspended, renewed with more vigor than ever. In this connection it may not be amiss to state that Mr. Holmes has been in the grocery business, without a change of site, longer than any other grocer in Jeffersonville. His store is very heavily stocked with commodities of a high grade, and he caters to the best class of people in Jeffersonville.

On May 12, 1887, Mr. Holmes wedded Emma Beck, daughter of Cornelius and Harriet Beck, of Jeffersonville. The father of Mrs. Holmes was always very active in politics, and held the office of County Commissioner for several terms. He was acting in that capacity when the county seat was moved from Charleston to Jeffersonville. He has also been a member of the Jeffersonville City Council.

By his first wife, for he was married twice, Mr. Holmes had one son, Clyde Holmes, who is a traveling salesman for the Peaslee-Gaulbert Company, of Louisville, Kentucky. Mrs. Holmes died in July, 1889. Mr. Holmes, in 1891, married Ella Beck, a sister of his first wife, and to them were born two children, Richard, now aged nine years, and Emmogean, the latter being in the sixth year of her age. Mr. Holmes believes that secret orders exert a great influence for good, and he is an active member of the Odd Fellows. He also has firm religious convictions, and he and his wife are members of the Port Fulton Methodist Episcopal church. The interests of Mr. Holmes are by no means confined to the grocery business. He has funds invested in mines and stone quarries, is a shareholder in the Peyton Lumber & Realty Company, stock in the Princess Amusement Company, of Indianapolis, also in the Ben Harrison Gold & Copper Company, the Apex Mining Company, one-fourth interest in the U. S. T. Mining Company, and one-half interest in the Delmar Skating Rink. Some time ago he took stock in the Bloomington & Bedford Stone Company.

With these diversified interests it may well be imagined that Mr. Holmes is an unusually busy man. He has the reputation, however, of keeping a watchful eye on his business affairs, and his investments have usually been a source of revenue. Notwithstanding his close attention to the material things of life he is a man of social proclivities, and both he and his wife go much in society, where they are always warmly welcomed.

H. MONROE FRANK.

The study of such a life as Mr. Frank's cannot fail of interest as he is representative in his sphere of activity and has contributed in no small measure to the prosperity of the city in which he was born and reared and which always has been his home and the scene of his operations. H. Monroe Frank was born September 11, 1852, and is a brother of Adolph Frank, whose sketch appears elsewhere in these pages in connection with which the reader will also find a brief general outline of the family history.

As stated above Mr. Frank first saw the light of day in Jeffersonville in the public schools of which he received his educational training. Actuated by a desire to devote his life to commercial pursuits, he entered at the age of seventeen upon an apprenticeship to learn the dry goods business and in due time mastered the basic principles of the same, besides becoming a very efficient salesman. His ambition, however, was not to hold a subordinate position but to engage in business for himself and become an employer instead of an employee. Accordingly after acquiring a practical knowledge of the dry goods trade he started in March, 1888, an establishment of his own at his present location, 355 Spring street, beginning with limited capital and in a modest way, but it was not long until his patronage grew to such proportions as to enable him to increase his stock and enlarge the building in which he met his customers.

Mr. Frank has spared no pains or expense in his efforts to please his customers and make his store the leading one of its kind in the city, both of which desires have long since been realized, as his present large and fully equipped establishment, the only exclusively dry goods house in the city, abundantly attests, carrying a stock conservatively estimated in excess of fifteen thousand dollars, and giving steady employment to five clerks, a force which he is frequently obliged to increase during busy and special seasons. Mr. Frank's early training and subsequent careful study of the dry goods business have been greatly in his favor in building up the large and lucrative trade which he now commands.

On the 22d day of October, 1885, Mr. Frank was united in marriage with Novella Fry, daughter of John F., and Mary E. Fry, of Utica township, representatives of two of the oldest and most respected pioneer families of Clark county. The Frys have been actively identified with this part of the state ever since its original settlement, where a number of them have become prominent in public affairs and acquired considerable wealth and a high social status. John F. Fry, father of Mrs. Frank, was for many years an enterprising and successful farmer of the above township, but is now living a retired life in Jeffersonville. Two children have been born to Mr. and Mrs. Frank, the older of whom, Homer M., after being graduated from the Jeffersonville high school, entered DePauw University, where he earned an honorable record as a student; Graham M., the second in order of birth, is pursuing his studies in the public schools of his native city, and, like his brother, has a bright and promising future before him.

Mr. Frank and family are members of the Wall Street Methodist Episcopal church, and deeply interested in the success of the same, being among the most active and influential workers in the Sunday school, the Epworth League and other lines of endeavor, Mr. Frank holding at this time the position of trustee in the organization. He is an ardent member of the ancient and honorable order of Masonry, belonging to Clark Lodge, No. 40, and is also identified with Myrtle Lodge of the Knights of Pythias, in which he holds the title of past commander. In politics he has been a life-long Democrat, as was also his father, and with a single exception all of his brothers are pronounced in their allegiance to the same party. He keeps well informed on the great questions and issues of the day, notwithstanding which he has never aspired to office, having no time to devote to such matters and little taste for public life. With the exception of serving a short time as Police Commissioner he has held no public position though well qualified by nature and training for any office within the power of his fellow citizens to bestow. He has been a member of the board of directors of the Carnegie Public Library of Jeffersonville ever since it was established.

Mr. Frank was among the first to urge the necessity of such an institution and from the time it was under the management of the township board to its present permanent standing he labored assiduously with others in its behalf, who communicated with Mr. Carnegie and induced great capitalists to contribute the liberal fund for the erection of the fine building in which it now has a home. He has always used his influence in many other ways to arouse and promote an interest in the enterprise of the city and anything for the conservation of the public good has met with his hearty co-operation and endorsement, giving freely of his time and means. He was one of the organizers of the Jeffersonville Commercial Club and has served as its president for the past five years, having been re-elected to that position four times.

DAVID COHEN, M. D.

Dr. Cohen is a native of the city in which he resides and an honorable representative of one of its prominent families. Louis Cohen, his father, was born in Germany, but came to the United States in early life and lived for some time at Newbern, North Carolina. Leaving that place a number of years ago he located at Jeffersonville, Indiana, where he worked for some time at his trade of cigar making, subsequently engaging in the real estate business, which he still carries on and in which he has achieved marked financial success. Jeanette Graumer, wife of Louis Cohen and mother of the doctor was born in Louisville, Kentucky, and departed this life in the city of Jeffersonville. She was an estimable lady of high social standing and sterling worth, and is affectionately remembered, not only by her immediate friends, but by all who came within the influence of her gracious personality. The family of Louis and Jeanette Cohen consisted of seven children, four sons and three daughters, the doctor being the third in order of birth. Maurice, the oldest son, is engaged in the shoe business in Jeffersonville and is also secretary and treasurer of the Memphis & Sellersburg Canning Company, in which he owns a controlling interest; Herman is manager of a clothing store in Jeffersonville, and principal owner of the same, being one of the leading merchants of the city and widely known in business circles; George, a lawyer by profession, is a resident of Chicago, where he has built up a large and lucrative practice; Hulda married Lesser Jacobs and lives in Versailles, Kentucky; Nannie, who is unmarried, is secretary of the canning company with which her brother is connected; and Dollie, the youngest of the number, is still a member of the home circle. By a subsequent marriage with Anna Eppstein, Mr. Cohen is the father of four children, namely Blanche, Melvin, Sultan and Armond.

Dr. David Cohen was born December 3, 1882, and grew to maturity in Jeffersonville, receiving his preliminary mental discipline in the public schools. Later he entered the Louisville University to prosecute his medical studies and in due time completed the prescribed course, graduating in the year 1903, with an horable record. Shortly after receiving his degree he effected a co-partnership with Dr. E. N. Flynn, of Jeffersonville, with whom he practiced three years and at the expiration of that time was made assistant physician at the Indiana State Reformatory to the duties of which position he devoted one year. Since severing his connection with the latter institution the doctor has been alone in the practice, the meanwhile building up a large and eminently successful professional business and forging rapidly to the front among the leading physicians of the city.

Doctor Cohen keeps abreast of the times in all matters relating to his chosen calling. He is a member of the American Medical Association, the Indiana State Medical Society, the Third District Medical Society, in which he holds the office of secretary, and the Medical Society of Clark county, of which he is now the secretary and treasurer, taking an active interest in the deliberations of these several bodies and keeping pace with the advanced professional thought they inculcate.

Doctor Cohen recently took a post-graduate course in the Bellevue Medical Hospital of New York City, where he made a specialty of genito and urinary diseases. He is a member and medical examiner of the Modern Woodmen of Jeffersonville, and holds a similar position with several other fraternal organizations, including the Pathfinders, Knights and Ladies of Honor and Knights and Ladies of Security.

Doctor Cohen maintains an abiding interest in all worthy enterprises for the material advancement of the city and is thoroughly informed on the leading questions of the times, being a Democrat in politics and an influential worker in the party, but not a partisan, much less a seeker after the honors and emoluments of office or public place. With other members of his family he is connected with the Reformed Jewish Synagogue in Louisville, and is not only one of the accomplished and popular leaders of his nationality in the city, but numbers his friends and admirers by the scores among all classes, irrespective of nationality or creed.

EBERTS BROTHERS.

This widely known and influential firm composed of Jacob and Conrad Eberts, operate the flouring mills at Henryville and Charleston and do a large and continually growing business, being among the most enterprising and progressive men of those places, besides holding worthy prestige in other lines of trade and enjoying an honorable reputation in commercial circles throughout Indiana and the neighboring state of Kentucky. As the name indicates, the Eberts family is of German origin, the father, Conrad Eberts, Sr., having been born in Hesse, Darmstadt, of which Grand Duchy and two sons are also natives.

In the year 1853 the elder Eberts, with his two sons and widowed mother, immigrated to the United States, landing in May of that year at New Orleans and proceeded thence to St. Louis, Missouri, where Conrad, Jr., remained during the ensuing thirteen years.

Conrad Eberts, Jr., was born on the 5th day of August, 1844, and was nine years of age when he became a resident of the country with which his subsequent life has been so closely identified and in which he has achieved such signal success as an enterprising, broad-minded man of affairs. Leaving St. Louis in 1866, he went to Cincinnati, but after spending a brief time in that city, proceeded to Louisville, Kentucky, where he worked at his trade of currier and leather dresser for many years. At the breaking out of the Civil war he joined the First Missouri Infantry, with which he served for a period of thirteen months, at the expiration of which time he resumed his trade and continued the same at various places, until 1870, when, in partnership with his brother, Jacob, he engaged in the tannery business at Shepherdsville, Kentucky.

The firm of Eberts Brothers, after remaining three years at the latter place, purchased a plant at Henryville, Clark county, which they operated with gratifying success until its destruction by fire in 1884, when they erected a flouring mill in the same town, which also fell a victim of the flames within less than three years after its completion. Nothing daunted by these disasters, they located at Jeffersonville and immediately began rebuilding but upon a more extensive scale. In January, 1887, the new mill was finished and in operation since which time the business has grown rapidly in magnitude and importance, until their milling interests are now the largest of the kind in Clark county, the daily output of the plant at Jeffersonville averaging three hundred barrels of high-grade flour, for which there is a wide demand by both the local and general trades. They also own and operate a second mill at Charlestown, with a daily capacity of one hundred barrels, both plants being thoroughly equipped by the latest and most approved machinery for the manufacture of flour by the roller process, the two properties representing a capital considerably in excess of sixty-five thousand dollars, and affording steady employment to about twenty-four men every working day of the year.

In addition to the large and increasing business interests of the Eberts Brothers at Jeffersonville and Charlestown, they also own and operate a one hundred barrel mill at North Vernon, Indiana, valued at twenty thousand dollars, and an ice plant at the same place, conservatively estimated at fifteen thousand dollars, besides doing a successful coal business with a stock ranging from three thousand dollars to five thousand dollars, their various enterprises being extensively patronized and giving them a reputation in business circles second to that of no other man or firm in Southern Indiana similarly engaged. To meet the steadily growing demand for their products the Eberts Brothers are obliged to operate their mills at their full capacity, the number of men employed in these and their other lines of effort averaging about fifty.

While maintaining somewhat of a conservative policy and making no special efforts to give their business undue publicity, the character of the output and honorable dealing on the part of the proprietors furnishing their best advertisement. The Eberts Brothers have contributed largely to the material advancement of Clark county and to the upbuilding of the towns where their interests are located.

Conrad Eberts was married at St. Louis in the year 1875 to Margaret G. Lall, a native of that city, the union being blessed with four children, namely: Olga C., wife of Charles Gallrein, a shoe merchant of Jeffersonville; Edward C.; Minnie, wife of Horner F. McNaughton, manager of the business at North Vernon; and Otto J., a student in the manual training school of Louisville. Edward C., the elder son, is a young man of intelligence and business standing, being at this time general manager of the large and growing interests of the firm. He married Estella Schwaninger and has an interesting family of three children.

Jacob Eberts, whose life, like that of his brother, has been closely interwoven with the business and industrial interests of Clark county and who, as already indicated, is now associated in some of the largest business enterprises in this part of the state, was also a soldier in the Civil war, enlisting at St. Louis in 1861 and serving for a period of four years and five months; three months with the Fourth Missouri Infantry, thirteen months in the First Regiment, United States Reserve Corps, Missouri Volunteer, and three years and one month in the Second Missouri Battery, spending his last five months in the army on the frontier, guarding the settlers against the hostile Indians. He witnessed the construction of the first five miles of the Union Pacific Railroad, saw the building of the first locomotive on the Iron Mountain Railroad System, besides participating in many daring adventures and thrilling experiences during his long and strenuous period of service in behalf of his adopted country. He married Eliza Baumbarger, of Henryville, and is the father of three living children, Carrie, wife of George B. Parks, County Attorney of Clark county; John J., who is engaged in business at El Paso, Texas, and Edith, who is still with her parents.

Both Jacob and Conrad Eberts belong to the Free and Accepted Masons, the Knights of Pythias, and in religious matters are zealous and respected members of the German Reformed church, taking an active interest in the congregation to which they belong and contributing liberally to its material support. Politically they are Republicans, but not partisans, nor have they ever asked for office at the hands of their fellow citizens or aspired to leadership.

Conrad Eberts, Sr., spent the closing years of his life in Jeffersonville, where his death occurred at the ripe old age of eighty-one; his mother, who accompanied him to the city, departed this life when eighty-four years old.

CHARLES F. ANTZ.

Like many of America's progressive men of affairs, Mr. Antz is of foreign birth, being a native of Oberdam Winesburg, Wurtemburg, Germany, where he first saw the light of day on December 2, 1850. His father, Charles F. Antz, was a man of high standing and wide influence in his town, having been a successful lawyer for a number of years and later a judge of the highest court of his province, which office he was holding at the time of his death in the year 1853. Subsequently in 1854 the widowed mother and her two children, a son and a daughter, came to the United States and located in Louisville, where for some years she was obliged to rely upon the hardest kind of manual labor in order to rear her children respectably and provide for their education. Later she became the wife of Charles Schifler, of Jeffersonville, a very worthy man who came to this city in 1860 and made it his place of residence until his death in the year 1885, Mrs. Schifler departing this life on the 3d day of November, 1907. The two children born to her first marriage were Katie, who died in 1880, and Charles F., whose name introduces this sketch. By her marriage with Mr. Schifler she had three children, two daughters, the older being Mrs. Emma Quick, the younger Mrs.

Carrie, both living in Jeffersonville, and a son, Louis Schifler, died in 1904, at the age of thirty-six years.

Charles F. Antz was but four years of age when brought to the United States and from that time until attaining his majority he spent the greater part of his life in Jeffersonville, receiving the meanwhile a practical education in the city schools, though his opportunities in this direction were rather limited. In 1862 he engaged to drive a government train in conveying soldiers and war supplies to the scene of action and later drove an express wagon until the year 1867, when he resigned his position and entered the Ohio Falls Car Works to learn the moulder's trade. Applying himself closely to his work he made such rapid progress that at the age of twenty he was considered one of the most efficient moulders in the city, his wages at that time ranging from six to eight dollars per day. He continued his trade until the panic of 1873, when his trade was rendered no longer profitable and he accepted employment as a hod-carrier in the building of the quarter-master's department, United States Army, on the completion of which job he returned in 1883 to his work in the foundry, where he remained during the ensuing years commanding high wages the meantime and filling one of the most important positions in the moulding department. Severing his connection with the foundry in March, 1884, he made a trip to San Antonio, Texas, where he purchased two car loads of Texas ponies, which he brought to Jeffersonville and sold at a handsome profit, which marked the beginning of his career as an enterprising and successful trader and business man. During the several following years he traded and sold in various parts of Indiana, Missouri and Illinois, coming in contact with the people and acquiring a practical knowledge of business which proved valuable to him, not only at the time, but afterwards. On retiring permanently from his trade he melted his tools, declaring that never again would he enter a foundry as a workman, a resolution to which he has adhered strictly ever since.

Shortly after his business experience in the states above mentioned, Mr. Antz engaged in the saloon business in Jeffersonville and during the ensuing fifteen years devoted his attention to that line of trade, meeting with encouraging financial success and becoming known as a progressive man of affairs. In 1890 he was one of the nine men who incorporated the Jeffersonville Ice Company, an enterprise which continued under the original management until 1897, when he bought out the last of the stockholders' interests and became sole proprietor. Since taking possession of the plant he has added greatly to its capacity and built up a large and lucrative business, the present daily output being twenty-seven tons of excellent high grade ice, all of which finds ready sale in the city, the factory being taxed to the utmost to supply the constantly increasing demand. The improvement in the plant have kept pace with the steady growth of the business and under the judicious oversight of

the present proprietor it has become a very valuable property. one of the largest and best of the kind in the southern part of the state. with encouraging
prospects of still greater growth in the future.

Financially Mr. Antz's success has been commensurate with the energy
and sound business ability displayed in the management of his affairs, being
at this time one of the substantial and well-to-do men of the city, with a sufficiency of material wealth to place him in independent circumstances. In addition to his manufacturing plant and other business interests he owns a beautiful and commodious modern brick dwelling erected in 1902 on the lot adjoining the ice plant and is well situated to enjoy the results of his many years
of well directed profit. The former presiding spirit of the comfortable and
luxurious home was the amiable lady to whom he was joined in the bonds of
wedlock in the year 1872, and who previous to that time was Elizabeth Green-
agle, a native of Wayne county, New York. To Mr. and Mrs. Antz were
born five children, namely: William C., who is engaged in the ice business
in Jeffersonville; Anna M., her father's housekeeper; Edith who has charge
of the books in her father's establishment; George, who holds a position in
the factory, and Walter, a student in the Manual Training School of Louisville. William C., the oldest of the family, is married and is the father of
two children, Gertrude and Kenneth, his wife having formerly been Daisy
Akers, daughter of Charles Akers, of Jeffersonville. Mrs. Antz, who was an
exemplary wife and mother, and a devoted member of the German Lutheran
church, departed this life on the 5th day of September, 1904, since which
time the household has been looked after and successfully managed by the
daughter, Anna, a young lady of high social standing.

Politically Mr. Antz is a Democrat and as such has taken an active part
in county and municipal affairs, representing the third ward four years in the
City Council and proving an able and untiring worker while a member of that
body. At the age of twenty-one he was initiated into the local lodge of the
Knights of Pythias and has been an active member of the fraternity from that
time to the present. He is also identified with the uniform rank of the order,
besides holding membership with the Benevolent and Protective Order of
Elks and Independent Order of Odd Fellows, in both of which societies he
has been from time to time honored with important official positions. He
was one of the organizers of the society known as the Knights and Ladies
of Washington, and has been prominent in the affairs of the same.
holding at this time the office of treasurer of the supreme body in the United
States. In his religious belief he subscribes to the Lutheran creed, himself
and family being members of the church of that name in Jeffersonville.

Mr. Antz is interested in various business enterprises in Jeffersonville and
elsewhere, being a stockholder in the New Albany Ice Company and in the
American Machine Company of Louisville, besides owning considerable valu-

able real estate in these cities to say nothing of his large private means, all of which bear witness to his mature judgment and sound financial ability. He is in the best sense of the term a self-made man as few started in life with poorer prospects.

THE MERIWETHER FAMILY.

Those who read the history of the United States, including the period of discovery, the subsequent settlement, the colonial times and eventually the great work of development that followed the establishment of the Union, will frequently come across the name Meriwether. Sometimes it is a soldier fighting the battles of England against the French and Indians, then a patriot taking part in the struggle for independence; bleeding at the crossing of the Delaware, starving at Valley Forge, suffering the privations of the march through the western wilderness under the banner of George Rogers Clark. Then we find these heroic descendants of worthy sires, filling high places in the state, as representatives of the Federal government, members of the Legislature or Congress, governors, administrators and promoters of the great industrial enterprises. The Meriwethers were especially conspicuous during the formative period of the Republic, and we hear of them in Kentucky and Indiana, when the Indians were still on the war path, when the woodsman's ax awakened the echoes in the lonely glens, before the buffalo had crossed the Mississippi, and while Daniel Boone was endeavoring to plant the white man's standard in the regions of the Blue Grass. It was one of this patriotic family that Jefferson selected to lead his celebrated exploring expeditions to the mouth of the Columbia river, an expedition that resulted in acquiring the Oregon country for the United States, and which made possible that American possession of the Rocky Mountain regions, with its romantic and dramatic developments, that give such fascination to the era of discovery and settlement in the times of Bonneville, Bridges, Sublette, and other heroic spirits. During ten generations of North American history there has not been a time when some man with Meriwether blood in his veins was not acting a conspicuous part in the great drama unfolded by the occurrences of the last three centuries.

It was Nicholas Meriwether, born in Wales, in 1678, to whom this country is indebted for the red blood that enriches so many men and women during the troublous years that succeeded the first settlements on the Atlantic. Nicholas, his namesake, and one of three sons, reared a family of children and became a man of vast wealth. He owned one tract of land near Charlottesville, Virginia, that included seventeen thousand nine hundred and fifty-two hundred acres and many other thousand acres in other sections, besides

horses and immense numbers of cattle. This Nicholas, of the second generation, lived to the advanced age of ninety-seven years, was a figure of consequence during the period of his activities and left descendants well worthy of
his name. One of his sons was Col. David Meriwether, who married Anne
Holmes, and became the direct ancestor of the famous Meriwether Lewis,
who went with Clark across the continent in 1803-4, on what was perhaps
the most momentous exploring expeditions in the history of the world.

Another of his descendants was Col. Nicholas Meriwether, who was one
of four American soldiers that bore General Braddock from the fatal field at
Fort DuQuesne, when Washington was serving in his first important military expedition, as a subordinate officer of the Virginia troops. Still another Meriwether was with George Rogers Clark in his daring campaigns
against Vincennes and Kaskaskia. The roll of governors of Kentucky, filled
with glorious and heroic names, shows a Meriwether as one of the earliest and
most enterprising of the state's executives. William Meriwether, a son of
Colonel David, married Martha Wood and died in 1790 on a large farm near
Louisville. His son, William, married Sarah Oldham and after making two
or three trips from the Virginia home, finally settled near Louisville in 1784.

It was the son of the latter, Dr. Samuel Meriwether, who settled in Jeffersonville in 1813 and through his descendants became interwoven through
all its subsequent local history. He served during the War of 1812 as a surgeon in the Northwest Territory and subsequently became chief of the land
office at Jeffersonville and receiver of the public moneys. He was a leader in
founding the Presbyterian church at Jeffersonville, buying ground for the
site and otherwise contributing liberally to the enterprise. He was the first
and for many years the only elder and clerk, holding the flock together in
the face of many discouragements until it became a large and flourishing
congregation. His sacrifices for the church and his stalwart Christian character are commemorated for a marble tablet in the edifice which he helped to
build and to which he devoted so much of his time and energy.

In 1813 Doctor Meriwether married Mary Lewis, by whom he had five
children, one son and four daughters. One daughter became Mrs. J. H.
McCampbell and mother of Mrs. Joseph M. Hutchinson. The son, Waller,
Lewis, was born at Jeffersonville, Indiana, April 23, 1824, and during a long
life was actively and influentially connected with the development of that city.
For thirty-five years he was engaged in business as a druggist, and became the
owner of considerable real estate, including the beautiful homestead in Clarksville, fronting on the Falls of the Ohio, which he built for a family residence.
He was a member of the Presbyterian church and respected by all who knew
him as an upright citizen. On December 10, 1846, he married Rebecca Keigwin, member of a very prominent family. She was the daughter of James
Keigwin, Sr., a sister of Col. James Keigwin, Jr., and an aunt of James S.

Keigwin. Mr. Meriwether died November 17, 1905. Only two children by this marriage are now living, Nora Elva, who married J. M. Glass, a former Mayor of Jeffersonville, is now a resident of Los Angeles, California.

Henry K. Meriwether, the surviving son, was born March 16, 1852, and grew up in Jeffersonville and after leaving school occupied a position in the First National Bank until his twenty-second year, when he went to Cincinnati and engaged in the ice cream business, which he was compelled to abandon on account of ill health. In 1878 he settled on a farm at Olney, Illinois, where he has since spent most of his time, though he still retains his home at Jeffersonville. He devotes his Illinois farm to stock raising, making a specialty of Hereford cattle and finds his chief pleasure in agricultural pursuits. In 1877 he married Caroline, daughter of John C. Lewis, a county official at Cincinnati, and has three sons. Walter Lewis, who is married, lives on his father's farm at Olney; Samuel Eber is a resident of Los Angeles, and Henry Keigwin, familiarly called Harry, is also on the Illinois farm. The Jeffersonville branch of the Meriwether family has worthily sustained the reputation of an historic ancestry, by bearing bravely their share of life's burdens. In whatever department their lot was cast, as farmers, business men, officials of the county, members of the church, as plain citizens or officers they have always been found equal to the requirements and challenging both the respect and good will of the community in which they lived.

GEORGE W. LUSHER.

George W. Lusher was born in Floyd county, Indiana, near New Albany, August 27, 1846, being one of three children born to Michael and Mary (Knasel) Lusher. Michael Lusher, father of George W., was born in Switzerland in 1812 and came to this country with his parents when he was five years old. He was active in the affairs of life, making a success of whatever he attempted. His wife was born in Baden, Germany, on the Rhine river in 1832. She immigrated to America with her parents when seven years old. They attended the public schools of Floyd county and were married in 1844. The other children besides George W. born to them were Carrie and M. D. Lusher, the former being deceased, and the latter a farmer of Jefferson county, Kentucky.

George W. Lusher attended the common schools in his native community until he was eighteen years old, receiving a good education, but being ambitious for higher learning he entered the Hartsville Academy where he remained until he was twenty-two years old and where he made a brilliant record for scholarship.

After leaving school he decided that his true calling and inclination lay along the peaceful lines of the husbandman, consequently he at once began farming on the land where he has ever since resided, giving it his undivided care and attention with the result that he has today one of the finest and best improved farms to be found in Utica township, highly improved in every respect, well drained and well fenced, and the soil produces as abundant crops as ever in the history of the place, which consists of one hundred and four acres, upon which general farming and truck growing are carried on with the care and skill that ever insures success and which yields the owner not only a comfortable living from year to year, but also enables him to lay up an ample competency for his declining years. The products raised here find a ready market near home, his vegetables especially being eagerly sought for, being always regarded as first class.

The residence of Mr. Lusher is a large brick structure that is well arranged for comfort and convenience, being substantial and well equipped with modern appliances, also nicely furnished. The other buildings on the place are up-to-date in every respect, so that all in all, Mr. Lusher has one of the most desirable places to be found in this locality.

George W. Lusher was united in marriage on May 8, 1872, to Mildred A. Gilmore, a native of Floyd county, Indiana, a member of a fine old family. The following children have been born to this union: Lena Byron, wife of Fielding L. Wilson, of Jeffersonville; Maud J., wife of E. M. Frank; Charles died when twenty years of age; Edna is now living at home. Mrs. Lusher is a talented woman, and she was a student of DePauw University.

In his fraternal relations Mr. Lusher is a member of the Masonic Order, Clark Lodge No. 40. He is a member of the Christian church and a liberal subscriber of the same. In politics he is a Democrat.

Mr. Lusher has ever been known as a loyal citizen and has done his share in aiding the march of progress and development in this county, and surrounded by everything conducive to his comfort and happiness he has the unbounded esteem and confidence of a community for the material, social and moral advancement of which so much of his life and interest have been devoted and no man in Clark county is held in higher esteem than he.

WILLIAM E. COLLINGS.

Originally from Ireland the ancestors of the Collings family were early emigrants to America and settlers in various other states, and when William E. Collings and his family floated down the Ohio river they found no town on either side of the Falls of the Ohio in Kentucky or Indiana. They had to stop at the Falls because the water was too low to get over and they made a settle-

WILLIAM E. COLLINGS.

ment in Clark county, the first family to locate there. The head of this pioneer household had a son named Kearnes and he also left a son of the same name, who was born in Clark county in 1823, on a farm, a portion of which is where the town of Underwood now stands. He died March 3, 1894, in the same house where he first saw the light of day and in which he spent seventy-two years of his life. His father bought the one hundred sixty acres from the government at two dollars and twenty-five cents per acre, which is still in the possession of his grandson, and the latter has a valued souvenir in shape of the original sheepskin patent received from the government. Indians were still plentiful in Southern Indiana when the Collings settlers arrived and some of them were killed in the frequent fights that occurred. William E. Collings was an Indian fighter of note and was engaged against the band that perpetrated the Pigeon Roost massacre. Everybody carried a gun in those days as a protection from wolves and other wild animals and one of these guns, handed down through three generations, is preserved as a precious heirloom by the owner, William C. Collings, a cousin of our subject. Kearnes Collings the second, was a well known man in Clark county and a farmer and timber man by occupation and prominent as a member of the Baptist church. The Underwood branch of this denomination was organized in his house and he became a charter member both there and at Vienna. He was a great church worker and gave the ground on which two churches were built. He married Elizabeth Partin, who was born in Tennessee in 1847. By this union there were eight children, but by two previous marriages eight other children were born to Kearnes Collings.

William E. Collings, eldest of the children by his father's last marriage, was born at Underwood, Indiana, July 24, 1871. He inherited a part of the old homestead entered by his grandfather and cleared and improved by his father. In addition to farming he learned the carpenter's trade and has divided his time between these two occupations. On July 31, 1892, he was married to Maggie M., daughter of William H. and Cynthia (Mendenhall) Glessner, the former of Morgan and the latter of Marion counties, Indiana. Mrs. Collings is a native of the last named county, where her birth occurred July 20, 1873. Mr. and Mrs. Collings have three children, Charles W., born January 17, 1895, and died January 26th, in the same year; Ruth G., born January 21, 1897, and Cynthia E., born January 21, 1902. Mr. Collings is justly proud of the patriotic record of his ancestors, some of whom served in the War of the Revolution, also the War of 1812, and in the Civil war of 1861. He also has just reason for recalling with pride the services of his direct line as pioneers in settling and civilizing Clark county. The farm he owns has been in the family for nearly a hundred years and no name is more highly respected in Clark county than that of Collings. Mr. Collings inherited his politics as well as his religion, being the latest representative of a long line of Baptist church people,

40

while his wife affiliates with the Methodists. They live in a comfortable home in Underwood and cordially entertain all the friends who visit them.

SAMUEL NOBLE WOOD.

Among the self-made men in Clark county whose efforts have been influential in promoting the welfare of the community in which he lives, is Samuel Noble Wood, who has won success in life because he has worked for it and has exercised those qualities that always win out if properly and persistently applied, as has been done in his case.

Mr. Wood was born in Utica township, August 9, 1849. He is the son of Napoleon B. and Lucinda (Hay) Wood. They were natives also of Clark county, being among the pioneer families here.

Samuel Wood received his early education in the common schools of his native community, where he applied himself as best he could and laid a good foundation for his subsequent mental development, which has been done by coming in contact with the business world and by home reading. After casting about for some time during his boyhood days in an effort to find just what line of work was best suited to his tastes he eventually became a stone contractor, which line of business he is still conducting in a most satisfactory manner, having handled some big jobs in Clark county. He understands thoroughly this line of work and has been very successful owing to his close application to business and his desire to please his patrons which he invariably does, always turning out high class work at reasonable charges. He is known as one of the leading stone contractors in this locality.

Mr. Wood was married April 24, 1879, with Mary E. Todd. She was born at Paris, Indiana, the daughter of William Todd, a representative citizen of Jennings county, this state, the wedding occurring at Paris. Mrs. Wood's mother was known as Mary Cleland, a native of Madison, Indiana. Mrs. Wood was one of a family of the following children: Mary, Lizzie, deceased; William, who married Florence Wells; Stella, who married a Mr. Carlock; Bertha is living at home; Fletcher is deceased.

Mr. Wood is a Socialist. He has never held political office, however, he takes considerable interest in local political affairs, and is liberal in his religious views, being a well read man and keeps abreast of the times and is an interesting conversationalist. In his fraternal relations he is a member of the Knights of Pythias. The Wood family is well and favorably known in Clark county, having always borne good reputations and taken an active part in local affairs for the general welfare of the community.

JOHN MACKAY.

Death came to Mr. Mackay after he had retired from active life and was living quietly amid the scenes of his early manhood, and was, in his declining years, enjoying the fruits of a career that was marked by few idle moments. Very peaceful indeed were the latter years of his long and honorable life, as he was absolutely free from the cares that overburden many men in their old age. It was a consolation to him to know that he had reared a family of children who had thrived and prospered and had been guilty of no act that might cast dishonor upon the family name. This venerable man was one of the best known citizens of Utica, having made it his home for more than half a century.

John Mackay was born in Jefferson county, Kentucky, in 1831, and came to Utica seventeen years later, and engaged in farming with his cousin, M. P. Howes, working very hard and saving his money. He was married February 20, 1861, to Julia Morrison, a native of Utica township. and daughter of William and Sarah Morrison, being one of a family of nine children, three of whom died in infancy. The survivors are Ephraim, who is married; John, who wedded Miss M. Gibson; Mrs. Samantha (Morrison) Worthington; James married Ellen Goodwin; William remained single.

Mr. and Mrs. Mackay were the parents of four children, namely: Mrs. Mollie Marsh; a son. William; Mrs. Cora Emmerich, and John Floyd Mackay, who married Nora Colvin.

Mr. Mackay died November 13, 1905. While a Democrat all his life he took no part in politics beyond casting his vote, and never held, or aspired to any public office, his interest being centered in his agricultural pursuits. He was not a member of any secret order, but attended church regularly, being a Methodist. There was a strong bond of affection between the deceased and his wife. He was a man of high character and sterling worth, and his demise was greatly deplored by the community which looked upon him as a man it could ill afford to lose.

OSCAR DIX.

To conduct successfully a mercantile business requires not only a knowlededoe of articles handled, but a broad conception of human nature, and the skill so to manipulate affairs as to bring about a satisfactory relation between merchant and consumer. Prominent among the merchants of Utica, Indiana, is the firm of Dix Brothers, dealers in general merchandise, and now for many years rated as among the town's most progressive business men. The members of the firm are Oscar and George B. Dix.

Oscar Dix was born at Utica on the 5th of April, 1876, the son of James and Margaret (James) Dix, both of whom were born in Clark county. Samuel Dix, grandfather of Oscar Dix, was a native of Virginia, and after coming to Indiana was married to a Miss Swartz, of Utica.

Oscar was educated in the local school and after completing the work there decided later to prepare himself thoroughly for business. He accordingly went to Louisville and completed the course at Bryant and Stratton's Business College. Following this he returned to Utica and soon entered into business, continuing therein up to the present time.

On September 6, 1900, Mr. Dix was united in marriage to Leanora Cleffmann, who was born at Florence, Indiana, on the 21st of November, 1875. She is the daughter of Henry Cleffman, a native of Germany. Mr. and Mrs. Dix are the parents of one child, Dorothy, born January 25, 1904. They are members of the Christian church and stand well in the community. Mr. Dix is a Democrat in politics, and has served his party as a member of the Township Advisory Board.

JAMES W. TAYLOR.

James W. Taylor, well known in Port Fulton and Jeffersonville, and throughout Clark county in general, has arisen to his present high standing in the community through his own innate ability and personal worthiness. His career is a direct refutation of the charge made nowadays that men of worth and merit have not the scope and opportunity in our present complex business life to develop themselves without injury to their own individuality. While yet a comparatively young man, he is successful in business life and a factor in the political affairs of his county. He is the present paymaster of the American Car & Foundry Company, an office which he fills with distinction and credit to himself. He has also for many years been proprietor of the Excelsior Laundry in Jeffersonville and has brought that concern to a high state of perfection. He is in addition treasurer of the town of Port Fulton, having held the office for four years.

James W. Taylor was born in Port Fulton on the 19th of December, 1870, and was the son of Thomas and Catherine (Sweeney) Taylor. Thomas Taylor was born in Wales, and in his boyhood lived near London, England. In 1837, having meanwhile emigrated, he settled in Jeffersonville, where he carried on a butchering trade for a great many years. He died in 1894. Mrs. Catherine Taylor was a sister of the Sweeney brothers, the shipyard and foundry men. To Mr. and Mrs. Thomas Taylor four boys and two girls were born. They are all living with the exception of one boy. Benjamin is in Mobile, Alabama, as representative of the American Car & Foundry Company. Thomas B. is at Thomasville, Georgia, having previously resided at Mobile and Birmingham for the past ten years. He is engaged in the lumber trade as a buyer for the Chicago Lumber and Coal Company. Catherine Taylor, one of the daughters of Mr. and Mrs. Thomas Taylor, is secretary to the district manager of the car works in Jeffersonville. She has held her present position for about fifteen years and is said to be a woman of unusual business ability. Her sister, Mary C. Taylor, is a stenographer in the general offices of the Louisville & Nashville Railroad at Louisville, Kentucky.

James W. Taylor was educated in the public schools and the high school at Jeffersonville. He also graduated at the Louisville Business College. Upon leaving school he was for the period of eight years a clerk for the Pennsylvania Railroad. He then changed to the American Car and Foundry Company, the firm with which he is now paymaster, a position which has been his since 1907. Prior to that time he was with the same company for about five years as assistant auditor and paymaster.

In July, 1904, he succeeded Cheney and Williams in the proprietorship of the Excelsior Laundry, an industry which for the term of twenty years and up to quite recently was the only one of its kind in Clark county. Mr. Taylor has directed and concentrated all that business resourcefulness with which he is credited in an effort to bring the Excelsior Laundry to a greater state of efficiency. In this he has admirably succeeded, and it is now well equipped to meet the competition of the most up-to-date concerns of its kind.

James W. Taylor has always been the friend of the fraternal societies. He belongs to the Elks and Red Men, being a past exalted ruler of the former. In religious life he is a practical and influential member of St. Augustine's Catholic church. He is a Democrat, and he is looked upon by the party leaders as a coming power in county politics. He is an able accountant, a levelheaded, practical business man whose success has been due to his own efforts, and a man who possesses amiable and kindly traits.

GEORGE B. DIX.

The second member of the firm of Dix Brothers, George B. Dix, was born at Utica on the 21st of September, 1878. The facts regarding his parentage are given under the article headed Oscar Dix on another page of this work.

George received his early education in the Utica public schools, and after reaching maturity entered into business as a partner with his brother Oscar. Much of the success of the firm is owing to his close attention to business and his ability to interpret the demands of the trade. He holds liberal views on religious questions and votes with the Democratic party. He is a member of the Masonic fraternity and is a popular figure in the social life of the community.

The firm of Dix Brothers has now been doing business for twelve years. Their stock is complete, their prices popular and their equipment second to none. They are obliging to their trade and are able to meet all the demands made by the exactions of competition and progress. They enjoy a large patronage and hold a high place in the esteem of neighbors and friends.

MATTHEW COLVIN.

The family of Matthew Colvin, made up as it was of thirteen children, will stand as an example of plenitude both in numbers and in domestic spirit. After all there is a charm that gathers about the home life of a large family. There is a feeling of kinship and a spirit of fellowship that is not found elsewhere in life. The circle of children gathered about the evening fire awakens in the breast a bond of fellowship never to be broken and one that years may make dimmer but can never efface. The contest of mind with mind and the many calls for sympathy and brotherly kindnesses are not without their influence in shaping the disposition and temperament of boys and girls in the most impressionable period of their lives.

Matthew Colvin was born in Mercer county, Kentucky, on January 4, 1845. He was the son of Elisha and Margaret (Curry) Colvin, both natives of Kentucky, as were also the grandparents of our subject, Abraham J. and Sarah Colvin. Abraham Colvin reached the age of seventy-five years. The maternal grandparents of Mr. Colvin were James and Jane Curry, also natives of the Blue Grass state.

Mr. Colvin was educated in the district schools of Mercer county, Kentucky, and upon reaching maturity began life as a farmer. When about forty-five years of age he came to Indiana and continued to farm after his arrival.

Matthew Colvin chose as his companion in life, Lorenda Tatum, who was born in Jessamine county, Kentucky. Their union took place in 1867 and as stated above, resulted in the birth of thirteen children. as given below: Elisha Thomas, husband of Mary Carmany; Joseph, married to Ellen Driscol; William Ivory, deceased; Ruth, wife of Granville Hooper; Georgia Ann, wife of William Ross; Lucy, wife of William Bruner; Jennie, wife of John Mackay; Maggie and Sarah, deceased; Martha, living with her parents; Mary, wife of Edward Zable; Ophelia, deceased; and Emma, at home.

Mr. and Mrs. Colvin are members of the Christian church as are almost all of the children. The parents are held in high esteem, not only by their children, but by friends and neighbors as well. The home is often the scene of happy social gatherings and the spirit of welcome and genial hospitality is a strong characteristic known far and wide, and heartily appreciated.

WILLIAM GOODWIN.

Many of the early settlers of Clark county were descended from ancestors that came to the Middle West from Maryland and Virginia. These made their way for the most part through the Cumberland Gap into Kentucky, branching later into the territory north of the Ohio river, as opportunity afforded. Prominent among these families coming to Clark county is the one from whom our subject is descended.

William Goodwin was born on the farm where he now lives, in Utica township, Clark county, on May 20, 1846. His father, Isaac Goodwin, was born in the county also in 1818, and died September 19, 1883. Amos Goodwin, William's grandfather, was born in Virginia, in 1789, and died in August, 1863, having attained the age of seventy-three years. His wife, Amelia (Dunn) Goodwin, grandmother of William, was born in Jefferson county, Kentucky, in 1793, and died in 1885, having reached the age of ninety-two years.

William Goodwin was one of a family of seven children, as follows: Amelia Ann, deceased; William, of this review; Amos married Miss A. Sharp and is now deceased; Beverly died at the age of thirteen years; Maria, wife of Dr. W. N. McCoy; Charles died at the age of seventeen years, and Mary Bell, wife of John D. Sharp.

Mr. Goodwin received his early education in the neighboring district school, but as he advanced toward maturity he was possessed with the ambition to acquire a more liberal training, and accordingly attended the Northwestern Christian University, at Indianapolis, later known as Butler College. He also took up a period of study at Kentucky University at Lexington, Kentucky. After these years of study he addressed himself to the wholesome task of running the farm, and his subsequent career demonstrated his ability to bring intelligent and scientific thought to bear upon the problems of the soil.

On the 15th of February, 1888, Mr. Goodwin was married to Lena Goodwin, to whom was born one child that died in infancy. She was the oldest daughter of Columbus C. Goodwin, a native of Clark county, and was one of a family of thirteen children.

Mr. Goodwin affiliates with the Republican party and has always taken a firm stand for thoroughness and a conscientious discharge of all public duties. From 1896 to 1900 he served as Clerk of the Circuit Court, giving general satisfaction to all with whom his duties involved connection. He has also served two terms as Township Trustee and was for seven years postmaster at Utica. In all of his public life he has made a clean record and has left the affairs of the several offices in excellent condition.

His farm of three hundred and fifty-six acres keeps Mr. Goodwin, for the most part, engaged. He has shown in its management the same business sagacity that characterized his public career, and has applied a most intelligent and sane judgment in its management. He is a member of the Masonic fraternity and is a most worthy exponent of the principles laid down by the order. The Goodwin home possesses a most wholesome atmosphere of social welcome and domestic happiness.

CHARLES SHARP GOODWIN.

From 1900 to 1904 Utica township, Clark county, Indiana, was served in the official capacity of Assessor by the youngest incumbent to that office in the history of the township. This was none other than Charles Sharp Goodwin, who was nominated for the office before he was twenty-one years of age, reaching his majority in time to fulfill the requirements of the law. Although the office is one that is humble in its scope, yet it requires good judgment and close application to bring about satisfactory service and in this Mr. Goodwin was eminently successful.

Mr. Goodwin was born on the 21st of June, 1879, in Utica township, on the farm where he resides at the present time. He is the son of Amos and Alice (Sharp) Goodwin, who are among the highly respected citizens of the township. The family consisted of five children, viz: Maggie, wife of Charles Litzler; Iva, deceased; Lena, wife of Homer Holman; Charles, of this review; and Ella, who is unmarried.

Charles was educated in the neighboring district school and after completing the work of the grades took a two years' high school course. As a student he was apt and industrious and was generally well liked by companions and teachers. After leaving high school Mr. Goodwin began farming and has continued in that line up to the present time. In this he has achieved success, bringing to bear on his work the benefits of his training and experience. He does not waste time on day-dreams or theories, but drives steadily at the vital duties that come to hand and as a result is enabled to make a splendid showing without any waste of time or energy. He operates the farm on which he lives, consisting of fifty-one acres, and also controls a farm of one hundred and fifty acres in the neighborhood state of Kentucky. No doubt future years will be for him years of opportunity and achievement.

On April 29, 1903, Mr. Goodwin was united in marriage to Maud Fry, an estimable young lady of good education and excellent tastes. This union has been graced with one son, Charles, who was born on the 4th of June, 1905.

Mr. Goodwin votes with the Republican party and advocates a strict observance of the principles of honesty and the fair discharge of all official duties and obligations. He is a member of the Independent Order of Odd Fellows, belonging to Utica Lodge, No. 112, and is a faithful exponent of the principles of that noble organization.

PETER H. BOTTORFF.

Although bent with the weight of years the mind of Mr. Bottorff is as bright and active as that of many men still in the middle journey of life, and he relates with a keen relish incidents of the days when Indiana. and especially the southern section of the state, was practically a trackless forest. This venerable man's memory of the stirring events, and the hardships that confronted the men and women of those early times is very vivid. He has seen a great commonwealth grow from an almost inpenetratable wilderness, his family having been one of the eight original settlers of Utica township, Clark county, and it was there that Peter H. Bottorff first saw the light more than eighty-one years ago. having been born in Utica township, October 19, 1827. His parents were Peter and Sarah (Fry) Bottorff, the former a native of Pennsylvania, and the latter from the state of Kentucky. The date of the birth of the father was December 17, 1791, while the mother was born August 17, 1799. Peter H. Bottorff was one of a family of nine children, three of whom are living, Abraham, eighty-eight years old; Sarah Ann, eighty-six years old, and the subject of this review.

Mr. Bottorff secured little or no education, as schools were very scarce in the days of his boyhood, and such as did exist were decidedly crude, the course of study being confined to reading, writing and spelling, with a smattering of arithmetic. He began to work on his father's farm very early in life, accumulating sufficient money to enable him to become a land owner himself after he had attained his majority. He is at the present time the possessor of one hundred and thirty acres of very productive soil. He was married three times, his first wife being Clarissa Ann Crump, by whom two children were born, namely: William Peter and Mary Alice. His second marriage was with Hannah Carr, by whom one child was born, which died in infancy.

Later they adopted a son ten years old, Albert Carr Bottorff. He has reached manhood's estate, having been born December 25, 1879. He is married and the father of two children. His present wife was known as Eliza Crandall in her maindenhood and was the widow of James Bottorff.

Mr. Bottorff is a member of the Methodist church. He has been a deacon in this church for many years and is also an ordained elder of that body, having been a local preacher of that denomination and accomplishing much good. During early and mature years he was a hard worker, one of the most active in the neighborhood and second to none in the township in skill and speed with a cradle. He does not belong to any fraternal order. In politics he is a Democrat, and never held but one public office, that of Supervisor.

DAVID ALDEN SPANGLER.

Many of our families are constantly changing their place of residence and the family traditions and warm associations clinging about the old home are entirely wanting. Close observers think this is a serious defect in our modern life and should be met and adjusted as rapidly as possible in order to conserve the best interests of our community life. But we are already old enough as a nation to be as well provided with a stable population as are many other nations of today, and it is to be hoped that the keeping of the family homestead by members of the same family will be more common in the future that it has been in the past.

This thought leads us to mention the fact that the man whose name heads this review, was born on the farm where he now lives, having never left the old homestead. He was born on New Year's day in 1851, and was the son of James and Clarissa (Smith) Spangler, the former having been born in Clark county, Indiana, and the latter in New York state.

David Alden Spangler received his early education in the district schools in the neighborhood, and showed many excellent traits as a student when a boy. As he grew to manhood he resolved to widen his general training as a preparation for life, and finally decided to go to Moore's Hill College. After returning from there he went back to the farm and later took up the study of law under Judge J. K. Marsh, of Jeffersonville, a leading authority on legal matters. He was admitted to the bar, but never practiced, for, upon the death of his father, he was looked to as the proper one to manage the farm, which duty he assumed in 1882. This farm of one hundred acres bears the marks of thrift and good management. Mr. Spangler has given it his entire time and thought, with results that are noticeable to the most casual observer. Mr. Spangler is a member of the Methodist church and the Masonic fraternity.

JACOB LENTZ.

Jacob Lentz was born on May 12, 1860, the son of Jacob and Mahala Lentz, the former being a native of Pennsylvania, and the latter of Clark county, Indiana. They were the parents of ten children, three of whom besides Jacob are still living. They are Frank, who was married to Amanda Gilman, of Kentucky; Fannie, who became the wife of Bruner Daily; and Mary, who was married to D. Tuttle.

Mr. Lentz's early days were spent upon the farm, where he acquired his habits of industry and steady application to work. His opportunities for education were limited both on account of the lack of good school facilities and also on account of the short periods of time that could be given over to the work of education and school training. However, he made the most of his common school course that he was privileged to obtain and has made the education thus acquired instrumental for self-culture and development after coming to maturity. As soon as he reached manhood he began farming on his own responsibility and has continued at that occupation ever since.

His domestic career began with his marriage to Emma Howes, an accomplished lady and daughter of Mitchell and Eliza (Parks) Howes, the former being a native of New York and the latter of Kentucky. Four children were born to this union, three of whom survive. They are, Bernice E., who has become the wife of Cornelius Kennedy; Frank has become the husband of Carrie Ross; the third child, Charles, married Ethel McCoy; the fourth child, Bertha, being deceased.

Although a member of no particular church Mr. Lentz sees something of good in all churches and stands ready and willing to further the interests of righteousness and justice in his neighborhood in every way that he can. He is independent in his views in church questions of a doctrinal nature. In politics he adheres to the Republican party although he has always advocated the need of placing great emphasis on the sovereignty of the ballot, and makes of it an instrument for the advancement and uplifting of the cause of good government.

WALTER J. HOLMAN.

Walter J. Holman was born in Clark county, Indiana, near Utica, September 29, 1870, and, unlike many of his contemporaries, never sought his fortune in other fields, but early in life concluded that the best opportunities for him were to be found right at his door, consequently he has remained in his native county, with the result that his labors have been crowned with success. He is the son of Andrew Jackson Holman, who was born and reared in this county, spending his life here in such a manner as to gain the respect and plaudits of his fellow men. The mother of the subject was known in her maidenhood as Rozella Worrall, who was born near Utica. Isaac Holman, who was born in Virginia, was Walter J.'s paternal grandfather, and Thomas Worrall, who was born in Kentucky, was his maternal grandfather, whose wife's name was Eliza, and who was also born in Kentucky.

Walter J. Holman lived at his birth place until he was five years old, when his parents moved, taking him to the farm four miles from Jeffersonville, where he now resides and where he and his brother, H. A. Holman, carry on the various departments of farming with that discretion and industry that insures them a comfortable living from year to year. The farm consists of eighty acres, well tilled and highly improved, and on which a comfortable dwelling and convenient out buildings stand.

Mr. Holman received a fairly good common school education at Utica. He was united in marriage on December 5, 1900, with Carrie Wright, who represented a well known and influential family, and to this union two children, one of whom is deceased, were born. The living child is named W. B. Holman, whose date of birth occurred September 22, 1901. Mrs. Carrie Holman was born in Jefferson county, Kentucky, in 1874, and came to Clark county, Indiana, with her parents after she had reached maturity, meeting Mr. Holman after coming to her new home, and her domestic life was harmonious and happy for a brief period of four years, when she was called to her reward on April 7, 1904. Mr. Holman was again married September 23, 1908, to Myrtle Swartz, a native of Utica township, and daughter of George W. Swartz, a sketch of whom appears elsewhere in this volume.

Fraternally Mr. Holman is a member of the Modern Woodmen, and in his church relations he subscribes to the Christian denomination. Politically he is a Democrat, and he has never aspired to public office, being contented to spend his time on his farm and to lead a quiet life at home.

ISAAC N. HOLMAN.

Isaac N. Holman was born December 27, 1834, in Utica township, Clark county, and he died August 27, 1905. His education was obtained in the local schools after which he became a farmer, which work he followed in a successful manner for a period of six years. But believing that he was best suited to a business career he launched into general mercantile pursuits and followed this until his death, building up a good trade and maintaining a neat and well managed store at Utica.

He was the son of Andrew Holman, who was born in Utica township, and his mother was known in her maidenhood as Levina Bowman. They were people of influence in their community.

Isaac N. Holman was married to Julia A. Poillon on November 9, 1856. She was born July 21, 1835, in Utica township, Clark county, and she was educated in Louisville. They were married in Utica. Mrs. Holman is one of two children, her brother, John Poillon, having married a Miss Snyder, and they are living in Jeffersonville.

Julia A. Poillon was the daughter of Alexander C. Poillon, who married Harriet A. Middlecoff. The former was born in Utica, New York, in 1801 and died in 1890, and the latter was born in 1811 and died in 1901, her birthplace being Lancaster, Pennsylvania.

To Mr. and Isaac N. Holman the following children were born: Nettie, who remained single, died at the age of twenty-three years; Richard married a Miss Howes; Annie married Alonzo Brindle.

In religious matters Mr. Holman adhered to the beautiful principles of Unitarianism, and in politics he was a Republican but never aspired to public office. In his fraternal relations he was a member of the Independent Order of Odd Fellows. He was a man whom everyone liked and respected for he was courteous and honorable in his dealings with his fellow men.

GEORGE WILEY SWARTZ.

All classes recognize the fact that this venerable citizen of Clark county stands in the foremost rank of her worthy and substantial business men, being the owner of one of the finest landed estates in this county, and who, in the golden evening of his age can quietly enjoy his declining years, conscious that his life has not been spent in vain and that he has nothing to regret or retract.

George Wiley Swartz, as the name would indicate, is of German descent, and he was born in Utica township, this county, December 26, 1827. That was during the pioneer period when the beautiful banks of the Ohio were yet covered with giant trees of the primeval forest and the first settlers were combating the red men, the obstacles of a new soil, and it is interesting to hear Mr. Swartz recite the many stirring happenings of those early days. Believing that this was one of the best countries on earth, he preferred to risk his chances at home, and he has seen this locality develop through the various gradations from the wilderness to its present solid prosperity.

He is the son of George Swartz, a Methodist minister, who was also born in Utica township, spending his long and useful life in this locality, becoming known as one of the greatest pioneer defenders of the Gospel, having been born January 13, 1803, and called to his reward August 11, 1890, at the advanced age of eighty-seven years. His wife was known in her maidenhood as Nancy Fry, a native of Jefferson county, Kentucky, where she was born March 29, 1804, and after a long and beautiful Christian life passed to her rest September 10, 1888.

George W. Swartz's paternal grandfather was John Swartz, who was born November 1, 1767, and his grandmother, Elizabeth Swartz, was born January 20, 1775, in Pennsylvania.

George W. Swartz was one of a family of twelve children, of which he is now (1909) the only surviving member. He received what education he could in the primitive schools of his native township. After spending his youth attending school and assisting in the work about the home place Mr. Swartz launched in the mercantile business in 1845, in Jeffersonville, Indiana, handling a stock of dry goods, but believing that a freer and more successful life existed for him in agricultural pursuits he moved to a farm in 1863 in Utica township, where he has since resided, developing it into one of the model farms of the southern part of the state. It consists of nearly two hundred acres of fertile land, and it is in a high state of improvement, and on it stand a beautiful residence and splendid out buildings and in its fields roam all kinds of carefully selected live stock.

Mr. Swartz has been twice married, his first wife having been Elizabeth Butler, whom he married March 29, 1853, and who bore him four children, named in order of birth as follows: Sally, who died February 18, 1894; Belle, Kate, Anna, who died in childhood. The subject's first wife was born December 25, 1828, and passed to her rest October 25, 1861. He was married to Maria Lentz on August 26, 1862. She was born in Utica township, Clark county, April 17, 1836, and she was called to the other shore July 8, 1902. Four children were also born to this second union, namely: Charles, who is a farmer living on a part of his father's land; William, who is a teamster; Ella, deceased, and Myrtle.

Mr. Swartz is a member of the Masonic fraternity, also the Odd Fellows, having become a member of the former when a young man. In religious matters he subscribes to the Methodist creed, and in politics is a Democrat.

NICHOLAS LENTZ.

Nicholas Lentz was born in Utica township, Clark county, Indiana, December 27, 1830, and he has preferred to spend his days in his native community. His birth occurred on the same farm where he is now (1909) living, having lived here until 1847, when he went into the harness and saddle business at Louisville, at which he made a success, but gave it up when his mother died and returned to the farm, having lived with his father and ministering to his wants in his old age for ten years prior to his death, having bought the home place and managed it on his own account. His father, a man of influence and high integrity, was Samuel Lentz, who was born in Philadelphia, in 1802, who came to Utica township, this county, when he was fifteen years old. The subject's mother, Eleanor Shafer, a kindly and industrious woman, was born in Germany and came to America when she was thirteen years old and married Samuel Lentz in Utica, this county. The father was called to his rest in 1875, having been preceded to the silent land by his wife in 1865. They were the parents of ten children, four of whom are living at this writing as follows: Katherine, Ellen, Christian and Nicholas.

Nicholas Lentz spent his early youth much in the same manner as other boys in his community, attending what schools the times afforded and in working on the old homestead during the remainder of the year until he reached man's estate. He delights to tell of the early days, remembering the wild game which was in abundance and also most distinctly the Indians but who were then fast passing away from this locality.

Mr. Lentz has always carried on general farming. His farming property consists of two hundred and twenty-five acres on the home place, another farm adjoining of two hundred and twenty-five acres, fifty-one acres in another farm and another farm two miles away of two hundred and seventy acres, all of the seven hundred and seventy acres under a high state of cultivation and well improved. The fields are well drained and well fenced, mostly with wire, in fact, everything about these farms shows thrift, prosperity, and that a man of modern agricultural ability has managed them. Mr. Lentz has also always handled some live stock of an excellent quality, being a good judge of all kinds of stock, especially horses and cattle. Early in his business career he assumed a debt of fifteen thousand dollars, but that was long ago paid, and he has been remarkably successful in his dealings in the business world. On his lands are to be found as substantial and modern buildings as anywhere in the county, and he lives in an up-to-date residence, having every convenience. The grounds in which it is located are well kept.

The domestic life of Nicholas Lentz dates from 1862, when he was married to Margaret Carr, the representative of an influential family, and after a most congenial married life of forty-three years, passed to her rest in 1905.

Five children were born to Mr. and Mrs. Lentz, named in order of their birth as follows: Samuel, Oma, Walter and Webster. Elden, the oldest of the family, died in infancy.

Mr. Lentz has never held public office, being content to devote his time and attention to home life and his private business. He is a Democrat.

Fraternally he belongs to the Masonic Order and the Odd Fellows and is liberal in his religious views.

He has led an eminently useful life in his community and his influence has ever been exerted on the side of right and morality.

CAPT. HENRY ORMSBY HOFFMAN.

Capt. Henry Ormsby Hoffman was born in Allegheny county, Pennsylvania, September 2, 1847, the son of George and Sarah (Hutchinson) Hoffman, both natives of Allegheny county, in the old Keystone state, where their successful and influential lives were spent, both reaching an advanced age, and rearing a family of five sons and one daughter, all living at this writing except two of the sons. Their names follow: Samuel, William, John, George, Sarah and Henry.

Mr. Hoffman was educated in the public schools of his native county, and he remained at home until he was twenty-one years of age, when he departed from his parental roof and entered river traffic, emigrating to Jeffersonville, Indiana, and becoming a river pilot, soon evincing an adaptability for this work that placed him in the front rank of pilots, even performing his duties with as much caution and discretion as the oldest men in this line of work on the Ohio, and he has been engaged in the navigation and coal business nearly all his life, having made a marked sucess of both. He was a pilot around the Louisville harbor for twelve years.

Mr. Hoffman is the owner of one hundred and ninety-seven acres of land at his homestead which are under a high state of cultivation. The improvements of the place are first class in every respect and a general air of thrift is plainly discernible. The Hoffman residence is one of the most modern and elegantly furnished of any farm house in this part of the state and surrounding it are elegant grounds well laid out and tastily maintained. Mr. Hoffman also owns a valuable farm in Mercer county, Pennsylvania.

The domestic life of Mr. Hoffman dates from 1871, when he was united in the bonds of wedlock with Angeline Stewart, a native of Pennsylvania. She was a woman of gracious demeanor, who, after a happy wedded life of thirty-four years, was called to her rest in October, 1905. To Mr. and Mrs. Hoffman three daughters were born, namely: Nellie, Irene and Ruth, all well educated, and of a charming personality.

In his fraternal relations Mr. Hoffman is a member of the Knights of Pythias and the Benevolent and Protective Order of Elks. His political affiliations are with the Democratic party, the principles of which he has ever sought to foster when an occasion demanded. However, he has never found much time nor inclination to deal extensively in politics. Religiously he subscribes to the Christian faith and is a liberal supporter of his local church.

BENJAMIN F. SWARTZ.

The emigrant ancestors of the large and well known family of this name in Clark county were members of the German yeomanry who did so much during the nineteenth century to populate and push forward the development of the United States. John and Elizabeth (Oldweider) Swartz, who were born in Germany shortly before the American revolution, emigrated in early life and located in Pennsylvania. From that commonwealth they came to Indiana in time to be numbered among the first settlers of Clark county, and from them have descended a long and constantly ramifying line which by its inter-marriages, is connected with a wide social circle in Southern Indiana. The original arrivals were among the founders of the second Methodist church, South, in Indiana, known as the New Chapel Methodist Episcopal church of Utica circuit, Clark county. They were the parents of four sons: Jacob, John, George and Leonard, all of whom with the exception of the second became local Methodist preachers. Jacob was the father of A. A. Swartz, president of the First National Bank of Jeffersonville. Rev. George Swartz married Nancy Fry, of Jefferson county, Kentucky, daughter of George Fry, who was born in Virginia in 1796. A son by this marriage was John Franklin Swartz, who married Alice A Cole. Benjamin F. Swartz, a child of this union, was born in Clark county, Indiana, in May, 1865. He was reared on a farm and attended the old Fry school near Watson. He became a farmer after reaching maturity and was engaged in agricultural pursuits until the early nineties. About 1891 Mr. Swartz removed to Louisville and engaged in the wholesale commission business, dealing chiefly in fruits and vegetables. Subsequently he admitted C. L. Drane into partnership and the business was continued under the firm name of B. F. Swartz & Company. In 1905 Mr. Swartz brought his family to Jeffersonville and re-established himself in a large home on East Chestnut street. As previously stated the entire Swartz family of the older days were pioneer Methodists and to this religious faith most of the descend-ants have adhered. The subject of our sketch joined many years ago and has for a number of years been regarded as one of the pillars of Methodism. He is also a member of the Travelers' Protective Association, but beyond this has not extended his fraternal relations.

On February 3, 1884, Mr. Swartz was married to Cora Charlton, daughter of Jeremiah and Lizzie (Charlton), the former of Scotland, the latter's parents were natives of Ireland and of Protestant faith. Mr. and Mrs. Swartz have an only daughter, Elsa Charlton, and the family enjoy general esteem in the social, religious and business circles of the city.

JOHN H. HOFFMAN.

John H. Hoffman was born in Alleghany county, Pennsylvania, in 1844. His ancestors were Pennsylvania Germans, Scotch and Irish, who were established in America several generations ago. He was reared and educated in his native county. He came to Jeffersonville, Indiana, in 1859, but returned to Pittsburg in 1861, and feeling that her services were needed in the Union army, enlisted in Company I, Sixty-third Pennsylvania Volunteer Infantry, in which he served with distinction for a period of three years in the army of the Potomac, having taken part in all the engagements of that historic army. He was wounded in the second battle at Bull Run, but returned to the front in time to take part in the first battle after the great engagement at Antietam. So gallant was his conduct that he was promoted to sergeant of his company. He was discharged at Pittsburg in 1864.

Mr. Hoffman ran a steamboat between Pittsburg and Nashville for one year, after which he located again in Jeffersonville. He was in the coal landing business from 1868 to 1891, when he sold out to the combine, after having become known as one of the leading coal men in this locality. After selling out Mr. Hoffman had charge of the business of the Monongahela Coal & Coke Company on the Indiana side of the river at Port Fulton. He became the owner of one of the finest farms in Clark county, comprising one hundred and twenty acres of well improved and highly productive land which under skillful management became a model twentieth century farm, on which stands one of the best residences in this part of the state, of beautiful architecture, convenient, and having all modern appliances and equipment. It is located about a mile and a half above Port Fulton, overlooking the Ohio river.

Mr. Hoffman's domestic life dated from 1874, when he was united in marriage with Mattie Cook, a lady of culture, who is a native of Clark county, and the scion of a well known and representative family, her parents being Mitchell and Elizabeth (Ballam) Cook. One son and two daughters were born to this union, namely: Bertha, who was called to her rest on March 29, 1896, at the early age of twenty-one years, much to the profound sorrow of a host of friends and acquaintances who prized her talent and amiability; Bessie, the living daughter, a genteel young lady, is a member of the home circle, being much admired for her accomplishments Samuel R., the son, is engaged in the automobile business at Denver, Colorado. He married Nellie Holmes, the representative of an aristocratic family of Indianapolis.

Mr. Hoffman was a Republican in his political views, and was well fortified in his opinions in the political world, however, he never spent much time in local conventions or elections, but preferred to merely cast his vote for the men whom he deemed would best serve the public good. He was liberal in his religious views, believing that to do good comprises all religion. His family are Episcopalians. Fraternally he was a member of the Independent Order of Odd Fellows, Encampment, also the Masons, Royal Arch degree, Knights Templar and the thirty-second degree, and the Shriners. As might be expected from his war record he was a consistent member of the Grand Army of the Republic. He never held any official position.

In every relation of life Mr. Hoffman proved himself the possessor of such qualities as are bound to win in any line of effort and he won and retained the esteem of all who knew him as a result of his honesty of purpose, kindness of heart and courtesy of manner. His death occurred December 3, 1908.

OLIVER P. GRAHAM, M. D.

The family of this name in Clark county feel a native pride in their genealogy, which is ancient and honorable. The name, spelled in various ways, is constantly found in the old chronicles of England and Scotland and later in connection with the history of the New World. In the fifth century a noted warrior named Graeme fought so valiantly and effectively at the Roman wall in England that ever afterward it was called Graham's Wall, or Graham's Dyke. In the twelfth century, Sir William de Graham, of Scotland, ancestor of the great house of Montrose, in England, was a member of the Scotch nobility, and a close relative of King David I. His grandson, Sir John Graham, was called the "right hand" of Wallace, in whose arms he died at the battle of Falkirk. Many other illustrious Grahams, including lords, earles, marquis and finally the Duke of Montrose, most of them were soldiers for Scotland and later Scotch Covenanters. Under the Stuarts many of them were driven out by religious persecution and settled in the northern part of Ireland. In 1812 Duncan and Margaret Graham, descendants from the Covenanters, came from Ireland to America while the war with England was in progress. They had five sons: John, William, Duncan, James and Andrew. James was born in Ireland in 1780, and in 1815 married Sarah Cavan, who was born in Maryland in 1794. In 1822 James Graham and wife removed to Ohio and a year later to Madison, Indiana, settling ten miles west of that place, near Kent. Still later they established a home in Saluda township, Jefferson county, where they ended their days. They had seven children: William, Margaret, Eliza, Andrew, Mary, Jane and Susan. William married

Catherine G. Patterson, whose lineage is traceable to a Revolutionary ancestry. Major Giles, a soldier of the patriot army under Washington, had a daughter named Mary, who married James Fisher, a soldier of the War of 1812. After his death she married Robert Patterson and by him became the mother of Catherine G., wife of William Graham. To the latter were born eight children, whose careers are thus briefly sketched in the family records: Margaret Jennie married Harvey C. Allison, editor of the Franklin (Indiana) Jeffersonian, and died in 1866; Robert L. married Julia M. Mitchell, of Decatur county, in 1872, and resides near Maxon, Kansas; Thomas A. became a physician at Jeffersonville, practicing medicine there for thirty-three years, probably visiting more homes in Clark county than any other man of his time. He was a member of the City Council, served two terms in the Indiana Legislature and took an active interest in public affairs until his death in 1901. He married Belle D. Haymaker, of Eminence, Kentucky. James M., the fourth child, married Anna O. Walker and lives near Mount Hope, Kansas. John A. was a druggist in Jeffersonville and a leading member of the Presbyterian church. He married Cora B. Fry and died June 1, 1901, leaving one son, Roy Allen. Ella G. married Dr. J. L. Reeves, of Edwardsport, Indiana, a member of the Legislature and otherwise prominent. She died in 1884. Emma D. maried Frank R. Allen, member of the wholesale grocery firm of Boniface, Webber and Allen, at Jeffersonville. He has charge of the branch house of his firm at Bedford, Indiana, and makes his home at that place. He was the father of three children, two of whom are living.

Oliver P. Graham, the eighth and youngest of his father's children, was born at New Washington, Indiana, March 29, 1864. His father died in 1872, and about ten years later his mother moved to Jeffersonville in company with her son. He attended school for awhile and took a course in Hanover College, and then entered the medical department of the University of Louisville, from which he was graduated in February, 1890. Shortly thereafter he began practice in Jeffersonville and has continued without intermission until the present time. He has an extensive practice in the city and surrounding country and is regarded as one of the ablest and most successful of Clark county's physicians. He stands in the front rank in his profession and is popular with his fellow practitioners, taking an active part in anything that concerns the progress and growth of medicine as a science as well as the welfare of the institutions devoted to the protection of the public health. A close reader and student, he follows the latest discoveries, experiences and theories concerning sanitation, hospital work and other branches of medical practice. Dr. Graham is a member of the State and County Medical societies, and the American Medical Association. His fraternal relations are with the Clark Lodge, No. 40, Free and Accepted Masons, Horeb Chapter Royal Arch Masons and Jeffersonville Commandery, Knights Templar. He also belongs to the Elks,

Hope Lodge, No. 13, Knights of Pythias, Jefferson Lodge, Independent Order of Odd Fellows, and Hoosier Camp Modern Woodmen of America, of which he is a charter member.

On December 11, 1906, Doctor Graham married Julia B., daughter of Thomas Paswater, a Justice of the Peace for Jeffersonville township. They have one son, Thomas Garland Graham, who was born October 29, 1908.

THOMAS J. LINDLEY.

The name above is familiar to everyone in Clark county as that of one of Jeffersonville's best and most successful business men. Left an orphan at an early age, deprived of the paternal advice so essential in boyhood, he overcame all obstacles and long before he had reached middle life had fully established himself in the commercial and financial world. In all of his undertakings, and they have been many, he has exhibited the same good judgment, the firm grasp on the laws of trade and fluctuations of the market, which are indispensable to the man who hopes to keep abreast with this progressive age. The result is that he has "made good" in every respect and enjoys high standing among those at the head of Jeffersonville's industrial development. Mr. Lindley was born in Lawrence county, Arkansas, in 1858. His parents were Abraham and Maria (Curtis) Lindley, the former of Quaker ancestry and both born in Illinois, of Pennsylvania parents. After marriage in their native state they removed to New Orleans and later to Arkansas, where the father established a large pork packing plant, occupying an entire block. This section was overrun during the Civil war by soldiers of both armies and business suffered much from these disturbing factors. Abraham Lindley died in 1865, and his wife six years later, after which Thomas J., then thirteen years old, came to Jeffersonville to make his home with a sister.

After leaving school he entered the employment of William H. Lawrence in the hardware business and remained with him until 1882, Mr. Lawrence having failed in business. Mr. Lindley obtained a position with the Perrin & Gaff Manufacturing Company as assistant shipping clerk. This firm was contractors at the Indiana Prison, South, making and supplying builders' hardware. After remaining with them three months Mr. Lindley formed a partnership with A. F. McNaughton and purchased the business of Mr. Lawrence, the location of which was a few doors south of Chestnut on Spring street, in Jeffersonville. In August, 1883, Mr. Lindley bought the interest of his partner and continued the business at the former location until 1892, when he built the block at the northeast corner of Spring and Maple streets, to which he removed his plant. In 1894 he established a farm implements and seeds business two doors from his hardware business and in 1896 added lumber to his other enterprises, the building for this trade being located on Maple street, east of the hardware store.

In 1884 Mr. Lindley married Estella M., daughter of William Thias, of Jeffersonville. They have four children, Claude, Frank, Clara and Grace. Mr. Lindley is a director of the First National Bank, trustee of Clark Lodge, No. 40, Free and Accepted Masons, and a member of Myrtle Lodge, No. 19, Knights of Pythias.

EPENETUS HOWES.

An examination into the ancestral records of the residents of Southern Indiana, or any other district contiguous to the Ohio river, reveals a very interesting intermingling of various streams of settlers during pioneer days. The movement of the emigrants from Virginia and the Carolinas was largely through the Cumberland Gap into Kentucky and Tennessee, spreading from there like a fan in the Middle West. Another stream crossed from Maryland, Pennsylvania, New Jersey and Southern New York and descended the Ohio river, dropping off here and there to find themselves homes in the virgin wilderness. Still another stream moved from New England through the Mohawk Basin in New York state, traveling westward along the lake route to the agricultural regions farther on. Thus we find the Ohio Basin peopled with settlers who ranged from homes sometimes widely removed from one another. Clark county, Indiana, received its major portion from the southern stream, but there have come into this section goodly numbers from the states farther north. Among others, we make mention of the parents of the subject of this review, Epenetus Howes, who was born in Utica township, Clark county, Indiana, in June, 1849. He was the son of M. P. and Eliza (Parks) Howes, the former a native of New York state and the latter of Kentucky. They joined the stream that flowed steadily to the west and made their way down the usual route, stopping at last in the promising district of Clark county.

Epenetus Howes received his education in the township schools of Utica township and as soon as opportunity afforded turned his attention to fruit growing, devoting considerable care to this industry and in the course of time became an expert in the business. He has decided views on the question relating to the culture, production and development of high grade fruit and is recognized as a standard of authority on many questions coming up at the present time. The fame of Southern Indiana as a fruit section has become a matter of more than local importance and it is to such men as Mr. Howes that the credit for these praiseworthy achievements should be given.

Mr. Howes was united in marriage September 29, 1870, to Virginia Cammack, who was born in Louisville on December 29, 1851. This union was blessed with the following children: Bettie, Fannie, deceased, and Julian E. The last named holds an important appointment in the post-office of Louisville, and he is reflecting considerable credit upon his parents as a result of close application to business and a polite and pleasant demeanor.

Mr. and Mrs. Howes are members of the Christian church, and are held in high esteem by their many friends and acquaintances.

EDGAR MITCHELL LENTZ.

In the southern part of Indiana we find natural scenery which, though not stupendous, is yet fascinating. It is in such a locality that we come upon the country residence belonging to Edgar Mitchell Lentz, whose home lies high above the beautiful stream whose meanderings are visible for miles as it lapses peacefully on towards its destination.

Mr. Lentz was born at Utica, Indiana, October 4, 1860. His father, Louis Lentz, who died in 1893, at the age of sixty-three years, was a farmer and was at one time a Justice of the Peace in Kentucky. The mother of our subject was Mary E. Parks, who was born in 1824 and passed to her reward in 1873, twenty years before the death of her husband. The other children of the family, besides Edgar M., were Samuel, deceased; Osa W., Mamie E., and Ella, the latter dying when a child.

On February 10, 1892, Mr. Lentz was joined in marriage to Nannie Barbara Zinck, who was born at Utica, Indiana, on the 19th day of June, 1862. She was the daughter of John C. and Nancy (Summers) Zinck, the former being a native of Germany, born in 1816, and the latter of Clark county, Indiana, born in 1825. Her father was one of the industrious type so well known in this country as being among the best class of immigrants that have come to us from foreign lands. He was originally a cabinet-maker, but later turned his attention to farming. The other children of this family are: Marietta, now living in Chattanooga, Tennessee; George Leonard, who has a general store at Utica; Elizabeth Eleanor; Charles Henry, John Edward, Alice Alma and Ida Ammon.

John George Summers, grandfather of Mrs. Lentz, wife of our subject, is deserving of mention for his patriotic spirit and courageous conduct, having served as a drummer boy in the Continental Army during the Revolution. Later, on account of meritorious conduct, he was promoted to positions of greater responsibility, and fulfilled his obligations with praiseworthy integrity. He was a pioneer settler in this section of the county. Henry Summers, Mrs. Lentz's uncle, was for many years a minister of the Methodist Episcopal church.

The following children have been born to Mr. and Mrs. Lentz: Alma Lorean, born August 29, 1893; Ruth Ashmore, October 12, 1895, and Allen Graham, March 7, 1899.

Mr. Lentz has made farming his chief occupation. He is a member of the Masonic fraternity and affiliates with the Democratic party.

WILLIAM C. PFAU.

Among the prosperous business houses of Jeffersonville, none is better known than Pfau's Cut Rate Drug Store at 329 Spring street, owned and operated by William C. Pfau, one of the city's progressive citizens. Mr. Pfau was born in this city on the 24th of March, 1868, being the second son of George and Barbara (Fuhrman) Pfau, both natives of Germany. The former was one of the early business men of the city, having emigrated hither in an early day and was one of the number that laid the foundation for the later growth and prosperity of this thriving community. He has now retired from active business and with his wife is spending his days surrounded by the scenes made familiar through many years of pleasant associations. His business interests are being taken care of by two of the sons, George, Jr., and Alfred C. Pfau.

William C. Pfau was educated in the city schools, continuing in the regular work until he reached the junior year of the city high school. He then took up the study of pharmacy under Prof. C. Lewis Diehl, at the College of Pharmacy at Louisville, Kentucky. This preceptor has the degree of Master of Pharmacy, only three of which are extant in the United States. Mr. Pfau completed his course, graduating on March 7, 1890, and has since been in professional work. He started in business at his present location in January, 1893, and has continued there without interruption up to the present time.

His drug store is a model of its kind, being one of the best equipped in the southern part of the state. It stands for honest prices, being the pioneer institution in the city among what are known as the "Cut Rate Stores." Mr. Pfau was the originator of the "cut rate" idea here and promoted the system in such a way as to enlist the co-operation of the local dealers, so that its inauguration was consummated without friction.

Turning to the domestic side of Mr. Pfau's biography, we find that he was first joined in marriage on October 4, 1893, to Nellie Bly Russell, of Lebanon, Kentucky, daughter of A. Knox Russell and wife, who are now residents of Louisville. After three years of this happy domestic union, death summoned Mrs. Pfau to her reward. She was the mother of one daughter, Madeline Charlotte. Mr. Pfau was married again on November 16, 1898, taking as his companion Viola Schrader, of New Albany, daughter of John and Mary (Hough) Schrader, both natives of New Albany. Mrs. Mary Schrader died when Viola was still an infant. No children have been born of this last union.

In political questions Mr. Pfau usually espouses the Republican cause, but he lays no claim to political aspirations. The religious element of the home, community and personal life is not without attention on the part of our subject and his wife. They are affiliated with the German Lutheran and Episcopal churches respectively. He is a member of the Benevolent and Protective Order of Elks, being on the charter roll of the local lodge, No. 362. He is also a member of the Independent Order of Odd Fellows, being past grand master of the Jeffersonville Lodge, No. 272. The lodge finds him a most excellent supporter and an enthusiastic exponent of all that these orders represent. The Pfau home is one of the most attractive ones in the city, and is known to intimate friends as a center of warm associations and uplifting influences.

CORNELIUS BECK.

The ancestry of the Beck family is one of unusual interest and is deserving of conspicuous notice as the following random items from the various life records of the subject's forebears will show. Cornelius Beck, whose date of birth is given as March 17, 1826, having been born on what in now known as the Wormald place on the Charlestown Pike, near Jeffersonville, was the son of Daniel and Esther (Sigmond) Beck. Felix Sigmond, father of the latter, was an uncle of the famous Gen. Marquis de LaFayette, making the subject's mother a cousin of that distinguished Frenchman.

When an infant Cornelius Beck was left an orphan, and after reaching the age of six years he was reared by Isaac Prather, a well known member of the numerous Prather family in Utica township. Cornelius began to learn the blacksmith trade near the village of Prather when fifteen years of age. Possibly a year later, when about sixteen years old, he came to Jeffersonville and went to work for his brother-in-law, Joshua Phipps, making edge tools. He assisted in forging the first iron used on the old Jeffersonville, Madison and Indianapolis Railroad, now a part of the Pennsylvania System. Later he went into the cooperage business and after a short time began clerking for Reuben Dedrick in a store, which position he resigned after two or three years, and went into partnership in a wholesale and retail grocery business with Dan Dedrick, a nephew of his former employer. In 1870 Mr. Beck purchased the interest of his partner and continued the business alone until his death, which occurred July 1, 1896, having died very suddenly. He made a pronounced success of his chosen line of work, building up a very extensive trade and giving every evidence of a thorough business man. His death was very much regretted by the entire community for his had been a life of industry, integrity and resulted in good to the public. His store was located on Spring street.

Cornelius Beck was united in marriage with Harriett Christy in 1857. Her father was Francis M. Christy and her mother was known in her maidenhood as Rosalinda Burett, daughter of Solomon Burett, who enlisted in the Revolutionary cause, under General La Fayette at Valley Forge and served with distinction in his command. Long after this, in the year 1824, when La Fayette made an address at Jeffersonville, he recognized his old and dear friend, Solomon Burett, and embraced and kissed him in the presence of a large audience, Mr. Burett being probably the only veteran of the Revolutionary war then living in Jeffersonville. He was buried in the old cemetery at the foot of Mulberry street in Jeffersonville. The Buretts were known as bright, highly educated people, William Burett, of Massachusetts having been a very versatile and prolific author. Solomon Burett and Felix Sigmond, La Fayette's relative, were both natives of France.

Cornelius Beck had the distinction of serving as a soldier in the Mexican war, having enlisted in Company C, Fourth Indiana Regiment, at New Albany, May 31, 1847, serving under Capt. Morgan L. Payne.

The family of Mr. and Mrs. Cornelius Beck consisted of the following children: Hattie, Emma, Ella, Stephen A. Douglas, Esther Rosalind, Anna Cornelia, Eugenia and Irene Virginia.

Cornelius Beck was a man who ever availed himself of an opportunity to serve his fellow citizens. He was several times Councilman in Jeffersonville and always looked as carefully to the interests of the city as if he were managing his own private affairs; he also served as County Commissioner from 1872 to 1878, contributing to the removal of the court-house from Charlestown to Jeffersonville. He was one of the oldest members of Jefferson Lodge, Independent Order of Odd Fellows. He was a regular attendant on the services of the Maple Street Methodist Episcopal church, South, and a liberal supporter of the same financially, and left behind him a noble heritage— a good name.

JESSE E. COLEMAN.

Mr. Coleman is a man of simple and unaffected tastes and has for many years been a trusted employe of the Walton boiler manufacturing concern. He is descended on his mother's side from one of Southern Indiana's most prominent pioneers, while his father's ancestry were staunch participants in the War of the Revolution.

Jesse E. Coleman was born in Leavenworth, Crawford county, Indiana, on the 22d of December, 1866, and was the son of Charles W. Coleman and his wife, whose maiden name was Mary Gray. Mrs. Coleman was the daughter of Thomas Gray, who settled in Crawford county early in the nineteenth century and was the prominent pioneer above referred to. A member of the Coleman family served through the Mexican war, and our subject's father was a member of Company E, First Indiana Cavalry, the first cavalry regiment to go to the front from Indiana during the Civil war. While yet a boy Jesse E. Coleman's parents moved to Jeffersonville, Clark county, and here he availed of the opportunity of attending the public schools. Before becoming of age he associated himself with the boiler manufacturing concern of C. J. Walton, now known as C. J. Walton & Son, and has continued ever since with the same firm. For nearly a quarter of a century his business ability and trustworthiness have been well tested and today he holds a high place among the older employes of the plant.

The Walton Boiler Manufactory was first started in 1836 by Joseph Mitchell and was one of the first plants of its kind in the South. It made a specialty of steamboat boilers and furnished many for boats from the Howard shipyards. The Waltons control a widespread business extending to lumber mills in Florida and sugar plantations in Louisiana. The steel trust recently bought thirty-five boilers from the firm for use in their business in Alabama.

In December, 1888, Mr. Coleman married Josephine M. Runyon, daughter of Joseph and Ann Runyon, of Jeffersonville. Mrs. Runyon, whose maiden name was Ann Morgan, was the granddaughter of Ebenezer Morgan, one of Jeffersonville's early settlers. At the time of his arrival we are told that there were but three houses in the vicinity. He contemplated purchasing the tract of land on which the Galt house now stands on the Louisville side of the river, but owing to some unsatisfactory flaw in the title he contented himself by buying land on the Jeffersonville side. Ebenezer Morgan made his way from Connecticut, his native state, all the way on foot. Mrs. Runyon's father, Sylvester P. Morgan, was a Virginian and came of the opposite side of the family from Ebenezer; the two Morgan families being only related by marriage. He was a prominent citizen of Jeffersonville, and was a relative of Daniel Morgan of Revolutionary fame. A sister of Mrs. Coleman, Dr. Sallie Keller Runyon, is one of the best known lady dentists practicing in Southern Indiana. Her early life was spent on the family farm, and she attended the public schools in Jeffersonville and graduated from high school there. She then became a teacher for the space of eleven yars, until 1893, in the local public schools. At that time she resigned and entered the Ohio Dental College at Cincinnati. She graduated from the institution in 1896 and located in Louisville, where she has practiced with considerable success ever since. In September, 1897, she opened her present office at 723

Third avenue, Louisville, which has been her headquarters ever since. For about ten years she was the only woman practicing denistry in Louisville and deserves much credit for succeeding so well in so large a city, where though practically unknown, she successfully overcame the Southern prejudice against women in public life.

Jesse E. Coleman and his wife have one son, Charles Walton Coleman. Mr. Coleman was formerly one of the most active members of the local Presbyterian church and when a few years ago he removed across to Louisville, he continued his religious activity in connection with the Warren Memorial church of which he is an officer.

CLAYTES McHENRY MARBLE.

A brilliant and varied career as an educator, and accomplished as a scholar in many branches of learning, have made Professor Marble both a useful and interesting man. If it be true that the greatest benefactor is he who makes intelligent citizens by educating the people, he has strong claims to this high recognition. His whole adult life has been devoted to this high calling and the record will show that he has done his work well. The genealogy of this gentleman indicates a long line of worthy ancestors on both sides of the house. The paternal grandfather was Nathan Marble, one of the pioneer citizens of Ohio. His son, Ephraim P., married Elizabeth McHenry, descended from a Scottish emigrant, who came to America at a very early day. Isaac McHenry moved to Westmoreland county, Pennsylvania, shortly after marriage with his first wife, Mary, who died after giving birth to an only son, named Joseph. The second wife of Isaac McHenry was Elizabeth O'Neal, who became the mother of twelve children, including one named James. The latter married Eliza S. W. Gard, whose father served two terms in the Indiana Legislature. He took part in the War of 1812, being among the number surrendered to the British by General Hull at Detroit. James and Eliza (Gard) McHenry were the parents of Elizabeth, who afterwards became Mrs. Marble and the mother of our subject. In 1841 members of the McHenry family took the lead in rather a novel temperance movement which would hardly be possible in the changed conditions of modern times. The pastor of the Baptist church in Switzerland county was, it seems, an indulger in intoxicants to a degree that shocked the moral sentiment of some of his congregation. A faction of the church opposed going to extremes with their bibaceous pastor, but the McHenrys, unable to get rid of the minister, boldly led the way to the organization of another church, which stood for absolute temperance, and this was the last heard of the hard-drinking preacher in that section of the state.

Claytes McHenry Marble was born at Rising Sun, Indiana, February 22, 1857. He passed through the common schools finishing in the high school at Rising Sun, and then entered the National Normal University, where he. was graduated in 1885 with the degree of Bachelor of Philosophy. In 1900 the University of Chicago conferred on him the degree of Bachelor of Pedagogy and seven years later he received from Hanover College the degree of Master of Arts. Beginning in 1878 he taught for five years in the common schools of Ohio county, and for two years held the office of County Superintendent of Schools. Later he was elected principal of the Poseyville (Indiana) schools and served in that capacity for one year. After his third term in college he served two years as principal of the Rising Sun high school. In 1887 he was chosen principal of the Jeffersonville high school, and after holding this office until February 27, 1904, was appointed superintendent of the city schools, which position he has held up to the present time. His long tenure of these important positions furnishes ample proof of Professor Marble's efficiency and popularity. He is a man of easy address, amiable manner and entertaining conversation.

In August, 1887 Professor Marble married Louise Haines, daughter of Hugh S. and Abigail (Haines) Espey, and by this union there are two children, Hugh McHenry and Abby May. The family are members of the Wall Street Methodist church, and Professor Marble's fraternal relations are with the Odd Fellows, Clark Lodge 40, Free and Accepted Masons, the Golden Cross and Modern Woodmen.

ARTHUR LOOMIS.

Though of New England origin, the Loomis family became identified with Southern Indiana before the Civil war and the name has been made famous by the genius of several of those who bore it. A talent for mathematics ran through the whole male line and it has been in the arts based on this noble science that they have achieved their best results. Dr. John Loomis, progenitor of the Clark county branch of this notable family, was born in Massachusetts, but came to Indiana nearly fifty years ago. He descended from a long line of ancestors, many of whom were prominent in the various walks of life, and few families have more just reason to boast of their genealogy. In the sketch of Doctor Loomis, appearing elsewhere in this volume, fuller particulars will be found in this subject. Arthur Loomis, son of the doctor, was born at Westfield, Massachusetts, and in youth was brought by his parents to Clark county, Indiana. After the usual routine in the public schools he learned engineering and architecture. His real career began when in 1876 he entered an architect's office in Louisville to learn the details and technique of the profession to which he had determined to devote his life. By 1891 he was able to become a partner in this establishment under the firm name of Clark & Loomis. Since the death of the senior partner in 1908, Mr. Loomis has continued his business alone. Though his office is in Louisville, he makes his residence in Jeffersonville, and has an exhaustive acquaintance in both cities. His achievements in architecture have not only been extensive but distinguished. In Jeffersonville he designed the Episcopal church, the public library, the Citizens' Bank, the Trust Building and the new cell-house at the Indiana Reformatory, this declared by experts to be the largest and most modern establishment of the kind in the United States. It contains six hundred cells, is original in design and embodies the very latest ideas and discoveries connected with prison architecture. To Mr. Loomis' skill and taste Jeffersonville is also indebted for the new school-house on Spring Hill and many of her finest residences. He also made the plans for some of the principal buildings in Louisville. Among them are included the Louisville Medical College, Levi Brothers' store building, Bacon & Sons' large department store, St. Paul's Evangelical church, the German Reformed Evangelical church, St. Matthew's, St. Peter's, and the First Presbyterian church at Fourth and York streets. Mr. Loomis also designed the Todd building, the largest office building at the time of construction in Kentucky, and the first steel frame fire-proof structure in Louisville. The fire-proof storage building on Green street stands as a monument to Mr. Loomis's architectural ability, as it combines in a remarkable degree artistic excellence with utility of service. Perhaps, however, the most striking example of his achievements is the new Whiteside Bakery, which is a marvel of the ornamental combined with the useful, and of the beautiful in its adaption with the practical. It is indeed a wonderful plant, which must be seen to be appreciated, and if Mr. Loomis had done nothing else, this great building would be sufficient to perpetuate his name. The Armstrong residence, on Third avenue, is regarded as one of the best examples of Italian Renaissance in the city. Another gem in the architectural wreath that adorns the brow of Mr. Loomis is a beautiful stone structure, the Conrad residence, situated in St. James Court. Mr. Loomis was associated as architect with Carrere H. Hastings, of New York, in building the J. Ross Todd residence at Cherokee Park. The style is Italian Renaissance, and it is easily the finest residential establishment in the limits of the Kentucky metropolis. Mr. Loomis is erecting the residence for Capt. Clyde Howard, of Jeffersonville, on Third avenue, Louisville, which will be of unusual design and attraction.

On December 9, 1902, Mr. Loomis married Carrie B., daughter of Capt. J. C. Dorsey, for many years superintendent of the Jeffersonville and Louisville Ferry Company. Mr. Loomis is a member of the American Institute of Architects, president of the Louisville Chapter of American Architects, and was a delegate in 1908 to their national convention at Washington. He stands high in the Masonic circles, having reached the thirty-second degree, being past eminent commander of Jeffersonville Commandery, Knights Templar, and past high priest of Horeb Chapter, Royal Arch Masons. He is also an honorary member of Louisville Lodge, No. 400, Free and Accepted Masons.

HIRAM E. HEATON.

The Heatons can trace their genealogy into the far distant past and may justly boast of an ancestry which was honorable and distinguished in their respective callings. As early as the beginning of the eighteenth century they were domiciled in Pennsylvania, and several became leading men of affairs in their community. Isaac, son of Samuel Heaton, was born in 1731, and became the father of a son afterwards known as Col. John Heaton. The latter was born in 1760, accumulated wealth and laid off parts of the town of Jefferson in 1814. He married Sarah Morgan and to this union was born John Heaton, Jr., eventually to become the founder of the family name in the West. He married Nancy, daughter of Isaac Weaver, who was born in 1756, became a man of wealth and held many high offices in Pennsylvania during the earlier decades of the nineteenth century. He and others of his name were honored by their neighborhood with official trusts of importance. John Heaton, Jr., of Sullivan county, where he was a miller and merchant, achieved high repute. His son, Hiram W. Heaton, removed to Jeffersonville in the early fifties and engaged in the mercantile business, which he followed with success for many years. He was noted for his honesty, his word being as good as his bond with all who knew him and was equally famed for his Christian morality, and liberal handed generosity. He gave at least a tenth of his income to the church and charitable causes, his whole life being such as to gain him an unusual esteem and affection. He married Hulda, daughter of Thomas Jefferson Howard, a prominent and influential citizen of Clark county, whose wife, Elizabeth Helmer, was descended from Revolutionary ancestry. She was the daughter of George Frederick and Elizabeth (Thum) Helmer, both of Herkimer county, New York. Her paternal grandfather was Lieut. George Helmer, who served through the Revolutionary war and was wounded at the battle of Oriskany, for which he received a pension for life. He served in the company of Captain Small, under Col. Peter Bellinger, commander of a regiment of New York state troops. His parents came from Holland long before 1740.

Hiram E. Heaton, son of Hiram W., was born at Jeffersonville, Indiana, January 1, 1858, and was educated in the local schools. Following the example of his father and grandfather, he had a yearning for commercial pursuits and took a course calculated to equip him for success in that line. For seven years he was employed as bookkeeper and cashier for the Perrin, Gaff Manufacturing Company, contractors at the old Indiana State Prison, South, their specialty being the production of hollow-ware and hardware of various kinds. In 1882 he accepted a position as cashier of the First National Bank and has since continued in this employment. Mayor Burtt appointed him City Comptroller and he was for five years a member of the Clark County Council, holding the position of president of that body for some time and resigning in September, 1908. He is a member of the Democratic party and though not an extreme partisan always takes an active interest in public affairs. For at least thirty years Mr. Heaton has been a member of the Presbyterian church and is president of the board of deacons. For seventeen years he has been a member of Jefferson Lodge, No. 3, Independent Order of Odd Fellows, and holds the office of trustee. He is also a member of Myrtle Lodge of the Knights of Pythias.

On April 5, 1881, Mr. Heaton married Minnie E., daughter of William and Esther Smart, the former a native of Kelso, near Edinburgh, Scotland. For a long time he was located at North Madison, Indiana, as master mechanic of the Pennsylvania Railroad Company. Mr. and Mrs. Heaton have two daughters and a son: Jeanette F., the eldest, is the wife of William S. Whiteside, manager of the Whiteside bakery, of Louisville, and has two children, William S. and Hiram H. Minnie Hutchinson Heaton, the second daughter, is a teacher in the public schools of Jeffersonville. Hiram H. Heaton, the only son, is assistant bookkeeper and stenographer at the Howard shipyards.

WILLIAM MORROW, Sr.

The biographer is greatly pleased to give the life history of the well remembered pioneer citizen whose name appears at the head of this sketch, than whom a more whole-souled, sterling and public-spirited man it would have been hard to find within the borders of Clark county, and whose friends were limited only by the circle of his acquaintance.

He was one of those far-seeing men who realized the great future of Clark county, and did what he could in its development. William Morrow, Sr., was born in Bourbon county, Kentucky, February 8, 1794. He was the son of William Morrow, a native of Scotland, who emigrated to America when seventeen years of age, locating in Bourbon county, Kentucky. He married Sarah Patton, and they emigrated to Ohio in 1806, where he owned a farm in Highland county, on which he lived the remainder of his life, dying in 1846. While a resident of Kentucky he became the first

WILLIAM MORROW.

Sheriff of Bourbon county. Being opposed to slavery he left that state and located in Ohio.

William Morrow, Sr., was reared in Highland county, Ohio, and came to Indiana in 1820, settled in Charlestown, where he resided during the remainder of his life. He was a successful business man and for several years was a magistrate. He left ample property for his children, his death having occurred in 1873. He was a devout member of the United Presbyterian church. In politics he was a Whig and later a Republican. He was an influential man in this community and had hosts of friends. To his first wife, Margaret Adair, seven children were born. Mrs. Elizabeth A. Wright is the only surviving child of her father's second marriage, with Jane Manley, who bore him four children. Mrs. Wright was born in Charlestown, Indiana, on the lot where she now resides, May 24, 1847. She was reared in Charlestown, where she received her education. She was united in marriage December 3, 1889, to John D. Wright, who was born in Highland county, Ohio, October 27, 1831. He was reared in the Buckeye state. After his marriage he lived in Charlestown, Indiana, until his death. He farmed in Ohio on an excellent place which our subject now owns. He was successful as a business man and was known to be scrupulously honest, industrious and a man of pleasing address. He was a member of the Presbyterian church, having been an elder in the same. In politics he was a Republican and was always ready to lend his aid in furthering any movement looking to the advancement of his community, whether political, educational or moral. He was one of the organizers, a stockholder and president of the Charlestown Bank at the time of his death, which occurred September 6, 1904.

Mrs. Wright's beautiful, commodious and elegantly furnished home stands at Main and Cross streets, where her friends often gather and where true hospitality and good cheer are ever unstintingly dispensed. She is justly proud of the record of her ancestors who were true American patriots. William Morrow, her father, was a soldier in the War of 1812, and John Morrow, Mrs. Wright's brother, was a soldier in the Civil war. He died in 1907 in Charlestown, being survived by four children, three sons and one daughter.

Mrs. Wright is a lady of tact and culture, pleasant to meet, and she holds high rank socially among the people of Clark county.

CHARLES F. SWARTZ.

The career of Charles F. Swartz is that of a man who has depended largely upon his own personal efforts to attain that goal which most men are seeking, success. Possessed of a large fund of energy, and indomnitable will he has forged rapidly to the front in his avocation, that of an agriculturalist,

42

being today one of the most prosperous farmers in Utica township, Clark county.

Mr. Swartz was born in Utica township, March 8, 1865, being a son of George W. Swartz, a sketch of whom appears elsewhere. He acquired a fair education in the local schools. Immediately after his graduation he began active work on the farm, and he has given his undivided attention to the cultivation of the soil ever since. He was twice married, his first wife being Mrs. Ellen Worrall, whom he espoused in 1887. This union was devoid of children, and Mrs. Swartz died June 8, 1905. Nearly two years later, April 10, 1907, he wedded Mrs. D. V. Scott, who had two children by her first marriage. These children were Marvin and Catherine Scott. By her second marriage one child, Charles W., was born to her.

Mr. Swartz is a Methodist and takes considerable interest in religious affairs, as does also his wife. He has always been a consistent Democrat, although he does not participate actively in politics. He joined the Masons some years ago, and is also a member of the Modern Woodmen, being high in the councils of both organizations. Mr. Swartz has the reputation of being a public-spirited citizen in every sense of the word. He has a very extensive acquaintance throughout Clark county.

THOMAS J. PIERS.

Although modest and unassuming, with no disposition to boast of his attainments, Thomas J. Piers, through hard study has acquired a most complete knowledge of the profession upon which he launched at an early age, and his services have been sought by many big firms in different parts of the country. It is a profession that requires a steady hand and a clear brain. Mr. Piers has traveled extensively, and he is a man of broad ideas. The fact that he is the chief of an important department of a big manufacturing company is a sure indication that he is thoroughly competent and trustworthy. Although he is not a native of Jeffersonville he has spent a large portion of his life here.

Thomas J. Piers was born in Louisville, Kentucky, the son of Joseph and Margaret (Gregory) Piers. His mother was the daughter of Smith Gregory, of Louisville, who was a prominent Mason, having been one of the organizers and the first worshipful master of Preston lodge, Free and Accepted Masons, one of the oldest and largest Masonic lodges in Louisville. He was generally known as a man of most loveable character, being generous and charitable almost to a fault. It was while the subject was an infant that his parents removed to Jeffersonville. He attended the public schools and procured a fair education. He entered the employment of the Jeffersonville car works and learned pattern-making. From there he went to the drafting room of the Henry Voigt Machine Company, of Louisville, and took up the study of mechanical engineering. Desiring a wider experience, he remained there but a year, going east, where he secured employment with different large manufacturing concerns. He spent five or six years in that section, on steam pump and gas engine work, and at the end of that time returned to Jeffersonville a proficient designer of machinery which knowledge is of great use to him in the position that he now occupies, as chief draftsman of the B. F. Avery & Sons Plow Company, of Louisville. Mr. Piers devoted about two years to locomotive work in the shops of the Louisville & Nashville Railroad, and also traveled for an electrical house of Dayton, Ohio. Since he has been in the employ of the Avery company he has produced a number of very creditable designs, and is looked upon as a valuable man by his employers. He retained his residence in Jeffersonville, except while on his eastern tour.

Mr. Piers is a member of Clark Lodge, No. 40, Free and Accepted Masons, Horeb Chapter, No. 66, Royal Arch Masons; Jeffersonville Commandery, No. 27, Knights Templar, also Kosair Temple of the Mystic Shrine, of Louisville. Besides this he belongs to the Jeffersonville lodge of Elks, serving as exalted ruler in 1908 and 1909, and representing his lodge at the session of the Grand Lodge, held at Los Angeles in July, 1909. As an evidence of his popularity in the last named organization he has prior to being elected exalted ruler, filled all of the chairs in the lodge. Mr. Piers is an unmarried man, with pronounced social proclivities.

CAPTAIN ADDISON BARRETT.

Although he practically spent the years of his manhood in high official positions in the service of the government, with a small army of subordinates subject to his orders, Captain Barrett was the true type of a modest and unostentatious man. He believed in discipline, but never abused his power by resorting to tyranny in the discharge of the functions of his office, and when all that was mortal of him was laid to rest the men who had worked under him joined with his loved ones in passing eulogies upon his high character. He was a descendant of old Puritan ancestors, and from them inherited the qualities that form the foundation of a noble life. In his early youth he showed a desire to follow the varying fortunes of a soldier's career, and no sooner had he attained his majority than he entered the army.

Capt. Addison Barrett was born at Cambridgeport, Massachusetts, May 5, 1841, the son of Samuel and Ann Juliet (Eddy) Barrett. His mother was the daughter of Zachariah and Sally (Edson) Eddy. When Captain Barrett was twenty-one years of age, August 16, 1862, he was appointed sergeant in the general service of the United States army in the War Department at Washington, D. C. He served in this capacity until April 1, 1863, when he was made a civilian clerk in the office of the adjutant-general. On December 21, 1864, he was appointed captain and commissary of subsistence of the volunteers, United States army. Further honors came to him September 14, 1865, when he was breveted major of volunteers. This promotion came to him as a fitting reward for meritorious services. He was mustered out the following year. His next appointment was that of captain and military storekeeper in the quartermaster's department, this appointment being dated back to July 28, 1866. In August of that year he was married to Marion Harrison, daughter of Lieutenant W. M. Harrison, a native of Georgia. Six children were born to them, of whom four are living. Horace, the first born, died in early manhood; Harold E. lives at Silver Hills, New Albany, and is married to Corene G. McNaughton; they have two children, Margaret and Annelle; Mr. Barrett is manager of the Henry Voigt Machine Company, of Louisville. Addison Barrett, Jr., married Minnie Howes, and upon his death had one child, Addison Barrett. Miss Marion married James H. Armstrong, who is connected with the Howard Ship Building Company, and they have one child, James Barrett Armstrong. Ernest H. Barrett married Annie Zimmerman, daughter of the Reverend Zimmerman, a German minister, and they are the parents of a daughter, Corene. Samuel Barrett and wife, whose maiden name was Ethel Perry, have a daughter, Helen. Both Ernest and Samuel are residents of San Diego, California.

In 1872 Mr. Barrett was ordered to take charge of the military stores of the quartermaster's department at Jeffersonville, and during his twenty-two years' service in that office he distinguished himself by his industry, and the skill that he displayed in conducting the operations of the department. His long service in itself is mute testimony to his competency. In July, 1891, Captain Barrett sustained a great affliction in the death of his wife. On December 26, 1893, he was united in marriage to Mrs. Anna Laura Ferguson, widow of Walter Ferguson, a son of the eminent jurist, Judge C. P. Ferguson. In 1894 the subject was ordered to San Francisco, where he filled the same office that he had occupied in Jeffersonville. Two years later he was stricken with a severe attack of pneumonia, and died at his residence in Almeda. The esteem in which he was held in Almeda is indicated by the following from the Almeda press:

"Captain Barrett was a man of such noble character and sterling worth that more than a passing notice seems necessary. During his residence here he became greatly endeared to all with whom he came in contact, and displayed such qualities of mind and heart that his example will serve as an inspiration to a noble life and character, to those with whom he was associated.

The Presbyterian church will keenly feel the loss of so valuable a member. He held the office of elder, besides being a trustee, the only one who held both of these positions. As president of the Boys' Brigade, his influence and example have been of benefit to the boys and young men whom he has met every week for instruction and counsel. Those who knew him best say that a more perfect example of a Christian gentleman is seldom met with."

In Jeffersonville, where Mr. Barrett lived much longer than at Almeda, he was no less esteemed. He was for many years an elder in the church in that city. In view of the character of the position that he held with the government, he studiously avoided any political entanglements. Physically he was a fine specimen of vigorous manhood. He was much beloved by his associates, and took a kindly interest in his fellow men, more than one human being owing his rescue from a debased life to Captain Barrett. He was intensely religious, but for a long time refused the office of elder, fearing that he was not worthy of the honor.

JACOB S. SMITH.

The family name of the subject is certainly very closely associated with the pioneer history of Utica township, Clark county, since not only he, but his father and mother were both products thereof, and helped blaze the way for future generations. Mr. Smith, like his father before him, has devoted his life to farming, and has had a very large degree of success, for fertility and productive capacity the land he tills being unexcelled in Clark county. He is warmly attached to the place of his nativity, having never lived anywhere else in his sixty years of life, with the exception of two years spent in Illinois.

The date of the birth of Jacob S. Smith was March 9, 1849. He is one of a family of twelve children, of whom only seven are living. Including the subject they are: Ezra L., Simon L., Mrs. Sarah Spaulding, Mrs. Mary McFarland, Mrs. Susan Gant, and Mrs. Rebecca Worman. Both Mrs. Gant Mrs. Worman reside in Missouri, while Mrs. McFarland is a resident of Illinois.

The parents of these children were James and Mary (Swartz) Smith, natives of Utica township. The grandfather and grandmother of the subject also lived here. Mr. Smith secured a limited education in the township schools at the end of which time he took up farming, and that has been his avocation ever since. He was married February 14, 1877, to Belle Young, of Charlestown, Indiana, and four children were born to them, Daisy, Ruby, Arthur and Earl.

Mr. Smith resides on one hundred and sixteen acres of fine farm land in

Jefferson township, which each year yields bountiful harvests. He is very progressive, and his place is fitted with many modern appliances in the way of agricultural implements of the latest design. He is a member of but one secret order, the Knights of Pythias, and belongs to the Methodist church. He has always voted the Republican ticket, but does not give a great deal of attention to politics, as he is a very busy man. Any project contemplating the advancement of the interests of his locality finds in Mr. Smith a hearty supporter, and that accounts for his great popularity in that section of Clark county.

WILLIAM OSCAR SWEENEY.

From a father who was one of the most prominent figures in the business circles of Jeffersonville William Oscar Sweeney inherited those traits that mark the character of the man who attains success in a wordly way. One of the secrets of his success lies in the fact that he gives close personal attention to his affairs, instead of leaving it to the supervision of others, as many men engaged in his line are often wont to do.

The birth of Mr. Sweeney occurred at Greencastle, Indiana, in 1859, his parents being Patrick H. and Amelia J. (Lane) Sweeney, who, when William O. was fourteen years of age, moved to Jeffersonville. His father immediately upon arriving there engaged in the contracting business, doing considerable municipal work. In 1870 he began contracting on a large scale, erecting a number of public buildings. His first venture in that line was in Johnson county, Indiana, where he built the court-house. It was not long before he had attained a wide reputation, and he took his son into his employ as superintendent of construction on his various public works. They built jails, court-houses, asylums and school-houses all over the state, the Rose Polytechnic at Terre Haute being among the buildings they erected. When the state-house at Indianapolis was in the course of construction Patrick H. Sweeney acted as stone inspector. He built altogether thirty-two court-houses in Indiana, besides many others outside of the state. From 1870 until 1890 they moved about to different parts of the country, where they had contracts. During five years of that period William O. Sweeney was in the South supervising the construction of government boats. In the winter of 1889 he returned to Jeffersonville, and a year later, January 2, 1890, he married Hettie Miner, of Lewisville, Henry county, Indiana. She is the descendant of pious Quaker stock. One son was born to Mr. Sweeney and his wife, namely, Patrick H. Shortly after his marriage Mr. Sweeney and his father resumed street contracting at Jeffersonville, and were kept busy up to the time of the latter's death in 1900. After this sad event William O. continued the contracting business alone, building macadam streets, sewers, bridges and turn-pikes. It is his theory that in the contracting business time is money, and therefore he wastes very few of the precious moments. He has the credit of doing some remarkably quick work, having built ten squares, fifty-six feet wide, of street in fifty-six days. He sometimes employes three hundred men. When he was engaged in government work on the Ohio Falls he used two hundred and ninety teams. He has recontracts of streets that his father built many years ago, and has constructed the masonry for practically all the first class bridges in Clark county, besides having put in nearly all the sewers that have been built in Jeffersonville in the last few years.

On November 1, 1908, Mr. Sweeney and T. J. Lindley. and their sons, organized a corporation under the name of the W. O. Sweeney Company for the purpose of enlarging the scope of the business. Mr. Sweeney is president of the organization.

Mr. Sweeney is equipped with a good education. He attended the public schools, and graduated after a four years course at St. Joseph's College. Bardstown, Kentucky. He is a member of the Elks lodge.

RICHARD MELDRUM HARTWELL.

Mr. Hartwell has reason to be proud of his ancestry, being descended from a very old English family. He is the son of Samuel Adams and Charlotte (Meldrum) Hartwell. He was born at Louisville, Kentucky, August 28, 1850. Through the veins of the Hartwells flows the blood of William Hartwell, who came to America from England in 1636, and settled at Concord, Massachusetts. Through his father's maternal line he is descended from Capt. Seth Walker, who took part in the battle of Bunker Hill, and also distinguished himself in an engagement in the harbor of Portsmouth, between an American vessel and a British armed ship, in which his superior officer was killed by a cannon ball. Lieutenant Walker assumed command, and conducted the engagement to a successful termination, although he was seriously injured. He retired with the rank of captain. Samuel Adams Hartwell was the son of Jonathan and Elizabeth B. (Walker) Hartwell. His mother was the daughter of Capt. Seth Walker.

Mr. Hartwell attended the public schools of Louisville, and after completing a course there he attended an academy at Lake Forest, Illinois. Samuel Adams Hartwell was largely interested in the Ohio Falls Car and Locomotive Company of Jeffersonville, and here in July, 1868, Richard M. secured employment in a clerical capacity, taking up his residence in Jeffersonville a year later. So satisfactorily and faithfully did he perform his duties that in

September, 1876, he was made secretary and treasurer of the company. He continued in that capacity until he became imbued with a desire to go into business for himself. Filled with this determination he resigned after a term of service covering a period of eighteen years. In 1887 he purchased an interest in the firm of H. Verhoef, one of the largest firms of grain dealers in Louisville, with which he is still identified. Mr. Verhoef, senior member of this firm, owned the first elevator south of the Ohio river.

On September 9, 1873, Richard M. Hartwell was married to Bettie Heaton, of Jeffersonville, who was the daughter of Hiram W. and Huldah (Howard) Heaton. The latter is the daughter of Thomas Jefferson Howard, a former well known citizen of Clark county, and a member of the Indiana Legislature in the early days when he rode to Indianapolis on horseback. Through her maternal grandmother Mrs. Hartwell traces her ancestry back to Revolutionary stock. Her grandmother was Elizabeth Helmer, daughter of George Frederick Helmer, of Herkimer county, New York. His father, George Helmer, was of Dutch parentage, and was a lieutenant in Captain Small's company in a New York regiment, commanded by Col. Peter Bellinger.

The first child born to Mr. and Mrs. Richard M. Hartwell, Charlotte Amelia, died in infancy. They have two daughters and one son, all of whom are married. Clara Hartwell became the wife of J. Halbert Lewman, of Jeffersonville, while Mary M. is the wife of Harry Bowden Warren, and lives in Louisville. The son, William Crichton Hartwell, married Madelaine Dunlop, of Louisville, and they are residents of that city.

Mr. Hartwell is a keen business man who is highly respected and admired by his associates in commercial circles of Louisville.

WALTER IRWIN.

There is no question that in the death of Walter Irwin the city of Jeffersonville lost one of its most valued citizens. In a residence in this community covering a period of nearly twenty years, Mr. Irwin greatly endeared himself to all with whom he came in contact. One of the beautiful traits of his character was his devotion to home ties.

Walter Irwin was born at New Market, twenty miles north of Toronto, Canada, in 1843. His father was Jared Irwin, who was prominent in official life in Canada. The former received a thorough education, graduating from the Toronto University in 1865. After finishing his education he went to Columbus, Indiana, taking a position of ticket agent at that point for the Pennsylvania Railroad, and his advancement through various departments was rapid until 1875, when he was made paymaster of the line. His next step in the way of promotion was to the office of cashier of the road, which position he held until the offices of the company were removed to Pittsburg. He then was made secretary and treasurer of the Louisville Bridge Company, which is operated by the Pennsylvania Railroad. He held this important office for the remainder of his life. On October 20, 1880, he was married to Annie M. Howell, of Jeffersonville. She was the daughter of Martin Howell, a well known business man. Her mother's maiden name was Eleanor Pearson, her parents having settled in Jeffersonville in 1845. The father was a very highly respected man in his home city. Mr. and Mrs. Irwin, who had no children of their own, adopted four little ones, who were the children of the latter's brother, and treated them with the most tender affection. Two of them died in early childhood. The survivors are Annie Marshall Irwin and William Robert Irwin.

When quite a young man Mr. Irwin became a member of the Masonic lodge, and he always took an active interest in its affairs. He belonged to the Presbyterian church, of which his parents before him were members. There were few men who had a greater love for their home and family. They held a place in his heart high above all other interests, being practically his world.

Death came to Walter Irwin February 15, 1899. Physically he was a man of handsome presence. His passing recalled no memories of an unpleasant nature, for his life had been honorable. He was descended from the Scotch Covenanters. who were driven into Ireland by religious persecution, and he had many of the traits of those fearless men and women. Despite his dignity he was possessed of a most sunny and genial disposition that seemed to make itself felt wherever he went.

THEODORE S. JENNINGS. M. D.

In the noble profession that he has followed for more than two decades Doctor Jennings has done much toward alleviating the ills and suffering of his fellow men, and consequently holds a high place among the medical practitioners of the city of Louisville. Kentucky. Although his practice is confined to that city he retains his residence in Clark county, where, because of his many sterling qualities and his genial and kindly disposition he is greatly esteemed. The early years of Doctor Jennings' life were spent in mercantile pursuits, but his paramount desire was to become a physician, and that he was peculiarly adapted for that profession is apparent from the success that has attended his efforts. The city of Greencastle. Indiana, was his birthplace. and the date thereof, June 7, 1850. He was the son of Theodore C.

Jennings, who first started the Cataract Flouring and Woolen Mills in Owen county. When seventeen years of age he left home with the intention of making his own way in the world. He came to Utica and secured a clerical position in the establishment of Theodore Rose, who was then the leading merchant of the little town. It was a busy place in those days, owing to the fact that a large force of men were employed in the quarries, getting stone for the big bridge being built by the Pennsylvania Railroad Company. Later he spent four years at the Indiana State University, at Bloomington. In the year of 1872 he returned to Utica, and purchased the establishment of his former employer, continuing in this business until 1875. In 1876 he opened the first drug store in Utica, and remained there until 1881, when he sold out and went to Jeffersonville. He took charge of the drug store of Lewman Brothers, in that city, and was manager thereof until October, 1884. During that year he removed to Louisville and attended medical college, graduating with high honors February 25, 1887. He has engaged in the practice of medicine in that city ever since, with remarkable success.

On November 26, 1872, Dr. Theodore S. Jennings married Maggie Summers, daughter of Charles Summers, who was, at that time, a well known lime burner at Utica. She died May 25, 1880, having become the mother of three children, Annie, James and Maggie. Doctor Jennings remained a widower until October 11, 1883, when he wedded Maud Fogle, of Penick, Kentucky. Three children were the fruit of this marriage, Nellie, Robert and William. Robert died in January, 1908.

Doctor Jennings is a member of the Masonic lodge at Louisville, and also of the Odd Fellows at Utica. He still has a warm spot in his heart for Utica, the place where he first entered upon the battle of life, and that is why he still retains his membership in the lodges at that place. He is an active member of the Christian church, and during his residence at Utica was superintendent of the Sunday school, also being at the head of the Christian Sunday School Association of Clark and Floyd counties.

Doctor Jennings has a most sympathetic nature and many unostentatious acts of charity may be placed to his credit. A little incident that throws light on his high character is related of him. While engaged in the drug business at Utica, he, like other pharmacists of that time, sold liquor along with other drugs. One night a crowd of well known young men of the community purchased a quantity of whisky for consumption on a fishing trip. Some time after they had departed with the intoxicants the doctor's conscience began to trouble him, and late in the night he arose from a sleepless couch, and walking through the darkness two miles to where the party had pitched their tent, he refunded the amount of the purchase and compelled them to return the whisky.

JOHN F. CRUM.

The family of this name originated in North Carolina, but by migration became identified with Clark county, Indiana, in 1802. The first arrival was Mathias Crum, who, after tarrying a while in Kentucky, decided to cross the river for permanent residence. He brought with him a son, then only one year old, and a native of Kentucky, who grew up to be William Spangler Crum, and a farmer of some local prominence. His mother's maiden name was Margaret Spangler, sister of David Spangler, grandfather of the gentleman of the same name whose sketch appears elsewhere in this volume. William S. left a son named Andrew Jackson Crum, who married Mary E., sister of Abram Fry, whose sketch is given on another page. By this union there were eight children, five sons and three daughters, Oscar, Fannie (deceased); Sallie, wife of T. D. Jacobs, who died April 10, 1897; William A., John F., Abram L., Benjamin O., and Olive B., who married C. W. Baird.

John F. Crum, fifth in the above list, was born near Prather, in Clark county, Indiana, June 7, 1865. He grew up on his father's farm, attended the Charlestown high school and Central Normal College, later completing a course in surveying and civil engineering. He had a natural talent for these studies and was a graduate with honors, January 12, 1886. After completing his education Mr. Crum took charge of a farm recently bought by his father a short distance east of New Chapel church. Mr. Crum now owns the one hundred and ten acres on which he resides, south of Watson, and two hundred and thirty-six acres on Silver creek, near Straw's mills, in Utica township. In 1894 and again in 1896 Mr. Crum was elected Surveyor of Clark county, being the only Republican ever so honored. He is well educated, progressive, public-spirited and hospitable. He is a member of the Farmers' Institute No. 1, composed of the progressive agriculturists of his community.

On October 23, 1889, Mr. Crum was married to Paulina, daughter of Wyatt E. Willey, whose sketch appears elsewhere. They have the following children: Elsie, Andrew Jackson, Wyatt Willey, Nelson and Harold.

Benjamin Oren Crum, brother of John F., was born in Utica township, Clark county, Indiana, May 17, 1869. He remained on the home place until eighteen years old and then went to Jeffersonville to work in the Gathright flouring mill at the Falls of the Ohio. Some two and a half years later he returned to the home neighborhood. Previous to this experience he had educated himself in the high school at Charlestown and normal at Mitchell, taking a course in commercial work on the side. In 1904 Mr. Crum bought the Fox farm near Watson and some four years later removed his family to that place for permanent residence. He owns one hundred and ninety-five acres of good farming land, on which is a neat residence and necessary out buildings. He is a member of the Odd Fellows and the Union Chapel Methodist Episcopal church. On January 4, 1891, Mr. Crum married Clara, daughter of John and Cynthia E. Peden. The former was a son of Joseph Peden, a prominent man at Memphis, where he ran a mill. He was a Quaker and lived to the remarkable age of ninety-four years. To Mr. and Mrs. Crum four children have been born: Alma Ruth, the eldest, died when two years old; the others are Oren Talmage, Dexter Huber, and Lucy Lorene. The mother, who was born January 17, 1867, died July 7, 1908.

THEODORE J. KIGER.

The family of this name is of German origin and has been identified with various states of the Union for more than a hundred years. Joseph Kiger, the emigrant founder, was a native of Germany and emigrated to this country before 1800. Settling in Kentucky he was there married to Maria Barbara, daughter of Adam Calfhead and some years later determined to try his fortunes in Indiana. Crossing the Ohio river he eventually landed in Clark county, where he entered land in the northern part of Utica township. His son, John F. R. Kiger, inherited the estate and lived on his farm during his whole life, eventually dying peacefully on his homestead, north of Prather. In early manhood he married Rebecca, daughter of William S. Crum, and sister of A. J. Crum. (Further particulars of this family will be found in the sketch of John Crum.) By this union there were seven children, of whom those living are as follows: James Marion, Joseph William, John Franklin; Anna, now Mrs. Anderson, and the subject of this sketch.

Theodore Kiger, youngest of this family, was born near Prather, in Clark county, Indiana, in 1870. He owns about seventy acres of farming land, nearly all of which is under cultivation. Mr. Kiger's specialty is the breeding of Jersey cattle and he takes great pride in his herd, all of which is registered stock. The fine butter made by his wife from the milk of these cows enjoys a great local reputation and much of it is sold in the nearby markets.

Mr. Kiger is hospitable at his home and loves to talk of current events, on which he keeps well informed. He is also able to impart much information about farming, especially the best methods of breeding and feeding live stock. The family are members of the Methodist Episcopal church, and much esteemed by their neighbors. E. O. Kiger, son of Joseph William Kiger, lives nearby with his mother. J. D. Kiger, who lives three and a half miles northeast of Charlestown, is a son of James Davis Kiger and grandson of Joseph, the first of the family who came from Germany. The connection possesses all the characteristics that cause the Germans to be so highly esteemed as citizens in this country. Frugality, intelligence in conducting their business and sociability with friends and neighbors are the good qualities seldom found lacking in the German-American citizen, whether he be on a farm, in a store, a restaurant, hotel-keeper or baker.

JAMES EDGAR BROWN.

Jonas Warren Brown, the founder of the family of this name in Clark county, was a native of Ohio and came to Indiana during the second quarter of the last century. He married Elvira Ann, daughter of James Collins, of Charlestown, and to this union we are indebted for the popular citizen whose life and career constitute the subject of this sketch. James Edward Brown was born near Charlestown, Clark county, Indiana, July 1, 1848. Having lost his mother by death when four years old, he was taken in charge by Mrs. Sarah J. W. Sullivan, a maternal aunt, who reared him with tenderness and affection until he reached manhood's estate. This aunt was originally Miss Collins, who married Daniel McDonald, and after his death became the wife of a minister named Sullivan. James Edgar Brown was reared on the farm where he now lives and which he owns by inheritance and in youth went through the usual educational experiences of the district schools. Later he entered as a pupil in old Asbury, now DePauw University, at Greencastle, and remained there long enough to acquire a fair college education. After leaving college he engaged in farming and has devoted his whole life to agricultural pursuits. He is a Methodist and a member of the Independent Order of Odd Fellows.

On March 3, 1870, Mr. Brown was married to Clara M. Bennett, a descendant of one of the old and highly respected pioneer families. Her father, Joshua Selvey Bennett, was born in Clark county, Indiana, of North Carolina parentage, married Indiana Davis, and was the chief factor in building the village of Prather, which was named after its first postmaster. To Mr. and Mrs. Brown four children have been born, two sons and two daughters, all of whom are living, and well settled in life. Emmons Warren Brown, the eldest, removed to Boise, Idaho, where he married Edith Ellis, daughter of a prominent banker of that place. Four children have been born to them: George, Olive, Arnett, and Jonas, the latter deceased. Daisy W., the eldest daughter of James Edgar Brown, is the wife of Winnie C. Lewman, a contractor, whose sketch appears elsewhere in this volume. Samuel Edward Brown, the third child, still makes his home with his parents. Bessie Ann Brown, the youngest, was married August 5, 1903, to S. J. Swartz, who was for many years in the undertaking business at Jeffersonville. The latter first married a Miss Conway, who died November 24, 1901, leaving two children, Bessie Alberta and Ralph C. The founders of this family were John and Elizabeth (Old-weiler) Swartz, who were born in Germany before the American Revolution, and after coming to this country first settled in Pennsylvania, whence they removed to Indiana about the beginning of the nineteenth century. They located in Clark county on a farm situated in Utica township and became leaders in founding the New Chapel Methodist Episcopal church, which is now the oldest existing congregation in Indiana Methodism. Jacob Swartz, son of this pioneer couple, was the father of Thomas J. and A. A. Swartz, the latter a well known banker of Jeffersonville. Thomas J. married Eleanor Lentz and their son became the husband of Bessie Brown, as recorded above. S. J. Swartz, like his ancestors before him for several generations, is a member of the Methodist Episcopal church and also holds membership in the Independent Order of Odd Fellows, Masons, Knights of Pythias and Modern Woodmen.

EMERY SYLVESTER.

Indiana was still a territory covered all over with virgin forest when Purdue Sylvester left Wilmington, Delaware, to seek a new home in the western wilderness. Following the usual route across the mountains and down the Ohio river, he eventually landed in Clark county, which at that time presented few attractions for the agriculturist. He entered a large tract of land in Jeffersonville township on what subsequently became known as the Hamburg Pike, and here he went through all the rugged experiences incident to pioneer life in that early day. He married Rachael Scott, whose parents moved in among the first settlers, and owned land on the Middle Road in Utica township. Emery Sylvester, a child by this union, was born on the paternal farm, about four miles north of Jeffersonville, January 11, 1816, which was the year of the state's admission into the Union. He worked on the farm as he grew up but had poor opportunities for education, as schools at that time were few and far between. However, he learned all about farming, as it was carried on in those days, acquired industrious habits, and came to know the value of work as an element of success in life. He remained with his parents until the eighteenth year of his age when in language of the country, he "struck out for himself." Going up to Jeffersonville he learned the plasterer's trade and followed it for a livelihood for a few years, after which he returned to the farm and continued in agricultural pursuits during the rest of his life. Though he never sought office, his neighbors insisted on electing him a Justice of the Peace and he discharged his official duties so well that he was kept in the same position for twenty years. He was a good citizen who led a quiet, unobtrusive life, paid his debts and enjoyed general esteem in the community where he resided. He died March 3, 1885, without an enemy in the world, and with a consciousness in his last hours that he had done his duty in all the relations of life. In 1839 when twenty-three years old, Mr. Sylvester married Caroline McClintock, member of one of the old, esteemed pioneer families of the county. Her grandfather, John McClintock, came from Ireland, when twelve years of age accompanied by two brothers, one of whom, named Samuel, settled near the Charlestown Pike, north of Jeffersonville. John prospered after reaching manhood, and when he died was the owner of several hundred acres of farm land in Jeffersonville township. He left a son, known as John McClintock, Jr., who in 1809 married Mary Provine, a native of Tennessee, and became one of the county's substantial citizens. He owned a large farm, five miles north of Jeffersonville, on the road that runs from Utica township west to Blackstone's mill, near Cementville. It was his daughter who became the wife of Emery Sylvester and shared his joys as well as his sorrows, for nearly fifty years. She survived him about four years and passed away March 8, 1889. Six children were born of this union: Mary, Charlotte, Caroline, Emery, John and Commodore C. The last named died in childhood, and both of the other sons passed away in their twentieth years. The three daughters own the home place, consisting of two hundred and fifteen acres of land and have made their residence there since the death of their mother. The Sylvesters and McClintocks being among the earliest settlers, have been known in Clark county for over a hundred years, and no families have enjoyed greater esteem. One of the proud recollections cherished by the latest generation of Sylvesters is that the grandfather, John McClintock, Jr., was a soldier with Gen. William Henry Harrison at the celebrated battle of Tippecanoe.

WILLIAM W. SMITH.

This family is of English origin and has had representatives in the United States for fully seventy years. Edward Smith came from England in 1840 and settled near Memphis. With him was a son named Christopher, who on reaching maturity married Sarah, daughter of John Dietz, a soldier in the War of 1812. William W. Smith was a child by this union, and was born near Sellersburg, Clark county, in 1844. He remained on his father's farm until 1862, when he enlisted in Company A, Eighty-fourth Regiment, Indiana Volunteer Infantry, which afterwards became a part of the Army of the Cumberland. With his command he participated in the battle of Stone River, Chickamauga, Franklin, Nashville, Dallas, Georgia, and Resaca, besides many minor engagements. After his muster out, June 15, 1865, he returned to Sellersburg and engaged in farming, which he has followed continuously until the present day. He has owned three farms, but disposed of all except one in Charleston township, and the one on which he resides in Utica township. His house deserves especial mention as one of the historic relics of the county and a curious reminder of pioneer days. It is a two-story brick, looking rather modern to the casual passer, but dating from 1815, when it was erected by a man named Bowen. The rooms are unusually large and the wide fireplace with a crane is surmounted by a mantel nearly ten feet long. An old "Dutch oven" of ancient pattern, recalls the cooking devices of our great-grand-mothers. About a mile north of Mr. Smith's place stood an old cabin, which was for a long time known as the last house from the river until the traveler reached Vincennes.

In 1867 Mr. Smith married Nancy Ann Bottorff, whose genealogy is presented in the biography of her brother, Moses E. Bottorff, in this volume. The children born to Mr. and Mrs. Smith, seven in number, are thus recorded in the family archives: Elmer D., a baker, at Riverside, California, is married and has four children; Lewis C. is a resident of New Albany; Christopher C. is a dentist at Riverside, California; Katie is the wife of Wallace Jacobs, has four children and resides on the Utica and Salem road; Jason C., next to the youngest, is unmarried; Nellie R., wife of Howard Fry, has one child, and resides at Port Fulton. One of the seven children of Mr. Smith died at an early age. The mother dying in 1901 Mr. Smith was married in 1904 to Julia A., daughter of Samuel and Susan (Beadels) Bottorff. She is a grand-daughter of Henry Bottorff, a native of Germany, who founded the family of that name in Clark county. Mr. Smith is a member of the Grand Army of the Republic and of the Methodist church, to which his wife also belongs.

MOSES E. BOTTORFF.

The family of this name is one of the oldest and most respected in Clark county, with which its members have been connected during the vicissitudes of a century. Henry Bottorff, the founder, born in Germany, December 3, 1780, came to the United States before 1810. He owned a grist mill on Muddy Fork, where the Speed's Cement mill now stands, and which after his death in 1859, was continued by his sons, Samuel and Lewis. The latter was born in 1810 and became a well known figure during his long and active life, which came to a close October 19, 1896. For some years he was engaged in the milling business, but afterwards ran flatboats down to New Orleans, selling cider and other farm products. Subsequently he abandoned this for farming and to this substantial occupation he devoted all of his later years. On July 16,

1842, he married Mary C. Congleton, by whom he had six children: Marietta, Nancy Ann, wife of William Smith; Peter, who died October 17, 1885; Irene R., wife of James Wier, Justice of the Peace at Sellersburg for thirty-five years; Lewis, who married Emma Kramer, resides at Speed.   Moses E. Bottorff, the youngest child, was born on his father's farm in Charlestown township, Clark county, Indiana, in 1856, and remained under the parental roof until about twenty-two years old.   On October 24, 1878, he married Amanda, daughter of John and Erthusa (Carr) Hill.   The latter was a niece of Col. Joseph Carr, who was a colonel under General Harrison at the battle of Tippecanoe.   Mr. and Mrs. Bottorff have five children: Elbert, who married Clara Pass, lives on his father's farm in Charlestown township; Lulu; Myrtle Irene, who married Charles M. Sage, son of County Assessor, Erasmus T. Sage; and James L., an unusually promising young man.   He was appointed by Governor Hanly, Justice of the Peace, when only a little over twenty-one years old, and is entering on the practice of law and holds the position of telegraph operator on the Louisville branch of the Baltimore & Ohio Southwestern Railway, at Watson.   Clarence C., the youngest son, is still at home with his parents.   By a previous marriage of his father Mr. Bottorff has several half brothers and sisters.   These were James, George, and Sarah Catherine, wife of Dr. Joseph McCormick.   James was a soldier under Grant and present when the terms for surrendering Vicksburg were being arranged by the two commanding generals.   Among the interesting landmarks in this neighborhood is a stone house now owned by Calvin Bottorff, built in 1817, out of material of a still earlier structure, on a site about a quarter of a mile away.   A short distance west is another stone house, said to have been built in 1800 by Ephraim Arnold, and sold by him later to a Scotchman named Purdy.   There is a tradition that it was erected as a refuge from the Indians and wild beasts in the pioneer period and that at one time it sheltered sixteen families.   Mrs. Rachael Bowen, of Charlestown, who is authority on things relating to the old days, talks interestingly concerning old houses and the people who occupied them in the distant past.

THOMAS DOUDEN JACOBS.

The reader of Clark county history will often find the names of Prather, Lentz and Jacobs and closer inspection in the biographical branch will disclose the fact that these families, by intermarriages for several generations, have left descendants that constitute some of the best citizenship of the various townships.   Thus we find that Eliphalet Douden Jacobs married Catherine, daughter of Thomas W. and Elizabeth (Lentz) Prather and all these recall names familiar in the pioneer period.   Thomas Douden Jacobs, a son by this

43

union, was born at Jeffersonville, Clark county, Indiana, March 29, 1857. When he was three years old his parents removed to their farm three miles from Jeffersonville on the Plank Road. After a residence there of eleven years, they changed locations by moving to the old Thomas W. Prather farm, between Watson and Utica, which was the homestead of Mr. Jacobs' mother. He remained there until March 10, 1880, when he married Belle, daughter of Tilford Prather. The latter was a son of Samuel and grandson of Basil Prather, founder of the family in Clark county. Clarence Newton Jacobs, the only fruit of this union, married Bertha, daughter of Edwin LaDuke, of Utica township, and is a resident of Port Fulton. His mother died October 9, 1889. After his marriage in 1880, Mr. Jacobs moved to the farm in Utica township now occupied by Isaac Jacobs. In December, 1890, he married Sallie, daughter of A. J. Crum, who lives in Utica township on the Charlestown Pike. Of the three children by this second marriage only one is living, her name being Minnie Olive. The mother died April 10, 1897, and after this bereavement, Mr. Jacobs sold his farm above mentioned and built a residence on the other place at the crossing of the Plank and Sellersburg, Utica roads. This farm consists of one hundred and sixty-one acres of good soil which Mr. Jacobs has cultivated carefully and kept in excellent condition in every respect. The house is large and home-like, well furnished and possessing all the modern conveniences for comfort.

On September 20, 1898, Mr. Jacobs married Ethel, daughter of Abram Fry, of Utica township, a sketch of whose family appears elsewhere in this volume. Of their four children, one named Mary died in infancy, the others being Margaret, Elizabeth and Virginia. Mr. and Mrs. Jacobs are members of the New Chapel Methodist church, and also belong to Farmers' Institute No. 1, in Utica township. Mr. Jacobs is regarded as one of the county's progressive farmers and his home is the abode of hospitality and cheerful greeting to friends.

JEFFERSON AND DAVID L. PRATHER.

The family of this name has been identified with Clark county for more than a hundred years and borne a conspicuous part in its development. Devoted chiefly to farming, its members have found time for other activities and the county history will show them always ready to bear their full share of responsibilities in the civil, religious and political activities of their respective communities. Basil Prather, the founder of the family, came to the county about the beginning of the last century and was one of the sturdy old pioneers who left their impress upon this section of Southern Indiana during the formative period of the state. He was one of the founders of New Chapel church, the second Methodist meeting house established in Indiana and the oldest existing religious society in the state. He left a son who became well known in after life as Judge Samuel Prather, in his time one of the county's most substantial citizens. He married a Miss Holman, by whom he had a son named Sion, the latter married Catherine, daughter of David Lutz, who came from North Carolina before the year 1800. His father, Henry Lutz, a native of Germany, found his way north to the then Indiana Territory and established a home in the wild woods of Clark county, subsequently known as Charlestown township. A fuller sketch of this early pioneer appears on another page of this volume. Sion and Catherine (Lutz) Prather were the parents of four children: Jefferson, David, Alvin and Tilford. Alvin joined the Union army in the Civil war and was killed at the battle of Stone River. Tilford reached maturity, married Indiana Bennett and died in 1907, leaving one child.

Jefferson Prather, the third in order of birth of these four children, was born on the paternal farm in Utica township, Clark county, Indiana, in 1840. In 1865 he married Annie, daughter of William and Mary (Hikes) Gibson, who came from Kentucky to Clark county in what the historians call an "early day." Mrs. Prather died September 26, 1906, after becoming the mother of two sons, Rolla and Morris; Rolla removed to California some years ago and settled in Fresno county, where he has a family consisting of a wife and four children. Morris was married in the fall of 1908 to a Missouri lady and makes his home with his parents. Mr. Prather's farm consists of one hundred and eighteen acres, a part of the old homestead which fell to him after his father's death. David L. Prather, his younger brother, was born in 1844, and remained on the home place until his marriage to Rebecca, daughter of John Glossbrenner, one of the early pioneers of Utica township, now a resident of Jeffersonville. By this union there were seven children. Jesse R. married Hattie Pass, and lives with his uncle Jefferson. Elmer, Durward and Herbert still remain with their parents. Royd Alvin died December 17, 1908.

Mr. Prather was elected County Commissioner on the Democratic ticket in 1892, and made an excellent official during his term of service. At his father's death the north part of the old homestead, consisting of seventy-four acres, and the residence fell to his share and here he has since lived the simple and wholesome life that comes from agricultural pursuits. He and his brother Jefferson are members of the Cement Lodge of the Independent Order of Odd Fellows. Aside from its value as farmland, the old Prather homestead, now occupied by these worthy brothers, is of interest to archæologists. The ground is thickly strewn with Indian arrowheads and other relics of the red men, skeletons having been found which are known to have belonged to the original occupants of this part of Indiana. Still earlier and more interesting relics are remains of the Mound builders, going back to pre-historic times. Three mounds, with indications of a fourth have been found on the Prather place.

They are arranged in a semi-circle, connected by a strip of black earth overlying the natural soil. Two burial mounds yielded potsherds, stone-pipes, boneneedles, pestles, axes, a color cup and stone from which red color was made, spear and arrow heads in great variety, besides skeletons of this vanished race, lying on a quantity of charcoal.

WILLIAM H. DEIBEL.

The family of this name in Clark county is of German origin. Peter Deibel, a native of Germany, emigrated from that country in the early forties, and, after spending a few years in Kentucky, crossed the Ohio river into Indiana. Early in the fifties he bought the first farm west of New Chapel church. He married Magdalene Foreman, also a native of Germany, who came to this county about the time of his own arrival. Eight children were born to them, of whom the five living are Henry, William H., Mary, wife of George Edward Crum, of Jeffersonville; Katie, wife of George Sweeney, of the same city; Christina, wife of G. N. Prather, a resident of Johnson county, Indiana; John, died aged six years; Minnie, wife of William Miller, died in Oldham county, Kentucky, leaving three children; Peter died in Jeffersonville, leaving three children, Rudolph, Peter and Isabelle. . William H. Deibel, the fifth child of his parents, was born on his father's farm in Clark county, Indiana, December 24, 1862. He attended the public schools in his neighborhood and after reaching manhood became a farmer. He owns a place of fifty-one acres of the good farming land of Utica township, where the soil is underlaid with limestone. He is enterprising as a manager, up-to-date in his methods and aims to keep well informed in matters pertaining to agriculture. His home is the abode of hospitality and all who call either on business or pleasure are given a cheerful greeting. He joined the Masonic Order in 1896, and is also a member of the Odd Fellows and Modern Woodmen. On April 21, 1897, Mr. Deibel married Paulena, daughter of Charles and Mary (Fichter) Holzbog, of DuBois county, Indiana. They have three children: Marie Paulena, Lulu Loretta and Charles William. The family are members of the New Chapel Methodist Episcopal church and enjoy excellent standing in the community.

Henry Deibel, eldest son of Peter and Magdalena (Foreman) Deibel, was born on his father's farm in Clark county, Indiana, in 1854. As he grew up he attended the schools of his neighborhood and also those of Jeffersonville. While a young man he spent a couple of years in Illinois, and then returned to Jeffersonville to take a job at the car works, where he remained about one year. On December 25, 1885, Mr. Deibel was married to Mary, daughter of Michael and Mary (Kansinger) Dietrich, the former one of the pioneers of the county and a resident of the community about four miles north of Jeffersonville. Mr. and Mrs. Deibel are the parents of the following children: Otis married and settled at Franklin, Indiana, and has two children; Ida May, wife of James Stanforth, resides in Jeffersonville; Matilda married Rufus Rogers, of Jeffersonville, and has one daughter; Lora, also lives at the county seat, while William, Magdalene, Eva Lee, Henrietta, Buford, Bertha and Louisa, are all at home with their parents. After his marriage Mr. Deibel lived two years on the old Falker farm, but in the fall of 1887 purchased thirty-three acres of land on the Plank Road, about five miles out from Jeffersonville, where he has since made his residence. Recently he bought the old Wormald tract of fifty-seven acres, adjoining his home place, and is comfortably fixed for farming on a large scale. Mr. and Mrs. Deibel are members of the Lutheran church at Jeffersonville, and he belongs to the Odd Fellows and Modern Woodmen.

THE DUNBAR FAMILY.

Though Scotland has contributed much valuable material to the citizenship of America, she has sent over few worthier families than the Dunbars. The "Head of the House," as the term is used in old Scotia, was William Dunbar, who was born in 1806 and reared a family of lusty sons, destined at a later day to make their marks in the United States. John was born in Scotland in 1830, James in 1846 and William in 1848. John reached the United States in 1852, and five years later was joined by the family. Coming to New Albany, Indiana, about 1854, John Dunbar became superintendent of the gas works, which position he held until his death, in 1870. In 1854 he returned to Scotland and married Margaret Whitson, bringing his bride to New Albany, where they made their home. Of their nine children five died in early childhood, the four still living being James W., Mrs. George W. Robb, Alexander and Lundy. James W. is superintendent of the gas department of the United Gas and Electric Company of New Albany and Jeffersonville. He married Nannie, daughter of Morris McDonald, and is a resident of New Albany. Mrs. Robb was formerly the wife of Professor Borden, whose sketch appears elsewhere in this volume. Alexander and Lundy are both citizens of Indianapolis. William Dunbar, uncle of these children and one of the three brothers who came to this country in the fifties, now a resident of California, was the father of Horace Dunbar, well known as a lawyer in Jeffersonville and now mining editor of the Salt Lake Tribune. James Dunbar, the second of the emigrant brothers, died without marrying. Though the Dunbars are rather of Floyd than Clark county, their business connections and social relations have brought them in touch with the affairs of both counties and made them well known throughout Southern Indiana. All of them developed an aptitude for business in the prosecution of which they displayed the Scotch skill, application and industry which are the chief factors in gaining success in any calling.

FLOYD J. REDDING.

The family of this name is of Kentucky origin and its members have long been identified with the farming interests of Clark county, though not figuring in public life, but pursuing the even tenor of their way, they have borne their full share of the burdens and responsibilities of developing the county and giving it its high standing in the state. John Redding, founder of the family in Clark county, was a native of Oldham county, Kentucky, but crossed the river in early manhood in search of an opportunity to better his fortunes. Securing employment with Abram Fry, he worked for him several years as a farm hand and during that time a romance such as we read about in the story books, developed and had an important influence over his subsequent life. The yellow fever plague which devastated New Orleans shortly after the Civil war was of widespread damage to thousands of families and many persons came north to escape its fatal effects. Among those stricken was a family named McDonald, and as a result of the death of her parents, little Mary was left an orphan of tender years. Abram Fry knew them, and out of sympathy adopted this child, who in time became a permanent member of his household. As she grew up she became a good friend of John Redding; this friendship ripened into love and in due time they were married. Of the four children resulting from this union three are living: Emma is the wife of J. Ellis Potter, a sketch of whom appears elsewhere in this volume; Ella L., another daughter, makes her home with her brother, who is the subject of this sketch. The father died in January, 1877, and the mother in February, 1900.

Floyd J. Redding, the only surviving son, was born on his father's farm on the Plank Road, three miles from Jeffersonville, Indiana, July 22, 1874. He was but a little over two years old when he lost his father, but enjoyed the care of an affectionate mother until he reached manhood's estate. On March 11, 1903, he was married to Nellie, daughter of Edwin and Lauara (Swartz) Dunn, of Utica. Mrs. Redding's mother was a daughter of Franklin Swartz, whose father was the John Swartz that became so well known as a leader in the establishing of the New Chapel Methodist church in pioneer days. The Dunns have been well known residents of Utica township for many years. Mr. and Mrs. Redding have two children, Ruth Alene and John Edwin. The family, like their ancestors before them for many decades, are members of the New Chapel church, which since the early settlement of the county has been one of the bulwarks of Methodism. Mr. Redding is a quiet, unassuming man of frugal and industrious habits who enjoys the esteem of all his neighbors.

JACOB H. GIBSON.

It was while Kentucky was earning its name as the "Dark and Bloody Ground," that William Mac Gibson came in from Winchester, Virginia, and cast his lot with the western wilderness. He located in Nelson county, some thirty-five miles south of Louisville, in 1792, and there reared his family. His son, who was given the same name as himself, was born at Bardstown, in 1810, and when seventeen years old he began teaching school on the pike about five miles from Louisville. In that neighborhood was a family whose members figured conspicuously in the early history of the locality. George Hikes, its founder, came from Harrisburg, Pennsylvania, in 1790, and settled at Gilman's Point, two miles from Louisville, when the latter was a village of log cabins, and he became the owner of twelve hundred acres of land. He had six children and left each of them two hundred acres, which eventually increased into landed estates of great extent and value. Jacob Hikes, one of the sons, was a child when his father moved in and after growing up, in connection with his brother, established large nurseries near Louisville. He owned hundreds of acres of land and many slaves, which he freed and sent to Liberia, paying all their expenses and enough besides to support them for a year. Five hundred acres of his land was located near Charlestown, in Clark county, Indiana, and another tract of two hundred and fifty acres was situated near Mitchell. He also owned a fuller mill, a distillery on the Bear Grass creek and held ten thousand dollars' worth of stock in the Bardstown Pike Company. He made the first writing paper that was made in Louisville and altogether was one of the most important men in Northern Kentucky during the days of his activity. He married a daughter of Frederick Geiger, who was with General Harrison at the battle of Tippecanoe and received a slug bullet in his body which he carried to his dying day. John, a brother of Jacob Hikes, was also in this battle though he seems to have escaped without injury. While William M. Gibson was teaching in the neighborhood, he became acquainted with Mary L. Hikes, a daughter of Jacob, to whom he was subsequently married, and to this union we are indebted for the subject of our sketch.

Jacob H. Gibson was born in 1841, on his father's farm four miles south of Charlestown, Indiana. His rearing and schooling did not differ materially from the average country boy of that day, his training being such as to fit him for agricultural pursuits. The Civil war broke out when he was about twenty years old and being patriotic in impulse and filled with youth's natural ardor he was anxious to become a soldier in the army that was to fight for the restoration of the Union. With this end in view he enlisted in Company D, Fourth Regiment, Indiana Cavalry, and with his command became a part of the forces engaged in the great task of re-opening the Mississippi. The Fourth Regiment served under Wilson, Rosecrans and Thomas, took part in the campaigning from Chattanooga to Atlanta and later joined the great march to the sea under Sherman, winding up at Macon, Georgia. Being discharged in July, 1865, Mr. Gibson returned to the old homestead to receive the plaudits of his friends and relatives. He engaged in farming, has met with success and at present owns one hundred acres of land, on which is located a comfortable farm home, surrounded by all that a reasonable man can desire.

In December, 1869, Mr. Gibson married Sallie, daughter of Adam and Mary (Lutz) Howard, representatives of old pioneer families. Her grandfather, George Howard, came to Kentucky in the latter part of the eighteenth century and as early as 1800 owned a flouring and saw mill at Fisherville. About the year 1832 he located in Charlestown township, Clark county, Indiana, where he owned a square mile of land. The Lutz family, from which Mrs. Gibson was descended on her mother's side, came from North Carolina about 1801 and were people of consequence in their day. Mr. and Mrs. Gibson have two children, Mrs. Stella Dettmer and Mrs. Carrie Lawrence, the latter a resident of Utica township, south of Watson.

JOHN HENRY GOEDEKER.

This representative farmer lives in section 19, within a distance of six miles of Borden, Clark county. He has already reached his sixty-third year and his life story tells of a career unremittingly spent in an effort to bring about the success which justly rewards his later years. His married life has brought him a large family, the greater portion of whom he has the pleasure of seeing prosperously settled in good circumstances. An early life not without its quota of vicissitudes and set-backs of a minor nature, from the experience of which he profited, enables him to appreciate the present years of tranquillity.

John H. Goedeker was born on the 13th of February, 1846, in Wood township, being the son of John H. and Mary K. (Richter) Goedeker. Both parents were natives of Hanover, Germany. John H. Goedeker, senior, came to America in the early thirties of the previous century. He sojourned in Baltimore, Maryland; Cincinnati, Ohio, and Lexington, Kentucky. His marriage is supposed to have taken place in Cincinnati, and he ultimately settled in Wood township, Clark county, in the early days of that locality. The elder Goedeker settled down as a farmer at the time of his settling in Wood township, and his death, after an industrious life, occurred at the age of sixty-five; his wife, our subject's mother, died about twenty years ago. Our subject is the second eldest of ten children, of whom he was the eldest boy. He became a shoemaker in his youth, learning the trade in Louisville about the time of the war. Sometime afterwards owing to ill health he quit his shoemaker's bench and embarked in general farming, which he has followed ever since. In the year 1870 his marriage with Mary J. Huber, the eldest daughter of Ignatius and Mary Huber, took place. Mrs. Goedeker was born in Wood township and had two brothers and five sisters. Her father was an old resident of the township, and her grandfather Huber was one of its earliest settlers.

Mrs. Goedeker has borne her husband eleven children. In regular order they were: Ignatius, born April 9, 1871; Francis, born May 27, 1873; Katherine, born March 11, 1875; John H., born August 18, 1877; Charles J., born October 26, 1879, died in infancy; Joseph H., born January 20, 1881, died July 10, 1882; Hannah M., born April 13, 1883; Henry Ludwig, born February 13, 1885; Edward H., born November 14, 1887; Florentine, born 27th of October, 1889, deceased; and Anna J., born December 12, 1891. Ignatius married Gertrude Schaffer, has five children, and lives in Charlestown. Frances married William Shalk, has one child, and lives at Otisco. Katherine is the wife of Peter Missie, has two children, and lives at Otisco. John H. married Frances Tomling, deceased. His second wife, Frances Missie, has borne him two children; they live at Charlestown. Hannah M. married Theodore Trindeitmer; they live in Carr township and have two children. Henry Ludwig lives in Charlestown and both Edward H. and Anna Josephine are still at home.

John H. Goedeker and his family belong to the Catholic faith and are members of St. John's church, in Wood township. In politics he is an unswerving Democrat and a man who has never aspired for political office; he was once elected Justice of the Peace for his district, but did not serve. Part of the land he now owns is part of the old Goedeker homestead. In his boyhood days the place was mostly timber land and he took a prominent part in improving the place. He has a substantial and cheerful home and enjoys the friendship and good will of his neighbors.

HARRY DODSWORTH PEET.

Among the emigrants who came over from England in the early forties was a young girl named Elizabeth Dodsworth. Her parents located at Cincinnati and there she subsequently met her "fate" in the person of a young countryman who reached America from his native England about 1845 and took up his abode in Louisville. In due time they became acquainted, learned to love each other and finally became man and wife. In 1853, not a great while after their union, John Peet, and wife crossed the river into Clark county, secured land in Silver Creek township, and in time had a good farm home, where they lived in comfort and reared their children in the paths of rectitude. They had five children in all, four of whom survive. One of them, Harry D., subject of this sketch, was born at Louisville, January 29, 1852, and he was still an infant when his parents decided to become residents of Indiana. He grew up on the farm in Silver Creek township and was taught by his father the value of industry as well as principles of morality, from which he has never departed during all the years of his subsequent life. After finishing in the local schools Mr. Peet became a pupil in the male school at Bardstown, Kentucky, where he spent two years in acquiring the ground work of an academical education. From this seminary he went to the Indiana State University at Bloomington, where he spent two more years in earnest application to the higher branches taught at that famous seat of learning. Not as yet satisfied he took a finishing course of a more practical nature in a commercial college at Cincinnati. After completing his studies Mr. Peet returned to his Clark county home and entered upon the serious affairs of life. One year was spent on a farm in Wabash county, but soon deciding that the old place was the best he came back to Clark county and located on a tract of land half a mile north of New Chapel. During the next twenty years Mr. Peet met with the usual ups and downs of a farmer's life, but on the whole has prospered and has considerable to show as the result of his toil and good management. He now owns three tracts of land, one of ninety-two acres and others of fifty-two and twenty-six acres, all of which is the fine agricultural soil for which Clark county is noted. In the early part of 1907 Mr. Peet built a new residence, half a mile west of New Chapel, and here he has since made his home. It is situated in the border of a natural grove near Watson, and is one of the cosiest country homes imaginable. Everything indicates taste and love of the beautiful as well as the ornamental and an old hospitality and cordiality of greeting to friends are characteristic of this pleasant abode.

On September 26, 1876, Mr. Peet married Ella, daughter of William Lentz, and they have three children. Mary Edith, the eldest, married Herbert Fry and has four children; she resides on a farm near New Chapel. John L., the eldest son, who recently married Mamie Childers, of West Virginia, is a civil and mining engineer employed by the government in the Phillipines.

Harry D., Jr., the youngest son, is at home with his parents. Mr. Peet is a member of the New Chapel Methodist Episcopal church and holds the position of secretary of the board of trustees, which makes him custodian of the old records that date back to early pioneer days. He has been a lifelong abstainer and earnest advocate of temperance, which convictions naturally made him a member of the Prohibition party, to whose cause he has devoted his best energies for years, without hope of other reward than the plaudits of a good conscience.

CHARLES EDWIN McKINLEY.

Charles Edwin McKinley is a well known member of the Indiana branch of the illustrious McKinley family, and a relation of our martyred President of that name. In common with the other members of his family he boasts a Scotch-Irish line of ancestry, in which the Scotch strain predominated. The family was of Scotch Covenanter origin and as the descendants of sturdy and religious men the family history in this country has upheld its ancient traditions. He is a business man of acknowledged ability and as a citizen he has not gone without recognition.

Charles Edwin McKinley was born at Pleasant Ridge, Wood township, four and a half miles south of Borden, in the vicinity of the old burial ground, on May 7, 1862. He was the son of William McKinley, and his wife, whose maiden name was Nancy Bell. Our subject's grandfather, Thomas McKinley, was a son of the head of the Indiana branch of the McKinley family.

Charles Edwin was educated in the public schools of Wood township and on arrival at the proper age began life as a farmer. For eighteen years he farmed and marketed farm and dairy produce and had a large array of private customers in New Albany. In this line he was very successful and he still retains his farm at Pleasant Ridge. In October, 1906, he established himself as head of the well known McKinley Hotel, at Borden, which was started some years before by Edwin McKinley. He also opened an adjoining store and carried on a general mercantile business. At the present time he conducts the McKinley Hotel, a livery stable, and a general store, on an extensive scale and in a first class manner. In addition he has been since 1907 president of the Borden State Bank.

Mr. McKinley married on the 17th of September, 1885, Jemima E. Bell, the daughter of well known townsfolk. Their marriage proved very happy and they have reared a family of four sons and four daughters, namely: Francis M., Sarah F. (known to her friends as Fannie); Jessie E., John H., Clarence D., Georgia E., Harry Goebel, and Iva Mildred McKinley. All are well educated and accomplished.

Our subject was a member of a family composed of one girl and ten boys. In politics he is a Democrat. He is reckoned as one of the leading men of his party in Clark county. He was Trustee of Wood township from 1895 to 1900.

EDGAR I. COOMBS.

As a successful agriculturist and trusted official Mr. Coombs has discharged ably and conscientiously the duties devolving upon him, and his aim has ever been to measure up to the highest standard of excellence.

Edgar I. Coombs was born near his present place of residence on the 1st day of January, 1852, and his entire life has been spent within the township over which he now exercises official jurisdiction. His childhood and youth were spent amid the peaceful rural scenes of his native place and as a farmer's boy he learned the lesson of industry and the respect for moral worth which had such potent influence in forming his character, and directing his life into proper channels. At the proper age he entered the public schools and after acquiring a knowledge of the branches taught therein, later he turned his attention to agricultural pursuits and in due time engaged in gardening, which he followed for several successive years. By industry, consecutive effort and excellent management he early laid a solid foundation for the future and so conducted his affairs as to accumulate a handsome property, owning at this time considerable valuable real estate in Utica township, and occupying a conspicuous place among the well-to-do men of his own community. After acquiring a sufficiency of this world's goods to place him in independent circumstances, he discontinued active pursuits and for some time past has been living practically a retired life, although still interested in agriculture and keeping in touch with the affairs of the times.

Mr. Coombs is a Democrat in politics and one of the leaders of his party in Utica township, being an able and judicious adviser in its councils and an earnest and influential worker in the ranks. He has always taken a keen interest in public questions and the great issues on which men and parties divide, and his opinions concerning the same, which are intelligent and well founded, carry weight and command respect. As a reward for valuable services rendered his party as well as by reason of his fitness for the place, he was elected in 1904, Trustee of Utica township, the duties of which office he has since discharged in an able and business like manner, creditable to himself and satisfactory to the people of his jurisdiction. An indication of his popularity is afforded by the fact of his having carried the election in the above year by the largest majority ever given a candidate in the township of Utica.

Mr. Coombs is a believer in revealed religion and for a period of twenty-five years has been a devoted member of the Christian church and an active worker in the congregation at Utica, in which for some years he has held the office of trustee. In his fraternal relations he is an Odd Fellow.

The domestic life of Mr. Coombs dates from December 7, 1880, when he was united in marriage with Catherine Oglesby, daughter of Thomas B. Oglesby, late of Jeffersonville township, the union being blessed with one child, a son by the name of Carl C. Coombs, a young man of high intellectual attainments. After completing the public school course young Coombs entered the Kentucky University at Lexington, where he made an enviable record as a student. On leaving that institution he took up the legal profession, and after a course in the law school of Louisvile was admitted, in 1906, to the Clark County Bar.

DANIEL MILBURN DOW.

It has been almost a century since the first member of the Dow family placed a foot upon the prolific soil of Wood township, Clark county. Daniel M. Dow now lives within a half mile from the spot where his eyes first opened upon the world. He is justly proud of his ancestors, who had no little part in the making of the history of this Republic, and than whom none were more closely identified with that of Southern Indiana. The blood of one who helped wrest his native land from the grasp of an oppresser surges through the veins of our subject.

Mr. Dow was born in Wood township, in 1854, his parents being Henry D. and Elizabeth (Beggerly) Dow. The former was born within the precincts of the same township in 1824, being the son of Henry and Mercy (Kinney) Dow, who came to Wood township in 1818. The former was born in Connecticut, May 13, 1794, his wife in the same state June 24, 1791. The grandfather of the subject died November 3, 1873, and the grandmother July 22, 1874. The death of his father occurred October 27, 1898, while his mother passed away May 25, 1902, having been born in Kentucky, September 26, 1823.

The children born to Henry and Mercy (Kinney) Dow were as follows: Hannah, born in Plainfield, Connecticut; Martha, born February 5, 1817, also in that city; Lucy, born July 30, 1818, on the way to Clark county, Indiana; Sallie, born September 20, 1820, in Clark county; Henry D., born April 19, 1824, Clark county; Rhoda, born September 13, 1826, Clark county; Lydia, born July 14, 1829, Clark county; Rebecca, born May 24, 1832, Clark county.

The following children were those of H. D. and Elizabeth (Beggerly) Dow: Sallie Ann, born August 11, 1845, died May 30, 1849; Lydia A., born January 10, 1848, died in infancy; Laura A., born January 22, 1850, married to John B. Goss, living in the state of Washington, has five children; Henry E., born June 2, 1852, died March 29, 1853; Daniel M. (subject), born March 1, 1854; George W., born July 17, 1856, married Anna Hurst, and lives in Davis county, has five children; Alice J., born September 28, 1858, married James Pearce, and lives in Clark county; Mary A., born May 5, 1862, married to Willard Todd, and lives in Wood township, has two children; Elizabeth C., born February 11, 1864, married N. S. Martin, of Washington county, and has five children.

H. D. Dow, father of these children, was a farmer and breeder of stock. He took an active part in politics and was a hard worker on election day, but never held or sought public office. He was an adherent of the Republican party, and he belonged to the Christian church, of which he was an elder for many years.

Daniel M. Dow was married to Philena B. Walker, of Washington county, November 9, 1876, the parents of the bride being James H and Phœbe Ann Walker. The following children were born to them: Stella B., born June 25, 1878, at home; Linna M., born April 30, 1881, and married James E. Cooley, had five children, and died in 1908; Mrs. Alice G. (Dow) Miller, living in Wood township; Mary B., born August 21, 1892, living at home.

Mr. Dow was educated in the common schools of Wood township. He is a Republican and a member of the Christian church. He spends very little time in politics, devoting his entire attention to farming and stock raising. He lives in the house that his grandfather built in 1838, and which was rebuilt by his father in 1878. The grandfather manufactured the brick with which he built the structure, and at that time it was considered one of the finest dwellings in the county. Mr. Dow has cleared a great deal of land himself, and made many improvements on his farm, which is in section 12.

Elizabeth Beggerly was the daughter of Jonathan B. and Casender Bailey. The former was born in Kentucky, August 2, 1802. The same state was the birthplace of his wife, the date thereof being April 3, 1804. Her parents emigrated to Clark county when she was but two years old. They were the parents of the following children: Elizabeth Ann, born September 26, 1823; Susan and Nancy (twins), born July 10, 1825; William P., born August 9, 1827; Eliza, born October 25, 1829; James O., born May 12, 1832; Isaac J., born December 29, 1833; Lewis and Melvina (twins), born August 20, 1836; Clinton, born November 29, 1839; Benona G., born April 6, 1842.

In the parlor door of the Dow home there is a notch where grandfather Dow was hanged by the neck until nearly dead by four highwaymen to make him divulge the hiding place of his money. As it was they secured from him the sum of sixteen hundred dollars and four horses. This was during the days of the Civil war, and the robbers, supposed to be part of Morgan's band, were captured later, and five hundred dollars of the stolen money and the horses returned to the owner. The Dows had the first grist mill in that part of Indiana, and one of the first steam mills. In the early days all of the flour was bolted by hand. An uncle of the subject was the owner of one of the first saw mills in the state.

JOHN MILTON HALLET.

The subject of this sketch lives upon the soil upon which he was born three quarters of a century ago, and in the house that his father built when John Milton Hallet was in the first year of his age. His parents penetrated the wilderness of Indiana when its trackless forests were filled with hostile Indians and when ferocious animals menaced them every step of the way, but with that dauntless courage which characterized the early settler, they had no thought of turning back, but pushed on to their journey's end.

John Milton Hallet, one of the oldest and most prosperous citizens of Wood township, Clark county, was born in Wood township, May 6, 1833, the son of Samuel and Cynthia (Geer) Hallet. His father was born August 6, 1790, in New London, Connecticut, and moved to Wood township in 1819, where he engaged in agricultural pursuits. He was known as "Squire" Hallet, having served as Justice of the Peace for many years, and was very active in politics. He was the second postmaster of the little town of Borden, then known as New Providence. Like his father, who had fought in the War of the Revolution, he was a soldier, serving his country well throughout the War of 1812. He was a most pronounced Whig, and died in Wood township in 1852. The mother of the subject, like her husband, was a native of Connecticut, being the daughter of Israel and Mary (Newton) Geer. The year of her birth was 1794, and she was married in 1814. The following children were born to the parents of the subject: William S. B., born in Connecticut, April 4, 1815, died in Borden, July 31, 1860; Margaret Wood, his wife, died March 16, 1841; George W., born in Connecticut, April 4, 1840, died at Borden, September 25, 1841; Thomas B., born in Clark county, May 28, 1821, died in Morrilton, Arkansas, 1868; Rhoda M., his wife, died January 24, 1848; Emeline, who was born in Clark county, August 20, 1823, died in New Albany in 1885; Henry, born in Clark county, January 21, 1826, died in November, 1853; Mary Ann, born July 13, 1828, died April 28, 1855; Elizabeth, born in Clark county, is still living near Borden, and is the wife of Robert Huston; John Milton, born May 6, 1833, still living in Wood township; Norman, born May 9, 1837, died October 28, 1841. The parents on both sides of the house had members of their families in the War of the Revolution and the War of 1812.

The father of the subject, in connection with his agricultural pursuits, engaged in the nursery business and set out one of the first orchards in the county, two or three of the old trees still standing upon the land upon which the subject lives. He was always foremost in school and church work, being a public-spirited man, and naturally very popular. As stated in the introductory of this sketch, the house where his son, John Milton Hallet, now resides, was built by him in 1834. He purchased the land in that year, cleared and improved it until it was considered one of the best pieces of farm land in the county. Mr. Hallet burned the brick to build his dwelling upon land close to where his son now lives.

John Milton Hallet was married to Cynthia Kelly June 14, 1855, and she died March 29, 1856, a little less than one year after she had become a bride. The result of this union was one child, who was born in 1856, and died in her infancy. On October 2, 1861, the widower contracted a second alliance, marrying Louisa Martin. Their children were Edwin Stanton, born September 4, 1862, who married Emma K. Pierce and now lives in St Louis, where he is chief engineer in the government service; Linnie E., born October 19, 1864, is living at home; Thomas B., born September 27, 1866, who is also at home, is a school teacher at Henryville, having graduated from the Michigan University, and has taught school for thirteen years; John M., Jr., born June 22, 1874, lives at home. The mother of these children died March 16, 1904.

Mr. Hallet started in life with a very scant education, but despite that handicap has been very successful. Besides being a farmer he is a breeder of fine Jersey cattle. He has a fine place, three miles and a half from Borden, and owns land in sections 5 and 7, living in the last named section. He is a member of the Christian church, and a Republican.

CAPTAIN JAMES T. DUFFY.

The career of the well remembered gentleman whose name forms the caption of this biographical memoir, was a strenuous and varied one, the distinction which he attained in different spheres of activity entitling him to honorable mention among the leading men and representative citizens of his day and generation in the county with which his life was so closely identified, and to him is due the credit of giving prestige to the family name, an old and honored one in the Emerald Isle, and adding to the brightness of an escutcheon which shines with peculiar luster in communities long noted for the high standing and distinguished achievements of its business and public men, and although his life record has been brought to a close by the inevitable fate that awaits all mankind, his influence still pervades the lives of a wide circle of friends and acquaintances who reverence his memory.

Capt. James T. Duffy was born in Cootehill, County Cavan, Ireland, in 1844, the son of Thomas and Ellen (Clark) Duffy, both natives of Ireland, where they were reared and married, and in which country the latter died about 1846, after becoming the mother of five children, four boys and one girl, of whom James T. was the youngest. Thomas Duffy was a druggist in the northern part of Ireland, maintaining in connection with his brother, a drug store in Cootehill, County Cavan. The latter came to New York about 1845, and a year later, after the death of his wife, Thomas Duffy came to the United States bringing his children to join their relative in the new world. They landed in New Orleans and ascended the Mississippi and Ohio rivers, intending to go to New York, but Thomas Duffy was stricken with typhoid fever and died in Cincinnati, leaving five orphan children, practically penniless and among strangers. The oldest child, Michael, who was then nineteen years of age, finally located in Pittsburg, Pennsylvania, where he secured work and became a very successful business man, eventually carrying on an extensive coal business. James T., the youngest of the children, lived in Cincinnati and later in Pittsburg with his brother, until he reached the age of sixteen years, having worked in the coal mines. When the war between the states came on he espoused the Union cause and showed his patriotism for his adopted country by enlisting in a Pennsylvania regiment, in which he faithfully served until the close of the war, proving himself a soldier of intrepid courage and gallantry although a mere youth. He was a bugler, but was found in the thickest of many sanguinary engagements, always ready to obey the orders of his commanding officer. He saved all his wages during these years, and appropriated the same to the laudable undertaking of securing an education to which he directed his attention after being mustered out of the army. That he possessed a great amount of fortitude and a spirit which no obstacle could daunt, is shown in his efforts to obtain a mental training that would guide him to subsequent success in later years. Devoting ten hours a day to the arduous duties that befall the lot of a miner, he gave but five hours to sleep, spending the remainder of the twenty-four in study. This careful application to miscellaneous subjects, coupled with an innate capacity for obersvation and assimilation, rendered him a well educated man, and his conversation was at once learned and interesting.

Having made trips to Jeffersonville on tow boats in connection with the movement of coal he observed the splendid advantages here of future business possibilities, and in 1866 in partnership with Patrick Bonner, he established a coal business in Jeffersonville. They engaged in shipping coal and holding quantities on the river for the local market. Being far-sighted, able to see with remarkable accuracy the outcome of commercial transactions, Mr. Duffy saw the advantages of obtaining possession of landings along the river and as soon as practicable bought different ones. The business of this firm grew to

44

extensive proportions, owing principally to the careful management and wise discretion exercised by Mr. Duffy, this firm handling practically all the coal that came down the Ohio river for distribution in this locality. They also engaged in towing on the river, which necessitated the ownership of many boats, some of which they purchased, but constructed the major part themselves and became very wealthy in due course of time. In 1881 Mr. Duffy purchased the landing known as the "Pumpkin Patch," which extends quite a distance along the water front, about two miles above Port Fulton. At that time Mr. Duffy also purchased about one hundred acres of land at this point, on which he made his home. later buying more land, developing a very fine farm of over two hundred acres. Everything about the place showed thrift and prosperity, being highly improved and under an excellent state of cultivation. Much stock of fine quality and variety was to be found here, and a magnificent dwelling was erected in the midst of attractive surroundings, one of the most attractive country homes in the state. It is modern in every detail, commodious. commanding a beautiful view of the Ohio river and it has always been a place where the numerous friends of the family delighted to gather, where free hospitality and good cheer ever prevailed and culture and refinement ever centered.

Besides his extensive farming and coal interests Captain Duffy also managed other large enterprises with that soundness of judgment and wise foresight that stamped him as no mediocre man of affairs, but truly a wizard of finance. with remarkable ability as an organizer and promoter. In the year 1901 he established the sand business at Louisville, now carried on by his sons in a manner which stamps them as worthy descendants of their father and men to whom the future augurs many notable achievements in the world of business. This industry grew to extensive proportions, and Captain Duffy acquired considerable property in Louisville, owning a number of business blocks in connection with other property and becoming well known to business circles on both sides of the river, by whom he was regarded as a most ex traordinary business man, very frugal, but generous toward his fellows. He extended a helping hand to many and had never a word of criticism for anyone, in fact, he often did favors for those who had shown him no quarter in his earlier years of business struggles. He was a great home man. During business hours the captain was deeply absorbed in whatever he had in hand, but he left his business cares and worries behind when he closed his office and after reaching his cozy home enjoyed to the utmost the seclusion and quiet of his family and home environment, which was always harmonious and congenial.

In later years Captain Duffy became a large stockholder in the Louisville Ice Company and he established the ice plant in Jeffersonville. He at one time owned large interests in French Lick Springs, Indiana, but sold out to Thomas

Taggart, of Indianapolis. He was regarded as one of the leading and best known river men in the country, at one time having control of the coal harbor business at this point and at the time of his death he had numerous interests, including the Cincinnati Packet Company, the Louisville & Evansville Packet Company, and the Louisville & Jeffersonville Ferry Company. He was also interested in the Jeffersonville City Railway.

Captain James T. Duffy was always a man of fine personal appearance, enjoying good health, principally due, no doubt, to his temperate habits, never using tobacco or liquors in any form, and his lamented death was untimely, having been sick but a short time. He was taken to the hospital at Rochester, Minnesota, where he died from the effects of an operation, November 24, 1905, his demise being a matter of keen regret throughout the country, newspapers all over the United States giving eulogistic and extended notices of his death. His funeral was from the St. Augustine church in Jeffersonville.

An interesting chapter in the history of Captain Duffy is that bearing on his happy domestic life, which began September 21, 1871, when he was united in the bonds of wedlock with Miss Nora V. Robinson, of Jeffersonville; the ceremony having been performed in the rectory of the cathedral in Louisville, the Rev. Father Bouchet, subsequently vicar-general, officiating. Mrs. Duffy was the daughter of Hamilton Robinson, a sketch of which well known pioneer appears in another part of this volume. Eight children blessed the union of Mr. and Mrs. James T. Duffy, two of whom are deceased, Sarah and Mary; John Thomas and James Thomas are still members of the family circle; Nora is the wife of Dr. C. F. C. Hancock, of Jeffersonville, and Marguerite Fay is the wife of O. H. Wathen, of Louisville; James Hamilton married Miss Emma Howard; Leta married Dr. C. W. Shropshire, of Birmingham, Alabama. Mrs. Duffy is a woman of gracious personality and has long been a leader in social circles in Jeffersonville, where she is held in high esteem as are also her children, whose daily lives reflect the wholesome home environment and uplifting influence in which they were reared. She always took a great interest in the affairs of her husband and much of his business prosperity was no doubt due to her encouragement and counsel. She took an especial interest in the development of their fine farm and presides with rare dignity over the attractive Duffy residence.

James T. Duffy was a devout Catholic all his life, and in his political relations he supported the Democratic party, although he never sought public office, preferring to devote his entire attention to his private business affairs and to his home. However, his interest in the welfare of Jeffersonville and community was deep seated and abiding and he gave liberally toward the support of all movements calculated to improve the material, social and moral interests of the same.

By reference to the foregoing review the life of Captain Duffy appears

to have been a very strenuous one, filled to repletion with duty ably and faithfully performed and characterized throughout by a devotion to principle, above
reproach and a sense of honor defying adverse criticism. He has a capacity
for large undertakings and his eminently interesting career not only com-
mended him to the people of his own county and state, but gave him a reputation much more than state wide and an honorable name among the leading
men of his day. He was a man of fine sensibilities and a high sense of justice
and honor, it being his aim to be on the right side of every question with
which he had anything to do and to lose sight of self or selfish interests in
the noble endeavor of striving for the greater good of the greater number.
Broad-minded, public-spirited, fervidly patriotic and taking liberal views of
men and affairs he impressed his individuality upon the community and county as an enterprising, large-hearted, progressive American citizen of the best
type, while among his immediate friends he will always be remembered as a
man without pretense and a courteous gentleman whose integrity and loyalty
would bear the closest scrutiny.

COLUMBUS J. BOTTORFF.

That he has attained a competency through his individual efforts is naturally a matter of pride with Mr. Bottorff. His opportunities to store his mind
with knowledge were limited, but he procured a fair education in the township
schools, and early in life began to perform the arduous duties that devolve
upon the boy who is reared on a farm. Mr. Bottorff has been very successful
in agricultural pursuits, his crops, as a rule, being abundant. He is a native
of Jackson county, where he was born February 13, 1851, coming to Jeffersonville with his parents when but an infant. He was married long after
he reached manhood's estate, taking unto himself a wife in May, 1893.

The father of the subject, William Jackson Bottorff, was born in Clark
county, near Charlestown, while his mother was a native of Kentucky. There
were four children besides himself, William E., Ida, who married David Hostetter, and is now dead; Samantha, wife of Wallace James, and Lily, wife of
John Collins.

The land owned by C. J. Bottorff consists of one hundred and fifty acres,
and he engages in general farming. He is a Seventh Day Adventist, and politically a Democrat. He never held office, and is not a member of any
fraternal order.

Mr. Bottorff is a very genial man of sterling honesty, and in his dealings
with his neighbors observes the golden rule. He is thoroughly practical and
has broad views upon all subjects in which the people of today are interested.

WILLIAM ADAMS.

Owing to the great number of changes that take place in the population of our counties it is now only occasionally that we come upon a person of advanced age that has been born upon native soil. One, however, is to be found in William Adams, who was born in Clark county, this state, on May 16, 1836. His ancestry includes in its roll some of the sturdy settlers of Kentucky, where were born his parents, Martin and Jane (Davis) Adams, who were among the earliest pioneers of Clark county. They were staunch Presbyterians and each lived to the advanced age of ninety-two years. Of this family there are still surviving besides William two brothers and one sister, the brothers living at this time in Indiana and the sister in Denver, Colorado.

The domestic life of Mr. Adams has not been one of the uninterrupted smoothness inasmuch as his home has been repeatedly invaded by visits from the death angel. His first wife, Charlotte Kisler, was not permitted to live to see her children grow to maturity, but five of these are still living. The three children of the second wife, Sarah S. Swartz, have also joined their mother in the great beyond. Following this Mr. Adams was married to a sister of his second wife, Eliza Swartz, after whose death he was joined in marriage to Sarah Heuser. The children now living refered to above are Anna Belle Scott, Jennie Gilmore, Elizabeth Ogg, Martin A. and Minnie Smith.

Mr. Adams is well known as a splendid business man and an aggressive, public-spirited citizen. He has been called upon by his fellow citizens to serve them in many public capacities. In 1880 he served as Township Assessor and filled the office in a praiseworthy manner. In 1895 he demonstrated his ability as a party figure, assisting to bring about a complete change in the political complexion of county affairs, the usual Democratic majorities being wiped out and the county offices placed into the hands of the Republicans. In waging this fight Mr. Adams used as his instrument the columns of the New Albany Tribune.

Mr. Adams is a loyal Methodist in his religious affiliations, as were also his wives. He has for a long term of years been a most faithful and helpful worker in promoting the growth and progress of church life in the community. He has been a member of the board of trustees of the New Chapel Methodist church since 1883, and served as president of the same for twenty years. He was also president of the building committee, which constructed one of the finest church edifices in Clark county in 1883, every dollar for the same passing through his hands, for which a strict and satisfactory account was given.

The farm now occupied by Mr. Adams consists of one hundred and thirty-one acres, and has been his home since 1857. Two of his children, Mrs. Gilmore and Mrs. Scott, occupy nearby farms to that of their father. In addition to this farm Mr. Adams owns tracts of land in Utica and Washington townships. He is a man well preserved, is keenly alert to the questions of the day. He has lived to see many changes in the community where he has maintained his residence for over fifty years. There are only two heads of families now occupying the same houses they did in 1857 in his neighborhood. He recalls the days before the use of coal for fuel on the river. Andrew Van Dike, a pioneer wood hauler, furnished the ferry with its fuel in those days, and in after years assisted Mr. Adams in threshing grain.

AMOS B. STACY.

Among the well-to-do and progressive farmers of Clark county, Indiana, must be mentioned Amos B. Stacy, who operates a farm of two hundred and forty-two acres in Jeffersonville township. He was born in the city of Jeffersonville in 1844, and received his early education in the public schools of that town. He is the son of Amos B. and Elizabeth N. Stacy, both born "on the banks," as they say, of Southern Indiana. The family consisted of thirteen children, a number which, whether "lucky" or not, is one that is rarely equalled by the families of the present day. Amos B. was the second in the order of birth, and nine of the number are still living. The names of the children are herewith appended: Hulda, wife of John W. Crandall; Margaret, wife of David R. House; Jonas D., unmarried and now in Colorado; William O. and John H., the latter in Cripple Creek, Colorado; Edward D., living at Upper Sandusky, Ohio; Katie A., wife of James H. Walker, and both now deceased; Anna D., deceased, wife of John C. Enteman; Emma R., deceased; Howard N., living in Albuquerque, New Mexico; Augusta, deceased; Gaudaloupe V., in Los Angeles, California.

Mr. Stacy after finishing his schooling in the Jeffersonville schools, decided to leave the city for life on the farm and brought with him the experience and training obtained through close contact with business affairs in the town. He made use of his training in broadening his outlook on life, and in fully preparing himself for the task of operating a farm in such a way as to bring about profitable results. In this he has demonstrated his ability to measure up to the requirements, for he has been eminently successful as a farmer. He has made a close study of the problems of the soil and understands fully how to manage the rotation of crops so that the best results may be obtained with the least exhaustion of the soil. In conjunction with this he has developed good judgment in the selection of seeds and their varieties, demonstrating that this is a very important factor in achieving successful production.

Mr. Stacy is a member of the Methodist denomination and contributes

willingly to its support, maintaining at all times a quiet and unassuming attitude. Politically he adheres to the tenets of the Democratic party, but does
not place party above principle. From 1886 to 1888 he served as Supervisor,
but beyond this has not consented to run for public office of any kind, preferring rather to act his part as a citizen by ruling his life in harmony with the
requirements of unimpeachable patriotism.

FRANK KEISER.

Mr. Keiser is now reaping the reward of a career of industry, having
embarked upon the battle of life with little or no capital, and now being the
owner of one of the most productive truck farms in Clark county. Landing
on the shores of America from a foreign country, without even a smattering
of the English language he was confronted with many difficulties, but he had
come to the new world filled with a determination to better his condition, and
persevered until he had realized his ambition to become a land owner.

Frank Keiser was born August 31, 1855, at Frankfort-on-the-Main,
Germany, and came to this country when in the twenty-fourth year of his age,
after having served three years in the army of the Fatherland. He was the
son of Wilhelm and Marie (Hoch) Keiser. The former was also a native of
Frankfort-on-the-Main, while the mother of the latter was born at Naples-
town, Germany. Frank Keiser attended the schools of his native country for
several years, and then learned the butcher's trade, at which he worked in
Baltimore shortly after his arrival in the United States. He did not remain
in the East long, however, but started out in the direction of the setting sun,
having been informed that there were great opportunities for energetic young
men in the Middle West. For twenty years he lived in Louisville, being engaged in the meat business, but he never lost his desire to become a cultivator
of the soil, and nine years ago he purchased his present place, which is located
on the middle road, near Jeffersonville, and which consists of one hundred
acres, and is very productive.

Frank Keiser was married in 1886, in Louisville, to Emma Foreman, of
Jasper, Indiana. Mr. and Mrs. Keiser are the parents of six children, Charles,
William, Maggie, Lily, Rose and Frank. The first named is a resident of
Kansas, while the others make their home with their parents. The subject is
a member of the German Lutheran church, and he is very faithful in his atten-
ance upon religious services, as are also the members of his family. Politically
he is a Democrat, but does not actively participate in politics, nor has he ever
filled any public office. Mr. Keiser and his wife are highly esteemed by their
neighbors.

HARVEY JOINER.

Lovers of art and readers of pages devoted to this subject in the press will readily recognize in this name one of the best known painters of the Middle West. From earliest boyhood Harvey Joiner developed a taste for art and a most commendable ambition to succeed as a painter which no discipline could repress and no misfortune entirely check. By persistence and the exercise of his natural talent he not only achieved a fair measure of fame but success in a financial way, though as usual with artists perhaps not equal to his deserts. He is a son of Oscar and Elizabeth (Tophouse) Joiner, the former of whom located in Charlestown in 1840 and engaged in the cooperage business. Harvey Joiner was born in Charlestown, Clark county, Indiana, April 8, 1852, and in due time beame a pupil at 'Possum Trot school near his native place. Even at this early period the innate inclination manifested itself in pictures drawn on the blackboard or any other receptive surface, the teacher being unable to curb the irrepressible instinct or interest the embryonic artist in routine studies.

As a boy he made his own colors from poke-berry juice, milkweed, wash bluing, pot-black and pounded grass, which combination he used like water colors. His first effort in oil was made at Artic Springs, of the Louisville water works, painted on a piece of pine board. This crude sketch he gave away and lost track of, but he afterward regretted its loss, and would now prize it highly as a souvenir of his early days. About this time he held out between two opinions, being undecided between a theatrical and artistic career, though he had some ability in both lines. The love of drawing finally prevailed and he abandoned all ambition to shine in the Court of Thespis. His first serious efforts consisted in drawing sketches of negro characters dancing Jim Crow on the plantations of the South. Here he spent three years sketching and steamboating, the beautiful surroundings giving many ideas for the accumulations of material for subsequent landscape and woodland scenes. In 1873 Mr. Joiner made his first serious sketch in oil and located the next year in St. Louis, where he began painting portraits with Hoffman, the noted German artist. Later he established a studio in the Courier-Journal building at Louisville, Kentucky, which, for twenty-seven years was a mecca for the art loving world. Visitors came for miles to attend his annual exhibitions which did much to cultivate a taste for art in the South. His methods are peculiar to himself. He paints most of his woodland scenes at a single sitting, first making a sketch in brown and laying all color upon another until the entire picture is completed. He has made a special study of sunlight effect and his beautiful beechwoods scenes give a distinction to Mr. Joiner's work that is not equalled by the work of any other artist. The daily press of Louisville has teemed with praise of his contributions to the world of art and his worth as a leader in educating the public taste. His first figure picture, six by ten feet, was completed in 1877, the same being a life-size painting in oil and now hangs in the Christian church at Utica, Indiana, the subject presenting "Ruth Gleaning in the Field of Boaz." It was a very creditable effort though done in his early career. Since 1896, when he exhibited at the Nashville Centennial Exposition, Mr. Joiner has held annual exhibitions of his landscape paintings and of late has confined his attention exclusively to painting beechwood scenes in Kentucky and Indiana. After having resided in Jeffersonville since 1864, Mr. Joiner located in Louisville in 1902. On August 29, 1907, his studio was entirely destroyed by fire and ninety-eight pictures were consumed in the flames, which, in part, consisted of an accumulation of thirty years. Practically all the sketches he had done from his boyhood, including newspaper and magazine notices, and a mailing list of five thousand names including patrons from San Francisco to New York, were irreparably lost. Among the paintings lost was a marine scene of compelling interest, showing a limp and lifeless figure of a beautiful girl in the semi-nude left by the receding tide on the barren rocks. Mr. Joiner's studio is at present located in the Equitable Building, Louisville, Kentucky.

In 1878 Mr. Joiner married Nettie Kane, daughter of Capt. John W. Kane, both now deceased. Two children were born to this union, Mrs. Earl Lewman, a resident of Charlestown township, Clark county, and Harvey, an only son, being employed at Denver, with the Colorado Fuel & Iron Company, also the Rocky Mountain Timber Company. He inherited his father's artistic temperament but has made no serious effort to develop his talents along that line. In the last fifteen years Mr. Joiner's paintings have become widely known and are owned by art patrons in all the principal cities of the United States.

JOHN TALLEY.

John Talley was born in Columbia, South Carolina, February 14, 1833. His father, Stephen Talley, was born in England, and came to America when still a young man. After arriving here he married Eliza Brown, who was born in South Carolina, and was of German extraction.

Stephen Talley deserves mention as one of our country's patriotic sons, who, although English born, nevertheless took up arms in the American cause during the War of 1812, and fought nobly and well in behalf of the land of his adoption. He was a member of Company C, of the Second South Carolina Infantry, under the command of Captain Hancock.

When John Talley was seven years old his parents removed to Georgia and there he grew to manhood. He received such education as the community afforded, being reared in Gordon county, near the city of Rome. After reaching maturity he learned the blacksmith's trade, and continued to make his home in the vicinity of Rome until after the close of the war.

Mr. Talley participated in the Civil war, and, being a resident of the South, his views were in harmony with the cause of the Confederacy. He became a member of the Sixty-fifth Georgia Infantry under the command of that intrepid and invincible hero of Southern soil, Stonewall Jackson. For some time also Mr. Talley was employed at Bragg's Arsenal No. 2, and gave to the cause he espoused the best service that he could command.

The war being concluded Mr. Talley removed from his Southern home and took up his quarters at Jeffersonville, Indiana. In 1858 he was joined in marriage to Emily Jane Conoly, who was a most estimable companion and mother. She departed this life in April, 1908. To this union were born eight children, four of whom still survive. They are: John, who was married to Maggie Houston; Eugene, being still at home; Dennis, who became the husband of a Miss Smith; and Effie, who is also at home.

Mr. Talley holds liberal views on all religious questions and believes in a large charity for all mankind. Politically his inclinations favor the Democratic cause, his convictions being at all times his guide. He holds no prejudice toward those whose opinions do not coincide with his own, but he adheres strictly to what seems to him to be the right attitude to take on all public questions. He has had no desire to fill public office of any kind. He is a Mason, having his membership in the Clark Lodge, No. 40, at Jeffersonville.

DANIEL J. BOWER.

Upon a comfortable and well equipped farm in Jefferson township, Clark county, Indiana, lives the interesting character whose name forms the caption of this biography. Mr. Bower was born near New Washington on the 3d of January, 1830. He was the son of Daniel and Elizabeth (Hostetter) Bower, the former having been born in North Carolina, in 1800, and the latter in Kentucky, in 1802.

Our subject's father was a man of considerable daring and possessed great skill as a rifleman. The exigencies of the times created a great demand for men of that type to oppose the hostilities of the Indians, and Mr. Bower took an active part in the Black Hawk war and after his death his widow, who survived him. received a pension in recognition of Mr. Bower's services to the country. He was long connected with the militia.

Mr. Bower attended the district schools of the neighborhood and also the Charlestown school when conducted by Zebulon Sturgus. In addition to this he benefited by the rigid discipline and the stern duties of his daily life, and grew to manhood with a good educational equipment.

On December 22, 1859, Mr. Bower was united in marriage to Elizabeth Walford, who was born on the 7th of June, 1834. The house in which she was born stood upon the site of the present court-house in Louisville. She received a good general education in the district schools of Indiana and Kentucky and has proved to be a most estimable companion and competent mother. Her family of six children are: Minnie Alice, Annie Alene, Virginia Elizabeth, George Franklin (deceased), Catherine May and Cora Lee.

As a member of the community Mr. Bower has commanded the confidence and trust of his neighbors and friends. For many years he has been Justice of the Peace and filled the place with credit and with entire satisfaction to his constituents. He also served as Deputy Assessor for two terms. He and his family are members of the Christian church and are held in high esteem by the membership on account of their loyalty to their faith and the sincerity of their daily life. In politics Mr. Bower affiliates with the Democratic party. He takes great pride in his family and has given his children all the opportunities that could be afforded. Three of his daughters, Virginia, Catherine and Cora, graduated from the Jeffersonville high school and later taught school. They are now married and each is presiding over a comfortable home.

AARON P. SCOTT.

A five mile drive to the east from Jeffersonville brings the visitor to the well kept and attractive country residence of Aaron P. Scott, whose family is one of the best known in this section of the county and is one that has been connected in a most intimate manner with the advancement and progress of the community along all important lines.

Mr. Scott was born in Utica township on the 22d day of March, 1856, the son of William Wascomb and Mary (Seamster) Scott, the former a native of Utica township anl the latter of Marion county, Kentucky. They were people whom everybody was glad to have for neighbors, being at once obliging and free, lending a helping hand without question or hesitancy whenever opportunity afforded.

Mr. Scott received such education as the schools of the neighborhood afforded, but, not stopping with this, he has broadened his outlook on the affairs of life until he is a recognized authority on all such topics as are of general interest to the citizens of any community. He has long been officially connected with the township schools, having at all times taken a deep interest in its educational affairs, and he has always stood for progress. At the present time he is a member of the County Council, and is regarded as an invaluable counsellor in the disposition of the perplexing problems which so often confront that body.

Mr. Scott was married to Anna Belle Adams, daughter of William and Charlotte Adams, sketch of whom will be found on another page of this work. Mrs. Scott's paternal grandfather, Col. Martin Adams, was a man of considerable note in the early days of the Middle West. When sixteen years of age he was sent to the frontier as a scout and guardsman against the Indian foes. Many tribes were hostile and treacherous and a high degree of skill and courage were necessary to successfully combat the foe on their own ground. According to the customs of the times, made necessary by circumstances, he dressed in buckskin trousers which, when once put on, were worn for something like six months. In the case of Col. Martin Adams, he wore his buckskin trousers as long as his growth would permit, hence when longer wear became impossible, on account of size, he submitted to the odd operation of having his trousers cut from his body.

Mr. and Mrs. Scott have become the parents of three children: Addie, born on the 25th day of August, 1880, became the wife of Carl C. Canter, who is connected with the management of the Jeffersonville Reformatory. She died December 3, 1908, leaving two children, Frances Marie and Ruth Estella; Lottie May was born on the 2d day of January, 1888, and William Martin first saw the light on January 3, 1898.

Mr. Scott affiliates with the Democratic party, but takes his stand on the principles of justice and fairness, believing with Rutherford B. Hayes that "He serves his party best who serves his country best." He and his wife are loyal supporters of the Methodist church, and are well known for their charitable spirit.

HENRY HANKA.

Mr. Hanka is entitled to rank among the successful self-made men of Wood township, Clark county, who, by energy and enterprise, have wrought wisely and well not only to make a comfortable home and surroundings for themselves but also to make this one of the leading localities in the state.

Henry Hanka was born in Floyd county, Indiana, May 5, 1869, the son of Benjamin and Caroline (Stumbler) Hanka. The former was born in Franklin county, Indiana, and he came to Floyd county when about sixteen years old, where he has since resided. He has been a cooper by trade, but he has followed farming for many years and is still living on a farm in Floyd county, being known as one of the pioneer berry growers of Floyd county, in fact, he was one of the first growers of small fruit in this part of the state. Caroline Stumbler was born about 1838, in Floyd county, the daughter of Jacob and Elizabeth (Martin) Stumbler. She died about 1880. Henry Hanka had eight brothers and one sister, only five of whom are living.

The subject received his education in the common schools of Floyd county. He has been a farmer and fruit grower all his life, having started life for himself when he was married, May 17, 1904, to Elnora Martel, of New Albany, daughter of Conrad, and Mary (Steller) Martel. Her parents live in New Albany, their family consisting of seven children, five girls and two boys. Mr. Martel is a shoemaker by trade.

Mr. Hanka devotes considerable time and attention to the growing of vegetables and all kinds of garden truck, besides fruit growing and general farming, and he makes a great success of all these lines, always finding a ready market for what he produces. He has a beautiful home five miles from Borden. He has been living in Clark county for several years. He is a bright young German, well known in this community, known as one of the extensive truck and berry growers. He has always been a Democrat and is a Catholic in his religious belief, belonging to St. John's church, in Wood township.

Benjamin Hanka, father of the subject, was born April 15, 1842, in Franklin county, Indiana, the son of Joseph Hanka, who was born in Germany, and who came to the United States when a young man. He married Elizabeth Burman, who was also a native of Germany. Joseph Hanka was about forty years old when he died, in Franklin county. His wife died in Louisville, Kentucky, at the age of fifty-seven years. The following children were born to Mr. and Mrs. Benjamin Hanka: Joseph, who died at the age of two years; John, Henry, of this review; Jacob, Elizabeth died when twelve years old, Benjamin, Jr., Antone, Frank was five years old at his death, Adam and Lena.

Benjamin Hanka was the originator of strawberry culture in this section of the country. He started in the strawberry business here about twenty-six or twenty-seven years ago. He came to Floyd county about forty-one years ago and has resided in this locality ever since. He is a Demorat, a Catholic and a well known and highly respected man in the county as are all the Hankas.

MATTHIAS FISCHER.

Among the highly honored veterans of the war between the states and the prosperous farmers of Wood township, Clark county, the subject of this sketch deserves to be enrolled.

Matthias Fischer was born October 28, 1837, at Oberstedten, by Frankfort-on-the-Main, near Homburstch, Forderha, Germany, the son of Matthias F. and Elizabeth (Rocke) Fischer, the former having been born in 1800 in the same place as the subject. He was a miller in the Fatherland before coming to the United States in 1853, having brought his family with him by way of New York, direct to Clark county, Indiana. He bought land in Wood township, where he farmed until his death, October 5, 1871. He went back to Germany twice on business after coming to the United States. He often told of his first trip to this country, which was made in an old-fashioned sailing vessel, which took sixty-four days to make the trip. He was a hard working man and made all the improvements on the two hundred acres of land which he secured in this township. He devoted his life in this country to farming and stock raising, exclusively. He was the only member of his family who ever came to America. He was a well known man in Clark county and had a good business. He transported most of his farm products to Louisville where he found a ready market. He was a well educated man, a Democrat and a member of the Reformed Lutheran church. His parents died when he was very young.

Matthias Fischer went to Louisville, Kentucky, soon after he arrived in America and learned the cooper's trade, at which he worked until 1862. He had received a fairly good education in Germany, but never attended school in this country. He espoused the cause of the National government during the dark days of the Civil war and enlisted in 1862, in the Twelfth Indiana Battery, Heavy Artillery, and served faithfully until the close of the war. He was in the battles of Huntsville, Alabama, and was at Fort Negley for about nine months. His next engagement was at Chickamauga, then Missionary Ridge and later the battle of Nashville. He lost his hearing in one ear from the concussion of the heavy guns and he gets a pension from the government which he so ably served.

Mr. Fischer was married after his return from the army, in 1865, on November 23d, to Helen Hooffman, who was born June 3, 1843, the daughter of Jacob and Margaret (Dietz) Hooffman. Mrs. Fischer was born in Niederdorfelten, Germany, and she came to the United States in 1865. Her parents died when she was young.

Following are the names of the brothers and sisters of the subject: Christian, born October 10, 1825, died February 5, 1894; Elizabeth, born November 29, 1827; Louis, born February 22, 1832, died August 24, 1905; John E., born December 22, 1834, died February 12, 1900; Frederick, born October 4, 1835, died August 25, 1863; Henry lives in Wood township; Phillip is deceased; Mary, born in 1839, lives in Ohio; Eliza, born in 1838, lives in Shelby county, Kentucky.

Four children have been born to Mr. and Mrs. Matthias Fischer, as follows: Elizabeth, born August 14, 1866, married Lemuel Fordyce, who is deceased; she is living in Wood township. Her children are George and Augusta. Augusta, the second child, was born January 18, 1869, married Christopher Miller, and they have two sons, Edwin and Lawrence, and they are living in Harrison county, Indiana. George M., who was born January 14, 1873, is married and has these children, Nellie, Jacob, Glen, Bertha and Leno. Emma, born January 7, 1879, married Nicolas Miller; they also live in Harrison county and are the parents of one child, named Lillian. George M. married Jennie Fordyce. They live in Wood township.

Mr. Fischer went to farming after his marriage on sixty-five acres of land, in Wood township, section 8, and he developed a good farm, being a diligent worker and a careful manager. He has made a success of his agricultural and stock raising pursuits and is now living retired in Borden, having ceased active business operations five years ago. In his political relations he supports the principles of the Republican party. He is a member of the Methodist Episcopal church. He belongs to Mitchell Post, No. 424, Grand Army of the Republic, of Borden. His is a fine old German family.

ABRAHAM FRY.

Mr. Fry has long been considered one of the leading pioneer agriculturists of Clark county, his farm being a model in every respect and under his management it has been developed from the rudely improved virgin ground to a most highly productive place, which has from year to year yielded a splendid income, so that our subject has laid up a competency for his old age.

Abraham Fry was born in Utica township, Clark county, Indiana, in 1833, the date of his birth falling on September 17th, having been reared near where he now resides, for, unlike many of his early contemporaries who left their parental roof-tree early in life to seek precarious fortunes in other states, Mr. Fry decided to remain at home. His father, John Fry, a native of Kentucky, was a man of influence and high integrity. The mother of the subject, known as Sarah Swartz in her maidenhood, was reared in Utica township, where she attended school and where she married John Fry in about 1822, and became the mother of twelve children, five sons and seven daughters, of whom Abraham is the third living child.

Abraham Fry spent his boyhood days working on his father's farm and attending the public schools, where he applied himself in such a manner as to gain a good education, which has later in life been supplemented by home reading. Not being in position to leave his home and business to take part in the great Civil war, but feeling that it was necessary to do what he could in assisting to suppress the rebellion, Mr. Fry hired a substitute who went to the front in his stead. He began farming on his father's place, having purchased his present farm about 1856, therefore it has received his care and attention for over a half century, during which time it has been carefully managed so that the soil is as productive today as when he first assumed control of it, and as the years passed by the place assumed a more pleasing aspect as to improvements in a general way. It consists of one hundred and ninety-eight acres, worth two hundred dollars per acre. On it stand many substantial and convenient buildings, including a very fine and nicely furnished residence, which ranks well with the best of farm houses in the county.

Mr. Fry has been twice married, his first marriage having been solemnized with Sarah E. Parks, and to this union two children were born, one of whom, Floyd J., is now living in 1908. His second marriage was with Margaret A. Mann, in 1860, to whom the following children have been born: Horace, deceased; Mrs. Emma P. Johnson, Frank A., Mrs. Cora B. Graham, Mrs. Ethel M. Jacobs, Walter T., Mrs. A. Redding, Harry J. and Mrs. Grace M. Richardson.

Mr. Fry is a Democrat in his political beliefs, being well grounded in the principles of his party, and while he has never sought the emoluments of public office he has ever been ready to assist in placing the ablest men possible in the local offices where the public weal is to be considered. In his religious relations he is a faithful member of the Methodist church, having long taken a delight in this denomination. Fraternally Mr. Fry is a Mason, being a member of the Knights Templar, and judging from his daily walk one would conclude very readily that he believes in carrying out the sublime doctrines of this worthy order and the creed of his church as well, for, being a representative of one of the oldest and best families of Clark county he has ever sought to be worthy to bear their honored name.

JAMES K. GIBSON.

One of the well known farmers of Wood township, Clark county, Indiana, is James K. Gibson, who was born here November 15, 1846, and it has been Mr. Gibson's good fortune to be able to spend his life on the old homestead where he still resides. He is the son of James and Hannah (Peck) Gibson, the former having been born in Carr township, this county, in 1817. The parents of the subject's father came from North Carolina. They were living in Clark county at the time of the Pigeon Roost massacre, when the whole settlement went to Fort Clark, in this county, for protection. Grandfather Gibson was an Indian fighter himself. He often repaired to an old blockhouse not far from where the subject now lives. James K. Gibson's grandparents were of Scotch-Irish descent. Grandfather Burrell Gibson and one brother, William, came to America together, the former coming to Clark county, Indiana, being among the first white settlers.

James Gibson died in 1889. He was a farmer and stock raiser and a man of influence in his community, many of his sterling qualities having been inherited from his father and transmitted in turn to the subject of this sketch. James Gibson took a prominent part in political affairs and held several township offices, and he was Constable for several years. He had no chance to get an education in those early days, but he was a strong man mentally as well as physically. Both the subject's father and grandfather entered land in Clark county, and the land where James K. now lives was entered by his uncle, the government giving him the deed for land signed by President John Quincy Adams. James K. Gibson has the deed to his father's land, which is signed by President Franklin Pierce. James Gibson was one of eleven children. His wife, Hannah Peck, was born in Wood township, this county, in 1822, the daughter of Rufus and Naomia (Alexander) Peck, the former a native of Rhode Island, and the latter of Connecticut. She was one of a family of four children. Her parents died when they were young.

James K. Gibson received what education he could in the old log subscription schools, the school-room being equipped with log benches, hewn from trees from the surrounding forests. Mr. Gibson has been a farmer all his life, having assisted his father in his youth to improve the farm and clear the land, and he has continued to make improvements on the same until his place now ranks with any in the township. It is located in section 1, southwest quarter, two miles from the village of Borden. He is a hard working man and his labors have been amply repaid by Mother Nature for he is in easy circumstances and has a good home and pleasant surroundings.

Mr. Gibson was united in marriage in 1885 to Indiana Goss, daughter of John Goss. She was born in Wood township, this county, June 4, 1852. One child has blessed this union, John L. Gibson, whose date of birth is April 23, 1886. He married Myrnie Rose, of Wood township. He is a school teacher of more than ordinary ability and he and his wife are highly respected people.

In his political relations Mr. Gibson is a supporter of the Democratic party. He was at one time Supervisor of Wood township and made a most excellent official, according to his neighbors. He is at this writing a member of the Advisory Board of the township. Mr. Gibson belongs to the Christian church.

GEORGE JACKSON, Sr.

There is little doubt that a life of activity, especially if lived near the great heart of Mothern Nature in the woods and fields is conducive of longevity. In his own person the subject of this sketch, who has now passed into the silent land exemplified it. From youth his life was one of great activity as a huntsman and pioneer farmer in Clark county and he was a vigorous and

45

very active man even down to his last years, and his father reached nearly the century milestone. There can be no doubt that it is the sluggard, not the toiler, who dies early in life.

George Jackson, Sr., was born in Clark county, Indiana, May 4, 1828, the son of Zephaniah and Fannie Jackson. The subject's parents were among the very first pioneers of Clark county. Their children were as follows: Katie, Mary Ann, William, Thomas, John, Henry, Harrison, Zephaniah, Jeremiah and George, the subject of this biographical memoir.

George Jackson was a woodsman, as already intimated, a great hunter of deer, wild turkey and all kinds of wild game. He was also a tan-bark maker. During his youth in this county the land was all timbered, and all the heavy work was then done with ox teams. He was educated in the subscription schools, which he attended for a few months during the winter, but never had an opportunity to attend free schools. He was a member of the Methodist church and was a Republican, but never sought political preferment. He married Matilda Starr, in Clark county, but the date is not known, George and two brothers having married three Starr sisters. Seven children were born to Mr. and Mrs. George Jackson, namely: William Riley, who lives in Wood township, married Anna Spurgeon and they are the parents of eleven children; John T., who is now deceased, married Liza Jane Goss, who lives in Wood township, the mother of eight children; Caroline, who married Perry Spurgeon, is the mother of seven children and lives in Clark county; Lewis A. is living at home; Emeline, who married Samuel Pixley, is the mother of five children and is living in Jeffersonville; George W.; Amanda, who married John Ross, lives in Clark county, became the mother of four children, all now deceased. Matilda Starr, wife of the subject, is the daughter of John and Nancy (Bailey) Starr, natives of Kentucky, and early pioneers of Clark county. The wife of the subject was one year old when she was brought to Clark county by her parents. She remembers the early condition of the country in his girlhood days, how wild it was, and also tells of the exciting life of her father, who was among other things, an Indian fighter. She is still living in 1909, aged seventy-six years. George Jackson died April 11, 1903. He was a man of many sterling qualities and was widely and favorably known in this locality.

George W. Jackson, Jr., was born March 4, 1863, in Wood township, Clark county, and he was educated in the common schools of this district, assisting with the work on the place in the meantime until he reached maturity, when he was married to Linnie Spurgeon, who was born in Washington county, Indiana, August 4, 1870. Five children have been born to this union, namely: Grace, born June 30, 1891, died when fourteen months old; Everett, born November 24, 1892; Ethel, born June 6, 1894; Marshall, born July 29, 1896, died May 16, 1899; Goldie, born May 18, 1905.

George W. Jackson, Jr., has been in poor health for several years and although he is a skilled carpenter and plasterer by trade, he is at present unable to work on account of ill health. He has been engaged for some time in the growing of small fruits and the mercantile business. He has a nice little general store and has a fair trade, the store being located on his place on the Salem road, about five miles from Borden. He keeps a good stock of carefully selected goods and he is known to be honest in all his dealings with his fellow men. He is a member of the Methodist Episcopal church, and he supports the Republican party. He has a nice family and he is very proud of his father's record as a hunter, and he seems in every way to be a worthy descendant of such a man of mettle.

William R. Jackson, who married Anna Spurgeon, is a farmer of Wood township. His wife is the daughter of Archie and Mary Spurgeon, who were among the pioneers of Clark county, and both deceased. W. R. Jackson and wife are the parents of eight children, who grew to maturity: Ferris, Icy, wife of Andrew Taylor; Calvin, deceased; Martie, Cephus, Archie, Raymond and Eleanor. Mr. Jackson is a Republican in politics and he and his wife are members of the Methodist church.

DAVID O. BLANKENBAKER.

Thus far the career of David O. Blankenbaker has been one of great activity and signal usefulness and he bears an unsullied reputation in both business and social circles. He was born in Washington county, Indiana, January 10, 1862, the son of Samuel Blankenbaker. His mother was known in her maidenhood as Nancy Jane Terrell. Samuel Blankenbaker was born in 1840 and died January 20, 1904. Nancy Jane Terrell was born in 1835 and died at an advanced age. The subject's grandparents were among the first white settlers in Washington county, having settled in Harrison township in that county upon their arrival from Kentucky. Samuel Blankenbaker was a farmer in Washington county, having been born and reared there. He died in Clark county about thirty years ago. He was a Republican but took no part in politics. He was a member of the Methodist church. His people came from Kentucky as far back as known. The subject's mother was the daughter of Thaddeus Terrell, who was one of the early pioneers of Clark county, where he was well known as a dealer in horses, being regarded as a very shrewd man. He was also an extensive tobacco raiser.

David O. Blankenbaker is one of seven children, four boys and three girls. He married Emma E. Thompson, who was born August 18, 1863, the daughter of Solomon and Esther (Want) Thompson, a well known family in their community. Solomon Thompson was born in 1827 and died January 5, 1905.

Esther Want died November 24, 1873. She was born in 1829. Her maternal grandparents were from Germany while her father's people were Hoosiers as far as known. Seven children have been born to the subject and wife, as follows: Newton Samuel, born December 10, 1885, died June 7, 1906; Alfonso Solomon, born January 1, 1887, married Dora Lee Masters, and they live in Illinois; George E. was born January 10, 1889, and is living at home; Benjamin F., born November 1, 1895, is living at home; John B., born November 1, 1897, is also living at home; Herman C., born August 17, 1899, is living at home; Iva E., born December 14, 1903; Lilly B., born July 7, 1904.

David O. Blankenbaker has lived in Clark county for the past thirty years, during which time he has been a very active man, engaged principally in agricultural pursuits. He was a farmer and fruit grower up to eight years ago, when he went into the mercantile business on the Blue River road, about three and one-half miles from Borden. He has a neat little store well stocked with a good quality of goods and he has built up an extensive trade with the surrounding community. He is regarded by all who know his as industrious and honest in his dealings with his fellow men. In politics he is a Republican and he belongs to the Methodist Episcopal church, where he is a familiar figure in the gatherings of that congregation. He is a well informed man, havnig been educated in the common schools of Clark county and he has since read a great deal at home. He has a host of friends in this community and no enemies, for his life has been led along safe and honorable lines.

HENRY PACKWOOD.

Henry Packwood is one of the old and representative farmers of Clark county. He has persevered in the pursuit of a persistent purpose and gained a satisfactory reward. He was born in Clark county, Indiana, February 26, 1836, the son of Samuel and Phoebe (Heaton) Packwood, the former born March 5, 1808, in Patrick county, Virginia, who came to Clark county, Indiana, with his father, William Packwood. Samuel Packwood was a farmer, a Democrat, and he died in Wood township in 1896. The Packwoods were among the first settlers in this part of the county. Samuel Packwood entered land in sections 32 and 33, which was wild and heavily timbered at that time, but he cleared the land and made extensive improvements on it. The village of Salem at that time was larger than New Albany and most of the trading in this locality was done there. Phoebe Heaton was born in Pennsylvania in 1812 and died in 1904. She first came to Washington county, Indiana, and then to Clark county when quite young. She and Samuel Packwood were married in Clark county June 14, 1832. Ten children were born to them, namely: John, born December 1, 1834, died about 1886, in Texas; Henry, of this review; Emily and Ellen (twins), were born October 11, 1838, and Emily died when ten years old; William, who was born in 1840, died at the age of twenty-one years; Samuel, born in 1844, lives in Lawrence county, Indiana; Thomas was born March 10, 1846, and died when forty-two years of age; Jesse, born in 1849, lives at Borden; Elizabeth, born in 1851, lives in Wood township; James, born in 1857, lives in Wood township.

Henry Packwood received only a limited education in the subscription schools of the early days. He can remember when there was plenty of game and wild animals in this township, the country being very wild when he was a boy. He has no military record, but three of his brothers were soldiers in the Civil war. He built the first frame school-house in Wood township. He started in life for himself when he was married to Katherine Warman, when he was about twenty-three years old. She was the daughter of Abraham and Mary Warman. Her people were among the early settlers in this part of the county, having come from Kentucky. Two children have been born to Mr. and Mrs. Henry Packwood, namely: Laura, born October 19, 1863, lives at home; Ellen, born May 26, 1867, died in 1888. Mr. Packwood's second wife was Rebecca Nicholson, the daughter of Joseph and Mary Nicholson. Rebecca was born in 1839 and she passed to her rest in Wood township in 1900. Two children were born to the subject by his second marriage, Joseph E., born September 4, 1875, married Bertha Gorman; they live in Wood township and are the parents of one child. Charles H., the second child, was born September 8, 1877, lives with the subject.

Henry Packwood has been a farmer and a small fruit grower most all his life. He has lived to see the township cleared of its wilderness and he is a well preserved old man, although he has been a hard worker all his life. He has made all the improvements on the place where he now lives, in Wood township, section 27. He has developed a valuable farm. Mr. Packwood served eighteen years as Trustee of his township in a most praiseworthy manner. He also served six years as County Commissioner. He is a Democrat. He and his family are members of the Church of Christ, and no family in the township bear a better reputation for honor, industry and hospitality than his.

GEORGE W. BELL.

The gentleman whose name appears above is one of the honored residents of Wood township, Clark county, being a native born of Clark county, where he was elected to spend his entire life, believing that greater advantages were to be had here than elsewhere, and the success he has achieved through his persistent labors in farming would lead one to believe that he made a wise decision.

George W. Bell was born in Wood township April 20, 1838, the son of Elias and Jemina (McKinley) Bell, the former having been born in 1808, in Pennsylvania, who came to Clark county in 1812, settling in Wood township. Elias Bell was the son of Thomas and Rachael (Dunbar) Bell. Grandfather Bell entered part of the land where George W. now lives and where Elias Bell lived until his death, in 1860. He was an extensive stock raiser and dealer. He was a very religious man and was a deacon in Pleasant Ridge church, which he helped establish, which is located about one mile from where George W. Bell lives. This church was established in about 1847 or 1848. It was first an old log house. Hiram Green was among the first men to preach there. Elias Bell, Joe Nicholson and Jerry McKinley were the first trustees of this church. Elias Bell was one of the best known and most influential men of this community in his day. Jemina McKinley was born about 1810 in Kentucky and she died in Wood township, Clark county, in 1888. Nine children were born to them, our subject being the only survivor.

George W. Bell helped to clear off a great deal of the land on his father's farm when he was young, the country being heavily timbered. He received a limited education in the subscription schools, having never attended the free schools.

Mr. Bell was married to Fanny McCutchen January 5, 1864. She was born December 11, 1842, in Floyd county, to which county her people came from Kentucky in the early days, having the Indians for neighbors. She was the mother of five children, namely: Charles H., born October 3, 1866, lives in Wood township; William J., born January 21, 1868, married Lulu Brown; they live in Wood township and are the parents of three children; Elias J., the third child, was born December 1, 1871, married Lilly Morris; they have three children and make their home with the subject. Ida, the fourth child, who was born January 13, 1873, married Gilbert Gillispie, lives in Indianapolis, and is the mother of three children; George T., who was born June 10, 1879, married Carrie Scott, and they are living in Floyd county.

Mr. Bell has been a farmer all his life on the same place, which he has greatly improved and made it yield abundant crops. He has a pleasant and comfortable home, four miles south of Borden, on the Greenville road, his land being located in section 22.

Mrs. Bell passed to her rest October 21, 1894. The subject has been Assessor of Wood township for five years, giving entire satisfaction to his constituents in this capacity. He has also held some other minor offices in the township. He is a Democrat and a member of the Christian church at Pleasant Ridge. He is known as a man of honesty, industry and force of character, and he has many friends in this county.

JOSEPH NICHOLSON, Sr.

One of the progressive and well known agriculturists of Wood township, Clark county, is the gentleman whose name initiates this paragraph, who has spent more than a half century, his entire life, in fact, in this locality, consequently everybody here not only knows but respects him, for his life has been one of integrity as well as of industry.

Joseph Nicholson was born in Wood township, March 14, 1841, on the same place where he now lives, the son of Joseph M. and Mary (Graves) Nicholson, the former a native of Randolph county, North Carolina, where he was born in 1795, from which state he came to Crawford county, Indiana, in 1816, settling among the pioneers in October of that year. He lived in Orange county for a while and then came to Clark county, in 1832, settling on the place where the subject now lives, in section 21, being a prominent farmer and tobacco raiser for those early days, and later launched in the dairy business. He was a Democrat and was Trustee of the township for one term. He was reared a Quaker, but he became a member of the Christian church. He marketed all his tobacco in Louisville. He also found a market in New Albany, where he sold his dairy products. He died in March, 1876. He made several trips to New Orleans to sell stock. He was the son of Zachariah and Mary (Harvey) Nicholson, who settled in Crawford county, Indiana, in 1816. Mary Graves was the daughter of Benjamin and Mary (Fincher) Graves. Mary Graves was born in 1800, in Randolph county, North Carolina. The subject is the youngest of thirteen children. He assisted with the farm work when a boy and attended the subscription schools of sixty day terms, receiving only a limited education.

Mr. Nicholson likes to tell of the days of his boyhood and recount the stories told by his father of the first settlers, there being many deer and bear when he first came here.

When about twenty-three years old Joseph Nicholson was united in marriage with Mary Goss, who was born in Clark county, her parents being pioneers of Wood township. Mary was born in November, 1841, the daughter of John and Mary (McKinley) Goss. John Goss was born in 1816 in Clark county. Nancy McKinley was born about 1820.

Mr. Nicholson was a hard worker in his youth, the country being wild and covered with brush he did much in assisting to clear the land. When five years old he made a trip to North Carolina and back with his parents in a wagon. It took fifteen days each way to make the trip.

Mr. Nicholson lives five and one-half miles from Borden, in section 21. He has an excellent farm which he has spent his life in improving until it is today quite productive and well kept. He has a comfortable home with beautiful surroundings, which stands back from the road for some distance. He is a good manager and his fields yield bounteously under his skillful care.

Three children have been born to Mr. and Mrs. Joseph Nicholson, namely: John W. is single and living at home; Leanora is single and living at home; Charles A., born April 3, 1876, died in 1900.

Mr. Nicholson has been a farmer all his life and has devoted much attention to stock raising, always keeping a good variety of excellent stock, mostly hogs and Jersey cattle. This family has borne an excellent reputation since the first members settled here upwards of a hundred years ago.

JOHN BERNARD KOETTER.

Among the sterling Germans who have done so much for the upbuilding of Clark county, establishing good homes and taking an interest in public affairs, lending what assistance they could in the promotion of movements looking to the general good, the subject of this sketch, who is now deceased, must be mentioned for he was long an honored resident of this locality.

John Bernard Koetter was born in Prussia, January 16, 1826, about twenty miles from the Rhine river. He came to the United States in 1845, locating in Cincinnati, where he remained seven years and where he married, in 1852, to Bernadina Bergman. She was born June 5, 1827, in Oldenberg, Germany, and she came to the United States in 1850, locating in Cincinnati. He followed cabinet-making while he lived in Cincinnati. He left that city and came to Clark county to engage in farming in Wood township, in section 22. The land was pretty well settled up when he came here. He hauled all his produce to New Albany and Louisville, where he found a market. He was one of Wood township's best known men, but he was not a public man. He stayed close at home and was a money maker. He was a Democrat, but never an office seeker. It was 1852 when he came to this county. He died in September, 1894, while living in Wood township. He was a strict Catholic. His wife makes her home with William F., her son. She is a fine old lady, and in comparatively good health for one of her advanced years. She has an excellent memory. The wife of the subject was the daughter of John and Elizabeth (Rosemeier) Bergman. Her father died in Germany when about sixty years old, and her mother died in Cincinnati when seventy-six years old.

Seven children have been born to the subject and wife, as follows: Henrietta, age fifty-five, married Bernard Schmidt; Anna, age fifty-three, married Herman Voor, and they have six children, three living and three dead; they live in Louisville; John Bernard, Jr., died at the age of twenty-three years, in 1881; Joseph I., who married Ida Vanolman, died in 1900, at the age of thirty-eight years; John H., who is forty-four years old, married Barbara Engel, lives in Wood township and they have five children living and three dead; William

F., who is forty-one years old, married Katie Verst, daughter of Henry Verst, who lives in Floyd county. Her mother was Caroline (Tennis) Verst, who has been deceased for twenty-five years. William F. and wife have four children, namely: Mary B., born May 16, 1900; Joseph B., born May 21, 1903; Edward John, born May 29, 1905; Anna Roseline, born July 26, 1908.

William F. Koetter has a well improved farm in Wood township and one of the finest homes in the township, much of which he has made himself, being a man of thrift and good judgment. His farm is located in section 14, four and one-half miles from Borden. He is like his father in a business way. He keeps good stock. He is well known in this locality and is a man of excellent business principles and is honest and straightforward in his dealings.

BENJAMIN SCHMIDT.

Among the sterling class of German citizens who have done so much toward the upbuilding of the great Hoosier state, none in Clark county deserve special mention more than Benjamin Schmidt, who is one of her best agriculturists and honored citizens, having been born in Prussia, April 4, 1845, the son of Harmon and Mary (Krier) Schmidt, his father having been a farmer in the old country. The subject's grandfather and grandmother on his father's side of the house lived to advanced ages, reaching nearly ninety years. Harmon Schmidt lived to be between seventy and eighty years of age and his mother died at the age of seventy-three. They were Catholics. They never came to America. However, two brothers and one sister of Benjamin came to this country. One of them, Henry Schmidt, lives in Covington, Kentucky; the subject's sister, Theresa, who married Frank Vinker, lives in Covington, Kentucky. Benjamin is the third of five children. His brothers and sisters that came to this country are all living. They represent a typical and substantial old German family.

Benjamin Schmidt came to the United States in 1865, first locating in Covington, Kentucky, later coming to Clark county, Indiana. He has been living on his present place for a period of thirty-one years. He is a carpenter by trade, but he quit carpentering about fifteen years ago and has since devoted his attention almost exclusively to his farm, which is located four miles south of Borden, in section 11. He has a good farm, which he has made equal to any in the community through hard work and careful management until it produces excellent crops and yields a good income. He has cleared a great deal of the land and his fields show that a man of industry and sound judgment has had their management in hand. He has a substantial dwelling and a convenient barn. He keeps stock and poultry of various kinds.

Mr. Schmidt was married in 1873 to Henrietta Koetter, daughter of Barney and Dina Koetter. Her father was born in Germany in the Rhine river country. Her parents were among the first settlers of Clark county. She was born in Cincinnati, August 15, 1853, and came to Clark county, Indiana, when four years old. Being the oldest of the family she had to stay at home and assist with the household duties and therefore did not receive much education. The subject was educated principally in Germany. To Mr. and Mrs. Benjamin Schmidt the following children have been born: Benjamin, Jr., born on July 6, 1875, married Lizzie Lightheart; they are the parents of three children and are living in Floyd county. Joseph, the second child, was born August 4, 1878, married Agnes Gill; they have two children and are living in Floyd county, this state. Henry, the third child of the subject, was born January 17, 1881, and died at the age of seventeen years; Dina and Frances (twins), were born June 30, 1883. The former married Jacob Engel; they live in Kansas City and are the parents of two children. Frances, who married Theodore Verst, lives in Floyd county, and they are the parents of two children. Herman, who was born December 14, 1886, is single; John, who was born March 27, 1888, is also single; Phillip, who was born January 4, 1890, is single; Rosa, who was born July 17, 1892, is living at home. The subject's wife has two brothers and one sister.

In his political relations Mr. Schmidt supports the Democratic ticket, having always been affiliated with this party, but he has never sought public office. He and his family are faithful Catholics and belong to St. John's church of Wood township   They all bear good reputations.

JONATHAN WADE.

This venerable agriculturist is one of the sterling characters of Clark county who have come down to the present from the pioneer era, and no man has done more in his community for the upbuilding of the same than has Mr. Wade.

Jonathan Wade was born in Wood township, Clark county, December 18, 1832, on the place where he now lives, the son of Lindsey and Margaret (Carlisle) Wade, the former a native of Randolph county, North Carolina, where he was born in November, about 1812. He was brought to Clark county, Indiana, by his mother when about three years old, settling in the wilds, with Indians and wild beasts as neighbors. Lindsey Wade was the son of James and Belle Wade. He was a farmer and stock dealer until his death, in 1887. He was a well known man in this county. He was a Democrat, but never would accept public office. The country was very wild in

Lindsey Wade's time. Land here was taken up about 1819. It was all timber. The land where Lindsey Wade lived when the subject was born was first settled by a family named Clark. The father of the subject dealt extensively in horses. The subject's mother was brought to this county by an uncle, James Johnson, from Pennsylvania. Her parents died when she was an infant. The mother and father of Jonathan Wade were born in the same month and the same year, only one day's difference. The mother died in 1895. To Mr. and Mrs. Linsey Wade six children were born, only three of whom are living; besides Jonathan his brother, Henry, is living in Floyd county, and his sister, Elizabeth, who married a Mr. Stolzer, is living in New Albany.

Jonathan's education was limited, but he attended the old time subscription schools, taught in log houses, and he educated himself, after he was married, by night study. He started in life for himself when he married, May 9, 1854, Elizabeth Nicholson, who was born June 6, 1832, in Wood township, Clark county, the daughter of Joseph and Mary (Graves) Nicholson. Mary Graves was born December 29, 1799, in Randolph county, North Carolina. Joseph Nicholson was born January 30, 1794, in North Carolina. Their parents were from England. Joseph and Mary Nicholson came to Clark county, Indiana, about 1817. Joseph Nicholson died in March, 1876, and his wife passed away in April, 1888. Mrs. Joseph Nicholson brought cotton seed from North Carolina, which she planted here and used the cotton she grew from it to spin a bed cover that the subject's wife still owns. The cotton was picked by Mrs. Nicholson and carded by hand.

The following children have been born to Mr. and Mrs. Jonathan Wade: Lindsey, born May 31, 1855, married Rebecca Clark, who lives in Wood township, and they are the parents of four children; Mary, born February 28, 1857, married James Keas, and her second marriage was with J. B. LaDue. Mary had one child by her first husband and two by her second. She lives in Kansas. Richard H., the subject's third child, was born July 15, 1859, and married Nora Schreiber. They live in Michigan and are the parents of five children living and two deceased. Margaret R., the subject's fourth child, was born January 19, 1861, and died when two years and eight months old; Carrie, born November 28, 1864, married Frank Rush, living in California, and they are the parents of one child; Henrietta, born in April in 1866 or 1867, is married and is living in Peru, Indiana; Eliza, born February 5, 1869, married Will Schleicher, living in Wood township, this county, and they are the parents of one child living and three died in infancy; Omega, born March 26, 1871, married Jacob Smith, living in New Albany, and they are the parents of four children; Sarah, born August 30, 1873, married Robert H. Clark, living in Louisville, Kentucky, and they are the parents of two children; Byron J., born July 5, 1877, married Minnie Hunt. They live with the subject of this sketch and are the parents of three children.

Jonathan Wade has spent his life in Wood township farming and stock raising which he has made a success. He has always been a great lover of horses and some good ones are to be found on his place at all times. He is regarded as a good farmer in every sense of the word. He is a loyal Democrat, and has been Trustee and has held several other township offices. He and his wife are members of the Christian church. The subject has been an elder and a deacon in the same for many years. He has a beautiful and comfortable home in section 23, six miles from Borden. They are fine people of the old-fashioned type. They still use the old-time fire-place and burn wood in it.

JOHN W. HUNT.

The Hunt family has been known in this section of Indiana from early pioneer days and it has always borne an excellent reputation and its members have done their full share in the development of Clark and the adjoining county of Floyd, and John W. Hunt is a worthy descendant of his well known ancestors. He was born May 30, 1865, in Floyd county, Indiana, the son of William and Sarah (Smith) Hunt. They are still living in Floyd county, their ages in 1909 being about seventy-one and sixty-eight, respectively. William Hunt has been a farmer all his life. He was born June 26, 1836, in Floyd county, the son of James Hunt, who was born March 3, 1791. He was a farmer and blacksmith by trade. He married Massa Fitzpatrick. They were both natives of Virginia. The latter was born June 11, 1800, and died in 1881. James Hunt died March 7, 1853. The father of William Hunt came to Clark county in 1836. He was one of the early settlers of Floyd county. The subject's father entered government land in Floyd county. William Hunt married Sarah Smith in 1860. She was born June 25, 1842. the daughter of Reuben and Elizabeth (Shaver) Smith. She was born in Floyd county, but her people were natives of Kentucky, being early settlers in Floyd county. William Hunt had three brothers and four sisters. In politics he was a Democrat. He received his education in the old log school-houses, having never attended the free schools.

The following are the names of the children born to Mr. and Mrs. William Hunt: Elizabeth, who married Robert Meeks, is the mother of one child and lives in New Albany; John W., of this review; Norris, who married Katie Cochran, is the mother of three children and lives in Floyd county; Jacob C. is a school teacher and makes his home with the father of the subject, in Floyd county; Ella married John Stone and she is the mother of one child, making her home in New Albany; Minnie, who married Byron Wade, is the mother of three children and is living in Clark county; Charles is living with the parents of these children, in Floyd county.

John W. Hunt started in life for himself when about sixteen years old, having attended the Floyd county public schools for a few years prior to that time. He has always been a farmer. He has become a fruit grower on quite a large scale. He has an excellent farm, which is kept well improved and everything shows careful management. He has made most of the improvements on his place. He has a comfortable and nicely kept house upon one of the highest knobs in this locality. He deserves a great deal of credit for what he has accomplished for he has done it all unaided, having started life in a small way when merely a boy, but he has the qualities that always make for success when rightly applied.

Mr. Hunt was united in marriage with Emma E. Fenwick, daughter of Thomas and Margaret (Jenkins) Fenwick, well known people of Floyd county. Mrs. Hunt is one of six children. Her father is still living, but her mother has joined the great majority in the silent land.

John W. Hunt lived all his life in Floyd county up to about eighteen years ago, when he came to Clark county, locating in section 13, where his present splendid home is located. He and his wife are the parents of three children, namely: William T., born December 26, 1891; John Albert, born March 10, 1894; Clara, born February 12, 1897.

Mr. Hunt has always been a Democrat, and he is prominent in politics in this part of the county. He is at this writing ably serving his community as Township Trustee, the first office he has ever tried to secure. He is regarded by all who know him as a man of honest principles.

JOSEPH ROSENBERGER.

Joseph Rosenberger is of the second generation of Germans in this country, having been born in Harrison county, Indiana, January 20, 1849, the son of John Adam and Anna M. Rosenberger, the former having been born November 30, 1800, in Germany, who came to the United States when thirty-seven years old, he and his bride having come here to get married and they immediately settled in Harrison county, Indiana. He was a blacksmith by trade but always followed farming in this country. They were Catholics in their religious life. Joseph, who is the seventh of ten children, was three years old when his parents came to Wood township, Clark county. They settled on the place where the subject now lives. John Adam Rosenberger died on this place October 5, 1890. The country roundabout was very wild when they came here, mostly all in timber, which necessitated the clearing off of all their land. There was much wild game and animals here then. The farm of the subject once lay in the great peach belt, but principally small fruits are raised on it now.

John Adam Rosenberger was a Democrat but not a public man, having spent all his time at home looking after his farm.

The mother of our subject was born in the same part of Germany that her husband came from, her birth having occurred in 1811. She came to America with her husband, as already indicated, and she passed to her rest March 30, 1891.

Joseph Rosenberger's education was obtained principally in the subscription schools, taught in log houses of the early days. He has been a hard working farmer all his life and he has prospered by reason of his close application to his work and his careful management, having always worked on the old home place, where his father settled. His farm is under a high state of cultivation, well fenced and carefully kept in every respect and it yields abundant crops. He is quite a grower of small fruits on the "knobs." He has a very comfortable home in section 14, four miles from Borden.

Mr. Rosenberger was united in marriage in 1873, to Frances Huber, who was born November 1, 1852, in Wood township, the daughter of Ignatius Huber, who was born in 1824, in Baden, Germany. He was three years old when he came to the United States, and he devoted his life to farming. Mrs. Rosenberger's mother's name in her maidenhood was Anna Mary Ast, who was born in Bairn, Germany, about 1824, and died in 1894. Her father died in 1885. The subject's wife is the second child of a family of seven children. The following children have been born to Mr. and Mrs. Joseph Rosenberger: John William, the oldest child, married Rosa Youcom, and they are the parents of three children and live in Wood township; Anna Mary, born September 9, 1877, is single; Mary Elizabeth, born September 5, 1879, married Herman Faska, to whom three children have been born, and they are living in Floyd county; Phillomina, born September 15, 1881, died in infancy, September 3, 1882; Mary Katherine, born July 17, 1885, died October 4, 1886; Clara F., born October 22, 1887, is still a member of the home circle; Mary Rosina, born September 24, 1890, lives at home; John Edward, born June 9, 1894.

Mr. Rosenberger and family are people of excellent standing in Wood township, where they have many loyal friends.

CLAUDE BURTON McBRIDE.

Persistance and courage in the face of difficulties are necessary factors to success, and energy and determination must lend their aid if one would succeed in the face of competition and gain prosperity in this age of feverish activity, when all are striving for the same goal. Realizing this fact our subject early in life determined upon a career which has brought ultimate success early and won for him the esteem of a wide circle of acquaintances in Clark county.

Claude Burton McBride first saw the light of day March 19, 1883, three miles north of Jeffersonville. He is the son of Isaac and Emma (Hale) McBride, the former the son of John McBride, also natives of Clark county, in fact, this county has been the home of the McBrides for many generations and few families have been more closely identified with its growth than this one, for we find that one, Isaac McBride, the subject's great-grandfather, came to this county in the early pioneer days from Pennsylvania, locating near Henryville. He was a very active Presbyterian and did a most commendable work religiously in the early settlement here. He had a brother who distinguished himself as a scout in Gen. George Rogers Clark's expedition against Fort Vincennes. John McBride, grandfather of our subject, was one of the few men of that day who was interested in a county public school system and rode to Charlestown on horseback to cast his vote in favor of the project at the time the election for Clark county was held at that place for the establishment of free public schools in Indiana.

Emma Hale was the daughter of Isaac Hale, who came to Clark county from the New England states and worked on the Ohio river as a deck hand for some time, later turning his attention to farming and was quite successful, developing an excellent farm by hard work and good management for he was poor when a boy and was compelled to help support a widowed mother.

Claude Burton McBride grew up on the old Hale homestead, where he was born, assisting with the work about the place, attending the McBride school in the meantime, later taking a course in Borden College, where he made a very commendable record, fitting himself for a teacher, which line of work he had long desired to follow. consequently soon after completing his education in the local schools he began teaching, and so constant was his progress that in September, 1908, he was appointed to the responsible position of principal of the Ohio Falls school, which place he filled with much credit to himself, and the entire satisfaction to both pupil and patron, giving every evidence of a well educated instructor and possessing the many other pre-requisites for this line of work, and showing that a future in the same awaited him with signal results.

Mr. McBride in his fraternal relations is a member of Tabor Lodge, No. 92, Independent Order of Odd Fellows, also Hope Lodge, Knights of Pythias; and Jefferson Lodge, Free and Accepted Masons, in all of which he takes an abiding interest. He is a member of the Presbyterian church, having adhered to the faith of a long line of ancestors. Politically he is a Democrat and takes an active part in local affairs. He is a prepossessing, gentlemanly young man and is popular in his community.

Q. ROBERT HAUSS, A. M., M. D.

Clark county, Indiana, has been and is signally favored in the class of the professional men that have added to its prestige in all lines and in this connection Dr. Q. Robert Hauss demands representation, and stands admittedly in the front rank of her medical practitioners, being known also as a public-spirited man of high ideals and unswerving integrity, so that he naturally has won the confidence and esteem of all who know him.

Doctor Hauss was born September 22, 1864, in Liberty, Union county, Indiana, the son of Carl Frederick and Anna Marie Hauss, who emigrated to America from Germany in 1852. They were people of honor and sterling worth, and reared their children in a wholesome atmosphere, there being nine in number, of whom our subject was the youngest in order of birth. He received his early education in the public schools of Brownsville and Liberty, and selecting medicine as his life work matriculated in the Eclectic Medical Institute in 1885, and graduated with honors three years later. In addition to this he took a two years' clinical course of instructions in the Cincinnati Hospital, and a special private course under the late Professor McDermott, an eminent oculist and aurist, at that time a member of the faculty of the Pulte-Homeopathic Medical College. Thus being so well prepared for his chosen field of endeavor it is no wonder that eminent success should attend his efforts, and that he has taken first rank among the medical men in the southern part of Indiana, a locality long noted for the high order of its medical talent. The doctor located in Sellersburg immediately after graduation, succeeding his brother, Dr. A. P. Hauss, who removed to New Albany. His success was instantaneous and his practice soon extended over a wide range of country. To meet the demands of his surgical work the doctor established a private hospital in 1898. Although a building of nine rooms and well euipped, it is inadequate and a much larger building is under consideration.

An interesting chapter in the life record of Doctor Hauss is that bearing on his domestic relations, which dates from October 10, 1888, when he was united in the bonds of wedlock with Frances E. Hall, a representative of a well known family at Brownsville, Indiana. This union has resulted in the birth of five children, four of whom survive, namely: Robert, who is at present fourteen years of age; Frances, twelve; Mildred, ten, and Russell, eight.

Doctor Hauss has for many years been prominently connected with the Indiana Eclectic Medical Association and was president of this organization in 1905. He is also a member of the National Eclectic Medical Association, and is a special contributor to some of the leading publications of the Eclectic School of Medicine.

During 1898 he was made a member of the board of trustees of Moore's Hill College and has served in this capacity to the present time. He received

Q. ROBERT HAUSS.

the degree of Master of Arts from this institution in 1901. He is an official member of the Methodist Episcopal church, a Mason, and a member of the Eastern Star and a state director of the Indiana Children's Society. He is justly proud of being an honorary member of Jeffersonville Post, No. 86, Department of Indiana Grand Army of the Republic. In all of the above organizations and associations, Doctor Hauss takes an abiding and active interest and he makes his influence felt in all of them. In temperament the doctor is artistic and appreciates the beautiful in music, nature and art. He is proficient in music and devotes as much attention to it as his many exacting duties will permit. He is congenial, affable and public spirited, and his attractive home is always a place of hospitality and good cheer, where numerous friends of the doctor and his estimable wife frequently gather.

PETER P. RENN.

Among the stury German element who have done so much toward the development of Clark county, none deserve more credit than the Renn family for members of the same have labored here since the days of the wilderness, the first member of the family to migrate hither being Peter Renn, Sr., who was one of the first settlers of this part of the county, in the vicinity of Sellersburg, there being only three or four settlers in Carr township when he located here in the midst of the heavily timbered land, which he set about at once to clear and make a home. Indians still roamed the forest depths and much wild game could be found. New Albany and Louisville were the only trading points then, and oxen were used principally in farm work. His son, Peter Renn, father of our subject, assisted in clearing the land, engaging in general farming. He was also one of the first store keepers in St. Joe, becoming known as one of the leading Germans in the county. He was born in Germany and came to the United States in about 1838, having hailed from the famous Rhine country. The voyage to America consumed thirty-seven days. He was married in the Fatherland before coming to the United States. He was educated in that country. He was a devout Catholic and one of the men who started the movement to build the St. Joseph Hill Catholic church; although interested in worthy movements for the general good, he was not a public man. His death occurred in Clark county, in 1893.

The mother of our subject was known in her maidenhood as Mary Smith, also a native of Germany, where she was born in 1811, and she passed away at the age of fifty-six years. Two children were born to the parents of the subject while living in Germany and three while they were residents of the United States, Peter P., of this review, having been born in McKeesport,

46

Pennsylvania, December 17, 1840, and he came to Clark county with his parents when one year old. It fell to his lot to assist in improving the farm here, consequently he had little chance to attend school, however, he got what education he could in the common schools. He began life for himself in 1862, when he began farming of his own accord, and he has devoted his attention since that time exclusively to agricultural pursuits, now owning the old Prather farm, in section 128. Although this is one of the oldest farms in this locality, it is still a very valuable one, owing to the systematic management of the subject, and it produces excellent crops from year to year. Mr. Renn has a beautiful home surrounded by attractive lawns, trees, etc., at St. Joe.

The married life of Mr. Renn dates from February 2, 1862, when he was united in the bonds of wedlock with Barbara Schafer, daughter of Jacob and Magdalene Schafer. She was a native of Pennsylvania, born in 1842. Her people were also early pioneers in Clark county, Indiana. Mrs. Renn passed to her rest in 1899, after becoming the mother of the following children: Peter, deceased; Matthew M., who is chief engineer at the Louisville & Nashville shops in Louisville, Kentucky; Joseph, who is a member of the priesthood; Jacob, Benjamin, George, Annie, John F. and Francis X.

Peter P. Renn is a member of the Catholic church at St. Joe. His life is exemplary in every respect and he has ever supported those measures which are calculated to uplift and benefit humanity, and his life work has been a success, owing to hard work and good habits. In politics he is a Democrat.

DAVID S. COOK.

There are few industries more important, especially in connection with the building trades than the manufacture of cement, whose expansion in this country is of recent origin and has been on a gigantic scale. The men who have developed it deserve especial credit as part of the force behind the wonderful growth of the United States, as the work requires expert knowledge and all the qualities which make men valuable in the mechanical arts. In this line it is no more than his just due to say that David S. Cook has made a record that is creditable to himself and achieved results of great value to his employers as well as the community where he has lived so long and to which he has devoted his energies and best abilities. He is of Scotch origin, his parents, William and Margaret Cook, having been natives of the land made famous by Burns and Scott. They married in Scotland, emigrated to America in 1852 and after spending a few years in New York removed to Chillicothe, Ohio. They made their home in this historic city until some time after the Civil war, when they located in Louisville, Kentucky, for permanent abode.

David S. Cook, son of this worthy couple, was born during their residence at Chillicothe, February 9, 1857, and received his education in the public schools of Louisville. When fourteen years old he secured employment with the Louisville Cement Company and here he obtained his first experience in the line of business which was destined to prove his life work. During the ten or twelve years following his apprenticeship, he was connected with various plants and by taking advantage of his opportunities to learn, advanced rapidly in knowledge concerning every feature of cement manufacture. In the fall of 1883 he temporarily abandoned his chosen calling and spent two years as a locomotive engineer on the Texas & St. Louis Railroad. He soon longed for his old occupation, however, and in the fall of 1885 returned to Indiana to accept a position as superintendent of the Speed Cement Mill, located ten miles north of Louisville, on the Pennsylvania Railroad, at Speed Station. When Mr. Cook took charge of this mill the capacity was about three hundred barrels of natural hydraulic cement per day, but largely through his instrumentality and energetic supervision, this plant has been made the largest of its kind in the United States. When it was found that Portland cement could be manufactured in this country, he immediately began experimenting on the new material and in 1905 entered upon the erection of the Speed Portland cement plant at Speeds. This mill, strictly modern and up-to-date, is at the present time manufacturing two thousand barrels per day and this product has gained wide notoriety throughout the central states as the celebrated Speed brand of Portland cement. Mr. Cook is a fine sample of the American mechanic, to whom the great Republic owes so much of its rapid progress and prosperity. He is entirely self-educated, owing little or nothing to schools, but much to home study, systematically and wisely directed. Beginning in poverty, at the very bottom of the ladder, with no reliance but his own brains, hands and character, he has gained all his promotions by merit and ability. Unassuming in manner, quiet and courteous in demeanor, he has the faculty of making friends and thus enjoys the loyal co-operation of the large force of men who work under his direction.

In 1879 Mr. Cook was married to Ruth, daughter of Samuel Hinton, a native of Indiana, and from this union resulted four children: Harry W., David, Jesse and Scott. The eldest, who gave promise of future usefulness, died in 1902 while in his senior year at Purdue University. David L. and Jesse C. are both students at Purdue University and by their application to their tasks and their general bearing give assurance of eventually becoming useful men. Mr. Cook is domestic in his tastes, proud of his boys and fond of his family, to which he devotes most of his leisure and in whose company he finds his chief enjoyment. As a citizen he is interested in progress and entertains high ideals concerning those things which most benefit a community. His highest ambition is to aid in elevating the moral tone and advancing educational movements of all kinds. As a result of this his name is always mentioned in connection with all kinds of gatherings of social importance in Silver Creek township, where he has made his residence for many years.

JOHN MORTON MELOY, M. D.

About the year 1838 the Tuttle family left their home at Rochester, New York, and came to Clark county, settling in the vicinity of Memphis. About the same time the Meloys came in from the northwestern part of Pennsylvania and found a location near Charlestown. William H. Meloy and Emily C. Tuttle, children of these respective families, were each about two years old when their parents removed to this section, grew up as neighbors and on reaching maturity were married. Shortly afterward they went to Marshall county, Indiana, and established a home near Plymouth, but in January, 1870, returned to the neighborhood of Memphis and spent the next four years in that part of Clark county. In 1874 they removed to Lexington, the old county seat of Scott county, and remained in that section until 1884.

John Morton Meloy, son of this couple, was born near Plymouth, Indiana, August 30, 1862, and was a little over seven years old when his parents returned to Clark county. His primary education was obtained during the residence in Scott county, where there were good public schools and a normal in summer. In the spring of 1884 he went to Illinois and worked on a farm until October, when he entered the Central Normal School at Danville, Indiana, and spent a year and a half in that institution. He then taught a few years in the Clark county schools and in January, 1889, became a student in the Kentucky School of Medicine at Louisville, from which he was graduated with the class of June, 1890. The following fall he took a course of instruction at the Louisville University and on January 6, 1891, began the practice at Sellersburg. With the exception of about four months, Doctor Meloy has been secretary of the Sellersburg Board of Health ever since the town government was organized over eighteen years ago. During President's McKinley's administration he was appointed a member of the Pension Board of Examining Surgeons, and has held this position continuously for twelve years. During this period he has held membership of the Sellersburg School Board and been one of the active spirits in forwarding the cause of education. He is medical examiner for a large number of life insurance companies and local surgeon for the Louisville & Northern Railway and Lighting Company. He is a member of Buckner Lodge, No. 631, Free and Accepted Masons, Sellersburg Lodge, No. 702, Independent Order of Odd Fellows, of the Knights of Pythias and Camp No. 3269, Modern Woodmen. Doctor Meloy is popular, both as a man and physician. He has made his own way in the world and done well whatever duty fell to him for performance.

In October, 1889, Doctor Meloy was united in marriage with Ella O., daughter of Jacob C. Nichols, former citizen of Charlestown and brother of the late Doctor Nichols, of Sellersburg. Their children are as follows: Helen J., Hazel F., Hollis A., Hortense E., Lorene M. and Hugh O., all born in Sellersburg except Helen J., whose place of birth was on a farm in Union township.

HON. JAMES MADISON REYNOLDS, M. D.

Proximity and easy access caused the Indiana Territory to gain many recruits in pioneer times from the older state of Kentucky. Men by thousands crossed the river to enter the new and fertile lands lying north and thus it came about that Southern Indiana was extensively settled by families which had tarried awhile in "the daughter of Virginia," but became restless and eventually pressed their fortunes across the border. It was in an early day in the history of Clark county when the Reynolds family found a location in Union township and joined their confreres in helping to subdue the wilderness. At that time all was wild, the primeval forests covering all the land that stretched from the Ohio river hundreds of miles toward the Great Lakes. The story of the conquest of this region has often been told and the stirring incidents formed the most fascinating features of the history of Indiana. Every newcomer added his mite to the general movement and shares the glory which prosperity has been willing to accord to that great army of conquest known as "early pioneers." The original Reynolds family left a son by the name of James Madison Reynolds, who married Catherine Smith, who came with her parents from England when she was a small child. To their union we are indebted for the popular physician and politician who constitutes the subject of this sketch.

James Madison Reynolds, Jr., was born on his father's homestead, in Union township, Clark county, Indiana, February 22, 1855. His early experiences were those of a farm boy, with its hardships, its struggles and endless work which, though trying at the time was always afterwards recognized as an excellent training for life. He learned the valuable lesson of self-discipline, learned also that work was honorable as well as beneficial and laid the foundations which enabled him to become a useful man in after life. The common schools of those days were not all that might be desired, but such as they were young Reynolds availed himself of them and obtained a fair education in the fundamental "three R's." He was an ambitious boy, however, and by no means content to stop with the acquisitions of the district schools. By graduation from the high schools at Salem he was qualified to enter the profession of teaching and spent in this occupation several years, which proved valuable as an educator, besides giving him funds for future expenses. His ambition, formed at an early age, was to become a physician, and even while teaching he was preparing himself for this noble calling. In 1874 he entered the Louisville University, and two years later was the proud possessor of a degree, granted by the Medical College of Ohio at Cincinnati. Locating at Memphis he entered immediately into practice, but in 1884 attended the Bellevue Hospital Medical College of New York, from which he was graduated in the spring of 1885. Returning to Memphis he resumed practice and has continued the same up to the present time. He has been successful and is recognized as one of the leading physicians of his part of the county. In 1890 Doctor Reynolds was appointed a member of the Board of Pension Exanimers, at Charlestown, and served in this capacity for four years. Meantime he had been elected Township Trustee and devoted four years of his time to the duties of that office. In 1894 Doctor Reynolds was nominated as a candidate for Joint Representative from the counties of Clark, Scott and Jennings, on the Republican ticket. This district had usually been overwhelmingly Democratic, but it was a year of Republican tidal waves all over the country and Doctor Reynolds got the benefit of being sent to Legislature by a substantial majority. In 1900 he was again elected Trustee of Union township, and, owing to Legislative extension of the term served five years. In this important office he gave satisfaction, transacting its duties in such a way as to disarm criticism.

In 1874 Doctor Reynolds married Matilda A., daughter of Eden Coombs, Sr. He has long been a member of the Christian church and for fifteen years has served as one of its trustees. As a physician he keeps abreast of the times, holding membership in the Clark County Medical Society and the Indiana and the American Medical Associations. His fraternal relations are confined to membership in the order of the Modern Woodmen of America.

JOSEPH C. MORGAN.

The subject of this sketch is deserving of mention in this work, if for no other reason, because of the valiant service of three years he rendered his country during the internecine strife of the early sixties. Joseph C. Morgan was born in Laporte county, Indiana, November 20, 1843, the son of Luther L. and Betsy (Hough) Morgan, the former having been born March 1, 1809, in the old Nutmeg state (Connecticut), having come to the state of Indiana about 1836, following the carpenter's trade here for a period of about seven years, when he went to Michigan and engaged in farming, also worked at his trade there, dying in that state in April, 1862. Betsy Hough, mother of the subject, was born in 1806 in Otsego county, New York. Her wedding with Mr. Morgan occurred in Michigan in March, 1835, and to this union four children were born, three boys and one girl, all deceased except Joseph C., of this review. Mrs. Luther L. Morgan passed away September 16, 1881.

Joseph C. Morgan received his early education in the common schools of Michigan, assisting with the work at home in the meantime, never leaving his parental roof-tree until the breaking out of the war between the states, when his patriotism prompted him to enlist in the Union army, on August 7, 1862, in Company H, Nineteenth Michigan Infantry, and he was on detached service most of his enlistment of three years. He was a clerk in the quarter-master's department part of the time, and later he was sent to Chicago, where he did guard duty. An older brother enlisted in the same regiment with Joseph C., and was killed in 1863 at the battle of Spring Hill, Tennessee.

Upon being mustered out at the close of the war Mr. Morgan returned to Michigan and engaged in farming. On May 20, 1873, he was united in marriage, in the city of Grand Rapids, to Cornelia Doty, who was born in 1854, in New York. After becoming the mother of one child, Mrs. Bertha McGee, now living in Battle Creek, Michigan, the subject's first wife passed to her rest in 1876, and Mr. Morgan was again married, his last wife being Louisa Devoe, whom he married in Nebraska in the year 1883. They lived in Nebraska for about twelve years, this union resulting in the birth of four children, an equal number of boys and girls, namely: Adelle, born January 11, 1885; Ray, born August 22, 1886; Ellis, born in 1888; Beda, born in 1889. Mr. Morgan's second wife was called to her rest in 1906.

Mr. Morgan's life work has been successful for he has always been a hard worker. He learned the carpenter's trade when young and worked at it most of the time he spent in the West. But he has devoted his time to farming since coming to Clark county, this state, some eight years ago. He lives on a farm in section 67, located on the interurban line, two miles from Sellersburg. He has built a very comfortable house and made many other substantial improvements on the place since coming here until it now ranks with the best farms of this township and he is reaping from year to year, excellent results from his toil.

Mr. Morgan took a great deal of interest in political affairs while living in Michigan, but since his removal to Clark county he has not been active in political matters. He is a member of the Methodist Episcopal church, and he has gained the respect of all whom he has met since casting his lot in this county.

FERDINAND ENDERS, Sr.

Although a large number of foreign born citizens have located in Clark county, no class has done nearly so much in the general development of the same as has the Germans, who are among our best residents, being law-abiding, loyal and industrious. Belonging to this class is the gentleman whose life record is here briefly outlined.

Ferdinand Enders was born in Bavaria, Germany, in the year 1846, the son of August and Marthalene (Hedcer) Enders, spending their lives in the Fatherland, in fact, our subject was the only member of this family who ever came to the United States, he having made the trip in 1865, after receiving a common school training in his home country. He located in the city of Baltimore, Maryland, where he remained for a period of two years, then came to Clark county, Indiana, believing that greater opportunities were to be found in the Middle West than in the more effete East.

Although a proficient veterinary surgeon, having been trained in this work before leaving Germany, he never practiced it here. His father was also a veterinary surgeon, having practiced the same in the service of the German government.

Mr. Enders says that Clark county was somewhat wild and undeveloped when he came here. He has spent his entire life since his advent in Clark county working in the cement mills, the first mill for the manufacture of cement having been established here about forty-one years ago. He has thoroughly mastered this work and is one of the best authorities in this line that could be found in this country, and he has been eminently successful in the same. He is very ably serving as assistant superintendent of the Belknaps Cement Mills.

Ferdinand Enders was united in marriage in the year 1867, to Barbara Ehringer, who was born in Sellersburg, Indiana, March, 1848, the daughter of John and Barbara (Popp) Ehringer. Mrs. Enders' father was an early pioneer in Clark county, having served for a period of three years in the German navy before coming to the United States, having during that time visited the major portion of the civilized world and much wild country.

To Mr. and Mrs. Ferdinand Enders the following children have been born: Mary, who is at this writing forty-one years old, married Christopher L. Apple, living at Hamburg, Indiana, and they are the parents of nine children; Fred, thirty-eight years old, married Frances Capps, being the parents of two children and living at Hamburg; Annie, thirty-four years old, married William Ried; they are the parents of five children and live at Belknaps; John, who was born in 1876, married Susan Stroble, and they live in Louisville, Kentucky, and are the parents of one child; Edith, who was born August 7, 1879, married James Talkington; they are the parents of two children and live in Vansville, Indiana; Margurite, born in 1882, married Horace Warfort, and they are living in Cleveland, Ohio; Ferdinand, born in 1886, married Teresa Liefelt; they live in Silver Creek township, this county, and are the parents of one child; George, born in 1889, is living at home; one son of the subject is deceased, George T., who was born in 1873 and died when fifteen months old.

Mr. Enders is quite a musician and plays a number of instruments in a manner that has delighted hundreds, and his pleasant home is often the gather-ing place for the many friends of the family who are entertained by Mr. Enders' playing. In politics he is a Democrat and has served his township as Trustee, also has held several other township offices, and is one of the most influential men in the township. He is a member of the Catholic church at St. Joe.

PORTER C. BUTTORFF.

Few of the captains of industry have achieved or deserved greater success than this energetic and progressive citizen of Jeffersonville. He belongs to the class who possess an intuitive insight into the problems underlying manu-facturing on a large scale, and this, connected with a capacity for organizing, initiating new methods and utilizing the latest improvements while applying all the economics, have made Mr. Buttorff notable among the prosperous busi-ness men of the state. He has a natural capacity for large affairs, combined with unruffled patience in working out details, which are prime factors in achieving results in any line of manufacturing. Porter C. Buttorff was born at Nashville, Tennessee, April 12, 1866, his parents being Henry W. and Mary E. (Nokes) Buttorff. After the usual course in the public schools of Nashville, young Buttorff decided to fit himself for the world of practical busi-ness, by obtaining an education that would qualify him best for a calling where profit is the sure result of skill. With this end in view he became a student at the celebrated Technical Institute at Worcester, Massachusetts, with a determination to become proficient in mechanical engineering. By close application and diligence, he accomplished his object and when he left the school walls he knew how to do something and to do it well. He spent two years in New York City, and being a close observer, learned much from what he saw and heard in that busy mart of finance and commerce. Returning to Nashville, he took charge of a blasting furnace and spent two years to great advantage in studying the processes of making iron. He next became junior member of the Phillips & Buttorff Manufacturing Company, at Nashville, makers of stoves, tinware, general wholesale hardware and house furnishings, in which lines they were both manufacturers and jobbers. Although his enter-prises took him elsewhere Mr. Buttorff still remains a member of this pros-perous concern at the Tennessee capital.

It was in the spring of 1901 that Mr. Buttorff transferred his activities to Southern Indiana, which was destined to be the scene of his future operations and his permanent home. He had been called to take up the responsible task of managing and superintending the complicated work of the Indiana Manufacturing Company and the Indiana Chain Works, in both of which he became a heavy stockholder. These establishments employ about five hundred men at the Indiana Reformatory, the first making cast-iron, stoves and hollow-ware, and the other manufacturing chains of all kinds. November 25, 1899, Mr. Buttorff was married to Cornelia Johnson, of Nashville, and they have two sons, Henry and Gordon. He holds fraternal relations with Clark Lodge, No. 40, Free and Accepted Masons, and the family enjoy an extensive acquaintance in the highest social circles of Jeffersonville and Louisville. They live in a beautiful home on the banks of the Ohio, enjoying a fine view up and down the great river, the residence being roomy, handsomely furnished and supplied with every modern convenience. Mr. Bottorff's financial success has not spoiled him in the least. He is affable and approachable, of pleasing personality and popular with all who meet him, either socially or in business.

MAJ. GEORGE DALLAS HAND.

Of the many soldiers furnished by the Keystone state to the army of the Union during the deadly struggles of the Civil war, none served more gallantly than the subject of this sketch. He belonged to an old and influential family from which he inherited patriotism and all those social courtesies of distinguished gentlemen of the old school. Dr. George Chew Hand, who was prominent as a physician in Philadelphia, was married in early manhood to Susan Taylor, an accomplished lady of the same city, and by this union there was a son, christened George Dallas, in honor of one of the country's foremost statesmen. George Dallas Hand was born at Allentown, Pennsylvania, and received a liberal education as he grew up. Through the influence of political friends his father secured him an appointment as cadet at the Annapolis Naval Academy, where he graduated with honors previous to the Civil war. He entered civil life but was not so engaged very long when the firing on Fort Sumpter electrified the country, and started a blaze that was only extinguished by the complete submission of the seceding states. Hastening to offer his services he was made captain of a company of the Lochiel Cavalry, recruited in Pennsylvania, but later was promoted to the rank of major of artillery in command at Fort Delaware, Pennsylvania.

In 1862 Major Hand married Mildred Cosby Lyon, a scion of one of the best known families of Jeffersonville, and a lady of many admirable qualities.

Her parents were Sidney S. and Honora Vincent Lyon, widely known in the social circles of the Falls Cities. Blanche Vincent Hand, the fruit of this union, married A. H. Simmons, of Louisville. Major Hand died November 5, 1892, and since then his widow has resided with her sister in Jeffersonville. The latter, formerly Blanche Lyon, was married May 23, 1859, to William Wallace Caldwell, who afterwards became prominent both in military and civil life. He was born at Portsmouth, Ohio, August 3, 1834, a son of James Gordon and Sarah (Leonard) Caldwell, and was brought to Jeffersonville by his parents when still a boy. Unusually precocious and ambitious he was appointed postmaster of Jeffersonville when twenty-one years of age. At the breaking out of the Civil war he raised Company D, of which he was elected captain and which became a part of the Twenty-third Indiana Infantry and kept them six weeks at his own expense. Later he recruited the Eighty-first Regiment, Indiana Volunteer Infantry, of which he was appointed colonel by Governor Morton and for a time was acting brigadier-general. After the war he resided for a while at Lafayette, but later returned to Jeffersonville, and finally located at Indianapolis, where he was general agent for a number of fire insurance companies. After a retention of this place for ten years he removed to Chicago, and continued in the same line of employment there for nearly twenty years. Colonel Caldwell died in Chicago, November 2, 1891. By his marriage with Blanche Lyon he had three children, of whom Mildred D. died in Chicago at the age of seventeen years. William Lyon Caldwell, the only son, is a resident of Indianapolis. Jessie Caldwell, the surviving daughter, married M. J. Ries, of East London, South Africa, and is now residing with her husband in that remote country.

JOSEPH J. HAWES.

A strong and courageous character that meets all life's duties and dangers with fortitude is Joseph J. Hawes, well known throughout Clark county as a popular official and in business circles as a successful manufacturer and merchant. This section was decidedly wild if not "woolly," when his grandfather, old Jason Hawes, left his home in New York and floated down the Ohio in 1824. Landing at Utica, he moved on to Washington county, but in a few years returned south and settled near Memphis. About the same time a family by the name of McGuire moved in from Alabama, and a friendship sprang up between the children of the two households, which resulted in the marriage of Isaac Hawes and Elizabeth McGuire. The former was born in New York, in 1809, was about fifteen years old when his parents reached Clark county. After his marriage he operated a saw mill at Memphis for twenty-two years incidentally following as a side line. He had eight children, all of whom are dead but the subject of this sketch.

Joseph J. Hawes was born on his father's homestead, near Memphis, Indiana, in 1838. When about seventeen years of age he quit school to become a brakeman on the old New Albany & Salem Railroad, but after a year and a half in this work he went with the Louisville & Nashville Railroad in January, 1859, in a similar capacity. About the beginning of 1861 he was promoted to the position of conductor on that road and continued in that line until 1879. He still has the "traveling letters" used in those days instead of passes, as souvenirs of his railroad experience. After leaving the road he located on a farm and began manufacturing barrels and lumber at Blue Lick, but in 1887 removed his plant to Memphis. Here he branched out with several additions to his original enterprise, consisting of a saw mill, stave factory and planing mill, besides a creamery which he erected in 1890. He also conducted an extensive general merchandise business, employed the best men he could get for assistants and keeping his own accounts. He was postmaster at Blue Lick until 1887, and held the same office at Memphis until Cleveland's second term. In 1884 he was elected Trustee of Union township on the Republican ticket and was re-nominated in 1886. Though the Democrats held no convention they placed Mr. Hawes' name on their ticket, realizing the uselessness of opposing one who had given such satisfaction in office. In 1880 Mr. Hawes made the race for Sheriff and though unsuccessful, ran four hundred and eighty-four votes ahead of his ticket in a strongly Democratic county. In 1894 he was re-nominated and elected and two years later was re-elected without canvassing or asking for the office. When his term expired, August 22, 1899, none of his official acts were questioned nor was the slightest explanation needed as to his manner of fulfilling the duties imposed upon him by the people. About that time he completed the building of his flouring mill at Memphis.

One of Mr. Hawes' playmates in his boyhood days was an attractive little girl named Mary B. Dietz, daughter of T. M. and Abigail (Guernsey) Dietz. Between them there grew up a friendship which ripened into love, which only ended with the death of one of the parties. They were married December 31, 1863, at Blue Lick, and lived together in unbroken affection until November 18, 1900, when Mrs. Hawes was called to answer the summons which none can escape. Their thirty-five years of wedded life were singularly happy and as they had no children all their affections were concentrated upon each other. Mrs. Hawes was a noble woman, loved and esteemed by all who knew her. Exactly four months after her death a large portion of Memphis was destroyed by fire and Mr. Hawes lost his store buildings and stock, a big ware-room, with flour and other goods. Since then he has devoted his attention to the flour mill and farming business, being also interested in a co-operative creamery company, of which he is president. He is a member of the Jeffersonville Lodge of Elks, and Hope Lodge, Knights of Pythias, at Jeffersonville.

CLYDE HOWARD.

No name is more familiar in Clark county than that of Howard. It has been associated for years with one of the most important industries of the Falls Cities, and members of the family have figured conspicuously in the political and business history of this section. Some of them have been prominent in all the walks of life while others have filled useful situations in the less showy occupations. Among the latter is Clyde Howard, secretary and treasurer of the Howard Ship Yards Company, a position he has filled acceptably over sixteen years. He was born in Jeffersonville in 1868, and is a son of Capt. Edward J. and Laura A. Howard. He received his education in the common schools of his native city and went through the high school and also attended a private school in Louisville, Kentucky. His life work has been in connection with the ship yards, having reached his present position when he was twenty-four years old.

On January 29, 1896, Mr. Howard was married to Julia Thompson, a native of Jeffersonville, and daughter of J. M. Thompson. They have three daughters, Laura Jean, Frances Rebecca and Ailsie. The family live quietly and unobtrusively enjoying their home life and society of friends.

A. J. CALLOWAY.

The family of this name is of Irish origin and descended from an emigrant who came over during the last half of the eighteenth century. John Calloway, a native of Dublin and son of a wealthy merchant of that city, was still young when he joined the tide settling in for the American colonies and crossed the ocean in time to join the movement for independence. There is a tradition that he became a soldier in the patriot army and after the treaty of peace settled in Virginia, where he died soon afterward. His son, Joseph, when four years old, accompanied his widowed mother, who decided to try her fortunes north of the Ohio, which held out the inducement of cheap land and easily acquired homes for the adventurous. Settling in Washington county, Indiana, Joseph grew to manhood and there married Polly Sloan, whose parents were among the pioneers from North Carolina. A. J. Calloway, one of the children by this union, was born in Washington county, Indiana, March 11, 1844,

and remained with his parents until his seventeenth year, which he reached
about the time the country was convulsed by the firing on Fort Sumpter. The
excitement, great among all classes, was especially felt by the boys who longed
to become soldiers and participate in "the pride, pomp and circumstance of
glorious war." Young Calloway caught the fever, like the rest of them, and
became a member of Company H, Thirty-eighth Regiment, Indiana Volunteer
Infantry, with which he went to the front and served faithfully for three
years. His command became a part of the great Army of the Cumberland
and participated in all the long marches and hard-fought battles of that celebrated corps. Returning after the cessation of hostilities, Mr. Calloway went
to Michigan and found employment at Owasso, where he spent two years and
then came back to Washington county, and settled near Chestnut Hill. Two
years later he removed to Bartle post-office, but still not being satisfied came in
1875 to Flower's Gap, between Borden and Henryville, in Clark county, where
he bought one hundred and sixty acres of land. In 1882 he located at Wilson's Switch, conducted a store at that place for a year and then returned to
the Chestnut Hill locality in Washington county. On May 16, 1892, he
established himself permanently in business at Sellersburg, where he has a
repair shop and deals in jewelry and millinery. As a side line, he represents
two of the large fire insurance companies and altogether makes a good living,
besides a modest profit from his various employments. For many years he has
been a member of the Christian church, of the Masons and the Independent
Order of Odd Fellows.

While living in Michigan Mr. Calloway married Margaret Burgess, by
whom he had six children, all of whom are married and well settled in life.
One of his daughters, Mrs. Perrin, has a grandson named Maxwell Jones,
and this puts Mr. Calloway in the great-grandfather class, though he as yet
not a very old man. In January, 1878, his wife died and on May 31, 1881,
he married Nancy J., daughter of James W. and Martha J. Stewart, of Washington county. By this union there are four daughters: Martha Jane, Hattie
Belle, Ella Aretta and Tina Pearl.

CHARLES W. McCULLOCH.

When Hugh McCulloch reached Clark county as an emigrant from "Old
Scotia," there was little in the land that was inviting and little in the prospect
that was pleasing. Before leaving Scotland he had married an English woman
named Sarah Guest, and with her made the long voyage which brought them
to Southern Indiana, in 1820. Settling at New Albany, then a mere hamlet,
the new arrivals from northern Europe made a living in agricultural pursuits,

which in those days were attended by great hardships and privations. They were unable to accumulate much and when their son, John McCulloch, started life it was as a poor boy, with a bitter struggle before him against adversity and toil in its worst forms. Cutting cord-wood and pealing tanbark were samples of his occupations, but out of it all with true Scottish thrift, he managed to save something and with this he bought a small piece of land. Eventually he found himself the proud possessor of a saw mill at New Albany, which he ran with considerable success until 1865, when he went into the flour milling business, but after a few years his establishment was burned down and this caused his temporary retirement. In the seventies he located on a farm near Jeffersonville, and lived there until his death, which occurred June 13, 1895. As he was born near New Albany, January 3, 1821, his age when the final summons came was nearly seventy-four years. On April 10, 1856, he married Martha Ann Fry, daughter of an old Kentucky pioneer family. Her father, John Fry, who came from the vicinity of Louisville, was the son of George Fry, who was born in Virginia, November 13, 1796. John married Sarah, daughter of John and Elizabeth (Oldeweiler) Swartz, who came from Germany in pioneer times and located in Clark county, at a date that entitled them to rank as early settlers. They were religious people and among the leaders in establishing the second church in Indiana, the same being subsequently known as the New Chapel of the Methodist Episcopal church, in Utica township. John and Martha Ann McCulloch had these children: Charles W., John, Franklin and James R., deceased in infancy; Sarah F., wife of John R. Lancaster, postmaster of Jeffersonville, whose sketch appears elsewhere in this volume; Martha, wife of C. K. Boyer, who resides near the old farm; Edward M. and Walter.

Charles W. McCulloch, eldest of the children, was born at New Albany, Floyd county, Indiana, February 1, 1857. He received his early education in the public schools of New Albany and also attended the high school there. He early decided to devote his life to farming pursuits and at once began this line of work with a zeal that has subsequently led to eminent success. He is at present the owner of a large and valuable farm near Jeffersonville, which is highly improved with a fine residence and excellent outbuildings, everything indicating progressiveness, thrift and prosperity.

On April 21, 1880, he was married to Mary E., daughter of Nathaniel Strong and Melissa (Smith) Matthews, of Jeffersonville. Their children are, Arthur Nathaniel, born February 16, 1881, and died September 23, 1906; Charles Raymond, born September 12, 1883; Laura Ethel, born September 12, 1888.

Mrs. McCulloch was born January 2, 1858, in Illinois. Mr. McCulloch is a member of Hope Lodge, Knights of Pythias, Company 9, of the Uniform Rank, and Jeffersonville Lodge, No. 362, Benevolent and Protective Order of

Elks. In politics he is a Republican. He and family are members of the First Presbyterian church at Jeffersonville.

JOHN SCHELLER.

Southern Indiana obtained its share of the much desired German immigration which was at its full tide during the two decades preceding the Civil war. Wherever these Germans located they left their impress for good on the community and when they were present in numbers, their power for progress was marked. About sixty years ago New Albany received one of these families consisting of the father and several stalwart sons and a daughter. Among the sons was John G. Scheller, who was born in Bavaria, Germany, September 1, 1811. His first business venture was as a grocer, but later he became a farmer and real estate dealer. He was active in Democratic politics, prominent in various local connections, dealt largely in live stock, retired from business at the age of sixty and died November 14, 1896. He had learned surveying in his native land, where he also obtained a good education and his main object in coming to America was to escape army service, it being necessary to smuggle him out of the country to avoid the sharp-eyed forces looking for conscripts. In 1845 he married Nancy Ann McCurdy, who was born at Balle Castle, Ireland, in 1807, and died February 28, 1901. They had four children: Anna Jane, now Mrs. Brown; John, William and James.

John Scheller, the second child, was born at New Albany, Floyd county, Indiana, January 29, 1848. He received but a limited education in the poorly equipped schools available during his childhood, became a farmer in early manhood and has spent most of his adult life in agricultural pursuits. He has held many offices of trust and profit and discharged all their duties with efficiency and integrity. He served as postmaster of Sellersburg for eight years, president of the Town Board, treasurer of the School Board for many years and by election and re-election was County Commissioner for three terms. The last of his nine years of service in this responsible office expired on the first of January, 1909. Though he resides in Sellersburg, his farm, which lies just outside of the town limits, occupies the principal part of his attention. His life has been one of unusual activity and he is one of the best known men in the county.

On June 10, 1872, Mr. Scheller married Mary Jane, daughter of Alfred Farrabee, who came here from North Carolina. Her mother was a daughter of Moses Sellers, who gave the town of Sellersburg its name and he built the first house in the village, the fact that it was constructed of brick making it rather noteworthy for those days. Moses Sellers was a preacher and rail-splitter. but also engaged in the huckster business and had a big store at Sellers-burg. For years he enjoyed a large trade and by the time of his death had accumulated a considerable fortune. To Mr. and Mrs. Scheller five children have been born: Harry, deceased in infancy; Anna Belle, Maggie Ellen, Daniel and Nora. The family are members of the Christian church. Mr. Scheller is a member of the Independent Order of Odd Fellows and donated the lot on which their local hall stands. Owing to the vigor of its various members and their success in various callings to say nothing of their personal popularity the Schellers have long been regarded as one of the prominent and influential families of the county.

WILLIAM SAMPLE.

William Sample, of Henryville, Clark county, is a venerable citizen of the township in which he lives. His settlement in his present location dates from the close of the Civil war in which he took part and sustained a wound. Since that time he has become familiar to his neighbors as a man of rigid honesty; and as one who has ever been interested in the industrial progress and moral advancement of the community.

The subject of this biographical sketch was born on March 12, 1832, in Scott county, Indiana, and was the son of Robert and Jane (McClain) Sample. Both parents were of Kentucky families. Robert Sample was born in 1792, in the Blue Grass state and was a gunsmith by trade. He came to Indiana about the time of his marriage, located first in Ripley county, removing to Scott county and later to Jackson county, where he died in 1844. He took part in the War of 1812. In politics he was a pronounced Whig, but took no strenuous part in the politics of his day. His wife died in Scott county, having attained to her seventieth year. She and her husband had eleven children, of whom our subject was the eighth in order of birth.

William Sample began his career on his own resources at a very early age and from that time has been solely engaged in the farming business. In 1852 his marriage to Abigail Gray, the daughter of Orin C. Gray, of Scott county, took place. The Gray family came from New York to Scott county. Mrs. Sample was born on the 3d of February, 1836. She has led a happy life and has borne her husband ten children, namely: Alice, born October 24, 1853, died in infancy; Thomas B., born March 27, 1855, also died in infancy; Watson, born May 2, 1857, died June 12th of the same year; Annis, born June 15, 1858, died October 1, 1859; Alexander, born August 1, 1860, married Anna Cramer; they have one child and live in Indianapolis. Lilly, born April 11, 1863, married Martin Hosteter and lives in Monroe township; they

47

have seven children. Orin C. was born April 19, 1866, and was killed while coupling cars at Frankfort, Indiana, August 12, 1887. Charlotte R., born in May, 1868, married James Shear; they live in Scott county. Mary J. was born June 25, 1871, married Charles Whittinghill; they live in Memphis, Indiana, and have seven children. The youngest member of our subject's family, Eleanora S., was born September 29, 1875, married Alexander Carter, and lives with our subject.

In 1862 William Sample enlisted in the Union army at New Albany, Indiana, August 14th, under command of Captain Howard and Colonel Caldwell. Stone River and Chickamauga were the most important fights participated in; and in the latter engagement he received a wound which caused him to be confined in a hospital for a long period. At Perryville he received his baptism of fire and as his place on the field was amongst the scouts he was practically fighting all the time in skirmishes with the enemy. In consideration of his war services he is in receipt of a pension from the government.

At the close of the war Mr. Sample engaged in farming and stock raising in Clark county and in which he has been eminently successful. Educational facilities were slight in his youth and he did not have much schooling. In politics he is a Republican and a member of the Christian church. He is a well preserved man for his age though unable to participate actively in work any longer. He lives in comfortable surroundings on his land in section 241.

JOHN M. KIRK.

John M. Kirk, of Otisco, Clark county, Indiana, is well known as a prosperous farmer and cooper in his section of the county. He comes from an honorable line of ancestry; his great-great-grandfather coming to this country in the first emigrant ship that set out from Scotland prior to the Revolutionary war and he, together with eight of his sons, fought in that struggle. Our subjest is now close to his seventy-ninth year and has led a life of activity, which has ever gained the admiration of his friends and neighbors.

John M. Kirk was born on the 18th of September, 1830, in Washington county, Pennsylvania, and was the son of Jesse and Nancy (McSherry) Kirk. Jesse Kirk was born on the 1st of October, 1805, in the same county and became a farmer in the Kirk settlement in Western Pennsylvania. He was the son of a soldier of the Revolution who had served seven years in that historic conflict. After the Revolution he was given a section of land—the Kirk settlement referred to. It was settled by his comrades of the war as was also the surrounding territory. Even so far east as Western Pennsylvania the Indians caused much trouble in those days. When Jesse Kirk came to Clark county the surrounding country was in its state of primitive wilderness. Settlements were few and far between, and deer, wolves, and many kinds of wild animals roved at will through the timber. Jesse Kirk bought land in section 208 and made all the improvements on same. Though not a public man he was well known in his part of the county. He came here from Pennsylvania with a small colony of pioneers, coming from Wheeling to Charlestown, Indiana, on the river, and rode the rest of the way over the blazed trail. This was in the year 1846 and with them was his wife and the subject of our sketch. Jesse Kirk became a large farmer and stock raiser in Clark county and died in 1881. He was a well known man and a member of the Presbyterian church. His people were famous for their longevity; his mother lived to the age of one hundred and three, and his father reached the century mark previous to his death. Nancy (McSherry) Kirk was born in 1803 in the same settlement as was her husband, in Pennsylvania. Her parents were natives of Ireland. Her marriage took place in Washington, Pennsylvania, in 1828, and eight children were subsequently born, of whom John M. and three sisters survive. President Monroe, whose name is enshrined on the roll of those who have held, in the early days, office as chief executive of the nation, was a near relation of the Kirk family. He was an uncle of Jesse Kirk, our subject's grandmother being his sister.

John M. Kirk started on his own account in the farming and coopering business directly after his marriage to Mary Kemple. This event occurred in 1853. His wife was born in Ohio and was of Virginian extraction. Her parents were William and Leana (Davis) Kemple. Mrs. Kirk was born on January 7, 1834, and died several years ago. She bore her husband the following children: Leana, born in 1834, married Francis Prall; they have nine children and live in Henryville. Addie was born in 1855 and married Philip Hartman; they have three children and live in Clark county. Sarah Jane, born March 4, 1859, married John W. Huffman; they live in Clark county and have two children. Lucretia May was born September 1, 1861, and married Jacob Kahl; they live in Clark county and have five children. Rebecca, born October 31, 1863, died when young. Jesse, born May 25, 1865, married Emma Hughes; they live in Clark county. Alice Ebbie, born January 26, 1869, lives at home; and Cora, born January 20, 1872, married Alora B. Barber and lives in Louisville.

As previously stated Mr. Kirk is a cooper by trade. He owns land in section 226. In politics he is a Republican and voted for the first time for Franklin Pierce for the Presidency. In religion he is a member of the Presbyterian church. He did not get very much of an education in his youth, attending but four winter terms. This, however, did not hinder his achieving success in the school of practical experience. He is a well preserved man for his age and lives in security and comfort in the family homestead. Rheumatism in a

severe form precluded him from seeing active service in the Civil war much
to his regret. Had it been otherwise, this relative of the illustrious expounder
of "The Monroe Doctrine" would assuredly have taken a man's part in the
service of his country.

EDWARD L. PERRINE.

Edward L. Perrine, of Henryville, Clark county, is one of the most intelligent and experienced farmers in his section of the county and a man who
has taken an acute interest in the public affairs of the township. He is now in
his sixty-second year and during his career fought as a soldier in the Civil
war, taking part, among other engagements, in Sherman's famous march to
the sea. Outside of his farming activities he has been active in political circles
and has a large number of friends in Clark county.

The subject of our sketch was born in Scott county, Indiana, on the 5th
of November, 1846, and was the son of D. C. Perrine and his wife, whose
maiden name was Mahala Finley. D. C. Perrine was born in 1812, in Staten
Island, New York, and was a cooper by trade. In his twenty-second year he
came to Scott county, Indiana, where he married a short time after. He was
in the mercantile business in the county for a number of years. In the political
arena of his day he became a Whig and took an active part in the public life
of Scott county. He died in 1879 at New Albany, having retired from business in which he engaged in that city during his later years. Mahala Finley
was born in 1817, in Kentucky, and was the daughter of John and Matilda
Finley. She and her husband had eight children. D. C. Perrine was married twice and our subject was a son by the first marriage. The elder Perrine
was a great friend of old Major English, although they agreed to differ
politically.

When about fourteen years old Edward L. Perrine learned the shoemak-
ing trade and at the outbreak of the Civil war enlisted in Company D, Fifty-
third Indiana Infantry, under command of Capt. William Howard, of Jeffersonville, and Colonel Gresham. He figured in the Georgia campaign and
served until the close of the war, at which time he was in a hospital. On returning home, having obtained his discharge, he went to Hartsville University,
took a scientific course, and came to Monroe township, where he taught school
for sixteen years at the old Beckett school-house. At the close of his teaching
career he became a farmer on the place where he now lives, in section 257. He
married Mary Dieterlen, born on June 15, 1849, in Rochester, New York.
She was the daughter of Christian and Caroline Dieterlen. Her father died
when she was an infant, her mother remarried and came to Clark county about
1857. Edward L. Perrine and his wife have led a happy married life. The

following eleven children were born to them: Victor Hugo, born October 8, 1870, who married Nettie Monroe, has six children, and lives at Memphis, Indiana; Louisa was born February 18, 1872, and died October 24th of the same year; Minnie, born April 7, 1874, who married the Rev. Harvey Park, lives in Huntington county and has one child; Alice, born June 11, 1876, married Dr. Bine Whitlatch, located in Pierceville, Indiana, and they have one child; Rose, who was born April 18, 1878, married Lewis Monroe, living in Jeffersonville and they have four children; Ella, born May 6, 1880, who married James Doyle, has one child and they live in Oklahoma; Edward H. was born May 26, 1883, and resides at home; Millie, born March 14, 1885, also resides with her parents; Tomaline, born October 29, 1887, lives in Indianapolis; Charles F., born August 13, 1889, lives at home, and Arthur F., born April 3, 1893, died on the 6th of September, 1895.

Mr. Perrine is a Republican in politics. He was Assessor of the township for six years. In 1890 he stood as his party's candidate for Auditor, but suffered defeat. He is at present Deputy Sheriff under Oscar Johnson. He with the members of his family belong to the Methodist Episcopal church. He belongs to the Masonic Order. Edward L. Perrine owns a very fine family residence three miles east of Henryville. His land was formerly the property of a daughter of Gen. William Preston of the Confederate army. The Prestons were cousins of Gen. George Rogers Clark and owned the land which was known as Preston tract, No. 257, from the time of the survey here.

AARON N. WARMAN.

In the first quarter of the nineteenth century a young Englisman appeared among the pioneers of Southern Indiana. He was secretive as to his private affairs and no record was left of the time or place of his birth. He entered government land and later bought some school land and spent the working period of his life in clearing and improving his possessions. Scott and Clark counties, in which Aaron Warman figured, were at that time a wilderness filled with deer and other wild game, while wolves made night hideous by their dismal howling. The settlers, however, were of a sturdy race and nothing daunted them in their efforts to make homes and better their conditions. So Aaron Warman, full of English pluck and indomitable will, struggled on until he had his wild land reduced into respectable shape. He was inclined to be religious, was long an active member of the Methodist church and became well known in the section where he lived. He married Jane Cox, daughter of an old pioneer Kentucky family. Her father, John Cox, left her with her grandfather and went over into Indiana at the time of the celebrated Pigeon Roost massacre. He was an Indian fighter of note, having gained experience in "The Dark and Bloody Ground," and he helped to drive the red-skins out of Southern Indiana after the bloody scenes at Pigeon Roost. His father lived to the remarkable age of one hundred and ten years. About one year subsequent to the massacre his granddaughter, Jane, then a mere child, followed her father to the state north of the Ohio. By their marriage, in 1830, Aaron and Jane (Cox) Warman had sixteen children, consisting of fourteen boys and two girls.

Aaron N. Warman, the only survivor of the above mentioned large family, was born December 31, 1830, on the banks of the Ohio river, in Clark county, Indiana. There were no public schools in those days and like all other boys he had to pick up his learning as best he could. He began farming for himself at the age of eighteen and soon had a good farm, which he managed success-fully. At the breaking out of the Civil war he enlisted in Company K, Sixty-sixth Regiment, Indiana Volunteer Infantry, which was eventually as-signed to the command of Gen. John A. Logan. In the battle of Richmond his regiment suffered severely, the survivors being captured, paroled and sub-sequently exchanged. They were sent to Corinth and from there joined Sher-man in his campaign from Dalton to Atlanta, thence in the famous march to the sea, up the coast and on to Washington for the grand review. Mr. War-man was in nearly all the great battles of this campaign and saw much of arduous service during his three years as a soldier under the Union flag. After the war he served as postmaster at Underwood under Presidents McKinley and Roosevelt, meantime conducting a grocery business, but owing to advanc-ing years he resigned the office in 1906 to live a retired life. He has always been an active politician on the Republican side but never sought office. He recalls with pleasure that he helped to build the first school-house in Vienna township, Scott county. Religious in his temperament he has long been a mem-ber of the Methodist Episcopal church, in which he has been an enthusiastic worker and class leader for over fifty years and a licensed exhorter for more than thirty years. He is highly respected as one of the old-time pioneers of the county and one of the few remaining whose recollections reach back in the thirties long before the Mexican war. He received a pension as an hon-orable recognition of his devoted services during the Civil war and is a mem-ber of the Scottsburg Post, Grand Army of the Republic.

On February 19, 1852, Mr. Warman was married to Katherine C., daugh-ter of William and Cynthia (Collins) Anderson, who was born in Clark coun-ty, in 1832. They were the parents of ten children: Lorenzo D., James G., Zebulon G. (deceased), Jane Alice (deceased), William N., Mary, Aaron E., George Anna, Oliver (deceased), and Milford C. His first wife dying in 1902, Mr. Warman married in 1904 to Mary M. Guynn, who was born in Ger-many, August 21, 1849, and came to America when about four years old. Few men are better preserved for the evening of life than Mr. Warman.

JAMES CALVIN GLOSSBRENNER.

Not the least interesting among the many beautiful waterways of the Middle West is the Ohio, rushing at times in rapids, or gliding in a calmer mood around its many graceful windings. The bluffs and hills that grace its banks are marks of beauty, the fame of which has become a matter of more than local interest. Furthermore, when the season for overflows approaches, a new interest in the famous stream is at once awakened, for it is then that its turbulent waters become a menace to life and property.

On a beautiful spot overlooking this stream is the residence of James Calvin Glossbrenner, who, for the last ten years, has had an opportunity to become familiar with the varying moods of the river, being employed by the Jeffersonville & Louisville Ferry Company. Mr. Glossbrenner was born in Jeffersonville on the 16th of July, 1880, being the son of John and Rachael (Swartz) Glossbrenner, both of whom were natives of Clark county, Indiana. Our subject received his education in the city public schools and attended the high school until he reached the age of eighteen, at which time he entered the employ of the company mentiond above.

On the 10th of April, 1902, Mr. Glossbrenner was united in marriage to Shirley Canter, who was born in Utica township on the 11th day of April, 1880. She is the daughter of L. A. and Jennie (Brendel) Canter, both born in Clark county.

Mr. Glossbrenner and wife are members of the Presbyterian church and are held in high regard by their fellow workers, on account of their unobtrusive yet sincere devotion to the principles for which the denomination stands. In their social intercourse with friends and neighbors the same spirit is apparent and their beautiful home overlooking the river is often the scene of genial hospitality and social freedom.

Politically Mr. Glossbrenner espouses the Republican cause, but has had no aspirations for office or political prominence.

JOHN ELLIS POTTER.

John Ellis Potter was born in Jefferson township, Clark county, Indiana, on the 13th of August, 1869. He was the son of John T. and Matilda (Miller) Potter, both natives of Kentucky, where they grew to maturity and were married before coming to Indiana. Their family consisted of seven children besides our subject, viz: Frank, Molly, Clara, Ella, George, Sallie and William. Frank became the husband of Mary Dils; Clara and Ella died when young; George was married to Emma Smith; Sally became the wife of John Yarbrough; William departed this life when eighteen years of age.

John Ellis Potter was educated in the public schools of Clark county and later took a business course at the New Albany Business College. At the age of twenty-one he decided to make farming his occupation in life and accordingly assumed control of a farm of two hundred and seventy-five acres in Utica township which he has managed very successfully ever since.

On the 22d of April, 1891, Mr. Potter was united in marriage to Emma Redding, his wife at that time living in the same house in which the groom was born. His wife was the daughter of John and Mary Redding. She was one of three children, having one brother, Floyd, and one sister, Ella.

Mr. and Mrs. Potter are the parents of two children, viz: Ivy, born August 28, 1892, and Hallie, born September 5, 1894. Mr. Potter is liberal in his religious views and affiliates with the Republican party.

FAIRES COLWELL.

The West was decidedly wild when John Colwell left his Maryland home to make the long trip to Kentucky then chiefly famous for Indian affrays and the sturdy character of the men who were trying to reclaim the rich lands along the Ohio river from the warlike red men. Daniel Boone was still living when he reached the "Dark and Bloody Ground," though he had transferred his abode to the distant region beyond the Mississippi. Simon Kenton and Lewis Wetzel were at the height of their fame as Indian fighters and Henry Clay had already entered upon the career which was to make him nationally famous. From Kentucky after a residence of some years John Colwell crossed the river into the newer and more promising territory of Indiana, taking up his residence first in Dearborn county. From there he came to Clark county, which was destined to be his permanent residence. He entered land in Monroe township and became a farmer and stock raiser. He lived to a very advanced age, and was nearing the century mark when he passed away at the home where he had so long labored. In young manhood he had married Mary Burk, a native of Tennessee, where her parents had been early pioneers. She too was quite old at the time of her death. This venerable couple had twelve children, all of whom are dead but Faires and Rebecca, the latter, who lives with her brother, being over ninety-five years old and very feeble at this writing.

Faires Colwell, the only surviving son, was born in Dearborn county, Indiana, January 11, 1836. He was quite a young child when his parents came to Clark county and grew up amid the wild scenes characteristic of the country of that day. Settlements were sparse, neighbors lived far apart, everything was forest without roads or means of transportation away from the river. Game abounded and on this the settlers relied almost entirely for their meat. Education beyond the most meager attainments was out of the question for most of the pioneer boys, as schools were rare and of the rudest kind, kept up by spasmodic subscriptions and usually poorly taught by wandering pedagogues. So Faires was able to pick up but little book learning in his youth, though in after life he made up for this want by reading, attending public speakings and the observation of the world that is natural to the observant man. He engaged in farming in early manhood, and has devoted his entire life to agricultural pursuits.

On November 16, 1862, Mr. Colwell was married to Lucinda Allen, who was born in Monroe township in 1846. She was the daughter of James Allen and wife, who came to Clark county at an early period in its history. Two children were born to Mr. and Mrs. Colwell, both of whom are dead. Both the Colwells and the Burks were of Irish origin and as is often the case with that sturdy race were unusually long lived. Mr. Colwell after a long, laborious and blameless life is spending the evening of his life in repose, on the farm where he put in so many hard licks, during his working period. He has always ranked as a good citizen, doing his duty by his fellow men and obeying the laws of his country.

JOHN R. LANCASTER.

John Lancaster, father of our subject, was born in Lexington, Kentucky, located with his parents in Indiana at the age of seven years, his father being a farmer, also did some boating on the Ohio river. During the war Mr. Lancaster was intimately associated with Oliver P. Morton. He acted as private detective along the Ohio river, receiving his orders direct from Governor Morton. He was also captain of the Switzerland County Home Guards, and was prominent in the Morgan raid. Following this he was engaged in river traffic, which he followed until about 1873, when he went to Cass county, Missouri, and engaged in the grocery business which he followed up to the time of his death. The mother of John R. Lancaster, of this review, was a Johnson, her parents coming from England. She died at the age of seventy-four years. To them eight children were born, four boys and four girls, and all these are living but one.

John R. Lancaster, the only one of the family in Indiana, his brother and sisters all being in the West, was born in Switzerland county, Indiana, January 14, 1853. When his father came to Jeffersonville he went to work in the shoe store of S. Goldbach as a salesman and retained this position for about six years, then resigning he opened a shoe store for Calvin W. Prather and continued in charge of this establishment for two years. His next move was to enter into partnership with Jacob Loomis, which firm was later dissolved and the business continued for a number of years by Mr. Lancaster alone. He erected the building in which the store was conducted and it is still running under the ownership of B. A. Coll. In 1906 Mr. Lancaster was appointed postmaster of Jeffersonville, and a year later sold his shoe store in order that he might devote all of his time to his official duties.

On October 13, 1880, Mr. Lancaster married Sarah F., daughter of John McCulloch, a prominent and wealthy farmer residing northwest of Jeffersonville. Mrs. Lancaster's mother was Martha A. Fry, member of the family of that name that is so well known in Utica township. Her father was John Fry, a prominent citizen of the county. To Mr. and Mrs Lancaster three children have been born, the eldest of whom died in infancy. Ralph J., the second child, was a young man of good education and fine promise but while attending Purdue University was afflicted with a spinal trouble, which caused his death December 22, 1907, in the twentieth year of his age. Edwin R., the only survivor of Mr. Lancaster's little family, is employed in the plumbing business at Louisville, Kentucky. In politics Mr. Lancaster is a Republican and has always been active in the interest of his party, during campaigns. He is regarded as a wise counselor as well as an enthusiastic worker. In 1874 under the pastorate of Rev. J. M. Hutchinson he joined the congregation of the First Presbyterian church and has ever since been an enthusiastic and devoted member. He also takes interest in fraternity affairs, being a member of Jeffersonville Lodge, No. 340, Free and Accepted Masons, Hope Lodge, No. 13, Knights of Pythias, and the Benevolent and Protective Order of Elks. Mr. Lancaster enjoys local popularity.

SAMUEL LOGAN SCOTT.

The genealogy of the Scotts is traceable through old Southern families on both sides of the house, and they were honorably mentioned in connection with the pioneer development of Southern Indiana. John Scott, a native of Kentucky, came to Clark county, Indiana, at an early day and left his mark in the community where his active life was passed. About the time of his arrival, James McKinley, a native of Old Virginia, joined the ranks of settlers in Clark county, and figured conspicuously in subsequent years of growth. He was a cousin of the late President McKinley's father, and a man of high standing in all the relations of life. Herbert Scott, a son of John, married Nancy, the daughter of James McKinley, and thus brought about a union of two old pioneer families. Herbert Scott was born and reared in Clark county, became a farmer and spent his entire life in agricultural pursuits in the counties of Clark and Floyd. He survived until the advanced age of seventy-nine and his wife was seventy-four years old at the time of her death. They had fifteen children, nine sons and six daughters, all of whom grew to maturity and are still living except one.

Samuel Logan Scott, eighth in numerical order of this large family, was born near Borden, in Floyd county, Indiana, February 27, 1867. He was reared on the parental farm, attended the neighborhood schools and later was graduated from the high school department of Borden College, which was supplemented by a degree obtained by graduation from the college in 1889. With a view to preparation for educational work Mr. Scott entered the Ladoga Normal in 1890 and after graduating from that instiution practically completed the course at the Indiana State Normal. In the meantime he had for ten years been engaged in teaching in the schools of Clark county and for three years was superintendent of the schools at Clarksville. In 1897 he was elected superintendent of schools for Clark county and has been re-elected three times without opposition, which is a high tribute to popularity and efficiency. In 1902 he was nominated as a candidate for the office of State Superintendent of Public Instruction and although he led his ticket he went down in the general defeat which overtook his party that year. In recognition of his standing as an educator, Dr. Robert J. Aley, who was elected State Superintendent, in 1908, appointed Mr. Scott as first assistant in the office, but he declined the same, preferring to remain in his old position. In 1903 he served as a member of the board of inspectors for the Indiana State Normal, and was president of the County Superintendents' State Association in 1907. Mr. Scott is a member of the Masonic fraternity, and the Modern Woodmen.

In April, 1906, Mr. Scott was married to Emma Louise Schimpff, a native of Jeffersonville, and member of one of the city's prominent families. Her father, Charles Schimpff, is a well known business man and now filling the office of City Comptroller. Mr. and Mrs. Scott have one child, a daughter, and by a former marriage Professor Scott has two children, a son and a daughter. He is a member of the Christian church, while his wife's religious affiliations are with the German Lutheran.

WILLIAM J. MORRIS.

The family of this name in Jeffersonville is one of American and German origin, and has been identified with the city from a time shortly succeeding the Civil war. Edward E. Morris was born in Maryland, near Baltimore, in 1843, but while quite young the family moved to Pennsylvania, and later to Pottsville, in that state, where Mr. Morris lived until 1878. In 1878 Edward

E. Morris came to Jeffersonville and took employment with the Pennsylvania Railroad Company, with which he is still identified, at present serving it in the capacity of road foreman of engines. In 1862 he was married to Anna Catherine Marquardt, who was born in Wurtemberg, Germany, in 1842, and still survives. They had six children, of whom two survive:

Willliam J. Morris was born in Pottsville, Pennsylvania, July 20, 1868, and was ten years old when the family came to Jeffersonville. After completing the course in the public schools he secured employment with the Pennsylvania Company, and remained with the same for fifteen years as its general timekeeper. In January, 1901, he embraced an opportunity to go into business for himself, in which he has met with marked success. From the estate of George J. Liebel he purchased a jewelry and optical business, which by extensive improvement and enlargement has become one of the features of the city. The establishment contains the largest and most varied assortment of optical supplies in Jeffersonville. There is a complete equipment for the grinding of lenses, which is a decided innovation, as such features are practically unknown outside of the large cities. The department devoted to the optical work is equipped with a complete and modern outfit. Especial attention is given to instruments for testing the eye, and supplying its needs with the latest and most scientific improvements. In addition to the optical department, a full line of merchandise is carried, and all kinds of repair work is done—a first class watchmaker and clerk being employed as assistants. Mr. Morris has infused into his business a spirit of energy and up-to-dateness. and as a result his establishment is one that not only elicits compliments from all patrons, but is a decided credit to the city, and compares very favorably with the best to be found in the larger cities.

In 1888 Mr. Morris was united in marriage to Carrie Dale Willey, member of an old and highly respected family of this county. Her father, Dennis F. Willey, who died recently, served during the Civil war as an enthusiastic soldier for the Union, and was a man much esteemed during his later life. Mrs. Morris's mother, Mrs. Amanda F. Willey, is a resident of Charlestown, in this county. Mr. and Mrs. Morris have five children: Kathryne Dale, Mary Amanda, Anna Ruth, Carrie Willey and E. Elbridge, all of whom still remain at home with their parents.

Mr. Morris is a prominent member of the Masonic fraternity, being connected with Clark Lodge, No. 40, Free and Accepted Masons; Horeb Chapter, No. 66, Royal Arch Masons; and Jeffersonville Commandery, No. 27, Knights Templar, and is also a member of the Murat Temple, Ancient Arabic Order Nobles Mystic Shrine, of Indianapolis, Indiana. His political affiliation is with the Republican party. The family are members of the Methodist church, and attend services at the Wall Street church, of which Mr. Morris is chorister.

OLIVER CRONE.

The parents on both sides of the house of this worthy representative of the Crone family, were among the early pioneers of Indiana, Washington Crone, the father of Oliver, having come from the state of Virginia where he was born, to the Hoosier state when he was twelve years old, being accompanied by his parents. The grandfather of our subject entered land in Harrison county upon his arrival in the new country, which was then all a wilderness, the principal towns in this part of the country being Louisville and Corydon.

The date of Oliver Crone's birth is recorded as July 22, 1847, having first seen the light of day in Harrison county, this state, the son of Washington and Savilla (Riley) Crone, who lived on a good farm which they developed. Oliver was only eight years old when his father died. Oliver Crone's maternal grandfather had the distinction of serving in the War of 1812, under command of Gen. William Henry Harrison. Savilla Riley was born in Harrison county, this state, in 1827, and she passed to her rest in 1899. She and Washington Crone were married in Harrison county, and to them two children were born, Oliver and a daughter named Elizabeth, who died when three years of age.

The early education of Oliver Crone was obtained in the common schools of Harrison county, and in the County Academy; a year was also spent in the high school of New Albany. After his school days were over he started in life for himself when about twenty years old, taking up farming which he has continued with unabating success to the present time. Upon coming to Clark county he at once resumed farming and he has remained here, developing an excellent farm and making a good living by his habits of persistent toil and good management, his valuable property, one hundred and forty acres of which is in cultivation, the rest being as yet in timber, is located in sections 200, 216 and 217. He has made all the extensive improvements on the place which today render it well up to the standard farms of Carr township. On it is to be seen a fine house with attractive surroundings and convenient out-buildings. Considerable attention is devoted to stock raising, good breeds of various kinds of live stock being kept on the place from year to year.

Mr. Crone was united in marriage with Mary A. Whalen in 1869. She is the daughter of Charles P. and Margaret J. (Slider) Whalen, and her birth occurred in Clark county, October 23, 1850. Her father was born October 27, 1824, and after an eminently active and useful life, he passed to his rest in 1894. Margaret J. Slider was born October 3, 1828, and she joined her husband in the silent land in 1906. They were early pioneers of Clark county and were well known and influential people.

To Mr. and Mrs. Oliver Crone six children were born, named in order of birth as follows: Hattie, born December 29, 1869, married James W. Huffman; they are the parents of five children and they live in Clark county; Lizzie, born April 10, 1871, married William L. Beyl; they are the parents of two children, and also reside in this county; Alva, who was born October 8, 1874, died when four years of age; Charles P., born July 9, 1877, married Flora D. Beyl; they are residents of Clark county and are the parents of four children; Oliver W., who was born January 1, 1885, married Clara Tolan; they are the parents of one child and are living in this county; Mary Arnold, the youngest of the children, was born June 3, 1891. They have all received fairly good educations and are well situated in life.

Since 1876 Mr. Crone has been active in politics. He served in a very acceptable manner for a period of fifteen years, as Township Trustee of Carr township; he was Assessor for a period of six years, and at this writing he is County Commissioner. He served for four years as deputy Sheriff, under P. C. Donovan. He has three more years to serve as Commissioner, having begun his term of office in 1909. He is keeping up his excellent record, established long ago as a public servant; all the time he has served his constituents they have never had occasion to complain at any of his work. In politics he is a staunch Democrat.

In his fraternal relations Mr. Crone is a member of Lodge No. 94, Independent Order of Odd Fellows at Charlestown; also a member of Hope Lodge, No. 13, Knights of Pythias at Jeffersonville. Mrs. Crone and family are consistent members of the Methodist Episcopal church.

Our subject is one of the best known men in this section of Clark county, and he and his family are all popular with their neighbors, being people of the highest honor, courteous and kind-hearted.

HAMILTON ROBINSON.

The life of Mr. Robinson was such as to bear aloft the high standard which had been maintained by his ancestors who were among the early pioneers of this section of the Middle West, the life of the subject having been signally noble, upright and useful, one over which fell no shadow of wrong or suspicion of evil. Such was the type of men who laid the foundation and aided in the development of this and neighboring states, and to their memories will ever be paid a tribute of reverence and gratitude by those who have profited by their well directed endeavors and appreciated the lessons of their lives. In the early days when the great network of railways that now penetrate every section of the continent were not dreamed of, and steamboats practically had a monopoly on the transportation of both passengers and freight, Hamilton

Robinson was one of the best known men along the Ohio river from Louisville to New Orleans. He was born in Pennsylvania in 1810, the son of John and Nancy (Archibald) Robinson, natives of the old Keystone state, and of Irish and English extraction, respectively.

John Robinson grew to maturity in his native state, married and engaged in farming there, later removing to Kankakee, Illinois, where he engaged in farming on an extensive scale, owning large tracts of land, and was known as one of the most prominent and substantial of the pioneers in that locality, although he was called from his earthly labors there when yet a young man, aged thirty-seven years. His family consisted of four children, three sons and a daughter. His widow afterwards married Absalom Kent, this family having also been among the early pioneers of that part of Illinois.

Hamilton Robinson was but a child when his parents located in Illinois, and he was a small boy when his father died. When a mere lad he was apprenticed to the machinist's trade and when twenty years old he came to Jeffersonville, Indiana, and although having been well equipped to follow his trade his fondness for the life of a river man could not be overcome, and he gave up the machinist idea and won both fame and success from a financial standpoint, for many years his name having been a very familiar one on the steamers that plied the waters of the Ohio, during which time many interesting events transpired which he delighted to recount in his old age. Retiring from the steamboat business he established an iron foundry at Jeffersonville, which was conducted with gratifying results for a number of years. He later engaged in the milling business which also grew to large proportions under his capable management. In all his business life he showed rare innate ability and soundness of judgment, and was regarded as being very careful to guard the rights of others while advancing his own interests.

Mr. Robinson was married soon after coming to Jeffersonville, when about twenty years old, choosing as a life partner Sarah Lankiskis, a native of Lancaster, Pennsylvania, the daughter of John and Mary (Darst) Lankiskis, the former a native of Poland, while the latter was of sterling Pennsylvania Dutch stock. Sarah Lankiskis was a young girl when she came to Clark county, Indiana, with her parents, who were early settlers here, having located on the farm east of Jeffersonville, now owned by Mrs. Nora V. Duffy, a granddaughter. John Lankiskis, who died while living on this farm, is buried in a small burying ground near there. His widow, who survived him several years, died at Jeffersonville.

Hamilton Robinson and wife were the parents of the following children: John, James, Francis, Mary and Nora V., all deceased except the last named.

During the last years of his life Hamilton Robinson made his home with his daughter, Mrs. Nora V. Duffy, and from there he was called to his reward in 1896, having been preceded to the silent land by his wife by twenty years.

Early in life Mr. Robinson joined the Independent Order of Odd Fellows, being one of the oldest members of that order in Jeffersonville, having for years been very active in its affairs. He was a member of the Universalist church, and he was always a Democrat, although he never sought political emoluments at the hands of his party. Owing to his long life of fidelity to correct principles and his honesty, kindness and genuine worth he retained to the last the high esteem of all who knew him.

WILLIAM E. BOWER, Sr.

In examining the record of this honored pioneer of Washington township we find that laudable ambition for a competence was the potent force and incentive which led him forward, and that as a result of his strong purpose, determination and energy he has won a place among the substantial citizens of Clark county, being one of her representative farmers, having spent his long and useful life within her borders and played no inconspicuous part in the development of the general welfare of the section of his nativity.

William E. Bower, Sr., was born in Washington township, Clark county, October 19, 1833. Henry Bower, the great-grandfather of the subject, who died when eighty years old, was a native of Sweden, from which country he emigrated to the United States, locating in New York, later going to Pennsylvania, thence to North Carolina. He served as a soldier in the Revolutionary war throughout that sanguinary struggle. He and his wife were the parents of eleven children. One of these was Andrew, who was the father of W. E. Bower. He married Polly Lawrence, and they were the parents of seven children, namely: Henry, who died when a small boy; Andrew J., George W., William E., Eliza J., Mariah and Margaret C., who is the wife of James M. Bower. The father of the subject reached the age of ninety-four years, and his grandfather died at the age of eighty-four.

William E. Bower, Sr., our subject, was reared on the farm, just across the road from where he now lives and there he learned to swing the axe and use the spade, attending school some during the winter months. He lived with his parents until their death. He later bought one hundred and sixty acres of the old farm and seventy acres west of the old homestead and he has always been actively engaged in farming which he has made a success. He has remained unmarried. As the poet Gray has said, "His sober wishes never learned to stray," for he has remained closely at home, having never been in but two other states, Kentucky and Ohio. He has made a great success, now owning over five hundred acres of land and is worth twenty thousand dollars. He keeps his farm in good condition in every respect.

W. E. BOWER, Sr.

In his political relations Mr. Bower is a Democrat, and he served as Trustee of Washington township from April, 1865, to October, 1876, continuously, having been re-elected from time to time, rendering the utmost satisfaction in this capacity. He was secretary of the grange lodge.

Mr. Bower has lived a quiet, inoffensive and straightforward life, a life that has resulted in no harm to any one and he is considered one of the substantial men of his locality.

THOMAS F. PRALL.

The pioneer founders of this well known family of this name were Pennsylvanians, who came to Clark country about 1840. Thomas Prall, the first to identify himself with Southern Indiana interests, was a man of most excellent qualities, and noted for his patriotism and generosity. He bought and improved a lot of wild land, mostly timber, and at one time owned fifteen hundred acres. When the Eighty-first Regiment of Indiana Volunteer Infantry was organized, Mr. Prall gave each man a dollar and as the enlistment ran well up towards a thousand it will be seen that this involved a large sum of money. He acted as a secret scout for the Union army and at one time was captured and held as a spy, but managed to escape. As a member of the Cumberland Presbytery he was quite active in church work and gave liberally whenever money was needed for missionary or local charities. When at the age of sixty-four years he was killed by a stroke of lightning, while sitting on his horse. He was mourned as one of the county's most enterprising men.

Before leaving his native state of Pennsylvania he had married Rebecca Sibert, and had two children when they settled in Clark county, a few miles southeast of where Henryville now is. Their trading was done at Charlestown, the nearest point for the purpose in those days. Altogether there were thirteen children in this family and three of the sons served in the Union army. David was a member of the Twenty-first Regiment, under Captain Ferguson; Elymes belonged to the Twenty-eighth Regiment Mounted Infantry, and Houston, when only fifteen years old, joined the Fifty-second Regiment. The eldest son was killed by sharp shooters at Richmond, Virginia, during one of the many severe battles fought around that city.

Thomas F. Prall, the sixth child in this large family, was born in Clark county, Indiana, October 12, 1850. He grew up on his father's farm and later in life became a farmer himself and continued in agricultural pursuits during the larger part of his adult life. About nine years ago he came to Henryville and for seven years was engaged in the livery business at that place. He then established a store and since has devoted most of his time to mercantile

48

matters, in which he has met with success. He still owns the land in grant 225, which as a young man he purchased and improved. He has long been regarded as one of Monroe township's most substantial citizens and he has made a success of all enterprises in which he has embarked, from farming to merchandising. Though he obtained but a limited education in youth he has learned much by observation and contact with the world and exercises good business judgment in all his dealings with his fellow men. He is a member of the Presbyterian church and the local lodge of Knights of Pythias.

On April 6, 1873, Mr. Prall married Nancy L., daughter of John M. and Mary Kirk, of Clark county, where Mrs. Prall was born in 1854. Twelve children have been born to them: Monroe, the eldest, married Lulu Lutz, has five children and resides in Monroe township; Arthur, the second child, died in infancy; the third child in order of birth is Addie; Charles married Emma Campbell, has two children and is a resident of Henryville; Garfield, who married Sadie Frankey, has two children, also resides in Henryville; Jesse died in infancy; William, who married Edith Woodlock, has one child and makes his home in Henryville; and Mary died in infancy. The others are Pearl, Eva, Flora and Burton. William and Charles Prall are in the livery business at Henryville.

ROBERT M. HOWSER.

So far as can be ascertained the Howser family were of German extraction, but emigrated to America at an early day and settled in Pennsylvania. At a later period descendants removed into various states, and one branch founded a family in Jessamine county, Kentucky. There in the first half of the nineteenth century Elijah Howser was born. He grew up on a farm, learned the business and spent his whole life in agricultural pursuits. The methods were primitive in those days, there being much hard work and little profit. He was fond of politics and became well known as a politician in support of the Democratic party. He was, however, content to help others and never became an office-seeker himself. About 1857 he decided to cross the Ohio river and endeavor to better his fortunes in the young state of Indiana. He bought wild timber land in Clark county, brought his family over and spent the rest of his life in the arduous business of clearing and improving. It involved much hard work and endless struggle, but before his death, July 6, 1872, he had established a comfortable home, provided well for a large family and left a respectable name, as well as some property as an inheritance for his children. He was a member of the Christian church, observant of the rules of morality, industrious, law-abiding and in all respects a good neighbor and citizen. He married Nancy Bridgewater, descended from a substantial Virginia family, scions of which emigrated to Kentucky when that state was still wild and sparsely settled. Her union with Elijah Howser took place when they were still young and before her death, October 19, 1872, less than two months after her husband's death, she had become the mother of ten children, six of whom were boys and four girls. Of these five are still living, among the number being the subject of this sketch.

Robert M. Howser, fifth child in the family, was born March 14, 1844, in Oldham county, Kentucky. He remained with his parents until reaching his majority when he started out in the world to make a living for himself. He had obtained a fair education in the schools of Monroe township, was naturally industrious and intelligent and these accomplishments enabled him to hold his own in the struggles that confront all poor young men at their entrance into business. When his father came to Clark county, most of the land was still in timber and there were comparatively few improved farms. He had all the experiences of a pioneer boy in the wilderness and learned what it was to get up at four o'clock in the morning, grub or pile logs all day, drive oxen and occasionally go to mill for the family meal or flour. When he got land of his own he had to go through the same experiences and make all the improvements, but eventually he had a comfortable home and now may be said to live on "Easy Street," compared to the conditions prevailing in his youth. His place is within two and a half miles of Henryville, and his whole life has been devoted to the duties falling to the lot of a general farmer. Decidedly a home man, his chief pleasure is found in assembling around the fireside in the evening with his family. His politics are Democratic, but while he takes an interest in party affairs and helps his friends, he himself has never cared for office or sought to become a candidate. He has made a success of his affairs and is one of the well known men in this part of the county.

In 1889 Mr. Howser was married to Eva Watson, who was born in Henderson county, Kentucky, December 7, 1861. Her parents were John W., and Martha A. Watson, substantial people and of excellent families in the South. Mr. and Mrs. Howser have one child, Charles W., whose birth occurred October 1, 1890. The family are members of the Presbyterian church and have a large acquaintance in various parts of Clark county, by all or whom they are highly esteemed.

LAFAYETTE D. TOWNSEND.

On a home three miles west of Henryville, which is one of the finest in Monroe township, resides one of those quiet substantial business men, who benefit themselves by their industry and help to build up this community in enterprises that extend and encourage improvements. Partly as a farmer, but chiefly as a carpenter and contractor, Lafayette D. Townsend is well known as a citizen, neighbor and father of a large family, which he has reared to lives of usefulness. The name has been familiar in Clark county almost since its origin, as the pioneer ancestor was here among the first, when everything was still a wilderness, heavy growths of the primeval forest being seen on every hand and when settlements were to be found only along the rivers and here and there in the fertile valleys. George H. Townsend was born in New York state, June 11, 1811, and came to Clark county, about 1820. He entered land as was customary in those days, and put in the usual hard licks, clearing it of timber and underbrush. He devoted his whole life to farming, met with fair success in his calling, reared a large family and closed his blameless life at a ripe old age. He was married in Bartholomew county, Indiana, to Elizabeth Hart, who was born in Blount county, Tennessee, October 23, 1823, her father being a farmer named Thomas. By this union there were ten children, those living being named as follows, according to age: Nora J., Thomas M., Lafayette D., Addie, Ella, Elizabeth, Lillie Alice, Laura and Daisy.

Lafayette D. Townsend, third of the family, was born in Clark county, Indiana, December 27, 1852. At that time schools were few and poor and he was able to obtain but a limited education. The attendance was chiefly in the winter months, the building, the historic log cabin, with puncheon floor and slab seats, the presiding genius who handled the birch was usually some eastern pedagogue, much like Ichabod Crane, made famous by Washington Irving, in his "Legend of Sleepy Hollow." In the spring, summer and fall, all farm boys were needed for the out door work as assistants to their parents, and it was under circumstances of this kind that Mr. Townsend got his training for his future life. In due time he became owner of land and engaged in agricultural pursuits on his own account. He made all the improvements on his farm and had the satisfaction of seeing it gradually grow into a fine and productive farm home. Later he became a carpenter and contractor, to which calling he has devoted most of his energies. He put up many of the buildings in Monroe township and prospered by his trade. At present he is in the business of furnishing ties to the railroads, which has proved a profitable side line. He is recognized as one of the county's substantial men, being a member of the Methodist Episcopal church and a supporter of all causes calculated to upbuild and improve the community. His fraternal relations are confined to membership in the Masonic Order and he takes much interest in the affairs of his lodge.

On September 9, 1875, Mr. Townsend married Mary M. Buehler, who was born in Ohio, in 1855. Her parents were Rudolph and Mary (Wild) Buehler, the latter descended from Swiss immigrants, who came to this country about 1860. Her father was a tailor by trade, but spent most of his life in agricultural pursuits. Mr. and Mrs. Townsend have eleven children: Nora

Elizabeth, who was born June 30, 1876, married Jason Smith, of Utica township, and has one child; Annie, the second of the family, was born January 13, 1878; Lelah B., who was born April 18, 1880, is the wife of W. H. Freeman, Secretary of the State Board of Forestry, a resident of Indianapolis; Paul V., the eldest son, was born February 7, 1882, married Addie Burleson, is a resident of Monroe township and has one child; James, the second son, was born November 5, 1883; Charles B., born July 4, 1886, married Louisa Cummings, resides at Scottsburg and has one child; Lucy T. was born December 8, 1889; Herman R., September 6, 1890; Ruth Irene, June 28, 1892; Elmer L., May 18, 1895, and Hazel M., November 7, 1897. The family are highly esteemed and have a wide circle of friends and acquaintants all over the county. They who visit Mr. Townsend's hospitable home are sure of a cordial welcome and the good cheer that comes from kindliness of disposition and the accumulations of an industrious life.

MATTHEW H. DUNLEVY.

Matthew H. Dunlevy, son of Thomas A. and Catharine (Clegg) Dunlevy, was the oldest of a family of fourteen children. In Mr. Dunlevy we have the genuine type of the energetic successful business man of the kind that makes a community. He has been in many kinds of business, called on to do things and always did them well. The result has been success, social, political and financial, with an excellent home and other worldly goods to show as rewards for his efforts. Matthew H. Dunlevy was born September 30, 1859, at Blue Lick, in Clark county, Indiana. His only education was obtained in the public schools of Clark county, but on this basis, and by subsequent reading and observation he became a well informed man. It was in 1880, when twenty-one years old, that he came to Henryville to accept a clerkship with Amelia, widow of Henry Ballinger, where he remained for three years. His next venture was in the stock business, which he followed with varying success until 1886. Though still quite a young man, he had obtained sufficient prominency to be selected as postmaster to which office he was appointed by President Cleveland. He served from March 1, 1886, to June 30, 1889, and gave excellent satisfaction to all the patrons, and meantime carried on the mercantile business as a side line. The change of administration in 1888 caused him to be replaced by a Republican, and he resumed his old business of trading in stock. This he kept up until 1892, when the wheels of political fortune again brought Cleveland to the Presidency, and by him Mr. Dunlevy was appointed to his old place of postmaster August, 1893. He served until June 4, 1897, and by general concensus of public opinion he made the best postmaster that Henryville ever had. When McKinley came into the Presidency in 1896, Mr. Dunlevy was the first Democrat to "walk the plank" in his congressional district, on account of the political fight he made during the campaign, but office holding was not essential to his happiness and he lost no time in re-embarking in the mercantile business, which he has ever since followed. Active in various lines, always public-spirited and anxious to help in the development of his community, Mr. Dunlevy was one of the organizers of the Henryville State Bank, which began business March 17, 1904, and he is now one of the directors and vice-president of this popular institution. In 1902 Mr. Dunlevy was a moving spirit in establishing the Henryville Canning Factory, and in addition to these public services has helped to get lights for Henryville. To him was chiefly due the establishment of an exchange of the Cumberland Telephone and Telegraph Company, at Henryville, and he has been the agent during the five years the station has been opened. In company with R. R. Freeman, he secured the option and bought the land on which the State Forestry Reservation was subsequently established and in this way greatly benefited the county while doing something for himself.

Mr. Dunlevy is a prominent member of the Knights of Pythias, Modern Woodmen, the Odd Fellows and Rebekahs. He takes much pleasure in attending his various lodges, is prompt in attending to all duties assigned him by his societies, and altogether is one of the best known as well as most esteemed of Clark county's citizens. Though a life-long Democrat and taking an active interest in campaigns for his party, he has never sought office, though frequently influential in securing office for others. His general store at Henryville is one of the institutions of the town, and enjoys a large patronage.

In 1880 Mr. Dunlevy was married to Ida A. Gray, a native of Franklin county, Indiana, where she was born in 1859. Her parents were Jeduthen and Lucinda (Hardesty) Gray, the former a Union soldier, who was killed in September, 1862, at the battle of Antietam. Mr. and Mrs. Dunlevy have had seven children of whom five are living, and two died in infancy. Mary Ethel, born in 1881, married Clarence Hough and resides in Chicago; Grace C. was born in 1887; William T. in 1888, Homer in 1891 and Margaret in 1904.

JAMES H. WALKER, M. D.

Though Clark county numbers many bright physicians within her borders, there are none more interesting to talk to and none that stand higher professionally or socially than Doctor Walker. Finely educated, of wide experience and naturally affable, he makes a charming companion and one whom his acquaintances are always glad to meet again. Good blood always tells and worthy ancestors usually produce worthy descendants. The Walkers have reason to be proud of their lineage as their ancestors were with Lord Baltimore when he crossed the Atlantic to make his historic settlement of Maryland. They were English Catholics and deserve the glory of having favored the first statute for religious freedom ever adopted by an American colony. Descendants of these Maryland emigrants became early pioneers of Indiana and were among the first settlers of Martin county, having removed there from Kentucky. Peter M. Walker, born in 1845, is engaged in the flour mill business at Loogootee and one of the most prominent men of that Martin county town. He married Margaret Karl, who died at the age of thirty, after becoming the mother of four children. Her husband married again and by this union eight children were born.

James H. Walker, born March 14, 1868, in Martin county, Indiana, was the second of the four children by the first marriage and six years old when his mother died. After the usual course in the common and high schools of Loogootee, he taught for three years in Martin county. He then took up the study of medicine, entering the Kentucky School of Medicine, at Louisville, and was graduated in the class of 1891. Locating at Jeffersonville for the two years he subsequently went to Wisconsin, but after a twelve months' sojourn in that state returned to Clark county, in 1894. He soon gained a good patronage in Henryville and has been practicing with increasing success ever since. He is generally regarded as in the front rank of his profession and no local physician enjoys greater popularity. Like all men ambitious to shine in his calling Doctor Walker was not content with his original graduation but took and completed a course in the celebrated Medico-Chirurgical College, at Philadelphia. In addition to this he had the benefit of two post-graduate courses during the years from 1902 and 1904, inclusive. The practical was united with the theoretical by his experiences as a surgeon in the Second Division Hospital at Camp Meade, in Pennsylvania, and during the Spanish-American war he served with the Second Army Corps. Thus it will be seen that Doctor Walker is a thoroughly equipped physician not only because he studied hard in his younger days and got the benefit of the best schools, but by reason of the fact that he has always kept up his reading of the foremost medical journals, which keep him fully abreast of all the latest improvements, discoveries and appliances. Doctor Walker has a delightful home in Henryville, to which his many friends often gather with assurances of the most cordial hospitality and pleasing entertainment.

In 1897 Doctor Walker was married to Mary Ferguson, a lady of an old and esteemed family, who was born at Henryville, November 11, 1877. Her father, Dr. H. H. Ferguson, was quite prominent in Clark county, both as a citizen and physician. The fact that her grandfather laid off the town of Henryville, indicated that the family were among the earliest pioneers of the county. Doctor and Mrs. Walker have two bright children, a daughter and a son. Helen, born in 1898, and Robert, born in 1900.

JOHN E. ENLOW.

This name recalls a well known Kentucky family whose members were identified with the old state almost from its earliest history. Jacob Enlow, a native of Virginia, crossed the mountains when everything on this side was still a wilderness with only sparse settlements here and there. His son, Thomas K. Enlow, was born in Kentucky, in 1811, became a farmer when he reached his majority and in 1845 removed to Harrison county, Indiana, where he purchased land. That section was still in a wild condition and he had the usual trying experiences in clearing and improving his property. He was a prominent member of the Methodist church and an active worker in all its undertakings. In 1837 he was married at Mauckport, Indiana, to Amanda Gwartney, who was born in Corydon, Indiana, in 1821. Nine children were born to them, of whom two sons and two daughters survive.

John E. Enlow, one of the surviving children, was born in Hardin county, Kentucky, in 1842, and hence was three years old when his father removed to Indiana. When about seventeen years old he began teaching in Harrison county, and was thus engaged at the breaking out of the Civil war. In the fall of 1862 he enlisted in Company I, Thirty-fourth Regiment, Kentucky Volunteer Infantry, and served until the close of hostilities. He was on detached service in the provost marshal's office during the winter of 1862, and after leaving Louisville served as company clerk until September, 1863. He was present at the siege of Knoxville and went from there to Tazewell county, Tennessee, where he was laid up for a long time with typhoid fever. The command retreated from there to Cumberland Gap and in March, 1864, Mr. Enlow was sent to the hospital at Louisville and furloughed for sixty days. In July he became attached to the hospital boat "Ohio," at New Albany, Indiana, where he acted as chief clerk, later going in the same capacity to the provost marshal's office. At the close of the war he was mustered out at Louisville and resumed his old occupation of teaching school. After continuing at this for four years he went to Mauckport, and engaged in the milling business. A year later he engaged in the ice business at Louisville and so continued until 1880, when he came to Clark county, and located on a farm in Monroe township. His business since then has been farming, combined with the duties of pension agent. In May, 1907, he was appointed postmaster of Underwood, where he also carries on merchandising as a side line. Mr. Enlow is a member of the Underwood Baptist church and an ordained minister. He was a member of Underwood Post, 264, Grand Army of the Republic until their headquarters were destroyed by fire.

In November, 1865, Mr. Enlow was married to Alice Reynolds, who was born at Louisville, in 1844. Her parents were J. L. and Eliza (Woodruff) Reynolds, the former of Connecticut and the latter a native of New York. Mrs. Enlow's people drove from New York City to Louisville in a wagon. Mr. and Mrs. Enlow have three children living, Joseph T., born in 1866, is chief of the fire department in Jeffersonville; William, born in 1870, married Daisy Rogers, lives in Louisville and has two children; Laura W., born in 1885, married John E. Anderson, and resides at New Albany.

ELAM G. PRALL, D. D. S.

The Pralls were of the sturdy race known as Pennsylvania Dutch, and representatives of the family came to Indiana in the early part of the nineteenth century. They were among the first of the pioneers who settled in Clark county, making their appearance when this section was little more than a wilderness, with the Ohio river as the only highway.

Henry H. Prall, one of the descendants, obtained considerable local prominence and was a man of influence in Monroe township. He became the owner of land when everything was covered with timber of the original forest growth and went through the usual hardships and toil connected with clearing and improving wild land. Though farming was his main business and most of his time was devoted to agricultural pursuits he was active in the social, political and religious life of the community. A lifelong member of the Methodist church, he was ordained as a minister in that denomination and did much good in elevating the morals of the community. He was a close friend of Henry Ferguson, who laid out the town of Henryville and lent every assistance in his power to this public improvement. In fact, whenever any movement was set on foot calculated to benefit the people and aid the cause of progress, Henry H. Prall could be relied upon to lend a helping hand. He married Susan E. Lewellen, whose ancestors were Virginians and the family claimed relationship with John Quincy Adams, sixth President of the United States.

Elam G. Prall, son of Henry H., was born in Monroe township, Clark county, Indiana, September 7, 1865. He was educated in the county schools, proving an apt pupil and giving promise in boyhood of a successful career in life. He decided at an early date to adopt one of the professions, and after finishing his academic course entered the Indiana Dental College at Indianapolis. In due time he was graduated and his popularity and acquirements as a student brought him an office of a professorship. He accepted and had a chair in the college for five years. This was followed by the practice of dentistry at Indianapolis for several years, after which he removed to Dubois county. He remained there several years and then decided to return to his native county, opening an office in Henryville. He has met with success and enjoys a good practice in the town and surrounding country.

Doctor Prall has an inclination for fraternal societies and has risen to prominence and influence in several of the popular orders. He holds membership in the Knights of Pythias, Red Men, Modern Woodmen and Maccabees. He has been a representative to the Indiana Grand Lodges, both of the Knights of Pythias and the Red Men. Doctor Prall is an intelligent man, well informed not only in all matters connected with his profession but on current affairs.

In 1905 Doctor Prall married Anna Wermling, a native of Dubois county. Her parents were Henry and Barbara Wermling, who were of German descent. Her father died some years ago and the re-marriage of her mother caused the name of Wermling to disappear from the census rolls of the county. Mrs. Prall is a member of the Lutheran church.

JAMES DOTHITTE APPLEGATE.

The Applegate family has been one of prominence in the vicinity of which this history treats, since the pioneer days, and he whose life record is contained in the following paragraphs is a well known descendant of worthy ancestors. James Dothitte Applegate was born in Louisville, Kentucky, April 11, 1857, the son of John D. and Mary Ann (Applegate) Applegate, the former a native of Jeffersonville township, Clark county, and the latter a native of Louisville. Aaron Applegate, grandfather of the subject, was born on the 6th of October, 1779, and was joined in marriage to Mary Rebecca Ross, who was born on the 15th of April, 1781. To this union were born the following children: James Ross, born September 2, 1800; Cynthia, born on the 9th of May, 1802, in Jefferson county, Kentucky; Charles Ross, born on the 18th of September, 1805, died January 22, 1887; Mary Ann, born in Clark county, Indiana, on the 5th of May, 1808; David Floyd, born on November 19, 1810; John Dothitte, born February 16, 1812; Mary Jane, born February 9, 1816; George R., born June 9, 1818; John F. R., born March 23, 1820; Sarah M. R. S., born June 23, 1822. Aaron Applegate and wife were among the very earliest settlers of Clark county, having been natives of Virginia. They settled on the Utica pike, then a trail through the wilderness, above Jeffersonville. They came here from Kentucky, They later moved to the place where the subject of this sketch now lives, in Jefferson township, and where the father of the subject was born. The house on this place was built about 1808, and was one of the first two-story frame houses in the county. It was a meeting place where frequently circuit-riders from Indianapolis held services. During one of these meetings a herd of deer, attracted by the music, gathered in front of the house and during the prayer which followed, Aaron Applegate observed them, and quietly reached for his rifle and shot one before the prayer was ended. This startled the minister and stopped the meeting, all adjourning to the yard, where the minister assisted in dressing the deer. Mr. and Mrs. Aaron Applegate died on this place. John D. Applegate, father of the subject, was born and reared on this farm. Soon after his marriage he found employment as cooper in a tobacco warehouse in Louisville, later becoming the superintendent of the same place, where he remained for a number of years, until his health gave way and he returned to the old homestead, resuming farming. He was a man of thrift and accumulated a competency and died in Louisville, March 5, 1876. His wife also died in that city on February 10, 1874. They were the parents of twelve children, as follows: Mary Jane, born November 16, 1839; Josephine, born June 9, 1842; America, born March 22, 1844; Joseph, October 10, 1846; Sarah Ellen, February 14, 1848; Louisa B., November 29, 1850; Annie Elizabeth, March 16, 1852; Florence Ross, November 23, 1854; James D., of this review; Burge, September 3, 1859; Archie Clark, February 11, 1862; Julia B., September 11, 1865. Of the above, only four are now living.

James D. Applegate was reared on the old home farm and in Louisville, Kentucky. He received a liberal education. Preferring farm life he early devoted his attention to the same. He became heir to a part of the old homestead, and he later purchased the remaining portion of this place, which has now been in the possession of the family for over one hundred years. It consists of one hundred acres, well improved and although it has been in cultivation for a long time, the soil has retained its fertility, having been skillfully managed and it still produces abundant crops.

Mr. Applegate has been four times married, first on December 20, 1882, to Clara B. Whiteside, daughter of W. S. Whiteside, which union resulted in the birth of three children, one of whom is living—Frank; Mrs. Applegate died September 17, 1890. His second marriage was to Ida K. Anderson, daughter of George S. Anderson, the wedding occurring in November, 1893; she died August 2, 1898, leaving one child, Maude P. His third marriage was to Maggie May Terry, November 16, 1898; she was the daughter of Joshua Terry, and she passed to her rest without issue, on October 18, 1899. The subject's last wife was Lorena L. Robertson, daughter of Alexander Robertson, a member of a prominent family, this marriage occurring May 21, 1900.

In his political relations Mr. Applegate is a Democrat, and fraternally he belongs to Hope Lodge, No. 13, and the Uniform Rank, No. 9, Knights of Pythias, of Jeffersonville.

EP HAWES.

The ancestors of the subject on both sides of the house were early pioneers of Clark county, Indiana, having lived here when neighbors were no nearer than six or seven miles, but they were hardy people and long-lived, the paternal grandfather dying at the age of eighty-nine years and the mother of the subject reaching the advanced age of ninety-four years. The latter, who was known in her maidenhood as Nancy Kelly, was born in Ohio in 1804, and when about thirteen years old she came to Utica township, Clark county, where she witnessed the first steamboat that ever passed Utica on the Ohio river. She never resided outside of this county after coming here. Nathan Hawes, father of our subject, was born in 1802, in the state of New York, and he came to Clark county, this state, with his parents in 1817, settling in Utica, where he remained for two years, then went to Washington county and bought wild land which he improved, engaging in farming all his life. When about twenty-one years old, he returned to Clark county, and was a resident of the same until his death at the age of sixty-eight years. He and Nancy Kelly married in this county about 1827, and to them ten children were born, only three of whom are living, namely: Martha I., who married Jesse J. Coombs; Thomas J., and Ep, our subject.

When Nathan Hawes first came to Clark county, he settled on grant 220 in Union township. Charlestown was the principal town and voting place at that time. He bought a farm in grant 203 in 1852, where the subject now lives. He devoted practically all his time to his home, not being a public man. In politics he was a Whig. He operated the first horse-power threshing machine in this county, and his son, our subject, taking up the work, was the first to operate a steam threshing machine in Clark county.

Ep Hawes was born in Union township, Clark county, Indiana, December 7, 1839, and he has shown himself to be a worthy descendant of his sterling ancestors, according to the statement of those who have known him the longest and best. He got a good education in the free schools of the county, and early in life gave evidence of those habits of industry which have characterized his entire career, having been engaged in farming all his life in Union township, being known as one of the leading general farmers in this vicinity. He has an excellent farm which has been well tilled and his home is a pleasant one, where his neighbors delight to gather. This home is presided over by Mrs. Hawes, who was known in her maidenhood as Harriet Coleman, whom our subject married in 1864, at Edinburg, Indiana. She is the daughter of J. O. and Salina (Gates) Coleman, of Edinburg. Harriet Coleman was born at Salem, Connecticut, on July 21, 1844. Her people were all hardy New Englanders. J. O. Coleman was a colonel of state militia and a captain in the Civil war.

To Mr. and Mrs. Ep Hawes ten children were born, three of whom, Epsell, May and Lotta Belle, died within two days, having been stricken with diphtheria. They were all interred in the same grave. The names of the subject's children follow in order of birth: Jessie, born April 1, 1867, died when ten years old; Emma J., born September 12, 1868, died at the age of twenty-seven years; Gussie, born April 10, 1871, died in infancy; James K., born July 28, 1874, is a practicing physician at Columbus, Indiana; he married Myrtle Wisner, and they are the parents of four children: Elenore, born April 10, 1876, is living at home; May, born December 4, 1877, died September 27, 1885; Epsell, born July 28, died September 29, 1885; Samuel C., born July 27, 1882, married Myrtle Carr, and they became the parents of two children; he married a second time, his last wife, Jessie Carr, being a sister to his first wife; they are living at Memphis, Indiana. Lotta Belle, the ninth child of the subject, was born March 12, 1885, and died September 27, 1885; Arta C., born October 17, 1886, is a school teacher.

Ep Hawes is one of the best known men in that part of Clark county, where he has long resided, and no man in the county is more favorably known than he, for his life has been exemplary in many respects; among the most praiseworthy traits of his character being the fact that he has never used tobacco in any form, nor ever taken a drink of whiskey. In his fraternal relations he is a Mason, having been affiliated with that great order for a period of nearly forty years, having cast his lot with this fraternity at Charlestown, Indiana, in 1870. He is now a member of the Henryville lodge. He is a faithful member of the Christian church.

BALIE L. BURTT.

It has been said that success treads on the heels of every right effort, and amid all the theorizing as to the cause of success, there can be no doubt that this aphorism has its origin in the fact that character is the real basis of success in any field of thought and action. He of whom the biographer now writes has gained a substantial footing in his native community not by reason of the fact that someone has mapped out his life work for him or aided him in any material way, but because he has been a man of industry and honesty of purpose all his life and employed such methods as always make for success.

Balie L. Burtt was born September 27, 1864, in Utica township, Clark county, Indiana, the representative of an old and highly honored family. He was educated in the common schools of Utica township in which he made a splendid record, but not being satisfied with a common school education he entered Oberlin College, where he remained two years, standing high in his classes.

After leaving college Mr. Burtt decided that the free and untrammeled life of the agriculturist and horticulturist was the most attractive for a man of his tastes and he accordingly went to farming, which he has since continued with signal success. He has a highly productive and well improved farm of one hundred and ten acres, which is mostly used for the raising of fruits, being in orchard and grass. He is known in this part of the county as "the peach king," being one of the largest peach growers in Southern Indiana. He is a good manager and has a most desirable farm on which stands a good dwelling and other buildings.

Mr. Burtt was united in marriage with Lillace Holman, a native of Jeffersonville township, and the daughter of an excellent family. The date of their wedding was October 22, 1890. Mrs. Burtt was born December 10, 1866, in Utica township, where she attended the common schools, after which she took a course at Oberlin College.

Two children living and one dead have been born to the subject and wife, namely: Eli Ivan, born October 17, 1891, died January 8, 1892; Glen Eli, born November 11, 1895; Leta Kathryn, born November 25, 1903.

Mrs. Burtt is a member of the Christian church, and in politics Mr. Burtt is a Democrat. In his fraternal relations he is a Mason and a Woodman, and his daily life would indicate that he believes in living up to his lodge vows, for he is known as a man of upright principles in all his relations with his fellow men.

HENRY E. SMITH.

Among the many sturdy settlers from Kentucky that made their way across the Ohio river into Indiana in former years, were the parents of Henry E. Smith, who was born in Utica township, Clark county, Indiana, on the 25th of April, 1878. He was the son of George D. and Mary E. (Howes) Smith, both of whom were born on Kentucky soil, and were the parents of four children, two of whom, Alia and Mitchell, are at home. The third, Charles, was married to Lilly Eversole. Henry E., of this review, was the fourth in order of birth. He received his education in the local district school and as a boy proved to be a lad of steady habits and pleasant temperament. He made his schooling the instrument for wider study and self-culture, and after reaching maturity, entered into the Government service as a packer in the quartermaster's department, and has continued therein ever since. The same characteristics that marked him as a boy have clung to him in his maturer years, and his genial disposition has won for him many warm and appreciative friends.

Mr. Smith was joined in marriage to Mary Wallace, daughter of John and Lucy Wallace, the former being a native of Clark county, Indiana, while the latter was born in Kentucky. John and Lucy Wallace were the parents of five children, besides the wife of our subject. They were: Gertrude, Katie, Cora, Helen and Charles.

Mr. and Mrs. Smith have become the parents of four children, viz: Wallace F., Mary L., James H., and George D. They reside in Port Fulton.

Mr. Smith holds liberal religious views, and says that it has been his practice through life to place the emphasis on the spirit of one's conduct, rather than on the formal side of creed or doctrine. Politically he affiliates with the Republican party, but has made no effort at office-seeking or political prominence of any kind. He is a member also of the Knights of Pythias, in which he has shown an active spirit and has contributed freely of his time to promote the welfare of the order. Thus as a citizen and a neighbor he fills a useful place in the community life.

FRANK G. DOBBINS.

County Armagh in Ireland has contributed generously of her citizenship to the building up of the great Republic across the sea. When the great army of Irish immigrants came pouring in during the forties and fifties no part of the Emerald Isle was better represented than old Armagh and many of those who came from there "made good" after they reached the American shore. They are found in all the walks of life, in the mercantile world, in politics, in every branch of trade, in the great manufacturing and the railroad world. They are always proud of their native land, the "old sod" as they call it, and well they may be as, in the language of the famous Sergeant A. Prentiss, " it has contributed to the world more than its due share of wit and eloquence and its sons have fought successfully on all fields save their own." It was previous to the Civil war that the Dobbins family emigrated from Armagh and took up their residence in the East. As the result of the marriage of S. H. and Sallie (Garwood) Dobbins, there were several children and one of these is the young man whose name appears at the head of this sketch.

Frank G. Dobbins was born in Trenton, New Jersey, in 1872, and remained at the place of his nativity until after passing his majority. He attended the public schools of Trenton, where he laid the foundations of the education, which is indispensable to all those who enter upon the sharp struggle for existence in this country of great competition, no matter what the line of business selected. It was in 1895 that young Dobbins decided to come to the West and grow up with the country as was advised by old Horace Greeley unto all who were ambitious of success in life. Arriving at Madison, Indiana, he first found employment in a drug store, a line of work which appealed to his taste and fancy. After a brief sojourn in the old Ohio river town he transferred his residence to Bedford, and later came to Jeffersonville, where he found satisfactory relations and has since made his home. At the present time he is city salesman for the Peter Neat Richardson Drug Company, of Louisville, Kentucky, and is prospering satisfactorily in this employment. He is a young man of good address, of quiet demeanor and has the faculty of making and holding friends. As a salesman he has proved a success and he is popular both in the business and social circle in which he moves.

On April 28, 1903, Mr. Dobbins was united in marriage with Margaret Mitchell, a worthy young lady of Jeffersonville. She is the daughter of James R. and Ellen (Blizzard) Mitchell, the former of Henryville and the latter of Scottsburg. The only child of Mr. and Mrs. Dobbins is a bright little daughter whom they have named Helen Frances. The family are well known and highly esteemed in the younger social set to which they belong.

ABNER BIGGS.

Abner Biggs, who resides near Henryville, Clark county, is a widely known native-born citizen of this community. At the close of the Civil war he started on his career as a farmer in his present location, and during the years since then he has met with the success which his hard-working disposition deserved. His personality has at all times been marked with the qualities which engender a sense of trustfulness and mutual helpfulness among neighbors. As a conequence he has made many life-long friends. He is the son of one of the older pioneers who engaged in many a grim encounter with the Indians from behind the palisade of the old fort which stood east of the present town of Henryville in those primitive days. The elder Biggs was in the fort at the time of the Pigeon Roost massacre.

Abner Biggs was born January 28, 1844, in Monroe township on the farm on which he now lives. He is the son of Abner and Emily (Miller) Biggs. Abner Biggs, senior, was born about 1799. In early life he lived with his father on the old Indian trail northeast of Henryville. Later, as above stated, he became an Indian fighter and was known as a man of great nerve and a good shot. There were large numbers of Indians in the immediate neighborhood in his day, and on one occasion he came within a narrow margin of being kidnapped by them; the event being planned with all the craftiness of the aborigine. Abner Biggs, Sr., was also a farmer and stock raiser. In his youth he attended school in the old log subscription schools. He acquired timber land which included our subject's farm. In those days blazed trails through the woods were the only roads available and civilization throughout the entire Middle West was in its early stages. The mother of Abner Biggs was born February 6, 1802, in Clark county. Her marriage took place about 1820, and fifteen children were born to the union, Abner being the thirteenth in order of birth, and his brother, James, was the first person buried in Mount Zion cemetery. His father died in December, 1872, in Henryville, and his mother at the age of ninety-one, in 1893.

Abner Biggs started on his own way in life when about eighteen years of age. In the year 1865 he enlisted in the Union army at Jeffersonville, in Company H, One Hundred Forty-fourth Indiana Volunteers, under command of Colonel Riddle and Capt. Stephen Cole. While on their way to Richmond, Virginia, news of General Lee's surrender was brought. Soon after our subject was mustered out of service at Indianapolis. As a Civil war veteran he is a well known member of the Grand Army of the Republic, Post No. 461, at Henryville. On his return home he married in the year 1872, Mary Gray, who was born in 1850 in Clark county. She died April 13, 1891, having borne her husband eight children. They were: Claude L., who was born December 3, 1873, and died June 18, 1874; Jessie was born July 24, 1875, and married Matthew Clegg; they have four children and live in Monroe township. Edgar H. was born August 19, 1876, and lives in Jeffersonville; Herman, born March 14, 1878, married Hettie Wells, lives in Monroe township, and has two children; Alec G., born January 7, 1880, married Laura McClellan; they have one child and live in Monroe township. Bertha M., born December 13, 1882, married John Nash; she lives in Oklahoma, and has one child. Emma G. was born on March 7, 1885, and Anna J., who married Ernest Thomas, and lives in Clark county, was born June 7, 1886.

Our subject married secondly on October 11, 1896, Mamie Wells, who was previously married to John Pfister. Mamie (Wells) Pfister was born in 1867, February 20th, and was the daughter of Isaac and Lucy (Hall) Wells. She was born in Kentucky, her people being all Kentuckians, and came to Clark county when she was about five or six years old. Mrs. Biggs had two children by her first marriage, viz: Thomas F. Pfister, born December 28, 1886, and Annie May, born February 21, 1888, who died August 25, 1896. Mrs. Biggs has become the mother of one child, Claude R., born July 4, 1898, by her second marriage.

Abner Biggs is a Republican in politics and a staunch party supporter, though not himself desirous of public life. He received his education in the

49

schools of the county, and in religious life belongs to the Methodist Episcopal church. Though he himself did not see extended service in the Civil war, his brother, Robert, did, having served all through that conflict.

JAMES R. FERGUSON.

James R. Ferguson, retired farmer and veteran soldier, of Henryville, Clark county, is one of the older generation that has contributed so much to the progress and upbuilding of the community. His father, Colonel Ferguson, who died in 1868, was the founder of Henryville. He was the foremost man in getting the railroad through that part of the country and induced Ben Marsh, the engineer who surveyed the railroad, to survey and help him lay off the town of Henryville, which was afterwards named in his honor. Our subject is well versed in the blacksmith trade, having spent ten years of his life in that business; the remainder of his career, outside of his military experiences, was spent in farming pursuits in which he has been unquestionably successful. He and his wife live in retirement in Henryville in a manner fitting to their time of life.

James R. Ferguson was born on June 23, 1837, in Washington county, Pennsylvania, and was the son of Henry and Nancy (Young) Ferguson. Col. Henry Ferguson, as he became known in later life, was born in 1804, in the same county in Pennsylvania. He was a farmer and came to Clark county, Indiana, about 1842, and located on the present site of Henryville, owning all the land on which the town now stands. In order to induce the railroad authorities to open up Clark county, about 1848 or 1849 he both donated and sold them land. He helped to do the grading work on the road and was afterwards kept in the company's employ as paymaster, holding the position until his retirement from same. He retired from the service of the railroad in his fiftieth year. Colonel Ferguson was educated in the common schools of Pennsylvania, was a Democrat in politics, and belonged to the Presbyterian faith. He was a great friend of President Armstrong, of the Jeffersonville, Madison & Indianapolis Railroad, and was known all over the county. He was quite active in the political circles of his day, but never sought a public office. He was at one time colonel of a regiment of Pennsylvania militia, and was also employed by the state to collect all the old government arms in Clark, Scott, Floyd and Washington counties. He and James Allen hauled them to Indianapolis. He died in 1860, just before the war broke out His wife died in 1844, when our subject was quite young. James R. besides himself had five brothers and two sisters. He and his sister, Maria Calender, of Louisville, Kentucky, are the only survivors.

James R. Ferguson started for himself when about sixteen years old. He learned the blacksmith trade, at which he worked for ten years with good results. In the year 1861, at tne outbreak of the war, he enlisted in Company D, Forty-ninth Indiana Infantry, as a private, on September 19th. He fought in the battles of Cumberland Gap, Memphis, Tennessee; Vicksburg, and in the campaign around the last named district. He then participated in the Red River Expedition, came home on furlough, and was mustered out in 1865, at which time he held a commission as captain. From that time until a year ago he was a prosperous farmer.

In the year 1879 he married Mamie Connor, who was born on the 22d of November, 1850, and was the daughter of Mary and Bryan Connor. Her parents were natives of Ireland, though she herself was born in Maryland. Her mother died in Henryville and her father was killed in an accident on the Baltimore & Ohio Railroad, in Virginia, about 1856. Her mother, whose death occurred in 1885, was in her sixty-first year. Mrs. Ferguson and her husband have been blessed with the following children: Ray, born May 5, 1880; Earl R. was born December 4, 1881, and lives in California; Chester C., born May 13, 1885; Henry H. was born in February, 1887; Charles Blaine was born in 1890, January 11th, in Louisville, and James A. on December 31, 1893.

James R. Ferguson obtained his education in the common schools. He and his family are members of the Methodist Episcopal church. In politics he is a Republican and served as Assessor of the township for one term. He is a member of the Grand Army of the Republic, Post No. 461.

RICHARD J. ELROD.

Richard J. Elrod, of Henryville, Clark county, is one of Monroe township's representative farmers and a man of straightforward and honorable character. Ever since 1876 he has been associated with the district in which he lives and has met with marked success in the general farming line. He is now approaching his seventieth year and his long life of industry enables him to enjoy the declining period of his career in security. He was born on the 10th of August, 1840, in Washington county, and was the son of Stephen and Elizabeth (Wyman) Elrod. Stephen Elrod belonged to an old North Carolina family and was born there in 1793. He was a farmer, and in his young days came to Washington county, Indiana, where his marriage took place, and where his after life was spent. He became known as a raiser of hogs, cattle and sheep on a large scale. As a Justice of the Peace he was widely known as 'Squire Elrod. In his early life he obtained an education in the old log subscriptiqn schools. His death occurred in 1847 in Washington county. His wife, who was born in Germany, came to the United States when quite young with her parents, and settled in Washington county. She was born in 1798 and died in 1852. Twelve children, four girls and eight boys, were born to them, only four of their sons, including our subject, now surviving. They are: Eli and Robert, both living in Washington county; Thomas Benton lives in Oklahoma, and Richard J., the youngest living.

Richard J. Elrod has made his own way in the world since his eleventh year, at which period he became an orphan. In the year 1867 his marriage to Lucinda B. Walker took place. She was born in Washington county October 4, 1845, and was the daughter of William S. and Louisa Walker. To Richard and Mrs. Elrod one child, William D., was born in 1873. He married Laura Townsend; they live in Monroe township and have two children.

When thirty-three years of age our subject came to Clark county and resided in Monroe township, where he still lives in section 266. As a general farmer he was successful and used to bring his farm produce to Salem, which was the nearest large market town, in order to dispose of same. His education was obtained in the common schools of Washington county, and in his early days the country round was pretty well settled. In politics he is a Democrat. He has never sought political office, devoting the greater part of his time to home and farm life. His wife is a member of the Methodist Episcopal church. Previous to his present marriage he married in the year 1861, Katherine Swain, who died about eighteen months afterwards leaving him a daughter, Cora, born in 1862, who married Sheridan McGrew. They live in Holton, Kansas, and have two children.

JAMES A. CLEGG.

James A. Clegg, retired farmer of Henryville, Clark county, is a well known and respected member of the community in which he has lived and a man whose family has been actively associated with the prosperity and progress of that section of the state. His father was known throughout Clark county as a lawyer of ability and reputation, and a man of honorable character. Our subject was himself a participant in the Civil war, and at the close of his term of service was discharged with honor. Since that time he has been most successful in his farming pursuits.

James A. Clegg was born on February 2, 1839, in Wood township, Clark county, and was the son of Matthew and Martha C. (Allen) Clegg. Matthew Clegg was born in the year 1799 in Pennsylvania, and came to Clark county where he located, near Utica, when he was quite young. He lived there a short time and then moved on Silver Creek, at which place his parents, who also came to Clark county, both died. He got little regular education, but succeeded in educating himself through home study in his spare time. In this manner he took up the study of law and became one of the best pioneer lawyers of his day in Clark county. He became judge of the Criminal Court and was Prosecuting Attorney for many years. He participated in the Civil war as first lieutenant in Company M, Fifth Indiana Cavalry, emerging from the conflict as a captain after three years' service. Having been captured at Macon, Georgia, by the Southern troops he spent six months in Libby prison. Three sons, one of whom was our subject, served with him. James A. was in the same company with his father, a brother and two nephews. The brother, whose name was Matthew, died in Andersonville prison. Returning from the war the older Clegg went back to his law practice in this part of the county, and previous to his death in 1881, lived in Henryville for many years. His first marriage to Catherine Anderson occurred about 1835. They had two children, both of whom died when young. His second wife, Martha C. Allen, was the daughter of James and Mary (McBride) Allen. The second Mrs. Clegg's parents were married about 1837; her mother being born about the year 1819 or 1820 and was a native of Ohio. James A. Clegg is the second of a family of fourteen children. The death of both parents occurred on the same day, the 6th of February, 1881, in Henryville. The elder Clegg was one of the best known men in Clark county and well liked by everyone.

James A. Clegg started for himself at the time of his marriage in 1860, to Martha Dietz, who was born in 1840 in Monroe township. She was the daughter of John Frederick and Sarah (Lewis) Dietz. John F. Dietz was born on the 4th of October, 1788, and died March 15, 1874; his wife was born April 23, 1806, and died on the 5th of November, 1873. John F. Dietz was a farmer and an early pioneer. He came here in the Indian days with his parents. They had to go to the scattered block-houses on several occasions for protection from Indians, and met with much hardship in consequence. John F. Dietz was also known as a large fruit grower. His parents came from Philadelphia.

James A. Clegg enlisted in Company M, Fifth Indiana Cavalry, in 1862, at Jeffersonville. He joined as a private, and at the end of three years was mustered out as a sergeant. At the end of the war he became a farmer in Monroe township at which occupation he remained until ten years ago, when he retired and came to Henryville. He obtained his education in the subscription schools of Clark county. In politics he is a Republican and in religion he is a member of the Christian church. He is commander of the local post No. 461 Grand Army of the Republic at Henryville. The following children have been born to Mr. and Mrs. Clegg: Richard M., who was born September 19, 1861, married Ellen Cain; they live at Cainville, Missouri, and have two children. Mary A. was born July 7, 1865, and married John Copeland; they live at Manford,

Oklahoma, and have three children. Sarah C. Clegg was born July 28, 1868, and married Charles M. Clark; they live in Jeffersonville and have five children. John W. was born April 7, 1871, and lives in Oklahoma; Matthew S. was born May 13, 1873; he married Jessie Biggs; they live in Clark county and have four children. James A. was born on the 28th of June, 1876; he married, has one child and lives in Oklahoma, being an undertaker at Manford. Frank, the youngest child, was born August 3, 1879, and remains at home with his parents.

James A. Clegg, his wife and son live comfortably in their nice home at Henryville. Both the elder people are still well preserved and enjoy good health.

HON. CHARLES F. C. HANCOCK, M. D.

Though the medical profession of Southern Indiana contains a bright galaxy of physicians, there are none better known or more highly esteemed than Doctor Hancock. Though still in the prime of life he has accomplished much in the line of his profession and has before him a still more brilliant future. William Hancock, his father, was a Kentuckian by birth, but came early to Indiana and still lives at Memphis. He married Catherine Smith, who was born in England, but came to America when ten years old. By this union there were five children: George W. and Edward L. are residents of Seymour, Indiana; Mrs. Patience Gournsey also lives at Seymour; Mrs. Eugene Dunlevy is a resident of Memphis, and Mrs. Albert Puddell resides at Charlestown, Indiana. Dr. James N. Reynolds, a half-brother of the above mentioned, is a practicing physician at Memphis.

Charles F. C. Hancock, next to the youngest member of this family, was born at Memphis, Clark county, Indiana, February 3, 1867. He was a diligent pupil. In 1881 he entered the Seymour high school, and the following year became a student in Eikosi Academy, at Salem, graduating from the latter institution in the spring of 1883. He began the study of medicine under Doctor Reynolds, and in the intervals taught two terms of school. During this period he burned much "midnight oil" in his efforts to master the contents of the learned books put before him, many of his nights and most of his vacation periods being devoted to fitting himself for his exacting profession. In 1885 he entered the Medical Department of the University of Louisville, and a year later matriculated in the Medical College of Ohio at Cincinnati, from which he was graduated in the class of March, 1887. He formed a partnership for practice with the late Dr. E. J. Kempff, at Jasper, but one year later located at Jeffersonville, which has since been the theater of his operations. He has met with success and has steadily risen both in extent of practice and reputation as a general practitioner. Since 1892 he has been local surgeon for the Pennsylvania Railroad Company. He is a member of the Clark County Medical Society and the State Medical Association. His fraternal relations embrace membership in Clark Lodge, No. 40, Free and Accepted Masons; Horeb Chapter, Royal Arch Masons, and Jeffersonville Commandery, Knights Templar. Though wedded to his professional duties and realizing that medicine is a jealous mistress, the doctor occasionally takes an excursion into the realms of politics and proved his popularity in 1904, when he made a successful race for State Senator from this district on the Republican ticket. He served out his term acceptably, which embraced two sessions of the Legislature.

On October 27, 1897, Doctor Hancock was married to Nora Clark Duffy, member of a prominent and wealthy family of Clark county. Her parents were James T. and Nora (Robinson) Duffy, the former well known for many years in the business circles of Jeffersonville. Fuller particulars concerning him will be found in the sketch of James T. Duffy, appearing elsewhere in this volume. Doctor and Mrs. Hancock have five children: James D., James R., Catherine V., William and Charles F. C., Jr. Doctor Hancock is of quiet, unostentatious manners, of a frank and friendly nature and fond rather of his home and family than of society or any kind of display. Philantropic and kind hearted, he finds many opportunities to do favors on the quiet to his deserving and less fortunate brethren. On the whole it is not too much to pronounce him not only a skillful and successful physician, but a model citizen, friend and neighbor.

WALLACE LAWRENCE JACOBS.

This enterprising citizen lives in Utica township, Clark county, and is a representative of two pioneer families. His birth occurred November 7, 1874, only a short distance from his present home, and his parents, Isaac A. and Loretta (Lawrence) Jacobs, were born in the same township. Isaac A. Jacobs was a resident of Utica township all his life and he became known as a prosperous and influential farmer. The maternal grandfather of Wallace L. Jacobs, Albert Lawrence, was born in New Jersey and, coming to Indiana, settled in Clark county, where he passed his remaining years, dying at Jeffersonville at the age of eighty-four years. Wallace Lawrence Jacobs is the only child of his parents. He was reared as a farmer boy and received the advantages offered by the country schools, supplemented by one year in the high school at Utica. When twenty-one years of age he engaged in farming for himself and later purchased the place where he now lives, having prospered from the first. He owns fifty-two acres of well improved land, and the buildings thereon are such as his needs and comfort require.

Mr. Jacobs was united in marriage with Catherine A. Smith, November 22, 1898, she being a daughter of W. W. and Nancy (Bottorff) Smith, also natives of Utica township, Clark county. The children born unto Mr. and Mrs. Jacobs are four in number and their names are: Herbert W., Irwin A., Nanetta and Ruth R.

In politics Mr. Jacobs has supported the principles of the Republican party and both he and Mrs. Jacobs are members of the New Chapel Methodist Episcopal church, he being one of its trustees. This family is held in high esteem by their neighbors as a result of lives of industry, honesty and hospitality, causing them to rank among the township's valued citizens.

HARRY C. MONTGOMERY.

Harry C. Montgomery was born in Jeffersonville, Indiana, April 9, 1870, and while yet young in life has become Judge of the Clark Circuit Court. His father, a man of many sterling attributes, was John R. Montgomery, a captain and pilot on the Ohio and Mississippi rivers before, during and after the war between the states, whose life was brought to a close by the dread scourge of yellow fever, September 1, 1873. John R. Montgomery married Mary L. Mauzy, representative of an influential family. She is living at this writing in San Angelo, Texas, with two of her daughters, Mrs. Jessie Abbott and Mrs. May Wear. At an early age the Judge was compelled by circumstances to make his own way, successively as a newsboy, upholster's assistant, musician on the Ohio river steamboats; also as a school teacher in country schools of Clark county, and finally, in 1895, graduated from the University of Louisville, law department, as valedictorian of his class. He was admitted to the bar of Clark county and soon thereafter entered upon his chosen profession. He was always a close student and an original thinker, and he allowed no opportunity to advance his education to pass in his school days. In both the grade schools and in the Jeffersonville high school he held a distinctive and leading position among his classmates, and his record here and at the State University at Bloomington shows that he made a conscientious and careful application to his studies.

Judge Montgomery has never assumed the responsibilities of the married state.

The success at the bar of Judge Montgomery was instantaneous and has gradually increased. In 1896, after a practice of one year, his abilities were recognized by the citizens of this community and he was elected prosecutor of the Fourth Judicial Circuit, in which position he very ably and conscientiously served until 1900, in fact, it was the splendid discharge of his duties in this capacity, to a great extent, that made his election to the bench a certainty. In 1904 Mr. Montgomery was elected Judge of the circuit, which he had served so well in the capacity of prosecutor and he has given his constituents entire satisfaction in this office. Although one of the younger generation of lawyers of Clark county he has discharged his duties in an eminently just and conservative manner, for he came to the bench well qualified for its exacting duties and responsibilties, and from the beginning his judicial career was characterized by such a profound knowledge of the law and an earnest and scientious desire to apply it impartially that he was not long in gaining the respect and confidence of the attorneys and litigants and earning for himself an honorable reputation among the leading jurists of this part of the state. The Judge has ever kept in touch with he inerests of his city and county and is an ardent advocate and liberal patron of all worthy enterprises making for their advancement and prosperity. He is active in every movement for the good of his fellow men, and his popularity is bounded only by the limits of his acquaintance. As a lawyer he is easily the peer of any of his professional brethren in this locality, and the honorable distinction already achieved at the bar is an earnest of the still higher honors to be achieved in years to come, as he is just in the prime of manhood. Behind him lay his years of toil and adversity, the formative period of his life; but before him are higher honors and larger rewards, both in public and private life, for he is not only an accomplished lawyer, a skillful advocate, an honorable and just Judge, also a genial and courteous gentleman.

JAMES ERNEST BURKE.

In tracing the genealogy of the well known business man of Jeffersonville whose life record is presented in the following paragraphs the biographer finds that he is a worthy scion of sterling Irish ancestors on the paternal side, his father, James Burke, for many years a prominent contractor of this city, having been born in the Emerald Isle, and who in 1854, when a young man, immigrated to the United States, locating in Jeffersonville, Indiana, where his brother had previously settled. He was a carpenter by trade and he followed this and contracting on street work, wharves, railroad work, etc., for many years. He married Cornelia Crandle, a representative of a well established family of Troy, New York. James Burke died in Jeffersonville several years ago at the age of seventy-three years. He was an active worker in the Democratic party, and for his local services he was chosen City Treasurer, serving three terms; he also served in the City Council, proving himself to be an able exponent of the people's interests. His widow, whom he married in

New Orleans, survived him several years, dying at the age of sixty-eight. They were the parents of seven children, five of whom grew to maturity, three living at the present writing.

James Ernest Burke, the sixth child in order of birth in his father's family, was born in the city of Jeffersonville, January 17, 1865, and was reared in his native town. He received a common school education, and later, in order to fit himself for a business career, attended the Bryant and Stratton Business College in Louisville, Kentucky. After finishing his education he remained with his father as clerk and bookkeeper for several years while they were engaged in railroad construction work. In 1883 Mr. Burke purchased a wholesale and retail coal business of A. B. Howard & Company, and he has since carried on this enterprise with success, having built up a liberal trade with the surrounding community and proving himself to be a man of energy and good judgment in business affairs. He is located at the corner of Chestnut and Wall streets.

The domestic chapter in the life of James E. Burke dates from 1893, when he was united in marriage with Bertha C. Read, a native of Jeffersonville, the accomplished daughter of John F. and Eliza A. Read. After a brief and harmonious married life, Mrs. Burke was called to her rest in 1894.

Mr. Burke is a Democrat in his political relations, and fraternally he belongs to Jeffersonville Lodge, No. 362, Benevolent and Protective Order of Elks; also the Knights of Columbus, in which he has taken a deep interest, as he has in the former been past exalted ruler of the Elks. He is a member of St. Augustine Catholic church and a liberal supporter of the same.

JOHN A. H. OWENS.

A citizen of the United States can wear no greater badge of honor than the distinction of having served the government in the four years of war between the states. One of these defenders of the nation's integrity is the gentleman whose name appears at the head of this article, a well known citizen of Clark county, Indiana, and one of the local contributors to the history of this county.

John A. H. Owens was born in Scott county, Indiana, August 7, 1842, the son of Charles and Sarah (Whitson) Owens. The Owens family were native Hoosiers, the father was born in Charlestown township in Clark county, August 22, 1808. His wife was born July 16th, the same year in Utica township. There were eleven children in Grandfather Owens' family, the oldest having been born in 1788. They were all born in Clark county, Indiana. The paternal grandfather of our subject was born in Philadelphia, Pennsylvania, in 1768 and his wife was born in 1767. They emigrated to Indiana, coming down the Ohio river in boats. John Owens and Sarah Jackson, the subject's grandparents, married in Spring Station, Jefferson county, Kentucky, April 5, 1787. The Owens and Jacksons reached the Falls of the Ohio, or Bear Grass, as it was then known, about 1785. Here the grandparents of the subject were married. The maternal great-grandparents of the subject, John and Elizabeth Jackson, who were natives of Scotland, moved from Pennsylvania to Bear Grass, Kentucky, where they lived for many years, and in 1809 settled in Clark county, Indiana, where they died. They were buried in an old family grave yard, four miles east of Charlestown. John and Sarah Jackson Owens were the parents of the following children: David, born in Clarksville, Indiana, in 1788; John, born in 1790; Elizabeth, born in 1792; George, born in 1795; Harvey, born in 1797; James, born in 1798; William J., born in 1799; George Clark, born in 1802; Charles was born in 1804; Rebecca was born in 1806; Charles was born in 1808.

Charles and Sarah (Whitson) Owens were married May 9, 1837, and to them three children were born, two girls and one boy, namely: Philena was born May 11, 1838, and married a Mr. Johnson. She died in Potomac, Illinois, after becoming the mother of five children; Susan, the second child of Charles and Sarah Owens, was born March 2, 1840; she became the wife of Capt. Thomas R. Mitchell. She died in Charlestown, Clark county, Indiana, in May, 1899, after becoming the mother of four children, three of whom are living at this writing. John A. H., our subject, was the third child. For some time he lived with his uncle, William Owens. He received his education in the common schools of Clark county, Indiana. Although his text-book training was somewhat limited it was good for the times in which he was reared. He afterward entered the high school at Charlestown, and became a teacher, having taught in a very creditable manner from 1866 to 1879 in the country schools, during which time he became well known as an able educator and his services were in great demand.

Feeling that it was his duty to sever home ties, give up his teaching and assist in defending his country's integrity, when the great Rebellion broke out, our subject enlisted in Company I, Eighty-first Volunteer Infantry, and was transferred to the Marine Brigade March 1, 1863, from which he was discharged at Vicksburg, Mississippi, January 17, 1865, after being in the service two and one-half years.

Mr. Owens was married February 1, 1872, to Eliza Riley, who was born in Clark county, Indiana, March 19, 1845. Her family came to this county before 1820, not long after Indiana entered the Union. They have two children living, Charles, who was born December 30, 1873, is a barber in Charlestown, Indiana; Bessie C., who was born August 21, 1881, is a graduate of the Charlestown schools. She is single and living at home.

Mr. Owens devoted his life to farming after the war until 1881, when he moved to Charlestown and entered business there, making a success of the same, for he has always been known as a man of industry and one whom the people could trust.

In politics Mr. Owens is a Republican and he has ever taken a lively interest in political affairs and the advancement of his county's interests in any way. He faithfully and very acceptably served the city of Charlestown as postmaster under President Benjamin Harrison. He was elected Trustee of Charlestown township, and his work elicited the hearty approval of everyone concerned. Mr. Owens stands high in the estimation of the people of Clark county.

WINNIE CLARE LEWMAN.

The Lewmans may be described as a family of contractors as several members of it have achieved success in that line, while the activities of others extended into financial and commercial subjects. Moses T. Lewman, who was born in Clark county, subsequently became an influential citizen of Putnam county, where he did contracting work on a large scale and held the office of Sheriff. His first work at contracting was the construction of the Bethany Christian church on the Charlestown pike, near Charlestown. He was a successful man of affairs, and accumulated considerable property, but met an untimely death by drowning, in 1870, at a sea-side resort, near Savannah, Georgia. He married Naomi Lavina Conover, and became the father of a number of children, who are now located in various parts of the country. John B. and Harry L. are contractors. The former married Annabell Newman, the daughter of a Louisville plumber. Leon D., the third son, married Idoline Sparks, of Atlanta, Georgia, where he is engaged in banking and contracting. Nora, the eldest daughter, is the wife of a Mr. Moore, and resides at Seattle. Bessie, wife of J. R. Riggs, is a resident of Sullivan, Indiana. The wife of Harry was formerly Lelia Curtis, of California, whose mother was a member of the Holman family of Clark county.

Winnie Clare Lewman was born at Greencastle, Indiana, May 12, 1871, and received his education in the schools of his native city. After leaving Greencastle he was a student for some time at the Bardstown Male College and also Hanover. He returned from his studies to the farm at Prather and remained at home for several years. In 1894 he engaged in the seed business at Louisville, but after following this for a year he began contracting, which he has steadily followed since then. His work which has taken him to many parts of the South has included the construction of many large public buildings. He met with success and before he reached middle life was able to construct for himself a home, which in beauty of surroundings, fine finish and tasteful furnishings is something exceptional. This residence, erected in 1906, is located on the Charlestown pike, near Prather, and is one of the landmarks of the vicinity. Standing on high ground, with an extensive lawn in front, it commands a wide view, extending for many miles in every direction. The structure is surrounded by broad verandas, whose supporting columns are made of rough hewn native stone. The downstairs interior is finished in "mission oak," with fluted columns of the same material, marking the dividing line between the large double parlors. The upstairs rooms are of various finishes, one in light oak, another in mahogany, others of contrasting woods, and with furniture to match. Other luxuries of this home are the tile-floored bath room with all modern equipments, furnace, hot and cold water, chandeliers of beautiful design, lighted by electricity. An electric plant of most modern construction furnishes both lights and power. Being skilled in everything relating to the art of construction Mr. Lewman has exhibited his good taste in the selection of all the furniture and decorations, which enter harmoniously into the color scheme of the entire surroundings.

Mr. Lewman is a member of the Mutual Construction Company, a corporation of contractors which put up large public buildings throughout the South. His fraternal relations are with the Knights Templar and the Free and Accepted Masons. He also holds membership in Cement Lodge of the Odd Fellows at Prather.

On November 16, 1892, he was married to Daisy, daughter of James Edgar Brown, a sketch of whom appears elsewhere in this volume. Mr. and Mrs. Lewman have one child, a daughter named Vere, at present a student in the Jeffersonville schools.

THE GREEN FAMILY.

William Raleigh Green came from England about the year 1750, and settled near Poolesville, Montgomery county, Maryland. About the year 1770 he moved with his family to Iredell county, North Carolina, where his children grew up, married and most of them removed to homes farther west. Of these the names of Isaac, Thomas, William, John and Martha have been preserved.

William Green was born in 1761, grew up in Iredell county, and on March 17, 1796, was married to Chloe Ann Roby. In 1806 he moved to Kentucky and in 1809 came to Clark county, where he settled permanently, about four miles north of Jeffersonville. William Green died March 23, 1823, and his wife August 11, 1821. They are buried in the old Jacobs cemetery, about four miles northeast of Jeffersonville. The children of William Green and his wife, Chloe Ann Green, were as follows: John Willetts Green, born July 31, 1797; Thomas Wilkinson Green, born October 3, 1799; Martha Green, born November 15, 1801; Lurana Green, born January 7, 1804; Sarah Adeline Green, born July 19, 1807; Leonard Roby Green, born December 29, 1809; Mary Green, born March 11, 1812, and William Henry Green, born July 13, 1814. All grew up in Clark county. Thomas Wilkinson Green located near Worthington, Greene county, where he died February 16, 1880. Leonard Roby Green engaged in newspaper work in New Albany, where he owned and published the Weekly and Daily Bulletin. He sold out there in 1849 and died in Goliad, Texas, August 7, 1853. William Henry Green learned the printer's trade at the age of seventeen in the office of the New Albany Gazette and was engaged in newspaper work for more than fifty years, owning and publishing papers in New Albany, Connersville and Brookville, Indiana. He was Auditor of Fayette county, Indiana, for twelve years, and died at Shelbyville, Indiana, in 1907.

Isaac Green, eldest son of William Raleigh Green, was born August 21, 1755, and was married to Elizabeth Wilson, May 28, 1780. They remained permanently in Iredell county, North Carolina, where he died November 22, 1833. The children of Isaac and Elizabeth Green were: Zachariah, John, Thomas, William, Isaac, Hetty and Annie. Zachariah Green married Ann Jacobs and located in Wapello county, Iowa. John Green located in Kentucky. Thomas Green fought in the Seminole war, received a land warrant, and located in Morgan county, Indiana. Isaac Green remained at the old home in North Carolina. Hetty Green married John Summers and settled in Tennessee. Annie died young, and William Green located in Clark county, Indiana.

William Green was born March 15, 1790, in Iredell county, North Carolina. He was married December 19, 1816, to Celia Lewman and in 1819 in company with the Lewmans removed to Clark county, settling near Utica. He remained here a short time and then leased a tract of land near the old county farm. They lived here until 1833, when they purchased a tract of land near Memphis, which became their permanent home the same year.

William Green died December 5, 1867, and Celia Green died May 15, 1877. They with all their children are buried in Ebenezer cemetery, near Memphis.

The children of William and Celia Green were: Isaiah Green, born October 10, 1817, married Matilda Jane Perry, December 10, 1839, and died August 18, 1840. No descendants. Elizabeth Caroline Green, born April 9, 1823, married Francis Durment, March 25, 1847, and settled in Carr township; died March 31, 1907. Only two children grew up and married. Albert N. Durment married Mary King, of Carr township, and Jennie E. married George T Dunlevy, of Bluelick. All located in Carr township.

John Wesley Green, born December 25, 1830, died January 30, 1845. Nancy Ann Green born August 24, 1833, married Joseph Thomas Harrell, December 23, 1855, died August 10, 1860. No descendants.

George Washington Green was born April 9, 1837, married Catherine Whitesides November 16, 1859, and died December 22, 1898. George W. Green was highly educated and spent fourteen years teaching. In 1861 he was ordained a minister of the Church of God, or the Adventists. He served this church for many years, held many public discussions on the articles of faith peculiar to that church and traveled much as an evangelist. He later became a member of the Christian church, with which he remained a faithful member and minister until his death. He lived on the old homestead, near Memphis, and is buried at Ebenezer.

The children of George W. and Catherine Green were: Edwin Orville, born December 26, 1860; Annie Alice, born July 2, 1862; Ella Etta, born April 11, 1864; Alvin Ellis, born June 15, 1866; Oscar Otto, born August 20, 1868; Mary Lizzie, born May 23, 1870; Clara Daisy, born September 18. 1872; William Louis, born September 13, 1874; John Frederick, born March 23, 1877; Eva Myrtle, born June 11, 1880; Katie Lillian, born December 1, 1882; Charles George, born June 1, 1885.

Edwin Orville Green was educated in the common schools of Union township, and the Indiana State Normal School at Terre Haute; he taught for six years, and was principal of the schools at Raub, Benton county, in 1886-7, and at Memphis in 1887-8-9. He was appointed to the railway mail service June 8, 1889, and assigned to the New York and Chicago Railway postoffice with headquarters at Cleveland, Ohio. He was soon promoted and for many years has been clerk in charge of some of the largest exclusive mail trains in the world. He was married May 3, 1888, to Ella E. Townsend, of Blue Lick. Their children are Florence Catherine, born August 14, 1890; Bernice Edna, born August 15, 1893, and Amos Townsend Green, born September 11, 1898. He has recently purchased a large tract of land in Silver Creek township, near Sellersburg, and expects soon to make it his permanent home.

Alvin Ellis Green was married March 3, 1889, to Daisy Forest Townsend, of Blue Lick, and owns a fine farm in Union township, but at present follows the carpenter's trade in New Albany.

Clara Daisy Green was married December 26, 1897, to Joseph L. Shirley, a farmer of Union township. They reside near Memphis, and have three children, Lester Louis, Joseph Irvin and George Shirley.

William Louis Green was educated in the common schools of Union township and at Borden; taught school four years, and in 1896 he entered the Western Reserve Medical College of Cleveland, Ohio, where he graduated in 1900; served sixteen months as resident house physician in the Cleveland City Hospital, after which he located at Pekin, Washington county, Indiana, where he has since practiced with great success. · He was married April 8, 1901, to Jessie A. Scott, of Waucoma, Iowa. They have one son, William Thomas Green, and a daughter, Jean Catherine Green.

Katie Lillian Green was married October 26, 1904, to Virgil Johantgen, of Union township; they live in Jeffersonville, Indiana, and have one child, Inez Catherine Johantgen, born September 13, 1905.

Charles George Green was educated in the common schools of Union township and studied telegraphy at New Albany. He now holds a responsible position with the Northern Pacific, and is located at Missoula, Montana, where he was married June 1, 1907, to Adele Basset, a teacher in the Missoula public schools.

ISAAC F. WHITESIDE.

This biographical memoir has to do with a characer of unusual force and eminence, for Isaac F. Whiteside, whose life chapter has been closed by the fate that awaits us all, was for a long lapse of years one of the prominent citizens of the Falls Cities and one of Jeffersonville's most distinguished native sons. He assisted in every way possible bringing about the wondrous transformation from the primitive conditions of the early days to later day progress and improvement. While he carried on a special line of business in such a manner as to gain wide notoriety, he also belonged to that class of representative citizens who promote the public welfare while advancing individual success. There were in him sterling traits which command uniform confidence and regard, and his worthy personal attributes, enshrined in the hearts of hosts of friends, will long be honored.

Isaac F. Whiteside was born in Jeffersonville, Indiana, July 16, 1858, and was therefore only in the fifty-first year of his age when summoned to join the great phantom army on May 4, 1909, but although cut off in the zenith of his powers he left behind an inheritance of which his descendants may well be proud—the fruits of a successful career and a good name. His parents were William S. and Rebecca (Friend) Whiteside, the former a native of Charlestown, Indiana, and the latter a native of what is now Danville, Kentucky. His father passed away several years ago, but his mother, a woman of gracious personality and beautiful Christian character, is still living at Jeffersonville. They were the parents of eight children, Isaac F., of this review, being the fourth child in order of birth. After reaching as far as the third year in high school he cut short his educational career to become an actor in 1874, his inclination being towards elocution, and his talents were recognized by Benjamin Cassesay, of Louisville, under whom he studied, after which he was offered a position with the stock company at the old Macauley

theatre and he made his debut at the Academy of Music, Indianapolis, in 1875. From that time until 1877 he remained on the stage and assisted in supporting many of the greatest actors and actresses of that time, among them being Edwin Booth, John McCullough, the elder Sothern, John T. Raymond, Larence Barrett, Mary Anderson and William J. Florence. Ada Rehan was a member of the company to which Mr. Whiteside belonged. At one time he was a roommate of W. H. Gillette, the playwright.

After leaving the stage Mr. Whiteside became connected with his father in the grocery business in Jeffersonville, and in 1880 took charge in his own name. He proved to be an alert business man from the first and two years later built a bakery in connection with his grocery. Branching out further he purchased the produce business of J. S. Fry and established the firm of I. F. Whiteside & Brother, the junior member, Harry R. Whiteside, being placed in charge. In 1893 he abandoned the grocery and devoted his energies to the bakery and soon pushed his way into the Louisville market with such success that in 1895 he decided to move there and build a plant. Later he made additions and in the summer of 1908 opened what is probably the most extensive and best equipped bakery in the South and excelled by but few plants in size and none in equipment throughout the United States. It was opened to public inspection on Mr. Whiteside's fiftieth birthday anniversary, July 16, 1908. Mr. Whiteside had the novel experience in the winter of 1893 of sending his wagons and teams across the Ohio river on the ice. His bakery in Louisville was at first located at Fourteenth and Maple streets, later it was removed to Fourteenth and Broadway where the great plant described in detail on another page of this work is now located. Its emergence from the little plant across the river with an investment of about one hundred and fifty dollars recalls the maxim, "how tall oaks from little acorns grow." The fully developed plant has a capacity of one hundred and forty-four loaves per minute and employes one hundred men. Bread is daily shipped from this busy establishment as far southeast as Cumberland Gap, and as far south as Decatur, Alabama. The daily capacity foots up to the tremendous aggregate of one hundred and seventy thousand loaves.

Mr. Whiteside was one of the most indomitable of workers in the Falls Cities and it was the popular belief about him that he could make no error in a business way. He appeared to have an unerring sense of what was the right thing to do and the best course to pursue and he never lacked the necessary courage to carry through any resolution or scheme upon which he determined. To the last, although his business interests remained in Louisville, Mr. Whiteside retained his affection for his home city in whose welfare he never ceased to take a keen interest. It is also remembered with high appreciation by the people of Jeffersonville that it was to Mr. Whiteside's faith, courage and will that the city owes her first steps upon the road to improve-

50

ment upon which road she is now making rapid progress with confidence of a great future. The first granitoid walks and the first brick roadway were laid in Jeffersonville under the inspiration of Mr. Whiteside's counsel and are monuments to his determination since they were built in the face of much shortsighted opposition. Mr. Whiteside had faith in the future of his native city and the fact that the future looks brighter to Jeffersonville than the past is due in no small measure to the course he marked out and pursued for himself when he became Jeffersonville's chief magistrate in 1894. He had long been faithful in his support to the Republican party, but had never cared to take part in local politics until pursuaded to enter the mayoralty contest of the year mentioned above. He filled his four years of office with credit to himself and to the entire satisfaction of his constituents and all concerned and with benefit to the city at large. It was during his administration that the national encampment of the Grand Army of the Republic was held in Louisville and Mr. Whiteside saw to it that Jeffersonville did her just part in entertaining the visitors to this vicinity, even, it is said, outstripping Louisville, proportionately to her size, upon this occasion. Mr. Whiteside always retained his citizenship in Jeffersonville, and several years ago purchased the old and attractive Henry Peter property on West Front street and that remained his home until the last. Being hospitable and always desiring to entertain his friends, his home and social life were delightful. He was happy in his family relationship, warmly attached to his family and his pleasant home was always a place of harmony and good cheer. Mr. Whiteside's domestic life began when he had just passed his twentieth birthday, having married on August 13, 1878, Miss Louise F. Smith, daughter of John F. and Elmira Smith, the latter still living in Jeffersonville, and by this union there were two children, William S. Whiteside who is in the bakery business, having long been associated with his father, and he resides in Louisville. His sister, Miss Nora Whiteside, resides at home. Their mother was called to her rest in 1888, and two years later Mr. Whiteside married Katherine Beatty, daughter of John J. and Louise (Woodruff) Beatty, of Louisville, and this union resulted in the birth of two children, Sue May and Katherine, both members of the home circle. They and their mother are well known in social circles of this vicinity and are held in high esteem by a large circle of friends by reason of their culture, refinement and kindness.

Mr. Whiteside was never much of a secret order man, but was a member of Jeffersonville Lodge, No. 362, Benevolent and Protective Order of Elks, and he was not a member of any church, holding to no man-made creed. However, his daily life was exemplary and evinced religious principles. His mother is a Methodist and his inclination was toward Methodism.

Mr. Whiteside showed unusual fortitude and courage during his long illness and never complained. His death was announced to the citizens of

Jeffersonville by the tolling of bells and the various city buildings were draped in black as a mark of esteem for the honored dead. He was laid to rest in Cave Hill cemetery with universal regret.

WILLIAM E. BOTTORFF.

The subject of this sketch holds a conspicuous place among the successful business men and public-spirited citizens of Clark county and is an honorable representative of one of the oldest and best known pioneer families in the southern part of the state. He is a son of William J. and Eliza J. (Nett) Bottorff, whose sketch appears elsewhere in these pages, and dates his birth from the 19th day of May, 1857, having first seen the light of day on the old family homestead, in Charlestown township, where his ancestors located when the few sparse settlements of Clark county were but niches in the deep and well-nigh impenetrable forests. Reared amid the beautiful rural scenes by which his childhood home was surrounded and familiar with the rugged duties of the farm he grew up a strong and well developed lad and when his services could be utilized took his place in the fields where he was able to do a man's work long before reaching the years of maturity. Meanwhile in winter seasons he attended the district schools of the neighborhood and after finishing the branches taught therein entered the Charlestown Academy, where for two years he pursued the prescribed course.

Mr. Bottorff began his business career as a merchant, conducting for a period of thirteen years a general store and built up a large and lucrative patronage, during the greater part of which time he also had charge of the post-office at Vesta. For the purpose of educating his children he finally disposed of his mercantile interests and moved to Greencastle, but after a brief residence in that city went to New Albany, where he again embarked in general merchandising and millinery business, devoting especial attention to the latter line of trade, which he conducted for some time on a very extensive scale. Mr. Bottorff's commercial experience at New Albany was financially successful but after some years he sold his stock and returned to Clark county. He invested his capital in land, purchasing one hundred and eighty acres in Charlestown township, since which time he has devoted his attention very largely to his agricultural and real estate interests, meeting with gratifying success the meanwhile and earning an honorable reputation as an enterprising, far-seeing business man and praiseworthy citizen.

A Democrat interested in the success of his party and in touch with the leading questions and issues of the times he has never entered the political arena as a partisan or office seeker. He is essentially a business man and while ever striving for his own advancement he has also been mindful of the interests of his friends and fellow citizens.

Mr. Bottorff on September 13, 1881, was united in marriage with Sallie S. Sandifer, a native of Kentucky, and a graduate of the Midway Female School of that state.

Mr. and Mrs. Bottorff have four children, the oldest of whom, Minnie, born July 5, 1882, is a graduate of the Charlestown high school and now chief operator in the telephone exchange of the same city. Garnett E., born May 16, 1884, married Bertha Dellinger and lives in Owen township. Mary K. is the wife of James H. Taggart, of Charlestown township, and Earyl is still a member of the family circle.

HON. CURTIS W. BALLARD.

The career of the present Clerk of Clark county's Circuit Court affords a practical illustration of the truth of the statement made by Shakespeare when he said "The purest treasure mortal times afford is spotless reputation, that away, men are but gilded loam or painted clay." Through right living Mr. Ballard has gained the confidence of the people of his adopted county and a distinctive evidence of this popular esteem was given in 1906 in his election to the important office which he now so ably fills.

Curtis W. Ballard is a Kentuckian by birth and a worthy member of an old and highly respected family of Shelby county, that state. His father, William Jordon Ballard, also a native of Kentucky, and for a number of years an honored resident of the above county, served with a creditable record in the Civil war as a private in Company A, Fifteenth Kentucky Volunteer Infantry, and shortly after retiring from the army entered the railway postal service, to which he gave about thirty of the best years of his life. When a young man he married Mary Moody, who was born and reared in the Blue Grass state, and in due time became the father of two sons and one daughter, the latter deceased, the older of the sons being the subject of this review. The younger, John Ballard, is a merchant of Jeffersonville, and one of the well known and successful business men of that city. After spending a number of years in the state of his birth William J. Ballard moved his family to Jeffersonville, Indiana, where he made his home until about 1875, when he returned to Kentucky, but about 1887 again changed his place of abode to Jeffersonville and since that time has been living in this city and taking an active interest in the public affairs of the same.

Curtis W. Ballard was born in Shelby county, Kentucky, on the 13th day of October, 1868, and spent his childhood and youth under the grateful influences of rural scenes. As soon as old enough for his services to be utilized to advantage he bore his full share in the cultivation of the family homestead and during the time spent on the farm received a good education in the schools of his native county, prosecuting his studies at intervals until a youth in his teens.

When twenty years of age Mr. Ballard severed home ties for the purpose of making his own way in the world, and for some time thereafter was employed in a foundry at Jeffersonville, where by diligent attention to duty he not only became familiar with the business in its every detail but in due time rose to the responsible position of foreman. After spending ten years in that capacity and acquiring a profound knowledge of the trade and great skill as a mechanic he resigned his position to make the canvass for the Legislature, having been duly nominated for the office by the Democracy of Clark county and triumphantly elected on November 6, 1904.

Mr. Ballard proved an able and creditable representation and during his one term of service spared neither labor nor pains in looking after the interests of his constituents and the welfare of the state. He was placed on a number of important committees, where his judgment and counsel carried weight and commanded respect and in the general deliberations and debates on the floor of the chamber he bore an active and conspicuous part. At the close of his term he resumed his trade and continued the same until 1906, when he again entered the political arena as an important candidate for official honors, having been nominated in the spring of that year for the office of Clerk of the Clark County Circuit Court and defeating his opponent by a decisive majority at the ensuing election the following November.

Mr. Ballard entered upon the discharge of his duties as Clerk in February, 1908, and thus far has fully realized the high expectations for his friends and the public and justified the Democracy in the wisdom of their choice, proving a capable and courteous official. When a young man Mr. Ballard laid a substantial foundation for a life of usefulness and the firmness of his purposes is carrying to conclusion all of his undertakings, has enabled him to achieve a larger measure of success than the majority attain.

Politically he yields allegiance to the Democratic party as before indicated, the success of which in his own county is partly due to his judicious counsel and able leadership. He keeps in touch with the leading questions and issues of the day. In the broadest sense of the term he is a self-made man and he occupies a place of influence.

Mr. Ballard takes much interest in secret fraternal work and belongs to a number of organizations and societies, in all of which he has been honored with positions of trust and importance besides taking an active interest in the wider field of general state and national work. He is a charter member of the lodge of Red Men in Jeffersonville, and a past official in the same; he belongs to the Benevolent and Protective Order of Elks and the Independent Order of Odd Fellows. Although reared under the influence and teachings of the Christian church, with which his family were identified, he is a member of the Methodist church.

REV. JOHN SIMONSON HOWK, D. D.

Pastor of the First Presbterian church of Jeffersonville, and one of the most learned and popular divines of his church in Indiana, is he whose name appears above, who is a native of Floyd county, this state, and a son of the late Hon. George Vail Howk, of New Albany, formerly a Judge of the Supreme Court and a jurist of national repute. The Howk family is of German origin, but settled in Massachusetts early in the eighteenth century and engaged in agricultural pursuits. Isaac Howk, the subject's grandfather, was born in that state, received a liberal education in Williams College and in 1817 located at Charlestown, Indiana, where he engaged in the practice of law. His wife, Elvira Vail, was a daughter of Dr. Gamaliel Vail, who moved from New England to Indiana Territory in 1806, and settled in Clark county.

Hon. George V. Howk was reared in Charlestown, graduated from Asbury University in 1846, studied law with Hon. Charles Dewey, a Judge of the Indiana Supreme Court, and was admitted to the bar in 1847, beginning the practice of his profession in New Albany, where he soon arose to eminence in his chosen calling. He filled various official positions and was long prominently before the public, serving as City Judge of New Albany, Common Pleas Judge, Circuit Judge and Representative to the General Assembly. In 1876 he was chosen one of the Judges of Indiana Supreme Court, which distinguished position he held twelve years with credit to himself and to the honor of the state, and in which he achieved national repute as a learned and profound jurist. Judge Howk was twice married, the first time in 1848 to Eleanor, daughter of Judge Charles Dewey, of Charlestown, and in 1854 to Jane Simonson, daughter of Gen. John S. Simonson, of the United States army. The subject of this sketch is the only survivor of the family of eight children, born of these marriages. Charles D. and George V. Howk, Jr., brothers of the subject, were lawyers at New Albany, both dying in early manhood, and a sister, Jennie, also grew to years of maturity, the others dying in infancy and childhood. Judge Howk was one of the leading Democrats of Indiana, and for many years filled a large place in public view. His professional and judicial careers were eminently honorable and distinguished and his life for many years closely identified with the history of his native state, made him distinctively one of the noted men of his day. He died at his home in New Albany January 13, 1892.

Rev. John Simonson Howk was born May 28, 1863, and spent his early life in New Albany, receiving his elementary education in the public schools of the city. Manifesting an ardent desire for more thorough intellectual training, he was prepared for college under the tutorship of Miss Suda May, and in due time entered DePauw University, where he prosecuted his studies until 1883, when he was graduated with the Degree of Bachelor of Arts. Subsequently in 1886 he received from the same institution the Degree of Master of Arts, and having taken up the study of theology in the meantime, and achieved high standing as a scholar and much more than ordinary success in the ministry, he was granted in the year 1896 the Degree of Doctor of Divinity, by his alma mater. Animated by a laudable ambition to attain the highest possible efficiency in his holy calling, he afterwards took a two years' post-graduate course in philosophy and ethics under Rev. Dr. McCosh, at Princeton University, and in 1888 he was graduated with an honorable record from the Princeton Theological Seminary, thus laying broad and deep a substantial foundation for his subsequent career in one of the noblest and most responsible fields of endeavor.

At one time Doctor Howk seriously contemplated entering the lagal profession and to this end studied law under his father, and in due time was admitted to the bar, but after a year's practice he abandoned the business to devote his life to the Christian ministry. On May 17, 1887, he was licensed by the New Albany Presbytery, and on June 19th of the year following, was ordained by the Presbytery of New Castle, since which time he has given himself unreservedly to his chosen calling, his first charges being the churches at Rehoboth and Pitts Creek, Maryland, where he labored with great acceptance from 1888 to 1898 inclusive. In the latter year he was chosen minister of the church at East Palestine, Ohio, but after a residence of a little more than a year at that place he resigned the pastorate to take charge of the First Presbyterian church of Jeffersonville, of which he was duly installed pastor on the 19th day of October, 1899, and to which he has since ministered with marked ability and happy results as the growth of the congregation in all lines of activity abundantly attests. Doctor Howk's labors in Jeffersonville have been highly creditable to himself and satisfactory to his congregation, presenting a series of successes which have tended greatly to the strengthening of the church temporally and spiritually, and making it one of the most prosperous Presbyterian organizations in the southern part of the state. Fruitful in expedients, he has introduced a number of reforms calculated to arouse the latent energies of the members and develop their usefulness along practical lines, not the least of which was a Presbyterian Brotherhood he established five years before the national organization of the same name went into effect. This society, which has fully realized the object for which intended, has been of almost inestimable value by keeping alive an interest in religious and benevolent work, while at its sessions many subjects of vital importance to the church as well as ways and means for the general dissemination of the cause of Christ, are considered and discussed. He was also instrumental in organizing the Thomas Posey Post, Presbyterian Brotherhood Cadets, for the purpose of enlisting the interest of the boys of his congregation by means of Bible study, athletics, physical training, healthful amusements, etc., the success of the enterprise more than meeting his expectations and proving a sure safeguard against the many alluring temptations and evils to which the youth and young men of cities are subjected.

During the past nine years Doctor Howk has been secretary of the home missionary work of the New Albany Presbytery, and as such has been untiring in his efforts to advance its interest and plant churches and Sunday schools in destitute fields. He was a commissioner of the General Assembly in 1893 and 1903 respectively, and for several years served as chairman of the Sunday school work of the Baltimore Synod, comprising the states of Delaware, Maryland and the District of Columbia. He keeps in close touch with his denomination and everything relating thereto, is influential in its public assemblages and stands high in the esteem of his fellow ministers and co-workers, besides enjoying the confidence of the public irrespective of faith or creed. While loyal to the church of his choice, the faith and practice of which he justifies by reason and history, showing that its object and aim both appeal to and receive the sanction of all fair-minded persons, he is by no means narrow in his views, perceiving good in all religious organizations and being ready at all times to co-operate with his brother ministers of other bodies in the laudable work of the world's evangelization.

Doctor Howk is not unknown in the domain of literature, having contributed a number of articles, chiefly of a religious and historical character, to the different magazines and periodicals. While pastor of the old church at Rehoboth, Maryland, he discovered and secured the history of the first Presbyterian organization on the American continent, which appears to have been established as early as 1683, by Rev. Francis Makenzie, who ministered to the little band of worshipers for many years. Collecting all available data bearing on this church, the doctor wrote a very interesting history of the birthplace of Presbyterianism in the United States, the sketch proving one of the most valuable additions to church literature in recent years. He has also written not a few poems of decided merit and a number of hymns which have appeared from time to time in various religious and secular journals, all of his literary productions finding ready publishers and appreciative readers.

The doctor's fraternal relations include the Phi Gamma Delta college fraternity, Jeffersonville Lodge, No. 240, Free and Accepted Masons; R. S. Taggart Camp, Sons of Veterans of East Palestine, Ohio, and the Indiana Society, Sons of the American Revolution, being eligible to membership in the last named organization through his great-great-grandfather, Colonel William Edmonson, who was second in command at King's Mountain and distinguished himself by bravery and gallantry in that and other battles. His maternal grandfather, Gen. John S. Simonson, was a soldier in the War of 1812 and the war with Mexico, and bore a distinguished part in the Civil war from 1861 to 1866, besides serving a number of years in the frontier against various hostile Indian tribes. He was a soldier by profession, rose by successive promotions from private to the rank of general and was noted for fearlessness and bravery in action as well as for strict discipline as a commander.

Doctor Howk was married at New Albany to May Lorraine Collins, daughter of Henry H. and Mary (Scribner) Collins, both residents of New Albany, and representatives of the early pioneer families of that city and well and favorably known in social and religious circles. Mrs. Howk was reared and educated in her native city, graduating from the high school with the class of 1886. Doctor and Mrs. Howk have two daughters, Margaret, born March 12, 1890, at Pocomoke, Maryland, and Mary Simonson, whose birth occurred at the same place on March 31st of the year 1895, both being students at Hanover College. Doctor Howk has been a trustee of Hanover College since 1905, and his interest and activity in educational work is secondary only to his ministerial and religious duties.

Since October, 1908, Doctor and Mrs. Howk have moved to Hanover to be with their children, and Doctor Howk has engaged in general evangelistic work.

JOHN C. ZULAUF.

The fact that this name appears in the city directory of Jeffersonville is due to a somewhat romantic episode, involving a rather interesting chapter in the history of Southern Indiana. Many years before the Civil war a wealthy citizen of Switzerland, by the name of Fischli, pre-empted a large amount of land near Seymour, and owned other extensive tracts near Jeffersonville. At that time the law of Indiana prohibited the inheritance of land by foreign heirs, and at the death of the original owner the estate escheated to the school fund of the commonwealth by provision of the statute. To recover lands John Zulauf, a distant relative of Fischli, was employed to come to America. He was born in Switzerland, in 1818, and obtained a collegiate education, spoke six languages and altogether was an unusually well informed man. He spent several years in clerical occupations in some of the factories and banks in different parts of Europe, including one year in the bank at Marseilles, France, and several years in the large manufactories at Birmingham,

England. His employment as attorney for the Fischli heirs brought him to Clark county, in 1846, and the extent and complications of the business necessitated his remaining in this country for many years. Realizing that he had become a fixture he opened a lace and silk importing store on Fourth street, Louisville, in 1848, and was appointed Swiss consul to the western states. By the exercise of much diplomacy as well as skill and legal ability, he managed after a protracted struggle against powerful and influential opposition to save the Fischli estate for the heirs. During these complicated transactions and delays he often returned to his native land and while there, in 1857, was married to Wilhelmina Schoch, daughter of a prominent government official of Bavaria. In 1861 he brought his wife and eldest daughter to Jeffersonville, but a year or two later, when the Northern and Southern armies were closing on Louisville, he sent his family back to Switzerland. The entire family returned from Europe in 1865 and settled permanently in Jeffersonville, where the father died in 1873.

John C. Zulauf, one of his father's four children, was born in Switzerland, October 26, 1864, soon after his mother's return from the United States. His father did not see him until he was about a year old, when he was brought back to Jeffersonville with the rest of the family, of which he was the first son. He grew up in Jeffersonville and in 1885 was graduated from DePauw University, with the degree of Bachelor of Arts. In 1886 he received the degree of Bachelor of Laws from the Louisville Law School and subsequently took a special course in the law department of Harvard University. Admitted to the bar in 1887 he entered actively into the practice of his profession at Jeffersonville, continuing alone until 1888, when he formed a partnership with Judge George W. Howk, of the Supreme Court of Indiana, with offices in New Albany and Jeffersonville. In 1894 he became vice-president of the Citizens' National Bank, was elected president of that institution in 1904 and three years later was made president of the Citizens' Trust Company. In many ways he has been prominent in the business affairs of Clark and Floyd counties, being recognized as a public-spirited citizen of great energy and enterprise and excellent judgment. He was a director of the Louisville and Jeffersonville Bridge Company, and made several trips to Washington to obtain rights of way for the bridge across the river at the most suitable landing place on the Jeffersonville side. He was president and business manager of the Ohio Falls Street Car Company, organized to construct and run a line in Jeffersonville and composed of Louisville and Jeffersonville capitalists. Mr. Zulauf has also been quite prominent in politics, as a Republican. In 1892 he was candidate for Joint Senator from Clark, Scott and Jennings county, but owing to the great preponderance in the opposition majority was defeated. In 1904 he was chairman of the Republican District Committee, and in 1906 was a member of the Republican State Central

Committee. In 1908 he was a delegate to the Republican National Convention at Chicago, that nominated Taft and Sherman.

In 1896 Mr. Zulauf married Agnes, daughter of Dr. W. D. and Matilda (Koehler) Hutchings, of Madison, Indiana. They have two daughters, Agnes and Elizabeth. The family's religious affiliations are with the St. Paul's Protestant Episcopal church, of which Mr. Zulauf has been vestryman since 1888.

WILLIAM A. RUBEY.

Of sterling New England ancestry and inheriting many of the sturdy qualities for which the people of that historic section of the country have been distinguished, the subject of this sketch although young in years has achieved success in the dual capacity of professional and business life. William A. Rubey, attorney at law and secretary of the Denhard, Rubey Company, dealers in furniture and a kindred line of goods, is a native of the old and time-honored town of Bridgeport, Connecticut, where his birth occurred on the 23d of September, 1872, being the third of a family of seven children whose parents, Albert B. and Fannie E. (Hoyt) Rubey, were also born and reared in the Nutmeg state.

Albert B. Rubey is a merchant and manufacturer at Bridgeport, Connecticut, and one of the leading business men and representative citizens of that city. Of his family of two sons and five daughters, all but one of the latter are living, their names being as follows: Georgie, wife of O. V. Smith, of Milford, Connecticut; William A., of this review; Lena M. died in her twenty-second year; Sarah, now Mrs. Edwin R. Hampton, lives at New Haven, Connecticut, where her husband is practicing law; Elizabeth married Harry C. Gates and resides at Bridgeport; Albert B. is engaged in the automobile business at Springfield, Massachusetts, and Ethel, now Mrs. Walter Griffith, is still under the parental roof.

The early life of William A. Rubey was cast in pleasant places. As soon as old enough he entered the schools of his native city, where under the direction of capable teachers, he made commendable progress and attained high standing as a close and diligent student. He remained in the state of his birth until eighteen years of age, at which time (1891) he came to Louisville, Kentucky, moving to Jeffersonville, Indiana, in 1900, to prosecute his legal studies in the Jefferson School of Law, Louisville, which institution he attended until completing the prescribed course and receiving his degree. With a mind well disciplined by intellectual and professional training he was admitted in 1907, to the Clark county bar, and soon won recognition as one of the enterprising and capable young lawyers in a city noted for the high order of its professional talent. Two years before engaging in the practice of law, however, he became interested in a mercantile enterprise which, under the firm name of the Denhard & Rubey Company, was incorporated in 1905, and which jointly managed by the original proprietors is still carried on, being at this time the largest and most successful furniture house in Jeffersonville, as well as one of the leading commercial concerns in the southern part of the state. It is ably conducted by the solid business men whose names the company bears, the stock which represents a heavy investment of capital, consisting of a large and complete line of furniture from the simplest and cheapest to the most ornate and expensive, also full lines of all kinds of house furnishing materials, no pains nor expense being spared to satisfy the most critical demand on the part of customers. By honorable dealing and a sincere desire to please the proprietors have gained the confidence of the public and the business has grown steadily in magnitude; is now widely and favorably known in commercial circles and its reputation is second to that of no other enterprise of the kind in the country.

Aside from his professional and commercial interests Mr. Rubey is connected with the Casino Amusement Company, of which he is now secretary and treasurer and in the management of which he takes an active and influential part. In this as in other enterprises he has met with well earned success, by the people appreciating his efforts to provide them a commodious and pleasant place in which to meet, and a series of high class amusements for their entertainment.

In his political affiliations Mr. Rubey is a Democrat and an influential worker in his party, while the Episcopal church represents his religious creed. He is a leading member of Lodge, No. 362, Benevolent and Protective Order of Elks, in which he holds the title of past exalted ruler, and his name also adorns the records of other local lodges, including the Improved Order of Red Men, Knights of Pythias, K. of T. M., of the World, in which he fills the office of record-keeper. In addition to the organizations mentioned he belongs to the Century Road Club of America, and to the National Automobile Association, besides being identified with various other enterprises of a social, literary and benevolent nature in all of which he has been honored from time to time with important official positions, to say nothing of his liberal contributions for their maintenance.

Mr. Rubey was happily married on September 6, 1894, to Ida M. Denhard, of Jeffersonville, daughter of Edwin L. Denhard, his business partner, and proprietor of one of the largest furniture establishments in the city of Louisville, Kentucky. Mrs. Rubey is a native of Louisville, received a liberal education in the city schools of the same and made her home in that city until her marriage. Five children have been born to Mr. and Mrs. Rubey, namely: Florence, Ruth, Wallace, Edward and Elmore, the last two, Edward and

Elmore, being dead, the remaining residing with their parents, constituting a happy and contented household.

FRANK SPEAR ARMSTRONG.

The subject of this sketch was born in Jeffersonville, November 18, 1868. Captain Armstrong's family is among the oldest, if not the oldest family in Clark county, and from the earliest time has held a very prominent position in the history of the county. His great-grandfather, Col. John Armstrong, was the last commandent at Fort Steuben, long before Jeffersonville existed. He was a captain in the First United States Regiment, Colonel Harmar, at the close of the Revolution and had seen extended and meritorious service during that conflict, being in four general engagements, including the battle of Monmouth and the siege of Yorktown. After leaving the service of the United States he returned to Clark county and was one of the most prominent men in our early history. He settled on a tract of land opposite the Grassy Flats, where his remains now lie buried and where his monument still stands.

Col. John Armstrong's son, William Goforth Armstrong, made Bethlehem his home until 1841. He served eleven years in the Indiana House of Representatives and two years in the Senate, and was receiver of public moneys in the land office at Jeffersonville under William Henry Harrison. He was one of the principal promoters of the Jeffersonville, Madison & Indianapolis Railroad and it was due greatly to his energy that the road was finished, in 1852, and trains run through to Indianapolis. He was the first president of this road, retiring in 1853. His son, John R. Armstrong, Capt. Frank S. Armstrong's father, was closely connected with the business and commercial life of Jeffersonville until ill health compelled him to go to the West. He died in Jeffersonville, in June, 1878, at the age of thirty-four. Of unsullied character and possessing ability of a high order, he filled a large place in the business circles of his community and elsewhere, and in his untimely death the city of Jeffersonville lost a leading citizen who promised to rise to still higher positions of honor and trust.

Lucy M. Howard, daughter of James Howard, the boat builder, who became the wife of John R. Armstrong, was reared in Clark county, and like her husband possessed many amiable qualities of head and heart as well as a strong and beautiful character, which endeared her to the large circle of friends with whom she was wont to associate. She measured up to the highest standard of intelligent and cultured womanhood and exerted a refining and elevating influence upon all with whom she came in contact; she departed this life in Jeffersonville, in the year 1900, being the mother of three children:

Howard Armstrong, who died in infancy; James H. Armstrong and Capt. Frank S. Armstrong, whose name introduces this article.

Frank Spear Armstrong was educated in the public schools of Jeffersonville and at old Rugby, in Louisville. He graduated from the West Point Military Academy in the class of 1891, and was assigned to the Ninth Cavalry at Fort Robinson, Nebraska. This regiment was transferred to Fort Grant, Arizona, in October, 1898. Lieutenant Armstrong served on recruiting service in the South during the war with Spain, but returned to his regiment when it was ordered to China, in 1900. He sailed for the Taku Forts at the mouth of the Pei Ho river, August 16, 1900, but the Chinese troubles becoming of less importance, the regiment was ordered to Neuva Caeceres, Southern Luzon, Philippine Islands, where it served for two years, returning to the United States in 1902 to garrison Fort Walla Walla, Washington. Two years later the regiment was ordered to Fort Riley, Kansas. Lieutenant Armstrong was commissioned first lieutenant July 1, 1898, and captain February 2, 1901. August 30, 1904, he married Jennie Dimmick, the daughter of Major Dimmick, of the Fifth United States Cavalry, and has two sons, Frank and John.

At present Captain Armstrong is serving his second tour of duty in the Philippines, at Camp McGrath, but the regiment is soon to return to this country and will be stationed at Fort Russell, Wyoming. Since his connection with the service he has written several text books on different phases of army life.

JAMES HOWARD ARMSTRONG.

James Howard Armstrong, the youngest of three sons of John R. and Lucy M. (Howard) Armstrong, and brother of Frank S. Armstrong, whose sketch appears in another part of this volume, was born September 6, 1870, in Jeffersonville, Indiana, and received his early education in the city schools, the discipline thus acquired being afterwards supplemented by a more advanced and thorough training at Wabash College at Crawfordsville, Indiana, graduating in June, 1893. Impressed with a desire to enter the legal profession he subsequently commenced the study of law and in due time became a student in the law department of the University of Louisville, where he graduated in 1899.

His habits of industry and other qualities which guarantee advancement early brought him to the favorable consideration of his fellow citizens and while still a young man he rose to a prominent place in the confidence of the public and made his influence felt in the affairs of the city and county. From 1901 to 1903 inclusive, he served as Deputy Treasurer of Clark county and discharged the duties of the position in an able and satisfactory manner, but before the expiration of his time he was induced to accept a position with the historic Howard Ship Yards, of Jeffersonville, which were established in 1835, by his grandfather, James Howard, and which have been continued in the family name ever since that time, being one of the leading enterprises of the kind on the Ohio and Mississippi rivers and contributing much to the industrial advancement of the city.

For some years past Mr. Armstrong has also been associated with E. M. Frank in the real estate and insurance business, the firm under the name of Armstrong & Frank being widely and favorably known and commanding extensive and lucrative patronage in Jeffersonville, Louisville and other cities and also dealing quite largely in farm properties throughout Clark and neighboring counties and doing all the legal business in their line besides a successful and growing general office practice.

Mr. Armstrong in the year 1901 was married to Marion Barrett, of Jeffersonville, the accomplished and popular daughter of Capt. Addison Barrett, of the United States army, who had been connected with the Quarter Master's Department in this city. Mrs. Armstrong was educated in Jeffersonville and at Alameda, California, and is a lady of varied culture whose friends are as the number of her acquaintances and whose gracious presence and many social attractions have made their home a favorite resort for the best society circles of the community. She has borne her husband one child, James Barrett, and she belongs to the First Presbyterian church of Jeffersonville, in which Mr. Armstrong holds the position of elder.

JOHN A. MITCHELL.

About one hundred years ago there came to Clark county, Indiana, Andrew Mitchell, grandfather of the subject of our sketch, being among the earliest settlers in this vicinity. Andrew Mitchell was born in Virginia, and after coming to Indiana was noted for his public spirit and energetic leadership. The old stone house on the Amos Martin farm was built by Mr. Mitchell in 1814, and the land occupied by the Salem church and cemetery was donated by him for these purposes.

A. J. Mitchell, father of our subject, was born near the Salem church on July 15, 1815. He was married to Elnora Mitchell, and they became the parents of eight children, two of whom are still living, these being John A., of this review, and one brother, Filmore.

John A. Mitchell worked on the farm during his younger days and had but a limited opportunity for education. What he did learn, however, he has made good use of and he has demonstrated the value of a good practical judgment in the administration of affairs connected with the making of his own way in the world.

Among other commendable traits of character, patriotism has been one of the most prominent in Mr. Mitchell's make-up. He enlisted in August, 1862, in Company I, of the Eighty-first Indiana Volunteer Infantry. In February, 1863, he was transferred to the First Battalion of Cavalry, Company B, of the Mississippi Marine Brigade, continuing with that company until June 2, 1863, when he was discharged from the service on account of disabilities resulting from exposures and severe service. The meager pension of twelve dollars per month is but a slight recognition of the unselfish service which Mr. Mitchell has rendered in defense of his country.

On March 25, 1868, Mr. Mitchell was joined in marriage to Margaret Martin, daughter of John Martin. She was born near Salem church, on the 10th of June, 1843, and has become the mother of four children: William S. is deceased; Ida M., is the wife of John A. Noe, now a resident of Jeffersonville; William E. married Virginia Crum, and they are now living in Charlestown township; Marion M. was married to Cecil Manix, now residing in this township.

Mr. Mitchell and family are members of the Methodist church, and the religious training of the family has been one phase of the home life that has been strongly emphasized. Though a life-long Republican, Mr. Mitchell has not sought prominence in the party ranks and has been content to fill his station in the world by practicing the virtues of good citizenship in his daily walk. He practices not only those virtues bearing on the spiritual side of human character, but also the ones that make for a strong and robust physical frame. He has passed his sixty-seventh milestone on the journey, but is still a vigorous man, is never sick, and is able to manage the affairs of his one-hundred-two-acre farm in a marvelous manner. He is a close observer and is able to discuss the merits and failings of modern theories as to farming in a most intelligent and conclusive manner.

WALTER S. HIKES.

Walter S. Hikes, one of the leading business men of Charlestown, Indiana, is a Hoosier by birth, having first seen the light of day at Utica, Indiana, on the 25th of November, 1861. His father, George G. Hikes, was a native of Kentucky, having been born in that state in 1812. The grandfather was a native of Pennsylvania, and after coming west became an extensive land owner, a part of which reverted to George G. Hikes, as an heir. The latter was engaged for many years as a nurseryman, having followed the business while still at the parental homestead. He was joined in marriage to Anna E. Putnam, and this union was graced with two children, one of whom, Edward B., died at the age of five years, leaving Walter S., of this review, as the sole heir to the family estate.

Walter S. was reared on the farm and received in addition to the training afforded by this wholesome environment a good education. He completed the common school course and after that was for three years a student in the Sturgus Academy at Charlestown.

In 1876 death came to George G., father of our subject, and with this came the responsibility of managing the affairs of the estate; this Walter did in conjunction with his mother, and under the arrangement the business side of their home affairs was closely and carefully managed, so that growth and development were among the characteristics of the household history. This joint management continued until the mother was joined in marriage to James Howard.

On March 16, 1883, Walter S. Hikes was married to Mary Bowen, daughter of Festus W. and Elizabeth (Lewman) Bowen, pioneer settlers of Clark county, Indiana. She was educated in the public schools of the county, and has been a most admirable help-mate and a competent and conscientious mother. Six children were born of this union, four of whom survive. The children in order of birth were: Edward, deceased; Olive, Ethel, Bessie, Dorothy and Mamie, the latter also deceased. Olive and Ethel are graduates of the Charlestown high school.

Mr. Hikes is engaged in the handling of lumber and real estate in Charlestown, but retains his management of his large farm in connection with his other duties. Although a Republican in politics he has never sought for political preferment, choosing rather to live his part as a conservative and upright citizen. He is a member of the Presbyterian denomination, acting in the capacity of an elder in the church. Mr. Hikes is also a member of the Odd Fellows, belonging to Charlestown Lodge, No. 94. His friends and neighbors are coming more and more to recognize his sterling worth and unwavering integrity.

LOUIS BADGER.

Louis Badger, of Charlestown, Clark county, has had a prosperous business career, and has been a successful holder of public offices entrusted to him at different times. He has fought and bled for his country. He is one of the older generation of men whose careers embraced many of the critical periods which this land of ours experienced, periods which were gloriously tided over by the self-reliance and undaunted courage of such men as he.

51

Mr. Badger was born in the vicinity of Charlestown, Clark county, on September 10, 1845, and was the son of C. G. and Lourena (Green) Badger, the former a native of Germany, and the latter of Clark county. C. G. Badger was born in the "Fatherland," on June 30, 1819, and his wife on March 7, 1824. He came to this country at the age of seventeen and went from Charlestown to New Orleans, returning again to Charlestown, where on the edge of the city he operated a blacksmith shop, and at the same time engaged in farming pursuits. He was a Democrat and active in party work. About the year 1859 he was elected Auditor of Clark county, and served for eight years. He was also Treasurer of his county, serving in that capacity when the county seat was located at Charlestown. His name was put forward for Auditor of State on one occasion, but was defeated for the nomination. He died on the 27th of January, 1887. He was a man of great attainments and his success in public life was achieved over the obstacle of foreign birth and the difficulties of language. At his death he was reputed to be a man of some wealth.

To C. G. Badger and his wife were born thirteen children; eight boys and five girls. Eight are still living, five of the boys and three of the girls. They are: Emily, wife of William Masiner, of Charlestown; Belle, wife of Charles Reich, of Charlestown; Lucinde, wife of Harry Reil, of Alexandria, Indiana; Edward B. Badger, of Wichita, Kansas; Louis, of Charlestown; C. G., Jr., of Jeffersonville, Indiana; Charles, of Clinton county, Iowa; George, of Jeffersonville, Indiana.

In his young days Louis Badger assisted his parents in working the farm, and later hired out to neighboring farmers by the month. In winter time he went to school, attending Prof. Z. B. Sturgus' school in Charlestown, where he obtained a good education. In 1863 he enlisted in Company D, of the Fourth Indiana Cavalry, and the Seventy-seventh Regiment for service in the Civil war. During the conflict he was wounded in the engagement at Dug Gap, Georgia, on May 9, 1864. His wound proved to be of so serious a nature that he could no longer be of service, and was accordingly discharged July 28, 1865. He is now in receipt of thirty dollars a month pension money.

Shortly after the close of the war he was appointed Deputy Sheriff of Clark county, under Thomas Bellins, and served in that capacity for two years. In 1867 his marriage with Adora Grabe took place. Since that time nine children have been born to them, of whom there are seven living, five boys and two girls. Charles G. was born May 25, 1868; Nora B. on February 8, 1870; Oscar is deceased; Centennial J. was born May 27, 1876; Robert L. in December, 1880; M. A. in 1884; Jesse E. April 14, 1886; Edith O. in 1887, and George L. on May 25, 1890.

In politics Mr. Badger is a Democrat and he has been an active worker in the interest of his party for a great many years. He served as postmaster in Otisco from 1883 to 1887, and was elected in 1890 Trustee of Oregon township and served in that office for four years. He was in business as a huckster for ten years, and spent five years in the business at Otisco. Seven years of his life at a later period were spent on a farm in Oregon township. In 1903 he sold his farm and returned to Charlestown and entered the harness business in which he is now engaged.

Fraternally Louis Badger is an active member in many orders. He is a Mason of the Blazing Star Lodge, No. 226. He belongs to the Independent Order of Odd Fellows Lodge, No. 714 at Marysville, and has of late become connected with the Banner Lodge, No. 15, in Jeffersonville, in which he carries two thousand dallars' worth of insurance. He leads a quiet, domestic life.

HENRY S. LUTZ.

Among the highly respected citizens of Charlestown a few words are due the subject of this sketch, Henry S. Lutz, proprietor of the Interurban livery barn. He was born on December 6, 1845, in Charlestown township, Clark county, Indiana, the son of George and Sarah (Royer) Lutz, who were also natives of this county. Our subject's grandparents emigrated to Indiana from North Caolina as early as 1800. They followed farming and braved the dangers incident to pioneer life and carved a homestead out of the virgin wilderness. The hardships were such as were common to the life of the times, but they succeeded in establishing themselves on a good farm and ended their days in their newly adopted state.

George Lutz, father of Henry S., was a man of modest and quiet demeanor, but was well liked by his neighbors, being ready at all times to accommodate his friends in every possible way. He made no efforts to become prominent in any way and steadily refused to enter into the political arena, so free and open to all the people. He was the father of seven children, two sons and five daughters, as follows: Benjamin F., second lieutenant of the Twelfth Indiana Battery, who lost his life during the Civil war, on the field of battle, thus giving himself as a ransom for the preservation of the integrity of the flag; Clara became the wife of Samuel Tolan, both of whom have now gone to their reward; Laura is the wife of Alexander Young, of Jeffersonville, Indiana; Ellen, widow of George Gibson, is now a resident of Jeffersonville, Indiana; Sarah is the wife of James K. Bennett, of New Albany, Indiana; Anna is the widow of A. B. Bennett, of Jeffersonville, Indiana.

Henry S. Lutz was reared upon the home farm, which lies three miles from Charlestown. He received his education in the neighboring district schools, but the discipline of life on the farm was not lost upon him, for he appropriated to himself such a fund of experiences that he has had no difficulty in going forward with his own business affairs with the success that crowns loyal and untiring efforts.

On December 15, 1868, Mr. Lutz was married to Sarah Sharp, daughter of James Sharp, of Charlestown. After their union the young couple made their home with Mr. Sharp's parents and continued so until the latter's death, after which Mr. Lutz sold his farm and removed to Charlestown. The children born to theme are Anna, wife of James W. Teeple, of Charlestown; Benjamin, a railroad engineer at Spokane, Washington; James, a practicing physician at Louisville, Kentucky; Mamie G. is at home.

Mr. and Mrs. Lutz and family are members of the Christian denomination and they have been of inestimable service in the work of the church. Mr. Lutz is a member of Cement Lodge, No. 494, Independent Order of Odd Fellows, of Charlestown, Indiana. He has passed through all the chairs and has twice served his fellows at the grand lodge held at Indianapolis. He affiliates with the Republican party, but does not place party above principle, preferring to remain in the background when it comes to seeking for offices or honor. In 1903 he removed to Charlestown, beginning the livery business as stated above.

CARL BRAYFIELD.

Carl Brayfield is well known and respected throughout Clark county. For the space of thirty-six years he has been actively engaged in newspaper work; one of the rank and file of that army whose business it is to sketch the history of current events, and whose arduous labors, ephemeral-like, find a resting place within the dusty files of the newspaper office. His early training admirably fitted him for his life task, and a successful career as a writer, a traveling correspondent and as editor and publisher has been his. As may be surmised he is also well versed in the art of the practical printer, and is intimately acquainted with all the details of that trade. Carl Brayfield comes of families whose genealogical trees have their roots in the distant past.

Mr. Brayfield was born in Daviess county, Indiana, on the 10th of October, 1850, and was the son of John and Sarah (Milholland) Brayfield. Both parents belonged to old and respected families. John Brayfield was originally a native of Mason county, Kentucky. He traced his descent from an English family who came to the United States as early as 1640, and settled in Virginia. Grandfather John Brayfield removed from Virginia to Maryland, and there married, coming to Kentucky in 1793. His son, John Brayfield, Jr., father of Carl, was born in Kentucky about the year 1810, and moved into the state of Indiana about the year 1834. Of our subject's mother's family it may be mentioned that the maternal great-grandfather, Emanuel Van Trees, of Dutch extraction, settled in Daviess county, Indiana, about 1816, having come from New York. He was by profession a civil engineer.

Carl Brayfield received a good early training and was educated in the common and private schools. In the year 1872, at the age of twenty-two years, he entered the newspaper business, and since that time, for thirty-six years his pen has rarely been idle. He has been through all the phases of newspaper work and is a fluent and lucid writer. He has been most successful and in the executive position of editor and publisher he has full scope for his abilities.

His marriage took place at the age of twenty-three on July 12, 1873, when he took for his companion through life an accomplished young person, Kate Bower, a native of Washington county, Indiana. She was the daughter of George W. and Martha (Turner) Bower, well known people in their section of the country. Mr. Brayfield's married life has been a very happy domestic one, although no children have been born to him. In religious life they belong to the church of Christ faith and are diligent and influential in the affairs of their church. In politics Carl Brayfield is a Democrat and an upholder of the best traditions of his party. In the newspaper field in his own county he has been of much assistance to his party.

Carl Brayfield is as yet a young man, comparatively speaking, and long years of activity in his chosen sphere are yet in store for him. He is a man respected and well thought of in township and county, and is acknowledged to be a keen-minded, energetic and far-seeing member of the community. His personality embraces all the attributes of the successful and aggressive business man. He is of a kindly genial disposition and is a favorite with a large circle of friends and acquaintances.

DR. CADWALLADER JONES.

Dr. Cadwallader Jones, of Charlestown, Clark county, is one of those professional men who have arrived at their present success solely through their own efforts. Energy and ambition characterized him from the time of his earliest school attendance in the district schools of his native township, and during his years at the Blue River Academy, when his enthusiasm and industry overcame every obstacle and brought him his well earned medical doctor degree. He has a reputation second to none as a professional man and citizen in Charlestown, where his professional and public services are in constant demand.

Doctor Jones, who has the militant blood of North Carolina in his veins, was born in Bartholomew county, Indiana, on the 12th of October, 1849. He was the son of William and Elizabeth (Stalker) Jones. His grandfather Jones, a native of North Carolina, came to Washington county, Indiana, in 1811, and there entered forty acres, on which he farmed during the remainder of his life, dying late in life on his farm. William Jones, our subject's father, moved to a farm about a mile south of Jonesville, Bartholomew county. Jonesville received its name from a Ben Jones, an early settler, who was a relation of our subject's family. William Jones married, lived on a farm and died there in 1855. Mrs. Jones married secondly a Mr. Parker, also deceased, while she is still living, in Washington county, Indiana; having arrived at the age of eighty in 1908. Mrs. Jones had five children, three girls and two boys, three are living: Anne, the wife of Calvin Hinkle, of Washington county; E. E. Jones, a resident of Colorado; and Cadwallader, of this review.

At the age of six years Doctor Jones was left fatherless and went six years later to live with his grandfather Jones, who arranged for his education at the district school. In the spring of 1871 he entered the Blue River Academy and remained there for two and a half years when, owing to his financial circumstances, he was obliged to supplement his income by teaching and other means, but still continuing his studies. In 1876 he entered the medical department of the University of Louisville and graduated two years later with the Doctor of Medicine degree. He then went into practice for four years at Borden and at New Washington for five and a half. He located in Charlestown on November 2, 1887, where, for one year, he practiced with the late Dr. David H. Coombs, after which he entered practice for himself. When the building, which contained the office in which he had located for eighteen years, burned down he moved on October 5, 1907, in with Doctor Work, with whom he is located at present. Doctor Jones is a Republican in politics and served as a member of the Pension Board under the Harrison administration. In Cleveland's time he was out of office, but was re-appointed under President McKinley, and still holds the office (1908). In 1886 he was nominated for Auditor of Clark county by the Republican party, during his residence in Washington township. His popularity in his residential township may be gauged from the fact that the Democratic majority there which averaged one hundred five was reduced to fifteen votes.

On December 25, 1877, Doctor Jones married Laura Harned and has had six children born to him, all but two of whom are graduates of the local high school. They were named: Lunsford, Bessie, Mamie, Anna, Leslie and Flossie. The first Mrs. Jones died in August, 1893. Doctor Jones married secondly on October 12, 1894, Leah Lander.

Our subject is a prominent and popular Mason and a member of Blazing Star Lodge, No. 226, in which he has held every office and of which he is a past master. He is an influential and practical member of the Presbyterian belief and holds the office of deacon in the local Presbyterian church.

Doctor Jones attended the National Republican Convention of 1892, in Minneapolis, as an alternate delegate. Outside of his professional duties the doctor is a sincere lover of outdoor sports, particularly in the art of the gun and rod. As a hunter and a fisherman he stands second to very few in the community. He is also a man who has traveled through the country extensively and has been within the borders of fourteen different states. He is a man of culture, with a high reputation for honesty as a citizen, and is acknowledged to be a skilled practitioner.

JOSEPH L. CARR.

Joseph L. Carr, superintendent of the Clark county infirmary, is a figure well known in the civic life of the county. He comes of a military family, for the Carrs for many generations have been prominently identified with military history in the state of Indiana. They have also made a name for themselves in other walks of life. Gen. John Carr, a member of the family, represented the Charlestown district several terms in Congress. Andrew Jackson Carr, the father of Joseph L., was a veteran of the Mexican war and a citizen of worth and influence. Joseph L. Carr is a worthy scion of the family. He is a man of probity and uprightness and in his sphere in public life he has won the confidence of all with whom he has come in contact. He has been Assessor of Charlestown township for six years, an office which he filled with credit to himself. He was appointed superintendent of the county infirmary in 1905, and at the close of his term, owing to the skill he displayed in conducting his duties he was re-appointed. Two of his sons, in keeping with the traditions of the family, fought for their country in the Spanish-American war.

Joseph L. Carr was born in Charlestown township, Clark county, on the 6th of February, 1852, and was the son of Andrew Jackson Carr and Sarah Whiteman, his wife. Andrew Jackson Carr was also born in Charlestown township, Clark county. He was a soldier of the Mexican war, who went through the most critical stages of that conflict. He was also a civic figure of importance and served as Treasurer of Clark county for the period of four years. He also served as private secretary to Governor Whitcomb, and was later a representative of Clark county to the state Legislature. He was a farmer by occupation and a wealthy man. His death occurred in 1885. In his lifetime Andrew Jackson Carr was an influential man in the Masonic fraternity in his part of the county. He was a genial and kind-hearted man and was well known in his township for his liberality and charitable traits.

He and his wife had four children born to them, of whom Joseph L. was the eldest. The two other sons, Richard and George Dunlap, are deceased. Mary Neal, a daughter, resides in Denver, Colorado. The mother of these children died on the old homestead in Charlestown township in November, 1902.

Joseph L. Carr was reared in Charlestown township. He attended the district school in his youth and afterwards worked on the farm of his father. He is now in his fifty-sixth year and has lived an industrious and active life. In politics he is an avowed Democrat and a loyal supporter of his party. For six years he was Assessor of Charlestown township, after which he was appointed superintendent of the county infirmary, in which capacity he served for nearly eight years. He married Ida E. Baldock, daughter of George W. Baldock, of Charlestown township. His marriage, which has proved a happy one, brought him seven children, namely: Emmett R., who served as a soldier in the Spanish-American war; Benjamin F., who also served three years in the army, taking part in the Spanish-American war; Josie E., who is the wife of Wesley Buck, of Pomeroy, Ohio; Bessie I. is the wife of Clyde Hawes, of Utica township; Sadie S., Georgia E., Ella D., all three are at home with their parents.

Joseph L. Carr and all the members of his family are members of the Christian church and are active and faithful in all things pertaining to the further success of the local congregation of their faith. Mr. Carr has now held his position as superintendent of the county infirmary for the period of nearly twelve years.

EDWIN B. BENTLEY.

Edwin B. Bentley, of Charlestown township, Clark county, is a well known farmer in the township in which he lives, and is one of those men whose lives, placid and well-ordered, are an open book to their neighbors. He comes of an old and respected family, the Bentleys of Ashbourne, Derbyshire, England. He has lived the life of an honest, energetic and industrious farmer, one who has never looked for nor expected anything beyond the return which his labors justly merited.

He was born in Cincinnati, Ohio, on the 15th of July, 1860, the son of Francis W. and Catherine (Taylor) Bentley. The former was born on the Solan Young farm, in Charlestown township, in 1831. Our subject's grandfather, James T. Bentley, was born in Ashbourne, Derbyshire, England, and came to this country in 1820. He lived in the South until 1829, when he came to Clark county, Indiana. In New Orleans he married Mary A. Johnson, of Boston, Massachusetts, in the year, 1826, and with the proceeds of both their savings they started a dairy farm and owned slaves, who afterwards came with them to Indiana. About the year 1833 they bought the farm which Edwin B. now owns. Here James T. Bentley remained until his death, which occurred in 1878. He was a man of pleasant disposition, and was well and favorably known. He and his wife had four children, namely: Mary Anna, Mary Elizabeth, Francis Wilson and Sarah Mariah.

Francis W. Bentley was reared upon his father's farm and received his education in the Clark County Academy. In the year 1856 he married Catherine Taylor, a native of Cincinnati, Ohio. Mrs. Bentley was born on the 24th of May, 1838, and was educated in Cincinnati, where she attended private school. She further pursued her studies at the Shelbyville (Kentucky) Female College, at which she graduated in the year 1855. She and her husband had four children, namely: John T., born March 4, 1857, who died March 1, 1904; James T., born August 20, 1858, lives in Kansas; Edwin B., who is the subject of this sketch, and Frank T., a resident of Chicago, who was born May 2, 1862. Francis W. Bentley died on the 3d of February, 1888, and was a man well liked. He belonged to the Presbyterian church and was a deacon of that church. He was politically a Republican, though he never took an active part in politics.

Edwin B. Bentley was reared upon the family farm in Charlestown township, and attended the schools of the district and the Barnett Academy at Charlestown. He married on December 29, 1891, Lena V. Reeves, a daughter of M. D. Reeves, of Charlestown. Mrs. Bentley went to school at Charlestown, and like her husband, attended the Barnett Academy. Both she and her husband are members of the local Presbyterian church, in which he is an elder. They have no children.

Fraternally Mr. Bentley has interested himself in two organizations. He is a member of the Knights of Pythias Lodge, and of the Modern Woodmen of America. In politics he is a Republican. He owns a farm of one hundred and seventy acres which is worth sixty dollars an acre. He has an up-to-date dairy on his farm, the milk from which nets him a good revenue.

JOSEPH M. HAYMAKER.

Joseph M. Haymaker, of Charlestown township, Clark county, is well known throughout his township and county as a breeder of shorthorn cattle and as a large land owner. He is a prosperous member of the community and has been markedly successful in all the ventures with which he has connected himself.

Mr. Haymaker was born in Oregon township, Clark county, in the year 1844, and was the son of John Haymaker and Anna Crum, his wife. To his parents eight children were born, namely: John W., Eliza J., Katherine, George W., Isaac N., James M., Amanda, and the subject of our sketch. There are only three members of the family now living, namely: Isaac N., Amanda, and our subject, Joseph M. In the year 1874 Joseph M. Haymaker married Sallie Beggs, who was born in Charlestown township on the 17th of December, 1849. Six children have been born of their marriage. They are: Nettie B., William M., deceased; Anna F., Lulu M., John G., and Carrrie F.

Mrs. Haymaker comes of an old and honored family. She was the daughter of the late John Beggs, who father, James, was the son of Judge John Beggs, of Rockingham county, Virginia, and who came to Indiana in 1797. Her mother was Louisa Work, the daughter of Samuel Work, whose father, Henry Work, came to Indiana in 1804. Mrs. Haymaker's ancestors were prominent in the public and private life of the country for over a century. Mrs. Haymaker and the members of her family are members of the Christian church and are all influential and practical church workers.

The subject of our sketch is a member of Blazing Star Lodge, No. 226, of the Free and Accepted Masons of Charlestown. In political affairs he is a Democrat and a staunch upholder of his party. He is a successful breeder of shorthorn cattle and owns seven hundred acres of excellent farming land on a part of which stands a stone house still in a good state of preservation, which was built in 1811 by its owner, the Hon. James Beggs, president of the Legislative branch of the territory, and a great-great uncle of Mrs. Haymaker. Joseph M. Haymaker is a stockholder of the bank of Charlestown and is interested in that concern to a considerable extent. He also holds stock in the First National Bank of Jeffersonville, Indiana.

Joseph M. Haymaker and his wife live on section No. 57, on a bluff overlooking the classic Ohio river, seventeen miles above the Falls, and in the shadow of a monument erected to the memory of Col. John Armstrong, a hero of Revolutionary fame. They are now advanced in years and can well afford to enjoy the declining period of life surrounded by all the comforts of a prosperous home in that picturesque portion of Charlestown township. The Haymakers have made many staunch friends in the course of their long lives and have a host of acquaintances who sincerely wish them prolonged life.

JAMES CARR.

The name of James Carr, pioneer resident and wealthy farmer of Charlestown township, is one that carries great weight and influence when mentioned in connection with the progress of Clark county. Beyond and above his material wealth, James Carr is entitled to the respect of his fellow citizens, for he is the descendant of an illustrious family, his grandfather, Thomas Carr, being one of the original framers of the constitution of Indiana, and a man who was a native of Pennsylvania and one of the first to note the possibilities of the Hoosier state.

James Carr was born on grant No. 154, Charlestown township, Clark county, October 18, 1827, and was the son of Joseph and Nancy (Drummond) Carr. Joseph Carr was a native of Pennsylvania, where he was born February 7, 1796, and his wife in Kentucky. Joseph Carr's father, the grandfather of our subject, came from Pennsylvania and arrived in Indiana in 1806 in Charlestown township. Here he lived until his death. He served one term in the Indiana Legislature. Joseph Carr married Nancy Drummond about the year 1818, and they were the parents of twelve children, of whom there are four now living. James Carr was reared upon the grant above mentioned. He helped his parents and attended the district schools. His father died at the age of forty-eight, about the year 1844, and James had to lend his help in managing the farm, which he did until his thirty-fifth year, or some time near 1862. He then married Sarah M. Stricker, daughter of William Stricker, of Charlestown township. Mrs. Carr was born on July 9, 1842. Her father was born in Frederick county, Virginia, and came with his parents when he was but six years old to Clark county, Indiana. He married Phoebe A. Bower, and had nine children, three of whom are still living. Mrs. Carr worked during her youth as a country girl and many times worked in the fields for her father. She, however, got a good common school education. William Stricker as he advanced in life became a financier and the owner of two thousand acres of land. When he first started he bought one hundred one acres of land and even went in debt to obtain it. In his earlier years it was his custom to personally take his farm produce to New Orleans via the river, and on arrival there he used to sell his boat as well as his farm produce, and walk back home. As time went on and as prosperity came to him he became of great benefit to the community. He helped the poor and needy and, though not a member of any church, was a liberal subscriber to those of all denominations. He was known to raise a large amount of stock. His death occurred in 1886; while his wife lived to a very old age. His estate at the time of his death was estimated to be worth something like one hundred thousand dollars.

James Carr and Sarah M. Stricker were the parents of the following children: Emma, the wife of Charles D. Nicholson, of New Albany, Indiana; Charles Carr, of Charlestown township; William J., also of Charlestown township; Nancy Ann, the wife of John P. Nicholson, of Oldham county, Kentucky; Mamie M., who died at the age of sixteen; John T. Carr, who is at home; Katie S., who became the wife of Frank Bottorff, is deceased; and an infant that died at the age of fourteen months. They as well as their parents are members of the Christian church at Stony Point on Silver Creek.

In politics Mr. Carr is an ardent Democrat. He is the owner of sixteen hundred acres of land, one thousand of which lie within the borders of Clark county. In 1880 he built the fine residence in which he and his family reside. It consists of eleven large rooms firmly built upon a picturesque site on five hundred and twenty acres of land, three miles northwest of Charlestown, Indiana.

James Carr has many friends among all classes in the community. He has always possessed many characteristics which have been known to engender mutual good will and fellowship, and this no doubt is the secret of much of his popularity. He is now leading a life of semi-retirement in keeping with his years, although he is still hale and hearty and one in whose veins the fires of youth have not burned themselves out.

WILLIAM J. BARNETT.

William J. Barnett, of Charlestown township, Clark county, is a well known and respected native born resident of the township in which he lives. He is now the prosperous owner of as fine a farm as there is in Charlestown township, the soil of which is estimated to be at least worth seventy dollars an acre, and the high state of perfection which the property has reached is due mainly to his own industrious efforts. William J. Barnett had the advantages of a first class education in his youth and was excellently fitted to meet the needs of life in his chosen avocation. He comes of a family, the members of which always possessed the characteristics of industry and adaptability.

William J. Barnett was born near Charlestown, Indiana, on the 1st of September, 1853, and was the son of Allen and Edith (Jacobs) Barnett, the former a native of Pennsylvania, and the latter of Clark county. Allen Barnett was a mechanic of more than ordinary skill. He patented the first cooking stoves of the fire above the oven variety. He made some money by this and came to Clark county from Louisville, Kentucky, and dealt in land. He entered much land from the government not only in Indiana, but in Illinois and Iowa. The time of his coming to Clark county was in the spring of 1840, when he located near Charlestown. He married Edith Jacobs in Clark county, his marriage with her being his second. Nine children were born to them, seven of whom are still living. At the time of his death Allen Barnett owned a large amount of land. During his life he was a member of the Presbyterian faith and was a trustee of the local Presbyterian church, of which he was ever a liberal financial supporter. At the close of the Civil war he became a Republican in politics. Allen Barnett's children were:

Samuel J., Edward A., William J., our subject; Clarence C.. Barton A., Ella S., wife of J. L. Cole; and Edith R., the wife of Judge W. H. Watson. All are living.

William J. Barnett was reared upon the parental farm near Charlestown and helped on the farm, attending the common school in winter time. At the close of his common school education he entered DePauw University, at Greencastle, Indiana, but owing to ill health he had to retire. He afterwards married Sallie O. Swartz, who was born in Cincinnati, Ohio, on the 11th of March, 1854. Mrs. Barnett in addition to a common school education had the advantages of an academy training. Their married life was happy and they were blessed with three children. They were named: Nellie B., born March 30, 1879, who is the wife of H. B. Smith; Arthur S., born March 25, 1882, and died August 15, 1908; and Charles A., born June 1, 1885, who is stenographer of a large concern in Kansas City, Missouri. Mrs. Barnett passed to her reward February 18, 1894.

Our subject and the members of the family belong to the Methodist Episcopal faith. He is steward and one of the trustees of the Charlestown Methodist Episcopal church and an influential and active church attendant.

In politics William J. Barnett has consistently stood for the Republican party, but he has taken no active interest in machine work. He lives quietly with his family in the substantial family residence and has a host of friends and well wishers.

FRANK P. McCORMICK.

Frank P. McCormick, of Charlestown township, Clark county, comes of a Virginian family of Irish extraction while from his mother he has inherited the rich red blood of old Kentucky. He is a believer in the strenuous life, and he is not one of those whose preachings belie their practice. Day in and day out for many years he has led a life of energetic endeavor. He is now in a position to enjoy the full fruition of his labors and can leisurely spend the declining years of his life in peacefulness, and without surrendering his independence or self-respect, upon his well stocked farm.

He was born in Charlestown township, Clark county, on grant No. 77. He was the son of Joshua and Christina (Brentlinger) McCormick. Joshua, McCormick was also born in Clark county and was of Irish extraction. Grandfather McCormick came here at a very early date, presumably from Virginia, and lived and died on the present McCormick land. Joshua McCormick married Christina Brentlinger, of Kentucky. They owned about five hundred acres of land and reared many children. Their names were: William E. McCormick. C. B. McCormick, Theodoscia, wife of Doctor Miller, of Princeton, Kentucky; J. B. McCormick, F. P. McCormick, and Willie, Stella and Millie McCormick, the last three dying when young. Frank P. McCormick is the only member of the family now left in Clark county. Here he grew up, obtaining his education at the district schools.

In after life he married Nannie Bowen, of Charlestown township, Clark county. Mrs. McCormick came of an old and respected Clark county family, and was born in September of the year 1875. She obtained a good common school education and was well fitted to be the wife of a well-to-do farmer, and the mother of children. Two children were born to Frank McCormick and wife. They are H. L. McCormick, born in June, 1901, and Clifton K., born in November, 1907.

Frank P. McCormick resides on his father's farm, the Joshua McCormick estate, of which he is the superintendent. He owns forty acres of prime land. He has been quite a large raiser of mules, and has the distinction of having the finest span of mules to be seen in Clark county. He also raises large numbers of sheep, hogs and cattle.

In politics Mr. McCormick is a Republican, and though he has never taken an active part in the political doings of township or county, nevertheless he is an enthusiastic partisan of the party with which his sympathies lie.

Both Frank P. McCormick and his wife are considered first class neighbors and have many sincere friends in Charlestown township. They live an ideal home life, and they are good, religious, industrous and strictly honest members of the community.

DR. JOSIAH L. TAGGART.

Dr. Josiah L. Taggart, late of Owen township, Clark county, was extensively engaged for over twenty years in breeding short-horn cattle, and he was most successful in raising stock of this description. His father, the late Dr. William Taggart, very successfully combined the exacting duties of an extensive medical practice with farming and stock raising interests on a large scale. Both father and son enjoyed much confidence and friendship in public as well as private life; and the much lamented deaths of these noted doctors were serious losses both to their family and friends.

The subject of our sketch was born in Owen township, Clark county, on the 27th of August, 1847, and was the son of Dr. William and Mary (Crawford) Taggart. The Taggart family were natives of Ireland, Dr. William Taggart being born in the Emerald Isle. He came with his parents to America when about eight years old, and located with them in Tennessee, later coming to Indiana. Dr. William Taggart was a graduate of Louisville University, and a prominent medical practitioner. He lived on his farm and practiced, and in 1848 he removed to Charlestown in order to obtain better educational facilities for his children, remaining there until 1856, when he returned to his farm in Owen township. Here he had an extensive practice and became wealthy. To himself and his wife there were born six boys and three girls, of whom there are now living two boys and three girls.

Josiah L. lived on the farm and attended the common schools of the district and the Charlestown school. He became a teacher and taught school for a period of ten years. In 1865 he entered the Indianapolis Medical College and graduated at that institution in 1869. He then went to Washington territory and practiced there for eighteen months. On February 11, 1886, he married Nannie Haymaker, a daughter of Dr. G. W. Haymaker, of Charlestown. Mrs. Taggart was born in New Market, Clark county, and was educated in the common schools. Doctor and Mrs. Taggart lived a very happy married life, and one child was born to them, Ethel, who is a student at Hanover College.

In politics the subject of our sketch was a Republican and was elected Trustee of Owen township in 1904, an office which he held four years. He was a member of the Presbyterian faith and subscribed liberally towards the church. Mrs. Taggart is also a member of that church. Dr. J. L. Taggart had two hundred and fifty acres of choice land, on which he carried on his breeding and raising operations. In addition to the short-horn cattle which he raised, and of which he brought the first imported stock of that kind to Clark county, he also interested himself extensively in the raising of sheep.

When Doctor Taggart came into the trusteeship the tax levy was one dollar and seven cents. This he succeeded in reducing to sixty-four cents, and during his term of office all indebtedness of the township was wiped out. Dr. J. L. Taggart died May 16, 1909. He was a man of irreproachable character and loved by all.

JOHN W. BOTTORFF.

The subject of this sketch has passed more than half a century, or his entire life, in the community of which this history treats and his habits have been such that during its entire span of years no one has spoken anything disparaging regarding them, and during this interval he has continued his efforts and labors in an untiring and well directed way, and is today carrying on general farming and stock raising in such a manner as to stamp him well abreast of the leading agriculturists of Clark county.

John W. Bottorff was born in Washington township, Clark county, April 23, 1853, the son of Fletcher and Mary J. (Robinson) Bottorff, the former a native of Kentucky, who came to Indiana when a boy and located in Washington township where he worked a farm and where he married Mary J. Robinson, and to them were born: Emma J., the wife of John M. Bower, deceased; Orie B., who is single; John W., our subject; Sudie E., who is single.

Fletcher Bottorff was a prosperous farmer and the owner of one hundred and eighty-six acres here and one hundred and sixty acres in another section. These farms now belong to his heirs. He died March 19, 1887, and his wife passed away in February, 1901. They were people of many commendable traits, and lived honorable lives.

John W. Bottorff was reared on the farm where he now lives and attended the district schools of his own neighborhood and later entered a college at Eminence, Kentucky, where he remained one year, when he returned to Clark county and began farming which he has since continued with uniform success.

Mr. Bottorff married Belle Bower, a sister of John M. Bower, and a daughter of Tobias Bower. No children have been born to Mr. and Mrs. Bottorff. The latter is a member of the Christian church.

Our subject manages a good farm in such an able manner as to gain a comfortable living from year to year, and he always keeps some good stock of various kinds. In politics he is a loyal Democrat and has long taken considerable interest in the affairs of his party, desiring to see the best men possible placed in the local offices. He was elected Commissioner from the Third district, November 3, 1908, and will take office January 1, 1910. His election is regarded by his fellow citizens as a most fortunate one. He will succeed David Watson, of Oregon township, in this office.

JUDGE GEORGE H. D. GIBSON.

There is no more widely known or influential citizen in Charlestown than Judge George H. D. Gibson, ex-Judge of the Clark county Circuit Court. He is the scion of an old and highly respectable family, and the son of a father who achieved success in many diverse callings and who was also a lawyer of distinction. The subject of our sketch has undoubtedly inherited all the legal acumen and forensic ability of his honored parent, together with his characteristics of courage, self-reliance and self-control. During his term on the bench of the Circuit Court Judge Gibson gave every evidence of his fitness for the office which he held. A man in whom the judicial temperament is highly developed, his verdicts displayed a nicety of distinction, a clearness of thought, and an impartiality which dispelled all doubts and logically settled all difficulties. In private practice at the present time he enjoys a large and extensive clientele.

Judge Gibson was born in Charlestown, Indiana, on the 9th of September,

George H. D. Gibson.

1851, and was the son of Thomas W. and Mary W. (Goodwin) Gibson. Thomas W. Gibson was born in Philadelphia, Pennsylvania, and was brought when but six years old to Lawrenceburg, Indiana. At the age of sixteen he entered the United States Academy at West Point and at the expiration of three years he was appointed midshipman in the United States Navy. He served three years on the United States sloop "Vandalia," cruising near the West Indies. After an active career in the navy he retired in 1836, and returned to Lawrenceburg, where he studied law with George H. Dunn. In 1837 he moved to Charlestown, and in 1838 was united in marriage with Mary W. Goodwin, the daughter of Col. Amos Goodwin. After his marriage Thomas W. Gibson practiced law at Charlestown until 1846, when in that stirring period he raised Company I, Third Indiana Vounteers. He became captain of his company and participated in the battle of Buena Vista in the Mexican war. In 1847 he returned to Charlestown, and in 1848 was elected to the Indiana Legislature on the Democratic ticket. He became a member of the Constitutional Committee in 1851, and afterwards served as an Indiana Senator. In 1852 he moved his law office to Louisville, Kentucky, but continued to reside in Charlestown until his death, which occurred in 1876, on the 30th of November of that year. Thomas W. Gibson reached a high pinnacle of success as a lawyer. He was a man of remarkable attainments and was a well known writer, having written several novels which were widely read. During the war period he was brought into considerable prominence and served as provost marshal in Louisville during the most critical periods of the Civil war. He also commanded a regiment for a short time in the defense of that city, and in after times his prowess as a fighter threatened to eclipse his fame as an attorney.

Thomas W. Gibson had a family of three boys and three girls, of whom one girl and two of his sons are now deceased. They were: Lydia D. Gibson, who married B. F. Walter; Amelia A. Gibson died single; Lieutenant Thomas W. Gibson, of the Eighth United States Cavalry, died single; Sarah G. is the wife of McDowell Reeves; Charles H. Gibson is an attorney-at-law in Louisville, and George H. D. Gibson, our subject.

Judge Gibson was reared in Charlestown and received his early education at the Barnett Academy in Charlestown. He spent four years in the Kentucky Military Institute and graduated in 1873. He then studied law at Louisville and graduated at the Louisville Law University in 1874. He immediately opened an office in Charlestown and was in 1876 elected Prosecuting Attorney. In 1877 he removed his law office to Louisville, Kentucky, but later returned to Charlestown, and in 1881 was elected to the Indiana Legislature. He was again returned by election to the session of 1883. In 1892 he was elected Judge of the Clark county Circuit Court, an honored office which he held with distinction until 1898. While still on the judicial bench he bought a farm

52

to which he later retired and engaged extensively in stock farming with mucn success until 1908, when he sold his farm and reopened his law practice in Charlestown.

He married in July, 1896, Virginia C. Van Hook, who came of a well known family. His matrimonial happiness was of brief duration, however, for Mrs. Gibson died in July, 1908, an occurrence which was a sad blow to her husband.

Judge Gibson, needless to say, is an influential and prosperous man. He is a large stock holder in and a director of the First National Bank, an institution whose destiny he has taken no small share in bringing to its present success.

Judge Gibson is yet but fifty-seven years old, and it is safe to say that his already successful career is but a stepping stone to greater things.

JOHN McMILLIN.

John M. McMillin, of Charlestown township, Clark county, is a prosperous and industrious farmer and an influential citizen, and there are a few men who are more prominently associated with the financial and business life of the community than he. He has shown himself to have inherited the dominant characteristics of the McMillin family, whose name has been associated with Charlestown township for nearly a hundred years. They were a Pennsylvania family of Scotch-Irish origin and were an industrious people, careful to husband their resources and endowed with a marked facility for successfully manipulating their financial affairs. The Indiana head of the family, William McMillin, fought in the War of 1812, at the close of which he settled in Kentucky and later moved to Charlestown, Clark county. He was grandfather of the resident of Charlestown township whose name heads this sketch.

John M. McMillin was born in Charlestown township, Clark county, on the 9th of February, 1856, and was the son of William C. and Mary F. (Brentlinger) McMillin. Grandfather William McMillin, referred to above, was a native of Pennsylvania, of Scotch-Irish descent. He was by trade a cabinetmaker and served in the War of 1812, then settled in Kentucky, and later came to Indiana. He worked at his trade in Charlestown until 1841, at which time he bought a farm of one hundred and fifty acres in grant No. 99, on which he lived until 1880, when his death occurred. His wife had died previously, in 1854. They were the parents of five children, all boys, namely: William C., John M., Thomas, George and Robert. All the members of the family migrated to Illinois with the exception of William C., the father of our subject, who remained on the old place in grant No. 99, until his death, which occurred in 1897. His wife is still living, her seventy-seventh birthday taking place in 1908. William C. McMillin was a man with a great talent for making money and the owner of many acres of land. He was of much importance to the township financially and was known as a liberal-hearted man. When the bank of Charlestown was organized in 1891 he became its second vice-president and an influential stockholder. Though he attended church and was a practical Christian he never belonged to any particular church, but was a liberal supporter of many. In politics he was a Republican. He and his wife were the parents of two children: John M. (our subject), and William E., who is now one of the instructors in the carpentry department of the Jeffersonville Reformatory.

John M. McMillin was reared on the family homestead and in his youth was a regular school attendant and consequently got a good education. In after life he married Jennie B. Stierheim, born in the year 1859, whose father was a native of France. The couple have led a happy married life and one son has been born to them, H. R. McMillin, Deputy Sheriff of Clark county. Their son was reared on the family farm and received a good common school education. The McMillins belong to the Presbyterian church at Charlestown, in which our subject is a deacon.

In the fraternal world John M. McMillin is a member of the Modern Woodmen of America and carries insurance in that organization. In politics he is a Republican. His farm embraces some three hundred and sixty acres of choice land and is well cultivated and stocked. As was his father, he is also a stockholder of the bank of Charlestown. He has met with much success in his financial ventures and this, no doubt, is to be attributed to his powers of judgment and discrimination. He is a director of the well known Charlestown Canning Factory. He and his wife and son are popular in all circles in Charlestown township and have the reputation of being hospitable and kindly neighbors.

THE TOWNSEND FAMILY.

Among the early settlers of Union township was the family of Isaac Townsend, who came to Clark county in 1817. Isaac Townsend was born in Bradford county, Pennsylvania, October 10, 1790, and was the son of Uriah and Dorothy Townsend. Uriah Townsend was a son of Elijah Townsend and Dorothy, a daughter of Rudolph Fox, who was among the earliest pioneers of Bradford county, Mr. Fox having located there in 1770. In 1793 Uriah Townsend with his family moved to Yates county, New York, locating in the town of Jerusalem, near Pennyan. Here Isaac Townsend grew up and was married in 1810, to Meliscent Guernsey, daughter of Daniel Guernsey. They resided in Yates county until 1817, when Mr. Townsend resolved secure a home in Indiana. Traveling overland to what was then known as Olean Point, they embarked and floated down the Alleghany and Ohio rivers to Utica, where they landed, and Clark county became their permanent home. They settled in the Blue Lick country, within the present limits of Union township. Mr. and Mrs. Townsend were both Methodists and lived quiet and happy lives. Mrs. Townsend died May 8, 1871, and Mr. Townsend June 17, 1875. They are buried with all their children except one, in Mountain Grove cemetery, three miles west of Henryville. The children of Isaac and Meliscent Townsend were: George Harmon, Elizabeth, Uriah, Julia, Isaac Monroe, Guernsey and Desire.

George Harmon Townsend was born in Yates county, New York, June 11, 1811, came with his parents to Clark county in 1817, and grew up in the Blue Lick country. He became quite wealthy and was one of the first trustees of Union township. He was married September 13, 1832, to Sarah Maria Thompson. The children of George Harmon and Sarah Maria Townsend were: Phila Ann Townsend, born June 27, 1833; married to John S. Dunlevy February 9, 1857. They settled in Monroe township and had three children—Ann Eliza, George Townsend, and Simeon Crawford Dunlevy. Burritt Leroy Townsend, born April 15, 1835; married to Mary E. Biggs, March 22, 1860. .Their children are: Ida, Emma, Annie, Hobart, Robert, Franklin, Byron and Pauline. They live in Cumberland county, Illinois. Isaac Franklin Townsend was born January 31, 1837; married to Julia F. Hart, March, 1861. They live in Smith county, Kansas, and have four children: William B., Charles Hart, Lelah M., and George Franklin. Angeline Townsend was born May 31, 1842; married to John King, October 22, 1862. They located in Carr township and their children are: George Washington, John Franklin, Thomas Leroy, Lafayette Sampson, Charles Walter, Clela Dailey, Hamilton Ferguson, and Annie Ella.

Sarah Marie Townsend died June 10, 1845, and on August 31, 1847, George Harmon Townsend was again married, to Elizabeth Hart, of Bartholomew county. The children of George Harmon and Elizabeth Townsend are: Lenora Jane Townsend was born June 7, 1849; married to Henry H. Carr, November 3, 1866. He died and she was married a second time to John W. Batty. They live in the Blue Lick country and have four children—Ralph Covert, John Byron, Estelle Pink, and Helen Townsend. Thomas Matson Townsend was born March 7, 1851; married to Matilda Reed, September 30, 1869. They live in Silver Creek township and their children are—Henry Augustus, Annie Laura, Cora Alice, Thomas Lafayette, George Harmon, Ella Reed, Frank Smith, and Martha Rave. Lafayette Demarcus Townsend was born December 27, 1852; married to Mary M. Buehler, September 9, 1875. They live in the Blue Lick country, and their children are—Nora Elizabeth, Annie Blanche, Lelah Belle, Paul Vernon, James Edwin, Charles

B., Lucy Forest, Herman Ray, Ruth J., Elmer L., and Hazel M. Sarah Addie Townsend was born August 30, 1859; married to James Frederick Whitesides, September 14, 1876. They reside near Memphis and their children are—Nora America, Catherine Ella, Goldie Lillie, Homer Townsend, Pearl Indiana, Mabel Elizabeth, James Otto, Mary Addie, and Daisy Grace. Ella Elizabeth Townsend was born September 2, 1861; married to Edwin Orville Green, May 3, 1888. They reside in Cleveland, Ohio, and their children are—Florence Catherine, Bernice Edna, and Amos Townsend Green. Lillie Alice Townsend was born November 24, 1863; married to James Madison Hawes, September 6, 1882. They live in Jeffersonville, and their children are—Bessie Beatrice, Edith Nathan, Blanche Townsend, Myrtle Foster, and Katharine Jeanette. Laura Pink Townsend was born February 23, 1868; married to Marcellus Mayfield, July 1, 1888. They live in Royal Center, Indiana, and their children are—Clyde Townsend, Hollis Earl, and Lecta Geneva. Daisy Forest Townsend, born June 19, 1870; married to Alvin E. Green, March 3, 1889. They reside in New Albany, Indiana, and have no children.

George Harmon Townsend died February 22, 1889, after a long and useful life. His wife, Elizabeth, having preceded him, died April 23, 1879. They with the first wife are buried in Mountain Grove cemetery.

Of the other children of Isaac and Meliscent Townsend: Elizabeth Townsend married Almond Roberts and located in Monroe township. Their children were—Wesley, Millie, Emily, Julia, Marintha, Huldah, and Nancy. Uriah Townsend married Elizabeth ————, and settled in Union township. Their children were—Nancy, Minerva, and Elizabeth. Julia Townsend married Joseph Johnson and lived in the Blue Lick country. They left no descendants. Isaac Monroe Townsend married Julia Ann Harris and lived in Union township. Their children were—James Allen, Huldah and Elam. Dr. Terry Monroe Townsend, formerly of Jeffersonville, but now living in New York City, is a son of Elam Townsend. Desire Townsend married Joseph Biggs and lived in Monroe township. They left no descendants. Guernsey Townsend married and moved to Clinton county, Indiana, where he brought up a large family, and lived to a good, ripe old age. He is the only one of the children not buried in Mountain Grove cemetery.

Other members of the Townsend family in the Blue Lick country are of the same lineage, through John Townsend, a brother of Isaac Townsend. They are: Sophia Townsend, who married Parady Payne, and lived in Monroe township. Their children are—William, James, Lillie, George F., Blanche, Charles, Arthur, Kate, and John. James Townsend married Serena Trotter, and resided in Monroe township. Their children are—Albert, James, and Charles Townsend. Rexie Townsend married Thompson M. Dietz, and lived in the Blue Lick country. Their children are—Florence, Ruth, Grace, Fanny, Thompson M., Walter, and Bryan Deitz.

JACOB P. BARE.

Jacob P. Bare was for many years prior to his death a skilled agriculturist and a well-to-do resident of Charlestown township, Clark county. He was one of those unassuming men who find ample scope for their abilities in performing industriously and consistently the duties which providence placed before them. He lived to a ripe age, conscious of a life well spent in an effort to rightly rear and to enrich his family, and enjoying the friendship and unfailing loyalty of a large circle of friends. He was born on the 17th of September, 1823, near Washington, Indiana. His father was a Virginian. In his sixth year our subject came with his parents to Owen township, Clark county, in which county the remainder of his life was spent. He married Ann M. Baird on the 24th of December, 1846. She was the daughter of John and Sarah (Martin) Baird. Jacob and his wife were the parents of nine children. In regular order they were: John H., born on May 13, 1848; Almira M. on September 24, 1849; William H. on the 25th of May, 1851; H. T., born May 20, 1853; Sarah A. on the 13th of April, 1855; Robert A. and Charles (twins), born August 23, 1857; Ida V., born September 13, 1859, and Harriet E. December 27, 1862. Our subject and his wife on their marriage settled on the farm where Mrs. Bare still lives and where he afterwards died on the 4th of October, 1891. The farm contains two hundred acres of choice land. Jacob Bare was a deeply religious man through life and was a deacon of the local Presbyterian congregation; his entire family also belong to that faith. In politics he was a Republican. His death was a loss to the community at large as well as to his family, and an overwhelming blow to his sorrowing wife, on whom the duty developed of caring for her children. From her husband's death in 1891 to the present day, Mrs. Anna M. Bare has admirably demonstrated her fitness as the head of the family. During that time she has shown herself to be possessed of a natural ability and talent to deal with all the problems which have faced her. She is now past the age of eighty-two years, and lives a life of much less strenuousness than was her custom hitherto. She was born near Lexington, Kentucky, on August 30, 1826, and was, as we have stated, the daughter of John and Sarah (Martin) Baird. Her father was born near Coleraine, Londonderry county, Ireland, in 1789. In the year 1810, at the age of twenty-one, he crossed the intervening ocean to the United States and landed in Philadelphia, Pennsylvania, where for some time he worked in a factory, and in that city married Sarah Martin, a native of the place. They then came to Tennessee and later to Kentucky, resided for some time in Ohio and finally came to Clark county, where they settled in Owen township. Here he erected a building for a woolen factory, and was in his ninety-third year at the time of his death. John Baird and his wife were the parents of the following children: William, John, Henry, Sarah, Eliza, Ann M.,

George W., James A., Robert and Martha H. The only survivors of the family in 1908 were Ann M. and Martha H. Ann M. was sixteen years old when she came to Owen township and she obtained a good common school education. On her marriage to Jacob P. Bare, the subject of our sketch, she went to live on her present farmstead. Here her family, whom we have already enumerated, grew up and here her husband died.

Mrs. Ann M. Bare is widely known and respected and lives peaceably in her advanced years with her son, Charles E., and her daughter, Elizabeth. Three of her children, Sarah, William H. and Harrison F., are deceased.

JOHN M. BOWER.

It is a rare privilege to spend one's life in the house in which one was born. The subject of this sketch has lived under the same roof for a period of sixty-two years, and judging from the success he has made in his life work, he was wise in remaining at home, rather than seek uncertain fortune in other states as so many of his contemporaries did, many of them to their regret.

John M. Bower was born in Washington township, Clark county, Indiana, February 17, 1847, the son of Tobias and Mary A. (Piercy) Bower, the former a native of North Carolina, and the latter of Virginia. Tobias Bower came from the old Tar state with his father, and located in section 1, Washington township, this county, in 1810, and here he was reared and worked on a farm attending such schools as there were in those pioneer days. The Piercy family came to this county in an early day, settling on Fourteen Mile creek. Tobias Bower and Mary A. Piercy were married in Washington township, and here they lived and died, the former at the age of sixty-eight years, the latter surviving until she was ninety-four. They were the parents of the following children: Edward T. was a soldier in Company I, Eighty-first Indiana Volunteer Infantry, having been wounded at the battle of Nashville, living only twenty-one days afterward when he died in the service of his country; William A. was in the same company and was wounded at the battle of Stone River, Tennessee, and also died in twenty-one days after, while in the service of the Union; James S. was the next in order of birth; Carrie is the wife of Benton Wilson; Julia became the wife of William Snider, of Utica; Jennie is the wife of J. C. Lewman, of Louisville, Kentucky; Belle is the wife of John W. Bottorff; Alice A. married P. F. Shilling and they live at New Washington, Clark county.

John M. Bower, of this review, was born and reared upon the farm where he now lives, as already intimated. He worked about the place in his boyhood and attended the neighboring schools in the meantime, having remained with his parents until he married Emma J. Bottorff in 1878. She was called to her rest in May, 1903, after becoming the mother of three children, two of whom are living, namely: May died when ten years old; Jennie is the wife of Ed Patterson; Sudie is single; both she and Jennie graduated in the common schools.

Mr. Bower has been a successful farmer and is regarded as a very capable manager, and a good judge of live stock. He is the owner of a valuable landed estate consisting of three hundred acres. It is well improved and everything about the place shows careful management and thrift. The old home is beautifully located, surrounded by fine old trees, and everything to make home pleasant and attractive. Mr. Bower always keeps some good stock on the place, and he carries on a general farming with much satisfaction. He is fond of all kinds of stock and keeps good horses, cattle and sheep. Mr. Bower is a stockholder in the First National Bank of Charlestown. He has shipped many horses from time to time. He has found time to travel some and is a man of good judgment and well informed on general topics.

In his political relations Mr. Bower is a loyal Democrat and he very ably served his township as Trustee for a term of five years. He is one of the substantial and well known citizens of this part of the county.

WILLIAM H. LONG.

Among the representative citizens of Oregon township, Clark county, few have attained as distinctive prestige as Mr. Long, who is carrying on a general merchandise business at New Market, and in a perusal of the following biography it will be seen that he is a man of proper ideals regarding private, social and civic life, and that the esteem in which he is held and the success which he has won, are due rewards for the consistent life he has led.

William H. Long was born in Charlestown township, Clark county, September 15, 1847, the son of Morgan and Isabelle (Martin) Long, the former having been born in Virginia, but was reared in Kentucky, his ancestors having come to America from Ireland.

William H. Long was reared in Charlestown township, this county, where he worked on the farm and attended the common schools, receiving such education as was possible in these early days. When the dark clouds of Civil war darkened our national horizon, he was not satisfied to let his fellow countrymen alone defend the flag consequently in the spring of 1864, before he was eighteen years old, he enlisted in Company K, One Hundred and Thirty-seventh Indiana Regiment, and did guard duty, never having an occasion to engage in any of the great battles. He receives a pension.

Mr. Long married Samantha Cortner, the youngest of a family of thirteen children. She was born in Oregon township, where she received her early schooling. To this union four children have been born, namely: Edmund E. is married and lives at Prather, Indiana, where he is clerking in the Union National Bank. He is a graduate of the Borden high school, and of a business college in Louisville, Kentucky; Maggie is the wife of William Cartright, of Charlestown township; Ada, the third child, who became the wife of Morgan Bower, is deceased; Harrison R., who was born in 1892, is living at home.

Mr. Long is a faithful member of the Presbyterian church at New Market, being one of the deacons in the same. Mrs. Long was also a member of this church. In politics he is a Republican, and in 1904 was elected Trustee of Oregon township, in a township that is about ninety Democratic. He took office January 1, 1905, and he retired January 1, 1909. He made one of the best local officials the township has ever had, according to his constituents. When Mr. Long came into office the township was in debt seven hundred dollars. This has been paid and he built a good school-house at No. 1, in the township, which is also paid for, and the rate is lower now than it has been.

Mr. Long has been a general merchant at New Market for the past thirteen years, during which time he has built up a good trade with the surrounding country, for he is honest in his dealings with his fellow men, and he keeps a good quality of goods. He has a fine home in New Market, well furnished and modern, where he lives with his boy, Mrs. Long having passed to her rest in February, 1908.

BENTON B. BOWER.

The subject of this sketch has enjoyed the privilege of living nearly his entire life under the same roof, having devoted his life to agricultural pursuits, being the owner of a good farm in Washington township, while he is honored as one of the useful citizens of the same and as an able exponent of its farming interests.

Benton B. Bower was born in Washington township, Clark county, May 8, 1857, the son of John A. and Mary (Coombs) Bower, the former being the son of Col. Daniel W. Bower, an officer in the War of 1812. Col. Daniel W. Bower was a native of North Carolina, who came to Indiana and purchased one thousand acres of land when it was cheap, entering most of it from the government. He married Elizabeth Hostettler, who was a native of North Carolina.

There were eight children in this family, namely: Adam, John A., Corydon C., Daniel, George B., Mary A., Elizabeth and Catherine B. John

A. Bower, father of the subject, was reared in Washington township, this county, where he married Mary J. Coombs, the daughter of William and Margaret (Myers) Coombs. They settled in Silver Creek township in which they lived until 1858, when they moved to Coles county, Illinois, in which place they lived the remainder of their lives.

John A. Bower attended the early schools in his boyhood days in his native vicinity. He married Mary Coombs, the daughter of a prosperous farmer, her parents being members of the Christian church, the former being an elder in the same. He was a strong Democrat. He died November 16, 1903, and she passed to her rest in October, 1903. Three children were born to them. Orrie D., who became the wife of F. J. Stutsman, is now deceased. They resided in Chicago. Benton B., our subject, was the second in order of birth, and Daniel W. was the youngest. Benton B. was reared on the old home place on which he worked when a boy attending the district schools in the meantime, later, took a course in the Charlestown Academy, where he received a sufficient education to enable him to teach, and he taught with success in this county for two years. He was in the merchandise business at New Washington for five years during which time he built up a good trade. Disposing of his goods here he was in the merchandise business at Indianapolis for two years, but tiring of the exacting life of a large city he preferred to live in the country and returned to his native community, buying a good farm of ninety-one acres, which he now owns and on which he carries on a general farming with much success, being the owner of the old homestead which he has greatly enhanced in value by is careful management and extensive improvemnts.

Mr. Bower was united in marriage in May, 1893, with Laura A. Jackson, and to this union one child, Harold M., was born in February, 1894. Mrs. Bower passed to her rest in 1897, and Mr. Bower was married a second time October 19, 1906, his last wife being Leora Blackford, who was born in Jefferson county, Missouri, December 9, 1870, the daughter of John W. Blackford. She was educated in the district schools and the normal school at Indianapolis, and also at Danville, Indiana. She was a teacher in the district schools and later in the primary schools at Hanover, Utica and New Washington. No children have been born to this union.

Mr. Bower is a member of the Christian church. In politics he is a Democrat, and has long taken considerable interest in his party's affairs. He was postmaster at New Washington during one of Cleveland's administrations, and he proved to be a very faithful public servant. He finds time to devote some attention to music, having been a student of this art while in Indianapolis, and he is regarded as an excellent performer on musical instruments, having taught music with success. He has made several instruments. Both Mr. and Mrs. Bower are intelligent and friendly people, and they are highly respected by all who know them.

GEORGE W. SWENGEL.

Among the representative citizens of Clark county, Indiana, the subject of this sketch has long been prominent, being a well known and successful business man and a factor of value in the development of the section of the county in which he lives, having formerly been engaged in the mercantile business, but of late years he has devoted his energies to farming pursuits, but whatever he has turned his hand to he has made a marked success.

George W. Swengel was born in Jackson county, Indiana, March 19, 1850, the son of Charles and Catherine (Kiser) Swengel. Charles Swengel, grandfather of the subject, was a native of Maryland, having come from that state to Circleville, Ohio. He married Virginia Kensel. They were the parents of these children: Michael, John, Samuel, Charles, Elizabeth, Sophia and Catherine.

Charles Swengel, father of the subject, was reared on a farm in Pickaway county, Ohio, where he grew to manhood, attending what schools there were in his neighborhood in that early day. He married Sarah Kiser in 1848. To that union three children were born. Charles Swengel was first married to Katherine Kiser, to which union five children were born. This wife died and he married her sister. One of Charles Swengel's children, Mary, is the wife of Joseph Ryan, a resident of Elizabethtown, Bartholomew county, Indiana.

George W. Swengel was born and reared in Jackson county, this state, having grown to manhood on the farm and he attended the district schools of that county, being enabled to teach at the age of seventeen. He successfully followed this line of work for four years. He then engaged in the mercantile business until 1901, building up an extensive trade in the same, but desiring to lead the freer life of the husbandman, he then went on a farm in Washington township, where he has since resided. He has a good farm which he manages with success, carrying on general farming and keeping about him some good stock.

Mr. Swengel was married to Rose I. Haymaker September 23, 1879, who was born at New Market, Indiana, in 1857, the daughter of Dr. George W. Haymaker, brother of Capt. Isaac N., Joseph M. and J. W. Haymaker. Dr. George Haymaker married Foster Henley, daughter of Noah and Lousana (Munday) Henley. Noah was the son of Jesse Henley, who came to Indiana in 1806 from North Carolina. Jesse Henley married Catherine Fouts. He was the owner of twenty-eight hundred acres of land in Clark county. He died in 1829, his wife having died in 1806. He again married a Miss Bower.

Mr. and Mrs. George W. Swengel are the parents of the following children: Carl H., born January 28, 1881; Lulu B., born July 20, 1884; Jessie F., born March 26, 1887; Margaret R., born April 16, 1890; George W., Jr., born December 25, 1891; Helen T., born April 21, 1895; Kenneth, born August 1, 1897. Five of these children are living at this writing (1909).

The Kiser family emigrated to Indiana from Brownsville, Pennsylvania, where the subject's maternal grandfather was engaged in the mercantile business, having moved from there to Ohio. Grandmother Kiser, whose maiden name was Landis, was a native of Philadelphia, Pennsylvania.

Mr. and Mrs. Swengel are members of the Christian church. In politics Mr. Swenger is a Democrat, and has long taken considerable interest in the affairs of his party. He at one time served as postmaster of Sellersburg, Indiana, during Cleveland's administration. His father was also interested in political affairs and was Commissioner of Jackson county, Indiana. Our subject is known as a man of sound practical ideas, honest in his purpose and is regarded as an excellent neighbor and citizen.

F. M. CARR, M. D.

The venerable and honored physician whose name initiates this review, is one of the best known and useful men in Oregon township, Clark county, his practice having long ago pervaded the entire county, his fame having been augmented as the years increased until today his name is a household word throughout the locality.

Dr. F. M. Carr was born in Charlestown township, Clark county, Indiana, January 3, 1831, the son of Absalom and Jane (Weir) Carr. Thomas and Hannah (Coombs) Carr were the grandparents of the subject, Thomas Carr having come to this country from Fayette county, Pennsylvania in 1806, and settled on Sinking Fork of Silver creek, in Charlestown township. He was of Irish descent. The subject's great-grandfather came from Ireland and landed at Annapolis, Maryland, with one sister and one brother, this being the first advent of the Carr family in America; one of these brothers went to Tennessee and the other remained in Maryland. Doctor Carr is a descendant of the Carr who settled in Pennsylvania. Jane Weir was born in Virginia May 1, 1792, and was reared in Kentucky. She came to Indiana in 1810.

Absalom Carr and Jane Weir were married in Union township in October, 1812, and they resided in Charlestown township until in the thirties, then moved to Washington county, Indiana, where they lived until about 1838, when they moved to Washington township, Clark county, where they remained the rest of their days, the father of the subject dying in 1876, and his wife preceded him to the silent land in 1862. They were the parents of ten children, namely: Thomas J. lived to be eighty-one years old and died in Missouri; Hulda, who became the wife of Felix Huston, died in Illinois in 1857; Julia married Thomas McClosky in 1836; Susan became the second wife of Phelix Huston; Martha died early in life, having remained single; Mary, who also remained single, is deceased; A. W., who died in Scipio, Indiana, married Martha Goforth; F. M., our subject, was the next in order of birth; Joseph married Elizabeth Cartner, both deceased; John married Nancy J. Amick, both deceased.

Dr. F. M. Carr was born in Charlestown township, and he went with his parents to Washington county, this state, and back to Clark county when they returned. He worked on his father's farm until 1852. He attended school at Charlestown, read medicine in New Washington, Indiana, having early decided that his talents lay along the lines of medical science, and he made rapid progress in the same from the first. He attended a medical college at Louisville, Kentucky, graduating in 1855. In the same year he commenced practice in New Market, Clark county, and practiced continuously until 1906, when he retired. During those long years of faithful service, he built up an extensive patronage, as already indicated, and became known as one of the most successful practitioners in the county.

Doctor Carr was united in marriage with Martha E. Cortner, December 25, 1854. They are the parents of seven sons, all living, namely: J. P., superintendent of schools at Vicksburg, Mississippi; J. W., who is a telegraph operator at Colwich, Kansas; M. W. lives in Corydon, Indiana; S. E. is a drug clerk in Jeffersonville, this state; F. W. is a lawyer in Charlestown, Indiana; C. L. lives at home; Manton M. lives in Corydon, this state.

Doctor Carr is a member of the Presbyterian church and has been an elder in the same for many years. In politics he has always been a Democrat, and he cast his first vote for President Franklin Pierce in 1852. He served as Trustee of Oregon township for five years. J. P. Carr served as Superintendent of county schools from 1883 to 1887. S. E. Carr served in the same capacity for four years. F. W. Carr also served as Clerk of Clark county for a period of four years.

Doctor Carr is a man of wonderful memory and it is interesting to hear his instructive and entertaining conversation on the development of this locality, and scenes and conditions as they existed in the early days and he is the historian of Oregon township. Doctor Carr has a comfortable home with beautiful surroundings.

HENRY H. RATTS.

Among the enterprising and progressive men of Washington township, Clark county, whose efforts have been lent to the prestige of the agricultural industry of this locality, is the subject of this review, whose long life has been passed within her borders.

Henry H. Ratts was born in Washington township, Clark county, Indiana, March 9, 1842, the son of Jacob and Lucintha (Fouts) Ratts, the former a native of North Carolina, who came with his father, Henry Ratts, when Jacob was eighteen years old. Jacob Ratts married Lucintha Fouts. Grandfather Fouts also came from North Carolina. Jacob Ratts and wife were the parents of seven children, three boys and three girls growing to maturity, namely: Thomas L., David F., Mary A., Sarah J., Henry H. and Margaret E. The three living in 1909 are David F., Henry H. and Margaret E.

Our subject was reared on the farm on which he worked when a young man and attended the district schools in the meantime until he was eighteen years old, when he quit school, but remained at home until he was thirty.

He rented the farm and was married in 1872 to Anna Rodgers, who was born and reared in this county. They at once moved to where they now live, and have since remained in the same home, being the owners of a valuable farm consisting of two hundred and thirty acres of land, which is well improved. The land has always yielded rich harvests of various kinds. Mr. Ratts has a substantial and comfortable dwelling and convenient out buildings. He always keeps plenty of good stock on the place, and he is regarded by his neighbors as an up-to-date farmer in every respect.

To Mr. and Mrs. Ratts six children have been born, namely: Harry, Thomas, Olive, Jacob, Roy and Cynthia. Thomas was killed.

The subject and wife are members of the Christian church at New Washington, this county, and the former is one of the trustees of the same. They take considerable interest in church work. In politics Mr. Ratts is a Democrat, but he has never taken a very active part in political movements. He is a man of much force of personality and stability of character, and he has made a success as a result of his close application to his farm work.

JOSIAH C. CRAWFORD.

Among those of the farming element in Clark county whose labors have been rewarded with proportionate fruits is he whose name appears above, who is the owner of a well improved landed estate in Owen township.

Josiah C. Crawford was born in Owen township, Clark county, Indiana, January 26, 1861, the son of Josiah and Phœbe H. (Crosby) Crawford, the former a native of this county. William Crawford, grandfather of the subject, was a native of Virginia and one of the early settlers of Clark county, Indiana. He was the father of five children, all deceased. The Crosbys were natives of Massachusetts, from which state they emigrated to the West. The family originated in England. Josiah Crawford, the subject's father, was a man of considerable prominence in his day, having been a graduate from Hanover College, and a Presbyterian preacher, traveling over a large circuit in Southern

Indiana. He passed to his rest in 1892. He and his noble wife were the parents of seven children, all now deceased but the subject of this sketch, Josiah C., who was reared on grants Nos. 104 and 105, and he began working on the farm at an early age, in the meantime attending the district schools. Not being satisfied with a common school education, he entered Hanover College and graduated with the class of 1896, receiving the degree of Bachelor of Arts, having made a splendid record in that institution.

Our subject was united in marriage with Anna Bowyer, a native of this township, the date of their wedding occuring October 9, 1887. She is a graduate of the common schools. They have farmed continuously since their marriage, their fine farm of two hundred acres being located in Owen township, which is well managed and highly improved under the direction of our subject, who is one of the most progressive agriculturists of this locality, carrying on general farming with that energy and sound judgment that always insures success.

To Mr. and Mrs. Crawford nine children have been born, one of whom is deceased, namely: Sophronia, Nellie, Mary, deceased; Alma and Alice are twins; Charles, Helen, Esther and Margaret.

Mr. and Mrs. Crawford are faithful members of the Presbyterian church. In politics our subject is a loyal Republican, but he prefers to devote his attention to his farm rather than seek political preferment at the hands of his fellow citizens. He is a member of several college orders, and is known in his community as a man of excellent mental endowment, integrity and industry, and his nicely furnished home is a place of generous hospitality.

EDWARD M. GRAVES.

Edward M. Graves first saw the light of day February 5, 1865, on the fertile acres which he now owns in Owen township, Clark county, and he is regarded as one of the most progressive agriculturists in that community. He is a man of advanced ideas, and his farm is occupied with the most modern machinery. As a lad he showed a great aptitude for learning, and his advancement in such studies as he pursued in the township schools was rapid, although in connection with his studies he did much work upon the farm. He settled down in the old homestead, and as a result of his energy can today point with pride to a fine farm.

He is the son of Charles and Elvira A. (Rogers) Graves. Charles Graves was born in Washington township in 1821, while his wife came into the world in 1823. David Graves, the father of Charles, came to Indiana in the days when the southern portion of the Hoosier state was practically a wilderness.

Charles Graves and Elvira A. Rogers were married in Washington township. After a short residence in Oregon they returned to their old home, and purchased a farm in the west half of section 22. Here they lived happily until 1894, when Mrs. Graves died. Ten children were born to them, six of whom are living, namely: James M., John O., Willie, Samuel D., Thomas, Cyrus, Lottie, Rhoda, Laura and Edward M.

Edward M. Graves was united in marriage July 24 1892, to Hattie L. Moore, the daughter of William Moore, who was a native of England. To them were born four children, three of whom survive, viz: Isoline, Alzena and Alberta.

Ever since he attained manhood's estate Mr. Graves has been a staunch adherent of the Republican party, but that he is popular with the voters of the community in which he has so long resided is evidenced by the substantial plurality that he received in the fall election of 1908, when he was the candidate of his party for the office of Township Trustee, and received several votes over the regular majority. He entered upon the duties of this office January 1, 1909.

Mr. Graves not only gives close attention to the cultivation of his land, producing some of the finest corn and wheat that is shipped out of Clark county, but is also extensively engaged in the stock business, which in the last few years he has found very profitable. He has made a close study of this line of business, and has the reputation of being one of the best judges of live stock in Owen township. Therefore Mr. Graves experiences no difficulty in finding a ready market for the products of his stock farm, which is well drained and consists of one hundred forty-eight acres.

JOHN W. CLAPP.

John W. Clapp is a native of Clark county, Indiana, where he first saw the light of day March 7, 1849, the son of William and Catherine (Amick) Clapp, the former who was a native of Indiana, was the son of Valentine Clapp, who emigrated to the Hoosier state from North Carolina, from which state the Amick family also came, being among the first settlers in this part of the state. William Clapp and Catharine Amick were married in Clark county. having lived and died on the farm where the subject now lives. They were the parents of the following children: J. W., Lois M., James V., William W., L. M., Henry P., Robert A., Sarah, the wife of J. D. Robinson; Maggie A., the wife of O. G. Thomas; Zella, the wife of M. Mosser, lives in Illinois.

John W. Clapp was reared on the farm adjoining the one on which he now lives, having been born there, and he early began working on the same, attending the district schools in the meantime, for a few months each winter, having remained with his parents until he was twenty-four years old. He was married February 27, 1873, to Margaret A. Searles, and five children were born to the subject and wife, namely: Lulu M., the wife of Fon Jones; Ira D. was killed; Clarence V. lives in Illinois; Julia F. is the wife of Ira Bowles, of Illinois. The subject's wife passed to her rest December 18, 1885, and Mr. Clapp was married again, his second wife having been known in her maidenhood as Emma J. Himnlhever, whom he married June 10, 1886. Three children have been born to this union, namely: Amza R., Clyde C., and Ine E., all single. This wife was called to her rest September 18, 1906, and the subject was married to Lillie B. Sanders, widow of John M. Sanders. She was born in Clark county, November 29, 1861.

Mrs. Clapp is a member of the Methodist Episcopal church, while the subject belongs to the United Brethren church. In politics he is a Democrat.

Mr. Clapp is the owner of a fine farm of two hundred and seventeen acres of land in grant No. 213, which he has improved until it ranks with the best farms in the county. In fact he has devoted his life to the improvement and cultivation of this one farm and he has been amply repaid for his labor. He has a good old substantial dwelling and convenient barns, sheds, etc. Besides managing his farm he runs a threshing machine and husker with much success. and no man in Oregon township keeps better stock than he, especially cattle and hogs, the latter being the Poland-China breed. In 1901 he met with an unfortunate accident which resulted in losing his left hand in a shredder. He is well known throughout this locality and is regarded as a man of excellent business ability.

ANDREW M. FISHER.

The subject has spent his long life in Clark county, where he has labored for the general good of his community as well as for his own interests. He is the owner of a very valuable farm in Washington township, and is classed among the prosperous, self-made men of this county.

Andrew M. Fisher was born in Washington township, Clark county, this state, December 8, 1841, the son of John and Elizabeth (Fouts) Fisher. Jacob Fouts, the grandfather of the subject, came to Clark county prior to 1800, from North Carolina. He married Mary Dugan, and to that union four boys and five girls were born, Elizabeth being one of their number, she being the mother of our subject. John Fisher, father of Andrew M., was born in North Carolina in 1802. He was the son of George Fisher, who came to Clark county, Indiana, in 1813, settling in Washington township, living neighbors to the Fouts family. John Fisher and Elizabeth Fouts were married in 1828, and

53

they became the parents of these children: William, Sarah J., James L., Isabelle A., Jacob H., Allen, Andrew M. and Mary C. Five of these children are living in 1909.

Andrew M. Fisher was reared on the farm where he now lives in section 19, township 2, range 9 east, assisting with the work about the place in his youth and attending the district schools of Washington township during the winter months. He assisted in clearing the land and improving the home place until he was twenty years of age. He obtained a fairly good schooling for those early days.

Our subject was married to Ellen Taff, who was a daughter of James Taff. She was a native of Jefferson county, Indiana, and was educated in the common schools of that county, and to this union six children were born: Frank M., born November 9, 1884, a graduate of Hanover College; Emery L., born in 1893, is a graduate of the common schools.

Mr. Fisher owns five hundred acres of land, all in Washington township, where he carries on farming and stock raising in a general way. He is regarded by his neighbors as one of the leading agriculturists of this locality, keeping his farm in splendid condition and stocked with various kinds of live stock of excellent grade. He has a beautiful home, an excellent barn, and in fact, everything about the place shows thrift. At the organization of the New Washington Bank in 1907, Mr. Fisher was made vice-president and one of the directors, and he is performing his duties with rare care and foresight. He is a fine type of the modern business man, alert, progressive and honorable.

W. A. BRITAN.

The subject of this sketch, who has lived in Clark county for more than half a century, in fact all his life, has been a witness of the great development which has characterized this section, and indeed has borne his full part in making the community in which he resides one of the choice sections in this part of the state.

W. A. Britan first saw the light of day in Clark county, Indiana, May 15, 1853, the son of Dr. W. W. and Jane A. (Dickey) Britan, the latter a daughter of Rev. John M. Dickey, a pioneer preacher in the Presbyterian church of Indiana. Dr. W. W. Britan was a native of Massachusetts, having graduated from a medical school and he was also a student at Andover. He practiced medicine and also engaged in farming, owning the old Dickey farm of one hundred and ten acres. To the subject's parents eleven children were born, six of whom are now living, W. A., our subject, being the sixth in order of birth. Mr. and Mrs. Britan were people of much sterling worth.

Our subject was reared on the farm where he assisted with the work about the place and acquired many valuable attributes of mind and character, in the meantime attending the comon schools in that vicinity until he received enough education to enable him to begin teaching in the common schools, having taught several terms with much success.

In 1878 Mr. Britan was married to Emma Taylor, daughter of Simpson Taylor and six children have been born to this union, three of whom are living at this writing, 1909, namely: Charles D., Leroy T. and Elizabeth J., all single. Elizabeth J. is a student at Hanover College, where she is making a splendid record.

Mr. Britan is the owner of a fine farm, which he has greatly improved by hard work and careful management, carrying on general farming in a most successful manner, keeping some good stock and poultry about the place from year to year. He has a commodious and comfortable residence, surrounded by an attractive lawn. He is regarded as a wide-awake farmer, a careful manager.

The subject's wife passed to her rest October 10, 1905. Mr. Britan takes quite an active part in religious movements, also educational, being a member and an elder of the New Washington Presbyterian church. He has long been an active worker in the Sunday school, and is now vice-president of the Clark County Sunday School Association, in which he does a commendable work, making his influence felt throughout the county. He is also active in the farmers' institute work, being regarded as one of the leading spirits in that plausible movement in the county. He is held in high esteem by all who know him, for his educational ability, his integrity and industry.

THOMAS W. SAMPLE.

Among the honored veterans of the Civil war and the leading farmers of Washington township, Clark county, the subject of this sketch is numbered.

Thomas W. Sample was born in Jefferson county, Indiana, July 12, 1848, the son of John F. and Mary (Pender) Sample. Jacob Sample, grandfather of the subject, was a native of either Kentucky or Virginia, and he came to Jefferson county, Indiana, in an early day. He had married Rachael Harberson, and they were the parents of these children: Elizabeth, Mary, Nancy, John F. and Jacob. John F., the subject's father, was born and reared, married and died in Jefferson county. He was a farmer, and married Mary Pender and lived on the same farm until his death. He was born November 19, 1818, and died January 16, 1902. His wife was born October 28, 1817, and died January 27, 1896. John F. Sample was a prosperous farmer and left some property. His wife was a member of the Methodist Episcopal church. He was a Whig and later a Republican. He enlisted in Company K, Sixth Indiana Regiment, in 1861, and served for three years. Seven children were born to the subject's parents, namely: Alex, born February 23, 1841, died February 15, 1847; Jacob, born February 8, 1843, died December 29, 1870, having served one hundred days in the One Hundred and Thirty-seventh Indiana Regiment in the Civil war, and he re-enlisted in the One Hundred and Forty-sixth Indiana and served until the close of the war; Martha J. was born December 15, 1845, and died August 26, 1866; Thomas W., the subject of this sketch; James O., born April 2, 1851, died December 21, 1872; Nancy A., born December 1, 1853, died June 19, 1883; Jessie B., born October 13, 1857, died February 16, 1875. All these children are now deceased except Thomas W., who was reared on the old farm in Jefferson county, where he assisted with the work about the place, and where he attended the district schools, receiving as good an education as possible in those early days in the common schools. He was one of the patriotic men who followed the footsteps of his father and enlisted in Company E, Twenty-second Indiana Regiment, December 16, 1863, when only fifteen years and six months old and he served faithfully until the close of the war, having taken part in the following battles: Tunnel Hill, Georgia, May 7, 1864; Resaca, Georgia, May 14, 1864, where he was wounded in the right shoulder; Rome, Georgia, May 17, 1864; Dallas, Georgia, May 27 1864; Big Shanty, June 16, 1864; Kenesaw Mountain, June 27, 1864; Vining Hill, July 7, 1864; Chattahoochee River, July 12th; Peach Tree Creek, July 19th; Sandtown Road, August 7th and 8th; Jonesboro, September 1st; Savannah, December 21st, all in 1864; Black River, North Carolina, May 10, 1865; Bentonville, May 19, 1865. He was with Sherman in his march to the sea. He receives a pension of twenty-four dollars.

At the close of the war the subject returned to Jefferson county and resumed farming, also worked as a carpenter, and he gained some notoriety as a violinist, having possessed natural talent from youth. Mr. Sample was married January 1, 1874, to Delilah Montgomery, who was born in Clark county, Indiana, October 21, 1849, the daughter of Alexander and Catherine (Baker) Montgomery. The Montgomery people were pioneers of Washington township where the grandfather of the subject's wife entered a large tract of land. She attended graded schools after graduating from the common schools and followed teaching for some time with success. Part of her education was gained in the National Normal School at Lebanon, Ohio. Jacob Baker was the grandfather of Mrs. Sample. He came here from Harrisburg, Pennsylvania. William Montgomery, her grandfather, was born in Virginia. Alexander Montgomery was the son of William Montgomery, whose children are given as follows: John, born April 16, 1782; May, born December 28, 1783; William, born September 5, 1785; James, born September 1, 1787; Robert, born July 23, 1789; Thomas, born May 21, 1791; Jane, born March 16, 1793; Ag-

.nes, born February 25, 1795; Johnson, born January 26, 1798; David, born August 1, 1800; Samuel, born October 1, 1803; Mathew, born March 3, 1805; Alexander, born August 2, 1808.

The following children were born to Alexander Montgomery and wife: Joseph, William, Johnson, Jacob, Mary J., Nathaniel, Catherine, Alexander and Delilah.

Jacob Baker was the grandfather of Mrs. Sample. He died September 1, 1840. His children were: Catherine, born June 2, 1807, died January, 1887; Henry, born April 27, 1809, died in 1891; Mary, born October 6, 1811, died in 1865; Joseph, born September 15, 1813, died November 10, 1905; Frederick, born January 18, 1816, died December 4, 1904; Charles, born May 14, 1818, died in 1894; Susana, born December 25, 1820; John B. was born June 19, 1823; Hannah, born January 18, 1826, and died in 1866.

When Mr. and Mrs. Sample were married they moved to Washington township in March, 1875, locating on a part of the old Montgomery homestead, which was then in the woods. He has cleared and improved this land until he has one of the best farms in the neighborhood which yields good crops from year to year under Mr. Sample's skillful management. He has sixty-three acres. He is regarded as a first class mechanic and fixes all kinds of musical instruments, and is regarded by all who know him as a man of rare talent.

His children are: Sylvia B., who was born December 3, 1874, and who graduated in music, is the wife of Lambert E. Barnes, of Owensville, Indiana; Mary A., born July 1, 1877, is a teacher in the Gibson county, Indiana, schools at Owensville; James M., born December 4, 1880, graduated in medicine at the Medical College of Louisville, Kentucky, in June, 1907, and he is married to Pearl Reed, and is located at Austin, Scott county, Indiana.

Mr. and Mrs. Sample are members of the Universalist church. The former is a member of the New Washington Lodge, No. 167, Free and Accepted Masons being past master of the same. He is also a member of the Grand Army of the Republic and Sons of Veterans. He was a social member of the Woodmen lodge. In politics he is a Republican and he served in a very able manner as postmaster of New Washington from 1898 to 1904.

JOHN L. MAGRUDER.

The subject of this sketch is now engaged in the banking business at New Washington, Clark county, where he has maintained his home for some time. He has been prominently identified with industrial enterprises of importance and the name which he bears has long been one which has stood for progressiveness while he is a scion of an old and influential southern family, being a native of the Blue Grass state.

John Magruder, cashier of the new Washington State Bank, was born in Bullitt county, Kentucky, August 2, 1868, the son of Levi and Mary (Straney) Magruder. He was reared on the farm in that state and received his early educational training in a log school-house near his home. Later he entered the Pitt's Point Academy, where he took an academic course and made a splendid record for scholarship. Believing that the profession of teaching held peculiar advantages for him, he left that institution in 1888 and began teaching, having taught one term of school in his own town and county, when he went to Louisville, Kentucky, where he worked for six months, then going to Pleasureville, Kentucky, and entered a normal school, remaining there for ten months, during a part of 1889 and 1890. In June, of the latter year, he began farming and in 1891 he entered the National Normal School at Lebanon, Ohio, where he remained for two years, having graduated from the scientific course with the degree of Bachelor of Science. He was then principal of the schools at Smithville, Kentucky, for two years, rendering high grade services, for which he was heartily thanked by the board. He then taught with equal success for two years in New Haven, Nelson county, Kentucky; also for two years at Lotus, that state.

Our subject then turned his attention to farming, which he followed with great satisfaction for several years, and for three years engaged in trading on an extensive scale. In 1903 he sold his farm and moved to Grant county, Kentucky, and in 1904 he bought a hotel, which he ran in connection with the agency for the Louisville & Nashville Railroad and Adams Express Company for four years, when he sold out and moved to Clark county, Indiana, locating in New Washington, where he at once began making preparations for the organization of the New Washington State Bank, which he succeeded in organizing and forming a strong board of directors, August 17, 1907, with a capital stock of twenty-five thousand dollars, with the following officers as directors: H. F. Schowe, president; A. M. Fisher, vice president; John L. Magruder, the subject, cashier; Dr. R. S. Taggart, S. K. Pech, A. R. Miles, J. C. Bower, N. H. Linthicun, T. R. Stevens and T. N. Manaugh. Under the direction of the subject this bank has become popular in the community of New Washington, and is regarded as one of the strongest institutions of its kind in the southern part of the state and it is well patronized.

The happy domestic life of Mr. Magruder began in 1900, when he married Minnie Powell, a native of Dry Ridge, Grant county, Kentucky, the representative of a well known family in that community. To this union one winsome daughter, Lucille, was born in 1902.

Mr. Magruder is a member of the Catholic church, while Mrs. Magruder attends the Methodist Episcopal church, of which she is a member. In his political relations Mr. Magruder affiliates with the Democratic party, however, he has not aspired to office nor taken a very active part in his party's affairs, but he is interested in the political, moral and material development of his community and lends what aid he can in movements looking to such ends.

WILLIAM P. CORTNER.

There is much that is commendable in the life record of Mr. Cortner, for he has been found true to duty in every relation, whether it was in following the stars and stripes on many a sanguinary battle field of the South; or in the every day affairs of private life.

William P. Cortner was born in Oregon township, Clark county, Indiana, February 24, 1842, the son of Elias and Lucy (Amick) Cortner, the former a native of Guilford, North Carolina, where he was born in 1821. John Cortner, the grandfather of the subject, was also born in North Carolina. He came to Clark county, Indiana, in 1823, settling in Oregon township, where he farmed and spent the remainder of his days, and was buried at New Market. Elias Cortner was reared on the farm. When he reached his majority he married Lucy Amick, who was born in Oregon township, September 24, 1821, the daughter of Peter Amick, a native of North Carolina, and who married Margaret Black, also a native of the old Tar state, and to them the following children were born: Levi, Gideon, Riley, Alfred, Elizabeth, Polly, Peggy, Sarah, Catharine, Nancy and Lucy.

John Cortner married Elizabeth Amick and they were the parents of these children: Abraham, Daniel, George, Elias, Phama and Polly. To Elias and Lucy (Amick) Cortner the following children were born: William P., our subject and John M., who died when a small boy.

The subject of this sketch was reared in Oregon township, working on the home place and attending the district schools during the winter months, having worked on the farm until he was twenty years old, when he felt the call to serve his country during the dark days of the sixties, and he enlisted in Company G, Ninety-third Indiana Regiment, August 28, 1862. His first battle of importance was the Siege and fall of Vicksburg, July 4, 1863. He was in the battle at Jackson, Mississippi, July 17, 1863. He was never wounded but suffered from being overheated. He gets a pension. On May 10, 1864, he was disabled and he went into Missouri. He was discharged in June, 1865. After the war he returned to Clark county and resumed farm work.

The subject was married to Angeline D. Turner in 1866, and to this union five children were born, namely: William M., born December 1, 1867, died September 13, 1900, having been killed by an accident: Alonzo B. was born April 7, 1870, and he married Effie M. Carr; Clella B. was born June 24, 1872; Harley H. was born July 9, 1881; Alma M. was born November 16, 1885, and died in 1887. Mrs. Cortner passed to her rest November 15, 1903.

Mr. Cortner is a member of the Presbyterian church, being an elder in the same. In politics he is a Republican and served as Trustee of Oregon township from 1886 to 1890, having been elected when the township was seventy Democratic. This shows his unquestioned popularity in his own community. The township was in debt when he assumed this office, but after four years and three months of service he turned the township over to his successor free from debt.

Mr. Cortner is the owner of one hundred and eighty acres of good land in grant No. 197 in Oregon township. It has been well improved by the subject who is regarded as one of the leading agriculturists of this community. He has a good dwelling house, barn and other buildings, and he always keeps good stock. He is well known in Oregon and adjoining townships as an industrious and straightforward citizen.

JOHN V. CLAPP.

This representative citizen of Oregon township is a native of Clark county, Indiana, and has passed here his entire life, aiding in whatever way possible in the moral, civic and material development of this community. He is the owner of a well improved farm, and he is one of the prominent man in this part of the county.

John V. Clapp was born in Oregon township, Clark county, near New Market, May 10, 1853, the son of Henry and Nancy J. (Smith) Clapp, the former a native of North Carolina, who came from that state to Oregon township, settling near New Market. The subject's parents had each been married before their wedding, Nancy Smith having been married to a Mr. Jerard, by whom she became the mother of two children. Henry Clapp had been married to a Miss Amick, two children having been born to this union. Fourteen children were born to the subject's parents which made them a family of eighteen children including those they had by former marriages. Daniel and Riley were the children of Henry Clapp by his first wife. Sarah and Tilford Jerard were the children born to Mrs. Clapp by her first husband. The following children were born to the subject's parents: James H., William P., Elijah, Uriah, Alex, Alfred, deceased; John V., Mary J., Elizabeth, Julia, Charity, Joseph. James F. and William L. were soldiers in the Union army, and Riley died in the service. The parents of the subject finally located near Marysville, where they both died.

John V., the subject of this sketch, was reared on a farm and assisted his father with the work about the place, attending the district schools of Oregon township.

Our subject was married to Mrs. Mattie W. Ramsey, of Lexington, Indiana, who was born near that city, the daughter of James Pattison, of near Lexington. She is a graduate of the State Normal of Indiana. She became a competent teacher and is still following this profession in the local schools, where she is regarded as a woman of excellent attainments, and she gives entire satisfaction to all concerned. One child was born to her by her first marriage, who is named Georgia Ramsey, who married Melville Rice.

John V. Clapp has been crippled for the past twenty-five years. Both he and his wife are members of the Christian church at Marysville, Indiana, the subject being one of the trustee of the same, and a member of the official board. He is a member of the Marysville Lodge No. 714, Independent Order of Odd Fellows, being the organizer of the lodge here, being past noble grand, having been the first in this lodge and also the first representative to the Grand Lodge. This lodge now has one hundred members. The members own the property in which the lodge is housed and it is in good condition. In his political relations Mr. Clapp is a Democrat, having long been interested in the success of his party and was twice County Recorder, having served in this capacity in a most able and praiseworthy manner. He was elected Trustee of Oregon township and served as such from 1884 to 1888. He was postmaster of Marysville during President Cleveland's administration.

Mr. Clapp has been a successful man financially. He served as agent for the Baltimore & Ohio Railroad for nine years, having been agent at Nabb for a period of two years. This road regarded him as one of their most faithful and able employees. Mr. Clapp is one of the well known men of this section of Clark county.

ALLEN A. HUTSEL.

The subject of this review is a gentleman of high standing in Bethlehem township, Clark county, where he manages a well improved farm and to whom has not been denied a fair measure of success.

Allen A. Hutsel has spent his life in this community, being a native of Bethlehem township, Clark county, where he was born, September 4, 1863, the son of Chesterfield and Sarilda (Giltner) Hutsel, both natives of Bethlehem township. It is believed that Jacob Hutsel, grandfather of the subject, emigrated to Indiana from Virginia. The subject's parents were married in Bethlehem township, and they lived in this township until about 1878 when they moved to adjoining county of Floyd where they still reside. To them eight children were born, six of whom are still living, Allen A. being the only one living in Clark county. Chesterfield Hutsel was in the saw-mill business for many years, finally his mill burnel and he lost all.

Allen A. remained with his father until he was twenty-one years of age, assisting him with his work and attending the common schools in the meantime until he received a fairly good education. When he was twenty-one years old the wife of his uncle, Allen H. Giltner, died and the subject went to live with him where he remained for several years.

Allen A. Hutsel married Frances Burkett, a native of Harrison county, Indiana, who passed to her rest July 13, 1891. To this union one child was born who died in infancy. On November 1, 1892, Mr. Hutsel was again married, his last wife being Lillian Taff, daughter of James S. and Ellen Taff, of Washington township. No children have been born to this union.

Mr. Hutsel bought the Bohney farm of one hundred acres, which was considerably depleted when he took possession of it, but being an excellent manager and a hard worker he has built it up until the soil now produces excellent crops of all kinds and the place presents a fine appearance, showing that a man of excellent ability as an agriculturist has its management in hand. Mr. Hutsel is also a stock raiser, always keeping about him some excellent breeds, his short horn cattle being especially noted in this vicinity. He is also a breeder in Percheron horses and has an interest in a fine stallion. He also has charge of the Allan A. Giltner farm which he successfully manages.

Politically Mr. Hutsel is a strong Republican but he does not find time to take an active part in political affairs very largely, being a very busy man with his land and stock. In religious matters he is a supporter of the Christian church, holding his membership at Bethel in the congregation of which he is held in high favor.

MRS. ADDIE BOWER.

Mrs. Addie Bower, of Bethlehem township, Clark county, is a woman possessed of remarkable executive powers and this has been demonstrated by the way she has handled the affairs of herself and family when the two life companions she had chosen at different times were taken from her. Mrs. Bower comes of an old family, the McIntires, of Virginia, and, doubtless, many of the prominent traits of character she possesses are inherited from a sturdy Virginian source. Mrs. Bower manages her farm of one hundred and sixty-one acres with admirable skill. She has a very imposing home in which she lives as happily as her duties and the cares which fall upon the head of a family will allow her. She is surrounded and helped by her children whose presence is a source of much comfort to her.

Mrs. Addie Bower was born in Bethlehem township in 1856, and was a daughter of Shedrick and Nancy (Brenton) McIntire. Her father was born and reared in the township, his father having come from Virginia to Indiana in the early years of Clark county. The elder McIntire reared a large family. Shedrick McIntire and Nancy Brenton married in Bethlehem township, and there they lived the greater part of their lives. Shedrick died at the age of seventy-two, and his wife at the age of seventy-four. Their marriage brought them twelve children. They were: Isabella, Harland W., Charles M., Addie, William A., Eliza, Luella, Alvira, Florence, Emma, Annie and Jesse. Nine are still living.

Addie McIntire was born within two miles of where she now resides. In her young days she attended the district school, but her education was of a limited description, as she had been needed at home. On March 1, 1881, she married Jacob Schlichter and their union resulted in the birth of three children: Jacob, Lawrence and Edith, who married William Ross, and lives in this township. Jacob Schlichter died in the year 1887. Three years afterwards the subject of our sketch married secondly William A. Bower, the marriage ceremony taking place on August 27, 1890. Her husband was born in New Washington township in 1861, and was educated in the district school of that township. Her second marriage brought her three more children: Vallie, born in 1891, Vada H., born in 1892, and Eva, in 1895.

All the members of Mrs. Addie Bower's family are members of some Protestant church, four Methodists and one a Presbyterian, and one a member of the Christian church. Her late husband was a trustee of the local church as well as a steward. William A. Bower's death occurred in Bethlehem on July 27, 1908, and was of a tragic nature, as he was killed by two men named Wilson. In politics, Mrs. Bower's late husband was a Democrat. He was a popular member of the community and his death was lamented by a large number of friends and acquaintances.

At the present time Mrs. Bower's three young daughters are at home with her. She is a hard-working woman and one who has earned the good will of all with whom she has come in contact.

THOMAS R. STEVENS.

Thomas R. Stevens is a native born resident of Bethlehem township, Clark county. He has carried on farming operations on an extensive and modern scale for the last eleven years. To his avocation he brought natural talents of a high order which had been tested, developed, and fortified by a classical and scientific education obtained in some of the best institutions in the country.

At the time he started on his farm it was in a rather run-down condition and it owes its present high state of cultivation and improvement directly to his masterful and skilled supervision.   Thomas R. Stevens raises much stock of a high quality and which it is his custom to ship, when they reach the proper state of perfection, direct to the markets in Louisville and Cincinnati.

He was born in Bethlehem township, Clark county, Indiana, on the 23d of July, 1871, and was the son of A. T. and Mary (Ray) Stevens. A. T. Stevens was also a native of Bethlehem township.   Thomas Stevens, the grandfather of our subject, was born and reared in London, England.   He married Mary Stevens, a native of the same country and city, and he and his wife emigrated to the United States about the year 1818, and in the course of a short time bought a farm in Bethlehem township, Clark county, Indiana.   The remainder of his life was spent in different places in Clark county, and his death occurred in Louisville, Kentucky.   His son, A. T. Stevens, married Mary Ray at Louisville, and afterwards came to Bethlehem township where he built a house on the land on which he still lives.   Two children were born to A. T. Stevens; Alfred G., who died at the age of seven months, and Thomas R. Stevens, of this review.

Thomas R. Stevens was reared by a stepmother and grew to manhood on the family farm.   He attended the district school and at the age of sixteen, entered Hanover College, graduating with the degree of A. B. in the classic course in the year 1893, being then in his twenty-second year.   He thereupon entered the School of Pharmacy at Philidelphia, Pennsylvania, in 1894, and graduated in 1896; he held a position in a drug store while studying in Philadelphia.   In May, 1897, he retired from his position in Philadelphia and returned to his native township in Indiana.   In the year 1899 he married Mattie Wilson, of Louisville.   His wife, who was a daughter of James Buford Wilson, of Lebanon, Kentucky, was born on the 16th of October, 1880.   Her father was for many years, after leaving Lebanon high school teacher in Louisville.

To Thomas R. Stevens and wife four children have been born.   They are: Thomas R., Junior, born on the 12th of November, 1904; Dorothy E., born July 18, 1908; the two other children died in infancy.

Shortly after his marriage the subject of our notice moved to his farm which contained one hundred and eighty-five acres.   He is a scientific farmer, modern and progressive in every respect, who has concentrated and devoted all his energies to obtain the best results from his agricultural labors.   He has accomplished this to his own satisfaction and profit.

Thomas R. Stevens is an important man in the affairs of the locality. He has a large circle of friends whose confidences he has succeeded in winning.   He is a Republican in his political sympathies though he has not been very active as a party man.   He is a member of the Pythian and Red Men lodges, being a charter member of the Knights of Pythias fraternity. He is a member of the New Washington Masonic Lodge, No. 167. He is a deacon of the local Presbyterian church and a religious and moral man. In March, 1907, at the organization of the State Bank at New Washington he became a stock holder and a member of its directorate.

JOHN A. GLASS.

John A. Glass, of Bethlehem township, Clark county, is a well educated and cultured citizen as well as a farmer of prominence in the community in which he resides. Jointly with his sister, Clara, he is the owner of five hundred and thirty acres of land as good as any in the township, and on which the paternal homestead stands. The Glass family were originally of North Carolina, and were for many generations prominently identified with that historic southern state. John A. Glass has the reputation in his native township of industriousness and temperate habits. Had he followed the teaching profession to which he devoted some years of his life, it is probable that he would have made a name for himself as an educator of note. As it is he is content to lead the life of a farmer.

John A. Glass was born in Bethlehem township and was the son of John A. and Eliza (Cortner) Glass. John A. Glass, senior, was born near New Washington, Clark county, Indiana, on the 11th of January, 1827. His father, David Glass, was a settler in Clark county, having migrated to Indiana from North Carolina at an early date. Our subject's mother, Eliza (Cortner) Glass, was born August 11, 1837. The Cortners were also of North Carolina, and were neighbors of the Glass family in that state, who afterwards also migrated to Indiana. John A. Glass, senior, and Eliza Cortner married on May 31, 1857, at New Market, in Oregon township. They came to Bethlehem township about the year 1861, where they farmed. They moved to Charlestown in 1877, as they desired to have better educational advantages for their children. Five children were born to them, two of whom are now living. Two, Edward and Alice, died in infancy; David died at the age of twenty years, and the two survivors are the subject of our review, and his sister, Clara. John A. Glass, senior, died on May 10, 1895, while his wife died previously on July 27, 1880. John A. Glass was known over Clark county in his lifetime as an excellent farmer. He was a Democrat in politics and belonged to the Christian church, of which he was an influential member. Altogether, he was an admirable citizen, an affectionate father and a man with a large number of friends.

John A. Glass and his sister, Clara, passed through the Charlestown schools together. John A. took the Bible course and graduated at the Kentucky University at Lexington. He was reared upon the family farm and attended the district schools. He studied at the Charlestown schools and then attended the Butler University for two years, at the end of which time he had to give up on account of a breakdown in his health. He afterwards taught school for two years in Bethlehem township and attended the Lexington (Kentucky) Bible College, graduating in 1897.

On April 12, 1899, Clara H. Glass married Dr. W. H. Willyard, and has one daughter, Dorcas H. Willyard. Mrs. Willyard lives with her brother, the subject of our sketch, in the old homestead on the family acres. Dr. W. H. Willyard is now in Peru, Indiana, and engaged in the practice of medicine, where he expects to move his family.

John A. Glass is a Prohibitionist in politics and adheres to the tenets of his party in everyday life and is a consistent voter on the ticket at election time. He is a member of the Christian church and is influential and active in religious affairs.

JOHN BYRN.

John Byrn, well known farmer, of Bethlehem township. Clark county, is a man now well advanced in life who has ever been a valuable asset in the community in which he has resided. An industrious farmer, he has ever worked assiduously for the family which has been his privilege to raise. He has given his children a good education, and has brought them to maturity conscious of their duties in life and well equipped to take their part as citizens. John Byrn is a man of strong religious convictions and his activity in religious work has often been felt in the local Methodist Episcopal church of which he is a trustee. It has been his privilege, also, to fight for his country in the Civil war. In the fight at Vicksburg he was wounded. He is a Grand Army man.

Mr. Byrn was born in New Albany, Floyd county, Indiana, on January 2, 1844, and was the son of Michael and Amelia A. (Hay) Byrn. Michael Byrn was a native of Ireland who came to America when a boy and, when old enough, worked on a farm and learned the carpenter business in which he became proficient at an early age. Adaron Hay, the father of Mrs. Byrn, was an Englishman who came to this country and followed farming pursuits during his life. He owned a large tract of land in Floyd county, Indiana.

Michael Byrn and Amelia Hay were the parents of three children: John, of this review, Joseph H., and a child that died in infancy. Joseph H. Byrn enlisted as a soldier in the Thirteenth Cavalry in which he remained for two years. He is now dead.

John Byrn was reared on a farm in Floyd county, Indiana, and on arriving at the proper age helped his parents. He attended school and at the age of eighteen he joined Company D of the Fifty-ninth Indiana Regiment on February 20, 1862. They camped at New Albany, Indiana, from where they were transported to New Madrid, Missouri, where the regiment engaged the enemy for the first time. From that time forth our subject participated in several of the big fights. He was at Chattanooga and Missionary Ridge, and was wounded at the siege of Vicksburg. He suffered from the effects of the injury for about five months, at the end of which time he rejoined his regiment. He was then detailed for special duty on the staff at General McPherson's headquarters and thus spent the remaining two years of his military life. At the close of the war he returned to Floyd county, Indiana, where he remained for a very short time coming to Clark county, Indiana, where his mother had located, and there he farmed for two years. He then married Susan M. Varble on the 22d of October, 1867. She was born in Clark county, Indiana, on the 29th of December, 1849, and was the daughter of George Varble. She spent all her life, with the exception of one year, in the county. She was educated in the district school and was left motherless at an early age.

John Byrn and his wife became the parents of five children: George D., born June 11, 1871, died November 26, 1903; Minnie, born May 22, 1875, is the wife of O. W. Simonton; Mary, born November 12, 1877, died July 30, 1901; she was the wife of George B. Headley and left one daughter, Edith, born November 20, 1882, is unmarried as is also Maime, born November 30, 1886. At his marriage, not being able to purchase a farm, John Byrn rented land for several years and then bought the farm owned by George Varble which consisted of one hundred and eighty-three acres, twenty acres of which has been sold. The Byrn farm lies in section No. 6. Our subject and his wife have been prosperous in their farming pursuits. In religion they are members of the Methodist Episcopal church. The Byrn family attend the local New Hope church. John Byrn is a Republican in politics and has for many years followed the fortunes of his chosen party.

H. C. FORWARD.

H. C. Forward, Civil war veteran and prosperous farmer, of Bethlehem township, Clark county, has been connected with the district in which he lives all through life. He has now reached the age of sixty-six years and is in a position to lead a life of leisure and enjoy the fruits of his labors. When the spectre of war spread itself over the land H. C. Forward was among the first in his township to volunteer for action and passed through the thick of that dread conflict valorously bringing credit on himself. At the close of the war he returned to his native township and resumed his work, and his prosperity has increased with his years.

He was born in Bethlehem township, Clark county, on the 8th of February, 1842, and was the son of J. Nathan and Elizabeth (Long) Forward. His father was born in Trumbull county, Ohio, and came to Clark county in 1833, where he settled in Bethlehem township. He was a carpenter by trade and married Elizabeth Long, who was a native of Kentucky. He was the father of the following children: H. C., Francis, Ellen, Chancy R., Urshel died August, 1908; Samuel, Abigail, Walter, Laura, Jane, Alwilta and Huldah; one child died in infancy.

H. C. Forward was reared upon the farm in Bethlehem township and when old enough helped on the farm. He had but little chance of education, and on the outbreak of the Civil war he enlisted in the Thirteenth Indiana Cavalry on the 18th of November, 1863. The engagement at Nashville was the largest in which he took part though his term of service extended until the close of the war. His brother, Samuel, also took part in the conflict, as a soldier. He died in the Andersonville prison.

On his discharge from the army our subject returned home, and since that time has engaged in farming operations in his native township. On April 8, 1869, his marriage took place. He took for his wife Anna E. Allen, also a native of Clark county. They have not, however, had any children. H. C. Forward is a member of the local post, Grand Army of the Republic, in which he is a prominent member. In politics he is a Republican though not a strenuous party man. He receives a pension from the government for his war services. He owns fifty-six acres of land, which he has brought to its present state of cultivation and improvement through his own efforts.

MORDICAI B. COLE.

The family of this name settled in Maryland at a very early date, the genealogy extending back to the middle of the eighteenth century. We first hear of Thomas Cole, who was born in Baltimore county, Maryland, December 25, 1754, and died September 12, 1808. He married Aletha Ford, born February 15, 1768, in Maryland, and died March 16, 1848. By this union, which occurred in May, 1786, there were several children: Mordicai Cole, the oldest, ond son, was born March 6, 1802, and died October 6, 1889; Thomas Cole, the third son, was born October 8, 1803, and died February 25, 1823. Christopher Cole married Mary Fouts, one of the twelve children of Lewis and Sarah (Dougan) Fouts, the former born April 10, 1778, and died March 28, 1864. His wife was born July 25, 1783, and died August 12, 1852. Their children were: Thomas, Isabel, Mary, Elizabeth, Eleanor, Jane, Sarah, Catherine, Andrew, Harriet, Thomas, Douglas and Rebecca. Their births occurred during the years 1801-27 and all of them have long since passed away. The marriage of Christopher Cole and Mary Fonts occurred in 1822, and they were the parents of Mordicai B. Cole, who was born after his fathe and mother had removed to Clark county. Christopher Cole was a native of Maryland, and removed with his parents to near Steubensville, Ohio, and later to Clark county, where he was married. He became a pioneer merchant at New Washington, engaging in this line of business for many years during the early history of Clark county. In 1841 he was appointed to the office of sergeant-at-arms at Washington, D. C., and he served in that capacity until 1860. He then returned to Charlestown, Indiana, where his family had resided during his absence at the national capital. He lived in retirement after this until his death in 1889.

Mordicai B. Cole was born in New Washington, Indiana, July 7, 1825, the son of Christopher Cole. He was reared in that town and when young his parents located in Charlestown, where he received a common school education. When twenty years old he engaged in the mercantile business at Charlestown. He built up a large trade and in a few years became one of the leading merchants of Clark county, as well as one of the best known men in this locality. In later years he was associated with his sons and still later his son-in-law, G. T. Beeler, became a partner and after the death of Mr. Cole continued the business. Mr. Cole was continuously in business in Charlestown for fifty-nine years at the time of his death, July 7, 1904, probably the longest record of any man in the county in this respect. He was prominent in business circles, and his name was known to all classes throughout the county. He was one of the organizers of the Bank of Charlestown in 1891, and was elected as first president and he very ably served in the same capacity until his death. He was a public-spirited man and always contributed to the upbuilding of the town in any way possible. He was the most successful merchant Charlestown ever had. He started with a small capital and became wealthy through the skillful management of his business affairs. He was a member of the Christian church and for many years an official in the same and one of its most liberal supporters. He was a member of the Independent Order of Odd Fellows, at Charlestown, during his entire mature life, and was prominent in the same. In politics he was formerly a Whig, later a Republican. He never held office or aspired to positions of public trust, preferring to devote his time exclusively to his business affairs.

Mordicai B. Cole married Margaret E. Long, a native of Clark county, the accomplished, cultured daughter of John Long, and the representative of

54

an old and influential family here. Mr. and Mrs. Cole were the parents of five children, who grew to maturity, namely: John Christopher, Edward W., Eva, James L. and Albert M. Mrs. Cole, a very estimable lady, survives her husband, making her home at the old family residence at Charlestown.

FRANK F. DEAN.

Frank F. Dean has been located on his present farm in Owen township since the year 1900, coming from Bethlehem township, where he had been located since 1884. He is widely known throughout Clark county as an expert fruit grower and an agriculturist of merit. He passed through the Civil war and emerged unscathed from the conflict.

The subject of our sketch was born in Jefferson county, Indiana, on the 25th of April, 1843. He was the son of Argus and Abigail (Stowe) Dean. Argus Dean, a man of broad culture and the writer of several books on river and harbor topics, was born in Ohio in 1810. He engaged in the quarry business and was later a large fruit grower. He was appointed at one time on the Harbor and River Commission by Governor Porter, of Indiana, and accordingly wrote upon the subject. Argus Dean and his wife were the parents of the following children: William S., Frank F., Charles E., Mary L., Hiram P. and Abbie J.

Frank F. was raised on a farm in Jefferson and Clark counties, near Bethlehem, and at the proper age he attended school. He enlisted in Company H, Thirty-ninth Indiana Regiment, in October, 1861. This regiment was afterwards known as the Eighth Indiana Cavalry. Our subject served all through the Civil war and was mustered out in the year 1865, receiving a commission as second lieutenant. He participated in the following engagements: Middletown, Stone River, Shiloh, Cumberland Gap, Chickamauga, Jonesboro, Waynesboro, Averysboro, Brown's Cross Road, and a number of other battles of minor importance. At the close of the war he returned to Clark county and afterwards went to Missouri, where he engaged in the fruit business for five years. There he married Eliza Zumault, of Missouri. He then moved to Cincinnati and engaged in selling peaches for his father and brother during the season, and there he obtained an appointment as postal clerk in the railway mail service on the road from Cincinnati, Ohio, to Grafton, West Virginia, on the Baltimore & Ohio Railroad, which he held for eleven years. He resigned in 1884 and located in Bethlehem township, and in 1900 moved to Owen township, where he has engaged in the fruit raising business, raising peaches and apples. He and his wife are the parents of two children. They are: Minnie A., the wife of Charles E. Pernett, of Bethlehem township, and

Frank, who married a daughter of J. F. Rice, of Owen township, named Lucy. Both children are well settled and prosperous.

The subject of our sketch was a prominent member of the local Grand Army of the Republic Post at Otto, now disbanded. In politics he is a Republican, his earliest vote for the Presidency being cast for General Grant, and his latest for William Howard Taft. Frank F. Dean enjoys a peaceful domestic life, where he has all the comforts suitable to his advanced years. He was Justice of the Peace from 1886 to 1900. In 1900 he was nominated for Representative on the Republican ticket against Reuben Daily, and ran about two hundred ahead of most of the ticket. In 1892 he was a candidate for Joint Senator of Clark and Jefferson counties. In 1904 he was Republican candidate for County Commissioner. All these nominations came to him unsolicited.

JOHN CHRISTOPHER COLE.

John Christopher Cole was born at Charlestown, Indiana, October 7, 1849. He was educated in the place of his nativity. His father conducted a dry goods store at Charlestown, and in this he got his business training as a clerk. He remained under the parental roof until February, 1882, when he removed to Bloomington, Illinois, in company with his brother, Edward W. Cole. In partnership they purchased the dry goods and carpet business of J. E. Houtz & Company, which they proceeded to enlarge and extend. The Cole brothers became well known as merchants throughout that part of Illinois, and for over twenty-seven years conducted a successful business. In January, 1909, the Cole brothers sold their stock of merchandise and retired from active business, but they continued to reside in Bloomington, Illinois.

On December 9, 1874, John Christopher Cole was married to Cora E. Bottorff, who was born March 9, 1855, in Clark county, Indiana. Her parents were John T. and Margaret Bottorff, members of the old and well established families of this section. The four children of Mr. and Mrs. Cole are William Gordon, Margaret Thomas, Nina and Louise.

FRANK W. CARR.

In an analysis of the character of this well known citizen of Charlestown, Clark county, Indiana, who has for many years stood at the forefront of the legal profession, we find the qualities of reliability in business, and conscientiousness in the discharge of the duties of private and public life.

Frank W. Carr was born in Oregon township, Clark county, July 17, 1866, the son of Dr. F. M. Carr, long a prominent physician of this locality. After practicing medicine in Oregon township for fifty years, he is now living in retirement. Frank W. Carr is a member of a family of seven living at this writing. J. P. was a student at Hanover College and the University of Indiana. He served for five years as superintendent of Clark county schools. He is at present superintendent of schools of Vicksburg, Mississippi. J. W. is a telegraph operator in Kansas. M. W. is a barber at Corydon, Indiana. S. E. was a student at Hartsville University and at the school at Danville. He served as county superintendent of schools of Clark county for two terms. He is now a druggist. C. L. is a resident of Oregon township. M. M. is a barber at Corydon. Frank W., our subject, attended the public schools and later attended the Danville (Indiana) Central Normal School, where he graduated from the teacher's course. He later took a partial course in the scientific department and later graduated from the law department with high honors.

Mr. Carr taught school in a very acceptable manner for several terms in a town school and began the practice of law in 1896 in Charlestown, Indiana, where he practiced with marked success for a period of two years, when he was elected Circuit Clerk of Clark county by the Democratic party and served one term from 1900 to 1904 in a manner that elicited nothing but words of commendation from everyone.

On October 11, 1904, the happy domestic life of Mr. Carr began, when he was united in marriage with Nevada Bottorff, who was a native of Clark county, having been born in Oregon township, the representative of an influential family. One child has brightened the home of the subject and wife, Marion B., who was born June 14, 1907.

Mr. Carr has made a pronounced success of his profession, his office is always a busy place and he is known as an able counselor and advisor, his name having become known throughout Southern Indiana as one that stands at the head of the legal profession.

Our subject is a member of the Presbyterian church, being one of the elders in the same. He served as a commissioner to the Presbyterian general assembly in 1909.

Mr. Carr is a member of the old and honored Masonic fraternity, the lodge at New Washington, Indiana. Also the Independent Order of Odd Fellows, having passed the chairs of the same and represented his lodge in the Grand Lodge. He is also a member of the Modern Woodmen of America and has represented this district at the head camp, Dubuque, Iowa. He was made permanent chairman of the first state camp at Indianapolis. Shortly after the expiration of his term of office as Circuit Clerk, Mr. Carr removed to Charlestown where he resumed the practice of law, maintaining an office by himself. Alive to all that interests and benefits the public or makes for the benefit of his fellowmen, Mr. Carr's efforts have been strenuous and fruitful of happy results.

JAMES LEE COLE.

A well known and influential business man of Charlestown, Clark county, Indiana, is James Lee Cole, who was born here March 17, 1861, the son of Mordicai B. Cole, a sketch of whom appears elsewhere in this volume. He was reared in Charlestown, his native town, educated in the public schools, and at Barnett Academy, one of the old and well known private educational institutions of Charlestown in the early days. After he finished school he purchased his father's farm adjoining Charlestown, and he has carried on general farming very successfully ever since. He owns two hundred and twenty acres under excellent improvements, and which has been so skillfully managed that it is just as productive as when he first took possession of it. He has a fine and commodious residence, good out buildings and he keeps some excellent stock of various kinds, dealing extensively in Jersey cattle, and no small part of his yearly income is derived from his successful handling of live stock, of which he is regarded by his neighbors as a splendid judge.

In 1885 Mr. Cole established a creamery on his farm and it soon grew into an extensive business. He purchased large quantities of cream in addition to that furnished by his own cattle. This was operated quite successfully by Mr. Cole until 1900, when he closed his creamery. He also engaged in the farm implement business in Charlestown for a period of ten years, under the firm name of Cole & McMillin.

In August, 1906, Mr. Cole was elected president of the Bank of Charlestown, and he continues in this position, ably managing the affairs of this, one of the soundest institutions of its kind in the state. He is also a director and stockholder in the same.

Mr. Cole's domestic life began March 20, 1883, when he married Ella S. Barnett, who was born in 1862, in Charlestown township, the daughter of Allen and Edith (Jacobs) Barnett, also natives of Clark county, and representatives of old and well established families. To Mr. and Mrs. Cole two daughters have been born: Laura, the wife of Cortland S. Hughes, a well known and extensive contractor; Nita, the second child, a graduate of Butler University, Indianapolis, is still a member of the home circle.

In politics Mr. Cole is a Republican, but he has never taken much interest in party affairs, preferring to devote his time exclusively to business. In his fraternal relations he is a member of the Knights of Pythias and the Modern Woodmen of America, at Charlestown.

Personally Mr. Cole is a gentleman of unblemished reputation. He is essentially cosmopolitan in his ideas, a man of the people, and in the best sense of the word a representative type of the strong, virile American manhood, which commands and retains respect by reason of inherent merit, sound sense and correct conduct. He has so impressed his individuality upon the community where his life has been spent as to win the confidence and esteem of his fellow citizens. Measured by the accepted standard of excellence, his career, though strenuous, has been eminently honorable and useful, and his life fraught with great good to the people of Clark county, according to those who know him best, although he is unconscious of this, being unostentatious and unassuming, at the same time courteous and kind, and always considerate of the welfare of others, and ever ready to aid in any manner possible the up-building of his native community.

WILLIAM J. BOTTORFF.

More than eighty-five years have dissolved in the mists of the past since the well known and representative citizen whose name appears above, first saw the light, during all of which time he has lived in Clark county, and the greater part of the time figured prominently in the affairs of the community in which he resides. The Bottorffs were among the early pioneers of this part of the state, the subject's grandfather migrating from Pennsylvania to Jefferson county, Kentucky in the latter part of the eighteenth century. He was a Presbyterian minister, and settled near Louisville. It is supposed that he was killed by wild beasts while on a journey through the wilderness to perform a marriage ceremony, as his horse returned and portions of his clothing were afterward found. John Bottorff, the subject's father, a Pennsylvanian by birth, was seventeen years old when the family moved to Kentucky and in the year 1800 he came to Clark county, settling on a farm in what is now Charlestown township, and from that time until his death, a number of years later, he was one of the leading farmers and influential citizens of Clark county. He was a true type of the sturdy pioneer of the period in which he spent his early manhood, strong, industrious and energetic, and took an active interest in the improvement of the country, and the development of its resources. To him belongs the credit of literally fulfilling the scriptural injunction to "multiply and replenish the earth," having been twice married, and the father of twenty-three children, nine by the first and fourteen by the second wife.

John Bortorff with his two companions has long been sleeping the sleep of the just, and of the large and interesting family that formerly gathered around the hearthstone, eight survive, all except one brother and two sisters living within two miles of Charlestown, and five of the number having passed the ripe old age of eighty years. This is certainly a remarkable record, and it is doubtful whether another family in the state can produce as many living representatives, ranging in age from seventy to ninety years.

The following are the names and dates of birth of the surviving children of John Bottorff: Louis, born in the year 1817; Gabriel, March 29, 1819; Sophia, November 5, 1820; William J., of this review, May 3, 1824; L. D., February 17, 1826; Joshua, January 27, 1831; Lucinda A., August 20, 1833, and Mary A., who was born on June 21, of the year 1834.

William J. Bottorff whose birth is noted above is a son of his father's second wife, whose maiden name was Elizabeth Stonecipher. He was born on the family homestead in Charlestown township and like the majority of boys in a new and sparsely settled country was reared to habits of industry and at an early age learned by practical experience the true meaning of hard work. When old enough to wield an axe he was assigned his task in the woods, and from early morn until late in the evening, labored at clearing away the forest and undergrowth and tilling the soil for cultivation. Blessed with strong, vigorous physical powers and splendid health he nobly did his share in clearing and developing the farm and being an adept with the axe he was enabled while still a youth to do a man's part at any kind of labor in which that implement was required. Owing to his laborious duties he had little leisure to attend school, nevertheless he made the most of his opportunities and in due time obtained the rudiments of an education which supplemented by reading and close observation in later years made him an intelligent and well informed man.

In addition to farming the subject's father operated for some years a combination saw and grist mill, in and about which young William was required to work during the winter months, devoting the rest of the year to labor in the clearing and cultivating of the fields. Although deprived of many privileges and obliged to earn his bread by the sweat of his brow, he grew up to strong and well developed young manhood. He not only passed his minority on the home farm assisting in its cultivation but remained with his father five years longer and it was not until he chose a wife and helpmeet and set up a domestic establishment of his own that he left the parental roof. This important event occurred in the spring of 1850, and the one who agreed to take his name, preside over his home, and share his life and fortune was a most estimable and popular young lady by the name of Eliza J. Nett, a native of Jefferson county, Kentucky, where she was born in the year 1834. Meantime Mr. Bottorff had entered a tract of land in Jackson county, Indiana, and some months previous to his marriage he erected a log cabin of the conventional type to which in due time he brought his bride and began life for himself, his father assisting him in the momentous undertaking to the extent of one cow and four sheep. After clearing twenty acres of his land he sold it and purchased a place in Owen township, Clark county, where in due time he cleared about one hundred and fifty acres and developed one of the finest and most productive farms in the locality. He not only cut the timber and split the rails to enclose the three hundred and sixty acre tract which he now owns, but at odd times made rails for a number of his neighbors having become an expert in this particular kind of work as well as skilled in all lines of labor in which implements of woodcraft were required.

By industry and excellent management Mr. Bottorff succeeded in making his farm one of the best in the county and his reputation as a successful and enterprising agriculturist soon made his name widely and favorably known. In connection with tilling the soil he has devoted considerable attention to live stock and always made it a rule to keep on a sufficient number of cattle and hogs to consume the produce of his farm, besides buying and shipping from time to time to Cincinnati and other leading markets of the Middle West. He has worked hard in his time frequently form sixteen to eighteen hours a day, but of recent years has been in a situation to enjoy the fruits of his many years of toil and take life easy, being at this time not only in independent circumstances but the possessor of a handsome fortune which places him in the front ranks of the financially solid and well-to-do men of Clark county. His beautiful and attractive homestead in Owen township, one of the most valuable farms in the county, nearly all of which was cleared and made ready for tillage by the labor of his own hands, represents a value considerably in excess of twenty thousand dollars in addition to which he owns a comfortable and commodious modern residence in Charlestown where he moved in 1897, and where he is now spending the evening of a long and useful life in honorable retirement.

On state and national issues he has always been an unwavering supporter of the Democratic party, but in local affairs he votes for the best qualified candidates irrespective of political ties.

Mr. Bottorff and his good wife are the parents of eight children, four of whom are living and whose names and dates of birth are as follows: Columbus, February 13, 1851; William E., May 19, 1857; Mattie, April 19, 1865; Lettie, August 8, 1867.

Mr. Bottorff gave his children the best educational advantages the schools of the county afforded. Mr. and Mrs. Bottorff have lived to see their descendants to the fourth generation and now rejoice in a happy family circle of four children, thirteen grandchildren and their five great-grandchildren, in all of whom are reproduced many of the amiable qualities and sterling characteristics of the venerable old couple whom they delight to love and honor. Religiously Mr. Bottorff and wife have been active members of the Methodist Episcopal church since the year 1865. He has held at intervals important official positions in the local church to which he belongs and for a number of years has been one of the pillars of the same.

LEWIS C. BAIRD.

Lewis C. Baird was born in Jeffersonville, Indiana, July 3, 1869. The Baird family is one of the older ones in the city of Jeffersonville, being residents here in 1837. The material side, the Howard family, were residents in Jeffersonville in 1835. The early youth of the subject of this sketch was passed in Louisville, Kentucky, Augusta, Georgia, in West Virginia, and in Dallas and Waxahatchie, Texas. He was educated in the public schools of Jeffersonville until the spring of 1887 when he withdrew, being a junior in the high school at the time, to prepare for admission to the United States Naval Academy at Annapolis. He entered the class of '92, U. S. N. A., and remained a midshipman until June, 1891, when he resigned. In 1892 he was commissioned captain in the First Regiment Indiana National Guard, serving at such until 1895, commanding his company in the field during the miners' riots in Sullivan county in 1894. In 1898 he was commissioned captain in the One Hundred Sixty-first Indiana Volunteer Infantry, war with Spain, and served with his regiment in the Army of Occupation of the Province of Havana.

Captain Baird was made a Mason in Clark Lodge No. 40, Free and Accepted Masons, at Jeffersonville September 19, 1895, and was raised to the sublime degree of a Master Mason November 21, 1895. He was master of Clark Lodge in 1900, 1901, and 1902, and is at present secretary. For thirteen years he was lay reader of St. Paul's Episcopal church, of which he is a member, and is at present a member of and the clerk of the vestry. For a number of years he has been engaged in the practice of his profession of civil and landscape engineering in Louisville, being the civil engineer at Cave Hill cemetery at the present time. On June 1, 1896, he was united in marriage with Miss Martha H. Johnson, the eldest daughter of the Hon. S. S. Johnson of the Clark County Bar.

Captain Baird is a member of the Jeffersonville Commercial Club and takes a keen interest in the development of the city and county.

THE SHARPLESS FAMILY.

John Sharpless was baptized August 15, 1624; died April, 1685; married April 27, 1662, to Jane Moor. He was the first of the Heaton ancestors in this country, and was the son of Jeffrey Sharpless, of Wybunbury, Chester, England. He died near Chester, Pennsylvania. He had a grant of land from William Penn on April 5, 1682, paying twenty pounds, or $100, for one thousand acres. John Sharpless, with a forethought unusual in American immigrants of that period, instead of disposing of all his possessions, reserved the lease of the house and lands which he held at Blakenhall, probably with the idea that, if dissatisfied with his new home he would have one to return to in England.   He, therefore, made his will before emigrating and left it behind him in the custody of his executors.   He was a tenant of Sir Thomas Delves, the lord of the manor, from whom he held a lease for ninety-nine years, and that he was able to retain this after the purchase he had made in Pennsylvania and the necessarily considerable expense of transporting so large a family there, speaks well for his thrift and proves conclusively that he was in comfortable circumstances.   Although he called himself a "yeoman" he was entitled to a coat-of-arms and was born to command.   His will, disposing of a large amount of property, is still extant.

James Sharpless, born in England, first month, 5th day, 1670-1, died in Chester, Pennsylvania, about 1746, married Mary Edge first month, 3d day, 1697-8; then married Mary Lewis twelfth month, 20th day, 1699-1700; died in 1753.   The certificate of his marriage to Mary Lewis is still in existence—also his will.   The ideas in those days of distributing much property does not accord with our times.

Rachael Sharpless, born the 9th day of the 5th month, 1708, was married 8th month, 17th day, to James Dell.   He also had much property, land and money.   Her daughter, Sarah Dell, married Isaac Weaver 7th month, 20th day, 1750.   She died aged eighty-two years; he died aged eighty-nine years.

Isaac Weaver was assessed in Nether Providence, 1764, with one hundred ninety acres and buildings, seventy acres of uncultivated land, nine horses, six cattle and five sheep.

Isaac Weaver, Jr., born in Nether Providence, 3d month, 1st day, 1756, died in Green county, Pennsylvania, 5th month, 22d day, 1830, and was buried upon his own farm upon Sactile Run.   He married Abigail Price. Isaac Weaver, Jr., was educated in Philadelphia and while a young man taught school for several years.   He also fought in the Revolutionary war. He received a good education for that day and was a very fine penman.   In person he was large, being six feet four inches in height and weighing about two hundred forty pounds.   He possessed great physical strength, was very erect and in appearance handsome, stately and dignified.   He was a man of unswerving integrity and served in both houses of the State Legislature of Pennsylvania.   In 1800 he was Speaker of the Assembly, in 1802 State Treasurer and carried money from Lancaster to Washington City on horseback, filling the office with credit to himself and honor to the state.   He was four times elected Senator from the district composed of Washington and Green counties, in 1806, 1812, 1816, 1820 and in 1817 was Speaker of the Senate. His wife, Abigail Price, was the daughter of David Price and Ann Husband Price, of Cecil county, Maryland, and was descended from Barnabas Wilcox, who gave three of his daughters to colonial mayors of Philadelphia.

His daughter, Nancy Weaver, daughter of Isaac Weaver, Jr., born June 17, 1797, married John Heaton.

WYATT EMORY WILLEY.

The family of which the subject of this review is an honorable representative has figured for over a century in the annals of Clark county and before migrating to Indiana was well known in the colony of Connecticut where the original ancestors settled a number of years prior to the War of Independence. Brazilla Willey, the first of the name to seek a home in the West was a native of Connecticut and when a young man served two terms of enlistment in the War of the Revolution, at the close of which he located in his native state where he remained until migrating to Southern Indiana nearly one hundred years ago. Arriving at his destination in 1811 he settled a short distance above Jeffersonville near the site now occupied by the Zulauf residence, but the following year moved to the tract of land northwest of Memphis where he built his cabin and stockade to which he brought his family the same year. Mr. Willey was a fine mechanic and made three trips to New Orleans making the return journey on foot and meeting with not a few thrilling experiences on the way. Owing to the failure of his partner, a Mr. Bowman of Jeffersonville, his last trip was far from being successful, but to reimburse him for the loss sustained that gentleman subsequently deeded him the two hundred acres northwest of Memphis referred to which at that time was valued at a little more than the government price per acre but which in the end proved fortunate indeed to the possessor. Southern Indiana being on the frontier and exposed to the depredations of hostile Indians, the settlers took the precaution to protect their cabins by surrounding them with well constructed stockades and well it was that they did so for it was not long after the completion of Mr. Willey's fortification that the terrible Pigeon Roost massacre occurred in which so many settlers and their families fell victims to the ruthless savages and which for a long time caused great uneasiness on the frontier. When Mr. Willey moved to his possession it was a wilderness but with the energy characteristic of the true pioneer he resolutely addressed himself to the task of its improvement and in the course of a few years had a goodly portion cleared and under cultivation. Meantime as opportunities permitted he continued his mechanical work which consisted principally of building boats for the river trade, the material used in the construction of these crafts being whipsawed and but little iron required. In 1813 he built a boat sixty-feet in length on Silver creek which he floated to the river when the water rose, and sold at a good price. Several years later he constructed another boat near the mouth of the same creek which was propelled by steam forced through a pipe projecting from the stern into the water, this being one of the earliest attempts to utilize steam as a motive power on water.   In addition to boats, a number of which he constructed and disposed of Mr. Willey built a grist and saw mill combined on the Blue river which burned when nearing completion but he immediately rebuilt it which he operated about two years and then sold the same.   He furnished the lumber for the Collins Mill on the Kentucky side of the Falls.   He was a man of great energy and ability and his mechanical skill proved of immense service to his own and other localities.   When quite young he united with the Methodist Episcopal church and not long after moving to Indiana entered the ministry of the same and discharged the duties of his holy office for many years first as a local preacher and later on the regular work of the circuit.

Brazilla Willey died in 1851 and is buried in the cemetery at Bowery Chapel, a church about one mile west of Memphis which he organized and to which he ministered from time to time for a number of years besides erecting the building in which the society worships.   The children of Mr. Willey were as follows: Allen, Brazilla, Elam, Dennis, John W., John F., Martha A., Clarissa Ann, who married James S. Tricker; Mary Elizabeth, wife of Lewis Tuttle; and Damrus who died in childhood.   At the breaking out of the War of 1812, Allen the oldest son, who was in Canada, was conscripted into the British army and for a time forced to serve against his own country.   When a favorable opportunity presented itself, however, he deserted, crossing Lake Erie in a canoe, a hazardous trip of three days, and after a long journey and somewhat strenuous experience in the wilderness on foot finally arrived at the family home where a royal welcome awaited him.   He was a well educated man for those days and was a rival for the nomination as first Governor of Indiana against Jonathan Jennings.

For many years the Willeys were quite numerous in Clark county and prominent in the affairs of their respective communities, but some time prior to the War of the Rebellion all of the name except John Fletcher Willey moved to other parts and are now with their descendants scattered over various states.

John Fletcher Willey, who was the youngest son of Brazilla Willey, was born in Cincinnati in 1809 and was brought to Clark county when an infant two years old.   Like his father he was a man of intelligence and great energy, a believer in progress and few citizens of Clark county have done so much as he to promote the material interest of their places of residence or been more influential in advancing the moral and social condition of the people.   He was one of the first men in the county to engage in horticulture on more than a nominal scale and for a number of years he ranked among the largest and most successful fruit growers of Southern Indiana besides earning a wide reputation among horticulturists of his own and other states. He was a public spirited man and a representative citizen and ever endeavored to keep bright and untarnished the escutcheon of the esteemed old family of which he was for many years the honored head. He died in Wood township in 1899, at the age of ninety years.

WYATT E. WILLEY.

This enterprising farmer and gallant ex-soldier of one of the great wars in the annals of time is a son of John F. and Pauline (Garner) Willey, the latter a daughter of Shieveral Garner, whose antecedents came to America many years ago from France.

Wyatt Willey is a native of Clark county, Indiana, born March 2, 1841, in Utica township, and combines many of the estimable qualities and sterling characteristics for which his family for many generations have been distinguished. He was reared on the farm. In the fields in the summer seasons and attending the district schools in the winter he spent his time until the breaking out of the great rebellion, when with the spirit of patriotic zeal which characterized so many of the loyal young men throughout the north he laid aside his implements of husbandry for the death dealing weapons of war. In the month of December, 1861, when but a few months past his twentieth year he enlisted in Company H, Thirty-eighth Indiana Infantry, which in due time was attached to the Fourteenth Arm Corps and with his comrades he was soon experiencing all the realties of war on the march, in camp and on the field of battle. The first engagement in which he participated was fought near Louisville, Kentucky, following which he took part in some of the most noted battles which made his period of service historic including Perryville, Stone River, Hoover's Gap, Chickamauga, Missionary Ridge, the various engagements of the Atlanta campaign following which he marched with Sherman to the sea, thence to Goldsboro, North Carolina, and on March 19 and 20, 1865, took part in the battle of Bentonville. After the surrender of Johnston's force at Raleigh he proceeded with his command to Washington, D. C., where in the presence of President and other high officials of the civil and military departments of the government, he took part in the grand review, the closing scene in the long and sanguinary struggle which it is hoped will make rebellion in the country hereafter forever impossible.

From the national capitol Mr. Willey was sent with his regiment to Louisville, Kentucky, where, on July 23, 1865, he received an honorable discharge after three years, seven months and seventeen days of strenuous and honorable service in defense of the National Union.

On leaving the army Mr. Willey returned to Clark county, and shortly thereafter resumed the peaceful pursuits of civil life in Utica township where he has since lived and prospered devoting his attention the meanwhile to the ancient and honorable vocation of husbandry in which he has achieved most gratifying success. He has a beautiful and well improved farm of one hundred seventy-four acres, the greater part in a high state of cultivation and he also gives considerable time to horticulture which returns him no small part of his income. Mr. Willey cultivates the soil according to modern methods and is a man of practical ideas. He has broadened his mind and added very materially to his mental discipline by reading and intelligent observation in addition to which he has also traveled quite extensively over various parts of the United States visiting many interesting places. In politics he is a Republican but has never asked for office, nevertheless he is well read on the questions of the day and keeps abreast of the times on all matters of public interest.

Mr. Willey on January 24, 1866, was united in the bonds of wedlock with Eleanora T. Steelman, the marriage resulting in the following children: Charles E., born May 5, 1868; Paulina, August 30, 1870, and James F., who first saw the light of day on April 26, 1874; Charles E., the oldest of the family, married May Cooper and lives in Louisville, Kentucky. James F. chose a wife in the person of Sue Watts, and resides in the city of Jeffersonville. Paulina is now Mrs. John F. Crum, and makes her home in Utica township where she was born and reared. Mr. Willey is a Methodist in his religious faith and from early life has been an earnest and devout member of the church and a liberal contributor to its support. He has held the office of steward, class leader and trustee and for some years has been the superintendent of the Sunday school, besides being interested in various lines of religious and charitable work. Mrs. Willey is also a member of the church and a leader in some of its departments.

HENRY J. LUTZ.

Few families in Clark county can trace so old a genealogy as that of which the above named gentleman is descendant in the third generation. Henry Lutz, the original founder, was born in Germany, but came to America during the later part of the eighteenth century. He settled first in North Carolina, but before 1800 joined the tide then setting in toward the Northwest Territory, and reached Clark county in the vanguard of the early pioneers. He located in Utica township, entered a tract of wild land which by dint of hard work incident to settlers in the wilderness he eventually converted into a respectable farm. This property has ever since been in possession of his descendants, until recently, who by intermarriages with other offshoots of the first comers, now constitute a wide and influential family connection. Joseph A. Lutz, one of the sons of Henry, married Mary I., daughter of Jacob Daly, and niece of D. W. Daly, of Charlestown. Henry J. Lutz, a child by this union, was born in Utica township, Clark county, Indiana, in 1847. As he grew up he attained an elementary education in the neighborhood schools, supplemented by courses at Hanover College and the Kentucky State University, in Lexington. The death of his parents compelled a shortening of his college career and a return home where he took charge of the farm. In 1886 he bought a farm of two hundred twenty acres a mile northwest of Charlestown to which he moved after a commodious house and suitable out-buildings had been erected. To the cultivation and care of this place he gave his attention until 1908, when he retired from active work and located at Charlestown to spend the rest of his days in a beautiful concrete house, designed and constructed under his own directions. He is a member of the Christian church, and the Independent Order of Odd Fellows, being regarded as one of the county's substantial citizens in all the relations of life.

In 1870 Mr. Lutz married Rhoda B., daughter of William and Mary Gibson, of Utica township, whose family history will be found in the sketch of Jacob Gibson. They have seven children; Adella, Burdette C., Harry, Nora, Clarence P., Fred and Carl. Burdette, who is practicing law in Jeffersonville, was elected to the State Legislature in 1906 on the Democratic ticket. Harry, who married Pearl Huffstetter, lives on a farm in Charlestown township on the Bethlehem pike. He has three bright little daughters and is regarded as a progressive young farmer. Clarence married Mamie Harris and is traveling through the South for the Bell Telephone Company. Fred married Maggie, daughter of William Duesser, and Carl took for his wife, May, daughter of Alois Bastian. Fred and Carl are living on the farm northeast of Charlestown, which their father bought some years ago and recently turned over to their management.

GEORGE T. JACOBS.

The present solid prosperity enjoyed by Clark county may be attributed largely to the early settlers, who became later the prosperous and honored citizens of this locality and prepared the way for those who should come after them, leaving a rich inheritance to their children. Among those who have continued the great work brought to a high state by these pioneers, those of the aftermath, is the subject of this sketch.

George T. Jacobs was born November 14, 1852, in Clark county, the representative of an old and highly respected family who was identified with the pioneer work of this section.   He received his education in the local schools after which he began farming and has continued this line of work up to the present in a most satisfactory manner.   He is the owner of a fine farm of three hundred and ten acres, which he has improved until it ranks with any in the county.   He has a good dwelling and outbuildings, and on his place may be found stock of various kinds, in fact, Mr. Jacobs is a modern farmer in every respect and he owes his success to his indomitable energy and close application to business.

Our subject was united in marriage to Mrs. Kate H. Peet on September 21, 1876.   She is a native of Silver Creek township, where she was born in 1853 and where she received her education in the common schools.

The home of Mr. and Mrs. Jacobs has been blessed by the birth of three children, namely: Mrs. Dr. E. O. Sage, of Louisville, Kentucky; Ivan A., who lives in Jefferson township on a farm; Katie E., who is still a member of the home circle.

Mr. and Mrs. Jacobs are Methodists in their religious affiliations.   Fraternally the subject is a member of the Independent Order of Odd Fellows. He is independent in politics and has never aspired to public office, although he takes a keen interest in all matters pertaining to the good of his community and county whether political, material, educational or moral, and he and his wife are regarded as people of excellent worth whom everybody properly respects.

JAMES A. JOHNSON.

The family of this name in Clark county is descended on the paternal side from old North Carolina stock, and like all true sons of the old Tar State, are justly proud of their lineage.   We first hear of Baker Johnson, a native of Rowan county, North Carolina, who caught the western fever in early life and reached Southern Indiana in 1820.   He first located in Utica township, but in 1828 moved to a place in grant 73, a mile and a half south of Charlestown.   Tilghman Johnson, his son, was born in Rowan county, North Carolina, and was but an infant when brought by his father to the wilds of lower Ohio.   He became a man of prominence, accumulated property and owned the first government bond amounting to one thousand dollars ever purchased in Clark county.   He was a first cousin of President Andrew Johnson, and a good type of the rugged characters who did the work of development in this state during the trying days of the pioneer period.   He lived to an advanced age, his death occurring September 3, 1907, after a useful and strenuous life.

In early manhood he married Mary Neely, a woman of individuality, and marked strength of character, whose career covered the period of early settlement, concerning which she talked most entertainingly. Her father was Alexander Neely, a native of Maine, who made the long trip to the West at a time when it involved many hardships, as well as many dangers. His wife, Sarah Lanard, was born in 1792, and was one of the first white babies born in Utica township. She was fond of telling how she went over the Ohio Falls in a skiff when there was only one log house to be seen on either side of the river.

James A. Johnson, a grandson of this worthy couple, was born on his father's farm in Charlestown township, Clark county, in October, 1846. He made his home with his parents until the completion of his twenty-fourth year, when he spent considerable time in traveling through the West and other parts of the country. Eventually he settled down in his native county as a farmer and he has devoted all of his adult life to agricultural pursuits. He has, however, figured considerably in local politics and the record he made is one to be proud of. In 1894 he was elected County Commissioner on the Republican ticket and served three years so acceptably that on his retirement in 1898, he received an unusual testimonial from his official associates. This was in the shape of a resolution passed by his fellow-officers in the court-house, commending Mr. Johnson for his honest and fearless devotion to the interests of the people. This was ordered to be spread of record in the Commissioners' Court and constitutes a personal tribute which falls to but few men, under similar subjects. It was, of course, a gratifying surprise to the recipient and will be a proud inheritance for his descendants to the remotest generations. Mr. Johnson's party twice gave him the nomination of County Treasurer, and he has held several minor offices such as Justice of the Peace and others.

In 1872 Mr. Johnson married Alice, daughter of Felix C. and Sophia L. (Haas) Young. The grandparents were Alexander and Elizabeth (Blizzard) Young, being old residents of Utica township. Mr. and Mrs. Johnson have two children, Olive and Clare. The former is married to G. C. Martin, and lives in Charlestown, and has two children. Clare is a member of the home circle. Mr. Johnson is trustee of the Methodist church.

HON. LOUIS SPRIESTERSBACH.

The subject of this review enjoys distinctive prestige among the enterprising and public spirited citizens of Clark county, Indiana, and who has earned the right to be called one of the progressive men of this locality, is the gentleman whose name appears at the head of this sketch at this writing performing the duties of Mayor of Charlestown.

55

Louis Spriestersbach is a native of the town where he has spent his life, and where his useful talents have been employed, having been born in Charlestown, this county, December 10, 1864, the son of George and Catherine (Wagner) Spriestersbach. His father was born in Germany and immigrated to America in 1852. He first settled in Louisville, Kentucky, and two years later came to Charlestown, Indiana, where he was married. He started a blacksmith shop, which he conducted in a very successful manner. He is living in Charlestown at this writing, retired from business. His wife was called to her reward in 1896, after a faithful and worthy career. They were the parents of ten children, six of whom are still living.

Our subject was reared in Charlestown, where he attended the public schools, later attending the Barnett Academy, where he applied himself in a manner that resulted in a fairly good education. After leaving school he decided to follow the footsteps of his father and become a blacksmith, consequently he set about learning this trade under his father's able instruction, and when his father retired Louis took over the shop and conducted it with marked success until 1897 when he associated with his brother, Julius, in the implement and hardware business. The store continued to grow in magnitude and was patronized from all parts of the county resulting in a very lucrative business. Our subject has made a financial success all unaided and in an honorable manner. He is a stockholder and one of the directors of the Bank of Charlestown.

Our subject was married September 21, 1899, to Lottie Leonora Jacobs, of Jeffersonville, Indiana, a native of Greencastle, this state. She is a graduate of the Jeffersonville high school. She was born in 1876. One son has been born to this union, George Gordon, whose date of birth is recorded as March 22, 1908. Both our subject and wife are members of the Presbyterian church, and are liberal contributors to the same.

Mr. Spriestersbach in his fraternal relations is a member of the Independent Order of Odd Fellows No. 94, having passed the chairs of the same and represented this lodge in the Grand Lodge of Indiana.

In politics he is a Democrat and is well grounded in his convictions, being ever ready to further the interests of his party by lending his aid in placing the best possible men in local offices. He was elected Mayor of Charlestown in 1904, having taken charge of the office January 1, 1905. He has done a very great deal in improving the town. Among the many things he secured for Charlestown was the building of uniform sidewalks of the best cement for the principal streets.

Our subject is honest in all his business dealings and always ready to do his part in promoting the well-being of the community at large and because of his sterling attributes of character he is held in high regard in the county where his useful life has been spent.

JAMES D. KIGER.

During the last century one of the most significant facts in the movements among civilized nations was the great influx of immigrants into America from European shores. One condition in many of the European countries that led to this movement of their citizens to other lands was the strict military requirements made necessary by the war-like attitude of the powers toward each other. Many of the best people made it a point to bid farewell to the home-land in order to avoid a long term of military service either in active warfare or in the regular militia. Among other countries thus affected, Austria was one, being often engaged in open warfare with neighboring powers, or continuing for the most part under hostile relations with some one of them. One of their citizens that emigrated to America early in the century was Joseph Kiger, the grandfather of the subject of the present review, James D. Kiger, of Clark county, Indiana. Joseph Kiger was born on June 10, 1783, near Vienna, Austria, and after coming to America, was joined in marriage, February 22, 1820, to Maria B. Calfshead, who was born in Bourbon county, Kentucky, August 15, 1795. They were the parents of the following children: Casper, Catherine L., Christina, John F., James D., Sarah A. and Mary J. Of this family Christina attained the greatest age, having reached her eighty-third year before death overtook her.

James D. Kiger, our subject, was born in Charlestown township, Clark county, Indiana, on the 24th of November, 1857. His father, James D., was born in Utica township, same county, on the 14th of March, 1829. His mother, Lucy J. (Bottorff) Kiger, became a widow before our subject was born, and later she was again married.

James remained at home until he was nineteen years of age, and received a common school education. He was a boy of steady habits, industrious and economical. Whenever opportunity offered, he worked out and saved his earnings, and in this way as he grew to manhood he acquired the habit of frugality, which has characterized him in his later years.

On May 3, 1882, he was married to Elizabeth K. Spriestersbach, daughter of George Spriestersbach. Elizabeth was born in Charlestown, on the 13th of July, 1861, and received her education in the public schools of her native city. They began their married life on the farm where they now live, which embraces two hundred eighty-eight and one-half acres. This farm shows the fruits of good management and close application to work. The improvements are all first class, the soil is kept in excellent condition and the crops are such as any producer may well be proud of.

In conjunction with the farming of the lands, Mr. Kiger has devoted some attention to stock raising. In this he has also had singular success, for he has given close study to the problem of getting good results with the minimum of expense.

Four children have been born of this union, viz: Georgia B., born February 28, 1883; Jessie M., born June 8, 1885, Claude M., born December 23, 1887, and John P., born August 15, 1891. Jesse and Claude graduated from the Charlestown high school, the former in 1905 and the latter in 1907. Claude is now at Purdue University taking the agricultural course, having shown an aptitude for this branch of study, and a strong desire to do research work. John P. died October 17, 1893, and Georgia B. died April 8, 1896.

Mr. and Mrs. Kiger are members of the Presbyterian church, and are loyal supporters of the cause, giving freely not only of their means but their time, as well. Mr. Kiger has for many years been one of the deacons in the church. Although politically a Democrat, Mr. Kiger does not place party above principle, and stands first of all for a just and economic administration of all public affairs.

WILLIAM W. FARIS.

The gentleman whose name furnishes the caption for this article is one who is well known in Clark county, and is held in high esteem for his sterling characteristics and unassuming demeanor. Mr. Faris was born in Charlestown township, on the 22d of September, 1872. He was the son of Dr. W. W. and Sarah (Coombs) Faris, and the grandson of Capt. John Faris. The latter was a participant in the Indian wars of the Middle West, and became famous as an Indian fighter. He took part in the battle of Tippecanoe, under Gen. William Henry Harrison, and was an efficient sharp-shooter and frontier scout. He married Rebecca Work and to them were born Willis, Mrs. Dr. John Baird, Mrs. Faris, of Princeton, Indiana; Robert (deceased) and Dr. W. W. Faris, father of our subject. Doctor Faris attended the Chestnut Street Medical College of Louisville, Kentucky, having previously graduated from the Sturgus Academy of Charlestown. He followed teaching for several years, and became interested in civil engineering. This latter subject became so attractive to him that he began to make it a special study, and in time gave up the practice of medicine almost entirely. He served as County Surveyor of Clark county for twenty years, and took up the management of a farm in conjunction with his official duties. He became the owner of about six hundred acres of land and became well fixed financially. His death occurred March 5, 1895. He is still survived by his wife. The three children of this family were: John M., Jesse C., and our subject. William W. was educated in the neighboring district schools and later attended the Charlestown high school, from which he graduated in 1891. He then entered Hanover College, and was in attendance there until he reached the sophomore year.

August 14, 1895, our subject was married to Nannie Barnes, daughter of

Hon. Willis L. Barnes. She was born on the 4th of June, 1876, and is a woman of excellent tastes and good education. Two children have been born of this union, viz: Jesse C., born June 25, 1896, and Arthur W., born August 13, 1902. The members of this family are affiliated with the Christian denomination.

Mr. Faris operates his own farm of one hundred eighty acres, and also the parental estate upon which his mother still resides. His home is a splendid illustration of what can be accomplished by judicious management and untiring energy, and is recognized as a model farm by his friends and neighbors. He is a man of few words and affiliates with the Democratic party, but has never had any aspirations for political prominence. As a citizen, his conduct has been that of a loyal patriot, standing at all times for those views that make for the welfare of the community at large.

Mr. Faris's brother, John M., is connected with the United States War Department, and is storekeeper, now stationed at Fort Benjamin Harrison at Indianapolis.

THOMAS JEFFERSON LEWMAN.

Descended from a line of hardy pioneers, Thomas J. Lewman is an excellent representative of that type of men who have made themselves masters over circumstances. He was born in Charlestown township, Clark county, Indiana, on the 26th of October, 1846, being the son of Milas and Nancy (Prather) Lewman, and grandson of Moses Lewman. Milas Lewman was born in North Carolina in 1807, and was twelve years old when he came to Indiana, with his parents, making his home in Utica township, this county. The means of the family were quite limited, their only worldly possessions being the few things that were brought in the wagon in which they made their overland journey.

The family of Moses Lewman consisted of four boys, John, Silas, Milas and Isaiah, and three girls, Celia, Elizabeth and Nancy. These children were thrown largely upon their own responsibility, Moses Lewman having died two years after arriving in Clark county, and were thus made to stand face to face with the problem of making their own way in the world. In this way they all made a most commendable showing, as the mother was permitted to see the day when all of her children were comfortably settled in homes of their own. This did not come easy, as anyone familiar with such undertakings will admit, for it meant years of hard work, steady application and untiring grit. The mother, Elizabeth (Cash) Lewman, died in Utica, at the advanced age of ninety-five years.

Milas Lewman, father of our subject, was especially known among his neighbors as industrious and economical, making every move count and wasting no time on theories or speculations. He was a man of considerable independence of thought, and after making up his mind as to what he deemed right, did not hesitate to stand upon his own convictions. Up to the time of the Civil war, he had been a Democrat in politics, but he then saw fit to change his views, and cast his influence from that time on with the Republican party. He passed to his reward on November 19, 1887, having been preceded by his wife in 1886. The latter was the daughter of Judge Samuel Prather, a man widely known for his efficiency on the bench.

Milas and Nancy Lewman were the parents of five children, viz: Samuel P., deceased; Thomas J., our subject; Elizabeth R., wife of Phestus Bowen, of Charlestown township; Edith, wife of William P. Hughes, and Nancy, widow of James Smith.

Our subject was reared on the farm where he now lives. He helped to clear much of the land and had a hand in bringing a large part of it under cultivation. His boyhood experiences were not unlike those common to the times. He attended the district school in the winter time, and received a good common school education. Upon reaching maturity he was married to Mary E. Steelman, daughter of James Steelman. She was born at Cincinnati, Ohio, in 1854 and came to Indiana in 1856. Her father died May 5, 1909, in Charlestown township, having acquired the advanced age of ninety-five years.

Mr. Lewman and wife are the parents of two children: Cash A., born March 7, 1885, and Frank S., born October 14, 1887. The former has been joined in marriage to Susan M. Bottorff.

The religious affiliations of this family have been with the Christian denomination. Mr. Lewman is an elder in the Bethany church of Charlestown township, and has been for years superintendent of the Sunday school. In politics he is identified with the Republican party, but he has never aspired to office, feeling that his time was all needed in giving proper attention to his business affairs. He takes great pride in his home, making that the chief object of his thought and care. A visit to his residence will convince one at once that he has succeeded in this to a most satisfactory degree, having all the conveniences and improvements that are needed for the comforts of his remaining years.

EDWARD COVERT.

The history of this family presents the characteristics of industry, honesty, frugality and patriotism, all of which are strongly marked in Edward Covert, who is a native of Clark county, Indiana, where he was born November 20, 1843, being descended from a line of ancestors noted for an enterprising spirit that hesitated at no difficulties, however numerous and formidable.

Luke Covert, great-great-grandfather of our subject, was born in New Jersey, whither his ancestors had come when emigrating to America from Northern Holland. They sailed aboard the Puritan, which name was given the bay and river where the passengers landed in 1650 and founded the little town which afterward assumed the same name. Luke Covert ended his days in New Jersey, and was laid away in the land of his adoption. His son, Daniel Covert, great-grandfather of our subject, was a gunsmith in Washington's army, and contributed loyal and patriotic service to the cause of continental independence. His home lay in the neighborhood of historic Monmouth, famous as one of the spots upon which was waged the conflict in behalf of the American cause. In fact Daniel Covert owned part of the land on which the battle was fought.

After the close of the Revolutionary war the family removed to the West, emigrating first to Ohio, later to Kentucky, and finally coming to Clark county, Indiana, in 1797, where Daniel Covert died in 1803. His son, Peter Covert grandfather of our subject, resided in Clark county as a farmer for many years. He reached a ripe old age, going to his reward on April 15, 1857. He reared a large family, one of whom, Henry, was the father of our subject, and was married to Mary Cortner, January 5, 1843. To this union were born six children, ,as follows: Edward; Sarah, who became the wife of S. W. Evans; Elijah, of Jennings county, Indiana; Emaline, deceased wife of John W. Hanlin; Addie, born in 1856, wife of James W. Hart, living now in Scott county, and Julia, now deputy post mistress at Otisco, Indiana.

Our subject was reared upon the farm and received such education as was afforded by the district schools of the vicinity, taking later some work at the Sturgus Academy. While at the academy the Civil war was in progress and Edward joined the cause of the Union, in 1865 becoming a member of the One Hundred Forty-eighth Indiana Volunteer Infantry. He remained in the service till the close of the war, his principal duties consisting of guarding railroad bridges and sharing the vicissitudes incident to the life of the men who took up their station in behalf of the flag. The war being concluded, Mr. Covert returned to his home and embraced the opportunity afforded to continue his education at the Charlestown high school.

On December 26, 1872, our subject was joined in marriage to Mary C. Beckett, a most estimable young lady, members of whose family were pioneers in the county. She was called to her reward December 19, 1906, and was without children.

Mr. Covert has affiliated with the Democratic party and for many years had charge of the local post-office. He has also served as Justice of the Peace, for seven years. For twenty years he has had charge of the local railroad agency, and express agent for twenty-eight years. In connection with these duties he has carried on to a limited extent his trade as a cobbler.

He is a member of the Methodist church, taking an active part in the church and Sunday school work. He is especially fond of music, and on account of natural talent has been called on to look after the musical affairs pertaining to the church activities.

JOSEPH M. HAAS.

The biographies of the veterans of the Civil war are always interesting. This is due in part, no doubt, to the share they had in one of the mightiest conflicts of modern times, and also to the period of our country's history in which they grew to manhood. Here in the Middle West the life of the times preceding the rebellion seems more romantic and full of variety and incident than the years following the war and since those days are fast receding into the perspective of time, they are rapidly becoming surrounded with the twilight effect that lends charm to even the most commonplace of incidents.

On November 24, 1836, there was born in Lexington, Scott county, Indiana, Joseph M. Haas. His father, Ezra Haas, was born at Woodstock, Virginia, and came to Scott county, Indiana, when quite a young man. He was a tanner by trade and a very industrious citizen. He removed later, about 1850, to Clark county, where he ended his days. Joseph's mother, Mary (Schwitzer) Haas, was of Irish descent, and was the mother of nine children, only two of whom, our subject and a brother, James A., are surviving. Both of these sons participated in the Civil war, Joseph joining the Fourth Indiana Cavalry and James enlisting in the Twelfth Indiana Battery.

Our subject enlisted in 1862 and served until the close of the war. The pioneer experiences of his boyhood had developed in him the spirit of courage and presence of mind under danger and he went into the field of battle without hesitancy or thought of personal concern. He participated in many of the historic conflicts, among others being the ones at Chattanooga and Chickamauga. At Nashville he received a compound fracture in the left limb, which disabled him for a while, but he took his place among his comrades as soon as able. The cavalry to which he belonged became a part of the Army of the Cumberland and experienced the vicissitudes incident to the memorable campaigns waged by that noted body of men.

After the war closed Mr. Haas returned to the family homestead in Clark county and devoted himself to farming and stock raising. Through untiring industry and diligent application he has made for himself an attractive home in Charlestown township. This, with a small government pension, places within his reach the comforts of life and he is content to live out the remainder of his days in the sunshine of the old Hoosier state

Mr. Haas was never married and for many years made his home with one of his sisters. Although a Republican, he has made no effort to enter the political arena, being content to live the life of an exemplary citizen. He has always had a fondness for hunting and in early days when wild game was still abundant nothing gave him more satisfaction than to shoulder his rifle and take to the woods. At one time he made an overland trip to Missouri, and Iowa, and made hunting one of the features of the excursion. This experience afforded him much enjoyment, and one over which he delights to reflect.

As a member of the Grand Army of the Republic, Mr. Haas has shown the same genuine loyalty that has characterized him in all of his associations, and he holds a secure place in the esteem of neighbors and associates.

WILLIAM M. DEUSER.

William M. Deuser, of Charlestown, Clark county, is a man of some sixty-five years. All his life has been associated with the township in which he lives, and it is no exaggeration to say that he knows every nook and corner of it and every one of the older inhabitants. Through life he has worked hard and industriously and can now enjoy the eventide of life at the expense of very little energy. He is still robust and hearty, allowing for the advance of age.

William M. Deuser was born in Charlestown on June 6, 1843, being the son of Jacob and Barbara (Schleichten) Deuser. Both were native born Germans who about the year 1833 settled in Charlestown, and here they met one another and married. Jacob Deuser helped to build the Charlestown court house and upon its completion he moved onto a farm in the township a short distance from Charlestown. Here he and his wife lived the remainder of their lives. Mrs. Deuser survived her husband, her death taking place two years later. Ten children were born to them, of whom there are nine living, and all but one live in the vicinity of Charlestown. They are: George, William M., Christenia, Amelia, Maggie, Jacob, Jr., Charles, Joseph, Eva and Maggie, the latter (deceased). Jacob Deuser was a man who had the reputation of being a money maker. He owned at one time about three hundred acres of land. He afterwards went to Missouri but later returned to Charlestown, where he died. In religion he was a member of the Presbyterian church while his wife was a member of the Catholic faith. Jacob Deuser was all through life a Democrat in politics.

William M. Deuser was reared in and around Charlestown and labored there on his father's farm. He attended the country school and also school at Louisville and obtained a fair education. On reaching manhood he married Mary Lori, and one child, William, resulted from the marriage. William has now entered upon a successful career in the hardware business in Louisville, Kentucky. In after years he married secondly, Barbara Deutchman and to this union were born the following children: George, now in the flour business in Charlestown; Charles, a barber, in Chattanooga, Tennessee; Lillian Margaret, wife of Fred Lutz, of Charlestown; and Dortha. All belong to the Presbyterian church.

In politics our subject is a Democrat and an active and faithful party worker. During the Civil war period he was not inactive. When war was declared he volunteered and went into service as a carpenter in which capacity he served for about two years.

William M. Deuser owns fourteen acres of choice land just outside of Charlestown on which he resides. He has the reputation, as had his father before him, of being a good business man. He is a man of means and has been quite successful in his farming pursuits. He is an intelligent type of farmer. He has traveled extensively, and the impressions made upon him by the outside world have been turned to good account by his observant mind. The fact that his children are coming to the front in their vocations has added much to the happiness of his later years. Mrs. Deuser is a constant companion to her husband and her attention and help have been of much importance to him.

S. P. KELLY.

S. P. Kelly, farmer and notary public of Bethlehem township, Clark county, is a man of much influence and a widely respected resident of the district in which he lives. He is the descendant of an old Virginia family, one of whom in the person of his grandfather, Samuel Kelly, migrated to Kentucky, coming thence to Clark county, Indiana, where he settled and was the first man buried in Ross cemetery; his interment taking place on the 6th of November, 1806. The Kelly family were militant Whigs until the birth of the Republican party. Since that time all members of the family have consistently followed the fortunes of the party at present in power. S. P. Kelly has traveled outside his own state, is of an observant disposition, and, consequently, a cultured and well posted citizen. He has for many years been prominently connected with the most influential fraternal organizations of the state, and has a host of friends in fraternal circles and throughout Clark county.

The subject of our notice was born in Bethlehem township in the house in which he now lives on the 22d of November, 1850. He was the son of Samuel and Harriett Kelly, the latter a cousin of her husband. Samuel Kelly was born in Bethlehem township, Clark county, Indiana, and he grew up in the immediate neighborhood of Bethlehem township. Grandfather

Samuel Kelly was born in Virginia, and, as we have already stated, came to Kentucky and afterwards to Clark county, Indiana, where he entered land in quarter-section No. 35, southwest, township No. 2, range No. 9 east. Samuel and Harriett Kelly had the following children born to them: S. P. Kelly, John H., Emma and Harriett A. Our subject and his sister, Harriett A., are the only surviving members.

S. P. Kelly was reared on the farm and helped his parents in the farm work. In wintertime he attended the district school and got a fair common school education. He married Sarah A. Matthews, who was born in Bethlehem township on the 25th of April, 1853. Five children were born of their marriage as follows: Ellen M., who is the wife of Ira C. Dean, lives in Bethlehem township; Clara E. is the wife of Charles Jameson, of Bethlehem township; Hattie F. is unmarried and lives at home; Ira M. is also unmarried and lives at home. Hattie is a graduate of the district common school.

For seventeen years after his marriage our subject conducted a flour mill. He then came back on the family farm of one hundred and sixty acres which he now owns. He has been most successful in his farming pursuits. He is a respected member of the community and a trustee of the local Presbyterian church of which he and his family are active members. He is a member of the New Washington lodge, Free and Accepted Masons, No. 167. He belongs to Bethlehem Lodge, No. 498, Knights of Pythias, and the Red Men of the Abenaki Tribe, No. 367. S. P. Kelly and his wife are members of the Pocahontas Council, No. 260, and Mrs. Kelly is a member of the Pythian Sisters, No. 325, of which she is the treasurer. Our subject is a charter member of all the lodges with which he has been associated with the exception of the Red Men. He is a member of the K. of R. and S. since its inception. He became chief of records of the local Red Men lodge on the night of its initiation.

In politics S. P. Kelly follows the example of his family and is a staunch Republican. In local affairs he is a member of the Advisory Board and its secretary. He has been a notary public since July 1, 1890.

F. V. HOLLOWAY.

F. V. Holloway, of Bethlehem township, Clark county, is a well known farmer and a public man of worth and influence in the community. He has been for almost twenty-three years a resident of the county in which he lives, having come to Bethlehem township in the year 1885. Previous to that time he had spent his years in the state of Missouri, where he made a name for himself both in private and public life.

He was born in Cass county, Missouri, on the 27th of October, 1837, the son of Thomas and Martha (Secrest) Holloway. His father was born in Tennessee in 1809, and went to Missouri in 1834, remaining there until his death which occurred in 1895. Grandfather Holloway was an upright and honorable man and a native of Virginia of Scotch descent. Our subject's mother's family, the Secrests, were of German extraction, and natives of North Carolina. Martha Secrest married in Blount county, Tennessee, and went from there with her husband to Cass county, Missouri, in 1834. Eight children were born to them, seven of whom grew to maturity. The subject of our sketch, and two sisters are the surviving members of the family; one sister is married to a Mr. Foster in Missouri.

F. V. Holloway was reared upon his father's farm and assisted on the farm until his marriage, which took place in his twenty-second year. He received a common school education in the schools of his township in Missouri. He married Mary J. Cooper, of Missouri, and had a family of eight children. They are: James T., who died at the age of eight years; Ella F., who is the wife of James Hocker, of Missouri; Minnie, the wife of D. K. Elder, of Chicago, Illinois; Charles W., a resident of Kansas City, Missouri; May, who is the wife of Harry King, of Louisville, Kentucky; B. F. Holloway is a farmer in Bethlehem township; A. F. lives near New Washington, Clark county, and is a farmer; and W. G. is single and lives at the family residence. All received a good common school education. F. V. Holloway's first wife died in 1883, and he has since married three times. His second wife died in 1899, and his third in 1903. He had no children by either. He married Anna M. Robertson, his present wife, on the 14th of September, 1908. She was born in Jeffersonville, Indiana.

In his religious life F. V. Holloway has been a consistent member of the Presbyterian church since 1854, and is an elder in the local church in Bethlehem township. His wife is also a member of the same faith. Our subject is well known in Masonic circles and is a member of New Washington Lodge, No. 164, Free and Accepted Masons, having been a member for forty-nine years. He is also a member of Arcana Council, Harrisonville, Missouri, and is a member of the Royal Arch Chapter and the Gouley Commandery at Butler, Missouri. He served as master of Lodge No. 254, Free and Accepted Masons, at Butler, Missouri, for three years, and was district deputy grand master of Missouri for two years.

F. V. Holloway came from Missouri to Clark county with his family in 1885. In politics he has been a life-long Democrat. He was County Treasurer of Bates county, Missouri, for four years, two terms. In 1898 he was elected Justice of the Peace of Bethlehem township and is serving in that capacity at the present time. The township usually is known to go Republican by twenty-eight votes, but, nevertheless, our subject was elected by a majority of eighteen although a Democrat. This, needless to say, speaks well for his popularity and worth as a citizen. He owns four hundred and eighty-three acres of prime land in the township which is worth a good figure. He is a stockholder in the State Bank at New Washington.

Turning back to the public record of our subject in Missouri, it might be mentioned that he was elected Treasurer of Bates county, Missouri, by a majority of two hundred votes on his first term. On his second term he got the appointment by a seven hundred and fifty majority. And this although the county is known to be Republican. He was candidate for Commissioner from the district on two occasions.

F. V. Holloway is now advanced in years and he can point with pride to his record as a man, as a father of a family, and as a public spirited citizen.

JAMES A. BAIRD.

James A. Baird, who was part owner of the Baird Woolen Mills, came to Owen township, Clark county, with his father as a boy. From that time onward, through the years of his life, he was the recipient of his neighbors' friendship and good will. He established himself firmly in the industrial life of the community, and was a man of uprightness and probity; and one who never swerved from the settled path of duty.

The subject of our sketch was born in Lexington, Kentucky, in the year 1828. At the time of their arrival in Clark county his father built a woolen mill at the juncture of the cross-roads a short distance from the present family residence. James A. assisted his father in running the mill from his boyhood and made the venture a pronounced success. The mill was known as the Baird woolen mill and, in later years, after the death of the elder Baird, it was changed to Baird Brothers, the name by which it went ever afterwards.

James A. Baird married Martha Burton on the 19th of February, 1868, and a very happy domestic life was entered upon. Mrs. Baird is still living and is a comparatively young woman. She comes of an old and respected family, the Burtons of Virginia. She was born in Henry county, Kentucky, on May 9, 1852, and was the daughter of Laban and Sarah (Harris) Burton. Her parent, Laban Burton, was born in Virginia in 1807, came with his family to Kentucky, and lived in Henry and Madison counties. He married Sarah Harris, of Henry county, Kentucky, and had eight children, four of whom were living in 1909. They are: Everrel, wife of Russel Brent, living in Owen county, Kentucky; Sarah, wife of T. J. McMillin, living in Illinois; Linzey, living in Rosedale, Indiana, and the wife of the subject of our sketch. Mrs. Martha Baird was reared upon her father's farm and on arrival at a proper age attended private school and got a common school education.   During her married life she has reared a family of nine children.   Almost all are now married and in prosperous circumstances.   They are: Sarah A., born January 14, 1869, who is the wife of Marshall Cravens and is living in North Carolina; Mary S., born July 22, 1870, is the wife of John Goforth, living in Clark county; Maggie B., born December 22, 1871, married Jesse L. Roberts, of Henry county, Kentucky; Carrie G., born September 12, 1873, lives in Kentucky and is unmarried; Relda A., born September 17, 1875, is the wife of Frank Stroker, of Henry county, Kentucky; William A., born October 28, 1877, married Claudie Dellinger (Mrs. William A. Baird was the daughter of William S. Dellinger); Cora E. was born October 29, 1879, and married Joseph Green, of Henry county, Kentucky; Daisy H. was born September 9, 1882, and married William Dowden, of Henry county, Kentucky, and John G., born December 11, 1888, is unmarried and lives with his mother. All the girls, with the exception of Carrie G. and Mary S. were teachers. Both the boys and the girls were high school graduates; John G. was a graduate of the common school. Mrs. Baird and her son attend the local Methodist Episcopal church.

The Baird farm consists of one hundred and twenty acres of land in sections No. 27 and 28, Owen township.   Mrs. Baird is a woman of a charitable disposition and as a neighbor she is considerate for others and hospitable. James A. Baird died December 11, 1904.

EDWARD S. PERNETT.

Edward S. Pernett, postmaster and well known business man of Bethlehem, Bethlehem township, has made a name and a reputation both as a citizen and as a progressive business man. Born in the year 1860 he is but forty-eight years of age and has been connected with the business life of Bethlehem since his twenty-third year. His career during the past twenty-five years might well be called a series of victories over the usual obstacles which face the business man relying on his own resources and with very little capital. Edward S. Pernett started with a capital of something like eighty dollars; he is today worth thousands.   His success in life has been due to nothing beyond the efforts which he put forth and the success-making characteristics which have marked him.

The subject of this notice was born on the 23d of January, 1860, in Bethlehem, and was the son of Samuel and Naomi (Bowman) Pernett. Samuel Pernett was born in Mount Sterling, Switzerland county, Indiana, and was brought at the age of four years to Bethlehem.   He attended the common schools of the township and afterwards graduated at Hanover College.   At the age of twenty-four he entered the merchandise business and remained in that business in Bethlehem until his death, which occurred on the 19th of October, 1873. He was a successful man and became wealthy. His father, David Pernett, was a merchant and a hotel keeper. The business interests which he controlled were burned down in a disasterous conflagration which occurred in 1854.

Samuel Pernett married Naomi Bowman in his twenty-second year and became the father of Edward S., David E., Charles E., John S., Emma, and Eva Pernett.

Edward S. Pernett received a business training in his father's store and obtained a common school education. In the year 1883 he started in business in Bethlehem for himself in the general mercantile line on a shanty boat on the Ohio river with a stock worth eighty dollars. He prospered and added to his stock and later went into a building of his own with stock worth six thousand dollars. He was most successful in his new place of business and remained there until the 6th of November, 1908, when the place was destroyed by fire.

In the year 1884 the subject of our sketch married Estella A. Stewart who was born in Bethlehem township. Mrs. Pernett in her young days had a common school education and got a good home rearing. She bore her husband two children. Nellie was born in 1886, and is the wife of Halstead Murret, of Indianapolis. Inez, born in the year 1894, is a graduate of the common school and is unmarried. Edward S. Pernett, his wife, and his family are members of the Methodist Episcopal church and are active in church work. He is trustee of the local Methodist Episcopal church. He is active also in fraternal affairs and is a member of the New Washington Lodge, No. 167, Free and Accepted Masons, and the Knights of Pythias. He is a member of the Red Men's lodge at Bethlehem. He built the local Pythian hall in the year 1902, being a charter member of same. In political affairs he is a Republican and has been active in local affairs. He served three terms as Trustee of his township. He is the present postmaster of Bethlehem, an office which he has filled for the past sixteen years.

Edward S. Pernett is part owner of the steamer "Alma" plying up and down the river, and at the organization of the State Bank at New Washington he became a large stock holder. He owns real estate at Elwood, Indiana, and he has also invested money in other interests of a minor character. As an important and trustworthy citizen he has been called upon at various times to act as administrator of several substantial estates and he has always acted in this capacity in creditable and satisfactory manner. He is an administrator of the J. M. Stewart estate. Mr. Stewart being our subject's father-in-law.

ALLEN A. GILTNER.

Allen A. Giltner, of Bethlehem township, Clark county, needs no introduction to the people of the township in which he was born and reared and among whom he has lived, and very little to the people of Clark county in general. He is now in the seventy-fifth year of his existence and his record as a farmer is one to be proud of. He came of a sturdy race of farmers, agriculturists in Kentucky and Tennessee, and he brought from them all their tenacity of purpose and all their shrewdness and natural ability in grappling with land problems. Allen Giltner, living in semi-retirement under the roof that sheltered his father and mother before him, has the satisfaction of feeling that his present state of security has been obtained at the price of his own self-sacrificing efforts and in spite of obstacles that would dishearten one less courageous.

The subject of our sketch was born on the farm on which he now lives in Bethlehem township, section No. 1, north range 10 east, on the 6th of February, 1833, and was the son of Daniel and Elnora (Cummings) Giltner. Daniel Giltner was a native-born Kentuckian, the Giltner family coming from Pennsylvania to Kentucky, where Daniel Giltner was born in the January of 1802. Mrs. Giltner's family, the Cummings, came from Tennessee, and her mother and father married in Clark county and lived on the land which now belongs to our subject. Mrs. Daniel Giltner was born in 1820. She and her husband reared six children, four of whom are now living, in 1909. They are: Allen A., Nathan, Sarilda (deceased), Thomas, Huldah and Stephen.

Allen A. Giltner was reared upon the farm on which he now resides and on arrival at the proper age he helped to clear and improve the family farm. His education was rather limited as there were no free schools, but he, however, managed to obtain a fair school education and studied algebra. He remained upon the farm until his twenty-first year with his parents, and at that time began to farm his share of the land. He married Margaret J. Matthews in May, 1857. Mrs. Giltner was born about September 28, 1836, and was a native of the township. She bore her husband one child that died in infancy. Mrs. Giltner died on the 2d of August, 1884. As their only child died in infancy they adopted Myra M. Conn, who is now the housekeeper and careful attendant of the subject of our sketch. Allen A. Giltner rented land for some time after his marriage and later bought the old homestead of one hundred and sixty acres which is worth sixty dollars an acre. He has been very prosperous; in recent years he has rented his land. He is a Republican and has been somewhat active in politics. He served as Assessor of the township for sixteen years. He is a man of well ordered life and religious convictions, and, though he is not connected with any church, he favors the Presbyterian belief.

ALBERT R. MILES.

Albert R. Miles is a prosperous farmer and an influential citizen of Bethlehem township, Clark county, where he is known as a raiser of stock and a farmer who has made the most of the possibilities of his large farm. He comes of German stock, his father having come from the Fatherland in his young days to the United States like hundreds of other German youths eager to become rich and opulent in this western land. On his mother's side our subject is of French extraction, and, as he combines within him German and French ancestry, he inherits many of the welcome traits of both races. Albert R. Miles has reared a sturdy and intellectual family and in the person of his wife he has a life companion of even temperament and affability.

The subject of our sketch was born in Jefferson county, Indiana, on the 22d of November, 1855, and was the son of John R. and Rebecca F. (Coughlin) Miles. John R. Miles was born in Germany in 1822, and left his native land ostensibly to avoid service in the German army and came to America. He came up the Mississippi and Ohio rivers and landed in Cincinnati, Ohio, and later came to Jefferson county, Indiana, where he lived until his death. He was a blacksmith by trade and later in life became a prosperous farmer. Rebecca F. Coughlin was born in Louisville, Jefferson county, Georgia, on the 13th of November, 1833. Mrs. John R. Miles bore her husband ten children, seven of whom are now living in 1909. Mary is the wife of C. H. Jones, of Kentucky; Henry is deceased, having been killed by a train in California; Albert R. is the subject of our sketch; Louisa is the wife of Andrew MaNaugh, of Jefferson county, Indiana; Fred W. Miles is in Kansas and is unmarried; Lana is the wife of N. D. Rankins, of Jefferson county, Indiana; Herman and Iva are deceased; L. B. Miles lives in Kansas, and C. H. Miles lives in Clark county, Indiana.

Albert R. Miles was reared on the farm in Jefferson county and helped his parents in the farm duties. At the proper age he entered the district school and got a good common school education. At the age of twenty-two years he started out for himself. He worked for some time by the month in a peach orchard and made seventy-five cents and a dollar a day. At the time of his marriage he had saved three hundred dollars. This event occurred in 1881, when he espoused Ellen Giltner, a daughter of Enoch and Malinda (Hutsel) Giltner. Mrs. Miles was educated in the county schools and obtained a sound common school training. She and her husband have had three children born to them. They are: E. J. Miles, born January 9, 1886, who graduated from the common schools, No. 3, of Bethlehem township and from the Borden College, after which he entered the State University at Bloomington, graduating at that institution with the degree of Bachelor of Arts. He then studied at Swathmore College, Pennsylvania, where he obtained the degree of Master of

56

Arts. He is now entered at the Chicago University, and this is his first year at that institution. Irvin R. Miles, the third child, was born on March 31, 1897; Earl S., second child, born July 29, 1888, is a graduate of the common schools.

The subject of our sketch owns five hundred and fourteen acres of choice land in Bethlehem township situated on the banks of the picturesque Ohio river about twenty miles below Madison. He and his wife and family are members of the Christian church at Painville, Jefferson county, Indiana. Albert R. is a member of the Pythian Lodge No. 13, at Jeffersonville, Indiana. In politics he is a Democrat. When the State Bank at New Washington was organized in 1908, our subject, who subscribed for a substantial amount of stock in the undertaking, was chosen to be a member of its first directorate, and is still director in the bank.

STEPHEN H. GILTNER.

Stephen H. Giltner, of Bethlehem township, Clark county, is a substantial farmer, and a member of the Giltner family, whose name has been entwined with the history of Bethlehem township and the county for many years. He owns one of the best stocked and most highly cultivated farms in the township, brought to its present high state of efficiency through his painstaking efforts. His farm embraces one hundred and ninety-eight acres in all. In everyday life Stephen H. Giltner is a simple and unassuming member of the community, who is content to labor as best he may for the interests of himself and his family.

He was born in the township in which he still lives, on the 19th of December, 1853, and was the son of Enoch and Malinda (Hutsel) Giltner. Enoch Giltner was born in Kentucky in 1822, and came in 1826 with his parents to Bethlehem township, where they settled in the vicinity of Otto, and where he was reared. Abraham Giltner, our subject's grandfather, bought the farm that is now owned by the Henry Giltner heirs. He married in Kentucky, in which state he afterwards died. His son, Enoch was raised in Bethlehem township, and received a common school education. In after years he married Malinda Hutsel and their entire life was spent in Bethlehem township. Enoch Giltner was a devout and active member of the Christian church, and was an elder in the local congregation of that faith for many years. He was a Republican in politics and an industrious and wealthy farmer who, at one time owned two hundred and forty acres. He reared a family of eleven children; the living members, all of whom but two reside in Clark county, are: Jacob, Stephen H., subject of this review; Ellen, John, Alvin and Stella. Enoch Giltner died in Bethlehem township in 1899, in February of that year, and his wife in July, 1905.

Stephen H. Giltner was reared in the neighborhood in which he lives, and attended the district school in early life during the winter months and obtained a fair common school education, considering the school facilities of that the time. He remained at home until his twenty-second year, at which time he went to Illinois and worked for two years as a farm hand, after which he returned to his native township. On the 1st of March, 1882, he married Anna E. Taff, a native of Clark county. She was born on the 13th of January, 1859, and was the daughter of J. S. Taff, who was by profession a school teacher. Mrs. Giltner attended the district school and passed through the Normal Training School at New Washington, and became a teacher. Their marriage brought Stephen and Mrs. Giltner two children, one of whom died in infancy, and the other, Frank L., born February 25, 1888, a graduate of the New Albany high school, is a teacher in the township.

The Giltners are members of the Christian church of Bethel, Stephen H. being an elder in the same, as well as a liberal supporter. In politics Mr. Giltner is a Republican, but he has always kept himself from active participation in political matters, contenting himself with giving his vote and his sympathies to the party of his choice.

The Giltner family live in the comfortable farm house on their farm, where friends and acquaintances are ever assured of a warm welcome and genuine hospitality.

FRANK X. KERN.

Frank X. Kern, now of Indianapolis, Indiana, and a former merchant of Jeffersonville, this state, also of the former city, was born at Wurtemburg, Germany, December 3, 1850, a descendant of a prominent and honored old family of that province, where he remained under the parental roof in his youth, and where he received a good elementary education in his native language, remaining there until 1864, when he formed a small colony and sailed for the United States, leaving the old homestead and parents and friends behind to seek a home and live from under monarchial rule. He arrived at Louisville, Kentucky, the same year, where he commenced the struggle of life on his own account. He soon adopted the American ideas and grew to manhood, enjoying the free privilege of an American boy, taking an interest in all that pertained to state and national affairs, and he has ever since been proud of his American home, his adopted country, to which he has ever been loyal, and he has never since visited his Fatherland. His parents have since passed to their reward. His father, a well-to-do man, engaged in the manufacturing of chinaware, having been in business for many years, and he was well known and highly respected by all. The original Kern family were Catholics in their religious belief, but the younger generations left that faith and became Presbyterians, Methodists and other denominational adherents.

When Frank X. Kern arrived in Louisville, he was fourteen years old, and he first worked in a confectionary, where he had a splendid opportunity for picking up American ideas. Later he began the barber business, learning the trade thoroughly, becoming a proficient artist in this line, and he remained in Louisville until 1869, when he went to Jeffersonville and continued his business, soon building up a large practice. During that time he was patronized by many distinguished men, one particular customer being Hon. John Reed, Sr., who was a prominent lawyer for thirty years, and one of the leading men of the state. Mr. Kern continued his business at Jeffersonville in a most successful manner until 1882, when he engaged in the retail grocery business, building up a liberal patronage, continued until 1896, when he took a partner and embarked in the wholesale grocery business, which was continued successfully for a period of two years, when he sold out and in the same year came to Indianapolis and again engaged in the retail grocery business in which he continued a few years.

When Mr. Kern came to Jeffersonville in 1869, he found a thrifty little town, which had just begun to develop, and being able to see the great future possibilities of the place, he joined the ranks of progressive citizens and helped push all enterprises. In politics he chose the principles of Democracy, of which he has ever since been a strong supporter, and while in Jeffersonville he was a conspicuous figure in all local organizations. He was elected and very ably served two terms as City Councilman, and later he was a candidate before the nominating convention for City Treasurer. He was regarded by the leaders of the party as a strong supporter and good campaigner. Through his political activity and business enterprises he became well known throughout Clark county, where his integrity and honor are above reproach.

Mr. Kern was married at Jeffersonville in 1873 to Louisa Pfau. She was born in the same province in Germany that Mr. Kern came from. She came to America with her brothers and sisters. Her parents died in the Fatherland. Her father was connected with lumbering and logging. He was well known in his community and highly respected there. Mrs. Kern's brothers and sisters are: George, William, Caroline, who married in this country, her husband being Herman Gallrein. These three children all reside in Jeffersonville. Louisa, the fourth child, is the wife of our subject; Christian lives in Chicago, where Lewis also resides; Jacob is a resident of Louisville, Kentucky.

To Mr. and Mrs. Frank X. Kern five interesting children have been born, namely: John A. is in the money-lending business in Louisville; Otto P. is a bookkeeper in the Union National Bank, in Indianapolis; Louisa, now Mrs. Malcomb C. Porter. Mr. Porter is in the real estate business in Indianapolis; Clara married Lester Van Cleve, of the Indianapolis Star; Lillian is still a member of the family circle.

Mr. Kern has given all his children a liberal education and they are all fairly well situated in reference to this world's affairs.

WILLIAM H. BARRATT.

William H. Barratt, of Charlestown township, Clark county, is a native-born resident of the township in which he lives. He has been known all through his long life as an honest and industrious farmer. He passed through the Civil war and who, though wounded in the conflict, still lives in the ripeness of his years.

He was born in Charlestown township on the 27th of February, 1840, the son of George and Anna (Hultz) Barratt. George Barratt came from England with his wife, who was also a native of that country. He and his wife landed in New York and he began his career in the United States as a farmer. He finally came from New York to Indiana, and on a farm in Charlestown township he lived the remainder of his life. George Barratt and his wife were the parents of eleven children, six of whom are living at the present time.

William H. Barratt was reared upon the farm in Charlestown township, where in summer time he helped his parents, and attended school in winter. He remained under the parental roof until 1862, at which time he enlisted in Company I, Eighty-first Indiana Volunteers, remaining with his regiment until 1865 or the close of the war. His company was on the field at the battle of Perryville, Kentucky, but did not figure in the engagement. At Stone River, however, members of this company were active participants and again at Atlanta, Georgia. His regiment then returned to Nashville, Tennessee, where they engaged and dispersed the enemy. In one engagement Mr. Barratt was wounded on the second day of the fight, and had to be taken from the field, and was accordingly unable to join his regiment until their return to Nashville, Tennessee. He was discharged in June, 1865, and received a pension. Upon his discharge he returned home to Clark county and remained with his parents for two years. In 1868 he married Sarah Ann Weir, who was born in Washington county, Indiana, on the 6th of December, 1847. She was the daughter of David Weir, who was a farmer. To William H. Barratt and his wife were born the following children: John S., born December 14, 1869; Charles O., born April 15, 1871; Rosa, on April 18, 1874; William, on January 3, 1878;

Cora, on October 16, 1883, and Dora, November 13, 1887. Dora graduated from the common schools of Clark county in the year 1904.

Mr. Barratt, his wife and the members of his family are all members of the Methodist Episcopal church at Otisco. Politically William H. Barratt is a Republican and although a sincere admirer of his party, he has never been very active in local political affairs. He is a popular member of the Grand Army of the Republic, Post No. 402, at Henryville, Indiana. His farm consists of ninety-two acres and is in grant No. 93, Charlestown township. He has lived on this farm since his marriage, and it owes its present prosperous condition to his efforts.

SAMUEL D. SULLIVAN.

Samuel D. Sullivan, of Charlestown township, Clark county, is the owner of one hundred and nine acres of land, and a farmer whose reputation is of the highest. During the period of his life in Charlestown township he has achieved a high standing as a citizen. He was born in Scott county, Indiana, on the 4th of February, 1861, being the son of William C. and Mary (Bridgewater) Sullivan. Grandfather Dennis Sullivan was a native of Maryland, who emigrated to Trimble county, Kentucky. He sojourned for a few years in Indiana and later returned to Kentucky, where he died at the advanced age of eighty years. His son, our subject's father, William C. Sullivan, was born in Kentucky, and on coming to Indiana, was bound to Elisha English, of Scott county, with whom he remained until his eighteenth year. From that time until his marriage he hired out by the month with neighboring farmers in Scott county. After his marriage he went to Missouri, traveling overland in a wagon, and sometime afterwards returned to Indiana. In 1871 he came to Clark county, where he settled and remained until his death. He and his wife reared a large family of fourteen children, of whom eight boys and one girl grew to maturity.

Samuel D. Sullivan was reared on the parental farm and attended the district school, receiving a common school education. At the age of twenty-one years he started out for himself as a carpenter and a farm worker. His marriage to Eveline Campbell, daughter of Richard and Priscilla (Barratt) Campbell, took place on December 21, 1892. Mrs. Sullivan was born in Charlestown township on grants Nos. 192 and 193, where she now lives, on October 26, 1869. She was educated in the district school and obtained a fair education. Samuel D. Sullivan and his wife have had two children, Elsie, born November 24, 1893, and Rubie, born May 23, 1899. All the family are members of the Methodist Episcopal church at Otisco, of which our subject is one of the trustees.

In politics Mr. Sullivan is an unswerving Republican, although he has never taken a hand in local politics preferring to lead a private life. His farm embraces the old homestead of Mrs. Sullivan's parents, and their land, which amounted to sixty-two acres. The farm land is as good as any in the township, and is valued at about forty dollars an acre. Under the supervision and painstaking efforts the land has been brought to the highest point of perfection.

CHARLES P. MELOY, M. D.

Dr. Charles P. Meloy, physician and surgeon, of Otisco, Clark county, Indiana, is but forty-eight years of age and a comparatively young man in the medical profession yet he has succeeded in building for himself a large and lucrative practice at Otisco. He is a man who is well equipped for his life work, having had the advantage of an education and training in medicine of the highest order. He is a college and university graduate and to his profession, apart from his training, he has brought inherent natural ability of a more than average depth. In public life he has not been inactive and he is a figure of some prominence in all township and county gatherings of a civic nature. He was born on the 27th of September, 1860, in Charlestown township, Clark county, the son of John Q. and Cynthia (Campbell) Meloy. The Campbells, his mother's family, were prosperous pioneers in Clark county.

Dr. Charles P. Meloy was the third member of a family of nine children, three boys and six girls. At the age of six years he became a resident of Charlestown, and here he entered upon his school studies. His teachers were Kate Mitchell and Marion Leiter. Having completed his school course at Charlestown, he entered Hanover College in 1876, where he spent two years, leaving there in 1878. In 1879 he took a sophomore course at Depauw University, and entered the office of Dr. James E. Oldham in 1879, and there commenced the study of medicine. After one year with his preceptor he entered the Ohio Medical College at Cincinnati for one term, 1880 to 1881. He then went into the grocery business to obtain money to pursue his medical studies and he later went west and finally completed his medical course at the Louisville Medical College. In 1896-97 he began the practice of medicine and moved to Otisco, where he has practiced ever since.

Doctor Meloy is well versed in fraternal work and believes in fraternal organization as a potent agency for good in the community. He is a member of the Independent Order of Odd Fellows and the Knights of Pythian lodges at Charlestown. He is a past grandmaster in the Independent Order of Odd Fellows. He also belongs to the Modern Woodmen, and was the first head consul at its inception in 1903, and carries insurance in the organization.

Being a Republican he has served as chairman and secretary of the Republican Central Committee, and has been a candidate for Sheriff and Joint-Senatorship. As a Republican he is a man to be reckoned with in the political life of the party in Clark county.

Doctor Meloy married Anna Seward and three children have been born to them. Cora M., born November 24, 1897; Martin R., born September 27, 1900, and Fay, who was born June 17, 1906.

Doctor Meloy is a lover of outdoor sports and pastimes, and a good horseman; he is the possessor of two good horses.

SARGENT W. EVANS.

Sargent W. Evans is an old and respected native-born citizen of Otisco, Clark county. He comes of a Welsh family that settled in North Carolina in 1806 in the personage of his grandfather and grandmother Evans. He owes his present wealth and social position solely to his own individual efforts.

The citizen of Otisco, of whom we speak, was born in the town of which he is a resident on the 11th of October, 1843, and was the son of Absalom and Mary (Gunter) Evans. Samuel Evans, grandfather of our subject, married and brought his young wife from Wales, Britain, to North Carolina in 1806. They were not well supplied with worldly goods, and Samuel lived the remainder of his life in North Carolina. After his death his wife and family came to Clark county, Indiana, and settled in Charlestown in 1831. Mrs. Samuel Evans afterwards died in the neighborhood of what is now Otisco. To Grandfather Evans and his wife were born the following family: Sargent, Solomon, Absalom, Robert, Rachael, Elizabeth and Mary.

Absalom Evans was single when he came to Clark county. Here he married Mary Gunter, who was born in Kanawha county, West Virginia, and who came with her father, William Gunter, when a child and settled in Charlestown township. Absalom Evans was a farmer and reared eleven children. They were: John, Sarah E., Eliza E., Sargent W., Mary E., Martha A., James C., Zerilda C., Perlina, Hannah H. and Alice E. There are but four living in 1909, all of whom live in Otisco.

Sargent W. Evans was reared on his father's farm on which when old enough he helped, occasionally going to school. His father died when he was but fourteen years old, and though he was not yet eighteen at the outbreak of the Civil war, he enlisted in Company B, Eighty-first Indiana Regiment, under Captain A. J. Howard, of Jeffersonville, Indiana. He received his baptism of fire at the engagement at Perryville, Kentucky, on the 8th of October, 1862, and remained in the vicinity of the Cumberland district until May, 1863, when he was discharged, owing to disability. He returned home, where he remained until February, 1865, when he re-enlisted, this time in the One Hundred and Forty-eighth Indiana Regiment, in which he served until the close of the war. He then returned to his native Clark county, where he still lives. On the 21st of February, 1867, his marriage to Sarah E. Covert took place. His wife was born in Oregon township, June 22, 1845, and was the daughter of Henry and Mary Covert. Mrs. Evans went to the district school in her township and obtained a fair education. At the time of their marriage Sargent W. Evans and his wife were not in good financial circumstances. He built a house previous to his marriage on his father's farm, near Otisco, and there he and his wife lived until 1872, when he removed to Otisco. In Otisco he and his brother, James C., built the store building in 1872, where he now does business, and, having borrowed one thousand five hundred dollars to start them, they ran the store jointly until 1876, when our subject bought out his brother's interest. On November 26, 1908, Sargent W. Evans celebrated the thirty-sixth year of his business life in his store. To Mr. and Mrs. Evans the following children were born: Lillie D., born on May 16, 1870; Henry C., born December 19, 1871; W. W. Evans, born October 25, 1873; C. M. Evans, born August 19, 1875; Richard, on December 6, 1879; Harriett B., on April 6, 1881, and Julia on March 1, 1883. Richard is the only deceased member of the family, his death occurring on the 3d of August, 1884.

Sargent W. Evans since he became active in the life of Otisco has been a money maker and something of a benefactor to the town. He built a cooper shop, which in 1876 was destroyed by fire. In 1896 he built a fine flouring mill which ran successfully for nine years, at which time it was also destroyed by fire. In 1902 he erected a canning factory, in which tomatoes, principally, are canned, and which accordingly gives the neighboring farmers a local market for products of this kind. Our subject in addition to his own business concern superintends this industry himself. He is a Knight of the Golden Cross in fraternal life, and carries insurance in the order of which he is a prominent local member. In politics he is a Democrat, though he has never held any political office. He was a candidate for the office of Sheriff of Clark county on his party's ticket, but was defeated for the nomination. At the November election of 1908 he supported William Jennings Bryan for the third time for the Presidency.

CHARLES M. BOTTORFF, M. D.

The name of Dr. Charles M. Bottorff, of Charlestown, Clark county, is almost synonymous with a high degree of medical skill and with accuracy in the compounding of drugs and in the making-up of prescriptions. Doctor Bottorff has been a medical practitioner in Charlestown for very many years and the years in their onward course have seen him achieve a standard of success commensurate with his ability. His drug-store, to which he has given much of his time and attention, is always replete with an up-to-date stock of merchandise.

Dr. Charles M. Bottorff was born in Washington township, Clark county, Indiana, on the 1st of October, 1860, and was the son of Cyrus and Eliza Josephine (McGee) Bottorff. Cyrus Bottorff was also a native of Clark county, but his father, John Bottorff, was a native of Pennsylvania, who migrated to Kentucky, and thence to Clark county, Indiana, at a very early date. John Bottorff reared a large family and was twice married. His son, Cyrus, was born in Clark county. He had three children: William P., a farmer of Washington township; Charles M., and Nora, who is single, and who lives at the edge of Charlestown.

Doctor Bottorff was reared upon the parental farm and received his education principally in winter time. In the summer months farm work demanded his attention. In this manner he attended the district school in Washington township until his nineteenth year. In 1880 he entered Hanover College, and emerged a graduate in 1886, with the Bachelor of Arts degree. In the spring of 1887, he entered the Kentucky School of Medicine from where he graduated in June, 1888, with the degree of Medical Doctor. In the fall of 1888 he began the practice of medicine in two different places, and in 1890 bought a stock of drugs in Charlestown, and in connection with this store he practiced ever since, gradually devoting the greater part of his time to his drug business.

On the 6th of June, 1890, he married Katie Piatt, a native of Boone county, Kentucky. Miss Piatt had formerly been a classmate and a co-graduate of Doctor Bottorff, at the Hanover College. Eight children have been born to them, five of whom are now living.

Doctor Bottorff and his wife and family are members of the Presbyterian church, and are actively interested in church work. He is a member of the Knights of Pythias. He was also a member of the United Order of the Golden Cross, an organization which has an insurance feature, and in which he carries a substantial policy on his life. In civic and social affairs he is well to the fore in Charlestown and vicinity.

D. H. COOMBS, M. D.

Dr. D. H. Coombs is a well known figure in the daily life of Charlestown, Clark county, Indiana, and, we might add that the name of Coombs has been inseparably associated with the medical profession in Charlestown for nearly sixty years. His father, whose death took place in 1896, was for many years Charlestown's premier physician, and an esteemed, respected and genial citizen.

Dr. D. H. Coombs has inherited all the professional ability of his father and has also had the advantage of the rapid strides and advancement made in the therapeutic and surgical sciences in recent years. Doctor Coombs is a man well fitted in temperament and training for his life work, and he has already a reputation which extends beyond the borders of Clark county.

He was born in Charlestown, Indiana, on October 17, 1870, the son of Dr. D. H. and Sarah (Goodwin) Coombs. His father, Dr. D. H. Coombs, senior, was born in the township in 1824 and died in the year 1896. The late Doctor Coombs was a graduate of Jeffersonville Medical College. He was a first-class doctor and was a practitioner in Charlestown for years. He was well-to-do and prominent in local affairs. He was a Republican in politics and an influential member of the Masonic fraternity. Our subject's mother's family were also old and esteemed residents of Clark county and prosperous citizens. Dr. D. H. Coombs was twice married. Seven children born of his first marriage survived infancy; three of whom still live, namely: Amos, who lives in Vincennes, is a traveling salesman; Jesse is the wife of Walter Bowen, of Charlestown, and D. H. is the third.

Dr. D. H. Coombs attended the graded schools at Charlestown, and completed the course there. He went from there to Hanover College, where he took a three years' literary course in 1888. He then entered the Louisville Medical College, graduating in 1894. He at once began to practice as an assistant to his father, and remained in that role until 1896, when his father died. Since then he has practiced with growing success on his own account. In 1902 his marriage to Mayme Beeler took place. His wife is the daughter of a prominent merchant, George T. Beeler. Mrs. Coombs received her education at Oxford, Ohio, and in the schools of Charlestown. To their marriage has been born one child, Margaret, born February 26, 1906. Doctor and Mrs. Coombs and their little one lead a very happy domestic life, and are influential in social circles in Charlestown.

Doctor Coombs has for years been active in fraternal work. He is a member of the Masonic fraternity; prominent in the Knights of Pythias, and a past chancellor of that influential order; he is also a member of the Modern Woodmen. In all the orders with which he is associated he has a great many staunch friends. In the political world the doctor as a member of the Republican party has taken quite an animated interest in the local political arena, and were political preferment to hold a place in his ambitions at any time, there is hardly a doubt but that they would be swiftly realized. Doctor Coombs is a member of the Christian church congregation. He is a very active man and popular in his profession, and one whose disposition gains for him the confidence of all. He is a member of the Clark County and American Medical societies, and is a past presdent of the former. He is as yet a young man, and judged by present standards, his future success seems to be assured.

JAMES HOWARD.

James Howard, of Charlestown, Clark county, Indiana, was a well known citizen of the community in which he lived a long and upright life, which has now closed. Few men in Charlestown were more widely known or had a wider circle of friends and acquaintances. His career was one in which the characteristics of industry and honesty were admirably blended, and in such a way as to command the respect of all classes. He died in Charlestown May 7, 1909, in his eighty-fourth year of his life, of which all but the first ten years were spent in Charlestown.

He was born in Jefferson county, Kentucky, on the 22d of March, 1826, and was the son of George and Catherine (Hoke) Howard. George Howard was of English descent, and a native of Maryland. He came to Indiana with his family in the year 1836, where he remained ever afterwards. George Howard's wife's family, the Hokes, are presumed to be of Pennsylvanian origin.

James Howard was reared on the family farm and was of much assistance to his parents, obtaining such education as was to be had at the neighboring schools in his day. In the year 1849 he married Marietta Fry, and after a happy married life his wife died in the year 1888. They had five children, namely: Amanda C., George F., James N., Laura and Eva. Two years afterwards, on January 8, 1890, our subject married Mrs. Anna Hikes, widow of George G. Hikes, and a member of an old and illustrious New England family. The second Mrs. Howard's maiden name was Putnam. She was the daughter of Elbridge G. and Eunice (Wolton) Putnam. The Putnam family came to Salem, Massachusetts, from across the broad Atlantic about the year 1634. The American descendant of the family was named John Putnam. The Putnam ancestry came down to Mrs. Howard through successive sons: Thomas Putnam, who was a son of John; Edward, a son of Thomas; Isaac, a son of Edward; Nathan, a son of Isaac. Zadock Putnam was the great-grandfather of Mrs. Howard and was one of those who figured prominently in the Revolutionary war, and fought at the battle of Lexington. Elbridge, Mrs. Howard's father, was the son of John Putnam, and a grandson of Zadock. Mrs. Howard came with her father to Louisville, Kentucky, in the year 1838, and lived there with him until his removal to Kankakee county, Illinois, where he farmed until his death. Mrs. Howard attended the schools in Louisville, where she obtained a good education and was afterwards a teacher for a short time. In 1856 she married George G. Hikes. She had two children: Edwin, born December 9, 1858, and Walter S., born November 25, 1861. Edwin died on June 3, 1860. George G. Hikes died October 27, 1877. January 8, 1890, Mrs. Howard entered upon her present married life. Mrs. Howard is now in her seventy-sixth year, having been born on the 4th of November, 1832.

In politics James Howard was a Democrat and a man who took a great interest in the political progress of his party. In religious life he was a member of the Christian church and active in church affairs. His widow belongs to the Presbyterian faith.

W. F. WORK, M. D.

The subject of this sketch is among the leading representatives of the medical profession in Clark county, Indiana, for earnest, persistent labor and close application have been so co-ordinated with distinctive technical ability as to gain him marked prestige in his chosen profession, his residence being in the attractive and quiet little city of Charlestown, where his circle of friends is coincident with that of his acquaintance, having for many years successfully practiced medicine throughout the county in such a manner as to gain the unqualified confidence and respect of everyone who knows him.

Dr. W. F. Work is a native of Clark county, Indiana, having been born here August 27, 1850, the son of William and Mary (Fouts) Work, and he has spent his entire life in this county, where he has prospered. The Work family came to America from Ireland as early as 1720, settling in Philadelphia and Lancaster county, Pennsylvania. The great-grandfather of the subject, Henry Work, came to Jefferson county, Kentucky, in 1800, and lived there until 1802, in which year his death occurred. The subject's great-grandmother came to Clark county in 1802 and settled at Work's Landing, on the Ohio river, which derived its name from the Work family. She was the mother of three children, Samuel, Henry and Sarah. The daughter was the wife of a Mr. Parr. Samuel was the grandfather of the subject of this sketch. He married Elizabeth Henley and they reared ten children. William H. Work, father of the subject; Andrew J., Jesse H., Alexander C. and Samuel M. were their sons, and their daughters' names follow: Clarissa, Malinda, Elizabeth, Louisa and Sarah. All are now deceased but Sarah, who married a Mr. Eversole, and who now lives in Illinois. William H. married Mary Fouts. They were the parents of Henry F., Mary Elizabeth, and W. F. Henry F. is a farmer in Washington township, Clark county; Mary E. is the wife of William H. McIlvaine, of Henry county, Kentucky. William F. Work was reared on the farm, and at an early age he attended the district schools and in the summer months worked on the farm until he was about seventeen years old, when he entered Hanover College, taking a three years' literary course. Believing that a medical profession was best suited to his tastes he began the study of medicine, making rapid progress from the first with Dr. S. M. Work, of Charlestown, Indiana. He entered the medical college at Cincinnati, Ohio, from which he graduated in 1875, having made a splendid record there for scholarship.

After leaving school our subject began practice in Charlestown, then he graduated from a medical college in Louisville, Kentucky, in 1885. He began practice in 1875, his success having been achieved from the very first and his business steadily grew until he had a very liberal patronage, taking high rank as a physician and surgeon. Doctor Work has not been in active practice since 1902.

Doctor Work was happily married September 27, 1876, to Ella Dedrick, the daughter of Reuben Dedrick, a wholesale grocer of Jeffersonville. She was a graduate of St. Mary's College at Madison, Indiana. The date of her birth was March 19, 1859, and after a happy wedded life she was called to her rest in July, 1904. To Doctor Work and wife two children were born: Ruby, who is the wife of L. L. Robinson, of Jeffersonville, and William H., who was born March 19, 1883, and was married to Leona Coombs, daughter of the late Dr. David Coombs, also of Charlestown. He is a graduate of the linotype school of Chicago, and is employed on The Louisville (Kentucky) Herald. Our subject was married in 1905 to Mrs. Graham, widow of Dr. T. A. Graham, of Jeffersonville.

Doctor Work in his fraternal relations is a member of Blazing Star, No. 226, Horeb Chapter; Commandery, No. 66, at Jeffersonville; Jennings Lodge, Knights of Pythias. He is past master of the Free and Accepted Masons. In politics he is a Democrat, however, he has never taken a leading part in his party's affairs. He is a member of the Clark County Medical Society, the State Medical Society, also the Mississippi Medical Society, in all of which he holds high rank. He is a very pleasing man to meet, bearing a reputation for honesty of purpose and always ready to do what he considers his just share in promoting the welfare of his county.

HON. WILLIS L. BARNES.

The Hon. Willis L. Barnes, of Charlestown, Clark county, needs very little introduction to the people of Southern Indiana. Situated as he is at present he is in a position to enjoy a leisurely existence and engage in pursuits of a studious and scientific nature, which have always had an attraction for him, but which were necessarily denied him in the ceaseless activity of his public life. Success has crowned his business ventures, and his political aspirations have all been fulfilled. As Joint-Senator of Clark, Scott and Jennings counties he was of value to the community at large, and a powerful acquisition to the standard of his party.

He was born in Jefferson county, Indiana, on April 3, 1840, the son of McGannon and Rebecca (Fouts) Barnes, and came of sturdy stock. His grandfather, John Barnes, was a native of Culpeper county, Virginia, and of English and Irish ancestry. Hon. Thomas J. Hanley, formerly member of Congress from the Third district of Indiana, was an uncle of our subject, and a pioneer of Clark county. John Barnes was a substantial farmer and a pioneer of Jefferson county, Indiana. His wife, whom he married in Indiana, was originally named Sarah Law. He settled down, farmed extensively, and died in Jefferson county. His son, McGannon Barnes, moved to Washington township, Clark county, in 1860, and became a leading farmer in that section. He died late in life, July 5, 1894, aged eighty-five years. His wife died in the year 1887. Their family consisted of the following children: John C. Barnes, of Illinois; Jacob F. (deceased); Thomas B., of Washington township, Clark county; William E., also of Washington township; George D. (deceased); Edward C. (deceased), and Willis L.

The Hon. Willis L. Barnes was reared on his father's farm, and upon his arrival at the customary age helped and assisted in the farm work. In winter time he attended the district schools. He received sufficient education to become a teacher through attending Hanover College, and was for several terms a teacher in Clark county and in Kentucky. He was naturally inclined towards mechanical pursuits and therefore switched himself into the saw-mill industry, in which business he interested himself for several years, and built his own mill. He then began to figure in political life, being a Democrat. In 1884 he was nominated for the Legislature and served in the session of 1885, and, upon being again nominated and elected by an increased majority, served in the session of 1887. In 1885 he was appointed chairman of the Committee on Claims, and acted in the same capacity in the session of 1887; he was also prominent in other committees. In 1888 and 1889 he was nominated and elected deputy warden of the Jeffersonville prison. His political worth was not, however, appreciated until he had been nominated and elected a joint Senator of Clark, Scott and Jennings counties, when he filled the office with much credit and dignity in the sessions of 1891-1893. Since then he has led a comparatively retired life. He is a civil engineer and surveyor and does much work of this nature. He is an astronomer of no small ability, and is the possessor of a good telescope, with lens of the approved type, and with which he makes many astronomical investigations. Mr. Barnes has devoted much time of later years to the study of astronomy, and has recently developed an improved method of determining the elements of double-star systems, by which the intricate process is reduced to a mathematical and geometrical formula, and has received the endorsement of the highest authorities engaged in that branch of stellar astronomy.

In 1874 he married Lydia Buxton, of Jefferson county, Indiana. They have a family of five children. The family residence at Halcyon's Hill is capacious and substantial and an ideal home, and there, in fitting surroundings, Mr. Barnes enjoys his retirement.

The Hon. Willis L. Barnes has the reputation of a gentleman of the highest type, cultured and courteous. He is a member of the Universalist church.

EDWARD C. HUGHES.

Edward C. Hughes, attorney-at-law, of Charlestown, Indiana, is a lawyer of prominence in his native township. He comes from that stock from which America has ever drawn her foremost lawyers—the tillers of the soil. His grandfather came to Clark county in its early days and engaged in agricultural pursuits. We find his father following the same vocation, and Edward C. began life in the same strenuous fashion.

Edward C. Hughes was born in Charlestown township, Clark county, on the 28th of October, 1864, the son of Hiram K. and Nancy J. (Lewman) Hughes. Grandfather Eleven Hughes was of English birth, born in the year 1795. In after life he emigrated and settled in Kentucky. He fought as a soldier in the War of 1812, and was captured by the enemy on the defeat of Dudley. He escaped, however, by running the gauntlet through the Indian lines and came back to his home in Bourbon county, Kentucky. He settled in Clark county, Indiana, in 1830, and in that county the remainder of his life was spent in farming. Grandfather Hughes was known through life to be a man of sturdy and upright character. He belonged to the Methodist church and was a Democrat in politics.

Hiram K. Hughes was a lad when he came to Clark county, Indiana, with his father, from Bourbon county, Kentucky. He assisted in working the parental farm, and in after years married Nancy J. Lewman. His wife was born and reared in Utica township, Clark county. Six children were born of the marriage, of whom there are three dead and three living. The surviving members of the family are: W. Clay Hughes, who is a well-to-do farmer; Court S. Hughes, who is a contractor in Florida, and Edward C.

Edward C. Hughes was reared upon his father's farm, assisting in the farming work as best he could in summer and in winter time attended the district school. He later took up his studies at the Charlestown high school, and afterwards entered Depauw University. He graduated in the law department of that institution on June 13, 1894. In September of the same year he opened a law office at Charlestown, and later in the same year was appointed County Attorney, an office in which he served for four years. At the present time he is the chairman of the Clark County Council, and while in this capacity has been instrumental in reducing the tax levy of the county.

Edward C. Hughes is a close student of fraternal work and is a member of many orders, including the Independent Order of Odd Fellows, having passed the chairs in that organization. He is a past master in the local Masonic lodge, and takes an interest in local religious affairs, being an active member of the Christian church.

Attorney Hughes married Maude Robertson, the daughter of John S. and Matilda (Beggs) Robertson, who are among the oldest residents of the county. The marriage took place on the 10th of April, 1901. Mr. Hughes is a business man of ability and firmness. In politics he a good type of the present-day Democrat, anxious and active for the success and further progress of his party. His financial ventures have been lucky and he is beginning to experience the prosperity which his energetic years have merited.

JAMES NOBLE WOOD.

James Noble Wood was born in South Carolina, December 26, 1768, and was married to Margaret Smith September 27, 1794, at Clarksville, Indiana. He died at Utica, Indiana, March 25, 1826, aged fifty-eight years.

Margaret Smith was born in the state of Pennsylvania March 5, 1777, and she died at Utica, Indiana, March 5, 1854.

From Clarksville, Indiana, on Christmas day, 1795, James Noble Wood and several friends went to what is now Utica, Indiana, eight miles above Clarksville, in a pirogue, taking with them the few tools necessary to fell and shape the timber and build a log cabin; this they did in one day. It was built about ninety yards above what is now the northernmost street of Utica. The cabin was near the river bank, as was the two-story log house built later, and nearer the town. His nearest neighbor lived on Harrod creek, Kentucky, two and a half miles from the Ohio river. The only building in what is now Jeffersonville was the block-house occupied by soldiers. In the spring of 1796, he, with his wife, moved into the cabin. Their table was the top of a poplar stump, having felled a tree, four feet in diameter for clapboards for the roof and puncheons for the floor; later enough of the timber was cut away to form a well-shaped center table.

Wood employed two men to assist in clearing a few acres of land in the river bottom, planting corn and vegetables. In December the men wished to go to Shippingsport, Kentucky, to remain during the winter months. They hunted two days, killed several bears and a few deer and sold the game at Shippingsport. Game was then very plentiful.

A few years later Wood built a ferry boat of poplar, immense poplar trees being then abundant. About this time many families from the Carolinas were moving into what is now the state of Indiana, at that time known as

57

Knox county, Virginia. Wood made big money with his ferry boat, and soon added more boats. He sold corn at one dollar per bushel. If an emigrant had a lame or worn-out horse he would sell or trade. Soon a stock of horses were on hand, and became a part of the business. Wood also sold a great deal of whiskey.

Later Judge John Miller, of Utica, New York, settled here, purchasing land adjoining what later was the southern part of Utica. Miller built a large two-story log house, with hall and ell, yet occupied and in good repair. Joseph Miller, late of New Albany, Indiana, was a son of Judge Miller. Joseph Miller was a well known river pilot, between Louisville and New Orleans. Judge Miller built and operated ferryboats between Utica and Harrod's Creek, Kentucky, making good money in the business. Miller, Wood, and a Mr. Bright, of Philadelphia, Pennsylvania, laid out the town of Utica. Part of the town was owned by Wood, by deed of gift from his mother's half brother, Capt. Robert George, of Arlington Springs. Virginia. Captain George served under Gen. George Rogers Clark in what was known as the Illinois Regiment, which was present at the capture of Vincennes, Indiana, Kaskaskia, Illinois, and St. Louis, Missouri, and also at points on the lower Mississippi river. It appears that Captain George spent his years of capability in military service. There is no tradition as to whether he was or was not at Braddock's defeat in 1758. His brother, William George, of Arlington Springs, Virginia, owned much land and many slaves. He made his home with James Noble Wood during the remainder of his life, although he held patents for two bodies of land of one thousand acres each, in Kentucky. He gave nothing to either of his two sisters, claiming that their husbands failed to take up arms against the crown during the Revolutionary war. The two sisters, with their husbands, lived in this vicinity for several years and the descendants of both families were good citizens. Some of them have held good county offices in Clark county, yet the old captain held to his prejudice and gave the two thousand acres of land in Kentucky, and the three hundred and sixty acres in and adjoining Utica to the sons of his half sister, Margaret Sharon, the widow George having married a man of that name, wife of James Wood. James Wood had to leave his home in South Carolina after striking an English soldier with a blacksmith's hammer. Captain George considered striking an English soldier deserved reward. Ann Wood, born in 1796, often told of the peculiarities of Captain George. He died about the year 1807; buried in Utica cemetery.

Of eleven children born to James Noble Wood and his wife, six died before reaching the age of seven years, one died at the age of seventy-five years, one at eighty-four, one at eighty-seven, two at eighty-nine, four were in fairly good health until within a week or two of death; one was feeble for two or three years. It appears that malarial fever was so common and malignant that only the strong survived.

James Noble Wood was presented to General Lafayette in Louisville, and had a little conversation with him. He met Aaron Burr also in Louisville. Moses Wood, a brother, joined the expedition under Burr, and was captured by the United States troops while descending the Ohio. George Wood, a brother, settled in what is now Wood township, this county. Some of his descendants live in that township today. Ann Wood, a sister, married Samuel Hay, of Lancaster county, Pennsylvania. Hay was appointed and served as Sheriff while Indiana was yet a territory. Court was held at Vincennes. Jane Wood, a sister, married John Douthett, a native of Pennsylvania. He served many years as Recorder of Clark county. Another sister married William Ferguson, a cousin, and lived some time in the vicinity of Utica.

James Noble Wood lost much through his friends, and sold some land before his death. His two sons, Robert George Wood, born in 1803, and Napoleon B. Wood, born in 1813, inherited his estate and through recklessness lost the greater part of it. Some of the descendants of Robert G. Wood live in Utica, others in Kentucky. Some of the descendants of Napoleon Wood live in Utica; others in Kentucky. Robert G. Wood died April 18, 1878.

James Wood, father of James Noble Wood, was born of Scotch parentage. No record as to date of birth is at hand, and he may have been born in Scotland and possibly in America. He married Margaret Sharon, half sister to Capt. Robert George, of Arlington Springs, Virginia. The tradition of the family is that James Wood during the Revolutionary war was located sixty miles from Charlestown, South Carolina. He kept a country store, cooper shop and blacksmith shop, being a blacksmith by trade. He organized a company of thirty men favorable to the colonial cause, a home guard, the American general commanding the military district ordered Wood to report at headquarters, which he did. The general (probably Gen. Francis Marion) offered Wood a commission, provided he would be mustered into the service, and also bring as many men as possible. Wood failed to accept. Immediately following the battle of Eutaw Springs (in which the Americans were sorely defeated) two British cavalrymen on jaded mounts stopped at the blacksmith shop to have horse shoeing done. They told of the battle; of the British victory and American defeat, and said that soon there would not be a rebel in South Carolina. One horse was shod; his rider mounted and rode away. Later Wood struck the remaining soldier with his blacksmith hammer, the result of the blow is not known. In less than an hour Wood, with wife and children, a bed and covering, a few pots and pans and some food, were in an ox wagon, driving northward. He drove all night and all of the next day, when he stopped for the night the oxen and wagon were always headed southward, in order to deceive pursuers. He reached Virginia, remaining there until the close of the war. He then returned home and sold both personal and realty, and prepared to move to the Falls of the Ohio.

About 1786 Wood reached the Falls of the Ohio, bought land and culti-vated it. It was located between Shippingsport and Portland. He later sold this land and moved near Utica. His bones lie about the center of Jefferson street and about half way in the square between Eleventh and Twelfth street, Louisville, Kentucky, the street having been cut through the cemetery. He died September 24, 1816. His wife, Margaret Sharon, died October 19, 1801, and is buried beside him.

Margaret Smith, wife of James Noble Wood, in the year 1785, together with two sisters in charge of the their father and mother, left the state of Pennsylvania, in a house boat, their destination being the Falls of the Ohio. In another boat were Mrs. Smith's sister and her husband. With several boats they reached the blockhouse where Cincinnati now stands, known then as Fort Washington. They turned their cattle out to browse. The brother-in-law, an Indian fighter, went after the cattle, but came back without them, reporting signs of Indians. Smith, also an Indian fighter, disregarding the advice of the brother-in-law, took his rifle and started to get the cattle, the bells being plainly heard. (The bells were probably rung by the Indians.) Shortly after rifle shots were heard, the soldiers pushed out into the timber, found Smith dead and scalped. He had been struck by several bullets. Smith was an athlete and excelled in jumping. A survey of the surroundings showed that he had run some distance and had reached a ravine, or gully. The marks showed that he had jumped, falling dead on the opposite side of the gully. The soldiers de-cided that the force of the bullets carried him across, as they struck him while in the air, as no one could possibly have jumped that distance. The brother-in-law returned to Pennsylvania with his family.

Nancy Smith, the widow, determined to go on to the Falls of the Ohio. During the trip a storm at night separated her boat from the fleet. When morning came she was alone with her children, pulling to the middle of the river. She rowed to overtake the fleet during the day. She was fired upon by Indians, several bullets striking the boat. The children were told to lie flat on the floor, while the mother pulled for the opposite shore, keeping the boat be-tween her and the Indians, and was soon out of danger. She soon overtook the other boats and reached Clarksville in safety. One of her daughters mar-ried a Mr. Ware, of Clarksville; a son born to them, was for many years a Falls pilot. A sister, Nancy, while washing clothes at a spring at the outskirts of Clarksville, was fired upon by Indians, receiving seven wounds. One Indian rushed forward and scalped her. He then turned to run, made a few steps and turned, threw his tomahawk at her but missed her. By that time men were in sight, rushing to the scene with arms in hand. The Indian made his escape. Years afterward, at Vincennes, Indiana, an Indian in conversation with whites remarked that he had never killed a white man, but had killed a white squaw at the Falls of the Ohio, and pointed to a scar on the calf of his leg, where she had bitten him while being scalped. When told that the white squaw was living and was the mother of several children, he answered "Ugh! Kill 'um next time." Nancy was about sixteen years of age at the time of the scalping, and later she married a Mr. Pittman. Pittman was a Virginian, had served in a military organization, known as The Rangers. Their service was in Indiana Territory, and he probably had served under General Clark. He received patent for five hundred acres of land, this he sold for a trifling sum, as did many others. After being discharged from the service he remained in Clarksville awaiting for the spring time weather before starting for his Virginia home, bidding acquaintances and Clarksville farewell. He mounted his horse, crossed the river below the Falls and as he led his horse off the boat, the horse fell, injuring him so badly as to make him useless. Pittman returned to Clarksville and later married Nancy Smith and several years after, with his wife and children, left in a flat boat. They floated down the Mississippi, and years after were located on Fairchild's Island, near Vicksburg, Mississippi. The mother of Mrs. Julia Mackay, *nee* Morrison, of Utica, had in her possession for several years, a lock of white hair, coarse as the mane of a horse, taken from the new growth of the scalp on the head of Nancy Smith. William Morrison, father of Mrs. Mackay, fought under General Jackson at the battle of New Orleans. He settled in Utica about the year 1823, dying there in 1867. He deserves a place in frontier history.

Nancy Smith, mother of Margaret, wife of James Noble Wood, died August 10, 1828, aged one hundred and two years. At the age of ninety-six she bought a new spinning wheel. A neighbor wished to borrow it and the old lady refused to loan, saying "I've owned several wheels. Other people borrowed and wore them out. I intend to wear this out myself."

THOMAS WEST FREEMAN.

The Freemans were of English origin and the emigrant ancestors came over before the Revolutionary war, settling in Massachusetts. Charles B. Freeman, one of the descendants, was born in the old Bay state, August 20, 1776, shortly after the Declaration of Independence was adopted. He was one of four orphans apprenticed to learn trades and he learned that of carpentry, which was his line of work throughout his life. He was reared by a Congregational minister, who came from England to do missionary and philanthropic work. He came to Indiana about 1818, and settled at Vevay, being one of the earliest pioneers of that section. The state at that time was little more than the original wilderness full of wild game and still inhabited by various Indian tribes. He married Elizabeth Haskell, who was born in

Massachusetts in 1784, her father being Job Haskell, of English descent. The marriage took place in their native state, and there were seven children born to them. Thomas West Freeman, of this review, was born in Philadelphia, Pennsylvania, December 16, 1816, and was but two years old when his parents came to Indiana. As he grew up he learned the carpenter's trade and followed that occupation until he was fifty years old. He learned his letters in one of the old fashioned school-houses, his teacher being the mother of Edward Eggleston, the famous author of "The Hoosier School Master." He came to Clark county about 1868, and bought timber land in Monroe township, which he cleared and improved. In 1840. Mr. Freeman was married to Eliza Ogle, who was born in Switzerland county, Indiana, December 22, 1816. Her father and mother were among the first settlers of that section and went through all the hardships and dangers of pioneer life. They became the parents of ten children, most of whom are now dead. Ida, who was born in 1851, married George Lewellen, and resides at Columbus, Indiana; Eliza, born in 1853; Ramey, born in 1860, married Emma Dunlevy, lives in Monroe township and has two children; John W., one of the sons, enlisted in the army at the beginning of the Civil war, and died at Stone River. As he was under age, his father drew a pension on his account. Mr. Freeman retired from active business many years before his death, and made his home with his son, Ramey, in Monroe township. For some time he was the oldest man in the township, and one of the oldest in the county, his age having corresponded with that of Indiana as a state. He was an interesting relic of a bygone age and loved to talk about the old pioneer days. He remembered the Indians very well after they had become peaceful and mingled freely with the white people. He enjoyed the reputation of having been a good neighbor and a good citizen during his long life. After giving up the carpenter's trade he devoted his time to farming with success in that line. The death of Thomas West Freeman occurred on May 7, 1909.

JOSEPH CLARK.

The emigrant ancestor of this family was a native of County Down, Ireland, who came to America when a small boy, where he found a temporary home in Pennsylvania, but later joined the tide of emigration setting in towards the West and eventually found a location in Southern Indiana. He was one of the earliest pioneers of Scott county, the state at that time being little more than an unbroken wilderness. He reared a family after the primitive methods of those days when toil and hardship were the experience of every one. Among his children was a son by the name of William, who was born a few years before the settlement in Scott county, and went through all the privations of a boy on a pioneer farm. After he grew up he became a farmer and devoted his life to agricultural pursuits. He was a Democrat and quite active in local politics, but never aspired to office. He died in 1844. His first wife was Mahala Taylor, a native of Kentucky, where her ancestors were early settlers. She was quite young when her parents came to Indiana. She died after becoming the mother of three children; there were also three children by her husband's second marriage. All but one are still living, four in Clark county and a sister in Indianapolis.

Joseph Clark, eldest of the family, was born in Scott county, Indiana, in January, 1836. He remained at home until his twenty-third year, when he branched out in business for himself as a farmer and dealer in timber. For seventeen years he devoted his time to getting out cross-ties and did a large business in this line. He made the ties that were used in the building of the Belt Railroad at Indianapolis, also furnishing the timber for the bridges and other purposes on that line. In fact he was one of the pioneer lumber men of Southern Indiana, and no man in the state better understands the "ins and outs" of this business. At the same time he carried on his farming operations. When he began business Clark county was practically all woods, being covered with the fine growth of the original forests. There was an abundant harvest for the woodsmen, and Mr. Clark reaped his share of the trade, although it involved much hard work and considerable financial risk. He remembers when there were no roads, only blazed trails, through this section. Charlestown was the only village of any importance in the vicinity. As was customary in all the families of those days, his mother made his clothes from flax grown on the farm. The schools were few and far between, and of the most primitive character, being kept up by meager subscription, while the teacher "boarded around." Mr. Clark put in a month or two during the winter months, but is unable to recall that he got any benefit from his irregular attendance, except a slight grounding in the three "R's." The land he bought after reaching manhood was entirely wild, covered with timber and the clearing and improving involved much toil and some labor. Those now living on the smiling and highly cultivated farms of Clark county with their rural mail delivery and telephones can little realize what the first settlers had to contend with. Mr. Clark is a Presbyterian in religion, a Republican in politics, and in every respect has been a model citizen. Blessed with a powerful constitution, he was able to endure much of the hardest kind of work, and few men of his years are better preserved.

In 1859 Mr. Clark was married to Mary Ann Woods, a native of Ohio. Her parents were Jesse and Jane Woods, natives of Kentucky, who lived for a time in Clark county. Mr. and Mrs. Clark became the parents of an interesting family, their children being well situated in life.

ANDREW J. HOLMAN.

One of the substantial agriculturists in Jeffersonville township, Clark county, is Andrew J. Holman, whose life, covering a period of sixty-eight years, has been spent in this county, the greater portion of the time within sight of the spot where his father was born and where his grandfather, Isaac Holman, settled in 1802. Mr. Holman has been very successful in his avocation, and a broad expanse of highly cultivated soil is evidence of the careful attention that he has bestowed upon his possessions. The subject is a man of most genial disposition and affable manners, which has been the means of his having formed many warm friendships throughout the county. Mr. Holman has been a hard worker all his life, but is still a very hale and hearty man for his years.

As heretofore stated, he is a native of Utica township, having been born there April 4, 1841. His father was Isaac N. Holman, who lived to quite a ripe old age. The subject married October 12, 1864, to Rosetta Worrall, and four children were born to the couple. They were Mrs. Bailey L. Burtt, Walter J. Holman, Homer A. and Sol.

Mr. Holman has participated in politics to a large extent during his life, being an ardent and active Democrat. He has held but one political office, that of Township Supervisor. He is a member of the Christian church, and belongs to the Odd Fellows. His record in both business and politics is an honorable one, the people of the community having implicit confidence in him.

WALTER ERLE McCULLOCH.

One of the well known and enterprising agriculturalists of Jeffersonville township, Clark county, who is deserving of mention in a work of this character, owing to his upright life and his public-spirit, is Walter Erle McCulloch, son of Mr. and Mrs. John McCulloch. He was born on the farm where he now resides in Jeffersonville township on Friday, August 13, 1876. Here he was reared. He attended the public schools in New Albany, also DePauw preparatory college in New Albany and, having applied himself in a very careful manner he received a good education. Being the youngest of the family he came into possession of the old homestead and he has lived here, carrying on farming on an extensive scale in such a manner as to stamp him an agriculturist of the best type. He is the owner of a very fine landed estate consisting of five hundred and twenty-five acres, located about midway between Jeffersonville and New Albany on the interurban traction line. In 1907 he surveyed and platted thirty-five acres, making one hundred and forty-nine lots, and since then he has sold over one hundred of the same. He named this suburb Midway, being ambitious to make this the finest

suburban residence district of this section.   It is about ten minutes' ride to
Jeffersonville and New Albany and only thirty minutes to Louisville.   It has
modern advantages in the way of electric lights, telephone, and inside of
two years water and gas will be accessible.   Mr. McCulloch has constructed
twelve up-to-date houses on these lots, and is making a sale of houses and
lots on popular small payments down and monthly payments without interest
or taxes until the agreed amount has been paid in full, and a deed is given
in case of death without further payment and cost.   Mr. McCulloch was the
instigator and builder of the McCulloch boulevard, which extends from
McCulloch Pike (built by his father at a cost of seventeen thousand and five
hundred dollars) to Howard Park on the south.   He also carries on farming
extensively, having over three hundred acres in cultivation.   The land is all
highly improved, showing that a man of good judgment has its management
in hand, and the McCulloch residence is modern, beautiful of design and
elegantly furnished.   He is an admirer of good stock and always keeps some
high grade horses, cattle and hogs.

Mr. McCulloch's domestic life began on October 19, 1898, when he
was united with Edith H. Schwaninger, a native of Jeffersonville, the accomplished daughter of Abraham and Sarah (Carwardine) Schwaninger, the
former a native of Switzerland and the latter of London, England.   The
father of Mrs. McCulloch was City Judge of Jeffersonville for several years
and also served as Mayor, filling these offices with credit to himself and to
the satisfaction of all concerned.   His death occurred in Jeffersonville on
October 17, 1906.   His widow resides with her daughter, Mrs. McCulloch.
She is a woman of gracious personality.   To Mr. and Mrs. McCulloch three
interesting children have been born, namely: Kenneth, Ruth Agnes and
Howard Schwaninger.

Mr. McCulloch in his fraternal relations is a member of New Albany
Lodge, No. 270, Benevolent and Protective Order of Elks.   In politics he
is a staunch Republican.   He is a member of the Third Presbyterian church
at New Albany, while his wife belongs to the Episcopal church in Jeffersonville.
They are both popular in social circles and are held in high esteem by a
wide circle of friends owing to their hospitality and affability.

OMER L. MILLER.

A scion of worthy pioneer ancestors is Omer L. Miller, Deputy United
States Revenue Collector, with offices in the Federal Building, Indianapolis,
well known at Jeffersonville, Clark county, Indiana, who was born at Galena,
Floyd county, this state, January 19, 1871.   He was reared to the honest

toil of the farm and received a good elementary education at the district schools and later attended a business college. He is the oldest of two children born to James L. and Clara (Thurman) Miller, both natives of Floyd county, Indiana, the former having been born in 1841, the son of Jacob and Isabelle (Smith) Miller, both of Pennsylvania, where they were married, soon after moving to the then new Eldorado, settling in Floyd county, this state, and engaged in farming in a most successful manner for those early times, and there they spent the remainder of their lives, honored by all who knew them. The names of their large family follow: George W.; James L., father of the subject of this review; Elmer, Charles W.; Anna, now Mrs. John Sheets; Caroline, who married George W. McKinley; Harriet (Mrs. Mosier); Jennie (Mrs. McKinley); Belle (Mrs. Hancock).

James L. Miller was born and reared in Floyd county. During his early youth he worked on the home farm. While yet in his teens thoughts of the great rebellion aroused his patriotism and he resolved to do something in the restoration of the Union, consequently he enlisted in the Federal army three times before the close of the war, his father having taken him from the service twice, but later decided not to interfere and allowed him to go to the front. He enlisted in the One Hundred and Forty-fourth Regiment, Indiana Volunteer Infantry, in which he served until the close of the war. He was always on duty and in the front ranks, but he was never wounded nor made a prisoner. He received an honorable discharge after the close of hostilities. He returned home and resumed farming. Later he married and began farming on his own account, which he continued successfully for a number of years, finally leaving the farm and moving to Jeffersonville, where he worked in the railroad car shops, becoming a skilled finisher on passenger coaches. When free mail delivery was inaugurated in Jeffersonville he entered the service and he delivered the first letter by the free delivery system in that city, and he is still in the city service in 1909. Although a strong Republican he has never aspired to offices outside of his present appointment. He is a worthy member of the Grand Army of the Republic. He is widely known and highly respected in Jeffersonville and vicinity. His wife is the daughter of Henry C. Thurman, of Virginia, a prominent and honored early settler of Indiana. Although dying at middle age, he had become an extensive land owner. He was survived by a large family of children, the mother of our subject being the youngest child. Following are the names of the Thurman children: Henry, William, John, Phillip, Robert, Barney, Elizabeth, Sarah, Laura, Harriet and Clara, mother of our subject. She is a worthy member of the Presbyterian church while her husband subscribes to the Unitarian denomination. To James L. Miller and wife two children were born, Omer L., of this review; and Nettie, the wife of H. Hazzard.

Omer L. Miller remained at home during his youth assisting his father.

When he reached manhood he began work at the Jeffersonville Car Works and later took a business course, after which he engaged in the grocery business in Jeffersonville, beginning in 1890, and he continued in that line successfully until 1906, when he received the appointment as Deputy Revenue Collector (Internal) for the United States, for the port of Indianapolis. He then closed out his business and moved to Indianapolis, for the purpose of assuming charge of his newly assigned duties. He has charge of fifty-nine men acting in different capacities, store keepers, gaugers, etc. He also has charge of the bonded spirits department, and full charge of the various departments of the government at the Indianapolis branch of the revenue department, and he is handling the same with accuracy and dispatch, showing that he is a man of apt business acumen.

From boyhood he has always taken a great deal of interest in politics, being a loyal Republican, and while he was at Jeffersonville he was active in the ranks, and he keeps well posted on curent events of state and national import, but he has never aspired to elective office. For many years he was prominently connected with the business interests of Jeffersonville and vicinity, being favorably known throughout Clark county.

Omer L. Miller was married on October 3, 1897, to Clara E. Tatspaugh, who was born in New Albany, Indiana, in 1875, a lady of intelligence and culture, the daughter of John and Julia Tatspaugh, who still live in New Albany. Mr. Tatspaugh is a railroad engineer, having been prominent in railroad circles for many years. He is a member of the Christian church. He is the father of two children, Cora, now Mrs. Beatte; and Clara, wife of Omer L. Miller, who is the father of one winsome daughter, born August 5, 1899. Her name is Marjorie.

Both Mr. and Mrs. Miller are members of the Presbyterian church. They moved their membership from Jeffersonville to Indianapolis when they moved to the latter city.

HARRY C. SHARP, M. D.

This distinguished physician, one of the most eminent socialogists of the age and a reformer of high degree, is a native of Clark county, whose fame he has done so much to extend. His birth occurred in Charlestown, Indiana, December, 1869, his parents being James K., and Margaret J., (Ferguson) Sharp, the latter a sister of the well known Judge C. P. Ferguson. After graduating from the high school in 1888, he entered the medical department of the University of Louisville and there obtained his degree in 1893, locating at Henryville, this county, and began active practice of his profession. In 1895 he removed to Seymour, Indiana, and in October of that year was appointed physician of the Indiana State Prison, South. In connection with others he framed and secured the passage of a bill that changed this prison to the Indiana Reformatory, working it before the Legislature, though he knew the passage would cost him his place as official physician. He was, however, re-appointed by Governor Mount and has ever since given the institution the benefit of his rare talents. He offered his resignation to take effect on October 1, 1908, but on urgent request consented to remain until the subsidence of the epidemic of typhoid fever then prevalent at the Reformatory, subsequently removing to Indianapolis, where he continues the practice of his profession. During his tenure at the Reformatory he had charge of about sixty-five hundred inmates, the usual average being some twelve hundred and fifty at one time. Dr. Sharp has received many evidences of esteem from fellow members of his profession and has been showered with honors, but his greatest claim to distinction is due to the leading part he took in instituting a great and epoch-making reform in the treatment of degenerates. It has long been recognized by the medical profession and sociologists that many, if not most of the insane, epileptic, ibecile, idiotic, sexual pervert, and many confirmed drunkards, prostitutes, tramps, habitual criminals and chronic paupers are by heredity degenerates. In other words they have defects that cannot be cured. If allowed to become parents their posterity increases the same defects and their number increases at a ration far greater than that of the total population. The question was how to stop this growth of degeneracy, what method would be most effective with least hardship. In studying out this vital problem, Dr. Sharp reached a remedy that is destined to enroll his name high among the benefactors of his race. He formed and took a leading part in passing through the Legislature a bill that is destined to have far-raching importance. In effect it provides that when degenerates are confined in state institutions, the proper authorities, under prescribed safeguards, may cause to be performed on them a surgical operation, known as vasecotomy, a simple easy and not very painful operation, that prevents procreation. Dr. Sharp has operated on two hundred and fifty such, with full opportunity to study the results and is highly pleased with the outcome. He says the results, unlike those of castration, are physicially, mentally and morally beneficial to the patient and the patients themselves favor and recommend the operation to their friends as being for their good. He has never observed any unfavorable symptoms, but the great result achieved is the prevention of the multiplication of degeneracy. It is a distinction to Clark county that this great reform began here and was instituted by one of her citizens. Other states are now following the way pointed out by Dr. Sharp, and the discovery will undoubtedly spread over the whole civilized world as one of the most valuable achievements in the science of sociology.

Dr. Sharp recently received letters of inquiry from Germany relative to this subject. The German government, through the efforts of repesentative citizens and philanthropists, has taken up the matter of changing the laws of that country in regard to degenerates and criminals and is in correspondence with the doctor for the purpose of incorporating into the German code a law similar to that of Indiana. The originator is destined to rank with Koch and Pasteur as a benefactor to the human race and Clark county will receive the glory reflected upon her by one of her most distinguished citizens.

Dr. Sharp has held many positions of honor and trust, among them being the president of the Third District Medical Society, and the vice-president during 1906-7 of the Indiana Medical Association. He was councilor of the third Councilor District of the last mentioned association and Indiana member of the committee on medical legislation of the American Medical Association. In 1908 he read a paper before the American Anti-Tuberculosis Association at its annual meeting in Chicago, which gained for him much favorable comment and wide distinction as a physician of learning and original thought upon the subject of that dread disease. In his discussion he took the advanced ground that rarely if ever death was due to the direct results of tuberculosis, but in almost every instance to complications therefrom. This position has since been indorsed by practically the entire profession. He is a member of the Jeffersonville Lodge of Free and Accepted Masons, and Lodge No. 362 of the Elks, of which he was exalted ruler in 1907. His religious affiliations are with the Unitarian church and his standing both socially and professionally is of the highest rank.

ELISHA CARR.

Elisha Carr belongs to one of the old pioneer families of Clark county. His great-grandfather, John Carr, came to this country from Ireland when ninetten years of age. He was accompanied by a brother and sister, but his father and mother both died on the ocean voyage to America. The young people landed at Annapolis, Maryland.

Later we find his son, Thomas Carr, and wife moving from Westmoreland county, Pennsylvania, to Clark county, Indiana, in 1806. He settled on what is known as the Sinking Fork of Silver creek, a tract of land embracing five hundred acres, which he purchased for one thousand six hundred sixty-six dollars.

He was a man of influence in his time, and became a member of the famous constitution convention which sat under the great elm tree in Corydon, Indiana, and framed the state constitution in 1816. Later he was for two years a member of the General Assembly of the state, and was also an officer in one of the regiments serving in the Indian wars. He was present at Colonel Crawford's defeat. His death occurred in 1822.

One of the eleven children of Thomas Carr was Joseph Carr, who was born February 7, 1796. On February 26, 1818, he married Nancy Drummond and they established their home where the residence of Elisha Carr is at this time. From this union came twelve children, and when the youngest of these, Elizabeth Carr, was but seven months of age, Joseph Carr died, leaving to his widow, Nancy Carr, the care of twelve children.

It was a great task for a mother to thus rear so large a family in those pioneer days. However, she proved to be a careful and successful manager, both in regard to her family and in the conduct of the estate. It may be of interest to say that of the twelve children, eleven attained their majority, one daughter having died in her eighth year.

One of these sons, Elisha Carr, who was born December 3, 1838, acquired the home farm from the various heirs, after the death of his mother, Nancy Carr. He still holds this farm, comprising now the land on which his grandfather, Thomas Carr, settled in 1806. It is one of the most beautiful homes in Southern Indiana.

Mr. Carr has been in every way a successful farmer and stock raiser. May 22, 1878, he was married to Mary Hess, of Cadiz, Henry county, Indiana. Her father, Milton T. Hess, and his wife, Elizabeth Shively, were born in Monongahela county, Virginia, and were brought by their parents to Indiana about the year 1830, entering farms near where Mount Summit is now situated.

Mr. and Mrs. Carr have one daughter, Miss Lucile Carr, and it was for the purpose of placing her in Butler College that they left their home on the farm and moved to Irvington, suburb of Indianapolis, in 1900. Mr. Carr still manages his farm in Clark county, however, making frequent visits to it from his home in Indianapolis.

MISS LILLIAN HARMON.

The many friends of this affable and estimable lady will no doubt be glad to learn more of her personal history than has heretofore been shown the public through the medium of a sketch similar to that which here follows, for she has shown herself to be capable, alert and possessing many commendable attributes of character, which have won for her the esteem of all with whom she has come in contact. She is the present efficient postmistress of Marysville.

Miss Lillian Harmon was born in Oregon township, Clark county, the daughter of Daniel and Rachael C. (Bower) Harmon. Her ancestors are of sturdy German stock, seven brothers of the Harmon family having come to America from the Fatherland, four of whom settled in New York and three in Virginia; one of the three, William, was the son of the one that later emigrated to Indiana and settled in Clark county, and he was the grandfather of Lillian Harmon. William Harmon married Elizabeth Stoner, and they were the parents of Daniel Harmon, the subject's father, their family consisting of the following children: William, John, Silas, Joseph, Daniel, Elizabeth, Mary and Sarah.

To the subject's parents the following children were born: May, wife of A. H. Hemphry, of Marysville; Lillian the subject of this sketch; Milton E.; Myrtle is the wife of Jacob Shields, of Lexington, Indiana. These children all received every care at the hands of their worthy parents, who were people of sterling qualities and they are all held in high respect wherever they have gone.

Miss Lillian Harmon was reared on the farm in Oregon township, where she did her share of the household duties and attended the district school, having graduated from the common school and rapidly developed into a lady of culture and refinement as well as an innate individuality that has shown her to be a woman of rare business ability.

Our subject moved to Marysville in 1891, and she was appointed postmistress in 1906, in which capacity she is serving in 1909 in a manner that has won the praise of everyone concerned.

She is a member of the Christian church, and she was honored by being elected district superintendent of the Christian Endeavor work in this district, faithfully serving in this capacity for a period of four years. She takes a great interest in religous and educational movements, and has become widely known in this line of work.

THE WHITESIDE BAKERY.

Truly a wonderful plant—one of the finest in the United States—is that of the Whiteside Bakery, where the famous "Mother's Bread" is made, and which was established by the late Isaac F. Whiteside, a sketch of whom appears in another part of this history.

The building is a beautiful structure, reflecting much credit upon the architect, Arthur Loomis. It is Moorish or Spanish in design. In the large tower which looms high over the lower part of the building is an immense clock, which strikes every hour during the twenty-four, and at night it is especially imposing, for then the characters describing the circle and declaring the hours stand forth in letters of fire, and read, "Mother's Bread." The hands of this enormous clock are also illuminated as soon as twilight comes on. It is a master time-piece and controls, electrically, all the other clocks around the building.

The building was formally opened and dedicated July 16, 1908, the fiftieth birthday of Mr. Whiteside. It is a concrete and fire-proof structure and is a real marvel among bakeries. It is located at the corner of Broadway and Fourteenth street, Louisville, Kentucky, on the tracks of the Pennsylvania Railroad. This has a great advantage since it does away with any re-handling of materials—these coming direct from the cars to the consumer.

The flour in barrels is taken from the cars, placed directly into the large iron chutes leading to different parts of the basement storage room. The sifting and cleaning are done mechanically in the basement. A "worm" elevator runs the flour to the second floor, where great mixing machines mix the dough, going from the sifters and blenders on to the dough mixers, and into the sanitary dough troughs. These are portable and can be wheeled with their contents into the cooling room.

From this room the dough descends through iron chutes into dough dividers, thence into the "merry-go-round." The next step in the preliminary process takes place in the moulding machine, where the dough is formed into loaves for the baking pan. These loaves are placed on large portable cars and wheeled into the steam rooms, where they remain about half an hour to raise. This is quite different from the home method, where the bread has to be "set" over night for the "raising" process.

Now that it is time to begin baking the loaves are wheeled to the ovens. The oven room in the Whiteside Bakery would be a joy to any baker, and is perhaps the finest one extant. It is long and well lighted with nine ovens down each side. These have a combined capacity of one hundred forty thousand loaves daily. The ovens, which are faced with white enameled tile, are fired from the rear with coke, which is brought in by an overhead trolley. After a proper time the bread is wheeled out of the opposite side of the steam box which opens into one hundred and twenty corridors between two rows of ovens.

During the whole time of baking, pilot lights show the condition of the bread. When it is finished it is delivered to the shipping room. Twenty doors leading to as many wagons lead from this room. These wagons are lined up in a covered paved court. Delivery of the bread begins at 12:30 in the morning and the last wagons leave the court at 1:45 a. m., to serve the community with breakfast rolls and bread.

Praise is due the architect for the splendid arrangement of lights, ventilation and extreme cleanliness, for the sanitary condition of the bakery is as near perfect as is possible. Just above the front of the ovens is a wall, slightly protruding over and between it and the oven tops is a space which permits the heat to pass out, to prevent overheating the workers, as is often the case in bakeries. Much care had to be taken in the arrangement of the skylights, etc., in order to produce the proper amount of light—light enough to prevent seeing into the darker ovens and yet enough in which to work comfortably and to show every spot of dirt that might accumulate; but the proper results were obtained by the minute arrangement of upright sky-lights over the middle of the corridor from end to end.

Bath-rooms of the most improved design occupy one part of the building. Every employee is compelled to bathe before commencing work, and is furnished by the company a freshly laundered linen suit each day before beginning work, and all workers are required to wash their hands when returning from any place about the building where there might be a chance to collect the least particle of dirt.

The mechanical appliances throughout the plant are of the very latest design. But little of the work is done by hand, the machinery even dividing and weighing each loaf automatically, and the least possible waste of energy is avoided in the plant, and to fully appreciate the genius of the architect one must go through the plant and observe how perfectly the various departments coincide, making one splendid system.

The entire building is lighted with electric lights, each light being enclosed in a glass globe for sanitary purposes, the fixtures being absolutely dust-proof. The flour sifters and blenders, as well as the machines in the moulding room, are driven by motors attached to the ceiling. A tiny motor is also used in the testing laboratory, the Whiteside Bakery being a model both among bakeries and as to electrical installations.

DAVID W. WATSON.

This name is well known in Clark county, where our subject was born, and where his ancestors also maintained their homes, being numbered among the representative pioneers here, and Mr. Watson is not only recognized as one of the leading agriculturists of Oregon township, where he has a valuable farm property, but he has also been prominent in public affairs of a local nature and has been incumbent of offices of distinctive trust and responsibility, and he has been signally faithful to his duties of citizenship.

David W. Watson was born in Oregon township, Clark county, Indiana, December 28, 1853, the son of John and Catherine (Amick) Watson. John Watson was also born in Oregon township, this county, his birth occurring

58

March 17, 1827, the son of Robert Watson, who was of Scotch-Irish descent. John Watson is living at this writing (1909). John Watson and Catherine Amick were married in Oregon township February 5, 1849. They are elderly people of much stability of character, and are making their homes with David W., their son. They are the parents of Ann, the wife of William McNew, of Scott county, Indiana; D. W., of this review, being the second in order of birth; Amanda, the wife of Daniel Smith, of Scott county, this state.

David W. Watson was reared on the farm in this county, having assisted with the work about the place until he reached man's estate, attending the district schools in the meantime until he was seventeen years old, but he remained under his parental roof until he was married to Mary Taflinger, who was born in Oregon township, Clark county, August 20, 1858, the daughter of Joseph and Hester Taflinger. She was reared on a farm and received her education in the district schools. The subject and wife moved on the farm where they now live, which is in Clark's grant No. 279, soon after their marriage, and they have a valuable farm, consisting of three hundred and seven acres, which is highly improved. Mr. Watson carries on general farming, being regarded by his neighbors as a first class agriculturist in every respect. He was formerly in the lumber business in which he prospered. He has a substantial home well located with attractive surroundings.

Mr. and Mrs. Watson are the parents of fourteen children, named as follows: Catherine, born September 25, 1875, the wife of Charles Bonsett; John, born November 27, 1876, married Ida Boley; Bertha, born August 19, 1878, is the wife of Edward Zimmerman; Bert E. was born November 27, 1879, married Amelia Deiterlen; William I., born September 22, 1881, married Catherine Gladdin; Elmer, born September 14, 1883, is single and living in Illinois; Lunetta, born October 9, 1885, is the wife of John Deiterlen; Dudley, born December 3, 1887, is a teacher and is unmarried; Nellie was born January 28, 1890, and is single; Jessie, born July 14, 1892; Alta, born October 17, 1894; David, born May 13, 1897; Mamie, born September 15, 1899, is deceased; Walter was born August 6, 1900.

Mr. and Mrs. Watson are members of the Methodist Episcopal church of this neighborhood. Mr. Watson is a member of English Lodge, Free and Accepted Masons, also of the Marysville Lodge, Independent Order of Odd Fellows, of which he is a past grand master.

In his political relations Mr. Watson is a Democrat, and he has taken considerable interest in the affairs of his party. He was elected Trustee of Oregon township in 1900, and faithfully served in this capacity until 1904, and while incumbent of this office he was nominated and elected Commissioner of the Third district, and two years later, in 1906, was re-elected and is at this writing serving in that capacity in a manner that stamps him as a man of excellent business qualities. His term expires January 1, 1910. During his term as Trustee he built the graded school at Marysville, this county, and it was during Mr. Watson's term that the magnificent county infirmary was built, which is a credit to Clark county. For this manifestation of interest in public affairs and his honest dealings with his fellow men, Mr. Watson is held in high favor with all who know him.

DANIEL W. BOWER.

Daniel W. Bower, Commissioner of the Second District of Clark county, and prosperous and influential farmer of Charlestown township, has done much during his career to increase the material and moral welfare of the township in which he resides. He has been instrumental in obtaining many of the progressive innovations which have become associated with the townships with which he has been connected in recent years. During his term of office the Board of Commissioners built the new county infirmary at the cost of twenty-five thousand dollars, which is a credit to the county, and of much assistance to many of the inhabitants. He has been successful as a farmer, lives in a beautiful spot on the banks of the Ohio, and leads a peaceful domestic life.

He was born in Oregon township on the 29th of June, 1860, the son of John A. and Mary Jane (Coombs) Bower. John A. was born in Owen township, Clark county, his father, who was the grandfather of our subject, having come to Indiana from South Carolina at a very early date and settled in Clark county, where he lived the remainder of his life. The elder Bower was interested in the manufacture of flat boats and he followed the old custom of piloting them down the river to New Orleans from which place, having effected a sale, he would back to Indiana overland. It was during one of these trips that he took sick at Natchez, Mississippi. Grandfather Bower was the father of eight children. They were: George, John A., Daniel, Adam, Elizabeth, Kittie, Anna and Eliza. All grew to maturity. John A. Bower was born in the old log school-house where he received his early education. During his life time he was a successful farmer and served as Justice of the Peace. He married Mary J. Coombs, a cousin of the late Doctor Coombs, of Charlestown. He and his family were members of the Christian church. Three children were born to John A. Bower: Orrie, born in 1852, who was the wife of Frank J. Stutsman and is now deceased; Benton B., who was born in 1857, is a farmer in Oregon township; the third was Daniel W., of this review.

Daniel W. Bower was reared on the old farmstead in Oregon township, worked on the farm, and went to the district school, where he got a common school education. He married Belle Graebe on November 10, 1882. Mrs.

Bower was born and reared in Owen township, where she attended the district school. At the time of his marriage both Daniel W. Bower and his wife were in rather poor circumstances. They moved to Illinois and farmed there for awhile, returning thence to Nabb, in Washington township. In 1892, he bought the farm he now owns which contains in all one hundred and sixty acres of bottom land and one hundred and fifty-three of the old homestead. He has been quite successful financially in all agricultural ventures. In 1904 he erected a fine residence on the banks of the Ohio, eighteen miles above Louisville.

To Mr. and Mrs. Daniel W. Bower were born seven children, five of whom are at home and all have a good common school education. His wife and family are members of the Presbyterian church, while he belongs to the Christian church.

Daniel W. Bower is a member of the Independent Order of Odd Fellows, Lexington Lodge, No. 405. He also belongs to the Modern Woodmen of America, and the Red Men. In politics he has ever been a Democrat and has been active in the affairs of his party in this county. He served as Trustee of Owen township from the year 1900 to 1904. He was then Commissioner, and served one term, being elected the second time in 1906. He is the present Commissioner of his district. In past years he has worked strenuously for gravel roads in the county, as he is a firm believer in their efficiency.

PARADY PAYNE.

Parady Payne, of Henryville, Clark county, needs slight introduction to the people of his township and county. He is one of the oldest settlers now living on Blue Lick road. He is the proprietor of the widely known Blue Lick Springs, which are justly famous for the medicinal properties of the water.

He was born on the 28th of May, 1830, in Lawrenceburg, Kentucky, and was the son of Thomas B. and Mary (Coffman) Payne. Thomas B. Payne was of English descent and was by occupation a riverman, being for many years associated with the steamboat business. He died in Kentucky at a ripe old age, never having come to Indiana. His wife was of German descent. She was one of the earliest pioneers in this section of the county, and died aged sixty-seven years. Of their family our subject was the only boy of three children born to them; one of his sisters still survives in Crothersville. Parady Payne came to Clark county when about four years old. Some time about his sixth year his mother became a widow. The old salt trail, still visible on the subject's farm, and the deer trail lay across the land, while every night in those early days it was necessary to bar the doors of their log cabins to keep out the wolves. This section of the state was almost a wilderness then and on one occasion during this period a five hundred acre tract of land of which our subject's farm was a part was bartered for an old flint-lock gun.

Parady Payne's education was obtained in the subscription schools in the old log school-houses; he never attended a free school. In the year 1844 he started to make his own way in the world. He ventured into the cafe business, and was for many years connected with the steamboat service on the Ohio. In 1853 his marriage took place, his wife Sophia Townsend, being the daughter of John F. Townsend and Celesta Ferris, his wife, natives of New York. Mrs. Payne was born in Staten, New York, and her marriage ceremony was performed on March 20th, of the above-mentioned year, in Michigan. They then came to Monroe township, Clark county, Indiana, which has ever since been their home. The children born to them were: William H., born in 1855, married Nora Sprague; they live in New York, and have two children, both boys. James M., born in 1856, married Mattie Russell; they live in Nebraska, and have six children. Lilly C., born 1858, married Daniel Guernsey; they have two children, and live with the subject. George F., born in 1860, is a doctor in Louisville. He graduated from the Louisville Hospital College of Medicine. He married Addie Guernsey, and has four children. Charles, born in 1862, married Katie Hawes; they live in Clark county, and have four children. Henry H., born in 1864, died when young. Blanche, born in 1866, died when nineteen years old. Arthur B., born in 1866 (twin brother of the last named), married Lizzie Manning; they live in Clark county, and have six children. A child, Eleanor, died in infancy. Katie, born in 1868, married F. W. Carney; they live in Charlestown. John Byron Payne, born in 1870, is the youngest member. He married Rose Gray; they live in Louisville, and have one child.

Parady Payne is a Democrat. He is secretary of the Township Advisory Board. He is also interested in the cemetery association, and president of the finance committee of the township. His land is contained in sections No. 265-266.

HENRY FISCHER.

Among the energetic and prosperous agriculturists of Clark county, whose efforts have benefited alike themselves and their community, is the subject of this sketch, who is one of the best known men in his locality, being an American by adoption only, for Mr. Fischer was born in Germany, June 22, 1845, the son of Mathias and Elizabeth (Rockey) Fischer, the former having been born in the Fatherland and came to the United States in 1853, locating in Clark county, Indiana, on the farm where the subject now lives in section 5. He was a farmer and miller in the old country. He made the voyage to

America in an old sailing vessel, the trip requiring nearly four months. He made two or three return trips to Europe. He followed farming until his death, October 5, 1871. He was a member of the German Reformed church, and a good Democrat, and although often solicited by his friends to accept public office, he would not do so. He became well known in this county. Mathias Fischer and wife were the parents of ten children. This family first came to New York, where they remained about six months, then came to Clark county. Mathias Fischer was born February 1, 1802, died October 25, 1871. His wife was born December 22, 1805, and died May 12, 1883. The former received his education in Germany. He was a well informed man, and a good farmer, his land lying in section 5, Wood township, where he bought a farm when he came here. It was all timber and in the wilderness, but he cleared it all off and made extensive improvements.

Henry Fischer, our subject, still lives on the old home place, where the Fischer family was reared. At the age of twenty-three he married Ozena Fordyce, and after her death he maried Mary Temple October 10, 1872. She was the daughter of Frank and Magdalene (Siler) Temple. Her father came from Germany and her mother from Switzerland. She is the oldest of nine children.

The following children have been born to the subject and wife: Clara Matilda, born August 14, 1873, married Hite Henry Heistand, and they are living in Hammond, Indiana; Flora Amelia, born September 21, 1875, married Louis P. Wagoner; they are living in Harrison county, this state and are the parents of two children; Walter Henry, born January 31, 1878, married Laura Jameson; they also live in Harrison county, and are the parents of one child; Elmer Milton, who was born July 11, 1880, married Iva Haddox, and is living at home; Anna Nora, born October 7, 1882, is single and living at home; Hettie Pearl, born June 12, 1884, married Joseph Bowman, of Harrison county, and they are the parents of three children; Edgar Emil, born June 18, 1886, is single; Jesse Gilbert, born May 18, 1889, is single; Carl Leon, was born October 18, 1893.

The subject has been a farmer all his life and he has also been interested in the flour mill business, and is now interested in the mercantile business in Harrison county. He has been a hard working man and now as the twilight of old age approaches, he finds himself well fixed in reference to this world's affairs. All his time is taken is looking after his farm and other business, consequently he takes little interest in politics, merely voting the Republican ticket when elections come. He is a well informed man, having received some education in Germany and some in America. He delights to tell of his boyhood days and the early experiences of his father in this county, when he used to haul the products of his farm to New Albany and Louisville to market, using oxen to do the heavy hauling.

Following are the brothers and sisters of the subject: Christian, born October 10, 1825, died February 5, 1894; Elizabeth, born November 29, 1837, is now deceased; Louis, born February 22, 1832, died August 24, 1905; John E. born December 22, 1834, died February 12, 1900; Ferdinand, born October 4, 1835, died August 25, 1862; Mathias lives in Borden; Philip is deceased; Mary, who was born in 1839, lives in Ohio; Eliza, born in 1838 lives in Shelby county, Kentucky.

Mr. Fischer is known as a man of good business principles and is an excellent neighbor and has many friends throughout the county.

Index

to

Baird's History

of

Clark County

Index of Names

ABBETT
James, 238
Margaret, 238
ABBOT
John, 51
ABBOTT
A. Q., 117
Asa, 93
J. B., 107
U. G., 252
ACKERMAN
Frank, 273
ACTON
A. J., 404
ADAIR
S. L., Jr., Dr.,
421, 422
S. Z., Jr., Dr.,
Samuel, Dr., 421,
422
ADAMS
C. Graham, Rev.,
235
John, 235, 276, 316
Thomas H., 177
William, 54 (Bio. 693)
AIKEN
Josiah, 142
AKERS
Simon, 55
ALBEN
Hugo, 226
ALDRIDGE
A.G., 253
Hiram, 382
ALLEN
Benjamin, "Elder", 277
David, 362
James, 52
R.H. (Rev.), 261
Stephen, 223
Thomas, 250
ALLHANDS
David, Dr., 423
David S., Dr., 421
ALLMOND
A.T., 236
Bettie, 235
ALMSTEAD
A.E., 225
ALPHA
George W., 202
AMES
C.R., 256
Edward R., 245, 248
AMICK
Gideon, 263
Levi, 263
Margaret, 263
Mary, 263
Peter, 263
Sophia, 263
ANDERSON
Albert L., 490
C.C., 277
Charles C., 92, 96
George F., 216, 217
James, 56
John, 142
Moses G., 111
ANDREWS
Francis E., Prof., 437

ANGST
Jacob, 278
ANSON
Silas, 404
ANTHONY
D.C., 302
ANTZ
Charles F., 618
APPLEGATE
Aaron, 245
James D., 762
John, 220
Thomas, 89
ARMER
D.S., Dr., 416
ARMSTRONG
Frank S., 797
Frank Spear, Capt.,
141, 210
James, 244, 353
James H., 359
James Howard, 798
John, Capt., 138, 140
John, 65
Lucy, Mrs., 357
William, 390
William G., 93, 100,
107, 108
ASBURY
C.E., Mrs., 359
Charles E., Rev., 131
ASH
Maggie, Miss, 274
P.J., 171
Robert, Rev., 230
ASHTON
Charles, 202
John, 140
ASHWORTH
Moses, 243, 248
ASTOR
Richard, 63
ATHAN
J.S., 419
James S., Dr., 419
ATHON
James S., Dr., 424
ATTERBURY
J.G., Rev., 267
AUDRAN
Ernest, Rev.. 272
AULT
Frank, Miss,
249
AUSTIN
Edward A., 216
John, 101
Thomas R., Rev.,
232
BACHMAN
John A., 278
BACON
Thomas B., Rev.,
233
BADEN
Theodore Stephen, Fat-
her, 270
BADGER
Louis, 801
Millard A., 220

BAGGERLY
Evan, 396
Isaac, 56, 63
BAILEY
A.Q., Rev., 236
David, 166
J.W., 222, 223
BAILY
Francis, 140
BAIN
George W., 228
BAIRD
Harry, 223
J.F., 264
J.F., Rev., 317
James A., 877
James W., 369
L.C., 409
L.C., Capt., 128, 130,
207, 208, 213, 235,
236
Lewis C., Mrs., 403
Martha Howard, Mrs.,
249
William, 264
BAKER
Aaron, 223
Barzillai, 60, 142
Chris, 124
D., 396
E.D. (Hon.), 396
James, 55, 63
Jesse, 56, 63
Robert M., 255
BALDWIN
Amos G., Rev., 229
John H., Dr., 418
John Hutchinson, 583
BALL
William J., 101
BALLARD
Curtis W., Hon., 788
BAMBER
Alfred H., 131
BAMFORD
W.H., Rev., 234, 235,
236
BANKS
David C. (Rev.), 263
BANNISTER
Henry, 289
BARE
Jacob P., 170, 264,
(Bio. 822)
Joseph, 264
Polly, 264
Thomas, Lt., 188
BARMORE
D.S., 123
David S., 327, 353
BARNABY
H.S., 323, 329
Matthew, 55
BARNARD
M., 382
BARNES
G.L., 427
Francis, 230
Willis, 128
Willis L., Hon., 894

DAVIS continued
 157, 210
 John S., 294, 297, 309
 Joseph, 151
 O.F., 223
 Solomon, 93, 396, 421
 Thomas T., 287
 W.A., 132
 William A., 539
DAWSON
 Kate W., 228
DAYES
 Phillip, 268
DAYTON
 Jonathan, 57
DEAIRK
 D.W., 224
 Henry, 224
DEAN
 Charles W., 547
 Frank F., 850
 Frank L., 404
 James D., 223
 William S., 405
DEIBEL
 William H., 676
DEITY
 John, 52
DE LA HARLANDIERE
 Celestine, Bishop, 272
DELAHUNT
 John L., 213, 217, 219
DELTON
 Claiborn M., 176
DENBO
 Robert, 143
DENNY
 John, 92
DENZLER
 Gustave Adolph, 564
DEPAW
 John, 148
DE ST. PALAIS
 Bishop, 271, 272
DEUSER
 William M., 873
DEWEY
 Charles, 286, 291, 292,
 296, 302
 Charles, Jr., 302
 Park, 302
DICKEY
 J.H., 320
 John M. (Rev.), 262,
 263, 264, 265
 N.S. (Rev.), 265
DICKMAN
 Joseph, Rev., 273, 274
DIETZ
 Henry C., 176
DIFFENDERFER
 S.B., 115
DILGER
 Henry F., 458
DITZLER
 Jacob, 257
DIX
 George B., 629
 Oscar, 627
DIXON
 John, 221

DIXON continued
 William H., 221
DOBBINS
 Frank G., 767
DODD
 Edward, 223
 Eleas, 223 (2)
 Louis, 223
DOES
 Charles, 269
DOLAN
 Matthew, 275
DOLD
 Edward, 216
DOLPH
 E.L., Rev., 228, 248,
 249
DONAGAN
 Elizabeth, 50
DONAHUE
 John, 275
 Thomas, 272
DONALDSON
 Peter C., 538
DONOVAN
 P.C., 235
DORSEY
 Josiah, Mrs., 249
DOUBET
 Joseph C., 520
DOUGLAS
 L.A., 302
DOW
 Daniel Milburn, 685
 Henry, 64
 Henry, Sr., 64
DOWLING
 Alexander, 294, 302,
 309
DOWNS
 Thomas, 48, 49, 284
DOYLE
 Philip, Father, 271
 William, Rev., 271
DOYON
 M.R., Major, 408
DRAKE
 Francis, Sir, 229
DREYER
 William, 280
DRISCOLL
 John D., 316
DRYDAN
 David M., 174
DRYDEN
 David M., 167
 David M., 329
DRUMMOND
 James, 151
 Joseph C., 170
DUERSON
 Thomas, Dr., 420
 William, 211, 212
DUFFY
 Ham, 365
 James H., 580
 James F., Capt., 688
 Oscar H., 598
DUGAN
 Henry, Capt., 533
DUNBAR

DUNBAR continued
 Butler, 78
 Family, 677
 Horace, 213
DUNCAN
 M.E., 385
DUNHAM
 Cyrus L., 291, 300,
 302, 311
 George A., 218
DUNLAP
 John F., 203
DUNLEVEY
 Dave, 223
 M.H., 222, 223
DUNLEVY
 C.S., 269
 Matthew H., 757
DUNN
 George C., 300
 George D., 302
 George G., 296
 George H., 101
 William McKee, 300
DUNWOODY
 James, 198
DURBIN
 W.F., Col., 406
DURFY
 Joseph, 64
DUSTIN
 Moody, 329
 Moody, Jr., 198
EASTMAN
 Harvey E., 218
 Harvey G., 213,
 219
EBERTS
 Conrad, 616
 Jacob, 616
EDDY
 D. T. M., 246
 L. E., 421
 Thomas M., Rev.,
 249
EDWARDS
 Isaac, 238
EGGLESTON
 A. L., 222
EHLE
 John, 279
EISMANN
 C. J., 223
EKIN
 James E., Col.,
 165
 Josiah, 142
ELROD
 C.L., 318
 J.W., 215
 Richard, Jr., 771
EMERKE
 E., 400
 H.C., 399, 400
ENDERS
 Ferdinand, Sr., 728
ENGLISH
 James E., 405
 Levi, 228
 William E., 130
ENGSTROM

LEMMON continued
  Walter Lewis, 556
LEMON
  James, 70, 142, 370
  Thomas D., 212
LENTZ
  Edgar Mitchell, 647
  Jacob, 635
  Nicholas, 399, 638
LEONARD
  Somerville E., 101
LEPPERT
  John C., 541
LESLIE
  Lyman, 289
LEVER
  John, 250
LEWELLEN
  P.R., 268
  Thomas, 268
LEWELLN
  M. J., 268
LEWIS
  Felix, 121, 246, 315
  Felix R., 363
  John, 257
  John, Sr., 52
  Nimrod, 404
  Pe eg, 64
  U. B., 216
  W. B., 359
  William, Mrs., 359
  William, Rev., 268
LEWMAN
  G. W., 235
  George W., 317
  J. C., 235
  J. L., Mrs., 235
  John, 55
  John C., 218
  Thomas J., 645
LIENKAEMPER
  Ben E., Rev., 279
  W. G., Rev., 279
LIESEN
  Father Joseph, 272
LINCOLN
  Abraham, 243
LINDLEY
  Eli M., 467
  John F., 103
LINDSEY
  Isaac, 255
  Robert, 386
LINES
  William E., 217
LINGEN
  Joe, 386
LINGENFELTER
  Esther F., 257
  J. R., 257
LINGLE
  Samuel, 179
LINTHICUM
  N. H., 320
LISTON
  Elizabeth, 246
LITTELL
  Abram, 90
  A. G., 215
  family, 54

LITTELL continued
  Mary, 276
  Spencer, 395
  Thomas, 104
  Thomphson, 56, 63
LITTLE
  Absalom, 56, 59, 90
  Amos, 63
LIVINGSTONE
  Robert, 325
LOCK
  George, 251
LOCKMILLER
  G. M., 214
LODER
  Benjamin, 101
LOGAN
  John A., Gen., 192
LOHEIDE
  Carl, 280
  Fredric, 280
LONG
  Anenj, 92
  Dennis, 118, 123
  E. C., 220
  John W., 92
  Theodore S,, 552
  William H., 824
LOOMIS
  Arthur, 132, 218, 234,
    358, 379, 426, 653
  Carrie, 132
  Clara J., Miss, 357,
    359, 360
  Jacob, 219
  John, Dr., 418
  John, 599
  John C., 228
  John, Mrs., 359, 360
LORIMER
  George C., 240
LOTSPRECH '
  Ralph, 243
LOUDEN
  A. M., 253
LOVELACE
  Samuel, 257
LOVERING
  Amos, 101, 154, 290,
    291, 294, 299
LUALLEN
  George, 405
LUGENBEEL
  W. E., Dr., 397
LUITZ
  Father Clements, 272
LUKE
  Eva, 131
LUKENBILL
  Edwin, 266
  Lizzie, 266
LUSHER
  George W., 623
LUTZ
  Alban, 170
  B. C., 302
  Ben, 169
  Benjamin, 198
  Benjamin F., 170
  David, 56
  David, Sr., 256

LUTZ continued
  Henry S., 803
  Oscar F., 170, 320
  Samuel, 320
LYLE
  Hugh, 212
LYON
  S. S., Major, 186
  Sidney S., 108
  Victor, 57, 125
  Victor W., 58
LYONS
  Granville, 257
LYSLE
  Hugh, Dr., 419
MC ALLISTER
  Daniel, 92
MC BRIDE
  C. R., Dr., 414
  Claude B., 718
MC CAFFERTY
  Andrew, 395
MC CAMPBELL
  Harvey, 96, 141
  J. H., 126, 262, 316,
    383
  James, 60
  Samuel, 107, 260
  William L., 316
MC CAULEY
  C. A. H., Col., 165
  Eli, 290
  John S., 166
MC CAWLEY
  Edward, 208
  Tom, 188
MC CLEARY
  John L., 405
MC CLELLAN
  Neil, 200
MC CLINTOCK
  John, Jr., 143
MC CLOUD
  Islam, 52
MC CLUNG
  James, 260
MC CLURE
  Alexander, 53
  Daniel, 300
  David, Dr., 416
  David, Mrs., 357
  T. J., 269
  William T., 268
MC COMB
  William, 404
MC COMBE
  Andrew, 85
MC CONNELL
  F. C., Rev., 241
MC CORMACK
  John C., 200, 202
MC CORMICK
  Frank P., 813
MC CORY
  John, 405
MC COY
  Christiana, 239
  Eliza, 239
  Enoch A., 405
  Isaac, Rev., 239
  J. A. C., 170, 179

MC COY continued
  James, 395
  James L., 405
  John, 142, 144, 148,
    238, 290
  Theo, 217
  Theodore, Rev., 268
  W. N., Dr., 415
  William H., 237, 239
MC CRAE
  John, Rev., 268
MC CREADY
  James, Rev., 262
MC CULLOCH
  Charles W., 734
  George, 395
  Hugh, 292
  J. F., 317
  Walter Erle, 904
MC CULLUM
  Henry H., 183
MC DANIELS
  Daniel H., 107
MC DEITZ
  J. F., 100
MC DIETZ
  Thomas, 100
  Thompson, 105
MC DONALD
  Joseph E., 289, 297,
    301
  Peter, 63
  William, 275
MC FARLAND
  James, 143
MC GARRAH
  Francis, 277
  Mary, 277
MC GEE
  Robert, 266
MC GHEE
  C. R., Rev., 264
  Clark, Rev., 264
  James, 264
  Martha, 264
  Tamar, 264
  William, 264
MC GINNIS
  William, 251
MC GREADY
  James, 260
MC GREGAR
  James, 531
MC GUIRE
  A., Rev., 243
MC HENRY
  John J., 318
MC HOLLAND
  J. B., 91
MC KEE
  James A., Rev., 264
  Joseph A., 213
MC KENNA
  E. W., 363
MC KENSIE
  George, 257
MC KILLIP
  M. E., 260, 268
MC KINLEY
  Charles E., 319
  Charles Edwin, 683

MC KINLEY continued
  George, 319
  J. H., 319
  James, 55, 63, 78
  Jesse E., 215
  John, 55
  Richard A., 225
  Samuel, 545
  Sylvanus, 319
  William, 104
MC KOSSKY
  Peter, 107
MC MAHAN
  William, 255
MC MILLAN
  William, 263
MC MILLIN
  John, 818
MC NAUGHT
  John, 143
MC NULTY
  Catherine, 264
MC RUNNELS
  John, 251
MC WILLIAMS
  John A., 405
MABURY
  Hiram, 316
  Woods, 316
MACKEY
  John, 627
MADDOCK
  Laura, 289
MAGILL
  C. W., 91
MAGRUDER
  J. L., 320
  John L., 837
MALCOME
  W. D., Rev., 266, 268
MALINDER
  John, 251
MALONEY
  Father Daniel, 270
MALOTT
  Joseph, 289
MANAUGH
  T. N., 320
MANN
  Baily, 93
MANNY
  Theobald, 272
MAPLE
  William, 179
MARBLE
  Claytes McHenry,
    652
MARKLE
  C. M., Supt., 397
MARRA
  James, 272, 542
MARSH
  Asa, 239
  B. F., 108
  James K., 294, 302
  John K., 132, 434
MARSHALL
  Humphrey, 75, 291
  James M., Col., 165
  John, 303
  Joseph C., 296

MARSHALL continued
  Joseph G., 291, 300,
    301, 302, 305, 307
  Thomas, 75
MARTIN
  Adam, Col., 65
  Enoch, Rev., 263, 265
  George W., 592
  J. E., 257
  Rodger 300
MASTERS
  Frank, 222
MASTIN
  Frank, 223
MATHES
  Charles, 151
MATHEWS
  J. M., 386
MATT
  Lucius, Rev., 272
MATTEG
  William, 280
MATTHEWS
  E. M., 223
  George, 93, 396
  J. L., 259
  John, 263
  William K., 170
MATTOCK
  J. W. L., 111
MAUPIN
  William, 251
MAUZY
  John M., 568
MAYBURY
  Woods, 107, 108
MAYFIELD
  F. M., 302
  Frank M., 491
MEIBOOM
  H., Rev., 279
MEIBOON
  J. Henry, 408, 608
MEIGS
  M. C., Maj.-Gen.,
MELCHER
  Christian,
MELOY
  C. P., Dr., 225
  Charles P., 887
  John M., 217, 227
  John Morton, M.D.,
    724
MERCER
  T. C., 177
MERIWETHER
  Family, 621
  John, 211
  Mary, 412
  Samuel, 371
  Samuel, Dr., 412, 414
MERRIWETHER
  James, 164
  James B., 175, 177,
    302
  Samuel, 81, 91, 100,
    107, 141, 145, 230,
    260, 261, 262
MESHAC
  James, 399
METZGAR

RICHARDS continued
  Daniel, 372
RICHARDSON
  W. A., 107
RICHARDS
  Lewis E., 544
RICKARD
  George M., 536
RICKETS
  D., 382
RICKETTS
  Dillard, 111, 308,
    316
RIDER
  Matthew, 142
RIDDLE
  George W., 178, 193
RIEKE
  H., Rev., 279
RIETH
  Daniel, 278
RIGGLES
  Benjamin, 220
RIGSBY
  Charles R., 553
RITTER
  John A., 179
ROBB
  David, Capt., 243
ROBERTS
  George, 143
ROBERTSON
  Charles, 55, 63
  Eli, 142
  Hezekiah, 55, 243,
    290
  J. S., 317
  Nathan, 56, 242, 243
  Robert, 59, 85, 142,
    144, 148
ROBINSON
  A. G., Col., 165
  B. H., 405
  George, 404
  Hamilton, 96, 750
  Henry, 66
  Ira, 230
  Ira, Mrs., 230
  J. V., 404
  Jacob, 400
  Lee L., 391
  S. L., 212
  Theophilias, 266
  William, 66
  William E., 391
ROCKSTROH
  I. L., 278
RODGERS
  Andrew, Dr., 419
  H. D., 404
ROE
  Phillip J., 157
ROEDER
  Ludwig, 279
ROERK
  B. F., 405
ROGERS
  Charles, Mrs., 358
  O. W., 222
ROLAND
  J. B., 173

ROLAND continued
  John, 90
ROLLER
  Lewis F., 216
ROSE
  Joel, 253
  John, 71
  T., 400
  W. E., 222
ROSENBERGER
  Joseph, 717
ROSS
  Charles, 256
  George, 396
  J. M., 96
  James, 60
  James M., 157, 204
  John F., 286, 287,
    288
  John T., 320
ROSSEAU
  Lovell H., 160
ROSSLER
  Charles, 222
ROTH
  Charles, 258
ROWAN
  John, Hon., 83
ROWE
  Austin, 104
ROWLAND
  Jesse, 49
ROYSE
  Henry H., 101
ROZZLE
  Nelson, 245
RUBEY
  William A., 795
RUBY
  W. A., 224
RUCKER
  Shadrick, 255
RUDDELL
  Alexander, 94
  J. M., 168
  James, 391
RUDDLE
  Charles, 224
  I. N., Dr., 417
  Jacob, 253
RUEHL
  John, 278
RUHLIN
  George, Col., 165
RULE
  L. V., Rev., 268
  Lucien, Rev., 269
RUNCIE
  James, Rev., 232
RUNYAN
  David N., 175
  E. G., 223
  Eli, 223
  Francis M., 212
RUSK
  Robert, 143
RUSSELL
  James R., 214
  John, 65
  Robert L., 215
  William, Col., 149

RUTER
  C. W., 255
RUTLEDGE
  Emmaus, 255
  John, 251
RUTTER
  Calvin, 250, 251
  John, 250
RYAN
  J. S., 170
  James, 169, 405
RYANS
  Edward Arthur, 548
SAGE
  Erasmus T., 215
  George, 61
  H. T., 121
  Harry T., 216, 217
SAME
  Frank H., 563
  Harry, 308
  W., 279
SAMPEL
  William, 405
SAMPLE
  Alexander, 222
  Thomas W., 835
  William, 737
SAMUELS
  Conway C., 275
  William L., Dr., 418
SAMPLE
  Thomas W., 214
SANDERS
  John P., 221
SARGEANT
  Winthrop, 139
SARGENT
  Melsin, 250, 251
SAUNDERS
  Louis, 559
SAVITZ
  George, 315, 316
  George F., 100
SAXTON
  Rufus, Col., 165
SAYER
  Lewis A., 422
SCANLAND
  J. R., 385
SCHEER
  G. A., 224
  George A., 218
SCHELL
  Eugene, Lt., 200
  Eugene M., 202
  Francis M., 158
  James, 158
  Pink, 205
SCHELLER
  John, 736
SCHMIDT
  Benjamin, 713
SCHIMPFF
  A. R., 391
  Charles A., 279, 473
  Rudolph, 453
SCHLAEFER
  John, 279
SCHLEICHER
  Ernest, 405